T0142357

Lecture Notes in Computer Science   13846

Founding Editors

Gerhard Goos
Juris Hartmanis

Editorial Board Members

The series Lecture Notes in Computer Science (LNCS), including its subseries Lecture Notes in Artificial Intelligence (LNAI) and Lecture Notes in Bioinformatics (LNBI), has established itself as a medium for the publication of new developments in computer science and information technology research, teaching, and education.

LNCS enjoys close cooperation with the computer science R & D community, the series counts many renowned academics among its volume editors and paper authors, and collaborates with prestigious societies. Its mission is to serve this international community by providing an invaluable service, mainly focused on the publication of conference and workshop proceedings and postproceedings. LNCS commenced publication in 1973.

Lei Wang · Juergen Gall · Tat-Jun Chin ·
Imari Sato · Rama Chellappa
Editors

Computer Vision – ACCV 2022

16th Asian Conference on Computer Vision
Macao, China, December 4–8, 2022
Proceedings, Part VI

 Springer

Editors
Lei Wang (iD)
University of Wollongong
Wollongong, NSW, Australia

Juergen Gall (iD)
University of Bonn
Bonn, Germany

Tat-Jun Chin (iD)
University of Adelaide
Adelaide, SA, Australia

Imari Sato
National Institute of Informatics
Tokyo, Japan

Rama Chellappa (iD)
Johns Hopkins University
Baltimore, MD, USA

ISSN 0302-9743   ISSN 1611-3349 (electronic)
Lecture Notes in Computer Science
ISBN 978-3-031-26350-7   ISBN 978-3-031-26351-4 (eBook)
https://doi.org/10.1007/978-3-031-26351-4

This Springer imprint is published by the registered company Springer Nature Switzerland AG
The registered company address is: Gewerbestrasse 11, 6330 Cham, Switzerland

Preface

The 16th Asian Conference on Computer Vision (ACCV) 2022 was held in a hybrid mode in Macau SAR, China during December 4–8, 2022. The conference featured novel research contributions from almost all sub-areas of computer vision.

For the main conference, 836 valid submissions entered the review stage after desk rejection. Sixty-three area chairs and 959 reviewers made great efforts to ensure that every submission received thorough and high-quality reviews. As in previous editions of ACCV, this conference adopted a double-blind review process. The identities of authors were not visible to the reviewers or area chairs; nor were the identities of the assigned reviewers and area chairs known to the authors. The program chairs did not submit papers to the conference.

After receiving the reviews, the authors had the option of submitting a rebuttal. Following that, the area chairs led the discussions and final recommendations were then made by the reviewers. Taking conflicts of interest into account, the area chairs formed 21 AC triplets to finalize the paper recommendations. With the confirmation of three area chairs for each paper, 277 papers were accepted. ACCV 2022 also included eight workshops, eight tutorials, and one grand challenge, covering various cutting-edge research topics related to computer vision. The proceedings of ACCV 2022 are open access at the Computer Vision Foundation website, by courtesy of Springer. The quality of the papers presented at ACCV 2022 demonstrates the research excellence of the international computer vision communities.

This conference is fortunate to receive support from many organizations and individuals. We would like to express our gratitude for the continued support of the Asian Federation of Computer Vision and our sponsors, the University of Macau, Springer, the Artificial Intelligence Journal, and OPPO. ACCV 2022 used the Conference Management Toolkit sponsored by Microsoft Research and received much help from its support team.

All the organizers, area chairs, reviewers, and authors made great contributions to ensure a successful ACCV 2022. For this, we owe them deep gratitude. Last but not least, we would like to thank the online and in-person attendees of ACCV 2022. Their presence showed strong commitment and appreciation towards this conference.

December 2022

Lei Wang
Juergen Gall
Tat-Jun Chin
Imari Sato
Rama Chellappa

Organization

General Chairs

Gérard Medioni	University of Southern California, USA
Shiguang Shan	Chinese Academy of Sciences, China
Bohyung Han	Seoul National University, South Korea
Hongdong Li	Australian National University, Australia

Program Chairs

Rama Chellappa	Johns Hopkins University, USA
Juergen Gall	University of Bonn, Germany
Imari Sato	National Institute of Informatics, Japan
Tat-Jun Chin	University of Adelaide, Australia
Lei Wang	University of Wollongong, Australia

Publication Chairs

Wenbin Li	Nanjing University, China
Wanqi Yang	Nanjing Normal University, China

Local Arrangements Chairs

Liming Zhang	University of Macau, China
Jianjia Zhang	Sun Yat-sen University, China

Web Chairs

Zongyuan Ge	Monash University, Australia
Deval Mehta	Monash University, Australia
Zhongyan Zhang	University of Wollongong, Australia

AC Meeting Chair

Chee Seng Chan   University of Malaya, Malaysia

Area Chairs

Aljosa Osep   Technical University of Munich, Germany
Angela Yao   National University of Singapore, Singapore
Anh T. Tran   VinAI Research, Vietnam
Anurag Mittal   Indian Institute of Technology Madras, India
Binh-Son Hua   VinAI Research, Vietnam
C. V. Jawahar   International Institute of Information Technology,
                                   Hyderabad, India
Dan Xu   The Hong Kong University of Science and
                                   Technology, China
Du Tran   Meta AI, USA
Frederic Jurie   University of Caen and Safran, France
Guangcan Liu   Southeast University, China
Guorong Li   University of Chinese Academy of Sciences,
                                   China
Guosheng Lin   Nanyang Technological University, Singapore
Gustavo Carneiro   University of Surrey, UK
Hyun Soo Park   University of Minnesota, USA
Hyunjung Shim   Korea Advanced Institute of Science and
                                   Technology, South Korea
Jiaying Liu   Peking University, China
Jun Zhou   Griffith University, Australia
Junseok Kwon   Chung-Ang University, South Korea
Kota Yamaguchi   CyberAgent, Japan
Li Liu   National University of Defense Technology,
                                   China
Liang Zheng   Australian National University, Australia
Mathieu Aubry   Ecole des Ponts ParisTech, France
Mehrtash Harandi   Monash University, Australia
Miaomiao Liu   Australian National University, Australia
Ming-Hsuan Yang   University of California at Merced, USA
Palaiahnakote Shivakumara   University of Malaya, Malaysia
Pau-Choo Chung   National Cheng Kung University, Taiwan

Qianqian Xu	Key Laboratory of Intelligent Information Processing, Institute of Computing Technology, Chinese Academy of Sciences, China
Qiuhong Ke	Monash University, Australia
Radu Timofte	University of Würzburg, Germany and ETH Zurich, Switzerland
Rajagopalan N. Ambasamudram	Indian Institute of Technology Madras, India
Risheng Liu	Dalian University of Technology, China
Ruiping Wang	Institute of Computing Technology, Chinese Academy of Sciences, China
Sajid Javed	Khalifa University of Science and Technology, Abu Dhabi, UAE
Seunghoon Hong	Korea Advanced Institute of Science and Technology, South Korea
Shang-Hong Lai	National Tsing Hua University, Taiwan
Shanshan Zhang	Nanjing University of Science and Technology, China
Sharon Xiaolei Huang	Pennsylvania State University, USA
Shin'ichi Satoh	National Institute of Informatics, Japan
Si Liu	Beihang University, China
Suha Kwak	Pohang University of Science and Technology, South Korea
Tae Hyun Kim	Hanyang Univeristy, South Korea
Takayuki Okatani	Tohoku University, Japan/RIKEN Center for Advanced Intelligence Project, Japan
Tatsuya Harada	University of Tokyo/RIKEN, Japan
Vicky Kalogeiton	Ecole Polytechnique, France
Vincent Lepetit	Ecole des Ponts ParisTech, France
Vineeth N. Balasubramanian	Indian Institute of Technology, Hyderabad, India
Wei Shen	Shanghai Jiao Tong University, China
Wei-Shi Zheng	Sun Yat-sen University, China
Xiang Bai	Huazhong University of Science and Technology, China
Xiaowei Zhou	Zhejiang University, China
Xin Yu	University of Technology Sydney, Australia
Yasutaka Furukawa	Simon Fraser University, Canada
Yasuyuki Matsushita	Osaka University, Japan
Yedid Hoshen	Hebrew University of Jerusalem, Israel
Ying Fu	Beijing Institute of Technology, China
Yong Jae Lee	University of Wisconsin-Madison, USA
Yu-Chiang Frank Wang	National Taiwan University, Taiwan
Yumin Suh	NEC Laboratories America, USA

Yung-Yu Chuang   National Taiwan University, Taiwan
Zhaoxiang Zhang   Chinese Academy of Sciences, China
Ziad Al-Halah   University of Texas at Austin, USA
Zuzana Kukelova   Czech Technical University, Czech Republic

Additional Reviewers

Abanob E. N. Soliman
Abdelbadie Belmouhcine
Adrian Barbu
Agnibh Dasgupta
Akihiro Sugimoto
Akkarit Sangpetch
Akrem Sellami
Aleksandr Kim
Alexander Andreopoulos
Alexander Fix
Alexander Kugele
Alexandre Morgand
Alexis Lechervy
Alina E. Marcu
Alper Yilmaz
Alvaro Parra
Amogh Subbakrishna
    Adishesha
Andrea Giachetti
Andrea Lagorio
Andreu Girbau Xalabarder
Andrey Kuehlkamp
Anh Nguyen
Anh T. Tran
Ankush Gupta
Anoop Cherian
Anton Mitrokhin
Antonio Agudo
Antonio Robles-Kelly
Ara Abigail Ambita
Ardhendu Behera
Arjan Kuijper
Arren Matthew C.
    Antioquia
Arjun Ashok
Atsushi Hashimoto

Atsushi Shimada
Attila Szabo
Aurelie Bugeau
Avatharam Ganivada
Ayan Kumar Bhunia
Azade Farshad
B. V. K. Vijaya Kumar
Bach Tran
Bailin Yang
Baojiang Zhong
Baoquan Zhang
Baoyao Yang
Basit O. Alawode
Beibei Lin
Benoit Guillard
Beomgu Kang
Bin He
Bin Li
Bin Liu
Bin Ren
Bin Yang
Bin-Cheng Yang
BingLiang Jiao
Bo Liu
Bohan Li
Boyao Zhou
Boyu Wang
Caoyun Fan
Carlo Tomasi
Carlos Torres
Carvalho Micael
Cees Snoek
Chang Kong
Changick Kim
Changkun Ye
Changsheng Lu

Chao Liu
Chao Shi
Chaowei Tan
Chaoyi Li
Chaoyu Dong
Chaoyu Zhao
Chen He
Chen Liu
Chen Yang
Chen Zhang
Cheng Deng
Cheng Guo
Cheng Yu
Cheng-Kun Yang
Chenglong Li
Chengmei Yang
Chengxin Liu
Chengyao Qian
Chen-Kuo Chiang
Chenxu Luo
Che-Rung Lee
Che-Tsung Lin
Chi Xu
Chi Nhan Duong
Chia-Ching Lin
Chien-Cheng Lee
Chien-Yi Wang
Chih-Chung Hsu
Chih-Wei Lin
Ching-Chun Huang
Chiou-Ting Hsu
Chippy M. Manu
Chong Wang
Chongyang Wang
Christian Siagian
Christine Allen-Blanchette

Christoph Schorn
Christos Matsoukas
Chuan Guo
Chuang Yang
Chuanyi Zhang
Chunfeng Song
Chunhui Zhang
Chun-Rong Huang
Ci Lin
Ci-Siang Lin
Cong Fang
Cui Wang
Cui Yuan
Cyrill Stachniss
Dahai Yu
Daiki Ikami
Daisuke Miyazaki
Dandan Zhu
Daniel Barath
Daniel Lichy
Daniel Reich
Danyang Tu
David Picard
Davide Silvestri
Defang Chen
Dehuan Zhang
Deunsol Jung
Difei Gao
Dim P. Papadopoulos
Ding-Jie Chen
Dong Gong
Dong Hao
Dong Wook Shu
Dongdong Chen
Donghun Lee
Donghyeon Kwon
Donghyun Yoo
Dongkeun Kim
Dongliang Luo
Dongseob Kim
Dongsuk Kim
Dongwan Kim
Dongwon Kim
DongWook Yang
Dongze Lian

Dubing Chen
Edoardo Remelli
Emanuele Trucco
Erhan Gundogdu
Erh-Chung Chen
Rickson R. Nascimento
Erkang Chen
Eunbyung Park
Eunpil Park
Eun-Sol Kim
Fabio Cuzzolin
Fan Yang
Fan Zhang
Fangyu Zhou
Fani Deligianni
Fatemeh Karimi Nejadasl
Fei Liu
Feiyue Ni
Feng Su
Feng Xue
Fengchao Xiong
Fengji Ma
Fernando Díaz-del-Rio
Florian Bernard
Florian Kleber
Florin-Alexandru
    Vasluianu
Fok Hing Chi Tivive
Frank Neumann
Fu-En Yang
Fumio Okura
Gang Chen
Gang Liu
Gao Haoyuan
Gaoshuai Wang
Gaoyun An
Gen Li
Georgy Ponimatkin
Gianfranco Doretto
Gil Levi
Guang Yang
Guangfa Wang
Guangfeng Lin
Guillaume Jeanneret
Guisik Kim

Gunhee Kim
Guodong Wang
Ha Young Kim
Hadi Mohaghegh
    Dolatabadi
Haibo Ye
Haili Ye
Haithem Boussaid
Haixia Wang
Han Chen
Han Zou
Hang Cheng
Hang Du
Hang Guo
Hanlin Gu
Hannah H. Kim
Hao He
Hao Huang
Hao Quan
Hao Ren
Hao Tang
Hao Zeng
Hao Zhao
Haoji Hu
Haopeng Li
Haoqing Wang
Haoran Wen
Haoshuo Huang
Haotian Liu
Haozhao Ma
Hari Chandana K.
Haripriya Harikumar
Hehe Fan
Helder Araujo
Henok Ghebrechristos
Heunseung Lim
Hezhi Cao
Hideo Saito
Hieu Le
Hiroaki Santo
Hirokatsu Kataoka
Hiroshi Omori
Hitika Tiwari
Hojung Lee
Hong Cheng

Hong Liu
Hu Zhang
Huadong Tang
Huajie Jiang
Huang Ziqi
Huangying Zhan
Hui Kong
Hui Nie
Huiyu Duan
Huyen Thi Thanh Tran
Hyung-Jeong Yang
Hyunjin Park
Hyunsoo Kim
HyunWook Park
I-Chao Shen
Idil Esen Zulfikar
Ikuhisa Mitsugami
Inseop Chung
Ioannis Pavlidis
Isinsu Katircioglu
Jaeil Kim
Jaeyoon Park
Jae-Young Sim
James Clark
James Elder
James Pritts
Jan Zdenek
Janghoon Choi
Jeany Son
Jenny Seidenschwarz
Jesse Scott
Jia Wan
Jiadai Sun
JiaHuan Ji
Jiajiong Cao
Jian Zhang
Jianbo Jiao
Jianhui Wu
Jianjia Wang
Jianjia Zhang
Jianqiao Wangni
JiaQi Wang
Jiaqin Lin
Jiarui Liu
Jiawei Wang

Jiaxin Gu
Jiaxin Wei
Jiaxin Zhang
Jiaying Zhang
Jiayu Yang
Jidong Tian
Jie Hong
Jie Lin
Jie Liu
Jie Song
Jie Yang
Jiebo Luo
Jiejie Xu
Jin Fang
Jin Gao
Jin Tian
Jinbin Bai
Jing Bai
Jing Huo
Jing Tian
Jing Wu
Jing Zhang
Jingchen Xu
Jingchun Cheng
Jingjing Fu
Jingshuai Liu
JingWei Huang
Jingzhou Chen
JinHan Cui
Jinjie Song
Jinqiao Wang
Jinsun Park
Jinwoo Kim
Jinyu Chen
Jipeng Qiang
Jiri Sedlar
Jiseob Kim
Jiuxiang Gu
Jiwei Xiao
Jiyang Zheng
Jiyoung Lee
John Paisley
Joonki Paik
Joonseok Lee
Julien Mille

Julio C. Zamora
Jun Sato
Jun Tan
Jun Tang
Jun Xiao
Jun Xu
Junbao Zhuo
Jun-Cheng Chen
Junfen Chen
Jungeun Kim
Junhwa Hur
Junli Tao
Junlin Han
Junsik Kim
Junting Dong
Junwei Zhou
Junyu Gao
Kai Han
Kai Huang
Kai Katsumata
Kai Zhao
Kailun Yang
Kai-Po Chang
Kaixiang Wang
Kamal Nasrollahi
Kamil Kowol
Kan Chang
Kang-Jun Liu
Kanchana Vaishnavi
　　Gandikota
Kanoksak Wattanachote
Karan Sikka
Kaushik Roy
Ke Xian
Keiji Yanai
Kha Gia Quach
Kibok Lee
Kira Maag
Kirill Gavrilyuk
Kohei Suenaga
Koichi Ito
Komei Sugiura
Kong Dehui
Konstantinos Batsos
Kotaro Kikuchi

Kouzou Ohara
Kuan-Wen Chen
Kun He
Kun Hu
Kun Zhan
Kunhee Kim
Kwan-Yee K. Wong
Kyong Hwan Jin
Kyuhong Shim
Kyung Ho Park
Kyungmin Kim
Kyungsu Lee
Lam Phan
Lanlan Liu
Le Hui
Lei Ke
Lei Qi
Lei Yang
Lei Yu
Lei Zhu
Leila Mahmoodi
Li Jiao
Li Su
Lianyu Hu
Licheng Jiao
Lichi Zhang
Lihong Zheng
Lijun Zhao
Like Xin
Lin Gu
Lin Xuhong
Lincheng Li
Linghua Tang
Lingzhi Kong
Linlin Yang
Linsen Li
Litao Yu
Liu Liu
Liujie Hua
Li-Yun Wang
Loren Schwiebert
Lujia Jin
Lujun Li
Luping Zhou
Luting Wang

Mansi Sharma
Mantini Pranav
Mahmoud Zidan
  Khairallah
Manuel Günther
Marcella Astrid
Marco Piccirilli
Martin Kampel
Marwan Torki
Masaaki Iiyama
Masanori Suganuma
Masayuki Tanaka
Matan Jacoby
Md Alimoor Reza
Md. Zasim Uddin
Meghshyam Prasad
Mei-Chen Yeh
Meng Tang
Mengde Xu
Mengyang Pu
Mevan B. Ekanayake
Michael Bi Mi
Michael Wray
Michaël Clément
Michel Antunes
Michele Sasdelli
Mikhail Sizintsev
Min Peng
Min Zhang
Minchul Shin
Minesh Mathew
Ming Li
Ming Meng
Ming Yin
Ming-Ching Chang
Mingfei Cheng
Minghui Wang
Mingjun Hu
MingKun Yang
Mingxing Tan
Mingzhi Yuan
Min-Hung Chen
Minhyun Lee
Minjung Kim
Min-Kook Suh

Minkyo Seo
Minyi Zhao
Mo Zhou
Mohammad Amin A.
  Shabani
Moein Sorkhei
Mohit Agarwal
Monish K. Keswani
Muhammad Sarmad
Muhammad Kashif Ali
Myung-Woo Woo
Naeemullah Khan
Naman Solanki
Namyup Kim
Nan Gao
Nan Xue
Naoki Chiba
Naoto Inoue
Naresh P. Cuntoor
Nati Daniel
Neelanjan Bhowmik
Niaz Ahmad
Nicholas I. Kuo
Nicholas E. Rosa
Nicola Fioraio
Nicolas Dufour
Nicolas Papadakis
Ning Liu
Nishan Khatri
Ole Johannsen
P. Real Jurado
Parikshit V. Sakurikar
Patrick Peursum
Pavan Turaga
Peijie Chen
Peizhi Yan
Peng Wang
Pengfei Fang
Penghui Du
Pengpeng Liu
Phi Le Nguyen
Philippe Chiberre
Pierre Gleize
Pinaki Nath Chowdhury
Ping Hu

Ping Li
Ping Zhao
Pingping Zhang
Pradyumna Narayana
Pritish Sahu
Qi Li
Qi Wang
Qi Zhang
Qian Li
Qian Wang
Qiang Fu
Qiang Wu
Qiangxi Zhu
Qianying Liu
Qiaosi Yi
Qier Meng
Qin Liu
Qing Liu
Qing Wang
Qingheng Zhang
Qingjie Liu
Qinglin Liu
Qingsen Yan
Qingwei Tang
Qingyao Wu
Qingzheng Wang
Qizao Wang
Quang Hieu Pham
Rabab Abdelfattah
Rabab Ward
Radu Tudor Ionescu
Rahul Mitra
Raül Pérez i Gonzalo
Raymond A. Yeh
Ren Li
Renán Rojas-Gómez
Renjie Wan
Renuka Sharma
Reyer Zwiggelaar
Robin Chan
Robin Courant
Rohit Saluja
Rongkai Ma
Ronny Hänsch
Rui Liu

Rui Wang
Rui Zhu
Ruibing Hou
Ruikui Wang
Ruiqi Zhao
Ruixing Wang
Ryo Furukawa
Ryusuke Sagawa
Saimunur Rahman
Samet Akcay
Samitha Herath
Sanath Narayan
Sandesh Kamath
Sanghoon Jeon
Sanghyun Son
Satoshi Suzuki
Saumik Bhattacharya
Sauradip Nag
Scott Wehrwein
Sebastien Lefevre
Sehyun Hwang
Seiya Ito
Selen Pehlivan
Sena Kiciroglu
Seok Bong Yoo
Seokjun Park
Seongwoong Cho
Seoungyoon Kang
Seth Nixon
Seunghwan Lee
Seung-Ik Lee
Seungyong Lee
Shaifali Parashar
Shan Cao
Shan Zhang
Shangfei Wang
Shaojian Qiu
Shaoru Wang
Shao-Yuan Lo
Shengjin Wang
Shengqi Huang
Shenjian Gong
Shi Qiu
Shiguang Liu
Shih-Yao Lin

Shin-Jye Lee
Shishi Qiao
Shivam Chandhok
Shohei Nobuhara
Shreya Ghosh
Shuai Yuan
Shuang Yang
Shuangping Huang
Shuigeng Zhou
Shuiwang Li
Shunli Zhang
Shuo Gu
Shuoxin Lin
Shuzhi Yu
Sida Peng
Siddhartha Chandra
Simon S. Woo
Siwei Wang
Sixiang Chen
Siyu Xia
Sohyun Lee
Song Guo
Soochahn Lee
Soumava Kumar Roy
Srinjay Soumitra Sarkar
Stanislav Pidhorskyi
Stefan Gumhold
Stefan Matcovici
Stefano Berretti
Stylianos Moschoglou
Sudhir Yarram
Sudong Cai
Suho Yang
Sumitra S. Malagi
Sungeun Hong
Sunggu Lee
Sunghyun Cho
Sunghyun Myung
Sungmin Cho
Sungyeon Kim
Suzhen Wang
Sven Sickert
Syed Zulqarnain Gilani
Tackgeun You
Taehun Kim

Takao Yamanaka
Takashi Shibata
Takayoshi Yamashita
Takeshi Endo
Takeshi Ikenaga
Tanvir Alam
Tao Hong
Tarun Kalluri
Tat-Jen Cham
Tatsuya Yatagawa
Teck Yian Lim
Tejas Indulal Dhamecha
Tengfei Shi
Thanh-Dat Truong
Thomas Probst
Thuan Hoang Nguyen
Tian Ye
Tianlei Jin
Tianwei Cao
Tianyi Shi
Tianyu Song
Tianyu Wang
Tien-Ju Yang
Tingting Fang
Tobias Baumgartner
Toby P. Breckon
Torsten Sattler
Trung Tuan Dao
Trung Le
Tsung-Hsuan Wu
Tuan-Anh Vu
Utkarsh Ojha
Utku Ozbulak
Vaasudev Narayanan
Venkata Siva Kumar
    Margapuri
Vandit J. Gajjar
Vi Thi Tuong Vo
Victor Fragoso
Vikas Desai
Vincent Lepetit
Vinh Tran
Viresh Ranjan
Wai-Kin Adams Kong
Wallace Michel Pinto Lira

Walter Liao
Wang Yan
Wang Yong
Wataru Shimoda
Wei Feng
Wei Mao
Wei Xu
Weibo Liu
Weichen Xu
Weide Liu
Weidong Chen
Weihong Deng
Wei-Jong Yang
Weikai Chen
Weishi Zhang
Weiwei Fang
Weixin Lu
Weixin Luo
Weiyao Wang
Wenbin Wang
Wenguan Wang
Wenhan Luo
Wenju Wang
Wenlei Liu
Wenqing Chen
Wenwen Yu
Wenxing Bao
Wenyu Liu
Wenzhao Zheng
Whie Jung
Williem Williem
Won Hwa Kim
Woohwan Jung
Wu Yirui
Wu Yufeng
Wu Yunjie
Wugen Zhou
Wujie Sun
Wuman Luo
Xi Wang
Xianfang Sun
Xiang Chen
Xiang Li
Xiangbo Shu
Xiangcheng Liu

Xiangyu Wang
Xiao Wang
Xiao Yan
Xiaobing Wang
Xiaodong Wang
Xiaofeng Wang
Xiaofeng Yang
Xiaogang Xu
Xiaogen Zhou
Xiaohan Yu
Xiaoheng Jiang
Xiaohua Huang
Xiaoke Shen
Xiaolong Liu
Xiaoqin Zhang
Xiaoqing Liu
Xiaosong Wang
Xiaowen Ma
Xiaoyi Zhang
Xiaoyu Wu
Xieyuanli Chen
Xin Chen
Xin Jin
Xin Wang
Xin Zhao
Xindong Zhang
Xingjian He
Xingqun Qi
Xinjie Li
Xinqi Fan
Xinwei He
Xinyan Liu
Xinyu He
Xinyue Zhang
Xiyuan Hu
Xu Cao
Xu Jia
Xu Yang
Xuan Luo
Xubo Yang
Xudong Lin
Xudong Xie
Xuefeng Liang
Xuehui Wang
Xuequan Lu

Xuesong Yang
Xueyan Zou
XuHu Lin
Xun Zhou
Xupeng Wang
Yali Zhang
Ya-Li Li
Yalin Zheng
Yan Di
Yan Luo
Yan Xu
Yang Cao
Yang Hu
Yang Song
Yang Zhang
Yang Zhao
Yangyang Shu
Yani A. Ioannou
Yaniv Nemcovsky
Yanjun Zhu
Yanling Hao
Yanling Tian
Yao Guo
Yao Lu
Yao Zhou
Yaping Zhao
Yasser Benigmim
Yasunori Ishii
Yasushi Yagi
Yawei Li
Ye Ding
Ye Zhu
Yeongnam Chae
Yeying Jin
Yi Cao
Yi Liu
Yi Rong
Yi Tang
Yi Wei
Yi Xu
Yichun Shi
Yifan Zhang
Yikai Wang
Yikang Ding
Yiming Liu

Yiming Qian
Yin Li
Yinghuan Shi
Yingjian Li
Yingkun Xu
Yingshu Chen
Yingwei Pan
Yiping Tang
Yiqing Shen
Yisheng Zhu
Yitian Li
Yizhou Yu
Yoichi Sato
Yong A.
Yongcai Wang
Yongheng Ren
Yonghuai Liu
Yongjun Zhang
Yongkang Luo
Yongkang Wong
Yongpei Zhu
Yongqiang Zhang
Yongrui Ma
Yoshimitsu Aoki
Yoshinori Konishi
Young Jun Heo
Young Min Shin
Youngmoon Lee
Youpeng Zhao
Yu Ding
Yu Feng
Yu Zhang
Yuanbin Wang
Yuang Wang
Yuanhong Chen
Yuanyuan Qiao
Yucong Shen
Yuda Song
Yue Huang
Yufan Liu
Yuguang Yan
Yuhan Xie
Yu-Hsuan Chen
Yu-Hui Wen
Yujiao Shi

Yujin Ren
Yuki Tatsunami
Yukuan Jia
Yukun Su
Yu-Lun Liu
Yun Liu
Yunan Liu
Yunce Zhao
Yun-Chun Chen
Yunhao Li
Yunlong Liu
Yunlong Meng
Yunlu Chen
Yunqian He
Yunzhong Hou
Yuqiu Kong
Yusuke Hosoya
Yusuke Matsui
Yusuke Morishita
Yusuke Sugano
Yuta Kudo
Yu-Ting Wu
Yutong Dai
Yuxi Hu
Yuxi Yang
Yuxuan Li
Yuxuan Zhang
Yuzhen Lin
Yuzhi Zhao
Yvain Queau
Zanwei Zhou
Zebin Guo
Ze-Feng Gao
Zejia Fan
Zekun Yang
Zelin Peng
Zelong Zeng
Zenglin Xu
Zewei Wu
Zhan Li
Zhan Shi
Zhe Li
Zhe Liu
Zhe Zhang
Zhedong Zheng

Zhenbo Xu
Zheng Gu
Zhenhua Tang
Zhenkun Wang
Zhenyu Weng
Zhi Zeng
Zhiguo Cao
Zhijie Rao
Zhijie Wang
Zhijun Zhang
Zhimin Gao
Zhipeng Yu
Zhiqiang Hu
Zhisong Liu
Zhiwei Hong
Zhiwei Xu

Zhiwu Lu
Zhixiang Wang
Zhixin Li
Zhiyong Dai
Zhiyong Huang
Zhiyuan Zhang
Zhonghua Wu
Zhongyan Zhang
Zhongzheng Yuan
Zhu Hu
Zhu Meng
Zhujun Li
Zhulun Yang
Zhuojun Zou
Ziang Cheng
Zichuan Liu

Zihan Ding
Zihao Zhang
Zijiang Song
Zijin Yin
Ziqiang Zheng
Zitian Wang
Ziwei Yao
Zixun Zhang
Ziyang Luo
Ziyi Bai
Ziyi Wang
Zongheng Tang
Zongsheng Cao
Zongwei Wu
Zoran Duric

Contents – Part VI

Deep Learning for Computer Vision

Biomedical Image Analysis

HiCo: Hierarchical Contrastive Learning for Ultrasound Video Model Pretraining

Chunhui Zhang[1,2] , Yixiong Chen[3,4] , Li Liu[3,4(✉)] , Qiong Liu[2] ,
and Xi Zhou[1,2]

[1] Shanghai Jiaotong University, Shanghai 200240, China
[2] CloudWalk Technology Co., Ltd., Shanghai 201203, China
[3] The Chinese University of Hong Kong (Shenzhen), Shenzhen 518172, China
liuli@cuhk.edu.cn
[4] Shenzhen Research Institute of Big Data, Shenzhen 518172, China

Abstract. The self-supervised ultrasound (US) video model pretraining can use a small amount of labeled data to achieve one of the most promising results on US diagnosis. However, it does not take full advantage of multi-level knowledge for learning deep neural networks (DNNs), and thus is difficult to learn transferable feature representations. This work proposes a hierarchical contrastive learning (HiCo) method to improve the transferability for the US video model pretraining. HiCo introduces both peer-level semantic alignment and cross-level semantic alignment to facilitate the interaction between different semantic levels, which can effectively accelerate the convergence speed, leading to better generalization and adaptation of the learned model. Additionally, a softened objective function is implemented by smoothing the hard labels, which can alleviate the negative effect caused by local similarities of images between different classes. Experiments with HiCo on five datasets demonstrate its favorable results over state-of-the-art approaches. The source code of this work is publicly available at https://github.com/983632847/HiCo.

1 Introduction

Thanks to the cost-effectiveness, safety, and portability, combined with a reasonable sensitivity to a wide variety of pathologies, ultrasound (US) has become one of the most common medical imaging techniques in clinical diagnosis [1]. To mitigate sonographers' reading burden and improve diagnosis efficiency, automatic US analysis using deep learning is becoming popular [2–5]. In the past decades, a successful practice is to train a deep neural network (DNN) on a large number of well-labeled US images within the supervised learning paradigm [1,6]. However, annotations of US images and videos can be expensive to obtain and sometimes infeasible to access because of the expertise requirements and time-consuming reading, which motivates the development of US diagnosis that requires few or even no manual annotations.

In recent years, pretraining combined with fine-tuning has attracted great attention because it can transfer knowledge learned on large amounts of unlabeled or weakly labeled data to downstream tasks, especially when the amount

© The Author(s), under exclusive license to Springer Nature Switzerland AG 2023
L. Wang et al. (Eds.): ACCV 2022, LNCS 13846, pp. 3–20, 2023.
https://doi.org/10.1007/978-3-031-26351-4_1

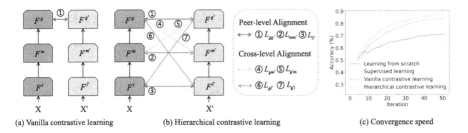

(a) Vanilla contrastive learning   (b) Hierarchical contrastive learning   (c) Convergence speed

Fig. 1. Motivation of hierarchical contrastive learning. Unlike (a) vanilla contrastive learning, our (b) hierarchical contrastive learning can fully take advantage of both peer-level and cross-level information. Thus, (c) the pretraining model from our proposed hierarchical contrastive learning can accelerate the convergence speed, which is much better than learning from scratch, supervised learning, and vanilla contrastive learning.

of labeled data is limited. This has also profoundly affected the field of US diagnosis, which started to pretrain models from massive unlabeled US data according to a pretext task. To learn meaningful and strong representations, the US video pretraining methods are designed to correct the order of a reshuffled video clip, predict the geometric transformation applied to the video clip or colorize a grayscale image to its color version equivalent [7,8]. Inspired by the powerful ability of contrastive learning (CL) [9,10] in computer vision, some recent studies propose to learn US video representations by CL [3,11], and showed a powerful learning capability [11,12]. However, most of the existing US video pretraining methods following the vanilla contrastive learning setting [10,13], only use the output of a certain layer of a DNN for contrast (see Fig. 1(a)). Although the CL methods are usually better than learning from scratch and supervised learning, the lack of multi-level information interaction will inevitably degrade the transferability of pretrained models [3,14].

To address the above issue, we first propose a hierarchical contrastive learning (HiCo) method for US video model pretraining. The main motivation is to design a *feature-based* peer-level and cross-level semantic alignment method (see Fig. 1(b)) to improve the efficiency of learning and enhance the ability of feature representation. Specially, based on the assumption that the top layer of a DNN has strong semantic information, and the bottom layer has high-resolution local information (*e.g.*, texture and shape) [15], we design a joint learning task to force the model to learn multi-level semantic representations during the CL process: minimize the peer-level semantic alignment loss (*i.e.*, ① global CL loss, ② medium CL loss, and ③ local CL loss) and cross-level semantic alignment loss (*i.e.*, ④, ⑤ global-medium CL losses, and ⑥, ⑦ global-local CL losses) simultaneously. Intuitively, our framework can greatly improve the convergence speed of the model (*i.e.*, providing a good initialized model for downstream tasks) (see Fig. 1(c)), due to the sufficient interaction of peer-level and cross-level information. Different from existing methods [16–20], this work assumes that the knowledge inside the backbone is sufficient but underutilized, so that simple yet effective peer-level and cross-level semantic alignments can be used to enhance feature representation other than designing a complex structure. In addition, medical images from different classes/lesions may have significant local similarities (*e.g.*, normal and infected individuals have similar regions of tissues and organs unrelated to disease), which is more severe than natural images. Thus, we follow the popular label smoothing strategy to design a *batch-based* softened objective function during the pretraining to avoid the model being over-confident, which alleviates the negative effect caused by local similarities.

The main contributions of this work can be summarized as follows:

1) We propose a novel hierarchical contrastive learning method for US video model pretraining, which can make full use of the multi-level knowledge inside a DNN via peer-level semantic alignment and cross-level semantic alignment.
2) We soften one-hot labels during the pretraining process to avoid the model being over-confident, alleviating the negative effect caused by local similarities of images between different classes.
3) Experiments on five downstream tasks demonstrate the effectiveness of our approach in learning transferable representations.

2   Related Work

We first review related works on supervised learning for US diagnosis and then discuss the self-supervised representation learning.

2.1   US Diagnosis

With the rise of deep learning in computer vision, supervised learning became the most common strategy in US diagnosis with DNN [1,3,21–23]. In the last decades, numerous datasets and methods have been introduced for US image classification [24], detection [25] and segmentation [26] tasks. For example, some US image datasets with labeled data were designed for breast cancer classification [27,28], breast US lesions detection [25], diagnosis of malignant thyroid nodule [29,30], and automated measurement of the fetal head circumference [31]. At the same time, many deep learning approaches have been done on lung US [32,33], B-line detection or quantification [34,35], pleural line extraction [36], and subpleural pulmonary lesions [37]. Compared with image-based datasets, recent video-based US datasets [1,3] are becoming much richer and can provide more diverse categories and data modalities (*e.g.*, convex and linear probe US images [3]). Thus, many works are focused on video-based US diagnosis within the supervised learning paradigm. In [1], a frame-based model was proposed to correctly distinguish COVID-19 lung US videos from healthy and bacterial pneumonia data. Other works focus on quality assessment for medical US video compressing [38], localizing target structures [39], or describing US video content [2]. Until recently, many advanced DNNs (*e.g.*, UNet [40], DeepLab [41,42], Transformer [43]), and technologies (*e.g.*, neural architecture search [44], reinforcement learning [45], meta-learning [46]) have brought great advances in supervised learning for US diagnosis. Unfortunately, US diagnosis using supervised learning highly relies on large-scale labeled, often expensive medical datasets.

2.2 Self-supervised Learning

Recently, many self-supervised learning methods for visual feature representation learning have been developed without using any human-annotated labels [47–49]. Existing self-supervised learning methods can be divided into two main categories, *i.e.*, learning via pretext tasks and CL. A wide range of pretext tasks have been proposed to facilitate the development of self-supervised learning. Examples include solving jigsaw puzzles [50], colorization [8], image context restoration [51], and relative patch prediction [52]. However, many of these tasks rely on ad-hoc heuristics that could limit the generalization and robustness of learned feature representations for downstream tasks [10,13]. The CL has emerged as the front-runner for self-supervision representation learning and has demonstrated remarkable performance on downstream tasks. Unlike learning via pretext tasks, CL is a discriminative approach that aims at grouping similar positive samples closer and repelling negative samples. To achieve this, a similarity metric is used to measure how close two feature embeddings are. For computer vision tasks, a standard loss function, *i.e.*, Noise-Contrastive Estimation loss (InfoNCE) [53], is evaluated based on the feature representations of images extracted from a backbone network (*e.g.*, ResNet [22]). Most successful CL approaches are focused on studying effective contrastive loss, generation of positive and negative pairs, and sampling method [9,10]. SimCLR [10] is a simple framework for CL of visual representations with strong data augmentations and a large training batch size. MoCo [9] builds a dynamic dictionary with a queue and a moving-averaged encoder. Other works explores learning without negative samples [54,55], and incorporating self-supervised learning with visual transformers [56], *etc.*

Considering the superior performance of contrastive self-supervised learning in computer vision and medical imaging tasks, this work follows the line of CL. First, we propose both peer-level and cross-level alignments to speed up the convergence of the model learning, compared with the existing CL methods, which usually use the output of a certain layer of the network for contrast (see Fig. 1). Second, we design a softened objective function to facilitate the CL by addressing the negative effect of local similarities between different classes.

3   Hierarchical Contrastive Learning

In this section, we present our HiCo approach for US video model pretraining. To this end, we first introduce the preliminary of CL, after that present the peer-level semantic alignment and cross-level semantic alignment, and then describe the softened objective function. The framework of HiCo is illustrated in Fig. 2.

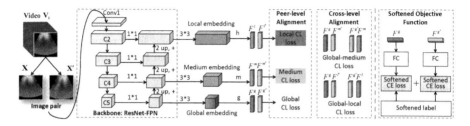

Fig. 2. Overall framework of the proposed HiCo, which consists of peer-level semantic alignment, cross-level semantic alignment, and softened objective function. 1) We extract two images from each US video as a positive sample pair. 2) We use ResNet-FPN as the backbone to obtain the local, medium and global embeddings, followed by three projection heads h, m and g. 3) The entire network is optimized by minimizing peer-level semantic alignment loss (*i.e.*, local CL loss, medium CL loss and global CL loss), cross-level semantic alignment loss (*i.e.*, global-medium CL loss and global-local CL loss), and the softened CE loss.

3.1 Preliminary

The vanilla contrastive learning learns a global feature encoder Φ and a projection head g that map the image X into a feature vector $\mathbf{F} = g(\Phi(X)) \in \mathbb{R}_d$ by minimizing the InfoNCE loss [53]:

$$\mathscr{L}_{nce}(\mathbf{F}_i, \mathbf{F}_j) = -\log \frac{exp(sim(\mathbf{F}_i, \mathbf{F}_j)/\tau)}{\sum_{k=1}^{2N} \mathbb{1}_{[k \neq i]} exp(sim(\mathbf{F}_i, \mathbf{F}_k)/\tau)}. \tag{1}$$

where $(\mathbf{F}_i, \mathbf{F}_j)$ are the global feature vectors of the two views of image X, N is the batch size. $sim(\mathbf{F}_i, \mathbf{F}_j) = \mathbf{F}_i \cdot \mathbf{F}_j / (\|\mathbf{F}_i\|\|\mathbf{F}_j\|)$ denotes the cosine similarity, $\mathbb{1}_{k \neq i} \in \{0, 1\}$ is an indicator function evaluating to 1 iff $k \neq i$, and τ is a tuning temperature parameter.

In practice, Φ is a DNN (*e.g.*, ResNet [22]) and the objective function is minimized using stochastic gradient descent. The two feature vectors of the one image are a positive pair, while the other $2(N-1)$ examples within a mini-batch are treated as negative examples. The positive and negative contrastive feature pairs are usually the global representations (*e.g.*, the output from the last layer of a DNN) that lack multi-scale information from different feature layers, which are important for downstream tasks. In addition, having a large number of negative samples is critical while minimizing the InfoNCE loss. Hence, a large batch size (*e.g.*, 4096 in SimCLR [10]) is required during the pretraining.

To address the above problem, we explore multi-level semantic alignments for CL, peer-level and cross-level ones (see Fig. 2). Specifically, we use ResNet-FPN as the backbone. For each image pair, we extract two local feature vectors ($\mathbf{F}^l$ and $\mathbf{F}^{l'}$), two medium feature vectors ($\mathbf{F}^m$ and $\mathbf{F}^{m'}$) and two global feature vectors ($\mathbf{F}^g$ and $\mathbf{F}^{g'}$) from Conv2 (C2), Conv4 (C4) and Conv5 (C5), respectively. We then optimize the peer-level and cross-level alignments simultaneously.

3.2   Peer-level Semantic Alignment

Fine-grained Contrast. The $\mathbf{F}^l$ and $\mathbf{F}^{l'}$ encode the fine-grained local information (*e.g.*, edges and shapes) of original images. Such fine-grained information is useful for US diagnosis, but is usually ignored in existing CL algorithms. To leverage the fine-grained information, we define the local CL loss $\mathcal{L}_{ll'}^{local}$ as

$$\mathcal{L}_{ll'}^{local} = \frac{1}{2N} \sum_{i=1}^{N} (\mathcal{L}_{nce}(\mathbf{F}_i^l, \mathbf{F}_i^{l'}) + \mathcal{L}_{nce}(\mathbf{F}_i^{l'}, \mathbf{F}_i^l)), \tag{2}$$

where N denotes the batch size, $\mathcal{L}_{nce}(\cdot)$ is the InfoNCE loss [53].

Medium-Grained Contrast. Considering that $\mathbf{F}^m$ and $\mathbf{F}^{m'}$ capture medium-grained information of original images, we therefore define the medium CL loss $\mathcal{L}_{mm'}^{medium}$ as

$$\mathcal{L}_{mm'}^{medium} = \frac{1}{2N} \sum_{i=1}^{N} (\mathcal{L}_{nce}(\mathbf{F}_i^m, \mathbf{F}_i^{m'}) + \mathcal{L}_{nce}(\mathbf{F}_i^{m'}, \mathbf{F}_i^m)), \tag{3}$$

Notably, we find that medium-grained information demonstrate complementary superiority relative to fine-grained and global information, further improving model performance (see Sect. 4.2 Table 1).

Coarse-Grained Contrast. Owing to $\mathbf{F}^g$ and $\mathbf{F}^{g'}$ capture coarse-grained global information of original images, we hope to reach a consensus among their representations by maximizing the similarity between global embeddings from the same video, while minimizing the similarity between the global embeddings from different videos. Thus, the global CL loss $\mathcal{L}_{gg'}^{global}$ can be defined as

$$\mathcal{L}_{gg'}^{global} = \frac{1}{2N} \sum_{i=1}^{N} (\mathcal{L}_{nce}(\mathbf{F}_i^g, \mathbf{F}_i^{g'}) + \mathcal{L}_{nce}(\mathbf{F}_i^{g'}, \mathbf{F}_i^g)), \tag{4}$$

3.3   Cross-Level Semantic Alignment

Global-Local Contrast. We regard the global feature vector $\mathbf{F}^g$ as the *anchor* of the local feature vector $\mathbf{F}^{l'}$, because it contains the global semantic information of the original image and shares some semantic content with the local feature vector. Thus, we define the global-local objective $\mathcal{L}_{gl'}$ to make the local feature vectors move closer to the global ones as

$$\mathcal{L}_{gl'} = \frac{1}{2N} \sum_{i=1}^{N} (\mathcal{L}_{nce}(\mathbf{F}_i^g, \mathbf{F}_i^{l'}) + \mathcal{L}_{nce}(\mathbf{F}_i^{l'}, \mathbf{F}_i^g)), \tag{5}$$

The $\mathcal{L}_{g'l}$ can be calculated similarly. Then, the global-local CL loss can be written as $\mathcal{L}_{local}^{global} = \mathcal{L}_{gl'} + \mathcal{L}_{g'l}$.

Algorithm 1. Hierarchical Contrastive Learning

Input: US videos $\mathbf{V}$, backbone Φ, projection heads g, m, h, linear classifier f_θ, hyperparameters λ, α, β, max epoch e_{max}, batch size N.
Output: pretrained backbone Φ.
1: random initialize Φ, g, m, h, and f_θ
2: **for** $e = 1, 2, ..., e_{max}$ **do**
3:      **for** random sampled US videos $\{\mathbf{V}_i\}_{i=1}^N$ **do**
4:          # extract two images from each US video as a positive sample pair.
5:          random sample $\{(\mathbf{x}_i^{(1)}, \mathbf{x}_i^{(2)}), \mathbf{y}_i\}_{i=1}^N$ into mini-batch
6:          **for** $i \in \{1, ..., N\}$ **do**
7:              # Augment image pair for each US video.
8:              random cropping, resizing, ipping, and color jitter
9:              # Get local, medium and global embeddings.
10:              $\mathbf{F}_i^l = h(\Phi(\mathbf{x}_i^{(1)})), \mathbf{F}_i^{l'} = h(\Phi(\mathbf{x}_i^{(2)}))$;
11:              $\mathbf{F}_i^m = m(\Phi(\mathbf{x}_i^{(1)})), \mathbf{F}_i^{m'} = m(\Phi(\mathbf{x}_i^{(2)}))$;
12:              $\mathbf{F}_i^g = g(\Phi(\mathbf{x}_i^{(1)})), \mathbf{F}_i^{g'} = g(\Phi(\mathbf{x}_i^{(2)}))$;
13:              # Get outputs of the linear classifier.
14:              $\mathbf{o}_i = f_\theta(\mathbf{F}_i^g), \mathbf{o}_i' = f_\theta(\mathbf{F}_i^{g'})$
15:      # peer-level semantic alignment
16:      **for** $i \in \{1, ..., N\}$ **do**
17:          calculate the local CL loss $\mathcal{L}_{ll'}^{local}$ by Eq. (2)
18:          calculate the medium CL loss $\mathcal{L}_{mm'}^{medium}$ by Eq. (3)
19:          calculate the global CL loss $\mathcal{L}_{gg'}^{global}$ by Eq. (4)
20:      # cross-level semantic alignment
21:      **for** $i \in \{1, ..., N\}$ **do**
22:          calculate the global-local CL loss $\mathcal{L}_{local}^{global}$ by Eq. (5)
23:          calculate the global-medium CL loss $\mathcal{L}_{medium}^{global}$
24:      calculate the overall CL loss $\mathcal{L}^{con}$ by Eq. (6)
25:      calculate the softened CE loss $\mathcal{L}^{soften}$ by Eq. (8)
26:      $\mathcal{L} = \mathcal{L}^{con} + \beta\mathcal{L}^{soften}$
27:      update Φ, g, m, h, and f_θ through gradient descent
28: **return** pretrained Φ, discard g, m, h, and f_θ

Global-Medium Contrast. Similar to the global-local CL loss, the global-medium CL loss can be written as $\mathcal{L}_{medium}^{global} = \mathcal{L}_{gm'} + \mathcal{L}_{g'm}$.

Therefore, the overall CL loss of HiCo is formulated as

$$\mathcal{L}^{con} = \lambda(\mathcal{L}_{ll'}^{local} + \mathcal{L}_{mm'}^{medium} + \mathcal{L}_{gg'}^{global}) + (1 - \lambda)(\mathcal{L}_{local}^{global} + \mathcal{L}_{medium}^{global}), \quad (6)$$

where λ is a trade-off coefficient, the first three terms $\mathcal{L}_{ll'}^{local}$, $\mathcal{L}_{mm'}^{medium}$ and $\mathcal{L}_{gg'}^{global}$ represent the peer-level semantic alignment objective functions, while the last two terms $\mathcal{L}_{local}^{global}$ and $\mathcal{L}_{medium}^{global}$ represent the cross-level semantic alignment objective functions.

3.4   Softened Objective Function

The one-hot label assumes there is absolutely no similarity between different classes. However, in medical imaging, the images from different classes may have some local similarities (*e.g.*, the tissues and organs unrelated to diseases). Thus, we propose the softened objective function to alleviate the negative effect caused by local similarities. We first define the corresponding softened label $\widetilde{\mathbf{y}}_i$ as

$$\widetilde{\mathbf{y}}_i = (1 - \alpha)\mathbf{y}_i + \alpha/(N - 1), \tag{7}$$

where $\mathbf{y}_i$ is the original one-hot label, α is a smoothing hyper-parameter, and N is the number of videos in a training batch. Then the softened cross-entropy (CE) loss $\mathcal{L}^{soften}$ with corresponding softened label $\widetilde{\mathbf{y}}_i$ is formulated as

$$\mathcal{L}^{soften} = \frac{1}{2N} \sum_{i=1}^{N} (CE(\mathbf{o}_i, \widetilde{\mathbf{y}}_i) + CE(\mathbf{o}'_i, \widetilde{\mathbf{y}}_i)), \tag{8}$$

where $\mathbf{o}_i = f_\theta(\mathbf{F}_i^g)$, $\mathbf{o}'_i = f_\theta(\mathbf{F}_i^{g'})$, and f_θ is a linear classifier.

Finally, the total loss can be written as

$$\mathcal{L} = \mathcal{L}^{con} + \beta\mathcal{L}^{soften}, \tag{9}$$

where the parameter β is used to balance the total CL loss and softened CE loss. The whole algorithm is summarized in Algorithm 1.

4   Experiments

4.1   Experimental Settings

Network Architective. In our experiments, we apply the widely used ResNet18-FPN [57] network as the backbone. Conv2 to Conv5 are followed by a convolution layer with kernel size of 1*1 to obtain intermediate feature maps. In the FPN structure, we double upsampling the intermediate feature maps, and then add them to the intermediate feature maps of the previous layer. The intermediate feature maps are followed by a convolution layer with kernel size of 3*3 to obtain local embedding, medium embedding, and global embedding, respectively. All convolution layers are followed by batch normalization and ReLU. The projection heads h, m, and g are all 1-layer MLP. After the projection heads, the local, medium, and global embeddings are reduced to 256-dimensional feature vectors for CL tasks. The linear classifier is a fully connected (FC) layer.

Pretraining Details. We use the US-4 [3] video dataset (lung and liver) for pretraining and fine-tune the last 3 layers of pretrained models on various downstream tasks to evaluate the transferability of the proposed US video pretraining models. During the pretraining process, the input images are randomly cropped and resized to 224*224, followed by random flipping and color jitter. The pre-training epoch and batch size are set to 300 and 32, respectively. The parameters of models are obtained by optimizing the loss functions via an Adam optimizer with a learning rate 3×10^{-4} and a weight decay rate 10^{-4}. Following the popular CL evaluations [10], the backbone is used for fine-tuning on downstream tasks, projection heads (h, m, and g) and linear classifier (f_θ) are discarded when the pretraining is completed. The $\tau = 0.5$ is a tuning temperature parameter as in SimCLR [10]. We empirically set $\lambda = 0.5$, indicating that peer-level semantic alignment and cross-level semantic alignment have equal weights in the CL loss. The smoothing parameter α set to 0.2 indicates slight label smoothing. The β is empirically set to 0.2, indicating that the CL loss dominates the total loss. All experiments were implemented using PyTorch and a single RTX 3090 GPU.

Downstream Datasets. We fine-tune our pretrained backbones on four US datasets (POCUS [1], Thyroid US [29], and BUSI-BUI [27,28] joint dataset), and a chest X-ray dataset (COVID-Xray-5k [58]) to evaluate the transferability of our pretraining models. For fair comparisons, all fine-tuning results on downstream datasets are obtained with 5-fold cross-validation. The POCUS is a lung convex probe US dataset for pneumonia detection that contains 2116 frames across 140 videos from three categories (COVID-19, bacterial pneumonia and the regular). The BUSI contains 780 breast tumor US images from three classes (the normal, benign and malignant), while BUI consists of 250 breast cancer US images with 100 benign and 150 malignant. Thyroid US [29] dataset contains thyroid images with 61 benign and 288 malignant. Note that the BUSI, BUI and Thyroid US datasets are collected with linear probes. The COVID-Xray-5k is a chest X-ray dataset that contains 2084 training and 3100 test images from two classes (COVID-19 and the normal). In our fine-tuning experiments, the learning rate, weight decay rate and epoch are set to 10^{-2}, 10^{-4} and 30, respectively. The performance is assessed with Precision, Recall, Accuracy or F1 score.

4.2 Ablation Studies

In this section, we verify the effectiveness of each component in our approach on the downstream POCUS pneumonia detection task, and all the models are pretrained on the US-4 dataset.

Peer-Level Semantic Alignment. The impact of peer-level semantic alignment is summarized in Table 1. We reimplement the self-supervised method Sim-CLR [10] with ResNet18 (w/o FPN) as our baseline. We can find that the baseline cannot achieve satisfying performance (85.6%, 87.0% and 86.9% in terms of Precision, Recall and Accuracy, respectively). The effectiveness of fine-grained contrast, medium-grained contrast and coarse-grained contrast can be verified by comparing backbones pretrained using $\mathcal{L}_{ll'}^{local}$, $\mathcal{L}_{mm'}^{medium}$, $\mathcal{L}_{gg'}^{global}$ with the baseline, which contribute to the absolute performance gains of 1.4%, 2.7% and 3.2% in terms of Accuracy. In addition, better or comparable results can be achieved when using two

Table 1. Impact of peer-level semantic alignment. The models are pretrained on US-4 and fine-tuned on POCUS dataset.

$\mathcal{L}_{ll'}^{local}$	$\mathcal{L}_{mm'}^{medium}$	$\mathcal{L}_{gg'}^{global}$	Precision (%)	Recall (%)	Accuracy (%)
			85.6	87.0	86.9
✓			87.6	87.5	88.3
	✓		87.9	90.2	89.6
		✓	90.5	89.8	90.1
✓	✓		89.3	89.5	90.1
✓		✓	91.0	90.7	90.5
	✓	✓	91.9	92.3	91.9
✓	✓	✓	91.3	92.3	92.0

Table 2. Impact of cross-level semantic alignment. The models are pretrained on US-4 and fine-tuned on the POCUS dataset.

$\mathcal{L}_{medium}^{global}$	$\mathcal{L}_{local}^{global}$	Precision (%)	Recall (%)	Accuracy (%)
		85.6	87.0	86.9
✓		88.0	89.6	89.4
	✓	90.4	91.1	90.8
✓	✓	89.4	90.8	90.9

contrasts (*e.g.*, coarse-grained contrast and medium-grained contrast) than a single contrast (*e.g.*, coarse-grained contrast). Considering the excellent performance of backbones when using only the global CL loss (*i.e.*, an Accuracy of 90.1%), and using both the global CL loss and the medium CL loss (*i.e.*, an Accuracy of 91.9%), we argue that coarse-grained global information is very important to improve the transferability of pretrained US models. The best performance is achieved when all three peer-level semantic contrasts are used.

Cross-Level Semantic Alignment. The impact of cross-level semantic alignment is summarized in Table 2. In previous experiments, we find that global information is pivotal to CL tasks. Therefore, when performing cross-level semantic alignment, we regard the global feature as an *anchor*, and only consider aligning the local features and the middle-level features with the global features (*i.e.*, global-local contrast and global-medium contrast). From Table 2, we can observe that consistent performance gains are achieved by conducting global-local contrast and global-medium contrast in terms of Precision, Recall and Accuracy. When global-local contrast and global-medium contrast are performed at the same time, our pretrained model can achieve the best performance in terms of Accuracy (*i.e.*, 90.9%). However, using the proposed peer-level semantic alignment can achieve the best Accuracy of 92.0% as shown in Table 1. Therefore, it is difficult to learn better transferable representations by using cross-level semantic alignment alone. Next, we will demonstrate that using the peer-level semantic alignment and cross-level semantic alignment at the same time can bring significant performance gains.

Table 3. Ablation study of each component in our approach. The models are pretrained on US-4 and fine-tuned on POCUS dataset.

$\mathcal{L}_{ll'}^{local}$	$\mathcal{L}_{mm'}^{medium}$	$\mathcal{L}_{gg'}^{global}$	$\mathcal{L}_{medium}^{global}$	$\mathcal{L}_{local}^{global}$	$\mathcal{L}^{soften}$	Precision (%)	Recall (%)	Accuracy (%)
						85.6	87.0	86.9
✓						87.6	87.5	88.3
✓	✓					89.3	89.5	90.1
✓	✓	✓				91.3	92.3	92.0
✓	✓	✓	✓			92.2	93.2	93.2
✓	✓	✓	✓	✓		93.5	94.2	94.4
✓	✓	✓	✓	✓	✓	94.6	94.9	94.7

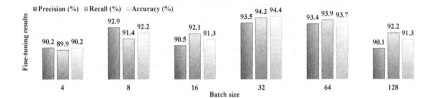

Fig. 3. Impact of batch size. Fine-tuning results obtained on POCUS dataset with different batch sizes.

Ablation Study of Each Component. The impact of each component in our approach is summarized in Table 3. We can see that each component can bring a certain performance improvement to our final method, which verifies the effectiveness of each component. An interesting observation is that our method (an Accuracy of 94.4%) without using labels can surpass the current state-of-the-art semi-supervised method USCL (an Accuracy of 94.2%) and supervised method (an Accuracy of 85.0%) on POCUS dataset (see Tables 3 and 4). This result demonstrates the superiority of peer-level semantic alignment and cross-level semantic alignment for learning transferable representations. In addition, the softened objective function can further facilitate the performance of our approach (from 94.4% to 94.7% in terms of Accuracy).

Impact of Batch Size. The effect of batch size is shown in Fig. 3. We can observe that as the batch size increases, the overall performance demonstrates a trend from rising to decline, where the best overall performance is achieved when the batch size is 32. Compared with existing state-of-the-art CL algorithms that rely on large batch sizes (more negative samples), *e.g.*, 1024 in MoCo [9], 2048 in SimCLR [10], to achieve convergence, our proposed method is easier to optimize. In this way, we can train the model in fewer epochs and steps to obtain a given accuracy. We argue that the multi-level contrast promotes the effective and sufficient interaction of information from different layers of a DNN, thus we can use a smaller batch size.

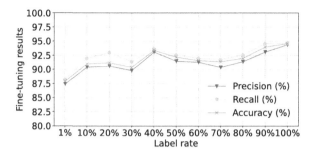

Fig. 4. Impact of the label rate. Fine-tuning results obtained on POCUS dataset with different label rates.

Impact of Label Rate. The effect of label rate is shown in Fig. 4. We pretrain eleven models on US-4 dataset with different label rates. We find that the performance of models gradually improve with the increase of label, as more label can bring stronger supervision signals to promote the process of pretraining.

4.3   Comparison with State-of-the-Art Methods

To verify the effectiveness of our approach, we compare the proposed HiCo with supervised ResNet18 backbones (*i.e.*, "ImageNet" pretrained on ImageNet dataset, "Supervised" pretrained on US-4 dataset), and other backbones pretrained on US-4 dataset with semi-supervised methods (*i.e.*, Temporal Ensembling (TE) [59], Π Model [59], FixMatch [60], USCL [3]) and self-supervised methods (*i.e.*, MoCo v2 [13], SimCLR [10]).

POCUS Pneumonia Detection. On POCUS, we fine-tune the last three layers to verify the transferability of pretrained backbones on the pneumonia detection task. The results are summarized in Table 4. We report the Accuracy of three classes (*i.e.*, COVID-19, pneumonia and the regular), total Accuracy and F1 scores on POCUS. The proposed HiCo achieves the best performance in terms of total Accuracy (*i.e.*, 94.7%) and F1 (94.6%) scores, which are significantly better than other supervised, semi-supervised and self-supervised methods. HiCo also obtains the best Accuracy on COVID-19 and pneumonia classes, and the second-best Accuracy on the regular. USCL achieves the best Accuracy on the regular, which is a semi-supervised CL method with a carefully designed sample pair generation strategy for US video sampling. Compared with USCL, HiCo makes full use of the peer-level and cross-level knowledge from the network via multi-level contrast, which presents a stronger representation capability.

BUSI-BUI Breast Cancer Classification. The fine-tuning results on BUSI-BUI joint dataset are summarized in Table 4. Among the compared methods, HiCo provides the best Accuracy (*i.e.*, 86.0%). Compared with "Supervised", HiCo obtains an absolute gain of 14.7% in terms of Accuracy. We also observe

Table 4. Comparison of fine-tuning results on POCUS and BUSI-BUI classification datasets. Top two results are in bold and underlined.

Method	POCUS					BUSI-BUI
	COVID-19	Pneumonia	Regular	Accuracy (%)	F1 (%)	Accuracy (%)
ImageNet [61]	79.5	78.6	88.6	84.2	81.8	84.9
Supervised [3]	83.7	82.1	86.5	85.0	82.8	71.3
TE [59]	75.7	70.0	89.4	81.7	79.0	71.8
Π Model [59]	77.6	76.4	88.7	83.2	80.6	69.7
FixMatch [60]	83.0	77.5	85.7	83.6	81.6	70.3
MoCo v2 [13]	79.7	81.4	88.9	84.8	82.8	77.8
SimCLR [10]	83.2	89.4	87.1	86.4	86.3	74.6
USCL [3]	<u>90.8</u>	<u>97.0</u>	**95.4**	<u>94.2</u>	<u>94.0</u>	<u>85.5</u>
HiCo (Ours)	**97.1**	**100.0**	<u>92.5</u>	**94.7**	**94.6**	**86.0**

Table 5. Comparison of fine-tuning results on Thyroid US Images dataset. "Supervised", "LFS", and "VCL" denote the backbones pretrained with supervised learning, learning from scratch, and vanilla contrastive learning, respectively.

Method	Precision (%)		Recall (%)		Accuracy (%)
	Benign	Malignant	Benign	Malignant	
Supervised	81.3	89.0	42.6	97.9	88.3
LFS	79.3	88.1	37.7	97.9	87.4
VCL	89.3	88.8	41.0	99.0	88.8
HiCo (Ours)	**91.2**	**89.7**	**49.2**	**99.7**	**90.5**

that our HiCo does not demonstrate significant superiority to "ImageNet" like on POCUS dataset. This is because our pretraining dataset US-4 is captured with convex probes, while BUSI-BUI joint dataset is captured with linear probes. The domain gap between convex and linear probes damages the performance of backbones pretrained on convex probe US data including our HiCo.

4.4   Transferability to Thyroid US Images

We further evaluate the transferability of HiCo on Thyroid US classification dataset. We compare HiCo with the other three backbones pretrained using supervised learning (*i.e.*, Supervised), learning from scratch (*i.e.*, LFS), and vanilla contrastive learning (*i.e.*, VCL). For fair comparisons, all the backbones are pretrained on US-4 dataset and fine-tuned the last three layers. The results are shown in Table 5. We report the Precision and Recall of two classes (*i.e.*, the benign and malignant) and the total Accuracy. We find that HiCo has the consistent best performance on the classification of two classes, and its total Accuracy of 90.5% is also significantly better than the other three methods.

4.5   Cross-Modal Transferability to Chest X-ray

The goal of this work is to design an effective method for US video model pre-training. To test our approach's transferability, we also apply our approach to

Table 6. Comparison of fine-tuning results on COVID-Xray-5k chest X-ray dataset. "Supervised", "LFS", and "VCL" denote the backbones pretrained with supervised learning, learning from scratch, and vanilla contrastive learning, respectively.

Method	Precision (%)		Recall (%)		Accuracy (%)
	COVID-19	Normal	COVID-19	Normal	
Supervised	94.2	94.5	90.6	96.7	94.4
LFS	87.2	94.2	90.5	92.1	91.5
VCL	92.2	94.9	91.5	95.4	93.9
HiCo (Ours)	**94.5**	**97.7**	**96.2**	**96.7**	**96.5**

a Chest X-ray classification dataset (*i.e.*, COVID-Xray-5k). This experiment can verify the cross-modal transferability of our approach. The detailed results about Supervised, LFS and VCL are listed in Table 6. From Table 6, we can see that our HiCo achieves the best performance of two classes (*i.e.*, COVID-19 and the normal) and total Accuracy. Specifically, HiCo outperforms the LFS, VCL and Supervised by 5.0%, 2.6% and 2.1%, respectively. Although our approach is designed for US video model pretraining, the above results demonstrate its excellent cross-modal transferability.

5   Conclusion

In this work, we propose the hierarchical contrastive learning for US video model pretraining, which fully and efficiently utilizes both peer-level and cross-level knowledge from a DNN via multi-level contrast, leading to the remarkable transferability for the pretrained model. The advantage of our proposed method is that it flexibly extends the existing CL architecture (*i.e.*, the vanilla contrastive learning framework) and promotes knowledge communication inside the network by designing several simple and effective loss functions instead of designing a complex network structure. We empirically identify that multi-level contrast can greatly accelerate the convergence speed of pretrained models in downstream tasks, and improve the representation ability of models. In addition, a softened objective function is introduced to alleviate the negative effect of some local similarities between different classes, which further facilitates the CL process. Future works include exploiting more general frameworks for multi-level contrast and other applications for US diagnosis.

Acknowledgments. This work is supported by the National Natural Science Foundation of China (No. 62101351), the Guangdong Basic and Applied Basic Research Foundation (No.2020A1515110376), Shenzhen Outstanding Scientific and Technological Innovation Talents PhD Startup Project (No. RCBS20210609104447108), the National Key R & D Program of China under Grant (No.2021ZD0113400), Guangdong Provincial Key Laboratory of Big Data Computing, and the Chinese University of Hong Kong, Shenzhen.

References

1. Born, J., et al.: Accelerating detection of lung pathologies with explainable ultrasound image analysis. Appl. Sci. **11**, 672 (2021)
2. Gao, Y., Maraci, M.A., Noble, J.A.: Describing ultrasound video content using deep convolutional neural networks. In: 2016 IEEE 13th International Symposium on Biomedical Imaging, pp. 787–790 (2016)
3. Chen, Y., et al.: USCL: pretraining deep ultrasound image diagnosis model through video contrastive representation learning. In: de Bruijne, M., et al. (eds.) MICCAI 2021. LNCS, vol. 12908, pp. 627–637. Springer, Cham (2021). https://doi.org/10.1007/978-3-030-87237-3_60
4. Liu, L., Lei, W., Wan, X., Liu, L., Luo, Y., Feng, C.: Semi-supervised active learning for COVID-19 lung ultrasound multi-symptom classification. In: 2020 IEEE 32nd International Conference on Tools with Artificial Intelligence (ICTAI), pp. 1268–1273. IEEE (2020)
5. Gao, L., et al.: Multi-modal active learning for automatic liver fibrosis diagnosis based on ultrasound shear wave elastography. In: 2021 IEEE 18th International Symposium on Biomedical Imaging (ISBI), pp. 410–414. IEEE (2021)
6. Su, H., Chang, Z., Yu, M., Gao, J., Li, X., Zheng, S., et al.: Convolutional neural network with adaptive inferential framework for skeleton-based action recognition. J. Vis. Commun. Image Represent. **73**, 102925 (2020)
7. Jiao, J., Droste, R., Drukker, L., Papageorghiou, A.T., Noble, J.A.: Self-supervised representation learning for ultrasound video. In: 2020 IEEE 17th International Symposium on Biomedical Imaging, pp. 1847–1850 (2020)
8. Zhang, R., Isola, P., Efros, A.A.: Colorful image colorization. In: Leibe, B., Matas, J., Sebe, N., Welling, M. (eds.) ECCV 2016. LNCS, vol. 9907, pp. 649–666. Springer, Cham (2016). https://doi.org/10.1007/978-3-319-46487-9_40
9. He, K., Fan, H., Wu, Y., Xie, S., Girshick, R.: Momentum contrast for unsupervised visual representation learning. In: Proceedings of the IEEE/CVF Conference on Computer Vision and Pattern Recognition, pp. 9729–9738 (2020)
10. Chen, T., Kornblith, S., Norouzi, M., Hinton, G.: A simple framework for contrastive learning of visual representations. In: International Conference on Machine Learning, pp. 1597–1607. PMLR (2020)
11. Jiao, J., Cai, Y., Alsharid, M., Drukker, L., Papageorghiou, A.T., Noble, J.A.: Self-supervised contrastive video-speech representation learning for ultrasound. In: Martel, A.L., et al. (eds.) MICCAI 2020. LNCS, vol. 12263, pp. 534–543. Springer, Cham (2020). https://doi.org/10.1007/978-3-030-59716-0_51
12. Zhang, Y., Jiang, H., Miura, Y., Manning, C.D., Langlotz, C.P.: Contrastive learning of medical visual representations from paired images and text. arXiv preprint arXiv:2010.00747 (2020)
13. Chen, X., Fan, H., Girshick, R., He, K.: Improved baselines with momentum contrastive learning. arXiv preprint arXiv:2003.04297 (2020)
14. Gao, J., et al.: Accurate temporal action proposal generation with relation-aware pyramid network. Proceed. AAAI Conf. Artif. Intell. **34**, 10810–10817 (2020)
15. Ren, S., He, K., Girshick, R., Sun, J.: Faster R-CNN: towards real-time object detection with region proposal networks. IEEE Trans. Pattern Anal. Mach. Intell. **39**, 1137–1149 (2016)
16. Xu, H., et al.: Seed the views: hierarchical semantic alignment for contrastive representation learning. In: IEEE Transactions on Pattern Analysis and Machine Intelligence (2022)

17. Lee, S., Lee, D.B., Hwang, S.J.: Contrastive learning with adversarial perturbations for conditional text generation. In: 9th International Conference on Learning Representations. ICLR (2021)
18. Li, M., et al.: Keywords and instances: a hierarchical contrastive learning framework unifying hybrid granularities for text generation, pp. 4432–4441 (2022)
19. Li, D., Zhang, T., Hu, N., Wang, C., He, X.: HiCLRE: a hierarchical contrastive learning framework for distantly supervised relation extraction, pp. 2567–2578 (2022)
20. Wang, X., et al.: HELoC: hierarchical contrastive learning of source code representation. arXiv preprint arXiv:2203.14285 (2022)
21. Schmarje, L., Santarossa, M., Schröder, S.M., Koch, R.: A survey on semi-, self-and unsupervised techniques in image classification. arXiv preprint arXiv:2002.08721 (2020)
22. He, K., Zhang, X., Ren, S., Sun, J.: Deep residual learning for image recognition. In: CVPR, pp. 770–778 (2016)
23. Gao, J., Sun, X., Ghanem, B., Zhou, X., Ge, S.: Efficient video grounding with which-where reading comprehension. In: IEEE Transactions on Circuits and Systems for Video Technology (2022)
24. Chi, J., Walia, E., Babyn, P., Wang, J., Groot, G., Eramian, M.: Thyroid nodule classification in ultrasound images by fine-tuning deep convolutional neural network. J. Digit. Imaging **30**, 477–486 (2017)
25. Yap, M.H., Yap, M.H., et al.: Automated breast ultrasound lesions detection using convolutional neural networks. IEEE J. Biomed. Health Inform. **22**, 1218–1226 (2017)
26. Huang, Q., Luo, Y., Zhang, Q.: Breast ultrasound image segmentation: a survey. Int. J. Comput. Assist. Radiol. Surg. **12**(3), 493–507 (2017). https://doi.org/10.1007/s11548-016-1513-1
27. Al-Dhabyani, W., Gomaa, M., Khaled, H., Fahmy, A.: Dataset of breast ultrasound images. Data Brief **28** 104863 (2019)
28. Rodrigues, P.S.: Breast ultrasound image. Mendeley Data, V1, (2018). https://doi.org/10.17632/wmy84gzngw.1
29. Pedraza, L., Vargas, C., Narváez, F., Durán, O., Muñoz, E., Romero, E.: An open access thyroid ultrasound image database. In: SPIE, vol. 9287 (2015)
30. Nguyen, D.T., Kang, J.K., Pham, T.D., Batchuluun, G., Park, K.R.: Ultrasound image-based diagnosis of malignant thyroid nodule using artificial intelligence. Sensors **20**, 1822 (2020)
31. Li, P., Zhao, H., Liu, P., Cao, F.: Automated measurement network for accurate segmentation and parameter modification in fetal head ultrasound images. Med. Biol. Eng. Comput. **58**(11), 2879–2892 (2020). https://doi.org/10.1007/s11517-020-02242-5
32. Kalafat, E., et al.: Lung ultrasound and computed tomographic findings in pregnant woman with covid-19. Ultrasound Obstet. Gynecol. **55**, 835–837 (2020)
33. Long, L., Zhao, H.T., Zhang, Z.Y., Wang, G.Y., Zhao, H.L.: Lung ultrasound for the diagnosis of pneumonia in adults: a meta-analysis. Medicine **96**(3), e5713 (2017)
34. Kerdegari, H., et al.: Automatic detection of b-lines in lung ultrasound videos from severe dengue patients. In: 2021 IEEE 18th International Symposium on Biomedical Imaging, pp. 989–99 (2021)
35. Wang, X., Burzynski, J.S., Hamilton, J., Rao, P.S., Weitzel, W.F., Bull, J.L.: Quantifying lung ultrasound comets with a convolutional neural network: initial clinical results. Comput. Biol. Med. **107**, 39–46 (2019)

36. Carrer, L., et al.: Automatic pleural line extraction and covid-19 scoring from lung ultrasound data. IEEE Trans. Ultrason. Ferroelectr. Freq. Control **67**, 2207–2217 (2020)
37. Xu, Y., et al.: Boundary restored network for subpleural pulmonary lesion segmentation on ultrasound images at local and global scales. J. Digit. Imaging **33**, 1155–1166 (2020)
38. Razaak, M., Martini, M.G., Savino, K.: A study on quality assessment for medical ultrasound video compressed via HEVC. IEEE J. Biomed. Health Inform. **18**, 1552–1559 (2014)
39. Kwitt, R., Vasconcelos, N., Razzaque, S., Aylward, S.: Localizing target structures in ultrasound video-a phantom study. Med. Image Anal. **17**, 712–722 (2013)
40. Ronneberger, O., Fischer, P., Brox, T.: U-Net: convolutional networks for biomedical image segmentation. In: Navab, N., Hornegger, J., Wells, W.M., Frangi, A.F. (eds.) MICCAI 2015. LNCS, vol. 9351, pp. 234–241. Springer, Cham (2015). https://doi.org/10.1007/978-3-319-24574-4_28
41. Chen, L.C., Papandreou, G., Kokkinos, I., Murphy, K., Yuille, A.L.: Semantic image segmentation with deep convolutional nets and fully connected CRFs. arXiv preprint arXiv:1412.7062 (2014)
42. Chen, L.-C., Zhu, Y., Papandreou, G., Schroff, F., Adam, H.: Encoder-decoder with atrous separable convolution for semantic image segmentation. In: Ferrari, V., Hebert, M., Sminchisescu, C., Weiss, Y. (eds.) ECCV 2018. LNCS, vol. 11211, pp. 833–851. Springer, Cham (2018). https://doi.org/10.1007/978-3-030-01234-2_49
43. Cao, H., et al.: Swin-Unet: Unet-like pure transformer for medical image segmentation. arXiv preprint arXiv:2105.05537 (2021)
44. Weng, Y., Zhou, T., Li, Y., Qiu, X.: NAS-Unet: neural architecture search for medical image segmentation. IEEE Access **7**, 44247–44257 (2019)
45. Huang, R., et al.: Extracting keyframes of breast ultrasound video using deep reinforcement learning. Med. Image Anal. **80**, 102490 (2022)
46. Gong, B., et al.: Diagnosis of infantile hip dysplasia with D-mode ultrasound via two-stage meta-learning based deep exclusivity regularized machine. IEEE J. Biomed. Health Inform. **26**, 334–344 (2021)
47. Korbar, B., Tran, D., Torresani, L.: Cooperative learning of audio and video models from self-supervised synchronization. In: Advances in Neural Information Processing Systems 31 (2018)
48. van den Oord, A., Li, Y., Vinyals, O.: Representation learning with contrastive predictive coding. arXiv (2018)
49. Ye, M., Zhang, X., Yuen, P.C., Chang, S.F.: Unsupervised embedding learning via invariant and spreading instance feature. In: Proceedings of the IEEE/CVF Conference on Computer Vision and Pattern Recognition, pp. 6210–6219 (2019)
50. Noroozi, M., Favaro, P.: Unsupervised learning of visual representations by solving jigsaw puzzles. In: Leibe, B., Matas, J., Sebe, N., Welling, M. (eds.) ECCV 2016. LNCS, vol. 9910, pp. 69–84. Springer, Cham (2016). https://doi.org/10.1007/978-3-319-46466-4_5
51. Chen, L., Bentley, P., Mori, K., Misawa, K., Fujiwara, M., Rueckert, D.: Self-supervised learning for medical image analysis using image context restoration. Med. Image Anal. **58**, 101539 (2019)
52. Doersch, C., Gupta, A., Efros, A.A.: Unsupervised visual representation learning by context prediction. In: Proceedings of the IEEE International Conference on Computer Vision, pp. 1422–1430 (2015)

53. Gutmann, M., Hyvärinen, A.: Noise-contrastive estimation: a new estimation principle for unnormalized statistical models. In: Proceedings of the Thirteenth International Conference on Artificial Intelligence and Statistics, JMLR Workshop and Conference Proceedings, pp. 297–304 (2010)
54. Grill, J.B., et al.: Bootstrap your own latent-a new approach to self-supervised learning. Adv. Neural. Inf. Process. Syst. **33**, 21271–21284 (2020)
55. Chen, X., He, K.: Exploring simple Siamese representation learning. In: Proceedings of the IEEE/CVF Conference on Computer Vision and Pattern Recognition, pp. 15750–15758 (2021)
56. Chen, X., Xie, S., He, K.: An empirical study of training self-supervised vision transformers. In: Proceedings of the IEEE/CVF International Conference on Computer Vision, pp. 9640–9649 (2021)
57. Lin, T.Y., Dollár, P., Girshick, R., He, K., Hariharan, B., Belongie, S.: Feature pyramid networks for object detection. In: Proceedings of the IEEE Conference on Computer Vision and Pattern Recognition, pp. 2117–2125 (2017)
58. Minaee, S., Kafieh, R., Sonka, M., Yazdani, S., Soufi, G.J.: Deep-covid: Predicting covid-19 from chest X-ray images using deep transfer learning. Med. Image Anal. **65**, 101794 (2020)
59. Laine, S., Aila, T.: Temporal ensembling for semi-supervised learning. In: ICLR (2017)
60. Sohn, K., et al.: FixMatch: simplifying semi-supervised learning with consistency and confidence. arXiv:2001.07685 (2020)
61. Russakovsky, O., et al.: ImageNet large scale visual recognition challenge. Int. J. Comput. Vision **115**, 211–252 (2015)

APAUNet: Axis Projection Attention UNet for Small Target in 3D Medical Segmentation

Yuncheng Jiang[1,2,3], Zixun Zhang[1,2,3], Shixi Qin[1,2,3], Yao Guo[4],
Zhen Li[1,2,3(✉)], and Shuguang Cui[1,2,5]

[1] FNii, CUHK-Shenzhen, Shenzhen, Guangdong, China
{yunchengjiang,zixunzhang}@link.cuhk.edu.cn, lizhen@cuhk.edu.cn
[2] SSE, CUHK-Shenzhen, Shenzhen, Guangdong, China
[3] SRIBD, CUHK-Shenzhen, Shenzhen, Guangdong, China
[4] Shanghai Jiao Tong University, Shanghai, China
[5] Pengcheng Laboratory, Shenzhen, Guangdong, China

Abstract. In 3D medical image segmentation, small targets segmentation is crucial for diagnosis but still faces challenges. In this paper, we propose the **A**xis **P**rojection **A**ttention UNet, named **APAUNet**, for 3D medical image segmentation, especially for small targets. Considering the large proportion of the background in the 3D feature space, we introduce a projection strategy to project the 3D features into three orthogonal 2D planes to capture the contextual attention from different views. In this way, we can filter out the redundant feature information and mitigate the loss of critical information for small lesions in 3D scans. Then we utilize a dimension hybridization strategy to fuse the 3D features with attention from different axes and merge them by a weighted summation to adaptively learn the importance of different perspectives. Finally, in the APA Decoder, we concatenate both high and low resolution features in the 2D projection process, thereby obtaining more precise multi-scale information, which is vital for small lesion segmentation. Quantitative and qualitative experimental results on two public datasets (BTCV and MSD) demonstrate that our proposed APAUNet outperforms the other methods. Concretely, our APAUNet achieves an average dice score of 87.84 on BTCV, 84.48 on MSD-Liver and 69.13 on MSD-Pancreas, and significantly surpass the previous SOTA methods on small targets.

Keywords: 3D medical segmentation · Axis projection attention

1 Introduction

Medical image segmentation, which aims to automatically and accurately diagnose lesion and organ regions in either 2D or 3D medical images, is one of the

---

Y. Jiang and Z. Zhang—Equal contributions. Code is available at github.com/zx33/APAUNet.

Supplementary Information The online version contains supplementary material available at https://doi.org/10.1007/978-3-031-26351-4_2.

L. Wang et al. (Eds.): ACCV 2022, LNCS 13846, pp. 21–36, 2023.
https://doi.org/10.1007/978-3-031-26351-4_2

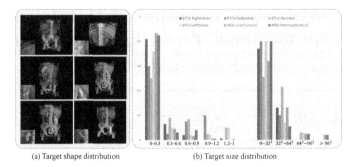

(a) Target shape distribution   (b) Target size distribution

Fig. 1. Target shape samples and size distribution of MSD and synapse multi-organ segmentation dataset. (a) 6 example organs from synapse multi-organ segmentation dataset. (b) The target size distribution. The x-axis is the target size interval, and the y-axis is the proportion (%) of corresponding samples to the whole dataset. The left part shows the relative proportion (%) of the target size to the whole input, while the right part shows the absolute size of the target with a interval step of 32 voxels. It can be observed that the relative target sizes of most samples in all the 6 categories are less than 0.6% with various shapes.

critical steps for developing image-guided diagnostic and surgical systems. In practice, compared to large targets, such as organs, small targets like tumors or polyps are more important for diagnosis, but also prone to be ignored. In this paper, we focus on 3D medical image segmentation (CT/MRI), with an emphasis on small lesions. This task is challenging mainly due to the following two aspects: 1) severe class imbalance of foreground (lesions) and background (entire 3D scans); 2) large variances in shape, location, and size of organs/lesions.

Recent progress in medical image segmentation has mainly been based on UNet [1], which applies a U-shaped structure with skip-connections to merge multi-scale features. However, due to the inductive bias of the locality of the convolutions, the U-shaped networks still suffer from the limited representation ability. Some studies utilized a coarse-to-fine segmentation framework [2]. These approaches refine the final segmentation in the fine stage, by shrinking input features to the region of interest (ROI) predicted in the coarse stage. Also, instead of using vanilla 3D convolutions, some works tried to explore a 2.5D fashions [3], which performed 2D convolutions on xy-axis at the low-level layers of the network and 3D convolutions on the high-level layers. Other works attempted to use an ensemble of 2D and 3D strategies, which fuses the 2D predictions from different views with 3D predictions to get better results [4] or refine the 2D predictions using 3D convolutions [5]. Besides, inspired by the great success of Transformers, some works explored the feasibility of applying self-attention into medical images by integrating CNN-based architectures with Transformer-like modules [6–8] to capture the patch-level contextual information.

Although previous methods have achieved remarkable progress, there are still some issues: 1) The 2.5D or the ensemble of 2D and 3D methods still suffer from the limited representation ability since the 2D phases only extract features from two axes while ignoring the information from the other axis, which worsens the

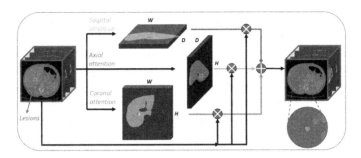

Fig. 2. In our APAUNet, we first project the 3D features into three orthogonal 2D planes to capture local contextual attentions from the three 2D perspectives, and then fuse them with the original 3D features. Finally, we adaptively fuse the features by weighted summation.

final segmentation prediction. Also, the two-stage designs are difficult for end-to-end training and require more computational resources. 2) Transformer-like models require higher computational cost on self-attention, and thus, have limited applications in 3D scenarios. Moreover, these models only learn the attentive interactions between patches, yet ignoring the local pattern inside the patch. 3) In addition, the imbalance between target and background has been ignored, which is vital for 3D medical segmentation. As shown in Fig. 1, on MSD challenge and BTCV datasets, the majority samples of the tumour target and small organ target are smaller than 0.6% to the whole 3D scans with various shapes.

In this paper, we propose an Axis Projection Attention (APA) UNet, named APAUNet, which utilizes an orthogonal projection strategy and a dimension hybridization strategy to overcome the aforementioned challenges. Specifically, our APAUNet follows the established design of 3D-UNet but replaces the main and functional component, the 3D convolution based encoder/decoder layers, with our APA encoder/decoder modules. In the *APA encoder*, the initial 3D feature maps are projected to three orthogonal 2D planes, i.e., *sagittal*, *axial*, and *coronal* views. Such a projection operation could mitigate the loss of critical information for small lesions in 3D scans. For instance, the original foreground-background area ratio of 3D features is $O(1/n^3)$ before the projection, but after projection, the ratio can be promoted to $O(1/n^2)$. Afterwards, we extract the local contextual 2D attention along the projected features to perform the asymmetric feature extraction and fuse them with the original 3D features. Eventually, the fused features of three axes are summed as the final output by three learnable factors, as shown in Fig. 2. Correspondingly, our *APA decoder* follows the same philosophy as the APA encoder but takes input features from two resolution levels. In this way, the decoder can effectively leverage the contextual information of multi-scale features. Furthermore, we also utilize an oversampling strategy to ensure the occurrence of foregrounds in each batch during the training process.

In summary, our contributions are in three-fold: (1) We propose the Axis Projection Attention UNet. APAUNet utilities the orthogonal projection strategy to enhance the asymmetric projection attention and feature extraction. (2) We introduce a novel dimension hybridization strategy to fuse 2D and 3D attention maps for better contextual representation in both encoder and decoder blocks. Besides, we further leverage a multi-resolution fusion strategy into decoder blocks for context enhancement. (3) Extensive experiments on Synapse multi-organ segmentation (BTCV) [9] and Medical Segmentation Decathlon (MSD) challenge [10] datasets demonstrate the effectiveness and efficiency of our APAUNet, especially on small targets.

2   Related Work

2.1   CNN-Based Medical Image Segmentation

CNNs, serving as the standard model of medical image segmentation, have been extensively studied in the past. The typical U-shaped network, U-Net [1], which consists of a symmetric encoder and decoder network with skip-connections, has become a common choice for medical image analysis. Afterwards, different variations of U-Net were proposed, such as Res-UNet [11], and Dense-UNet [12]. Besides, there are also some studies using AutoML to search for UNet architectures or an ensemble of 2D and 3D features, e.g., C2FNAS [13] uses a two stages NAS to search for the 3D architecture, and [4] utilizes meta learner to learn the ensemble of 2D and 3D features. Although these architectures have achieved remarkable progress in various 2D and 3D medical image segmentation tasks, they lack the capability to learn the global context and long-range spatial dependencies, even though followed by down-sampling operations. Thus, it leads to the degraded performance on the challenging task of small lesion segmentation.

2.2   Attention Mechanism for Medical Imaging

Attention mechanisms have been widely applied to segmentation networks, which can be categorized into two branches. The first branch is the hard attention, which typically uses a coarse-to-fine framework for segmentation tasks. [2] exploited two parallel FCNs to first detect the ROI of input features, then conducted the fine-grained segmentation over these cropped ROI patches for volumetric medical image segmentation. RA-UNet [14] introduced a residual attention module that adaptively combined multi-level features, which precisely extracted the liver region and then segmented tumours in this region. However, these hard attention methods usually need extensive trainable parameters and can be difficult to converge, which are not efficient for 3D medical segmentation tasks. The second branch is the adoption of the self-attention mechanism. One of the early attempts was the Attention U-Net [15], which utilized an attention gate to suppress irrelevant regions of the feature map while highlighting salient features. UTNet [6] adopted efficient self-attention encoder and decoder to alleviate the computational cost for 2D medical image segmentation. UNETR [7] further employed a pure transformer by introducing a multi-head self-attention mechanism into the 3D-UNet structure, taking advantage of both Transformers and CNNs to learn the sequential global features. Nonetheless, considering the class imbalance issue of small lesions and large variants of organs, the methods mentioned above are not effective enough. To this end, our work aims at developing an efficient approach, thoroughly taking advantage of the attention mechanism for specifically small lesion segmentation in 3D scans.

2.3 Small Target Segmentation

Segmentation of small objects, with limited available features and imbalanced sample distribution, is a common challenge in computer vision tasks, especially for medical images. Many previous studies have explored the solutions for natural images. For example, improved data augmentation methods [16,17] were proposed to increase the diversity of data and enhance the model generalization ability. In addition, advanced feature fusion techniques were adopted to better capture the small objects [18]. However, few works investigate this issue for medical images, and the obtained performance is usually less superior. For instance, [19] utilized a reinforcement learning (RL) based search method to construct the optimal augmentation policy for small lesions segmentation. UNet 3+ [20] exploited the full-scale skip-connections to extract small-scale features efficiently. C2FNAS [13] and DINTS [21] used Neural Architecture Search (NAS) to find an appropriate network for small features extraction. MAD-UNet [22] stacked multi-scale convolutions with attention modules to reduce the effects of intra-class inconsistency and enrich the contextual information. Nonetheless, these approaches are neither superior in performance nor computationally efficient, which motivates us to make an in-depth investigation of small object segmentation in 3D medical scans.

3 Methodology

Figure 3 illustrates the overall architecture of our APAUNet. Following the idea of 3D-UNet, our APAUNet consists of several axis projection attention (APA) encoder/decoder blocks with five resolution steps. In this section, we first introduce the macro design of the APA encoder/decoder in Sect. 3.1, and then dig into the detailed block design in Sect. 3.2.

3.1 Axis Projection Attention (APA) Encoder and Decoder

The axis projection attention (APA) Encoder aims to extract contextual information of multiple resolution levels from different perspectives. The structure of APA Encoder is depicted in Fig. 3 (left part).

In practice, given a 3D medical image $I \in \mathbb{R}^{C \times H \times W \times D}$, the APA Encoder extracts multi-level features at different resolution scales $X^i \in \mathbb{R}^{C_i \times \frac{H}{2^i} \times \frac{W}{2^i} \times \frac{D}{2^i}}$.

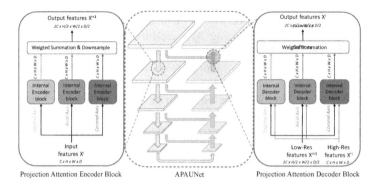

Fig. 3. The overview of APAUNet. Taking 3D scans as the input, our APAUNet exploits the 3D-UNet as the backbone. The yellow and green arrows denote the axis projection attention (APA) encoder and decoder blocks, respectively. For the left part, within one APA encoder block, we use three parallel internal encoder (IE) to construct the 2D attention on each projected orthogonal planes to filter the redundant background features and then adaptively fuse the features from the three perspectives. Correspondingly, for the right part, each APA decoder block merges the multi-scale features progressively to generate segmentation results. (Color figure online)

For the i-th level, the input feature X^i is fed to three *Internal Encoder (IE) blocks* in parallel to capture the contextual attention from three different perspectives. In order to capture the features of small targets more effectively, the original 3D features will be projected to three orthogonal 2D planes to extract the 2D spatial attention. And then, the learned 2D attentions and 3D feature maps are aggregated to enhance the feature representation. After obtaining fused features of the three axes, we use three learnable parameters $\beta_{i,a}$ to obtain the weighted summation of the enhanced features:

$$Y^i = \sum_{a=1}^{3} \beta_{i,a} \cdot \text{IE}(X^i, a), \sum_{a=1}^{3} \beta_{i,a} = 1 \tag{1}$$

where $\text{IE}(\cdot)$ is the operation of IE block and a denotes the three orthogonal axes. This aggregation function can further help the network adaptively learn the importance of different projection directions to achieve asymmetric information extraction. Afterwards, another $1 \times 1 \times 1$ convolution and $2 \times 2 \times 2$ average pooling are applied to perform the down-sampling operation to get X^{i+1}, the input features of next level.

Similarly, the APA Decoder modules are used to extract and fuse multi-resolution features to generate segmentation results. The detailed design is shown in Fig. 3 (right part). The APA Decoder block has a similar structure to the APA Encoder block, but takes two features with different resolutions as the input.

To be more specific, features of both low and high resolutions are fed into the APA Decoder block simultaneously, where the low resolution feature maps $X^{i+1} \in \mathbb{R}^{2C \times \frac{H}{2} \times \frac{W}{2} \times \frac{D}{2}}$ from the APA Decoder at the $(i + 1)$-th level and the

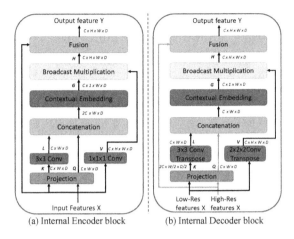

(a) Internal Encoder block   (b) Internal Decoder block

Fig. 4. The detailed structure of Internal Encoder/Decoder (IE/ID) block used in the APA Encoder/decoder along the *sagittal* (H) view respectively. (a) The IE block. (b) The ID block. They share a similar structure design while the ID block takes two inputs from different resolution levels.

high resolution feature maps $X'^i \in \mathbb{R}^{C \times H \times W \times D}$ from the APA Encoder at the i-th level. Afterwards, the *Internal Decoder (ID) block* aggregates both high and low resolution features to generate 2D contextual attentions from the three perspectives, then the 3D feature maps are fused with the 2D attentions to obtain 3D contextualized features, similar to that in the APA Encoder. To this end, the small-scale foreground information is better preserved, avoiding losing the crucial features. Finally, we take the weighted summation of three 3D contextualized features as the output features to next level.

3.2 Internal Encoder and Decoder Blocks

Inspired by the Contextual Transformer (CoT) [23], we adopt 3×3 convolutions in our internal blocks to mine the 2D context information and follow the design of the attention mechanism in CoT blocks. Meanwhile, we introduce several refinement strategies to tackle the challenges of 3D medical images, especially for small lesions. The detailed structure of internal blocks are illustrated in Fig. 4.

Orthogonal Projection Strategy. In the IE block, to better filter the irrelevant background and amplify the critical information of small lesions, we first project the input 3D features to three 2D planes. In particular, the 3D input feature $X \in \mathbb{R}^{H \times W \times D \times C}$ is projected to the *sagittal, axial* and *coronal* planes of the Cartesian Coordinate System to generate keys (K) and queries (Q), whereas the values (V) keep the 3D shape. Taking the *sagittal* view as an example, the input X is projected to 2D to get keys and queries: $K, Q \in \mathbb{R}^{C \times W \times D}$, while $V \in \mathbb{R}^{C \times H \times W \times D}$ is obtained by a single $1 \times 1 \times 1$ convolution. Here we adopt the summation of global average pooling (GAP) and global max pooling (GMP) along the desired axis (H in this case) as the projection operator:

$$K = Q = \text{GAP}_H(X) + \text{GMP}_H(X) \tag{2}$$

The projected K, Q are then used to learn different 2D contextual attentions along three orthogonal dimensions to better capture the key information of small lesions.

Dimension Hybridization Strategy. After the orthogonal projection, a 3×3 group convolution with a group size of 4 is employed on K to extract the local attention $L \in \mathbb{R}^{C \times W \times D}$, which contains the local spatial representation related to the neighboring keys. After that, we concatenate the local attention L with Q to further obtain the attention matrix $G \in \mathbb{R}^{C \times 1 \times W \times D}$ by two consecutive 1×1 2D convolutions and dimension expend:

$$L = h(\text{GConv}_{3 \times 3}(K)) \tag{3}$$

$$G = \text{Unsqueeze}(\text{Conv}_{1 \times 1}(h(\text{Conv}_{1 \times 1}([L, Q])))) \tag{4}$$

where GConv is the group convolution, $h(\cdot)$ denotes the normalization activation function, $[\cdot, \cdot]$ denotes the concatenation operation, and Unsqueeze$(\cdot)$ is the dimension expend operation. The attention matrix G encodes not only the contextual information within isolated query-key pairs but also the attention inside the keys.

Next, based on the 2D global attention G, we calculate the hybrid attention map $H \in \mathbb{R}^{H \times W \times D \times C} = V \odot G$, where $\odot$ denotes the broadcast multiplication, rather than the local matrix multiplication operation used in the original CoT blocks. This is because we empirically discovered that the local matrix multiplication operation does not contribute to any performance improvement under our 2D–3D hybridization strategy and consumes more GPU memory during training. Finally, the obtained hybrid attention maps are fused with the input feature X by a selective attention [24] to get the output features Y. The complete structure of the IE block is illustrated in Fig. 4(a).

Multi-resolution Fusion Decoding. In the ID block, in order to better obtain the multi-scale contextual information from the multi-resolution features, we integrate the upsampling operation into the attention extraction process. The design of ID block is similar to the IE block introduced above but takes two inputs from different resolution levels, where the high resolution features $X' \in \mathbb{R}^{C \times H \times W \times D}$ from the encoder are taken to produce the queries and the low resolution features from the previous decoder $X \in \mathbb{R}^{2C \times \frac{H}{2} \times \frac{W}{2} \times \frac{D}{2}}$ are taken to generate the keys and upsampled values. Then a $3 \times 3 \times 3$ transpose convolution is applied to upsample the keys to obtain the local attention L. Thus the decoder could fully capture the hybrid attention from various scales. The subsequent contextual extraction operations are similar to the IE block. And finally, we fuse the hybrid attention maps with the high resolution features X' to generate the output features Y. The detailed design of the ID block is illustrated in Fig. 4(b).

3.3 Loss Function

Following the previous methods [25, 26], we jointly use the Dice loss and the Cross Entropy loss to optimize our network. Specifically,

$$\mathcal{L}_{total} = \mathcal{L}_{dice} + \mathcal{L}_{CE} \tag{5}$$

$$\mathcal{L}_{dice} = 1 - \frac{2}{C} \sum_{j=1}^{C} \frac{\sum_{i=1}^{N} X_{ij} Y_{ij}}{\sum_{i=1}^{N} X_{ij} + \sum_{i=1}^{N} Y_{ij}} \tag{6}$$

$$\mathcal{L}_{CE} = -\frac{1}{N} \sum_{i=1}^{N} \sum_{j=1}^{C} (Y_{ij} \log X_{ij}) \tag{7}$$

where N denotes the total number of voxels, C is the number of target classes, while X and Y are the softmax output of the prediction and the one-hot ground truth, respectively.

4 Experiments

4.1 Datasets and Implementation Details

Our APAUNet is evaluated on two 3D segmentation datasets: Synapse multi-organ segmentation dataset (BTCV) [9] and Medical Segmentation Decathlon (MSD) challenge [10]. The synapse multi-organ segmentation dataset includes 30 cases of CT scans. Following the settings of [27, 28], we split 18 cases for model training while the rest 12 cases are used as test set. We report the 95% Hausdorff Distance (HD95) and Dice score (DSC) on 8 organs (aorta, gallbladder, spleen, left kidney, right kidney, liver, pancreas and stomach) following [27, 28]. While for MSD challenge we choose task 3 (Liver Tumours CT segmentation) and task 7 (Pancreas Tumour CT segmentation), since they contains more small targets. The Liver dataset contains 131 3D CT volumes with ground truth labels of both small liver tumours and large liver regions. While for the Pancreas dataset, it contains 282 3D CT volumes with labels of medium pancreas and small pancreas tumour regions. Since the MSD online test server is temporarily closed for submissions recently, we use the 5-fold cross-validation to evaluate our APAUNet on MSD datasets. Besides, we also reproduce the comparison methods on MSD with the same settings if the results on these datasets are not reported/evaluated in their original papers.

We implement our APAUNet on PyTorch and MONAI. For data preprocessing on MSD, we employ the method introduced in nnU-Net [29], which crops the zero values and re-samples all cases to the median voxel spacing of their respective dataset. Besides, the third-order spline interpolation is used for image data and the nearest-neighbor interpolation for the corresponding segmentation mask. During the training stage, we use a batch size of 2 and an input patch size of $(96 \times 96 \times 96)$, where the patches are sampled from the original volumes. Specifically, to address the problem that the foreground targets are hard to be randomly cropped,

Table 1. Segmentation results on the synapse multi-organ segmentation dataset. Note: Aor: Aotra, Gall: Gallbladder, LKid: Kidney (Left), RKid: Kidney (Right), Liv: Liver, Pan: Pancreas, Spl: Spleen, Sto: Stomach. All the results are obtained from the corresponding papers, except nnUNet.

Method	Average		Aor	Gall	LKid	RKid	Liv	Pan	Spl	Sto
	HD95	DSC								
TransUNet	32.62	77.49	87.23	63.13	81.87	77.02	94.08	55.86	85.08	75.62
CoTr	27.38	78.08	85.87	61.38	84.83	79.36	94.28	57.65	87.74	73.55
UNETR	23.87	79.57	89.99	60.56	85.66	84.80	94.46	59.25	87.81	73.99
MISSFormer	19.20	81.96	86.99	68.65	85.21	82.00	94.41	65.67	**91.92**	80.81
nnFormer	15.80	86.56	92.13	70.54	86.50	86.21	96.88	83.32	90.10	**86.83**
nnUNet	13.69	86.79	**93.20**	71.50	84.39	**88.36**	**97.31**	82.89	91.22	85.47
APAUNet	**11.26**	**87.84**	92.88	**75.26**	**88.47**	87.80	95.33	**85.47**	90.88	86.59

Table 2. Segmentation results (Dice score) on the MSD Liver and Pancreas Tumour datasets. The results of nnU-Net and C2FNAS are from the MSD leaderboard, while other methods are reproduced/implemented by ourselves on fold-1, including our APAUNet. (* denotes the average score with the standard deviations of 5-fold cross-validation.) Latency (s) is measured by a sliding window inference on GPU.

Method	Liver			Pancreas			Latency
	Organ	Cancer	Average	Organ	Cancer	Average	
UNet3+	87.32	70.10	78.71	75.30	46.00	60.65	39.65
HFA-Net	92.65	65.83	79.24	80.10	45.47	62.78	24.80
UTNet	92.51	69.79	81.15	80.30	49.68	64.99	18.16
UNETR	90.52	66.47	78.50	80.47	51.30	65.88	13.46
CoTr	90.20	69.88	80.04	77.9	50.20	64.05	21.77
nnU-Net	95.24	**73.71**	**84.48**	79.53	52.27	65.90	–
C2FNAS	94.91	71.63	83.27	80.59	52.87	66.73	–
APAUNet	**96.10**	72.50	84.30	**83.05**	**55.21**	**69.13**	**13.36**
APAUNet*	95.56 ±0.35	71.99 ±0.81	83.78 ±0.35	82.29 ±1.73	54.93 ±1.64	68.61 ±1.63	–

we adopt an over-sampling strategy as introduced in [29] to enforce that more than half of the samples in a batch contain the foreground targets. All the patches are randomly flipped as data augmentation. We use the SGD with an initial learning rate of 0.1, a momentum of 0.9, and a weight decay of $4e-5$ with cosine annealing. The models are trained for 500 epochs in total with a 50-epochs warm-up. All the models are trained on an NVIDIA V100 GPU.

4.2   Comparisons with Other Methods

We first evaluate our APAUNet against several state-of-the-art methods, including TransUNet [28], CoTr [8], UNETR [7], MISSFormer [27], and nnFormer [30]. The results are shown in Table 1. Our APAUNet achieves the best average dice score of 87.84 and the best average HD95 score of 11.26, and outperforms the second best method nnFormer by 4.54 and 1.28 on these two metrics respectively. For the class-wise results, our APAUNet also achieves the best dice scores in five of the categories and surpasses the second best method by 0.75–4.72, while is only 1.55, 1.04 and 0.24 lower on Liver, Spleen and Stomach.

While on MSD datasets, we compare our APAUNet with HFA-Net [31], UTNet [6], UNETR [7], UNet3+ [20], CoTr [8], C2FNAS [13] and nnUNet [29]. Since the MSD online leaderboard submission is temporarily closed at the time of the experiments, we focus on comparing our algorithm with the first 5 methods which are reproduced under the same settings, and also compare the 5-fold results with C2FNAS and nnUNet for reference. Table 2 shows the overall results of these methods. On Liver Tumour dataset, our APAUNet achieves a dice score of 96.10 on organ segmentation and 72.50 on cancer segmentation, which outperforms the second best method by 3.45 (HFA-Net) and 2.40 (UNet3+) on the dice score respectively. Also, the average dice score of our APAUNet is 84.30, which is 3.15 higher than UTNet. Similarly, the results of our APAUNet consistently outperform those of other methods on Pancreas dataset. Comparing with C2FNAS and nnUNet, our APAUNet surpasses both methods on all scores except Liver-cancer and Liver-average, where nnUNet uses additional test time augmentation, model ensembling and post-processing for better results. The results demonstrate the effectiveness of our APAUNet. More detailed results of 5-fold cross validation are shown in appendix.

4.3 Results on Small Cases

To verify the effectiveness of our APAUNet on small cases, we count the results of small targets with size less than 0.6% on Liver, Pancreas and BTCV. Figure 5 shows the performance of our APAUNet and comparison methods. We observe that our APAUNet surpasses the second best results by 3.9–12.6 in absolute dice scores. Concretely, on the interval of 0–0.1%, our APAUNet achieves dice scores of 51.3, 55.1 and 49.4 on three datasets respectively, and has an improvement of 27.9%, 14.3% and 27.1% compared to the second best methods. Similarly on the interval of 0.1–0.3%, the dice scores of our APAUNet are 16.6%, 14.9% and 15.2% higher than the second best methods respectively. These exciting results further highlights the superiority of our APAUNet, especially on small target segmentation.

4.4 Visualization Results

In this part, we visualize some segmentation results of our APAUNet and compare with UNETR, UTNet, CoTr and HFA-Net on the Liver Tumour dataset in Fig. 6 and on the Pancreas Tumour dataset in Fig. 7. It can be observed that all the methods have good performance on large organ segmentation with a dice score of over 90 on liver and over 75 on pancreas. While on small lesions, UNETR, UTNet, CoTr and HFA-Net could only locate the position and are still unsatisfactory in the segmentation of both the boundary and the size. In comparison,

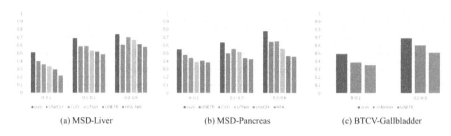

(a) MSD-Liver	(b) MSD-Pancreas	(c) BTCV-Gallbladder

Fig. 5. Statistical results of small cases on MSD and BTCV datasets. Note that since most targets are concentrated in the range of 0–0.3%, in order to show the results more clearly, we divide 0–0.3% into two intervals of 0–0.1% and 0.1–0.3%. And also, the split validation set of BTCV does not contain any targets with size of 0.3–0.6%.

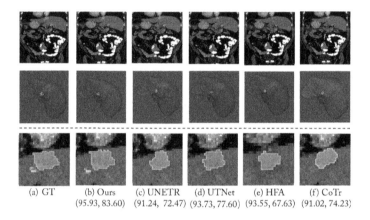

(a) GT	(b) Ours	(c) UNETR	(d) UTNet	(e) HFA	(f) CoTr
	(95.93, 83.60)	(91.24, 72.47)	(93.73, 77.60)	(93.55, 67.63)	(91.02, 74.23)

Fig. 6. Visualization of our proposed APAUNet and other methods on Liver. The upper two rows are the overall of segmentation results and the view of foreground targets, while the last row is an enlarged view of the segmentation results of small lesions. The dice scores (*organ*, *tumour*) are given under each method.

our APAUNet gets clearer and more accurate boundaries and sizes, further verifying the substantial advantage of APAUNet in medical image segmentation, especially for small targets.

4.5 Analysis and Ablation Studies

In this section, a variety of ablation studies are performed to thoroughly verify the design our APAUNet and validate the performance under different settings. More ablation results can be found in appendix.

2D–3D Hybridization Strategy. To verify the effectiveness of our 2D–3D hybridization strategy, we conduct several ablation experiments. First, we replace the 2D operators in the original CoT block with 3D operators, which is a pure 3D version of CoTNet (CoT-3D). For the pure 2D version (CoT-2D), we project

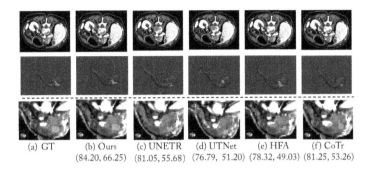

(a) GT   (b) Ours   (c) UNETR   (d) UTNet   (e) HFA   (f) CoTr
(84.20, 66.25) (81.05, 55.68) (76.79, 51.20) (78.32, 49.03) (81.25, 53.26)

Fig. 7. The visualization results of our APAUNet and comparison methods on Pancreas.

Table 3. Ablation experiments on the 2D–3D hybridization strategy, projection operators and the weighted importance. Avg, Max and Conv refer to the avgpooling, maxpooling and convolution operations, respectively. It can be seen that the effectiveness of the design of our APAUNet.

Method	Liver			Pancreas		
	Organ	Cancer	Avg	Organ	Cancer	Avg
CoT-2D	82.66	59.08	70.87	74.30	43.28	58.79
CoT-3D	91.08	63.26	77.17	75.40	46.28	60.84
Conv	85.20	68.81	77.00	80.24	51.33	65.78
Max	87.34	69.95	78.65	80.47	53.28	66.87
Avg	95.89	71.68	83.79	82.39	**55.48**	68.94
Mean	95.63	71.55	83.59	81.67	54.30	67.99
APAUNet	**96.10**	**72.50**	**84.30**	**83.05**	55.21	**69.13**

all the K, Q and V to 2D planes. The results are shown in Table 3. Compared with CoT-3D, our APAUNet achieves an improvement of 7.13 and 8.29 on average dice scores. Different from natural images, 3D medical CT scans contain more excessive background information that hinders the learning of contextual attention, while our 2D–3D hybridization strategy can filter the redundant information to enhance the performance. Also, APAUNet outperforms CoT-2D by a large margin, which indicates that it is suboptimal for the model to utilize only 2D attentions for 3D segmentation tasks.

Projection Operations. For the choice of projection operators, we conduct several experiments to figure out the best choice in {avgpooling, maxpooling, convolution}. For the fair comparison of the channel-wise operation of pooling, here we use a depth-wise convolution to perform the projection operation. Experiment results are shown in Table 3. Unexpectedly, the results of using convolution are the worst, despite its learnable parameters that make it more flexible than the pooling operators. We conjecture that the convolution lacks the ability to capture important information and is easily disturbed by the noise due to the high proportion of background information in medical images, even though with large kernel sizes. Fortunately, pooling operators could directly process the global information. Specifically, avgpooling involves all parts of the image to get the global statistics and maxpooling focuses only on the most salient part. By combining the complementarity of avgpooling and maxpooling, better performance can be achieved. Hence, we adopt the summation of avgpooling and maxpooling as the projection operation in our APA Encoder and Decoder.

Weighted Importance of Projection. Recall that there are three learnable weights during the fusion of features generated from different projection directions. Here, we conduct an experiment to study the effect of these weights. The results are shown in Table 3. Compared to the average mean, our APAUNet could gain an extra improvement of 0.47–1.38 on both datasets with the learnable weighted importance, which shows the feasibility of our asymmetric feature extraction on different projection axes. At the same time, this interesting phenomenon shows that the amount of information contained in different perspectives in the 3D structure is different, which motivates us to discover better 2D–3D fusion strategies. More detailed experimental results can be found in the appendix.

5   Conclusion

In this paper, we propose a powerful network for the 3D medical segmentation task, called Axis Projection Attention Network (APAUNet). In order to deal with the highly imbalanced targets and background, we leverage an orthogonal projection strategy and dimension hybridization strategy to build our APAUNet. Extensive experiments on the BTCV and MSD datasets demonstrate the promising results on 3D medical segmentation tasks of our APAUNet, and the superior results on small targets show the effectiveness of our APA Encoder/Decoder blocks. In our experiments, we also show that the importance of different perspectives is different, which motivates us to look deeper into the projection strategy and dimension hybridization pattern. For the future work, we would like to enhance the performance of small target segmentation by exploring more advanced projection techniques and designing more efficient dimension fusion strategies.

Acknowledgements. This work was supported in part by the National Key R&D Program of China with grant No.2018YFB1800800, by the Basic Research Project No. HZQB-KCZYZ-2021067 of Hetao Shenzhen HK S&T Cooperation Zone, by NSFC-Youth 61902335, by Shenzhen Outstanding Talents Training Fund, by Guangdong Research Project No.2017ZT07X152 and No.2019CX01X104, by the Guangdong Provincial Key Laboratory of Future Networks of Intelligence (Grant No.2022B1212010001), by zelixir biotechnology company Fund, by the Guangdong Provincial Key Laboratory of Big Data Computing, The Chinese University of Hong Kong, Shenzhen, by Tencent Open Fund, and by ITSO at CUHKSZ.

References

1. Ronneberger, O., Fischer, P., Brox, T.: U-net: convolutional networks for biomedical image segmentation. In: Navab, N., Hornegger, J., Wells, W.M., Frangi, A.F. (eds.) MICCAI 2015. LNCS, vol. 9351, pp. 234–241. Springer, Cham (2015). https://doi.org/10.1007/978-3-319-24574-4_28

2. Zhu, Z., Xia, Y., Shen, W., Fishman, E., Yuille, A.: A 3D coarse-to-fine framework for volumetric medical image segmentation. In: 2018 International conference on 3D vision (3DV) (2018)

3. Wang, G., et al.: Automatic segmentation of vestibular schwannoma from T2-weighted MRI by deep spatial attention with hardness-weighted loss. In: Shen, D., et al. (eds.) MICCAI 2019. LNCS, vol. 11765, pp. 264–272. Springer, Cham (2019). https://doi.org/10.1007/978-3-030-32245-8_30

4. Zheng, H., et al.: A new ensemble learning framework for 3D biomedical image segmentation. In: Proceedings of the Thirty-Third AAAI Conference on Artificial Intelligence and Thirty-First Innovative Applications of Artificial Intelligence Conference and Ninth AAAI Symposium on Educational Advances in Artificial Intelligence, pp. 5909–5916 (2019)

5. Xia, Y., Xie, L., Liu, F., Zhu, Z., Fishman, E.K., Yuille, A.L.: Bridging the gap between 2D and 3D organ segmentation with volumetric fusion net. In: Frangi, A.F., Schnabel, J.A., Davatzikos, C., Alberola-López, C., Fichtinger, G. (eds.) MICCAI 2018. LNCS, vol. 11073, pp. 445–453. Springer, Cham (2018). https://doi.org/10.1007/978-3-030-00937-3_51

6. Gao, Y., Zhou, M., Metaxas, D.N.: UTNet: a hybrid transformer architecture for medical image segmentation. In: de Bruijne, M., et al. (eds.) MICCAI 2021. LNCS, vol. 12903, pp. 61–71. Springer, Cham (2021). https://doi.org/10.1007/978-3-030-87199-4_6

7. Hatamizadeh, A., et al.: UneTR: transformers for 3D medical image segmentation. In: Proceedings of the IEEE/CVF Winter Conference on Applications of Computer Vision (2022)

8. Xie, Y., Zhang, J., Shen, C., Xia, Y.: CoTR: efficiently bridging CNN and transformer for 3D medical image segmentation. CoRR abs/2103.03024 (2021)

9. Landman, B., Xu, Z., Igelsias, J., Styner, M., Langerak, T., Klein, A.: MICCAI multi-atlas labeling beyond the cranial vault-workshop and challenge. In: Proceedings of MICCAI Multi-atlas Labeling Beyond Cranial Vault-Workshop Challenge, vol. 5, p. 12 (2015)

10. Simpson, A.L., Antonelli, M., Bakas, S., Bilello, M., Farahani, K., et al.: A large annotated medical image dataset for the development and evaluation of segmentation algorithms. arXiv preprint arXiv:1902.09063 (2019)

11. Xiao, X., Lian, S., Luo, Z., Li, S.: Weighted res-unet for high-quality retina vessel segmentation. In: 2018 9th International Conference on Information Technology in Medicine and Education (ITME) (2018)

12. Li, X., Chen, H., Qi, X., Dou, Q., Fu, C.W., Heng, P.A.: H-denseunet: hybrid densely connected unet for liver and tumor segmentation from CT volumes. IEEE Trans. Med. Imaging (2018)

13. Yu, Q., et al.: C2fnas: coarse-to-fine neural architecture search for 3D medical image segmentation. In: Proceedings of CVPR (2020)

14. Jin, Q., Meng, Z., Sun, C., Cui, H., Su, R.: Ra-unet: a hybrid deep attention-aware network to extract liver and tumor in CT scans. Front. Bioeng. Biotechnol. (2020)

15. Oktay, O., Schlemper, J., Folgoc, L.L., Lee, M., Heinrich, M., et al.: Attention u-net: learning where to look for the pancreas. arXiv preprint arXiv:1804.03999 (2018)
16. Zhang, H., Cisse, M., Dauphin, Y.N., Lopez-Paz, D.: Mixup: beyond empirical risk minimization. In: International Conference on Learning Representations (2018)
17. Yun, S., Han, D., Oh, S.J., Chun, S., Choe, J., Yoo, Y.: Cutmix: regularization strategy to train strong classifiers with localizable features. In: Proceedings of ICCV (2019)
18. Chen, L.C., Papandreou, G., Kokkinos, I., Murphy, K., Yuille, A.L.: Deeplab: semantic image segmentation with deep convolutional nets, atrous convolution, and fully connected CRFs. IEEE Trans. Pattern Anal. Mach. Intell. (2017)
19. Xu, J., Li, M., Zhu, Z.: Automatic data augmentation for 3D medical image segmentation. In: International Conference on Medical Image Computing and Computer-Assisted Intervention (2020)
20. Huang, H., Lin, L., Tong, R., Hu, H., Zhang, Q., et al.: Unet 3+: a full-scale connected unet for medical image segmentation. In: Proceedings of ICASSP (2020)
21. He, Y., Yang, D., Roth, H., Zhao, C., Xu, D.: Dints: Differentiable neural network topology search for 3D medical image segmentation. In: Proceedings of CVPR. (2021)
22. Li, W., Qin, S., Li, F., Wang, L.: Mad-unet: a deep u-shaped network combined with an attention mechanism for pancreas segmentation in CT images. Med. Phys. (2021)
23. Li, Y., Yao, T., Pan, Y., Mei, T.: Contextual transformer networks for visual recognition. arXiv preprint arXiv:2107.12292 (2021)
24. Li, X., Wang, W., Hu, X., Yang, J.: Selective kernel networks. In: Proceedings of the IEEE/CVF Conference on Computer Vision and Pattern Recognition, pp. 510–519 (2019)
25. Çiçek, Ö., Abdulkadir, A., Lienkamp, S.S., Brox, T., Ronneberger, O.: 3D U-net: learning dense volumetric segmentation from sparse annotation. In: Ourselin, S., Joskowicz, L., Sabuncu, M.R., Unal, G., Wells, W. (eds.) MICCAI 2016. LNCS, vol. 9901, pp. 424–432. Springer, Cham (2016). https://doi.org/10.1007/978-3-319-46723-8_49
26. Xie, E., et al.: Segmenting transparent object in the wild with transformer (2021)
27. Huang, X., Deng, Z., Li, D., Yuan, X.: Missformer: an effective medical image segmentation transformer. arXiv preprint arXiv:2109.07162 (2021)
28. Chen, J., et al.: Transunet: transformers make strong encoders for medical image segmentation. CoRR abs/2102.04306 (2021)
29. Isensee, F., et al.: NNU-net: self-adapting framework for u-net-based medical image segmentation. arXiv preprint arXiv:1809.10486 (2018)
30. Zhou, H.Y., Guo, J., Zhang, Y., Yu, L., Wang, L., Yu, Y.: NNFormer: interleaved transformer for volumetric segmentation. arXiv preprint arXiv:2109.03201 (2021)
31. Zheng, H., et al.: HFA-net: 3D cardiovascular image segmentation with asymmetrical pooling and content-aware fusion. In: Shen, D., et al. (eds.) MICCAI 2019. LNCS, vol. 11765, pp. 759–767. Springer, Cham (2019). https://doi.org/10.1007/978-3-030-32245-8_84

Multi-View Coupled Self-Attention Network for Pulmonary Nodules Classification

Qikui Zhu[1], Yanqing Wang[2(✉)], Xiangpeng Chu[4], Xiongwen Yang[3,4], and Wenzhao Zhong[4]

[1] Department of Biomedical Engineering, Case Western Reserve University, Cleveland, OH, USA
[2] Department of Gynecology, Renmin Hospital of Wuhan University, Wuhan, China
yanqingwang543@gmail.com
[3] School of Medicine, South China University of Technology, Guangzhou, China
[4] Guangdong Provincial Key Laboratory of Translational Medicine in Lung Cancer, Guangdong Lung Cancer Institute, Guangdong Provincial People's Hospital, Guangdong Academy of Medical Sciences, Guangzhou, China

Abstract. Evaluation of the malignant degree of pulmonary nodules plays an important role in early detecting lung cancer. Deep learning-based methods have obtained promising results in this domain with their effectiveness in learning feature representation. Both local and global features are crucial for medical image classification tasks, particularly for 3D medical image data, however, the receptive field of the convolution kernel limits the global feature learning. Although self-attention mechanism can successfully model long-range dependencies by directly flattening the input image to a sequence, which has high computational complexity. Additionally, which unable to model the image local context information across spatial and depth dimensions. To address the above challenges, in this paper, we carefully design a Multi-View Coupled Self-Attention Module (MVCS). Specifically, a novel self-attention module is proposed to model spatial and dimensional correlations sequentially for learning global spatial contexts and further improving the identification accuracy. Compared with vanilla self-attention, which has three-fold advances: 1) uses less memory consumption and computational complexity than the existing self-attention methods; 2) except for exploiting the correlations along the spatial and channel dimension, the dimension correlations are also exploited; 3) the proposed self-attention module can be easily integrated with other frameworks. By adding the proposed module into 3D ResNet, we build a classification network for lung nodules' malignancy evaluation. The nodule classification network was validated on a public dataset from LIDC-IDRI. Extensive experimental results demonstrate that our proposed model outperforms state-of-the-art approaches. The source code of this work is available at the https://github.com/ahukui/MVCS.

Keywords: Pulmonary nodules · Self-attention · Multi-View Coupled Self-Attention

L. Wang et al. (Eds.): ACCV 2022, LNCS 13846, pp. 37–51, 2023.
https://doi.org/10.1007/978-3-031-26351-4_3

1 Introduction

The accurate and earlier identification of malignant lung nodules from computed tomography (CT) screening images is a critical prerequisite for early detecting and diagnosing lung cancer [2,8]. Deep learning-based methods [17,18,26,33] have obtained promising results in lung nodules' malignancy identification research with their effectiveness in learning feature representation. For example, Lyu et al. [14] developed a multi-level convolutional neural network (ML-CNN) which consists of three CNNs for extracting multi-scale features in lung nodule CT images to assess the degree of malignancy of pulmonary nodules. Xie et al. [27] proposed a novel Fuse-TSD lung nodule classification algorithm that uses texture, shape and deep model-learned information at the decision level for distinguishing malignant from benign lung nodules. Murugesan et al. [15] created a simple yet effective model for the rapid identification and U-net architecture based segmentation of lung nodules. This approach focuses on the identification and segmentation of lung cancer by detecting picture normalcy and abnormalities. Although these methods have achieved remarkable results, there is still room for improvement in exploiting lung nodules information. Since the receptive field of the convolution kernel used in layer is always small and limited, which also limits the global feature learning during feature extraction and further limits the global information absorbed. However, both local and global features are critical for the malignancy assessment of pulmonary nodules. Assisting the model to obtain global context information from input data can further improve the performance of identification (Fig. 1).

Recently, the self-attention mechanism, particularly for Transformer [4], has been recognized as an effective way to exploit the global information and has been successful in natural language processing and 2D image analysis [31], due to the effectiveness of modeling long-range dependencies. For example, Li et al. [13] proposed an induced self-attention based deep multi-instance learning method that uses the self-attention mechanism for learning the global structure information within a bag. Guo et al. [7] proposed a separable self-attention network for video representation learning by investigating the relationship between spatial attention and temporal attention through a sequential self-attention structure. Inspired by PCA, Du et al. [5] proposed an interaction-aware self-attention to further use non-local information in feature maps. By constructing a spatial feature pyramid, the proposed model improves attention accuracy and classification accuracy. Zhang et al. [30] proposed an attention residual learning convolutional neural network model for skin lesion classification in dermoscopy images, which jointly uses the residual learning and novel attention learning mechanisms to improve the discriminative representation ability of DCNNs. However, the existing self-attention module meets two-fold challenges: 1) which builds the dependencies merely by computing the correlations along spatial dimensions and

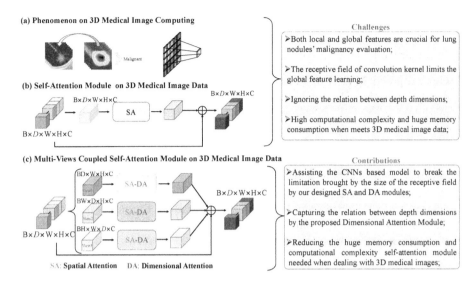

Fig. 1. The distinguishing between the self-attention module and our proposed Multi-View Coupled Self-Attention module.

ignores the relation between depth dimensions; 2) which has high computational complexity and huge memory consumption when meets the date with high spatial size, especially for 3D medical images, as the computational complexity of the self-attention is quadratic with respect to the number of tokens. The above phenomena limit the effectiveness of a vanilla self-attention module [24] in the domain of 3D medical image analysis.

To overcome the above challenges, in this study, we propose a novel self-attention module for assisting the model to model long-range dependencies and extract global information on 3D medical image data. Specifically, we propose a Multi-View Coupled Self-Attention module (MVCS) for completing the above functions with less memory consumption and computational complexity. In our design, different from the vanilla self-attention module, three independent spatial self-attentions are collaborate utilized to investigate the long range dependencies among pixels from three views for modeling the global spatial contextual and dimensional correlation information. Inside MVCS, both local and global spatial contextual information is captured with less memory consumption and computational complexity. Its advance has three-fold: 1) MVCS could model spatial and dimensional correlations sequentially for learning global spatial contexts; 2) MVCS uses less huge memory consumption and computational complexity than the existing self-attention methods when dealing with 3D medical image data; 3) MVCS can be easily integrated with other frameworks. By adding the proposed module into 3D ResNet, we build a nodule classification network for nodules' malignancy evaluation. The nodule classification network was validated on a public dataset LUNA16 from LIDC-IDRI. Extensive experimental results demonstrate that our proposed model has performance comparable to state-of-the-art approaches.

Summary, our detailed contributions are as follow:

– Our proposed MVCS module solves the problem that the relation between depth dimensions be ignored by a specific designed dimensional attention module.
– Our proposed MVCS module has less memory consumption and computational complexity compared with the vanilla self-attention module when dealing with 3D medical image data.
– Our proposed MVCS module can be easily integrated with other frameworks. By adding the proposed module into 3D ResNet, we build a nodule classification network for nodules' malignancy evaluation. Extensive experimental results demonstrate that our proposed model has performance comparable to state-of-the-art approaches on the public LUNA16 dataset.

2   Related Works

2.1   Pulmonary Nodules Classification

Lung cancer is consistently ranked as the leading cause of tumor-associated deaths all around the world in the past several years due to its aggressive nature and delayed detection at advanced stages. According to the statistics, estimated 10-year postoperative disease-specific survival (DSS) rates were 100% and 100%, and overall survival (OS) rates were 95.3% and 97.8% of patients with resected adenocarcinoma in carcinoma in situ (AIS) and minimally invasive adenocarcinoma (MIA) of the lung [8], respectively. Additionally, the 5-year survival for patients who present with advanced-stage IV non-small cell lung cancer is less than 10%, this percentage increases to at least 71% if the diagnosis is made early [2].

In recent years, deep learning-based methods [32,34] have obtained promising results on the identification of malignant nodules. For instance, Kumar et al. [11] proposed an autoencoder framework to extract lung nodule deep features for lung nodule classification. Shen et al. [18] proposed a hierarchical Multi-scale Convolutional Neural Networks (MCNN) to capture nodule heterogeneity by extracting discriminative features from alternatively stacked layers for lung nodule classification. Xie et al. [26] proposed a Multi-View Knowledge-Based Collaborative (MV-KBC) deep model to classify benign-malignant nodules under limited data. Shen et al. [17] proposed a domain-adaptation framework that learns transferable CNN-based features from nodules without pathologically-confirmed annotations to predict the pathologically-proven malignancy of nodules. Jiang et al. [9] presented a novel attentive and ensemble 3D Dual Path Networks for pulmonary nodule classification via contextual attention mechanism and a spatial attention mechanism. Shi et al. [20] proposed a Semi-supervised Deep Transfer Learning (SDTL) framework for benign-malignant pulmonary nodule diagnosis by utilizing a transfer learning strategy. Additionally, an iterated feature-matching-based semi-supervised method is proposed to take advantage of a large available dataset with no pathological results and a similarity metric function is adopted to iteratively optimize the classification network.

Although deep learning-based methods have obtained promising results in the study of malignant tumor identification of nodules, the limitations from the CNN itself always affect the performance of the model. First, CNN-based models employ kernel with a fixed and small size, such as 3×3, 5×5, for feature extraction, which hardly extracts global information. Under this configure, only local features can be extracted in each stage of CNNs based model. However, both local and global features are crucial for classification tasks, especially for benign-malignant nodules classification that requires the whole 3D information. Second, effective modeling of long-range dependencies among pixels and making the model pay more attention to the region of interest is essential to capture global and significant contextual information. Therefore, it is still important to improve nodules learning networks to efficiently learn nodules information and further improve the performance of evaluation.

2.2   Self-attention

Recently, the self-attention mechanism including Transformer [4] emerges as an active research area in the computer vision community and has shown its potential to be a viable alternative to CNNs in medical image analysis. For example, Dong et al. [3] proposed a new image polyp segmentation framework, named Polyp-PVT, which utilizes a pyramid vision transformer backbone as the encoder to explicitly extract more powerful and robust features. Zhang et al. [31] combined Transformers and CNNs in a parallel style and proposed a novel paralleling-branch architecture, where both global dependency and low-level spatial details can be efficiently captured in a much shallower manner. Wang et al. [25] proposed an fNIRS classification network based on Transformer, named fNIRS-T, which could explore the spatial-level and channel-level representation of fNIRS signals to improve data utilization and network representation capacity. Shi et al. [22] proposed a unified framework based solely on the attention mechanism for skeleton-based action recognition. The proposed model employed a novel decoupled spatial-temporal attention to emphasize the spatial/temporal variations and motion scales of the skeletal data, resulting in a more comprehensive understanding of human actions and gestures. Wang et al. [23] designed a novel framework Attention-based Suppression and Attention-based Enhancement Net to better distinguish different classes based on attention mechanism and weakly supervised learning for the fine-grained classification of bone marrow cells. Fang et al. [6] proposed a novel attention modulated network based on the baseline U-Net, and explores embedded spatial and channel attention modules for adaptively highlighting interdependent channel maps and focusing on more discriminant regions via investigating relevant feature association. Li et al. [12] proposed a parallel-connected residual channel attention network with less parameters and a shorter prediction time to enhance the representation ability for remote sensing image SR.

However, the existing self-attention module have huge memory consumption and high computational complexity when meeting data with large spatial sizes, especially for 3D medical images. And the relation between depth dimensions of 3D medical images is also ignored. Thus, effective modeling of long-range dependencies among pixels from both spatial and depth dimensions and making the model pay more attention to the region of interest can overcome the limitations of CNNs in capturing global and significant contextual information, and further improve the performance of the model.

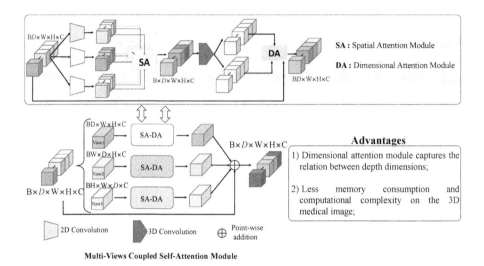

Fig. 2. Diagram of our proposed Multi-view Coupled Self-Attention Module. The proposed method which consists of two separable self-attention: 1) **Spatial Attention**; 2) **Dimensional Attention**.

3   Method

In this section, we first discuss Multi-View Coupled Self-Attention Module in detail, and then give an overview of our proposed pulmonary nodules classification framework.

3.1   Multi-View Coupled Self-Attention Module

Given the input data $X \in \mathbb{R}^{B \times D \times H \times W \times C}$ with a spatial resolution of $H \times W$, depth dimension of D (number of slices), C channels and B batch size. The vanilla self-attention maps X into query, key and value embeddings using three $1 \times 1 \times 1$ convolutions, which are denoted as $X_q \in \mathbb{R}^{B \times D \times H \times W \times C'}$, $X_k \in \mathbb{R}^{B \times D \times H \times W \times C'}$ and $X_v \in \mathbb{R}^{B \times D \times H \times W \times C'}$. The three embeddings are then reshaped to the sizes of $DHW \times C'$, $C' \times DHW$ and $DHW \times C'$, respectively. Afterward, the similarity matrix $M \in \mathbb{R}^{DHW \times DHW}$, which models the long-distance dependency in a global space, is calculated by using $X_q \times X_k$. Finally, the attention map in each location is generated by normalized M through the softmax function.

As the computational complexity of the self-attention is quadratic with respect to the number of tokens. Although the typical self-attention can successfully model long range dependencies by directly flattening the input image to a sequence, which has high computational complexity. Additionally, this simple strategy makes self-attention unable to model the image local context information across spatial and depth dimensions. To address the above challenges, we carefully design a Multi-View Coupled Self-Attention Module (MVCS), which extracts a comprehensive representation of each volume from 2D three views. The main structure of our proposed MVCS is illustrated in Fig. 2, which consists of two separable self-attention:1) **Spatial Attention**; 2) **Dimensional Attention**, to exploit the correlations along the spatial and channel dimension, respectively. The details of the two separable self-attention are described as follows.

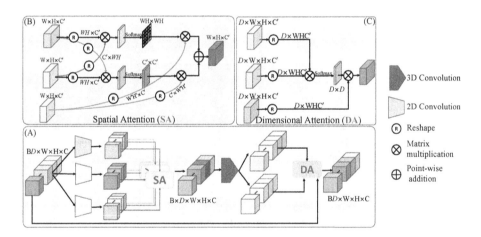

Fig. 3. The details of **Spatial Attention** and **Dimensional Attention**. **Spatial Attention** explores the dependencies along the spatial and channel dimension for computing position-wise attention and channel-wise attention. **Dimensional Attention** is attached after spatial attention, which builds the range correlations along the third dimension for exploiting the dimension correlations.

3.2 Spatial Attention

The input feature X is first converted to three view $X^0 \in \mathbb{R}^{BD \times W \times H \times C}$, $X^1 \in \mathbb{R}^{BH \times W \times D \times C}$, $X^2 \in \mathbb{R}^{BW \times H \times D \times C}$. Each view is mapped into spatial key, query, and value embeddings denoted as X_k^t, X_q^t, and X_v^t using 2D 1×1

convolutions, where t is view index. Then, the embeddings are used to generate spatial attention maps independently. Inside the spatial attention, both position-wise attention and channel-wise attention are computed as shown in Fig. 3(A). Given the embeddings X_q^t and X_k^t, which are first reshaped to the size of $HW \times C'$ and $C' \times HW$. The spatial similarity matrix $M_S^t \in \mathbb{R}^{HW \times HW}$ is generated by $X_q^t \times X_k^t$, which model long range dependencies from spatial view. The channel similarity matrix $M_C^t \in \mathbb{R}^{C' \times C'}$ is generated by $X_k^t \times X_q^t$, which explores the dependencies along the channel dimension. The spatial attention maps for view t are then calculated as:

$$X^t = soft\max(M_S^t) \times X_v^t + soft\max(M_C^t) \times X_v^t \tag{1}$$

3.3 Dimensional Attention

Dimensional attention is attached after spatial attention, which builds the range correlations along the third dimension. The structure of dimensional attention is illustrated in Fig. 3(B). Similar to spatial attention, the input feature X is first mapped into spatial key, query, and value embeddings denoted as $X_k \in \mathbb{R}^{B \times D \times W \times H \times C}$, $X_q \in \mathbb{R}^{B \times D \times W \times H \times C}$, and $X_v \in \mathbb{R}^{B \times D \times W \times H \times C}$ using $3 \times 1 \times 1$ convolution instead. The similarity matrix $M_D^t \in \mathbb{R}^{D \times D}$ along the third dimension is then calculated by reshaped X_q, X_k.

$$X^t = soft\max(M_D^t) \times X_v^t \tag{2}$$

Summary, the generated output feature can be described as:

$$\mathrm{X} = \sum_{t=0}^{2} (soft\max(M_S^t) + soft\max(M_C^t) + soft\max(M_D^t)) \times X_v^t \tag{3}$$

Summary of the Advantages: 1) our proposed MVCS module solves the problem that the relation between depth dimensions be ignored by the dimensional attention module. 2) our proposed MVCS module breaks the limitation brought by the size of the receptive field and assists the model to extract both local and global information in each stage. 3) solving the challenges that huge memory consumption and computational complexity self-attention module needed when dealing with 3D medical images. 4) Last but not least, the proposed MVCS module is portable for other tasks models.

3.4 Pulmonary Nodules Classification

Following previous works [21,28], we also employ a 3D CNN as the backbone in this work. We choose 3D ResNet framework as our baseline. Meanwhile, we insert Multi-View Coupled Self-Attention (MVCS) module into different layers to create our proposed Multi-View Coupled Self-Attention Network as shown in Fig. 4. In this architecture, MVCS module assists the model to capture both global and local contextual information in different stages to further improve the performance of the model. Remarkably, MVCS module can also be easily added in other 3D based architecture.

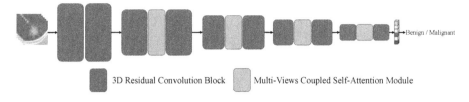

Fig. 4. Overview of multi-view coupled self-attention network for pulmonary nodules classification. The 3D ResNet framework as baseline.

4 Experiment

4.1 Datasets and Implementation Details

To comprehensively evaluate the classification performance of our model, the LUNA16 dataset is employed in our experiments. Especially, LUNA16 dataset is a subset of LIDC-IDRI database from the Cancer Imaging Archive. Inside LUNA16 dataset, the CTs with slice thickness greater than 3mm, the annotated nodules of size smaller than 3mm, slice spacing inconsistent or missing slices from LIDC-IDRI dataset are removed, and explicitly gives the patient-level 10-fold cross validation split of the dataset. Finally, there are totally 1004 nodules left, in which 450 nodules are positive and 554 nodules are negative.

All the lung nodules were cropped from raw CT images for training and testing. Then, 3D nodule patch with size $32 \times 32 \times 32$ pixels was cropped from CT images around the centers of the lung nodules. Afterward, each 3D nodule patch is normalized by the z-score standardization method. The mean and std values are set as -400 and 750, respectively. During training, randomly adding Gaussian noise, horizontal flip, vertical flip, z-axis flip the data are utilized for data augmentation. We implement our framework by using Pytorch and two GTX 2080Ti GPUs. Adam optimizer with a minibatch size of 48 was applied for optimization. The learning rate and weight decay were set to 1e−4 and 0.01, respectively. Additionally, linear warmup with cosine annealing was also used for learning rate adjusting.

Following the settings in [9,35], we also evaluate our method on folds 1–5 and the average performance of 5 folds as final results. The metrics of the AUC, Specificity, Sensitivity, Accuracy, Precision, and F1-score were calculated for comprehensively evaluating the classification performance of model. Sensitivity (Recall) denotes the percentage of correctly predicted malignant nodules and is crucial for CAD; Accuracy evaluates the percentage of correctly predicted malignant/benign nodules; Precision is the percentage of correctly predicted benign nodules; F1-score evaluates the trade-off between Sensitivity and Precision. Defined as follows:

$$Accuracy = \frac{TP + TN}{TP + FN + TN + FP} \tag{4}$$

$$Sensitivity = \frac{TP}{TP + FN} \tag{5}$$

$$Specificity = \frac{TN}{FP + TN} \tag{6}$$

$$Precision = \frac{TP}{TP + FP} \tag{7}$$

$$F1 - score = \frac{2TP}{2TP + FP + FN} \tag{8}$$

where True-Positive (TP) is the number of correctly predicted malignant nodules; False-Positive (FP) denotes the number of predicted malignant nodules that are actually benign; True-Negative (TN) represents the number of correctly predicted benign nodules; False-Negative (FN) is the number of predicted benign nodules that are actually malignant.

Table 1. Quantitative evaluation results of proposed models and other state-of-the-art methods on LUNA16 dataset.

	Accuracy [%]	Sensitivity [%]	Specificity [%]	Precision [%]	AUC [%]	F1-score [%]
HSCNN [16]	84.20	70.50	–	–	85.60	–
3D CNN [29]	87.40	89.40	85.20	–	94.70	–
Multi-crop CNN [19]	87.14	77.00	93.00	–	93.00	–
Local-Global [1]	88.46	88.66	–	87.38	95.62	88.37
Deep+visual features [27]	88.73	84.40	90.88	82.09	94.02	83.23
Dual Path Networks [9]	90.24	92.04	–	–	–	90.45
DeepLung [35]	90.44	81.42	–	–	–	–
NASLung [10]	90.77	85.37	95.04	–	–	89.29
Our	91.25	89.10	93.39	91.59	91.25	90.19

4.2   Experimental Results

Compared with Other State-of-the-Art Methods: We compare our proposed model with state-of-the-art methods, including Multi-crop CNN [19], Vanilla 3D CNN [29], DeepLung [35], Ensemble 3D Dual Path Networks [9], and NASLung [10], where all models use the same dataset with the same number of samples.

The results of our proposed method and compared methods are shown in Table 1. As it can be seen from the Table 1, our proposed model achieves the highest Accuracy and Precision compared with other state-of-the-art methods, which represents our model possesses more powerful nodules representation learning capability and can classify benign and malignant features accurately. And MVCS could further boost the diagnosis accuracy and justify the diagnosis process. The results confirmed two aspects of feature learning for lung nodule classification. First, building the dependencies correlations along both spatial and depth dimensions could assist the model to extract the feature representation. Second, absorbing the global spatial contextual information could further improve the performance of the model.

Table 2. Quantitative evaluation results of 3D ResNet with various configures on LUNA16 dataset (the 5th fold).

	Accuracy [%]	Sensitivity [%]	Specificity [%]	Precision [%]	AUC [%]	F1-score [%]
Baseline	82.61	83.78	81.82	75.61	82.80	79.49
SANet	85.87	78.39	90.91	85.29	84.63	81.69
*VSANet	86.96	83.78	89.09	83.78	86.44	83.78
DANet	88.04	91.89	85.45	80.95	88.67	86.08
MVCSNet	92.39	94.59	90.91	87.50	92.75	90.91

Effectiveness Analysis Using MVCS: To demonstrate the effectiveness of the proposed MVCS, we analyze the influence of each part on the classification results by adding the split MVCS module inside the base network. Three other baseline methods and one vanilla self-attention based method are included as follows (Notably, in this section, we use the 5th fold as the testing dataset and all the other folds as the training dataset.):

(1) 3D ResNet (baseline): The classification is achieved by directly using 3D ResNet without attention mechanism. The classification results as a baseline.

(2) 3D ResNet + Spatial Attention (SANet): Different from (1), here the classification is acquired by inserting Spatial Attention into 3D ResNet.

(3) 3D ResNet + Dimensional Attention (DANet): Dimensional Attention is inserted into 3D ResNet for evaluating the effectiveness of Dimensional Attention.

(4) 3D ResNet + MVCS (MVCSNet): Our proposed model.

(5) 3D ResNet + Vanilla Self-Attention (VSANet): To compare the effectiveness of the self-attention module, we also insert the vanilla self-attention module which directly flattens the feature maps to model long-range interactions and spatial relationships into ResNet3D.

The Table 2 lists the classification performance of the methods described above. From the Table 2, we can notice that the innovations in our framework bring significant enhancements. The baseline (3D ResNet) has a poor performance. The major reason is that the typical convolution block construed by stacked convolution layers cannot fully learn nodules' representation. The spatial attention module assists the baseline model to obtain a 3.26%, 9.09%, 9.68%, 1.83% and 2.20% improvement on Accuracy, Specificity, Precision, AUC and F1-Score, respectively. When utilizing dimensional attention, the Accuracy, Sensitivity, Specificity, Precision, AUC and F1-Score achieve 5.43%, 8.11%, 3.63%, 5.34%, 5.87% and 6.59%, respectively. Those improvements proved the effectiveness of the two attention modules in modeling long-range dependencies among pixels and capturing global and significant contextual information. What's more, when using these two modules in combination, the Accuracy, Sensitivity, Specificity, Precision, AUC and F1-Score are increased by 9.78%, 10.81%, 9.09%, 11.89%, 9.95% and 11.42% due to the multi-view information adaptive fusion. Above extensive experiments with promising results reveal the power of the MVCS module and its significance in improving the performance of the model.

Meanwhile, in this section, we also compare the effectiveness of the vanilla self-attention module with our proposed MVCS. From Table 2, we can notice that both the vanilla self-attention module and MVCS module could improve the performance of ResNet. Specifically, the vanilla self-attention module assists the baseline model to obtain a 4.35%, 7.27%, 8.17%, 3.64% and 4.29% improvement in Accuracy, Specificity, Precision, AUC and F1-Score, respectively. Compared with the vanilla self-attention module, MVCS obtains a higher improvement, 5.43%, 10.81%, 1.82%, 3.72%, 6.31% and 7.13% in Accuracy, Sensitivity, Specificity, Precision, AUC and F1-Score, respectively. And from the Table 2, we can notice that SANet obtains a similar performance to SANet, which proves that vanilla self-attention ignores the correlations along depth dimensions, and absorbs the global spatial contextual information from the depth dimension could improve the performance of the model. Additionally, those results confirmed three aspects of feature learning for lung nodule classification: 1) extracting the correlations along spatial and depth dimensions is advanced in nodule features learning. 2) the improvement over the vanilla self-attention module could be explained that exploiting the relation between depth dimensions is also significant. 3) less memory consumption and computational complexity are advanced in improving the performance of the model.

Memory Consumption and Computational Complexity: In this section, we compare our proposed MVCS with the vanilla self-attention module in the memory consumption and computational complexity. Given an input data $X \in \mathbb{R}^{D \times H \times W \times C}$ with size $D \times H \times W \times C$, the per-layer complexity of the vanilla self-attention module is $O(D^2 H^2 W^2 C)$ and the attention matric size is $DHW \times DHW$. The per-layer complexity of three views inside the MVCS is $O(D^2 H^2 C)$, $O(D^2 W^2 C)$, $O(H^2 W^2 C)$ and the attention matric size is $DH \times DH$, $DW \times DW$, and $HW \times HW$, respectively. We can notice that our proposed model significantly reduces memory consumption and computational complexity.

5   Conclusion

In this paper, we propose a Multi-View Coupled Self-Attention module to assists the CNNs based models to break the limitation brought by the size of the receptive field inside the convolutional layer. In specific, two types of self-attention mechanisms are designed to investigate the relationship between spatial attention and dimensional attention, and a view-complementary manner is proposed to model both local and global spatial contextual information. The proposed model solves two challenges in self-attention: 1) builds the dependencies merely by computing the correlations along spatial dimensions and ignoring the relation between depth dimensions; 2) huge memory consumption and high computational complexity in 3D medical image data. Additionally, our proposed module can be easily integrated with other frameworks. By adding the proposed module into 3D ResNet, we build a nodule classification network for nodules' malignancy evaluation. The nodule classification network was validated on a public dataset

LUNA16 from LIDC-IDRI. Extensive experimental results demonstrate that our proposed model has performance comparable to state-of-the-art approaches.

Acknowledgements. This work was supported by the National Natural Science Foundation of China (81872510); Guangdong Provincial People's Hospital Young Talent Project (GDPPHYTP201902); High-level Hospital Construction Project (DFJH201801); GDPH Scientific Research Funds for Leading Medical Talents and Distinguished Young Scholars in Guangdong Province (No. KJ012019449); Guangdong Basic and Applied Basic Research Foundation (No. 2019B1515130002).

References

1. Al-Shabi, M., Lan, B.L., Chan, W.Y., Ng, K.H., Tan, M.: Lung nodule classification using deep local-global networks. Int. J. Comput. Assist. Radiol. Surg. **14**(10), 1815–1819 (2019)
2. Bray, F., Ferlay, J., Soerjomataram, I., Siegel, R.L., Torre, L.A., Jemal, A.: Global cancer statistics 2018: Globocan estimates of incidence and mortality worldwide for 36 cancers in 185 countries. CA: Cancer J. Clinic. **68**(6), 394–424 (2018)
3. Dong, B., Wang, W., Fan, D.P., Li, J., Fu, H., Shao, L.: Polyp-PVT: polyp segmentation with pyramid vision transformers. arXiv preprint arXiv:2108.06932 (2021)
4. Dosovitskiy, A., et al.: An image is worth 16x16 words: transformers for image recognition at scale. arXiv preprint arXiv:2010.11929 (2020)
5. Du, Y., Yuan, C., Li, B., Zhao, L., Li, Y., Hu, W.: Interaction-aware spatio-temporal pyramid attention networks for action classification. In: Ferrari, V., Hebert, M., Sminchisescu, C., Weiss, Y. (eds.) ECCV 2018. LNCS, vol. 11220, pp. 388–404. Springer, Cham (2018). https://doi.org/10.1007/978-3-030-01270-0_23
6. Fang, W., Han, X.H.: Spatial and channel attention modulated network for medical image segmentation. In: Proceedings of the Asian Conference on Computer Vision (2020)
7. Guo, X., Guo, X., Lu, Y.: SSAN: separable self-attention network for video representation learning. In: Proceedings of the IEEE/CVF Conference on Computer Vision and Pattern Recognition, pp. 12618–12627 (2021)
8. Hussein, S., Cao, K., Song, Q., Bagci, U.: Risk stratification of lung nodules using 3D CNN-based multi-task learning. In: Niethammer, M., et al. (eds.) IPMI 2017. LNCS, vol. 10265, pp. 249–260. Springer, Cham (2017). https://doi.org/10.1007/978-3-319-59050-9_20
9. Jiang, H., Gao, F., Xu, X., Huang, F., Zhu, S.: Attentive and ensemble 3D dual path networks for pulmonary nodules classification. Neurocomputing **398**, 422–430 (2020)
10. Jiang, H., Shen, F., Gao, F., Han, W.: Learning efficient, explainable and discriminative representations for pulmonary nodules classification. Pattern Recogn. **113**, 107825 (2021)
11. Kumar, D., Wong, A., Clausi, D.A.: Lung nodule classification using deep features in CT images. In: 2015 12th Conference on Computer and Robot Vision, pp. 133–138. IEEE (2015)
12. Li, Y., Iwamoto, Y., Lin, L., Chen, Y.W.: Parallel-connected residual channel attention network for remote sensing image super-resolution. In: Proceedings of the Asian Conference on Computer Vision (2020)

13. Li, Z., Yuan, L., Xu, H., Cheng, R., Wen, X.: Deep multi-instance learning with induced self-attention for medical image classification. In: 2020 IEEE International Conference on Bioinformatics and Biomedicine (BIBM), pp. 446–450. IEEE (2020)
14. Lyu, J., Ling, S.H.: Using multi-level convolutional neural network for classification of lung nodules on CT images. In: 2018 40th Annual International Conference of the IEEE Engineering in Medicine and Biology Society (EMBC), pp. 686–689. IEEE (2018)
15. Murugesan, M., Kaliannan, K., Balraj, S., Singaram, K., Kaliannan, T., Albert, J.R.: A hybrid deep learning model for effective segmentation and classification of lung nodules from CT images. J. Intell. Fuzzy Syst. (Preprint), 1–13 (2022)
16. Shen, S., Han, S.X., Aberle, D.R., Bui, A.A., Hsu, W.: An interpretable deep hierarchical semantic convolutional neural network for lung nodule malignancy classification. Expert Syst. Appl. **128**, 84–95 (2019)
17. Shen, W., et al.: Learning from experts: developing transferable deep features for patient-level lung cancer prediction. In: Ourselin, S., Joskowicz, L., Sabuncu, M.R., Unal, G., Wells, W. (eds.) MICCAI 2016. LNCS, vol. 9901, pp. 124–131. Springer, Cham (2016). https://doi.org/10.1007/978-3-319-46723-8_15
18. Shen, W., Zhou, M., Yang, F., Yang, C., Tian, J.: Multi-scale convolutional neural networks for lung nodule classification. In: Ourselin, S., Alexander, D.C., Westin, C.-F., Cardoso, M.J. (eds.) IPMI 2015. LNCS, vol. 9123, pp. 588–599. Springer, Cham (2015). https://doi.org/10.1007/978-3-319-19992-4_46
19. Shen, W., et al.: Multi-crop convolutional neural networks for lung nodule malignancy suspiciousness classification. Pattern Recogn. **61**, 663–673 (2017)
20. Shi, F., et al.: Semi-supervised deep transfer learning for benign-malignant diagnosis of pulmonary nodules in chest CT images. IEEE Trans. Med. Imaging (2021). https://doi.org/10.1109/TMI.2021.3123572
21. Shi, F., et al.: Semi-supervised deep transfer learning for benign-malignant diagnosis of pulmonary nodules in chest CT images. IEEE Trans. Med. Imaging (2021)
22. Shi, L., Zhang, Y., Cheng, J., Lu, H.: Decoupled spatial-temporal attention network for skeleton-based action recognition. In: Proceedings of the Asian Conference on Computer Vision (2020)
23. Wang, W., et al.: Attention-based fine-grained classification of bone marrow cells. In: Proceedings of the Asian Conference on Computer Vision (2020)
24. Wang, X., Girshick, R., Gupta, A., He, K.: Non-local neural networks. In: Proceedings of the IEEE Conference on Computer Vision and Pattern Recognition, pp. 7794–7803 (2018)
25. Wang, Z., Zhang, J., Zhang, X., Chen, P., Wang, B.: Transformer model for functional near-infrared spectroscopy classification. IEEE J. Biomed. Health Inform. **26**(6), 2559–2569 (2022). https://doi.org/10.1109/JBHI.2022.3140531
26. Xie, Y., et al.: Knowledge-based collaborative deep learning for benign-malignant lung nodule classification on chest CT. IEEE Trans. Med. Imaging **38**(4), 991–1004 (2018)
27. Xie, Y., Zhang, J., Xia, Y., Fulham, M., Zhang, Y.: Fusing texture, shape and deep model-learned information at decision level for automated classification of lung nodules on chest CT. Inf. Fusion **42**, 102–110 (2018)
28. Xu, X., et al.: MSCS-deepLN: evaluating lung nodule malignancy using multi-scale cost-sensitive neural networks. Med. Image Anal. **65**, 101772 (2020)
29. Yan, X., et al.: Classification of lung nodule malignancy risk on computed tomography images using convolutional neural network: a comparison between 2D and 3D strategies. In: Chen, C.-S., Lu, J., Ma, K.-K. (eds.) ACCV 2016. LNCS, vol. 10118, pp. 91–101. Springer, Cham (2017). https://doi.org/10.1007/978-3-319-54526-4_7

30. Zhang, J., Xie, Y., Xia, Y., Shen, C.: Attention residual learning for skin lesion classification. IEEE Trans. Med. Imaging **38**(9), 2092–2103 (2019)
31. Zhang, Y., Liu, H., Hu, Q.: TransFuse: fusing transformers and CNNs for medical image segmentation. In: de Bruijne, M., et al. (eds.) MICCAI 2021. LNCS, vol. 12901, pp. 14–24. Springer, Cham (2021). https://doi.org/10.1007/978-3-030-87193-2_2
32. Zhu, Q., Du, B., Yan, P.: Boundary-weighted domain adaptive neural network for prostate MR image segmentation. IEEE Trans. Med. Imaging **39**(3), 753–763 (2019)
33. Zhu, Q., Du, B., Yan, P.: Self-supervised training of graph convolutional networks. arXiv preprint arXiv:2006.02380 (2020)
34. Zhu, Q., Wang, Y., Du, B., Yan, P.: Oasis: one-pass aligned atlas set for medical image segmentation. Neurocomputing **470**, 130–138 (2022)
35. Zhu, W., Liu, C., Fan, W., Xie, X.: DeepLung: deep 3D dual path nets for automated pulmonary nodule detection and classification. In: 2018 IEEE Winter Conference on Applications of Computer Vision (WACV), pp. 673–681. IEEE (2018)

Multi-scale Wavelet Transformer for Face Forgery Detection

Jie Liu$^{(\boxtimes)}$, Jingjing Wang$^{(\boxtimes)}$, Peng Zhang, Chunmao Wang, Di Xie, and Shiliang Pu$^{(\boxtimes)}$

Hikvision Research Institute, Hangzhou, China
{liujie54,wangjingjing9,zhangpeng45,wangchunmao,
xiedi,pushiliang.hri}@hikvision.com

Abstract. Currently, many face forgery detection methods aggregate spatial and frequency features to enhance the generalization ability and gain promising performance under the cross-dataset scenario. However, these methods only leverage one level frequency information which limits their expressive ability. To overcome these limitations, we propose a multi-scale wavelet transformer framework for face forgery detection. Specifically, to take full advantage of the multi-scale and multi-frequency wavelet representation, we gradually aggregate the multi-scale wavelet representation at different stages of the backbone network. To better fuse the frequency feature with the spatial features, frequency-based spatial attention is designed to guide the spatial feature extractor to concentrate more on forgery traces. Meanwhile, cross-modality attention is proposed to fuse the frequency features with the spatial features. These two attention modules are calculated through a unified transformer block for efficiency. A wide variety of experiments demonstrate that the proposed method is efficient and effective for both within and cross datasets.

1 Introduction

Due to the various image-editing software and publicly available deep generator models, it is easy to manipulate existing faces and make forged faces very realistic and indistinguishable from genuine ones. These photo-realistic fake faces may be abused for malicious purposes, raising severe security and privacy issues in our society. Therefore, it is extremely necessary to develop effective methods for face forgery detection. To defend against the possible malicious usage of face forgery, various face forgery detection methods have been proposed. Previous researchers [1,2] mainly designed methods based on texture artifacts caused by the face forgery techniques in the spatial domain. Due to the fast evolution of face forgery techniques, these artifacts are gradually concealed. Therefore, although these methods achieved high within-dataset detection accuracy, their performance dropped severely in the cross-dataset scenario, especially when confronted with new face forgery methods.

L. Wang et al. (Eds.): ACCV 2022, LNCS 13846, pp. 52–68, 2023.
https://doi.org/10.1007/978-3-031-26351-4_4

Table 1. EMD of multi-level frequency components. Cropping the face in the first frame of every video in FF++ dataset, and then calculating the EMD of the original images or sub-bands frequency features between the fake and corresponding real images. These sub-bands are obtained by three level discrete wavelet transform.

Level	Sub-bands	Deepfakes (DF)	Face2Face (F2F)	FaceSwap (FS)	NeuralTextures (NT)
–	Ori-Img	1.301	1.092	1.307	1.296
Level-1	LL	1.281	1.008	1.265	1.208
	LH	2.688	2.709	2.970	2.959
	HL	2.716	2.778	2.720	2.857
	HH	2.582	2.914	3.258	2.758
Level-2	LL	1.208	0.958	1.165	1.162
	LH	2.817	2.840	2.882	3.106
	HL	2.598	2.686	2.549	2.871
	HH	3.184	2.929	3.162	3.127
Level-3	LL	1.189	1.055	1.136	1.246
	LH	2.473	2.493	2.510	2.826
	HL	2.135	2.409	2.166	2.837
	HH	2.774	2.917	2.936	2.985

To make the algorithm generalize well to unseen forgery methods, recently, many face forgery detection methods attempt to aggregate information from frequency domains. Yu *et al.* [3] utilized channel difference images and the spectrum obtained by DCT to detect fake faces. Other researchers leveraged Discrete Fourier Transform (DFT) [4] and Discrete Cosine Transform (DCT) and block DCT [5] for frequency information extracting. However, these methods only utilized one level frequency information. And we found that multi-level frequency features have more discriminable details between real and fake images. Only using one level frequency may be less effective for extracting the abundant frequency information, which limits the expressive ability of the obtained features. As we all know, Discrete Wavelet Transform (DWT) is often used to obtain multi-level frequency, so we choose Haar DWT to extract frequency features. The filter f_{LL}, f_{LH}, f_{HL}, and f_{HH} of DWT are $\frac{1}{2}\begin{bmatrix} 1 & 1 \\ 1 & 1 \end{bmatrix}$, $\frac{1}{2}\begin{bmatrix} 1 & 1 \\ -1 & -1 \end{bmatrix}$, $\frac{1}{2}\begin{bmatrix} 1 & -1 \\ 1 & -1 \end{bmatrix}$, and $\frac{1}{2}\begin{bmatrix} 1 & -1 \\ -1 & 1 \end{bmatrix}$, and they are used to calculate the frequency (LL, LH, HL, HH) of an image I. The LL, LH, HL, and HH are defined as $LL = f_{LL} * I$, $LH = f_{LH} * I$, $HL = f_{HL} * I$, $HH = f_{HH} * I$. DWT divides an image into four frequency components with half resolution of the original image: a low-frequency component (LL) and three high-frequency components (LH, HL, HH). And the LL can be further decomposed into four frequency components recursively. In this way, we can get multi-level wavelet representations. Earth Mover's Distance (EMD) [6] is used to measure the dissimilarity between two multidimensional distributions, whose formula is defined in [6]. The total EMD distance of FF++

dataset is calculated by three level frequency components between the real and fake data, whose results are shown in Table 1. We observe that the distance of high-frequency information between real and fake facial images is bigger than low-frequency one at each level, which demonstrates that different level high frequencies are all useful so that fusing multi-level high frequencies can make the representations more expressive for face forgery detection.

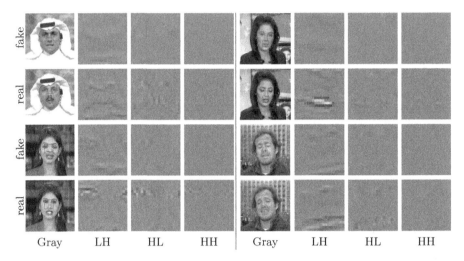

Fig. 1. High-frequency sub-bands are obtained by DWT. The images in the 1st and 3rd lines are fake images, and the others are real images. In this figure, we show the fake facial images and their corresponding real images. The 1st and 5th column are the gray images, and the column 2 to 4 and 6 to 8 are high frequency sub-bands corresponding to the cropped red box. The forged pixels have fewer high-frequency details (LH, HL, HH) compared with the real ones. (Color figure online)

We also visualize the examples of the real and fake high frequency by DWT in Fig. 1 and 2. In Fig. 1, we enlarge the local region of the first level DWT, so we can see that there are more details in low-level high frequency. Figure 2 shows the whole high-frequency sub-bands of the three-level DWT, and there is more global semantic information in high-level frequency. So the low-level and high-level high-frequency features are all important for facial forgery detection.

Taking the above considerations, we take the multi-scale analysis of wavelet decomposition into consideration and propose a multi-scale wavelet transformer framework for face forgery detection named MSWT. Specifically, we gradually aggregate the multi-scale wavelet features at different stages of the backbone network to take full advantage of multi-level high-frequency representation. To better fuse the frequency feature with the spatial features, frequency-based spatial attention is designed to guide the spatial feature extractor to concentrate more on forgery traces. Meanwhile, cross-modality attention is proposed to fuse

Gray   LH_L1 HL_L1 HH_L1 LH_L2 HL_L2 HH_L2 LH_L3 HL_L3 HH_L3

Fig. 2. The images in 1st and 2nd lines are the fake and the real facial images, respectively. Columns 2 to 10 are level 1, 2, and 3 high frequency (LH, HL, and HH) sub-bands by DWT. There is more details in lower levels, and more global semantic structure in higher levels.

the RGB spatial features and the frequency features. These two attention modules are calculated through a unified transformer block for efficiency named frequency and spatial feature fusion (FSF) module. The main contributions are summarized as follows:

- To make full use of frequency features, we are the first to utilize the multi-scale properties of wavelet decomposition to improve the feature fusion of spatial and frequency domains, and propose a multi-scale wavelet transformer framework for face forgery detection.
- To better capture the manipulation trace, frequency-based spatial attention is designed to guide spatial feature extractor to focus on forgery regions.
- To better fuse the frequency features with the RGB spatial features, cross-modality attention is introduced.
- Experiments demonstrate that the proposed method works well on both within-dataset and cross-dataset testing compared with other approaches.

2   Related Work

2.1   Forgery Detection

Forgery Detection Based on Spatial Feature. In order to resist manipulated faces and protect media security, many forgery detection algorithms have been proposed in academia. Because deep learning can learn good feature representation, some methods are proposed to extract RGB spatial features based on deep learning. These approaches mainly include consisrency-based [7], attention-based [8], and domain generalization methods [9]. Zhao *et al.* [8] proposed a method based on multi-attention and textural feature enhancement to enlarge artifacts in shallow features and capture discriminative details for face forgery detection, fusing the low-level and high-level features by attention maps. Zhao *et al.* [7] proposed patch-wise consistency learning between patches from the feature maps, which utilizes consistency loss to learn and optimize the consistency of the patches from real or fake regions. Wodajo *et al.* [10] proposed a convolutional vision transformer for deepfake video detection, and the network consists of a convolutional neural network (CNN) and a vision transformer (ViT). The ViT processes the features learned by CNN and then exports the classification results. Different from Wodajo et al. , we only utilize transformer encoder as the attention module to fuse high-frequency components and RGB spatial features.

Forgery Detection Based on Frequency. Because of the effectiveness of frequency information for forgery detection, some proposed networks combined the spatial features with frequency information. Li et al. [11] offered a single-center loss to learn the frequency-aware features and used the Discrete Cosine Transform (DCT) transform to get the frequency representation. Qian et al. [5] proposed F3-Net for face forgery detection, utilizing DCT and block DCT to calculate the global and block frequency information. Zhu et al. [12] also utilized frequency and spatial feature for forgery detection, with a two-stream architecture for RGB image and high-frequency component respectively. SPSL [4] was proposed by Liu et al. , in which DFT is applied to extract the phase spectrum as the high-frequency representation. However, these methods only use one level frequency information, discarding the valuable information in multi-level frequency information.

2.2   Wavelet in Computer Vision Tasks

For images, DWT obtains frequency and spatial components simultaneously, as shown in Fig. 1. Besides, wavelet transform has the characteristics of multi-resolution analysis, by which multi-scale frequency feature representation calculated by DWT has tremendous significance in computer vision tasks. For example, DWT is used in image depth prediction [13], image denoising [14,15], restoration [16], compression [17], and fusion [18,19], achieving good performance at that time.

3   Proposed Method

3.1   Overview of the Structure

For face forgery detection, we propose a multi-scale wavelet transformer architecture. The comprehensive framework is depicted in Fig. 3, which takes the RGB image and the multi-level high-frequency representations via DWT as inputs and fuses high-frequency features and the RGB spatial features with the proposed fusion module. According to the different input sources, the network is divided into the RGB branch which takes the RGB image as input, and the high frequency branches which take the wavelet-based high frequency representations as input. For the RGB branch, following most works, we take Xception [20] as the feature extractor. According to the resolution of feature maps, we split it into four convolutional feature extracting stages and one classifier, shown as the yellow and green blocks in Fig. 3.

For the high frequency branches, we take Haar wavelet [21] to get the multi-level high-frequency representations (shown as the red blocks in Fig. 3) as input

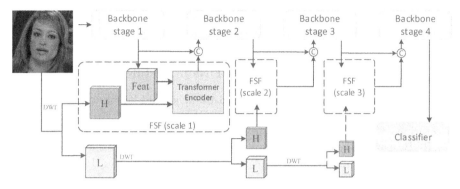

Fig. 3. The architecture of the proposed method. The backbone is Xception [20]. This backbone is split into four stages according to its features' resolution. The backbone extracts the features from the original image, and DWT is used to divide the input image into the low-frequency (L) and high-frequency (H) components at each channel (RGB). The frequency and spatial feature fusion (FSF) module as shown in the red dashed rectangle takes high-frequency information H and the spatial features $Feat$ extracted from the corresponding backbone stage as inputs. (Color figure online)

due to its simplicity and efficiency. DWT can divide a gray image into four frequency components which consist of one low-frequency (LL) and three high-frequency components (LH, HL, and HH) with half resolution of the original image. We do DWT for each channel of the RGB image respectively. Therefore, each frequency component consists of three channel maps corresponding to the red, green, and blue channel of the RGB image. As shown in the high frequency branch of Fig. 3, taking the three high-frequency components "H" as the frequency representations at the current level and using the low-frequency component "L" to do further wavelet decompositions, we can get the multi-level frequency representations. As analyzed in the introduction, frequency representations at different levels contain different useful information. In our method, we use high-frequency representations of the first three levels.

To fuse the information among different branches, we aggregate the information from the high frequency branches into the RGB branch using the proposed light-weight Frequency and Spatial Feature Fusion (FSF) module at three levels for efficiency, shown as the red dashed rectangle of Fig. 3. The information of the three high frequency branches is fused into the corresponding stages of the RGB branch to match their resolutions. Except for matching resolution, another reason is that, as analyzed in the introduction the low level frequency representations contain more details, while the high level frequency representations contain more global structure information, which has similar meanings to the features in the multiple stages of the RGB branch. The FSF module is based on the transformer and its details are described in the next Subsect. 3.2. Finally, the enhanced features are input into the classifier, and the whole network is optimized end-to-end using the cross-entropy loss.

3.2   Frequency and Spatial Feature Fusion Module

The structure of frequency and spatial feature fusion (FSF) module is shown in Fig. 4(a). It takes features $Feat$ from the RGB branch and high-frequency representations H at the corresponding level as inputs to fuse the high frequency and RGB spatial features. FSF module consists of two attention blocks. One block is used to enhance spatial feature maps $Feat$ with the high-frequency guided attention which is denoted as frequency-based spatial attention (FSA). The other block is used to fuse the high-frequency information into $Feat$ with cross-modality attention (CMA). Finally, the outputs of these two blocks are concatenated as the output of FSF module as shown in Fig. 4(a). The high-frequency representations H (LH, LH, HH) are obtained by DWT via the original image, while $Feat$ are RGB spatial features obtained from the RGB branch. To match the meaning of $Feat$, each part of H is first processed with the corresponding convolutional block. Then they are concatenated and fused with another convolution to get the output high-frequency feature maps F_H. This operation is defined as:

$$F_H = f_{combine} \left(Concat \left(f_{conv}^{LH} \left(LH \right), f_{conv}^{HL} \left(HL \right), f_{conv}^{HH} \left(HH \right) \right) \right) \qquad (1)$$

where f_{conv} is convolution block used to process the high-frequency features, and then the processed high-frequency features are concatenated with $Concat$. $f_{combine}$ fuses all high-frequency features with another convolution operation. The total operation process is shown in the blue dashed rectangle of Fig. 4(a).

On the other hand, to match the channel dimension of feature maps F_H, a down-channel convolution is performed on the RGB spatial features $Feat$. The down-channel feature is defined as:

$$F_S = f_{DownConv} \left(Feat \right) \qquad (2)$$

where $f_{DownConv}$ means the down-channel convolution operation.

The high frequency features F_H and spatial features F_S are fused using frequency-based spatial attention (FSA) and cross-modality attention (CMA), which are the yellow and the green rectangular boxes in Fig. 4(a). The first attention is used to guide the RGB spatial feature learning with high frequency information, and the second one is used to fuse information from high frequency features and spatial features. They are illustrated in the following subsection in detail.

Frequency-Based Spatial Attention. The area of the manipulated region usually contains the total face or an expression region. For example, the main region of the original face is replaced by another face when using Deepfake as the forgery method. Therefore, leveraging the long-term relationship is helpful to enhance the representation ability of the features. We take transformer to model this relation. However, using the spatial features F_S to calculate the self-attention may not be the best choice, since the self-attention based on F_S is more likely disturbed by the appearance details. Therefore, we propose to use F_H to calculate the attention, since the manipulated regions have similar high-frequency forgery traces. The architecture of frequency-based spatial attention is shown in the left rectangular box in the Fig. 4(b). First, the attention query Q_H^{FS} and key K_H^{FS} are calculated by embedding the high-frequency features F_H. And the value V_S^{FS} is obtained by embedding spatial features F_S. The output is named O_1, which is defined as:

$$O_1 = MHA\left(Q_H^{FS}, K_H^{FS}, V_S^{FS}\right) \tag{3}$$

where MHA is the multi-head attention of the vision transformer, and the superscript FS means the vector of Frequency-based Spatial Attention.

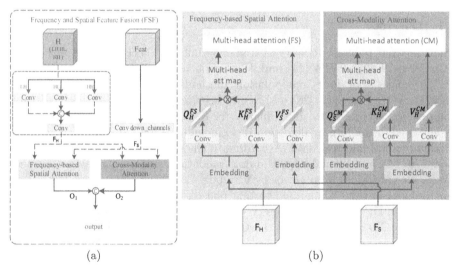

Fig. 4. (a) FSF module. (b) The architectures of frequency-based spatial attention (FSA) and cross-modality attention (CMA). The left block is FSA, in which Q and K are calculated with high-frequency features and V is obtained by spatial features. The right one is CMA, in which Q is calculated with spatial features, and the others are obtained with high-frequency features. (Color figure online)

Cross-Modality Attention. The cross-modality attention is used to fuse the information from the high-frequency representations and RGB spatial features. The architecture of cross-modality attention is shown in the right rectangular box in Fig. 4(b). The key K_H^{CM} and value V_H^{CM} are calculated by embedding the high-frequency features F_H, and the query Q_S^{CM} is obtained by embedding spatial features F_S. And the output of cross-modality attention is O_2, which is defined as follows:

$$O_2 = MHA\left(Q_S^{CM}, K_H^{CM}, V_H^{CM}\right) \tag{4}$$

where the superscript CM means the vector is in Cross-Modality Attention.

By the above two attentions, the features are enhanced through the frequency information from two different aspects. On the one hand, the features are enhanced by fusing the information of the relative regions in the spatial domain with high frequency guiding. On the other hand, the features are enhanced by fusing the information of the relative regions at the high frequency domain with cross-modality attention. Finally, we concatenate O_1 and O_2 as the output of FSF module, and then send them and the original RGB spatial features of this stage of RGB branch into the next RGB branch stage as shown in Fig. 3.

4   Experiments and Analysis

4.1   Datasets

There are four popular datasets used in experiments, FaceForensics++ (FF++) [22], Celeb-DF [23], FFIW [24], and WildDeepfake (WDF) [25] datasets. **FF++:** [22] It consists of four manipulation methods, which are DeepFakes [26], Face2Face [27], FaceSwap [28], and NeuralTexture [29]. And the videos have three compression settings: raw, high quality (c23), and low quality (c40). FF++ is widely used in the forgery detection task, including 1000 videos for each manipulation method and real data. According to the official split, we extract frames from 720, 140, and 140 videos as training, validation, and testing datasets respectively. We get frames from videos by FFmpeg. We use all frames and 300 frames (each video) in the training and testing phases. **Celeb-DF:** [23]. Li *et al.* proposed Celeb-DF dataset for forgery detection. Before long, they added more videos into Celeb-DF, and then the Celeb-DF V2 dataset appeared. Celeb-DF V2 is the most popular cross-dataset in forgery detection. Therefore, we also use Celeb-DF V2 as one of the cross-dataset evaluations. For each test video, we extract one frame for every five frames in each video. To evaluate methods in more realistic scenarios, two new public large-scale deepfake datasets in the wild **FFIW** [24] and **WDF** [25] are used for within- and cross-domain evaluations. FFIW is a large scale deepfake dataset with high quality, and the fake videos are photo-realistic and close to the real world. WDF collects videos purely from the internet which is more diverse and closer to the real-world deepfakes.

4.2   Experiment Details

We crop the face and resize them to 384×384 according to key points by MTCNN [32] as the input of the network. The model of RGB branch is initialized with the parameters pre-trained on ImageNet. In the training phase, we only use

Table 2. The results of within-dataset evaluation on FF++ dataset (video level). In this table, we show the results of each manipulation method (DF, FF, FS, and NT) based on c40. The last two columns show the results of c23 and c40 of FF++ dataset. The metrics are ACC and AUC.

Methods	DF_c40		F2F_c40		FS_c40		NT_c40		FF++_c23		FF++_c40	
	ACC	AUC	ACC	AUC	ACC	AUC	ACC	AUC	ACC	AUC	ACC	AUC
Two-branch [30]	–	–	–	–	–	–	–	–	96.43	–	86.34	–
MADFD [8]	–	–	–	–	–	–	–	–	–	98.9	–	87.2
Xception [20]	95.1	99.0	83.4	93.7	92.0	97.4	77.8	84.2	95.7	96.3	86.8	89.3
F3Net [5]	97.9	–	95.3	–	96.5	–	83.3	–	97.5	98.1	90.4	93.3
SPSL [4]	93.4	98.5	86.0	94.6	92.2	98.1	76.7	80.4	–	95.3	80.3	82.8
FADFL [11]	–	–	–	–	–	–	–	–	96.6	99.3	89.0	92.4
GFFD [31]	**98.6**	–	**95.7**	–	92.9	–	–	–	–	–	–	–
Ours	97.8	99.7	94.6	98.5	**98.2**	**99.1**	**86.6**	**93.8**	**98.6**	**99.8**	**94.9**	**98.6**

random horizontal flip as data augmentation, because we don't want other data augmentations to interfere with the final experimental results. The loss function of the model is cross-entropy loss. The batch size is set to 24. For training, we adopt AdamW [33] optimizer to optimize the total network, whose coefficients are set to 0.9 and 0.999 as default. The learning rate is initialized as 0.0001 and decreases by 0.5 with StepLR schedule for each 6×10^4 iterations, and the total number of iteration is 1.5×10^5. For attention layers, the number of heads is set to 1, 2, 5 empirically, and the embedding dimension is set to be 64, 128, 320 at attention level 1 to 3 respectively.

4.3   Results and Analysis

Metrics of the Results: In essence, face forgery detection is a two-class task, so we choose accuracy rate (ACC) and area under the receiver operating characteristic curve (AUC) to evaluate the performance of models. In the next tables, we calculate the frame and video level results in the cross-dataset evaluation. For video level, the same as other works [5,30,31], we average the prediction scores of all frames for each video as the final prediction of this video.

Within-Dataset Evaluation. The results of within-dataset evaluation are presented in Table 2, which includes different compression ratio (c23 (high quality) and c40 (low quality)) and four manipulation methods of FF++. We can see that our method achieves the best or comparable performance under different settings. It is notable that on the harder datasets, e.g. FF++ with low quality, especially FS and NT, we achieve more significant improvement which verifies the learned feature by our method is more effective for different forgery methods and robust with quality variation. Compared with GFFD using SRM to obtain high frequency features, our method outperforms it by 6.6% on FS, which shows multi-scale DWT is more effective for extracting the abundant high

Table 3. Cross-dataset evaluation on Celeb-DF V2 [23] dataset, whose model is trained on FF++ dataset. The ACC values of some methods are missing, so we mostly compare the performance with AUC.

Datasets	Celeb-DF V2 [23]			
Methods	Frame Level		Video Level	
	ACC	AUC	ACC	AUC
DDPGF [34]	–	56.90	–	–
Two-branch [30]	–	73.41	–	76.65 –
MADFD [8]	–	67.44	–	–
DGFFD [9]	63.40	64.10	–	–
F3-Net [5]	–	65.17	–	–
SPSL_c23 [4]	–	72.39	–	–
GFFD [31]	–	–	–	79.40
Xception	69.65	67.58	72.66	73.54
Ours	**72.69**	**74.55**	**76.37**	**80.65**

Table 4. The results of within-dataset evaluation on FFIW and WDF datasets (video level). In this table, FFIW-M [24] and ADDNet [25] mean the forgery detection methods proposed in FFIW [24] and WDF [25], respectively.

Datasets	FFIW		WDF	
Methods	ACC	AUC	ACC	AUC
MesoNet [35]	53.80	55.40	64.47	–
TSN [36]	61.10	62.80	–	–
C3D [37]	64.30	65.50	55.87	–
I3D [38]	68.80	69.50	62.69	–
FFIW-M [24]	71.30	73.50	–	–
ADDNet [25]	–	–	76.25	–
Xception	95.05	99.32	81.74	87.46
Ours	**95.70**	**99.48**	**82.72**	**89.96**

frequency information than these low-level filters. Compared with F3Net, SPSL, and FADFL adopting DFT or DCT to get frequency features, our method outperforms it by 5.3%, 15.8%, and 6.2% on FF++_c40, which verifies multi-scale DWT is more suitable for face forgery detection task due to its rich multi-scale high-frequency information. MADFD [8] utilized multiple attention maps and texture feature enhancement to capture local discriminative features. We utilize RGB and high frequency branches and fuse these features by FSF module. Compared with Two-branch and MADFD, it demonstrates that the proposed framework and FSF module are effective in capturing the forgery information. We also make a within-dataset evaluation on realistic scenarios i.e. FFIW and WDF datasets, whose results are shown in Table 4. Our results are the best. So, the proposed method is more suitable for diverse deepfakes and real-world face forgery detection.

Cross-Dataset Evaluation. Celeb-DF V2 dataset is often used as cross-domain evaluation, so we evaluate the model on Celeb-DF V2, whose results are shown in Table 3. Considering the diversity of realistic scenarios, we also make a cross-domain evaluation on WDF and FFIW datasets, whose results are shown in Table 5. From the Tables 3 and 5, we can observe that our method achieves the state-of-the-art performance on Celeb-DF V2, FFIW, and WDF datasets. Therefore, MSWT is robust and effective in within- and cross-dataset, which demonstrates that multi-scale structure and FSF module can learn more forgery details and make full use of high-frequency and spatial features.

Table 5. Cross-dataset evaluation on WildDeepfake (WDF) [25] and FFIW [24] datasets, whose model is trained on FF++ dataset.

Datasets	FFIW [24]				WDF [25]			
Methods	Frame Level		Video Level		Frame Level		Video Level	
	ACC	AUC	ACC	AUC	ACC	AUC	ACC	AUC
Xception	71.07	76.86	70.28	76.40	67.33	67.21	62.03	64.76
Ours	**73.11**	**81.54**	**76.10**	**82.68**	**68.55**	**68.71**	**63.28**	**67.30**

4.4 Ablation Study and Analysis

To demonstrate the effectiveness of the proposed framework, we do ablation studies both on frequency and spatial feature fusion (FSF) module and multi-scale high frequency representations. In the ablation study experiments, we use FF++ as the training dataset and test on FF++ and CelebDF datasets as within-dataset and cross-dataset evaluations.

Ablation Study on Frequency Fusion. The frequency and spatial feature fusion (FSF) module consists of a frequency-based spatial attention (FSA) and a cross-modality attention (CMA). Therefore, we keep single attention (FSA or CMA) to train the framework. To demonstrate the effectiveness of high-frequency features in FSA module, we utilize only RGB features to calculate attention, which is denoted as Xception+SA, and Xception+FSA means calculating the attention by frequency features. Besides, we train the Xception backbone by combining the high frequency sub bands into the corresponding stage directly without attention, named Xception+DWT in Table 6.

Table 6. The results of ablation study on frequency and spatial feature fusion (FSF) module. The metrics are ACC and AUC (frame-level).

Test type	Self Eval		Cross Eval	
Methods	FF++		Celeb-DF V2	
	ACC	AUC	ACC	AUC
Xception	95.73	96.30	69.65	67.58
Xception+DWT	96.85	99.35	71.45	69.22
Xception+SA	96.29	99.19	72.54	71.88
Xception+FSA	97.02	99.47	72.98	73.72
Xception+CMA	97.09	99.41	72.64	73.70
MSWT	**97.23**	**99.48**	**72.69**	**74.55**

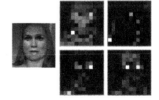

Fig. 5. Visualization of multi-head attention map in FSA and SA shown in the 1st and 2nd rows. We choose two patches (a manipulated patch shown in green box) and a real patch shown in red box) to illustrate the difference between attention maps calculated by FAS and SA respectively. (Color figure online)

Table 7. The results of ablation study on multi-level structure of DWT. The metrics are ACC and AUC (frame-level).

Test type	Self Eval		Cross Eval	
DWT_level	FF++		Celeb-DF	
	ACC	AUC	ACC	AUC
Level 1	97.07	99.40	72.14	72.17
Level 2	97.14	99.39	72.50	73.10
Level 3 (MSWT)	**97.23**	**99.48**	**72.69**	**74.55**

The results are shown in Table 6. We can observe that the result of Xception+DWT is better than Xception's, which means that the high frequency is useful for face forgery detection. Except for Xception, Xception+DWT which combines the high-frequency information directly has the worst results due to the misalignment between the frequency and RGB spaces. The results of Xception+SA are worse than Xception+FSA, which demonstrates that it is more effective to use the high frequency information to guide the attention calculation. The results of the method utilizing FSA or CMA are better than Xception+DWT, which demonstrates the effectiveness of the frequency-based spatial attention and cross-modality attention modules. The network with FSA and CMA achieves the best performance, which demonstrates that the two fusion modules are complementary.

To illustrate the influence of FSA and SA, we make a visualization of the attention in the 1st and 2nd second rows of Fig. 5. We can see that the attention map of the manipulated region (the green rectangle) calculated via frequency features has high values in the manipulated region. The attention map of the real region (the red rectangle) is sparse in the manipulated region. While the attention maps calculated via spatial features have little difference between the manipulated and real regions, which learns less distinguish forgery details. Therefore, when using frequency features to guide the attention calculation, it effectively extracts the discriminable information between the real and fake regions.

Ablation Study on Multi-scale High Frequency Structure. To illustrate the influence and effectiveness of the multi-scale high-frequency fusion, we do level-by-level experiments. We not only show the quantitative accuracy in Table 7, but also make a visualization of the attention map at each level shown in Fig. 6. In Table 7, level 1, level 2, and level 3 represent the number of DWT levels used in the framework.

The results of the multi-scale wavelet transformer are shown in Table 7. The performance of three-level frequency is the best compared with the results of levels 1 and 2, which demonstrates that multi-scale fusion is beneficial for face forgery detection. So the gradual aggregating fusion of multi-scale wavelet representation at different stages of the network can take full advantage of the frequency information.

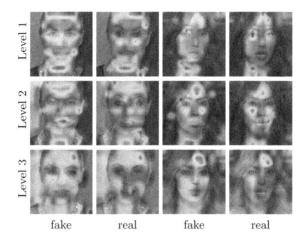

Fig. 6. Visualization of multi-level attention. The 1st and 2nd columns are fake images from DF and the corresponding real images. The third and fourth columns are fake images from NT and the corresponding real image. In this figure, the first to the third rows represent attention at level 1, 2, and 3 respectively.

We make a visualization on each level in Fig. 6, we use the method proposed in [39, 40] to generate the visualization maps. We choose two examples from ID replacement Deepfakes and expression modification NeuralTextures. The fake image from Deepfakes and the corresponding real image, the fake face from NeuralTextures and the corresponding real image are in the 1st to 4th columns of Fig. 6 respectively. The visualization maps show that the fusion module can learn more global information at the higher level, and at the first and second levels, the fusion module learns more details about the local region. So via multi-scale frequency representations and fusion, we can enhance the feature learning from both the global structure and the local details simultaneously, which is important to face forgery detection task.

5   Conclusion

Considering the multi-scale analysis property of DWT and making full use of frequency information, we extract the multi-level frequency representations via DWT and use these high frequency components to the proposed multi-scale wavelet transformer architecture for face forgery detection. We apply transformer as the attention block to integrate the high-frequency and RGB spatial features at multiple levels. Specifically, the frequency based spatial attention guides spatial features to focus on forgery regions. The cross-modality attention is used to better fuse the frequency features with the RGB spatial features. The various experiments demonstrate that the proposed framework is effective and robust on self and cross datasets compared with the existing methods.

References

1. Ferrara, P., Bianchi, T., De Rosa, A., Piva, A.: Image forgery localization via fine-grained analysis of cfa artifacts. IEEE Trans. Inf. Forensics Secur. **7**, 1566–1577 (2012)
2. Pan, X., Zhang, X., Lyu, S.: Exposing image splicing with inconsistent local noise variances. In: 2012 IEEE International Conference on Computational Photography, pp. 1–10. IEEE (2012)
3. Yu, Y., Ni, R., Zhao, Y.: Mining generalized features for detecting ai-manipulated fake faces. arXiv preprint arXiv:2010.14129 (2020)
4. Liu, H., et al.: Spatial-phase shallow learning: rethinking face forgery detection in frequency domain. In: Proceedings of the IEEE/CVF Conference on Computer Vision and Pattern Recognition, pp. 772–781 (2021)
5. Qian, Y., Yin, G., Sheng, L., Chen, Z., Shao, J.: Thinking in frequency: face forgery detection by mining frequency-aware clues. In: Vedaldi, A., Bischof, H., Brox, T., Frahm, J.-M. (eds.) ECCV 2020. LNCS, vol. 12357, pp. 86–103. Springer, Cham (2020). https://doi.org/10.1007/978-3-030-58610-2_6
6. Rubner, Y., Tomasi, C., Guibas, L.J.: The earth mover's distance as a metric for image retrieval. Int. J. Comput. Vision **40**, 99–121 (2000)
7. Zhao, T., Xu, X., Xu, M., Ding, H., Xiong, Y., Xia, W.: Learning to recognize patch-wise consistency for deepfake detection. arXiv preprint arXiv:2012.09311 (2020)
8. Zhao, H., Zhou, W., Chen, D., Wei, T., Zhang, W., Yu, N.: Multi-attentional deepfake detection. In: Proceedings of the IEEE/CVF Conference on Computer Vision and Pattern Recognition, pp. 2185–2194 (2021)
9. Sun, K., Liu, H., Ye, Q., Liu, J., Gao, Y., Shao, L., Ji, R.: Domain general face forgery detection by learning to weight. In: Proceedings of the AAAI Conference on Artificial Intelligence, vol. 35, pp. 2638–2646 (2021)
10. Wodajo, D., Atnafu, S.: Deepfake video detection using convolutional vision transformer. arXiv preprint arXiv:2102.11126 (2021)
11. Li, J., Xie, H., Li, J., Wang, Z., Zhang, Y.: Frequency-aware discriminative feature learning supervised by single-center loss for face forgery detection. In: Proceedings of the IEEE/CVF Conference on Computer Vision and Pattern Recognition, pp. 6458–6467 (2021)
12. Zhu, X., Wang, H., Fei, H., Lei, Z., Li, S.Z.: Face forgery detection by 3d decomposition. In: Proceedings of the IEEE/CVF Conference on Computer Vision and Pattern Recognition, pp. 2929–2939 (2021)
13. Ramamonjisoa, M., Firman, M., Watson, J., Lepetit, V., Turmukhambetov, D.: Single image depth prediction with wavelet decomposition. In: Proceedings of the IEEE/CVF Conference on Computer Vision and Pattern Recognition, pp. 11089–11098 (2021)
14. Malfait, M., Roose, D.: Wavelet-based image denoising using a Markov random field a priori model. IEEE Trans. Image Process. **6**, 549–565 (1997)
15. Pizurica, A., Philips, W., Lemahieu, I., Acheroy, M.: A joint inter-and intrascale statistical model for bayesian wavelet based image denoising. IEEE Trans. Image Process. **11**, 545–557 (2002)
16. Figueiredo, M.A., Nowak, R.D.: An em algorithm for wavelet-based image restoration. IEEE Trans. Image Process. **12**, 906–916 (2003)
17. Meyer, F.G., Averbuch, A.Z., Stromberg, J.O.: Fast adaptive wavelet packet image compression. IEEE Trans. Image Process. **9**, 792–800 (2000)

18. Shi, W., Zhu, C., Tian, Y., Nichol, J.: Wavelet-based image fusion and quality assessment. Int. J. Appl. Earth Obs. Geoinf. **6**, 241–251 (2005)
19. Pajares, G., De La Cruz, J.M.: A wavelet-based image fusion tutorial. Pattern Recogn. **37**, 1855–1872 (2004)
20. Chollet, F.: Xception: deep learning with depthwise separable convolutions. In: Proceedings of the IEEE Conference on Computer Vision and Pattern Recognition, pp. 1251–1258 (2017)
21. Haar, A.: Zur theorie der orthogonalen funktionensysteme. (erste mitteilung). Mathematische Annalen **69**, 331–371 (1910)
22. Rossler, A., Cozzolino, D., Verdoliva, L., Riess, C., Thies, J., Niessner, M.: Faceforensics++: learning to detect manipulated facial images. In: Proceedings of the IEEE/CVF International Conference on Computer Vision (2019)
23. Li, Y., Yang, X., Sun, P., Qi, H., Lyu, S.: Celeb-df: a large-scale challenging dataset for deepfake forensics. In: Proceedings of the IEEE/CVF Conference on Computer Vision and Pattern Recognition, pp. 3207–3216 (2020)
24. Zhou, T., Wang, W., Liang, Z., Shen, J.: Face forensics in the wild. In: Proceedings of the IEEE/CVF Conference on Computer Vision and Pattern Recognition, pp. 5778–5788 (2021)
25. Zi, B., Chang, M., Chen, J., Ma, X., Jiang, Y.G.: Wilddeepfake: a challenging real-world dataset for deepfake detection. In: Proceedings of the 28th ACM International Conference on Multimedia, pp. 2382–2390 (2020)
26. DeepFakes: Deepfakes github (2017). http://github.com/deepfakes/faceswap. Accessed 18 August 2020
27. Thies, J., Zollhofer, M., Stamminger, M., Theobalt, C., Nießner, M.: Face2face: real-time face capture and reenactment of rgb videos. In: Proceedings of the IEEE Conference on Computer Vision and Pattern Recognition, pp. 2387–2395 (2016)
28. FaceSwap: Faceswap github (2016). https://github.com/MarekKowalski/FaceSwap. Accessed 18 August 2020
29. Thies, J., Zollhöfer, M., Nießner, M.: Deferred neural rendering: image synthesis using neural textures. ACM Trans. Graph. **38**, 1–12 (2019)
30. Masi, I., Killekar, A., Mascarenhas, R.M., Gurudatt, S.P., AbdAlmageed, W.: Twobranch recurrent network for isolating deepfakes in videos. In: Vedaldi, A., Bischof, H., Brox, T., Frahm, J.-M. (eds.) ECCV 2020. LNCS, vol. 12352, pp. 667–684. Springer, Cham (2020). https://doi.org/10.1007/978-3-030-58571-6_39
31. Luo, Y., Zhang, Y., Yan, J., Liu, W.: Generalizing face forgery detection with highfrequency features. In: Proceedings of the IEEE/CVF Conference on Computer Vision and Pattern Recognition, pp. 16317–16326 (2021)
32. Zhang, K., Zhang, Z., Li, Z., Qiao, Y.: Joint face detection and alignment using multitask cascaded convolutional networks. IEEE Signal Process. Lett. **23**, 1499–1503 (2016)
33. Loshchilov, I., Hutter, F.: Fixing weight decay regularization in adam. ArXiv abs/1711.05101 (2017)
34. Sun, Z., Han, Y., Hua, Z., Ruan, N., Jia, W.: Improving the efficiency and robustness of deepfakes detection through precise geometric features. In: Proceedings of the IEEE/CVF Conference on Computer Vision and Pattern Recognition, pp. 3609–3618 (2021)
35. Afchar, D., Nozick, V., Yamagishi, J., Echizen, I.: Mesonet: a compact facial video forgery detection network. In: IEEE International Workshop on Information Forensics and Security, pp. 1–7. IEEE (2018)

36. Wang, L., Xiong, Y., Wang, Z., Qiao, Yu., Lin, D., Tang, X., Van Gool, L.: Temporal segment networks: towards good practices for deep action recognition. In: Leibe, B., Matas, J., Sebe, N., Welling, M. (eds.) ECCV 2016. LNCS, vol. 9912, pp. 20–36. Springer, Cham (2016). https://doi.org/10.1007/978-3-319-46484-8_2
37. Tran, D., Bourdev, L., Fergus, R., Torresani, L., Paluri, M.: Learning spatiotemporal features with 3d convolutional networks. In: Proceedings of the IEEE International Conference on Computer Vision, pp. 4489–4497 (2015)
38. Carreira, J., Zisserman, A.: Quo vadis, action recognition? a new model and the kinetics dataset. In: Proceedings of the IEEE Conference on Computer Vision and Pattern Recognition, pp. 6299–6308 (2017)
39. Chefer, H., Gur, S., Wolf, L.: Transformer interpretability beyond attention visualization. In: Proceedings of the IEEE/CVF Conference on Computer Vision and Pattern Recognition, pp. 782–791 (2021)
40. Chefer, H., Gur, S., Wolf, L.: Generic attention-model explainability for interpreting bi-modal and encoder-decoder transformers. In: Proceedings of the IEEE/CVF International Conference on Computer Vision, pp. 397–406 (2021)

Slice-Mask Based 3D Cardiac Shape Reconstruction from CT Volume

Xiaohan Yuan[1], Cong Liu[1], Fu Feng[1], Yinsu Zhu[2], and Yangang Wang[1(✉)]

[1] School of Automation, Southeast University, Nanjing, China
yangangwang@seu.edu.cn
[2] Department of Radiology, the First Affiliated Hospital of Nanjing Medical University, Nanjing, China

Abstract. An accurate 3D ventricular model is essential for diagnosing and analyzing cardiovascular disease. It is challenging to obtain accurate patient-specific models on scarce data via widely accepted deep-learning methods. To fully use the characteristics of medical volume-based images, we present a slice-mask representation to better regress the parameters of the 3D model. A data synthesis strategy is proposed to alleviate the lack of training data by sampling in the constructed statistical shape model space and obtaining the corresponding slice-masks. We train the end-to-end structure by combining the segmentation and parametric regression modules. Furthermore, we establish a larger left ventricular CT dataset than before, which fills the gap in relevant data of the healthy population. Our method is evaluated on both synthetic data and real cardiac scans. Experiments demonstrate that our method can achieve advanced results in shape reconstruction and segmentation tasks. Code is publicly available at https://github.com/yuan-xiaohan/Slice-mask-based-3D-Cardiac-Shape-Reconstruction.

Keywords: 3D reconstruction · Segmentation · Cardiac CT

1 Introduction

The heart is one of the vital organs of our body, and cardiovascular disease is the leading cause of death and morbidity worldwide [23]. The left ventricle (LV) is the most important chamber of the heart and main source of blood flow. However, current disease diagnosis and assessment are always guided by slice-based 2D images, making it difficult for clinicians to obtain intuitive patient-specific visualizations and resulting in inaccurate estimates of clinical metrics such as volume and ejection fraction. Therefore, boosting the limited 2D images

---

All the authors from Southeast University are affiliated with the Key Laboratory of Measurement and Control of Complex Systems of Engineering, Ministry of Education, Nanjing, China.

Supplementary Information The online version contains supplementary material available at https://doi.org/10.1007/978-3-031-26351-4_5.

L. Wang et al. (Eds.): ACCV 2022, LNCS 13846, pp. 69–85, 2023.
https://doi.org/10.1007/978-3-031-26351-4_5

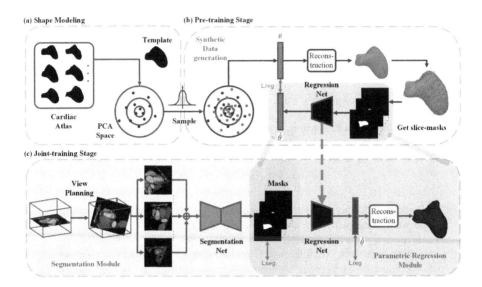

Fig. 1. The overall pipeline of the proposed framework. (a) Shape modeling. We first generate a cardiac atlas from the real meshes and construct a statistical shape model by PCA, resulting in low-dimensional parameter space. (b) In the pre-training stage, the parametric regression module is trained by generating massive synthetic data, consisting of reasonable model parameters and their corresponding slice masks. (c) Joint-training stage includes a segmentation module and a pre-trained parametric regression module. The input to the segmentation module is the set of view-planned slices, and the output is their masks, which are used as the input to the parametric regression module, finally obtaining the shapes.

with the prior of 3D heart shapes, and using it to instantiate cardiac models has important applications for surgical planning, morphological assessment, and educational purposes. Although recent years have witnessed the rapid progress of deep learning in the field of medical image analysis, especially for the segmentation and reconstruction tasks, the lack of scale of annotated datasets impedes the generalization of trained models for 3D heart reconstruction. In this paper, we focus on the problem of accurate 3D reconstruction of the left ventricle in response to the data-poor dilemma.

Generally, existing 3D medical reconstruction methods often require fine-scale segmentation masks, mainly focusing on the precursor task of medical image segmentation [12]. The methods of directly generating a mesh from masks depend highly on the segmentation quality and often produce surfaces with stair-step artifacts that are affected by the low resolution of medical images. To avoid the lack of mesh integrity, a model-driven strategy, as a parametric method, is often addressed. The segmented contour is fitted by the constructed statistical shape model (SSM) to complete the shape prediction [8,10,13], but the separated multi-stage iterative strategy will greatly increase the computational cost. Recently, a few pioneers have devoted the organ geometry reconstruction of point clouds or meshes directly from images or volume with the deep neural network [6,30,32]. These works are often derived from the field of computer vision and lack consideration of the characteristics of medical image data.

In this paper, to fully exploit the volume characteristics of medical images, our key idea is to slice the three-dimensional SSM model from different views into a set of two-dimensional mask images via the technique of computer graphics, where the masks are named as **slice-masks**. It is noted that the view we obtain is not a projection but a typical angle of slices in the volume, which is different from traditional multi-view reconstruction in the area of computer vision. In order to conveniently describe the anatomical cardiac model, the views of slices are predefined and chosen similar to the clinical strategy.

However, the scarcity of public datasets for cardiac CT images brings great difficulties to network training. To improve the variance of cardiac SSM parameters, we first construct the SSM space of the cardiac model and then sample the SSM parameters to synthesize massive 3D cardiac models that conform to the real anatomy, enlarging the size of the training set. The slice positions and 3D model landmarks can be easily defined in the SSM template model to obtain view-consistent slice-masks for all synthetic models. In such a manner, we can augment more slice-masks corresponding to the model without relying on the raw CT data.

With the obtained synthetic training data, the SSM parameter regression network is concatenated with a segmentation network to predict the SSM parameters. It is noted that these two modules might mismatch due to the imbalance of real and synthetic training data. To alleviate this circumstance, we propose a refining step to improve the accuracy of the segmentation module due to the anatomical constraints of the reconstruction task.

To further tackle the obstacle of data scarcity and fill the gap with normal human cardiac data, we increase the amount of real data by collecting a larger-scale healthy left ventricular CT dataset than most existing ones [14,31,35]. A more accurate low-dimensional parametric model is generated to facilitate the cardiac parameters regression and network training.

In summary, the main contributions of this work are as follows.

- Combining the characteristics of medical volume data with the anatomical knowledge of the heart, we use the proposed slice-mask representation to better regress the parameters of the 3D model. We synthesize massive models by sampling in a statistical shape model space and obtaining the corresponding slice-masks to alleviate the lack of training data.
- We design a training strategy for improving the accuracy of shape reconstruction and segmentation, where the end-to-end network consists of a segmentation module and a parameter regression module.
- We build a larger-scale CT atlas of the left ventricle than previous work, making up for the current scarcity of data, especially in healthy individuals.

2   Related Work

Parametric Shape Reconstruction. Traditional 3D medical reconstruction methods often require fine-scale segmentation masks, mainly focusing on the precursor task of medical image segmentation. Marching Cube algorithm [19] is then typically utilized to generate a mesh of segmented regions from the contours delineated from each layer of the image volume. Operations such as smoothing [3,15] are often performed at the last step. Such methods cannot ensure the integrity of the mesh. Therefore, a model-driven strategy is often addressed, which usually completes the shape prediction by constructing a statistical shape model (SSM) to fit the initial contour of the segmentation [8,10,13]. Some methods for shape prediction based on segmentation graphs introduce shape priors into the segmentation tasks in the previous stage to ensure better results in the downstream reconstruction [5,7,18,36]. For example, in the case of image artifacts, the constructed 3D cardiac shape can be ensured to have anatomical significance. [26] enforced robustness of shape prediction by simultaneously performing semantic segmentation, which is performed by regression of signed distance maps, trained using a loss function incorporating both distance and overlap measures. Other methods improve the reconstruction performance by directly introducing shape prior knowledge into the reconstruction task [1,4,27,33]. Most recently, with the development of deep learning, methods combining SSM with a convolutional neural network (CNN) can achieve better results. Zhou et al. [33] borrowed the PointOutNet [9] to learn the relationship between a 2D image and a 3D SSM in a single stage for 3D shape prediction. Regression of shape coefficients using a CNN was performed by Bhalodia et al. [4] and Adams et al. [1] extended this work to a probabilistic approach to determine the credibility of the model output by quantifying uncertainty. Probabilistic surface prediction with a PCA shape prior was also performed by Tóthová et al. [27], the input of the network is three orthogonal standard MR views. Attar et al. [2] proposed a deep neural network using both CMR images and patient meta-data to directly predict 3D cardiac shape parameters instead of a pixel-wise classification across each 2D slice. This method uses the promising ability of SSM to simplify shape complexity. However, it needs over 3000 CMR image volumes with manual delineations to construct reference 3D shapes for training, and the patient metadata is often challenging to obtain.

Nonparametric Shape Reconstruction. Shape reconstruction methods in the form of a nonparametric model are generally based on deep learning. They can directly predict the surface mesh of cardiac structures from image or volume data. A series of works on recovering 3D shapes from 2D images have emerged in computer vision, usually consisting of an encoder that extracts image features and an encoder-decoder that generates grids [20,29,32]. PointOutNet [9] can generate unordered 3D points from a single RGB image cloud and 3D-LMNet [20] can utilize an image encoder to map a 2D image into a 3D point cloud latent space learned by an auto-encoder. Ye et al. [32] proposed a network that directly reconstructs LV from the volume of 2D CT slices and generates its segmentation masks from the predicted 3D point cloud. Wang et al. [29] used information extracted from single-view 2D medical images to predict the displacement of control points to learn the spatial deformation of lung organs. In recent years, graph convolutional neural networks have also shown promise for surface mesh reconstruction [16,30]. According to the volumetric properties of medical images,

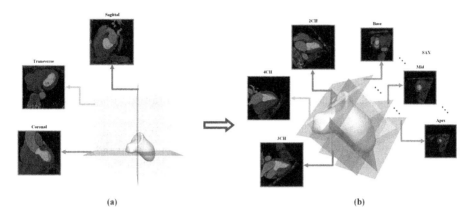

(a)   (b)

Fig. 2. Visual representation of the relative relationship between slice positions and ventricular model. Shapes with different color planes represent different views. On the left are the slices directly imaged by CT, and on the right are the slices we selected according to the view planning.

Wickramasinghe et al. [30] extended the Pixel2Mesh [28] from 2D images to 3D surface meshes, taking 3D volumes as input to solve the reconstruction problem of CT liver. Kong et al. [17] proposed a network that learns to deform a template grid into a volume of input image data by predicting the displacement of a multi-resolution control point grid.

3   Method

Figure 1 provides an overview of the proposed framework. First, we build a 3D model atlas of the left ventricle by manually segmenting and generating the meshes, then construct a low-dimensional parameter space using principal component analysis (PCA) (see Sect. 3.1). By sampling in the latent space, we make corresponding slice-masks for numerous reasonable samples generated, which are used to train the parametric regression network (see Sect. 3.2). After obtaining the pre-training weights of the parameter regression network, we add it to the joint architecture and optimize it with the segmentation network (see Sect. 3.3).

The joint architecture consists of two modules: the input CT volume is sliced into planes after view planning and used as the input to the segmentation module. The segmentation output will be used as the input to the parameter regression module, which directly estimates the model parameters.

3.1   Shape Modeling

Building an atlas is the first step in modeling the shape and constructing the parameter space. Benefiting from the high-resolution features of CT, we manually delineate each layer of the CT volume, so that the generated 3D model has sufficiently high fidelity. Suppose that the heart model training set $\mathbb{D} = \{\mathbf{D}_1, \mathbf{D}_2, \cdots, \mathbf{D}_M\}$ has M models, and different models have different vertices. The parametric model is mainly determined by the shape parameter $\alpha \in \mathbb{R}^K$. Since there is a large difference in the size of the heart at end-diastole and end-systole, to decouple it from shape, we add a size parameter $\beta \in \mathbb{R}^1$. As long as the overall parameter $\theta = [\alpha, \beta] \in \mathbb{R}^{K+1}$ is obtained, a heart model can be reconstructed.

We first use the Iterative Closest Point (ICP) algorithm to align each model with the template, and use the method proposed in [25] to deform the template onto each model to obtain a set of heart models with the same topology $\mathbb{S} = \{\mathbf{S}_1, \mathbf{S}_2, \cdots, \mathbf{S}_M\}$, and $\mathbf{S}_i \in \mathbb{R}^{3 \times N}, i \in 1 \cdots M$, where N is the number of vertices of the template. After the atlas is constructed, its parameter latent space can be obtained through statistical analysis. We use Principal Component Analysis (PCA) to construct the shape parameters of the model on the set $\mathbb{S}$ which is just gained by the registration. Map the shape $\mathbf{S}_i$ to vector $\mathbf{s}_i = [x_1, y_1, z_1, \cdots, x_N, y_N, z_N]^T \in \mathbb{R}^{3N}$, then let $\mathbf{S}_{map} = [\mathbf{s}_1, \mathbf{s}_2, \cdots, \mathbf{s}_M]^T \in \mathbb{R}^{M \times 3N}$ and the mean shape $\bar{\mathbf{s}} = \frac{1}{M} \sum_{i=1}^{M} \mathbf{s}_i$. Through the singular value decomposition (SVD) of $\mathbf{S}_{map}$:

$$\mathbf{S}_{map} = \mathbf{U} \sum \mathbf{V}^T, \tag{1}$$

we get $\mathbf{V} \in \mathbb{R}^{3N \times K}$ that fully defines the linear function below:

$$\mathcal{B}(\theta) = \beta \cdot \mathcal{M}(\bar{\mathbf{s}} + \mathbf{V}\alpha), \tag{2}$$

where $\theta = [\alpha, \beta] \in \mathbb{R}^{K+1}$ denotes the shape coefficients, and the operator $M(\mathbf{s}) : \mathbb{R}^{3N} \mapsto \mathbb{R}^{3 \times N}$ maps the vector to the shape. The function $\mathcal{B}(\theta)$ produces the shapes of different hearts.

3.2   Data Synthesis Strategy

Based on the parametric models that have been proposed, we analyze the parameter distribution of real data and generate multivariate Gaussian distribution centered on real samples for sampling. The resampled parameters can obtain different hearts from the original training set while maintaining anatomical consistency and fidelity. We will introduce the parametric regression network and how to obtain the slice-masks for each generated model.

Parametric Regression Network. In this work, we regard the CT heart modeling problem as a multi-view reconstruction problem and hope to regress the parameters directly from the slice-masks.

Typically, raw CT images are scanned in standard planes of the body (transverse, sagittal, and coronal). However, due to the unique shape and location of the heart, it cannot be simply expressed by the standard axis of the human body (as shown in Fig. 2(a)). Most existing methods do not consider the view problem but directly use the entire volume or images with the original view as input.

The former will bring the challenge of memory computing, and the latter cannot effectively contain the critical information for reconstructing the structure. Therefore, we propose to extract as much information as possible from a few slices from different perspectives. The process of obtaining these slices from the raw CT volume is called view planning, and the masks obtained from this series of slices are named slice-masks. The selection of slice locations is based on the anatomical structure of the heart: long-axis views (two-chamber (2CH), three-chamber (3CH), and four-chamber (4CH) heart) and short-axis views (SAX). We use the above-mentioned unique perspectives for the heart, equivalent to setting the "camera" in a place that can represent heart information more abundantly. The parameter regression network seeks the mapping relationship between slice-masks and parameter space, which significantly reduces the information redundancy caused by useless background. Figure 2(b) shows the relative position relationship between the position of each slice and the ventricular model. It can be seen visually that these perspective views cover the whole heart, and the segmented slices obtained in this way can comprehensively describe the shape of the ventricle.

For the parametric regression network, the input is 13 concatenated slice-masks (3 long-axis views and 10 short-axis views). Considering that the model parameters are generated by PCA operation, the coefficient corresponding to the eigenvector with a larger variance contribution is more important and can better reflect the topology of the model. Therefore, we use the weighted two-norm function to analyze the model parameters output by the network, which is,

$$L_{reg} = \lambda_1 \cdot \sum_{i=1}^{K} (\alpha_i - \hat{\alpha}_i)^2 \cdot w_i + \lambda_2 \cdot (\beta - \hat{\beta})^2 \tag{3}$$

For supervision, where the weight w_i is positively related to the variance ratio of the feature vector, α_i and $\hat{\alpha}_i$ is the true value and predicted value of the shape parameter in the ith dimension, respectively. β and $\hat{\beta}$ is the true value and predicted value of the model size, respectively. λ_1 and λ_2 represent the influence of the shape term and the size term, respectively.

Acquisition of Slice-Masks. According to the structural characteristics of the proposed regression network, the training data it needs is the pair of the slice-masks and the ground-truth parameters, so we propose a method to acquire the slice-masks of any generated model.

We will design the slices according to the given rules for each model to obtain the masks (See Supplementary Material for details). To plan the views directly, it is necessary to find the positional relationship between these slice-masks and the model. It is worth noting that the equations of slice planes are determined by several landmarks on the model, such as the apex (AP), the center of the mitral valve (MV), and the center of the aortic valve (AV). These anatomical landmarks are related to the vertices of the shape, and there is a one-to-one correspondence between the vertices of each parametric model. So as long as there are three landmark indexes, one slice of the model can be directly determined. We ask professional doctors to manually determine a series of landmarks on the template model and then propagate it to any other generated shapes. Thus, we can obtain the slice-masks of the synthetic models and train the parameter regression network from these.

3.3   Training Strategy

Considering the scarcity of CT data and its annotations, direct training in the architecture of a joint network will cause specific difficulties. So we design a strategy for staged training. We first train the parameter regression network separately using the synthetic data to enhance its generalization performance. We place the pre-trained parametric regression network after the segmentation network and estimate the parameters directly from the former segmentation results. However, the pre-trained subnetwork uses perfect masks sliced from the ground-truth model during its training phase. The masks estimated from the segmentation network often contain artifacts that interfere with the parameter estimation. Therefore, combining the two networks and fine-tuning the parameter estimation network to adapt to this situation is necessary.

Here, the process of view planning for CT volume is similar to that of MR standard [24] (See Supplementary Material for details) to obtain the input of the segmentation network. We choose 2D UNet as the architecture, using cross-entropy loss L_{seg}. When two networks are coupled, exploiting their respective tasks to promote each other: adding segmentation guidance to reconstruction and adding reconstructed anatomical constraints to segmentation can lead to improved performance on both tasks. The network is optimized by a joint loss as follows:

$$L_{joint} = \lambda \cdot L_{seg} + \mu \cdot L_{reg} \qquad (4)$$

where L_{seg} is the segmentation loss and L_{reg} is the parametric regression loss. Their details will be further introduced in later sections, and λ and μ are the weights of them.

4   Experiments

4.1   Data

Table 1. A brief review of previous literature on CT cardiac atlases.

Methods	Size	Subjects
Ecabert et al. [8]	13	patients
Ordas et al. [22]	100	healthy/patients
Hoogendoorn et al. [13]	138	patients
Ours	**225**	**healthy**

Table 1 compares different studies built on CT cardiac atlases. The scale of the existing atlases is so small to directly build a parametric model and the statistical shape modeling method usually relies on the database of a healthy population. In order to fill the gap in relevant data and lay the foundation for in-depth research on the function of healthy hearts, we recruited more than 50 volunteers for cardiac CT scans.

Our raw cardiac CT images were collected in Jiangsu Province Hospital, and the whole volume of data covered the entire heart structure, ranging from the upper abdomen to the aortic arch. Five professional doctors were organized to label and review and finally obtained more than 200 left ventricular models of different phases. Different time phases reflect different states of heart movement, which increases the diversity of data.

4.2 Implementation Details and Evaluation Metrics

The segmentation module adopts the UNet structure [24], the input is 13 slices, and the size of each slice is scaled to 192×192. The parameter regression module adds fully connected layers to the encoder architecture of UNet, and finally outputs $(50+1)$ parameters. To facilitate network regression, we normalize each dimension of the parameters. We use 3090Ti GPU for training, Adam optimizer with batch size 4, and initial learning rate set to 1e-4. In the joint loss, the weight of the segmentation loss λ is 1, and the weight of the parameter regression loss μ is 10.

For the segmentation task, we use the Dice Similarity Coefficient (DSC), intersection over union (IOU), and Hausdorff Distance (HD) for evaluation. For the reconstruction task, we use Mean Surface Distance (MSD) and Chamfer Distance (CD) for evaluation.

4.3 Ablation Study

We divided the data into a "real training set" (149 objects, which serves as a prior for building a parametric model, whose parameters are treated as ground-truth), and a "real test set" (76 objects, ground-truth without parameters). The synthetic data was also divided into a "synthetic training set" (3000 objects) and a "synthetic test set" (500 objects).

Data Synthesis Strategy Effectiveness. To demonstrate the data synthesis strategy, we trained the parameter regression network using only real data as the training set and adding synthetic data as the training set, respectively. As shown in Fig. 2, both can achieve overfitting on the real training set, which shows that the idea of the network regressing parameters from a few segmentation masks is feasible. After adding the generated data to the training set, the performance on the synthetic test set is very obvious: the network after data augmentation shows better generalization performance.

Table 2. Results of the parameters MSE loss (Lreg) and mean surface distance (MSD) with or without synthetic data training, respectively. *R-Train* is to train on the real dataset, and *R+S-Train* is on both the real dataset and synthetic dataset; *R-Test* is the real test set, and *S-Test* is the synthetic test set.

Training set	Lreg		MSD	
	R-Test	S-Test	R-Test	S-Test
R-Train	0.001	0.015	0.927	1.557
R+S-Train	**0.0003**	**0.002**	**0.669**	**0.625**

Table 3. Results of different inputs to the regression network. *Tran* represents the raw transverse slices, *SAX* and *LAX* are the short-axis and long-axis slices after view planning, respectively. The number in parentheses indicates the number of slices of the input network.

Input	Tran(13)	SAX(10)	LAX(3)	SAX+LAX(13)
MSD	2.292±1.393	1.793±0.887	1.012±0.460	**0.926±0.354**
CD	4.693±2.92	3.585±1.669	2.083±0.775	**1.960±0.606**

Slice-Masks Selection. We compared the effects of different slice-masks as inputs on the reconstruction results, as shown in Table 3. Using the raw transverse images obtained directly from CT is the choice of most existing work, but a small number of these views can not achieve ideal results. The selection of slice position is crucial, and LAX contains the most information because it is obtained according to the characteristics of heart structure. Taking both SAX and LAX perspectives as the input of the network can enhance the information obtained by the network.

Joint Optimization Effectiveness. We verified the effectiveness of the joint optimization of the segmentation module and the parametric regression module. As shown in Fig. 3, whether the pre-training model is added or not affects the segmentation loss and parameter regression loss, respectively. In general, the loss of the joint network decreases with or without the addition of a pre-trained model. Adding one pre-training module will make the loss of another module drop more smoothly and speed up the training. Comparing the two loss images, it can be found that the regression loss is more volatile than the segmentation loss because our training of the parametric regression module alone is more "ideal", assuming that the inputs are all accurate segmentations. In practice, the segmentation estimated from the segmentation network is often not that imperfect. Therefore, it can be seen from Fig. 4(a) that if the segmentation module and the parameter regression module are entirely separated and optimized separately, the accuracy of the parameter regression will be significantly affected by the segmentation results, which reflects the advantages of the joint network. By optimizing simultaneously, this incongruity can be neatly balanced.

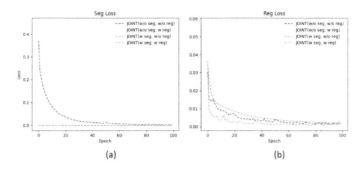

Fig. 3. Jointly optimized training. (a) and (b) are the curves of segmentation loss and parametric regression loss during training, respectively. Each figure shows the results of four training modes, where *seg* is the segmentation pre-training model, and *reg* is the parameter regression pre-training model.

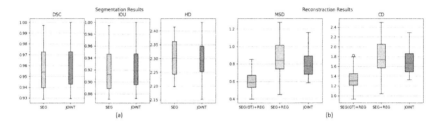

Fig. 4. The effectiveness of joint optimization. (a) and (b) are the performance results of different models on segmentation and reconstruction tasks, respectively. Among them, *SEG* is the segmentation model, *SEG(GT)+REG* represents that the input of the parameter regression module are the ground-truth masks, *SEG+REG* represents that the two modules are trained separately, and *JOINT* is the joint model.

The supervision of the parameter regression module will promote the improvement of segmentation accuracy, and the addition of the segmentation module can force the parameter regression module to learn parameters from imperfect segmentation, as shown in Fig. 4(b).

4.4 Comparison Experiments

- Raw images as input (**R-FCN**): We refer to the method from [2] and directly use the raw images as input to obtain shape parameters.
- Template fitting approach (**TF**): We use a two-stage method like [21] by minimizing the point-to-point distance between the obtained surface contour and the template mesh.
- Template fitting approach (**Voxel2Mesh**): A surface reconstruction method [30] based on GCN for 3D medical volumes.
- UNet and its variant versions: The classical medical image segmentation network (**UNet**) proposed by [24]. An encoder-decoder network (**UNet++**) with deep supervision and dense skip pathways [34]. A Context Encoder Net-

Table 4. Results on the reconstruction task.

Methods	MSD (mm)	CD (mm)	Runtime (s)
R-FCN	2.004 ± 0.920	4.014 ± 1.693	**0.040**
TF	0.867 ± 0.353	1.874 ± 0.673	20.056
Voxel2Mesh	2.127 ± 0.664	4.321 ± 1.215	4.868
Ours-UNet++	1.021 ± 0.577	2.135 ± 1.192	0.113
Ours-CE-Net	0.937 ± 0.328	1.936 ± 0.564	0.085
Ours-UNet	$\mathbf{0.862 \pm 0.341}$	$\mathbf{1.806 \pm 0.590}$	0.106

Table 5. Results of the segmentation task on the specific views.

Methods	DSC(%)	IOU(%)	HD(mm)
R-FCN	0.876 ± 0.063	0.787 ± 0.097	2.687 ± 0.237
TF	0.938 ± 0.023	0.907 ± 0.042	2.324 ± 0.341
UNet++	0.917 ± 0.114	0.864 ± 0.129	2.416 ± 0.482
Ours-UNet++	0.920 ± 0.144	0.867 ± 0.153	2.413 ± 0.608
CE-Net	0.945 ± 0.022	0.900 ± 0.037	2.368 ± 0.207
Ours-CE-Net	0.946 ± 0.022	0.900 ± 0.039	2.359 ± 0.233
UNet	0.948 ± 0.025	0.886 ± 0.037	2.397 ± 0.194
Ours-UNet	$\mathbf{0.952 \pm 0.025}$	$\mathbf{0.907 \pm 0.041}$	$\mathbf{2.321 \pm 0.347}$

work (**CE-Net**) to capture more high-level information and preserve spatial information for 2D medical image segmentation [11].

- **Ours**: Based on the above proposed UNet and its variants, our proposed parametric regression network is subsequently connected. To speed up the convergence, we train the parametric regression network with real and synthetic data and the segmentation network with real images and masks, respectively. The two networks are then concatenated to optimize the overall structure.

Results on the Reconstruction Task. Table 4 are the quantitative results of various methods on the reconstruction task, and our method is comparable to the TF method in accuracy. Combined with Table 5, it can be seen that the performance of the upstream segmentation task inevitably affects the results of the downstream reconstruction task. The segmentation network in our framework can be replaced with any SOTA structure; if the segmentation result is accurate enough, a better reconstruction effect can be obtained. The purpose of our joint optimization strategy is to minimize this effect.

Visualizations and error distributions reconstructed by several methods are presented in Fig. 5. For the R-FCN and Voxel2Mesh, a large amount of training data must be used to achieve good results, and the lack of raw CT data greatly restricts it. Since, in the training phase, we use synthetic data that does not depend on the raw images, avoiding this dilemma and achieving better results under the same conditions. In addition, taking the overall volume as the input of the network requires down sampling to meet the memory needs, which will lose

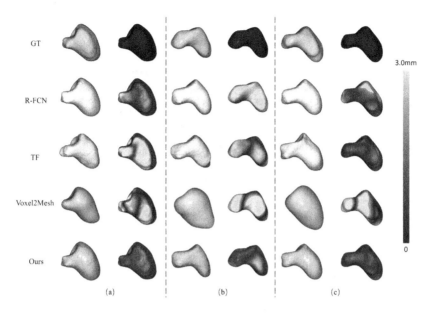

Fig. 5. Reconstruction results. Each alphabetical number represents an example, the first column of each example is the visualization, and the column row is the error distribution.

detailed information. Although the error of the classical TF method is also tiny, it depends highly on the first step segmentation. The iterative process will take more time, reflecting the end-to-end efficiency of deep learning. In comparison, our inference speed is several times faster than iterative methods.

Results on the Segmentation Task. As shown in the Table 5, the combination of Unet and regression module (Ours-UNet) achieves the best performance among all methods. Compared with the results of various optimization methods and their jointly optimized versions, the latter has a specific improvement in the segmentation effect. It shows that the supervision of the downstream parameter regression module can improve the performance of the upstream segmentation task. Figure 6 shows the visualization results of different methods. Our method can fit the contour of the ground-truth (due to the superposition of the two colors, it will appear almost white in the figure), while R-FCN and TF are pretty different from the ground-truth as a whole, sacrificing many details. Although the pixel classification-based method of UNet can also achieve high accuracy in numerical results, it is prone to some evident and non-physical flaws from the details shown in the orange box. Because a pure segmentation network only predicts from a few slices, it cannot incorporate the overall shape prior. In contrast, our method eliminates these flaws, balances the integrity of the model-based method with the fineness of classification-based segmentation, optimizes the overall contour, and performs numerically the best.

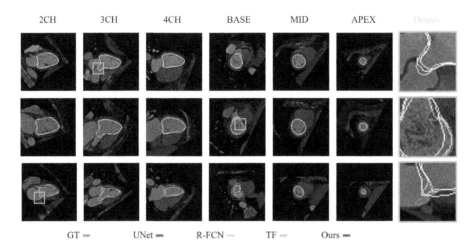

Fig. 6. Segmentation results on the specific views. Each row shows an example, and each column represents a different view from left to right: 2CH, 3CH, and 4CH slices on LAX; basal, middle, and apex slices on the SAX. The different colored outlines in the figure denote the results of different methods. The last column shows an enlarged version of the orange box in the figure. (Color figure online)

5   Conclusion

Obtaining an accurate ventricular model from medical images is of great clinical value. Given the challenge that the network cannot be well-trained due to the lack of publicly labeled cardiac images, according to the characteristics of medical volume data, we propose a slice-mask representation. We alleviate the shortage of training data by sampling in the constructed parameter latent space and increasing the network's generalization performance. The segmentations network is connected with the pre-trained parameter regression network for end-to-end joint optimization to reduce the impact of the imperfection of the upstream task on the downstream task. We evaluate our proposed method on synthetic data and real cardiac scans. The results show that our method can achieve advanced shape reconstruction and segmentation tasks. We hope our dataset can support related fields, and we will expand our method to more organs in the future.

Acknowledgements. This work was supported in part by the Natural Science Foundation of Jiangsu Province (No. BK20220127), the National Natural Science Foundation of China (No. 62076061), the "Young Elite Scientists Sponsorship Program by CAST" (No. YES20200025), and the "Zhishan Young Scholar" Program of Southeast University (No. 2242021R41083).

References

1. Adams, J., Bhalodia, R., Elhabian, S.: Uncertain-DeepSSM: from images to probabilistic shape models. In: Reuter, M., Wachinger, C., Lombaert, H., Paniagua, B., Goksel, O., Rekik, I. (eds.) ShapeMI 2020. LNCS, vol. 12474, pp. 57–72. Springer, Cham (2020). https://doi.org/10.1007/978-3-030-61056-2_5
2. Attar, R., et al.: 3D cardiac shape prediction with deep neural networks: simultaneous use of images and patient metadata. In: Shen, D., et al. (eds.) MICCAI 2019. LNCS, vol. 11765, pp. 586–594. Springer, Cham (2019). https://doi.org/10.1007/978-3-030-32245-8_65
3. Augustin, C.M., et al.: Anatomically accurate high resolution modeling of human whole heart electromechanics: a strongly scalable algebraic multigrid solver method for nonlinear deformation. J. Comput. Phys. **305**, 622–646 (2016)
4. Bhalodia, R., Elhabian, S.Y., Kavan, L., Whitaker, R.T.: DeepSSM: a deep learning framework for statistical shape modeling from raw images. In: Reuter, M., Wachinger, C., Lombaert, H., Paniagua, B., Lüthi, M., Egger, B. (eds.) ShapeMI 2018. LNCS, vol. 11167, pp. 244–257. Springer, Cham (2018). https://doi.org/10.1007/978-3-030-04747-4_23
5. Boussaid, H., Rouet, L.: Shape feature loss for kidney segmentation in 3d ultrasound images. In: BMVC (2021)
6. Cai, J., Xia, Y., Yang, D., Xu, D., Yang, L., Roth, H.: End-to-End Adversarial Shape Learning for Abdomen Organ Deep Segmentation. In: Suk, H.-I., Liu, M., Yan, P., Lian, C. (eds.) MLMI 2019. LNCS, vol. 11861, pp. 124–132. Springer, Cham (2019). https://doi.org/10.1007/978-3-030-32692-0_15
7. Duan, J., Bello, G., Schlemper, J., Bai, W., Dawes, T.J., Biffi, C., de Marvao, A., Doumoud, G., O'Regan, D.P., Rueckert, D.: Automatic 3d bi-ventricular segmentation of cardiac images by a shape-refined multi-task deep learning approach. IEEE Trans. Med. Imaging **38**(9), 2151–2164 (2019)
8. Ecabert, O., et al.: Automatic model-based segmentation of the heart in CT images. IEEE Trans. Med. Imaging **27**(9), 1189–1201 (2008)
9. Fan, H., Su, H., Guibas, L.J.: A point set generation network for 3d object reconstruction from a single image. In: Proceedings of the IEEE Conference on Computer Vision and Pattern Recognition, pp. 605–613 (2017)
10. Frangi, A.F., Rueckert, D., Schnabel, J.A., Niessen, W.J.: Automatic construction of multiple-object three-dimensional statistical shape models: application to cardiac modeling. IEEE Trans. Med. Imaging **21**(9), 1151–1166 (2002)
11. Gu, Z., et al.: Ce-net: context encoder network for 2d medical image segmentation. IEEE Trans. Med. Imaging **38**(10), 2281–2292 (2019)
12. Habijan, M., Babin, D., Galić, I., Leventić, H., Romić, K., Velicki, L., Pižurica, A.: Overview of the whole heart and heart chamber segmentation methods. Cardiovasc. Eng. Technol. **11**(6), 725–747 (2020)
13. Hoogendoorn, C., et al.: A high-resolution atlas and statistical model of the human heart from multislice ct. IEEE Trans. Med. Imaging **32**(1), 28–44 (2012)
14. Karim, R., et al.: Algorithms for left atrial wall segmentation and thickness-evaluation on an open-source ct and mri image database. Med. Image Anal. **50**, 36–53 (2018)
15. Kong, F., Shadden, S.C.: Automating model generation for image-based cardiac flow simulation. J. Biomech. Eng. **142**(11) (2020)

16. Kong, F., Shadden, S.C.: Whole heart mesh generation for image-based computational simulations by learning free-from deformations. In: de Bruijne, M., Cattin, P.C., Cotin, S., Padoy, N., Speidel, S., Zheng, Y., Essert, C. (eds.) MICCAI 2021. LNCS, vol. 12904, pp. 550–559. Springer, Cham (2021). https://doi.org/10.1007/978-3-030-87202-1_53

17. Kong, F., Wilson, N., Shadden, S.: A deep-learning approach for direct whole-heart mesh reconstruction. Med. Image Anal. **74**, 102222 (2021)

18. Lee, M.C.H., Petersen, K., Pawlowski, N., Glocker, B., Schaap, M.: Tetris: template transformer networks for image segmentation with shape priors. IEEE Trans. Med. Imaging **38**(11), 2596–2606 (2019)

19. Lorensen, W.E., Cline, H.E.: Marching cubes: a high resolution 3d surface construction algorithm. ACM siggraph computer graphics **21**(4), 163–169 (1987)

20. Mandikal, P., Navaneet, K., Agarwal, M., Babu, R.V.: 3d-lmnet: Latent embedding matching for accurate and diverse 3d point cloud reconstruction from a single image. arXiv preprint arXiv:1807.07796 (2018)

21. Medrano-Gracia, P., et al.: Large scale left ventricular shape atlas using automated model fitting to contours. In: Ourselin, S., Rueckert, D., Smith, N. (eds.) FIMH 2013. LNCS, vol. 7945, pp. 433–441. Springer, Heidelberg (2013). https://doi.org/10.1007/978-3-642-38899-6_51

22. Ordas, S., Oubel, E., Sebastian, R., Frangi, A.F.: Computational anatomy atlas of the heart. In: 2007 5th International Symposium on Image and Signal Processing and Analysis, pp. 338–342. IEEE (2007)

23. Organization, W.H.: The world health report 2002: reducing risks, promoting healthy life. World Health Organization (2002)

24. Ronneberger, O., Fischer, P., Brox, T.: U-Net: convolutional networks for biomedical image segmentation. In: Navab, N., Hornegger, J., Wells, W.M., Frangi, A.F. (eds.) MICCAI 2015. LNCS, vol. 9351, pp. 234–241. Springer, Cham (2015). https://doi.org/10.1007/978-3-319-24574-4_28

25. Sumner, R.W., Schmid, J., Pauly, M.: Embedded deformation for shape manipulation, pp. 80-es (2007)

26. Tilborghs, S., Dresselaers, T., Claus, P., Bogaert, J., Maes, F.: Shape constrained cnn for cardiac mr segmentation with simultaneous prediction of shape and pose parameters. arXiv preprint arXiv:2010.08952 (2020)

27. Tóthová, K., Parisot, S., Lee, M., Puyol-Antón, E., King, A., Pollefeys, M., Konukoglu, E.: Probabilistic 3D surface reconstruction from sparse MRI information. In: Martel, A.L., Abolmaesumi, P., Stoyanov, D., Mateus, D., Zuluaga, M.A., Zhou, S.K., Racoceanu, D., Joskowicz, L. (eds.) MICCAI 2020. LNCS, vol. 12261, pp. 813–823. Springer, Cham (2020). https://doi.org/10.1007/978-3-030-59710-8_79

28. Wang, N., et al.: Pixel2mesh: 3d mesh model generation via image guided deformation. IEEE Trans. Pattern Anal. Mach. Intell. **43**(10), 3600–3613 (2020)

29. Wang, Y., Zhong, Z., Hua, J.: Deeporgannet: on-the-fly reconstruction and visualization of 3d / 4d lung models from single-view projections by deep deformation network. IEEE Trans. Visual Comput. Graphics **26**(1), 960–970 (2020). https://doi.org/10.1109/TVCG.2019.2934369

30. Wickramasinghe, U., Remelli, E., Knott, G., Fua, P.: Voxel2Mesh: 3D mesh model generation from volumetric data. In: Martel, A.L., Abolmaesumi, P., Stoyanov, D., Mateus, D., Zuluaga, M.A., Zhou, S.K., Racoceanu, D., Joskowicz, L. (eds.) MICCAI 2020. LNCS, vol. 12264, pp. 299–308. Springer, Cham (2020). https://doi.org/10.1007/978-3-030-59719-1_30

31. Wolterink, J.M., et al.: An evaluation of automatic coronary artery calcium scoring methods with cardiac ct using the orcascore framework. Med. Phys. **43**(5), 2361–2373 (2016)
32. Ye, M., Huang, Q., Yang, D., Wu, P., Yi, J., Axel, L., Metaxas, D.: PC-U Net: learning to jointly reconstruct and segment the cardiac walls in 3D from CT Data. In: Puyol Anton, E., Pop, M., Sermesant, M., Campello, V., Lalande, A., Lekadir, K., Suinesiaputra, A., Camara, O., Young, A. (eds.) STACOM 2020. LNCS, vol. 12592, pp. 117–126. Springer, Cham (2021). https://doi.org/10.1007/978-3-030-68107-4_12
33. Zhou, X.-Y., Wang, Z.-Y., Li, P., Zheng, J.-Q., Yang, G.-Z.: One-stage shape instantiation from a single 2D image to 3D point cloud. In: Shen, D., Liu, T., Peters, T.M., Staib, L.H., Essert, C., Zhou, S., Yap, P.-T., Khan, A. (eds.) MICCAI 2019. LNCS, vol. 11767, pp. 30–38. Springer, Cham (2019). https://doi.org/10.1007/978-3-030-32251-9_4
34. Zhou, Z., Rahman Siddiquee, M.M., Tajbakhsh, N., Liang, J.: UNet++: a nested U-net architecture for medical image segmentation. In: Stoyanov, D., et al. (eds.) DLMIA/ML-CDS -2018. LNCS, vol. 11045, pp. 3–11. Springer, Cham (2018). https://doi.org/10.1007/978-3-030-00889-5_1
35. Zhuang, X., et al.: Evaluation of algorithms for multi-modality whole heart segmentation: an open-access grand challenge. Med. Image Anal. **58**, 101537 (2019)
36. Zotti, C., Luo, Z., Lalande, A., Jodoin, P.M.: Convolutional neural network with shape prior applied to cardiac mri segmentation. IEEE J. Biomed. Health Inform. **23**(3), 1119–1128 (2018)

Improving the Quality of Sparse-view Cone-Beam Computed Tomography via Reconstruction-Friendly Interpolation Network

Yanli Wang, Lianying Chao, Wenqi Shan, Haobo Zhang, Zhiwei Wang[✉],
and Qiang Li[✉]

Wuhan National Laboratory for Optoelectronics,
Huazhong University of Science and Technology, Wuhan, China
{zwwang,liqiang8}@hust.edu.cn

Abstract. Reconstructing cone-beam computed tomography (CBCT) typically utilizes a Feldkamp-Davis-Kress (FDK) algorithm to 'translate' hundreds of 2D X-ray projections on different angles into a 3D CT image. For minimizing the X-ray induced ionizing radiation, sparse-view CBCT takes fewer projections by a wider-angle interval, but suffers from an inferior CT reconstruction quality. To solve this, the recent solutions mainly resort to synthesizing missing projections, and force the synthesized projections to be as realistic as those actual ones, which is extremely difficult due to X-ray's tissue superimposing. In this paper, we argue that the synthetic projections should restore FDK-required information as much as possible, while the visual fidelity is the secondary importance. Inspired by a simple fact that FDK only relies on frequency information after ramp-filtering for reconstruction, we develop a Reconstruction-Friendly Interpolation Network (RFI-Net), which first utilizes a 3D-2D attention network to learn inter-projection relations for synthesizing missing projections, and then introduces a novel Ramp-Filter loss to constrain a frequency consistency between the synthesized and real projections after ramp-filtering. By doing so, RFI-Net's energy can be forcibly devoted to restoring more CT-reconstruction useful information in projection synthesis. We build a complete reconstruction framework consisting of our developed RFI-Net, FDK and a commonly-used CT post-refinement. Experimental results on reconstruction from only one-eighth projections demonstrate that using RFI-Net restored full-view projections can significantly improve the reconstruction quality by increasing PSNR by 2.59 dB and 2.03 dB on the walnut and patient CBCT datasets, respectively, comparing with using those restored by other state-of-the-arts.

Keywords: Sparse-view computed tomography (SVCT) reconstruction · FDK algorithm · Reconstruction-friendly projections · Interpolation · Ramp-filter loss

---

Y. Wang and L. Chao—Co-first authors.

L. Wang et al. (Eds.): ACCV 2022, LNCS 13846, pp. 86–100, 2023.
https://doi.org/10.1007/978-3-031-26351-4_6

1 Introduction

Cone Beam Computed Tomography (CBCT) is one of the key imaging techniques for various clinical applications, e.g., cancer diagnosis [11], image-guided surgery [5] and so on. The principle of reconstructing CBCT is first to take hundreds of 2D X-ray projections at regular intervals within a certain angle range, e.g., 360 °C, and then to utilize a Feldkamp-Davis-Kress (FDK) [24] algorithm to reconstruct a 3D CT image from those projections. Although CBCT enjoys lots of merits such as fast speed and large range, its brought ionizing radiation [4] is harmful to patients, which hinders long-term intensive usage [3]. Using fewer projections, that is, widening the sampling angle interval, is a crucial means of lowering CBCT's radiation dose, which is known as sparse-view CBCT [2]. However, sparse-view CBCT's dose reduction comes with a price of lost structures and streaking artifacts in CT images, which severely degrades reconstruction quality.

To improve the quality of sparse-view CBCT, several post-refinement methods [14,26,32] have been studied, and mainly focused on developing deep learning approaches to refine those FDK-reconstructed sparse-view CBCT images. Their objective is typically minimizing a voxel-wise L_2 distance between the refined sparse-view and original full-view CBCT images, however, this often yields over-smoothed refinement results. To overcome the over-smoothness problem [8,29], Liao et al. [19] used a VGG-based perceptual loss to minimize the L_2 distance between features extracted from the refined sparse-view CBCT image and its full-view counterpart, which was claimed to well preserve the high-frequency information in CT images. However, the VGG-network used in [19] was trained for natural image classification but not for CT image refinement, which may impair the perceptual loss's capability in CT data. Therefore, Li et al. [18] utilized a customized perceptual loss, which is based on a trained self-supervised auto-encoder network using CT data. This expanded the network's representational ability for further improving the post-refinement performance. Although some progress has been made, such CT post-refinement is disengaged from the CBCT imaging device/system, thus may ignore the valuable information contained in those raw X-ray projections. That is, the lost structures or streaking artifacts in sparse-view CBCT are hard to be rectified solely by a post-refinement without touching the raw projections.

Recently, a joint strategy has been proposed by two works [6,15], and it successively processes X-ray projections and CT images before and after FDK-reconstruction. Specifically, Hu et al. [15] developed a hybrid-domain neural network (HDNet), which, in the projection domain, first utilizes a non-parametric linear interpolator to restore the full-view projections, and then introduces a convolutional neural network (CNN) as a pixel-to-pixel translator to refine those linearly interpolated projections. However, the linear interpolator hardly handles rotating, and the caused interpolation errors are too difficult to be corrected. By comparison, Chao et al. [6] developed a DualCNN which utilized a projection domain interpolation CNN (PDCNN) to learn a direct interpolation of those missing projections from the sparse ones. PDCNN restores the full-view projections in a multi-step manner, i.e., the number of projections doubles in each step by synthesizing the middle in every two consecutive ones. Both HDNet and PDCNN bother forcing an identical appearance between the restored and original full-view X-ray projections by minimizing the voxel-wise distance. Thanks to the rotating projection and X-ray's tissue superimposing, such objective is extremely difficult to achieve.

If those restored full-view projections are not necessarily perfect, but just accurate to contain FDK-required information for reconstruction, the learning difficulty could be significantly alleviated, and the CNN efficacy is thus maximized. To this end, a straightforward idea is to have FDK differentiable, making CT reconstruction errors be back-propagated to guide the projection synthesis. However, this end-to-end manner involves concurrently processing hundreds of 2D projections and high-dimensional 3D CT images, bringing an unbearable huge computing cost inevitably.

In this paper, we develop a Reconstruction-Friendly Interpolation Network (RFI-Net) to trade off the computational efficiency, and introduce a novel Ramp-Filter Loss (RF-Loss) to have RFI-Net focus on learning the FDK-required projection information. Specifically, RFI-Net is implemented with a 3D-2D attention network architecture, which includes a 3D feature extractor, an inter-projection fusion module, and a 2D projection generator, as shown in Fig. 2. First, sparse 2D projections in a wide-angle range are stacked as a 3D volume that is encoded into a 3D feature map via the 3D feature extractor. Then, the inter-projection fusion module integrates features along the angle dimension for converting the 3D feature map to a 2D feature map. Lastly, the 2D projection generator decodes the 2D map into projections on missing angles.

RF-Loss is motivated by the FDK principle that only information of projections filtered by a ramp-filter will be used for reconstruction. Therefore, RF-Loss computes and minimizes the frequency difference between the restored and actual projections after ramp-filtering, and the ramp-filter in RF-Loss is set to be identical with that in FDK. With no need to optimize the CT reconstruction, RFI-Net is still aware of generating reconstruction-friendly full-view projections, rather than just mimicking the superficial appearance.

The main contributions of this work are as follows:

- We develop a CNN-based interpolator named RFI-Net, which can capture wide-angle range inter-projection relations, and synthesize reconstruction-friendly full-view projections, improving the quality of reconstructed sparse-view CBCT.
- We introduce a novel RF-Loss, which encourages RFI-Net's synthesized projections to contain FDK-required frequency information, without resorting to a computation-intensive end-to-end learning fashion.
- We build a complete reconstruction framework, which consists of a trained RFI-Net, FDK, and a commonly-adopted CT post-refinement. By enjoying those reconstruction-friendly projections synthesized by RFI-Net, our framework is experimentally demonstrated to increase PSNR by 2.59 dB and 2.03

dB on sparse-view CBCT reconstructions for the walnut and patient CBCT datasets under one-eighth dose, respectively, comparing with other state-of-the-arts.

2   Methods

Figure 1 presents the built complete CBCT reconstruction framework. First, RFI-Net synthesizes reconstruction-friendly full-view 2D projections from those sparse ones. Then, FDK reconstructs a 3D CT image from the synthesized full-view projections. Finally, a post-refinement network (Post-Net) is employed to further refine the FDK-reconstructed CT image. In the following, we detail RFI-Net and Post-Net, and explain our proposed RF-Loss for training.

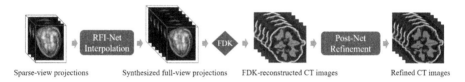

Sparse-view projections   Synthesized full-view projections   FDK-reconstructed CT images   Refined CT images

Fig. 1. Our built complete framework for sparse-view CBCT reconstruction.

2.1   RFI-Net Architecture

As shown in Fig. 2, RFI-Net is implemented with a 3D-2D attention network, which contains three components, i.e., a 3D feature extractor, an inter-projection fusion module and a 2D projection generator. Given full-view projections with the total number of N, the *quarter* dose sparse-view projections can be constructed as $\{P_{4i-3}|i = 1, 2, \ldots, N/4\}$, where N is 600 as the number of full-view projections and P_1 can be also denoted as P_{N+1}. Our goal is to restore the three missing projections $\{P_{4i-2}, P_{4i-1}, P_{4i}\}$ between every two adjacent sparse-view projections, i.e., P_{4i-3} and P_{4i+1}.

The 3D feature extractor stacks consecutive projections $\{P_{4i-3}, \ldots, P_{4(i+D-1)}\}$ sampled within a wide-angle range into a 3D volume, and encodes it into a 3D feature map F_{3D} with the size of $C \times H \times W \times D$, where C and D are the number of feature channels, input sparse-view projections, respectively, and we set D to 4 in this work, where H and W represent the size of X-ray projection. Specifically, the 3D feature extractor employs 3D ResUNet [31] as the backbone and has three main advantages: (i) the residual path can avoid gradient vanishing in the training phase; (ii) the skip connection [25] between encoder and decoder can fuse low-level features and high-level features to well express the projection information; (iii) the 3D kernels jointly capture the angle and spatial information of projections.

The inter-projection fusion module consists of a reshape operation, a 2D convolution layer and a channel attention module, which bridges the 3D feature

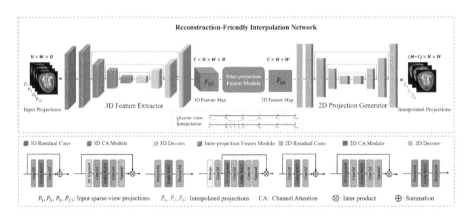

Fig. 2. The RFI-Net architecture. For example, sparse-view projections P_1, P_5, P_9, P_{13} are stacked and input into RFI-Net, and the missing projections $\hat{P}_6$, $\hat{P}_7$, $\hat{P}_8$ between P_5 and P_9 are synthesized.

extractor and the 2D projection generator. This fusion module first reshapes the 3D feature map F_{3D} to a 2D map with the size of $CD \times H \times W$ by merging the angle and channel dimensions, and then employs a 2D convolution layer to generate the final 2D feature map F_{2D} with size of $C \times H \times W$. The channel attention module finally measures the inter-dependencies between the feature channels and allows the module to focus on useful ones.

The 2D projection generator has the similar architecture with the 3D feature extractor, and replaces the 3D kernels with the 2D ones. The output size of the generator is $(M-1) \times H \times W$, where $M-1$ represents the number of missing projections for $1/M$ dose-level. We adjust M according to different dose-levels, e.g., $M = 4$ for *quarter* dose and $M = 8$ for *one-eighth* dose. Finally, the result of the generator is sliced along channel into individual synthesized projections with the total number of $M - 1$.

Note that, channel attention (CA) module [9] is embedded into each layer of the 3D-2D network architecture. In the CA module, global average pooling [20] is first used to enlarge the receptive field by compressing the spatial features. Then the following two convolution layers are utilized to capture the non-linear inter-channel relationships. Finally, sigmoid activation function is used to introduce non-linearity.

2.2   RF-Loss of RFI-Net

In FDK algorithm, projections are not directly back-projected to reconstruct CT images, but filtered by the ramp-filter in the frequency domain beforehand. The ramp-filter is a correction filter that can redistribute the frequency information by suppressing the low-frequency information but encouraging the pass of high-frequency information [22]. Motivated by this, we design RF-Loss to make RFI-Net mainly focus on the ramp-filtered frequency information in projections.

RF-Loss $\mathcal{L}_{RF}$ minimizes the frequency-wise error between the synthesized $\{\hat{P}_t | t = 1, 2, ..., M - 1\}$ and ground-truth $\{P_t^{GT} | t = 1, 2, ..., M - 1\}$ projections, which can be formulated as:

$$\mathcal{L}_{RF} = \frac{1}{M-1} \sum_{t=1}^{M-1} \left| RF(\hat{P}_t) - RF(P_t^{GT}) \right| \tag{1}$$

where $RF(*)$ represents the frequency representations after ramp-filtering. Specifically, we first convert a projection P_t into its frequency representation $F_t(u, v)$ by calculating the 2D Fast Fourier Transform (FFT) as follows:

$$F_t(u, v) = \sum_{x=0}^{H-1} \sum_{y=0}^{W-1} P_t(x, y) \times \left[\cos 2\pi (\frac{ux}{H} + \frac{vy}{W}) - i \sin 2\pi (\frac{ux}{H} + \frac{vy}{W}) \right] \tag{2}$$

where $u = 0, 1, ..., H - 1, v = 0, 1, ..., W - 1$, H and W are the height and width of the projection, and (x, y) denotes the position in the spatial domain. $P_t(x, y)$ is the pixel intensity at position (x, y). In the frequency domain, the projection is decomposed into cosine and orthogonal functions for constituting the real and imaginary parts of the complex frequency value. After applying the 2D FFT, a ramp-filter weight matrix $\alpha(u, v)$ [30] is used to multiply with the complex frequency value $F_t(u, v)$ as follows:

$$RF(P_t) = |\alpha(u, v) \times F_t(u, v)| \tag{3}$$

$\mathcal{L}_1$ loss [28] is also used to minimize the pixel-wise error between the interpolated projections and the references. The total loss $\mathcal{L}_{RFINet}$ can be formulated as:

$$\mathcal{L}_{RFINet} = \mathcal{L}_1 + \gamma \mathcal{L}_{RF} \tag{4}$$

where γ is the weighting parameter to balance the two losses and is set to 0.1 in our experiments.

2.3   Post-Net Architecture

In the reconstruction domain, we modified a simple 3D UNet [1] as the post-processing network to further refine the pre-processed CT images.

As shown in Fig. 3, Post-Net contains four convolutional blocks to extract rich features and four deconvolution blocks to restore the image contents. The artifacts distribution is generated through the last layer, and the final high-quality CT images are produced by subtracting the predicted artifacts distribution from the pre-processed CT images. The size of kernels used in Post-Net is $3 \times 3 \times 3$. A joint loss [7] that includes a perceptual loss and a SSIM loss is used for optimizing the Post-Net. Perceptual loss [16] makes Post-Net retain the high-frequency information in CBCT images to avoid the over-smoothness problem. SSIM loss [33] makes Post-Net well preserve the delicate structures in CT images. The joint loss $\mathcal{L}_{PostNet}$ can be formulated as:

$$\mathcal{L}_{PostNet} = \beta \mathcal{L}_{perc} - \mathcal{L}_{ssim} \tag{5}$$

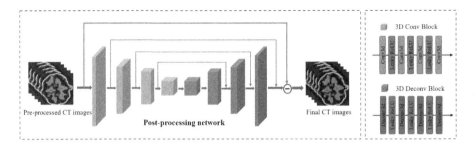

Fig. 3. Post-processing network architecture.

where $\mathcal{L}_{perc}$ and $\mathcal{L}_{ssim}$ denote the perceptual loss and SSIM loss, respectively. β is the weighting parameter to balance the two losses. $\mathcal{L}_{perc}$ and $\mathcal{L}_{ssim}$ are detailed in reference [7]. In the training of Post-Net, the input includes nine consecutive slices and the weighting parameter β in Eq. 5 is set to 200/3.

3 Experiment

3.1 Dataset

Our experiments are validated on two CBCT datasets:

(i) **Walnut dataset**: This is a public CBCT dataset provided for deep learning development [10]. In this dataset, 42 walnuts were scanned with a special laboratory X-ray CBCT scanner, with raw projection data. For each walnut, we take 600 projections evenly over a full circle as the full-view projections, and explore sparse-view CBCT reconstruction under the *quarter* and *one-eighth* dose by using only 150 and 75 projections, respectively. The CBCT reconstruction uses the FDK algorithm in ASTRA toolbox [27]. For each walnut, the size of the projection image is 972×768, and the reconstructed CT volume is $448 \times 448 \times 448$. The first five walnuts are used for test, the sixth for validation, and the rest for training.

(ii) **Patient dataset**: This dataset includes 38 real normal-dose 3D CT images provided by the TCIA data library [21], and the corresponding full- and sparse-view 2D projections are simulated by forward-projecting the CT images using the ASTRA toolbox. The number of full-view projections is 600, and the size of simulated projection is 972×768, and the size of the reconstructed CT volume is $n \times 512 \times 512$, where n is the slice number for each patient. Five patients are used for test, one patient for validation, and the rest for training.

3.2 Implementation Details

Our networks are implemented with Pytorch [23] ver. 1.9, Python ver. 3.7, and CUDA ver. 11.2. The Adam [17] solver with momentum parameters $\beta_1 = 0.9$

Table 1. Abbreviations of different comparison methods.

Abbreviations	Descriptions
FVCT	Full-view + FDK (as ground truth)
SVCT	Sparse-view + FDK (as baseline)
CNCL [13]	Sparse-view + FDK + Post-refinement by CNCL
SI-UNet [12]	Linear interpolation and 2D U-Net enhancement + FDK
HDNet [15]	Linear interpolation and 3D U-Net enhancement + FDK + Post-refinement by 3D U-Net
DualCNN [6]	PDCNN interpolation + FDK + Post-refinement by IDCNN
Ours	RFI-Net interpolation + FDK + Post-refinement by Post-Net

and $\beta_2 = 0.99$ is used to optimize RFI-Net with the learning rate of 2e−4. The number of training epochs and batch size are set to 150 and 1, respectively. All networks are trained using a NVIDIA GPU GTX3090 of 24 GB memory.

3.3   Evaluation Metrics and Comparison Methods

We use three evaluation metrics, including the root mean square error (RMSE), peak signal-to-noise ratio (PSNR), and structural similarity (SSIM), to quantify the difference or similarity between the full-view CBCT and improved sparse-view CBCT by different methods. The comparison methods are listed in Table 1. CNCL and DualCNN released their source codes. SI-UNet and HDNet were reimplemented by us by following their methodological descriptions.

3.4   Comparison with State-of-the-Arts

We first evaluate all methods on reconstructing sparse-view CBCT by using the quarter number of projections, i.e., 1/4 dose, and the evaluation results of the three metrics on the walnut and patient datasets are shown in Table 2.
endtable
From this table, we can have two major observations:

(i) The sparse-view CBCT reconstructed by our method has the highest quality compared with those by other state-of-the-arts. For walnut data, our method decreases RMSE by approximately 16%, increases PSNR by approximately 6%, and increases SSIM by approximately 11%, compared with the second-best method DualCNN. For patient data, the three quality metrics are improved by approximately 18%, 5% and 2%, respectively;

(ii) The reconstruction quality only using RFI-Net's restored full-view projections without any post-refinement is consistently better than those by projection interpolation only (SI-UNet, HDNet*, PDCNN) or post-refinement only (CNCL) methods, and even comparable to those by the two methods (HDNet, DualCNN), which jointly consider both projection interpolation and post-refinement.

Table 2. Quantitative quality on the walnut and patient datasets of **1/4** dose sparse-view CBCT with respect to the full-view CBCT. Best results are in bold. Methods with the marker '*' discard the post-refinement.

Methods	Walnut dataset			Patient dataset		
	RMSE	PSNR(dB)	SSIM	RMSE	PSNR(dB)	SSIM
SVCT	0.128	16.517	0.207	0.025	28.493	0.610
SI-UNet	0.039	26.374	0.662	0.016	31.218	0.870
HDNet*	0.035	27.236	0.686	0.018	30.246	0.804
DualCNN*(PDCNN)	0.034	27.568	0.713	0.012	33.764	0.900
Ours*(RFI-Net)	0.032	28.305	0.790	0.010	35.594	0.924
CNCL	0.038	26.444	0.548	0.014	33.442	0.874
HDNet	0.032	27.854	0.671	0.014	33.016	0.874
DualCNN	0.031	28.347	0.722	0.011	34.683	0.916
Ours	**0.026**	**30.148**	**0.799**	**0.009**	**36.413**	**0.934**

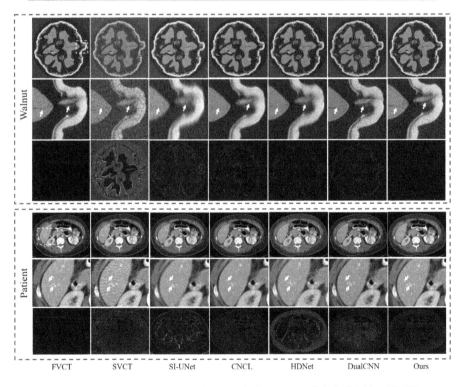

Fig. 4. Visual effects for the first walnut and the patient labeled L273 CBCT reconstruction with **1/4** dose sparse-view projections. For each dataset, the first row shows the representative slices; the second row shows the corresponding magnified ROIs; the third row shows the absolute difference images between the optimized slices and full-view slice.

Figure 4 visualizes the reconstructed sparse-view CBCT of the walnut and patient datasets under 1/4 dose by different methods. As can be seen, SVCT without any improvement contains severe streaking artifacts and hazy structures. SI-UNet, which considers projection interpolation only, suppresses the artifacts to some extent, but still suffers from the lost structures. CNCL, which considers post-refinement only, excessively smooths the reconstructed CBCT image, losing inner textures. HDNet and DualCNN achieve a relatively better visual quality compared with the projection interpolation only and post-refinement only methods, but an unsatisfactory reconstruction result on those delicate structures in Fig. 4. In comparison, our method accurately restores structures without losing inner textures, especially for those tiny structures indicated by the red arrows in the walnut and patient, and thus yields the cleanest difference map with respect to FVCT, as shown in the third rows of the walnut and patient in Fig. 4.

We further explore a more extreme case that reconstructs sparse-view CBCT using only one-eighth projections, i.e., 1/8 dose. Table 3 presents quantitative assessments. Figure 5 presents the visual examples of the walnut and patient datasets for different methods.

Table 3. Quantitative quality on the walnut and patient datasets of **1/8** dose sparse-view CBCT with respect to the full-view CBCT. Best results are in bold. Methods with the marker '*' discard the post-refinement.

Methods	Walnut dataset			Patient dataset		
	RMSE	PSNR (dB)	SSIM	RMSE	PSNR (dB)	SSIM
SVCT	0.184	13.623	0.131	0.048	22.805	0.437
SI-UNet	0.046	24.400	0.555	0.024	27.169	0.774
HDNet*	0.044	24.956	0.576	0.023	27.806	0.773
DualCNN*(PDCNN)	0.040	25.906	0.620	0.018	29.749	0.833
Ours*(RFI-Net)	0.037	27.074	0.727	0.015	32.194	0.873
CNCL	0.048	23.580	0.424	0.019	30.045	0.818
HDNet	0.038	26.202	0.582	0.018	29.979	0.831
DualCNN	0.037	26.224	0.633	0.017	30.829	0.865
Ours	**0.029**	**28.814**	**0.742**	**0.014**	**32.863**	**0.891**

Besides the consistently superior performance of our method over others just like the case of 1/4 dose, we can also have two new observations:

(i) Our method shows more improvement at 1/8 dose compared with 1/4 dose. On the walnut data, PSNR is improved by 2.59 dB at 1/8 dose and 1.80 dB at 1/4 dose comparing with the second-best method DualCNN. On the patient data, PSNR is improved 2.03 dB and 1.73 dB under the 1/8 and 1/4 dose, respectively. This suggests that our method may be useful for the ultra-sparse-view acquisition;

(ii) Comparing with SI-UNet and HDNet*, which only consider projection interpolation, RFI-Net can achieve a better reconstruction quality even with the
dose halved. Specially, on the walnut data, with only 1/8 dose, the quality
of sparse-view CBCT reconstructed by our method is still comparable to
the 1/4 dose sparse-view CBCT reconstructed by HDNet and DualCNN in
terms of RMSE and PSNR, and even better in terms of SSIM.

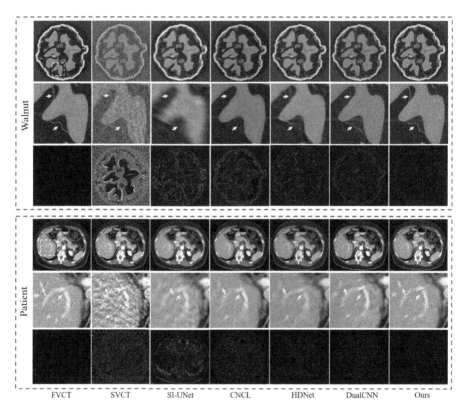

Fig. 5. Visual effects for the first walnut and the patient labeled L299 CBCT reconstruction with **1/8** dose sparse-view projections. For each dataset, the first row shows
the representative slices; the second row shows the corresponding magnified ROIs; the
third row shows the absolute difference images between the optimized slices and full-
view slice.

3.5   Ablation Study

In this section, we investigate the effectiveness of RFI-Net in two aspects:
(1) using different training losses, and (2) considering interpolation only, post-

Table 4. The investigation results by (1) using different training losses, and (2) different processing domains. Best results are in bold.

	Settings	Test images	RMSE	PSNR(dB)	SSIM
Loss	$\mathcal{L}_1$	Projections	**0.008**	39.320	0.955
	$\mathcal{L}_1+0.1^*\mathcal{L}_{RF}$		**0.008**	**39.680**	**0.958**
	$\mathcal{L}_1+1.0^*\mathcal{L}_{RF}$		0.009	38.553	**0.958**
	$\mathcal{L}_1+10.0^*\mathcal{L}_{RF}$		0.010	37.859	0.957
	$\mathcal{L}_{RF}$		0.010	37.869	**0.958**
	$\mathcal{L}_1$	CT images	0.038	26.664	0.692
	$\mathcal{L}_1+0.1^*\mathcal{L}_{RF}$		**0.037**	**27.074**	**0.727**
	$\mathcal{L}_1+1.0^*\mathcal{L}_{RF}$		**0.037**	26.956	0.725
	$\mathcal{L}_1+10.0^*\mathcal{L}_{RF}$		0.038	26.794	0.724
	$\mathcal{L}_{RF}$		**0.037**	27.026	0.726
Domain	Post-Net	CT images	0.048	22.463	0.487
	RFI-Net		0.037	27.074	0.727
	RFI-Net+Post-Net		**0.029**	**28.814**	**0.742**

refinement only, and both of them. All investigations are performed on the 1/8 dose sparse-view CBCT reconstruction of walnuts. The results are shown in Table 4.

Ablation Study on RF-Loss. To validate the effectiveness of the proposed RF-Loss, we train five versions of RFI-Net: one only using $\mathcal{L}_1$ loss, one only using $\mathcal{L}_{RF}$ loss and the remaining three using different coefficients on $\mathcal{L}_{RF}$. We assess the interpolated projections shown in the first five rows, and their reconstructed CT images shown in the 6th-10th rows of Table 4.

As can be seen, our method achieves the best performance on both projections and CT images when the coefficient of $\mathcal{L}_{RF}$ is set to 0.1. Besides, increasing the coefficient of $\mathcal{L}_{RF}$ or using single $\mathcal{L}_{RF}$ somewhat slightly degrades the projection quality in terms of RMSE and PSNR metrics, but improves the CT image quality reconstructed from these projections in terms of all the three metrics, especially for SSIM. These results indicate that RF-Loss can indeed interpolate the missing projections containing the FDK-required information. This is exactly what we expected since we are concerned with the high-quality CT images rather than visually similar projections.

Ablation Study on Domain. Furthermore, we build two new complete reconstruction frameworks which use either RFI-Net only or Post-Net only. The quantitative comparison results are presented in the last three rows of Table 4.

As can be seen, without those reconstruction-friendly projections interpolated by RFI-Net, Post-Net produces the reconstructed CT images with the lowest quality especially in terms of SSIM. This verifies that CT post-refinement has limited capability of further reducing the radiation dose, because it is difficult to restore the structures already lost in the reconstruction process. Only using those RFI-Net interpolated projections for reconstruction has already achieved a promising reconstruction quality by improving the SSIM value to that over 70%, while the quality can be further improved with the assistance of a post-refinement by Post-Net.

4 Conclusion

In this paper, we build a sparse-view CBCT reconstruction framework, which can be deeply embedded in the low-dose CBCT systems. This framework consists of three parts: (i) our developed RFI-Net to restore reconstruction-friendly projections from those sparse ones; (ii) FDK to translate 2D X-ray projections into a 3D CT image; (iii) a post-refinement network named Post-Net to further refine the quality of the reconstructed CT image. We also carefully design a novel loss named RF-Loss to help RFI-Net focus on learning FDK-required information of projections. Therefore, our method is expected to significantly improve the quality of sparse-view CBCT with no need to train the entire framework in an end-to-end manner. Experimental results demonstrate that no matter reducing the dose by four or eight times, the sparse-view CBCT reconstructed by our method has the highest quality in all comparison methods, with well persevering delicate structures and presenting the closest quality to that of the full-view CBCT images.

Acknowledgements. This work was supported in part by National Key R&D Program of China (Grant No. 2022YFE0200600), National Natural Science Foundation of China (Grant No. 62202189), Fundamental Research Funds for the Central Universities (2021XXJS033), Science Fund for Creative Research Group of China (Grant No. 61721092), Director Fund of WNLO, Research grants from United Imaging Healthcare Inc.

References

1. Baid, U., et al.: Deep Learning Radiomics Algorithm for Gliomas (DRAG) model: a novel approach using 3d unet based deep convolutional neural network for predicting survival in gliomas. In: Crimi, A., Bakas, S., Kuijf, H., Keyvan, F., Reyes, M., van Walsum, T. (eds.) BrainLes 2018. LNCS, vol. 11384, pp. 369–379. Springer, Cham (2019). https://doi.org/10.1007/978-3-030-11726-9_33
2. Bian, J., Siewerdsen, J.H., Han, X., Sidky, E.Y., Prince, J.L., Pelizzari, C.A., Pan, X.: Evaluation of sparse-view reconstruction from flat-panel-detector cone-beam CT. Phys. Med. Biol. **55**(22), 6575 (2010)
3. Brenner, D.J., Hall, E.J.: Computed tomography-an increasing source of radiation exposure. N. Engl. J. Med. **357**(22), 2277–2284 (2007)
4. Callahan, M.J., MacDougall, R.D., Bixby, S.D., Voss, S.D., Robertson, R.L., Cravero, J.P.: Ionizing radiation from computed tomography versus anesthesia for magnetic resonance imaging in infants and children: patient safety considerations. Pediatr. Radiol. **48**(1), 21–30 (2018)

5. Casal, R.F., et al.: Cone beam computed tomography-guided thin/ultrathin bronchoscopy for diagnosis of peripheral lung nodules: a prospective pilot study. J. Thorac. Dis. **10**(12), 6950 (2018)
6. Chao, L., Wang, Z., Zhang, H., Xu, W., Zhang, P., Li, Q.: Sparse-view cone beam CT reconstruction using dual CNNs in projection domain and image domain. Neurocomputing **493**, 536–547 (2022)
7. Chao, L., Zhang, P., Wang, Y., Wang, Z., Xu, W., Li, Q.: Dual-domain attention-guided convolutional neural network for low-dose cone-beam computed tomography reconstruction. Knowledge-Based Systems, p. 109295 (2022)
8. Chen, Z., Qi, H., Wu, S., Xu, Y., Zhou, L.: Few-view CT reconstruction via a novel non-local means algorithm. Physica Med. **32**(10), 1276–1283 (2016)
9. Choi, M., Kim, H., Han, B., Xu, N., Lee, K.M.: Channel attention is all you need for video frame interpolation. In: Proceedings of the AAAI Conference on Artificial Intelligence, vol. 34, pp. 10663–10671 (2020)
10. Der Sarkissian, H., Lucka, F., van Eijnatten, M., Colacicco, G., Coban, S.B., Batenburg, K.J.: A cone-beam x-ray computed tomography data collection designed for machine learning. Sci. Data **6**(1), 1–8 (2019)
11. Ding, A., Gu, J., Trofimov, A.V., Xu, X.G.: Monte Carlo calculation of imaging doses from diagnostic multidetector CT and kilovoltage cone-beam CT as part of prostate cancer treatment plans. Med. Phys. **37**(12), 6199–6204 (2010)
12. Dong, X., Vekhande, S., Cao, G.: Sinogram interpolation for sparse-view micro-CT with deep learning neural network. In: Medical Imaging 2019: Physics of Medical Imaging. vol. 10948, pp. 692–698. SPIE (2019)
13. Geng, M., et al.: Content-noise complementary learning for medical image denoising. IEEE Trans. Med. Imaging **41**(2), 407–419 (2021)
14. Han, Y., Ye, J.C.: Framing u-net via deep convolutional framelets: application to sparse-view CT. IEEE Trans. Med. Imaging **37**(6), 1418–1429 (2018)
15. Hu, D., et al.: Hybrid-domain neural network processing for sparse-view CT reconstruction. IEEE Trans. Radiation Plasma Med. Sci. **5**(1), 88–98 (2020)
16. Johnson, J., Alahi, A., Fei-Fei, L.: Perceptual losses for real-time style transfer and super-resolution. In: Leibe, B., Matas, J., Sebe, N., Welling, M. (eds.) ECCV 2016. LNCS, vol. 9906, pp. 694–711. Springer, Cham (2016). https://doi.org/10.1007/978-3-319-46475-6_43
17. Kingma, D.P., Ba, J.: Adam: a method for stochastic optimization. arXiv preprint arXiv:1412.6980 (2014)
18. Li, M., Hsu, W., Xie, X., Cong, J., Gao, W.: Sacnn: self-attention convolutional neural network for low-dose CT denoising with self-supervised perceptual loss network. IEEE Trans. Med. Imaging **39**(7), 2289–2301 (2020)
19. Liao, H., Huo, Z., Sehnert, W.J., Zhou, S.K., Luo, J.: Adversarial sparse-view CBCT artifact reduction. In: Frangi, A.F., Schnabel, J.A., Davatzikos, C., Alberola-López, C., Fichtinger, G. (eds.) MICCAI 2018. LNCS, vol. 11070, pp. 154–162. Springer, Cham (2018). https://doi.org/10.1007/978-3-030-00928-1_18
20. Lin, M., Chen, Q., Yan, S.: Network in network. arXiv preprint arXiv:1312.4400 (2013)
21. McCollough, C., et al.: Low dose CT image and projection data [data set]. The Cancer Imaging Archive (2020)
22. Pan, X., Sidky, E.Y., Vannier, M.: Why do commercial CT scanners still employ traditional, filtered back-projection for image reconstruction? Inverse Prob. **25**(12), 123009 (2009)
23. Paszke, P.: An imperative style, high-performance deep learning library. Adv. Neural Inf. Process. Syst (32), 8026

24. Rodet, T., Noo, F., Defrise, M.: The cone-beam algorithm of feldkamp, davis, and kress preserves oblique line integrals. Med. Phys. **31**(7), 1972–1975 (2004)

25. Ronneberger, O., Fischer, P., Brox, T.: U-Net: convolutional networks for biomedical image segmentation. In: Navab, N., Hornegger, J., Wells, W.M., Frangi, A.F. (eds.) MICCAI 2015. LNCS, vol. 9351, pp. 234–241. Springer, Cham (2015). https://doi.org/10.1007/978-3-319-24574-4_28

26. Shen, T., Li, X., Zhong, Z., Wu, J., Lin, Z.: R^2-Net: recurrent and recursive network for sparse-view CT artifacts removal. In: Shen, D., Liu, T., Peters, T.M., Staib, L.H., Essert, C., Zhou, S., Yap, P.-T., Khan, A. (eds.) MICCAI 2019. LNCS, vol. 11769, pp. 319–327. Springer, Cham (2019). https://doi.org/10.1007/978-3-030-32226-7_36

27. Van Aarle, W., Palenstijn, W.J., Cant, J., Janssens, E., Bleichrodt, F., Dabravolski, A., De Beenhouwer, J., Batenburg, K.J., Sijbers, J.: Fast and flexible x-ray tomography using the astra toolbox. Opt. Express **24**(22), 25129–25147 (2016)

28. Wang, Q., Ma, Y., Zhao, K., Tian, Y.: A comprehensive survey of loss functions in machine learning. Annal. Data Sci. **9**(2), 187–212 (2022)

29. Yang, Q., Yan, P., Kalra, M., Wang, G.: Ct image denoising with perceptive deep neural networks. arxiv 2017. arXiv preprint arXiv:1702.07019 (2017)

30. Zeng, G.L.: Revisit of the ramp filter. In: 2014 IEEE Nuclear Science Symposium and Medical Imaging Conference (NSS/MIC), pp. 1–6. IEEE (2014)

31. Zhang, Y., et al.: Clear: comprehensive learning enabled adversarial reconstruction for subtle structure enhanced low-dose CT imaging. IEEE Trans. Med. Imaging **40**(11), 3089–3101 (2021)

32. Zhang, Z., Liang, X., Dong, X., Xie, Y., Cao, G.: A sparse-view CT reconstruction method based on combination of densenet and deconvolution. IEEE Trans. Med. Imaging **37**(6), 1407–1417 (2018)

33. Zhao, H., Gallo, O., Frosio, I., Kautz, J.: Loss functions for image restoration with neural networks. IEEE Trans. Comput. Imaging **3**(1), 47–57 (2016)

CSS-Net: Classification and Substitution for Segmentation of Rotator Cuff Tear

Kyungsu Lee[1] , Hah Min Lew[2] , Moon Hwan Lee[1] , Jun-Young Kim[3(✉)] ,
and Jae Youn Hwang[1(✉)]

[1] Daegu Gyeongbuk Institute of Science and Technology, Daegu 42988, South Korea
{ks_lee,moon2019,jyhwang}@dgist.ac.kr
[2] KLleon R and D Center, Seoul 04637, South Korea
hahmin.lew@klleon.io
[3] Daegu Catholic University School of Medicine, Daegu 42472, South Korea
dr.junyoung@gmail.com

Abstract. Magnetic resonance imaging (MRI) has been popularly used
to diagnose orthopedic injuries because it offers high spatial resolution
in a non-invasive manner. Since the rotator cuff tear (RCT) is a tear
of the supraspinatus tendon (ST), a precise comprehension of both is
required to diagnose the tear. However, previous deep learning studies
have been insufficient in comprehending the correlations between the ST
and RCT effectively and accurately. Therefore, in this paper, we propose
a new method, *substitution learning*, wherein an MRI image is used to
improve RCT diagnosis based on the knowledge transfer. The *substitution learning* mainly aims at segmenting RCT from MRI images by using
the transferred knowledge while learning the correlations between RCT
and ST. In substitution learning, the knowledge of correlations between
RCT and ST is acquired by substituting the segmentation target (RCT)
with the other target (ST), which has similar properties. To this end,
we designed a novel deep learning model based on multi-task learning,
which incorporates the newly developed substitution learning, with three
parallel pipelines: (1) segmentation of RCT and ST regions, (2) classification of the existence of RCT, and (3) substitution of the ruptured ST
regions, which are RCTs, with the recovered ST regions. We validated
our developed model through experiments using 889 multi-categorical
MRI images. The results exhibit that the proposed deep learning model
outperforms other segmentation models to diagnose RCT with $6 \sim 8\%$
improved IoU values. Remarkably, the ablation study explicates that
substitution learning ensured more valid knowledge transfer.

1 Introduction

In modern society, owing to the frequent incidence of rotator cuff tears (RCT)
that occur in the supraspinatus tendon (ST) of people regardless of their age,

L. Wang et al. (Eds.): ACCV 2022, LNCS 13846, pp. 101–114, 2023.
https://doi.org/10.1007/978-3-031-26351-4_7

the demand for orthopedic diagnosis and surgery has increased recently [1]. RCT ruptures the shoulder joint, hindering movement of the shoulder [2,3]. However, to minimize resections, it is required to comprehend the precise location and size of RCTs and the mechanism behind them, prior to a surgical operation [4]. To this end, magnetic resonance imaging (MRI) has been established as an indispensable imaging tool owing to its non-invasive diagnostic capability to provide detailed anatomic structures. Using MRI, skilled surgeons have been able to localize RCTs and comprehensively analyze the tear. However, inter-clinician reliability and time-consuming manual segmentation have produced limitations in MRI-based diagnosis [5,6]. In contrast, advances in artificial intelligence have promoted the utilization of computer-assisted diagnosis (CAD) system in the medical imaging field [7–9]. Particularly, deep learning-based RCT diagnosis has been studied for the precise diagnosis of RCTs in terms of classification and segmentation. Kim *et al.* [10] detected the existence of RCT and classified the sizes, particularly a partial or full tear by adopting weighted combination layers. Shim *et al.* [11] exploited 3D CNN on volumetric MRI data to classify the existence of RCT and visualized the location of RCT using a gradient-weighted class activation mapping (Grad-CAM) [12].

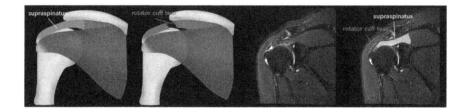

Fig. 1. Anatomical structure and MRI images of ST and RCT.

However, as illustrated in Fig. 1, the RCT region occupies a significantly smaller number of pixels in MRI images than the ST region, thus resulting in *class-imbalance problem*. Since the non-diseased regions correspond to most of the pixels, the trained network is biased toward the normal regions and converges to local minima [13,14]. In addition, since the RCT regions are sparse, the deep learning models could not learn enough knowledge related to RCT. To this end, researchers have used two major strategies; (1) a model-centric approach and (2) a data-centric approach. A novel loss function or network is proposed for the model-centric approach to resolving the biased state. The focal loss proposed by Lin *et al.* [15] was applied to resolve the class imbalance problem by assigning weights to the imbalanced class. Lee *et al.* [16] proposed a modified loss function to mitigate class imbalance in the diagnosis of RCTs from ultrasound images. However, previous studies and conventional algorithms for the class-imbalance problem have exhibited limited performance due to class imbalanced problem. Since these model-centric approaches could not dramatically improve the accuracy with low-quality datasets, the data-centric approach should be accompanied by the model-centric approaches [17]. Recently, generative adversarial neural networks (GANs) [18] have been proposed as a useful tool for a data-centric approach. Several studies have demonstrated that data augmentation using GANs improves the accuracy of the diagnosis [19,20]. Particularly, data augmentation using GANs that mask lesions in synthetic images has been shown to be very useful even for medical applications [21–23]. However, because these synthetic images are not completely accurate, their use in the medical field remains debatable.

Therefore, to ensure the reliability of the generated medical images and improve diagnostic accuracy despite the class-imbalance problem, we propose a novel learning method of substitution learning for image translation as well as the corresponding network, denoted as the classification, substitution, and segmentation Network (CSS-Net). Initially, to ensure the generation of reliable medical images compared to GANs, substitution learning is newly developed using Discrete Fourier Transform (DFT) in the CSS-Net. Next, to improve the class-imbalance problem, wherein the knowledge related to RCT is limited due to sparse RCT information, we adopted the knowledge transfer-based method to CSS-Net to learn abundant knowledge of RCT from other tasks and other related classes. Since RCT is originally a part of ST and the RCT is meanwhile given from the tear of ST, there should be correlations between RCT and ST. At this moment, we were motivated that the knowledge about correlations between RCT and ST could be informative for other tasks, such as segmentation of RCT.

To this end, we designed the multi-task learning-based deep learning network, including segmentation and classification tasks. The simple transfer learning-based network could not still improve the segmentation accuracy drastically. Therefore, we were motivated to use image translation to extract or capture features/knowledge of correlations between RCT and ST. Since the GAN models have the aforementioned limitations, we devised a new translation method: Since DFT can extract features regardless of the location, a new translation method adopts DFT in this study. As a result, substitution learning is motivated by the knowledge transfer that exploits the correlations between ST and RCT, and DFT is employed due to its feature extraction process regardless of the target objects' locations. Therefore, the CSS-Net based on multi-task learning includes three pipelines; (1) as the main task, the segmentation task of RCT and ST regions. (2) the classification task for determining the presence or absence of RCTs, and (3) the substitution task based on DFT that substitutes ruptured ST (RCT) images with normal ST images.

To summarize, the main contributions are summarized as follows:

– **Substitution learning**: In terms of data augmentation, substitution learning achieves reliable data manipulation using DFT compared to GANs which utilize intensity-based feature maps.
– **Multi-task learning**: In terms of knowledge transfer, the CSS-Net improves the segmentation performance with the interactions between three modules of substitution, classification, and segmentation.

– **Diagnostic performance**: In terms of segmentation, the CSS-Net achieves 10% improved RCT diagnostic performance compared to the baseline model using proposed modules, and $6 \sim 8\%$ improved RCT diagnostic performance.

2   Methods

This section illustrates the detailed architecture of the CSS-Net and its design principle. First, we introduce the architecture of the CSS-Net with the individual pipelines for multi-task learning. Then, the detailed descriptions of the substitution learning in the CSS-Net follow. Table 1 summarizes the mathematical notation to construct the CSS-Net.

Table 1. Mathematical notations for the CSS-Net. Here, $[G^{seg}(C = c)]_{h,w} = 1$ iff $[G^{seg}]_{h,w,c} = 1$ else 0.

Notation	Dimension	Element	Related notations	Description
I	$\mathbb{R}^{H \times W}$	$[I]_{h,w} \in [0,1]$	H: height of I W: width of I	Input MRI image
$M_{seg}(I)$	$\mathbb{R}^{H \times W \times 3}$	$[M_{seg}(I)]_{h,w,c}$ $= p \in [0,1]$	$M_{seg}(I)\|_c \in \mathbb{R}^{H \times W}$ $M_{seg}(I)\|_{h,w} \in \mathbb{R}^C$	Prediction by segmentation module
G^{seg}	$\mathbb{R}^{H \times W \times 3}$	$[G^{seg}]_{h,w,c}$ $= g \in \{0,1\}$	$G^{seg}(C = c) \in \mathbb{R}^{H \times W}$	Ground truth in segmentation task
$M_{clf}(I)$	$\mathbb{R}^2$	$M_{clf}(I) = \begin{pmatrix} p_0 \\ p_1 \end{pmatrix}$	$M_{clf}(I)\|_c = p_c \in [0,1]$ $\sum_c M_{clf}(I)\|_c = 1$	Prediction by classification module
G^{clf}	$\mathbb{R}^2$	$G^{clf} = \begin{pmatrix} p_0 \\ p_1 \end{pmatrix}$	$G_c^{clf} = p_c \in \{0,1\}$	Ground truth in classification task
DFT			$DFT : \mathbb{R}^{H \times W} \to \mathbb{R}^{H \times W}$	DFT function
$IDFT$			$IDFT : \mathbb{R}^{H \times W} \to \mathbb{R}^{H \times W}$	Inverse DFT function
S			$S : \mathbb{R}^{H \times W} \to \mathbb{R}^{H \times W}$	CNNs in M_{sl}
$M_{sl}(I)$	$\mathbb{R}^{H \times W}$	$[M_{sl}(I)]_{h,w} \in [0,1]$	$I' = IDFT(X')$ $X' = S(DFT(I * G(C = 2)))$	Substituted image
CL			$CL : \mathbb{R}^{H \times W} \times \mathbb{R}^{H \times W} \to \mathbb{R}$	Content loss function

2.1   Multi-Task Learning Architecture

Fig. 2 (a) describes the overall architecture and pipeline of the CSS-Net, which includes the substitution (M_{sl}), classification (M_{clf}), and segmentation (M_{seg}) modules based on convolutional neural networks (CNNs). The CSS-Net aims to predict the multi-categorical segmentation masks of the background (BG), ST, and RCT. To this end, the CSS-Net is mainly designed for the segmentation task

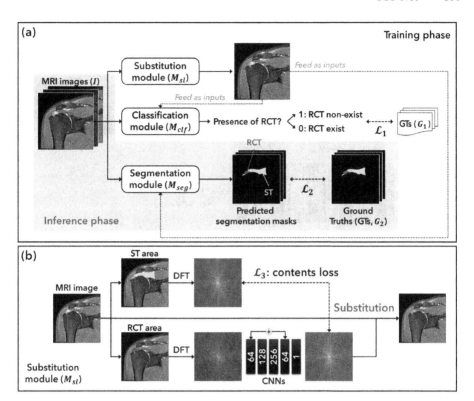

Fig. 2. (a) Overall pipeline of CSS-Net. Each module is optimized using the corresponding loss functions in the training phase. In the inference phase, the CSS-Net predicts the segmentation masks of ST and RCT using only the segmentation module. (b) Detailed architecture of the substitution learning module.

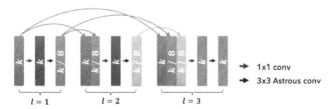

Fig. 3. Dense Block in the CSS-Net. Since ST and RCT occupy a small area, it is required to enlarge receptive fields to comprehend the correlations between RCT and ST. To this end, the Astros convolutions are utilized.

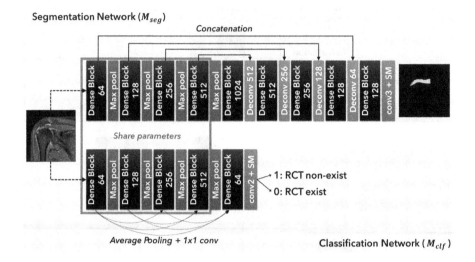

Fig. 4. Detailed architecture of M_{seg} and M_{clf} in the CSS-Net. M_{seg} and M_{clf} are designed based on U-Net and VGGNet, respectively. Convolution blocks in original models are replaced with DenseBlock.

(main task). In addition, despite the feasibility of single utilization of M_{seg}, to enhance the feature extraction during the optimization, two supplementary tasks and modules are appended; the classification module (M_{clf}) and the substitution learning module (M_{sl}). Figures 3 and 4 illustrate the detailed architecture of the CSS-Net. Note that, several convolutions are shared between M_{seg} and M_{clf} to transfer the learned knowledge related to RCT as illustrated in Fig. 4.

2.2 Segmentation Task

As the main task, M_{seg} aims to generate one-hot labeled segmentation masks that include three categories of $\{0, 1, 2\}$, where 0, 1, and 2 indicate BG, ST, and RCT classes, respectively. M_{seg} is constructed based on the U-Net [24], Atrous convolution in DeepLab [25], and the dense connectivity [26], which is a CNN structure shared with M_{clf} (Fig. 3). The segmentation network M_{seg} extracts the features of the input MRI images ($I \in \mathbb{R}^{H \times W}$), and then generates the segmentation outputs ($M_{seg}(I) \in \mathbb{R}^{H \times W \times 3}$). Here, $M_{seg}(I)$ is the probability-based segmentation mask, and thus $\sum_{c}^{\{0,1,2\}} M_{seg}(I)|_c = 1 \in \mathbb{R}^{H \times W}$, where c indicates class-wise notation. In addition, the pixel at the location (h, w) is classified as $\underset{c}{\operatorname{argmax}}\left(M_{seg}(I)|_{h,w}\right)$. Note that M_{seg} is trained with M_{clf} and M_{sl} during training, but the single M_{seg} is used during inference.

2.3 Classification Task

As the supplementary task, M_{clf} classifies the existence of the RCT in I as a binary classification, wherein the classification category is 0 or 1, where 0 and 1 indicate the absence and presence of RCT in I. Here, M_{clf} is designed using the dense connectivity [26] and shares parameters with M_{seg}. The M_{seg} extracts features of I and then outputs the classification results $(M_{clf}(I) \in \mathbb{R}^2)$. Since $M_{clf}(I)$ is also probability-based matrix, $\sum_c^{\{0,1\}} M_{clf}(I)|_c = 1 \in \mathbb{R}$, and is determined as $\underset{c}{\operatorname{argmax}}(M_{clf}(I))$. M_{clf} transfers the learned knowledge about the RCT by sharing parameters between M_{seg} and M_{clf}, and this knowledge improves the performance of M_{seg}.

2.4 Substitution Learning

M_{sl} substitutes the RCT region, which is a ruptured ST area in the MRI images, for a normal ST style. The substituted images are then utilized as additional inputs for M_{seg} and M_{clf}, in terms of data augmentation. Figure 2(b) describes the detailed pipeline of M_{sl}. First, I is binary-masked using the corresponding ground truth $(G = G^{seg})$ with the two outputs $(I*G(c = 1))$ and RCT $(I*G(c = 2))$, where $*$ indicates the Hadamard product. The individual masked regions are then converted into the frequency-domain as shown in Figs. 2(b) and 5(a). Here, the DFT is formulated as follows:

$$F[x, y] = \frac{1}{HW} \sum_h^H \sum_w^W I[h, w] e^{-j2\pi\left(\frac{h}{H}y + \frac{w}{W}x\right)}, \quad j = \sqrt{-1} \tag{1}$$

where, F is the output mapped into the frequency domain, e is Euler's number, and H and W are the height and width of I, respectively. Subsequently, a simple CNN architecture (S) with identical mapping transfers the DFT-converted output of the RCT, which is $D = DFT(I*G(c = 2))$, as $D' = (S \circ DFT)(I*G(c = 2))$. The inverse DFT (IDFT) is applied to D', and the substituted images $IDFT(D')$ is finally generated. In summary, the substituted image (I') is calculated as $I' = M_{sl}(I) = (IDFT \circ S \circ DFT)(I * G(c = 2))$. As illustrated in Fig. 5(b), the generated images by SL are more reliable than those of GANs.

2.5 Loss Functions of CSS-Net

As illustrated in Fig. 2, the CSS-Net includes three loss functions of classification loss $(\mathcal{L}_1)$, segmentation loss $(\mathcal{L}_2)$, and substitution loss $(\mathcal{L}_3)$. Here, $\mathcal{L}_1$ and $\mathcal{L}_2$ are based on the cross-entropy loss function. In particular, the KL-divergence of $M_{clf}(I)|_c$ is compared to that of the corresponding ground truth G^{clf}, and thus $\mathcal{L}_1 = \sum_c G_c^{clf} \log M_{clf}(I)|c$. Likewise, $\mathcal{L}_2 = \sum_{h,w,c}[G^{seg}]_{h,w,c} \log[M_{seg}(I)]_{h,w,c}$. Additionally, the content loss (CL) is utilized to compare the similarity between the substituted RCT and the normal ST, which is regarded as ground truth, in the frequency-domain. In particular, $(S \circ DFT)(I * G(C = 2))$ is compared to $I*G(C = 1)$, and thus $\mathcal{L}_3 = CL(S(DFT(I*G(C = 2))), I*G(C = 1))$. Moreover, the CSS-Net has additional constraints if the RCT does not exist in I, then the substituted images are the same as the original image, and thus $I = M_{sl}(I)$. Therefore, $G_0^{clf}|I - M_{sl}(I)|_1$ is constrained, where $f(x) = |x|_1$ is l_1 loss. Besides, since the RCT is not in substituted image, $M_{clf}(M_{sl}(I))|_0 = 1$ is constrained (Table 2).

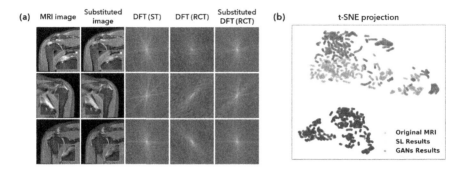

Fig. 5. (a) MRI, substituted, and corresponding DFT images. (b) t-SNE projection of MRI (green), SL images (red), and GANs images (blue). Distribution of substituted images is more similar to MRI than that of medical style GANs [27] (Color figure online).

Table 2. Loss functions for training CSS-Net. $\mathcal{L}_{total} = \sum_{i=1}^{5} \alpha_i \mathcal{L}_i$. Here α_i is a scale factor and trainable. The initial values of α_i is 1.0 except for $\alpha_4 = 0.01$. *CE* and *CL* are cross-entropy and content loss.

Loss function	Definition	Description
$\mathcal{L}_1$	$\sum_c G_c^{clf} \log M_{clf}(I)\|c$	CE for classification task
$\mathcal{L}_2$	$\sum_{h,w,c}[G^{seg}]_{h,w,c} \log[M_{seg}(I)]_{h,w,c}$	CE for segmentation task
$\mathcal{L}_3$	$CL(S(DFT(I * G(C=2))), I * G(C=1))$	CL for substitution task
$\mathcal{L}_4$	$G_0^{clf}\|I - M_{sl}(I)\|_1$, and $\|x\|_1$ is l_1 loss	If RCT not in I, then $I = M_{sl}(I)$
$\mathcal{L}_5$	$1 - M_{clf}(M_{sl}(I))\|_0$	RCT is not in $M_{sl}(I)$

3   Experiments and Results

3.1   Dataset Construction and Environmental Set-up

The data collection has been conducted in accordance with the Declaration of Helsinki, the protocol was approved by the Ethics Committee of the Institutional Review Board of Daegu Catholic University Medical Center, and the clinical

Table 3. Total number of samples and ratio in each segmentation class.

	Total	Fold 1	Fold 2	Fold 3	Fold 4	Fold 5	Avg. # pixels per images (%)	
Total patients	42	9	9	8	8	8		
Total images	889	196	192	166	174	161		
BG	612	127	131	119	128	109	Background (BG)	99.20%
BG + ST	123	31	33	13	17	29	Supraspinatus tendon (ST)	0.76%
BG + ST + RCT	152	38	28	34	29	23	Rotator cuff tear (RCT)	0.04%

Table 4. Training environment for the CSS-Net.

Parameter	Value	Parameter	Value	Parameter	Value
Image Size	512	Resolution	16bits	Augmentation	Flip
Optimizer	Adam	Learning rate	1e-3	Batch size	16
β_1 in Adam	0.9	β_2 in Adam	0.99	ϵ in Adam	1e-7
CPUs	2 Xeons	GPUs	8 Titan-Xps	RAM	256GB
Layer	Value			Layer	Value
Normalization	Group Normalization ($G = 16$)			Activation	ReLU

trial in this paper has been in accordance with ethical standards. In total, 889 images were obtained from 42 patients with shoulder pains. Table 3 illustrates the detailed description of the dataset. In the acquired dataset, the number of images on ST is 123, and that on both the ST and RCT is 152. The other images did not include the ST or RCT. The acquired dataset were divided into 5 folds for the k-fold cross-validation to guarantee the robustness of the experiments, such that each fold contained at least 160 images. MRI images originating from a single patient were only included in single folds. In addition, the experimental environment and the hyper-parameters to train deep learning models are illustrated in Table 4.

Table 5. Comparisons between ours with state-of-the-art models.

	mIoU	IoU-BG	IoU-ST	IoU-RCT	Sensitivity-RCT
U-Net	0.65 ± 0.01	0.93 ± 0.01	0.62 ± 0.02	0.38 ± 0.05	0.68 ± 0.02
DeepLabV3+	0.69 ± 0.01	0.94 ± 0.02	0.66 ± 0.03	0.41 ± 0.04	0.71 ± 0.02
IteR-MRL	0.71 ± 0.01	0.97 ± 0.01	0.69 ± 0.02	0.43 ± 0.06	0.80 ± 0.03
SA-RE-DAE	0.72 ± 0.01	0.97 ± 0.01	0.72 ± 0.02	0.45 ± 0.05	0.78 ± 0.02
Seg + Clf + SL	$\mathbf{0.75 \pm 0.01}$	$\mathbf{0.98 \pm 0.01}$	$\mathbf{0.74 \pm 0.02}$	$\mathbf{0.51 \pm 0.03}$	$\mathbf{0.88 \pm 0.04}$

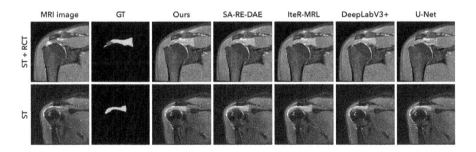

Fig. 6. Representative segmentation results using deep learning models.

3.2   Comparison with State-of-the-Art Models

Table 5 illustrates the quantitative analysis of the proposed CSS-Net compared with other deep learning models. U-Net and DeepLabV3+ were employed because of their popularity in segmentation tasks. In addition, the SA-RE-DAE [28] and IteR-MRL [29] were utilized as state-of-the-art segmentation and multi-task models. The experimental results demonstrated that all models achieve high scores in segmenting BG. Expecting the RCT, the CSS-Net significantly outperforms the other models. It showed at least a 6% IoU-RCT compared to the other models. In particular, the CSS-Net achieved 10% ∼ 20% improved sensitivity in RCT segmentation, suggesting that the CSS-Net with substitution learning could be utilized as an excellent diagnostic tool to localize RCT, as shown in Fig. 6.

3.3   Analysis of Our Model

Since the CSS-Net was designed based on multi-task learning that includes segmentation, classification, and substitution learning, an ablation study was conducted by using each task (Seg, Seg + Clf, Seg + SL, and Seg + Clf + SL). Additionally, because substitution learning was comparable with GANs, CSS-Net, which replaced the substitution module with Style-GAN [27] was also compared. Table 6 illustrates the ablation study of the CSS-Net. The results exhibited that the multi-task learning of segmentation and classification could slightly improve the segmentation of the RCT (Seg and Seg + Clf). In contrast, generative tasks, including GAN and SL, could significantly improve the performance of the CSS-Net. Here, the CSS-Net with SL and Clf tasks improve at 8% IoU-RCT than the baseline. However, the SL-based generative task was preferred in teaching intensity- and frequency-domain knowledge rather than GAN-based style transfer. The results implied that informative knowledge in SL could be transferred into the Seg task.

Table 6. Ablation study of CSS-Net.

	mIoU	IoU-BG	IoU-ST	IoU-RCT	Sensitivity-RCT
Seg (baseline)	0.68 ± 0.01	0.96 ± 0.01	0.65 ± 0.03	0.41 ± 0.04	0.69 ± 0.02
Seg + Clf	0.69 ± 0.01	0.95 ± 0.01	0.67 ± 0.03	0.44 ± 0.05	0.74 ± 0.02
Seg + SL	0.71 ± 0.01	0.96 ± 0.01	0.70 ± 0.04	0.46 ± 0.03	0.78 ± 0.02
Seg + GAN	0.71 ± 0.03	0.96 ± 0.02	0.70 ± 0.06	0.47 ± 0.11	0.75 ± 0.05
Seg + Clf + GAN	0.73 ± 0.02	0.97 ± 0.02	0.72 ± 0.05	0.49 ± 0.09	0.81 ± 0.05
Seg + Clf + SL	**0.75 ± 0.01**	**0.98 ± 0.01**	**0.74 ± 0.02**	**0.51 ± 0.03**	**0.88 ± 0.04**

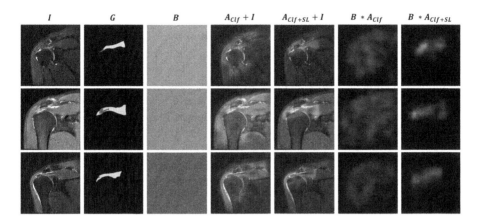

Fig. 7. Representative results of Guided Grad-CAMs. Left→Right: MRI images (I), Ground truth (G), Guided-backprop (B), Overlay of I and Grad-CAM (A_{Clf}) by the *Clf*-network which has only classification module, Overlay of I and Grad-CAM (A_{Clf+SL}) by the *Clf+SL*-network which has classification and substitution module, Guided Grad-CAM ($B*A_{Clf}$) by the *Clf*-network, and Guided Grad-CAM ($B*A_{Clf+SL}$) by the *Clf+SL*-network.

4   Discussion and Future Work

4.1   Explainability

To analyze the effectiveness of substitution learning on other tasks, we compared the Grad-CAM [12] of the CSS-Net with and without an SL module in the RCT classification. Figure 7 illustrates the Grad-CAM and Guided Grad-CAM samples. The results demonstrated that the Grad-CAMs generated by the CSS-Net without the SL module ($A_{clf} + I$) widely exhibited attentions nearby shoulders. On the contrary, the Grad-CAMs generated by CSS-Net with the SL module ($A_{clf+sl} + I$) exhibited an integrated attention distribution similar to that by ground truth of ST (G). The results implied that the CSS-Net with the SL module extracted the features maps of RCT from the ST- and RCT-related areas rather than the entire image. Therefore, it was concluded that the substitution learning improved RCT-related feature extraction by learning the correlations between ST and RCT.

4.2   Limitations and Improvements

One of the main reasons for low IoU-RCT values was the imbalanced pixel distribution in the dataset. Since the BG pixels occupied approximately 99%, whereas the RCT pixels occupy 0.04%, misprediction of the BG significantly affected the accuracy of the RCT regions. Although substitution learning improved segmentation performance by reliable data manipulation than GANs and by transferring the informative knowledge into the segmentation modules, the imbalanced problem could be further improved. Additionally, since the multi-task deep learning models demanded heavy memory utilization owing to their large number of CNNs, a long training time and high memory cost are required to optimize the deep learning models. However, we improved the prediction time by eliminating other tasks except for the segmentation task in the prediction phase. Therefore, the CSS-Net costs the same prediction time as the baseline but it offered high performance in segmentation. Furthermore, we have mainly focused on segmenting the ST and the RCT. However, substitute learning could be further extended to diagnose any diseases that are significantly imbalanced by learning the correlations between normal and disease regions using substitution (abnormal to normal).

5   Conclusions

We introduced integrated multi-task learning as an end-to-end network architecture for RCT segmentation in MRI images. We also proposed a novel substitution learning using DFT to augment data more reliably for the imbalanced dataset, as well as to improve accuracy by knowledge transfer. We employed the SL instead of GANs-based approaches since the SL was demonstrated as more reliable than GANs with even low computation costs. Our results showed that the CSS-Net produced a superior segmentation performance owing to the abundant knowledge transfer from the classification and substitution tasks to the segmentation task, outperforming other state-of-the-art models. It showed a 10% higher IoU value than the baseline model, and even at least 6% higher IoU values than those shown by other state-of-the-art models. Further experiments should be conducted for clinical applications that require reliable data augmentation and high performance.

Acknowledgments. This work was partially supported by the Korea Medical Device Development Fund grant funded by the Korea government (the Ministry of Science and ICT, the Ministry of Trade, Industry and Energy, the Ministry of Health & Welfare, the Ministry of Food and Drug Safety) (Project Number: RS-2022-00141185). Additionally, this work was supported by the Technology Innovation Program(2001424, Development of an elderly-friendly wearable smart healthcare system and service for real-time quantitative monitoring of urination and defecation disorders) funded By the Ministry of Trade, Industry & Energy(MOTIE, Korea). Ground truths were generated by one MRI imaging specialist and one of lab members, and reviewed by two orthopedic surgeons. The code and the dataset are released in the public repository[1]([1] https://github.com/kyungsu-lee-ksl/ACCV2022-Substitution-Learning.git).

References

1. Moosikasuwan, J.B., Miller, T.T., Burke, B.J.: Rotator cuff tears: clinical, radiographic, and us findings. Radiographics **25**, 1591–1607 (2005)
2. Davidson, J.J., Burkhart, S.S., Richards, D.P., Campbell, S.E.: Use of preoperative magnetic resonance imaging to predict rotator cuff tear pattern and method of repair. Arthrosc. J. Arthroscopic Relat. Surg. **21**, 1428–e1 (2005)
3. Shin, Y.K., Ryu, K.N., Park, J.S., Jin, W., Park, S.Y., Yoon, Y.C.: Predictive factors of retear in patients with repaired rotator cuff tear on shoulder MRI. Am. J. Roentgenol. **210**, 134–141 (2018)
4. Kukkonen, J., Kauko, T., Virolainen, P., Äärimaa, V.: The effect of tear size on the treatment outcome of operatively treated rotator cuff tears. Knee Surg. Sports Traumatol. Arthrosc. **23**, 567–572 (2015)
5. Khazzam, M., et al.: Magnetic resonance imaging identification of rotator cuff retears after repair: interobserver and intraobserver agreement. Am. J. sports Med. **40**, 1722–1727 (2012)
6. Medina, G., Buckless, C.G., Thomasson, E., Oh, L.S., Torriani, M.: Deep learning method for segmentation of rotator cuff muscles on MR images. Skeletal Radiol. **50**, 683–692 (2021)
7. Mazurowski, M.A., Buda, M., Saha, A., Bashir, M.R.: Deep learning in radiology: an overview of the concepts and a survey of the state of the art with focus on MRI. J. Magn. Reson. Imaging **49**, 939–954 (2019)
8. Roth, H.R., et al.: Federated whole prostate segmentation in MRI with personalized neural architectures. In: de Bruijne, M. (ed.) MICCAI 2021. LNCS, vol. 12903, pp. 357–366. Springer, Cham (2021). https://doi.org/10.1007/978-3-030-87199-4_34
9. Astuto, B., et al.: Automatic deep learning-assisted detection and grading of abnormalities in knee MRI studies. Radiol. Artif. Intell. **3**, e200165 (2021)
10. Kim, M., Park, H.m., Kim, J.Y., Kim, S.H., Hoeke, S., De Neve, W.: MRI-based diagnosis of rotator cuff tears using deep learning and weighted linear combinations. In: Doshi-Velez, F. (eds.) Proceedings of the 5th Machine Learning for Healthcare Conference. Vol. 126 of Proceedings of Machine Learning Research, pp. 292–308. PMLR (2020)
11. Shim, E., et al.: Automated rotator cuff tear classification using 3D convolutional neural network. Sci. Rep. **10**, 1–9 (2020)
12. Selvaraju, R.R., Cogswell, M., Das, A., Vedantam, R., Parikh, D., Batra, D.: Grad-CAM: visual explanations from deep networks via gradient-based localization. In: Proceedings of the IEEE International Conference on Computer Vision, pp. 618–626 (2017)
13. Hesamian, M.H., Jia, W., He, X., Kennedy, P.: Deep learning techniques for medical image segmentation: achievements and challenges. J. Digit. Imaging **32**, 582–596 (2019)
14. Milletari, F., Navab, N., Ahmadi, S.A.: V-Net: fully convolutional neural networks for volumetric medical image segmentation. In: 2016 Fourth International Conference on 3D Vision (3DV), pp. 565–571. IEEE (2016)
15. Lin, T.Y., Goyal, P., Girshick, R., He, K., Dollár, P.: Focal loss for dense object detection. In: Proceedings of the IEEE International Conference on Computer Vision, pp. 2980–2988 (2017)
16. Lee, K., Kim, J.Y., Lee, M.H., Choi, C.H., Hwang, J.Y.: Imbalanced loss-integrated deep-learning-based ultrasound image analysis for diagnosis of rotator-cuff tear. Sensors **21**, 2214 (2021)

17. Northcutt, C., Jiang, L., Chuang, I.: Confident learning: estimating uncertainty in dataset labels. J. Artif. Intell. Res. **70**, 1373–1411 (2021)
18. Goodfellow, I., et al.: Generative adversarial nets. In: Advances in Neural Information Processing Systems. **27** (2014)
19. Antoniou, A., Storkey, A., Edwards, H.: Data augmentation generative adversarial networks. arXiv preprint arXiv:1711.04340 (2017)
20. Mariani, G., Scheidegger, F., Istrate, R., Bekas, C., Malossi, C.: BAGAN: data augmentation with balancing GAN. arXiv preprint arXiv:1803.09655 (2018)
21. Shin, H.-C., et al.: Medical image synthesis for data augmentation and anonymization using generative adversarial networks. In: Gooya, A., Goksel, O., Oguz, I., Burgos, N. (eds.) SASHIMI 2018. LNCS, vol. 11037, pp. 1–11. Springer, Cham (2018). https://doi.org/10.1007/978-3-030-00536-8_1
22. Calimeri, F., Marzullo, A., Stamile, C., Terracina, G.: Biomedical data augmentation using generative adversarial neural networks. In: Lintas, A., Rovetta, S., Verschure, P.F.M.J., Villa, A.E.P. (eds.) ICANN 2017. LNCS, vol. 10614, pp. 626–634. Springer, Cham (2017). https://doi.org/10.1007/978-3-319-68612-7_71
23. Sandfort, V., Yan, K., Pickhardt, P.J., Summers, R.M.: Data augmentation using generative adversarial networks (cycleGAN) to improve generalizability in CT segmentation tasks. Sci. Rep. **9**, 1–9 (2019)
24. Ronneberger, O., Fischer, P., Brox, T.: U-Net: convolutional networks for biomedical image segmentation. In: Navab, N., Hornegger, J., Wells, W.M., Frangi, A.F. (eds.) MICCAI 2015. LNCS, vol. 9351, pp. 234–241. Springer, Cham (2015). https://doi.org/10.1007/978-3-319-24574-4_28
25. Chen, L.C., Zhu, Y., Papandreou, G., Schroff, F., Adam, H.: Encoder-decoder with atrous separable convolution for semantic image segmentation. In: Proceedings of the European Conference on Computer Vision (ECCV), pp. 801–818 (2018)
26. Huang, G., Liu, Z., Van Der Maaten, L., Weinberger, K.Q.: Densely connected convolutional networks. In: Proceedings of the IEEE Conference on Computer Vision and Pattern Recognition, pp. 4700–4708 (2017)
27. Kazuhiro, K., et al.: Generative adversarial networks for the creation of realistic artificial brain magnetic resonance images. Tomography **4**, 159–163 (2018)
28. Khan, S.H., Khan, A., Lee, Y.S., Hassan, M., et al.: Segmentation of shoulder muscle MRI using a new region and edge based deep auto-encoder. arXiv preprint arXiv:2108.11720 (2021)
29. Liao, X., et al.: Iteratively-refined interactive 3D medical image segmentation with multi-agent reinforcement learning. In: Proceedings of the IEEE/CVF Conference on Computer Vision and Pattern Recognition, pp. 9394–9402 (2020)

PathTR: Context-Aware Memory Transformer for Tumor Localization in Gigapixel Pathology Images

Wenkang Qin[1], Rui Xu[1], Shan Jiang[2], Tingting Jiang[1], and Lin Luo[1,3(✉)]

[1] Peking University, Beijing, China
{qinwk,xurui}@stu.pku.edu.cn, {ttjiang,luol}@pku.edu.cn
[2] Beijing Institute of Collaborative Innovation, Beijing, China
jiangs@bici.org
[3] Southern University of Science and Technology, Shenzhen, China

Abstract. With the development of deep learning and computational pathology, whole-slide images (WSIs) are widely used in clinical diagnosis. A WSI, which refers to the scanning of conventional glass slides into digital slide images, usually contains gigabytes of pixels. Most existing methods in computer vision process WSIs as many individual patches, where the model infers the patches one by one to synthesize the final results, neglecting the intrinsic WSI-wise global correlations among the patches. In this paper, we propose the PATHology TRansformer (PathTR), which utilizes the global information of WSI combined with the local ones. In PathTR, the local context is first aggregated by a self-attention mechanism, and then we design a recursive mechanism to encode the global context as additional states to build the end to end model. Experiments on detecting lymph-node tumor metastases for breast cancer show that the proposed PathTR achieves the Free-response Receiver Operating Characteristic Curves (FROC) score of 87.68%, which outperforms the baseline and NCRF method with +8.99% and +7.08%, respectively. Our method also achieves a significant 94.25% sensitivity at 8 false positives per image.

1 Introduction

Pathology is the gold standard of clinical medicine, especially for cancer diagnosis. With the rapid development of digital slide scanners, digital pathology, where glass slides are digitized into whole slide images (WSIs), has emerged as a potential new trend. To distinguish the hierarchical morphological characteristics such as glands, cells, stroma, and nucleus, pathology slides are usually scanned with magnification at 200 multiple or 400 multiple, which produces extra large digital images of gigapixels.

Although the images can be stored and rendered in a multi-resolution pyramid manner, it brings considerable challenges to computer vision algorithms.

W. Qin and R. Xu—These authors contributed equally to this work.

© The Author(s), under exclusive license to Springer Nature Switzerland AG 2023
L. Wang et al. (Eds.): ACCV 2022, LNCS 13846, pp. 115–131, 2023.
https://doi.org/10.1007/978-3-031-26351-4_8

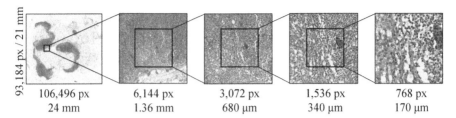

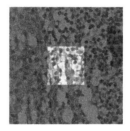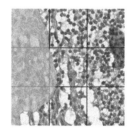

(a) A WSI is a very large gigapixel image with comprehensive pathological information that can be viewed in multiple scales. In a whole-slide-scale global view, it is difficult to recognize the details of tumor cells such as the shape of nucleus, which only presents a very small field of view at a high-resolution scale.

(b) Left: in a small patch that fits the regular neural network size (e.g. 224x224), although the details of nucleus are magnified can be viewed clearly, it is difficult to judge whether it contains tumor cells due to the lack of context patches surrounding it. Center: providing the context patches makes the task easier to detect tumor cells in the current patch. Right, the ground truth of the tumor area, which labeled as yellow.

Fig. 1. Overview of the challenges in tumor localization in gigapixel WSIs.

Taking a common task of tumor localization as an example, where the algorithm is to point out the suspicious locations in WSIs as boxes or heatmap, the input WSI usually is with a high resolution like $100,000 \times 100,000$ pixels. It is hard to infer such a high-resolution image by deep learning models.

There are several works [1–5] first divide WSIs into many patches. A deep learning model is used to classify patches, and these patch-level classification results are then organized into a heatmap to assist pathologists in tumor localization. The limitation of these methods is that the receptive field obtained by each patch is small, so the model may not be able to obtain enough spatial information (see Fig 1).

Some research works [6] referring to use both local and global spatial contexts only involve patch-level globel contexts, without utilizing *the spatial context information all-over the WSI* which reflects more structural disease characteristics. Some methods explore the effectiveness of local spatial information, such as [2] and its derivatives [3–5]. These methods aggregate some local patch information, and the results show that the model can obtain more accurate diagnosis results. In NCRF [2], neural conditional random fields are introduced to correlate the tumor probabilities of a central patch and its surrounding eight patches. This method effectively improves the tumor detection results on WSI and obtains a smoother heatmap. Some other derivative works, such as [3,4], try to change the local patch of fixed position to the local patch of deformable position as deformable convolution did. In [5], Shen et al. explored the patch sampling strategy, and by modifying the patch sampling strategy, they obtained higher performance and faster inference speed on tumor localization. However, how the more global context can be exploited has not been explored.

Vision Transformers exhibit remarkable ability to reflect contextual relevance in computer vision area. By introducing a self-attention mechanism, different input tokens can perceive each other's information. Several works in Sect. 2 use the Transformer to handle local and global contexts for video and language data. Inspired by them, our model utilizes Transformer to tackle with the large-scale WSI spatial context for tumor localization.

We proposed the Transformer-based model, PathTR, to combine local and global context within an end-to-end framework, especially to solve the large-scale context overflow issue. In our model, different patches' features are first extracted by the CNN backbone network. Then the features of a central patch and its surrounding features are further input into a Transformer encoder after adding positional encoding. At each layer of the Transformer Encoder, the context between different patches are accumulated through the self-attention layer. Through this simple approach, the local spatial context is more effectively utilized, and the tumor localization performance is effectively improved as described in Table 3. The next question is how to obtain larger spatial context information, even the spatial context information of the entire WSI. One of the simplest ways is that all the information on the entire WSI is input into the Transformer to obtain global perception. However, this method is difficult to implement because too many patches need to be input.

We further design a recursive mechanism to aggregate context over the entire WSI similar to RNN concept. During model initialization, as shown in Fig. 2, we add several additional hidden states for global information aggregation in addition to the input patch features. These hidden states are designed as tokens of the same dimension as the input local contextual features. After each round of Transformer outputs, we update these hidden states to continuously aggregate the global context. Due to the introduction of the recursive mechanism, the order of patch input will affect the encoding of the hidden state. How serialize the patches on 2D space into a 1D sequence may affect the performance of the model. We further explored how the model's results are affected by different serialization methods, including row-wise, column-wise, and zigzag serialization. The results show that our model is robust to input order and achieves similar performance under different serialization methods.

We evaluated our model on the Camelyon 16 [7] tumor localization task, and the results show that our method significantly outperforms previous work, achieving FROC scores of 87.68%. It is worth noting that by introducing global context, our method can achieve 94.25% sensitivity under 8 average false positives per WSI. This result will be very beneficial for clinical applications, which are very sensitive to false positive numbers.

Overall, our main contributions are as follows:

1. We explored how to better utilize the local and global context information in WSI by introducing the self-attention mechanism and the recursive context management mechanism. The recursive mechanism encodes the local context into a hidden state, thereby obtaining the global WSI perception capability for the first time in the tumor localization task;
2. We explored the influence of input order, position encoding and other factors on this method, and the results show that our model is very robust to input order and other factors;
3. Our method achieves significant progress on the tumor localization task on the Camelyon 16 dataset, and reaches the state-of-the-art results. We hope our work can bring the clinical application of AI one step further in histopathology-assisted diagnosis.

2   Related Works

Tumor Localization.   Since IEEE International Symposium on Biomedical Imaging (ISBI) held the Camelyon challenge [7] in 2016, which first released a dataset of histopathological images with detailed annotations, there have been many excellent works trying to solve tumor localization and achieved good performance. Wang *et al.*[1] won the Camelyon 2016 championship, and then Liu *et al.*[8] from Google Brain achieved better performance under the same pipeline. And in [9], it was applied to the real world, and the possibility of its application in clinical practice was explored. Many subsequent methods used the same pipeline to explore under different settings and different tasks, for example. However, the pipeline used in the above method has the disadvantage of lack of context. Liu *et al.*[2] from Baidu Research used Conditional Random Field (NCRF) to explore spatial local context aggregation for the first time. Some follow-up work [10–15] used this method and explored this method on different tasks. Basically, these methods have not taken broader-concept context correlation into consideration, either in the context size or the feature-domain point of view.

Context Aggregation.   Context Aggregation has been widely used in many tasks in the field of large-volume text and video [2,10,11,13,16–20], and have achieved excellent performance. The tumor localization task in gigapixel pathology images explored brings new challenges of a large spatial size of contexts. In [21], Alexander *et al.*tried to use local and global to get global context of staining. Chomphuwiset *et al.* [22] uses Bayes networks to classify the patches around. In [23], the superpixel algorithm was used for segmentation and classification in low resolution as a global context. Our work analyze the characteristics of pathology images and introduce the framework to aggregate local and global morphological features as context, which has good potential to generalize.

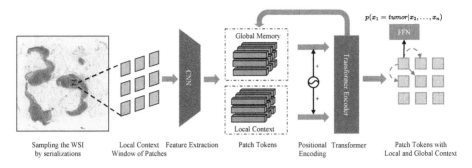

Fig. 2. An overview of our proposed PathTR. We sample WSIs into spatially adjacent patches, extract the feature representations of these patches through a convolutional neural network, and then perform context aggregation between patches through the Transformer [24]. We also save the features of all the inferred patches into the global memory. The global memory tokens also participate in the spatial context aggregation between patches to improve tumor localization performance.

3   Method

In this section, we first describe the pipeline we use for tumor localization on WSIs, and focus on how PathTR improves the pipeline. In particular, we introduced how our proposed local context module and global memory module aggregate the local context and the global memory into different patches. The overall structure of the model can be represented as shown in Fig. 2.

3.1   Preliminary

Pipeline of Tumor Localization.   Since most areas in the pathological images are background areas, and the background areas does not contain any tissue. We only randomly sample the normal patches and tumor patches from the foreground of the pathological image. To obtain the foreground mask, we use Otsu's method [25]. After obtaining the foreground mask, some points are sampled in the foreground area and use these points as the center point to crop out some patches in the normal area and the tumor area, and then train a binary classifier to diagnose the patches.

In the test phase, the trained model is tested by the sliding window manner on the foreground of the WSIs in the test set to obtain the tumor probability of each patch, and organize the probabilities of all patches into a heatmap as the output.

Problem Formulation.   The above classifier treats the tumor probabilities of different patches as independent of each other. So independently calculates the probability of each patch.

$$p(x_i = tumor) = f(x_i), x_i \in \mathbb{X} \tag{1}$$

where $p(x_i = tumor)$ represents the probability that a patch is a tumor, and $\mathbb{X}$ is the set of all patches. This inductive bias, which assumes that all patches are independent, is not that reasonable in pathological images, because whether each patch is a tumor is not only related to the current patch, but also to the surrounding patches, as shown in the Fig. 1b. In [2], which introduces a neural conditional random field after CNN to correlate the context of P patches around a patch at probability level. They try to fit the conditional probability function Eq. (2).

$$p(x_i|x_1, \ldots, x_{i-1}, x_{i+1}, \ldots, x_P) = f(x_1, \ldots, x_P),$$
$$P = p, x_1, \ldots, x_P \in \mathbb{X} \tag{2}$$

This enables some local context information, there are two issues in doing so. First, the window size of the local context P is difficult to determine in advance. If an excessive P is introduced, it will cause the model to be unable to infer due to hardware limitations. If the introduced P is too small, it will lead to inaccurate results because of a lack of context. Secondly, it performs context post-fusion after obtaining the probabilities of each patch *at the probability level*, which loses a lot of information about the patches' features.

To alleviate these two issues, we try to introduce local and global contexts at the feature level for feature aggregation. That is to say, our goal is to try to fit the Eq. (3).

$$p(x_i|x_1, \ldots, x_{i-1}, x_{i+1}, \ldots, x_n) = f(x_1, \ldots, x_n),$$
$$x_1, \ldots, x_n \in \mathbb{X} \tag{3}$$

3.2   Local and Global Context Aggregation

Different from the traditional pipeline sampling process, some non-adjacent patches may be randomly sampled. In PathTR, some windows are sampled in WSIs, and each window contains P patches (specifically, $P = 9$ in our experiment). When training, each sample is a window instead of a patch, that is to say, PathTR input $x \in \mathbb{R}^{N \times P \times C \times W \times H}$, where N, C, W, and H represent batch size, number of channels, width and height respectively. By this way, we can easily introduce local context. Similar to recurrent neural network (RNN), we retain the features of all the inferred patches into the global memory module to obtain a larger context. By introducing local context and global memory mechanism, we have solved the problems faced by models such as NCRF [2] above.

Local Context Aggregation.   Features extract network backbone is utilized, denoted as $f_{feat}(x) : \mathbb{R}^{N \times C \times W \times H} \rightarrow \mathbb{R}^{N \times M}$, to extract the features of these images, where M is the feature dimension. When patches are in f_{feat}, there is no correlation between different patches of different batches. Technically, x will be reshaped into $x \in \mathbb{R}^{NP \times C \times W \times H}$. After obtaining the features of all patches, we use the features aggregation network, denoted as $f_{aggr}(x) : \mathbb{R}^{N \times M} \rightarrow \mathbb{R}^{N \times M}$ to aggregate the features of different patches in the local context.

The features obtained by the P patches of the ith inference as an input tokens sequence, and add positional encoding,

$$z^i = [f_{feat}(x_1^i); f_{feat}(x_2^i); \ldots; f_{feat}(x_P^i)] + E_{pos},$$
$$f_{feat}(x_p^i), E_{pos} \in \mathbb{R}^{P \times M}, \tag{4}$$

input it into the feature aggregation network $f_{aggr}(x)$, which is a Transformer encoder [24] in our implementation. For each Transformer encoder layer, it is aggregated of multi-head self-attention (MSA) and multilayer perceptron (MLP), and uses layer normalization to normalize the intermediate results, as described in Eqs. (5) to (7). The self-attention in each layer provides the ability to aggregate the local context as Eq. (5).

$$h_i = MSA(LN(z_{i-1})) + z_{i-1}, \qquad\qquad i = 1 \ldots L \tag{5}$$
$$l_i = MLP(LN(h_i)) + h_i, \qquad\qquad i = 1 \ldots L \tag{6}$$
$$f_{aggr}(z^i) = l_L, \tag{7}$$

where $z^i = [z_1^i; z_2^i; \ldots, z_n^i]$, and finally output the fused features $f_{aggr}(x) \in \mathbb{R}^{NP \times M}$. Refer to [24] for details of Transformer.

Global Context Aggregation. The local context size P is required to determine whether a patch is a tumor is difficult to determine in advance. In order to make full use of the context, we have introduced a global memory module to record and aggregate the global contexts continuously. In pathological images, it is unrealistic to increase the size of the local context P unlimitedly, since its size is limited by the hardware. The local context in pathological images is far more important than the global context, but the global context has a role that cannot be ignored. Because global information may describe the overall information such as tissue and stain distribution of WSI. We save the global context by storing the inferred local context in the global memory module. That is, after the local context of the current patch is inferred by the model, the output tokens are encoded into the global memory module and wait to participate in the follow-up inferences. At the time of the ith inference, the information of $(i-1)P$ patches has been saved in the global memory module. With the patches in the local context module, a total of iP features of patches will be involved. This process can be formalized as follows:

$$y_i, z_{global}^{i+1} = f_{aggr}(z^i) = f_{aggr}([z_{local}^i; z_{global}^i]), \tag{8}$$

where $z_{local}^i = [z_1^i; z_2^i; \ldots, z_n^i]$, and $y_i, z_{global}^{i+1} \in \mathbb{R}^{NP \times M}$. Finally, we use a linear classifier to classify each patch embedding y_i.

The local context module and global memory module together constitute the core of PathTR. In order to illustrate how PathTR aggregate patches in different windows, context are progressively aggregated through the attention mechanism. For the patches currently input into the local context module, first use the feature network $f_{feat}(x)$ to get their feature tokens, and then aggregate through self-attention in Transformer [24]. Finally, the tokens in the local context module will aggregate the information in all past patches encoded in the global memory.

3.3 Robustness

Since our model uses self-attention and recursion, our model may be sensitive to positional encoding or input order of images. We design different positional encodings and image serializations to verify the robustness of our model.

Positional Encoding. Since Transformer [24] is not sensitive to spatial location, we have adopted the method of adding positional encoding to solve this problem as the convention. We tried three different position encoding methods to test our model. The first is the simplest version, which does not add any positional encoding. The second is to set a learnable parameter $E_{pos} \in \mathbb{R}^{P \times M}$. The third follows [24], we use sine positional encoding to encode, as follows:

$$E_{pos}(pos, 2i) = sin(\frac{pos}{temp^{2i/d_{model}}}) \tag{9}$$

$$E_{pos}(pos, 2i + 1) = cos(\frac{pos}{temp^{2i/d_{model}}}) \tag{10}$$

Serialization.   The windows have to be converted into a sequence to input into PathTR. Obviously, the aggregation context in the global memory module is related to the input order of patches. In order to ensure that the most relevant context is aggregation in the global memory module as much as possible when judging whether a patch is a tumor, we tested three serializations to input windows into PathTR, including row-wise serialization, column-wise serialization, and zigzag serialization. Row-wise serialization and column-wise serialization respectively represent the input of sampled windows into PathTR row by row and column by column. In order to make every time input into the global context in PathTR center around the local context as much as possible, we imitated the JPEG encoding process [26] and adopted zigzag serialization to achieve this goal. This method ensures spatially adjacent patches are still as close as possible after the serialization. As shown in Fig. 3.

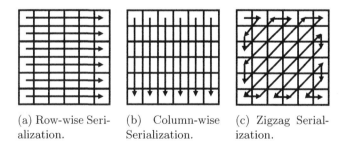

(a) Row-wise Serialization.   (b) Column-wise Serialization.   (c) Zigzag Serialization.

Fig. 3. Serialization.

4 Experiments

4.1 Dataset

We conducted the experiments based on the Camelyon 16 dataset [7], which includes 160 normal and 110 tumor WSIs for training, 81 normal and 49 tumor WSIs for testing.[1] Table 1 describes the distribution of the Camelyon 16 WSIs. All WSIs were annotated carefully by the experienced pathologist, from which we can get pixel-level ROIs from the annotation mask. We conducted all the experiments on the largest scale, 40X magnification. Otsu algorithm [25] had been applied to exclude the background regions of each training WSI. Following the setting in [2]. We just randomly selected foreground patches during the training stage. Normal_001 to Normal_140 and Tumor_001 to Tumor_100 were selected for training, while other WSIs in the rest of the training set was used for validation. We also applied hard negative samples mining to select more patches from the tissue boundary regions as [2].

Table 1. Number of WSIs in the Camelyon 16 dataset [7]. Tumor means the number of slides including tumor regions in the training set. And Normal means the slides without any tumor region in the training set. Two slides in the test set are excluded because of the errors of annotations following [8]. So there are only 128 slides will be used in test set.

Institution	Tumor	Normal	Test
Radboud UMC	90	70	80
UMC Utrcht	70	40	50
Total	160	110	130

4.2 Implementation Details

We implement PathTR with PyTorch-1.8.0 and train the model with NVIDIA GeForce GTX 1080 Ti GPU. As our implementation is based on the open-source codebase [2], the methods such as patches generation and non-maximum suppression are similar to the NCRF [2]. At training time, we fetch 768×768 pixel windows from the training set, which are cropped as 3×3 grid of 256×256 pixel patches to feed the ResNet [27] backbone during the forward propagation. We train with Adam with a weight decay of 10^{-4} and initial learning rates of 10^{-3}. Our Transformer model is loaded with pre-trained weights from [28]. As shown in the Table 4, we report results with two different backbones: a ResNet-18 and a ResNet-34 [27].

The Transformer encoder [24] is trained with a default dropout of 0.1. At training time, we try to select numbers of Transformer [24] encoder layers as 6 for default. And we compare the performance with sine, learned, and none

---

[1] The need for informed consent was waived by the institutional review board of Radboud University Medical Center (RUMC). [7].

positional encoding in ablation experiments. At the test stage, we use variant window grid size (baseline is 3×3) to aggregate the context at different scales of the surrounding regions. And we apply three types of serialization methods as described in Sect. 3.3, which are referred to as row-wise, column-wise and zigzag serialization.

In the ablation experiments, we use a training schedule of 20 epochs with a learning rate drop by a factor of 10 after 10 epochs, where a single epoch is a pass over all training patches once. Training the baseline model for 20 epochs on two 1080Ti GPUs takes about 24 h, with 5 patches per GPU (hence a total batch size of 10). PathTR takes 0.01s per patch and about one hour per WSI at the inference time. So the total inference time of 130 WSIs in the test set is about 5 days using just one 1080Ti GPU.

4.3   Evaluation

Besides comparing the average accuracy and AUC with other methods, we also adopt the two important metrics, Free-response Receiver Operating Characteristic Curves (FROC) and sensitivity@nFP in the performance evaluation, because in clinical diagnosis the false negative rate is worth more attention [29].

The calculation of FROC score [29] is similar to that of Area Under Curve (AUC). We need to report the coordinates and confidence of tumors. If the coordinates are not in any tumor, it is judged as a false positive. If the reported coordinates successfully hit a tumor, it is considered as a successful judgment that a certain tumor exists. We can get the number of false positives and the tumor recall rate under different confidence thresholds. The FROC score [29] then be defined as the average sensitivity in the case of an average of 1/4, 1/2, 1, 2, 4, and 8 false positives for all WSIs on the test set.

4.4   Main Results

The proposed PathTR achieves the accuracy and AUC on par with other the state-of-the-art methods (Table 2). We further evaluate the FROC scores [29] of PathTR with local context module and global memory module setups and compare them with that of the baseline and of NCRF [2]. In addition, the test time augmentation is taken to improve the FROC score of our model on the test set following NCRF [2]. That is, in the test stage, the input patch is flipped or rotated, then PathTR is used for inference on augmented patches, and finally the multiple probability values are averaged to obtain the final tumor probability. Due to the introduction of spatial context, our method reduces false positive regions well, our method achieves a significant improvement in FROC score.

Table 3 shows the comparison with the Vanilla Pipeline and NCRF [2]. Our FROC score reaches 87.68% with test time augmentation and 94.25% sensitivity at 8 false positives per WSI. For comparison, a human pathologist attempting exhaustive search achieved 73.2% sensitivity. [8]

In order to compare the results from different models, the FROC curves of baseline, NCRF [2] and PathTR are presented in Fig. 4a. In Fig. 4b, the

Table 2. Performance comparison of ACC and AUC.

Methods	ACC(%)	AUC
Baseline	96.79	0.9435
NCRF [2]	97.97	0.9725
Google [8]	–	0.9670
TransPath [6]	89.91	**0.9779**
PathTR	**98.19**	0.9757

improvement brought by different modules in PathTR are shown. With any false positives, the sensitivity has improved after the introduction of our local context module and global memory module.

Table 3. Performance comparison with the state of the art. We test the results of adding a local context module and a global memory module to the baseline. At the same time we use test time augmentation to get better performance. We show the sensitivity achieved by our model at different false positives, as well as the FROC score. All models use grid size of 3×3, sine positional encoding, and row-wise input sequence, and with 6-layer Transformer encoder [24].

Methods	Local	Global	Sensitivity (%)						FROC (%)
			@.25FPs	@.5FPs	@1FP	@2FPs	@4FPs	@8FPs	
Vanilla Pipeline [2]			66.98	71.90	77.20	81.80	84.95	89.28	78.69
NCRF [2]	✓		68.14	74.33	79.20	84.07	87.61	90.27	80.60
Wang et al.[1]			77.3	77.8	81.3	82.7	82.7	82.7	80.74
MSC-Net [4]	✓		–	–	–	–	–	–	80.78
DCRF [3]	✓		–	–	–	–	–	–	80.17
DP-FTD [5]	✓		–	–	–	–	–	–	81.7
DCRF-FTD [5]	✓		–	–	–	–	–	–	82.1
Ours (without global context)	✓		72.57	80.53	86.73	88.94	91.15	92.92	85.47
Ours	✓	✓	**76.55**	**83.63**	**88.94**	**90.27**	**92.48**	**94.25**	**87.68**

4.5   Ablation Study

Local and Global Module.   The local context module and global memory module are the core modules of PathTR aiming to aggregate a larger context, The local context module contains some spatially adjacent patches and completes the context aggregation in the Transformer [24]. The global memory module implicitly encodes the information of all past patches. We conduct ablation experiments in order to investigate the necessity of local context module and global memory module with different backbone networks.

As shown in Table 3, by introducing the local context module, the FROC is raised from the baseline 78.69% up to 84.59%, which is an improvement of 5.90%, proving the important role of local context feature-level fusion. Then introducing the global memory module receives a further improvement of 1.47% and reaches 86.06%. It demonstrates that global memory module can also contribute further improvement with a careful design.

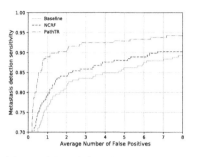 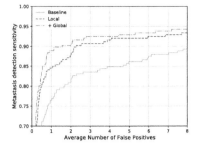

(a) FROC of baseline, NCRF and PathTR results.

(b) FROC comparison among baseline, our local context module and our global memory module.

Fig. 4. FROC of baseline, with local context and global memory module.

We also explored whether the local context module and global memory module can achieve consistent improvements under different backbones. As shown in Table 4, we use ResNet-18 and ResNet-34 as the backbone.

Transformer Layers. For aggregating the features from all patches of each window, we have taken Transformer encoder [24] to aggregate the local context and global memory. We set Transformer layers [24] from 2 to 8 with the interval of 2, since the experimental is too expensive for us. Table 5 shows the sensitivity at 8 false positives and FROC with different numbers of layers.

Table 4. Performance of global and local modules with different patch feature extraction backbone. Sensitivity is shown at 8 false positives per slide (same below). The FROC of baseline is reproduced by us, which is 78.25% in [2]

Methods	Backbone	Sensitivity (%)	FROC (%)
baseline	ResNet-18	89.28	78.69
+ Local	ResNet-18	93.36	84.59
+ Global	ResNet-18	93.81	86.06
baseline	ResNet-34	-	74.44
+ Local	ResNet-34	91.40	84.54
+ Global	ResNet-34	91.59	82.74

Running Time and Computational Cost. We test the inference times and FLOPs(on Nvidia GTX 1080Ti) of the Baseline, NCRF and PathTR to compare the computation overhead, as shown in Table 6. All input sizes are fixed as $9 \times 3 \times 224 \times 224$ (9 patches with 224×224 pixels).

Context Size. The implementation of PathTR determines that the size of local context and global memory are identical. We call this as context size. In PathTR, the capacity of local context depends on the context size we take (in other words,

Table 5. Performance comparison with different numbers of Transformer encoder layers (using the same sine positional encoding and row-wise serialization). [24]

Methods	TF layers	Sensitivity (%)	FROC (%)
Local	2	90.10	84.14
Local	4	90.97	84.07
Local	6	**93.36**	**84.59**
Local	8	89.39	82.70
+ Global	2	90.47	85.56
+ Global	4	91.03	85.74
+ Global	6	**93.81**	**86.06**
+ Global	8	93.36	84.36

Table 6. Speed Comparison.

Methods	Params (M)	Inference time (patches/second)	GFLOPs
Baseline	11.18	144	16.367
NCRF	11.18	120	16.367
PathTR	30.09	73	16.709

the number of grids). The feature space of global memory will also increase with the increase of context size. With the increase of context size, there can be a wider context in the local context, and global memory can encode more global semantics. We tested three context sizes of 2×2, 3×3 and 3×6, as shown in Table 7. The results show that larger context size generates better but not significant performance gain.

Table 7. Performance of global memory module with different context size at test stage.

Methods	Context size	Sensitivity (%)	FROC (%)
PathTR	2×2	91.79	85.20
PathTR	3×3	**93.81**	86.06
PathTR	3×6	92.18	**86.10**

Robustness. Because of the recursive mechanism used in our model, all the local context is aggregated in global memory, and different input sequences may result in different results. Three serialization methods were used in our ablation experiments, as described in Sect. 3.3. The results are shown in Table 8. The three serialization methods achieved similar results, with Zigzag serialization slightly higher than row-wise and column-wise. This suggests that PathTR is not sensitive to input order, and that global memory plays a different role in the model than local context. Probably retaining more high-level semantic information, such as WSIs staining, instead of low-level semantic information, such as morphology.

Table 8. Performance of PathTR with variant serialization method. Zigzag serialization gains a slight FROC increment than other methods.

Methods	Serialization	Sensitivity (%)	FROC (%)
PathTR	Row-wise	**93.81**	86.06
PathTR	Column-wise	92.79	85.91
PathTR	Zigzag	93.80	**86.20**

The location of each patch in the local context is indispensable for clinical diagnosis, thus the order of tokens is needed to be fed into the local context and global memory tokens.

Two types of positional encoding are utilized in PathTR. Sine positional encoding is used to generate fixed position information. Learned positional encoding is added to allow the Transformer [24] to learn a set of appropriate positional information representations during the training process. The results are shown in Table 9.

Table 9. Performance of global and local modules with different positional encoding (all with 6-layer Transformer).

Methods	PE	Sensitivity (%)	FROC (%)
Local	None	90.76	82.20
Local	Learned	91.59	83.33
Local	Sine	**93.36**	**84.59**
Local + Global	None	91.50	83.30
Local + Global	Learned	92.04	**86.43**
Local + Global	Sine	**93.81**	86.06

5 Conclusion

This paper presents the PathTR method for tumor localization in gigapixel pathology images. We first introduce the Local Context Module to aggregate the local context surrounding a center patch. And then we bring in the global context of the whole slide images by introducing a recursive mechanism. The proposed PathTR can make full use of the locality of the image while retaining the global context, thus achieving a significant analysis capability of gigapixel images. We hope that our work can inspire more vision tasks that require analysis of gigapixel images to achieve better performance.

Acknowledgement. This research was supported in part by the Foundation of Shenzhen Science and Technology Innovation Committee (JCYJ20180507181527806). We also thank Qiuchuan Liang (Beijing Haidian Kaiwen Academy, Beijing, China) for preprocessing data.

References

1. Wang, D., Khosla, A., Gargeya, R., Irshad, H., Beck, A.H.: Deep learning for identifying metastatic breast cancer. ArXiv preprint abs/1606.05718 (2016)
2. Li, Y., Ping, W.: Cancer metastasis detection with neural conditional random field. ArXiv preprint abs/1806.07064 (2018)
3. Shen, Yiqing, Ke, Jing: A deformable CRF model for histopathology whole-slide image classification. In: Martel, Anne L.., Abolmaesumi, Purang, Stoyanov, Danail, Mateus, Diana, Zuluaga, Maria A.., Zhou, S. Kevin., Racoceanu, Daniel, Joskowicz, Leo (eds.) MICCAI 2020. LNCS, vol. 12265, pp. 500–508. Springer, Cham (2020). https://doi.org/10.1007/978-3-030-59722-1_48
4. Zhang, W., Zhu, C., Liu, J., Wang, Y., Jin, M.: Cancer metastasis detection through multiple spatial context network. In: Proceedings of the 2019 8th International Conference on Computing and Pattern Recognition, pp. 221–225 (2019)
5. Shen, Y., Ke, J.: Sampling based tumor recognition in whole-slide histology image with deep learning approaches. IEEE/ACM Trans. Comput. Biol. Bioinform. (2021)
6. Wang, Xiyue, Yang, Sen, Zhang, Jun, Wang, Minghui, Zhang, Jing, Huang, Junzhou, Yang, Wei, Han, Xiao: TransPath: transformer-based self-supervised learning for histopathological image classification. In: de Bruijne, Marleen, Cattin, Philippe C.., Cotin, Stéphane., Padoy, Nicolas, Speidel, Stefanie, Zheng, Yefeng, Essert, Caroline (eds.) MICCAI 2021. LNCS, vol. 12908, pp. 186–195. Springer, Cham (2021). https://doi.org/10.1007/978-3-030-87237-3_18
7. Bejnordi, B.E., et al.: Diagnostic assessment of deep learning algorithms for detection of lymph node metastases in women with breast cancer. JAMA **318**, 2199–2210 (2017)
8. Liu, Y., et al.: Detecting cancer metastases on gigapixel pathology images. ArXiv preprint abs/1703.02442 (2017)
9. Liu, Y., et al.: Artificial intelligence-based breast cancer nodal metastasis detection: insights into the black box for pathologists. Arch. Pathol. Laboratory Med. **143**, 859–868 (2019)
10. Shen, Yiqing, Ke, Jing: A deformable CRF model for histopathology whole-slide image classification. In: Martel, Anne L.., Abolmaesumi, Purang, Stoyanov, Danail, Mateus, Diana, Zuluaga, Maria A.., Zhou, S. Kevin., Racoceanu, Daniel, Joskowicz, Leo (eds.) MICCAI 2020. LNCS, vol. 12265, pp. 500–508. Springer, Cham (2020). https://doi.org/10.1007/978-3-030-59722-1_48
11. Ye, J., Luo, Y., Zhu, C., Liu, F., Zhang, Y.: Breast cancer image classification on WSI with spatial correlations. In: IEEE International Conference on Acoustics, Speech and Signal Processing, ICASSP 2019, Brighton, United Kingdom, 12–17 May 2019, pp. 1219–1223. IEEE (2019)
12. Vang, Yeeleng S.., Chen, Zhen, Xie, Xiaohui: Deep learning framework for multiclass breast cancer histology image classification. In: Campilho, Aurélio, Karray, Fakhri, ter Haar Romeny, Bart (eds.) ICIAR 2018. LNCS, vol. 10882, pp. 914–922. Springer, Cham (2018). https://doi.org/10.1007/978-3-319-93000-8_104
13. Zanjani, F.G., Zinger, S., et al.: Cancer detection in histopathology whole-slide images using conditional random fields on deep embedded spaces. In: Medical

Imaging 2018: Digital Pathology, vol. 10581, p. 105810I. International Society for Optics and Photonics (2018)

14. Kong, Bin, Wang, Xin, Li, Zhongyu, Song, Qi., Zhang, Shaoting: Cancer metastasis detection via spatially structured deep network. In: Niethammer, Marc, Styner, Martin, Aylward, Stephen, Zhu, Hongtu, Oguz, Ipek, Yap, Pew-Thian., Shen, Dinggang (eds.) IPMI 2017. LNCS, vol. 10265, pp. 236–248. Springer, Cham (2017). https://doi.org/10.1007/978-3-319-59050-9_19

15. Mahbod, Amirreza, Ellinger, Isabella, Ecker, Rupert, Smedby, Örjan., Wang, Chunliang: Breast cancer histological image classification using fine-tuned deep network fusion. In: Campilho, Aurélio, Karray, Fakhri, ter Haar Romeny, Bart (eds.) ICIAR 2018. LNCS, vol. 10882, pp. 754–762. Springer, Cham (2018). https://doi.org/10.1007/978-3-319-93000-8_85

16. Oh, S.W., Lee, J., Xu, N., Kim, S.J.: Video object segmentation using space-time memory networks. In: 2019 IEEE/CVF International Conference on Computer Vision, ICCV 2019, Seoul, Korea (South), October 27 - November 2, 2019, IEEE (2019) 9225–9234

17. Woo, S., Kim, D., Cho, D., Kweon, I.S.: Linknet: Relational embedding for scene graph. In Bengio, S., Wallach, H.M., Larochelle, H., Grauman, K., Cesa-Bianchi, N., Garnett, R., eds.: Advances in Neural Information Processing Systems 31: Annual Conference on Neural Information Processing Systems 2018, NeurIPS 2018, December 3–8, 2018, Montréal, Canada. (2018) 558–568

18. Wu, C., Feichtenhofer, C., Fan, H., He, K., Krähenbühl, P., Girshick, R.B.: Long-term feature banks for detailed video understanding. In: IEEE Conference on Computer Vision and Pattern Recognition, CVPR 2019, Long Beach, CA, USA, June 16–20, 2019, Computer Vision Foundation / IEEE (2019) 284–293

19. Xu, J., Cao, Y., Zhang, Z., Hu, H.: Spatial-temporal relation networks for multi-object tracking. In: 2019 IEEE/CVF International Conference on Computer Vision, ICCV 2019, Seoul, Korea (South), October 27 - November 2, 2019, IEEE (2019) 3987–3997

20. Chen, Y., Cao, Y., Hu, H., Wang, L.: Memory enhanced global-local aggregation for video object detection. In: 2020 IEEE/CVF Conference on Computer Vision and Pattern Recognition, CVPR 2020, Seattle, WA, USA, June 13–19, 2020, IEEE (2020) 10334–10343

21. Wright, A.I., Magee, D., Quirke, P., Treanor, D.: Incorporating local and global context for better automated analysis of colorectal cancer on digital pathology slides. Procedia Computer Science 90 (2016) 125–131 20th Conference on Medical Image Understanding and Analysis (MIUA 2016)

22. Chomphuwiset, P., Magee, D.R., Boyle, R.D., Treanor, D.E.: Context-based classification of cell nuclei and tissue regions in liver histopathology. In: MIUA. (2011)

23. Zormpas-Petridis, K., Failmezger, H., Roxanis, I., Blackledge, M.D., Jamin, Y., Yuan, Y.: Capturing global spatial context for accurate cell classification in skin cancer histology. ArXiv preprint abs/1808.02355 (2018)

24. Vaswani, A., Shazeer, N., Parmar, N., Uszkoreit, J., Jones, L., Gomez, A.N., Kaiser, L., Polosukhin, I.: Attention is all you need. In Guyon, I., von Luxburg, U., Bengio, S., Wallach, H.M., Fergus, R., Vishwanathan, S.V.N., Garnett, R., eds.: Advances in Neural Information Processing Systems 30: Annual Conference on Neural Information Processing Systems 2017, December 4–9, 2017, Long Beach, CA, USA. (2017) 5998–6008

25. Otsu, N.: A threshold selection method from gray level histograms. IEEE Trans. Syst. Man Cybern. **9**, 62–66 (1979)

26. Wallace, G.K.: The jpeg still picture compression standard. Commun. ACM **34**, 30–44 (1991)
27. He, K., Zhang, X., Ren, S., Sun, J.: Deep residual learning for image recognition. In: 2016 IEEE Conference on Computer Vision and Pattern Recognition, CVPR 2016, Las Vegas, NV, USA, June 27–30, 2016, IEEE Computer Society (2016) 770–778
28. Dosovitskiy, A., Beyer, L., Kolesnikov, A., Weissenborn, D., Zhai, X., Unterthiner, T., Dehghani, M., Minderer, M., Heigold, G., Gelly, S., Uszkoreit, J., Houlsby, N.: An image is worth 16×16 words: Transformers for image recognition at scale. In: 9th International Conference on Learning Representations, ICLR 2021, Virtual Event, Austria, May 3–7, 2021, OpenReview.net (2021)
29. Egan, J.P., Greenberg, G.Z., Schulman, A.I.: Operating characteristics, signal detectability, and the method of free response. J. Acoust. Soc. Am. **33**, 993–1007 (1961)

Region-of-interest Attentive Heteromodal Variational Encoder-Decoder for Segmentation with Missing Modalities

Seung-wan Jeong[1,2], Hwan-ho Cho[3], Junmo Kwon[1,2], and Hyunjin Park[1,2(✉)]

[1] Sungkyunkwan University, Suwon, Republic of Korea
{jsw93,skenfn1231,hyunjinp}@skku.edu
[2] Center for Neuroscience Imaging Research, Suwon, Republic of Korea
[3] Konyang University, Daejon, Republic of Korea
hhcho@konyang.ac.kr

Abstract. The use of multimodal images generally improves segmentation. However, complete multimodal datasets are often unavailable due to clinical constraints. To address this problem, we propose a novel multimodal segmentation framework that is robust to missing modalities by using a region-of-interest (ROI) attentive modality completion. We use ROI attentive skip connection to focus on segmentation-related regions and a joint discriminator that combines tumor ROI attentive images and segmentation probability maps to learn segmentation-relevant shared latent representations. Our method is validated in the brain tumor segmentation challenge dataset of 285 cases for the three regions of the complete tumor, tumor core, and enhancing tumor. It is also validated on the ischemic stroke lesion segmentation challenge dataset with 28 cases of infarction lesions. Our method outperforms state-of-the-art methods in robust multimodal segmentation, achieving an average Dice of 84.15%, 75.59%, and 54.90% for the three types of brain tumor regions, respectively, and 48.29% for stroke lesions. Our method can improve the clinical workflow that requires multimodal images.

Keywords: Segmentation · Missing modalities · Multimodal learning · Adversarial learning

1 Introduction

Segmentation of lesions in medical images provides important information for assessing disease progression and surgical planning. Accurate segmentation often requires multimodal 3D images with complementary information about the lesions. For example, brain tumors are usually diagnosed with multimodal

Supplementary Information The online version contains supplementary material available at https://doi.org/10.1007/978-3-031-26351-4_9.

magnetic resonance imaging (MRI) and different MRI modalities, such as T1-weighted (T1), contrast-enhanced T1-weighted (T1ce), T2-weighted (T2), and fluid attenuation inversion recovery (FLAIR), provide complementary information (e.g., edema, enhancing tumor, and necrosis/non-enhancing tumor) about the brain tumor. In addition, T1, T2, diffusion-weighted images (DWI), and FLAIR MRI are acquired for the diagnosis of subacute ischemic stroke. DWI and FLAIR modalities provide general information about stroke lesions, whereas T1 and T2 modalities provide information on vasogenic edema present in subacute stroke [29]. Therefore, compared to the use of single-modality MRI, segmentation with multimodal MRI [11, 13, 14, 16, 18–21, 27, 30, 40] helps to reduce uncertainty and improve segmentation performance.

Using multimodal data for segmentation is generally preferred, but modalities can often be missing in clinical practice. Some modalities may be missing due to limited patient tolerance, limited scan times, and corrupted images. In such cases, the missing modalities are not available for learning, which degrades the segmentation performance. Therefore, to fill the information gap of the missing modalities, an algorithm that effectively handles missing modalities is required. The simplest way to compensate for missing modalities is to impute missing modalities from other modalities using a method such as a k-nearest neighbor. However, this method cannot fully incorporate semantic information originally contained in the missing modalities. Many deep learning methods have recently been proposed to solve the problem of missing modalities [7, 12, 17, 24, 35, 36, 42]. These methods can be broadly grouped into two approaches. The first approach synthesizes missing modalities from available modalities and performs segmentation using complete modalities [24, 36]. These methods are computationally complex because many different models are required to handle different missing scenarios. The second approach involves learning a shared representation of the multimodal information for segmentation. The learned shared representation is common to multimodal data, and thus, it is possible to construct one model that scales well to handle many missing scenarios.

Existing methods based on the second approach primarily use procedures to complete the full modalities as auxiliary tasks to learn a shared representation that is robust to missing modalities. Although this strategy successfully solves the problem of missing modalities, as a result, information about segmentation can be lost, which can lead to degradation of segmentation performance. Therefore, in addition to the constraints related to the completion of the full modalities, it is necessary to impose constraints related to segmentation tasks, such as image structure and the region-of-interest (ROI).

In this paper, we propose a new robust multimodal segmentation framework called region-of-interest attentive heteromodal variational encoder-decoder (RA-HVED). Our framework uses a heteromodal variational encoder-decoder (U-HVED) based on a multimodal variational formulation as a backbone to demonstrate the competitive performance of ROI attentive completion. The main contributions of our method are threefold: (1) We propose a robust segmentation framework for missing modalities that focuses on ROI. To impose additional weights on the ROI, we introduce the ROI attentive skip connection module (RSM) and the ROI attentive joint discriminator. (2) We facilitate the learning of segmentation task-relevant shared representations by adding RSM that constrains the skip connection and an ROI attentive joint discriminator that strongly constrains modality completion. (3) We have conducted extensive experiments with missing modalities using brain tumor and stroke lesion datasets. Our method is more robust than previous methods for segmentation with missing modalities for the two datasets. In summary, our method can be applied to practical situations where data with missing modalities occur.

2   Related Works

2.1   Medical Image Synthesis

Medical image synthesis is a field that has recently been explored. Initially, methods based on convolutional neural network (CNN) have been commonly used for image synthesis. Li et al. [24] synthesized positron emission tomography (PET) images from MRI to improve the diagnosis of brain disease. Han [15] proposed a CNN method to synthesize the corresponding computed tomography (CT) images from an MRI. Since the first generation of CNNs, generative adversarial network (GAN)-based methods have achieved excellent performance in various medical image synthesis tasks. Nie et al. [31] synthesized CT images from MRI images using a context-aware GAN with high clinical utility. Costa et al. [10] generated a vessel tree using an adversarial autoencoder and synthesized a color retinal image from a vessel tree using a GAN. Wolterink et al. [38] used a GAN to obtain a routine-dose CT by reducing the noise of low-dose CT. Bi et al. [4] synthesized low-dose PET images from CT and tumor labels using a multichannel GAN. These methods are mostly intended for cases where one source modality is mapped to another target modality and thus are not suitable for multimodal settings where there may be more than one source and target modalities. Many studies on multimodal synthesis have recently been conducted to exploit the complementary information of multimodal data [5,23,34,37,41]. Wang et al. [37] synthesized full-dose PET images by combining low-dose PET images and multimodal MRI. Lee et al. [23] proposed CollaGAN for the imputation of missing image data. CollaGAN used a generator to produce a single output corresponding to each combination of multimodal inputs. CollaGAN used multiple cycle consistency to obtain the content of each combination, and the generation of the corresponding target modality was controlled by the one-hot-mask vector. However, this method cannot handle multiple missing modalities because it assumes that only one modality is missing at a time. Therefore, Shen et al. [34] proposed ReMIC for multiple missing modalities. Because ReMIC is a GAN framework that generates multiple images by separating the common content code of modalities and modality-specific style code, it can solve problems with missing multiple modalities. Furthermore, it has been shown that the learned content code contains semantic information and, therefore, can perform segmentation tasks well. Because the segmentation task was performed independently after synthesis, the segmentation task was not explicitly optimized, and the segmentation performance depended on the results of the synthesized modalities. Therefore, we propose a robust segmentation framework for multiple missing modalities that overcomes these limitations.

2.2 Segmentation with Missing Modalities

Many methods have been proposed to solve the problem of the missing modality in segmentation [7,12,17,24,35,36,42]. These methods can be broadly divided into two types. The first approach synthesizes missing modalities and then performs segmentation from a set of complete modalities [24,36]. This approach can be effectively used when only two modalities are considered. However, once the number of modalities exceeds three, it becomes complex because many different models are required to handle different missing scenarios. Subsequently, the synthesis of the missing modalities in multimodal (more than two modalities) situations was proposed, but it is still difficult to deal with multiple missing modalities. The second approach involves creating a shared feature space that encodes multimodal segmentation information. Because this method finds common information via a shared encoder, it is possible to create one model that scales well to handle many missing scenarios. As such, many studies have adopted the second approach [7,12,17,35,42]. Havaei et al. [17] proposed a heteromodal image segmentation (HeMIS) method to calculate the statistics of learned feature maps for each modality and used them to predict the segmentation map. Because the encoder of HeMIS could not fully learn the shared representation using simple arithmetic operations, Dorent et al. [12] proposed U-HVED based on a multimodal variational formulation. U-HVED proved to be robust to missing modalities and outperformed the HeMIS in evaluating the brain tumor dataset. Chen et al. [7] applied the concept of feature disentanglement to effectively learn the shared latent representations in missing modality settings. However, this method requires an additional encoder for feature disentanglement. Shen et al. [35] introduced adversarial loss to learn invariant representations by matching feature maps of missing modalities to feature maps of complete modalities. This model was designed to be robust to only one missing modality; thus, it cannot handle situations where more than two modalities are missing. Existing methods [7,12,17,35,42] have proposed robust models for missing modalities using modality completion as an additional auxiliary task in the main segmentation task.

Our model goes further and improves the performance of segmentation with missing modalities by imposing constraints related to the segmentation task on the modality completion.

3 Methods

Figure 1 shows an overview of our proposed framework. As the backbone of our method, we first introduce U-HVED, which learns the multi-scale shared rep-

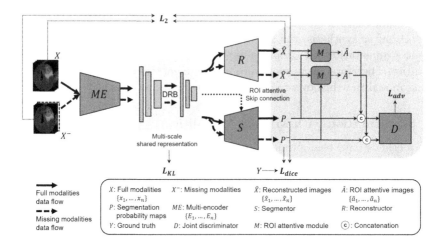

Fig. 1. Overview of our RA-HVED for robust multimodal segmentation. All modality-specific encoders $E_1, \ldots, E_n$ are included in the multi-encoder ME. The multi-scale shared representation from the multi-encoder ME flows into the reconstructor R for modality completion and segmentor S for image segmentation. The joint discriminator D computes adversarial loss using the concatenation $(\hat{A}, P)$ of the outputs from the two streams. ROI attentive images $\hat{A}$ are obtained using reconstructed images $\hat{X}$ and segmentation probability maps P.

resentation. This model extracts representations from encoders and fuses them into a shared representation of multimodal data. We also introduce a dimension reduction block (DRB) to efficiently learn the multi-scale shared representation. The shared representation is used in two streams for robust segmentation in different scenarios of missing modality. One stream generates the full modalities from the shared representation of the multimodal input, and the other performs the segmentation. At each level of the segmentor S, the encoder features are weighted by the segmentation-related regions using ROI attentive skip connections. Finally, we propose the ROI attentive module M and the joint discriminator D, which forces the reconstructor R to focus on the ROI.

3.1 Heteromodal Variational Encoder-Decoder

Dorent et al. [12] proposed U-HVED that combines U-net [33] and multimodal variational autoencoder (MVAE) [39] to perform segmentation from any subset of the full modalities. MVAE is a model developed in the context of conditionally independent modalities $X = x_1, \ldots, x_n$ when a common latent variable z is given. The authors of MVAE deal with the missing data by extending variational autoencoder (VAE) [22] formulation for multimodal inputs. The encoded mean μ and covariance Σ of each modality are fused into a common latent variable z of the multimodal data using the product of Gaussian (PoG) [6] (Supplementary Fig. 2(a)). If a modality is missing, the corresponding variation parameters are excluded (Supplementary Fig. 2(b)). The latent variable z estimated by sampling was decoded into the image space. Sampling was performed using a reparameterization trick [22]. U-HVED performs optimization by drawing random subsets in each iteration. VAE loss for the network optimization is as follows:

$$L_{VAE} = \mathbb{E}_{x^-}[D_{KL}[ME(x^-) \parallel N(0,1)] + \parallel \hat{x}^- - x \parallel] , \tag{1}$$

where x^- are the random missing modalities from input images x, $\hat{x}^-$ denotes the reconstructed images, D_{KL} is KL divergence, ME is a multi-encoder $E_1, \ldots, E_n$, and $N(0, I)$ is the normal distribution.

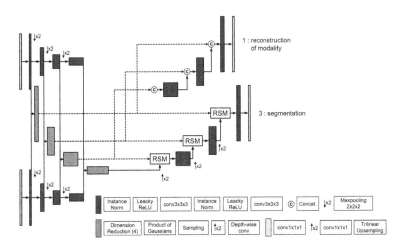

Fig. 2. Schematic visualization of our network architecture. Only two encoders, a segmentation decoder and a reconstruction decoder are shown. Each orange block stands for DRB. The size of the output channel of the decoder is 1 for the reconstruction of modality and 3 for segmentation. (Color figure online)

3.2 ROI Attentive Skip Connection Module

U-net [33] uses skip connections for successful segmentation. Generally, skip connection of U-net is a structure in which an input of a decoder and a feature of a corresponding encoder are concatenated. Since the decoder uses the encoder's features, it is easier to recover the lost detailed spatial information. Here, we propose an ROI attentive skip connection module (RSM) to emphasize the segmentation-related region in encoder features. Before applying RSM, a dimension reduction block for efficient representation learning is introduced.

Dimension Reduction Block. U-HVED learns multi-scale shared representation by applying MVAE to skip connections and the main stream of U-net. As the layer depth increases, the dimension of the representation increases, which makes learning the shared representation difficult. This problem is magnified in 3D medical images compared to 2D natural images because a two-fold magnification of the image leads to an eight-fold increase in the amount of data in 3D compared to the four-fold increase in 2D images. As the spatial size of the shared representation eventually increases, the expansion of the model becomes limited. To solve this problem, we propose DRB method that reduces the dimensions of the shared representation. DRB consists of dimension reduction and upsampling (Fig. 2). First, our DRB reduces the size of the spatial and channel by a 3 × 3 × 3 convolutional layer. Then, after sampling the representation, the representation is restored to the original dimension by a 1 × 1 × 1 convolutional layer, an upsampling layer, and depth-wise convolutional layer. DRB is applied to each modality at all levels. Ultimately, we obtain a shared representation with an 8-fold reduction in spatial size and a 2-fold reduction in channel size compared to the original U-HVED. This shared representation has a relatively small dimension compared to the original dimension, which enables efficient learning and facilitates 3D expansion of the model.

ROI Attentive Skip Connection. Our RSM does not simply concatenate input features when applying skip connection, but applies weights to encoder features using segmentation feature maps and then proceeds with concatenation. In Fig. 3, spatial features are obtained by using channel-wise average and max operations of the l-th segmentation feature f_l^S and l-th encoder features f_l^E. The concatenated spatial features are transformed into spatial attention weights by sequentially passing them through the depth-wise convolutional layer, the point-wise convolutional layer, and the sigmoid activation. Spatial attention weights are applied to the encoder features in a residual manner. The spatial attention weights of segmentation features f_l^S are obtained through the same process with only their own spatial features and are applied to the segmentation features f_l^S in a residual manner. Finally, the attentive segmentation and encoder features are concatenated.

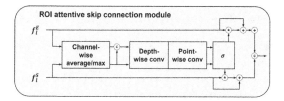

Fig. 3. Schematic visualization of our ROI attentive skip connection module. Using f_l^S, spatial attention weights are applied to each feature.

3.3   ROI Attentive Module and Joint Discriminator

Many studies [1,7,8,12,17,28,30,32,35,42] used an autoencoder or VAE as an auxiliary task to learn meaningful representations for segmentation. These methods have achieved success in accurate segmentation. However, the learned shared representation may be less relevant for segmentation because the network is simultaneously trained for image reconstruction and segmentation. Therefore, we introduce a joint discriminator D that combines ROI attentive images $\hat{a}$ and segmentation probability maps p to learn a shared representation that focuses on the segmentation task. The joint discriminator D enables learning of the shared representation by imposing additional constraints on the image reconstruction. ROI attentive images $\hat{a}$ are created by the ROI attentive module M (Eq. 2) using the reconstructed images $\hat{x}$ and their segmentation probability maps p as inputs. These values are calculated as follows:

$$\hat{a} = \hat{x} * \left(1 + \sum_k p_k\right) , \tag{2}$$

where p_k is the segmentation probability maps whose values are greater than 0.5 for segmentation class k. The ROI attentive module M emphasizes the ROI by using the average of the segmentation probability maps p in the reconstructed images $\hat{x}$ as a weight. Joint discriminator D is trained as an adversary by distinguishing between full and missing modalities with a focus on the ROI. The adversarial loss for joint discriminator D is defined as

$$L_{adv} = \mathbb{E}_{\hat{a}}[\log(D(\hat{a}, p))] + \mathbb{E}_{\hat{a}^-}[\log(D(\hat{a}^-, p^-))] . \tag{3}$$

Although it is possible to constrain the ROI in image reconstruction using only the joint discriminator D, we enforce stronger constraints on the ROI through the ROI attentive module M. Thus, our joint discriminator D strongly constrains the reconstruction network R to reconstruct images that focus on the ROI, making the shared representation more relevant to the segmentation task and more robust to missing modalities.

3.4   Segmentation

We choose a Dice loss for segmentation network $ME \circ S$ that consists of multi-encoder ME and segmentor S. Our goal is to successfully perform segmentation in all subsets of input modalities; thus, we use both Dice loss for full modalities x and missing modalities x^- to train a segmentation network $ME \circ S$.

$$L_{seg} = Dice(y, p) + Dice(y, p^-) , \tag{4}$$

where y is ground truth, and p represents is segmentation probability maps.

3.5   Training Process

As shown in Fig. 1, our goal is to learn a multi-scale shared representation for multiple encoders. In this context, segmentor S and reconstructor R are trained for segmentation and modality completion, respectively, using a multi-scale shared representation. Finally, through joint adversarial learning, segmentor S is forced to generate a segmentation map that is robust to missing modalities, and the reconstructor R is forced to generate images related to the segmentation task. The total objective function with trade-off parameters λ_1, λ_1 for the entire framework is as follows:

$$L = L_{seg} + \lambda_1 * L_{VAE} + \lambda_2 * L_{adv} .$$ (5)

4   Experiments

4.1   Data

BraTS. We evaluated our method using a multimodal brain tumor segmentation challenge (BraTS) 2018 dataset [2,3,26]. The imaging dataset included T1, T1ce, T2, and FLAIR MRI modalities for 285 patients with 210 high-grade gliomas and 75 low-grade gliomas. Imaging data were preprocessed by resampling to an isotropic 1 mm3 resolution, coregistration onto an anatomical template, and skull stripping. The ground truth of the three tumor regions was provided by manual labeling by experts. The clinical goal of BraTS 2018 dataset is to segment three overlapping regions (*i.e.*, complete tumor, tumor core, and enhancing tumor). We randomly divided the dataset into 70 % training, 10 % validation, and 20 % testing sets.

ISLES. The ischemic stroke lesion segmentation challenge (ISLES) 2015 dataset [25] provides multimodal MRI data. We selected the subacute ischemic stroke lesion segmentation (SISS) task between the two subtasks. The SISS dataset provides four MRI modalities consisting of T1, T2, DWI, and FLAIR for 28 patients. The imaging data were preprocessed by resampling to an isotropic 1 mm3 resolution, coregistration onto the FLAIR, and skull stripping. The infarcted areas were manually labeled by the experts. We randomly divided the dataset into 70 % training and 30 % testing sets.

4.2   Implementation Details

The network structure of RA-HVED is shown in Fig. 2. Our entire network takes the form of a 3D U-net [9]. A detailed network structure is referred in the supplementary material. We normalized the MRI intensity to zero mean and unit variance for the whole brain in each MRI modality. For data augmentation, we randomly applied an intensity shift for each modality and flipped for all axes. The 3D images were randomly cropped into $112 \times 112 \times 112$ patches and used during training. We used an Adam optimizer with an initial learning rate of 1e-4 and a batch size of 1. The learning rate was multiplied by (1-epoch/total_epoch)$^{0.9}$ for each epoch during 360 epochs. We set $\lambda_1 = 0.2$ and $\lambda_2 = 0.1$ through a grid search with 0.1 increments in $[0, 1]$ from the validation set. The missing modalities were constructed by uniformly drawing subsets, as is done in U-HVED [12] during training. All networks were implemented using the Pytorch library. To obtain the final inference result, we used the sliding window strategy, which is commonly used in patch-based networks. The stride of the sliding window is $28 \times 28 \times 28$ and equal to patch size / 4. After we obtained the final result, no postprocessing was done. The settings of the brain tumor dataset were used in the stroke dataset without any specific architectural changes or hyperparameter tuning. Our implementation is available here.[1]

4.3 Results of Segmentation with Missing Modalities

To evaluate the robustness of our method against the missing modalities, we compare our method (RA-HVED) to three previous methods in all scenarios of missing modalities: 1) U-HeMIS [12] is a U-net variant of HeMIS [17]-a first model for learning shared representations for missing modalities. 2) U-HVED [12], which combines MVAE and U-net, is compared because it is the base of

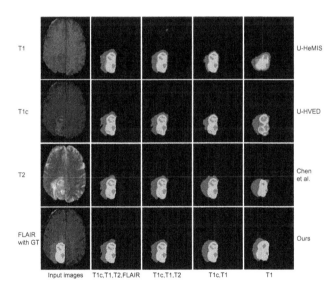

Fig. 4. Results of tumor segmentation produced by using different methods on the BraTS dataset. The first column is the input image of each modality, and each row shows segmentation results with missing modalities of comparison methods. GT: ground truth. Purple: complete tumor; Yellow: tumor core; Red: enhancing tumor. (Color figure online)

---

[1] https://github.com/ssjx10.

our method. 3) Chen et al. [7] is compared due to the strength of feature disentanglement in learning shared representations. It separates each modality into content and appearance codes. Then, segmentation is performed using the shared representation created by fusing the content codes.

Table 1. Comparison of segmentation performance with respect to all 15 missing modality scenarios on the BraTS 2018 dataset. The presence of modality is denoted by •, and the missing of modality is denoted by ○. All results are evaluated with a dice score (%).

Available Modalities				Complete tumor				Tumor core				Enhancing tumor			
F	T1	T1c	T2	U-HeMIS	U-HVED	Chen et al.	Ours	U-HeMIS	U-HVED	Chen et al.	Ours	U-HeMIS	U-HVED	Chen et al.	Ours
○	○	○	•	79.00	78.89	80.60	**81.47**	60.95	67.34	60.60	**67.82**	27.54	34.97	30.15	**36.93**
○	○	•	○	57.86	58.26	68.92	**71.83**	66.95	71.99	75.57	**77.93**	59.68	61.35	65.97	**68.97**
○	•	○	○	59.40	**68.38**	67.79	68.16	46.49	**58.60**	50.28	57.46	16.68	22.35	23.54	**28.75**
•	○	○	○	84.57	82.72	85.04	**88.21**	63.54	60.33	63.18	**65.62**	27.42	29.89	29.06	**36.96**
○	○	•	•	81.16	79.85	83.76	**84.63**	76.78	80.66	81.64	**81.68**	64.74	66.94	68.16	**70.29**
○	•	•	○	67.44	73.06	72.96	**75.27**	68.03	78.06	78.41	**80.35**	64.08	66.84	66.62	**69.97**
•	•	○	○	86.08	84.94	87.17	**88.84**	66.00	67.66	67.86	**70.73**	32.24	31.84	34.66	**38.12**
○	•	○	•	80.47	82.32	83.77	**83.97**	62.73	**72.76**	64.33	71.59	31.26	36.93	34.75	**39.19**
•	○	•	○	86.77	88.38	87.63	**88.94**	67.04	**71.94**	65.76	70.98	33.89	**40.69**	33.67	40.32
•	○	○	•	86.67	85.48	87.08	**89.45**	76.64	76.13	82.14	**83.17**	64.71	63.14	67.96	**69.76**
•	•	•	○	86.54	86.78	87.96	**89.12**	77.58	77.69	83.20	**84.14**	65.65	65.45	68.67	**70.87**
•	•	○	•	87.19	**88.59**	88.31	88.47	67.03	73.15	67.71	**73.58**	35.86	40.31	37.65	**41.71**
○	•	•	•	87.32	88.31	88.15	**89.31**	78.31	80.44	82.42	**82.65**	66.45	67.75	68.54	**69.89**
•	○	•	•	81.58	82.04	84.16	**84.89**	75.84	81.39	82.29	**82.59**	66.16	68.40	68.07	**70.54**
•	•	•	•	87.56	88.10	88.50	**89.64**	78.32	82.30	83.27	**83.62**	66.50	68.31	68.31	**71.28**
	Average			79.97	81.07	82.79	**84.15**	68.82	73.36	72.58	**75.59**	48.19	51.01	51.05	**54.90**

Results of BraTS. Table 1 shows the brain tumor segmentation results for various methods to deal with missing modalities. Our method outperforms the segmentation accuracy of previous methods for all three tumor regions in most missing modality scenarios. Our method achieved the highest average Dice of 84.15%, 75.59%, and 54.90% for the three nested tumor regions. The second robust method is Chen's approach, which achieves an average Dice of 82.79%, 72.58%, and 51.05%. We show that the Dice score increases more in the case of enhancing tumors than in other tumor regions. FLAIR and T2 modalities provide valuable information for complete tumors, and T1c modality provides crucial information for tumor cores and enhancing tumors. Because the T1 modality has relatively little information about the tumor compared to other modalities, it is difficult to obtain robust results when only the T1 modality is available. However, our method achieves similar or even higher accuracy than U-HVED, which shows high performance even in the case of the T1 modality alone. This indicates that the proposed method successfully learns shared representations. Inference times for other methods are referred in the supplementary Table 1.

Figure 4 shows a qualitative comparison of the various methods. As the number of missing modalities increases, the segmentation results of all methods gradually deteriorate. Nevertheless, our method provides more robust segmentation results than other methods and achieves accurate segmentation results even for the T1 modality, which contains relatively little information.

Table 2. Comparison of segmentation performance on the ISLES 2015 dataset.

Methods	U-HeMIS	U-HVED	Chen et al.	Ours
Average Dice score (%)	40.09	42.92	41.16	**48.29**

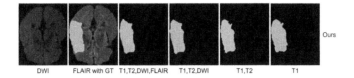

Fig. 5. Results of stroke lesion segmentation produced by our RA-HVED on ISLES.

Results of ISLES. The segmentation results for ISLES are shown in Table 2. On the average Dice score, our method shows a higher segmentation accuracy than other methods, reaching 48.29%. Chen's approach achieves a lower segmentation accuracy than U-HVED, in contrast to the results of the BraTS dataset. Figure 5 shows the results of stroke lesion segmentation using our method. Even when the number of missing modalities increases, our method provides robust segmentation results. Segmentation results for all missing scenarios and visualization of segmentation about other methods are referred in the supplementary material.

4.4   Results of Reconstruction with Missing Modalities

Our primary goal is to perform segmentation, but reconstruction of modalities can be performed during the process. Figure 6 shows the results of image reconstruction on FLAIR, the modality with the most information, for BraTS when modalities are missing. When all modalities are available, U-HeMIS and U-HVED produce images that are most like the corresponding image. However, other methods, including U-HVED, fail to produce tumor area details when the number of missing modalities increases. When only the T1 modality is available, the details of the tumor core are poorly generated. When all modalities are available, our method generates images similar to manual segmentation, although it is less similar to the corresponding image for the tumor region. Moreover, our method generates details of the tumor core better than other methods, even when the number of missing modalities increases. The reconstruction result for ISLES is referred in the supplementary material.

4.5   Ablation Study

We conduct an ablation study on RA-HVED with U-HVED as the baseline. In Table 3, we compare the methods using the average Dice score for all possible subsets of input modalities on the BraTS dataset. First, we confirm the effect

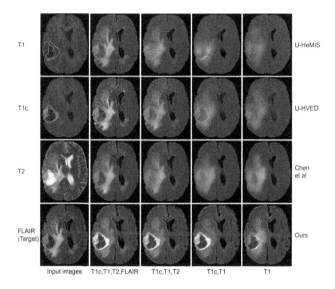

Fig. 6. Image reconstruction results generated by different methods on the BraTS dataset. The first column is the input image of each modality, and each row shows the reconstruction results with missing modalities of the comparison methods. Ground truth for segmentation is overlaid on T1. Purple: complete tumor; Yellow: tumor core; Red: enhancing tumor. (Color figure online)

Table 3. Ablation study of our key components. DRB : dimension reduction block, RSM : ROI attentive skip connection module, RJD : ROI attentive joint discriminator.

Methods	Average Dice Score (%)		
	Complete tumor	Tumor core	Enhancing tumor
(1) U-HVED	81.07	73.36	51.01
(2) U-HVED + DRB	81.34	73.03	51.36
(3) (2) + RSM	82.68	74.27	53.73
(4) (2) + RSM + RJD (RA-HVED)	**84.15**	**75.59**	**54.90**

of adding DRB to U-HVED when comparing (1) with (2). In Method (2), the dimension of the shared representation is decreased compared to (1), but the average Dice scores are similar. In method (3), RSM improves overall segmentation performance including enhancing tumor. In particular, the segmentation performance in enhancing tumor region is further improved because attention is imposed using segmentation features. Finally, in (4), an ROI attentive joint discriminator is added to (3) to provide stronger constraints to the ROI in the image reconstruction. The ROI attentive module is added to improve the segmentation performance in all tumor regions and achieve the highest Dice score in most scenarios with missing modalities. In particular, the average Dice increases by 4.5%

Table 4. Results on the effectiveness of ROI-based attention in RSM and ROI attentive joint discriminator.

Methods	Average Dice Score (%)		
	Complete tumor	Tumor core	Enhancing tumor
spatial-wise attention	83.16	74.24	53.69
joint discriminator	83.28	74.61	54.14
Ours (RA-HVED)	**84.15**	**75.59**	**54.90**

for (2) in the enhancing tumor. This shows that the proposed key components of RA-HVED efficiently learn the multi-scale shared representations.

In Table 4, we conduct experiments to prove the effect of ROI-based attention in RSM and ROI attentive joint discriminator. First, spatial-wise attention is applied to encoder features without the intervention of segmentation features in RSM (spatial attention in Table 4). Next, the joint discriminator replaces the ROI attentive joint discriminator (joint discriminator in Table 4). Both models achieve lower segmentation performance than RA-HVED. This indicates that ROI-based attention is important for learning segmentation-relevant shared representations.

5   Conclusion

In this study, we propose a novel and robust multimodal segmentation method that can function effectively when there are missing modalities. Our model efficiently learns segmentation-relevant shared representations through ROI attentive skip connection and joint adversarial learning that constrains the ROI in modality completion. We validate our method on a brain tumor and a stroke lesion dataset. Experimental results show that the proposed method outperforms previous segmentation methods on missing modalities. Moreover, we demonstrate the effectiveness of our key components in an ablation study. Our method can be applied to improve the clinical workflow that requires multimodal images.

Acknowledgements. This research was supported by the National Research Foundation (NRF-2020M3E5D2A01084892), Institute for Basic Science (IBS-R015-D1), Ministry of Science and ICT (IITP-2020-2018-0-01798), AI Graduate School Support Program (2019-0-00421), ICT Creative Consilience program (IITP-2020-0-01821), and Artificial Intelligence Innovation Hub (2021-0-02068).

References

1. Amyar, A., Modzelewski, R., Li, H., Ruan, S.: Multi-task deep learning based CT imaging analysis for Covid-19 pneumonia: classification and segmentation. Comput. Biol. Med. **126**, 104037 (2020)

2. Bakas, S., et al.: Advancing the cancer genome atlas glioma MRI collections with expert segmentation labels and radiomic features. Sci. Data **4**(1), 1–13 (2017)

3. Bakas, S., et al.: Identifying the best machine learning algorithms for brain tumor segmentation, progression assessment, and overall survival prediction in the brats challenge. arXiv preprint arXiv:1811.02629 (2018)

4. Bi, L., Kim, J., Kumar, A., Feng, D., Fulham, M.: Synthesis of positron emission tomography (PET) images via multi-channel generative adversarial networks (GANs). In: Cardoso, M.J., et al. (eds.) CMMI/SWITCH/RAMBO -2017. LNCS, vol. 10555, pp. 43–51. Springer, Cham (2017). https://doi.org/10.1007/978-3-319-67564-0_5

5. Cao, B., Zhang, H., Wang, N., Gao, X., Shen, D.: Auto-GAN: self-supervised collaborative learning for medical image synthesis. In: Proceedings of the AAAI Conference on Artificial Intelligence, vol. 34, pp. 10486–10493 (2020)

6. Cao, Y., Fleet, D.J.: Generalized product of experts for automatic and principled fusion of gaussian process predictions. arXiv preprint arXiv:1410.7827 (2014)

7. Chen, C., Dou, Q., Jin, Y., Chen, H., Qin, J., Heng, P.-A.: Robust multimodal brain tumor segmentation via feature disentanglement and gated fusion. In: Shen, D., et al. (eds.) MICCAI 2019. LNCS, vol. 11766, pp. 447–456. Springer, Cham (2019). https://doi.org/10.1007/978-3-030-32248-9_50

8. Chen, S., Bortsova, G., García-Uceda Juárez, A., van Tulder, G., de Bruijne, M.: Multi-task attention-based semi-supervised learning for medical image segmentation. In: Shen, D., et al. (eds.) MICCAI 2019. LNCS, vol. 11766, pp. 457–465. Springer, Cham (2019). https://doi.org/10.1007/978-3-030-32248-9_51

9. Çiçek, Ö., Abdulkadir, A., Lienkamp, S.S., Brox, T., Ronneberger, O.: 3D U-Net: learning dense volumetric segmentation from sparse annotation. In: Ourselin, S., Joskowicz, L., Sabuncu, M.R., Unal, G., Wells, W. (eds.) MICCAI 2016. LNCS, vol. 9901, pp. 424–432. Springer, Cham (2016). https://doi.org/10.1007/978-3-319-46723-8_49

10. Costa, P., et al.: End-to-end adversarial retinal image synthesis. IEEE Trans. Med. Imaging **37**(3), 781–791 (2017)

11. Cui, S., Mao, L., Jiang, J., Liu, C., Xiong, S.: Automatic semantic segmentation of brain gliomas from MRI images using a deep cascaded neural network. Journal of healthcare engineering 2018 (2018)

12. Dorent, R., Joutard, S., Modat, M., Ourselin, S., Vercauteren, T.: Hetero-modal variational encoder-decoder for joint modality completion and segmentation. In: Shen, D., et al. (eds.) MICCAI 2019. LNCS, vol. 11765, pp. 74–82. Springer, Cham (2019). https://doi.org/10.1007/978-3-030-32245-8_9

13. Feng, C., Zhao, D., Huang, M.: Segmentation of ischemic stroke lesions in multispectral MR images using weighting suppressed FCM and three phase level set. In: Crimi, A., Menze, B., Maier, O., Reyes, M., Handels, H. (eds.) BrainLes 2015. LNCS, vol. 9556, pp. 233–245. Springer, Cham (2016). https://doi.org/10.1007/978-3-319-30858-6_20

14. Halme, H.-L., Korvenoja, A., Salli, E.: ISLES (SISS) Challenge 2015: segmentation of stroke lesions using spatial normalization, random forest classification and contextual clustering. In: Crimi, A., Menze, B., Maier, O., Reyes, M., Handels, H. (eds.) BrainLes 2015. LNCS, vol. 9556, pp. 211–221. Springer, Cham (2016). https://doi.org/10.1007/978-3-319-30858-6_18

15. Han, X.: MR-based synthetic CT generation using a deep convolutional neural network method. Med. Phys. **44**(4), 1408–1419 (2017)

16. Havaei, M., et al.: Brain tumor segmentation with deep neural networks. Med. Image Anal. **35**, 18–31 (2017)

17. Havaei, M., Guizard, N., Chapados, N., Bengio, Y.: HeMIS: hetero-modal image segmentation. In: Ourselin, S., Joskowicz, L., Sabuncu, M.R., Unal, G., Wells, W. (eds.) MICCAI 2016. LNCS, vol. 9901, pp. 469–477. Springer, Cham (2016). https://doi.org/10.1007/978-3-319-46723-8_54

18. Isensee, F., Jäger, P.F., Full, P.M., Vollmuth, P., Maier-Hein, K.H.: nnU-net for brain tumor segmentation. In: Crimi, A., Bakas, S. (eds.) BrainLes 2020. LNCS, vol. 12659, pp. 118–132. Springer, Cham (2021). https://doi.org/10.1007/978-3-030-72087-2_11

19. Isensee, F., Kickingereder, P., Wick, W., Bendszus, M., Maier-Hein, K.H.: No new-net. In: Crimi, A., Bakas, S., Kuijf, H., Keyvan, F., Reyes, M., van Walsum, T. (eds.) BrainLes 2018. LNCS, vol. 11384, pp. 234–244. Springer, Cham (2019). https://doi.org/10.1007/978-3-030-11726-9_21

20. Jiang, Z., Ding, C., Liu, M., Tao, D.: Two-Stage Cascaded U-Net: 1st place solution to BraTS challenge 2019 segmentation task. In: Crimi, A., Bakas, S. (eds.) BrainLes 2019. LNCS, vol. 11992, pp. 231–241. Springer, Cham (2020). https://doi.org/10.1007/978-3-030-46640-4_22

21. Kamnitsas, K., et al.: Efficient multi-scale 3D CNN with fully connected CRF for accurate brain lesion segmentation. Med. Image Anal. **36**, 61–78 (2017)

22. Kingma, D.P., Welling, M.: Auto-encoding variational bayes. arXiv preprint arXiv:1312.6114 (2013)

23. Lee, D., Kim, J., Moon, W.J., Ye, J.C.: CollaGAN: collaborative GAN for missing image data imputation. In: Proceedings of the IEEE/CVF Conference on Computer Vision and Pattern Recognition, pp. 2487–2496 (2019)

24. Li, R., et al.: Deep learning based imaging data completion for improved brain disease diagnosis. In: Golland, P., Hata, N., Barillot, C., Hornegger, J., Howe, R. (eds.) MICCAI 2014. LNCS, vol. 8675, pp. 305–312. Springer, Cham (2014). https://doi.org/10.1007/978-3-319-10443-0_39

25. Maier, O., et al.: Isles 2015-a public evaluation benchmark for ischemic stroke lesion segmentation from multispectral MRI. Med. Image Anal. **35**, 250–269 (2017)

26. Menze, B.H., et al.: The multimodal brain tumor image segmentation benchmark (brats). IEEE Trans. Med. Imaging **34**(10), 1993–2024 (2014)

27. Mitra, J., et al.: Lesion segmentation from multimodal MRI using random forest following ischemic stroke. Neuroimage **98**, 324–335 (2014)

28. Moeskops, P., et al.: Deep learning for multi-task medical image segmentation in multiple modalities. In: Ourselin, S., Joskowicz, L., Sabuncu, M.R., Unal, G., Wells, W. (eds.) MICCAI 2016. LNCS, vol. 9901, pp. 478–486. Springer, Cham (2016). https://doi.org/10.1007/978-3-319-46723-8_55

29. Muir, K.W., Buchan, A., von Kummer, R., Rother, J., Baron, J.C.: Imaging of acute stroke. Lancet Neurol. **5**(9), 755–768 (2006)

30. Myronenko, A.: 3D MRI brain tumor segmentation using autoencoder regularization. In: Crimi, A., Bakas, S., Kuijf, H., Keyvan, F., Reyes, M., van Walsum, T. (eds.) BrainLes 2018. LNCS, vol. 11384, pp. 311–320. Springer, Cham (2019). https://doi.org/10.1007/978-3-030-11726-9_28

31. Nie, D., et al.: Medical image synthesis with context-aware generative adversarial networks. In: Descoteaux, M., Maier-Hein, L., Franz, A., Jannin, P., Collins, D.L., Duchesne, S. (eds.) MICCAI 2017. LNCS, vol. 10435, pp. 417–425. Springer, Cham (2017). https://doi.org/10.1007/978-3-319-66179-7_48

32. Ouyang, C., Kamnitsas, K., Biffi, C., Duan, J., Rueckert, D.: Data efficient unsupervised domain adaptation for cross-modality image segmentation. In: Shen, D., et al. (eds.) MICCAI 2019. LNCS, vol. 11765, pp. 669–677. Springer, Cham (2019). https://doi.org/10.1007/978-3-030-32245-8_74

33. Ronneberger, O., Fischer, P., Brox, T.: U-Net: convolutional networks for biomedical image segmentation. In: Navab, N., Hornegger, J., Wells, W.M., Frangi, A.F. (eds.) MICCAI 2015. LNCS, vol. 9351, pp. 234–241. Springer, Cham (2015). https://doi.org/10.1007/978-3-319-24574-4_28
34. Shen, L., et al.: Multi-domain image completion for random missing input data. IEEE Trans. Med. Imaging **40**(4), 1113–1122 (2020)
35. Shen, Y., Gao, M.: Brain tumor segmentation on MRI with missing modalities. In: Chung, A.C.S., Gee, J.C., Yushkevich, P.A., Bao, S. (eds.) IPMI 2019. LNCS, vol. 11492, pp. 417–428. Springer, Cham (2019). https://doi.org/10.1007/978-3-030-20351-1_32
36. van Tulder, G., de Bruijne, M.: Why does synthesized data improve multi-sequence classification? In: Navab, N., Hornegger, J., Wells, W.M., Frangi, A.F. (eds.) MICCAI 2015. LNCS, vol. 9349, pp. 531–538. Springer, Cham (2015). https://doi.org/10.1007/978-3-319-24553-9_65
37. Wang, Y., et al.: 3D auto-context-based locality adaptive multi-modality GANs for pet synthesis. IEEE Trans. Med. Imaging **38**(6), 1328–1339 (2018)
38. Wolterink, J.M., Leiner, T., Viergever, M.A., Išgum, I.: Generative adversarial networks for noise reduction in low-dose CT. IEEE Trans. Med. Imaging **36**(12), 2536–2545 (2017)
39. Wu, M., Goodman, N.: Multimodal generative models for scalable weakly-supervised learning. In: Advances in Neural Information Processing Systems, vol. 31 (2018)
40. Zhou, C., Ding, C., Wang, X., Lu, Z., Tao, D.: One-pass multi-task networks with cross-task guided attention for brain tumor segmentation. IEEE Trans. Image Process. **29**, 4516–4529 (2020)
41. Zhou, T., Fu, H., Chen, G., Shen, J., Shao, L.: Hi-Net: hybrid-fusion network for multi-modal MR image synthesis. IEEE Trans. Med. Imaging **39**(9), 2772–2781 (2020)
42. Zhou, T., Canu, S., Vera, P., Ruan, S.: Brain tumor segmentation with missing modalities via latent multi-source correlation representation. In: Martel, A.L., et al. (eds.) MICCAI 2020. LNCS, vol. 12264, pp. 533–541. Springer, Cham (2020). https://doi.org/10.1007/978-3-030-59719-1_52

Deep Learning for Computer Vision

Enhancing Fairness of Visual Attribute Predictors

Tobias Hänel[1]([⊠]), Nishant Kumar[1], Dmitrij Schlesinger[1], Mengze Li[2], Erdem Ünal[1], Abouzar Eslami[2], and Stefan Gumhold[1]

[1] Chair for Computer Graphics and Visualization, TU Dresden, Dresden, Germany
tobias.haenel@tu-dresden.de
[2] Carl Zeiss Meditec AG, Munich, Germany

Abstract. The performance of deep neural networks for image recognition tasks such as predicting a smiling face is known to degrade with under-represented classes of sensitive attributes. We address this problem by introducing fairness-aware regularization losses based on batch estimates of Demographic Parity, Equalized Odds, and a novel Intersection-over-Union measure. The experiments performed on facial and medical images from CelebA, UTKFace, and the SIIM-ISIC Melanoma classification challenge show the effectiveness of our proposed fairness losses on bias mitigation as they improve model fairness while maintaining high classification performance. To the best of our knowledge, our work is the first attempt to incorporate these types of losses in an end-to-end training scheme to mitigate biases of visual attribute predictors.

Keywords: Algorithmic fairness · Fair image classification · Deep neural networks · Visual attributes · Facial recognition · Disease diagnosis

1 Introduction

The manifestation of bias is evident in every aspect of our society, from educational institutions [15], to bank credit limits for women [30], to criminal justice for people of color [13]. The core problem is the inability of an individual to make ethically correct objective decisions without being affected by personal opinions. With the advent of recent machine learning (ML) algorithms trained on big data, there is a dramatic shift towards using such algorithms to provide greater discipline to impartial decision-making. However, ML-based algorithms are also prone to making biased decisions [4,27], as the reliability of data-based decision-making is heavily dependent on the data itself. For instance, such models are unfair when the training data is heavily imbalanced towards a particular class

---

Source code is available at https://github.com/nish03/FVAP.

Supplementary Information The online version contains supplementary material available at https://doi.org/10.1007/978-3-031-26351-4_10.

© The Author(s), under exclusive license to Springer Nature Switzerland AG 2023
L. Wang et al. (Eds.): ACCV 2022, LNCS 13846, pp. 151–167, 2023.
https://doi.org/10.1007/978-3-031-26351-4_10

of a sensitive attribute such as race [31]. A notable example by [4] shows that by assuming the ML model's target attribute as gender and the sensitive attribute as skin color, the classification error rate is much higher for darker females than for lighter females. A similar concern exists in the medical fraternity, where a recent work [22] studied the correlation between the under-representation of darker skin images with the classification error in predicting dermatological disease. Another work [23] showed a sharp decrease in classification performance while diagnosing several types of thoracic diseases for an under-represented gender in the X-ray image training data set. Therefore, it is critical to mitigate these biases in ML-based models for visual recognition tasks, to alleviate ethical concerns while deploying such models in real-world applications.

Recent studies focus on creating balanced data sets [19], or perform data augmentation [36] to remove imbalance with respect to the sensitive attributes. We argue that to make an ML model useful in real-life scenarios, it should achieve algorithmic fairness while still being trained on data sets that consist of real-world biases. In terms of algorithmic fairness, works such as [24,32,45] aim to learn the features in the data that are statistically independent of the sensitive attributes, while [2,18] focus on de-biasing the latent space of a generative model to achieve a fair outcome. We propose that to reduce bias w.r.t. the sensitive attributes, a model must satisfy the fairness notations by learning them during training. Additionally, none of the previous approaches attempted to utilize an inherent IoU-based fairness measure to train an ML model and achieve algorithmic fairness without loss in classification accuracy. Our overall learning scheme is presented in Fig. 1. The contributions of our work are as follows:

- We use classical fairness notations such as Demographic Parity (DP) and Equalized Odds (EO) to define the corresponding fairness loss terms and measure the deviations from the assumptions of the probabilistic independence w.r.t. sensitive attributes. We quantify these deviations by using mean squared error as well as the Kullback-Leibler divergence (KLD) between the learned probability distribution and the best-factorized distribution, leading to the mutual information (MI) between the variables in the learned model.
- We generalize the fairness notations such as DP and EO for categorical variables since the task is usually a multi-class problem in image classification. In the past, such notations were defined for binary variables only.
- We introduce a novel fairness loss based on the Intersection-over-Union(IoU) measure and study its relevancy for achieving fair classification results empirically. Our experiments show that it can simultaneously improve the model fairness and the baseline classification performance when the model is evaluated with fairness metrics.
- We exhaustively evaluate all introduced losses with facial attribute prediction on CelebA [25], age group estimation on UTKFace [49], and disease classification on the SIIM-ISIC Melanoma data set [36]. It was possible for all of these data sets to improve the model fairness with our method.

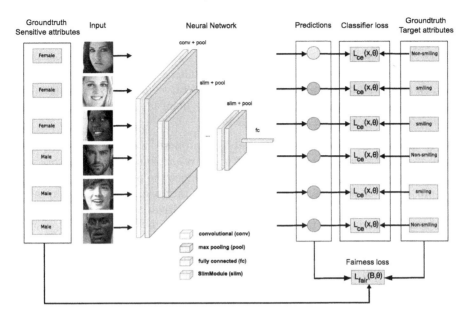

Fig. 1. The figure shows our new training procedure that improves the fairness of image classification models w.r.t. to sensitive attributes such as gender, age, and ethnicity. We add a weighted fairness loss to the standard cross-entropy loss during mini-batch gradient descent. It estimates the fairness of the model's predictions based on the sensitive attributes and the predicted and ground-truth target attributes from the samples within each batch.

2   Related Work

We discuss current methods that deal with bias mitigation in the data domain and provide an overview of works conducted to achieve fairness-aware facial and medical image recognition systems.

Mitigating bias in the data domain: The work [33] developed an audit process to highlight the fairness-driven concerns in facial recognition while [45] provided a benchmark for bias removal and highlighted key ethical questions for mitigating bias in vision data sets. Another study [22] estimated skin tones for images with skin disease and showed that the darker skin population is under-represented in the data set. In [11], the authors performed data augmentation to mitigate bias in facial image data sets. Multiple authors [19,28] presented new facial data sets with a balanced number of samples from different classes of sensitive attributes. The works such as [7,8,26] used image generation models to synthesize new facial images and used these images with standard pre-trained classifiers to investigate algorithmic performance bias based on sensitive attributes. Some authors [2,35] used the latent space of the Generative Adversarial Networks (GAN) to de-correlate the target and sensitive attributes, while [42] developed a tool that uses an image data set and its annotations as input and suggests actions to mitigate potential biases. The work [32] learned a GAN-based mapping of the source image to a target fair image representation by removing the semantics of target features such as eyes and lips from the sensitive attribute gender. The issue of unfair predictions due to biased data also exists in few-shot [50] and zero-shot [40] learning where [50] includes a constraint called decision boundary covariance, enabling independence of target and sensitive attributes while [40] maps the unlabelled target classes to a point in semantic space exterior to the point cluster of labeled source classes.

Fairness in facial recognition: A study [37] proposed a classifier that predicts target facial attributes using pre-learned sensitive attributes. Another work [51] calibrated the predicted target class labels to reduce the performance bias while [10] proposed separate fair classifiers for each target class. In [1], they used the cross-entropy loss between the predicted sensitive labels and the uniform distribution, causing the model to be confused and invariant to the sensitive attributes. Many authors [9,14,18,21,29,44] proposed adversarial learning to obtain a fair ML model. A study [12] presented channel-wise attention maps that adapt to diversity in facial features in every demographic group to obtain a fair classifier. A publication [43] used Q-learning to train an agent by rewarding less skew of the inter-class distance between the sensitive attribute such as race. In [17], they used a simple encoder-decoder network, [24,32] used adversarial learning of GAN, and [48] used a style transfer GAN to synthesize facial images independent of sensitive attributes such as gender and race. A work [16] ensured that the generated images from an image generation model have the same error rates for each class of the sensitive attributes. The authors of [47] introduced the False Positive Rate (FPR) as the penalty loss to mitigate bias. The authors in [46] showed that adversarial learning might worsen classification accuracy and fairness performance. They suggested a constraint that standard classification accuracy and fairness measures should be limited to the average of both metrics.

Fairness in disease diagnosis: In [23], they showed the problem of gender imbalance in medical imaging data sets, where the classification performance is less for disease diagnosis of the under-represented gender. A study [38] found that True Positive Rate (TPR) disparity for sensitive attributes such as gender, age, and race exists for all classifiers trained on different data sets of chest X-ray images. Another publication [5] highlighted some recent works to mitigate bias via federated learning (FL) [3,20,34]. FL enables multiple clients stationed at different geographical locations to train a single ML model with diversified data sets collaboratively. This method should help overcome the under-representation of individual classes of sensitive attributes in the data, resulting in unbiased models. However, data heterogeneity among the distributed clients remains a challenge for such FL-based models, which might degrade the performance.

In summary, past works did not thoroughly explore the theoretical insights into fairness-based regularization measures. They also did not apply them in experiments on visual data to obtain a model that has high classification performance on target attributes and is unbiased w.r.t. sensitive attributes.

3   Method

Let $x \in \mathcal{X}$ denote an image and $T = (x_1, x_2, \ldots, x_{|T|})$ be the training data consisting of $|T|$ images. Let $y_s \in \{1 \ldots K_s\}$ and $y_t \in \{1 \ldots K_t\}$ be *sensitive* and *target* attributes respectively. The latter is our classification target, whereas the former is the one, classification should not depend on. The asterisk will be used to denote the attribute ground truth values, e.g., $y_s^*(x)$ means the ground-truth value of the sensitive attribute for an x from T. We treat a trainable *classifier* as a conditional probability distribution $p_\theta(y_t|x)$ parameterized by an unknown parameter θ to be learned. In our work, we use Feed Forward networks (FFNs) as classifiers, which means θ summarizes network weights.

Next, we consider the joint probability distribution $p(x, y_t) = p(x) \cdot p_\theta(y_t|x)$, where $p(x)$ is some probability distribution, from which training data T is drawn. Noteworthy, the ground truths can also be considered as random variables, since they are deterministic mappings from $\mathcal{X}$, i.e., there exists a unique value $y_t^*(x)$ as well as a unique value $y_s^*(x)$ for each $x \in \mathcal{X}$. Hence, for the ground truths, we can also consider their statistical properties like joint probability distribution $p(y_s^*, y_t)$, independence $y_t \perp y_s^*$, or similar.

Demographic Parity. The notation reads $y_t \perp y_s^*$, i.e. the prediction should not depend on the sensitive attribute. Traditionally (for binary variables) a classifier is said to satisfy demographic parity if

$$p(y_t = 1|y_s^* = 1) = p(y_t = 1) \tag{1}$$

holds. A straightforward generalization to the case of categorical variables is to require the same for all possible values, i.e.

$$p(y_t = a|y_s^* = b) = p(y_t = a), \tag{2}$$

where $a \in \{1 \ldots K_t\}$ and $b \in \{1 \ldots K_s\}$. The above notation can be used to define a *loss* function, i.e. measure that penalizes the deviation of a given probability distribution p_θ from satisfying (2). One possible way is to penalize the sum of squared differences

$$L_{dp}^{l_2}(\theta) = \sum_{ab} \left[p_\theta(y_t = a|y_s^* = b) - p_\theta(y_t = a) \right]^2. \tag{3}$$

In fact, during the transition from (2) to (3) we compare the actual joint probability distribution $p_\theta(y_t, y_s^*)$ to the corresponding factorized (i.e. independent) probability distribution $p_\theta(y_t) \cdot p_\theta(y_s^*)$ using squared difference, i.e., interpreting probability distributions as vectors to some extent[1]. The squared difference is however not the only way to compare probability distributions. Another option

---

[1] Strictly speaking, it directly holds only if $p_\theta(y_s^*)$ is uniform, otherwise (3) corresponds to a squared difference between $p_\theta(y_t, y_s^*)$ and $p_\theta(y_t) \cdot p_\theta(y_s^*)$, where addends are additionally weighted by $1/p_\theta(y_s^*)^2$.

would be e.g., Kullback-Leibler divergence $D_{KL}(p_\theta(y_t, y_s^*)||p_\theta(y_t) \cdot p_\theta(y_s^*))$ which leads to the mutual information loss

$$L_{dp}^{mi}(\theta) = \sum_{ab} p_\theta(y_t = a, y_s^* = b) \cdot \log \frac{p_\theta(y_t = a, y_s^* = b)}{p_\theta(y_t = a) \cdot p_\theta(y_s^* = b)} =$$
$$= H(y_t) + H(y_s^*) - H(y_t, y_s^*), \tag{4}$$

where $H(\cdot)$ denotes the entropy. Note that we derived different losses (3) and (4) from the same independence requirements (2) using different distance measures for probability distributions.

Equalized Odds. It is assumed that the predicted target attribute and the ground truth sensitive attribute are *conditionally* independent given a fixed value of the ground truth target, i.e. $(y_t \perp y_s^*)|y_t^*$. Hence

$$p(y_t = a | y_t^* = b, y_s^* = c) = p(y_t = a | y_t^* = b) \tag{5}$$

should hold for all triples $a, b \in \{1 \dots K_t\}$ and $c \in \{1 \dots K_s\}$. Again, similarly to the previous case, we consider first the simple quadratic loss

$$L_{eo}^{l2}(\theta) = \sum_{abc} \left[p(y_t = a | y_t^* = b, y_s^* = c) - p(y_t = a | y_t^* = b) \right]^2. \tag{6}$$

It is also possible to measure the deviations of the current model $p_\theta(y_t, y_t^*, y_s^*)$ from the requirements (5) utilizing the corresponding mutual information as

$$L_{eo}^{mi}(\theta) = \sum_a \left[H(y_t | y_t^* = a) + H(y_s^* | y_t^* = a) - H(y_t, y_s^* | y_t^* = a) \right]. \tag{7}$$

Intersection-Over-Union. The above losses have a distinct statistical background since they rely on specific independence assumptions. In practice, however, we are often not interested in making some variables independent. Instead, the general goal could be phrased as "the classification performance should be similar for different values of the sensitive attribute". Hence, the core question is how to measure classifier performance adequately. We argue for the IoU measure because it can appropriately rate performance, especially for unbalanced data. For a target value a, the corresponding IoU is traditionally defined as

$$\text{IoU}_\theta(a) = \frac{p_\theta(y_t = a \wedge y_t^* = a)}{p_\theta(y_t = a \vee y_t^* = a)}, \tag{8}$$

where $\wedge$ and $\vee$ denote logical "and" and "or" respectively. The overall IoU is usually defined by averaging (8) over a, i.e.

$$\text{IoU}_\theta = \frac{1}{K_t} \sum_a \text{IoU}_\theta(a). \tag{9}$$

For a model $p_\theta(y_t, y_t^*, y_s^*)$ with target value a and sensitive value b, we extend (8) and define $\text{IoU}_\theta(a, b)$ as

$$\text{IoU}_\theta(a, b) = \frac{p_\theta((y_t = a \wedge y_t^* = a) \wedge y_s^* = b)}{p_\theta((y_t = a \vee y_t^* = a) \wedge y_s^* = b)}. \tag{10}$$

Now given (9), $\text{IoU}_\theta(b)$ for a particular value b of the sensitive attribute is

$$\text{IoU}_\theta(b) = \frac{1}{K_t} \sum_a \text{IoU}_\theta(a, b) \tag{11}$$

and the loss penalizes the deviations of these IoU-s from the overall IoU (9) as:

$$L_{iou}(\theta) = \sum_b \left[\text{IoU}_\theta(b) - \text{IoU}_\theta\right]^2. \tag{12}$$

Note that to define (8) to (12), we again used statistical interpretation of all involved variables, i.e., the joint probability distribution $p_\theta(y_t, y_t^*, y_s^*)$. This time however we do not explicitly enforce any independence in contrast to the demographic parity or equalized odds.

Optimization. All introduced losses are differentiable w.r.t. unknown parameter θ^2 because we use probability values for their computation. Hence, we can mix them with other losses simply and conveniently. In particular, if the classifier is e.g., an FFN, we can optimize them using error back-propagation. Second, it should be noted that all losses rely on low-order statistics, i.e., it is only necessary to estimate current $p_\theta(y_t, y_t^*, y_s^*)$ to compute them. For example, if the involved variables are binary, we only need to estimate 8 values. We assume that they can be reliably estimated from a data mini-batch of a reasonable size instead of computing them over the whole training data. This makes optimizing the introduced losses within commonly used stochastic optimization frameworks possible. To be more specific, the overall loss can be written as

$$L(\theta) = \sum_{x \in T} L_{ce}(x, \theta) + \lambda \cdot L_{fair}(T, \theta) =$$

$$= \mathbb{E}_{B \subset T} \sum_{x \in B} L_{ce}(x, \theta) + \lambda \cdot L_{fair}(T, \theta), \tag{13}$$

where the expectation $\mathbb{E}$ is over all mini-batches $B \subset T$ randomly sampled from the training data, L_{ce} is a "usual" classification loss, e.g., Cross-Entropy, λ is a weighting coefficient, and L_{fair} is one of the fairness losses introduced above. For the sake of technical convenience, we approximate (13) by

$$L(\theta) = \mathbb{E}_{B \subset T} \left[\sum_{x \in B} L_{ce}(x, \theta) + \lambda \cdot L_{fair}(B, \theta)\right]. \tag{14}$$

---

[2] We also assume that probabilities are differentiable w.r.t. parameters.

Impact on the Performance. We want to show a crucial difference between demographic parity and equalized odds. Imagine a hypothetical "perfect classifier" that always assigns probability 1 to the ground truth label. Hence, the requirements of demographic parity $y_t \perp y_s^*$ turn into $y_t^* \perp y_s^*$. It means that the perfect classifier can satisfy demographic parity only if the ground truth target and the ground truth sensitive attributes are completely uncorrelated, which is hard to expect in practice. It follows from the practical perspective that the classifier performance should decrease when we try to make the classifier fair in the sense of demographic parity.

On the other side, in our notations, the case of a perfect classifier can be written as

$$p_\theta(y_t, y_t^*, y_s^*) = p_\theta(y_t|y_t^*, y_s^*) \cdot p(y_t^*, y_s^*) = [\![y_t = y_t^*]\!] \cdot p(y_t^*, y_s^*), \tag{15}$$

where $[\![\cdot]\!]$ is 1 if its argument is true. Hence, without loss of generality

$$p_\theta(y_t, y_t^*, y_s^*) = [\![y_t = y_t^*]\!] \cdot p(y_t^*, y_s^*) = p_\theta(y_t|y_t^*) \cdot p(y_s^*|y_t^*) \cdot p(y_t^*). \tag{16}$$

It means that for a perfect classifier, the predicted target attribute and ground-truth sensitive attribute are conditionally independent, i.e., a perfect classifier automatically satisfies the requirements of equalized odds $(y_t \perp y_s^*)|y_t^*$. In practice, if the baseline classifier is already good enough, its performance should not worsen when we try to make the classifier fair w.r.t. equalized odds.

Considering the IoU-loss (12), it is easy to see that it is zero for a perfect classifier, just because all IoU values are equal to one in this case. Hence, as in the case of equalized odds, we do not expect a drop in classifier performance when we try to make it fair w.r.t. the IoU-loss.

Fairness and Calibration Properties. We consider a *linear squeezing* operation as follows. Let $y \in \{0, 1\}$ be a binary variable[3] and $p(y|x)$ a conditional probability distribution for an input x. The linear squeezing puts all probability values into the range $[0.5 - \alpha/2, 0.5 + \alpha/2]$ with $0 < \alpha < 1$ by applying

$$p'(y|x) = [p(y|x) - 0.5] \cdot \alpha + 0.5. \tag{17}$$

Firstly, this operation does not change the *decision* about y for a given x. The decision is made by thresholding $p(y|x)$ at the 0.5 level, which does not change after applying the linear squeezing. Secondly, it makes the classifier "less confident" about its decision because the output probabilities lie in a narrower range. At the same time, linear squeezing can be understood as mixing the original $p(y|x)$ and uniform distribution, since (17) can be rewritten as

$$p'(y|x) = p(y|x) \cdot \alpha + 0.5 \cdot (1 - \alpha). \tag{18}$$

Consider now the confusion matrix, i.e. $p(y_t, y_t^*)$, obtained by averaging over the training data, and the corresponding IoU-value (9) (for now we do not consider

---

[3] We discuss in detail only the case of binary variables and the IoU-loss for simplicity. The situation is similar for other cases.

the sensitive attribute). Let us assume evenly distributed ground truth labels for simplicity. So applying (18) to the output probabilities gives

$$p'(y_t, y_t^*) = p(y_t, y_t^*) \cdot \alpha + 0.25 \cdot (1 - \alpha). \tag{19}$$

For α close to 1, the IoU obtained from $p'(y_t, y_t^*)$ (i.e., squeezed by (19)) will be close to the original IoU (i.e. obtained from the original non-squeezed $p(y_t, y_t^*)$) for which we assume a rather high value since the classifier is essentially better than random chance. For α close to zero, the modified IoU converges to $1/3$. Hence, IoU differences (i.e. addends in (12)) vanish. To conclude, we can make the IoU-loss (12) alone arbitrarily small just by applying linear squeezing without changing the decision rule.

Note that the squeezing operation with a small α makes the primary loss, i.e., the cross-entropy, essentially worse since the log-likelihoods of the ground truth labels get smaller. In fact, the fairest classifier is a random choice decision, i.e., which does not depend on the input. It is fair and under-confident but poor in terms of the primary goal, i.e. classification accuracy, and w.r.t. the primary cross-entropy loss. To conclude, adding the IoU-loss to the primary objective (see (14)) pushes the solution towards being less confident. It may be a desired or an undesired behavior depending on whether the baseline classifier is already well-calibrated or not. For over-confident baseline classifiers, employing the IoU-loss should improve calibration properties. The calibration properties may get worse for already well-calibrated or under-confident baseline classifiers.

4   Experiments

We validate our contributions on three data sets. The first study of interest in 4.1 concerns the CelebFaces attributes (CelebA) data set [25] which contains more than 200K images of celebrities and manually annotated facial attributes. Secondly in 4.2, we investigate the UTKFace facial image data set [49] which contains over 20K images from a broad range of age groups. In addition to the facial images, we perform experiments with a data set from the SIIM-ISIC Melanoma classification challenge [36] in 4.3 that contains 33k+ skin lesion images. We focus on achieving a balanced target attribute prediction performance that does not depend on the sensitive attribute. We split each data set into a train, validation, and test partition to verify the results of our method. First, we train a baseline model (details in the supplementary material). To improve its fairness, we continue the optimization process by extending the cross-entropy loss with one of the weighted fair losses (see 14) and perform experiments with two different strategies for selecting λ in 4.4.

4.1   CelebA

For experiments with the CelebA data set, we use SlimCNN [39], a memory-efficient convolutional neural network, to predict whether a depicted person is

Table 1. Results of the experiments with manually selected weighing coefficients λ for CelebA facial attribute prediction. The task is to predict the binary target attribute $y_t = Smiling$. The experiments #1 to #6 use the sensitive attribute $y_s = Male$ for the evaluation of the fairness loss terms, while #7 to #12 use the sensitive attribute $y_s = Young$. The values in bold are the best results of each evaluation metric.

#	Loss	Acc	L_{iou} (12)	L_{eo}^{l2} (6)	L_{eo}^{mi} (7)	L_{dp}^{l2} (3)	L_{dp}^{mi} (4)
1	L_{ce}	0.902	8.73×10^{-4}	4.89×10^{-3}	5.12×10^{-3}	1.77×10^{-2}	8.46×10^{-3}
2	L_{iou}	**0.903**	7.32×10^{-5}	8.59×10^{-4}	4.26×10^{-4}	2.51×10^{-3}	1.20×10^{-3}
3	L_{eo}^{l2}	0.902	$\mathbf{1.35\times10^{-5}}$	$\mathbf{1.78\times10^{-4}}$	$\mathbf{7.71\times10^{-5}}$	$\mathbf{1.36\times10^{-4}}$	$\mathbf{6.45\times10^{-5}}$
4	L_{eo}^{mi}	0.899	2.37×10^{-5}	2.24×10^{-4}	1.03×10^{-4}	8.40×10^{-4}	4.00×10^{-4}
5	L_{dp}^{l2}	0.899	4.28×10^{-4}	3.75×10^{-3}	1.87×10^{-3}	1.57×10^{-4}	7.43×10^{-5}
6	L_{dp}^{mi}	0.901	5.28×10^{-4}	7.73×10^{-3}	3.96×10^{-3}	7.15×10^{-4}	3.40×10^{-4}
7	L_{ce}	0.901	1.34×10^{-3}	8.28×10^{-3}	4.93×10^{-3}	1.16×10^{-2}	3.48×10^{-3}
8	L_{iou}	0.901	4.15×10^{-5}	9.96×10^{-4}	3.06×10^{-4}	1.31×10^{-3}	3.96×10^{-4}
9	L_{eo}^{l2}	**0.902**	$\mathbf{1.01\times10^{-5}}$	$\mathbf{5.48\times10^{-5}}$	$\mathbf{1.65\times10^{-5}}$	$\mathbf{6.81\times10^{-5}}$	$\mathbf{2.08\times10^{-5}}$
10	L_{eo}^{mi}	0.901	1.64×10^{-5}	2.57×10^{-4}	7.40×10^{-5}	4.24×10^{-4}	1.29×10^{-4}
11	L_{dp}^{l2}	0.901	8.34×10^{-4}	6.93×10^{-3}	2.18×10^{-3}	1.58×10^{-4}	4.78×10^{-5}
12	L_{dp}^{mi}	0.901	5.63×10^{-4}	4.26×10^{-3}	1.33×10^{-3}	1.45×10^{-4}	4.44×10^{-5}

smiling or not. To evaluate how our method influences the fairness of this prediction task, we select the binary variables $Male$ and $Young$ (representing gender and age) as sensitive attributes y_s. We use the original train, validation, and test partitions in all experiments with this data set.

The results for the experiments with the best λ values are shown in Table 1 (details in the supplementary material). Each row shows the results from an experiment with a particular training loss. The columns list the corresponding prediction accuracy (Acc) and all fairness metrics on the validation partition. The model fairness improved for all experiments with this data set according to almost all proposed losses. The application of the fairness losses L_{iou} and the L_{eo}^{l2} did not lead to a reduction in the prediction accuracy. The L_{eo}^{l2} loss yielded the best fairness improvements according to all proposed fairness losses, while the L_{iou} loss could even improve the classification performance. However, the model training with other losses slightly decreased the classification accuracy. Furthermore, the L_{eo}^{mi} loss could improve model fairness w.r.t to all evaluated metrics, while the DP-based L_{dp}^{l2} and L_{dp}^{mi} losses could only improve their respective fairness losses. Next, applying any fairness loss did not deteriorate the model performance with the sensitive attribute $y_s = Young$.

4.2 UTKFace

The images in UTKFace have annotations of a binary gender variable (Female, Male), a multi-class categorical ethnicity variable (White, Black, Asian, Indian, and Others), and an integer age variable (0–116 Years). Commonly this data

Table 2. Quantitative outcomes with manually selected weighting coefficients λ for predicting the multi-class target attribute $y_t = Age\ group$ on the UTKFace facial image data set. Experiments #1 to #6 concern the sensitive attribute $y_s = Gender$ and #7 to #12 cover the sensitive attribute $y_s = Ethnicity$.

#	Loss	Acc	L_{iou} (12)	L_{eo}^{l2} (6)	L_{eo}^{mi} (7)	L_{dp}^{l2} (3)	L_{dp}^{mi} (4)
1	L_{ce}	0.847	1.45×10^{-3}	1.66×10^{-1}	1.23×10^{-1}	6.55×10^{-2}	4.21×10^{-2}
2	L_{iou}	0.852	$\mathbf{3.04\times10^{-4}}$	3.00×10^{-2}	2.89×10^{-2}	3.77×10^{-2}	2.18×10^{-2}
3	L_{eo}^{l2}	0.856	3.08×10^{-3}	8.11×10^{-2}	7.21×10^{-2}	4.85×10^{-2}	3.10×10^{-2}
4	L_{eo}^{mi}	**0.857**	9.82×10^{-4}	$\mathbf{2.88\times10^{-2}}$	$\mathbf{2.25\times10^{-2}}$	2.16×10^{-2}	1.36×10^{-2}
5	L_{dp}^{l2}	0.852	5.61×10^{-4}	3.59×10^{-2}	3.59×10^{-2}	9.39×10^{-3}	7.00×10^{-3}
6	L_{dp}^{mi}	0.848	7.78×10^{-4}	9.27×10^{-2}	6.40×10^{-2}	$\mathbf{5.33\times10^{-3}}$	$\mathbf{4.51\times10^{-3}}$
7	L_{ce}	0.846	2.06×10^{-2}	3.73×10^{-1}	1.81×10^{-1}	1.96×10^{-1}	5.48×10^{-2}
8	L_{iou}	0.847	6.62×10^{-3}	$\mathbf{9.75\times10^{-2}}$	8.60×10^{-2}	1.98×10^{-1}	4.53×10^{-2}
9	L_{eo}^{l2}	0.844	1.85×10^{-2}	2.50×10^{-1}	1.53×10^{-1}	1.91×10^{-1}	4.70×10^{-2}
10	L_{eo}^{mi}	**0.857**	1.53×10^{-2}	1.12×10^{-1}	1.08×10^{-1}	1.52×10^{-1}	4.21×10^{-2}
11	L_{dp}^{l2}	**0.857**	1.77×10^{-2}	1.48×10^{-1}	1.62×10^{-1}	8.85×10^{-2}	3.03×10^{-2}
12	L_{dp}^{mi}	0.854	$\mathbf{6.61\times10^{-3}}$	1.03×10^{-1}	$\mathbf{5.19\times10^{-2}}$	$\mathbf{3.26\times10^{-2}}$	$\mathbf{6.24\times10^{-3}}$

set is used to perform age regression. We derive a categorical age group variable (under 31 Years, between 31–60 Years, over 60 Years) from the original ages as our predicted target attribute. $y_s = Ethnicity$ and $y_s = Gender$ represent the sensitive attributes in the experiments. We quantify the performance of the trained model by the accuracy based on data from the validation partition. Preliminary experiments with SlimCNN [39] didn't produce satisfying accuracies. EfficientNet is an alternative convolutional network [41] that can scale the depth, width, and resolution of all filters with a single parameter (we use EfficientNet-B1). Since UTKFace does not have any partitioning information, we split the data set randomly into train, validation, and test partitions which contain 70%, 20%, and 10% of the samples.

Table 2 shows the quantitative results from the experiments with UTKFace. The interpretation of the rows and columns is the same as in Table 1. Again, the model fairness improved w.r.t. to almost all proposed fairness metrics for both sensitive attributes. In addition, applying any fairness loss led to an improvement in the prediction accuracy with the sensitive attribute $y_s = Gender$. Experiments with the sensitive attribute $y_s = Ethnicity$ also improved the prediction accuracy except when we applied the L_{eo}^{l2} loss.

4.3 SIIM-ISIC Melanoma Classification

The prediction target attribute in our experiments is a diagnosis, whether a lesion is malignant or benign. Each image has annotations of a binary gender variable (Male, Female) which we use as the sensitive attribute. The performance of the trained model is quantified with the area under the receiver operating

Table 3. Experimental results with manually selected weighting coefficients λ for predicting the binary target attribute $y_t = Diagnosis$ from skin lesion images with the SIIM-ISIC Melanoma classification data set. The experiments use the binary variable *Gender* as the sensitive attribute y_t.

#	Loss	AUC	L_{iou} (12)	$L_{eo}^{l_2}$ (6)	L_{eo}^{mi} (7)	$L_{dp}^{l_2}$ (3)	L_{dp}^{mi}(4)
1	L_{ce}	0.829	1.26×10^{-3}	6.22×10^{-2}	3.51×10^{-2}	3.54×10^{-4}	9.27×10^{-4}
2	L_{iou}	0.801	$\mathbf{5.71\times10^{-5}}$	$\mathbf{3.17\times10^{-2}}$	$\mathbf{1.67\times10^{-4}}$	$\mathbf{1.67\times10^{-4}}$	$\mathbf{1.32\times10^{-4}}$
3	$L_{eo}^{l_2}$	**0.869**	4.10×10^{-4}	8.52×10^{-2}	3.95×10^{-2}	7.60×10^{-4}	1.27×10^{-3}
4	L_{eo}^{mi}	0.854	7.54×10^{-4}	7.71×10^{-2}	4.38×10^{-2}	7.41×10^{-4}	1.43×10^{-3}
5	$L_{dp}^{l_2}$	0.804	6.62×10^{-4}	8.44×10^{-2}	4.86×10^{-2}	3.53×10^{-4}	8.89×10^{-4}
6	L_{dp}^{mi}	0.835	3.64×10^{-4}	4.71×10^{-2}	2.39×10^{-2}	4.52×10^{-4}	9.43×10^{-4}

curve (AUC) on the validation partition, which was the standard evaluation metric in this challenge. We use EfficientNet-B1 as the classification model in all experiments as with UTKFace. As the data set only contains annotations in the original train partition, we used these annotated images and randomly assigned them to train, validation, and test partitions consisting of 70%, 20%, and 10% of the original train samples. We used different transformations to augment the training data, which improved the baseline AUC score (details in the supplementary material). Since the data set only contains a small fraction of malignant samples, we used the effective number of samples [6] as a class weighting method to deal with this label imbalance. Each sample is assigned a normalized weight $\alpha_i = \frac{1-\beta}{1-\beta^{n_i}}$ according to the frequency n_i of the i-th class in the train partition. The hyper-parameter β adjusts these weights according to the label distribution in a particular data set, which we set to $\beta = 0.9998$. Table 3 shows the results of the experiments with the fine-tuned class-weighting. The application of the EO-based fairness losses $L_{eo}^{l_2}$ and L_{eo}^{mi} improved the AUC score considerably. Additionally, incorporation of our novel L_{iou} based fairness loss helped to improve the fairness of the model w.r.t the baseline for all of the proposed fairness-based evaluation metrics.

It is to be noted that our work is not comparable to closely related approaches. Some works [1,21] propose to remove biases w.r.t. sensitive attributes from the feature representation of the model. Our approach instead focuses on enabling the prediction accuracy of the target attribute to not depend on sensitive attributes. Recent works with similar tasks as ours propose loss functions based on distance [12] or cosine similarity [47] measures while we explore the inherent fairness-driven probabilistic measures as the loss functions in our experimental setup. Such loss functions were not studied before for visual data sets, so a reasonable comparison with methods such as [12,47] is also not possible.

4.4   Effect of λ on Fairness Vs Accuracy

We studied the effect of the coefficient λ on both model fairness and classification accuracy. Its value depends on the dataset, optimized loss, and whether

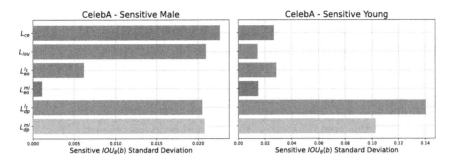

Fig. 2. Experimental results with the fairness loss weighting coefficient λ. The standard deviation of the $IoU_\theta(b)$ for different sensitive class labels b is used to quantify the model fairness. The prediction accuracy quantifies the classification performance.

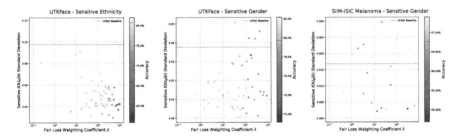

Fig. 3. Experimental results with the fairness loss weighting coefficient λ on UTKFace and SIIM-ISIC Melanoma. The standard deviation of the $IoU_\theta(b)$ for different sensitive class labels b is used to quantify the model fairness (less is fairer). The prediction accuracy quantifies the model performance. The blue lines show the baseline performance and fairness values.

achieving high accuracy is more relevant for a specific application or fairness. Note that setting $\lambda = 0$ reverts to the original image classification problem. We obtained the results for the initial experiments by heuristically searching for good weighting coefficients. We observed that starting with small λ-values is beneficial and studied whether the obtained model is fair. One could increase λ until the classification performance significantly decreases. Later, we performed hyper-parameter optimization (HPO) to find λ that leads to the best improvement in the model fairness with maintaining high classification accuracy.

Heuristic Search. We use the Bessel corrected standard deviation $\sigma_{IoU}(\lambda) = \sqrt{\frac{1}{K_s-1}\sum_{i=1}^{K_s}(IoU_\theta(b_i) - \overline{IoU_\theta(b)})^2}$ of the $IoU_\theta(b)$ (10) as a fairness evaluation measure and the prediction accuracy as a performance measure. The results for the manual selection of λ on CelebA can be seen in Fig. 2. The L_{iou} and L_{eo}^{mi} losses improved the fairness w.r.t. the baseline models (trained with the standard cross-entropy loss L_{ce}) for both sensitive attributes. In contrast, the $L_{eo}^{l_2}$ loss and the DP-based losses L_{dp}^{mi} and L_{dp}^{mi} improved the fairness only for the sensitive attribute $y_s = Male$.

Hyperparameter Optimization (HPO). We performed HPO of the weighting coefficient λ for the UTKFace and SIIM-ISIC Melanoma data sets with $\sigma_{IoU}(\lambda)$ as the minimization objective and searching λ within the range $[1 \times 10^{-1}, 1 \times 10^3)$. We use the validation partition for the HPO trials and evaluate the resulting models on the test partition. Due to time and resource constraints, we restrict our experiments to the novel IoU loss $L_{iou}(\theta)$ (12) with 60 HPO trials on the UTKFace data set and 20 trials on the SIIM-ISIC Melanoma classification data set. The results of these HPO experiments are shown in Fig. 3. We observe a clear trend for experiments on UTKFace with the sensitive attribute $y_s = Ethnicity$ (left figure), where the fairness of the baseline model is relatively low. With an exponentially increasing λ, there is a linear improvement in the model fairness and a linear decrease in the prediction accuracy. However, such a trend does not exist for experiments with UTKFace for the sensitive attribute $y_s = Gender$ (figure in the middle), where the baseline fairness is already good. Here, the model fairness and the prediction accuracy decrease linearly with exponentially increasing λ values. Additionally, there is more variation in the fairness improvements when λ is larger. In these experiments with UTKFace, there is a certain range of λ values (the region with yellow dots) that simultaneously improves the model fairness and prediction accuracy. The baseline fairness is already high for the SIIM-ISIC Melanoma data set with the sensitive attribute $y_s = Gender$ (right figure). Hence, the prediction accuracy and fairness improvement are independent of the λ value, as its effect on these metrics seems random.

5 Conclusion

In this work, we presented the theoretical intuition toward obtaining fair image classification models. We implemented various fairness metrics as standardized differentiable loss functions for categorical variables and compared their effectiveness in bias mitigation when compared to our novel IoU loss. Our experiments on publicly available facial and medical image data sets show that the proposed fairness losses do not degrade the classification performance on target attributes and reduce the classification bias at the same time. With this work and the publication of our source code, we provide a tool that encourages further work in this research direction. An interesting future work would be the visualization of relevant regions in the input image space that make the fair model less biased compared to the baseline model, trained with a standalone cross-entropy loss.

Acknowledgement. This work primarily received funding from the German Federal Ministry of Education and Research (BMBF) under *Software Campus* (grant 01IS17044) and the Competence Center for Big Data and AI *ScaDS.AI Dresden/Leipzig* (grant 01/S18026A-F). The work also received funding from Deutsche Forschungsgemeinschaft (DFG) (grant 389792660) as part of TRR 248 and the Cluster of Excellence *CeTI* (EXC2050/1, grant 390696704). The authors gratefully acknowledge the Center for Information Services and HPC (ZIH) at TU Dresden for providing computing resources.

References

1. Alvi, M., Zisserman, A., Nellaker, C.: Turning a blind eye: explicit removal of biases and variation from deep neural network embeddings. ECCV Workshops, Lecture Notes in Computer Science 11129 (2019)
2. Amini, A., Soleimany, A.P., Schwarting, W., Bhatia, S.N., Rus, D.: Uncovering and mitigating algorithmic bias through learned latent structure. In: Proceedings of the 2019 AAAI/ACM Conference on AI, Ethics, and Society, pp. 289–295 (2019)
3. Bercea, C.I., Wiestler, B., Ruckert, D., Albarqouni, S.: Feddis: disentangled federated learning for unsupervised brain pathology segmentation. arXiv preprint arXiv:2103.03705 (2021)
4. Buolamwini, J., Gebru, T.: Gender shades: intersectional accuracy disparities in commercial gender classification. Proc. Mach. Learn. Res. **81**, 77–91 (2018)
5. Chen, R.J., et al.: Algorithm fairness in AI for medicine and healthcare. arXiv preprint arXiv:2110.00603 (2021)
6. Cui, Y., Jia, M., Lin, T.Y., Song, Y., Belongie, S.: Class-balanced loss based on effective number of samples. In: Proceedings of the IEEE/CVF conference on computer vision and pattern recognition, pp. 9268–9277 (2019)
7. Denton, E., Hutchinson, B., Mitchell, M., Gebru, T.: Detecting bias with generative counterfactual face attribute augmentation. In: CoRR (2019)
8. Denton, E., Hutchinson, B., Mitchell, M., Gebru, T., Zaldivar, A.: Image counterfactual sensitivity analysis for detecting unintended bias. In: CVPR Workshop on Fairness Accountability Transparency and Ethics in Computer Vision (2019)
9. Dhar, P., Gleason, J., Roy, A., Castillo, C.D., Chellappa, R.: Pass: protected attribute suppression system for mitigating bias in face recognition. In: Proceedings of the IEEE/CVF International Conference on Computer Vision (ICCV), pp. 15087–15096 (2021)
10. Dwork, C., Immorlica, N., Kalai, A.T., Leiserson, M.: Decoupled classifiers for group-fair and efficient machine learning. In: Proceedings of the 1st Conference on Fairness, Accountability and Transparency, PMLR 81, 119–133 (2018)
11. Georgopoulos, M., Oldfield, J., Nicolaou, M.A., Panagakis, Y., Pantic, M.: Mitigating demographic bias in facial datasets with style-based multi-attribute transfer. Int. J. Comput. Vis. **129**, 2288–2307 (2021)
12. Gong, S., Liu, X., Jain, A.K.: Mitigating face recognition bias via group adaptive classifier. The IEEE Conference on Computer Vision and Pattern Recognition (CVPR), pp. 3414–3424 (2021)
13. Hetey, R.C., Eberhardt, J.L.: The numbers don't speak for themselves: racial disparities and the persistence of inequality in the criminal justice system. Current Directions Psychol. Sci. **27**(3), 183–187 (2018)
14. Hou, X., Li, Y., Wang, S.: Disentangled representation for age-invariant face recognition: a mutual information minimization perspective. In: IEEE/CVF International Conference on Computer Vision (ICCV), pp. 3672–3681 (2021)
15. Jacobs, J.A.: Gender inequality and higher education. Ann. Rev. Sociol. **22**, 153–185 (1996)
16. Jalal, A., Karmalkar, S., Hoffmann, J., Dimakis, A.G., Price, E.: Fairness for image generation with uncertain sensitive attributes. In: Proceedings of the 38th International Conference on Machine Learning (2021)
17. Joo, J., Karkkainen, K.: Gender slopes counterfactual fairness for computer vision models by attribute manipulation. In: Proceedings of the 2nd International Workshop on Fairness, Accountability, Transparency and Ethics in Multimedia (2020)

18. Jung, S., Lee, D., Park, T., Moon, T.: Fair feature distillation for visual recognition. In: Proceedings of the IEEE/CVF Conference on Computer Vision and Pattern Recognition (CVPR), pp. 12110–12119 (2021)
19. Karkkainen, K., Joo, J.: Fairface: face attribute dataset for balanced race, gender, and age for bias measurement and mitigation. In: Proceedings of the IEEE/CVF Winter Conference on Applications of Computer Vision, pp. 1548–1558 (2021)
20. Ke, J., She, Y., Lu, Y.: Style normalization in histology with federated learning. In: IEEE 18th International Symposium on Biomedical Imaging (ISBI), pp. 953–956 (2021)
21. Kim, B., Kim, H., Kim, K., Kim, S., Kim, J.: Learning not to learn: training deep neural networks with biased data. In: The IEEE Conference on Computer Vision and Pattern Recognition (CVPR), pp. 9012–9020 (2019)
22. Kinyanjui, N., et al.: Fairness of classifiers across skin tones in dermatology. Med. Image Comput. Comput. Assist. Interv. (MICCAI) **12266**, 320–329 (2020)
23. Larrazabal, A.J., Nieto, N., Peterson, V., Milone, D.H., Ferrante, E.: Gender imbalance in medical imaging datasets produces biased classifiers for computer-aided diagnosis. Proc. National Acad. Sci. **117**(23), 12592–12594 (2020)
24. Li, P., Zhao, H., Liu, H.: Deep fair clustering for visual learning. In: Proceedings of the IEEE/CVF Conference on Computer Vision and Pattern Recognition (CVPR), pp. 9070–9079 (2020)
25. Liu, Z., Luo, P., Wang, X., Tang, X.: Deep learning face attributes in the wild. In: IEEE International Conference on Computer Vision (ICCV), pp. 3730–3738 (2015)
26. McDuff, D., Song, Y., Kapoor, A., Ma, S.: Characterizing bias in classifiers using generative models. In: Proceedings of the 33rd International Conference on Neural Information Processing Systems (2019)
27. Mehrabi, N., Morstatter, F., Saxena, N., Lerman, K., Galstyan, A.: A survey on bias and fairness in machine learning. ACM Computing Surveys 54(6) (2021)
28. Merler, M., Ratha, N., Feris, R.S., Smith, J.R.: Diversity in faces. arXiv preprint arXiv:1901.10436 (2019)
29. Morales, A., Fierrez, J., Rodriguez, R.V., Tolosana, R.: SensitiveNets: learning agnostic representations with application to face images. IEEE Trans. Pattern Anal. Mach. Intell. **43**(6), 2158–2164 (2021)
30. Ongena, S., Popov, A.: Gender bias and credit access. J. Money, Credit and Banking 48 (2016)
31. O'Neil, C.: Weapons of math destruction: how big data increases inequality and threatens democracy. Crown Publishing Group (2016)
32. Quadrianto, N., Sharmanska, V., Thomas, O.: Discovering fair representations in the data domain. In: Proceedings of the IEEE/CVF Conference on Computer Vision and Pattern Recognition (CVPR), pp. 8219–8228 (2019)
33. Raji, I.D., Gebru, T., Mitchell, M., Buolamwini, J., Lee, J., Denton, E.: Saving face: investigating the ethical concerns of facial recognition auditing. In: Proceedings of the AAAI/ACM Conference on AI, Ethics, and Society, pp. 145–151 (2020)
34. Rajotte, J.F., Mukherjee, S., Robinson, C., et. al.: Reducing bias and increasing utility by federated generative modeling of medical images using a centralized adversary. In: Proceedings of the Conference on Information Technology for Social Good, pp. 79–84 (2021)
35. Ramaswamy, V.V., Kim, S.S.Y., Russakovsky, O.: Fair attribute classification through latent space de-biasing. In: Proceedings of the IEEE/CVF Conference on Computer Vision and Pattern Recognition (CVPR), pp. 9301–9310 (2021)

36. Rotemberg, V., Kurtansky, N., Betz-Stablein, B., et al.: A patient-centric dataset of images and metadata for identifying melanomas using clinical context. Sci. Data **8**(1), 34 (2021)

37. Ryu, H.J., Adam, H., Mitchell, M.: Inclusivefacenet: improving face attribute detection with race and gender diversity. Accountability, and Transparency in Machine Learning, Workshop on Fairness (2018)

38. Seyyed-Kalantari, L., Liu, G., McDermott, M., Chen, I.Y., Ghassemi, M.: Chexclusion: fairness gaps in deep chest x-ray classifiers. Pacific Sympsium On Biocomput. **26**, 232–243 (2021)

39. Sharma, A.K., Foroosh, H.: Slim-CNN: a light-weight CNN for face attribute prediction. In: 15th IEEE International Conference on Automatic Face and Gesture Recognition, pp. 329–335 (2020)

40. Song, J., Shen, C., Yang, Y., Liu, Y., Song, M.: Transductive unbiased embedding for zero-shot learning. In: 2018 IEEE/CVF Conference on Computer Vision and Pattern Recognition, pp. 1024–1033 (2018)

41. Tan, M., Le, Q.: EfficientNet: rethinking model scaling for convolutional neural networks. In: Proceedings of the 36th International Conference on Machine Learning 97, 6105–6114 (2019)

42. Wang, A., Liu, A., Zhang, R., et. al.: Revise: a tool for measuring and mitigating Bias in visual datasets. Int. J. Comput. Vis. 130, 1790-1810 (2022)

43. Wang, M., Deng, W.: Mitigate bias in face recognition using skewness-aware reinforcement learning. In: The IEEE Conference on Computer Vision and Pattern Recognition (CVPR), pp. 9322–9331 (2020)

44. Wang, M., Deng, W., Jiani Hu, J.P., Tao, X., Huang, Y.: Racial faces in-the-wild: reducing racial bias by deep unsupervised domain adaptation. In: IEEE/CVF International Conference on Computer Vision (ICCV), pp. 692–702 (2019)

45. Wang, Z., Qinami, K., Karakozis, I.C., et. al.: Towards fairness in visual recognition: effective strategies for bias mitigation. In: Proceedings of the IEEE/CVF Conference on Computer Vision and Pattern Recognition (CVPR), pp. 8916–8925 (2020)

46. Xu, H., Liu, X., Li, Y., Jain, A., Tang, J.: To be robust or to be fair: towards fairness in adversarial training. In: Proceedings of the 38th International Conference on Machine Learning (PMLR) 139, 11492–11501 (2021)

47. Xu, X., et al.: Consistent instance false positive improves fairness in face recognition. In: Proceedings of the IEEE/CVF Conference on Computer Vision and Pattern Recognition (CVPR), pp. 578–586 (2021)

48. Zhang, B.H., Lemoine, B., Mitchell, M.: Mitigating unwanted biases with adversarial learning. In: Proceedings of the 2018 AAAI/ACM Conference on AI, Ethics and Society (2018)

49. Zhang, Z., Song, Y., Qi, H.: Age progression/regression by conditional adversarial autoencoder. In: IEEE Conference on Computer Vision and Pattern Recognition (CVPR), pp. 5810–5818 (2017)

50. Zhao, C., Li, C., Li, J., Chen, F.: Fair meta-learning for few-shot classification. In: 2020 IEEE International Conference on Knowledge Graph (ICKG), pp. 275–282 (2020)

51. Zhao, J., Wang, T., Yatskar, M., Ordonez, V., Chang, K.W.: Men also like shopping: reducing gender bias amplification using corpus-level constraints. In: Proceedings of the 2017 Conference on Empirical Methods in Natural Language Processing, pp. 2979–2989 (2017)

Coil-Agnostic Attention-Based Network for Parallel MRI Reconstruction

Jingshuai Liu[1(✉)], Chen Qin[2], and Mehrdad Yaghoobi[1]

[1] IDCOM, School of Engineering, University of Edinburgh, Edinburgh, UK
{J.Liu,m.yaghoobi-vaighan}@ed.ac.uk
[2] Department of Electrical and Electronic Engineering, Imperial College London, London, UK

Abstract. Magnetic resonance imaging (MRI) is widely used in clinical diagnosis. However, as a slow imaging modality, the long scan time hinders its development in time-critical applications. The acquisition process can be accelerated by types of under-sampling strategies in k-space and reconstructing images from a few measurements. To reconstruct the image, many parallel imaging methods use the coil sensitivity maps to fold multiple coil images with model-based or deep learning-based estimation methods. However, they can potentially suffer from the inaccuracy of sensitivity estimation. In this work, we propose a novel coil-agnostic attention-based framework for multi-coil MRI reconstruction which completely avoids the sensitivity estimation and performs data consistency (DC) via a sensitivity-agnostic data aggregation consistency block (DACB). Experiments were performed on the FastMRI knee dataset and show that the proposed DACB and attention module-integrated framework outperforms other deep learning-based algorithms in terms of image quality and reconstruction accuracy. Ablation studies also indicate the superiority of DACB over conventional DC methods.

Keywords: MRI reconstruction · Coil agnostic · Attention network

1 Introduction

Magnetic resonance imaging (MRI) provides a non-invasive imaging tool and can be applied to visualize different types of tissues. However, the acquisition speed of MRI raw data is fundamentally limited due to both hardware and physiological constraints. One common practice to accelerate the process is to under-sample the measurements in k-space. However, the signals sampled below the Nyquist-Shannon rate suffer from aliasing artifacts in image domain. With the assumption that the target images can be expressed using sparse representations in image domain [9] or in some transformed space [13,20,28], compressed sensing (CS) methods solve the ill-posed problems via iterative model-based algorithms. Nevertheless, the sparsity prior can be difficult to hold in real-world

Supplementary Information The online version contains supplementary material available at https://doi.org/10.1007/978-3-031-26351-4_11.

scenarios and model complicated features [38], which restrains the growth of CS-based methods in modern MRI. The other method to reduce the acquisition time is parallel imaging (PI), which employs multiple coils to unfold the targets in image domain and exploits the coil correlations to generate clean reconstructions. GRAPPA is introduced in [11] which predicts the missing k-space data with the acquired multi-coil data, e.g. the auto-calibration signal (ACS) lines. It is still challenging to remove strong aliasing artifacts under low sampling rates, using traditional reconstruction methods.

In recent years, deep neural networks show superior performance in image super-resolution, de-noising, compressed sensing, and in-painting [2,35,37,40]. Many methods using neural networks to reconstruct MR images are proposed. The work in [19] uses magnitude and phase networks to perform residual learning of aliasing artifacts and achieve de-aliased outputs. The method in [33] retrieves promising reconstructions by maximizing the posteriori estimated via a pre-trained variational auto-encoder (VAE). The method in [3] predicts the missing k-space data from the sampled points using a neural network. Many PI methods conventionally incorporate the sensitivity maps in the reconstruction pipelines [1, 8], which can be pre-computed via model-based algorithms, e.g. ESPIRIT [34]. However, the reconstruction performance can be affected when the sensitivity estimation is inaccurate with few ACS lines at a high acceleration factor [32, 39]. A different class of methods have been proposed to jointly predict MR images and sensitivity maps. Deep J-Sense [4] unrolls an alternating optimization to jointly refine the reconstructed images and the estimated sensitivity maps. Joint-ICNet [16] merges deep learning networks with model-based methods and updates the sensitivity maps at each stage. Those methods rely on the sampled multi-coil data to estimate the coil sensitivities, which can be susceptible to coil configuration discrepancies and suffer from estimation errors.

In this paper, we introduce a novel multi-coil MRI reconstruction framework which incorporates spatial attention modules and interleaved data aggregation consistency blocks into a multi-level densely connected network structure. The proposed method is completely coil-agnostic when exhibiting data consistency in reconstruction steps, and therefore invulnerable to coil configurations. We show that it outperforms other state-of-the-art methods qualitatively and quantitatively. In ablations, we evaluate the effectiveness of model components and demonstrate the superior performance over other sensitivity estimation-based approaches. The implementation of our method is available at https:// github.com/JLiu-Edinburgh/CoilfreeMRI-ACCV2022. The main contributions are summarized below:

- we propose a coil-agnostic attention-based network for parallel MRI reconstruction;
- we develop a novel data aggregation consistency block (DACB) to explicitly utilize the multi-coil k-space consistency constraints without the estimation of sensitivity maps, where data consistency is performed with complex-valued measurements using a coil-invariant mapping to complex domain;
- we introduce a novel locality-aware spatial attention module (LoA-SAM) to achieve both adaptability and locality-aware spatial contexts and incorporate

multi-level dense connections to facilitate feature transmission at multiple levels, which shows to improve the performance;
- we perform extensive experiments on texture-rich FastMRI knee dataset to validate the efficacy of the proposed coil-agnostic method, showing its superior performance against the competing methods.

2   Related Works

2.1   Deep Neural Networks in MRI Reconstruction

Recently, deep neural networks have widely drawn attention and convolutional neural networks (CNN) achieved great success in computer vision tasks [18,29]. Many methods leverage the representations of neural networks to obtain gratifying achievements in MRI reconstruction. A deep cascade of CNNs was proposed in [30] to recover the aliased MR images. LPD-Net was introduced in [43] which converts the conventional CS problem into two easy sub-problems that are solved via a primal-dual network. The method in [23] adopts a CNN-based iterative framework to remove noise-like artifacts caused by under-sampling. A deep framework was proposed in [22] which fuses network structures with the conventional iterative optimization to provide more accurate solutions to CS-MRI problems. Generative adversarial networks (GAN) [10] produce photo-realistic images via an adversarial game between a generator and a discriminator. The method in [38] adopts a GAN-based framework to achieve sharp and realistic reconstructions. GANCS [25] leverages the interleaved null-space projections and deep residual blocks to remove the aliasing artifacts. The method in [41] uses a self-attention layer in the generator to capture the global information of high-level features. A GAN-based framework was proposed in [21] to ensure rich and natural textures using multi-level feature refinement and attentive selection. The methods in [6,26] incorporate the GAN prior in MRI reconstruction by optimizing the latent space of a pre-trained generative network.

Although deep neural network models recorded promising achievements in MRI reconstruction, how to produce high-fidelity reconstructions from highly under-sampled measurements still remains open, which can potentially limit the maximum acceleration factor in MRI scanning. We propose a locality-aware spatial attention module, which learns adaptive position-specific kernels to introduce more spatial diversities, and a GAN-based multi-level densely connected framework to boost the reconstruction performance in a fast MRI diet.

2.2   Sensitivity Encoding-Based Reconstruction

Coil sensitivity maps are widely employed for parallel MRI reconstruction. The method in [12] utilizes the pre-computed sensitivity maps to calculate the sensitivity weighted combination. The methods in [1,44] use the sensitivity maps in the interleaved data consistency layers. The weighted average block proposed in [8] merges the sensitivity maps concurrently with the preceding outputs in each reconstruction stage. However, the reconstruction performance can be severely affected by the inaccuracy of sensitivity estimation, particularly when very limited k-space points are sampled under high acceleration factors [16,32]. The work in [32] attempts to overcome this problem by predicting the sensitivity maps via a trainable network. Joint-ICNet [16] jointly updates the reconstructions and sensitivity maps. However, it can be affected by the estimation inaccuracy, e.g. caused by different machine configurations including coil deployment orders.

To avoid such issues, we propose a novel block to exploit generalized data consistency without using sensitivity maps, which yields superior performance over other approaches depending on coil sensitivity estimation.

3   Method

3.1   Problem Formulation

MRI reconstruction is traditionally modelled as follows:

$$\min_x \|A(x) - y\|^2 + \lambda R(x), \tag{1}$$

where A denotes the encoding operation involving the coil projection, the Fourier transform, and under-sampling in k-space, $y = \{y_i\}_i$ is the collection of multi-coil measurements, and $R(x)$ is a regularization. However, the iterative optimization methods can be computationally onerous. We instead leverage a trained neural network to provide an end-to-end solution. As illustrated in Fig. 1, the devised framework takes as input the under-sampled signals and reconstructs the target clean images via a network cascade. The framework utilizes a novel data aggregation consistency block (DACB) in a coil-agnostic manner and is characterized by locality-aware spatial attention (LoA-SAM) and multi-level dense connections.

3.2   Locality-Aware Spatial Attention Module (LoA-SAM)

Attention modules, e.g. the key constituent of transformers [36], are widely used to model the feature correlations and improve the representation capacity. However, the quadratic complexity hinders their implementations to high-resolution features which are closely linked with dense prediction tasks, e.g. image reconstructions. To avoid the substantial computational increase, we proposed a locality-aware spatial attention module (LoA-SAM) to capture the local contextual cues in an adaptive manner, which shows to achieve reconstruction gains. In this section, we introduce the structure of LoA-SAM.

Relative Feature Aggregation Block (RFA). We introduce a relative feature aggregation block (RFA) in this section, which captures the spatially relative information and potentially adds reconstruction performance gains. The input feature volume h of size $C \times H \times W$, where C is the number of channels and

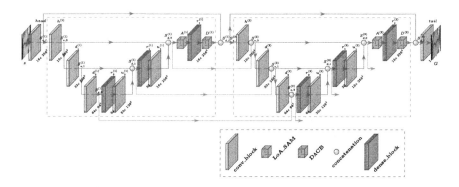

Fig. 1. Overview of the model architecture. The RSS input is first mapped via a head block and fed for a cascade of U-shaped sub-networks with multi-level dense shortcuts. The output features are fused to give the single-channel outcome via a tail block. For simplicity, only two sub-networks with three transitional levels are presented. The final framework has four sub-networks with four encoding-decoding levels

$H \times W$ refers to the spatial resolution, is respectively mapped to h_p and h_q by two branches, as illustrated in Fig. 2 (d). We shift h_p as follows,

$$ps(h_p; \Delta_i)(x) = h_p(x + \Delta_i), \tag{2}$$

where x denotes the spatial position, i.e. $h(x)$ is a vector formed with the elements across the channel axis at position x, and ps refers to the pixel-shift operator which spatially shifts the feature volume by $\Delta_i \in \{-L, .., 0, .., L\}^2$. Zero-padding is adopted for boundary pixels. L is selected to be 2 in our experiments. The relative direction vector $d(x; \Delta_i)$ at position x is given as follows,

$$d(x; \Delta_i) = ps(h_p; \Delta_i)(x) - h_q(x). \tag{3}$$

Each direction vector is combined with the corresponding relative similarity $s(x; \Delta_i)$ which is computed as follows,

$$s^*(x; \Delta_i) = 1 - sim(ps(h_p; \Delta_i)(x), h_q(x))$$
$$s(x; \Delta_i) = 1 - \frac{s^*(x; \Delta_i)}{\tau(\max_j(s^*(x; \Delta_j)) + \epsilon)}, \tag{4}$$

where sim denotes the Cosine similarity. The hyperparameter τ is practically set to 0.25, and ϵ is 10^{-6}. The feature aggregation $\hat{h}(x)$ is given by:

$$g(x; \Delta_i) = conv([d(x; \Delta_i), s(x; \Delta_i)])$$
$$\hat{h}(x) = conv([g(x; \Delta_i)]_i), \tag{5}$$

where $conv$ denotes a convolutional layer and $[\,]$ refers to the concatenation of feature maps along the channel axis.

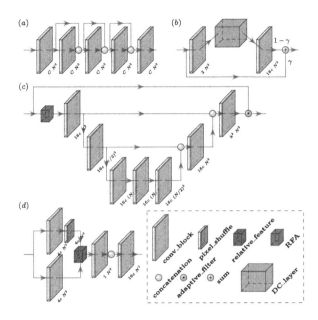

Fig. 2. Illustration of basic modules. C and N^2 indicate the channel and spatial sizes of output features. a) densely connected block, b) DACB, c) LoA-SAM, and d) RFA

Adaptive Spatial Attention Selection. The feature aggregation from RFA is passed to a tiny U-net, as shown in Fig. 2 (c), to predict the spatially varying kernels of size $k^2 \times H \times W$. The spatial attention selection is implemented by computing the weighted average of the neighboring positions:

$$\tilde{h}(x) = h(x) + \sum_{\delta \in \Delta} \omega(x, \delta) h(x + \delta), \tag{6}$$

where $\tilde{h}(x)$ is the output of LoA-SAM, Δ is the kernel grid, e.g. $\{-1, 0, 1\}^2$ for $k = 3$ in our experiments, δ is the moving footprint, and $\omega(\delta, x)$ denotes the predicted preference of position $x + \delta$. Different from [5,46] which predict the kernels of size $Ck^2 \times H \times W$ for adaptive filtering and introduce a substantial computational burden, LoA-SAM captures both the adaptive property and spatial diversity of attention patterns with reducing computational overheads.

3.3   Data Aggregation Consistency Block (DACB)

Data Consistency for MRI Reconstruction. We define two data consistency (DC) operators: the soft DC operator Ω^* and the hard DC operator Ω as follows,

$$\Omega^*(x; y, m) = F^{-1}(m \odot \frac{F(x) + \upsilon y}{1 + \upsilon} + (1 - m) \odot F(x))$$

$$\Omega(x; y, m) = F^{-1}(m \odot y + (1 - m) \odot F(x)), \tag{7}$$

where $x = f(h)$ denotes the prediction given by reducing the channels of h, v is a parameter, m refers to the sampling mask, F and F^{-1} are the Fourier transform and its inverse, and $\odot$ denotes the Hadamard multiplication. Ω^* is adopted in [1,15] and [27] updates the prediction by:

$$x \leftarrow x - \eta F^{-1}(m \odot F(x) - y). \tag{8}$$

The two update rules can be converted into a general form as below,

$$x \leftarrow \gamma x + (1 - \gamma)\Omega(x; y, m). \tag{9}$$

In parallel imaging scenarios, multi-coil signals can be combined and projected via sensitivity maps as follows,

$$s = \Phi(\{S_i\}; \{C_i\}) = \frac{\sum_i \bar{C}_i S_i}{\sum_j |C_j|^2}$$
$$S_i = \Psi(s; C_i) = C_i s, \tag{10}$$

where S_i denotes the i-th coil image, and C_i and $\bar{C}_i$ refer to the i-th sensitivity map and its conjugate. The output x is projected into the coil sensitivity via (10) and updated, e.g. use (9). The multiple images are then combined into a single view. The data consistency in (9) is eventually extended to be:

$$x \leftarrow \gamma x + (1 - \gamma)\Phi(\{\Omega(\Psi(x; C_i); y_i, m)\}; \{C_i\}), \tag{11}$$

where y_i denotes the measurement acquired by the i-th coil.

Data Consistency Block. Data consistency is widely used for multi-coil MRI reconstructions. The sensitivity maps were either estimated by model-based algorithms [1,8,12], or via trainable neural networks [16,32]. The former method requires extra computational cost and the reconstruction quality can be severely affected when the sampled ACS lines are not enough to guarantee the estimation accuracy. The latter approach transfers the estimation into end-to-end reconstruction pipelines, whereas it introduces extra parameter overheads and can be sensitive to machine configurations, e.g. coil number and deployment order, imposing restrictions on the generalization ability of reconstruction systems.

The focal point of consistency enforcement is to "correct" the intermediate reconstructions with the observed measurements. Instead of using sensitivity maps in data consistency operations, e.g. (11), we propose a simple yet effective block, named data aggregation consistency block (DACB), to tactfully perform approximated data consistency without sensitivity maps. Similar to the update rules in (9) and (11), we map the feature volume h into a 2-channel output, as illustrated in Fig. 2 (b), representing the complex-valued signal aggregation, and correct it using the summation of the measurements. Different from individually enforcing data consistency on each coil view and combining the outputs together using sensitivity maps, which is the conventional deep multi-coil MRI reconstruction method, we propose to leverage the linearity of the Fourier transform, i.e. the aggregation of the transforms equals the transformed aggregation, and adopt the summation operator instead of coil combination. To eliminate the impact of the bottleneck design, a shortcut is adopted at the feature level to take the advantage of residual learning. The data consistency is executed by,

$$h \leftarrow \gamma h + (1 - \gamma)f^*(\Omega(f(h); \sum y_i, m)), \tag{12}$$

where f and f^* are two convolutional layers used to fuse feature channels. DACB incorporates no sensitivity maps and can avoid defects caused by the inaccurate sensitivity estimation. This method is inherently robust to coil configurations due to the permutation-invariance property of the linear aggregation operation.

3.4   Framework Design

Multi-Level Dense Connections. We proposed a multi-level densely connected architecture which "reuses" the learned features at multiple levels via intra- and inter-connections. The illustrative diagram is displayed in Fig. 1 where two U-shaped sub-networks with three transitional levels are presented for simplicity. In order to enable information propagation between sub-networks and consecutively reuse the features, all preceding feature volumes at the same level are collected via skip-connections and combined with the current features, which forms the multi-level densely connected structure.

Network Architecture. In our experiments, each sub-network, shown in Fig. 1, has four transitional layers where the bottom level has $64c$ feature channels with $c = 2$. Densely connected layers [14], illustrated in Fig. 2 (a), are adopted at decoding levels. The LoA-SAM and DACB blocks are embedded at the top decoding levels. Two convolutional layers are used as the head and tail blocks to expand and reduce feature channels. Four sub-networks are used in our pipeline. The input zero-filled z is computed using Root-Sum-of-Squares (RSS):

$$z = \sqrt{\sum |F^{-1}(y_i)|^2}. \tag{13}$$

The output reconstruction G is a single-channel image.

3.5   Objective Function

The L_1 loss and structural similarity index (SSIM) [45] are used to measure the reconstruction errors. Moreover, we adopt an adversarial loss L_{adv} [24] to encourage rich and sharp details. Let G and s be the reconstruction and the RSS map of the fully sampled reference. The total loss is given by:

$$L = E_{\{(G,s)\}}[\lambda_{rec}((1 - \alpha)L_1(G, s) + \alpha L^{SSIM}(G, s)) + \lambda_{adv} L_{adv}], \tag{14}$$

where $\alpha = 0.64$, $\lambda_{rec} = 10$ and $\lambda_{adv} = 0.05$. We found that the least squares GAN [24] provides stable training. The discriminator in CycleGAN [47] is adopted.

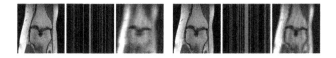

Fig. 3. First) fully sampled, second) mask, last) zero-filled at $8\times$ (*left*) and $4\times$ (*right*)

4 Experiments

4.1 Multi-Coil Reconstruction Comparisons

Implementations. We use the FastMRI multi-coil knee database [42] to conduct experiments, which contains rich textural and structural details. k-space raw data are acquired via 15 coils and converted to image domain via the inverse Fourier transform. Fixed random masks are used in under-sampling as shown in Fig. 3, where the reduction factors are respectively 8 and 4. The model was trained for 35 epochs with a batch size of 2, using an Adam optimizer [17] with $\beta_1=0.5$, $\beta_2=0.999$, and a learning rate of 10^{-5}, in PyTorch on a NVIDIA GTX 1080Ti. We compare our method with other deep learning approaches: VS-Net [8], ISTA-Net+ [44], DeepCascade [16,30], DC-CNN [31], FastMRI U-net [16,42], and Joint-ICNet [16]. The sensitivity maps are estimated via ESPIRIT [34] and used in VS-Net, ISTA-Net+, and DeepCascade. DC-CNN simultaneously reconstructs multiple coil views, FastMRI U-net uses image magnitude maps, and Joint-ICNet estimates coil sensitivities in the reconstruction pipeline. DeepCascade and U-net were also used in [16] as competing methods. The evaluation metrics are PSNR and SSIM, where higher values are better, and FID and KID [7], where lower values are preferred. More qualitative results, including $4\times$ accelerated reconstructions, are shown in Supplementary Material.

Results. The reconstructions using different methods are displayed in Fig. 4, where it shows that the proposed reconstruction framework produces superior results to other comparison methods. It generates more fine-grained textures and better preserves anatomic structures, which leads to more faithful and visually appealing reconstructions. From the last sample in Fig. 4, we observed that the reconstructions using VS-Net, ISTA-Net+, and DeepCascade suffer from artifacts, see the zoomed views. It is caused by the irregular artifacts in the estimated sensitivity maps, see Sect. 4.3 for more details. The quantitative comparisons presented in Table 1 show that our method consistently outperforms other competing approaches in terms of all evaluation metrics (p-value$\ll$0.05). Our model has fewer parameters than Joint-ICNet with faster inference speed, which potentially enables real-time reconstruction. Ablation studies are conducted to demonstrate that the superior performance is attributable to the proposed model components and structure, and not simply owing to the size of model.

4.2 Ablation Studies on Model Components

Framework Configurations. To perform ablation studies on model components: multi-level dense connections, LoA-SAM, and DACB, we implement the final pipeline, represented in (E), and its different variants in (A)-(D) and

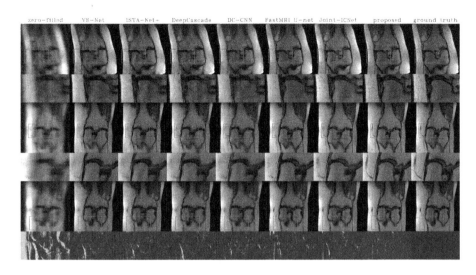

Fig. 4. Comparison results of 8× accelerated MRI reconstruction.

Table 1. Quantitative results of accelerated multi-coil knee MRI reconstruction. 4× accelerated reconstructions have the same runtime (s) and model size (MB) as 8×

	Method	PSNR↑	SSIM↑	FID↓	KID↓	Runtime↓	Size↓
8×	zero-filled	28.75	0.817	379.58	0.459	–	–
	VS-Net [8]	36.18	0.912	141.15	0.078	0.034	4.32
	ISTA-Net+ [44]	36.32	0.911	170.11	0.108	0.189	1.47
	DeepCascade [16,30]	35.82	0.909	146.17	0.081	0.083	1.73
	DC-CNN [31]	34.96	0.892	180.47	0.124	0.035	**1.11**
	FastMRI U-net [16,42]	36.19	0.922	145.58	0.095	**0.011**	10.59
	Joint-ICNet [16]	35.59	0.921	137.57	0.090	0.283	263.43
	proposed	**37.74**	**0.930**	**76.08**	**0.011**	0.112	159.11
4×	zero-filled	33.16	0.883	201.20	0.173	–	–
	VS-Net [8]	40.56	0.956	111.34	0.052	–	–
	ISTA-Net+ [44]	40.81	0.956	112.45	0.052	–	–
	DeepCascade [16,30]	40.57	0.956	109.46	0.050	–	–
	DC-CNN [31]	39.32	0.945	111.32	0.049	–	–
	FastMRI U-net [16,42]	39.37	0.951	108.52	0.055	–	–
	Joint-ICNet [16]	39.27	0.955	88.69	0.035	–	–
	proposed	**41.10**	**0.963**	**64.37**	**0.009**	–	–

(F). For fair comparisons, feature volumes of model (A) and (F) are repeated to approximate the parameter overheads of their counterparts with multi-level dense connections. For the same reason, the convolutional layers in DACB are maintained for (A)-(C). The U-net in LoA-SAM is only used for kernel prediction with limited parameters, while the reconstruction branch with a vast majority of parameters remains unchanged for a fair comparison. The model configurations and final performance are shown in Table 2.

Table 2. Ablations on model components at 8× acceleration

Method	ML-dense	LoA-SAM	DACB	PSNR↑	SSIM↑	FID↓	KID↓
(A)	×	×	×	36.53	0.921	89.83	0.025
(B)	√	×	×	37.06	0.926	85.39	0.024
(C)	√	√	×	37.33	0.926	84.16	0.022
(D)	√	×	√	37.53	0.929	80.14	0.017
(E) ours	√	√	√	**37.74**	**0.930**	**76.08**	**0.011**
(F)	×	√	√	37.11	0.927	82.13	0.018

Table 3. Ablations on data consistency blocks and data type at 8× acceleration. The proposed method performs no sensitivity estimation and is therefore free of ME-Arti

Method	Input	DC	Output	PSNR↑	SSIM↑	FID↓	KID↓	ME-Arti
(E)-CSM	complex	CSDC	complex	36.58	0.916	94.56	0.029	strong
(E)-CSM-a	complex	CSDC	single	36.83	0.920	87.46	0.022	weak
(E)-CSM-b	RSS	CSDC	single	36.99	0.925	83.95	0.020	trivial
(E) proposed	RSS	DACB	single	**37.74**	**0.930**	**76.08**	**0.011**	free

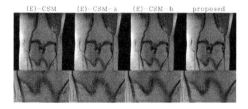

Fig. 5. Ablation results on data consistency blocks and data type at 8× acceleration.

Results. The results in Table 2 demonstrate that the proposed model components consistently improve the reconstruction performance in terms of evaluation metrics. Comparing model (B) and (E) with model (A) and (F), we found that the multi-level dense connections improve the reconstructions in all metrics. It can be observed that compared with model (B), both LoA-SAM and DACB which are respectively used in model (C) and (D) deliver performance gains in all evaluations. The complete model (E) consistently gives the best results, which indicates the efficacy of the proposed method and implies a positive synergy effect between LoA-SAM and DACB in improving reconstruction quality.

4.3 Ablation Studies on Data Consistency Methods

Implementations. We compare the proposed method with three variants to elucidate how the proposed DACB and RSS-based pipeline benefit the reconstruction performance. The first variant, dubbed (E)-CSM, has 2-channel inputs and outputs representing complex values. The pre-computed sensitivity maps

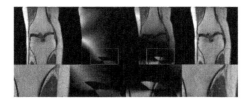

Fig. 6. Map estimation artifacts. First) RSS of fully sampled signal, second) positive component of the imaginary part of a sensitivity map, third) positive component of the imaginary part of the combined image, and last) reconstruction using (E)-CSM

Table 4. Ablation analysis on residual feature connection in DACB at 8× acceleration

Method	DC	PSNR↑	SSIM↑	FID↓	KID↓
(E) proposed	DACB	**37.74**	**0.930**	**76.08**	**0.011**
(E)-ResFree	ResFree	37.40	0.928	79.37	0.014

are used to combine multi-coil frames via (10). Data consistency is implemented using (11), which we refer to as CSDC. It is extended to be (E)-CSM-a and (E)-CSM-b by progressively adopting the single-channel magnitudes as output and input. The evaluation and visual results are presented in Table 3 and Fig. 5.

Results. From Table 3, we observed that the data type has considerable effects on the reconstruction results and DACB further contributes a performance gain. Comparing to (E)-CSM-b which uses the conventional sensitivity-based DC approach, the proposed method shows superior results, substantiating the efficacy of DACB. In Fig. 5, we found that (E)-CSM suffers from strong artifacts which can be alleviated by adopting (E)-CSM-a and -b. The proposed model avoids the sensitivity estimation and yields clean reconstructions. We postulate that the artifacts emanate from the sensitivity maps, when they are not appropriately estimated and the irregularities attend to the complex-valued inputs. Such artifacts can be propagated to the final reconstructions when the model fails to overcome them, which is demonstrated in the next subsection.

Map Estimation Artifacts (ME-Arti). We demonstrate how the artifacts in Fig. 5 are caused. The RSS map in Fig. 6 shows no artifacts. We found that such irregular shapes stealthily attend to separate image channels, representing complex-valued signals, and can be manifested by solely visualizing the values of the same sign, e.g. negative components. We display a sensitivity map and an image combined via (10) in Fig. 6, where the irregular shapes coincide with the artifacts in the reconstruction using (E)-CSM. It shows the impact of inaccurate sensitivity estimation and implies the usefulness of the proposed method.

Table 5. Ablation analysis on relative feature aggregation at $8\times$ acceleration

Method	RFA	PSNR↑	SSIM↑	FID↓	KID↓
(E) proposed	√	**37.74**	**0.930**	**76.08**	**0.011**
(E)-no-RFA	×	37.69	0.929	78.43	0.013

4.4　Ablation Analysis on Data Consistency Bottleneck Design

In Sect. 3.3, we postulate the negative impact of the bottleneck structure in conventional DC operations, i.e. channel reduction and expansion. To verify this, we remove the skip-connection in DACB and implement the update rule below,

$$h \leftarrow f^*(\gamma f(h) + (1 - \gamma)\Omega(f(h); \sum y_i, m)). \tag{15}$$

We denote by ResFree the update in (15), refer to the resultant model as (E)-ResFree, and present the comparisons in Table 4. We found that ResFree reduces PSNR and SSIM with a concomitant increase in FID and KID, which indicates the impact of the bottleneck structure in normal DC operations. It is shown that DACB is able to alleviate this issue and improve the model performance.

4.5　Ablation Analysis on Attention Feature

In this section, we testify the effectiveness of the relative feature aggregation (RFA) block in LoA-SAM. We implement a variant, dubbed (E)-no-RFA, which removes RFA and instead predicts the adaptive kernels directly from the input features. The comparison results are shown in Table 5, where the removal of RFA decreases PSNR and SSIM scores by a small margin and introduces moderately higher FID and KID. It shows that the relative information provided by RFA is preferable over the original features and enhances the capacity of LoA-SAM. Note that RFA uses simple mathematical operations. We leave it a future work to explore the potential benefits of more complex aggregation methods.

4.6　Robustness to Coil Configurations

As an alternative to model-based sensitivity estimation algorithms, neural networks can be used to predict the sensitivity maps, e.g. Joint-ICNet [16]. A different method is introduced in DC-CNN [31] which respectively performs data consistency for parallel coil images. However, such methods, as substantiated in the following, can be sensitive to machine configurations, which restricts models from generalizing to real-world scenarios. We randomly permute the coil orders in inference to demonstrate the robustness of the proposed pipeline to coil configurations. We compare it with Joint-ICNet and DC-CNN which take multi-coil images as input respectively to the sensitivity estimation network and the reconstruction model. Coil frame sequences are rolled by randomly sampled shift numbers. The FastMRI database provides limited diversities of coil orders.

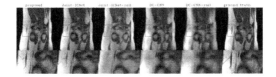

Fig. 7. Comparisons of 8× accelerated MRI reconstruction using coil permutation.

Table 6. Performance results of 8× accelerated multi-coil knee MRI reconstruction using random coil permutation

Method	Permutation	PSNR↑	SSIM↑	FID↓	KID↓
proposed	None/rolled	**37.74**	**0.930**	**76.08**	**0.011**
Joint-ICNet [16]	None	35.59	0.921	137.57	0.090
Joint-ICNet [16]	rolled	33.18	0.905	143.43	0.092
DC-CNN [31]	None	34.96	0.892	180.47	0.124
DC-CNN [31]	rolled	31.86	0.848	237.91	0.216

Nevertheless, the great majority follow the same configuration. The results are presented in Fig. 7 and Table 6. It is evident that the performance of both Joint-ICNet and DC-CNN can be severely affected by coil permutation, which shows their sensitivity to machine configuration discrepancies. The fact that the number of coils is required to be kept fixed is another problem which can violate the deployment of reconstruction models from training to real-world scanners. Leveraging the permutation-invariance of the RSS and measurement summation operators, the proposed method circumvents those issues and shows a strong invulnerability and generalization capacity.

5   Conclusion

In this study, we introduce a framework to circumvent the coil sensitivity estimation retrospectively required for multi-coil MRI reconstruction frameworks. We propose a coil-agnostic data aggregation consistency block to perform approximated data consistency and a spatial attention module to enhance the model performance. In experiments, it was demonstrated that the proposed framework outperforms other deep learning-based methods qualitatively and quantitatively. In ablation studies, the proposed coil-agnostic pipeline showed superior performance over conventional approaches in accelerated MRI acquisition settings. The future researches include applying our method to other anatomical structures and extending it to dynamic MRI reconstruction.

References

1. Aggarwal, H., Mani, M., Jacob, M.: MoDL: model-based deep learning architecture for inverse problems. IEEE Trans. Med. Imaging **38**(2), 394–405 (2019). https://doi.org/10.1109/TMI.2018.2865356

2. Ahmad, R., et al.: Plug-and-play methods for magnetic resonance imaging: using denoisers for image recovery. IEEE Signal Process. Mag. **37**(1), 105–116 (2020). https://doi.org/10.1109/MSP.2019.2949470

3. Anuroop, S., Jure, Z., Tullie, M., Lawrence, Z., Aaron, D., K.S., D.: GrappaNet: combining parallel imaging with deep learning for multi-coil MRI reconstruction. In: 2020 IEEE/CVF Conference on Computer Vision and Pattern Recognition (CVPR), pp. 14303–14310 (2020). https://doi.org/10.1109/CVPR42600.2020.01432

4. Arvinte, M., Vishwanath, S., Tewfik, A., Tamir, J.: Deep J-Sense: accelerated MRI reconstruction via unrolled alternating optimization (2021)

5. Bako, S., et al.: Kernel-predicting convolutional networks for denoising Monte Carlo renderings. ACM Trans. Graph. (TOG) **36**(4), 97 (2017)

6. Bhadra, S., Zhou, W., Anastasio, M.: Medical image reconstruction with image-adaptive priors learned by use of generative adversarial networks. Medical Imag. 2020: Phys. Med. Imag. **11312**, 206–213 (2020). https://doi.org/10.1117/12.2549750

7. Bińkowski, M., Sutherland, D., Arbel, M., Gretton, A.: Demystifying MMD GANs. In: International Conference on Learning Representations (2018)

8. Duan, J., et al.: VS-Net: variable splitting network for accelerated parallel MRI reconstruction. In: Shen, D., et al. (eds.) MICCAI 2019. LNCS, vol. 11767, pp. 713–722. Springer, Cham (2019). https://doi.org/10.1007/978-3-030-32251-9_78

9. Fair, M., Gatehouse, P., DiBella, E., Firmin, D.: A review of 3D first-pass, whole-heart, myocardial perfusion cardiovascular magnetic resonance. J. Cardiovasc. Mag. Reson. **17**, 68 (2015). https://doi.org/10.1186/s12968-015-0162-9

10. Goodfellow, I., et al.: Generative adversarial networks. Adv. Neural. Inf. Process. Syst. **27**, 2672–2680 (2014)

11. Griswold, M., et al.: Generalized autocalibrating partially parallel acquisitions (GRAPPA). Magn. Reson. Med. **47**(6), 1202–1210 (2002). https://doi.org/10.1002/mrm.10171

12. Hammernik, K., et al.: Learning a variational network for reconstruction of accelerated MRI data. Magn. Reson. Med. **79**(6), 3055–3071 (2017)

13. Hong, M., Yu, Y., Wang, H., Liu, F., Crozier, S.: Compressed sensing MRI with singular value decomposition-based sparsity basis. Phys. Med. Biol. **56**(19), 6311–6325 (2021)

14. Huang, G., Liu, Z., Van Der Maaten, L., Weinberger, K.Q.: Densely connected convolutional networks. In: 2017 IEEE Conference on Computer Vision and Pattern Recognition (CVPR), pp. 2261–2269 (2017)

15. Huang, Q., Yang, D., Wu, P., Qu, H., Yi, J., Metaxas, D.: MRI reconstruction via cascaded channel-wise attention network. In: 2019 IEEE 16th International Symposium on Biomedical Imaging (ISBI 2019), pp. 1622–1626 (2019). https://doi.org/10.1109/ISBI.2019.8759423

16. Jun, Y., Shin, H., Eo, T., Hwang, D.: Joint deep model-based MR image and coil sensitivity reconstruction network (Joint-ICNet) for fast MRI. In: Proceedings of the IEEE/CVF Conference on Computer Vision and Pattern Recognition (CVPR), pp. 5270–5279 (2021)

17. Kingma, D., Ba, J.: Adam: a method for stochastic optimization. In: 3rd International Conference on Learning Representations (ICLR) (2015). http://arxiv.org/abs/1412.6980
18. Krizhevsky, A., Sutskever, I., Hinton, G.: ImageNet classification with deep convolutional neural networks. In: Advances in Neural Information Processing Systems 25 (2012). https://proceedings.neurips.cc/paper/2012/file/c399862d3b9d6b76c8436e924a68c45b-Paper.pdf
19. Lee, D., Yoo, J., Tak, S., Ye, J.: Deep residual learning for accelerated MRI using magnitude and phase networks. IEEE Trans. Biomed. Eng. **65**(9), 1985–1995 (2018)
20. Lingala, S., Jacob, M.: Blind compressive sensing dynamic MRI. IEEE Trans. Med. Imaging **32**(6), 1132–1145 (2013)
21. Liu, J., Yaghoobi, M.: Fine-grained MRI reconstruction using attentive selection generative adversarial networks. In: ICASSP 2021–2021 IEEE International Conference on Acoustics, Speech and Signal Processing (ICASSP), pp. 1155–1159 (2021)
22. Liu, R., Zhang, Y., Cheng, S., Luo, Z., Fan, X.: A deep framework assembling principled modules for CS-MRI: unrolling perspective, convergence behaviors, and practical modeling. IEEE Trans. Med. Imaging **39**(12), 4150–4163 (2020). https://doi.org/10.1109/TMI.2020.3014193
23. Liu, Y., Liu, Q., Zhang, M., Yang, Q., Wang, S., Liang, D.: IFR-Net: Iterative feature refinement network for compressed sensing MRI. IEEE Trans. Comput. Imag. **6**, 434–446 (2020)
24. Mao, X., Li, Q., Xie, H., Lau, R., Wang, Z., Smolley, S.: Least squares generative adversarial networks. In: 2017 IEEE International Conference on Computer Vision (ICCV), pp. 2813–2821 (2017)
25. Mardani, M., et al.: Deep generative adversarial neural networks for compressive sensing MRI. IEEE Trans. Med. Imaging **38**(1), 167–179 (2019). https://doi.org/10.1109/TMI.2018.2858752
26. Narnhofer, D., Hammernik, K., Knoll, F., Pock, T.: Inverse GANs for accelerated MRI reconstruction. Wavelets Spars. XVIII **11138**, 111381A (2019). https://doi.org/10.1117/12.2527753
27. Pezzotti, N., et al.: An adaptive intelligence algorithm for undersampled knee MRI reconstruction. IEEE Access **8**, 204825–204838 (2020)
28. Ravishankar, S., Bresler, Y.: MR image reconstruction from highly undersampled k-space data by dictionary learning. IEEE Trans. Med. Imaging **30**(5), 1028–1041 (2011)
29. Sajjadi, M., Schölkopf, B., Hirsch, M.: EnhanceNet: single image super-resolution through automated texture synthesis. In: 2017 IEEE International Conference on Computer Vision (ICCV), pp. 4501–4510 (2017). https://arxiv.org/abs/1612.07919/
30. Schlemper, J., Caballero, J., Hajnal, J., Price, A., Rueckert, D.: A deep cascade of convolutional neural networks for dynamic MR image reconstruction. IEEE Trans. Med. Imaging **37**(2), 491–503 (2018). https://doi.org/10.1109/TMI.2017.2760978
31. Schlemper, J., et al.: Data consistency networks for (calibration-less) accelerated parallel MR image reconstruction. Abstract from ISMRM 27th Annual Meeting and Exhibition (2019)
32. Sriram, A., et al.: End-to-end variational networks for accelerated MRI reconstruction. In: International Conference on Medical Image Computing and Computer-Assisted Intervention, pp. 64–73 (2020)

33. Tezcan, K., Baumgartner, C., Luechinger, R., Pruessmann, K., Konukoglu, E.: MR image reconstruction using deep density priors. IEEE Trans. Med. Imaging **38**(7), 1633–1642 (2019). https://doi.org/10.1109/TMI.2018.2887072
34. Uecker, M., et al.: ESPIRiT-an eigenvalue approach to autocalibrating parallel MRI: where SENSE meets GRAPPA. Magn. Reson. Med. **71**(3), 990–1001 (2014)
35. Valsesia, D., Fracastoro, G., Magli, E.: Deep graph-convolutional image denoising. IEEE Trans. Image Process. **29**, 8226–8237 (2020)
36. Vaswani, A., et al.: Attention is all you need. In: Advances in Neural Information Processing Systems 30 (2017). https://proceedings.neurips.cc/paper/2017/file/3f5ee243547dee91fbd053c1c4a845aa-Paper.pdf
37. Wang, Y., Tao, X., Qi, X., Shen, X., Jia, J.: Image inpainting via generative multi-column convolutional neural networks. In: Advances in Neural Information Processing Systems, pp. 331–340 (2018)
38. Yang, G., et al.: DAGAN: deep de-aliasing generative adversarial networks for fast compressed sensing MRI reconstruction. IEEE Trans. Med. Imaging **37**(6), 1310–1321 (2018)
39. Ying, L., Sheng, J.: Joint image reconstruction and sensitivity estimation in SENSE (JSENSE). Magn. Reson. Med. **57**(6), 1196–1202 (2007)
40. Wang, X., et al.: ESRGAN: enhanced super-resolution generative adversarial networks. In: Leal-Taixé, L., Roth, S. (eds.) ECCV 2018. LNCS, vol. 11133, pp. 63–79. Springer, Cham (2019). https://doi.org/10.1007/978-3-030-11021-5_5
41. Yuan, Z., et al.: SARA-GAN: self-attention and relative average discriminator based generative adversarial networks for fast compressed sensing MRI reconstruction. Front. Neuroinform. **14**, 1–12 (2020). https://doi.org/10.3389/fninf.2020.611666
42. Zbontar, J., et al.: FastMRI: an open dataset and benchmarks for accelerated MRI. CoRR abs/1811.08839 (2018)
43. Zhang, C., Liu, Y., Shang, F., Li, Y., Liu, H.: A novel learned primal-dual network for image compressive sensing. IEEE Access **9**, 26041–26050 (2021). https://doi.org/10.1109/ACCESS.2021.3057621
44. Zhang, J., Ghanem, B.: ISTA-Net: iterative shrinkage-thresholding algorithm inspired deep network for image compressive sensing. In: IEEE Conference on Computer Vision and Pattern Recognition (CVPR), pp. 1828–1837 (2018)
45. Zhao, H., Gallo, O., Frosio, I., Kautz, J.: Loss functions for image restoration WTH neural networks. IEEE Trans. Comput. Imag. **3**(1), 47–57 (2017)
46. Zhou, S., Zhang, J., Pan, J., Xie, H., Zuo, W., Ren, J.: Spatio-temporal filter adaptive network for video deblurring. In: Proceedings of the IEEE International Conference on Computer Vision (2019)
47. Zhu, J., Park, T., Isola, P., Efros, A.: Unpaired image-to-image translation using cycle-consistent adversarial networks. In: 2017 IEEE International Conference on Computer Vision (ICCV), pp. 2242–2251 (2017). https://doi.org/10.1109/ICCV.2017.244

TriMix: A General Framework
for Medical Image Segmentation
from Limited Supervision

Zhou Zheng[1(✉)], Yuichiro Hayashi[1], Masahiro Oda[1], Takayuki Kitasaka[2], and Kensaku Mori[1,3(✉)]

[1] Nagoya University, Nagoya, Japan
zzheng@mori.m.is.nagoya-u.ac.jp
[2] Aichi Institute of Technology, Toyota, Japan
[3] National Institute of Informatics, Chiyoda City, Japan
kensaku@is.nagoya-u.ac.jp

Abstract. We present a general framework for medical image segmentation from limited supervision, reducing the reliance on fully and densely labeled data. Our method is simple, jointly trains *tri*ple diverse models, and adopts a *mix* augmentation scheme, and thus is called *TriMix*. TriMix imposes consistency under a more challenging perturbation, *i.e.*, combining data augmentation and model diversity on the tri-training framework. This straightforward strategy enables TriMix to serve as a strong and general learner learning from limited supervision using different kinds of imperfect labels. We conduct extensive experiments to show TriMix's generic purpose for semi- and weakly-supervised segmentation tasks. Compared to task-specific state-of-the-arts, TriMix achieves competitive performance and sometimes surpasses them by a large margin. The code is available at https://github.com/MoriLabNU/TriMix.

1 Introduction

Segmentation is fundamental in medical image analysis, recognizing anatomical structures. Supervised learning has led to a series of advancements in medical image segmentation [1]. However, the availability of fully and densely labeled data is a common bottleneck in supervised learning, especially in medical image segmentation, since annotating pixel-wise labels is usually tedious and time-consuming and requires expert knowledge. Thus, training a model with limited supervision using datasets with imperfect labels is essential.

Existing works have made efforts to take advantage of unlabeled data and weakly labeled data to train segmentation models [2] with semi-supervised learning (SSL) [3–5] and weakly-supervised learning [6–8]. Semi-supervised segmentation [9–11] is an effective paradigm for learning a model from scarce annotations, exploiting labeled and unlabeled data. Weakly-supervised segmentation aims to alleviate the longing for densely labeled data, utilizing sparse annotations,

---

Supplementary Information The online version contains supplementary material available at https://doi.org/10.1007/978-3-031-26351-4_12.

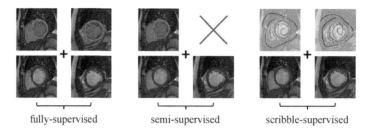

Fig. 1. Conceptual comparison of fully-supervised (using fully and densely labeled data), semi-supervised (using a part of densely labeled data and unlabeled data), and scribble-supervised (using data with scribble annotations) segmentation.

e.g., points and scribbles, as supervision signals [2]. In this study, in addition to semi-supervised segmentation, we focus on *scribble-supervised* segmentation, one of the hottest topics in the family of weakly-supervised learning. A conceptual comparison of fully-supervised, semi-supervised, and scribble-supervised segmentation is shown in Fig. 1.

Consistency regularization aims to enforce the prediction agreement under different kinds of perturbations, *e.g.*, input augmentation [3,9], network diversity [11,12], and feature perturbation [13]. Recent works [7,8,14–20] involving consistency regularization shows advanced performance tackling limited supervision. Despite their success in learning from non-fullness supervision, an impediment is that existing studies are *task-specific* for semi- and scribble-supervised segmentation. Driven by this limitation, a question to ask is: *Does a framework generic to semi- and scribble-supervised segmentation exist?* Although the two tasks leverage different kinds of imperfect labels, indeed, they have the same intrinsic goal: mining the informative information as much as possible from pixels with no ground truth. Thus, such a framework should *exist* once it can excellently learn representations from the unlabeled pixels.

Consistency regularization under a more rigorous perturbation empirically leads to an improved generalization [11]. However, lacking sufficient supervision, models may output inaccurate predictions and then learn from these under consistency enforcement. This vicious cycle would accumulate prediction mistakes and finally lead to degraded performance. Thus, the key to turning the vicious cycle into a virtuous circle is increasing the quality of model outputs when adopting a more challenging consistency regularization. From these perspectives, we hypothesize that an eligible framework should be endowed with these characteristics: **(i)** it should output *more accurate predictions*, and **(ii)** it should be trained with consistency regularization under a *more challenging perturbation*.

Based on the above hypothesis, we find a solution: we present a general and effective framework that, for the first time, shows its dual purpose for both semi- and scribble-supervised segmentation tasks. The method is simple, jointly trains *triple* models, and adopts a *mix* augmentation scheme, and thus is called *TriMix*. To meet the requirement of **(i)**, TriMix maintains triple networks, which have identical structures but different initialization to introduce *model perturbation* and imposes consistency to minimize disagreement among models, inspired by the original tri-training strategy [21]. Intuitively, more diverse models can extract more informative information from the dataset. Each model receives valuable information from the other two through intra-model communication and then generates more accurate predictions. To meet the requirement of (ii), the model diversity is further blended with *data perturbation*, which accompanies the mix augmentation scheme, to form a more challenging perturbation. We hypothesize that the tri-training scheme within TriMix well complements consistency regularization under the hybrid perturbation. This *self-complementary* manner enables TriMix to serve as a general learner learning from limited supervision using different kinds of imperfect labels. Our contributions are:

- We propose a simple and effective method called TriMix and show its generic solution for semi- and scribble-supervised segmentation for the first time.
- We show that purely imposing consistency under a more challenging perturbation, *i.e.*, combining data augmentation and model diversity, on the tri-training framework can be a general mechanism for limited supervision.
- We first validate TriMix on the semi-supervised task. TriMix presents competitive performance against state-of-the-art (SOTA) methods and surprisingly strong potential under the one-shot setting[1], which is rarely challenged by existing semi-supervised segmentation methods.
- We then evaluate TriMix on the scribble-supervised task. TriMix surpasses the mainstream methods by a large margin and realizes new SOTA performance on the public benchmarks.

2   Related Work

Semi-supervised learning (SSL) trains a model utilizing both labeled and unlabeled data. Existing SSL methods are generally based on pseudo-labeling (also called self-training) [5,25–27] and consistency regularization [3,4,28,29]. Pseudo-labeling takes the model's class prediction as a label to train against, but the label quality heavily influences the performance. **Consistency regularization** assumes predictions should be invariant under perturbations, such as input augmentation [3,9], network diversity [11,12], and feature perturbation [13]. Consistency regularization usually performs better than self-training and has been widely involved in the task of **semi-supervised segmentation** [14–18,30,31]. A more challenging perturbation empirically profits model generalization if the model could sustainably generate accurate predictions [11]. In this work, we introduce a hybrid perturbation harsher than its elements, *i.e.*, data augmentation, and model diversity.

Weakly-supervised segmentation learns a model using the dataset with weak annotations, *e.g.*, bounding boxes, scribbles, sparse dots, and polygons [2]. In this work, we utilize scribbles as weak annotations, which are mostly used in computer vision community, from classical methods [32,33] to current **scribble-supervised** methods [6–8,19,34–37], due to the convenient format. To learn

---

[1] Note that the concepts of one-shot learning [22–24] and semi-supervised learning should be *different*. We *borrow* the phrase "one-shot" to define a more challenging semi-supervised setting where only one labeled sample is available during training.

from scribble supervision, some methods [34–36] make efforts to construct complete labels based on the scribble for training. Other works like [37,38] explore possible losses to regularize the training from scribble annotations, and the scheme of [6] adds additional modules to improve the segmentation accuracy. Recently, consistency regularization is explored in several works [7,8,20,39].

Data augmentation generates virtual training examples to improve model generalization. Auto-augmentation methods [40–43] automatically search for optimal data augmentation policies and show higher accuracy than handmade schemes but with relatively higher search costs. In our study, we focus on the **mix augmentation** [44–50], which is one type of strong data augmentation and is more efficient than auto-augmentation methods. Mix augmentation mixes two inputs and the corresponding labels up in some way to create virtual samples for training. It has been widely applied in semi-supervised segmentation [9–11] as an effective way to import data perturbation and synthesize new samples during training. In [7], mix segmentation is firstly introduced to increment supervision for scribble-supervised segmentation.

Co-training and tri-training are two SSL approaches in a similar flavor, which maintain multiple models and regularize the disagreement among the outputs of models. Co-training framework [51,52] assumes there are sufficient and different views of the training data, each of which can independently train a model. Maintaining view diversity, in some sense, is similar to the data perturbation in SSL. Co-training has been extended to semi-supervised segmentation [18,53]. Unlike co-training, tri-training [21] does not require view difference. Instead, it introduces model diversity and minimizes the disagreement among various outputs. This strategy is similar to imposing consistency under the model perturbation in SSL. There are several variants of tri-training [54–57], but *none* are for semi- or scribble-supervised segmentation. In this work, we revisit tri-training and explore its potential and general solution for handling limited supervision when it meets mix augmentation.

3   Method

3.1   Overview

This paper proposes a simple and general framework, TriMix, to tackle semi- and scribble-supervised segmentation. The plain architecture of TriMix is illustrated in Fig. 2. TriMix adheres to the spirit of tri-training, simultaneously learning triple networks f_1, f_2, and f_3, which have identical structures but different weights $\mathbf{w}_1$, $\mathbf{w}_2$, and $\mathbf{w}_3$, to import network inconsistency. In addition, mix augmentation is adopted to introduce input data perturbation. Generally, assume a mini-batch $\mathbf{b} = \{\mathbf{x}, \mathbf{y}\}$ is fetched at each training iteration, where $\mathbf{x}$ and $\mathbf{y}$ are images and the corresponding ground truth. TriMix involves three steps to process a batch flow at each training iteration.

Step 1: first forward pass. For $i \in \{1, 2, 3\}$, each network f_i is fed with images $\mathbf{x}$ and outputs the prediction $\mathbf{p}_i$. A supervised loss $L_{sup}(\mathbf{p}_i, \mathbf{y})$ is then imposed between $\mathbf{p}_i$ and the ground truth $\mathbf{y}$.

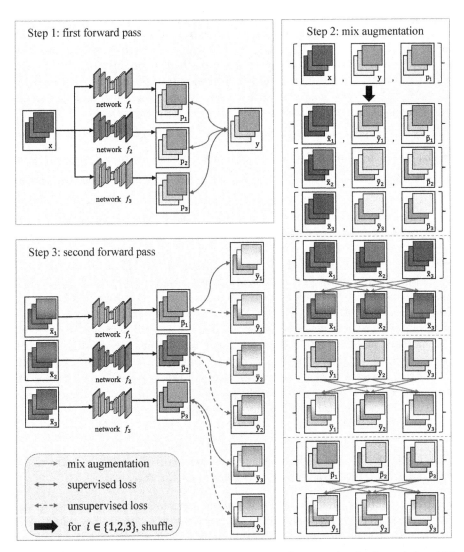

Fig. 2. Overview of TriMix. TriMix maintains triple networks f_1, f_2, and f_3, which have same architectures but different weights. Three steps are taken when given a mini-batch containing images $\mathbf{x}$ and ground truth $\mathbf{y}$ at each training iteration. **Step 1: first forward pass.** For $i \in \{1,2,3\}$, each network f_i outputs $\mathbf{p}_i$ for $\mathbf{x}$, with the supervision of $\mathbf{y}$. **Step 2: mix augmentation.** Three batches $\{\mathbf{x}, \mathbf{y}, \mathbf{p}_1\}$, $\{\mathbf{x}, \mathbf{y}, \mathbf{p}_2\}$, and $\{\mathbf{x}, \mathbf{y}, \mathbf{p}_3\}$ are randomly shuffled to obtain new batches $\{\tilde{\mathbf{x}}_1, \tilde{\mathbf{y}}_1, \tilde{\mathbf{p}}_1\}$, $\{\tilde{\mathbf{x}}_2, \tilde{\mathbf{y}}_2, \tilde{\mathbf{p}}_2\}$, and $\{\tilde{\mathbf{x}}_3, \tilde{\mathbf{y}}_3, \tilde{\mathbf{p}}_3\}$. Then each pair of these new batches are mixed up to form batches $\{\bar{\mathbf{x}}_1, \bar{\mathbf{x}}_2, \bar{\mathbf{x}}_3\}$, $\{\bar{\mathbf{y}}_1, \bar{\mathbf{y}}_2, \bar{\mathbf{y}}_3\}$, $\{\hat{\mathbf{y}}_1, \hat{\mathbf{y}}_2, \hat{\mathbf{y}}_3\}$. Squares with mixed colors indicate mixed samples. **Step 3: second forward pass.** For $i \in \{1,2,3\}$, each network f_i outputs $\bar{\mathbf{p}}_i$ for $\bar{\mathbf{x}}_i$, with the supervision of $\bar{\mathbf{y}}_i$. An unsupervised loss is calculated between $\bar{\mathbf{p}}_i$ and $\hat{\mathbf{y}}_i$. Note that $\hat{\mathbf{y}}_i$ can be soft (probability maps) or hard pseudo-labels (one-hot maps). (Color figure online)

Step 2: mix augmentation. With Step 1, we obtain three batches $\mathbf{b}_1 = \{\mathbf{x}, \mathbf{y}, \mathbf{p}_1\}$, $\mathbf{b}_2 = \{\mathbf{x}, \mathbf{y}, \mathbf{p}_2\}$, and $\mathbf{b}_3 = \{\mathbf{x}, \mathbf{y}, \mathbf{p}_3\}$. The goal is to mix up the pair of $(\mathbf{b}_2, \mathbf{b}_3)$, the pair of $(\mathbf{b}_1, \mathbf{b}_3)$, and the pair of $(\mathbf{b}_1, \mathbf{b}_2)$ to generate new batches. Similar to the mixing operation described in original papers [44,46], we first randomly shuffle $\mathbf{b}_1$, $\mathbf{b}_2$, and $\mathbf{b}_3$ to generate three new batches of $\tilde{\mathbf{b}}_1 = \{\tilde{\mathbf{x}}_1, \tilde{\mathbf{y}}_1, \tilde{\mathbf{p}}_1\}$, $\tilde{\mathbf{b}}_2 = \{\tilde{\mathbf{x}}_2, \tilde{\mathbf{y}}_2, \tilde{\mathbf{p}}_2\}$, and $\tilde{\mathbf{b}}_3 = \{\tilde{\mathbf{x}}_3, \tilde{\mathbf{y}}_3, \tilde{\mathbf{p}}_3\}$, in which $\tilde{\mathbf{x}}_1$, $\tilde{\mathbf{x}}_2$, and $\tilde{\mathbf{x}}_3$ have different image order, and each $\tilde{\mathbf{y}}_i$ and $\tilde{\mathbf{p}}_i$ correspond to $\tilde{\mathbf{x}}_i$ for $i \in \{1, 2, 3\}$. Afterward, we apply the mix augmentation to the pair of $\left(\tilde{\mathbf{b}}_2, \tilde{\mathbf{b}}_3\right)$, the pair of $\left(\tilde{\mathbf{b}}_1, \tilde{\mathbf{b}}_3\right)$, and the pair of $\left(\tilde{\mathbf{b}}_1, \tilde{\mathbf{b}}_2\right)$ to generate new batches of $\bar{\mathbf{b}}_1 = \{\bar{\mathbf{x}}_1, \bar{\mathbf{y}}_1, \hat{\mathbf{y}}_1\}$, $\bar{\mathbf{b}}_2 = \{\bar{\mathbf{x}}_2, \bar{\mathbf{y}}_2, \hat{\mathbf{y}}_2\}$, and $\bar{\mathbf{b}}_3 = \{\bar{\mathbf{x}}_3, \bar{\mathbf{y}}_3, \hat{\mathbf{y}}_3\}$ with mixed samples. Take the pair of $\left(\tilde{\mathbf{b}}_2, \tilde{\mathbf{b}}_3\right)$, for example. Each image of $\tilde{\mathbf{x}}_2$ is mixed with the image indexed in the same order in $\tilde{\mathbf{x}}_3$ to yield $\bar{\mathbf{x}}_1$, then $\tilde{\mathbf{y}}_2$ and $\tilde{\mathbf{y}}_3$, $\tilde{\mathbf{p}}_2$ and $\tilde{\mathbf{p}}_3$ are proportionally mixed to get $\bar{\mathbf{y}}_1$ and $\hat{\mathbf{y}}_1$. Squares with mixed colors in Fig. 2 indicate mixed samples.

Step 3: second forward pass. For $i \in \{1, 2, 3\}$, we feed each network f_i with mixed images $\bar{\mathbf{x}}_i$ to get the individual prediction $\bar{\mathbf{p}}_i$. Each $\bar{\mathbf{p}}_i$ is optimized to be close to the mixed ground truth $\bar{\mathbf{y}}_i$ with a supervised loss $L_{sup}(\bar{\mathbf{p}}_i, \bar{\mathbf{y}}_i)$. Besides, consistency is enforced between $\bar{\mathbf{p}}_i$ and the mixed pseudo-labels $\hat{\mathbf{y}}_i$, with an unsupervised loss $L_{unsup}(\bar{\mathbf{p}}_i, \hat{\mathbf{y}}_i)$. Note that $\hat{\mathbf{y}}_i$ could be soft (probability maps) or hard pseudo-labels (one-hot maps). A typical choice selected by most methods [4,14,17] is a soft pseudo-label, and an unsupervised loss L_{unsup}^p compares the *probability consistency* by the mean square error (MSE) equation. By contrast, several works, *e.g.*, [8,10] utilize a hard pseudo-label, where an unsupervised loss L_{unsup}^s calculates the *pseudo supervision consistency*.

To conclude, the total optimization objective of each network is

$$L_i = L_{sup}(\mathbf{p}_i, \mathbf{y}) + \lambda_1 L_{sup}(\bar{\mathbf{p}}_i, \bar{\mathbf{y}}_i) + \lambda_2 L_{unsup}(\bar{\mathbf{p}}_i, \hat{\mathbf{y}}_i), \qquad (1)$$

where $i \in \{1, 2, 3\}$ is the index pointing out items corresponding to network f_i, and λ_1 and λ_2 are hyperparameters to balance each term.

Default Settings. In this study, we adopt *pseudo supervision consistency*. We will show that TriMix potentially achieves better accuracy integrated with pseudo supervision consistency than probability consistency in Sect. 4.4. Besides, we utilize *CutMix* [46] as the mix strategy, similar to [9–11], but note that other kinds of mix augmentations should also fit our framework.

Inference Process. Triple networks with different weights are in TriMix. For a test sample, each network individually outputs a prediction. We will report the *average* result of them and report their *ensemble* result obtained by soft voting.

The below two sections will show how TriMix can be applied to semi- and scribble-supervised tasks, following the standard process from Step 1 to Step 3.

3.2 TriMix in Semi-Supervised Segmentation

Semi-supervised segmentation aims to learn a model by exploiting two given datasets: labeled dataset $\mathbf{D}_l = \{\mathbf{X}_l, \mathbf{Y}_l\}$, and unlabeled dataset $\mathbf{D}_u = \{\mathbf{X}_u\}$, where $\mathbf{X}$ and $\mathbf{Y}$ are images and the corresponding ground truth.

Assume a mini-batch of labeled data $\mathbf{b}_l = \{\mathbf{x}_l, \mathbf{y}_l\} \in \mathbf{D}_l$ and a mini-batch of unlabeled data $\mathbf{b}_u = \{\mathbf{x}_u\} \in \mathbf{D}_u$ are sampled at each training iteration. We illustrate the training detail of $\mathbf{b}_l$ and $\mathbf{b}_u$ in the following.

First, the mini-batch $\mathbf{b}_l$ contains the images and the corresponding ground truth, and TriMix can be optimized with $\mathbf{b}_l$ obeying the standard process as illustrated in Fig. 2. However, existing SSL methods, *e.g.*, [10,11] *rarely* introduce perturbations to the labeled data, even though it is beneficial for performance. Following previous methods, we optimize TriMix *only with Step 1* and eliminate the processes of Step 2 and Step 3 when using $\mathbf{b}_l$. Thus, for $i \in \{1, 2, 3\}$, assume each network f_i outputs perdition $\mathbf{p}_{l_i}$ for images $\mathbf{x}_l$, then only a supervised loss $L_{sup}(\mathbf{p}_{l_i}, \mathbf{y}_l)$ is calculated between $\mathbf{p}_{l_i}$ and the ground truth $\mathbf{y}_l$.

Second, the mini-batch $\mathbf{b}_u$ contains images $\mathbf{x}_u$ but no related labels. TriMix can still be optimized with $\mathbf{b}_u$ following the standard process as illustrated in Fig. 2 but *without supervised terms*. Specifically, for $i \in \{1, 2, 3\}$, each network f_i outputs individual prediction $\mathbf{p}_{u_i}$ for $\mathbf{x}_u$ with the first forward pass at Step 1. There is no supervised term at Step 1 for each $\mathbf{p}_{u_i}$, due to the lack of ground truth. At Step 2, three batches $\mathbf{b}_{u_1} = \{\mathbf{x}_u, \mathbf{p}_{u_1}\}$, $\mathbf{b}_{u_2} = \{\mathbf{x}_u, \mathbf{p}_{u_2}\}$, and $\mathbf{b}_{u_3} = \{\mathbf{x}_u, \mathbf{p}_{u_3}\}$, which contain no ground truth, can be mixed up to generate augmented batches $\bar{\mathbf{b}}_{u_1} = \{\bar{\mathbf{x}}_{u_1}, \hat{\mathbf{y}}_{u_1}\}, \bar{\mathbf{b}}_{u_2} = \{\bar{\mathbf{x}}_{u_2}, \hat{\mathbf{y}}_{u_2}\}$, and $\bar{\mathbf{b}}_{u_3} = \{\bar{\mathbf{x}}_{u_3}, \hat{\mathbf{y}}_{u_3}\}$, that have no mixed ground truth. At Step 3, each network f_i fed with mixed images $\bar{\mathbf{x}}_{u_i}$ is expected to output a similar prediction $\bar{\mathbf{p}}_{u_i}$ compared to $\hat{\mathbf{y}}_{u_i}$, with an unsupervised loss $L_{unsup}(\bar{\mathbf{p}}_{u_i}, \hat{\mathbf{y}}_{u_i})$.

To conclude, the total training objective of each network in this task is

$$L_i = L_{sup}(\mathbf{p}_{l_i}, \mathbf{y}_l) + \lambda L_{unsup}(\bar{\mathbf{p}}_{u_i}, \hat{\mathbf{y}}_{u_i}), \tag{2}$$

where items with $i \in \{1, 2, 3\}$ correspond to network f_i, and λ is a trade-off hyperparameter. Moreover, we use the *dice* loss [58] L_{dice} as both the supervised and unsupervised losses. Thus, Eq. (2) is re-written as

$$L_i = \underbrace{L_{dice}(\mathbf{p}_{l_i}, \mathbf{y}_l)}_{\text{sup}} + \underbrace{\lambda L_{dice}(\bar{\mathbf{p}}_{u_i}, \hat{\mathbf{y}}_{u_i})}_{\text{unsup}}. \tag{3}$$

3.3   TriMix in Scribble-Supervised Segmentation

Scribble-supervised segmentation trains a model from a given dataset $\mathbf{D}_s = \{\mathbf{X}_s, \mathbf{Y}_s\}$, where $\mathbf{X}_s$ and $\mathbf{Y}_s$ are images and the related scribble annotations.

Let $\mathbf{b}_s = \{\mathbf{x}_s, \mathbf{y}_s\} \in \mathbf{D}_s$ indicate a mini-batch fetched at every training itera-tion. Since $\mathbf{b}_s$ contains images and the corresponding ground truth in scribbles, we follow the standard process illustrated in Fig. 2 to train TriMix with $\mathbf{b}_s$. Let us say, for $i \in \{1, 2, 3\}$, each network f_i outputs its prediction $\mathbf{p}_{s_i}$ for $\mathbf{x}_s$ at Step 1, and we obtain mixed batches of $\bar{\mathbf{b}}_{s_1} = \{\bar{\mathbf{x}}_{s_1}, \bar{\mathbf{y}}_{s_1}, \hat{\mathbf{y}}_{s_1}\}, \bar{\mathbf{b}}_{s_2} = \{\bar{\mathbf{x}}_{s_2}, \bar{\mathbf{y}}_{s_2}, \hat{\mathbf{y}}_{s_2}\}$, and $\bar{\mathbf{b}}_{s_3} = \{\bar{\mathbf{x}}_{s_3}, \bar{\mathbf{y}}_{s_3}, \hat{\mathbf{y}}_{s_3}\}$ at Step 2. Then identical to Eq. (1), the training objective of each network f_i in scribble-supervised segmentation is

$$L_i = L_{sup}(\mathbf{p}_{s_i}, \mathbf{y}_s) + \lambda_1 L_{sup}(\bar{\mathbf{p}}_{s_i}, \bar{\mathbf{y}}_{s_i}) + \lambda_2 L_{unsup}(\bar{\mathbf{p}}_{s_i}, \hat{\mathbf{y}}_{s_i}), \tag{4}$$

where λ_1 and λ_2 are hyperparameters balancing each term.

Besides, since $\mathbf{y}_s$ and $\bar{\mathbf{y}}_{s_i}$ are scribble annotations, we apply the *partial cross-entropy* (pCE) function [38] L_{pce}, which calculates the loss only for annotated pixels as the supervised loss, following [7,8,38]. Formally, let $\mathbf{m}$ and $\mathbf{n}$ be the prediction and the scribble annotation, and $L_{pce}(\mathbf{m}, \mathbf{n})$ is defined as

$$L_{pce}(\mathbf{m}, \mathbf{n}) = -\sum_{j \in J} \sum_{k \in K} \mathbf{n}^{jk} \log \mathbf{m}^{jk}, \tag{5}$$

in which J is the set of pixels with scribble annotation, K is the number of classification categories. $\mathbf{m}^{jk}$ indicates the predicted value of k-th channel for the j-th pixel in $\mathbf{m}$, and $\mathbf{n}^{jk}$ is the corresponding ground truth of k-th channel for the j-th pixel annotation in $\mathbf{n}$.

Lastly, we use the *cross-entropy* (CE) loss L_{ce} as the unsupervised loss. Thus, Eq. (4) is re-written as

$$L_i = \underbrace{L_{pce}^{unmix}(\mathbf{p}_{s_i}, \mathbf{y}_s) + \lambda_1 L_{pce}^{mix}(\bar{\mathbf{p}}_{s_i}, \bar{\mathbf{y}}_{s_i})}_{\text{sup}} + \underbrace{\lambda_2 L_{ce}^{mix}(\bar{\mathbf{p}}_{s_i}.\hat{\mathbf{y}}_{s_i})}_{\text{unsup}}, \tag{6}$$

where the superscript $unmix$ denotes that labels for calculation are original and without the mix augmentation. The superscript mix indicates that labels and pseudo-labels for calculation are generated from the mix augmentation.

4   Experiments on Semi-Supervised Segmentation

4.1   Data and Evaluation Metric

ACDC Dataset. [59] consists of 200 MRI volumes from 100 patients, and each volume manually delineates the ground truth for the left ventricle (LV), the right ventricle (RV), and the myocardium (Myo). The original volume sizes are $(154 - 428) \times (154 - 512) \times (6 - 18)$ pixels. We resized all the volumes to $256 \times 256 \times 16$ pixels and normalized the intensities as zero mean and unit variance. We performed *4-fold* cross-validation. We validated our method under the 16/150 partition protocol. In each fold, we sampled 16 volumes among 150 as the labeled data, and the remaining ones were treated as unlabeled data.

Hippocampus dataset was collected by The Medical Segmentation Decathlon[2], is comprised of 390 MRI volumes of the hippocampus. We utilized the training set (260 volumes) for validation, which contains the corresponding ground truth of the anterior and posterior regions of the hippocampus. Volume sizes are $(31 - 43) \times (40 - 59) \times (24 - 47)$ pixels. We resized all the volumes to $32 \times 48 \times 32$ pixels. With this dataset, we challenged a more tough problem where only one labeled sample is available for training, *i.e., one-shot setting.* We conducted *4-fold* cross-validation, sampled 1 volume among 195 cases as the labeled data in each fold, and treated the rest as unlabeled data.

Evaluation Metric. Dice score and 95% Hausdorff Distance (95HD) were used to measure the volume overlap rate and the surface distance.

---

[2] http://medicaldecathlon.com/.

Table 1. Comparison with semi-supervised state-of-the-arts on ACDC dataset under 16/150 partition protocol. We report the average (standard deviation) results based on *4-fold* cross-validation. [†]: method with ensemble strategy.

Method	RV		Myo		LV		Avg.	
	Dice	95HD	Dice	95HD	Dice	95HD	Dice	95HD
Upper bound	81.6 (2.8)	4.2 (2.3)	79.5 (1.6)	2.0 (0.3)	89.6 (1.7)	2.2 (0.6)	83.6	2.8
Baseline	58.9 (2.3)	28.7 (8.3)	56.1 (3.3)	17.0 (3.1)	70.4 (2.5)	12.1 (5.3)	61.8	19.3
MT [4]	58.1 (3.1)	27.2 (9.3)	58.0 (3.8)	14.8 (1.4)	70.5 (4.0)	7.8 (3.6)	62.2	16.6
UA-MT [14]	54.5 (7.5)	35.4 (6.3)	58.6 (3.2)	17.9 (1.9)	72.1 (3.1)	10.3 (2.2)	61.7	21.2
CutMix-Seg [9]	57.4 (2.7)	36.1 (5.0)	59.3 (4.2)	18.8 (4.3)	71.8 (2.1)	14.2 (9.9)	62.8	23.0
STS-MT [28]	57.1 (4.1)	33.0 (5.4)	60.1 (3.3)	13.5 (2.5)	72.0 (2.7)	9.2 (3.1)	63.1	18.6
CPS [10]	74.6 (3.2)	7.0 (2.1)	72.5 (2.0)	5.0 (1.4)	84.8 (1.2)	5.5 (1.5)	77.3	5.9
UMCT [18]	58.2 (2.8)	29.1 (4.7)	60.4 (2.9)	16.4 (5.4)	74.6 (2.3)	11.1 (5.7)	64.4	18.9
UMCT[†] [18]	61.9 (2.0)	21.9 (4.6)	63.2 (3.5)	11.3 (5.4)	78.3 (1.1)	7.9 (5.0)	67.8	13.7
TriMix	73.9 (3.5)	7.9 (2.4)	72.8 (1.7)	4.3 (1.1)	85.8 (1.7)	4.7 (1.3)	77.5	5.6
TriMix[†]	**74.8 (3.6)**	**6.4 (2.0)**	**73.7 (1.9)**	**3.9 (1.1)**	**86.3 (1.7)**	**3.9 (1.2)**	**78.3**	**4.7**

4.2 Experimental Setup

Implementation Details. We adopted V-Net [58] as the backbone architecture. To fit the volumetric data, we extended CutMix [46] to 3D and set the cropped volume ratio to 0.2. We empirically set λ to 0.5 in Eq. (3). We trained TriMix 300 epochs using SGD with a weight decay of 0.0001 and a momentum of 0.9. The initial learning rate was set to 0.01 and was divided by 10 every 100 epochs. At each training iteration, 4 labeled and 4 unlabeled samples were fetched for the ACDC dataset, and 1 labeled and 4 unlabeled samples were fetched for the Hippocampus dataset.

Baseline and Upper Bound. We provided the baseline and upper bound settings for reference. We trained the backbone V-Net only with the partitioned labeled data and treated the result as the baseline setting. Besides, we regraded the result trained with the complete labeled data as the upper bound accuracy.

Mainstream Approaches. We implemented several SSL algorithms: Mean Teacher (MT) [4], Uncertainty-Aware Mean Teacher (UA-MT) [14], CutMix-Seg [9], Spatial-Temporal Smoothing Mean Teacher (STS-MT) [28], Uncertainty-Aware Multi-View Co-Training (UMCT) [18], and Cross Pseudo Supervision (CPS) [10], and compared TriMix to them. CutMix-Seg and CPS were incorporated with the 3D CutMix augmentation. UMCT was trained with three different views. We will report the student model results for MT, UA-MT, STS-MT, and CutMix-Seg. Since there is more than one trainable model within CPS and UMCT, we will report their average result among the trained models and the ensembled result for UMCT, the same as TriMix.

4.3 Experiment Results

Improvement over the Baseline. We investigated TriMix's effectiveness in exploiting the unlabeled data. As illustrated in Table 1 and Table 2, we note that

Table 2. Comparison with semi-supervised state-of-the-arts on Hippocampus dataset with one-shot setting. We report the average (standard deviation) results based on *4-fold* cross-validation. [†]: method with ensemble strategy.

Method	Anterior		Posterior		Avg.	
	Dice	95HD	Dice	95HD	Dice	95HD
Upper bound	84.4 (0.7)	1.5 (0.1)	82.6 (0.8)	1.4 (0.1)	83.5	1.5
Baseline	12.9 (2.8)	9.9 (1.7)	14.7 (5.3)	9.9 (1.5)	13.8	9.9
MT [4]	25.2 (5.9)	9.5 (1.2)	29.2 (7.2)	10.2 (1.6)	27.2	9.9
UA-MT [14]	23.3 (2.4)	8.5 (0.6)	34.7 (9.7)	9.3 (0.6)	29.0	8.9
CutMix-Seg [9]	29.7 (5.6)	7.5 (1.1)	41.5 (10.8)	8.9 (0.7)	35.6	8.2
STS-MT [28]	26.1 (2.5)	9.5 (1.1)	31.3 (9.5)	10.7 (1.3)	28.7	10.1
CPS [10]	55.1 (4.6)	5.9 (0.8)	56.8 (2.7)	4.5 (0.1)	56.0	5.2
UMCT [18]	30.3 (8.9)	6.9 (0.6)	26.0 (9.8)	5.4 (1.7)	28.2	6.2
UMCT[†] [18]	35.3 (12.0)	3.9 (1.0)	27.6 (11.2)	3.6 (1.2)	31.5	3.8
TriMix	70.0 (3.4)	3.0 (0.3)	67.0 (2.1)	3.2 (0.4)	68.5	3.1
TriMix[†]	**70.5 (3.6)**	**2.9 (0.4)**	**68.0 (1.7)**	**3.0 (0.3)**	**69.2**	**3.0**

TriMix significantly improve the baseline. Specifically, it gains +15.7% in Dice and -13.7 in 95HD on the ACDC dataset and +54.7% in Dice and -6.8 in 95HD on the Hippocampus dataset, demonstrating that TriMix can effectively mine informative information from the unlabeled data to improve generalization.

Comparison with SOTAs. For the ACDC dataset under 16/150 partition protocol (see Table 1), CutMix-Seg achieves better average results than MT and confirms its effectiveness with strong input perturbation. STS-MT employs the spatial-temporal smoothing mechanism and outperforms CutMix-Seg. UMCT is in a co-training style and takes advantage of multi-view information. It brings higher accuracy than STS-MT but can not achieve the performance of CPS. TriMix obtains the best results among the methods. For the Hippocampus dataset with the one-shot setting (see Table 2), the existing SSL methods generally improve the baseline, verifying how effectively they exploit the unlabeled data. TriMix greatly outperforms the other methods, producing meaningful accuracy. Notably, TriMix surpasses the second-best method CPS by +12.5% in Dice and -2.1 in 95HD. Validation of these two datasets reveals that TriMix is competitive with SOTAs under typical partition protocols and has strong potential for learning from extremely scarce labeled data.

4.4   Empirical Study and Analysis

Pseudo Supervision Consistency *vs.* Probability Consistency. We compared the pseudo supervision consistency (denoted by L^s_{unsup}) and probability consistency (denoted by L^p_{unsup}) on the ACDC and Hippocampus datasets under different partition protocols. Results are shown in Fig. 3. Overall, TriMix incorporated with L^s_{unsup} outperforms TriMix with L^p_{unsup} across all the partition protocols on the two datasets. Especially under the one-shot setting on the Hippocampus dataset, L^s_{unsup} surpasses L^p_{unsup} by +54.2% in Dice and -5.9 in 95HD, indicating that a one-hot label map plays a more crucial role than a probability

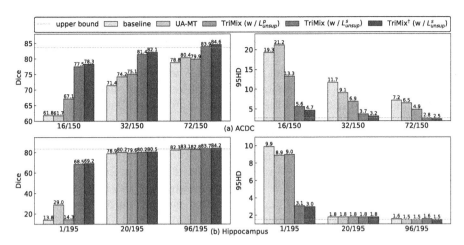

Fig. 3. Empirical study on different types of consistency regularization and various partition protocols with ACDC and Hippocampus datasets. L_{unsup}^s: an unsupervised loss that compares pseudo supervision consistency. L_{unsup}^p: an unsupervised loss that calculates probability consistency. [†]: method with ensemble strategy.

map as the expanded ground truth to supervise the other models within the framework TriMix. Previous works [5,8,10] have reported similar observations. Using hard pseudo-labels encourages models to be low-entropy/high-confidence on data and is closely related to entropy minimization [60]. Based on this ablation, we utilize the pseudo supervision consistency as the *default setting* for TriMix in semi- and scribble-supervised segmentation.

Robustness to Different Partition Protocols. We studied TriMix's robustness to various partition protocols on the ACDC and Hippocampus datasets. As shown in Fig. 3, TriMix consistently promotes the baseline and outperforms UA-MT across all the partition protocols, demonstrating the robustness and effectiveness of our method under different data settings. Moreover, TriMix surpasses the upper bound accuracy under the 72/150 partition protocol on the ACDC dataset and the 96/195 partition protocol on the Hippocampus dataset, revealing that TriMix can greatly reduce dependence on the labeled data.

Relations to Existing Methods. Among the semi-supervised methods for comparison, UMCT and CPS are the two most related methods to TriMix. UMCT is a co-training-based strategy to introduce view differences. Thus, TriMix resembles UMCT in some sense as both methods follow the spirit of multi-model joint training and encourage consistency among models. However, TriMix adopts a stricter perturbation than UMCT. Moreover, CPS can be regarded as a downgraded version of TriMix, in which two perturbed networks are trained to generate hard pseudo-labels to supervise each other. TriMix outperforms UMCT and CPS on the ACDC and Hippocampus datasets, demonstrating the superiority of our strategy, where consistency regularization under a more challenging perturbation is adopted in tri-training.

5   Experiments on Scribble-Supervised Segmentation

5.1   Data and Evaluation Metric

ACDC Dataset. [59] introduced in Sect. 4.1 was reused in this task, but with corresponding scribble annotations [6]. We resized all slices to the size of 256×256 pixels and normalized their intensity to [0,1], identical to the work [8].

MSCMRseg Dataset. [61] comprises of LGE-MRI images from 45 patients. We utilized the scribble annotations of LV, Myo, and RV released from [7] and used the same data partition setting as theirs: 25 images for training, 5 for validation, and 15 for testing. For data prepossessing, we re-sampled all images to the resolution of 1.37×1.37 mm, cropped or padded images to the size of 212×212 pixels, and normalized each image to zero and unit variance.

Evaluation Metric. Dice score and 95HD were utilized.

5.2   Experimental Setup

Implementation Details. We adopted the 2D U-Net architecture [62] as the backbone for all experiments in this task. The cropped area ratio was set to 0.2 when performing the CutMix augmentation. λ_1 and λ_2 in Eq. (6) were empirically set to 1. For the ACDC dataset, we used almost the same settings as in [8]. Specifically, we used SGD (weight decay = 0.0001, momentum = 0.9) to optimize TriMix for a total of 60000 iterations under a poly learning rate with an initial value of 0.03. The batch size was set to 12. We performed *5-fold* cross-validation. For the MSCMRseg dataset, we followed [7] to train TriMix 1000 epochs with the Adam optimizer and a fixed learning rate of 0.0001. We conducted *5 runs* with seeds 1, 2, 3, 4 and 5.

Baseline and Upper Bound. 2D U-Net trained with scribble annotations using the pCE loss [38] was regarded as the baseline setting. Furthermore, the upper bound accuracy was obtained using entirely dense annotations.

Mainstream Approaches. We compared TriMix with several methods, including training with pseudo-labels generated by Random Walks (RW) [33], Scribble2Lables (S2L) [19], Uncertainty-Aware Self-Ensembling and Transformation Consistency Model (USTM) [39], Entropy Minimization (EM) [60], Mumford-Shah Loss (MLoss) [63], Regularized Loss (RLoss) [37], Dynamically Mixed Pseudo Labels Supervision (simply abbreviated to DMPLS in this paper) [8], CycleMix [7], and Shape-Constrained Positive-Unlabeled Learning (ShapePU) [20].

5.3   Experiment Results

Improvement over Baseline. As shown in Table 3 and Table 4, TriMix significantly improves the baseline on the ACDC and MSCMRseg datasets, gaining +20.2% and +49.6% Dice scores, respectively, which proves that TriMix can learn good representations from sparse scribble annotations.

Table 3. Comparison with scribble-supervised state-of-the-arts on ACDC dataset. Other average (standard deviation) results are from [8]. Ours are based on *5-fold* cross-validation. [†]: method with ensemble strategy.

Method	RV		Myo		LV		Avg.	
	Dice	95HD	Dice	95HD	Dice	95HD	Dice	95HD
Upper bound	88.2 (9.5)	6.9 (10.8)	88.3 (4.2)	5.9 (15.2)	93.0 (7.4)	8.1 (20.9)	89.8	7.0
Baseline	62.5 (16.0)	187.2 (35.2)	66.8 (9.5)	165.1 (34.4)	76.6 (15.6)	167.7 (55.0)	68.6	173.3
RW [33]	81.3 (11.3)	11.1 (17.3)	70.8 (6.6)	9.8 (8.9)	84.4 (9.1)	9.2 (13.0)	78.8	10.0
USTM [39]	81.5 (11.5)	54.7 (65.7)	75.6 (8.1)	112.2 (54.1)	78.5 (16.2)	139.6 (57.7)	78.6	102.2
S2L [19]	83.3 (10.3)	14.6 (30.9)	80.6 (6.9)	37.1 (49.4)	85.6 (12.1)	65.2 (65.1)	83.2	38.9
MLoss [63]	80.9 (9.3)	17.1 (30.8)	83.2 (5.5)	28.2 (43.2)	87.6 (9.3)	37.9 (59.6)	83.9	27.7
EM [60]	83.9 (10.8)	25.7 (44.5)	81.2 (6.2)	47.4 (50.6)	88.7 (9.9)	43.8 (57.6)	84.6	39.0
RLoss [37]	85.6 (10.1)	7.9 (12.6)	81.7 (5.4)	6.0 (6.9)	89.6 (8.6)	7.0 (13.5)	85.6	6.9
DMPLS [8]	86.1 (9.6)	**7.9 (12.5)**	84.2 (5.4)	9.7 (23.2)	91.3 (8.2)	12.1 (27.2)	87.2	9.9
TriMix	87.7 (2.8)	8.9 (4.6)	86.4 (2.2)	4.3 (1.6)	92.3 (3.0)	4.4 (1.9)	88.8	5.9
TriMix[†]	**88.3 (2.6)**	8.2 (4.1)	**86.8 (2.2)**	**3.7 (1.5)**	**92.6 (2.7)**	**3.8 (1.8)**	**89.3**	**5.2**

Comparison with SOTAs. For the ACDC dataset (see Table 3), TriMix achieves the highest average accuracy in Dice and 95HD among all scribble-supervised methods and reaches the closest result to the upper bound accuracy. It is worth noting that TriMix obtains a gain of 1.6% in Dice over DMPLS and a reduction of 1.0 in 95HD than RLoss. For the MSCMRseg dataset (see Table 4), TriMix surpasses all mix augmentation-based schemes, *i.e.*, MixUp, CutOut, CutMix, PuzzleMix, CoMixUp, and CycleMix, as well as two SOTAs, *i.e.*, CycleMix, and ShapePU. TriMix outperforms CycleMix by +7.4% and ShapePU by +2.2% and even improves the upper bound accuracy by +11.9% in Dice. Evaluations of these two benchmarks reveal that TriMix shows stronger generalization learning from sparse annotations than SOTAs.

5.4   Empirical Study and Analysis

Ablation on Different Loss Combinations. We investigated the effectiveness of different loss combinations on the accuracy, as illustrated in Fig. 4. Only leveraging the original scribble annotations, L_{pce}^{unmix} brings the lower bound accuracy. L_{pce}^{mix} contributes to the performance and boosts the lower bound by +2.8% in Dice, showing that mix augmentation aids in *increasing scribble annotations* and thus improves accuracy. L_{ce}^{mix} contributes much more than L_{pce}^{unmix} and improves the lower bound by +41.0% in Dice, revealing that *pseudo supervision is essential* for TriMix. Besides, combining all losses yields the highest accuracy.

Relations to Existing Methods. TriMix is related to DMPLS and CycleMix. Specifically, DMPLS utilizes co-labeled pseudo-labels from multiple diverse branches to supervise single-branch output based on consistency regularization. CycleMix employs mix augmentation to increase scribble annotations and imposes consistency under the input perturbation. TriMix seems to be at the

Table 4. Comparison with scribble-supervised state-of-the-arts on MSCMRseg dataset. Other average (standard deviation) results in Dice score are from [7,20]. Ours are based on 5 runs. †: method with ensemble strategy.

Method	RV	Myo	LV	Avg.
Upper bound	68.9 (12.0)	72.0 (7.5)	85.7 (5.5)	75.5
Baseline	5.7 (2.2)	58.3 (6.7)	49.4 (8.2)	37.8
MixUp [44]	37.8 (15.3)	46.3 (14.7)	61.0 (14.4)	48.4
CutOut [45]	69.7 (14.9)	64.1 (13.6)	45.9 (7.7)	59.9
CutMix [46]	76.1 (10.5)	62.2 (12.1)	57.8 (6.3)	65.4
PuzzleMix [50]	2.8 (1.2)	63.4 (8.4)	6.1 (2.1)	24.1
CoMixUp [47]	5.3 (2.2)	34.3 (6.7)	35.6 (7.5)	25.1
CycleMix [7]	79.1 (7.2)	73.9 (4.9)	87.0 (6.1)	80.0
ShapePU [20]	80.4 (12.3)	83.2 (4.2)	91.9 (2.9)	85.2
TriMix	86.5 (0.6)	83.6 (0.4)	92.2 (0.3)	87.4
TriMix†	**87.7 (0.7)**	**84.7 (0.4)**	**93.0 (0.2)**	**88.5**

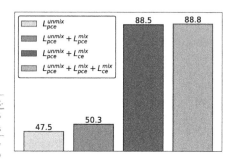

Fig. 4. Ablation study on different loss combinations on the ACDC dataset with scribble annotations using Dice score.

middle ground. It imports mix augmentation similar to CycleMix and enforces the consistency among various outputs with pseudo-label supervision, resembling DMPLS. TriMix incorporates valid features beneficial for scribble-supervised segmentation and achieves the new SOTA performance on two public benchmarks, *i.e.*, the ACDC and MSCMRseg datasets.

6   Discussion and Conclusion

This paper seeks to address semi- and scribble-supervised segmentation in a general way. We provide a hypothesis on a general learner learning from limited supervision: (i) it should output *more accurate predictions* and (ii) it should be trained with consistency regularization under a *more challenging perturbation*. We empirically verify the hypothesis with a simple framework. The method, called TriMix, purely imposes consistency on a tri-training framework under a stricter perturbation, *i.e.*, combining data augmentation and model diversity. Our method is competitive with task-specific mainstream methods. It shows strong potential training with extremely scarce labeled data and achieves new SOTA performance on two popular benchmarks when learning from sparse annotations. We also provide extra evaluations of our method in *appendix*.

Moreover, as suggested by [64], Deep Ensembles can provide a simple and scalable way for uncertainty estimation. TriMix maintains triple diverse networks, and such nature allows for its efficient uncertainty modeling. It is essential to estimate and quantify uncertainty for models learned from limited supervision, which is, however, rarely explored. It is also interesting to investigate whether TriMix can be applied to handle other types of imperfect annotations, *e.g.*, noise labels [2,65]. In addition, TriMix's mechanism is similar to that of the method BYOL [66], which employs two networks and enforces representation consistency between them. TriMix may be applicable for self-supervised learning, but it needs further evaluation. Last but not least, similar to multi-view co-training [18], TriMix is inherently expensive in computation. To make TriMix more efficient, we may investigate strategies such as MIMO [67] for TriMix in the future. The above avenues are regarded as our follow-up works.

Acknowledgement. This work was supported by JSPS KAKENHI Grant Numbers 21K19898 and 17H00867 and JST CREST Grant Number JPMJCR20D5, Japan.

References

1. Litjens, G., et al.: A survey on deep learning in medical image analysis. Med. Image Anal. **42**, 60–88 (2017)
2. Tajbakhsh, N., Jeyaseelan, L., Li, Q., Chiang, J.N., Wu, Z., Ding, X.: Embracing imperfect datasets: a review of deep learning solutions for medical image segmentation. Med. Image Anal. **63**, 101693 (2020)
3. Miyato, T., Maeda, S.I., Koyama, M., Ishii, S.: Virtual adversarial training: a regularization method for supervised and semi-supervised learning. In: TPAMI, vol. 41 (2018)
4. Tarvainen, A., Valpola, H.: Mean teachers are better role models: weight-averaged consistency targets improve semi-supervised deep learning results. In: NeurIPS (2017)
5. Sohn, K., et al.: FixMatch: simplifying semi-supervised learning with consistency and confidence. In: NeurIPS (2020)
6. Valvano, G., Leo, A., Tsaftaris, S.A.: Learning to segment from scribbles using multi-scale adversarial attention gates. In: TMI, vol. 40 (2021)
7. Zhang, K., Zhuang, X.: CycleMix: a holistic strategy for medical image segmentation from scribble supervision. In: CVPR (2022)
8. Luo, X., et al.: Scribble-supervised medical image segmentation via dual-branch network and dynamically mixed pseudo labels supervision. In: MICCAI (2022)
9. French, G., Laine, S., Aila, T., Mackiewicz, M., Finlayson, G.: Semi-supervised semantic segmentation needs strong, varied perturbations. In: BMVC (2020)
10. Chen, X., Yuan, Y., Zeng, G., Wang, J.: Semi-supervised semantic segmentation with cross pseudo supervision. In: CVPR (2021)
11. Liu, Y., Tian, Y., Chen, Y., Liu, F., Belagiannis, V., Carneiro, G.: Perturbed and strict mean teachers for semi-supervised semantic segmentation. In: CVPR (2022)
12. Ke, Z., Wang, D., Yan, Q., Ren, J., Lau, R.W.: Dual student: breaking the limits of the teacher in semi-supervised learning. In: ICCV (2019)
13. Ouali, Y., Hudelot, C., Tami, M.: Semi-supervised semantic segmentation with cross-consistency training. In: CVPR (2020)
14. Yu, L., Wang, S., Li, X., Fu, C.W., Heng, P.A.: Uncertainty-aware self-ensembling model for semi-supervised 3D left atrium segmentation. In: MICCAI (2019)
15. Wang, Y., et al.: Double-uncertainty weighted method for semi-supervised learning. In: MICCAI (2020)
16. Luo, X., Chen, J., Song, T., Wang, G.: Semi-supervised medical image segmentation through dual-task consistency. In: AAAI (2021)
17. Wu, Y., Xu, M., Ge, Z., Cai, J., Zhang, L.: Semi-supervised left atrium segmentation with mutual consistency training. In: MICCAI (2021)

18. Xia, Y., et al.: Uncertainty-aware multi-view co-training for semi-supervised medical image segmentation and domain adaptation. Med. Image Anal. **65**, 101766 (2020)
19. Lee, H., Jeong, W.K.: Scribble2label: Scribble-supervised cell segmentation via self-generating pseudo-labels with consistency. In: MICCAI (2020)
20. Zhang, K., Zhuang, X.: ShapePU: A new PU learning framework regularized by global consistency for scribble supervised cardiac segmentation. In: MICCAI (2022)
21. Zhou, Z.H., Li, M.: Tri-training: exploiting unlabeled data using three classifiers. Trans. Knowl. Data Eng. **17**, 1529–1541 (2005)
22. Zhao, A., Balakrishnan, G., Durand, F., Guttag, J.V., Dalca, A.V.: Data augmentation using learned transformations for one-shot medical image segmentation. In: CVPR (2019)
23. Wang, S., et al.: LT-Net: label transfer by learning reversible voxel-wise correspondence for one-shot medical image segmentation. In: CVPR (2020)
24. Tomar, D., Bozorgtabar, B., Lortkipanidze, M., Vray, G., Rad, M.S., Thiran, J.P.: Self-supervised generative style transfer for one-shot medical image segmentation. In: WACV (2022)
25. Lee, D.H., et al.: Pseudo-label: the simple and efficient semi-supervised learning method for deep neural networks. In: Workshop on Challenges in Representation Learning, ICML (2013)
26. Arazo, E., Ortego, D., Albert, P., O'Connor, N.E., McGuinness, K.: Pseudo-labeling and confirmation bias in deep semi-supervised learning. In: IJCNN (2020)
27. Berthelot, D., Carlini, N., Goodfellow, I., Papernot, N., Oliver, A., Raffel, C.A.: MixMatch: a holistic approach to semi-supervised learning. In: NeurIPS (2019)
28. Huang, T., Sun, Y., Wang, X., Yao, H., Zhang, C.: Spatial ensemble: a novel model smoothing mechanism for student-teacher framework. In: NeurIPS (2021)
29. Laine, S., Aila, T.: Temporal ensembling for semi-supervised learning. In: ICLR (2017)
30. Li, S., Zhang, C., He, X.: Shape-aware semi-supervised 3D semantic segmentation for medical images. In: MICCAI (2020)
31. Hang, W., et al.: Local and global structure-aware entropy regularized mean teacher model for 3D left atrium segmentation. In: MICCAI (2020)
32. Boykov, Y., Veksler, O., Zabih, R.: Fast approximate energy minimization via graph cuts. In: TPAMI, vol. 23 (2001)
33. Grady, L.: Random walks for image segmentation. In: TPAMI, vol. 28 (2006)
34. Lin, D., Dai, J., Jia, J., He, K., Sun, J.: ScribbleSup: scribble-supervised convolutional networks for semantic segmentation. In: CVPR (2016)
35. Bai, W., et al.: Recurrent neural networks for aortic image sequence segmentation with sparse annotations. In: MICCAI (2018)
36. Ji, Z., Shen, Y., Ma, C., Gao, M.: Scribble-based hierarchical weakly supervised learning for brain tumor segmentation. In: MICCAI (2019)
37. Tang, M., Perazzi, F., Djelouah, A., Ayed, I.B., Schroers, C., Boykov, Y.: On regularized losses for weakly-supervised CNN segmentation. In: Ferrari, V., Hebert, M., Sminchisescu, C., Weiss, Y. (eds.) ECCV 2018. LNCS, vol. 11220, pp. 524–540. Springer, Cham (2018). https://doi.org/10.1007/978-3-030-01270-0_31
38. Tang, M., Djelouah, A., Perazzi, F., Boykov, Y., Schroers, C.: Normalized cut loss for weakly-supervised CNN segmentation. In: CVPR (2018)
39. Liu, X., et al.: Weakly supervised segmentation of covid19 infection with scribble annotation on CT images. Pattern Recogn. **122**, 108341 (2022)
40. Cubuk, E.D., Zoph, B., Mane, D., Vasudevan, V., Le, Q.V.: AutoAugment: learning augmentation strategies from data. In: CVPR (2019)

41. Hataya, R., Zdenek, J., Yoshizoe, K., Nakayama, H.: Faster autoAugment: learning augmentation strategies using backpropagation. In: Vedaldi, A., Bischof, H., Brox, T., Frahm, J.-M. (eds.) ECCV 2020. LNCS, vol. 12370, pp. 1–16. Springer, Cham (2020). https://doi.org/10.1007/978-3-030-58595-2_1
42. Lin, C., et al.: Online hyper-parameter learning for auto-augmentation strategy. In: ICCV (2019)
43. Tian, K., Lin, C., Sun, M., Zhou, L., Yan, J., Ouyang, W.: Improving auto-augment via augmentation-wise weight sharing. In: NeurIPS (2020)
44. Zhang, H., Cissé, M., Dauphin, Y.N., Lopez-Paz, D.: mixup: beyond empirical risk minimization. In: ICLR (2018)
45. DeVries, T., Taylor, G.W.: Improved regularization of convolutional neural networks with cutout. arXiv (2017)
46. Yun, S., Han, D., Oh, S.J., Chun, S., Choe, J., Yoo, Y.: CutMix: regularization strategy to train strong classifiers with localizable features. In: ICCV (2019)
47. Kim, J., Choo, W., Jeong, H., Song, H.O.: Co-Mixup: Saliency guided joint mixup with supermodular diversity. In: ICLR (2021)
48. Verma, V., et al.: Manifold mixup: better representations by interpolating hidden states. In: ICML (2019)
49. Olsson, V., Tranheden, W., Pinto, J., Svensson, L.: ClassMix: segmentation-based data augmentation for semi-supervised learning. In: WACV (2021)
50. Kim, J.H., Choo, W., Song, H.O.: Puzzle mix: exploiting saliency and local statistics for optimal mixup. In: ICML (2020)
51. Blum, A., Mitchell, T.: Combining labeled and unlabeled data with co-training. In: COLT (1998)
52. Qiao, S., Shen, W., Zhang, Z., Wang, B., Yuille, A.: Deep co-training for semi-supervised image recognition. In: Ferrari, V., Hebert, M., Sminchisescu, C., Weiss, Y. (eds.) ECCV 2018. LNCS, vol. 11219, pp. 142–159. Springer, Cham (2018). https://doi.org/10.1007/978-3-030-01267-0_9
53. Peng, J., Estrada, G., Pedersoli, M., Desrosiers, C.: Deep co-training for semi-supervised image segmentation. Pattern Recogn. **107**, 107269 (2020)
54. Saito, K., Ushiku, Y., Harada, T.: Asymmetric tri-training for unsupervised domain adaptation. In: ICML (2017)
55. Chen, D.D., Wang, W., Gao, W., Zhou, Z.H.: Tri-net for semi-supervised deep learning. In: IJCAI (2018)
56. Zhang, T., Yu, L., Hu, N., Lv, S., Gu, S.: Robust medical image segmentation from non-expert annotations with tri-network. In: MICCAI (2020)
57. Yu, J., Yin, H., Gao, M., Xia, X., Zhang, X., Viet Hung, N.Q.: Socially-aware self-supervised tri-training for recommendation. In: KDD (2021)
58. Milletari, F., Navab, N., Ahmadi, S.: V-Net: Fully convolutional neural networks for volumetric medical image segmentation. In: 3DV (2016)
59. Bernard, O., et al.: Deep learning techniques for automatic MRI cardiac multi-structures segmentation and diagnosis: Is the problem solved? Trans. Med. Imaging **37**, 2514–2525 (2018)
60. Grandvalet, Y., Bengio, Y.: Semi-supervised learning by entropy minimization. In: NeurIPS (2004)
61. Zhuang, X.: Multivariate mixture model for myocardial segmentation combining multi-source images. In: TPAMI, vol. 41 (2018)
62. Ronneberger, O., Fischer, P., Brox, T.: U-Net: convolutional networks for biomedical image segmentation. In: MICCAI (2015)
63. Kim, B., Ye, J.C.: Mumford-shah loss functional for image segmentation with deep learning. Trans. Image Process. **29**, 1856–1866 (2019)

64. Lakshminarayanan, B., Pritzel, A., Blundell, C.: Simple and scalable predictive uncertainty estimation using deep ensembles. In: NeurIPS (2017)
65. Karimi, D., Dou, H., Warfield, S.K., Gholipour, A.: Deep learning with noisy labels: exploring techniques and remedies in medical image analysis. Med. Image Anal. **65**, 101759 (2020)
66. Grill, J.B., et al.: Bootstrap your own latent-a new approach to self-supervised learning. In: NeurIPS (2020)
67. Havasi, M., et al.: Training independent subnetworks for robust prediction. In: ICLR (2020)

Semi-supervised Breast Lesion Segmentation Using Local Cross Triplet Loss for Ultrafast Dynamic Contrast-Enhanced MRI

Young-tack Oh[1], Eunsook Ko[2(✉)], and Hyunjin Park[1,3(✉)]

[1] Sungkyunkwan University, Suwon, Republic of Korea
wpfl2034@g.skku.edu, hyunjinp@skku.edu
[2] Department of Radiology and Center for Imaging Science, Samsung Medical Center, Sungkyunkwan University School of Medicine, Seoul, Republic of Korea
mathilda0330@gmail.com
[3] Center for Neuroscience Imaging Research, Institute for Basic Science, Suwon, Republic of Korea

Abstract. Dynamic contrast-enhanced magnetic resonance imaging (DCE-MRI) and its fast variant, ultrafast DCE-MRI, are useful for the management of breast cancer. Segmentation of breast lesions is necessary for automatic clinical decision support. Despite the advantage of acquisition time, existing segmentation studies on ultrafast DCE-MRI are scarce, and they are mostly fully supervised studies with high annotation costs. Herein, we propose a semi-supervised segmentation approach that can be trained with small amounts of annotations for ultrafast DCE-MRI. A time difference map is proposed to incorporate the distinct time-varying enhancement pattern of the lesion. Furthermore, we present a novel loss function that efficiently distinguishes breast lesions from non-lesions based on triple loss. This loss reduces the potential false positives induced by the time difference map. Our approach is compared to that of five competing methods using the dice similarity coefficient and two boundary-based metrics. Compared to other models, our approach achieves better segmentation results using small amounts of annotations, especially for boundary-based metrics relevant to spatially continuous breast lesions. An ablation study demonstrates the incremental effects of our study. Our code is available on GitHub (https://github.com/yt-oh96/SSL-CTL).

Keywords: Semi-supervised segmentation · Tiplet loss · Ultrafast DCE-MRI

1 Introduction

Breast cancer is the most frequently diagnosed cancer in women and the main cause of cancer-related deaths [1]. Early detection of breast cancer can significantly lower mortality rates [2]. The importance of early detection has been

© The Author(s), under exclusive license to Springer Nature Switzerland AG 2023
L. Wang et al. (Eds.): ACCV 2022, LNCS 13846, pp. 203–217, 2023.
https://doi.org/10.1007/978-3-031-26351-4_13

widely recognized; therefore, breast cancer screening has led to better patient care [3,4]. Compared to commonly used mammography, dynamic contrast-enhanced magnetic resonance imaging (DCE-MRI) is increasingly being adopted owing to its higher sensitivity in dense breasts [5–7].

Breast DCE-MRI has many phases, including precontrast, early, and delayed phases. After contrast agent (CA) injection, each phase is recorded with a different delay time, up to a few minutes, from the initial CA injection to measure the distinct time-varying enhancement [8]. Each phase takes approximately 60-120 s to acquire. High-resolution T2 weighted and diffusion-weighted sequences have been routinely added for the complete MRI sequence. This leads to an increased scan time, ranging from 20 to 40 min [9]. Because a long scan time is associated with high cost, it is urgent to shorten the scan protocol for the widespread adoption of breast DCE-MRI [10–12].

Ultrafast DCE-MRI records an early inflow of CA and can obtain whole-breast images at several time points within 1 min after CA injection [13]. Conventional DCE-MRI is typically performed immediately after ultrafast sequencing. Within the first minute of ultrafast DCE-MRI, malignant breast lesions show altered patterns compared to that of benign tissue in terms of shorter enhancement, steeper maximum slope, and higher initial contrast ratio [14–17]. This implies that there could be lesion-differentiating information in ultrafast DCE-MRI.

Manual segmentation of breast lesions in DCE-MRI is troublesome; therefore, many computer-aided detection systems have been developed to automatically segment breast lesions [18,19]. These segmentation methods are increasingly adopting deep learning approaches [19,20]. There is limited literature on the application of deep learning methods for ultrafast DCE-MRI, possibly moving toward a short scan time for breast MRI imaging [5,19–21]. However, these methods are supervised learning approaches with high labeling costs.

In this study, we propose a semi-supervised segmentation method for breast lesions using ultrafast DCE-MRI with limited label data. In our method, we use a time difference map (TDM) to incorporate the distinct time-varying enhancement pattern of the lesion [21].Our TDM could locate enhanced regions, including the breast lesion, but could also enhance the blood vessel that receives the CA. To solve this problem, we introduce a distance-based learning approach of triplet loss to better contrast a lesion with a non-lesion area. Compared with various semi-supervised segmentation methods, our method can segment breast lesions well, even with a few labels. We obtained MRI data from 613 patients from Samsung Medical Center. Our method was evaluated using three metrics: dice similarity coefficient, average surface distance, and Hausdorff distance. The main contributions of our study are summarized as follows:

1. As labeled medical image data are difficult to obtain, we propose a semi-supervised segmentation method based on pseudo-labels.
2. We add TDM to explicitly model the distinct time-varying enhancement pattern of lesions.

3. We propose a local cross-triplet loss to discover the similarities and differences between breast lesions and non-lesion areas. This allows our model to focus on breast lesions with limited labeling data.

2   Related Work

Supervised Learning in DCE-MRI. Automatic segmentation technologies help with diagnosis and treatment planning tasks by reducing the time resources for manual annotation of breast cancer. In particular, deep learning algorithms show considerable potential and are gaining ground in breast imaging [22]. Several studies have proposed segmentation methods using conventional DCE-MRI. For example, Piantadosi et al. [23] proposed a fully automated breast lesion segmentation approach for breast DCE-MRI using 2D U-Net. Maicas et al. [24] used reinforcement learning to automatically detect breast lesions. Zhang et al. [25] proposed a breast mask to exclude confounding nearby structures and adopted two fully convolutional cascaded networks to detect breast lesions using the mask as a guideline. The aforementioned approaches worked well compared to those of the conventional machine learning approaches, they adopted conventional DCE-MRI with a long scan time.

Recently, the effectiveness of ultrafast DCE-MRI has been demonstrated [12–15], and studies using deep learning approaches in ultrafast DCE-MRI have been actively pursued. Ayatollahi et al. [19] detected breast lesions using spatial and temporal information obtained during the early stages of dynamic acquisition. Oh et al. [21] showed that ultrafast DCE-MRI could be used to generate conventional DCE-MRI, confirming the possibility of replacing conventional DCE-MRI with ultrafast DCE-MRI. These studies had shorter scan times for data acquisition than that of conventional DCE-MRI. However, because they adopted supervised learning, the labeling cost remained significant. Therefore, in this study, we propose a semi-supervised segmentation method using only a small amount of labeling data.

Semi-supervised Learning. Semi-supervised learning is widely used to reduce time-consuming and expensive manual pixel-level annotation [26,27].

Consistency regularization imposes a constraint on consistency between predictions with and without perturbations applied to inputs, features, and networks [28]. "Mean Teacher" [29] updates the model parameter values of the teacher model by the exponential moving average of the model parameter values of the student model. Based on "Mean Teacher" [29], "Uncertainty Aware Mean Teacher" [30] proposed a consistency loss such that learning proceeds only with reliable predictions using the uncertainty information of the teacher model.

Entropy minimization forces the classifier to make predictions with low entropy for an unlabeled input. This method assumes that the classifier's decision boundary does not traverse the dense area of the marginal data distribution [31]. "ADVENT" [32] proposed an entropy-based adversarial training strategy.

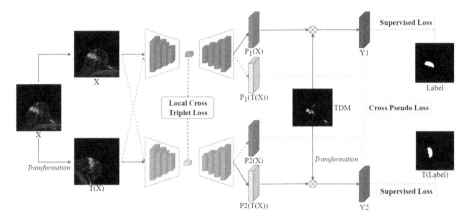

Fig. 1. An overview of the proposed method. The upstream model (purple) and downstream model (orange) receive both the original input (X) and transformed input $T(X)$. $P1$ and $P2$ are segmentation confidence maps derived from the two models. $Y1$ and $Y2$ are the final segmentation confidence maps with TDM applied. Flows corresponding to the blue dotted arrow for one model lead to pseudo-labels for the other model. The product sign means element-wise multiplication. (Color figure online)

"Pseudo-label" [33] implicitly performs entropy minimization because the intermediate prediction probability undergoes one-hot encoding [31]. The recently proposed "cross-pseudo supervision" [28] is a consistency regularization approach with perturbations of the network that provides input after different initializations for two networks of the same structure. For unannotated inputs, the pseudo-segmentation map of one network was utilized to supervise the other network. This can increase the number of annotated training data, resulting in more stable and accurate prediction results.

Our proposed model is based on "cross-pseudo supervision" [28] and introduces TDM and local cross-triplet loss to incorporate the time-varying enhancement pattern of ultrafast DCE-MRI and contrast lesions from non-lesions. Our model performs an input perturbation to enforce the consistency of the intermediate features. The proposed method achieves reliable segmentation with fewer annotations.

Deep Metric Learning. Deep metric learning maps an image to a feature vector in a manifold space through deep neural networks [34]. The mapped feature vector is trained using a distance function. Deep metric learning approaches typically optimize the loss functions defined on pairs or triplets of training examples [35]. The contrastive loss of pairs minimizes the distance from the feature vectors of the same class while ensuring the separation of the feature vectors of different classes [36]. Alternatively, triplet loss is defined based on three points: anchor point, positive point (i.e., a feature vector belonging to the same class as the anchor), and negative point (i.e., a feature vector belonging to a differ-

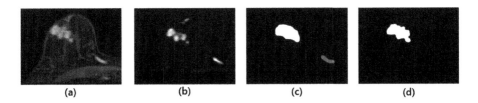

Fig. 2. Effects of time difference map (TDM). (a) Representative 1st phase image of ultrafast DCE-MRI. (b) TDM is computed as the difference between the last-phase image of ultrafast DCE-MRI and (a). (c) Example of the training result of "cross-pseudo supervision" (5% of the labeled data is used for training). This shows the focused regions for segmentation (white, cancer; red, vessel). (d) Ground truth. (Color figure online)

ent class than the anchor). This loss forces the distance of the positive pair to be smaller than that of the negative pair [37]. "CUT" [38], a recently proposed patch-based approach, defines negatives within the input image itself. This leads to efficient discrimination between the target and nontarget areas. Inspired by this method, we propose a local cross-triplet loss to discriminate breast lesions from non-lesions in the input image. This is discussed in detail in Sect. 3.2.

3   Methodology

This study aims to accurately segment breast cancer lesions with small annotation data based on pseudo-labels. First, TDM is defined to incorporate time-varying enhancement patterns in ultrafast DCE-MRI. Next, we discuss the drawbacks of TDM in our task, as well as the proposed loss terms to overcome the shortcomings using metric learning. An overview of the proposed method is shown in Fig. 1.

3.1   TDM

Ultrafast DCE-MRI has up to 20 phasic images, each taking 2-3 s, within 1 min after CA. Our ultrafast DCE-MRI sequence has 17 phases. We introduce the TDM to incorporate time-varying information. Lesions appear brighter than those in the normal regions of the breast. In general, as we traverse the time steps in the ultrafast sequence, the slope of the intensity change in the lesion is positive, while that in the normal region remains flat, close to zero. TDMs computed from consecutive phases or the averaged TDM are certainly possible, but for computational efficiency and the linear trend of enhancement, TDM is defined as the difference between the first and last (17th) phases in our ultrafast data following Oh et al. [21]. Our ultrafast DCE-MRI(V) are of dimension $H \times W \times D \times F\times$, where $D = 1$ and $F = 17$. Unlike color images, we have only one channel $D = 1$. TDM is defined as the difference between the last frame and the

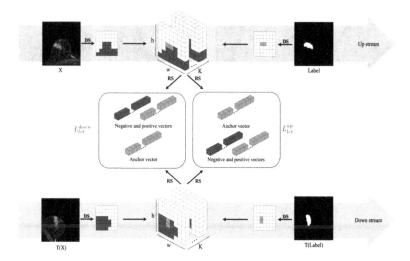

Fig. 3. Illustration of the proposed local cross-triplet loss. DS denotes downsampling, and RS denotes random spatial sampling. Anchor and positive points come from the positive group G_{pos} defined locally in the cancer region. Negative points come from the negative group G_{neg} defined locally in the non-cancer region. Cross-triplet comes from the loss defined across two streams. The loss is computed for each stream (M_{up}, M_{down}) and the two losses(L_{lct}^{up}, L_{lct}^{down}) are combined to obtain L_{lct}.

first frame. TDM can be obtained as follows:

$$V \in H \times W \times D \times F\times, D = 1, F = 17,$$
$$TDM = V[:,:,:,17] - V[:,:,:,1] \tag{1}$$

The TDM generated in this manner is multiplied by the prediction of the model so that the model could focus only on the enhanced regions, as shown in the final segmentation results (Fig. 1). However, the results show that the blood vessel region is enhanced in addition to the lesion (Fig. 2). This could be especially detrimental because our approach is limited to a small amount of label data. To overcome this problem, we propose a local cross-triplet loss.

3.2   Local-Cross Triplet Loss

Starting from D^l with N labeled images and D^u with M unlabeled images. our local cross-triplet loss L_{lct} is designed to avoid false detection in situations where there is a limited amount of label data available ($N <<< M$). The input image $X \in R^{H \times W}$, with height (H) and width (W), is mapped to anchor, positive, and negative points that are $h \times w$ K-dimensional vectors $\mathbf{z}, \mathbf{z}^+, \mathbf{z}^- \in R^K$ through the encoder of U-net [39] used as the backbone, where h,w are the height and width of the feature volume. respectively, We use h=7, w=7, K=256 for our setup.

The positive candidate group G_{pos} corresponding to the cancer region and the negative candidate group G_{neg} corresponding to the non-cancer region, are defined in the upstream model M_{up} and downstream model M_{down} of Fig. 3. G_{pos} is obtained by downsampling the given binary label mask to the size of the feature map. Similarly, G_{neg} can be obtained by downsampling the input image that contains the entire breast and others. However, background regions outside the breast lack the necessary information. Therefore, we set G_{neg} to exclude background and cancer regions (Fig. 3). Both groups are obtained from one given image, and thus, our design allows for effective local discrimination of breast lesions from non-lesions.

We adopt the local cross-triplet loss approach for both streams (M_{up} and M_{down}), The loss of M_{up} is as follows. "Locality" comes from how the triplet points are defined. Anchor and positive points come from the positive group G_{pos} defined locally in the cancer region. Negative points come from the negative group G_{neg} defined locally in the non-cancer region. "Cross-triplet" comes from the loss defined across two streams, where anchor points of one stream are compared with positive/negative points of the other stream. A K-dimensional vector $\mathbf{z}$ is chosen at random from G_{pos} of M_{up} to work as an anchor point and the K-dimensional vectors $\mathbf{z}^+$ and $\mathbf{z}^-$ are chosen at random from G_{pos} and G_{neg} of M_{down} to work as positive and negative points, respectively. Then, L_{lct}^{up} can be written as :

$$L_{lct}^{up}(\mathbf{z}, \mathbf{z}^+, \mathbf{z}^-) = -log[\frac{exp(\mathbf{z} \cdot \mathbf{z}^+/\tau)}{exp(\mathbf{z} \cdot \mathbf{z}^+/\tau) + exp(\mathbf{z} \cdot \mathbf{z}^-/\tau)}], \tag{2}$$

where τ is an important tuning parameter for supervised feature learning [38,40]. We set this value at 0.07, as in previous studies [38]. The loss for M_{down} can be calculated in the same manner as the loss for L_{lct}^{up}. We use the final L_{lct} obtained by combining L_{lct}^{up} and L_{lct}^{down} in the following manner.

$$L_{lct} = \frac{1}{2N} \left[\sum_{X \in D^l} L_{lct}^{up} + \sum_{X \in D^l} L_{lct}^{down} \right]. \tag{3}$$

3.3   Cross Pseudo Supervision Loss

In both labeled and unlabeled data, the loss for semantic segmentation consists of supervision loss L_s and cross-pseudo supervision loss L_{cps} [28]. Our models M_{up} and M_{down} for L_s use an original input image and a transformed input image as input, respectively. The segmentation confidence maps created in this manner are $P1(X)$ and $P2(T(X))$. The final segmentation confidence maps $Y1, Y2$ are created by applying the TDM and the transformed TDM introduced in Sect. 3.1. Standard pixel-wise cross-entropy for the confidence vectors $\mathbf{y}_{1i}, \mathbf{y}_{2i}$ at each i

position is as follows:

$$Y1 = P1(X) \odot TDM, y_{1i} \in Y1,$$
$$Y2 = P2(T(X)) \odot T(TDM), y_{2i} \in Y2,$$
$$L_s = \frac{1}{N} \sum_{X \in D^l} \frac{1}{H \times W} \sum_{i=0}^{H \times W} (l_{ce}(\mathbf{y}_{1i}, \mathbf{l}_{1i}))) + (l_{ce}(\mathbf{y}_{2i}, \mathbf{l}_{2i}))), \quad (4)$$

where T is the geometric transformation for the input perturbation, the circle dot is the element-wise multiplication, and $\mathbf{l}_{1i}$ and $\mathbf{l}_{2i}$ are one-hot vector corresponding to each pixel i of the ground truth $Label$, $T(Label)$.

The cross-pseudo supervision loss proposed in "cross-pseudo supervision" [28] is similar to the supervision loss above, but uses a pixel-wise one-hot label map created by the one-hot encoding of segmentation confidence maps from different stream models as the ground truth. The loss for the unlabeled data is as follows:

$$L_{cps}^u = \frac{1}{M} \sum_{X \in D^u} \frac{1}{H \times W} \sum_{i=0}^{H \times W} (l_{ce}(\mathbf{y}_{1i}, \mathbf{pl}_{2i}))) + (l_{ce}(\mathbf{y}_{2i}, \mathbf{pl}_{1i}))), \quad (5)$$

where $\mathbf{pl}_{1i}$, $\mathbf{pl}_{2i}$ are the hot vectors for each pixel i in a pixel-wise one-hot label map created using different stream models. Because pseudo supervision cannot access ground truth information, the addition of TDM might lead to focusing on unimportant regions, such as vessels, making the learning unstable. Therefore, we do not use the TDM when generating pseudo-supervision.

The cross-pseudo supervision loss L_{cps}^l for labeled data can be defined in the same manner. The cross-pseudo supervision loss for both labeled and unlabeled data is $L_{cps} = L_{cps}^u + L_{cps}^l$. The final objective function to which the trade-off weight λ is applied is as follows:

$$L = L_s + \lambda (L_{lct} + L_{cps}). \quad (6)$$

4   Experiments

4.1   Dataset

The institutional review board of Samsung Medical Center authorized this study, and the requirement for informed consent was waived. The total number of patients was 613, 500 as the training set, 50 as the validation set, and the remaining 63 as the test set. An expert manually segmented the breast lesions in the entire dataset. The following MRI protocol was used to acquire the imaging data. First, images of the precontrast phase were captured before CA injection. Following CA administration, ultrafast DCE-MRI images were collected for approximately 1 min, followed by conventional DCE-MRI images of the three phases recorded at 70 s intervals. There were three imaging acquisition settings available for ultrafast DCE-MRI, and the typical settings were as follows. The imaging

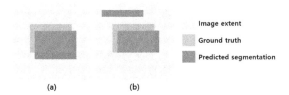

Fig. 4. Dice similarity coefficient (DSC) and its shortcomings. (a) and (b) have the same DSC, but (b) has two spatially disparate clusters that are inconsistent with the spatially continuous ground truth.

data were collected using a Philips 3T Ingenia CX scanner. Echo time, repetition time, and field-of-view were 2.1 ms, 4.1 ms, and 330×330 mm^2, respectively. In-plane resolution, slice thickness, and temporal resolution per phase were 1.0×1.0 mm, 1.0 mm, and 3.4 s, respectively. Because three settings were employed in the data collection process, $1.0 \times 1.0 \times 1.0$ resampling was used to unify them. Only images containing lesions were selected and further divided into left- and right-breast images by splitting them in half in the horizontal direction.

4.2   Implementation Details

To evaluate the effectiveness of the proposed approach, we compare ours with five models: 1) U-net [39]; 2) cross-pseudo supervision [28]; 3) mean teacher [29]; 4) uncertainty aware mean teacher [30]; and 5) entropy minimization [32]. The U-net is adopted to evaluate the fully supervised learning scenario, and the associated results using 100% labeled data represent the upper bound of our semi-supervised approach. All models, including ours, use a Vanilla U-net as their backbone. U-net-related codes are implemented using those proposed by Luo and Xiangde [41]. Our model is based on cross-pseudo supervision [28], which requires the application of geometric transforms to the input. Random rotation, flipping, and cropping are performed.

We train various models on four NVIDIA TITAN XP GPUs. For all experiments, the batch size is set to 24, and the maximum number of iterations is 15000. All codes are implemented using Pytorch1.8.0 and are available on GitHub [42].

4.3   Evaluation Metrics

We measure segmentation performance using three metrics: 1) dice similarity coefficient (DSC); 2) average surface distance (ASD); 3) Hausdorff distance (HD). DSC is the most representative metric based on the spatial overlap between the predictive segmentation and ground truth. However, it is insensitive to the spatial continuity of the segmentation results [43]. As shown in Fig. 4, one result is spatially continuous, while the other is spatially disparate. Both cases have the same DSCs, but the spatially continuous result is relevant

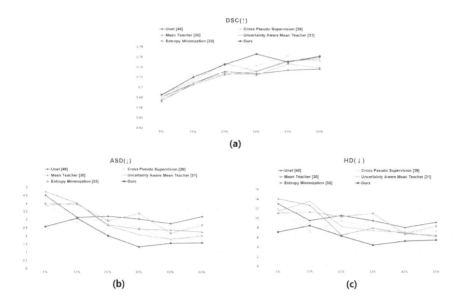

Fig. 5. Plots of segmentation performance metrics using varying portions (5%, 10%, 20%, 30%, 40%, and 50%) of labeled data. (a) Dice similarity coefficient (DSC). (b) Average surface distance (ASD). (c) Hausdorff distance (HD).

to the context of the breast lesion. Therefore, we further adopt the ASD and HD metrics based on the boundary distances. The ASD is the average of all distances from the point of the boundary of the predictive segmentation to that of the ground truth. HD is the maximum distance between a point in one of the two segmentation results and its nearest point in the other. Due to the spatially continuous nature of the breast lesion, it is important to have low ASD and HD, which penalize spatially disparate segmentation maps that are likely to be false positives.

4.4 Results

Figure 5 shows the performance metrics related to the increasing proportion of labeled data used for training. Because this study aims at an environment with limited labeled data, we show the results using up to 50% of the labeled data. As the proportion of labeled data approaches 100%, all models perform equally well, making the comparison pointless. DSCs are comparable among the methods; however, our model performs better than that of other methods for ASD and HD, which are more relevant for spatially continuous breast lesions.

We performed a 5-fold cross validation. Table 1 shows a detailed comparison of the models using 5% or 50% of the labeled data. Our model using 50% labeled data achieves a performance similar to that of the upper bound obtained from supervised U-net results using 100% labeled data. More importantly, our model

Table 1. Comparisons of a 5-fold cross validation performance between models using varying portions of labeled data. Values are given as mean (standard deviation) format. The supervised U-net results using 100% labeled data serve as the upper bound. CPS denotes cross-pseudo supervision [28], MT is the mean teacher [29], and UAMT is the uncertainty aware mean teacher [30].

Training	Model	Portion of labeled data	DSC(↑)	ASD(↓)	HD(↓)
Supervised	U-net [40]	5%	0.67923(±0.003)	5.06443(±0.535)	14.12663(±1.773)
		50%	0.74060(±0.008)	3.00268(±0.413)	8.74188(±0.889)
		100%	0.76279(±0.008)	2.09796(±0.389)	6.31361(±1.467)
Semi-supervised	CPS [29]	5%	0.68246(±0.01)	4.49830(±0.496)	12.59923(±0.755)
		50%	0.75389(±0.01)	2.01122(±0.348)	6.85415(±1.541)
	MT [30]	5%	0.67335(±0.01)	4.73847(±0.605)	12.74394(±1.652)
		50%	0.75394(±0.006)	2.14507(±0.061)	6.63480(±0.612)
	UAMT [31]	5%	**0.68503(±0.003)**	4.49306(±1.176)	12.23937(±2.481)
		50%	0.74427(±0.008)	2.53061(±0.391)	7.59957(±1.130)
	ADVENT [33]	5%	0.67719(±0.004)	4.93907(±0.686)	13.63126(±2.235)
		50%	0.74582(±0.006)	2.52074(±0.387)	7.82263(±1.191)
	Ours	5%	0.68412(±0.005)	**3.15440(±0.440)**	**8.60817(±0.947)**
		50%	**0.75422(±0.006)**	**1.80862(±0.167)**	**5.88411(±0.472)**

trained with only 5% of the labeling data shows similar performance in boundary-based metrics (ASD and HD) compared to the results of other models trained with 50% of the labeling data. This demonstrates that our proposed method does not detect false positives and segments spatially continuous breast lesions even with a small amount of labeling data.

Figure 6 shows representative segmentation results for various methods for different axial slices. All models use 5% of the labeled data. The U-net model uses 5% of the labeled data, while the others use 5% of the labeled data and 95% of the unlabeled data. Our method generally provides more accurate predictions than other comparative models. Furthermore, our model has fewer false positives, primarily due to enhanced blood vessels, and results in one spatially continuous cluster for the lesion. These results confirm that the loss terms of our approach are effective for the segmentation of breast lesions.

4.5   Ablation Study

An ablation study is conducted to demonstrate the incremental effects of the proposed contributions (Table 2). The cross-pseudo supervision model is used as the baseline model. 1) We apply TDM to incorporate the time-varying enhancement pattern of the lesion into the baseline model. DSC is improved because TDM can focus on enhanced regions (lesions and vessels), but the boundary distance-based metrics are not as favorable, possibly due to false positives owing to spatially disparate vessels. 2) This shortcoming of TDM is addressed with local cross-triplet loss, where spatially continuous lesions are explicitly encouraged. This results in improved performance for DSC, ASD, and HD. 3) In addition, we apply not only the network perturbation, but also the input perturbation by adopting geometric transformations, such as rotation, flipping, and cropping, to

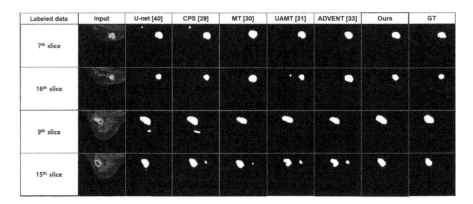

Fig. 6. Representative segmentation results for various models. All models use 5% of the labeled data. Rows 1 and 2 are different axial slice images from one patient. Rows 3 and 4 are the results for another patient.

better enforce the consistency of the intermediate features. Finally, the model to which all proposed techniques are applied shows good performance for all three metrics.

Table 2. Ablation study of the proposed method. The CPS denoting cross-pseudo supervision serves as the baseline, and the contributions of our approach are sequentially evaluated from top to bottom.

Model	Portion of labeled data	DSC($\uparrow$)	ASD($\downarrow$)	HD($\downarrow$)
CPS [29]	5%	0.68002	3.93187	11.90405
	50%	0.75182	2.0191	7.30482
+ TDM	5%	0.68121	4.84958	12.40415
	50%	**0.76322**	2.11603	7.07866
+ local-cross triplet loss	5%	0.68521	3.66874	9.49801
	50%	0.75707	2.02848	6.06029
+ **transformation (Ours)**	5%	**0.68560**	**2.57821**	**7.10232**
	50%	0.76240	**1.57659**	**5.48009**

5   Conclusion

As high-quality annotation is difficult to collect in the medical domain, an approach based on little or weak annotation is preferred. With only a small amount of annotation, we utilize the time-varying enhancement pattern of ultrafast DCE-MRI to segment breast lesions, and propose a loss to efficiently distinguish lesions from non-lesions. Our design allows the network to focus solely on breast lesions, reducing false positives using limited annotations. Compared to that of other models, our approach achieves significant qualitative and quantitative improvements. We plan to study a segmentation technique using a small number of weak annotations in the future. Rather than using TDM as self-attention, joint prediction across slices could be a more promising approach where the model can automatically figure out context by looking at consecutive slices.

Acknowledgments. This research was supported by the National Research Foundation (NRF-2020M3E5D2A01084892), Institute for Basic Science (IBSR015- D1), Ministry of Science and ICT (IITP-2020-2018-0-01798), AI Graduate School Support Program (2019-0-00421), ICT Creative Consilience program (IITP-2020-0-01821), and Artificial Intelligence Innovation Hub (2021-0-02068).

References

1. Sung, H., et al.: Global cancer statistics 2020: Globocan estimates of incidence and mortality worldwide for 36 cancers in 185 countries. CA Cancer J. Clinic. **71**, 209–249 (2021)
2. Maicas, G., Bradley, A.P., Nascimento, J.C., Reid, I., Carneiro, G.: Pre and post-hoc diagnosis and interpretation of malignancy from breast DCE-MRI. Med. Image Anal. **58**, 101562 (2019)
3. Lauby-Secretan, B., et al.: Breast-cancer screening-viewpoint of the IARC working group. N. Engl. J. Med. **372**, 2353–2358 (2015)
4. Morgan, M.B., Mates, J.L.: Applications of artificial intelligence in breast imaging. Radiol. Clinics **59**, 139–148 (2021)
5. Ayatollahi, F., Shokouhi, S.B., Mann, R.M., Teuwen, J.: Automatic breast lesion detection in ultrafast DCE-MRI using deep learning. Med. Phys. **48**, 5897–5907 (2021)
6. Gubern-Mérida, A., et al.: Automated localization of breast cancer in DCE-MRI. Med. Image Anal. **20**, 265–274 (2015)
7. Pisano, E.D., et al.: Diagnostic accuracy of digital versus film mammography: exploratory analysis of selected population subgroups in DMIST. Radiology **246**, 376 (2008)
8. Onishi, N., et al.: Ultrafast dynamic contrast-enhanced breast MRI may generate prognostic imaging markers of breast cancer. Breast Cancer Res. **22**, 1–13 (2020)
9. Mus, R.D., et al.: Time to enhancement derived from ultrafast breast MRI as a novel parameter to discriminate benign from malignant breast lesions. Eur. J. Radiol. **89**, 90–96 (2017)
10. Jing, X., Dorrius, M.D., Wielema, M., Sijens, P.E., Oudkerk, M., van Ooijen, P.: Breast tumor identification in ultrafast MRI using temporal and spatial information. Cancers **14**, 2042 (2022)
11. Kuhl, C.K.: A call for improved breast cancer screening strategies, not only for women with dense breasts. JAMA Netw. Open **4**, e2121492 (2021)
12. Mann, R.M., Kuhl, C.K., Moy, L.: Contrast-enhanced MRI for breast cancer screening. J. Magn. Reson. Imaging **50**, 377–390 (2019)
13. Abe, H., et al.: Kinetic analysis of benign and malignant breast lesions with ultrafast dynamic contrast-enhanced MRI: comparison with standard kinetic assessment. AJR Am. J. Roentgenol. **207**, 1159 (2016)
14. Kim, E.S., et al.: Added value of ultrafast sequence in abbreviated breast MRI surveillance in women with a personal history of breast cancer: a multireader study. Eur. J. Radiol. **151**, 110322 (2022)

15. Onishi, N., et al.: Differentiation between subcentimeter carcinomas and benign lesions using kinetic parameters derived from ultrafast dynamic contrast-enhanced breast MRI. Eur. Radiol. **30**, 756–766 (2020)
16. Honda, M., et al.: New parameters of ultrafast dynamic contrast-enhanced breast MRI using compressed sensing. J. Magn. Reson. Imaging **51**, 164–174 (2020)
17. Goto, M., et al.: Diagnostic performance of initial enhancement analysis using ultra-fast dynamic contrast-enhanced MRI for breast lesions. Eur. Radiol. **29**, 1164–1174 (2019)
18. Gubern-Mérida, A., et al.: Automated localization of breast cancer in DCE-MRI. Med. Image Anal. **20**, 265–274 (2015)
19. Ayatollahi, F., Shokouhi, S.B., Mann, R.M., Teuwen, J.: Automatic breast lesion detection in ultrafast DCE-MRI using deep learning. Med. Phys. **48**, 5897–5907 (2021)
20. Dalmis, M.U., et al.: Artificial intelligence-based classification of breast lesions imaged with a multiparametric breast MRI protocol with ultrafast DCE-MRI, t2, and DWI. Invest. Radiol. **54**, 325–332 (2019)
21. Oh, Y.T., Ko, E., Park, H.: TDM-stargan: Stargan using time difference map to generate dynamic contrast-enhanced MRI from ultrafast dynamic contrast-enhanced MRI. In: 2022 IEEE 19th International Symposium on Biomedical Imaging (ISBI), pp. 1–5. IEEE (2022)
22. Militello, C., et al.: Semi-automated and interactive segmentation of contrast-enhancing masses on breast DCE-MRI using spatial fuzzy clustering. Biomed. Signal Process. Control **71**, 103113 (2022)
23. Piantadosi, G., Sansone, M., Sansone, C.: Breast segmentation in MRI via U-Net deep convolutional neural networks. In: 2018 24th International Conference on Pattern Recognition (ICPR), pp. 3917–3922. IEEE (2018)
24. Maicas, G., Carneiro, G., Bradley, A.P., Nascimento, J.C., Reid, I.: Deep reinforcement learning for active breast lesion detection from DCE-MRI. In: Descoteaux, M., Maier-Hein, L., Franz, A., Jannin, P., Collins, D.L., Duchesne, S. (eds.) MICCAI 2017. LNCS, vol. 10435, pp. 665–673. Springer, Cham (2017). https://doi.org/10.1007/978-3-319-66179-7_76
25. Zhang, J., Saha, A., Zhu, Z., Mazurowski, M.A.: Hierarchical convolutional neural networks for segmentation of breast tumors in MRI with application to radiogenomics. IEEE Trans. Med. Imaging **38**, 435–447 (2018)
26. Van Engelen, J.E., Hoos, H.H.: A survey on semi-supervised learning. Mach. Learn. **109**, 373–440 (2020)
27. Cheplygina, V., de Bruijne, M., Pluim, J.P.: Not-so-supervised: a survey of semi-supervised, multi-instance, and transfer learning in medical image analysis. Med. Image Anal. **54**, 280–296 (2019)
28. Chen, X., Yuan, Y., Zeng, G., Wang, J.: Semi-supervised semantic segmentation with cross pseudo supervision. In: Proceedings of the IEEE/CVF Conference on Computer Vision and Pattern Recognition, pp. 2613–2622 (2021)
29. Tarvainen, A., Valpola, H.: Mean teachers are better role models: weight-averaged consistency targets improve semi-supervised deep learning results. In: Advances in Neural Information Processing Systems 30 (2017)
30. Yu, L., Wang, S., Li, X., Fu, C.-W., Heng, P.-A.: Uncertainty-aware self-ensembling model for semi-supervised 3D left atrium segmentation. In: Shen, D., et al. (eds.) MICCAI 2019. LNCS, vol. 11765, pp. 605–613. Springer, Cham (2019). https://doi.org/10.1007/978-3-030-32245-8_67

31. Berthelot, D., Carlini, N., Goodfellow, I., Papernot, N., Oliver, A., Raffel, C.A.: MixMatch: a holistic approach to semi-supervised learning. In: Advances in Neural Information Processing Systems 32 (2019)

32. Vu, T.H., Jain, H., Bucher, M., Cord, M., Pérez, P.: Advent: adversarial entropy minimization for domain adaptation in semantic segmentation. In: Proceedings of the IEEE/CVF Conference on Computer Vision and Pattern Recognition, pp. 2517–2526 (2019)

33. Lee, D.H., et al.: Pseudo-label: The simple and efficient semi-supervised learning method for deep neural networks. In: Workshop on Challenges in Representation Learning, vol. 3, pp. 896. ICML (2013)

34. Ge, W., Huang, W., Dong, D., Scott, M.R.: Deep metric learning with hierarchical triplet loss. In: Ferrari, V., Hebert, M., Sminchisescu, C., Weiss, Y. (eds.) ECCV 2018. LNCS, vol. 11210, pp. 272–288. Springer, Cham (2018). https://doi.org/10.1007/978-3-030-01231-1_17

35. Cakir, F., He, K., Xia, X., Kulis, B., Sclaroff, S.: Deep metric learning to rank. In: Proceedings of the IEEE/CVF Conference on Computer Vision and Pattern Recognition (CVPR) (2019)

36. Chopra, S., Hadsell, R., LeCun, Y.: Learning a similarity metric discriminatively, with application to face verification. In: 2005 IEEE Computer Society Conference on Computer Vision and Pattern Recognition (CVPR2005), vol. 1, pp. 539–546 (2005)

37. Do, T.T., Tran, T., Reid, I., Kumar, V., Hoang, T., Carneiro, G.: A theoretically sound upper bound on the triplet loss for improving the efficiency of deep distance metric learning. In: Proceedings of the IEEE/CVF Conference on Computer Vision and Pattern Recognition (CVPR) (2019)

38. Park, T., Efros, A.A., Zhang, R., Zhu, J.-Y.: Contrastive learning for unpaired image-to-image translation. In: Vedaldi, A., Bischof, H., Brox, T., Frahm, J.-M. (eds.) ECCV 2020. LNCS, vol. 12354, pp. 319–345. Springer, Cham (2020). https://doi.org/10.1007/978-3-030-58545-7_19

39. Ronneberger, O., Fischer, P., Brox, T.: U-Net: convolutional networks for biomedical image segmentation. In: Navab, N., Hornegger, J., Wells, W.M., Frangi, A.F. (eds.) MICCAI 2015. LNCS, vol. 9351, pp. 234–241. Springer, Cham (2015). https://doi.org/10.1007/978-3-319-24574-4_28

40. Wu, Z., Xiong, Y., Yu, S.X., Lin, D.: Unsupervised feature learning via non-parametric instance discrimination. In: Proceedings of the IEEE Conference on Computer Vision and Pattern Recognition (CVPR) (2018)

41. Luo, X.: SSL4MIS. https://github.com/HiLab-git/SSL4MIS (2020)

42. Oh, Y.T., Ko, E., Park, H.: SSL-CTL. https://github.com/yt-oh96/SSL-CTL (2022)

43. Yeghiazaryan, V., Voiculescu, I.D.: Family of boundary overlap metrics for the evaluation of medical image segmentation. J. Med. Imaging **5**, 1–19 (2018)

A Differentiable Distance Approximation for Fairer Image Classification

Nicholas Rosa[1]([✉])(iD), Tom Drummond[1,2](iD), and Mehrtash Harandi[1](iD)

[1] Monash University, Clayton, Australia
nicholas.rosa@monash.edu
[2] The University of Melbourne, Melbourne, Australia

Abstract. Naïvely trained AI models can be heavily biased. This can be particularly problematic when the biases involve legally or morally protected attributes such as ethnic background, age or gender. Existing solutions to this problem come at the cost of extra computation, unstable adversarial optimisation or have losses on the feature space structure that are disconnected from fairness measures and only loosely generalise to fairness. In this work we propose a differentiable approximation of the variance of demographics, a metric that can be used to measure the bias, or unfairness, in an AI model. Our approximation can be optimised alongside the regular training objective which eliminates the need for any extra models during training and directly improves the fairness of the regularised models. We demonstrate that our approach improves the fairness of AI models in varied task and dataset scenarios, whilst still maintaining a high level of classification accuracy. Code is available at https://bitbucket.org/nelliottrosa/base_fairness.

1 Introduction

In recent times, the use of Artificial Intelligence (AI) has permeated many processes that are used to make important decisions, such as filtering applicants for jobs, deciding if an applicant should receive credit and recognizing people in images [15,25]. Given this, it is essential to ensure that AI-driven models are not exhibiting behaviour which is morally or legally undesirable. In AI, data is a collection of attributes, which can either be explicit (*e.g.* labels) or implicit (*e.g.* information from an image). Some of these attributes are referred to as *protected* attributes as they should not be used to discriminate (*e.g.* gender, race or age). However, it has been shown numerous times that AI models which are naïvely trained are biased against one or more of these protected attributes, as they exhibit lower accuracy for some demographics [4,11,19]. This behaviour is discriminatory against these demographics and is *morally or legally undesirable*, or simply unfair. There are two common sources of unfair behaviour that can present itself in AI systems. The first source is biases that are present in

Supplementary Information The online version contains supplementary material available at https://doi.org/10.1007/978-3-031-26351-4_14.

the data used for training AI models. Biases in the data with respect to protected attributes can cause an AI model trained upon that data to discriminate against the protected attribute [2]. For example, if a dataset used to train a facial recognition model for unlocking doors, only contains images of men (*i.e.* bias with respect to gender) then the learned model will not accurately recognise and admit women (*i.e.* unfair behaviour). The second source of bias is due to some values or demographics of a protected attribute being inherently harder for AI to recognize than others. For example, it has been shown that even when training with a balanced dataset, faces with a darker skin tone are harder to recognize for facial recognition algorithms [28].

Various solutions to the fairness problem have been proposed. We focus on algorithmic in-processing methods for reducing the bias [5, 6, 8–10, 14, 29, 33]. In-processing aims to address the bias of a model by applying an extra objective during training which makes the model bias-aware and consequentially learns a fairer model. In-processing has proven to be quite effective at reducing the unfair behaviour of AI. However, in-processing methods often include extra models which can increase training cost and complexity [16]; use adversarial training [6, 8, 9, 33] which has proven to be notoriously unstable [24] or make assumptions about the representation space of the model which may not hold in all cases [10, 21, 32]. Creating fair AI models is particularly difficult in the computer vision domain as any problems with extra computational cost and complexity are exacerbated by the large models utilized. Additionally the high dimensionality of images means they can contain many implicit attributes, which are often highly correlated to each other and to protected attributes. Disentangling the implicit factors is extra challenging in these cases.

In this paper, we introduce **B**ias **A**ccuracy **S**tandard deviation **E**stimation or BASE, a novel fairness algorithm, which optimizes a differentiable approximation of the fairness metric *standard deviation of accuracy across demographics* (σ_{acc}) to learn an AI model which is fair with respect to *equalized odds* (EO). Models that exhibit a low standard deviation of accuracy across demographics or variance of demographics have the property of equal performance on a target task regardless of the demographic of the protected attribute. For example, a facial recognition model which has low variance of demographics for ethnicity, is equally likely to correctly recognize the identity of a person from an image regardless of their ethnicity. Reducing the variance of demographics of a model makes it fairer w.r.t. EO. However, for an AI model that is trained with gradient based optimization the variance of demographics is difficult to use. This is due to the accuracy of a single sample - an integral part of the variance of demographics (Sect. 2.3) - having an undefined gradient at 0 and being 0 everywhere else, which leads to zero influence on the model parameters. BASE overcomes this difficulty by instead using a sigmoid based approximation of accuracy which we call *soft-accuracy* inside the variance of demographics metric. This approach has multiple advantages. Firstly computational efficiency, for example, training a classifier on images with BASE incurs only the extra computation of calculating the variance of demographics. Compare this to training a classifier with knowledge distillation [16] or adversarial debiasing [33], where additional models are used which incur extra memory usage for the model parameters and gradients, alongside with extra computation for the forward pass of the additional model. Secondly, BASE makes no assumptions about the representation space. The model will automatically learn the representation space structure required to reduce the variance of demographics. Furthermore, due to its simplicity BASE can be combined with other solutions.

To summarize the main contributions of our work are:

- Provide a novel method for improving the fairness on AI models trained with gradient based optimization, that increases algorithmic simplicity and does not rely on training additional models (Sect. 3.1).
- Show that our method is competitive with and in some cases outperforms current state-of-the-art fair image classifiers when using either a biased dataset or an unbiased dataset (Sect. 4.4, Sect. 4.4).
- Show that our method increasingly outperforms the fairness of a naive classifier when exposed to increasingly biased training sets in which target and protected attributes are strongly correlated. Our method also achieves higher over-all accuracy on heavily biased datasets (Sect. 4.4).

2   Related Work and Preliminaries

Fair AI has received increasing attention in the past few years and a varied range of solutions has been proposed. Algorithmic methods for reducing the bias can be broken down into three main categories based upon when they apply their fairness constraint. *Pre*-processing methods aim to change the distribution of the data used for training such that a fairer model is produced. These methods include re-sampling, which changes the sampling rate of data during training to ensure each protected class is equally represented [1,23,26] and augmentation methods which add synthetic data to the dataset [3,22,31,34] to balance the protected classes. The second class of methods, *post*-processing methods, aim to adjust the prediction after the fact to compensate for the bias [30]. Pre-processing and post-processing have some major drawbacks. Pre-processing only addresses the bias in the dataset and the inherent difficulties of some demographics can still cause a biased model [28,29]. On the other hand post-processing methods require that protected attribute labels to be known at inference time or assume that the target and protected attribute are independent [30]. Our method is related to the final category of *in*-processing, which is discussed further below. In-processing methods typically run under a constrained optimization scheme where a loss penalty or a special construction of the AI model is used to reduce the bias during optimization.

2.1   In-processing for Fair Classification

Like many machine learning tasks, the fairness problem is difficult to optimize directly and adversarial training became a common method to create fair representations and predictors [6,8,9,29,33]. These methods use an adversarial model, or adversary, whose purpose is to learn the relationship between the predictor and the protected attribute. The output of the adversary is then used to enforce a fairness constraint upon the predictor. This is achieved either by gradient reversal of the adversary or by maximising the entropy of the adversaries predictions. If a strong adversary is unable to determine a relationship between the predictor and the protected attribute then fairness of the predictor can be guaranteed [33]

Other constrained optimization methods have been proposed and their approaches vary greatly. Gong *et al.* [10] minimize the variance of sample density across different demographics within the representation space. Cho *et al.* [5] use a kernel density estimate to approximate the conditional distributions used for measuring fairness in a differentiable manner. Hwang *et al.* [14] reduce the Wasserstein distance between protected groups within the representation space. Finally, in a work most similar to our own Shen *et al.* [27] use cross-entropy loss as a proxy for probability during training to optimise for fairness. Our method differs in two main aspects; our objective directly considers the two elements of the models output vector responsible for determining accuracy and we evaluate our work in the computer vision domain.

2.2   Problem Definition

The ultimate goal of fair machine learning is to create predictors which contain no bias. There is, however, many different forms of bias that can present themselves and as a consequence there are multiple different definitions of fairness. The three most common definitions are Demographic parity [33], Equalized Odds [12] and Equalized Opportunity [12]. In the following section A, $\hat{Y}$ and Y are random variables which represent the protected attribute, the output of a predictor and the true value of the target attribute respectively.

Demographic Parity. Demographic parity is the simplest form of fairness since it only considers the output of the predictor and the protected attribute. A predictor satisfies demographic parity when its output is independent of the protected attribute. That is $\forall a \in \mathcal{A}; \Pr(\hat{Y} = \hat{y} | A = a) = \Pr(\hat{Y} = \hat{y})$. However, this definition does not always allow for perfect classification [12]. If there is any correlation between the protected attribute and the target task then maintaining independence forces a reduction in performance. For example, if we learned a predictor for university admittance with age as a protected attribute, then achieving demographic parity would require our predictor to admit young children with the same probability as those who had just finished high school, regardless of each individuals suitability.

Equalized Odds. Equalized Odds is another definition of fairness that is more commonly applied for computer vision tasks. A predictor satisfies equalized odds when its output is conditionally independent of the protected attribute for all classes of the target class. That is $\forall y \in \mathcal{Y}, \forall a, a' \in \mathcal{A}, \Pr(\hat{Y} = y | A = a, Y = y) = \Pr(\hat{Y} = y | A = a', Y = y)$. This definition allows us to maintain performance as it is satisfied when a predictor achieves the same level of accuracy for each demographic of the protected attribute.

Equalized Opportunity. Equalized Opportunity is a special case of equalized odds for which there is a class of the target task $y_+ \in \mathcal{Y}$ that confers advantage, *e.g.*, to receive a loan or be hired for a job. It is a relaxation of equalized odds that is satisfied when the output of the predictor is conditionally independent of the protected attribute for only the advantageous class. That is $\forall a, a' \in \mathcal{A}, \Pr(\hat{Y} = y_+ | A = a, Y = y_+) = \Pr(\hat{Y} = y_+ | A = a', Y = y_+)$

Equalized odds and equalized opportunity are more practical definitions of fairness when applied to a computer vision problems because they still allow full predictive capability [12]. Further, since equalized opportunity is a relaxation of equalized odds, if equalized odds is achieved then equalized opportunity is also achieved. Therefore, in this work we aim to create predictors that satisfy equalized odds.

2.3   Distance Measures for Equalized Odds

Though the goal is to achieve true equalized odds, current methods are unable to achieve it [5,16,33]. Therefore, we need to use metrics to quantify how far a predictor is from true equalized odds. In this work we use three different metrics to measure the level of fairness of a predictor. The first two metrics use the difference in predictor output between different demographics of a protected attribute. This difference is called the *difference of equalized odds* (DEO).

$$\mathrm{DEO}(a, a', y) \triangleq \left| \Pr(\hat{Y} = y | A = a, Y = y) - \Pr(\hat{Y} = y | A = a', Y = y) \right| . \quad (1)$$

DEO can be directly used when the protected attribute is binary and can easily be extended for more demographics by aggregating DEO across the different target and protected attribute values. The methods used to aggregate DEO differ between various works in the literature. We use the aggregation methods from Jung *et al.* [16] who propose two different methods of aggregation, $\mathrm{DEO}_{\mathrm{max}}$ and $\mathrm{DEO}_{\mathrm{avg}}$ which are shown in Eqs.(2) and (3), respectively. $\mathrm{DEO}_{\mathrm{max}}$ can be used to understand the peak bias of an AI model and $\mathrm{DEO}_{\mathrm{avg}}$ can be used to understand the bias of a model in the majority of cases.

$$\mathrm{DEO}_{\mathrm{max}} \triangleq \max_{y}(\max_{a,a'}(\mathrm{DEO}(a, a', y))) . \quad (2)$$

$$\mathrm{DEO}_{\mathrm{avg}} \triangleq \frac{1}{|\mathcal{Y}|} \sum_{y}(\max_{a,a'}(\mathrm{DEO}(a, a', y))) . \quad (3)$$

Another fairness metric that is commonly reported, often in the Fair face recognition literature, is the standard deviation of accuracy across the demographics of the protected attribute, denoted by σ_{Acc}. This metric is shown in Eq. (5), where μ is the average accuracy across all the demographics. Note that

$\Pr(\hat{Y} = y | A = a)$ is equivalent to the accuracy of the predictor $\hat{Y}$ in the domain of demographic a.

$$\mu = \frac{1}{|\mathcal{A}|} \sum_{a \in \mathcal{A}} [\Pr(\hat{Y} = y | A = a)] \tag{4}$$

$$\sigma_{\text{Acc}} \triangleq \sqrt{\frac{1}{|\mathcal{A}|} \sum_{a} \left[\Pr(\hat{Y} = y | A = a) - \mu \right]^2} \tag{5}$$

All these metrics represent a distance from true equalized odds. In all cases this means that lower values indicate a fairer classifier.

3 Method

3.1 A Differentiable Approximation for Distance from Equalized Odds

The strategy used to train an AI model for classification uses a distance measure between the models output distribution and the true data distribution, referred to as the *loss* or *objective* function. Then a gradient optimization method is used to update the parameters of the model to reduce the distance measure. This is a simple but incredibly effective strategy. We aim to use the same strategy to increase the fairness of an AI model. We use $\sigma_{\text{Acc.}}$ as an objective function to reduce the distance from true EO.

In what follows, we use boldface fonts to denote vectors, *e.g.*, $\hat{\mathbf{y}} \in \hat{\mathcal{Y}}$ denotes the output vector of the model. We use $\hat{y}_t$ to show the element corresponding to the ground truth label y in $\hat{\mathbf{y}}$. Furthermore, $\hat{y}_m = \max(\hat{\mathbf{y}} \setminus \{\hat{y}_t\})$ represents the largest non ground truth element of $\hat{\mathbf{y}}$ and $\hat{\mathcal{Y}}_a$ represents the domain of demographic a for the protected attribute. Accuracy of a single sample $\hat{\mathbf{y}}$ is defined in Eq. (6).

$$\text{Acc}(\hat{y}_t, \hat{y}_m) \triangleq \begin{cases} 1 & \hat{y}_t > \hat{y}_m \\ 0 & \text{otherwise.} \end{cases} \tag{6}$$

In essence, if the element $\hat{y}_t$ is greater than all other elements, the model has correctly predicted the outcome for this sample and therefore, has an accuracy of one.

Since $\mathbb{E}_{\hat{\mathbf{y}} \sim \hat{\mathcal{Y}}_a}[\text{Acc}(\hat{y}_t, \hat{y}_m)] = \Pr(\hat{Y} = y | A = a)$, we substitute the expectation into Eqs. (4) and (5), which gives us Eqs. (7) and (8).

$$\mu = \frac{1}{|\mathcal{A}|} \sum_{a \in \mathcal{A}} \mathbb{E}_{\hat{\mathbf{y}} \sim \hat{\mathcal{Y}}_a}[\text{Acc}(\hat{y}_t, \hat{y}_m)] \tag{7}$$

$$\sigma_{\text{Acc}} = \sqrt{\frac{1}{|\mathcal{A}|} \sum_{a \in \mathcal{A}} \left[\mathbb{E}_{\hat{\mathbf{y}} \sim \hat{\mathcal{Y}}_a}[\text{Acc}(\hat{y}_t, \hat{y}_m)] - \mu \right]^2} \tag{8}$$

This is the objective we would like to optimize. However to be used for gradient based optimization that AI models are trained with an objective needs to be differentiable, which σ_{Acc} is not due to the undefined gradient at $\hat{y}_t = \hat{y}_m$ of $\mathrm{Acc}(\hat{y}_t, \hat{y}_m)$. Instead we approximate the accuracy using a sigmoid based soft accuracy function, shown in Eq. (9), which is a differentiable approximation of accuracy. The soft accuracy is characterised by κ, which is a hyper-parameter that describes the sharpness of the function. A higher value of κ leads to a closer approximation of accuracy with $\lim_{\kappa \to \infty} \mathrm{Acc_{soft}}(\hat{y}_t, \hat{y}_m) = \mathrm{Acc}(\hat{y}_t, \hat{y}_m)$, however this is paired with an increased sparsity of the gradient.

$$\mathrm{Acc_{soft}}(\hat{y}_t, \hat{y}_m) \triangleq \frac{1}{1 + e^{-\kappa(\hat{y}_t - \hat{y}_m)}} \tag{9}$$

We then substitute soft accuracy into σ_{Acc} for accuracy. This gives us the objective shown in Eq. (11).

$$\mu_{\mathrm{soft}} = \frac{1}{|\mathcal{A}|} \sum_{a \in \mathcal{A}} \mathbb{E}_{\hat{\mathbf{y}} \sim \hat{y}_a}[\mathrm{Acc_{soft}}(\hat{y}_t, \hat{y}_m)] \tag{10}$$

$$\sigma_{\mathrm{Acc_{soft}}} \triangleq \sqrt{\frac{1}{|\mathcal{A}|} \sum_{a \in \mathcal{A}} \left[\mathbb{E}_{\hat{\mathbf{y}} \sim \hat{y}_a}[\mathrm{Acc_{soft}}(\hat{y}_t, \hat{y}_m)] - \mu_{\mathrm{soft}}\right]^2} \tag{11}$$

This is the differentiable objective that we can optimize to obtain a fair predictor.

3.2   Training Objective

By itself the soft accuracy fairness objective does not learn to classify. In fact the easiest solution for a model to achieve equalized odds is to randomly classify each sample. Since it is important that the model still achieves high utility we combine the soft accuracy fairness objective with a cross entropy classification objective. This gives us the full objective which is shown in Eq. (12).

$$\mathcal{L} = \mathcal{L}_{\mathrm{ce}} + \gamma \sigma_{\mathrm{Acc_{soft}}} \tag{12}$$

The two losses, $\mathcal{L}_{ce}$ and $\sigma_{\mathrm{Acc_{soft}}}$, aim to achieve different objectives, which are classification performance and fairness respectively. Applying too much weight to one objective can harm the other. We use γ as a hyper-parameter to balance the utility of the model with the fairness. A higher value for γ will result in a fairer classifier, however at this can often come at the cost of classification performance. We experimentally determined the optimal value of γ for each dataset by performing a grid search. However, we observe an extensive search is not required and finding the correct order of magnitude results in good performance.

3.3   Balancing the Training Dataset

When calculating $\sigma_{\text{Acc}_{\text{soft}}}$ on a mini-batch the number of samples used to estimate the soft accuracy for each protected demographic is highly important. If
the number of samples for a particular demographic is too low then the variance
of the soft accuracy estimation will increase. Differences in variance between
the different demographics lead to instability of training gradients which has a
negative impact on performance. To counter this effect we simply oversample
the training dataset set such that each protected, target attribute pair is evenly
sampled. This is achieved by randomly duplicating samples from the undersampled pairs until all protected, target attribute pairs contain the same number of
samples. There exist more sophisticated methods [22,31] which could be used to
augment the training dataset and their use may lead to gains in performance.
However, we leave this investigation to future work.

4   Experiments

In the following section we thoroughly investigate and validate the capability of
our soft accuracy fairness objective.

4.1   Baselines

We compare our algorithm with four different baselines. The first is a naïve
classifier that is not aware of fairness in any regard. This baseline represents the
worst case scenario for fairness. Since one source of bias is an unbalanced dataset
we also include a naïve classifier which is trained by oversampling the dataset
such that it is balanced. We refer to this baseline as *Naïve Balanced*. The third
baseline is Adversarial Debiasing (AD) [33] which is used as a common benchmark method and the final baseline is the state-of-the-art in-processing method,
MFD [16]. The original MFD paper only provided results for the age task with
the UTKFace dataset. Additionally, the original MFD paper only implemented
a simple data augmentation scheme. We employed further data augmentations
which allowed our naïve classifier to achieve a much higher accuracy (74.7%
vs 83.1%). In the spirit of fair comparison, we apply their method code with
our datasets and augmentation scheme, this allows MFD to achieve comparable accuracy. Where applicable, results from the original paper are reported as
MFD$^{\diamond}$. Similarly, AD was originally implemented on non computer vision tasks,
we re-implement AD for evaluation on CV tasks. For both re-implementations
we perform a sweep of the bias loss hyper-parameter, discard hyper-parameter
choices that lead to a large reduction in accuracy and report the best results.

4.2   Datasets

We use three datasets for our experiments. UTKFace [17], CelebA [20] and Fairface [18]. UTKFace and CelebA are face image datasets commonly used to benchmark fairness. UTKFACE contains 20k samples with annotations of age, gender

and ethnicity. CelebA contains 200k images which are labelled with 40 binary attributes. The images from UTKFace and CelebA cover a large variation in position, facial expression, illumination, occlusion and resolution. Buolamwini and Gebru [4] note that collecting a balanced dataset should be the first step in a fairness solution. Therefore it is important that we also evaluate our method under these conditions, for which we use the Fairface dataset. Fairface is also a face image dataset. It contains 98k images with annotations of age, gender and ethnicity. Fairface was created in an effort to reduce racial bias in existing datasets and had a strong focus on reducing the imbalance of races in the dataset during its creation. As shown in Fig. 1, compared to UTKFace, the race labels in Fairface are much more balanced. Using these UTKFace, CelebA and Fairface we evaluate two scenarios. Where a task is trained with a balanced dataset and where the task is trained with a biased dataset. UTKFace provides the age labels as integers, instead of learning a regression problem we group ages together into classes. To allow comparison we follow the division used by Jung *et al.* [16] where ages are divided into three classes, less than 20, 20–39 and greater than 40. Fairface provides age labels in classes already, however they are heavily imbalanced with far fewer samples in the extreme young and old classes. To maintain Fairface as a balanced test set we divide the ages in four new classes to balance them. These four classes are 0–19, 20–29, 30–39 and 40+.

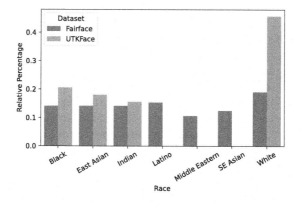

Fig. 1. The relative distribution of different races in the UTKFace dataset and Fairface dataset. UTKFace labels both East Asian and South East Asian faces together so these are shown under East Asian.

Skewed Fairface. Since it is imperative to understand how the performance of a fairness algorithm is related to the bias of a dataset, we present a protocol for controlling the bias within a dataset. We apply this protocol to Fairface to create a dataset which we name Fairface Skewed (FairfaceS). FairfaceS is characterised by a skew parameter (s) which can range from 0 to 1. The skew parameter describes the relative distribution of (target, protected) attribute pairs where a higher skew parameter leads to a dataset with a higher correlation between the target attribute and the protected attribute. The relative distribution is calculated by arranging the classes into a 2D array. Two diagonal corners are assigned the value of 1 and the other two diagonal corners are assigned the value of $1 - s$. Bilinear interpolation is then used to calculate the remaining values of the matrix. An example of the relative distribution for different skews is shown in Fig. 2. Fairface is then under-sampled such that the relative distribution of each (target, protected) pair matches that in the matrix. This protocol imposes an order on the class however, in the absence of a rigorous similarity metric between separate demographics and target attribute values we simply order the classes alphabetically.

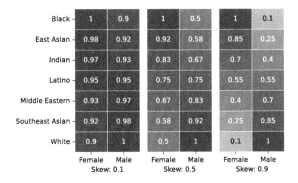

Fig. 2. The relative distribution of (protected, target) pairs in the FairfaceS dataset for different skew values.

As the skew value increases the mutual information between the protected attribute and the target attribute increases leading to an increase in the bias. Using FairfaceS allows us to evaluate how a fairness algorithm performs under varying degrees of dataset bias. Additionally, because FairfaceS uses genuine attributes that can be linked in complicated manners, rather than creating a bias with respect to augmentations such as grayscaling an image, it allows for greater understanding of how a system may behave in a real-world scenario.

Balanced Test Set and Triplicate Experiments. When evaluating the fairness of a model it is important that the test set have a uniform distribution of (protected, target) pairs. If a particular pair is undersampled or oversampled it will have a disproportionate impact on the results, e.g. if the White, Male pair is more prevalent in the test set then the accuracy on this pair will affect the average accuracy more. To ensure that our results do not include any bias toward a particular label pair we select samples for the test set such that each protected, target label pair is included in equal numbers. We also observed that whilst the target classification performance is stable over different training and test splits, the fairness varies by a large degree. To ensure robust results we perform our experiments on three different train test splits and report the mean and standard deviation. The exception is our experiments with CelebA, for which we use the official train, validation, and test sets as this allows us to compare to previous work. The results for CelebA are reported over three different random initializations.

4.3   Implementation Details

For all experiments we use a Resnet18 [13]. For experiments on UTKFace, Fairface and FairfaceS models are initialised from weights that were pretrained on Imagenet-1k [7]. Models in the CelebA experiments are randomly initialised. More details about the exact training procedure can be found in the supplementary material. MFD and AD are implemented according to their original papers. However, we follow Jung *et al.* [16] and remove the gradient projection from the original work to increase stability of training.

4.4   Classification Tasks

In this section we investigate the performance of our method on two tasks, age and gender classification.

Unbalanced Data. First we test the scenario in which the training data from the task is not balanced. This is the case for the majority of AI tasks unless special care has been taken during the creation of the dataset. For this experiment, we use the UTKFace and CelebA datasets. For UTKFace we use *race* as the protected attribute and test both age and gender as target attributes. For CelebA we use the *Male* attribute as the protected attribute and *Attractive* as the target attribute. The results are shown in Tables 1, 2 and 3, respectively. In both UTKFace scenarios all fairness methods improve fairness over a naïve classifier. The age classification task in harder than gender and is also much less fair, with the naïve classifier only achieving a σ_{Acc} of 8.5 compared to 3.0 for the gender task. In the highly unfair scenario with age as the target attribute, we observe that BASE achieves the best fairness for σ_{Acc} and DEO_{avg}, whilst achieving the highest over-all accuracy. It is only outperformed on DEO_{max} by MFD$^\diamond$ which does so with at a significantly lower over-all accuracy. Whilst the data for the gender task is still unbalanced, we observe that the naïve classifier can already achieve a better level of fairness leading us to believe this is a fairer task. For this task, BASE is competitive and achieves the second best accuracy and fairness. MFD achieves the greater fairness, however, this comes at the expense of a lower over-all accuracy. In the CelebA scenario BASE achieves the highest performance in all metrics. Again the fairness of the naï classifier is low for this scenario, showing that the CelebA task is unfair. These experiments show that BASE works best in an environment that is particularly unfair.

Table 1. Comparison of methods on UTKFace dataset with age as the target variable. Best results are **bold** and second best are <u>underline</u>. Results marked $\diamond$ are reported directly from [16].

Method	Acc. $\uparrow$	$\sigma_{\text{Acc}} \downarrow$	$\text{DEO}_{\text{max}} \downarrow$	$\text{DEO}_{\text{avg}} \downarrow$
Naïve Classifier	82.5 ± 1.5	8.8 ± 1.2	45.3 ± 2.5	25.8 ± 1.3
Naïve Classifier Balanced	83.3 ± 1.1	8.7 ± 1.3	43.4 ± 3.8	21.9 ± 2.2
MFD$^{\diamond}$ [16]	74.7 ± 0.7	-	$\mathbf{28.5 \pm 1.8}$	$\underline{17.8 \pm 1.4}$
MFD [16]	83.4 ± 0.5	$\underline{6.6 \pm 1.3}$	32.3 ± 3.5	18.3 ± 2.0
AD [33]	$\underline{83.6 \pm 1.4}$	7.3 ± 1.4	41.0 ± 5.6	21.2 ± 3.9
BASE *ours*	$\mathbf{83.8 \pm 0.6}$	$\mathbf{5.6 \pm 0.7}$	$\underline{29.0 \pm 2.6}$	$\mathbf{16.0 \pm 1.3}$

Table 2. Comparison of methods on UTKFace dataset with gender as the target variable. Best results are **bold** and second best are <u>underline</u>.

Method	Acc. $\uparrow$	$\sigma_{\text{Acc.}} \downarrow$	$\text{DEO}_{\text{max}} \downarrow$	$\text{DEO}_{\text{avg}} \downarrow$
Naïve Classifier	93.1 ± 0.7	2.8 ± 0.3	10.3 ± 3.2	7.2 ± 0.8
Naïve Classifier Balanced	$\underline{93.5 \pm 0.9}$	2.8 ± 0.6	10.0 ± 1.5	7.2 ± 1.3
MFD [16]	92.4 ± 0.4	$\mathbf{2.1 \pm 0.4}$	$\mathbf{8.0 \pm 1.0}$	$\mathbf{5.7 \pm 0.6}$
AD [33]	$\mathbf{93.9 \pm 1.1}$	2.6 ± 0.9	$\mathbf{8.0 \pm 2.6}$	6.2 ± 2.0
BASE *ours*	93.4 ± 0.3	$\underline{2.3 \pm 0.9}$	$\underline{9.0 \pm 1.0}$	6.2 ± 0.8

Table 3. Comparison of methods on CelebA dataset with attractive as the target variable. Best results are **bold** and second best are <u>underline</u>. Results marked $\diamond$ are reported directly from [21].

Method	Acc. $\uparrow$	$\sigma_{\text{Acc}} \downarrow$	$\text{DEO}_{\text{max}} \downarrow$	$\text{DEO}_{\text{avg}} \downarrow$
Naïve Classifier	79.6 ± 0.2	3.0 ± 3.5	26.3 ± 0.4	25.9 ± 0.6
Naïve Classifier Balanced	$\underline{80.1 \pm 0.2}$	$\underline{1.1 \pm 0.3}$	$\underline{3.5 \pm 0.4}$	2.1 ± 0.4
MFD$^{\diamond}$ [16]	78 ± 0.3	–	–	7.4 ± 0.3
FSCL$^{\diamond}$ [21]	79.1 ± 0.4	–	–	11.5 ± 0.3
FSCL+$^{\diamond}$ [21]	79.1 ± 0.4	–	–	6.5 ± 0.4
BASE *ours*	$\mathbf{80.7 \pm 0.1}$	$\mathbf{0.8 \pm 0.2}$	$\mathbf{3.0 \pm 0.7}$	$\mathbf{1.9 \pm 0.5}$

Balanced Data. Next, we test the scenario in which the training data for the task has been collected with a focus on ensuring that it is balanced with respect to the protected attribute. For this experiment, we use the Fairface dataset and *race* as the protected attribute. For the classification target attribute we test both age and gender. The results are shown in Tables 4 and 5, respectively.

In these two scenarios, we observe that the fairness of the naïve classifier is already high due to the balanced nature of the data. For both target attributes, the naïve classifier with balanced sampling achieves the best fairness for two

Table 4. Comparison of methods on Fairface dataset with age as the target variable. Best results are **bold** and second best are underline.

Method	Acc. ↑	$\sigma_{\text{Acc.}}$ ↓	DEO_{max} ↓	DEO_{avg} ↓
Naïve Classifier	67.4 ± 0.2	2.1 ± 0.5	23.6 ± 4.3	16.2 ± 0.4
Naïve Classifier Balanced	66.2 ± 0.4	$\mathbf{1.9 \pm 0.4}$	$\mathbf{12.4 \pm 0.8}$	$\mathbf{10.3 \pm 0.2}$
MFD [16]	$\underline{68.3 \pm 0.3}$	$\mathbf{1.9 \pm 0.2}$	14.6 ± 0.9	10.6 ± 1.4
AD [33]	$\mathbf{68.4 \pm 0.2}$	2.2 ± 0.2	21.3 ± 0.5	15.7 ± 0.9
BASE *ours*	$\mathbf{68.4 \pm 0.4}$	$\underline{2.0 \pm 0.04}$	14.8 ± 0.5	10.8 ± 1.2

Table 5. Comparison of methods on Fairface dataset with gender as the target variable. Best results are **bold** and second best are underline.

Method	Acc. ↑	$\sigma_{\text{Acc.}}$ ↓	DEO_{max} ↓	DEO_{avg} ↓
Naïve Classifier	93.4 ± 0.05	2.0 ± 1.6	7.5 ± 1.7	$\mathbf{6.3 \pm 0.8}$
Naïve Classifier Balanced	$\mathbf{93.6 \pm 0.05}$	1.9 ± 0.2	6.9 ± 0.3	$\underline{6.4 \pm 0.3}$
MFD [16]	93.4 ± 0.1	2.2 ± 0.05	7.7 ± 1.1	7.0 ± 0.4
AD [33]	$\mathbf{93.6 \pm 0.2}$	2.1 ± 0.1	7.3 ± 0.6	6.7 ± 0.4
BASE *ours*	$\underline{93.5 \pm 0.02}$	2.0 ± 0.1	7.0 ± 0.6	$\underline{6.4 \pm 0.4}$

of the three metrics. However, this comes at the cost of accuracy for the age task. For both tasks BASE achieves the second best results for $\sigma_{\text{Acc.}}$, with equal highest overall accuracy in the age task and the second best overall accuracy for the gender task.

Biased Data. Finally, we investigate how out method performs with an increasingly biased dataset. For this experiment we use the FairfaceS dataset (Sect. 4.2) with gender as the target variable. We evaluate a naïve classifier and BASE over a range of different skew parameters and observe the effect on accuracy and fairness. The results are shown in Fig. 3.

We observe that, as one would expect, as the skew increases and consequentially the bias in the dataset increases both accuracy and fairness decay for both methods. Additionally, at low levels of bias, whilst BASE is able to increase the fairness of the classifier in all metrics, this comes at the cost of overall accuracy compared to the naïve classifier. However, as the skew increases the accuracy of the naïve classifier decays at a greater rate than BASE. At extreme skew levels, BASE is even able to achieve a higher degree of overall accuracy. The same results can be seen with the fairness metrics. With the performance of the naïve classifier decaying at a higher rate than BASE. Even though BASE produces a more fair predictor at low skew levels, the performance gap only increases as the skew increases.

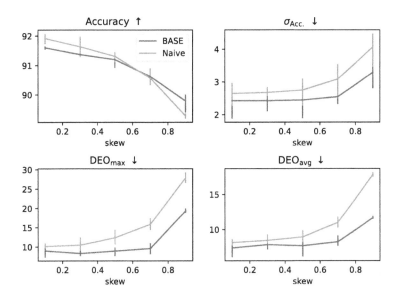

Fig. 3. The accuracy and fairness of a Naïve classifier and BASE over different skew parameters of the FairfaceS dataset. Error bars are the 95% confidence interval over 3-fold cross-validation.

5   Conclusion

In this work, we introduce a new fairness objective based upon optimising the standard deviation of soft accuracy across demographics of a protected attribute. Experimental results on UTKFace, CelebA, Fairface and FairfaceS show that our system is able to produce fairer AI models for computer vision tasks under widely varying conditions whilst being particular effective for more unfair scenarios and can even improve the overall accuracy compared to a naive model in heavily biased data-sets.

References

1. Amini, A., Soleimany, A.P., Schwarting, W., Bhatia, S.N., Rus, D.: Uncovering and mitigating algorithmic bias through learned latent structure. In: Proceedings of the 2019 AAAI/ACM Conference on AI, Ethics, and Society. AIES 2019, Honolulu, HI, USA, pp. 289–295. Association for Computing Machinery, New York (2019). https://doi.org/10.1145/3306618.3314243
2. Beutel, A., Chi, E.H., Chen, J., Zhao, Z.: Data decisions and theoretical implications when adversarially learning fair representations. In: FAT/ML (2017). https://arxiv.org/pdf/1707.00075.pdf

3. van Breugel, B., Kyono, T., Berrevoets, J., van der Schaar, M.: DECAF: generating fair synthetic data using causally-aware generative networks. In: Ranzato, M., Beygelzimer, A., Dauphin, Y., Liang, P.S., Vaughan, J.W. (eds.) Advances in Neural Information Processing Systems, vol. 34, pp. 22221–22233. Curran Associates, Inc. (2021). https://proceedings.neurips.cc/paper/2021/file/ba9fab001f67381e56e410575874d967-Paper.pdf

4. Buolamwini, J., Gebru, T.: Gender shades: intersectional accuracy disparities in commercial gender classification. In: Friedler, S.A., Wilson, C. (eds.) Proceedings of the 1st Conference on Fairness, Accountability and Transparency. Proceedings of Machine Learning Research, vol. 81, pp. 77–91. PMLR, February 2018. https://proceedings.mlr.press/v81/buolamwini18a.html

5. Cho, J., Hwang, G., Suh, C.: A fair classifier using kernel density estimation. In: Larochelle, H., Ranzato, M., Hadsell, R., Balcan, M.F., Lin, H. (eds.) Advances in Neural Information Processing Systems, vol. 33, pp. 15088–15099. Curran Associates, Inc. (2020). https://proceedings.neurips.cc/paper/2020/file/ac3870fcad1cfc367825cda0101eee62-Paper.pdf

6. Creager, E., et al.: Flexibly fair representation learning by disentanglement. In: Chaudhuri, K., Salakhutdinov, R. (eds.) Proceedings of the 36th International Conference on Machine Learning. Proceedings of Machine Learning Research, vol. 97, pp. 1436–1445. PMLR, Long Beach, California, USA, June 2019. http://proceedings.mlr.press/v97/creager19a.html

7. Deng, J., Dong, W., Socher, R., Li, L.J., Li, K., Fei-Fei, L.: Imagenet: a large-scale hierarchical image database. In: 2009 IEEE Conference on Computer Vision and Pattern Recognition, pp. 248–255. IEEE (2009)

8. Dhar, P., Gleason, J., Roy, A., Castillo, C.D., Chellappa, R.: PASS: protected attribute suppression system for mitigating bias in face recognition. In: Proceedings of the IEEE/CVF International Conference on Computer Vision (ICCV), pp. 15087–15096, October 2021

9. Gong, S., Liu, X., Jain, A.K.: Jointly de-biasing face recognition and demographic attribute estimation. In: Vedaldi, A., Bischof, H., Brox, T., Frahm, J.-M. (eds.) ECCV 2020. LNCS, vol. 12374, pp. 330–347. Springer, Cham (2020). https://doi.org/10.1007/978-3-030-58526-6_20

10. Gong, S., Liu, X., Jain, A.K.: Mitigating face recognition bias via group adaptive classifier. In: 2021 IEEE/CVF Conference on Computer Vision and Pattern Recognition (CVPR), pp. 3413–3423. IEEE, Nashville, June 2021. https://doi.org/10.1109/CVPR46437.2021.00342, https://ieeexplore.ieee.org/document/9577411/

11. Grother, P., Ngan, M., Hanaoka, K.: Face recognition vendor test part 3: demographic effects, December 2019. https://doi.org/10.6028/NIST.IR.8280

12. Hardt, M., Price, E., Price, E., Srebro, N.: Equality of opportunity in supervised learning. In: Lee, D., Sugiyama, M., Luxburg, U., Guyon, I., Garnett, R. (eds.) Advances in Neural Information Processing Systems, vol. 29. Curran Associates, Inc. (2016). https://proceedings.neurips.cc/paper/2016/file/9d2682367c3935defcb1f9e247a97c0d-Paper.pdf

13. He, K., Zhang, X., Ren, S., Sun, J.: Deep residual learning for image recognition. In: Proceedings of the IEEE Conference on Computer Vision and Pattern Recognition (CVPR), June 2016

14. Hwang, S., Park, S., Lee, P., Jeon, S., Kim, D., Byun, H.: Exploiting transferable knowledge for fairness-aware image classification. In: Ishikawa, H., Liu, C.-L., Pajdla, T., Shi, J. (eds.) ACCV 2020. LNCS, vol. 12625, pp. 19–35. Springer, Cham (2021). https://doi.org/10.1007/978-3-030-69538-5_2

15. Joseph, M., Kearns, M., Morgenstern, J.H., Roth, A.: Fairness in learning: classic and contextual bandits. In: Lee, D.D., Sugiyama, M., Luxburg, U.V., Guyon, I., Garnett, R. (eds.) Advances in Neural Information Processing Systems, vol. 29, pp. 325–333. Curran Associates, Inc. (2016). http://papers.nips.cc/paper/6355-fairness-in-learning-classic-and-contextual-bandits.pdf
16. Jung, S., Lee, D., Park, T., Moon, T.: Fair feature distillation for visual recognition. In: 2021 IEEE/CVF Conference on Computer Vision and Pattern Recognition (CVPR), pp. 12110–12119. IEEE, Nashville, June 2021. https://doi.org/10.1109/CVPR46437.2021.01194, https://ieeexplore.ieee.org/document/9578197/
17. Kamiran, F., Calders, T.: Classifying without discriminating. In: 2009 2nd International Conference on Computer, Control and Communication, pp. 1–6 (2009). https://doi.org/10.1109/IC4.2009.4909197
18. Karkkainen, K., Joo, J.: FairFace: face attribute dataset for balanced race, gender, and age for bias measurement and mitigation. In: Proceedings of the IEEE/CVF Winter Conference on Applications of Computer Vision, pp. 1548–1558 (2021)
19. Klare, B.F., Burge, M.J., Klontz, J.C., Vorder Bruegge, R.W., Jain, A.K.: Face recognition performance: role of demographic information. IEEE Trans. Inf. Forensics Secur. **7**(6), 1789–1801 (2012). https://doi.org/10.1109/TIFS.2012.2214212
20. Liu, Z., Luo, P., Wang, X., Tang, X.: Deep learning face attributes in the wild. In: Proceedings of International Conference on Computer Vision (ICCV), December 2015
21. Park, S., Lee, J., Lee, P., Hwang, S., Kim, D., Byun, H.: Fair contrastive learning for facial attribute classification. In: Proceedings of the IEEE/CVF Conference on Computer Vision and Pattern Recognition (CVPR), pp. 10389–10398, June 2022
22. Ramaswamy, V.V., Kim, S.S.Y., Russakovsky, O.: Fair attribute classification through latent space de-biasing. In: 2021 IEEE/CVF Conference on Computer Vision and Pattern Recognition (CVPR), pp. 9297–9306. IEEE, Nashville, June 2021. https://doi.org/10.1109/CVPR46437.2021.00918, https://ieeexplore.ieee.org/document/9578650/
23. Roh, Y., Lee, K., Whang, S.E., Suh, C.: FairBatch: batch selection for model fairness. In: ICLR (2021). https://openreview.net/forum?id=YNnpaAKeCfx
24. Roth, K., Lucchi, A., Nowozin, S., Hofmann, T.: Stabilizing training of generative adversarial networks through regularization. In: Guyon, I., et al. (eds.) Advances in Neural Information Processing Systems., vol. 30. Curran Associates, Inc. (2017). https://proceedings.neurips.cc/paper/2017/file/7bccfde7714a1ebadf06c5f4cea752c1-Paper.pdf
25. Schroff, F., Kalenichenko, D., Philbin, J.: FaceNet: a unified embedding for face recognition and clustering. In: 2015 IEEE Conference on Computer Vision and Pattern Recognition (CVPR), pp. 815–823 (2015). https://doi.org/10.1109/CVPR.2015.7298682
26. Shekhar, S., Fields, G., Ghavamzadeh, M., Javidi, T.: Adaptive sampling for minimax fair classification. In: Ranzato, M., Beygelzimer, A., Dauphin, Y., Liang, P.S., Vaughan, J.W. (eds.) Advances in Neural Information Processing Systems, vol. 34, pp. 24535–24544. Curran Associates, Inc. (2021). https://proceedings.neurips.cc/paper/2021/file/cd7c230fc5deb01ff5f7b1be1acef9cf-Paper.pdf
27. Shen, A., Han, X., Cohn, T., Baldwin, T., Frermann, L.: Optimising equal opportunity fairness in model training (2022). https://doi.org/10.48550/ARXIV.2205.02393, https://arxiv.org/abs/2205.02393

28. Wang, M., Deng, W.: Mitigating bias in face recognition using skewness-aware reinforcement learning. In: 2020 IEEE/CVF Conference on Computer Vision and Pattern Recognition (CVPR), pp. 9319–9328. IEEE, Seattle, June 2020. https://doi.org/10.1109/CVPR42600.2020.00934, https://ieeexplore.ieee.org/document/9156925/

29. Wang, T., Zhao, J., Yatskar, M., Chang, K.W., Ordonez, V.: Balanced datasets are not enough: estimating and mitigating gender bias in deep image representations. In: Proceedings of the IEEE/CVF International Conference on Computer Vision (ICCV), October 2019

30. Wang, Z., et al.: Towards fairness in visual recognition: effective strategies for bias mitigation. In: Proceedings of the IEEE/CVF Conference on Computer Vision and Pattern Recognition (CVPR), June 2020

31. Xu, D., Yuan, S., Zhang, L., Wu, X.: FairGAN: fairness-aware generative adversarial networks. In: 2018 IEEE International Conference on Big Data (Big Data), pp. 570–575 (2018). https://doi.org/10.1109/BigData.2018.8622525

32. Xu, X., et al.: Consistent instance false positive improves fairness in face recognition. In: Proceedings of the IEEE/CVF Conference on Computer Vision and Pattern Recognition (CVPR), pp. 578–586, June 2021

33. Zhang, B.H., Lemoine, B., Mitchell, M.: Mitigating unwanted biases with adversarial learning. In: Proceedings of the 2018 AAAI/ACM Conference on AI, Ethics, and Society, AIES '18, New Orleans, LA, USA, pp. 335–340. Association for Computing Machinery, New York (2018). https://doi.org/10.1145/3278721.3278779

34. Zietlow, D., et al.: Leveling down in computer vision: pareto inefficiencies in fair deep classifiers. In: Proceedings of the IEEE/CVF Conference on Computer Vision and Pattern Recognition (CVPR), pp. 10410–10421, June 2022

Class Concentration with Twin Variational Autoencoders for Unsupervised Cross-Modal Hashing

Yang Zhao[1], Yazhou Zhu[1], Shengbin Liao[2], Qiaolin Ye[3],
and Haofeng Zhang[1(✉)]

[1] School of Computer Science and Engineering, Nanjing University of Science and
Technology, Nanjing 210094, China
{zhao_yang,zyz_nj,zhanghf}@njust.edu.cn
[2] National Engineering Research Center for E-learning, Huazhong Normal
University, Wuhan 430079, China
[3] School of Information Science and Technology, Nanjing Forestry University,
Nanjing 210037, China

Abstract. Multi-modal deep hash learning is arguably one of the most commonly used unsupervised methods in cross-modal retrieval tasks. Most existing deep hashing methods focus on maintaining similarity information in the hash code learning step. Although accurate and compact binary representations are learned, these methods fail to encourage discriminative learning of features. In this paper, we propose a new method called Class Concentrated Variational auto-encoder (CCTV) to learn discriminative hash codes. The novelty of CCTV lies in two aspects. First, the proposed method focuses on the concentration of the mean vector of latent features. Based on the assumption that the features in the shared latent space produce multivariate Gaussian, CCTV updates the mean vectors and the cluster centroids of the latent features at the same time by minimizing the class concentration loss, so as to narrow the distance between the cluster centroids and the mean vectors, and further make the concentration more compact. Secondly, under the constraint of raw similarity information, CCTV is different from previous works, it uses the mean vector of latent features as the representation of the images to reduce the influence of variance, and then embeds them in the Hamming space. Our experimental evaluation on four multimedia benchmarks shows a significant improvement over the state-of-the-art methods. Code is available at: https://github.com/theusernamealreadyexists/CCTV.

Keywords: Cross-modal hashing · Visual-text retrieval · Class concentration · Twin variational autoencoder

1 Introduction

The past decades have witnessed the rapid growth of different types of contents on the Internet. The same events or objects can be described as diverse kinds of

L. Wang et al. (Eds.): ACCV 2022, LNCS 13846, pp. 235–251, 2023.
https://doi.org/10.1007/978-3-031-26351-4_15

data which can be referred as multi-modal data with heterogeneous properties. Huge volumes of these multi-modal data affects people's need for information and the ways they search on the Internet. One of the most popular tasks is cross-modal information retrieval, which aims to search relevant data of other different modalities with query data. For instance, using a caption to retrieve the related pictures in database.

Nowadays, cross-modal retrieval has attracted growing attention from researchers. The most difficult problem of cross-modal retrieval is how to measure the similarity between different modal features of data, which is known as heterogeneity gap. In order to support similarity relationship search, it is necessary to map the incomparable data into comparable features. Hence, learning representations for multi-modal data is considered as the fundamental step to extract features of various modalities. As proposed in [24], the main research effort is to design compact and accurate representations. During the learning process of representations modelling, the features of various modalities are mapped to so-called common latent embedding space, where the features of same object or event are pulled together and those of different objects or events are pushed away on the Euclidean distance basis. The challenge of learning accurate representation lays in deciding the correlation between two modalities. Intuitively, the learned feature is explicitly encouraged to maximize intra-class compactness and inter-class separability. What's more, the key problem for compactness, which makes the stage of representation succinct, is dependent on the dimension and discreteness of multi-modal features.

Hashing technology, which encodes continuous real-valued features into latent hash space, where relative samples have similar binary codes, is widely used in cross-modal retrieval due to its few storage, low Hamming distance computational complexity and fast retrieval speed. Motivated by hashing technology, [7,17,46,47] incorporate deep learning with hashing method and learn accurate and compact representations for multi-modal information. These methods have a common module called two-stream network which designs two networks for visual and textual data respectively. Supervised approaches [1,2,18,23,26,28,29,36,39,42] intuitively can perform better than unsupervised methods due to the constraint of labelled information in training step. However, labelled information is expansive and further limited in real world large scale retrieval application right now. Thus, it is realistic to pay attention to unsupervised hashing algorithms.

To date, pairwise similarity based unsupervised cross-modal hashing (UCMH) methods can achieve better performance than those methods directly embeds high-dimension feature into Hamming space, they preserve pairwise information to construct similarity constraint. Some of these approaches preserve the similarity information through graph structure [10,38,43,51]. Although these related works achieve breakthrough, there still exists two main problems in this task. Firstly, dense graph that basically contains pre-defined local neighbourhood information in a mini-batch get much redundant information, which means most of the graph neighbourhoods are useless and mislead the neighbour-

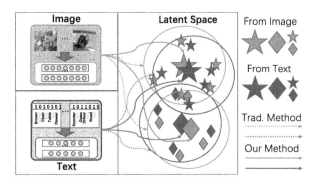

Fig. 1. Illustration of the difference between our method and traditional methods. Traditional methods try to project images and text directly into latent space, while our method projects them into their corresponding class centroids in latent space.

hood relationship in common Hamming space and consequently learn redundant hash codes, for example in Fig. 1, previous methods tries to directly map the features into latent or hamming space, where the variance of the features make the embeddings hard to separate. Secondly, previous methods fail to model the posterior distribution of the observed data and only adopt similarity information during training.

In light of these issues, we propose a novel unsupervised cross-modal hashing method called Class Concentration with Twin Variational autoencoders (CCTV). We train twin Variational Auto-Encoders (VAEs) models to encode and decode visual and textual modal features respectively. The given multi-modal data produces a distribution over the possible values of the latent features, and we directly concentrate the mean of the latent features with Deep Embedded Clustering (DEC) [44] method for updating the clustering centers and mapping at the same time. We align the distribution of two modalities by enforcing the mean of multi-modal data from the same cluster to produce the same posterior distribution. Consequently, by explicitly enforcing both the distribution of arithmetic mean of latent features and the distance between data point and each clustering center, the objects of same construction share the matched inter-modal distribution in common latent space, which generates much more accurate latent representation. Then we train a deep network to learn binary codes of latent features and minimize the reconstruction loss to learn compact representation. In general, our main contributions are as follows:

- We propose a novel deep learning framework that learns compact and accurate hash representation of multi-modal information via twin VAE models, which creatively align the mean vectors of each modality in latent space. This operation can circumvent the interference by the variances from the different features although in a same class.
- We approximate the intractable true distributions of inter-class and intra-class for class construction and jointly optimize the deep feature embedding and mean vector clustering.

– we have conducted extensive experiments on four popular datasets, and the results show that our method can achieve state-of-the-art performance.

2   Related Works

Due to its low computational complexity and fast retrieval speed, cross-modal hashing has attracted an increasing attention. It aims to mine the relationship between visual and textual modalities and embed data into common Hamming space. Similar to real-valued alternatives [5,16,30,52], cross-modal hashing methods can be also simply categorized into supervised methods [13,18,23,28,29,36,39]. and unsupervised methods. Since our method focuses on the unsupervised one, we only briefly introduce some related unsupervised methods in the following.

A large amount of unsupervised cross-modal hashing [12,13,21,34,43,48,51] have been proposed in the past few years. The earlier shallow schemes, *e.g.*, both Cross-view hashing (CVH) [20] and Inter-Media Hashing (IMH) [37], can be regarded as the extension of Spectral Hashing [41] from single-modal hashing to cross-modal hashing scenario. These methods learn hash functions by solving the eigenvalue decomposition with constructed similarity graph. Zhai *et al.* [49] presented the parametric local multi-modal hashing (PLMH), which designs a set of hashing function to generate several hashing space and accesses to non-linear global transformation. Ding *et al.* [8] employed matrix factorization methods and proposed Collective Matrix Factorization Hashing (CMFH), which bridges the modality gap by embedding different modal information into a latent common space. Zhou *et al.* designed Latent Semantic Sparse Hashing (LSSH) that extends CMFH in the manner of utilizing sparse coding in extracting latent feature process at the same time and restricts hash code learning subsequently. However, above shallow methods are week to extract the non-linear relevant information from different modalities for using hand-crafted features. As the progress of deep neural networks have made in exploring non-linear relationships, many methods [7,17,46,47] capture more semantic relevant features during binary code learning process. Most of them utilize similarity graphs generated from intrinsic data directly and obtain superior performances. Wang *et al.* [40] added an orthogonal regularizer to make the representation compact and accurate. [11] utilizes the adaptive tanh function which has concise derivation and can be used in objective function directly. [43] makes use of the matrix factorization with Laplacian constraint in training process to constraint the hash code generation, which consequently preserves the neighbour affinity information of original features in their own space.

Though impressive progress has been made by these models, there are still a few challenges to be solved that are mentioned in Sect. 1. In this paper, we focus on improving the retrieval performance of unsupervised deep cross-modal hashing. With the intention to model the posterior distribution of the observed data from both visual and textual modalities, we concentrate the mean of the latent

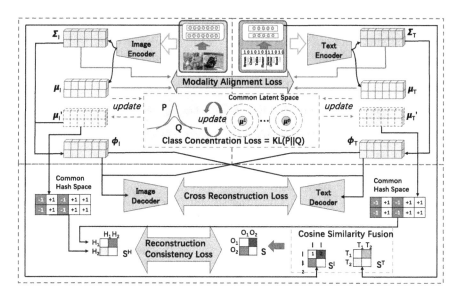

Fig. 2. The architecture of the proposed CCTV. The twin variational auto-encoder project both image and text into a common latent space, where the embeddings are aligned by their mean vectors and class discriminative information is raised by class concentration loss. Cross reconstruction and cross consistency are employed to constrain images and texts to have both their own semantic information and the semantic information of each other.

features with DEC clustering method which optimize the clustering centers iteratively, which tackles the problem of lacking label information and subsequently generate accurate representations.

3 Methodology

3.1 Preliminaries

We first introduce several definitions in our methods. With n equals to the amount of instances in each batch, the visual and textual features in each batch are denoted as $\boldsymbol{X}_I \in \mathbb{R}^{n \times d_I}$ and $\boldsymbol{X}_T \in \mathbb{R}^{n \times d_T}$ respectively. Here d_I and d_T represent the dimensions of image and caption features respectively. Furthermore, we aim to generate binary hash codes $\boldsymbol{B}_I$ and $\boldsymbol{B}_T$ by embedding continuous features into common latent hash space, where $\boldsymbol{B}_H \in \mathbb{R}^{n \times b}, (H \in \{I, T\})$ and b means hash code length. If two objects o_1 and o_2 are semantic similar, the hash codes generated by their features should be within a small Hamming distance.

Modelling the posterior distribution of the observed data can improves the performance of retrieval task. However, the lacking of labelled information before generating binary codes is not conducive to the construction of a prior constraints. Previous methods can be grouped into two categories in terms of how to conduct feature embedding. The first category methods, such as [49], preserve the affinity information of original features and use them to learn hash codes directly. They share the following common quantification loss function:

$$
\begin{aligned}
\mathcal{L}_q &= \|f_I(\boldsymbol{I}) - \boldsymbol{B}_I\|_F^2 + \|f_T(\boldsymbol{T}) - \boldsymbol{B}_T\|_F^2, \\
s.t. \boldsymbol{B}_H &\in \{+1, -1\}^{m \times l}, \boldsymbol{B}_H^T \boldsymbol{B}_H = m\boldsymbol{I},
\end{aligned}
\tag{1}
$$

where $f_I(\cdot)$ and $f_T(\cdot)$ are the embedding functions for visual and textual data respectively and $H \in \{I, T\}$. Equation (1) aims to reduce the gap between features and hash codes. The auxiliary constraint $\boldsymbol{B}_g^T \boldsymbol{B}_g = m\boldsymbol{I}$ aims to generate mutually independent hash codes.

Evolved from the first category, the second type of methods, such as [35], typically generate clustering centers with the method of deep clustering in common latent space, and further update the latent embedding. Both the design of construing matrices and the strategy of employing the matrices in training stage have an impact on the final performance. To be specific, the loss functions of these algorithms (optimizing objectives) are typically composed of two parts: $\mathcal{L}_q$ and clustering loss $\mathcal{L}_c$, the loss function can be formulated as follows:

$$
\mathcal{L} = \lambda \mathcal{L}_q + (1 - \lambda)\mathcal{L}_c, \quad s.t. \lambda \in [0, 1],
\tag{2}
$$

where λ is a hype-parameter to balance $\mathcal{L}_q$ and $\mathcal{L}_c$.

The goal of our model is to learn accurate and compact binary representations in a shared latent Hamming space for a combination of two modalities data. The basic module of CCTV is the VAE [19], which introduces a recognition model $q_\phi(\boldsymbol{z}|\boldsymbol{x})$ that is an approximation to the true posterior $P_\theta(\boldsymbol{z}|\boldsymbol{x})$, where $\boldsymbol{x}$ means original data point and $\boldsymbol{z}$ is the unobserved latent variable and produces the prior distribution. VAE approximates the prior over the latent variables to be the multivariate Gaussian $P_\theta(\boldsymbol{z}) = \mathcal{N}(\boldsymbol{z}; \boldsymbol{0}, \boldsymbol{I})$ and let the variational approximate posterior also be a multivariate Gaussian:

$$
\log q_\phi(\boldsymbol{z}|\boldsymbol{x}) = log\mathcal{N}(\boldsymbol{z}; \boldsymbol{\mu}, \boldsymbol{\sigma}^2 \boldsymbol{I}),
\tag{3}
$$

where $\boldsymbol{\mu}$ and $\boldsymbol{\sigma}$ is the mean and standard deviation of the approximate posterior, respectively.

From the perspective of coding theory, they are generated by non-linear encoder. Furthermore, the latent variable $\boldsymbol{z}$ is sampled using $\boldsymbol{z} = \boldsymbol{\mu} + \boldsymbol{\sigma} \odot \boldsymbol{\epsilon}$, where $\boldsymbol{\epsilon} \sim \mathcal{N}(\boldsymbol{0}, \boldsymbol{I})$ is an auxiliary variable with independent margin and $\odot$ means element-wise product. To learn the recognition model parameters ϕ and generative the model parameters θ simultaneously, the estimator can be written as:

$$
\mathcal{L}(\boldsymbol{\theta}, \boldsymbol{\phi}; \boldsymbol{x}) = D_{KL}(q_\phi(\boldsymbol{z}|\boldsymbol{x}) \| p_{\theta(\boldsymbol{z})}) - \mathbb{E}_{q_\phi(\boldsymbol{z}|\boldsymbol{x})}[log p_\theta(\boldsymbol{x}|\boldsymbol{z})],
\tag{4}
$$

where the first item is the Kullback-Leibler (KL) divergence between intractable true posterior and its approximation, and the second item is the lower bound on the marginal likelihood of data point.

3.2   Proposed Architecture

The overall pipeline of CCTV is shown in Fig. 2. We design a twin-VAE model to learn the conditional probability distributions over the latent variables, $q_{\phi_I}(z|x_I)$ for visual features and $q_{\phi_T}(z|x_T)$ for textual features using approximate posteriors, $q_{\theta_I}(z|x_I)$ and $q_{\theta_T}(z|x_T)$. The embeddings of data points from different modalities are supposed to share a common latent space.

Cross Reconstruction (CR) Loss. To minimize the information gap between the original data and latent feature in each modal, the twin-VAE reconstruction loss should include two single VAE (SV) loss for each modality:

$$\mathcal{L}_{SV} = \sum_{H \in \{I,T\}} D_{KL}(q_{\phi_H}(z|x_H)\|p_{\theta_H(z)}) - \mathbb{E}_{q_{\phi_H}(z|x_H)}[log p_{\theta_H}(x_H|z)], \quad (5)$$

where x_H means a specific original feature in X_H.

In addition to using single modal information reconstruction loss to constrain the latent space embedding process of data, it is also necessary to consider the alignment between different-modal data. That means using the modality-specific recognition model to approximate the true posterior in another modality. To be specific, the cross VAE (CV) loss is formulated as following:

$$\begin{aligned}\mathcal{L}_{CV} =& D_{KL}(q_{\phi_I}(z|x_I)\|p_{\theta_T(z)}) - \mathbb{E}_{q_{\phi_I}(z|x_I)}[log p_{\theta_T}(x_T|z)] \\ &+ D_{KL}(q_{\phi_T}(z|x_T)\|p_{\theta_I(z)}) - \mathbb{E}_{q_{\phi_T}(z|x_T)}[log p_{\theta_I}(x_I|z)].\end{aligned} \quad (6)$$

In the view of coding theory, the unobserved variables z is represented as a code with specific length. Given several data samples, they produce a possible distribution over the possible latent variables. Thus, same as VAE [19], we refer to the true conditional probability distributions over the latent variables, $q_{\phi_I}(z|x_I)$ and $q_{\phi_T}(z|x_T)$, as encoders and realize $q_{\theta_I}(z|x_I)$ and $q_{\theta_T}(z|x_T)$ with decoders. Since given an unobserved variable, it generates a corresponding distribution over the value of original data point. Here we combines the aforementioned object loss function and term them as cross reconstruction (CR) loss:

$$\mathcal{L}_{CR} = \mathcal{L}_{SV} + \mathcal{L}_{CV}. \quad (7)$$

Class Concentration (CC) Loss. Only reducing information loss can not generate discriminative latent representation. Thus, we propose a class concentration loss function. From the perspective of metric learning, after specifying the distance metric method, high-quality clustering results should narrow the gaps within the classes, and widen the gaps between the classes. This phenomenon shows that the data in each cluster has its own unique distribution. However, earlier deep unsupervised methods directly cluster data and did not consider the prior and posterior distribution of the data. Suppose that latent variables produce centered isotropic multivariate Gaussian distributions [19], we consider that each cluster refer to a unique Gaussian. Accordingly, the latent features in a cluster should share the same mean μ which has an interpretation as a vector.

Thus, the proposed method (CCTV) clusters the mean vectors $\{\boldsymbol{\mu}_i\}_{i=1}^n$ of latent features in order to generate latent features which are compact within a class and scattered between classes. For n latent points $\{\boldsymbol{z}_i\}_{i=1}^n$ with k clusters $\{\boldsymbol{c}_j\}_{j=1}^k$ in latent space, we are supposed to learn k clustering centers and update θ_I and θ_T, which are encoder learning parameters in an end-to-end fashion. To achieve this goal, we utilize the auxiliary target distribution mentioned in DEC [44]. The construction can be described in two steps. First, we assign a distribution for measuring the distance between mean vector of latent feature $\boldsymbol{\mu}_i$ and cluster centroid $\boldsymbol{c}_j$. Second, we calculate the KL divergence loss to update encoder parameters and cluster centers.

To be specific, we adopt t-distribution to measure the distance between mean vector of embedded feature $\boldsymbol{\mu}_i$ and cluster centroid $\boldsymbol{c}_j$, this step is formulated as:

$$A_{ij} = \frac{\left(1 + \|\boldsymbol{\mu}_i - \boldsymbol{c}_j\|^2 / \alpha\right)^{-(\alpha+1)/2}}{\sum_h \left(1 + \|\boldsymbol{\mu}_i - \boldsymbol{c}_h\|^2 / \alpha\right)^{-(\alpha+1)/2}}, \tag{8}$$

where α is the degree of freedom of t-distribution. Since A_{ij} give a distance measuring method, A_i can be regraded as a soft assignment. For instance, if A_{ij} has the largest value among other scalars over A_i, it means the possibility of $\boldsymbol{\mu}_i$ being assigned to cluster center $\boldsymbol{c}_j$ is the biggest.

Then, we construct auxiliary target distribution which can be written as following according to DEC:

$$B_{ij} = \frac{A_{ij}^2 / d_j}{\sum_h A_{ih}^2 / d_h}, \tag{9}$$

where $d_j = \sum_i A_{ij}$. This auxiliary target distribution can strengthen predictions and emphasize features with high confidence. What's more, the loss contribution of each centroid is standardized to prevent a large number of categories from distorting the hidden space. we try to refine the centroids by keeping cluster assignment distribution close to auxiliary target distribution. Thus, we adopt KL divergence loss as class concentration loss (CC) to reduce the distance between two distribution:

$$\mathcal{L}_{CC} = KL\left(\boldsymbol{A} \| \boldsymbol{B}\right) = \sum_i \sum_j A_{ij} \left(\log A_{ij} - \log B_{ij}\right), \tag{10}$$

so that we can cluster the mean vectors of latent variables to k points. As a result, latent features of same cluster share concentrated mean vector and still keep fine distribution characters with variance.

Modality Alignment (MA) Loss. The projected text and image also need to be matched in the latent space. Here, inspired by the concept of alignment for attributes and visual features in zero shot learning [33], we simultaneously align the mean vector and variance of VAE, and define the following modality alignment loss:

$$\mathcal{L}_{MA} = \frac{1}{n} \sum_{i=1}^n (\|\boldsymbol{\mu}_{Ii} - \boldsymbol{\mu}_{Ti}\|_2^2 + \|\Sigma_{Ii}^{\frac{1}{2}} - \Sigma_{Ti}^{\frac{1}{2}}\|_F^2)^{\frac{1}{2}}, \tag{11}$$

where, $\boldsymbol{\mu}_{Ii}$ and $\boldsymbol{\mu}_{Ti}$ represent the mean vectors projected from i-th pair of image and text respectively in a mini batch. Similarly, Σ_{Ii} and Σ_{Ti} stand for the corresponding variance matrices.

Reconstruction Consistency (RC) Loss. In this subsection, we utilize the original semantic matrices $\boldsymbol{S}_I$ and $\boldsymbol{S}_T$, which represents the original affinity relations of the input instances, to restrict the generation stage of hash code. Since it is hard to measure the distance between continuous feature and hash codes referring to Eq. (1), we consider to preserve the information of latent continues features indirectly by reducing the loss of information between the original information and the hash code in the manner of structuring affinity matrices. We calculate the similarity matrices in a mini batch from raw visual and textual modalities as:

$$S_{H(ij)} = \frac{\boldsymbol{X}_{H(i)}(\boldsymbol{X}_{H(j)})^T}{\|\boldsymbol{X}_{H(i)}\|\,\|\boldsymbol{X}_{H(j)}\|}, \tag{12}$$

where $H \in \{I, T\}$. Furthermore, we adopt manner of DJSRH [38] to get hybrid semantic affinity matrix $\boldsymbol{U} = f(\boldsymbol{S}_I, \boldsymbol{S}_T)$. To be concrete, $\boldsymbol{S}_I$ and $\boldsymbol{S}_T$ are merged in a trade-off method:

$$S = \omega S_I + (1 - \omega) S_T, \tag{13}$$

where $\omega \in [0, 1]$ is the weight of two affinity matrices. This algorithm coincides with the diffusion method in [9] which provides powerful evidence of effectiveness. Then, second order neighbourhood information is structured by $\boldsymbol{SS}^T$. Finally, similarity information across original affinity structure in two modalities is combined by the following manner:

$$U = \gamma S + (1 - \gamma)\frac{SS^T}{n}. \tag{14}$$

In latent Hamming space, relevant vertices have small Hamming distance. Thus, hash codes can be understood as discrete features. earlier unsupervised cross-modal algorithms directly generate hash codes using sign function with latent features. However, it is impossible to derive the result of sign function with respect to the input. Thus, we follow [3,11,38] and take a scaled tanh activation function into consideration:

$$b_i = tanh(\kappa\mu_i) \in [-1, +1]^{m \times d}, \kappa \in \mathbb{R}^+, \tag{15}$$

where κ is an auto-increasing parameter during training. With the increasing of κ, the result of Eq. (15) is close to the sign function and approximates the binary value of input feature.

Different from previous methods, CCTV is the first to embed the mean vectors μ to hash codes as far as we know. The purpose of hash learning is to map the continuous features into Hamming space where the relevant object share small Hamming distance. However, the noise of features in the original continuous space is harmful to generate concentrated distribution of data points.

Thus, we can narrow the binary features within same cluster in Hamming space by removing the noise of data points between the original continuous space. Since we utilize multivariate Gaussian as the prior distribution in latent space, the distance between data point and cluster centroid can be regarded as noise. Accordingly, it is beneficial to choose the mean of feature as the input of tanh function. Then, to calculate the similarity with neighbourhoods in Hamming space, the similarity function is defined as:

$$\mathcal{Z}(\boldsymbol{B}_{I(i)}, \boldsymbol{B}_{T(j)}) = \frac{\boldsymbol{B}_{I(i)}(\boldsymbol{B}_{T(j)})^T}{\|\boldsymbol{B}_{I(i)}\| \|\boldsymbol{B}_{T(j)}\|}, \tag{16}$$

where $\boldsymbol{B}_{I(i)}$ means the i-th row in $\boldsymbol{B}_I$ and $\boldsymbol{B}_{T(j)}$ means the j-th row in $\boldsymbol{B}_T$. The result of Eq. (16) is the cosine affinity score which represents the angular connection among discrete features. Minimizing the reconstruction error between the similarity matrix of hash code and the affinity matrix $\boldsymbol{U}$ of continuous features keeps their similarity consistency. Therefore, we define the formulation of reconstruction consistency (RC) Loss as the following manner:

$$\mathcal{L}_{RC} = \left\| \beta \boldsymbol{U} - \mathcal{Z}(\boldsymbol{B}_i^H, \boldsymbol{B}_j^H) \right\|_F^2, \tag{17}$$

where β is a trade-off parameter which makes reconstruction more flexible, referring to [38]. For instance, supposed that $U_{ij} = 0.7$, which means that ith instance and jth instance got 0.7 similarity score, then the similarity score of corresponding hash codes calculated from Hamming space need to be close to 0.7. $\beta > 1$ means the similarity score of hash codes pair need to lager than 0.7 and thus make the nodes in Hamming space compact, while $\beta < 1$ means the similarity score of hash codes pair need to smaller than 0.7 and accordingly make the nodes in Hamming space sparse. We empirically find that it is beneficial to set $\beta > 1$. And this phenomenon can be attributed to the fact that cosine similarity measures the similarity between two vectors by measuring the cosine of the angle between them.

Consequently, we provide our loss function of CCTV:

$$\mathcal{L} = \mathcal{L}_{SV} + \epsilon_1 \mathcal{L}_{CV} + \epsilon_2 \mathcal{L}_{CC} + \epsilon_3 \mathcal{L}_{MA} + \epsilon_4 \mathcal{L}_{RC}, \tag{18}$$

where ϵ_1, ϵ_2, ϵ_3 and ϵ_4 are hyper parameters to balance the total loss.

4   Experiments

4.1   Datasets

WIKI [31]: This dataset consists of 2,866 samples in total with 10 classes. Each image is described by a paragraph which represents related image, from 1 to 10. In our experiment, we randomly select 500 samples from the total dataset as the query set, and the remaining samples form the training set are composed as the retrieval database.

NUS-WIDE [6]: It consists of 269,648 multi-modal instances, each of which contains an image and the related captions with 81 class labels. Following previous methods, the top 10 largest categories is selected and totally contain over

Table 1. The mAP@all results on image query text $(I \rightarrow T)$ and text query image $(T \rightarrow I)$ retrieval tasks at various encoding lengths and datasets. The best performances are shown as bold. In this table, '*' on the right of methods' names means the scores are according to results in their own paper, and '−' means the score is not reported.

Task	Method	WIKI			MIRFlicker-25K			MSCOCO			NUS-WIDE		
		16bit	32bit	64bit	16bit	32bit	64bit	16bit	32bit	64bit	16bit	32bit	64bit
$I \rightarrow T$	CVH [20]	0.157	0.144	0.131	0.579	0.565	0.565	0.499	0.471	0.370	0.400	0.381	0.370
	CMFH [8]	0.173	0.169	0.184	0.580	0.572	0.554	0.442	0.423	0.492	0.381	0.429	0.416
	PDH [32]	0.196	0.168	0.184	0.544	0.544	0.545	0.442	0.423	0.492	0.368	0.368	0.368
	ACQ [15]	0.126	0.120	0.115	0.617	0.594	0.578	0.559	0.552	0.514	0.440	0.416	0.395
	IMH [37]	0.151	0.145	0.133	0.557	0.565	0.559	0.416	0.435	0.442	0.349	0.356	0.370
	QCH [42]	0.159	0.143	0.131	0.579	0.565	0.554	0.496	0.470	0.441	0.401	0.382	0.370
	UCH* [22]	–	–	–	0.654	0.669	0.679	0.447	0.471	0.485	–	–	–
	DJSRH [38]	0.274	0.304	0.350	0.649	0.662	0.669	0.561	0.585	0.585	0.496	0.529	0.528
	DGCPN [48]	0.226	0.326	0.410	0.651	0.670	0.702	0.469	0.586	0.630	0.517	0.553	0.567
	DSAH [45]	0.249	0.333	0.381	0.654	0.693	0.700	0.518	0.595	0.632	0.539	0.566	0.576
	JDSH [27]	0.253	0.289	0.325	0.665	0.681	0.697	0.571	0.613	0.624	0.545	0.553	0.572
	CCTV	**0.405**	**0.409**	**0.413**	**0.690**	**0.701**	**0.716**	**0.604**	**0.640**	**0.645**	**0.548**	**0.569**	**0.580**
$T \rightarrow I$	CVH [20]	0.342	0.299	0.245	0.584	0.566	0.566	0.507	0.479	0.446	0.405	0.384	0.372
	CMFH [8]	0.176	0.170	0.179	0.583	0.566	0.556	0.453	0.435	0.499	0.394	0.451	0.447
	PDH [32]	0.344	0.293	0.251	0.544	0.544	0.546	0.437	0.440	0.440	0.366	0.366	0.367
	ACQ [15]	0.344	0.291	0.247	0.628	0.601	0.580	0.565	0.561	0.520	0.445	0.419	0.398
	IMH [37]	0.236	0.237	0.218	0.560	0.569	0.563	0.560	0.561	0.520	0.350	0.356	0.371
	QCH [42]	0.341	0.289	0.246	0.585	0.567	0.556	0.505	0.478	0.445	0.405	0.385	0.372
	UCH* [22]	–	–	–	0.661	0.667	0.668	0.446	0.469	0.488	–	–	–
	DJSRH [38]	0.246	0.287	0.333	0.658	0.660	0.665	0.563	0.577	0.572	0.499	0.530	0.536
	DGCPN [48]	0.186	0.297	0.522	0.648	0.676	0.703	0.474	0.594	0.634	0.509	0.556	0.574
	DSAH [45]	0.249	0.315	0.393	0.678	0.700	0.708	0.533	0.590	0.630	0.546	0.572	0.578
	JDSH [27]	0.256	0.303	0.320	0.660	0.692	0.710	0.565	0.619	0.632	0.545	0.566	0.576
	CCTV	**0.535**	**0.557**	**0.564**	**0.679**	**0.703**	**0.714**	**0.615**	**0.654**	**0.662**	**0.549**	**0.574**	**0.584**

186 thousand instances and randomly choose 2,000 from them as query set, and employ the others as retrieval database.

MIRFlickr-25K [14]: The original training set and validation set contains more than 25 thousand samples from 38 categories. The class labels are represented as one-hot form where 1 represents the image belongs to this class while 0 is the opposite. We randomly choose 1,000 samples as the query set and set the others as the retrieval set.

MSCOCO [25]: The dataset contains more than 123 thousand images-caption pairs from real-world with 80 class labels. We randomly choose 2,000 from them as query set and the others as retrieval database.

4.2 Evaluation Metrics

To evaluate the efficiency of our method and the baseline approaches, we employ several frequently used evaluation metrics:

Mean Average Precision (mAP): mAP is a metric for evaluating the retrieval performance and its formal definition can be found in [50]. In addition, the performance of all baselines and the proposed method are evaluated on 16 bit, 32 bit and 64 bit hash codes.

Precision-Recall (P-R curve): This curve shows the precision and recall rates according to the retrieved images. It is worthy noting that the beginning plot of curve means the precision and recall rate of the retrieval under the condition that the binary codes of both query and returned items are the same.

4.3   Implementation Details

Our experiments follow previous methods to employ the fc7 layer of VGG-16 to extract the 4,096-dimensional deep features $X_I \in \mathbb{R}^{n \times 4096}$ from original images, while for original textual features we utilize the universal sentence encoder [4] to represent final textual features X_T whose dimension is 512. It is worth noting that to calculate the consistency loss as the manner of Eq. (17), we need to force the items in the same ranges. However, the cosine similarity ranges from -1 to $+1$, while the affinity value elements in U are non-negative, which can be obtained by Eq. (12) and Eq. (14). Therefore, we refine the S_H with $S_H \leftarrow 2S_H - 1, H \in \{I, T\}$. Additionally, we fix the batch size as 8 and employ the SGD optimizer with 0.9 momentum and 0.0005 weight decay. We experimentally take $\alpha = 1$, $\omega = 0.5$, $\gamma = 0.6$ and $\beta = 1.5$ for all four datasets. Then we set $\lambda = 0.6$, $\epsilon = \epsilon_2 = \epsilon_3 = \epsilon_4 = 0.1$ for NUM-WIDE, $\lambda = 0.9$, $\epsilon_1 = \epsilon_2 = \epsilon_3 = \epsilon_4 = 0.1$ for MiRFlickr, $\lambda = 0.3$, $\epsilon_1 = \epsilon_2 = \epsilon_3 = \epsilon_4 = 0.3$ for WIKI and $\lambda = 0.6$, $\epsilon_1 = \epsilon_2 = \epsilon_3 = \epsilon_4 = 0.1$ for MSCOCO.

4.4   Retrieval Performance

To evaluate the performance of the proposed method, we compare our CCTV with several recent competing methods, and record the result in Table 1. The results of the compared methods are obtained by using the codes released by themselves or reproduced according to the settings introduced in their original papers. It can be seen from the table that the proposed method can achieve satisfactory retrieval results on the four data sets. No matter the code length is 16, 32 or 64 bits, the performance of CCTV is higher than all other methods, especially on WIKI and MSCOCO. Specifically, the performance of CCTV's image retrieval text task on WIKI can be improved by about 20% compared with those unsupervised non-depth algorithms (the first six rows in Table 1). At the same time, the retrieval performance improves with the increase of the binary hash code length, which reflects another advantage of this method, that is, the more information the model obtains, the better the retrieval effect. This phenomenon demonstrates that the effective training method of the CCTV model reduces the loss caused by the lack of label information, so that the retrieval performance of the model still has certain advantages compared with other benchmark methods.

In addition, we also employ the P-R curves to evaluate the proposed method compared with other baselines. We choose a small-scale dataset WIKI and a large-scale dataset NUS-WIDE to illustrate the performance, and draw the P-R

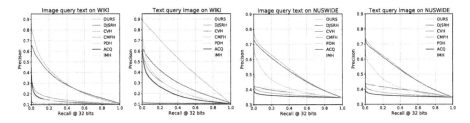

Fig. 3. P-R curves compared with other methods on NUS-WIDE and WIKI for 32 bits.

Fig. 4. Visualization of top 36 retrieved images by textual query on MSCOCO Dataset with random query text written on the top through. Returned samples with red boxes are false-positive candidates. (Color figure online)

curves of the 32-bit hash codes generated by different models. Figure 3 shows the result curves of image retrieving text (I2T) and text retrieving image (T2I). As can be seen from the figure, for the generated 32-bit hash code, the curves of our method lie high above those of the other methods, which means that our CCTV model can achieve satisfactory results on both datasets.

4.5 Visualization

In this subsection, we visually demonstrate the performance of our proposed method by using text retrieve images. We randomly select a query text from MSCOCO as an example, and display the top 36 retrieved images and visualize them in Fig. 4. Among the first 36 returned images, our method can obtain all the correct images based on the query, while at least one of the retrieved results from other methods is wrong. At the same time, it can be found that these incorrect returned results usually have a shape or color similar to the correct retrieved results, which means that they preserve too much redundant information from the training samples.

4.6 Ablation Study

To verify whether the proposed several modules are effective for improving the final performance, in this subsection we conduct ablation studies by removing them and record the experimental results. Since some modules are the core part

Table 2. The ablation studies of three proposed modules on WIKI and MIRFlickr.

Task	Modules	WIKI			MIRFlickr		
		16 bit	32 bit	64 bit	16 bit	32 bit	64 bit
$I \rightarrow T$	w./o. $\mathcal{L}_{CV}$	0.372	0.399	0.408	0.672	0.686	0.709
	w./o. $\mathcal{L}_{CC}$	0.386	0.404	0.410	0.673	0.692	0.709
	With All	0.405	0.409	0.413	0.690	0.701	0.716
$T \rightarrow I$	w./o. $\mathcal{L}_{CV}$	0.502	0.536	0.558	0.651	0.666	0.675
	w./o. $\mathcal{L}_{CC}$	0.531	0.553	0.561	0.666	0.679	0.680
	With all	0.535	0.557	0.564	0.679	0.703	0.714

of this method, such as modality alignment and reconstruction consistency, they cannot be removed. The verified modules are cross reconstruction module and the class concentration module, and we record the results of both $I \rightarrow T$ and $T \rightarrow I$ for 16, 32, 64 bits on WIKI and MIRFlicker in Table 2. This phenomenon reveals that the twin VAE module with reconstruction is dominant for the performance, and the final learned model is relatively close to only twin VAE. In addition, we can also find that the cross reconstruction and class concentration play very important roles.

5   Conclusion

In this paper, we have proposed a class concentration twin variational autoencoder to solve the problem of insufficient separability of hash codes in unsupervised cross-modal retrieval. A Twin VAE network is designed to generate the latent mean vector and variance, which are subsequently clustered by employing the class concentration loss to improve the degree of discrimination. In addition, reconstruction consistency loss is also applied to keep the graph similarity between hash codes and original features. Extensive experiments on four popular datasets are conducted and the results demonstrate that our method can achieve state-of-the-art performance. The ablation studies also verify that each module designed in this method contributes to the final performance.

Acknowledgements. This work was supported in part by the National Natural Science Foundation of China (NSFC) under Grants No. 61872187, No. 62077023 and No. 62072246, in part by the Natural Science Foundation of Jiangsu Province under Grant No. BK20201306, and in part by the "111" Program under Grant No. B13022.

References

1. Bronstein, M.M., Bronstein, A.M., Michel, F., Paragios, N.: Data fusion through cross-modality metric learning using similarity-sensitive hashing. In: CVPR, pp. 3594–3601 (2010)
2. Cao, Y., Long, M., Wang, J., Yu, P.S.: Correlation hashing network for efficient cross-modal retrieval. In: BMVC (2017)
3. Cao, Z., Long, M., Wang, J., Yu, P.S.: Hashnet: deep learning to hash by continuation. In: ICCV, pp. 5608–5617 (2017)
4. Cer, D., et al.: Universal sentence encoder. arXiv preprint arXiv:1803.11175 (2018)
5. Chen, H., Ding, G., Liu, X., Lin, Z., Liu, J., Han, J.: IMRAM: iterative matching with recurrent attention memory for cross-modal image-text retrieval. In: CVPR, pp. 12655–12663 (2020)
6. Chua, T.S., Tang, J., Hong, R., Li, H., Luo, Z., Zheng, Y.: Nus-wide: a real-world web image database from national university of Singapore. In: ICIVR, pp. 1–9 (2009)
7. Deng, C., Chen, Z., Liu, X., Gao, X., Tao, D.: Triplet-based deep hashing network for cross-modal retrieval. IEEE TIP **27**(8), 3893–3903 (2018)
8. Ding, G., Guo, Y., Zhou, J.: Collective matrix factorization hashing for multimodal data. In: CVPR, pp. 2075–2082 (2014)
9. Donoser, M., Bischof, H.: Diffusion processes for retrieval revisited. In: CVPR, pp. 1320–1327 (2013)
10. Gu, Y., Wang, S., Zhang, H., Yao, Y., Yang, W., Liu, L.: Clustering-driven unsupervised deep hashing for image retrieval. Neurocomputing **368**, 114–123 (2019)
11. Hu, D., Nie, F., Li, X.: Deep binary reconstruction for cross-modal hashing. IEEE TMM **21**(4), 973–985 (2018)
12. Hu, H., Xie, L., Hong, R., Tian, Q.: Creating something from nothing: unsupervised knowledge distillation for cross-modal hashing. In: CVPR, June 2020
13. Hu, M., Yang, Y., Shen, F., Xie, N., Hong, R., Shen, H.T.: Collective reconstructive embeddings for cross-modal hashing. IEEE TIP **28**(6), 2770–2784 (2018)
14. Huiskes, M.J., Lew, M.S.: The MIR Flickr retrieval evaluation. In: ACM MM, pp. 39–43 (2008)
15. Irie, G., Arai, H., Taniguchi, Y.: Alternating co-quantization for cross-modal hashing. In: CVPR, pp. 1886–1894 (2015)
16. Jia, C., et al.: Scaling up visual and vision-language representation learning with noisy text supervision. arXiv preprint arXiv:2102.05918 (2021)
17. Jiang, Q.Y., Li, W.J.: Deep cross-modal hashing. In: CVPR, pp. 3232–3240 (2017)
18. Jiang, Q.Y., Li, W.J.: Discrete latent factor model for cross-modal hashing. IEEE TIP **28**(7), 3490–3501 (2019)
19. Kingma, D.P., Welling, M.: Auto-encoding variational Bayes. arXiv preprint arXiv:1312.6114 (2013)
20. Kumar, S., Udupa, R.: Learning hash functions for cross-view similarity search. In: IJCAI (2011)
21. Li, C., Deng, C., Li, N., Liu, W., Gao, X., Tao, D.: Self-supervised adversarial hashing networks for cross-modal retrieval. In: CVPR, June 2018
22. Li, C., Deng, C., Wang, L., Xie, D., Liu, X.: Coupled cyclegan: unsupervised hashing network for cross-modal retrieval. In: AAAI, pp. 176–183 (2019)
23. Li, C., Chen, Z., Zhang, P., Luo, X., Nie, L., Xu, X.: Supervised robust discrete multimodal hashing for cross-media retrieval. IEEE TMM **21**(11), 2863–2877 (2019)

24. Li, X., Shen, C., Dick, A., Van Den Hengel, A.: Learning compact binary codes for visual tracking. In: CVPR, pp. 2419–2426 (2013)
25. Lin, T.-Y., et al.: Microsoft COCO: common objects in context. In: Fleet, D., Pajdla, T., Schiele, B., Tuytelaars, T. (eds.) ECCV 2014. LNCS, vol. 8693, pp. 740–755. Springer, Cham (2014). https://doi.org/10.1007/978-3-319-10602-1_48
26. Lin, Z., Ding, G., Hu, M., Wang, J.: Semantics-preserving hashing for cross-view retrieval. In: CVPR, pp. 3864–3872 (2015)
27. Liu, S., Qian, S., Guan, Y., Zhan, J., Ying, L.: Joint-modal distribution-based similarity hashing for large-scale unsupervised deep cross-modal retrieval. In: ACM SIGIR, pp. 1379–1388 (2020)
28. Luo, X., Yin, X.Y., Nie, L., Song, X., Wang, Y., Xu, X.S.: SDMCH: supervised discrete manifold-embedded cross-modal hashing. In: IJCAI, pp. 2518–2524 (2018)
29. Mandal, D., Chaudhury, K.N., Biswas, S.: Generalized semantic preserving hashing for n-label cross-modal retrieval. In: CVPR, pp. 4076–4084 (2017)
30. Peng, Y., Qi, J.: CM-GANs: cross-modal generative adversarial networks for common representation learning. ACM TOMM **15**(1), 1–24 (2019)
31. Rasiwasia, N., et al.: A approach to cross-modal multimedia retrieval. In: ACM MM, pp. 251–260 (2010)
32. Rastegari, M., Choi, J., Fakhraei, S., Hal, D., Davis, L.: Predictable dual-view hashing. In: ICML, pp. 1328–1336 (2013)
33. Schonfeld, E., Ebrahimi, S., Sinha, S., Darrell, T., Akata, Z.: Generalized zero-and few-shot learning via aligned variational autoencoders. In: CVPR, pp. 8247–8255 (2019)
34. Shen, H.T., et al.: Exploiting subspace relation in semantic labels for cross-modal hashing. IEEE TKDE (2020)
35. Shen, X., Zhang, H., Li, L., Zhang, Z., Chen, D., Liu, L.: Clustering-driven deep adversarial hashing for scalable unsupervised cross-modal retrieval. Neurocomputing **459**, 152–164 (2021)
36. Shi, Y., You, X., Zheng, F., Wang, S., Peng, Q.: Equally-guided discriminative hashing for cross-modal retrieval. In: IJCAI, pp. 4767–4773 (2019)
37. Song, J., Yang, Y., Yang, Y., Huang, Z., Shen, H.T.: Inter-media hashing for large-scale retrieval from heterogeneous data sources. In: ACM SIGKDD, pp. 785–796 (2013)
38. Su, S., Zhong, Z., Zhang, C.: Deep joint-semantics reconstructing hashing for large-scale unsupervised cross-modal retrieval. In: ICCV, pp. 3027–3035 (2019)
39. Sun, C., Song, X., Feng, F., Zhao, W.X., Zhang, H., Nie, L.: Supervised hierarchical cross-modal hashing. In: ACM SIGIR, pp. 725–734 (2019)
40. Wang, D., Cui, P., Ou, M., Zhu, W.: Learning compact hash codes for multimodal representations using orthogonal deep structure. IEEE TMM **17**(9), 1404–1416 (2015)
41. Weiss, Y., Torralba, A., Fergus, R., et al.: Spectral hashing. In: NeurIPS, vol. 1, p. 4. Citeseer (2008)
42. Wu, B., Yang, Q., Zheng, W.S., Wang, Y., Wang, J.: Quantized correlation hashing for fast cross-modal search. In: IJCAI, pp. 3946–3952. Citeseer (2015)
43. Wu, G., et al.: Unsupervised deep hashing via binary latent factor models for large-scale cross-modal retrieval. In: IJCAI, pp. 2854–2860 (2018)
44. Xie, J., Girshick, R., Farhadi, A.: Unsupervised deep embedding for clustering analysis. In: ICML, pp. 478–487 (2016)
45. Yang, D., Wu, D., Zhang, W., Zhang, H., Li, B., Wang, W.: Deep semantic-alignment hashing for unsupervised cross-modal retrieval. In: ICMR, pp. 44–52 (2020)

46. Yang, E., Deng, C., Li, C., Liu, W., Li, J., Tao, D.: Shared predictive cross-modal deep quantization. IEEE TNNLS **29**(11), 5292–5303 (2018)
47. Yang, E., Deng, C., Liu, W., Liu, X., Tao, D., Gao, X.: Pairwise relationship guided deep hashing for cross-modal retrieval. In: AAAI (2017)
48. Yu, J., Zhou, H., Zhan, Y., Tao, D.: Deep graph-neighbor coherence preserving network for unsupervised cross-modal hashing (2021)
49. Zhai, D., Chang, H., Zhen, Y., Liu, X., Chen, X., Gao, W.: Parametric local multimodal hashing for cross-view similarity search. In: IJCAI (2013)
50. Zhang, H., et al.: Deep unsupervised self-evolutionary hashing for image retrieval. IEEE Trans. Multimedia **23**, 3400–3413 (2021)
51. Zhang, J., Peng, Y., Yuan, M.: Unsupervised generative adversarial cross-modal hashing. In: AAAI (2018)
52. Zheng, Z., Zheng, L., Garrett, M., Yang, Y., Xu, M., Shen, Y.D.: Dual-path convolutional image-text embeddings with instance loss. ACM TOMM **16**(2), 1–23 (2020)

Meta-prototype Decoupled Training for Long-Tailed Learning

Siming Fu[1], Huanpeng Chu[1], Xiaoxuan He[1], Hualiang Wang[1], Zhenyu Yang[2], and Haoji Hu[1(✉)]

[1] College of Information Science and Electronic Engineering, Zhejiang University, Hangzhou, China
`{fusiming,chuhp,Xiaoxiao_He,hualiang_wang,haoji_hu}@zju.edu.cn`
[2] Shenzhen TP-LINK Digital Technology Co., Ltd., Shenzhen, China
`yangzhenyu@tp-link.com.cn`

Abstract. Long-tailed learning aims to tackle the crucial challenge that head classes dominate the training procedure under severe class imbalance in real-world scenarios. Supervised contrastive learning has turned out to be worth exploring research direction, which seeks to learn class-specific feature prototypes to enhance long-tailed learning performance. However, little attention has been paid to how to calibrate the empirical prototypes which are severely biased due to the scarce data in tail classes. Without the aid of correct prototypes, these explorations have not shown the significant promise expected. Motivated by this, we propose the meta-prototype contrastive learning to automatically learn the reliable representativeness of prototypes and more discriminative feature space via a meta-learning manner. In addition, on top of the calibrated prototypes, we leverage it to replace the mean of class statistics and predict the targeted distribution of balanced training data. By this procedure, we formulate the feature augmentation algorithm which samples additional features from the predicted distribution and further balances the over-whelming dominance severity of head classes. We summarize the above two stages as the meta-prototype decouple training scheme and conduct a series of experiments to validate the effectiveness of the framework. Our method outperforms previous work with a large margin and achieves state-of-the-art performance on long-tailed image classification and semantic segmentation tasks (e.g., we achieve 55.1% overall accuracy with ResNetXt-50 in ImageNet-LT).

Keywords: Meta-prototype · Decoupled training · Supervised contrastive learning · Feature augmentation

1 Introduction

Most real-world data comes with a long-tailed nature: a few head classes contribute the majority of data, while most tail classes comprise relatively few data. An undesired phenomenon is models [2,29] trained with long-tailed data perform better on head classes while exhibiting extremely low accuracy on tail ones.

© The Author(s), under exclusive license to Springer Nature Switzerland AG 2023
L. Wang et al. (Eds.): ACCV 2022, LNCS 13846, pp. 252–268, 2023.
https://doi.org/10.1007/978-3-031-26351-4_16

To address this problem, a large number of studies have been conducted in recent years, making promising progress in the field of deep long-tailed learning. Supervised contrastive learning (SCL) has been the main focus of many techniques for long-tailed learning. The mainstream insights work on supervised contrastive learning methods [17,43] which seek to learn class-specific feature prototypes to enhance long-tailed learning performance. DRO-LT [21] innovatively explores the idea of feature prototypes to handle long-tailed recognition in an open world. Following that, TSC [15] converges the different classes of features to a target that is uniformly distributed over the hyper-sphere during training.

Nevertheless, when a class has only few samples, the distribution of training samples may not represent well the true distribution of the data. The shift between test distribution and training distribution causes the offset of the prototypes in tail classes [21]. The above works are all based on the empirical prototype under imbalanced data, limiting the effectiveness of feature representation. Therefore, the sub-optimal prototypes become an issue in learning high-quality representations for SCL methods, which confuse optimization for improved long-tailed learning.

To alleviate the above issues, we propose the supervised meta-prototype contrastive learning which calibrates the empirical prototype under the imbalanced setting. Specifically, we extend meta-learner to automatically restore the meta-prototypes of feature embeddings via two nested loops of optimization, guaranteeing the efficiency of the meta-prototype contrastive learning algorithm. Our major insight here is to parameterize the mapping function as a meta-network, which is theoretically a universal approximator for almost all continuous functions, and then use the meta-data (a small unbiased validation set) to guide the training of all the meta-network parameters. The meta-prototypes provide more meaningful feature prototypes which are designed to be robust against possible shifts of the test distribution and guide the SCL to obtain the discriminative feature representation space.

To further ease the dominance of the head classes in classification decisions, we develop the calibration feature augmentation algorithm based on the learned meta-prototype in classifier training stage. Specifically, we utilize it as the 'anchor' of corresponding class which represents the mean of the class statistics under the imbalanced setting. In contrast to the typical methods which generate the new feature samples based on the class statistics of imbalanced training data, our meta-prototype calibrates the bias and provides the reasonable feature distribution of new feature samples for tail classes. The newly generated feature are sampled from the calibrated distribution and help to find the correct classifier decision boundary via improving the performance of severely under-represented tail classes.

We summarize the above processes as the meta-prototype decoupled training framework which includes calibrating the empirical prototype for SCL in the representation learning stage and enhancing feature embedding for tail classes based on learned meta-prototype in the classifier learning stage. We extensively validate our model on typical visual recognition tasks, including image classification on three benchmarks (CIFAR-100-LT [12], ImageNet-LT [18] and iNaturalist2018 [25]), semantic segmentation on ADE20K dataset [40]. The experimental results demonstrate our method consistently outperforms the state-of-the-art approaches on all the benchmarks.

Summary of Contributions:

- To the best of our acknowledge, we are the first in long-tailed learning to complete the meta-prototype to promote the representation quality of supervised prototype contrastive learning in the representation learning stage.
- On top of the learned meta-prototype, we develop the feature augmentation algorithm for tail classes to ease dominance of the head classes in classification decisions in the classifier learning stage.
- Our method outperforms previous works with a large margin and achieve state-of-the-art performance on long-tailed image classification and semantic segmentation tasks.

2   Related Work

Supervised Contrastive Learning. Existing supervised contrastive learning-based methods for long-tailed learning seek to help alleviate the biased label effect. DRO-LT [21] extends standard contrastive loss and optimizes against the worst possible centroids within a safety hyper ball around the empirical centroid. KCL [10] develops a new method to explicitly pursue balanced feature space for representation learning. TSC [15] generates a set of targets uniformly distributed on a hypersphere and makes the features of different classes converge to these distinct and uniformly distributed targets during training. Hybrid-SC [28] explores the effectiveness of supervised contrastive learning. It introduces prototypical supervised learning to obtain better features and resolve the memory bottleneck. The above works are all based on the empirical prototype under imbalanced data, which limits the effectiveness of feature representation. To alleviate the above issue, we introduce the meta-prototype to calibrate the empirical prototype, further constructing a discriminative feature space.

Meta-learning. The recent development of meta-learning [1,7] inspires researchers to leverage meta-learning to handle class imbalance. Meta-weight-net [22] introduces a method capable of adaptively learning an explicit weighting function directly from data. MetaSAug [14] proposes to augment tail classes with a variant of ISDA [30] by estimating the covariance matrices for tail classes. Motivated by these works, our method attempts to automatically estimate the meta-prototype of each class to calibrate the empirical prototype for high-quality feature representation.

Data Augmentation for Long-Tailed Learning. In long-tail learning, transfer-based augmentation has been explored. Transfer-based augmentation seeks to transfer the knowledge from head classes to augment model performance on tail classes. TailCalibX [26] and GLAG [38] explore a direction that attempts to generate meaningful features by estimating the tail category's distribution. RSG [27] dynamically estimates a set of feature centers for each class, and uses the feature displacement between head-class sample features and the nearest intra-class feature center to augment each tail sample feature. However, the estimated distribution of tail category and the intra-class feature center are biased or unreasonable due to the imbalanced size of training dataset. Our meta-prototype feature augmentation algorithm calibrates the bias and predicts likely shifts of the test distribution.

Decoupled Scheme for Long-Tailed Learning. Decoupling [9] is a pioneering work that introduces a two-step training scheme. It empirically evaluates different sampling strategies for representation learning in the first step, and then evaluates different classifier training schemes by fixing the feature extractor trained in the second step. Decouple [9] and Bag of tricks [37] decouple the learning procedure into representation learning and classification, and systematically explore how different balancing strategies affect them for long-tailed recognition. BBN [41] further unifies the two stages to form a cumulative learning strategy. MiSLAS [39] proposes to enhance the representation learning with data mixup in the first stage. During the second stage, MiSLAS applies a label-aware smoothing strategy for better model generalization. In our paper, our method also adopts the two-stage decoupled training scheme, which leads to better long-tailed learning performance.

3   The Proposed Methods

3.1   Problem Definition

For long-tailed learning, considering $\mathcal{D}^{tra} = \{x^i, y^i\}$, $i \in \{1, \cdots, K\}$ be the training set, where x^i denotes an image sample and y^i indicates its class label. Let K be the total numbers of classes, N_i be the number of samples in class i, where $\sum_{i=1}^{K} N_i = N$. A long-tail setup can be defined by ordering the number of samples per category, i.e. $N_1 \geq N_2 \geq \ldots \geq N_K$ and $N_1 \gg N_K$ after sorting of N_i. Under the long-tailed setting, the training dataset is imbalanced, leading to the poor performance on tail classes.

We train a network $\boldsymbol{\Psi}(\cdot; \boldsymbol{W})$ consisting of two components: (i) a backbone or representation network (CNN for images) that translates an image to a feature representation $z_i = \boldsymbol{\Psi}(x^i; w^E) \in \mathbb{R}^{1 \times d}$ and (ii) a classifier $w^C \in \mathbb{R}^{K \times d}$ at predicts the category specific scores (logits). As shown in Fig. 1, given a pair (x^i, y^i) sampled from a mini-batch $\mathcal{B} \subset \mathcal{D}^{tra}$, feature vector z_i is extracted by the feature extractor. z_i is projected onto the classifier to output the classification logit. Too few samples belonging to the tail classes result in inadequate learning of tail classes representations.

3.2   Supervised Meta-prototype Contrastive Learning in the Representation Learning Stage

Supervised contrastive learning introduces cluster-based prototypes and encourages embeddings to gather around their corresponding prototypes. Our

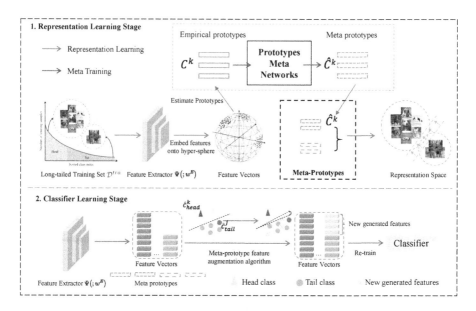

Fig. 1. Overview of our proposed method during the training period. **Upper box** introduces the meta-prototype, which consists of the following steps in sequence: sampling a mini-batch images $\mathcal{B}$ from training set $\mathcal{D}^{tra}$, learning features by the feature extractor $\boldsymbol{\Psi}(\cdot; \boldsymbol{w}^E)$, embedding features onto the hyper-sphere, estimating the prototypes for classes, and learning meta-prototypes for discriminative representation space. **Bottom box** introduces the meta-prototype feature augmentation algorithm which enriches the samples of tail classes to re-build the classifier decision boundaries.

original feature prototypes follow the MoPro [13], adopting the exponential-moving-average (EMA) algorithm during training by:

$$c_k \leftarrow mc_k + (1 - m)z_i, \quad \forall i \in \{i \mid \hat{y}_i = k\}, \tag{1}$$

where c_k is the prototype for class k and m is momentum coefficient, usually set as 0.999. Then given the embedding z_i^f, the prototypes are queried with contrastive similarity matching. The prototype contrastive loss [13,21] is defined as:

$$\mathcal{L}_{PC} = -\log \left[\frac{\exp\left(z_i^f \cdot c^k / \tau\right)}{\sum_{j=1}^{K} \exp\left(z_i^f \cdot c^j / \tau\right)} \right], \tag{2}$$

where τ is a hyper-parameter and usually set as 0.07 [11]. The neural network is denoted as $f(\cdot, \mathbf{W})$, and $\mathbf{W}$ denotes all of its parameters. Generally, the optimal network parameter $\mathbf{W}^*$ can be extracted by minimizing the training loss:

$$\mathcal{L}^{\text{train}}(\mathbf{W}; c^k) = \mathcal{L}_{CE}(\mathbf{W}) + \lambda \cdot \mathcal{L}_{PC}(\mathbf{W}, c^k), \tag{3}$$

where λ denotes the weighting coefficient to balance the two loss terms and $\mathcal{L}_{CE}$ is the cross-entropy loss. As aforementioned, the empirical prototypes of tail classes can be far away from the ground-truth prototypes due to the limited features of tail classes and large variances in data distribution between training and test datasets. Therefore, we aim to learn appropriate feature prototypes to perform reasonable feature representation learning.

The whole process of the meta-prototype constrastive learning is summarized in Algorithm 1. In the presence of imbalanced training data, our method calibrates the empirical prototypes by prototype meta network, denoted as $\mathcal{C}(\boldsymbol{c}^k; \Theta)$. $\boldsymbol{c}^k$ is the input of the meta network and Θ represents the parameters contained in it. The meta network consists of MLP, which maps the empirical prototype $\boldsymbol{c}^k$ into the meta-prototype $\hat{\boldsymbol{c}}^k$. The prototype meta network is an encoder-decoder network, where the encoder contains one linear layer with a ReLU activation function, and the decoder consists of a Linear-ReLU-Linear structure. The optimal parameter $\mathbf{w}$ is calculated by minimizing the following training loss:

$$
\begin{aligned}
\mathbf{W}^*(\Theta) &= \arg\min_{\mathbf{W}} \mathcal{L}^{\mathrm{train}}(\mathbf{W}; \boldsymbol{c}^k; \Theta) \\
&= \arg\min_{\mathbf{W}} \left\{ \mathcal{L}_{CE}(\mathbf{W}) + \lambda \cdot \mathcal{L}_{\mathrm{PC}}(\mathbf{W}, \mathcal{C}(\boldsymbol{c}^k; \Theta)) \right\}.
\end{aligned}
\tag{4}
$$

The parameters contained in the meta-network can be optimized by using the meta-learning idea. The optimal parameter Θ^* can be obtained by minimizing the following meta-loss:

$$
\Theta^* = \arg\min_{\Theta} \mathcal{L}^{meta}\left(\mathbf{W}^*(\Theta)\right),
\tag{5}
$$

where $\mathcal{L}^{\mathrm{meta}}(\mathbf{w}) = \mathcal{L}_{CE}\left(y_i^{(\mathrm{meta})}, f\left(x_i^{(\mathrm{meta})}, \mathbf{W}\right)\right)$ on meta-data. Specifically, following the meta-learning methods [14,22] for long-tailed learning, we conduct a small amount of balanced meta-data set (i.e., with balanced data distribution) $\left\{ x_i^{(\mathrm{meta})}, y_i^{(\mathrm{meta})} \right\}_{i=1}^{M}$ to represent the meta-knowledge of ground-truth sample-label distribution, where M is the number of meta-samples and $M \ll N$.

Online approximation. To estimate the optimal feature prototypes for different classes, we adopt a double optimization loop, respectively, to guarantee the efficiency of the algorithm. We optimize the model in a meta-learning setup by i). updating equation of the network parameter can be formulated by moving the current $\mathbf{W}^{(t)}$ along the descent direction of the objective loss in Eq. 4 on a mini-batch training data by

$$
\hat{\mathbf{W}}^{(t)}(\Theta) \leftarrow \mathbf{W}^{(t)} - \alpha \times \nabla_{\mathbf{W}^{(t)}} \mathcal{L}^{\mathrm{train}}(\mathbf{W}; \boldsymbol{c}^k; \Theta),
\tag{6}
$$

where α is the step size. ii). After receiving the updated network parameters $\hat{\mathbf{W}}^{(t)}(\Theta)$, the parameter Θ of the meta-network can then be readily updated by Eq. 5, i.e., moving the current parameter $\Theta^{(t)}$ along the objective gradient to be calculated on the meta-data by

$$
\Theta^{(t+1)} = \Theta^{(t)} - \beta \frac{1}{n} \sum_{i=1}^{n} \nabla_{\Theta^{(t)}} \mathcal{L}^{meta}\left(\hat{\mathbf{W}}^{(t)}(\Theta)\right),
\tag{7}
$$

Algorithm 1. The Meta-Prototype Contrastive Learning Algorithm.

Input: Training data $\mathcal{D}^{tra}$, meta-data set $\mathcal{D}^{meta}$, batch size n, m, max epochs T, epoch threshold T_{th}.
Output: Network parameter $\mathbf{W}^{(T)}$, meta-network parameter $\Theta^{(T)}$.

1: **for** epoch $= 0 : T_{\text{th}} - 1$ **do**
2:    Update $\mathbf{W}$ by $\mathcal{L}_{CE}$.
3:    Update c_k by Eq. 1.
4: **end for**
5: Initialize meta network parameters $\Theta^{(0)}$.
6: **for** epoch $= T_{\text{th}} : T - 1$ **do**
7:    $\{\, \boldsymbol{x}^i, y^i \,\} \leftarrow$ SampleMiniBatch (D^{tra}, n).
8:    $\{\boldsymbol{x}^{(\text{meta})}, y^{(\text{meta})}\} \leftarrow$ SampleMiniBatch (D^{meta}, m).
9:    Formulate the network learning function $\hat{\mathbf{W}}^{(t)}(\Theta)$ by Eq. 6.
10:   Update $\Theta^{(t+1)}$ by Eq 7.
11:   Update $\mathbf{W}^{(t+1)}$ by Eq 8.
12: **end for**

---

where β is the step size. iii) Then, the updated $\Theta^{(t+1)}$ is employed to ameliorate the parameter $\mathbf{W}$ of the network, constituting a complete loop:

$$\mathbf{W}^{(t+1)} = \mathbf{W}^{(t)} - \alpha \times \nabla_{\mathbf{W}^{(t)}} \mathcal{L}^{\text{train}}\left(\mathbf{W}^{(t)}; c^k; \Theta^{(t+1)}\right), \qquad (8)$$

Since the updated meta-network $\mathcal{C}(c^k; \Theta^{(t+1)})$ are learned from balanced meta-data, we could expect $\mathcal{C}(c^k; \Theta^{(t+1)})$ contribute to learning better network parameters $\mathbf{W}^{(t+1)}$.

3.3 Meta-prototype Feature Augmentation in the Classifier Training Stage

On the classifier training phase, the target of our work is to generate addition feature embeddings to further balance the over-whelming dominance severity of head classes in the representation space. It is natural to utilize the feature augmentation to calibrate the ill-defined decision boundary. Following the Joint Bayesian face model [3], typical feature augmentation methods [26,34,38] assume that the features $\mathbf{z}_i$ lies in a Gaussian distribution with a class mean μ_i and a covariance matrix Σ_i. The mean of a class is estimated as the arithmetic mean of all features in the same class by $\mu_k = \frac{1}{N_k} \sum_{i \in \mathcal{F}_k} \mathbf{z}_i$.

However, the means of Gaussian distribution for tail classes are biased due to sparse sample size of the tail categories and large variances for data distribution between train and test datasets. This bias causes the distribution of the generated data to deviate significantly from the data distribution of the validation set. It leads to significant performance drop, even the destruction of the original representational space. Therefore, as Fig. 2 illustrated, we leverage the meta-prototypes $\hat{c}_i$ as the 'anchor' to replace the typical class statistics μ_k to provide the reasonable feature distribution of new feature samples for tail classes.

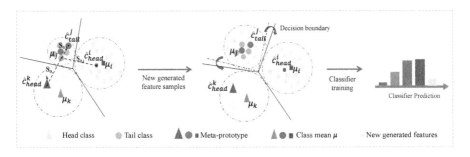

Fig. 2. Illustration of the feature augmentation process based on the learned meta-prototype $\hat{c}$. Tukey's Ladder of Power transformation function transfers the feature instance $\mathbf{z}_i$ into $\tilde{\mathbf{z}}_i$. Meta-prototypes replace the means μ of class statistics to calculate the neighbors $\mathcal{N}_i$ via $S_{i,k}$ and the calibrated distribution $\mu_{\tilde{\mathbf{z}}_i}$ and $\Sigma_{\tilde{\mathbf{z}}_i}$. Additional features for tail classes are sampled from the calibrated statistics so as to ease the dominance of the head classes in classification decisions.

Given a trained backbone (discussed in Sect. 3.2), we first pre-compute feature representations for the entire dataset. These features of true samples are denoted as $\mathcal{F} = \{\mathbf{z}_i\}_{i=1}^N$. $\mathcal{F}_k$ denotes features of images belonging to the category k. For each class, we sample $N_1 - N_K$ additional features, such that the resulting feature dataset is completely balanced and all classes have N_1 instances. Sampling is performed based on an instance specific calibrated distribution. Specifically, each $\mathbf{z}_{ik}$ (i^{th} feature from category k) is responsible for generating $s_{\text{new}} = \max\left\{[N_1/N_k - 1]_+, 1\right\}$ features, where $[\cdot]_+$ is the ceiling function.

Based on the learned meta-prototype, the features covariance for the corresponding class can be calculated as:

$$\Sigma_k = \frac{1}{N_k - 1} \sum_{i \in \mathcal{F}_k} \left(\mathbf{z}_i - \hat{c}^k\right)\left(\mathbf{z}_i - \hat{c}^k\right)^T, \tag{9}$$

where $\Sigma_k \in \mathbb{R}^{d \times d}$ denotes the full covariance of the Gaussian distribution for category k. Next, for each feature $\tilde{\mathbf{z}}_i$ belonging to tail classes k processed by Tukey's Ladder of Power transformation [24], we calculate the similarity degree with other classes k which have more training samples as $S_{i,k} = \tilde{\mathbf{z}}_i^\top \cdot \hat{c}^k / \|\tilde{\mathbf{z}}_i^\top\| \cdot \|\hat{c}^k\|$. We identify the set of M category indices that are neighbors $\mathcal{N}_i$ with the maximum cosine similarity. We calibrate the distribution of feature $\tilde{\mathbf{z}}_i$ as:

$$\mu_{\tilde{\mathbf{z}}_i} = (1 - \alpha) \cdot \tilde{\mathbf{z}}_i + \alpha \cdot \frac{1}{M} \sum_{k \in \mathcal{N}_i} \frac{e^{S_{i,k}}}{\sum_{j=1}^M e^{S_{i,j}}} \cdot \hat{c}^k$$

$$\Sigma_{\tilde{\mathbf{z}}_i} = (1 - \alpha)^2 \cdot \Sigma_i + \alpha^2 \cdot \frac{1}{M} \sum_{k \in \mathcal{N}_i} \frac{e^{S_{i,k}}}{\sum_{j=1}^M e^{S_{i,j}}} \cdot \Sigma_k + \beta, \tag{10}$$

where α is the hyper-parameter to balance the degree of the calibration and β is an optional constant hyper-parameter to increase the spread of the calibrated

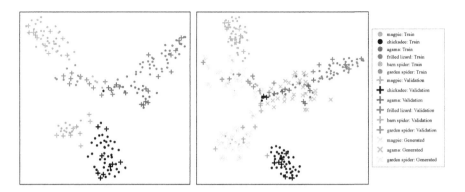

Fig. 3. t-SNE visualization of a few head and tail classes from ImageNet-LT. The plot on the left is before generation, and the plot on the right is after generation. We show 10 validation samples for each class and limit to 40 training + generated samples for ease of interpretation. Markers: · (dot) indicate training samples; + (plus) are validation samples; and × (cross) are generated features also shown with a lighter version of the base color. Best seen in colour.

distribution. We found that $\beta = 0.05$ works reasonably well for multiple experiments. We generate the new samples with the same associated class label and denote the new samples for category k as $\mathcal{F}_k^*$. This combined set of features is generated for all categories and used to train classifier. As shown in Fig. 3, we generate features using our meta-prototype feature augmentation and re-build the t-SNE visualization in the right plot. Compared with the left plot which is before generation, the right plot eases the interpretation and clarifies the feature boundaries. In addition, due to the meta-prototype, the newly generated features are close to validation samples, which further promote the performance of the classifier.

4   Experiments

4.1   Long-Tailed Image Classification Task

Datasets and Setup. We perform experiments on long-tailed image classification datasets, including the CIFAR-100-LT [12], ImageNet-LT [18] and iNaturalist2018 [25].

- CIFAR-100-LT is based on the original CIFAR-100 dataset, whose training samples per class are constructed by imbalance ratio (The imbalance ratios we adopt in our experiment are 10, 50 and 100).
- ImageNet-LT is a long-tailed version of the ImageNet dataset by sampling a subset following the Pareto distribution with power value 6. It contains 115.8K images from 1,000 categories, with class cardinality ranging from 5 to 1,280.

Table 1. Top 1 accuracy of CIFAR-100-LT with various imbalance factors (100, 50, 10). RL, DT, and DA indicate representation learning, decouple training, and data augmentation, respectively.

Type	Method	CIFAR-100-LT		
		100	50	10
Baseline	Softmax	38.3	43.9	55.7
RL	KCL [10]	42.8	46.3	57.6
	DRO-LT [21]	47.3	57.6	63.4
	TSC [15]	43.8	47.4	59.0
	Hybrid-SC [28]	46.7	51.9	63.1
DT	Decoupling [9]	43.3	47.4	57.9
	De-confound [23]	44.1	50.3	59.6
	MiSLAS [39]	47.0	52.3	63.2
	Bag of tricks [37]	47.8	51.7	–
DA	MetaSAug [14]	48.1	52.3	61.3
	TailCalibX [26]	46.6	50.9	61.1
	RSG [27]	44.6	48.5	–
	GLAG [38]	51.7	55.3	64.5
	Ours	**52.3**	**55.9**	**64.9**

- iNaturalist2018 is the largest dataset for long-tailed visual recognition. It contains 437.5K images from 8,142 categories. It is extremely imbalanced with an imbalance factor of 512.

Experimental Details. We implement all experiments in PyTorch. On CIFAR-100-LT, following [20], we use ResNet-32 [31] as the feature extractor for all methods. we conduct model training with SGD optimizer based on batch size 256, momentum 0.9 under three imbalance ratios (10, 50 and 100). For image classification on ImageNet-LT, following [5,8,23], we use ResNetXt-50 [31] as the feature extractor for all methods. We conduct model training with the SGD optimizer based on batch size 512, and momentum 0.9. In both training epochs (90 and 200 training epochs), the learning rate is decayed by a cosine scheduler [19] from 0.2 to 0.0. On iNaturalist2018 [25] dataset, we use ResNet-50 [31] as the feature extractor for all methods with 200 training epochs, with the same experimental parameters set for the other. Moreover, we use the same basic data augmentation (i.e., random resize and crop to 224, random horizontal flip, color jitter, and normalization) for all methods.

Comparison with State of the Arts. As shown in Table 1, to prove the versatility of our method, we employ our method on the CIFAR-100-LT dataset with three imbalance ratios. We compare against the most relevant methods

Table 2. Results on ImageNet-LT in terms of accuracy (Acc) under 90 and 200 training epochs. In this table, CR, DT, and RL indicate class re-balancing, decouple training, and representation learning, respectively.

Type	Method	90 epochs				200 epochs			
		Many	Med	Few	All	Many	Med	Few	All
Baseline	Softmax	66.5	39.0	8.6	45.5	66.9	40.4	12.6	46.8
CR	Focal Loss [16]	66.9	39.2	9.2	45.8	67.0	41.0	13.1	47.2
	BALMS [20]	61.7	48.0	29.9	50.8	62.4	47.7	32.1	51.2
	LDAM [2]	62.3	47.4	32.5	51.1	60.0	49.2	31.9	51.1
	LADE [8]	62.2	48.6	31.8	51.5	63.1	47.7	32.7	51.6
	DisAlign [35]	62.7	52.1	31.4	53.4	–	–	–	–
DT	Decoupling [9]	62.4	39.3	14.9	44.9	60.9	36.9	13.5	43.0
	MiSLAS [39]	62.1	48.9	31.6	51.4	65.3	50.6	33.0	53.4
	De-confound [23]	63.0	48.5	31.4	51.8	64.9	46.9	28.1	51.3
	xERM$_{TDE}$ [42]	–	–	–	–	68.6	50.0	27.5	54.1
RL	OLTR [17]	58.2	45.5	19.5	46.7	62.9	44.6	18.8	48.0
	DRO-LT [21]	–	–	–	–	64.0	49.8	33.1	53.5
	PaCo [5]	59.7	51.7	36.6	52.7	63.2	51.6	39.2	54.4
DA	RSG [27]	68.7	43.7	16.2	49.6	65.0	49.4	31.1	52.9
	SSP [32]	65.6	49.6	30.3	53.1	67.3	49.1	28.3	53.3
	Ours	**64.3**	**51.6**	**31.8**	**53.8**	**66.3**	**52.8**	**35.2**	**55.1**

and choose methods that are recently published and representative of different types, such as class re-balancing, decouple training and data augmentation. Our method surpasses the DRO-LT [21] under various imbalance factors, especially on the largest imbalance factor (52.3% vs 47.3%). Furthermore, compared with the data augmentation methods [38], our model achieves competitive performance (52.3% vs 51.7% with 100 imbalance factor).

Table 2 shows the long-tailed results on ImageNet-LT. We adopt the performance data from the deep long-tailed survey [36] for various methods at 90 and 200 training epochs to make a fair comparison. Our approach achieves 53.8% and 55.1% in overall accuracy, which outperforms the state of the art methods by a significant margin at 90 and 200 training epochs, respectively. Compared with representation learning methods, our method surpasses SSP by 0.7% (53.8% vs 53.1%) at 90 training epochs and outperforms SSP by 1.8% (55.1% vs 53.3%) at 200 training epochs. In addition, our method obtains higher performance by 1.1% (53.8% vs 52.7%) and 0.7% (55.1% vs 54.4%) than PaCo at 90 and 200 training epochs, respectively.

Furthermore, Table 3 presents the experimental results on the naturally-skewed dataset iNaturalist2018. Compared with the improvement brought by

Table 3. Benchmarking on iNaturalists2018 in Top 1 accuracy (%). RL, DT, and DA indicate representation learning, decouple training, and data augmentation.

Type	Method	iNaturalist			
		Many	Med.	Few	All
Baseline	Softmax	72.2	63.0	57.2	61.7
RL	Focal Loss [16]	–	–	–	61.1
	DRO-LT [21]	–	–	–	69.7
	OLTR [17]	59.0	64.1	64.9	63.9
	TSC [15]	72.6	70.6	67.8	69.7
	DisAlign [35]	69.0	71.1	70.2	70.6
DT	Decoupling [9]	65.6	65.3	65.5	65.6
	BBN [41]	49.4	70.8	65.3	66.3
DA	MetaSAug [14]	–	–	–	68.7
	GLAG [38]	–	–	–	69.2
	Ours	**72.8**	**71.7**	**70.0**	**71.0**

representation learning, decouple training and data augmentation approaches, our method achieves competitive result (71.0%) consistently.

4.2   Semantic Semgnetaion on ADE20K Dataset

To further validate our method, we apply our strategy to segmentation networks and report our performance on the semantic segmentation benchmark, ADE20K.

Dataset and Setup. ADE20K is a scene parsing dataset covering 150 fine-grained semantic concepts and it is one of the most challenging semantic segmentation datasets. The training set contains 20,210 images with 150 semantic classes. The validation and test set contain 2,000 and 3,352 images respectively.

Experimental Details. We evaluate our method using two widely adopted segmentation models (OCRNet [33] and DeepLabV3+ [4]) based on different backbone networks. We initialize the backbones using the models pre-trained on ImageNet [6] and the framework randomly. All models are trained with an image size of 512×512 and 80K/160K iterations in total. We train the models using the Adam optimizer with the initial learning rate of 0.01, weight decay of 0.0005, and momentum of 0.9. The learning rate dynamically decays exponentially according to the 'ploy' strategy.

Comparison with State of the Arts. The numerical results and comparison with other peer methods are reported in Table 4. Our method achieves 1.1% and 0.5% improvement in mIoU using OCRNet with HRNet-W18 when the iterations are 80K and 160K, respectively. Moreover, our method outperforms the baseline with large margin at 0.9% and 1.1% in mIoU using DeeplabV3+ with ResNet-50

Table 4. Performance of semantic segmentation on ADE20K. R-50 and R-101 denote ResNet-50 and ResNet-101, respectively.

Framework	Method	Backbone	80K iteration		160K iteration	
			mIoU	mAcc	mIoU	mAcc
OCRNet	Baseline	HRNet-W18	39.2	49.0	40.8	50.9
	Ours		**40.3**	**51.9**	**41.3**	**52.8**
DeepLabV3+	Baseline	R-50	43.8	54.5	44.9	55.0
	DisAlign [35]		–	–	45.7	**57.3**
	Ours		**44.7**	**55.1**	**46.0**	57.0
	Baseline	R-101	46.1	56.2	46.4	56.7
	DisAlign [35]		-	–	47.1	59.5
	Ours		**46.9**	**57.1**	**47.3**	**59.9**

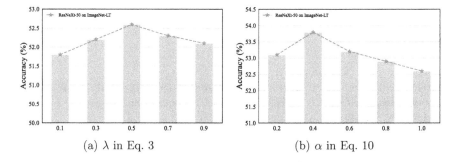

(a) λ in Eq. 3   (b) α in Eq. 10

Fig. 4. Ablation study on λ in Eq. 3 and α in Eq. 10.

when the iterations are 80K and 160K, respectively. Even with a stronger backbone, ResNet-101, our method also achieves 0.8% mIoU and 0.9% improvement than the baseline. Compared with DisAlign, our method still outperforms it on both in both mIoU and mAcc with various backbones consistently.

4.3   Ablation Study

We conduct ablation study on the ImageNet-LT dataset to further understand the hyper-parameters of our methods and the effect of each proposed component. All of them have trained with ResNetXt-50 by 90 epochs for a fair comparison.

λ **in Meta Training Loss.** One major hyper-parameter in our method is λ in Eq. 3, which adjusts the degree of adjustment in meta training loss. We set the hyper-parameter $\lambda \in \{0.1, 0.3, 0.5, 0.7, 0.9\}$. We study the sensitivity of the accuracy to the values of λ. Figure 4(a) quantifies the effect of the trade-off parameter λ on the validation accuracy. It shows that combining the $\mathcal{L}_{PC}$ and $\mathcal{L}_{CE}$ with optimal λ is 0.5 gives the best results.

Table 5. Ablation study on ImageNet-LT for different decouple methods.

CE	DRO-LT	KCL	MPCL	TailCalibX	MPFA	Many	Med.	Few	All
✓	✗	✗	✗	✗	✗	66.5	39.0	8.6	45.5
✓	✓	✗	✗	✗	✗	65.0	48.8	25.8	51.9
✓	✗	✓	✗	✗	✗	62.4	49.0	29.5	51.5
✓	✗	✗	✓	✗	✗	64.6	50.1	27.5	52.7
✓	✗	✗	✓	✓	✗	63.7	51.2	31.0	53.2
✓	✗	✗	✓	✗	✓	**64.3**	**51.6**	**31.8**	**53.8**

α **in Meta-Prototype Feature Generation.** In Eq. 10, we introduce a class-wise confidence score α which controls the degree of distribution calibration. We initialize α to 0.2 for each tail class and it changes adaptively during training. We set the hyper-parameter α in the interval from 0.2 to 1 with a stride of 0.2 and take the five sets of values to conduct ablation experiments as shown in Fig. 4(b). Overall, the larger α means more confidence to transfer the knowledge from head to tail classes. The optimal α for ImageNet-LT is 0.4.

Effectiveness of MPCL and MPFA. Table 5 verifies the critical roles of our adaptive modules for meta-prototype contrastive learning (MPCL) and meta-prototype feature augmentation (MPFA). The baseline only performs decoupled training pipelines without using any components of our methods. In representation learning stage, our MPCL module significantly surpasses the performance over the DRO-LT and KCL (52.7% vs 51.9% vs 51.5%). Moreover, in classifier training stage, our MPFA module further boosts the performance, especially in the tail classes (53.8% vs 53.2%). The results suggest the effectiveness of both the MPCL and MPFA components in improving the training performance.

5   Conclusion

In this paper, we have proposed a novel meta-prototype decoupled training framework to tackle the long-tail challenge. Our decoupled training framework includes calibrating the empirical prototype for SCL in the representation learning stage and enhancing feature embedding for tail classes based on learned meta-prototype in the classifier learning stage. The first module of our method completes the meta-prototype to promote the representation quality of supervised prototype contrastive learning. The second module leverages the learned meta-prototype to provide the reasonable feature distribution of new feature samples for tail classes. We sample features from the calibrated distribution to ease the dominance of the head classes in classification decisions. The experimental results show that our method achieves state-of-the-art performances for various settings on long-tailed learning.

Acknowledgments. This work is supported by the National Natural Science Foundation of China (U21B2004), the Zhejiang Provincial key RD Program of China (2021C01119), and the Zhejiang University-Angelalign Inc. R&D Center for Intelligent Healthcare.

References

1. Andrychowicz, M., et al.: Learning to learn by gradient descent by gradient descent. In: Advances in Neural Information Processing Systems, vol. 29 (2016)
2. Cao, K., Wei, C., Gaidon, A., Arechiga, N., Ma, T.: Learning imbalanced datasets with label-distribution-aware margin loss. In: Advances in Neural Information Processing Systems, vol. 32 (2019)
3. Chen, D., Cao, X., Wang, L., Wen, F., Sun, J.: Bayesian face revisited: a joint formulation. In: Fitzgibbon, A., Lazebnik, S., Perona, P., Sato, Y., Schmid, C. (eds.) ECCV 2012. LNCS, vol. 7574, pp. 566–579. Springer, Heidelberg (2012). https://doi.org/10.1007/978-3-642-33712-3_41
4. Chen, L.-C., Zhu, Y., Papandreou, G., Schroff, F., Adam, H.: Encoder-decoder with atrous separable convolution for semantic image segmentation. In: Ferrari, V., Hebert, M., Sminchisescu, C., Weiss, Y. (eds.) ECCV 2018. LNCS, vol. 11211, pp. 833–851. Springer, Cham (2018). https://doi.org/10.1007/978-3-030-01234-2_49
5. Cui, J., Zhong, Z., Liu, S., Yu, B., Jia, J.: Parametric contrastive learning (2021)
6. Deng, J., Dong, W., Socher, R., Li, L.J., Li, K., Fei-Fei, L.: Imagenet: a large-scale hierarchical image database. In: 2009 IEEE Conference on Computer Vision and Pattern Recognition, pp. 248–255 (2009)
7. Finn, C., Abbeel, P., Levine, S.: Model-agnostic meta-learning for fast adaptation of deep networks. In: International conference on machine learning. pp. 1126–1135. PMLR (2017)
8. Hong, Y., Han, S., Choi, K., Seo, S., Kim, B., Chang, B.: Disentangling label distribution for long-tailed visual recognition. In: Proceedings of the IEEE/CVF Conference on Computer Vision and Pattern Recognition, pp. 6626–6636 (2021)
9. Kang, B., et al.: Decoupling representation and classifier for long-tailed recognition (2019)
10. Kang, B., Li, Y., Xie, S., Yuan, Z., Feng, J.: Exploring balanced feature spaces for representation learning. In: International Conference on Learning Representations (2021)
11. Khosla, P., et al.: Supervised contrastive learning. Adv. Neural. Inf. Process. Syst. **33**, 18661–18673 (2020)
12. Krizhevsky, A., Hinton, G., et al.: Learning multiple layers of features from tiny images (2009)
13. Li, J., Xiong, C., Hoi, S.C.: Mopro: webly supervised learning with momentum prototypes. arXiv preprint arXiv:2009.07995 (2020)
14. Li, S., Gong, K., Liu, C.H., Wang, Y., Qiao, F., Cheng, X.: Metasaug: meta semantic augmentation for long-tailed visual recognition. In: Proceedings of the IEEE/CVF Conference on Computer Vision and Pattern Recognition, pp. 5212–5221 (2021)
15. Li, T., et al.: Targeted supervised contrastive learning for long-tailed recognition. In: Proceedings of the IEEE/CVF Conference on Computer Vision and Pattern Recognition, pp. 6918–6928 (2022)

16. Lin, T.Y., Goyal, P., Girshick, R., He, K., Dollár, P.: Focal loss for dense object detection. In: Proceedings of the IEEE International Conference on Computer Vision, pp. 2980–2988 (2017)
17. Liu, Z., Miao, Z., Zhan, X., Wang, J., Gong, B., Yu, S.X.: Large-scale long-tailed recognition in an open world. In: Proceedings of the IEEE/CVF Conference on Computer Vision and Pattern Recognition, pp. 2537–2546 (2019)
18. Liu, Z., Miao, Z., Zhan, X., Wang, J., Gong, B., Yu, S.X.: Large-scale long-tailed recognition in an open world. In: IEEE Conference on Computer Vision and Pattern Recognition (CVPR) (2019)
19. Loshchilov, I., Hutter, F.: SGDR: stochastic gradient descent with warm restarts. arXiv preprint arXiv:1608.03983 (2016)
20. Ren, J., Yu, C., Ma, X., Zhao, H., Yi, S., et al.: Balanced meta-softmax for long-tailed visual recognition. Adv. Neural. Inf. Process. Syst. **33**, 4175–4186 (2020)
21. Samuel, D., Chechik, G.: Distributional robustness loss for long-tail learning. In: Proceedings of the IEEE/CVF International Conference on Computer Vision (ICCV), pp. 9495–9504 (2021)
22. Shu, J., et al.: Meta-weight-net: learning an explicit mapping for sample weighting. In: Advances in Neural Information Processing Systems, vol. 32 (2019)
23. Tang, K., Huang, J., Zhang, H.: Long-tailed classification by keeping the good and removing the bad momentum causal effect. Adv. Neural. Inf. Process. Syst. **33**, 1513–1524 (2020)
24. Tukey, J.W., et al.: Exploratory data analysis, vol. 2. Reading, MA (1977)
25. Van Horn, G., et al.: The inaturalist species classification and detection dataset. In: Proceedings of the IEEE Conference on Computer Vision and Pattern Recognition, pp. 8769–8778 (2018)
26. Vigneswaran, R., Law, M.T., Balasubramanian, V.N., Tapaswi, M.: Feature generation for long-tail classification. In: Proceedings of the Twelfth Indian Conference on Computer Vision, Graphics and Image Processing, pp. 1–9 (2021)
27. Wang, J., Lukasiewicz, T., Hu, X., Cai, J., Xu, Z.: RSG: a simple but effective module for learning imbalanced datasets. In: Proceedings of the IEEE/CVF Conference on Computer Vision and Pattern Recognition, pp. 3784–3793 (2021)
28. Wang, P., Han, K., Wei, X.S., Zhang, L., Wang, L.: Contrastive learning based hybrid networks for long-tailed image classification. In: Proceedings of the IEEE/CVF Conference on Computer Vision and Pattern Recognition, pp. 943–952 (2021)
29. Wang, X., Lian, L., Miao, Z., Liu, Z., Yu, S.: Long-tailed recognition by routing diverse distribution-aware experts. In: International Conference on Learning Representations (2021)
30. Wang, Y., Pan, X., Song, S., Zhang, H., Huang, G., Wu, C.: Implicit semantic data augmentation for deep networks. In: Advances in Neural Information Processing Systems, vol. 32 (2019)
31. Xie, S., Girshick, R., Dollár, P., Tu, Z., He, K.: Aggregated residual transformations for deep neural networks. arXiv preprint arXiv:1611.05431 (2016)
32. Yang, Y., Xu, Z.: Rethinking the value of labels for improving class-imbalanced learning. In: Advances in Neural Information Processing Systems, vol. 33, pp. 19290–19301 (2020)
33. Yuan, Y., Wang, J.: OCNET: object context network for scene parsing (2018)
34. Zang, Y., Huang, C., Loy, C.C.: FASA: feature augmentation and sampling adaptation for long-tailed instance segmentation. In: Proceedings of the IEEE/CVF International Conference on Computer Vision, pp. 3457–3466 (2021)

35. Zhang, S., Li, Z., Yan, S., He, X., Sun, J.: Distribution alignment: a unified framework for long-tail visual recognition. In: Proceedings of the IEEE/CVF Conference on Computer Vision and Pattern Recognition, pp. 2361–2370 (2021)
36. Zhang, Y., Kang, B., Hooi, B., Yan, S., Feng, J.: Deep long-tailed learning: a survey. arXiv preprint arXiv:2110.04596 (2021)
37. Zhang, Y., Wei, X.S., Zhou, B., Wu, J.: Bag of tricks for long-tailed visual recognition with deep convolutional neural networks. In: Proceedings of the AAAI Conference on Artificial Intelligence, vol. 35, pp. 3447–3455 (2021)
38. Zhang, Z., Xiang, X.: Long-tailed classification with gradual balanced loss and adaptive feature generation (2022)
39. Zhong, Z., Cui, J., Liu, S., Jia, J.: Improving calibration for long-tailed recognition. In: Proceedings of the IEEE/CVF Conference on Computer Vision and Pattern Recognition, pp. 16489–16498 (2021)
40. Zhou, B., Zhao, H., Puig, X., Fidler, S., Barriuso, A., Torralba, A.: Scene parsing through ade20k dataset. In: Proceedings of the IEEE Conference on Computer Vision and Pattern Recognition. , pp. 633–641 (2017)
41. Zhou, B., Cui, Q., Wei, X.S., Chen, Z.M.: BBN: bilateral-branch network with cumulative learning for long-tailed visual recognition. In: Proceedings of the IEEE/CVF Conference on Computer Vision and Pattern Recognition, pp. 9719–9728 (2020)
42. Zhu, B., Niu, Y., Hua, X.S., Zhang, H.: Cross-domain empirical risk minimization for unbiased long-tailed classification. In: AAAI Conference on Artificial Intelligence (2022)
43. Zhu, L., Yang, Y.: Inflated episodic memory with region self-attention for long-tailed visual recognition. In: Proceedings of the IEEE/CVF Conference on Computer Vision and Pattern Recognition, pp. 4344–4353 (2020)

PEDTrans: A Fine-Grained Visual Classification Model for Self-attention Patch Enhancement and Dropout

Xuhong Lin[1], Qian Yan[1], Caicong Wu[1,2], and Yifei Chen[1,2(✉)]

[1] College of Information and Electrical Engineering, China Agricultural University, Beijing 100083, China
glhfei@126.com
[2] Key Laboratory of Agricultural Machinery Monitoring and Big Data Applications, Ministry of Agriculture and Rural Affairs, Beijing 100083, China

Abstract. Fine-grained visual classification (FGVC) is an essential and challenging classification task in computer visual classification, aiming to identify different cars and birds. Recently, most studies use a convolutional neural network combined with an attention mechanism to find discriminant regions to improve algorithm accuracy automatically. However, the discriminant regions selected by the convolutional neural network are extensive. Vision Transformer divides the image into patches and relies on self-attention to select more accurate discriminant regions. However, the Vision Transformer model ignores the response between local patches before patch embedding. In addition, patches usually have high similarity, and they are considered redundant. Therefore, we propose a PEDTrans model based on Vision Transformer. The model has a patch enhancement module based on attention mechanism and a random similar group patch discarding module based on similarity. These two modules can establish patch local feature relationships and select patches that are easier to distinguish between images. Combining these two modules with the Vision Transformer backbone network can improve the fine-grained visual classification accuracy. We employ commonly used fine-grained visual classification datasets CUB-200-2011, Stanford Cars, Stanford Dogs and NABirds to get advanced results.

Keywords: Fine-grained visual classification · Vision Transformer · Self-attention

1 Introduction

In deep learning, convolutional neural networks have been rapidly developed and used in various computer vision tasks. Fine-grained visual classification has long been a challenging task because it categorizes sub-classes within categories with little difference (for example, similar birds, dogs, and car types). In the early stages of the fine-grained visual classification model, researchers used expensive location-calibrated data to classify, relying on additional bounding boxes to

L. Wang et al. (Eds.): ACCV 2022, LNCS 13846, pp. 269–285, 2023.
https://doi.org/10.1007/978-3-031-26351-4_17

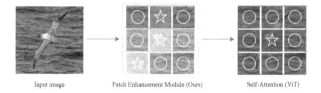

Input image   Patch Enhancement Module (Ours)   Self-Attention (ViT)

Fig. 1. Repeated and redundant patches are marked with a hollow circle, and local and global enhanced patches are marked with a hollow five pointed star.

locate detailed parts of the image [1,15]. However, with the development of the fine-grained visual classification network, researchers found that this calibration method was not the best because the annotator's notes might be incorrect and time and effort consumed. Thanks to the development of primary convolutional networks, new progress has been made in fine-grained visual classification networks and classification methods. Methods [18,38] represent weakly supervised learning, which avoids the use of expensive annotation data. Most of the current methods use weak supervision to solve this problem, effectively saving the labelling cost and producing good results. Transformer achieves good results in text tasks [3,4,26] and achieves the same results in visual classification tasks as deep convolutional networks [7]. Recently, it has been widely used in this field. Because the input of the visual converter is patch data, it can better find important parts in fine-grained visual classification.

Although the Vision Transformer model adds the position vector in the patch embedding stage, it only increases the relative position between patches and cannot establish the relationship between local patches. In addition, the model divides the input image into small patches, so there are many duplicate parts between patches. Effectively removing these duplicate patches can make the model better distinguish images. These problems are shown in Fig. 1, where the dotted box is the newly added Patch Enhancement Module. It more clearly presents enhanced local patches and redundant patches. Global and local enhanced patches can be more clearly distinguished.

This study proposes a fine-grained visual classification model for self-attention enhancement and random dropout patches to address these issues. We add two separate modules for the transformer to achieve better classification results, one is Patch Enhancement Module, and the other is Dropout Patch Module. The relationships between local patches can be established by the Patch Enhancement Module and make important patch information more prominent. The Dropout Patch Module uses the similarity between patches to select necessary patches and then classifies them using the most effective patches to avoid redundant information. The marked patches will be put into the transformer as new input and classified using the position token. Finally, we conduct extensive experiments on standard fine-grained Vision classification data sets and get better results than the convolutional neural network.

Our method is more effective than the existing methods and does not need additional annotation information. The main contributions we create in this paper are summarized as follows:

1. We use a method similar to channel attention to establishing the local relationship between patches. The patch information of effectively distinguishing images can be more significant through the self-attention mechanism, equivalent to the first selection of important feature regions.
2. Although patch information is beneficial to the search of important discrimination areas, there is a large amount of redundant information and high similarity in patches. We propose a method to drop out the repeated patches according to the information similarity, and the remaining patches will be easier to distinguish the images.
3. We conduct extensive testing on fine-grained classification data sets. The results show that the Vision Transformer accuracy is improved and advanced performance is achieved by adding the Patch Enhancement Module and the Dropout Patch Module.

2 Related Work

The second section introduces the related work and methods of fine-grained visual classification, channel attention, dropout method, and Vision Transformer.

2.1 Fine Grained Visual Classification Method

Zhang et al. [35] proposed a local-based Part-based R-CNN (Part R-CNN) fine-grained visual classification algorithm in 2014, which directly uses convolutional features for classification. Wei et al. [32] proposed the Mask CNN model, an end-to-end deep convolutional model, which is different from the Part R-CNN algorithm, which evaluates and screens the characteristics of deep convolution. Lin et al. [18] designed an effective Bilinear CNN model framework. Bilinear channel features extract the paired correlation between channels and then distinguish the subtle differences between images. This structure can obtain feature information of different granularity and then improve classification accuracy. Fu et al. [9] proposed a Recurrent Attention Convolutional Neural Network (RA-CNN) based on an attention mechanism that learns and discriminates region attention and region-based feature representation recursively and enhances each other. The progressive Multi-Granularity (PMG) model [8] adopts a progressive learning method and random patch puzzle to make different levels of networks can learn different feature information. Methods [34,36] rely on the attention mechanism to obtain more effective discrimination areas. The latest TransFG model [11] adds a Part Selection Module (PSM) to the Vision Transformer (ViT) [7] and applies it to fine-grained visual classification. The main fine-grained visual classification method is weakly supervised training based on image-level labeled data.

2.2   Channel Attention

Vaswani et al. [28] proposed a self-attention mechanism in 2017. Then, Hu et al. [13] Proposed a Sequence-and-Excitation Network (SENet), first embedded into the Residual Networks (ResNet) [12] model. The channel attention method improves the accuracy of the convolutional neural network and further extracts the effective features. Since then, Park et al. [23] Combined channel attention with spatial attention and proposed Bottleneck Attention Module (BAM) [23] and Convolutional Block Attention Module (CBAM) [33] models. The former is the parallel channel and spatial attention structure, and the latter is the serial structure. Wang et al. [31] designed a more efficient channel attention module, which uses a one-dimensional convolution to connect the features, avoiding using the full connection to reduce the dimension and lose unnecessary features. At the same time, the one-dimensional convolution is used to interact with local channels, which effectively reduces the complexity of the model.

2.3   Dropout

Regularization methods for dropping neural units have been applied in deep convolutional networks. These methods are generally divided into randomly dropping out information and self-attention methods. The initial Dropout method [24] was to suppress neurons with a certain probability, and later methods were to delete the entire feature map or patch. For example, the Spatial Dropout method [25] deletes channels randomly, and the Cutout method [5] deletes patches randomly from the input image. Similarly, the ADCM method [21] uses the method of randomly dropping out channels and location information to improve the performance of the attention method. ADL [2] is an attention-based dropout method in which attention-based drop masks are applied to feature maps to mask most discriminatory components and promote networks to learn important features that are easy to distinguish. In addition, the Channel Drop Block method is to remove a similar set of related channels to break similarities between channels [6].

2.4   Transformer

Transformer was originally applied in natural language processing and text translation fields and has greatly promoted its development [3,4,26]. Recently, more and more models based on Vision Transformer have been widely used in other computer vision tasks. Researchers have improved the model's accuracy by improving self-attention mechanisms to detect discriminant regions automatically [34,36] or to model parts [11,30]. The representation of computer vision direction is pure Vision Transformer [7], Swin Transformer [20], etc. Vision Transformer is the first time it has been used in the field of vision, followed by local or global connections through different hierarchical networks to extract features. The first Transformer model in the fine-grained visual classification task is the TransFG [11] model, which improves the performance of pure Vision

Transformer models in fine-grained visual classification by adding the Part Selection Module and redesigning the loss function. In our work, we also add part modules to the pure Vision Transformer model and apply them to fine-grained visual classification tasks.

3   Method

In this chapter, we will better explain our approach. The steps to construct the input data are described in Sect. 3.1. The entire PEDTrans model framework, the Patch Enhancement Module, and Module are shown in Sect. 3.2, which uses three different dropout strategies.

3.1   Patch Embedding

The input information of the Vision Transformer model is different from the traditional convolutional neural network because Transformer was originally used to solve text problems. Therefore we design image data as text vectors to be input into the Vision Transformer. The initial image area is marked $S = H * W$ and divided into patches of size $P * P$, so the number N of patches can be calculated from Eq. (1):

$$N = (H/P) * (W/P). \tag{1}$$

3.2   PEDTrans

Generally speaking, the size of the input image is set to a square, $H = W$. Patches are projected into D-dimensional vector space by a learnable linear projection. Since the original image is divided into patches that cannot represent relative location information, a learning position vector E_{pos} is added to x_p. In addition, a token for classification is added before the first token converted from the patch. The final vector is like Eq. (2):

$$Z_0 = \left[x_{class}; E(x_p^1); \cdots ; E(x_p^N) \right] + E_{pos}. \tag{2}$$

where E is the patch embedding projection, $E \in R^{(D*p^2*c)}$, c is the number of channels of the original image, and E_{pos} represents the learning position embedding. The embedded image is transmitted to the interior of the Vision Transformer model. First, a Layer Normalization (LN) process is applied, which is then fed to Multi-head Self-attention (MSA) Module and Multi-layer Perceptron (MLP) Module. For better classification, such encoders are repeated L times and use a shortcut connection structure in the ResNet model. The output from Layer i can be calculated according to Eq. (4).

$$z_l^{'} = MSA\left(LN\left(z_{l-1} \right) \right) + z_{l-1}. \tag{3}$$

$$z_l = MLP\left(LN\left(\left(z_l^{'} \right) \right) \right) + z_l^{'}. \tag{4}$$

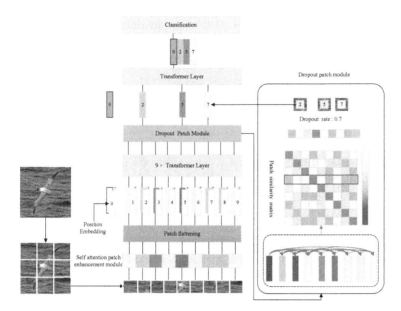

Fig. 2. PEDTrans: An image is divided into patches of the same size and enhanced by self-attention patches. Further, the linear projection embeds the patch into vector space, then combines it with the position embedding by addition. The Dropout Patch Module was designed to remove the duplicate and invalid patches before the last encoder to allow patch selection . The remaining patches are entered into the last encoder.

Following ViT, the original image is divided into N patches. The local relationship between patches helps the model select more effective patches. Although the patches add location information when embedded, the local patches' relationship is insufficient. We propose a Patch Enhancement Module for attention mechanism to enhance this local relationship. In addition, effective patches are a minority in a large number of patches. Redundant and duplicate patches can burden the classification results of models and mask patches that benefit classification. Our Dropout Patch Module can remove similar patches that are not good for classification. This section describes the details of our proposed PEDTrans. The framework of the whole model is shown in Fig. 2.

Patch Enhancement Module (PEM). In deep convolutional neural networks, the interaction between channels is very important. Different channels can get different weights through the attention mechanism, which enhances the characteristics of important channels. In Vision Transformer, patches are divided by the original image, ignoring the connections between local images. In addition, patch characteristics are critical to the final classification of the model, so using self-attention to enhance patch characteristics before converting patches

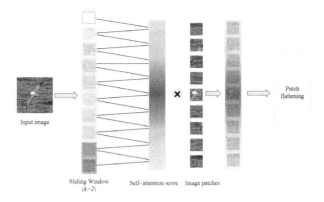

Fig. 3. This is a feature enhancement module with a sliding window length of 2. Each patch in the graph performs local information interaction through self-attention. Through this self-attention mechanism, different patches can obtain weights multiplied by the original feature map to obtain new enhanced feature patches.

to tokens increases the link between patches and makes important patches more effective in the final classification.

We propose a sliding window to establish local information connections. The framework of this module is shown in Fig. 3. Before the sliding window, we use global average pooling to process patches, and then use shared weights to learn the importance of local patches. Local attention weight is shown in Eq. (5).

$$\omega_i = s \left(\sum_{i=i-(k-1)/2}^{i+(k-1)/2} \omega_i * x_p^i \right). \tag{5}$$

$$x_p^i \in \Omega = \left\{ x_p^{i-(k-1)/2}, \cdots, x_p^i, \cdots, x_p^{i+(k-1)/2} \right\}. \tag{6}$$

where ω_i is the shared weight, s is the $Softmax$ function, and the set Ω consists of k patches are connected before and after the i-th patch. This method can be realized by fast one-dimensional convolution with kernel k, as shown in Eq. (7) :

$$\omega_i = s \left(Conv1D_k(mean(x_p^i)) \right). \tag{7}$$

where $Conv1D$ is a one-dimensional convolution, which can change the relationship between the upper and lower patches by adjusting the size of the k value to adjust the length of the sliding window. We do not use a structure similar to the ResNet model because we find that using a shortcut connection structure here does not increase performance very well. The general channel attention expression is represented by Eq. (8):

$$X_{out} = X_{in}^T W + X_{in}. \tag{8}$$

$$X_{out} = s \left(\frac{QK^T}{\sqrt{k}} \right) X_{in}. \tag{9}$$

However, we use a similar approach to self-attention in PEM to achieve feature enhancement, as shown in Eq. (9) where Q is obtained by the linear mapping of x^p and K is obtained by the global average pooling of x^p. k is the size of the sliding window. It can be understood more simply in Eq. (10).

$$X_{out} = X_{in}^T W. \tag{10}$$

More detailed results will be given in Chap. 4 of the ablation study and the reasons for the performance difference between the two will be analyzed.

Dropout Patch Module (DPM). This part contains three dropping strategies, namely, dropping out based on similarity, dropping out randomly and dropping out based on attention weight.

The Dropout Patch Module is implemented based on the correlation between patches to remove the most redundant patch and retain the most effective patches for final classification. We proposed that the Dropout Patch Module establishes a discarded patch combination by calculating the correlation coefficient matrix between patches. Figure 2 shows the details of the Dropout Patch Module in the PEDTrans module. Specifically, the input to Dropout Patch Module is a feature embedded $X_{in} \in R^{(N*P^2)}$ where N is the number of patches, and P^2 is the characteristic length of each embedded patch. Refer to Eq. (11) for the calculation process. We calculate the correlation matrix $M \in R^{(N*N)}$ between each patch, then drop out a patch by random selection and drop out patches that are too similar to the patch based on the calculated similarity matrix M and dropout rate γ.

The similarity matrix M of the Dropout Patch Module is calculated using the correlation measure in the bilinear pooling [18] algorithm, which measures the similarity between patches using the normalized cosine distance. Input features are first normalized, then similar matrices are constructed by matrix multiplication to obtain similar relationships between patches.

$$M = \mathcal{N}(X_{in}) \bullet \mathcal{N}(X_{in}^T) = \begin{bmatrix} 1 & M_{12} & \cdots & M_{1p} \\ M_{21} & 1 & \cdots & M_{2p} \\ \vdots & \vdots & \ddots & \vdots \\ M_{p1} & M_{p2} & \cdots & 1 \end{bmatrix}. \tag{11}$$

In Eq. (11), $\mathcal{N}$ is a normalization function, and the similarity matrix M is a symmetric matrix. That is, the diagonal element $M_{ii} = 1$. M_{ij} indicates how similar the i-th patch is to the j-th patch.

The algorithm 1 description indicates that the i-th patch is randomly selected for dropout, and if $M_{ij} > min(A)$, the j-th patch will be dropout where A is the most similar set to patch i, and its size is $N * \gamma$. In other words, the similarity between every two patches will be arranged in descending order, leaving only patches that are similar to $m_{(N*\gamma)}$ where $m_{(N*\gamma)}$ is the $N * \gamma$-th similarity. Dropout Patch Module contains only one super parameter: γ, which controls the percentage of similar patches discarded.

Algorithm 1: Dropout Patch Module

Data: Patches feature map X_{in}; Dropout rate γ
Result: The index of the reserved patch
1 Computing the correlation matrix M;
2 Randomly select a patch i;
3 Dropout patch i;
4 **while** $j \leq N$ **do**
5   **if** $M_{ij} > \min(A)$ **then**
6 | Dropout patch j;
7   **else**
8 | Retain patch j;
9   **end**
10 **end**

The above is the dropout strategy based on patch similarity. The following describes the random dropout strategy and the dropout strategy based on attention weight.

According to the description in Algorithm 1, the random dropout strategy is to randomly select $N * \gamma$ patches from N patches and return the remaining indexes. The self-attention weight dropout strategy relies on the self-attention score of each layer of patches to drop out, discards the $N * \gamma$ patches with the smallest weight, and returns the reserved index.

4 Experiments

This chapter introduces the detailed settings of the experiment in Sect. 4.1, including dataset, training hyperparameter settings, and hardware device information. Quantitative experimental analysis is given in Sect. 4.2. Ablation study is performed in subsequent Sect. 4.3. Qualitative analysis and experimental visualization are further given in Sect. 4.4.

4.1 Experiments Setup

Datasets. We tested the effectiveness of PEDTrans on several widely used fine-grained datasets, CUB-200- 2011 [29], Stanford Dogs [16], Stanford Cars [17], and NABirds [27] are datasets tested by general fine-grained visual algorithms to assess the performance of fine-grained visual algorithms very well, and they are challenging. Specific dataset information is shown in Table 1.

Experimental Details. We used most of the data enhancement methods in our experiments (clipping for training, central clipping for testing). First, we adjusted the image to $600 * 600$ and then clipped it to $448 * 448$. We use the pre-training model of the official ViT-B_16 in ImageNet21K. The parameters are set as follows: Batch size is 8, SGD optimizer is used, momentum is 0.9,

Table 1. Detailed statistics for CUB-200-2011, Stanford Dogs and Stanford Cars.

Datasets	Category	Training	Testing
CUB	200	5994	5794
Dog	120	12000	8580
Car	196	8144	8041
NABirds	555	23929	24633

learning rate is initialized to 0.02, cosine annealing is used as the scheduler of the optimizer. The loss function uses a cross-entropy function and contrast loss function. The Patch Enhancement Module sliding window super parameter k is 3, and the Dropout Patch Module dropout rate γ is 0.5. The experiments were trained with four Nvidia RTX 3080 GPUs using the deep learning framework Pytorch toolbox and Apex with FP16 training. In order to avoid the error caused by the experimental equipment, we conducted the experiment again according to the open source code and marked it with ∗.

Table 2. Comparison results of different methods on CUB-200- 2011, Stanford Dogs and Stanford Cars.

Method	Backbone	CUB	Cars	Dogs
RA-CNN [9]	VGG-19	85.3	92.5	87.3
MA-CNN [37]	VGG-19	86.5	92.8	–
P-CNN [10]	VGG-19	87.3	93.3	90.6
ResNet50 [12]	ResNet-50	84.4	–	–
Cross-X [22]	ResNet-50	87.7	94.6	88.9
PMG [8]	ResNet-50	89.6	95.1	–
FDL [19]	DenseNet-161	89.1	84.7	84.9
API-Net [38]	DenseNet-161	90.0	**95.3**	90.3
ViT [7]	ViT-B_16	90.7	93.7	91.7
FFTV * [30]	ViT-B_16	91.4	–	91.5
RAMS-Trans [14]	ViT-B_16	91.3	–	**92.4**
TransFG * [11]	ViT-B_16	91.3	94.8	92.3
PEDTans(ours)	ViT-B_16	**91.7**	95.1	**92.4**

4.2   Quantitative Analysis

Our specific experimental results are shown in Table 2 and Table 3. PEDTrans achieved 91.7% accuracy on CUB datasets. It is 1.0% higher than the original Vision Transformer (ViT) model, and it does not use the overlapping strategy in the TransFG model to improve accuracy. The overlap strategy improves accuracy by increasing the number of patches. Our method is 0.3% more accurate than

TransFG on the Stanford Cars dataset. It implements state-of-the-art (SOTA) on the data sets we tested and it is superior to most methods and has higher accuracy than the original Vision Transformer model. We obtained 92.4% accuracy on the Stanford dogs dataset, which is higher than 92.3% of the TransFG model and better than other convolutional neural networks. On the NABirds dataset, our model achieves an accuracy of 90.7%. In the experimental results, we use bold to represent the optimal results and underline to represent the suboptimal results.

Table 3. Comparison results of different methods on NABirds.

Method	Backbone	Acc
Cross-X [22]	ResNet-50	86.4
API-Net [38]	DenseNet-161	88.1
ViT [7]	ViT-B_16	89.3
TPSKG [14]	ViT-B_16	90.1
FFTV * [30]	ViT-B_16	89.5
TransFG * [11]	ViT-B_16	90.2
R^2-Trans [11]	ViT-B_16	90.2
PEDTans(ours)	ViT-B_16	**90.7**

4.3   Ablation Study

PEM: We performed an ablation study on PEDTrans to see how our framework affects classification accuracy. All the experimental results are implemented on the CUB dataset. We test these framework parts, including the Patch Enhancement Module and Dropout Patch Module. The impact of the Patch Enhancement Module is shown in Table 4.

A quantitative comparison between adding PEM and deleting PEM shows that the model's accuracy is improved by adding PEM. Specifically, the accuracy of the ViT results increased from 90.7% to 91.2%. We think that building the correlation of local information can increase the interaction between patches, which will help the model increase the ability to select different patches, enhance the characteristics of some patches, and improve the model's accuracy.

In the Patch Enhancement Module, we also tested the size of the sliding window and found that the best results at $k = 3$. The test results of sliding windows of different sizes are shown in Table 5. Sliding windows are too small to establish a good relationship between local patches and interact effectively, but too large windows can cause some valid patches to be masked by the best patches.

We try to use shortcut connections in this section, but we can not get good results. Typically, channel attention is a shortcut connection after a series of

Table 4. Ablation study on PEM and DPM on CUB-200-2011 dataset.

Datasets	Accuracy (%)
ViT	90.7
+PEM	91.2
+DPM	91.2
PEDTrans(ours)	91.7

Table 5. Ablation study on value of sliding window k on CUB-200-2011 dataset.

Value of k	Accuracy (%)
1	91.2
3	91.7
5	91.5
7	91.3

Table 6. Ablation study on shortcut connection on CUB-200-2011 dataset.

Method	Accuracy (%)
PEDTrans($XW^T + X$)	91.3
PEDTrans(XW^T)	91.7

feature extraction, but a multilayer convolution does not characterize our model. So, it is critical to multiply patches by the self-attention enhancement factor and get good results. The test results of these two connection modes are shown in Table 6.

DPM: We remove redundant patches from the last input level by adding a dropout patch module before the last encoder. The performance of ViT and ViT+DPM will be compared in this part, and compare three different dropout strategies in DPM. The test results are shown in Table 4. Specifically, the accuracy of ViT is 90.7%, and after adding DPM, the accuracy is improved by 0.5% to 91.2%. We believe that removing a large number of invalid, duplicate patches will make it easier for the model to obtain the most recognizable patches and thus improve the accuracy.

We also test the dropout rate γ in the dropout patch module with different 3 strategies and found that 50% dropout rate in DPM based on similarity is the best value, $\gamma = 0.5$. The input position information of the last encoder is shown in Fig. 4. The random dropout strategy (Blue Border) can get more scattered patches, while the self-attention score strategy (Yellow Border) can get more focused patches centered on the classification object. The similarity based dropout strategy (Red Border) is between the two. This strategy can achieve the best results. It not only drops out part of the background, but also eliminates some unimportant prospects. It has a certain regularization effect. It is calculated based on similarity, so even if the first patch selected randomly selects the foreground object, the module will keep the parts with differences because the parts of the object are different. More detailed results are shown in Table 7. Discarding too many patches will easily lose categorized patches, but discarding too few patches will not highlight important ones.

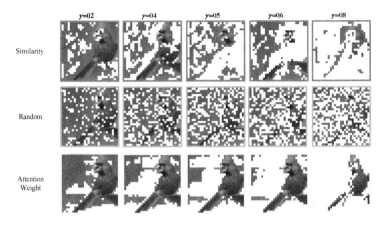

Fig. 4. Illustration of dropout rate. The visual images with different dropout rate are displayed, and the values of γ are 0.2, 0.4, 0.5, 0.6 and 0.8 respectively. (Color figure online)

We only added DMP during training, with an accuracy of 91.3%. DPM was added during training and testing, and the accuracy was 91.7%. Its more important role is to select the discrimination region, which is perfectly combined with patch in ViT.

Table 7. Ablation study on value of dropout rate γ on CUB-200-2011 dataset.

Value of γ	Similarity	Random	Attention-Weight
0.2	91.3	91.3	91.2
0.4	91.4	91.3	91.2
0.5	91.7	91.2	91.4
0.6	91.5	91.2	91.3
0.8	91.2	91.2	91.5

4.4 Analyze Visualization Results

We show the visualization of PEDTrans on four benchmarks in Fig. 5. We randomly selected two images from the four standard datasets we tested for visualization, and we drew an overall attention image based on the corresponding weight scales $(1, 2, 4, 8)$ of the last four layers of the network. The transparent white areas in the image are important areas from which we can see that our model can accurately capture the most easily distinguishable parts of the object under test, such as the mouth and eyes of a bird; The logo of the car, the lamp of the car, and the intake grille that BMW can recognize most easily; Dog's ears, eyes, etc.

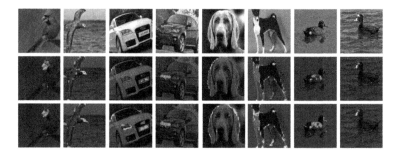

Fig. 5. Visualization results of PEDTrans in CUB-200-2011, Stanford Dogs, Stanford Cars and NABirds, where the first line are input images, while the second and third lines are partial attention maps generated by the ViT and PEDTrans. Best viewed in colour. (Color figure online)

5   Conclusion

This work proposes a fine-grained visual classification network based on the Vision Transformer model and has achieved advanced results on standard fine-grained visual classification datasets. We build relationships between patches through self-attention mechanisms like channel interactions in convolutional neural networks. Through this connection, we enhanced patches that help distinguish between images. Fine-grained visual classification networks are most important in finding patches that are easy to distinguish between images, so the Vision Transformer model is more helpful in choosing really effective patches, but most of the small patches are redundant. Duplicate patches can be effectively removed and play a certain role in regularization through our proposed Drop Patches module. The final visualization fully demonstrates the validity of our proposed model.

Acknowledgement. This work is partly supported by national precision agriculture application project (construction number: JZNYYY001).

References

1. Chai, Y., Lempitsky, V., Zisserman, A.: Symbiotic segmentation and part localization for fine-grained categorization. In: Proceedings of the IEEE International Conference on Computer Vision, pp. 321–328 (2013)
2. Choe, J., Shim, H.: Attention-based dropout layer for weakly supervised object localization. In: Proceedings of the IEEE/CVF Conference on Computer Vision and Pattern Recognition, pp. 2219–2228 (2019)
3. Dai, Z., Yang, Z., Yang, Y., Carbonell, J., Le, Q., Salakhutdinov, R.: Transformer-XL: attentive language models beyond a fixed-length context. In: Proceedings of the 57th Annual Meeting of the Association for Computational Linguistics, pp. 2978–2988 (2019). https://doi.org/10.18653/v1/P19-1285. https://aclanthology.org/P19-1285

4. Devlin, J., Chang, M.W., Lee, K., Toutanova, K.: BERT: pre-training of deep bidirectional transformers for language understanding. In: Proceedings of the conference, Association for Computational Linguistics. Meeting, pp. 4171–4186 (2019). https://doi.org/10.18653/v1/N19-1423. https://aclanthology.org/N19-1423

5. DeVries, T., Taylor, G.W.: Improved regularization of convolutional neural networks with cutout. arXiv preprint arXiv:1708.04552 (2017)

6. Ding, Y., Dong, S., Tong, Y., Ma, Z., Xiao, B., Ling, H.: Channel dropblock: an improved regularization method for fine-grained visual classification. arXiv preprint arXiv:2106.03432 (2021)

7. Dosovitskiy, A., et al.: An image is worth 16x16 words: transformers for image recognition at scale. In: International Conference on Learning Representations (2021)

8. Du, R., et al.: Fine-grained visual classification via progressive multi-granularity training of jigsaw patches. In: Vedaldi, A., Bischof, H., Brox, T., Frahm, J.-M. (eds.) ECCV 2020. LNCS, vol. 12365, pp. 153–168. Springer, Cham (2020). https://doi.org/10.1007/978-3-030-58565-5_10

9. Fu, J., Zheng, H., Mei, T.: Look closer to see better: recurrent attention convolutional neural network for fine-grained image recognition. In: Proceedings of the IEEE Conference on Computer Vision and Pattern Recognition, pp. 4438–4446 (2017)

10. Han, J., Yao, X., Cheng, G., Feng, X., Xu, D.: P-CNN: part-based convolutional neural networks for fine-grained visual categorization. IEEE Trans. Pattern Anal. Mach. Intell. **44**(2), 579–590 (2022). https://doi.org/10.1109/TPAMI.2019.2933510

11. He, J., et al.: TransFG: a transformer architecture for fine-grained recognition. arXiv preprint arXiv:2103.07976 (2021)

12. He, K., Zhang, X., Ren, S., Sun, J.: Deep residual learning for image recognition. In: Proceedings of the IEEE Conference on Computer Vision and Pattern Recognition, pp. 770–778 (2016)

13. Hu, J., Shen, L., Sun, G.: Squeeze-and-excitation networks. In: Proceedings of the IEEE conference on Computer Vision and Pattern Recognition, pp. 7132–7141 (2018)

14. Hu, Y., et al.: Rams-trans: recurrent attention multi-scale transformer for fine-grained image recognition. In: Proceedings of the 29th ACM International Conference on Multimedia, pp. 4239–4248 (2021)

15. Huang, S., Xu, Z., Tao, D., Zhang, Y.: Part-stacked CNN for fine-grained visual categorization. In: Proceedings of the IEEE Conference on Computer Vision and Pattern Recognition, pp. 1173–1182 (2016)

16. Khosla, A., Jayadevaprakash, N., Yao, B., Li, F.F.: Novel dataset for fine-grained image categorization: Stanford dogs. In: Proceedings CVPR Workshop on Fine-Grained Visual Categorization (FGVC), vol. 2, no. 1 (2011)

17. Krause, J., Stark, M., Deng, J., Fei-Fei, L.: 3D object representations for fine-grained categorization. In: Proceedings of the IEEE International Conference on Computer Vision Workshops, pp. 554–561 (2013)

18. Lin, T.Y., RoyChowdhury, A., Maji, S.: Bilinear CNN models for fine-grained visual recognition. In: Proceedings of the IEEE International Conference on Computer Vision, pp. 1449–1457 (2015)

19. Liu, C., Xie, H., Zha, Z.J., Ma, L., Zhang, Y.: Filtration and distillation: enhancing region attention for fine-grained visual categorization. Proceed. AAAI Conf. Artif. Intell. **34**(7), 11555–11562 (2020)

20. Liu, Z., et al.: Swin transformer: hierarchical vision transformer using shifted windows. In: Proceedings of the IEEE/CVF International Conference on Computer Vision, pp. 10012–10022 (2021)
21. Liu, Z., Du, J., Wang, M., Ge, S.S.: ADCM: attention dropout convolutional module. Neurocomputing **394**, 95–104 (2020)
22. Luo, W., et al.: Cross-x learning for fine-grained visual categorization. In: Proceedings of the IEEE/CVF International Conference on Computer Vision, pp. 8242–8251 (2019)
23. Park, J., Woo, S., Lee, J.Y., Kweon, I.S.: BAM: bottleneck attention module. British Machine Vision Conference, p. 147 (2018)
24. Srivastava, N., Hinton, G., Krizhevsky, A., Sutskever, I., Salakhutdinov, R.: Dropout: a simple way to prevent neural networks from overfitting. J. Mach. Learn. Res. **15**(1), 1929–1958 (2014)
25. Tompson, J., Goroshin, R., Jain, A., LeCun, Y., Bregler, C.: Efficient object localization using convolutional networks. In: Proceedings of the IEEE Conference on Computer Vision and Pattern Recognition, pp. 648–656 (2015)
26. Tsai, Y.H.H., Bai, S., Liang, P.P., Kolter, J.Z., Morency, L.P., Salakhutdinov, R.: Multimodal transformer for unaligned multimodal language sequences. In: Proceedings of the conference, Association for Computational Linguistics. Meeting, p. 6558 (2019)
27. Van Horn, G., et al.: Building a bird recognition app and large scale dataset with citizen scientists: the fine print in fine-grained dataset collection. In: 2015 IEEE Conference on Computer Vision and Pattern Recognition (CVPR), pp. 595–604 (2015). https://doi.org/10.1109/CVPR.2015.7298658
28. Vaswani, A., et al.: Attention is all you need. In: Advances in Neural Information Processing Systems 30 (2017)
29. Wah, C., Branson, S., Welinder, P., Perona, P., Belongie, S.: The caltech-UCSD birds-200-2011 dataset (2011)
30. Wang, J., Yu, X., Gao, Y.: Feature fusion vision transformer for fine-grained visual categorization. arXiv preprint arXiv:2107.02341 (2021)
31. Wang, Q., Wu, B., Zhu, P., Li, P., Hu, Q.: ECA-Net: efficient channel attention for deep convolutional neural networks. In: 2020 IEEE/CVF Conference on Computer Vision and Pattern Recognition (CVPR) (2020)
32. Wei, X.S., Xie, C.W., Wu, J., Shen, C.: Mask-CNN: localizing parts and selecting descriptors for fine-grained bird species categorization. Pattern Recogn. **76**, 704–714 (2018)
33. Woo, S., Park, J., Lee, J.-Y., Kweon, I.S.: CBAM: convolutional block attention module. In: Ferrari, V., Hebert, M., Sminchisescu, C., Weiss, Y. (eds.) ECCV 2018. LNCS, vol. 11211, pp. 3–19. Springer, Cham (2018). https://doi.org/10.1007/978-3-030-01234-2_1
34. Xiao, T., Xu, Y., Yang, K., Zhang, J., Peng, Y., Zhang, Z.: The application of two-level attention models in deep convolutional neural network for fine-grained image classification. In: Proceedings of the IEEE Conference on Computer Vision and Pattern Recognition, pp. 842–850 (2015)
35. Zhang, N., Donahue, J., Girshick, R., Darrell, T.: Part-based R-CNNs for fine-grained category detection. In: Fleet, D., Pajdla, T., Schiele, B., Tuytelaars, T. (eds.) ECCV 2014. LNCS, vol. 8689, pp. 834–849. Springer, Cham (2014). https://doi.org/10.1007/978-3-319-10590-1_54
36. Zhao, B., Wu, X., Feng, J., Peng, Q., Yan, S.: Diversified visual attention networks for fine-grained object classification. IEEE Trans. Multimedia **19**(6), 1245–1256 (2017)

37. Zheng, H., Fu, J., Tao, M., Luo, J.: Learning multi-attention convolutional neural network for fine-grained image recognition. In: 2017 IEEE International Conference on Computer Vision (ICCV) (2017)
38. Zhuang, P., Wang, Y., Qiao, Y.: Learning attentive pairwise interaction for fine-grained classification. Proceed. AAAI Conf. Artif. Intell. **34**(07), 13130–13137 (2020)

Three-stage Training Pipeline with Patch Random Drop for Few-shot Object Detection

Shaobo Lin[1(✉)], Xingyu Zeng[1], Shilin Yan[2], and Rui Zhao[1]

[1] Sensetime Research, Shanghai, China
{linshaobo,zengxingyu,zhaorui}@sensetime.com
[2] Fudan University, Shanghai, China

Abstract. Self-supervised learning (SSL) aims to design pretext tasks for exploiting the structural information of data without manual annotation, which has been widely used in few-shot image classification for improving the generalization of the model. However, few works explore the influence of SSL on Few-shot object detection (FSOD) which is a more challenging task. Besides, our experimental results demonstrate that using a weighted sum of different self-supervised losses causes performance degradation compared to using a single self-supervised task in FSOD. To solve these problems, firstly, we introduce SSL into FSOD by applying SSL tasks to the cropped positive samples. Secondly, we propose a novel self-supervised method: patch random drop, for predicting the location of the masked image patch. Finally, we design a three-stage training pipeline to associate two different self-supervised tasks. Extensive experiments on the few-shot object detection datasets, *i.e.*, Pascal VOC, MS COCO, validate the effectiveness of our method.

Keywords: Few-shot object detection · Self-supervised learning

1 Introduction

Deep Neural Networks (DNNs) have achieved great progress in many computer vision tasks [22,26,27]. However, the impressive performance of these models largely relies on a large amount of data as well as expensive human annotation. When the annotated data are scarce, DNNs cannot generalize well to testing data especially when the testing data belong to different classes of the training data. In contrast, humans can learn to recognize or detect a novel object quickly with only a few labeled examples. Few-shot learning, therefore, becomes an important research topic to learn from only a few examples. However, the generalization ability of the few-shot model is not satisfactory due to the lack of sufficient samples. Therefore, a novel strategy for improving the generalization power of a deep model is required.

Recently, self-supervised learning attracts many researchers' attention, because it can improve the generalization of the network without involving manual annotations. By designing pretext tasks to exploit the structural information

L. Wang et al. (Eds.): ACCV 2022, LNCS 13846, pp. 286–302, 2023.
https://doi.org/10.1007/978-3-031-26351-4_18

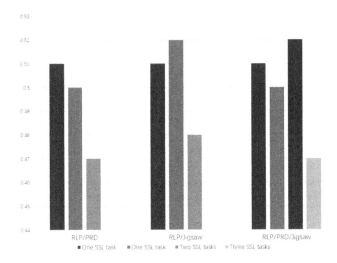

Fig. 1. Minimizing a weighted sum of multiple self-supervised losses can cause the degradation of performance compared to using only one self-supervised task. The adopted self-supervised learning (SSL) tasks include PRD, RLP, and Jigsaw. Y-axis means the novel AP50 on Pascal VOC.

of data itself, self-supervised learning aims to predict pseudo-labels only using the input images. Specifically, relative location prediction (RLP) [4] guides the model to learn the visual relative location in the image. MAE [14] re-constructs a high proportion of the masked patches. However, there is still a quality of the human vision, which is ignored by the current self-supervised learning. Specifically, if a region of an image is randomly cropped, human can easily identify the location of the significant change even the natural images have highly diversity. The reason is that the cropped patch can seriously effect the structural information of an image. To this end, we want to mask a random patch in an image, and use the model to predict the location of the masked patch. We call this method: patch random drop (PRD).

Some self-supervised tasks are gradually used to improve the performance of few-shot classification [1,9,20,28,29]. However, there are few works that introduce self-supervised learning into few-shot object detection which is a more challenging task. Self-supervised learning is to model the internal characteristics of a certain category or instance, which is applied to the whole image in few-shot classification. It is not suitable for the detection task, because object detection only cares about the positive samples. Using the self-supervised method like classification can make a model consider more about some changes of irrelevant background since there is a large region of background in an image, and thus cause the degradation of performance. In our work, by using the strategy of positive sample selection, we can introduce a self-supervised task into the few-shot object detection framework in such a simple way. Besides, we explore the integration of multiple self-supervised tasks in this framework.

When using multiple self-supervised tasks [28,29], the commonly used solution to associate the main task and auxiliary self-supervised tasks is optimizing the shared parameters by minimizing a weighted sum of the all losses. However, as the objectives of distinct tasks are different and the relationship between them is complicated, optimizing all losses can cause conflict. In few-shot object detection, we figure out that minimizing a weighted sum of the main tasks and several self-supervised tasks does not work, even worse than using a single self-supervised method as shown in Fig. 1. To solve this problem, we propose a novel three-stage training pipeline to associate two self-supervised tasks, including PRD and RLP. By using our proposed PRD, our method can outperform the baseline with a single self-supervised task, and achieves the state-of-the-art performance.

Our contributions can be summarized as three fold:

- We propose a novel self-supervised method: patch random drop (PRD) for few-shot object detection.
- To the best of our knowledge, we are the first to introduce multiple self-supervised tasks into few-shot object detection. We design a three-stage training pipeline for associating two different self-supervised methods, including PRD and RLP.
- Experiments evaluate the effectiveness of our approach on the few-shot object detection datasets, i.e., Pascal VOC, MS COCO.

2   Related Work

2.1   Few-shot Object Detection

There are two mainstream approaches in few-shot object detection, including meta-learning based and pre-train finetune-based methods.

Meta-learning Based Methods. Some works use meta-learning [7,17,19,33, 36], where a meta-learner is introduced to acquire class agnostic meta-knowledge which is transferred to novel classes. These methods usually extract meta-knowledge from a set of auxiliary tasks via the episode-based strategy [31], where each episode contains C classes and K samples of each class, i.e., C-way K-shot. With the help of a meta learner that takes the support images as well as the bounding box annotations as inputs, the feature re-weighting modules are applied to a single-stage object detector (YOLOv2) [17] and a two-stage object detector (Faster R-CNN) [36]. A weight prediction meta-model is introduced to learn the category-agnostic components from base class examples while predicting parameters of category-specific components from the few examples [33]. CME [19] uses a class margin equilibrium (CME) approach, with the aim to optimize both feature space partition and novel class reconstruction in a systematic way. Transformation Invariant Principle (TIP) [18] is proposed for various meta-learning models by introducing consistency regularization on predictions from the transformed images.

Pre-train Finetune-based Methods. Pre-train finetune-based approaches are the current one of the leading paradigms for few-shot object detection, which utilize a two-stage training pipeline to leverage the knowledge of base classes. TFA [32] is a simple two-stage fine-tuning approach, which significantly outperforms the earlier meta-learning methods. Following this framework, MPSR [35] adopts multi-scale positive sample refinement to handle scale variance problem. FSCE [30] proposes a simple yet effective approach to learning contrastive-aware object proposal encodings that facilitate the classification of detected objects.

2.2   Self-supervised Learning

Self-supervised methods have achieved great success in AI, including NLP and CV. In CV, self-supervised learning aims to construct some annotation-free pretext tasks to predict pseudo-labels only using the input images. The recent advances of self-supervised learning include two types: image generation and contrastive learning [1]. Image generation designs the pretext tasks to exploit semantic visual representation such as rotation prediction [10], relative location prediction [4], and jigsaw puzzle [25]. MAE [14] is a new image generation method via re-constructing a high proportion of the masked patches. Our proposed PRD belongs to this category. Contrastive learning [3,11,15] is training the feature representation of samples by bringing the features of positive pairs closer, and spreading the features of negative pairs apart. Momentum Contrast [15] trains a representation encoder by matching an encoded query to a dictionary of encoded keys via a contrastive loss. SimCLR [3] uses the normalized temperature-scaled cross-entropy loss as the contrast loss. BYOL [11] only relies on positive pairs to learn the feature representation.

When coming to few-shot learning with self-supervised tasks, [9] proposes a multi-task method combining the self-supervised auxiliary loss with the main few-shot classification loss. Conditional self-supervised learning (CSS) [1] is proposed to use prior knowledge to guide the representation learning of self-supervised tasks and introduces a three-stage training pipeline for few-shot image classification. There are some works [20,28] aim to combine multiple self-supervised tasks with a few-shot classification model via the weighted summation loss. However, [28] shows that the improvement from the association of rotation prediction and BYOL is limited when compared to only using rotation prediction or BYOL. The results of [29] indicate that combining multiple self-supervised tasks via the weighted summation loss even hurts the performance of few-shot classification in some cases. Due to the limited samples, the summation of multiple self-supervised losses can hurt the learning of key semantic information.

In few-shot object detection, few works explore the influence of SSL. Besides, our experiments demonstrate that using a weighted sum of different self-supervised losses causes performance degradation compared to using a single self-supervised task. To solve these problems, firstly, we introduce SSL into FSOD by applying SSL tasks to the cropped positive samples. Secondly, we propose a self-supervised method: patch random drop, for predicting the location of the masked image patch. Finally, we design a three-stage training pipeline to associate two different self-supervised tasks, including our proposed PRD and commnly used RLP. Our method can benefit from this training paradigm and learn a better semantic representation than that of a weighted summation loss. However, our goal is to use SSL to improve FSOD and we do not validate our methods on general object detection tasks.

3   Method

3.1   Preliminary

In few-shot detection, given a labeled base dataset $D_B = \{x_{Bi}, y_{Bi}\}$, there are C_B base classes with a large number of images in each class. Novel dataset $D_N = \{x_{Ni}, y_{Ni}\}$ with novel classes C_N consists of a few samples in each class, where xi and yi indicate training samples and labels, respectively. C_B and C_N do not have overlapping categories. The number of objects for each class in C_N is K for K-shot detection. The model is expected to detect objects in the test set with classes in $C_B \cup C_N$.

   Pre-train finetune-based methods adopt a simple two-stage training pipeline. In the pre-training stage, the model is trained on base classes to obtain a robust feature representation. In the fine-tuning stage, the pre-trained model is then fine-tuned on a balanced few-shot set which is composed of both base and novel classes $(C_B \cup C_N)$. Our proposed three-stage training pipeline is based on this framework.

3.2   Methodology

As illustrated in Fig. 2, the proposed training pipeline has three stages, in which the first stage is pre-training stage and the following two stages are fune-tuning stage. In the first stage, two models are pre-trained with two separate self-supervised tasks, including PRD and RLP, based on base classes, and then the backbone-P and backbone-R are got. In the second stage, the model pre-trained with PRD is finetuned on base and novel classes, obtaining a new backbone-P. In the third stage, the final model is re-initialized with the backbone-R and guided by the backbone-P based on base and novel classes. In all stages, we propose to use a positive selection module to crop the positive samples for the self-supervised tasks in our framework. When testing, the self-supervised heads and the positive selection module can be removed, thus our method is easy to deploy and use.

3.3   The Pre-training Stage

There are two parallel steps in the pre-training stage. The difference between these two steps is the using auxiliary task which is RLP or PRD. Patch random drop (PRD) is our proposed self-supervised task, which is achieved by masking a random patch in an image and using the model to predict the location of the masked patch.

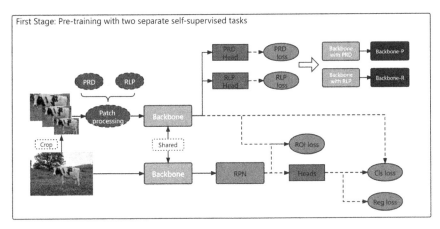

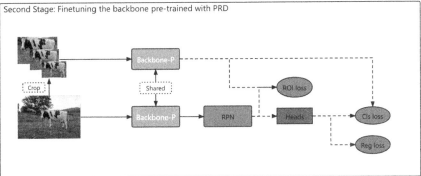

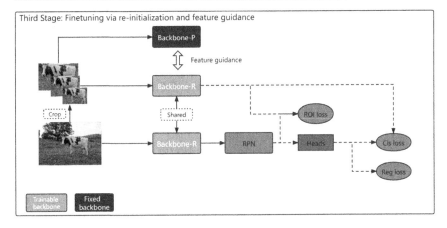

Fig. 2. Our three-stage training pipeline for few-shot object detection with two self-supervised methods, including PRD and RLP. In the first stage, two models are pre-trained with two separate self-supervised tasks based on base classes, and then backbone-P and backbone-R are got. In the second stage, the model pre-trained with PRD is finetuned on base and novel classes, obtaining a new backbone-P. In the third stage, the final model is re-initialized with the backbone-R and guided by the backbone-P based on base and novel classes.

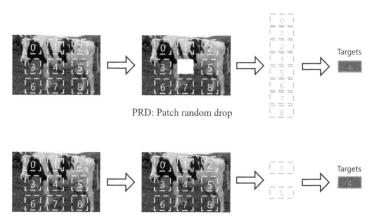

Fig. 3. The comparison between our PRD and RLP.

What Is PRD and Why Use PRD? The comparison between our PRD and RLP is shown in Fig. 3. RLP [4] is a self-supervised method for guiding model to learn the visual relative location in the image. It divides an image into 9 patches, and two patches are randomly selected as the inputs. The model is to predict the relative location of the two input patches. Similar to RLP, PRD divides an image into 9 patches. The masked patches are removed before model forwarding like MAE [14]. After removing the masked patch, the remaining patches are concatenated in order as the input of our model. The output of PRD head predicts the location of the dropped patch. The difference between PRD and MAE is the goal of model training. Specifically, PRD is predicting the location of the masked patch, while MAE is to re-construct the masked patches. The advantages of PRD to FSOD tasks include improving FSOD models and achieving better accuracy when associated with RLP. Moreover, PRD provides a new direction for designing more self-supervised methods by predicting the location of patches of our concern.

We consider the performance of applying RLP [4], Jigsaw Puzzle [25] and our PRD in our framework. In addition, we also do experiments on contrastive learning methods, such as simCLR and BYOL, and find them improvement is limited. MAE is not selected for implementation since it is designed for transformer. The combination of PRD and RLP can achieve better performance than others. Therefore, we build our framework with PRD and RLP.

It is worth noting that the proposed method is not a straightforward application of self-supervised learning in few-shot object detection. We propose to use the strategy of positive sample selection to obtain the foreground targets for self-supervised tasks. Besides, we explore the integration of multiple self-supervised tasks in our framework.

Pre-training with RLP. We train the model with the main few-shot object detection task and the RLP self-supervised task. The learned feature representation is backbone-R in the first stage of Fig. 2.

$$L_1 = L_{main} + w_1 * L_{RLP} \tag{1}$$

where L_{main} is the main few-shot object detection task defined as follows. L_{RLP} is the loss for relative location prediction. w_1 is the weight of L_{RLP}.

$$L_{main} = L_{roi} + L_{cls} + L_{reg} \tag{2}$$

where L_{roi} is applied to the output of RPN and the feature from the cropped positive samples. L_{roi} is to distinguish foreground from backgrounds, L_{cls} is a cross-entropy loss for the box classifier, and L_{reg} is a smoothed L1 loss for the box regressor.

Given a set of N training images $D = \{X_i\}_{i=0}^N$, the self-supervised training objective that RLP learns to solve is:

$$\min_\theta \frac{1}{N} \sum_{i=1}^N L_{RLP}(X^i, \theta, \eta) \tag{3}$$

θ and η are the learnable parameters of backbone and RLP head. The loss function L_{RLP} is defined as:

$$- |y_2 - y_1| * log(H_R(P_R|\eta)) \tag{4}$$

where $|y_2 - y_1|$ is the label for L_{RLP} and P_R is the predicted probability for the input. H_R is RLP head which is a fully-connected layer. P_R is computed as:

$$P_R = cat(F(g(X_i|y_1)|\theta), F(g(X_i|y_2)|\theta)) \tag{5}$$

where g is patch processing for RLP by randomly selecting two image patches according to the label y_1 and y_2 that $y_1, y_2 \in \{0, 1, 2, 3, 4, 5, 6, 7, 8\}$. $F(*)$ obtains the predicted probability for the input and θ is the learnable parameters of model F. Then the features from the two selected image patches are concatenated.

Pre-training with PRD. We train the model with the main few-shot task and the PRD self-supervised task. The learned feature representation is backbone-P in the first stage of Fig. 2. The loss L_2 in this step is computed as:

$$L_2 = L_{main} + w_2 * L_{PRD} \tag{6}$$

L_{PRD} is the loss of PRD task. w_2 is the weight of L_{PRD}.

Given a set of N training images $D = \{X_i\}_{i=0}^N$, the self-supervised training objective that PRD aims to solve is:

$$\min_\theta \frac{1}{N} \sum_{i=1}^N L_{PRD}(X^i, \theta, \eta) \tag{7}$$

θ and η are the learnable parameters of backbone and PRD head. The loss function of L_{PRD} is defined as:

$$- y * log(H_P(O|\eta)) \tag{8}$$

where y represents the location of the dropped patch which is the label for L_{PRD} and O is the predicted probability for the input. H_P is the PRD head with the learnable parameters η. H_P is a fully-connected layer. O is defined as:

$$O = F(g(X_i|y)|\theta) \tag{9}$$

where g is patch processing for PRD by dropping a random patch according to the label y that $\{y \in 0, 1, 2, 3, 4, 5, 6, 7, 8\}$, and remaining image patches are concatenated as the input. θ is the learnable parameters of backbone F.

3.4   The Fine-tuning Stage

In the second stage, we finetune the backbone pre-trained with PRD. The loss used in this stage is L_{main}.

In the third stage, we use the feature representation trained by our proposed PRD to guide the learning of the representation trained from RLP. The parameters of backbone-P are fixed and the parameters of backbone-R are trainable for prediction. The right order of the feature guidance is important which is proved in our experimental section. The loss of the third stage is L_f defined as:

$$L_f = L_{main} + w_3 * L_{FG} \tag{10}$$

L_{FG} is the loss for feature guidance, which is computed as following. Feature guidance is different from knowledge distillation which uses a large weight to ensure the consistency of features or probability value between the teacher model and the student model. When increasing w_3, the performance of the final model declines in our setting. By setting w_3 properly to guide the feature learning, our model can achieve better performance, thus our strategy is named by feature guidance.

$$L_{FG} = \sum_{i=1}^{K}(|F_p^i - F_r^i|^2) \tag{11}$$

where F_p and F_r are the feature representations from the backbone-P and backbone-R. K means the number of FPN levels.

The work which is most similar to our pipeline is CSS [1]. CCS also introduces self-supervised learning into a few-shot model and proposes a muti-stage training pipeline. However, the differences between our training pipeline and CSS are as follows. First, we are the first work to introduce the image-level self-supervised methods into few-shot object detection, in which the self-supervised tasks are applied to the cropped positive samples. Other methods use self-supervised learning to improve few-shot classification. Second, our work associates two different self-supervised methods and uses feature guidance to guide the learning of feature representation, while CSS only consider one self-supervised method and use a graph convolution network to generate a weight matrix for the final feature.

Table 1. Comparison with state-of-the-art few-shot object detection methods on VOC2007 test set for novel classes of the three splits. **Black** indicate state-of-the-art (SOTA).

Method/Shot		split 1			split 2			split 3		
		1	3	10	1	3	10	1	3	10
FRCN+ft [17]	ICCV2019	11.9	29	36.9	5.9	23.4	28.8	5.0	18.1	43.4
FRCN+ft-full [36]	ICCV2019	13.8	32.8	45.6	7.9	26.2	39.1	9.8	19.1	45.1
FR [17]	ICCV2019	14.8	26.7	47.2	15.7	22.7	40.5	21.3	28.4	45.9
MetaDet [33]	ICCV2019	18.9	30.2	49.6	21.8	27.8	43	20.6	29.4	44.1
Meta R-CNN [36]	ICCV2019	19.9	35	51.5	10.4	29.6	45.	14.3	27.5	48.1
TFA [32]	ICML2020	25.3	42.1	52.8	18.3	30.9	39.5	17.9	34.3	45.6
MPSR [35]	ECCV2020	41.7	51.4	61.8	24.4	39.2	47.8	35.6	42.3	49.7
CME [19]	CVPR2021	41.5	50.4	60.9	27.2	41.4	46.8	34.3	45.1	51.5
FSCN [21]	CVPR2021	40.7	46.5	62.4	27.3	40.8	46.3	31.2	43.7	55.6
Retentive R-CNN [8]	CVPR2021	42.4	45.9	56.1	21.7	35.2	40.3	30.2	43	50.1
HallucFsDet [37]	CVPR2021	47	46.5	54.7	26.3	37.4	41.2	40.4	43.3	49.6
FSCE [30]	CVPR2021	44.2	51.4	63.4	27.3	43.5	50.2	37.2	47.5	58.5
UPE [34]	ICCV2021	43.8	50.3	61.7	31.2	41.2	48.3	35.5	43.9	53.5
QA-FewDet [12]	ICCV2021	42.4	55.7	63.4	25.9	**46.6**	51.1	35.2	47.8	53.5
Meta faster-rcnn [13]	AAAI2021	43	**60.6**	**65.4**	27.7	46.1	**51.4**	40.6	**53.4**	58.6
FADI [2]	NIPS2021	50.3	54.2	63.2	30.6	40.3	48	**45.7**	49.1	**59.6**
Ours		**54.6**	56.5	61.4	**37.9**	44.4	47.6	42.8	46.6	51.2

4 Experiments

4.1 Datasets and Evaluation Protocols

We evaluate our methods on Pascal VOC [5,6] and MS COCO [23]. In PASCAL VOC, we adopt the common strategy [26,27] that using VOC 2007 test set for evaluating while VOC 2007 and 2012 train/val sets are used for training. Following [36], 5 out of its 20 object categories are selected as the novel classes, while keeping the remaining 15 ones as the base classes. We evaluate with three different novel/base splits from [36], named as split 1, split 2, and split 3. Each split contains 15 base categories with abundant data and 5 novel categories with K annotated instances for K = 1, 3, 10. Following [30,32,36], we use the mean average precision (mAP) at 0.5 IoU threshold as the evaluation metric and report the results on the official test set of VOC 2007. When using MS COCO, 20 out of 80 categories are reserved as novel classes, the rest 60 categories are used as base classes. The detection performance with COCO-style AP, AP50, and AP75 for K = 10 and 30 shots of novel categories are reported.

4.2 Implementation Details

Our baseline is TFA [32] combined with the positive sample selection strategy. TFA is the most basic and representative pretrain-finetune based method with

Table 2. Few-shot object detection performance on MS COCO. **Black** indicate the state-of-the-art (SOTA).

Method/Shot	novel AP		novel AP50		novel AP75	
	10	30	10	30	10	30
FR [17]	5.6	9.1	12.3	19	4.6	7.6
Meta R-CNN [36]	8.7	12.4	19.1	25.3	6.6	10.8
TFA [32]	10	13.7	–	–	9.3	13.4
MSPR [35]	9.8	14.1	17.9	25.4	9.7	14.2
CME [19]	15.1	16.9	24.6	28	16.4	17.8
Retentive R-CNN [8]	10.5	13.8	–	–	–	–
FSCN [21]	11.3	15.1	20.3	29.4	–	–
FSCE [30]	11.1	15.3	–	–	9.8	14.2
UPE [34]	11	15.6	–	–	10.7	15.7
QA-FewDet [12]	10.2	11.5	20.4	23.4	9.0	10.3
Meta faster-rcnn [13]	12.7	16.6	**25.7**	**31.8**	10.8	15.8
FADI [2]	12.2	16.1	22.7	29.1	11.9	15.8
Ours	**15.3**	**17.1**	24.9	28.4	**16.5**	**18.1**

a two-stage training pipeline. TFA can represent most of the pretrain-finetune based few-shot methods because they have the same training pipeline and the same model structure. In detail, we use Faster R-CNN [27] as our base detector and ResNet-101 [16] with a Feature Pyramid Network [22] as the backbone. All models are trained using SGD with a batch size of 4 and weight decay of 0.0001. A learning rate of 0.005 is used during all stages. For the three splits of PASCAL VOC, w_1 is 0.01, 0.05, and 0.01, w_2 is 0.005, 0.001, and 0.0001, and w_3 is 0.001, 0.00005, and 0.00005.

4.3   Comparison with State-of-the-Art Methods

To verify the effectiveness of our method, several competitive few-shot object detection methods are compared. The results are shown in Tables 1 and 2. Following [2,13,19,35], we use a single run with the same training images to get the results of different shots.

Results on PASCAL VOC. Following [30,32,36], we provide the average AP50 of the novel classes on PASCAL VOC with three splits in Table 1. Our method can outperform previous methods by a large margin in extremely low-shot settings (i.e. 1-shot). The effectiveness of our method is fully demonstrated.

Results on MS-COCO. We report the COCO-style AP, AP50, and AP75 of the 20 novel classes on MS-COCO in Table 2. Our method sets new state-of-the-art for 10 and 30 shots, under the same testing protocol and metrics.

Table 3. Components of our proposed training pipeline. RLP is training the model with relative location prediction. PRD is training the model with patch random drop. TTP is our three-stage training pipeline. When RLP and PRD are used together, a weighted summation loss is applied to associate these two losses. Removing PRD is using the baseline model for feature guidance. Removing RLP means adopting the baseline model as the initialization in the third stage.

Components			split 1			split 2			split 3		
RLP	PRD	TTP	1	3	10	1	3	10	1	3	10
–	–	–	48.3	52.8	59.6	35.6	42.1	47	40.6	45.2	50.3
✓	–	–	50.6	53.6	**62.9**	36.6	45.3	47.4	41.8	46	51.1
–	✓	–	50.3	54.4	60.7	36	43.6	46.9	41.4	44.2	49.6
✓	✓	–	46.6	53.5	57.9	32.4	43.5	47	41.5	44.6	49.9
–	✓	✓	51.7	55.6	59.3	36.9	43.2	46.5	40.1	42	49.1
✓	–	✓	54.1	56.4	61.3	37.3	**45.5**	47.2	39.8	46.4	50.2
✓	✓	✓	**54.6**	**56.5**	61.4	**37.9**	44.4	**47.6**	**42.8**	**46.6**	**51.2**

Table 4. The way of integrating self-supervised tasks: summation vs feature guidance. Sum is using a weighted summation loss. FG means feature guidance.

Method/Shot	split 1			split 2			split 3		
	1	3	10	1	3	10	1	3	10
Baseline	48.3	52.8	59.6	35.6	42.1	47	40.6	45.2	50.3
sum(PRD,RLP)	46.6	53.5	57.9	32.4	43.5	47	41.5	**46.8**	**52.4**
FG(PRD,RLP)	**54.6**	**56.5**	**61.4**	**37.9**	**44.4**	**47.6**	**42.8**	46.6	51.2

4.4 Ablation Study

Component Analysis. To show the effectiveness of our method, we first make a detailed comparison with the baseline by adding the components of our method. As shown in Table 3, each component can improve the performance of our baseline in most of settings on PASCAL VOC benchmark. To be specific, RLP improves baseline by 2.3, 0.8, 3.3 and 1, 3.2, 0.4 and 1.2, 0.8, 0.8 for K=1, 3, 10 on novel split1, split2, and split3. PRD improves baseline by 2, 1.6 1.1 and 0.4, 1.5, –0.1 and 0.8, –1, –0.6 for K=1, 3, 10 on novel split1, split2 and split3. If using PRD and RLP via a weighted summation loss, the performance become even worse than the baseline. By using our three-stage training pipeline, our method outperforms the baseline up to 6% and achieves better performance than the baseline with a single self-supervised task (RLP or PRD).

The Way of Integrating Self-supervised Tasks. We compare our feature guidance to integrating self-supervised tasks by a weighted summation loss. The results are shown in Table 4, in which using feature guidance is better than the weighted summation loss in almost all settings. In few-shot scenarios, due to the

Table 5. The order of the two models pre-trained with PRD and RLP. FG means feature guidance. FG(RLP, PRD) is using backbone-R to guide the learning of backbone-P. FG(PRD, RLP) is using backbone-P to guide the learning of backbone-R.

Method/Shot	split 1			split 2			split 3		
	1	3	10	1	3	10	1	3	10
Baseline	48.3	52.8	59.6	35.6	42.1	47	40.6	45.2	50.3
FG(RLP,PRD)	48.4	54.7	59.3	35.5	42.2	47.5	41	44.3	49.2
FG(PRD,RLP)	**54.6**	**56.5**	**61.4**	**37.9**	**44.4**	**47.6**	**42.8**	**46.6**	**51.2**

Table 6. PRD vs Jigsaw. FG means feature guidance. FG(Jigsaw, RLP) is using the backbone pre-trained with Jigsaw Puzzle to guide the learning of backbone-R.

Method/Shot	split 1			split 2			split 3		
	1	3	10	1	3	10	1	3	10
Baseline	48.3	52.8	59.6	35.6	42.1	47	40.6	45.2	50.3
+Jigsaw	52.2	56.4	60.9	35.3	41.9	46.2	39.3	45.6	50.2
+PRD	50.3	54.4	60.7	36	43.6	46.9	41.4	44.2	49.6
FG(Jigsaw,RLP)	52.4	53.6	60.6	36.4	**44.6**	47	40.5	**47.1**	**51.5**
FG(PRD,RLP)	**54.6**	**56.5**	**61.4**	**37.9**	44.4	**47.6**	**42.8**	46.6	51.2

lack of training samples, optimizing the model via a weighted summation loss may cause conflict, since the objectives of distinct tasks are different and the relationship between them is complicated.

The Order of Feature Guidance. In Fig. 2, we use backbone-P to guide the learning of backbone-R. If we use backbone-R to guide the learning of backbone-P, the results are shown in Table 5, indicating the position of these two models is important. The results show that the model pre-trained with PRD can provide better guidance, and the model pre-trained with RLP is suitable for initialization.

Visualization. Figure 4 shows the visual embeddings of using one self-supervised method and combining multiple self-supervised methods via a weighted sum of the losses or our FG (feature guidance). In Fig. 4(a) and b, the distributions of category "18" and "9" are easy to be confused, while the boundaries of the categories pairs, including "18"|"9", "16"|"18" and "17"|"10", are not clear in Fig. 4(c) demonstrates that simple combination of multiple self-supervised tasks is not a good choice for few-shot object detection. In Fig. 4(d), t-SNE [24] visualization of our method shows that our training pipeline with feature guidance can model the within-class similarity and build better classification boundaries, which demonstrate the effectiveness of our method.

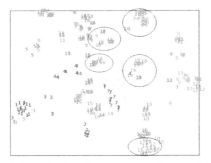 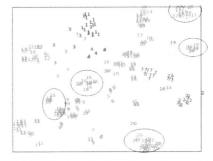

(a) t-SNE visualization from the model with PRD.

(b) t-SNE visualization from the model with RLP.

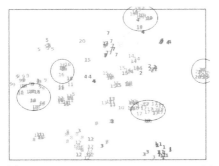 

(c) t-SNE visualization from the model with a weighted sum of PRD and RLP loss.

(d) t-SNE visualization from the model with our method.

Fig. 4. t-SNE visualization of the object proposal embeddings of cropped instances during the finetuning stage. The solid circles (16 to 20) denote novel categories during the fine-tuning stage. Others (1 to 15) are the base categories.

Comparison with Other Self-supervised Methods. We use Jigsaw Puzzle [25] to guide the learning of the third stage of our training pipeline. The results of using PRD is similar to Jigsaw Puzzle, which is shown in Table 6. By using feature guidance, our PRD can achieve better performance than Jigsaw Puzzle in most of settings.

5   Conclusions

In this paper, we study the influence of self-supervised learning on Few-shot object detection. Our experimental results demonstrate that using a weighted sum of the self-supervised losses can not achieve better accuracy than using a single task in FSOD. To solve these problems, firstly, we introduce self-supervised learning into FSOD by applying SSL tasks to the cropped positive samples. Secondly, we propose a novel self-supervised method: patch random drop (PRD), for predicting the location of the masked image patch. Finally, we design a three-stage training pipeline to associate two self-supervised methods, including PRD and RLP. Experiments evaluate the effectiveness of our approach on the few-shot object detection datasets, i.e., Pascal VOC, MS COCO.

References

1. An, Y., Xue, H., Zhao, X., Zhang, L.: Conditional self-supervised learning for few-shot classification
2. Cao, Y., et al.: Few-shot object detection via association and discrimination. In: Advances in Neural Information Processing Systems 34 (2021)
3. Chen, T., Kornblith, S., Norouzi, M., Hinton, G.: A simple framework for contrastive learning of visual representations. In: International Conference on Machine Learning, pp. 1597–1607. PMLR (2020)
4. Doersch, C., Gupta, A., Efros, A.A.: Unsupervised visual representation learning by context prediction. In: Proceedings of the IEEE International Conference on Computer Vision, pp. 1422–1430 (2015)
5. Everingham, M., Eslami, S.A., Van Gool, L., Williams, C.K., Winn, J., Zisserman, A.: The pascal visual object classes challenge: a retrospective. Int. J. Comput. Vision **111**(1), 98–136 (2015)
6. Everingham, M., Van Gool, L., Williams, C.K., Winn, J., Zisserman, A.: The pascal visual object classes (voc) challenge. Int. J. Comput. Vision **88**(2), 303–338 (2010)
7. Fan, Q., Zhuo, W., Tang, C.K., Tai, Y.W.: Few-shot object detection with attention-RPN and multi-relation detector. In: Proceedings of the IEEE/CVF Conference on Computer Vision and Pattern Recognition, pp. 4013–4022 (2020)
8. Fan, Z., Ma, Y., Li, Z., Sun, J.: Generalized few-shot object detection without forgetting. In: Proceedings of the IEEE/CVF Conference on Computer Vision and Pattern Recognition, pp. 4527–4536 (2021)
9. Gidaris, S., Bursuc, A., Komodakis, N., Pérez, P., Cord, M.: Boosting few-shot visual learning with self-supervision. In: Proceedings of the IEEE/CVF International Conference on Computer Vision, pp. 8059–8068 (2019)
10. Gidaris, S., Singh, P., Komodakis, N.: Unsupervised representation learning by predicting image rotations. arXiv preprint arXiv:1803.07728 (2018)
11. Grill, J.B., et al.: Bootstrap your own latent-a new approach to self-supervised learning. Adv. Neural. Inf. Process. Syst. **33**, 21271–21284 (2020)
12. Han, G., He, Y., Huang, S., Ma, J., Chang, S.F.: Query adaptive few-shot object detection with heterogeneous graph convolutional networks. In: Proceedings of the IEEE/CVF International Conference on Computer Vision, pp. 3263–3272 (2021)
13. Han, G., Huang, S., Ma, J., He, Y., Chang, S.F.: Meta faster R-CNN: towards accurate few-shot object detection with attentive feature alignment. arXiv preprint arXiv:2104.07719 (2021)
14. He, K., Chen, X., Xie, S., Li, Y., Dollár, P., Girshick, R.: Masked autoencoders are scalable vision learners. arXiv preprint arXiv:2111.06377 (2021)
15. He, K., Fan, H., Wu, Y., Xie, S., Girshick, R.: Momentum contrast for unsupervised visual representation learning. In: Proceedings of the IEEE/CVF Conference on Computer Vision and Pattern Recognition, pp. 9729–9738 (2020)
16. He, K., Zhang, X., Ren, S., Sun, J.: Deep residual learning for image recognition. In: Proceedings of the IEEE Conference on Computer Vision and Pattern Recognition, pp. 770–778 (2016)

17. Kang, B., Liu, Z., Wang, X., Yu, F., Feng, J., Darrell, T.: Few-shot object detection via feature reweighting. In: Proceedings of the IEEE International Conference on Computer Vision, pp. 8420–8429 (2019)
18. Li, A., Li, Z.: Transformation invariant few-shot object detection. In: Proceedings of the IEEE/CVF Conference on Computer Vision and Pattern Recognition, pp. 3094–3102 (2021)
19. Li, B., Yang, B., Liu, C., Liu, F., Ji, R., Ye, Q.: Beyond max-margin: class margin equilibrium for few-shot object detection. In: Proceedings of the IEEE/CVF Conference on Computer Vision and Pattern Recognition, pp. 7363–7372 (2021)
20. Li, H., et al.: Multi-pretext attention network for few-shot learning with self-supervision. In: 2021 IEEE International Conference on Multimedia and Expo (ICME), pp. 1–6. IEEE (2021)
21. Li, Y., et al.: Few-shot object detection via classification refinement and distractor retreatment. In: Proceedings of the IEEE/CVF Conference on Computer Vision and Pattern Recognition, pp. 15395–15403 (2021)
22. Lin, T.Y., Dollár, P., Girshick, R., He, K., Hariharan, B., Belongie, S.: Feature pyramid networks for object detection. In: Proceedings of the IEEE Conference on Computer Vision and Pattern Recognition, pp. 2117–2125 (2017)
23. Lin, T.-Y., et al.: Microsoft COCO: common objects in context. In: Fleet, D., Pajdla, T., Schiele, B., Tuytelaars, T. (eds.) ECCV 2014. LNCS, vol. 8693, pp. 740–755. Springer, Cham (2014). https://doi.org/10.1007/978-3-319-10602-1_48
24. Van der Maaten, L., Hinton, G.: Visualizing data using T-SNE. J. Mach. Learn. Res. 9(11), 2579–2605 (2008)
25. Noroozi, M., Favaro, P.: Unsupervised learning of visual representations by solving Jigsaw puzzles. In: Leibe, B., Matas, J., Sebe, N., Welling, M. (eds.) ECCV 2016. LNCS, vol. 9910, pp. 69–84. Springer, Cham (2016). https://doi.org/10.1007/978-3-319-46466-4_5
26. Redmon, J., Farhadi, A.: YOLO9000: better, faster, stronger. In: Proceedings of the IEEE Conference on Computer Vision and Pattern Recognition, pp. 7263–7271 (2017)
27. Ren, S., He, K., Girshick, R., Sun, J.: Faster R-CNN: towards real-time object detection with region proposal networks. IEEE Trans. Pattern Anal. Mach. Intell. 39(6), 1137–1149 (2016)
28. Simard, N., Lagrange, G.: Improving few-shot learning with auxiliary self-supervised pretext tasks. arXiv preprint arXiv:2101.09825 (2021)
29. Su, J.-C., Maji, S., Hariharan, B.: When does self-supervision improve few-shot learning? In: Vedaldi, A., Bischof, H., Brox, T., Frahm, J.-M. (eds.) ECCV 2020. LNCS, vol. 12352, pp. 645–666. Springer, Cham (2020). https://doi.org/10.1007/978-3-030-58571-6_38
30. Sun, B., Li, B., Cai, S., Yuan, Y., Zhang, C.: FSCE: few-shot object detection via contrastive proposal encoding. In: Proceedings of the IEEE/CVF Conference on Computer Vision and Pattern Recognition, pp. 7352–7362 (2021)
31. Vinyals, O., Blundell, C., Lillicrap, T., Wierstra, D., et al.: Matching networks for one shot learning. Adv. Neural. Inf. Process. Syst. 29, 3630–3638 (2016)
32. Wang, X., Huang, T.E., Darrell, T., Gonzalez, J.E., Yu, F.: Frustratingly simple few-shot object detection. arXiv preprint arXiv:2003.06957 (2020)
33. Wang, Y.X., Ramanan, D., Hebert, M.: Meta-learning to detect rare objects. In: Proceedings of the IEEE International Conference on Computer Vision, pp. 9925–9934 (2019)

34. Wu, A., Han, Y., Zhu, L., Yang, Y.: Universal-prototype enhancing for few-shot object detection. In: Proceedings of the IEEE/CVF International Conference on Computer Vision, pp. 9567–9576 (2021)
35. Wu, J., Liu, S., Huang, D., Wang, Y.: Multi-scale positive sample refinement for few-shot object detection. In: Vedaldi, A., Bischof, H., Brox, T., Frahm, J.-M. (eds.) ECCV 2020. LNCS, vol. 12361, pp. 456–472. Springer, Cham (2020). https://doi. org/10.1007/978-3-030-58517-4_27
36. Yan, X., Chen, Z., Xu, A., Wang, X., Liang, X., Lin, L.: Meta R-CNN: towards general solver for instance-level low-shot learning. In: Proceedings of the IEEE International Conference on Computer Vision, pp. 9577–9586 (2019)
37. Zhang, W., Wang, Y.X.: Hallucination improves few-shot object detection. In: Proceedings of the IEEE/CVF Conference on Computer Vision and Pattern Recognition, pp. 13008–13017 (2021)

Object Detection in Foggy Scenes by Embedding Depth and Reconstruction into Domain Adaptation

Xin Yang[1]([📧])(ⓘ), Michael Bi Mi[2], Yuan Yuan[2], Xin Wang[2], and Robby T. Tan[1,3](ⓘ)

[1] National University of Singapore, Singapore, Singapore
e0674612@u.nus.edu, robby.tan@nus.edu.sg
[2] Huawei International Pte Ltd, Singapore, Singapore
{yuanyuan10,wangxin237}@huawei.com
[3] Yale-NUS College, Singapore, Singapore
robby.tan@yale-nus.edu.sg

Abstract. Most existing domain adaptation (DA) methods align the features based on the domain feature distributions and ignore aspects related to fog, background and target objects, rendering suboptimal performance. In our DA framework, we retain the depth and background information during the domain feature alignment. A consistency loss between the generated depth and fog transmission map is introduced to strengthen the retention of the depth information in the aligned features. To address false object features potentially generated during the DA process, we propose an encoder-decoder framework to reconstruct the fog-free background image. This reconstruction loss also reinforces the encoder, i.e., our DA backbone, to minimize false object features. Moreover, we involve our target data in training both our DA module and our detection module in a semi-supervised manner, so that our detection module is also exposed to the unlabeled target data, the type of data used in the testing stage. Using these ideas, our method significantly outperforms the state-of-the-art method (47.6 mAP against the 44.3 mAP on the Foggy Cityscapes dataset), and obtains the best performance on multiple real-image public datasets. Code is available at: https://github.com/VIML-CVDL/Object-Detection-in-Foggy-Scenes.

Keywords: Domain adaptation · Object detection · Foggy scenes

1 Introduction

Object detection is impaired by bad weather conditions, particularly fog or haze. Addressing this problem is important, since many computer vision applications, such as self-driving cars and video surveillance, rely on robust object detection regardless of the weather conditions. One possible solution is to employ a pre-processing method, such as image defogging or dehazing [14,25] right before an object detection module. However, this solution is suboptimal, since bad weather

© The Author(s), under exclusive license to Springer Nature Switzerland AG 2023
L. Wang et al. (Eds.): ACCV 2022, LNCS 13846, pp. 303–318, 2023.
https://doi.org/10.1007/978-3-031-26351-4_19

(a) Input Image   (b) PBDA[21]

(c) **Our Result**   (d) Ground-Truth

Fig. 1. (a) Input dense fog image from Foggy Cityscapes [5]. (b) Result from PBDA [21], where many objects are undetected. (c) Ours, where more objects are detected. (d) Ground-truth, annotated from its corresponding clear image. Zoom in for better visualization.

image enhancement itself is still an open problem, and thus introduces a risk of removing or altering some target object information.

Recently, object detection methods based on unsupervised domain adaptation (DA) (e.g., [3,4,7]) have shown promising performance for bad weather conditions. By aligning the source (clear weather image) and the target (weather degraded image) distributions in the feature level, a domain adaptive network is expected to produce weather-invariant features. Unlike image pre-processing methods, domain adaptive detection networks do not require an additional defogging module during the inference stage, and can also work on both clear and foggy conditions. The DA methods, however, were not initially proposed for the adverse weather conditions, and hence align the source and target features based only on feature alignment losses, ignoring some important aspects of the target data, such as depth, transmission map, reconstruction of object instances of the target data, etc. This is despite the fact that for bad weather, particularly fog or haze, these aspects can be imposed. Sindagi et al. [21] attempt to fuse DA with adverse weather physics models, but do not obtain a satisfactory performance (39.3 mAP on Foggy Cityscapes, compared to 47.6 mAP of ours).

In this paper, we propose a DA method that learns domain invariant features by considering depth cues, consistency between depth from fog transmission, and clear-image reconstruction. Moreover, we involve the source and target data to train our whole network in a semi-supervised manner, so that our object detection module can be exposed to the unlabeled target data, which has the same type as data in the testing stage. Most existing DA methods aim to suppress any discrepancies between the source and target data in the feature space, and this includes any depth distribution discrepancies. However, depth information is critical in object detection [6,17,23], and thus the depth suppression will significantly affect the object detection performance. To resolve this, we propose a depth estimation module and its corresponding depth loss, so that the depth information in our features can be retained. This depth loss forces our DA backbone to retain the depth information during the DA process. Moreover, to further reinforce our DA backbone to retain the depth information, we also add a transmission-depth consistency loss.

When performing DA, the source and target images are likely to contain different object instances, and aligning two different objects with different appearances encourages the generation of false features. To address this problem, we fuse a reconstruction module into our DA backbone, and propose a reconstruction loss. Based on the features from our DA backbone's layers from the target (fog image), our reconstruction module generates a clear image. Our reconstruction loss thus measures the difference between the estimated clear image and the clear-image pseudo ground-truth of the target obtained from an existing defogging method. This reconstruction loss will then prevent false features generated during the feature extraction process. During the training stage, the DA model gradually becomes more robust to fog, and the predictions on the unlabeled target images become more reliable. This gives us an opportunity to employ the target data to train our object detection module, so that the module can be exposed to both source and target data and becomes less biased to the source data.

Figure 1 shows our object detection result, which incorporates all our losses and ideas into our DA backbone. As a summary, our contributions and novelties are as follow:

- Without imposing our depth losses, DA features are deprived from the depth information, due to the over-emphasis on source/target adaptation. This deprivation negatively affects object detection performance. Hence, we introduce depth losses to our DA backbone to retain the depth information in our DA features.
- We propose to reinforce the target transmission map to have consistent depth information to its corresponding depth estimation. This consistency loss constraints the transmission map and improves further the DA performance and the depth retention.
- We propose to integrate an image reconstruction module into our DA backbone. Hence, any additional false object features existing in DA features will be penalized, and hence minimized.

Our quantitative evaluations show that our method outperforms the state-of-the-art methods on various public datasets, including real image datasets.

2   Related Work

Object Detection in Foggy Scenes. Most existing object detection models require a fully-supervised training strategy [28]. However, under adverse weather conditions, having sufficient images and precise annotations is intractable. A possible solution is to utilize defogging algorithms. The defogged images are less affected by fog, and hence they can be fed into object detection models which are trained with clear images directly. However, defogging is still an existing research problem and thus limits the performance potential of this approach. Moreover, defogging introduces an additional computational overhead, hindering the real-time process for some applications. These drawbacks were discussed and analyzed in [19, 21, 26].

Domain Adaptation. DA methods were proposed to train a single network which can work on different domains. In DA, there will be labeled images from the source domain and unlabeled images from the the target domain. During the training stage, images from both domains will be fed into the network. The source images with annotations will be used for the training of object detection part. Meanwhile, a domain discriminator will examine which domain the extracted feature maps come from. The discriminator will be rewarded for accurate domain prediction, but the network will be penalized. Hence, the network is encouraged to extract domain invariant feature maps, i.e., fog free features. Since the feature maps are already domain invariant, the detection trained with the source labels can also detect objects from the target images. Additionally, once the network is trained, the domain discriminator is not needed anymore, hence no additional overhead in the inference stage.

There are a few existing DA methods that tried to perform DA between clear weather and fog weather. Some methods investigated where and how to put the domain discriminators, so that the DA can be more efficient whilst retain most object-related information [3, 4, 18, 20, 26]. [10, 12, 15, 21, 22, 27] aimed to designed a more suitable domain discriminator, using transmission maps, entropy, uncertainty masks, memory banks/dictionaries and class clusters. However, most of these methods focus on synthetic datasets, and ignores the fact where the weather-specific knowledge prior can also be integrated to better describe the domain discrepancy.

3   Proposed Method

Figure 2 shows the pipeline of our method, where clear images are our source input, and foggy images are our target input. For the source images, we have their corresponding annotations (bounding boxes and classes) to train our object detection module. For the target images, we do not have any annotations. In this DA framework, we introduce a few constraints: depth, consistency between the transmission and depth, and clear background reconstruction. The goal of adding these constraints is to extract features from both source (clear image) and target

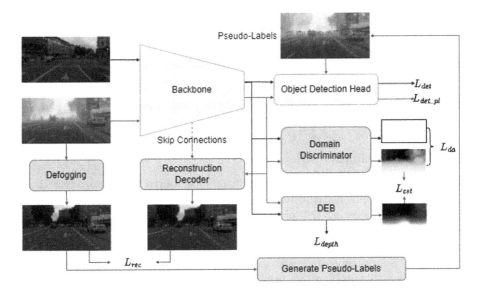

Fig. 2. The network consists of five parts. (1) Backbone extracts feature maps from the input images. (2) Object detection head localizes and categorizes object instances from the feature maps. (3) Domain discriminator and DEB encourage the backbone to extract fog-invariant features, and maintains the images' depth distributions. (4) Reconstruction decoder minimizes the fake object features generated by DA. (5) Pseudo-Labels involve target domain information in the pipeline, and apply consistency regularization between fog and defogged images. The green arrows represent source data-flow, and the red arrows represent target data-flow. Note, only the blue modules are needed in the testing stage. (Color figure online)

(fog image) that are robust for object detection. Moreover, we exploit the target predictions to train our object detection module, so that the module can be exposed to the unlabeled target data, and hence less biased to the source data.

Object Detection. For the object detection module, we employ Faster-RCNN [16], which consists of a backbone $\mathcal{F}$ for feature extraction, and an object detection head, $\mathcal{G}$. The loss for the object detection is defined as:

$$\mathcal{L}_{\mathrm{det}} = \mathcal{L}_{\mathrm{rpn}} + \mathcal{L}_{\mathrm{cls}} + \mathcal{L}_{\mathrm{bbox}}, \tag{1}$$

where, $\mathcal{L}_{\mathrm{rpn}}$ is the regional proposal loss, $\mathcal{L}_{\mathrm{cls}}$ is the classification loss, and $\mathcal{L}_{\mathrm{bbox}}$ is the localization loss.

Domain Adaptation. Our domain adaptation backbone shares the same backbone as that of the object detection module. For the domain discriminator, we use transmission maps as the domain indicator (i.e., the discriminator is expected to produce a blank map for source, and a transmission map for target). The corresponding loss can be defined as:

$$\mathcal{L}_{\mathrm{da}} = \|\mathcal{D}(\mathcal{F}(I_s))\|_2^2 + \|t - \mathcal{D}(\mathcal{F}(I_t))\|_2^2, \tag{2}$$

where, $\mathcal{F}$ is the backbone, $\mathcal{D}$ is the domain discriminator. I_s and I_t are the input images from the source domain and the target domain, respectively. t is the transmission map for the target image.

3.1 Depth Estimation Block (DEB)

In the DA process, it is unlikely that a pair of source and target images to have the same depth distribution, since they unlikely contain the same scenes. Thus, when the existing DA methods suppress the domain discrepancies, the depth information is also suppressed in the process. However, recent methods have shown that the depth information benefits object detection [6,17,23], which implies that suppression of depth can affect the performance of object detection.

To address this problem, we need to retain the depth information during the DA feature alignment. We introduce Depth Estimation Block (DEB), a block that generates a depth map based on the extracted features from our DA backbone. We define the depth recovery loss as follows:

$$\mathcal{L}_{\mathrm{depth}} = \|\mathrm{DEB}(\mathcal{F}(I_s)) - D_{gt}\|_2^2, \tag{3}$$

where, D_{gt} is the ground-truth depth map, which is resized to the same size as the corresponding feature map. $\mathcal{F}(I_s)$ represents the source feature maps, and DEB() is our DEB module. For datasets such as Cityscapes [5], they provide the ground-truth depth maps. For the other datasets which do not provide depth ground-truth, we need to generate the depth maps as a pseudo ground-truth using the existing depth estimation networks, such as [2,8,9]. Note, DEB is only trained on the source images. Unlike the transmission DA loss in Eq. (2), we backpropagate the depth loss over both our DA backbone and DEB to retain the depth information in our DA features. Figure 3 shows our depth estimations. Note that our goal here is not to have accurate depth estimation, but to retain depth cues in our features.

3.2 Transmission-Depth Consistency

In foggy scenes, we can model the transmission of light throughout the fog particles as $t = \exp(-\beta D)$, where t is the transmission, D is the depth, and β as the fog particles attenuation factor. As one can notice, there is a strong correlation between the transmission and depth. Hence, we reinforce our predicted transmission and depth to be consistent:

$$\mathcal{L}_{\mathrm{cst}} = \|Norm(-\log(\mathcal{D}(\mathcal{F}(I_t)))) - Norm(\mathrm{DEB}(\mathcal{F}(I_t)))\|_2^2, \tag{4}$$

where $\mathcal{D}(\mathcal{F}(I_t))$ is the generated transmission map from the domain discriminator, and $\mathrm{DEB}(\mathcal{F}(I_t))$ represents the estimated depth map. $Norm()$ represents a

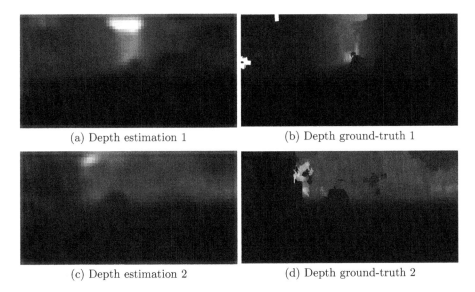

(a) Depth estimation 1   (b) Depth ground-truth 1

(c) Depth estimation 2   (d) Depth ground-truth 2

Fig. 3. Examples of the estimated depths in comparison with the ground-truths. Note that, the estimated depths look blurry as they have a low resolution (38×75). We can observe that the estimated depth maps (a) and (c) from DEB match the depth distribution patterns in the ground-truth depth maps (b) and (d), respectively, which indicates that our feature maps retain the depth information.

normalization operator. Like most defogging methods, we assume that β is uniform across the input target. Since the transmission and the depth values are the same only up to a scale, we normalize their values, and thus consequently cancel out β in the process. This consistency loss enforces the consistency between the depth encoded in the estimated transmission and the depth from our DEB, this constraint leads to more robust depth information in our features.

3.3   Reconstruction DA

Since DA methods use unpaired source and target that most likely contain different object instances, when the DA backbone aligns the features, the alignment will occur on two different object instances (e.g., car in the source, and motorbike in the target). Hence, when the DA backbone is suppressing such discrepancy, consequently it can generate false features, which can harm the object detection performance.

To address this problem, we regularize the generation of object features by fusing a reconstruction decoder into our DA backbone. This decoder reconstructs the features back to the clear background image. To train this decoder, we use either the clear image or the defogged image of the target image as the ground-truths. Since the reconstruction ground-truths have the same object instances as in the target images, the reconstruction loss will prevent our DA backbone from generating false instance features. Our reconstruction loss is defined as:

$$\mathcal{L}_{\text{rec}} = \left\| \mathcal{R}(\mathcal{F}(I_t)) - I^{de} \right\|_2^2, \tag{5}$$

where $\mathcal{R}$ is the reconstruction module and $\mathcal{R}(\mathcal{F}(I_t))$ represents the reconstructed target image. I^{de} is the clear/defogged target image, which we use as the ground-truth for the reconstruction. Only target images are involved in the reconstruction, as there are no fog distortions in the source images.

3.4 Learning from Target

In many DA cases, target data does not have ground-truths, and hence [3,4,10,15,18,20–22,26] use the source domain's knowledge to train the object detection module, right after the domain feature adaptation process. This means the object detection module is never exposed to the target data, which is likely to be different from the source data in terms of the appearances of the object instances (e.g., the shapes of road signs in one country are different from those of the road signs from another country, etc.). The main problem why many methods do not use target data in training the detection module is because the target data is unlabeled.

With the help from our DA module, our detection module's performance on the target data is improving over iterations. As the predictions on target become more accurate, we can select some reliable predictions as pseudo-labels to train our detection module. Hence, our training is split into two stages for each iteration: In the first stage, we generate pseudo-labels from the whole network; in the second stage, we do DA training involving the generated pseudo-labels. To obtain more reliable predictions in the first stage, we employ a defogging method to augment our target input. The augmented target input in the form of defogged image will enable our network to estimate the bounding boxes and class labels. If the network has high confidence with these estimates, it means the estimates can be considered as reliable and used as pseudo-labels. In the second stage, we feed the same target input to our network without augmentation, and let it to predict the bounding boxes and class labels. We then enforce these network's estimates to be consistent with the pseudo-labels. This process encourages the network to become more robust to fog, and to expose our object detection module to the target data. Note that, in the end of each iteration, we employ Exponential Moving Average (EMA) in our network to generate more reliable predictions.

Total Loss. Combining all the losses we introduced above, we can derive our overall loss as:

$$\mathcal{L} = \mathcal{L}_{\text{det}} + \lambda \mathcal{L}_{\text{da}} + a\mathcal{L}_{\text{depth}} + b\mathcal{L}_{\text{cst}} + c\mathcal{L}_{\text{rec}} + \mathcal{L}_{\text{det}}\_\text{pl}, \tag{6}$$

where, λ, a, b, c are the weight parameters to control the importance of the losses. $\mathcal{L}_{\text{det}}$_pl is the detection loss with pseudo-labels. Note that, in the testing stage, we only use our DA backbone and the detection module. In other words, all the additional modules (i.e., the domain discriminator, the depth estimation block, the reconstruction module or the pseudo-labels) does not affect the runtime in the testing stage.

4   Experimental Results

We compare our DA method with recent DA methods: [3,4,10,12,15,18,20–22,26,27], where the last two are published as recent as this year. To make the comparison fair, we use the same base of object detection, which is Faster-RCNN [24]. For the backbone, our method uses a pretrained ResNet-101 [24]. We set the confidence threshold τ to be 0.8 for all the experiments. More details of our blocks can be found in the supplementary material. Our overall network is trained end-to-end. We follow the same training settings as in [3,4,18,20,21], where the networks are trained for 60K iterations, with a learning rate of 0.002. We decrease the learning rate by a factor of 10 for every 20K iterations. The weights parameters λ, a, b, c are empirically set to be $0.1, 10, 1, 1$, respectively.

As for the datasets, the Cityscapes dataset is a real world street scene dataset provided by [5], and all images were taken under clear weather. Based on this dataset, [19] simulates synthetic fog on each clear image, and creates the Foggy Cityscapes dataset. We use the same DA settings as in [3,4,18,20,21], where 2975 clear images and 2975 foggy images are used for training, and 495 foggy images are used for evaluation.

Aside from the Cityscapes dataset, STF (Seeing Through Fog) [1], Foggy-Driving [19], and RTTS [13] are the datasets with real world foggy images used in our experiments. STF dataset categories its images into different weather conditions, we choose *clear weather daytime* as our source domain and *fog daytime* as our target domain. We randomly select 100 images from *fog daytime* as our evaluation set, and use the rest to train the network. For RTTS, we follow the same DA settings as in [20,21]. For FoggyDriving, it only contains 101 fog images, which is insufficient for DA training. Hence, we evaluate the DA models trained on Cityscapes/Foggy Cityscapes directly on these datasets.

4.1   Quantitative Results

The synthetic Foggy Cityscapes dataset has the ground-truth transmission maps, depth maps and the clear background of the target images for reconstruction, thus we can use the ground-truths directly in our training process, however for fair comparisons we do not use them. Instead we employ DCP [11] to compute the transmission maps, reconstruction maps, and use it as the defogging pre-processing module when involving target predictions. As for the depth, we employ Monodepth [8] to compute the pseudo ground-truths. We also employ DCP and Monodepth for real data that have no ground-truths of clear images, transmission maps, and depth maps. Note that, the methods we use to generate pseudo ground-truths (DCP and Monodepth) are not the state-of-the-art

Table 1. Quantitative results of Ours compared to the existing DA methods evaluated against Foggy Cityscapes testing set. AP (%) of each category and the mAP (%) of all the classes. Bold numbers are the best scores, and underlined numbers are the second best scores. Our mAP outperforms the best existing method over 3%.

Method		Backbone	Person	Rider	Car	Truck	Bus	Train	Motor	Bicycle	MAP
Baseline	Faster-RCNN	ResNet-101	32.0	39.5	36.2	19.4	32.1	9.4	23.3	33.2	28.1
DA Methods	DA-Faster [3]	ResNet-101	37.2	46.8	49.9	28.2	42.3	30.9	32.8	40.0	38.5
	SWDA [18]	VGG-16	29.9	42.3	43.5	24.5	36.2	32.6	30.0	35.3	34.3
	SCL [20]	ResNet-101	30.7	44.1	44.3	30.0	47.9	42.9	29.6	33.7	37.9
	PBDA [21]	ResNet-152	34.9	46.4	51.4	29.2	46.3	43.2	31.7	37.0	40.0
	MEAA [15]	ResNet-101	34.2	48.9	52.4	30.3	42.7	46.0	33.2	36.2	40.5
	UaDAN [10]	ResNet-50	36.5	46.1	53.6	28.9	49.4	42.7	32.3	38.9	41.1
	Mega-CDA [22]	VGG-16	37.7	49.0	52.4	25.4	49.2	46.9	34.5	39.0	41.8
	SADA [4]	ResNet-50-FPN	**48.5**	**52.6**	**62.1**	29.5	50.3	31.5	32.4	**45.4**	44.0
	CaCo [12]	VGG-16	38.3	46.7	48.1	33.2	45.9	37.6	31.0	33.0	39.2
	MGA [27]	VGG-16	43.9	49.6	60.6	29.6	50.7	39.0	38.3	42.8	44.3
	Ours	ResNet-101	39.9	51.6	59.0	**39.7**	**58.0**	**49.1**	**39.2**	45.1	**47.6**

Table 2. Quantitative results of Ours compared to the existing DA methods evaluated against the STF testing set. AP (%) of each category and the mAP (%).

Method		PassengerCar	LargeVehicle	RidableVehicle	mAP
Baseline	Faster-RCNN	74.0	54.1	25.7	51.3
DA Methods	DA-Faster	77.9	51.5	25.2	51.6
	SWDA	77.2	50.1	24.5	50.6
	SCL	78.1	52.5	20.7	50.4
	SADA	**78.5**	52.2	24.2	51.6
	Ours	**78.5**	**57.4**	**30.2**	**55.4**

methods, as we want to show that our DA's performances are not limited by the precision of the pseudo ground-truths.

The results on this dataset are provided in Table 1. The mAP threshold for all the models is 0.5. When comparing DA models, there are two important non-DA baseline models that need to be considered. One is the model trained on clear images but tested on foggy images, which we call Lowerbound. Any DA models should performance better than this Lowerbound model. In our experiment, Lowerbound is 28.12 mAP for Foggy Cityscapes dataset. The other model is both trained and tested on clear images, which we call Upperbound. Since it is not affected by fog at all, the goal of DA models is to approach its performance, but it is not possible to exceed it. In our experiment, Upperbound is 50.08 mAP for Foggy Cityscapes dataset. Table 1 shows that our proposed method performs better than any other DA methods.

For the real world datasets, we cannot compute Lowerbound's and Upperbound's performance, since we do not have the clear background of the foggy images. Thus, we can only compare our models with the performance of the other

Table 3. Quantitative results of Ours compared to the existing DA methods evaluated against the FoggyDriving testing set. mAP (%) of all the categories.

Method		mAP
Baseline	FRCNN	26.41
DA Methods	DA-Faster	31.60
	SWDA	33.54
	SCL	33.49
	SADA	32.26
	Ours	**34.62**

Table 4. Quantitative results of Ours compared to the existing DA methods evaluated against the RTTS testing set. AP (%) of each category and the mAP (%).

Method		Person	Car	Bus	Motor	Bicycle	mAP
Baseline	Faster-RCNN	46.6	39.8	11.7	19.0	37.0	30.9
DA Methods	DA-Faster	42.5	43.7	16.0	18.3	32.8	30.7
	SWDA	40.1	44.2	16.6	23.2	41.3	33.1
	SCL	33.5	48.1	18.2	15.0	28.9	28.7
	PBDA	37.4	**54.7**	17.2	22.5	38.5	34.1
	SADA	37.9	52.7	14.5	16.1	26.2	29.5
	Ours	**47.7**	53.4	**19.1**	**30.2**	**49.3**	**39.9**

DA methods. The results are presented in Tables. 2 to 4. Our model achieved a better performance on all the real world datasets. For FoggyDriving, we can observe that our model trained on synthetic dataset can also generalize well on the real world image datasets. Note that, the compared methods are not as many as the previous table, since some methods only provided their performances on the synthetic datasets, and we do not have their data or code to evaluate on the real world datasets.

4.2 Qualitative Results

The qualitative results are presented in Fig. 4. We evaluate our model on both synthetic and real world datasets, and compare it with DA-Faster [3] and SADA [4]. For the synthetic dataset, we also compare the model with Upperbound to visualize how close their predictions are. Note again that, Upperbound is the Faster-RCNN model trained on the clear training set and tested on the clear testing set. We can see that our method can detect more objects compared to DA-Faster. Both SADA and our method can detect most of the object instances in fog. However, we can see that SADA generated some false predictions. Our

(a) DA-Faster   (b) SADA   (c) **Our Result**   (d) Upperbound

(e) DA-Faster   (f) SADA   (g) **Our Result**   (h) Upperbound

(i) DA-Faster   (j) SADA   (k) **Our Result**

(l) DA-Faster   (m) SADA   (n) **Our Result**

(o) DA-Faster   (p) SADA   (q) **Our Result**

Fig. 4. Comparisons with DA-Faster [3], SADA [4], and Upperbound. The first two rows are the comparison on Cityscapes → Foggy Cityscapes. Our model detects more objects and reduces false positive predictions and approaches the Upperbound performance. The last three rows are the comparison on real world images. Our model has more true positive detections and less false positive detections. Different bounding box's colour represents a different confidence score.

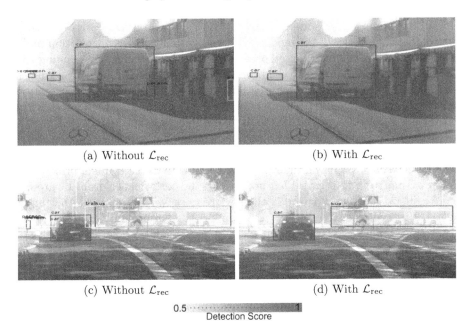

(a) Without $\mathcal{L}_{\mathrm{rec}}$ (b) With $\mathcal{L}_{\mathrm{rec}}$

(c) Without $\mathcal{L}_{\mathrm{rec}}$ (d) With $\mathcal{L}_{\mathrm{rec}}$

0.5 ·················· 1
Detection Score

Fig. 5. Ablation studies on our reconstruction loss. (a)(c): False positive predictions when there is no reconstruction, from model (DA+DEB+Consist). (b)(d): After we added our reconstruction loss. The false positive predictions are reduced.

Table 5. Ablation study of our model against the Foggy Cityscapes testing set. mAP is used to analyze the effectiveness of each loss.

DA	DEB	Consist	Reconst	PL	mAP
✓					42.6
✓	✓				43.3
✓	✓	✓			45.3
✓	✓	✓	✓		45.8
✓	✓	✓	✓	✓	47.6

method removed some false predictions, and thus the final object detection performance is approaching Upperbound.

4.3   Ablation Studies

Table 5 shows the ablation studies on Foggy Cityscapes to demonstrate the importance of each loss. The check mark indicates which losses are involved. In the table, DA represents the performance with domain discriminator only, DEB represents the depth recovery loss, Consist represents the transmission-depth consistency loss. Reconst represents the reconstruction loss using the pseudo ground-truth images generated from DCP [11]. We also provide Fig. 5 to show the comparisons between the models with and without our reconstruction module. PL means we include target predictions as pseudo labels for training. As one can notice, each of the losses improves the overall mAP. The network has a performance gain with only pseudo ground-truths of transmission maps, depth maps, and defogged images. This once again shows that our method works without the need of precise ground-truths. If we use the ground-truths of transmission maps, depth maps, and defogged images (which are actually available for Foggy Cityscape), our performance reaches overall 49.2 mAP. The weights of the losses are chosen to ensure that all the losses will contribute to the training properly. If we set a from 10 to 1, or we set b from 1 to 0.1, the performance drops by around 1 mAP. If we set c from 1 to 0.1, the performance drops by 2 mAP. Setting λ to be 0.1 is recommended by a few DA papers. The performance drops below 40 mAP if λ becomes too large. In our method, the weights are set empirically.

5   Conclusion

We have proposed a novel DA method with a reconstruction as a regularization, to develop an object detection network which is robust for fog or haze conditions. To address the problem that DA process can suppress depth information, we proposed the DEB to recover it. We proposed the transmission-depth consistency loss to reinforce the transmission map based DA to follow the target image's depth distribution. We integrated a reconstruction module to our DA backbone to reconstruct a clear image of the target image and reduce the false object instance features. We involved target domain knowledge into DA, by reusing reliable target predictions and enforcing consistent detection. We evaluated the framework on several benchmark datasets showing that our method outperforms the state-of-the-art DA methods.

References

1. Bijelic, M., et al.: Seeing through fog without seeing fog: deep multimodal sensor fusion in unseen adverse weather. In: Proceedings of the IEEE/CVF Conference on Computer Vision and Pattern Recognition, pp. 11682–11692 (2020)
2. Chen, P.Y., Liu, A.H., Liu, Y.C., Wang, Y.C.F.: Towards scene understanding: unsupervised monocular depth estimation with semantic-aware representation. In: Proceedings of the IEEE/CVF Conference on Computer Vision and Pattern Recognition, pp. 2624–2632 (2019)
3. Chen, Y., Li, W., Sakaridis, C., Dai, D., Van Gool, L.: Domain adaptive faster R-CNN for object detection in the wild. In: Proceedings of the IEEE conference on computer vision and pattern recognition, pp. 3339–3348 (2018)
4. Chen, Y., Wang, H., Li, W., Sakaridis, C., Dai, D., Van Gool, L.: Scale-aware domain adaptive faster R-CNN. Int. J. Comput. Vis. **129**(7), 2223–2243 (2021)
5. Cordts, M., et al.: The cityscapes dataset for semantic urban scene understanding. In: Proceedings of the IEEE Conference on Computer Vision and Pattern Recognition, pp. 3213–3223 (2016)

6. Ding, M., et al.: Learning depth-guided convolutions for monocular 3D object detection. In: Proceedings of the IEEE/CVF Conference on Computer Vision and Pattern Recognition Workshops, pp. 1000–1001 (2020)
7. Ganin, Y., Lempitsky, V.: Unsupervised domain adaptation by backpropagation. In: International Conference on Machine Learning, pp. 1180–1189. PMLR (2015)
8. Godard, C., Mac Aodha, O., Brostow, G.J.: Unsupervised monocular depth estimation with left-right consistency. In: Proceedings of the IEEE Conference on Computer Vision and Pattern Recognition, pp. 270–279 (2017)
9. Godard, C., Mac Aodha, O., Firman, M., Brostow, G.J.: Digging into self-supervised monocular depth estimation. In: Proceedings of the IEEE/CVF International Conference on Computer Vision, pp. 3828–3838 (2019)
10. Guan, D., Huang, J., Xiao, A., Lu, S., Cao, Y.: Uncertainty-aware unsupervised domain adaptation in object detection. IEEE Transactions on Multimedia (2021)
11. He, K., Sun, J., Tang, X.: Single image haze removal using dark channel prior. IEEE Trans. Pattern Anal. Mach. Intell. **33**(12), 2341–2353 (2010)
12. Huang, J., Guan, D., Xiao, A., Lu, S., Shao, L.: Category contrast for unsupervised domain adaptation in visual tasks. In: Proceedings of the IEEE/CVF Conference on Computer Vision and Pattern Recognition, pp. 1203–1214 (2022)
13. Li, B., et al.: Benchmarking single-image dehazing and beyond. IEEE Trans. Image Process. **28**(1), 492–505 (2018)
14. Liu, X., Ma, Y., Shi, Z., Chen, J.: GriddehazeNet: attention-based multi-scale network for image dehazing. In: Proceedings of the IEEE/CVF International Conference on Computer Vision, pp. 7314–7323 (2019)
15. Nguyen, D.K., Tseng, W.L., Shuai, H.H.: Domain-adaptive object detection via uncertainty-aware distribution alignment. In: Proceedings of the 28th ACM International Conference on Multimedia, pp. 2499–2507 (2020)
16. Ren, S., He, K., Girshick, R., Sun, J.: Faster R-CNN: towards real-time object detection with region proposal networks. Adv. Neural. Inf. Process. Syst. **28**, 91–99 (2015)
17. Saha, S., et al.: Learning to relate depth and semantics for unsupervised domain adaptation. In: Proceedings of the IEEE/CVF Conference on Computer Vision and Pattern Recognition, pp. 8197–8207 (2021)
18. Saito, K., Ushiku, Y., Harada, T., Saenko, K.: Strong-weak distribution alignment for adaptive object detection. In: Proceedings of the IEEE/CVF Conference on Computer Vision and Pattern Recognition, pp. 6956–6965 (2019)
19. Sakaridis, C., Dai, D., Van Gool, L.: Semantic foggy scene understanding with synthetic data. Int. J. Comput. Vis. **126**(9), 973–992 (2018)
20. Shen, Z., Maheshwari, H., Yao, W., Savvides, M.: SCL: towards accurate domain adaptive object detection via gradient detach based stacked complementary losses. arXiv preprint arXiv:1911.02559 (2019)
21. Sindagi, V.A., Oza, P., Yasarla, R., Patel, V.M.: Prior-based domain adaptive object detection for hazy and rainy conditions. In: Vedaldi, A., Bischof, H., Brox, T., Frahm, J.-M. (eds.) ECCV 2020. LNCS, vol. 12359, pp. 763–780. Springer, Cham (2020). https://doi.org/10.1007/978-3-030-58568-6_45
22. VS, V., Gupta, V., Oza, P., Sindagi, V.A., Patel, V.M.: MeGA-CDA: memory guided attention for category-aware unsupervised domain adaptive object detection. In: Proceedings of the IEEE/CVF Conference on Computer Vision and Pattern Recognition, pp. 4516–4526 (2021)
23. Vu, T.H., Jain, H., Bucher, M., Cord, M., Pérez, P.: DADA: depth-aware domain adaptation in semantic segmentation. In: Proceedings of the IEEE/CVF International Conference on Computer Vision, pp. 7364–7373 (2019)

24. Yang, J., Lu, J., Batra, D., Parikh, D.: A faster pytorch implementation of faster R-CNN. https://github.com/jwyang/faster-rcnn.pytorch (2017)
25. Zhang, H., Patel, V.M.: Densely connected pyramid dehazing network. In: Proceedings of the IEEE conference on computer vision and pattern recognition, pp. 3194–3203 (2018)
26. Zhou, Q., et al.: Self-adversarial disentangling for specific domain adaptation. arXiv preprint arXiv:2108.03553 (2021)
27. Zhou, W., Du, D., Zhang, L., Luo, T., Wu, Y.: Multi-granularity alignment domain adaptation for object detection. In: Proceedings of the IEEE/CVF Conference on Computer Vision and Pattern Recognition, pp. 9581–9590 (2022)
28. Zou, Z., Shi, Z., Guo, Y., Ye, J.: Object detection in 20 years: a survey. arXiv preprint arXiv:1905.05055 (2019)

Cluster Contrast for Unsupervised Person Re-identification

Zuozhuo Dai[1]([✉]), Guangyuan Wang[1], Weihao Yuan[1], Siyu Zhu[1], and Ping Tan[2]

[1] Alibaba Cloud, Singapore, Singapore
zuozhuo.dzz@alibaba-inc.com
[2] Simon Fraser University, Burnaby, Canada

Abstract. Thanks to the recent research development in contrastive learning, the gap of visual representation learning between supervised and unsupervised approaches has been gradually closed in the tasks of computer vision. In this paper, we focus on the downstream task of unsupervised person re-identification (re-ID). State-of-the-art unsupervised re-ID methods train the neural networks using a dictionary-based nonparametric softmax loss. They store the pre-computed instance feature vectors inside the dictionary, assign pseudo labels to them using clustering algorithm, and compare the query instances to the cluster using a form of contrastive loss. To enforce a consistent dictionary, that is the features in the dictionary are computed by a similar or the same encoder network, we present Cluster Contrast which stores feature vectors and computes contrastive loss at the cluster level. Moreover, the momentum update is introduced to reinforce the cluster-level feature consistency in the sequential space. Despite the straightforward design, experiments on four representative re-ID benchmarks demonstrate the effective performance of our method.

Keywords: Person re-ID · Unsupervised learning · Contrastive learning

1 Introduction

Deep unsupervised person re-ID aims to train a neural network capable of retrieving a person of interest across cameras without any labeled data. This task has attracted increasing attention recently due to the growing demands in practical video surveillance and the expensive labeling cost. There are mainly two approaches to address this problem. One is the purely unsupervised learning person re-ID, which generally exploits pseudo labels from the unlabeled data [14,15,17,30,47]. The other is the unsupervised domain adaptation person re-ID, which first pre-trains a model on the source labeled dataset, and then

Supplementary Information The online version contains supplementary material available at https://doi.org/10.1007/978-3-031-26351-4_20.

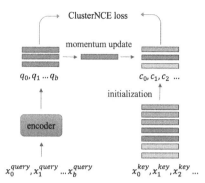

Fig. 1. The Cluster Contrast computes the contrastive loss in cluster level with momentum update. In the cluster level memory dictionary, the cluster feature is initialized as the averaged feature of the corresponding cluster and updated by the batch query instance. $x \in X$ is the training dataset. q is the query instance feature vector. c_k stands for the k-th cluster feature vector. Feature vectors with the same color belong to the same cluster.

fine-tunes the model on the target unlabeled dataset [12,29,48,51,59,67,68]. Generally, the performance of domain adaptation is superior to that of unsupervised learning because of the introduction of the external source domain. However, domain adaptation still suffers from the complex training procedure and requires that the difference between the source and target domain is not significant. In this paper, we focus on learning the person re-ID task without any labeled data, namely the purely unsupervised learning.

Recently, the unsupervised representation learning methods [1,2,5,6,19,20, 22,24,35,36,45,53,58] with contrastive loss [19] have gradually closed the performance gap with supervised pretraining in computer vision. Here, the contrastive loss [19] aims to compare pairs of image features so that the positive sample pairs are pulled together and the negative sample pairs are pulled away. Specifically, InstDisc [53] proposes an instance level memory bank for instance discrimination. It compares the query image features to all the instance features in the memory bank. Subsequently, the MoCo series [6,7,20] highlight the consistent memory dictionary in contrastive learning of visual representations. MoCo approximates the contrastive loss by sampling a subset of instances in the memory dictionary and uses the momentum-based moving average of the query encoder. Meanwhile, SimCLR [5] uses a large enough batch size to compute contrastive loss, which requires hundreds of TPU cores. Later on, SwAV [2] computes the contrastive loss in cluster level. It enforces the cluster assignment results rather than comparing sampling instance features. Since the cluster number is fixed in online clustering, SwAV does not require the large instance feature memory bank or large batch size to enforce the feature consistency.

Inspired by the great success of contrastive learning, recent works [4,14,15,17, 30,47,49,57,62,65] try to apply such ideology to the downstream re-ID tasks. In more details, such approaches exploit the memory dictionary and pseudo labels from clustering to train the neural network. At the beginning of each epoch, all the image features of the training data are extracted by the current neural network. Then, such image features are stored in a memory dictionary and a clustering algorithm, like DBSCAN [13] or K-means [34] is employed to cluster image features and produce pseudo labels. Meanwhile, the cluster ID is assigned to each image as the person identity. Finally, the neural network is trained with a contrastive loss such as triplet loss [23,41], InfoNCE loss [37], or other non-parametric classification loss [47] between the feature vectors of every instance inside the memory dictionary and the query instance. Since the instance features updated in one iteration are limited by the batch size, the instance features from the newly updated encoder network are not consistent with the previous ones. This problem of feature inconsistency in memory dictionary is especially serious in large-scale re-ID datasets like MSMT17 [51].

To enforce a consistent feature dictionary, we propose Cluster Contrast for unsupervised person re-ID. Remarkably, the ideology of Cluster Contrast is inspired by the contrasting cluster assignment technique from SwAV [2]. Different from SwAV which adopts an online clustering approach with a fixed number of clusters, we use an offline clustering method [14,17] which demonstrates superior clustering performance in re-ID tasks and remove un-clustered outliers. Then, a cluster-level memory dictionary is built and each dictionary key corresponds to a cluster which is represented by a single feature vector. More specifically, this cluster feature is initialized as the average feature of all the images from the same cluster and updated by the batch query instance features during training. Accordingly, we propose a cluster-level InfoNCE loss, denoted as ClusterNCE loss, which computes contrastive loss between cluster feature and query instance feature as illustrated in Fig. 1. Moreover, we apply the ideology of momentum update policy from MoCo [20] to the cluster level memory to further boost the feature consistency of cluster representations in the sequential space.

In summary, our proposed Cluster Contrast for unsupervised re-ID has the following contributions:

- We introduce the cluster-level memory dictionary which initializes, updates, and performs contrastive loss computation at the cluster level. The cluster feature embedding helps to alleviate the feature inconsistency problem.
- We apply the momentum updating policy to the cluster feature representation and further enforce the feature consistency in the memory dictionary.
- We demonstrate that the proposed unsupervised approach with Cluster Contrast achieves state-of-the-art performance on three purely unsupervised re-ID benchmarks.

2   Related Work

Deep Unsupervised Person Re-ID. Deep unsupervised person re-ID can be summarized into two categories. The first category is unsupervised domain adaptation re-ID, which utilizes transfer learning to improve unsupervised person re-ID [12,16,17,26,29,47,48,51,59,61,67,68]. The second category is pure unsupervised learning person re-ID [4,14,15,30,49,57,62,65], which trains model directory on unlabeled dataset. State-of-the-art unsupervised learning re-ID pipeline generally involves three stages: memory dictionary initialization, pseudo label generation, and neural network training. Previous works have made significant improvements either in parts or on the whole pipeline. Specifically, Lin*et al.* [30] treats each individual sample as a cluster, and then gradually groups similar samples into one cluster to generate pseudo labels. MMCL [47] predicts quality pseudo labels comprising of similarity computation and cycle consistency. It then trains the model as a multi-classification problem. SPCL [17] proposes a novel self-paced contrastive learning framework that gradually creates more reliable cluster to refine the memory dictionary features. OPLG [65] and RLCC [62] explore the temporal label consistency for better pseudo label quality. In addition to pseudo label, another stream of camera-aware methods [4,49] utilizes camera ID information as additional supervision signal to further improve the unsupervised re-ID performance. In this paper, we focus on purely unsupervised person re-ID, but our method can be easily generalized to unsupervised domain adaptation and camera-aware methods.

Memory Dictionary. Contrastive learning [1,2,5,6,19,20,22,24,35,36,45,53,58] can be thought of as training an encoder for a dictionary look-up task. Since it is too expensive in both memory and computation to compare all the image pairs within a dataset, several recent studies [1,20,22,24,37,44,54,70] on unsupervised visual representation learning present promising results through building dynamic dictionaries. Moco [20] builds a memory dictionary as a queue of sampled images. The samples in memory dictionary is replaced consistently on the fly to keep the feature consistency with the newly updated model. SimCLR [5] shows that the instance memory can be replaced by a large enough batch of instances. Similar to unsupervised visual representation learning, state-of-the-art unsupervised person re-ID methods also build memory dictionaries for contrastive learning [16,17,47,55]. During training, instance feature vectors in the memory dictionary are updated by the corresponding query instances features. Recently, SwAV [2] proposes an efficient online clustering method which approximates the contrastive loss of all image pairs by clustering centers, without requiring a large batch size or large memory bank. Inspired by SwAV [2] and Moco [20], we apply the ideology of cluster level contrastive learning and momentum update to the downstream unsupervised re-ID tasks and alleviate the problems of the large memory bank and memory dictionary inconsistency. Unlike SwAV in which the number of clusters is fixed, the proposed Cluster Contrast gradually selects reliable labels and dynamically refines the clustering results during training.

Loss Functions. In supervised person re-ID, the batch hard triplet loss has proved to be effective solutions to improve the re-ID performance [3,9,10,18,32, 42,46,63,69]. In unsupervised person re-ID, since there is no ground truth person identity and the pseudo labels are changing during training, non-parametric classification loss such as InfoNCE [37] are used as identity loss. Similar to InfoNCE,

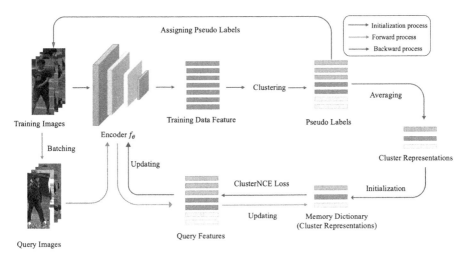

Fig. 2. The system pipeline of our unsupervised person re-ID method. The upper branch depicts the memory initialization stage. The training data features are assigned pseudo labels by clustering, where features of the same color belong to the same cluster. The lower branch represents the model training stage. Query features in iterative mini-batch are used to update the memory cluster representations with a momentum. The ClusterNCE loss computes the contrastive loss between query features and all cluster representations.

Tong *et al.* [55] designs an Online Instance Matching (OIM) loss with a memory dictionary scheme which compares query image to a memorized feature set of unlabelled identities. Wang and Zhang [47] introduce the memory-based non-parametric multi-label classification loss (MMCL), which treat unsupervised re-ID as a multi-label classification problem. In order to mitigate noisy pseudo labels, MMT [16] proposes a novel soft softmax-triplet loss to support learning with soft pseudo triplet labels. SPCL [17] introduces a unified contrastive loss including both source domain dataset and target domain dataset. In this paper, we apply InfoNCE loss between cluster feature and query instance feature on unsupervised re-ID.

3   Method

We first introduce our overall approach at a high level in Sect. 3.1. Then, we compare the multiple contrastive learning approaches for person re-ID with our proposed cluster contrast method in Sect. 3.2. Finally in Sect. 3.3, we explain the details of momentum update in Cluster Contrast along with its working theory.

3.1   Overview

State-of-the-art unsupervised learning methods [4,16,17,47] solve the unsupervised learning person re-ID problem with contrastive learning. Specifically, they

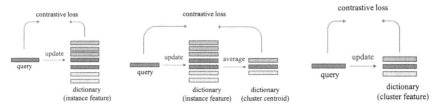

(a) Multi-label classi-   (b) Instance level InfoNCE loss   (c) ClusterNCE loss (ours)
fication loss

Fig. 3. Comparison of three types of memory-based non-parametric contrastive learning losses for re-ID. Different color features indicate different clusters. (a) computes the loss and updates the memory dictionary both at the instance level [47]. (b) computes the loss at the cluster level but updates the memory dictionary at the instance level [17]. (c) is our proposed approach and it computes the loss and updates the memory dictionary both at the cluster level.

build a memory dictionary that contains the features of all training images. Each feature is assigned a pseudo ID generated by a clustering algorithm. During training, the contrastive loss is minimized to train the network and learn a proper feature embedding that is consistent with the pseudo ID.

We focused on designing a proper contrastive learning method to keep the whole pipeline simple while obtaining better performance. An overview of our training pipeline is shown in Fig. 2. The memory dictionary initialization is illustrated in the upper branch. We use a standard ResNet50 [21] as the backbone encoder which is pretrained on ImageNet to extract feature vectors, and has basic discriminability though not optimized for re-ID tasks. We then apply the DBSCAN [13] clustering algorithms to cluster similar features together and assign pseudo labels to them. The cluster feature representation is calculated as the mean feature vectors of each cluster. The memory dictionary is initialized by these cluster feature representations and their corresponding pseudo labels. As shown in the lower branch, during the training stage, we compute the ClusterNCE loss between the query image features and all cluster representations in the dictionary to train the network. Meanwhile, the dictionary features are updated with a momentum by the query features.

To facilitate the description of methods, we first introduce the notations used in this paper. Let $X = \{x_1, x_2, \ldots, x_N\}$ denote the training set with N instances. And $U = \{u_1, u_2, \ldots, u_n\}$ denotes the corresponding features obtained from the backbone encoder f_θ, described as $u_i = f_\theta(x_i)$. q is a query instance feature extracted by $f_\theta(\cdot)$, where the query instance belongs to X.

3.2 Cluster Contrast

In this section, we analyze different contrastive learning methods to motivate our design of Cluster Contrast. As shown in Fig. 3 (a), the multi-label classification loss computes the loss in the instance level through an instance-wise contrastive loss. It stores all image feature vectors in the memory dictionary and computes multi-class score by comparing each query feature to all of them. The memory dictionary is updated by the query features after each training iteration.

In Fig. 3 (b), SPCL [17] computes the loss at cluster level through a cluster-wise InfoNCE loss. It can be defined as follows:

$$L_q = -\log \frac{exp(q \cdot c_+/\tau)}{\sum_{k=1}^{K} exp(q \cdot c_k/\tau)} \tag{1}$$

where τ is a temperature hyper-parameter, $\{c_1, c_2, \ldots, c_K\}$ are the cluster centroids and K stands for the number of clusters. It uses the cluster centroid as the cluster level feature vector to compute the distances between query instance q and all the clusters. c_+ is the positive cluster feature which q belongs to. The cluster centroids are calculated by the mean feature vectors of each cluster as:

$$c_k = \frac{1}{|\mathcal{H}_k|} \sum_{u_i \in \mathcal{H}_k} u_i \tag{2}$$

where $\mathcal{H}_k$ denotes the k-th cluster set and $|\cdot|$ indicates the number of instances per cluster. $\mathcal{H}_k$ contains all the feature vectors in the cluster k. But similar to multi-classification loss, it stores all image feature vectors in the memory dictionary. The stored image feature vectors are then updated by corresponding query image feature.

Both Fig. 3 (a) and Fig. 3 (b) update the feature vectors at an instance level, resulting in feature inconsistency problem. As shown in Fig. 4, the cluster size is unbalancedly distributed. In every training iteration, in a large cluster only a small fraction of the instance features can be updated due to the batch size limitation, whereas in a small cluster all the instances can be updated. Thus, the updating process is highly varied, and the contrastive loss computed by comparing all instance features is not consistent with the newest model. In each iteration, the network is constantly updated, which causes inconsistent oscillatory distribution of mini-batches. In contrast, we design our ClusterNCE loss as shown in Fig. 3 (c) using the following equation:

$$L_q = -\log \frac{exp(q \cdot \phi_+/\tau)}{\sum_{k=1}^{K} exp(q \cdot \phi_k/\tau)} \tag{3}$$

where ϕ_k is the unique representation vector of the k-th cluster. It updates the feature vectors and computes the loss both in the cluster level.

We can see that, our proposed algorithm uses unique feature vectors to represent each cluster category and remains distinct throughout the updating process, which is the most significant difference from the previous contrastive loss approaches. In the next section, we will discuss in detail how our method consistently updates the cluster representation to maintain the cluster consistency with the help of momentum update.

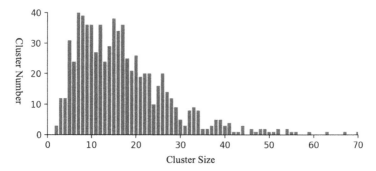

Fig. 4. The cluster size follows a normal distribution in Market1501 dataset.

3.3   Momentum Update

In this section, we present how to initialize and update the cluster level memory in the proposed Cluster Contrast method. The training details are presented in Algorithm 1.

Memory Initialization. Different from the instance level memory dictionary, we store each cluster's representation $\{\phi_1, \ldots, \phi_K\}$ in the memory-based feature dictionary. We use the mean feature vectors of each cluster to initialize the cluster representation, that is

$$\phi_k = \frac{1}{|\mathcal{H}_k|} \sum_{u_i \in \mathcal{H}_k} u_i \tag{4}$$

Equation 4 is executed when each epoch is initialized. And the clustering algorithm runs in each epoch, so K is changing as the model trains.

Memory Updating. During training, following [23], P person identities and a fixed number Z of instances for each person identity were sampled from the training set. Consequently, we obtain a total number of $P \times Z$ query images in the minibatch. We then momentum update the cluster representation iteratively by the query features in the minibatch by the Eq. 5 as illustrated in Fig. 3:

$$\forall q \in Q_k, \phi_k \leftarrow m\phi_k + (1 - m)q \tag{5}$$

where Q_k is the query features encoded from k-th cluster images and m is the momentum updating factor. m controls the consistency between the cluster feature and most updated query instance feature. As m close to 0, the cluster feature ϕ_k is close to the newest query feature. It is worth noting that all cluster representations are stored in the memory dictionary, so we calculate loss by comparing each query instance with all cluster representations in each iteration.

Algorithm 1: Unsupervised learning pipeline with Cluster Contrast

---

Require: Unlabeled training data X
Require: Initialize the backbone encoder f_θ with ImageNet-pretrained
ResNet-50
Require: Temperature τ for Eq. 3
Require: Momentum m for Eq. 5
for n in $[1, num\_epochs]$ **do**
    Extract feature vectors U from X by f_θ
    Clustering U into K clusters with DBSCAN
    Initialize memory dictionary with Eq. 4
    for i in $[1, num\_iterations]$ **do**
        Sample $P \times K$ query images from X
        Compute ClusterNCE loss with Eq. 3
        Update cluster feature with Eq. 5
        Update the encoder f_θ by optimizer
    end
end

Table 1. Statistics of the datasets used in the experimental section.

Dataset	Object	#train IDs	#train images	#test IDs	#query images	#total images
Market-1501	Person	751	12,936	750	3,368	32,668
MSMT17	Person	1,041	32,621	3,060	11,659	126,441
PersonX	Person	410	9,840	856	5,136	45,792
VeRi-776	Vehicle	575	37,746	200	1,678	51,003

4 Experiment

4.1 Datasets and Implementation

Datasets. We evaluate our proposed method on three large-scale person re-ID benchmarks: Market-1501 [64], MSMT17 [51], PersonX [43], and one vehicle ReID dataset, VeRi-776 [33]. Note that the DukeMTMC-reID [40] has been taken down for ethic issues. The Market-1501 and MSMT17 are widely used real-world person re-identification tasks. The PersonX is synthesized based on Unity [39], which contains manually designed obstacles such as random occlusion, resolution, and lighting differences. To show the robustness of our method, we also conduct vehicle re-identification experiments on the widely used real scene VeRi-776 datasets. The details of these datasets are summarized in Table 1.

Implementation Details. We adopt ResNet-50 [21] as the backbone encoder of the feature extractor and initialize the model with the parameters pre-trained on ImageNet [11]. After layer-4, we remove all sub-module layers and add global average pooling (GAP) followed by batch normalization layer [25] and L2-normalization layer, which will produce 2048-dimensional features. The

Table 2. Comparison with state-of-the-art methods on the object re-ID benchmarks. The purely unsupervised methods, unsupervised domain adaptation methods, and camera-aware unsupervised methods are considered for the comparison. The unsupervised domain adaptation method uses additional source domain labeled dataset and the camera-aware method uses the camera ID.

(a) Experiments on Market-1501 datasets

Methods	Market-1501				
	source	mAP	top-1	top-5	top-10
Purely Unsupervised					
SSL [31]	None	37.8	71.7	83.8	87.4
MMCL [47]	None	45.5	80.3	89.4	92.3
HCT [60]	None	56.4	80.0	91.6	95.2
CycAs [50]	None	64.8	84.8	–	–
UGA [52]	None	70.3	87.2	–	–
SPCL [17]	None	73.1	88.1	95.1	97.0
IICS [57]	None	72.1	88.8	95.3	96.9
OPLG [65]	None	78.1	91.1	96.4	97.7
RLCC [62]	None	77.7	90.8	96.3	97.5
ICE [4]	None	79.5	92.0	97.0	**98.1**
PPLR [8]	None	81.5	92.8	97.1	98.1
Ours	None	**83.0**	**92.9**	**97.2**	98.0
Unsupervised Domain Adaptation					
MMCL [47]	Duke	60.4	84.4	92.8	95.0
AD-Cluster [61]	Duke	68.3	86.7	94.4	96.5
MMT [16]	MSMT17	75.6	89.3	95.8	97.5
SPCL [17]	MSMT17	77.5	89.7	96.1	97.6
TDR [26]	Duke	83.4	94.2	–	–
Camera-aware Unsupervised					
CAP [49]	None	79.2	91.4	96.3	97.7
ICE(aware) [4]	None	82.3	93.8	97.6	98.4
PPLR(aware) [8]	None	84.4	94.3	97.8	98.6

(b) Experiments on MSMT17 datasets

Methods	MSMT17				
	source	mAP	top-1	top-5	top-10
Purely Unsupervised					
TAUDL [27]	None	12.5	28.4	–	–
MMCL [56]	None	11.2	35.4	44.8	49.8
UTAL [28]	None	13.1	31.4	–	–
CycAs [50]	None	26.7	50.1	–	–
UGA [52]	None	21.7	49.5	–	–
SPCL [17]	None	19.1	42.3	55.6	61.2
IICS [57]	None	18.6	45.7	57.7	62.8
OPLG [65]	None	26.9	53.7	65.3	70.2
RLCC [62]	None	27.9	56.5	68.4	73.1
ICE [4]	None	29.8	59.0	71.7	77.0
PPLR [8]	None	31.4	61.1	**73.4**	**77.8**
Ours	None	**33.0**	**62.0**	71.8	76.7
Unsupervised Domain Adaptation					
MMCL [47]	Duke	16.2	43.6	54.3	58.9
ECN [68]	Duke	10.2	30.2	41.5	46.8
MMT [16]	Market	24.0	50.1	63.5	69.3
SPCL [17]	Market	26.8	53.7	65.0	69.8
TDR [26]	Duke	36.3	66.6	–	–
Camera-aware Unsupervised					
CAP [49]	None	36.9	67.4	78.0	81.4
ICE(aware) [4]	None	38.9	70.2	80.5	84.4
PPLR(aware) [8]	None	42.2	73.3	83.5	86.5

(c) Experiments on PersonX datasets

Methods	PersonX				
	source	mAP	top-1	top-5	top-10
MMT [16]	Market	78.9	90.6	96.8	98.2
SPCL [17]	Market	78.5	91.1	97.8	99.0
SPCL [17]	None	72.3	88.1	96.6	98.3
Ours	None	84.7	94.4	98.3	99.3

(d) Experiments on VeRi-776 datasets

Methods	VeRi-776				
	source	mAP	top-1	top-5	top-10
MMT [16]	VehicleID	35.3	74.6	82.6	87.0
SPCL [17]	VehicleID	38.9	80.4	86.8	89.6
SPCL [17]	None	36.9	79.9	86.8	89.9
PPLR [8]	None	**41.6**	85.6	**91.1**	**93.4**
Ours	None	40.8	**86.2**	90.5	92.8

Gemeralized-Mean (GeM) pooling [38] can further improve the performance, which can be seen in appendix. During testing, we take the features of the global average pooling layer to calculate the consine similarity. At the beginning of each epoch, we use DBSCAN [13] for clustering to generate pseudo labels.

The input image is resized 256×128 for Market-1501, PersonX and MSMT17 datasets, and 224×224 for VeRi-776. For training images, we perform random horizontal flipping, padding with 10 pixels, random cropping, and random erasing [66]. Each mini-batch contains 256 images of 16 pseudo person identities and each person identity contains 16 images. In the case that a person identity has

Table 3. Our method is more robust to batch size changing.

Batch size	32		64		128		256	
	mAP	Rank-1	mAP	Rank-1	mAP	Rank-1	mAP	Rank-1
Baseline	62.5	80.3	65.5	82.7	71.5	86.7	73.1	87.3
Ours	79.0	90.4	80.2	91.2	81.8	92.0	83.0	92.9

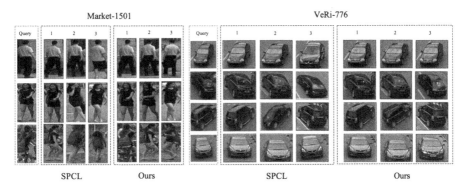

Fig. 5. The comparison of top-3 ranking list between SPCL [17] and our method on Market1501 and VeRi776 datasets. The correct results are highlighted by green borders and the incorrect results by red borders.

less than 16 images, images are sampled with replacement to compose 16 images. The momentum value m is set to 0.1 and the loss temperature τ is set to 0.05 for all datasets. We adopt Adam optimizer to train the re-ID model with weight decay $5e-4$. The initial learning rate is set to $3.5e-4$ with a warm-up scheme in the first 10 epochs, and then reduced to $1/10$ of its previous value every 20 epoch in a total of 50 epochs.

4.2 Comparison with State-of-the-Arts

We first compare our method to State-of-the-arts unsupervised learning methods which is the main focus of our method. From Table 2, we can see that our method is significantly better than all existing purely unsupervised methods, which proves the effectiveness of our method. Based on the same pipeline and DBSCAN clustering method, the mAP of our method surpasses the state-of-the-art purely unsupervised learning method by 2.5%, 2.6%, and 12.4% on person re-ID datasets Market-1501 [64], MSMT17 [51], and PersonX [43] dataset. Our method also performs comparable on vehicle re-ID dataset VeRi-776 [33]. And our method performs inferior to SOTA UDA and camera-aware unsupervised re-ID methods as they use additional source labeled dataset and camera id information. The Cluster Contrast can be easily generalized on UDA and camera-aware unsupervised re-ID methods. Details can be found in appendix.

Table 4. (a) We can see that the cluster level memory remarkably improves the performance and the momentum update strategy can further bring the improvement. (b) The performance is superior when a larger fraction of instances are updated on the baseline method. The statistics of both tables are obtained from the Market1501 dataset.

(a) Ablation study of effective components

Method	mAP	top-1
Baseline	73.1	87.5
+Cluster Memory	80.9	91.7
+Cluster Memory+Momentum	83.0	92.9

(b) Impact of cluster size

Cluster size	#Instance	Fraction	mAP	top-1
20	4	0.2	67.6	84.4
8	4	0.5	71.4	85.9
4	4	1.0	**76.5**	**89.0**

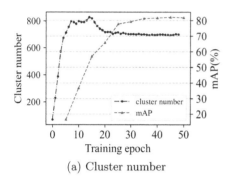

(a) Cluster number

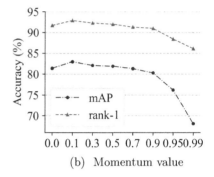

(b) Momentum value

Fig. 6. (a) We can see that the cluster number is dynamically changing as the model trains. (b) Our method performs comparably well when the momentum value is smaller than 0.9. All the statistics are obtained from the Market-1501.

4.3   Ablation Studies

In this section, we study the effectiveness of various components in Cluster Contrast method. We define the unsupervised learning pipeline with instance-level memory dictionary (Fig. 3 (b)) as the **baseline** method.

Cluster Memory. In Sect. 3.3, we argue that compared to instance-level memory, the cluster-level memory could update cluster feature more consistently. As shown in Fig. 3 (b), the instance-level memory maintains the feature of each instance of the dataset. In every training iteration, each instance feature in the mini-batch will be updated to its own memory dictionary. Since the cluster size is unbalancedly distributed, only a small fraction of the instance features could be updated in a large cluster when all instances in a small cluster are updated. Table 4a shows the effectiveness of Cluster Memory without momentum updating, where the instance feature is directly replaced by query feature.

The simplest solution is to increase the batch size similar to SimCLR [5]. As the batch size increases, more instance features could be updated inside one cluster. However, the batch size reaches its upper limit of 256 due to the GPU memory. To deal with the limitation of the GPU memory, we came up another

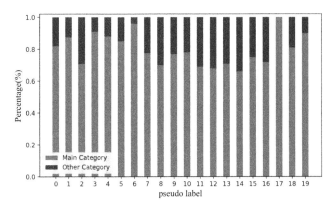

Fig. 7. We randomly select 20 categories from the Market1501 clustering results and calculate the percentage of different categories using ground truth labels.

solution that we restrict the cluster size to a constant number. Therefore, in every iteration a fixed fraction of the instance features could be updated. In this way, the instance feature vectors can be updated consistently with a small batch size. The results in Table 4b demonstrate that the performance of the baseline increases with the rising of the fraction of the updated instance features, until all instance feature vectors inside one cluster could be updated in a single iteration. In sum, we propose the Cluster Contrast, which can update the cluster feature representation in single iteration. As shown in Table 3, our method is more robust to batch size changing. And the Cluster Contrast is more memory efficient since the number of cluster features is an order of magnitude smaller than the number instance features.

Momentum Updating. SwAV optimizes the cluster feature end to end by gradient. Our method employs offline clustering so the cluster feature cannot be directly optimized. Instead we follow Moco to use the momentum updating strategy to update cluster representations to maintain the feature consistency. Table 4a shows the effectiveness of the momentum updating strategy. As shown in Eq. 5, the momentum value m controls the update speed of cluster memory. The larger the value of m, the slower the cluster memory update. We conducted experiments on the Market-1501 dataset to explore the influence of different m values on our method. As shown in Fig. 6 (b), it performs reasonably well when m is less than 0.9. When m is too large (e.g., greater than 0.9), the accuracy drops considerably. These results support us to build better cluster representation.

Cluster Feature Representation. As shown in Fig. 3 (b), the instance-level memory averages all instance feature vectors to represent the cluster feature. However, in unsupervised learning re-ID, the pseudo label generation stage would inevitably introduce the outlier instances, which are harmful to compute cluster centroid. In Fig. 7, we count the proportions of different real categories being clustered into the same category on the Market-1501 dataset. It shows there

Table 5. Comparison with unsupervised pretrained Resnet50 backbones

Method	Market-1501		MSMT17		PersonX		VeRi-776	
	mAP	top-1	mAP	top-1	mAP	top-1	mAP	top-1
Supervised	83.0	92.9	33.0	62.0	84.7	94.4	40.8	86.2
SwAV	**84.8**	**93.5**	**38.2**	**67.5**	**86.2**	**95.1**	**42.0**	**87.4**

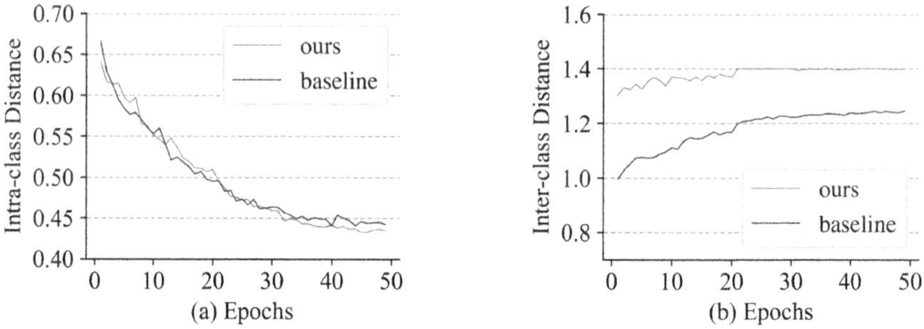

Fig. 8. Comparison of the intra-class distance and inter-class distance between our method and baseline method on Market1501 datasets.

still around 20% noisy instances when model training in finished. Our method can get better feature representation as shown in Fig. 8. The feature quality of our method measured by the intra-class distance and the inter-class distance are much better than the baseline method. From this we can speculate that better representation of features between classes is an important factor for our method to achieve better results (Table 5).

Compared with Unsupervised Pretrained Backbones. The pseudo-label based unsupervised re-ID methods [4,14,15,17,30,47,49,57,62,65] use the supervised ImageNet pretrained backbone for clustering initialization. In order to make the pipeline full unsupervised, we also evaluate our method with unsupervised pretrained backbone in Fig. 5. Thanks to the rich feature representation learned by the unsupervised SwAV method, our fully unsupervised re-ID pipeline with unsupervised backbone achieves better results on all four re-ID datasets.

5   Conclusion

In this paper, we present the Cluster Contrast for unsupervised re-ID, which stores feature vectors and computes contrast loss in cluster level memory dictionary. It unifies the cluster feature updating progress regardless the cluster size or dataset size. Momentum updating is used to further reinforce the cluster feature consistency. Experiments show demonstrate the effectiveness of our method.

References

1. Bachman, P., Hjelm, R.D., Buchwalter, W.: Learning representations by maximizing mutual information across views. arXiv preprint arXiv:1906.00910 (2019)
2. Caron, M., Misra, I., Mairal, J., Goyal, P., Bojanowski, P., Joulin, A.: Unsupervised learning of visual features by contrasting cluster assignments. In: Advances in Neural Information Processing Systems, vol. 33, pp. 9912–9924 (2020)
3. Chen, G., Lin, C., Ren, L., Lu, J., Zhou, J.: Self-critical attention learning for person re-identification. In: Proceedings of the IEEE/CVF International Conference on Computer Vision, pp. 9637–9646 (2019)
4. Chen, H., Lagadec, B., Bremond, F.: Ice: inter-instance contrastive encoding for unsupervised person re-identification. In: Proceedings of the IEEE/CVF International Conference on Computer Vision, pp. 14960–14969 (2021)
5. Chen, T., Kornblith, S., Norouzi, M., Hinton, G.: A simple framework for contrastive learning of visual representations. In: International Conference on Machine Learning, pp. 1597–1607. PMLR (2020)
6. Chen, X., Fan, H., Girshick, R., He, K.: Improved baselines with momentum contrastive learning. arXiv preprint arXiv:2003.04297 (2020)
7. Chen, X., Xie, S., He, K.: An empirical study of training self-supervised vision transformers. In: Proceedings of the IEEE/CVF International Conference on Computer Vision, pp. 9640–9649 (2021)
8. Cho, Y., Kim, W.J., Hong, S., Yoon, S.E.: Part-based pseudo label refinement for unsupervised person re-identification. In: Proceedings of the IEEE/CVF Conference on Computer Vision and Pattern Recognition, pp. 7308–7318 (2022)
9. Dai, Z., Chen, M., Gu, X., Zhu, S., Tan, P.: Batch dropblock network for person re-identification and beyond. In: Proceedings of the IEEE/CVF International Conference on Computer Vision, pp. 3691–3701 (2019)
10. Dai, Z., Chen, M., Zhu, S., Tan, P.: Batch feature erasing for person re-identification and beyond. arXiv preprint arXiv:1811.07130, $\mathbf{1}(2)$, 3 (2018)
11. Deng, J., Dong, W., Socher, R., Li, L.J., Li, K., Fei-Fei, L.: Imagenet: a large-scale hierarchical image database. In: 2009 IEEE Conference on Computer Vision and Pattern Recognition, pp. 248–255. IEEE (2009)
12. Deng, W., Zheng, L., Ye, Q., Kang, G., Yang, Y., Jiao, J.: Image-image domain adaptation with preserved self-similarity and domain-dissimilarity for person re-identification. In: Proceedings of the IEEE Conference on Computer Vision and Pattern Recognition, pp. 994–1003 (2018)
13. Ester, M., Kriegel, H.P., Sander, J., Xu, X., et al.: A density-based algorithm for discovering clusters in large spatial databases with noise. In: KDD, vol. 96, pp. 226–231 (1996)
14. Fan, H., Zheng, L., Yan, C., Yang, Y.: Unsupervised person re-identification: clustering and fine-tuning. ACM Trans. Multimedia Comput. Commun. Appl. (TOMM) $\mathbf{14}(4)$, 1–18 (2018)
15. Fu, Y., Wei, Y., Wang, G., Zhou, Y., Shi, H., Huang, T.S.: Self-similarity grouping: a simple unsupervised cross domain adaptation approach for person re-identification. In: Proceedings of the IEEE/CVF International Conference on Computer Vision, pp. 6112–6121 (2019)
16. Ge, Y., Chen, D., Li, H.: Mutual mean-teaching: pseudo label refinery for unsupervised domain adaptation on person re-identification. arXiv preprint arXiv:2001.01526 (2020)

17. Ge, Y., Zhu, F., Chen, D., Zhao, R., Li, H.: Self-paced contrastive learning with hybrid memory for domain adaptive object re-id. In: Larochelle, H., Ranzato, M., Hadsell, R., Balcan, M.F., Lin, H. (eds.) Advances in Neural Information Processing Systems, vol. 33, pp. 11309–11321. Curran Associates, Inc. (2020). https://proceedings.neurips.cc/paper/2020/file/821fa74b50ba3f7cba1e6c53e8fa6845-Paper.pdf

18. Guo, J., Yuan, Y., Huang, L., Zhang, C., Yao, J.G., Han, K.: Beyond human parts: dual part-aligned representations for person re-identification. In: Proceedings of the IEEE/CVF International Conference on Computer Vision, pp. 3642–3651 (2019)

19. Hadsell, R., Chopra, S., LeCun, Y.: Dimensionality reduction by learning an invariant mapping. In: 2006 IEEE Computer Society Conference on Computer Vision and Pattern Recognition (CVPR 2006), vol. 2, pp. 1735–1742. IEEE (2006)

20. He, K., Fan, H., Wu, Y., Xie, S., Girshick, R.: Momentum contrast for unsupervised visual representation learning. In: Proceedings of the IEEE/CVF Conference on Computer Vision and Pattern Recognition, pp. 9729–9738 (2020)

21. He, K., Zhang, X., Ren, S., Sun, J.: Deep residual learning for image recognition. In: Proceedings of the IEEE Conference on Computer Vision and Pattern Recognition, pp. 770–778 (2016)

22. Henaff, O.: Data-efficient image recognition with contrastive predictive coding. In: International Conference on Machine Learning, pp. 4182–4192. PMLR (2020)

23. Hermans, A., Beyer, L., Leibe, B.: In defense of the triplet loss for person re-identification. arXiv preprint arXiv:1703.07737 (2017)

24. Hjelm, R.D., et al.: Learning deep representations by mutual information estimation and maximization. arXiv preprint arXiv:1808.06670 (2018)

25. Ioffe, S., Szegedy, C.: Batch normalization: accelerating deep network training by reducing internal covariate shift. In: International Conference on Machine Learning, pp. 448–456. PMLR (2015)

26. Isobe, T., Li, D., Tian, L., Chen, W., Shan, Y., Wang, S.: Towards discriminative representation learning for unsupervised person re-identification. In: Proceedings of the IEEE/CVF International Conference on Computer Vision, pp. 8526–8536 (2021)

27. Li, M., Zhu, X., Gong, S.: Unsupervised person re-identification by deep learning Tracklet association. In: Ferrari, V., Hebert, M., Sminchisescu, C., Weiss, Y. (eds.) ECCV 2018. LNCS, vol. 11208, pp. 772–788. Springer, Cham (2018). https://doi.org/10.1007/978-3-030-01225-0_45

28. Li, M., Zhu, X., Gong, S.: Unsupervised Tracklet person re-identification. IEEE Trans. Pattern Anal. Mach. Intell. 42(7), 1770–1782 (2019)

29. Lin, S., Li, H., Li, C.T., Kot, A.C.: Multi-task mid-level feature alignment network for unsupervised cross-dataset person re-identification. arXiv preprint arXiv:1807.01440 (2018)

30. Lin, Y., Dong, X., Zheng, L., Yan, Y., Yang, Y.: A bottom-up clustering approach to unsupervised person re-identification. In: Proceedings of the AAAI Conference on Artificial Intelligence, vol. 33, pp. 8738–8745 (2019)

31. Lin, Y., Xie, L., Wu, Y., Yan, C., Tian, Q.: Unsupervised person re-identification via softened similarity learning. In: Proceedings of the IEEE/CVF Conference on Computer Vision and Pattern Recognition, pp. 3390–3399 (2020)

32. Liu, J., Ni, B., Yan, Y., Zhou, P., Cheng, S., Hu, J.: Pose transferrable person re-identification. In: Proceedings of the IEEE Conference on Computer Vision and Pattern Recognition, pp. 4099–4108 (2018)

33. Liu, X., Liu, W., Ma, H., Fu, H.: Large-scale vehicle re-identification in urban surveillance videos. In: 2016 IEEE International Conference on Multimedia and Expo (ICME), pp. 1–6. IEEE (2016)
34. MacQueen, J., et al.: Some methods for classification and analysis of multivariate observations. In: Proceedings of the Fifth Berkeley Symposium on Mathematical Statistics and Probability, Oakland, CA, USA, vol. 1, pp. 281–297 (1967)
35. Misra, I., Maaten, L.v.d.: Self-supervised learning of pretext-invariant representations. In: Proceedings of the IEEE/CVF Conference on Computer Vision and Pattern Recognition. pp. 6707–6717 (2020)
36. Van den Oord, A., Li, Y., Vinyals, O.: Representation learning with contrastive predictive coding. arXiv e-prints pp. arXiv-1807 (2018)
37. Oord, A.v.d., Li, Y., Vinyals, O.: Representation learning with contrastive predictive coding. arXiv preprint arXiv:1807.03748 (2018)
38. Radenović, F., Tolias, G., Chum, O.: Fine-tuning CNN image retrieval with no human annotation. IEEE Trans. Pattern Anal. Mach. Intell. **41**(7), 1655–1668 (2018)
39. Riccitiello, J.: John Riccitiello sets out to identify the engine of growth for unity technologies (interview). VentureBeat. Interview with Dean Takahashi. Retrieved January **18**(3) (2015)
40. Ristani, E., Solera, F., Zou, R., Cucchiara, R., Tomasi, C.: Performance measures and a data set for multi-target, multi-camera tracking. In: Hua, G., Jégou, H. (eds.) ECCV 2016. LNCS, vol. 9914, pp. 17–35. Springer, Cham (2016). https://doi.org/10.1007/978-3-319-48881-3_2
41. Schroff, F., Kalenichenko, D., Philbin, J.: Facenet: a unified embedding for face recognition and clustering. In: Proceedings of the IEEE Conference on Computer Vision and Pattern Recognition, pp. 815–823 (2015)
42. Song, J., Yang, Y., Song, Y.Z., Xiang, T., Hospedales, T.M.: Generalizable person re-identification by domain-invariant mapping network. In: Proceedings of the IEEE/CVF Conference on Computer Vision and Pattern Recognition, pp. 719–728 (2019)
43. Sun, X., Zheng, L.: Dissecting person re-identification from the viewpoint of viewpoint. In: Proceedings of the IEEE/CVF Conference on Computer Vision and Pattern Recognition, pp. 608–617 (2019)
44. Tian, Y., Krishnan, D., Isola, P.: Contrastive multiview coding. arXiv preprint arXiv:1906.05849 (2019)
45. Tian, Y., Krishnan, D., Isola, P.: Contrastive multiview coding. In: Vedaldi, A., Bischof, H., Brox, T., Frahm, J.-M. (eds.) ECCV 2020. LNCS, vol. 12356, pp. 776–794. Springer, Cham (2020). https://doi.org/10.1007/978-3-030-58621-8_45
46. Wang, C., Zhang, Q., Huang, C., Liu, W., Wang, X.: Mancs: a multi-task attentional network with curriculum sampling for person re-identification. In: Ferrari, V., Hebert, M., Sminchisescu, C., Weiss, Y. (eds.) ECCV 2018. LNCS, vol. 11208, pp. 384–400. Springer, Cham (2018). https://doi.org/10.1007/978-3-030-01225-0_23
47. Wang, D., Zhang, S.: Unsupervised person re-identification via multi-label classification. In: Proceedings of the IEEE/CVF Conference on Computer Vision and Pattern Recognition, pp. 10981–10990 (2020)
48. Wang, J., Zhu, X., Gong, S., Li, W.: Transferable joint attribute-identity deep learning for unsupervised person re-identification. In: Proceedings of the IEEE Conference on Computer Vision and Pattern Recognition, pp. 2275–2284 (2018)
49. Wang, M., Lai, B., Huang, J., Gong, X., Hua, X.S.: Camera-aware proxies for unsupervised person re-identification. In: AAAI, vol. 2, p. 4 (2021)

50. Wang, Z., et al.: Cycas: self-supervised cycle association for learning re-identifiable descriptions. arXiv preprint arXiv:2007.07577 (2020)
51. Wei, L., Zhang, S., Gao, W., Tian, Q.: Person transfer GAN to bridge domain gap for person re-identification. In: Proceedings of the IEEE Conference on Computer Vision and Pattern Recognition, pp. 79–88 (2018)
52. Wu, J., Yang, Y., Liu, H., Liao, S., Lei, Z., Li, S.Z.: Unsupervised graph association for person re-identification. In: Proceedings of the IEEE/CVF International Conference on Computer Vision, pp. 8321–8330 (2019)
53. Wu, Z., Xiong, Y., Yu, S.X., Lin, D.: Unsupervised feature learning via non-parametric instance discrimination. In: Proceedings of the IEEE Conference on Computer Vision and Pattern Recognition (CVPR), June 2018
54. Wu, Z., Xiong, Y., Yu, S.X., Lin, D.: Unsupervised feature learning via non-parametric instance discrimination. In: Proceedings of the IEEE Conference on Computer Vision and Pattern Recognition, pp. 3733–3742 (2018)
55. Xiao, T., Li, S., Wang, B., Lin, L., Wang, X.: Joint detection and identification feature learning for person search. In: Proceedings of the IEEE Conference on Computer Vision and Pattern Recognition (CVPR), July 2017
56. Xiao, T., Li, S., Wang, B., Lin, L., Wang, X.: Joint detection and identification feature learning for person search. In: Proceedings of the IEEE Conference on Computer Vision and Pattern Recognition, pp. 3415–3424 (2017)
57. Xuan, S., Zhang, S.: Intra-inter camera similarity for unsupervised person re-identification. In: Proceedings of the IEEE/CVF Conference on Computer Vision and Pattern Recognition, pp. 11926–11935 (2021)
58. Ye, M., Zhang, X., Yuen, P.C., Chang, S.F.: Unsupervised embedding learning via invariant and spreading instance feature. In: Proceedings of the IEEE/CVF Conference on Computer Vision and Pattern Recognition, pp. 6210–6219 (2019)
59. Yu, H.X., Zheng, W.S., Wu, A., Guo, X., Gong, S., Lai, J.H.: Unsupervised person re-identification by soft multilabel learning. In: Proceedings of the IEEE/CVF Conference on Computer Vision and Pattern Recognition, pp. 2148–2157 (2019)
60. Zeng, K., Ning, M., Wang, Y., Guo, Y.: Hierarchical clustering with hard-batch triplet loss for person re-identification. In: Proceedings of the IEEE/CVF Conference on Computer Vision and Pattern Recognition, pp. 13657–13665 (2020)
61. Zhai, Y., et al.: Ad-cluster: augmented discriminative clustering for domain adaptive person re-identification. In: Proceedings of the IEEE/CVF Conference on Computer Vision and Pattern Recognition, pp. 9021–9030 (2020)
62. Zhang, X., Ge, Y., Qiao, Y., Li, H.: Refining pseudo labels with clustering consensus over generations for unsupervised object re-identification. In: Proceedings of the IEEE/CVF Conference on Computer Vision and Pattern Recognition, pp. 3436–3445 (2021)
63. Zhang, Z., Lan, C., Zeng, W., Chen, Z.: Densely semantically aligned person re-identification. In: Proceedings of the IEEE/CVF Conference on Computer Vision and Pattern Recognition, pp. 667–676 (2019)
64. Zheng, L., Shen, L., Tian, L., Wang, S., Wang, J., Tian, Q.: Scalable person re-identification: a benchmark. In: Proceedings of the IEEE International Conference on Computer Vision, pp. 1116–1124 (2015)
65. Zheng, Y., et al.: Online pseudo label generation by hierarchical cluster dynamics for adaptive person re-identification. In: Proceedings of the IEEE/CVF International Conference on Computer Vision, pp. 8371–8381 (2021)
66. Zhong, Z., Zheng, L., Kang, G., Li, S., Yang, Y.: Random erasing data augmentation. In: Proceedings of the AAAI Conference on Artificial Intelligence, vol. 34, pp. 13001–13008 (2020)

67. Zhong, Z., Zheng, L., Li, S., Yang, Y.: Generalizing a person retrieval model hetero- and homogeneously. In: Ferrari, V., Hebert, M., Sminchisescu, C., Weiss, Y. (eds.) ECCV 2018. LNCS, vol. 11217, pp. 176–192. Springer, Cham (2018). https://doi.org/10.1007/978-3-030-01261-8_11

68. Zhong, Z., Zheng, L., Luo, Z., Li, S., Yang, Y.: Invariance matters: exemplar memory for domain adaptive person re-identification. In: Proceedings of the IEEE/CVF Conference on Computer Vision and Pattern Recognition, pp. 598–607 (2019)

69. Zhou, S., Wang, F., Huang, Z., Wang, J.: Discriminative feature learning with consistent attention regularization for person re-identification. In: Proceedings of the IEEE/CVF International Conference on Computer Vision, pp. 8040–8049 (2019)

70. Zhuang, C., Zhai, A.L., Yamins, D.: Local aggregation for unsupervised learning of visual embeddings. In: Proceedings of the IEEE/CVF International Conference on Computer Vision, pp. 6002–6012 (2019)

Revisiting Unsupervised Domain Adaptation Models: A Smoothness Perspective

Xiaodong Wang[1], Junbao Zhuo[2(✉)], Mengru Zhang[3], Shuhui Wang[2], and Yuejian Fang[1(✉)]

[1] School of Software and Microelectronics, Peking University, Beijing, China
wangxiaodong21s@stu.pku.edu.cn, fangyj@ss.pku.edu.cn
[2] Key Laboratory of Intelligent Information Processing,
Indian Institute of Computer Technology, CAS, Beijing, China
junbao.zhuo@vipl.ict.ac.cn, wangshuhui@ict.ac.cn
[3] MEGVII Technology, Beijing, China
zhangmengru@megvii.com

Abstract. Unsupervised Domain Adaptation (UDA) aims to leverage the labeled source data and unlabeled target data to generalize better in the target domain. UDA methods utilize better domain alignment or carefully-designed regularizations to increase the discriminability of target features. However, most methods focus on directly increasing the distance between cluster centers of target features, i.e., enlarging inter-class variance, which intuitively increases the discriminability of target features and is easy to implement. However, due to intra-class variance optimization being under-explored, there are still some samples of the same class are prone to be classified into several classes. To handle this problem, we aim to equip UDA methods with the high smoothness constraint. We first define the model's smoothness as the predictions similarity within each class, and propose a simple yet effective technique LeCo (impLicit smoothness Constraint) to promote the smoothness. We construct the weak and strong "views" of each target sample and enforce the model predictions of these two views to be consistent. Besides, a new uncertainty measure named Instance Class Confusion conditions the consistency is proposed to guarantee the transferability. LeCo implicitly reduces the model sensitivity to perturbations for target samples and guarantees smaller intra-class variance. Extensive experiments show that the proposed technique improves various baseline approaches by a large margin, and helps yield comparable results to the state-of-the-arts on four public datasets. Our codes are publicly available at https://github.com/Wang-Xiaodong1899/LeCo_UDA.

Supplementary Information The online version contains supplementary material available at https://doi.org/10.1007/978-3-031-26351-4_21.

1   Introduction

Deep learning methods have achieved great success on a wide variety of tasks, and show surprising performances even without labels [1–3]. However, when the training set and test set are drawn from different data distributions, the deep learning models would usually have poor generalization performance on the test set. To handle this problem, the Unsupervised Domain Adaptation (UDA) [5–7] technique was proposed. In the UDA scenario, the model is trained on a labeled source domain (training set) and an unlabeled target domain (test set) and required to perform well in the target domain, where the source and target distributions follow the Covariate Shift [8].

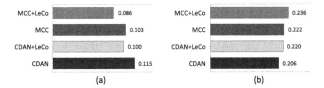

Fig. 1. Illustration of (a) the intra-class variance, and (b) the inter-class variance on VisDA-C [4]. Different colors indicate the results of different models. (Color figure online)

Recently, deep learning based UDA methods have almost dominated this field with promising results [9–16]. One direction is to learn domain-invariant feature. Methods [12,14] imposed adversarial training for better domain distribution alignment, and [15,16] employed the bidirectional alignment. The other direction is to add specific regularization items on the target data, which could obtain a striking performance [9–11] as the properties of target data are well exploited. For example, [9,10] added regularizations on classification responses for insuring larger prediction diversity or small prediction confusion. However, existing methods did not alleviate error accumulation well, and sometimes, the prediction confidence of wrongly classified examples also increases during training. Such accumulation of misclassification harms the learning process and affects those correctly classified examples with low prediction confidence. The above issue is very common in UDA methods, and recent methods like [15,16] expect to alleviate the accumulation problem by the better feature matching, or by using a target domain-oriented classifier [17] to generate more accurate pseudo labels. However, they relied on better models and did not explicitly reduce the sensitivity of models to sample disturbances, and are not generic.

In this paper, we revisit the UDA models in a new perspective: *smoothness*. Given some samples within a class or the augmented data of a sample, the model predictions should be similar. We define smoothness as the intra-class variance, which is a measure of how far a set of features (predictions) within a class is spread out from their average value. Obviously, the intra-class variance will be smaller if the predictions of the same class are more consistent. As shown in Fig. 1, compared with the CDAN [14], MCC [9] shows smaller intra-class variance and larger inter-class variance. Besides, when equipped with high smoothness, they both show smaller intra-class and larger inter-class variances.

However, smoothness is hard to insured in UDA, as the labels of the target samples are not available. Inspired by semi-supervised learning methods [18, 19] or self-supervised methods [1,2], we proposed a technique LeCo (impLicit smoothness Constraint). The key is to create new strongly perturbed samples which come from the same instance (of course the same class) as original samples of the target domain, so construct a large number of such pairs to estimate and reduce the intra-class variance, insuring the high smoothness. Specifically, two "views" of the same target sample under the weak and strong augmentations pass the same network to generate the two predictions, and we minimize the $L2$-distance of them on all class predictions, which is regarded as *naïve constraint*.

Furthermore, avoiding the hard-to-transfer samples to deteriorate the optimization, we quantify the uncertainty of samples using a novel *Instance Class Confusion* to condition the constraint. Instance class confusion of a certain sample is defined as the sum of all cross-class confusion by the class predictions of it. We consider the cross-class information and the probabilities of all classes, which is better to measure the transferability than only considering the probabilities of all classes [20]. We utilize the instance class confusion to condition the naïve constraint so that we can achieve a better training convergence for domain adaptation. Additionally, we provide theoretical analysis which reveals that our technique could approximate the more expected target risk.

We finally summarize our contributions as follows:

- We analyze the existing UDA methods with a novel perspective: **smoothness**. We introduce the reciprocal of intra-class variance as the indicator of smoothness. To promote the smoothness of models, we propose a simple yet effective technique named LeCo.
- LeCo could implicitly encourage the model to generate consistent predictions on the target domain. It is generic and can be applied to various UDA methods, reducing the intra-class variance effectively, also increasing the inter-class variance.
- We validate the effectiveness of LeCo on the image classification task of UDA. Extensive experiments demonstrate the effectiveness and we achieve results comparable to the state-of-the-arts on four public datasets.

2   Related Work

Domain adaptation aims to transfer source domain knowledge to the related but different target domain, and there are various settings in this field, such as Unsupervised Domain Adaptation [12,21,22], Semi-Supervised Domain Adaptation [23–26], Model Adaptation [27–29], Noisy Domain Adaptation [30,31] etc. Most of the works focus on UDA which is adopted in this paper. We also review regularization based methods and consistency learning based methods.

Unsupervised Domain Adaptation: The deep unsupervised domain adaptation methods have made a success without any labels in the target domain. These methods can be mainly divided into domain alignment methods and regularization-based methods. For the domain alignment methods, the early methods [21,22,32–34] are based on feature distribution matching. MMD [35] is often used [21,22] in the deep neural network to deal with the domain adaptation by aligning the distribution. For better aligning the distributions, JAN [33] considered the joint feature distributions, and CMD [34] proposed the new domain discrepancy metric. Due to the potential of GANs [36], various works [12,14,37–39] performed better domain alignment by using adversarial learning. DANN [37] firstly designed a novel adversarial pipeline. It imposed a domain classifier, and used adversarial training to learn domain-invariant representations. CDAN [14] conducted adversarial learning on the covariance of feature representations and classifier predictions. MCD [38] explicitly utilized two task-specific classifiers to measure the domain discrepancy and minimized it according to the $\mathcal{H}\Delta\mathcal{H}$ theory [6]. MDD [12] proposed a novel margin disparity discrepancy that firstly leveraged the scoring function and margin loss to bound the gap caused by domain shift. Recently, the bidirectional domain matching methods [15,16] exploited a novel and effective domain alignment strategy. Method [15] utilized mixup to augment intermediate domains for the bidirectional matching, while method [16] constructed virtual mirrors for both source and target domains.

Regularization Based Methods: Inspired by Semi-Supervised Learning (SSL), researchers [9–11,13,40] are more interested in exploring target data properties in UDA. Early, Entropy Minimization (EntMin) [20] is widely used in UDA and semi-supervised domain adaptation [14,28]. In recent years, some regularization based methods are proposed to hold the discriminability of the target domain. AFN [11] investigated that those task-specific features with larger norms are more transferable. BNM [10] proved that the batch nuclear-norm maximization can lead to the improvement on both the prediction discriminability and diversity, which works well in domain adaptation, SSL, and open domain recognition [41]. In [42], the authors proposed domain conditioned adaptation network, with a designed domain conditioned channel attention module to excite channel activation separately for each domain. In [43], a transferable semantic augmentation approach was proposed to enhance the classifier adaptation ability via implicitly generating source features toward target semantics. MCC [9] can be regarded as a regularization-based method that restrains the inter-class confusion of unlabeled data. These techniques can be considered as the self-training of target data, cooperating well with source supervised training. The regularization can also be the consistency regularization in self-ensembling [13,44] and achieved superior performance on VisDA-C [4].

Consistency Learning: We review related consistency learning methods in SSL and self-supervised learning. Consistency learning [44–46] or data augmentation [18,19] methods that have achieved good performance in SSL, as well as regularization methods [20,47]. Temporal ensembling [47] by constraining the consistency of different training epochs enabled the model to better learn unlabeled data. In [48], authors conceptually explored the regularization methods by comparing the gradient norms between regularization loss and cross-entropy loss in SSL. Our constraint is similar to FixMatch [18] using different augmentations [1,2], but we exploits all class predictions even the low confidence information which is shown to be effective for domain adaptation [15,49]. Our method utilizes all class predictions to maintain the consistency of two augmentations' predictions, rather than using the confidence thresholding. Nowadays, self-supervised learning makes a remarkable success due to large-scale data and instance discrimination learning. Contrastive learning methods [1,2] utilized two random augmentations for images and encouraged predictions to be consistent, which aim to learn the instance discrimination. Domain adaptation can be considered as a special case of SSL, where labeled and unlabeled data are drawn from different distributions. Methods in SSL aim to learn the consistency in a single domain, and the sparse labels or pseudo labels share the same domain with unlabeled data, whereas UDA is a cross-domain task. We focus on the intra-class consistency, which is related to the intra-domain consistency adopted in [50]. [50] attempted to use primary and auxiliary classifiers that share the same feature extractor to force the model to generate more similar predictions. We first use different augmentations to construct the inconsistency for each instance and reduce it, and then we use instance class confusion to guide the model to focus on more reliable instances which will be helpful for cross-domain training.

3   Method

3.1   Preliminaries

In UDA, we are given source domain data $\mathcal{D}_s = \{(x_i^s, y_i^s)\}_{i=1}^{n_s}$ of n_s labeled samples from $\mathcal{X}^s \times \mathcal{Y}^s$ and target domain data $\mathcal{D}_t = \{(x_i^t)\}_{i=1}^{n_t}$ of n_t unlabeled samples from $\mathcal{X}^t$. The two domains share the same K categories and their distributions follow the Covariate Shift [8]. Specifically, the input marginal distribution $P(\mathcal{X})$ changes $(P(\mathcal{X}^s) \neq P(\mathcal{X}^t))$ but the conditional $P(\mathcal{Y}|\mathcal{X})$ remains the same.

The model in our method is equipped with a feature extractor and a classifier. Here, the feature extractor ψ consists of the deep convolution networks and a bottleneck layer that is introduced to reduce the dimension of features, and the features are passed through the classifier f to generate predictions.

3.2   Recap of UDA Baselines

Domain-Alignment Methods. Explicit domain alignment methods [22,33] use the discrepancy metrics such as [34,35]. To better align the source and target domains, methods [12,14,37] utilize the adversarial training. Recently, bidirectional alignment shows great performances [15,16] in this field. These methods try to simultaneously optimize the source classification loss $\mathcal{L}_s$ and domain alignment loss $\mathcal{L}_{dom}$. First, using the randomly sampled batch labeled examples

$\{X^s, Y^s\}$ from the source domain $\mathcal{D}_s$ of size B, we can obtain the supervised classification objective:

$$\mathcal{L}_s = \frac{1}{B} \sum_{i=1}^{B} CE(Y_i^s, f(\psi(X_i^s))) \tag{1}$$

where the $CE(\cdot, \cdot)$ is the cross-entropy loss. As for the domain alignment methods using the discrepancy metrics such as the MMD [35], given the randomly sampled a batch of labeled examples $\{X^t\}$ from the target domain $\mathcal{D}_t$, the domain alignment loss $\mathcal{L}_{dom}$ is defined as below:

$$\mathcal{L}_{dom} = MMD(\psi(X^s), \psi(X^t)) \tag{2}$$

where $MMD(\cdot, \cdot)$ matches the feature distributions of $\mathcal{D}_s$ and $\mathcal{D}_t$. And the general optimization objective can be formulated as:

$$\min_{\psi, f} \mathcal{L}_s + \mathcal{L}_{dom} \tag{3}$$

As for the adversarial methods that introduce a domain discriminator D, if the inputs of D are the features, the domain alignment loss could be defined as below:

$$\mathcal{L}_{dom} = \frac{1}{B} \sum_{i=1}^{B} log(D(\psi(X_i^s))) + \frac{1}{B} \sum_{i=1}^{B} log(1 - D(\psi(X_i^t))) \tag{4}$$

And the optimization objective is formulated as:

$$\begin{aligned} \min_{\psi, f} \mathcal{L}_s + \mathcal{L}_{dom} \\ \max_{D} \mathcal{L}_{dom} \end{aligned} \tag{5}$$

Regularization-Based Methods. The properties of the target domain can be modeled by some regularization methods [9–11,20], which aim to enhance the discriminability of target samples. We denote the $\mathcal{L}_{reg}$ as the regularization loss in these methods. And $\mathcal{L}_{reg}$ often only depends on target features, which is defined as below:

$$\mathcal{L}_{reg} = \frac{1}{B} \sum_{i=1}^{B} \|\psi(X_i^t)\|_* \tag{6}$$

where the symbol $*$ can be replaced by the specific norm such as adaptive feature norm [11], nuclear norm [10], entropy [20], and class confusion [9]. And the general optimization objective in regularization based methods is formulated as:

$$\min_{\psi, f} \mathcal{L}_s + \mathcal{L}_{reg} \tag{7}$$

In this paper, we aim to equip both domain-alignment and regularization-based UDA methods with an effective technique about smoothness constraint. Our method can bring remarkable improvements to these methods.

3.3   Implicit Smoothness Constraint

We noticed that the prediction intra-class variance is relatively large, i.e. lower smoothness. The core problem is that the model is sensitive to image perturbations in the target domain, so it is prone to misclassify images of the same class to different classes. Therefore, to reduce the sensitivity of the model, we directly impose the model to generate more consistent predictions from original and perturbed images. Specifically, we impose the constraint that the predictions of weak and strong augmentations should be close enough. Although the idea is simple, it can effectively contribute to more consistent predictions.

We aim to enhance the smoothness of the domain alignment and regularization based models. Given the randomly sampled batch of unlabeled examples $\{X^t\}$ from target domain $\mathcal{D}_t$, we take two "views" of these examples by the weak augmentation (random flipping and cropping) and strong augmentation (RandAug [51]). We denote the weak and strong views as X_w^t and X_{str}^t, respectively.

Then, both the two views are passed through the feature extractor ψ and classifier f to generate the classification responses, respectively, as follows:

$$\hat{Y}_w^t = \sigma\left(f(\psi(X_w^t))\right), \hat{Y}_{str}^t = \sigma\left(f(\psi(X_{str}^t))\right) \tag{8}$$

where $\sigma(\cdot)$ is the softmax function. For each $x^t \in X^t$, we have the corresponding classification responses $\hat{y}_w^t \in \hat{Y}_w^t$, and $\hat{y}_{str}^t \in \hat{Y}_{str}^t$. The difference between $\hat{y}_w^t$ and $\hat{y}_{str}^t$ can be measured as below:

$$d(x^t) = \frac{1}{K}\left\|\hat{y}_w^t - \hat{y}_{str}^t\right\|_2^2 \tag{9}$$

where the $\|\cdot\|_2$ denotes L2-distance under K classes. Here we make full use of the low confident probabilities of all classes, rather than the most confident probability [18] to teach the strong one. We claim that more information including low confidence information [15,49] could promote the model transferability. Although we can not access the target labels, this can be regarded as an implicit smoothness constraint. Then, we can define the *naïve constraint* loss:

$$\mathcal{L}_{nc} = \frac{1}{B}\sum_{x^t \in X^t} d(x^t). \tag{10}$$

If we impose equal importance on all samples, we obtain the average on the sample level. Then, we can introduce the naïve constraint loss to both domain-alignment and regularization-based methods as follows,

$$\begin{aligned}
&\min_{\psi,f} \ \mathcal{L}_s + \mathcal{L}_{dom} + \lambda\mathcal{L}_{nc} \\
&\min_{\psi,f} \ \mathcal{L}_s + \mathcal{L}_{reg} + \lambda\mathcal{L}_{nc},
\end{aligned} \tag{11}$$

where λ denotes the tradeoff parameter.

Confusion Conditioning. The naïve constraint imposes equal importance for different samples. However, samples are not equally important, enforcing the optimization on all samples may harm the training convergence. Some methods [9,14] noticed this issue and utilized the entropy of samples to reweight the loss function. We should pay more attention to reliable samples, and noticed that the class confusion of a sample can be a good measure of the uncertainty of it. Different from the technique in [9], we model the class confusion on instance level, and then propose the *Instance Class Confusion*.

Given a target sample $x^t \in X^t$ and the corresponding classification response $\hat{y}^t \in \hat{Y}^t$, the class confusion matrix of x^t is defined as below:

$$M = \hat{y}^t \times \hat{y}^{t^\top}, \tag{12}$$

where $M \in \mathcal{R}^{K \times K}$. It is possible to walk from one class to another for each sample when it is easy to be misclassified, often asymmetrically, and we investigated that this category-normalization technique is the key to MCC [9]. Following MCC, the class confusion between class i and j is normalized as follows:

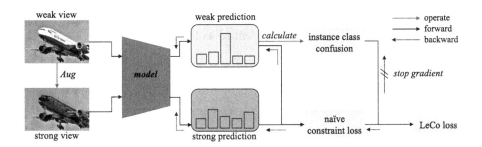

Fig. 2. Illustration of proposed LeCo framework.

$$\tilde{M}_{i,j} = \frac{M_{i,j}}{\sum_{j'=1}^{K} M_{i,j'}}. \tag{13}$$

Since normalized, it contains comprehensive information of confidence and cross-class, better reflecting the uncertainty than only considering the confidence such as entropy [20]. The *Instance Class Confusion* of a sample x^t is as below:

$$I(x^t) = \sum_{i=1}^{K} \sum_{j \neq i}^{K} \tilde{M}_{i,j}. \tag{14}$$

The lower instance class confusion indicates the lower uncertainty of this sample. We assume that discarding unlabeled samples with too low confidence will not lead to information loss but reduce the learning pressure of the model. So we condition the loss in Eq. (10) as below:

$$\mathcal{L}_{leco} = \frac{1}{B} \sum_{x^t \in X^t} \mathbb{1}(I(x^t) < \tau) d(x^t), \tag{15}$$

where $\mathbb{1}$ is the indicator function, and τ is the uncertainty threshold. We do not use the fixed threshold, because it can not properly reflect the changing uncertainty during training. We adopt an adaptive τ using the mean of the instance class confusion of mini-batch target samples. Finally, the proposed LeCo loss is pluggable to domain alignment and regularization based methods as follows:

$$\min_{\psi,f} \mathcal{L}_s + \mathcal{L}_{dom} + \lambda\mathcal{L}_{leco}$$
$$\min_{\psi,f} \mathcal{L}_s + \mathcal{L}_{reg} + \lambda\mathcal{L}_{leco}. \tag{16}$$

The illustration of proposed LeCo framework is shown clearly in Fig. 2.

4 Theoretical Guarantees

We present the theoretical analysis for the implicit smoothness constraint following the theory of [6]. Let $\mathcal{H}$ be the hypothesis class, given the source and target distribution S and T, and a ideal hypothesis $h^* = \underset{h \in \mathcal{H}}{argmin}\ \epsilon_S(h) + \epsilon_T(h)$. Source risk ϵ_S and target risk ϵ_T are defined as follows:

$$\epsilon_S(h) = \epsilon_S(h, y) = \mathbb{E}_{(x,y)\sim S}|h(x) - y|$$
$$\epsilon_T(h) = \epsilon_T(h, y) = \mathbb{E}_{(x,y)\sim T}|h(x) - y| \tag{17}$$

Given the two hypotheses h_1 and h_2, the disagreement under the data distribution D is defined as below:

$$\epsilon_D(h_1, h_2) = \mathbb{E}_{(x,y)\sim D}|h_1(x) - h_2(x)| \tag{18}$$

The target risk can be bounded following the theory of [6] as:

Theorem 1. For any hypothesis $h \in \mathcal{H}$, we have the target risk

$$\epsilon_T(h) \le \epsilon_S(h) + \epsilon_T(h^*) + \epsilon_S(h^*) + |\epsilon_T(h, h^*) - \epsilon_S(h, h^*)| \tag{19}$$

Generally, the hypothesis h uses the normal transforms (same as the weak augmentation in this paper), so $h(x) = h(w(x))$, $w(\cdot)$ is the weak augmentation. We define the different hypotheses h_1 and h_2 as below:

$$h_1 = h(w(x)), h_2 = h(s(x)) \tag{20}$$

where the $s(\cdot)$ is the strong augmentation in this paper.

In the Theorem 1, for a hypothesis h which is well trained in source domain S, the first item $\epsilon_S(h)$ is small enough. And the second and third items $\epsilon_T(h^*)$, $\epsilon_S(h^*)$ are small enough for the ideal hypothesis h^*. We bound the last item using the two hypothesis h_1 and h_2 as below:

$$|\epsilon_T(h, h^*) - \epsilon_S(h, h^*)| \le |\epsilon_T(h_1, h^*) - \epsilon_S(h_1, h^*)|$$
$$+ |\epsilon_T(h_2, h^*) - \epsilon_S(h_2, h^*)| \tag{21}$$

We using h_1 to approximate any hypothesis in $\mathcal{H}$, the proof of Eq. (21) is obvious. We jointly optimize the hypotheses h_1 and h_2 in our method. Hence, the domain discrepancy $|\epsilon_T(h, h^*) - \epsilon_S(h, h^*)|$ can be bounded using our optimization. We denote $\triangle(h_1, h_2)$ as $|\epsilon_T(h_1, h^*) - \epsilon_S(h_1, h^*)| + |\epsilon_T(h_2, h^*) - \epsilon_S(h_2, h^*)|$.

Because of the perturbation of strong augmentation, the risk of h_2 in target is close but larger than the h_1, and they share the source classifier, i.e., $|\epsilon_T(h_1, h^*) - \epsilon_S(h_1, h^*)| \leq |\epsilon_T(h_2, h^*) - \epsilon_S(h_2, h^*)|$. So we have the follow:

$$
\begin{aligned}
\triangle(h_1, h_2) &\leq 2 \; |\epsilon_T(h_2, h^*) - \epsilon_S(h_2, h^*)| \\
&\leq 2 \sup_{h, h' \in \mathcal{H}} |\epsilon_T(h, h') - \epsilon_S(h, h')| \\
&= d_{\mathcal{H}\triangle\mathcal{H}}(S, T)
\end{aligned}
\tag{22}
$$

The goal in UDA is to approximate the target risk $\epsilon_T(h)$, and then optimize it to a low value. The objective in our technique is to minimize $\triangle(h_1, h_2)$, which is more close to the supremum of $\mathcal{H}\triangle\mathcal{H}$ divergence, and this approximation does not undermine the UDA theory according to our experiments.

5   Experiment

5.1   Setup

Dataset. We apply our technique to various baselines and compare with many state-of-the-art methods on four public datasets, i.e., Office-31 [52], Office-Home [53], VisDA-C [4] and DomainNet [54]. Details about datasets can be found in supplementary material.

Implementation Details. Following the protocol for UDA in previous methods [9,10], we use the same backbone networks for fair comparisons. All baseline methods are reproduced in our codebase. All methods are trained with 10k iterations, and use same learning rate scheduler adopted in [10]. For DomainNet, we evaluated various methods following the settings in [55]. We fix the batch size as 36, and use the SGD optimizer. We set the same tradeoff as 1 for transfer loss both in domain-alignment and regularization-based methods. We choosed the best λ for LeCo loss by [56]. Each task was randomly repeated three times.

5.2   Results

We verify the effectiveness of applying our technique over various baselines, and compare with state-of-the-art methods on four public datasets. The results of Office-Home [53], VisDA-C [4], Office-31 [52], and DomainNet [54] are reported in Tables 1, 2, 3, and 4, respectively.

Office-Home. We evaluated various methods on the total of 12 tasks on Office-Home [53] shown in Table 1. We apply our LeCo to various methods including DANN [37], CDAN [14], BNM [10], and MCC [9]. For regularization-based

Table 1. Accuracy (%) on Office-Home for UDA using the ResNet-50 backbone.

Method	Ar→Cl	Ar→Pr	Ar→Rw	Cl→Ar	Cl→Pr	Cl→Rw	Pr→Ar	Pr→Cl	Pr→Rw	Rw→Ar	Rw→Cl	Rw→Pr	Avg
ResNet-50 [57]	34.9	50.0	58.0	37.4	41.9	46.2	38.5	31.2	60.4	53.9	41.2	59.9	46.1
DAN [22]	43.6	57.0	67.9	45.8	56.5	60.4	44.0	43.6	67.7	63.1	51.5	74.3	56.3
MCD [38]	48.9	68.3	74.6	61.3	67.6	68.8	57.0	47.1	75.1	69.1	52.2	79.6	64.1
EntMin [20]	51.0	71.9	77.1	61.2	69.1	70.1	59.3	48.7	77.0	70.4	53.0	81.0	65.8
AFN [11]	52.0	71.7	76.3	64.2	69.9	71.9	63.7	51.4	77.1	70.9	57.1	81.5	67.3
SRDC [58]	52.3	76.3	81.0	69.5	76.2	78.0	68.7	53.8	81.7	76.3	57.1	85.0	71.3
ATDOC [17]	58.3	78.8	82.3	69.4	78.2	78.2	67.1	56.0	82.7	72.0	58.2	85.5	72.2
FixBi [15]	58.1	77.3	80.4	67.7	79.5	78.1	65.8	57.9	81.7	76.4	62.9	86.7	72.7
Mirror [16]	57.6	77.6	81.6	71.9	77.8	78.7	72.0	56.3	82.5	77.9	61.3	85.3	73.4
DANN [37]	44.2	64.2	73.5	53.2	61.1	64.5	52.2	40.7	73.5	66.4	47.6	77.3	59.9
+LeCo	47.3↑	70.0↑	74.9↑	59.0↑	69.0↑	68.4↑	59.3↑	47.6↑	76.8↑	70.8↑	53.2↑	81.1↑	64.8↑
CDAN [14]	50.7	70.6	76.0	57.6	70.0	70.0	57.4	50.9	77.3	70.9	56.7	81.6	65.8
+LeCo	55.4↑	71.3↑	79.1↑	64.2↑	72.8↑	74.3↑	64.4↑	55.9↑	81.4↑	74.0↑	61.3↑	84.6↑	69.9↑
BNM [10]	57.3	74.1	80.6	66.2	76.1	76.8	65.8	51.9	81.1	73.0	59.3	83.4	70.5
+LeCo	59.3↑	74.8↑	80.9↑	66.8↑	77.0↑	76.7	67.0↑	53.8↑	81.1	74.2↑	60.6↑	83.8↑	71.3↑
MCC [9]	56.3	77.3	80.3	67.0	77.1	77.0	66.2	55.1	81.2	73.5	57.4	84.1	71.0
+LeCo	59.4↑	79.2↑	82.7↑	68.3↑	78.0↑	79.1↑	68.3↑	55.7↑	83.7↑	75.8↑	62.1↑	86.2↑	73.2↑

methods (BNM and MCC), our technique both improves the results, with average accuracy improvements of 0.8% and 2.2%, respectively. Compared with the SOTA Mirror [16], we help MCC to achieve the comparable average accuracy of 73.2% and achieves the best accuracy on 5 out of 12 tasks, bringing improvements to all tasks. Meanwhile, the proposed LeCo brings large margins to domain alignment methods. Based on methods DANN and CDAN, our method surprisingly improves the accuracies of all tasks, with the large average accuracy improvements of 4.9% and 4.1%, respectively. In general, the improvements to all baselines are shown in almost all tasks, demonstrating the robustness of LeCo.

Table 2. Accuracy (%) on VisDA-C for UDA using the ResNet-101 backbone.

Method	plane	bcycl	bus	car	horse	knife	mcycl	person	plant	sktbrd	train	truck	Mean
ResNet-101 [57]	67.7	27.4	50.0	61.7	69.5	13.7	85.9	11.5	64.4	34.4	84.2	19.2	49.1
DAN [22]	87.1	63.0	76.5	42.0	90.3	42.9	85.9	53.1	49.7	36.3	85.8	20.7	61.1
MCD [38]	87.0	60.9	83.7	64.0	88.9	79.6	84.7	76.9	88.6	40.3	83.0	25.8	71.9
AFN [11]	93.6	61.3	84.1	70.6	94.1	79.0	91.8	79.6	89.9	55.6	89.0	24.4	76.1
ATDOC [17]	93.7	83.0	76.9	58.7	89.7	95.1	84.4	71.4	89.4	80.0	86.7	55.1	80.3
BCDM [59]	95.1	87.6	81.2	73.2	92.7	95.4	86.9	82.5	95.1	84.8	88.1	39.5	83.4
FixBi [15]	96.1	87.8	90.5	90.3	96.8	95.3	92.8	88.7	87.2	94.2	90.9	25.7	87.2
CAN [60]	97.0	87.2	82.5	74.3	97.8	96.2	90.8	80.7	96.6	96.3	87.5	59.9	87.2
CAN+Mirror [16]	97.2	88.2	84.9	76.0	97.2	95.8	89.2	86.4	96.1	96.6	85.9	61.2	87.9
DANN [37]	90.4	36.1	84.5	40.7	55.9	63.6	80.9	56.5	78.9	58.9	70.3	21.6	61.5
+LeCo	93.4↑	30.0	87.5↑	55.2↑	89.4↑	93.0↑	88.3↑	41.3	80.1↑	38.5	68.7	19.1	65.4↑
CDAN [14]	91.8	73.8	83.6	57.6	82.2	76.9	88.4	76.9	88.9	83.0	76.1	36.1	76.3
+LeCo	95.0↑	72.1	88.8↑	78.6↑	92.0↑	93.4↑	91.1↑	77.1↑	91.5↑	87.4↑	78.6↑	27.7	81.1↑
BNM [10]	94.8	84.1	74.3	52.7	89.2	93.0	81.3	82.5	88.7	65.9	81.9	49.0	78.1
+LeCo	95.8↑	91.0↑	75.5↑	75.9↑	96.6↑	97.3↑	80.4	80.0	95.3↑	87.0↑	80.3	51.0↑	83.8↑
MCC [9]	93.7	82.2	75.3	62.3	91.6	87.7	84.8	79.3	88.1	87.5	81.8	54.4	80.7
+LeCo	96.4↑	86.4↑	83.2↑	90.6↑	96.2↑	96.9↑	90.9↑	80.3↑	95.5↑	92.0↑	85.8↑	40.8	86.3↑

VisDA-C. We report classification accuracy in the synthetic-to-real transfer task as shown in Table 2. We apply our LeCo to various methods including DANN [37], CDAN [14], BNM [10], and MCC [9]. It is noteworthy that the proposed LeCo achieved surprising improvements on these methods. We claim that due to the smaller number of categories, the intra-class variance can be effectively reduced by imposing our method. We can see that LeCo brings large improvements to these baselines in almost all tasks. Using our method, MCC can achieve a mean accuracy of 86.3%. It is worth noting that we get the highest accuracy of 90.6% on *car* class against the 90.3% of FixBi. However, the domain-alignment methods (FixBi, CAN and Mirror) beat our best result of 86.3%. Although our method achieved 4.5% improvement over MCC on average, it could lead to some class cluster overlap, resulting in a decrease in the accuracy of some classes. The reason is that our method does not explicitly reduce the inter-class variances, and results will be better if we cooperate with more powerful methods. Overall, our method can reasonably promote these baselines to reduce the intra-class variance, thus bringing considerable improvements.

Office-31. We compare various methods in this classic dataset. We apply our LeCo to methods DANN [37], BNM [10], CDAN [14], and MCC [9]. As shown in Table 3, each method could obtain improvements by imposing our method. These methods do not directly consider the optimization for intra-class variance, and left room for improvements. Our method aims to lower the intra-class variance by using implicit smoothness constraint. The results validate the effectiveness of our method. However, Mirror and FixBi got 91.7% and 91.4% accuracies, respectively, and both surpassed our best result of 90.0%. The reason may be that the images are fewer and the diversity of this dataset is relatively low, so it is hard to learn the instance discriminability, and the intra-class variances are lower naturally. We only achieve marginal improvements in this dataset.

DomainNet. Following the settings in [55], we compare various methods for 12 tasks among Clp, Pnt, Rel, and Skt domains on original DomainNet. The results are shown in Table 4. Our method improves the average accuracy of MCC [9] by 2.9%. Specifically, our method brings improvements to CDAN on all tasks. Our method also improves MCC on 10 of 12 tasks. And we achieve the best average accuracy of 52.6% on this public benchmark.

According to these extensive experiments, we believe that LeCo could exploit the underlying property of UDA

Table 3. Accuracy (%) on Office-31 for UDA using the ResNet-50 backbone.

Method	A→D	A → W	D→A	D→W	W→A	W→D	Avg
ResNet-50 [57]	78.3	70.4	57.3	93.4	61.5	98.1	76.5
DAN [22]	78.6	80.5	63.6	97.1	62.8	99.6	80.4
AFN [11]	87.7	88.8	69.8	98.4	69.7	99.8	85.7
BCDM [59]	93.8	95.4	73.1	98.6	73.0	100.0	89.0
ATDOC [17]	94.4	94.3	75.6	98.9	75.2	99.6	89.7
FixBi [15]	95.0	96.1	78.7	99.3	79.4	100.0	91.4
Mirror [16]	96.2	98.5	77.0	99.3	78.9	100.0	91.7
DANN [37]	85.7	90.2	68.3	97.6	66.4	99.2	84.6
+LeCo	86.8↑	90.8↑	70.9↑	98.0↑	73.2↑	100.0↑	86.6↑
BNM [10]	90.3	91.4	71.4	97.9	71.7	100.0	87.1
+LeCo	92.8↑	92.8↑	73.7↑	98.6↑	73.2↑	100.0	88.5↑
CDAN [14]	92.9	93.1	71.0	98.6	69.3	100.0	87.5
+LeCo	91.6	91.1	75.6↑	98.4	74.9↑	100.0	88.6↑
MCC [9]	95.6	96.1	73.8↑	98.1	73.6	100.0	89.5
+LeCo	95.4	96.2↑	73.8↑	98.5↑	75.9↑	100.0	90.0↑

about the intra-class variance, and then lead to promising performance from this perspective. Above all, our method is pluggable to various methods, and it brings remarkable improvements to these methods on different public datasets. Based on some widely-used baselines, we achieve comparable results against SOTA methods on four public datasets. These observations indicate that our technique is very effective for UDA setting.

Table 4. Accuracy (%) on DomainNet for UDA using the ResNet-101 backbone.

Method	Clp→Pnt	Clp→Rel	Clp→Skt	Pnt→Clp	Pnt→Rel	Pnt→Skt	Rel→Clp	Rel→Pnt	Rel→Skt	Skt→Clp	Skt→Pnt	Skt→Rel	Avg
ResNet-101 [57]	32.7	50.6	39.4	41.1	56.8	35.0	48.6	48.8	36.1	49.0	34.8	46.1	43.3
DANN [37]	37.9	54.3	44.4	41.7	55.6	36.8	50.7	50.8	40.1	55.0	45.0	54.5	47.2
BCDM [59]	38.5	53.2	43.9	42.5	54.5	38.5	51.9	51.2	40.6	53.7	46.0	53.4	47.3
MCD [38]	37.5	52.9	44.0	44.6	54.5	41.6	52.0	51.5	39.7	55.5	44.6	52.0	47.5
ADDA [61]	38.4	54.1	44.1	43.5	56.7	39.2	52.8	51.3	40.9	55.0	45.4	54.5	48.0
DAN [22]	38.8	55.2	43.9	45.9	59.0	40.8	50.8	49.8	38.9	56.1	45.9	55.5	48.4
JAN [33]	40.5	56.7	45.1	47.2	59.9	43.0	54.2	52.6	41.9	56.6	46.2	55.5	50.0
MDD [12]	42.9	59.5	47.5	48.6	59.4	42.6	58.3	53.7	46.2	58.7	46.5	57.7	51.8
CDAN [14]	39.9	55.6	45.9	44.8	57.4	40.7	56.3	52.5	44.2	55.1	43.1	53.2	49.1
+LeCo	40.0↑	56.5↑	46.6↑	45.3↑	58.2↑	41.6↑	56.9↑	53.1↑	46.0↑	55.5↑	44.3↑	53.3↑	49.8↑
MCC [9]	40.1	56.5	44.9	46.9	57.7	41.4	56.0	53.7	40.6	58.2	45.1	55.9	49.7
+LeCo	44.1↑	55.3	48.5↑	49.4↑	57.5	45.5↑	58.8↑	55.4↑	46.8↑	61.3↑	51.1↑	57.7↑	52.6↑

5.3 Ablation Study

Training Strategy. In the training process, the warm-up of supervised source training is important. For example, we set warm-up iteration to 3k on VisDA-C [4]. We show the classification accuracy of the synthetic-to-real task on VisDA-C during the training in Fig. 3 (a). The accuracy at 0% denotes the accuracy of the pre-trained ResNet-101 model, which has been finetuned with source labeled data. We compare the results of the MCC baseline and MCC+LeCo. In fact, during the warm-up phase, the differences only depend on the randomness of training. We can see that using our LeCo, the classification accuracy of the model is promoted stably. With our method, MCC outperforms the original baseline by a large margin.

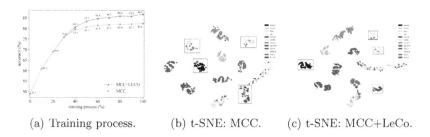

(a) Training process.   (b) t-SNE: MCC.   (c) t-SNE: MCC+LeCo.

Fig. 3. (a): Training process. The start point denotes that the pre-trained ResNet-101 which has been source-only finetuned on VisDA-C, a random experiment. (b) and (c) correspond to the t-SNE embedding visualization of MCC and MCC+LeCo on VisDA-C.

Feature Visualization. To better illustrate that LeCo can reduce the intra-class variance of target features, we visualize the features learned by MCC and

MCC+LeCo on VisDA-C. We employ the t-SNE method [62] for feature visualization. We randomly select 2000 samples across 12 categories from the real-world domain in VisDA-C, and extract the corresponding learned features. As shown in Fig. 3 (b), (c), compared with the MCC, our method better separate the target samples in the feature space. These class centers become more compact by using our method, especially the centers marked by black rectangles. The results indicate small intra-class variances by using our method.

Effects of the Components. We conduct the ablation study on the two components of LeCo. *NC* denotes the Naïve smoothness Constraint, and *Cond* denotes the naïve smoothness constraint conditioned by instance class confusion. We report the results on VisDA-C and Office-Home shown in Table 5. We analyze the effects of components of LeCo for CDAN [14] and MCC [9], and we observe stable improvements over the two datasets. Each component shows a positive effect, and proposed technique is verified to be very effective on various settings. In Table 5b, We also compare the common technique entropy (Ent) with the instance class confusion (ICC) as the condition way. The results show the large improvements of the latter, and prove that it is more suitable for our technique.

Table 5. Detailed ablations. (a) analyses the effectiveness of the components. (b) compares two condition ways. (c) analyses parameter sensitivity, and (d) evaluates different constraint types.

(a)								(b)		(c)				(d)			
VisDA-C				Office-Home				VisDA-C		VisDA-C		Office-Home		VisDA-C		Office-Home	
CDAN	NC	Cond	acc	CDAN	NC	Cond	acc	MCC	acc	method	acc	method	acc	λ	acc	λ	acc
✓			76.3	✓			65.8	+LeCo (Ent)	85.5	MCC	80.7	MCC	71.1	1	85.8	1	73.1
✓	✓		79.6	✓	✓		68.9	+LeCo (ICC)	**86.3**	+cos.	84.1	+cos.	71.2	2	85.6	2	**73.2**
✓	✓	✓	81.1	✓	✓	✓	69.9	Office-Home		+sup.	84.0	+sup.	69.0	3	**86.3**	3	72.8
MCC	NC	Cond	acc	MCC	NC	Cond	acc	MCC	acc	+L1	85.0	+L1	72.4	4	85.6	4	72.7
✓			80.7	✓			71.1	+LeCo (Ent)	72.5	+L2	**85.3**	+L2	**72.7**	5	85.1	5	71.8
✓	✓		85.3	✓	✓		72.7	+LeCo (ICC)	**73.2**								
✓	✓	✓	**86.3**	✓	✓	✓	**73.2**										

Choice of Constraint. The default choice of LeCo is using the L2-distance between the weak and strong predictions. We claimed that using the L2-distance considers the all class probabilities, and is better to transfer knowledge. We use other choices to construct the smoothness constraint, including L1-distance (L1), cosine distance (cos.), and weak supervising strong (sup.) [18]. The results are shown in Table 5c. For fair comparisons, we select the proper λ to tradeoff the implicit smoothness constraint loss. As we can see, cosine distance and weak supervising show less improvement, and even worse on Office-Home. Selected L2-distance show stable and considerable performance, so we think the L2-distance is a good choice for implicit smoothness constraint.

Parameter Sensitivity. We set the different values of the tradeoff for LeCo, i.e. the value of λ, and it is often sensitive in UDA scenario. In order to test the robustness, we simply change the values of $\lambda \in [1, 5]$ for MCC both on Office-Home and VisDA-C. The results are shown in Table 5d. On VisDA-C, the mean accuracy of the synthetic-to-real task is more sensitive to the tradeoff. On Office-Home, we find the accuracy sensitivity with regard to λ is relatively small. In a word, the proper trade-off of LeCo could bring large improvements to baselines.

6   Conclusion

In this paper, we investigated the previous methods in Unsupervised Domain Adaptation (UDA) from a new perspective: *smoothness*. We dived into the domain-alignment and regularization-based methods. These methods aim to increase the distance between cluster centers, i.e., enlarge inter-class variance, but also cause cluster overlapping and error accumulation. We propose a simple yet effective technique named LeCo (impLicit smoothness Constraint), to implicitly increase the smoothness of baseline models, i.e., lower intra-class variance. The keys are consistency on all class probabilities over weak and strong augmentations and a novel uncertainty measure named Instance Class Confusion to condition the consistency. LeCo guarantees the lower sensitivity to perturbations of samples. Extensive experiments demonstrate that LeCo is applicable to various domain-alignment and regularization-based baseline approaches.

Acknowledgement. The paper is supported in part by the National Key Research and Development Project (Grant No.2020AAA0106600), in part by National Natural Science Foundation of China: 62022083.

References

1. He, K., Fan, H., Wu, Y., Xie, S., Girshick, R.: Momentum contrast for unsupervised visual representation learning. In: Proceedings of the IEEE/CVF Conference on Computer Vision and Pattern Recognition, pp. 9729–9738 (2020)
2. Caron, M., et al.: Emerging properties in self-supervised vision transformers. In: Proceedings of the IEEE/CVF International Conference on Computer Vision, pp. 9650–9660 (2021)
3. He, K., Chen, X., Xie, S., Li, Y., Dollár, P., Girshick, R.: Masked autoencoders are scalable vision learners. arXiv preprint arXiv:2111.06377 (2021)
4. Peng, X., Usman, B., Kaushik, N., Hoffman, J., Wang, D., Saenko, K.: Visda: the visual domain adaptation challenge. arXiv preprint arXiv:1710.06924 (2017)
5. Ben-David, S., Blitzer, J., Crammer, K., Pereira, F.: Analysis of representations for domain adaptation. In: Advances in Neural Information Processing Systems, vol. 19 (2006)
6. Ben-David, S., Blitzer, J., Crammer, K., Kulesza, A., Pereira, F., Vaughan, J.W.: A theory of learning from different domains. Mach. Learn. **79**, 151–175 (2010)
7. Zhao, S., et al.: A review of single-source deep unsupervised visual domain adaptation. IEEE Trans. Neural Netw. Learn. Syst. (2020)
8. Shimodaira, H.: Improving predictive inference under covariate shift by weighting the log-likelihood function. J. Stat. Plann. Inference **90**, 227–244 (2000)

9. Jin, Y., Wang, X., Long, M., Wang, J.: Minimum class confusion for versatile domain adaptation. In: Vedaldi, A., Bischof, H., Brox, T., Frahm, J.-M. (eds.) ECCV 2020. LNCS, vol. 12366, pp. 464–480. Springer, Cham (2020). https://doi.org/10.1007/978-3-030-58589-1_28

10. Cui, S., Wang, S., Zhuo, J., Li, L., Huang, Q., Tian, Q.: Towards discriminability and diversity: batch nuclear-norm maximization under label insufficient situations. In: Proceedings of the IEEE/CVF Conference on Computer Vision and Pattern Recognition, pp. 3941–3950 (2020)

11. Xu, R., Li, G., Yang, J., Lin, L.: Larger norm more transferable: an adaptive feature norm approach for unsupervised domain adaptation. In: Proceedings of the IEEE/CVF International Conference on Computer Vision, pp. 1426–1435 (2019)

12. Zhang, Y., Liu, T., Long, M., Jordan, M.: Bridging theory and algorithm for domain adaptation. In: International Conference on Machine Learning, pp. 7404–7413 (2019)

13. French, G., Mackiewicz, M., Fisher, M.H.: Self-ensembling for visual domain adaptation. In: 6th International Conference on Learning Representations, ICLR 2018, Vancouver, BC, Canada, 30 April–3 May 2018, Conference Track Proceedings, OpenReview.net (2018)

14. Long, M., Cao, Z., Wang, J., Jordan, M.I.: Conditional adversarial domain adaptation. In: Advances in Neural Information Processing Systems: Annual Conference on Neural Information Processing Systems 2018, NeurIPS 2018, 3–8 December 2018, Montréal, Canada, vol. 31, pp. 1647–1657 (2018)

15. Na, J., Jung, H., Chang, H.J., Hwang, W.: Fixbi: bridging domain spaces for unsupervised domain adaptation. In: Proceedings of the IEEE/CVF Conference on Computer Vision and Pattern Recognition, pp. 1094–1103 (2021)

16. Zhao, Y., Cai, L., et al.: Reducing the covariate shift by mirror samples in cross domain alignment. In: Advances in Neural Information Processing Systems, vol. 34 (2021)

17. Liang, J., Hu, D., Feng, J.: Domain adaptation with auxiliary target domain-oriented classifier. In: Proceedings of the IEEE/CVF Conference on Computer Vision and Pattern Recognition, pp. 16632–16642 (2021)

18. Sohn, K., et al.: Fixmatch: simplifying semi-supervised learning with consistency and confidence. In: Advances in Neural Information Processing Systems: Annual Conference on Neural Information Processing Systems 2020, NeurIPS 2020, 6–12 December 2020, virtual, vol. 33 (2020)

19. Berthelot, D., Carlini, N., Goodfellow, I.J., Papernot, N., Oliver, A., Raffel, C.: Mixmatch: a holistic approach to semi-supervised learning. In: Advances in Neural Information Processing Systems: Annual Conference on Neural Information Processing Systems 2019, NeurIPS 2019, 8–14 December 2019, Vancouver, BC, Canada, vol. 32, pp. 5050–5060 (2019)

20. Grandvalet, Y., Bengio, Y., et al.: Semi-supervised learning by entropy minimization. CAP **367**, 281–296 (2005)

21. Tzeng, E., Hoffman, J., Zhang, N., Saenko, K., Darrell, T.: Deep domain confusion: maximizing for domain invariance. arXiv preprint arXiv:1412.3474 (2014)

22. Long, M., Cao, Y., Wang, J., Jordan, M.: Learning transferable features with deep adaptation networks. In: International Conference on Machine Learning, pp. 97–105 (2015)

23. Ma, N., et al.: Context-guided entropy minimization for semi-supervised domain adaptation. Neural Netw. **154**, 270–282 (2022)

24. Yao, T., Pan, Y., Ngo, C.W., Li, H., Mei, T.: Semi-supervised domain adaptation with subspace learning for visual recognition. In: Proceedings of the IEEE Conference on Computer Vision and Pattern Recognition, pp. 2142–2150 (2015)
25. Saito, K., Kim, D., Sclaroff, S., Darrell, T., Saenko, K.: Semi-supervised domain adaptation via minimax entropy. In: Proceedings of the IEEE/CVF International Conference on Computer Vision, pp. 8050–8058 (2019)
26. Kim, T., Kim, C.: Attract, perturb, and explore: learning a feature alignment network for semi-supervised domain adaptation. In: Vedaldi, A., Bischof, H., Brox, T., Frahm, J.-M. (eds.) ECCV 2020. LNCS, vol. 12359, pp. 591–607. Springer, Cham (2020). https://doi.org/10.1007/978-3-030-58568-6_35
27. Li, R., Jiao, Q., Cao, W., Wong, H.S., Wu, S.: Model adaptation: unsupervised domain adaptation without source data. In: Proceedings of the IEEE/CVF Conference on Computer Vision and Pattern Recognition, pp. 9641–9650 (2020)
28. Liang, J., Hu, D., Feng, J.: Do we really need to access the source data? Source hypothesis transfer for unsupervised domain adaptation. In: International Conference on Machine Learning, pp. 6028–6039 (2020)
29. Wang, X., Zhuo, J., Cui, S., Wang, S.: Learning invariant representation with consistency and diversity for semi-supervised source hypothesis transfer. arXiv preprint arXiv:2107.03008 (2021)
30. Shu, Y., Cao, Z., Long, M., Wang, J.: Transferable curriculum for weakly-supervised domain adaptation. In: Proceedings of the AAAI Conference on Artificial Intelligence, vol. 33, pp. 4951–4958 (2019)
31. Zhuo, J., Wang, S., Huang, Q.: Uncertainty modeling for robust domain adaptation under noisy environments. IEEE Trans. Multimedia (2022)
32. Zhuo, J., Wang, S., Zhang, W., Huang, Q.: Deep unsupervised convolutional domain adaptation. In: Proceedings of the 25th ACM International Conference on Multimedia, pp. 261–269. ACM (2017)
33. Long, M., Zhu, H., Wang, J., Jordan, M.I.: Deep transfer learning with joint adaptation networks. In: International Conference on Machine Learning, pp. 2208–2217 (2017)
34. Zellinger, W., Grubinger, T., Lughofer, E., Natschläger, T., Saminger-Platz, S.: Central moment discrepancy (CMD) for domain-invariant representation learning. In: 5th International Conference on Learning Representations, ICLR 2017, Toulon, France, Conference Track Proceedings, 24–26 April 2017. OpenReview.net (2017)
35. Borgwardt, K.M., Gretton, A., Rasch, M.J., Kriegel, H.P., Schölkopf, B., Smola, A.J.: Integrating structured biological data by kernel maximum mean discrepancy. Bioinformatics 22, e49–e57 (2006)
36. Goodfellow, I., et al.: Generative adversarial nets. In: Advances in Neural Information Processing Systems, vol. 27 (2014)
37. Ganin, Y., Lempitsky, V.: Unsupervised domain adaptation by backpropagation. In: International Conference on Machine Learning, pp. 1180–1189 (2015)
38. Saito, K., Watanabe, K., Ushiku, Y., Harada, T.: Maximum classifier discrepancy for unsupervised domain adaptation. In: Proceedings of the IEEE Conference on Computer Vision and Pattern Recognition, pp. 3723–3732 (2018)
39. Li, S., Lv, F., Xie, B., Liu, C.H., Liang, J., Qin, C.: Bi-classifier determinacy maximization for unsupervised domain adaptation. In: AAAI, vol. 2, p. 5 (2021)
40. Cui, S., Wang, S., Zhuo, J., Li, L., Huang, Q., Tian, Q.: Fast batch nuclear-norm maximization and minimization for robust domain adaptation. arXiv preprint arXiv:2107.06154 (2021)

41. Zhuo, J., Wang, S., Cui, S., Huang, Q.: Unsupervised open domain recognition by semantic discrepancy minimization. In: Proceedings of the IEEE/CVF Conference on Computer Vision and Pattern Recognition, pp. 750–759 (2019)
42. Li, S., Xie, B., Lin, Q., Liu, C.H., Huang, G., Wang, G.: Generalized domain conditioned adaptation network. IEEE Trans. Pattern Anal. Mach. Intell. (2021)
43. Li, S., Xie, M., Gong, K., Liu, C.H., Wang, Y., Li, W.: Transferable semantic augmentation for domain adaptation. In: Proceedings of the IEEE/CVF Conference on Computer Vision and Pattern Recognition, pp. 11516–11525 (2021)
44. Tarvainen, A., Valpola, H.: Mean teachers are better role models: weight-averaged consistency targets improve semi-supervised deep learning results. In: Advances in Neural Information Processing Systems, vol. 30 (2017)
45. Verma, V., Kawaguchi, K., Lamb, A., Kannala, J., Bengio, Y., Lopez-Paz, D.: Interpolation consistency training for semi-supervised learning. arXiv preprint arXiv:1903.03825 (2019)
46. Chen, Y., Zhu, X., Gong, S.: Semi-supervised deep learning with memory. In: Ferrari, V., Hebert, M., Sminchisescu, C., Weiss, Y. (eds.) ECCV 2018. LNCS, vol. 11205, pp. 275–291. Springer, Cham (2018). https://doi.org/10.1007/978-3-030-01246-5_17
47. Laine, S., Aila, T.: Temporal ensembling for semi-supervised learning. In: 5th International Conference on Learning Representations, ICLR 2017, Toulon, France, 24–26 April 2017, Conference Track Proceedings. OpenReview.net (2017)
48. Athiwaratkun, B., Finzi, M., Izmailov, P., Wilson, A.G.: There are many consistent explanations of unlabeled data: why you should average. In: 7th International Conference on Learning Representations, ICLR 2019, New Orleans, LA, USA, 6–9 May 2019. OpenReview.net (2019)
49. Zhang, Y., Li, J., Wang, Z.: Low-confidence samples matter for domain adaptation. arXiv preprint arXiv:2202.02802 (2022)
50. Zheng, Z., Yang, Y.: Unsupervised scene adaptation with memory regularization in vivo. In: Proceedings of the Twenty-Ninth International Conference on International Joint Conferences on Artificial Intelligence, pp. 1076–1082 (2021)
51. Cubuk, E.D., Zoph, B., Shlens, J., Le, Q.V.: Randaugment: practical automated data augmentation with a reduced search space. In: Proceedings of the IEEE/CVF Conference on Computer Vision and Pattern Recognition Workshops, pp. 702–703 (2020)
52. Saenko, K., Kulis, B., Fritz, M., Darrell, T.: Adapting visual category models to new domains. In: Daniilidis, K., Maragos, P., Paragios, N. (eds.) ECCV 2010. LNCS, vol. 6314, pp. 213–226. Springer, Heidelberg (2010). https://doi.org/10.1007/978-3-642-15561-1_16
53. Venkateswara, H., Eusebio, J., Chakraborty, S., Panchanathan, S.: Deep hashing network for unsupervised domain adaptation. In: Proceedings of the IEEE Conference on Computer Vision and Pattern Recognition, pp. 5018–5027 (2017)
54. Peng, X., Bai, Q., Xia, X., Huang, Z., Saenko, K., Wang, B.: Moment matching for multi-source domain adaptation. In: Proceedings of the IEEE/CVF International Conference on Computer Vision, pp. 1406–1415 (2019)
55. Jiang, J., Chen, B., Fu, B., Long, M.: Transfer-learning-library (2020). https://github.com/thuml/Transfer-Learning-Library
56. You, K., Wang, X., Long, M., Jordan, M.: Towards accurate model selection in deep unsupervised domain adaptation. In: International Conference on Machine Learning, pp. 7124–7133. PMLR (2019)

57. He, K., Zhang, X., Ren, S., Sun, J.: Deep residual learning for image recognition. In: Proceedings of the IEEE Conference on Computer Vision and Pattern Recognition, pp. 770–778 (2016)

58. Tang, H., Chen, K., Jia, K.: Unsupervised domain adaptation via structurally regularized deep clustering. In: Proceedings of the IEEE/CVF Conference on Computer Vision and Pattern Recognition, pp. 8725–8735 (2020)

59. Li, S., Lv, F., Xie, B., Liu, C.H., Liang, J., Qin, C.: Bi-classifier determinacy maximization for unsupervised domain adaptation. In: Thirty-Fifth AAAI Conference on Artificial Intelligence, AAAI 2021, Thirty-Third Conference on Innovative Applications of Artificial Intelligence, IAAI 2021, The Eleventh Symposium on Educational Advances in Artificial Intelligence, EAAI 2021, Virtual Event, 2–9 February 2021, pp. 8455–8464. AAAI Press (2021)

60. Kang, G., Jiang, L., Yang, Y., Hauptmann, A.G.: Contrastive adaptation network for unsupervised domain adaptation. In: Proceedings of the IEEE/CVF Conference on Computer Vision and Pattern Recognition, pp. 4893–4902 (2019)

61. Tzeng, E., Hoffman, J., Saenko, K., Darrell, T.: Adversarial discriminative domain adaptation. In: Proceedings of the IEEE Conference on Computer Vision and Pattern Recognition, pp. 7167–7176 (2017)

62. Van der Maaten, L., Hinton, G.: Visualizing data using t-SNE. J. Mach. Learn. Res. **9** (2008)

Staged Adaptive Blind Watermarking Scheme

Baowei Wang$^{(\boxtimes)}$ and Yufeng Wu

Nanjing University of Information Science and Technology, Nanjing 210044, China
wbw.first@163.com

Abstract. In traditional digital image watermarking methods, the stren-gth factor is calculated from the content of the carrier image, which can find a balance between the robustness and imperceptibility of encoded images. However, traditional methods do not consider the feature of the message and it is also unrealistic to calculate the strength factor of each image separately when faced with a huge number of images. In recent years, digital image watermarking methods based on deep learning have also introduced the strength factor. They assign the strength factor of each image to a fixed value to better adjust the robustness and imperceptibility of the image. We hope that the network can choose the most appropriate strength factor for each image to achieve a better balance. Therefore, we propose a staged adaptive blind watermarking scheme. We designed a new component - the adaptor, and used two stages of training by training different components in different stages, and improved the robustness and imperceptibility of watermarked images. By comparing the experimental results, our algorithmic scheme shows better results compared to current advanced algorithms.

Keywords: Strength factor · Adaptor · Staged training

1 Introduction

Traditional blind watermarking methods of digital watermarking is divided into two embedding methods: Spatial domain [1–3] and Frequency domain [4–7]. [1] was the first to embed digital image watermarking in the spatial domain. They proposed the basic concept of digital watermarking and encoded the message in the least significant bit (LSB) of the image pixel to realize the embedding of the message. This method is well hidden but the robustness is poor and the message is easy to be eliminated or detected by statistical measures. [4] chose to embed the message in the frequency domain, transform the carrier image into the frequency domain through DCT and modify the frequency domain components, so that the encoded image has higher robustness and confidentiality. Later studies found that embedding messages in DFT domain [5,8], DCT domain [6,9,10], DWT domain [7,11,12] and SVD domain [13,14] works better. [9,15,16] achieve a balance between the imperceptibility and robustness of image watermarking by controlling the strength factor of the watermark. The experimental results under different strength factors are calculated from different images. Finally, a suitable strength factor S is manually selected. These methods have poor applicability and cannot be applied to large-scale image strength factor calculations. Besides, analyzing the carrier image will ignore the unique characteristics of the message.

In recent years, deep learning has become an indispensable key technology in the field of image research. Among them, DNN-based digital watermarking schemes have made good progress [17–19]. Deep learning-based image watermarking methods can be roughly divided into two types of embedding methods. A mainstream method is end-to-end watermarking, which integrates the entire process into an overall network, that is, the process of embedding and extracting watermarks is completely handed over to DNN. The end-to-end solution can make all components closely related and interlocked, improving the embedding and extraction efficiency of the message. [17] proposed a relatively complete end-to-end robust blind watermarking classical network architecture for the first time. Given a masked image and a binary message, the encoder produces a visually indistinguishable encoded image that contains the message, which can be recovered by a decoder with a high degree of accuracy. Later model architectures related to deep learning watermark hiding are based on this and continue to improve it. The improved framework of [18] introduced the concept of the strength factor, multiplied the watermark W by the strength factor S to obtain the watermark to be embedded, and then directly added the watermark and the carrier image I_c to obtain the final encoded image I_{en}. The process is shown in Eq. (1):

$$I_{en} = S \times W + Ic \tag{1}$$

In view of the poor practicability of the current traditional digital watermarking strength factors and the inability to carry out the mass evaluation, the digital image watermarking algorithm based on deep learning remains in the stage of manual selection of strength factors Our proposed staged adaptive blind watermarking scheme can effectively solve the problems. We designed an end-to-end phased network framework and added a new component to the classic HiDDeN network architecture, named the adaptor. The adaptor exists independently of the network's main body, which can be understood as an auxiliary network. The function of the adaptor is to extract the important features of the carrier image and the message. At the same time, the staged training can fine-tune the decoder, so that we can improve the performance of different components in different stages of training.

2   Related Work

2.1   Deep Learning-Based Digital Image Watermarking

The rise of deep learning began in 2012. In order to prove the potential of deep learning, Hinton's research group participated in the ImageNet image recognition competition for the first time. It won the championship through the built CNN network AlexNet, and crushed the second place (SVM) classification performance. It is precise because of this competition that CNN has attracted the attention of many researchers. Many scholars applied deep learning to digital image watermarking until [20] first applied deep learning to digital image watermarking and proposed a new deep learning-based auto-encoder convolutional neural network (CNN) for embedding and extracting non-blind watermarking, and is far superior to traditional transform domain watermarking methods in imperceptibility and robustness. Subsequently, in 2018, [17] first proposed an end-to-end neural network-based blind watermark embedding scheme. The network architecture of HiDDeN is composed of four components: encoder, noise layer, discriminator, and decoder. The encoder can embed the message, the noise layer is used to improve the anti-attack ability of the watermark, and the discriminator is used to distinguish whether the input image has a watermark or not. The decoder is responsible for extracting the message in the encoded image. [18] proposed an adaptive diffusion watermarking framework composed of two residually connected fully convolutional neural networks, which took the image through DCT transformation as preprocessing and proposed a differentiable approximation of the JPEG attack. With the help of the confrontation network, the robustness of the watermark to JPEG attack is greatly improved. Not only that, but they also proposed for the first time to use a strength factor to control the strength of watermarking in the image. [21] hope to use a deep learning model to realize the application of digital image watermarking in real scenes. They simulated the distortion caused by real printing or display of images in the real world and subsequent image capture through an image perturbation module. The algorithm makes encoded images robust to image perturbations distorted by real printing and photography. [22] proposed a two-stage separable watermarking structure, which trains different components in the network in different stages, and finally achieves the optimal case of each component, which makes the watermarked image robust and imperceptible in terms of All achieved good results. [23] explored the research on the watermark based on the unknown distortion, and adopted the antagonistic training mode of the unknown distortion and the redundant channel coding mode to improve the robustness of the watermark against the unknown distortion. [19] proposed a new mini-batch method for simulated and real JPEG compression, which improved the noise layer of the attack simulation, after each batch training, from simulated JPEG, real JPEG, and no JPEG as one of the noise layers is randomly selected as the noise layer of the next mini-batch. The experimental results show that the end-to-end algorithm is very robust to JPEG and other attacks. According to the characteristics of [19] and [22]. This paper designs a staged and separable blind watermarking method based on an adaptive strength factor auxiliary network that can significantly improve the imperceptibility of encoded images.

2.2   Strength Factor

The strength factor S first emerged in traditional digital watermarking. [15] made a specific description of the estimation of the watermarking strength of the watermark in the article. Calculating the optimal S based on the content of the cover image is aimed to achieve a balance between robustness and imperceptibility. In many subsequent traditional watermarking methods, the evaluation method of the S has also been improved, but the robustness or imperceptibility will be reduced. At present, the digital watermarking methods based on deep learning have not conducted in-depth research on S [18,19]. S is regarded as a tool for experiments and the artificially assigned fixed value is used to control the watermarking strength of the watermark to change the robustness and imperceptibility.

2.3   Staged Separable Training

In order to overcome the situation that traditional end-to-end training is sensitive to hyperparameters, it is necessary to jointly train multiple components and the encoder needs to take into account the balance between robustness and imperceptibility during training, which can easily cause S to be overvalued. Extreme cases of too high or too low, and the selection of strength factor S is extremely unstable. We employ a staged training approach to help the model train and tune better. In stage one, the adaptor does not participate in training and the fixed S is 1, and only the encoder, discriminator, and decoder are trained, where noise is added for attack simulation to enhance the robustness of the encoded image. Thus, what we get is the best encoder capable of redundantly embedding a message into images. In the second stage, the parameters of the encoder are frozen to keep the weights unchanged, and the adaptor is added for training. The purpose is to enable the adaptor to comprehensively evaluate the carrier image and message to obtain an optimal S. The S should be the maximum value that can improve the image quality without reducing the bit error rate. After the attack simulation is performed, the encoder is fine-tuned to obtain the best decoder under noise attack. Compared with the traditional methods that use manual determination of watermarking strength, our staged training scheme can adjust the overall network in time while S changes.

3   Proposed Framework

3.1   Model Architecture

As shown in Fig. 1, the entire model architecture consists of five components: 1. Encoder, the encoder with parameters θ_{en} receives the message, carrier image, and S obtained by the adaptor, then outputs the encoded image with watermark. 2. Adaptor, the adaptor with parameters θ_{ad} outputs an S by receiving the carrier image and the reshaped message. 3. Noise layer, the noise layer receives the encoded image output by the encoder, performs attack simulation on it, and outputs the encoded image with noise. 4. Decoder, the decoder with parameters θ_{de} receives the noise image output by the noise layer and decodes it, and outputs the message contained in the watermark. 5. Discriminator, the discriminator with parameters θ_{di} receives the encoded image output by the encoder and discriminates whether the image is encoded. Next, each component will be described in detail.

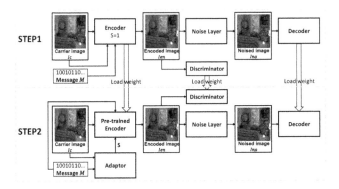

Fig. 1. The network model and training process of the network. The overall framework consists of an encoder, an adaptor, a noise layer, a decoder, and a discriminator. The training phase is divided into a no-adapter training phase and an adaptive factor overall fine-tuning phase.

Encoder. The encoder is divided into two parts: message processing and carrier image processing. First, the one-dimensional message $M \in \{0,1\}^L$ needs to be preprocessed for calculation. According to the calculation formula obtained in MBRS [19], we can reshape M into $M' \in \{0,1\}^{1 \times h \times w}$, after a 3×3 convolutional layer for preliminary feature extraction, n times of 2×2 upsampling operations with a stride of 2 are performed to make its size equal to the carrier image I_c, to make the message spread over the entire feature map. Finally, pass the diffused feature map through n SE blocks that do not change the shape of the feature map to obtain a more delicate message feature $I_m \in \mathbb{R}^{C \times H \times W}$. The message reshaping announcement is shown in Eq. (2):

$$L = h \times w = (H/2^n) \times (W/2^n) \quad I_m \in \mathbb{R}^{C \times H \times W} \tag{2}$$

where L is the message length (integer), h, w are the length and width of the reshaped message, and H, W are the length and width of the carrier image.

For the image processing part, I_c goes through a convolution layer and four SE blocks for feature extraction, and then the obtained image features $I_{cf} \in \mathbb{R}^{C \times H \times W}$ are concatenated with I_m to obtain the total feature I_g. Then, I_g are further extracted through a 3×3 dilated convolution to obtain features, and adding a receptive field is used to obtain more feature information. Finally, I_c combines S with I_m and encodes through a 3×3 dilated convolution. The encoded image is $I_{en} = I_c + S * I_m$. Since the encoder needs to make the encoded image I_{en} as similar to the carrier image I_c as possible, it chooses to use the mean square error between I_{en} and I_c as the loss function $\mathcal{L}_{en}$ to update the value of θ_{en}:

$$\mathcal{L}_{en} = \frac{1}{M \times N} \sum_{i=1}^{M} \sum_{j=1}^{N} (f(Ic) - f(Ien)) \tag{3}$$

where M, N is the image size.

Adaptor. The model architecture of the adaptor is shown in the Fig. 2. The adaptor is essentially an auxiliary network, which is frozen in the first stage and does not participate in training. The function of the adaptor is to determine the optimal S that the encoder should choose according to I_c and M. Regarding the optimal S, we think that *best* refers to the state where the decoder can correctly decode the message M in the watermark and reduce the embedding strength of the watermark to the greatest extent. In layman's terms, it is to fully exploit the potential of the image to enhance the imperceptibility without increasing the Bit Error Rate (BER). Usually, researchers use Peak Signal to Noise Ratio (PSNR) [24] and Structural Similarity (SSIM) [25] to evaluate watermark imperceptibility in digital image watermarking, so we judge watermark imperceptibility according to PSNR and SSIM. The formulas of PSNR and SSIM are shown in Eq. (4) and Eq. (5, 6, 7, 8):

$$PSNR = 10 \times \log_{10} \left(\frac{MAX^2}{MSE} \right) \tag{4}$$

where MAX is the maximum pixel value of the image, and MSE is the mean square error.

$$SSIM = \left[a(x,y)^\alpha \times b(x,y)^\beta \times c(x,y)^\gamma \right] \tag{5}$$

where x, y are samples, α, β are constants, μ is the mean, σ^2 is the variance, σ_{xy} is the covariance, k is a constant, and Eqs. (6, 7, 8) are the brightness, contrast, and structure of the image, respectively. Together they form SSIM.

$$a(x,y) = \frac{2\mu_x\mu_y + k_1}{\mu_x^2 + \mu_y^2 + k_1} \tag{6}$$

$$b(x,y) = \frac{2\sigma_x\sigma_y + k_2}{\sigma_x^2 + \sigma_y^2 + k_2} \tag{7}$$

$$c(x,y) = \frac{2\sigma_{xy} + k_3}{\sigma_x\sigma_y + k_3} \tag{8}$$

In the past, the effect of S was to achieve a balance between robustness and imperceptibility of the watermarked image. However, through our experiments, we found that each image has its unique S that can increase its imperceptibility. We redefine S as the embedding strength that maximizes the potential of image imperceptibility while maintaining robustness. The framework of the adaptor is shown in Fig. 2. The M of the extracted features is preprocessed by the same reshaping operation as in the encoder, and then through a convolutional layer, multiple upsampling and three SE blocks that do not change the feature size for feature extraction to obtain the feature $I_{am} \in \mathbb{R}^{C \times H \times W}$. The carrier image passes through a 3×3 convolutional layer and a SE block to obtain the feature $I_{acf} \in \mathbb{R}^{C \times H \times W}$, and after concatenating I_{am} and I_{acf} into a convolutional layer and three SE blocks for feature extraction. Finally, the optimal S is obtained by downsampling by an average pooling layer and sent to the encoder. Since the adaptor needs to be as imperceptible as possible while remaining robust, we will

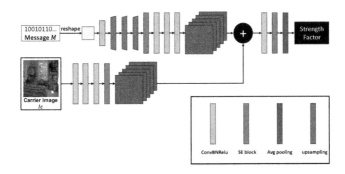

Fig. 2. Model architecture of the adaptor.

use a polynomial consisting of PSNR, SSIM, and BER as the loss function $\mathcal{L}_{ad}$ to update the value of θ_{ad}:

$$\mathcal{L}_{ad} = \lambda_{PSNR} \times (p_1 - PSNR) + \lambda_{SSIM} \times (1 - SSIM) + \lambda_{BER} \times BER \quad (9)$$

where $\lambda_{PSNR}, \lambda_{SSIM}, \lambda_{BER}, p_1$ is the weight factor.

Noise Layer. The encoded image produced by the encoder is not robust, but the noise layer can increase its resistance to attacks. I_{no} is obtained by attacking the encoded image I_{en}, so that encoder can robustly embed the message in a position that is not easily destroyed by the attack.

Decoder. In the decoder, we interpret the message M' from the noisy encoded image I_{no}, and the features are extracted through a 3×3 convolutional layer and downsampling by n SE blocks. To extract messages more accurately, we still use dilated convolution in the penultimate layer to improve the receptive field. Finally, we use a 3×3 convolution layer to change the feature map into a single channel, which can be obtained after reshaping message M'. Since the decoder needs to make M and M' as similar as possible, it chooses to use the mean square error between M and M' as the loss function $\mathcal{L}_{de}$ to update the value of θ_{en}:

$$\mathcal{L}_{de} = \frac{1}{M \times N} \sum_{i=1}^{M} \sum_{j=1}^{N} (f(M) - f(M')) \quad (10)$$

where M, N is the image size.

Discriminator. Even though the discriminator is only composed of 3 layers of 3×3 convolutional layers and one pooling layer for classification, its presence can improve the imperceptibility of images in constant adversarial. In this paper, we use 1 to represent that the image contains a watermark, and 0 to represent the carrier image. The discriminator uses the loss function $\mathcal{L}_{di}$ to improve the accuracy of the binary classification results by updating θ_{di}:

$$\mathcal{L}_{di} = \mathcal{L}_{di2} + \log\left(D_i\left(\theta_{di}, I_{en}\right)\right) \quad (11)$$

At the same time, to make the encoded image similar to the carrier image, the loss function $\mathcal{L}_{di2}$ is used to improve the image quality of I_{en} by updating θ_{en}:

$$\mathcal{L}_{di2} = \log\left(1 - D_i\left(\theta_{di}, I_{en}\right)\right) \tag{12}$$

3.2   Staged Training

Stage 1: The No-Adapter Training Stage. In the first stage of end-to-end encoder training, we uniformly set the adaptive factor to 1, to make the encoded image achieve higher robustness first, which is convenient for us to further fine-tune in the second stage. The encoded image is sent to the decoder for decoding after attack simulation, and the discriminator will also participate in the training. Use $\mathcal{L}_1$ as the total loss function to achieve the specified training goal:

$$\mathcal{L}_1 = \lambda_{en} \times \mathcal{L}_{en} + \lambda_{de} \times \mathcal{L}_{de} + \lambda_{di} \times \mathcal{L}_{di} \tag{13}$$

where $\lambda_{en}, \lambda_{de}, \lambda_{di}$ are weight factors.

Stage 2: The Overall Fine-Tuning Stage of the Adaptive Factor. Through the first stage of training, we get a strong encoder responsible for watermark embedding, after which the model moves to the adaptive fine-tuning stage. First, freeze the parameters of the encoder obtained by training in stage 1. In this stage, the adaptor is added to the training, and the decoder is fine-tuned in a targeted manner to discover the most suitable S that the encoded image can accept. Loading the model weights obtained from the first stage as pre-trained weights can significantly speed up the training speed of the second stage. For stage two, we use $\mathcal{L}_2$ as the loss function to find the optimal S:

$$\mathcal{L}_2 = \lambda_{di} \times \mathcal{L}_{di1} + \lambda_{de} \times \mathcal{L}_{de} + \mathcal{L}_{ad} \tag{14}$$

where $\lambda_{di}, \lambda_{de}$ are weight factors.

3.3   Why Use Staged Training

In our early experiments, we did try end-to-end training. However, the results were very bad. Specifically, because of the existence of strength factors, the model needs to modify too many super parameters. If we want to get a higher image quality, it will make the model set the strength factor directly to 0, that is, no watermark is embedded to ensure that the image is not damaged. On the contrary, if we pursue a lower bit error rate, the image will directly set the strength factor to a very high level, which will greatly damage the carrier image itself. To sum up, we hope to reduce the modification of super parameters, and finally adopt the phased training method of freezing parameters.

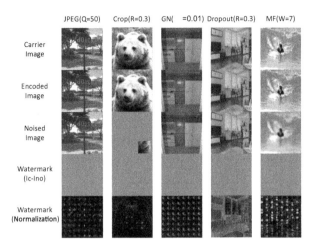

Fig. 3. Experimental results under various noise attacks. From top to bottom, the images are carrier image, encoded image, noise image, watermark, and normalized watermark. Since the pixel of the watermark itself is basically at a low value, The human eye is difficult to observe, and we normalize it to facilitate observation.

4 Experiment

Experimental Details. We randomly select 10,000 128 × 128 images from the COCO dataset as the training set, and also randomly select 5,000 128 × 128 images from the COCO validation set as the validation set, and 5,000 128 × 128 images as the test set. The model framework is implemented using PyTorch and trained and validated on NVIDIA RTX 4000. Each piece of message M is composed of random 0, 1 with a length of 64. For the real JPEG compression in the noise layer, we use the official JPEG compression API to call. After repeated testing, in one stage of training, we choose $\lambda_{en} = 1, \lambda_{de} = 10, \lambda_{di} = 0.0001$. In the second stage, $\alpha, \beta, \gamma = 1, \lambda_{PSNR} = 0.75, \lambda_{SSIM} = 6, \lambda_{BER} = 10000, p_1 = 100$, in order to get better training results, we also set the values of λ_{de}, the updated value is $\lambda_{de} = 15000$. To improve the convergence performance, the two-stage gradient descent method uses Adam optimizers instead of Stochastic Gradient Descent(SGD) optimizer, which has high computational efficiency and low memory usage, and sets its learning rate to 10^{-3}. At the same time, the size of the mini-batch training is 4, and each stage is trained for 100 epochs. For specific training, we train 18 specific decoders at different intensities using 5 traditional noises.

For combinatorial training, we train only one combinatorial decoder using a different traditional noise attack on each mini-batch.

Metrics. We employ robustness and imperceptibility, which are now commonly used in digital image watermarking evaluation, to evaluate our model performance. Robustness We use the bit error rate (BER) to measure, imperceptibility is the quality of the image, we use and values to measure. We chose to compare

Table 1. Comparison of experimental results of JPEG compression under different Q.

JPEG	Q = 30				Q = 50				Q = 70			
Metric	BER	SSIM	PSNR	S	BER	SSIM	PSNR	S	BER	SSIM	PSNR	S
MBRS [19]	0.61%	0.937	35.14	1	0.031%	0.947	36.41	1	0.044%	0.947	38.14	1
Ours	**0.51%**	**0.953**	**37.63**	0.87	**0.016%**	**0.963**	**38.42**	0.76	**0.037%**	**0.970**	**40.96**	0.74

Table 2. Comparison of experimental results for different Crop ratios.

Crop	R = 0.3				R = 0.5				R = 0.7			
Metric	BER	SSIM	PSNR	S	BER	SSIM	PSNR	S	BER	SSIM	PSNR	S
HiDDeN [17]	31.46%	0.921	34.24	1	24.5%	0.943	35.77	1	15.8%	0.950	37.56	1
MBRS [19]	25.6%	0.943	37.36	1	10.5%	0.946	37.69	1	0.90%	0.963	40.40	1
Ours	**24.7%**	**0.945**	**37.56**	1.08	**10.4%**	**0.968**	**40.86**	0.97	**0.86%**	**0.972**	**41.92**	0.91

PSNR and SSIM with almost close BER to evaluate the performance of our model.

Baseline. Our experiments refer to MBRS [19], so we will add it to the comparison, not only that, HiDDeN [17] will also be our comparison object. Due to the fact that [23] is biased towards agnostic distortion, and our model has a strong pertinence to the known distortion. This is unfair, so we did not include it in the experimental comparison.

4.1 Robustness and Imperceptibility of Encoded Images to Non-differentiable Noise

JPEG compression is a commonly used lossy compression method for digital images. JPEG compression is implemented in five steps, color mode conversion, data sampling, DCT transformation, quantization frequency coefficients, and encoding. Since quantization makes the inverse gradient 0, JPEG is non-differentiable. The selection of the quality factor Q in the quantization operation is important. The larger the Q, the higher the compression degree, but the image quality will be reduced. In the experiment, we choose Q = 10, 30, 50, 70, and 90 to test against JPEG compression attacks. Because [17,18,22] did not conduct experiments on these quality factors, and the anti-JPEG compression The capability is also far inferior to MBRS [19], so we only compare with [19].

As can be seen from Table 1, the PSNR and SSIM values increase with increasing Q, while the BER decreases accordingly. As Q increases and image quality improves, S also tends to choose smaller values to reduce the strength of the embedded watermark. Our model improves PSNR and SSIM by about 2 and 0.02 on average, respectively, which fully demonstrates the potential of watermarked images to get better.

4.2   Robustness and Imperceptibility of Encoded Images to Differentiable Noise

Common differentiable noises include Crop, Dropout, Gaussian noise, and Median blur.

Cropping refers to randomly cropping an image from top/bottom and left/right and then complementing the areas where the image is lost with black pixels. We choose the cropping ratio as 0.3, 0.5, and 0.7 for testing. Cropping can do a lot of damage to the information embedded in the image. In the Table 2, Adapter chooses a value greater than 1 as S for more robust watermarking, which can improve SSIM and PSNR. This fully shows that after adjusting the watermark strength, the entire model still has room for adjustment.

Dropout removes random pixels from noisy images and replaces them with pixels from the cover image, we use dropout with ratios of 0.3, 0.5, and 0.7 for testing. As shown in the Table 3, since the damage of the replacement attack to the image is much smaller than that of the crop, the S selected by this scheme is all less than 1, and the watermark information can be hidden with a lower watermark strength to obtain higher imperceptibility. It can be seen that compared with the second best MBRS [19], the average SSIM is improved by about 0.01, and the PSNR is also improved by about 2, which greatly enhances the imperceptibility of the image.

Gaussian noise refers to a class of noise whose probability density function obeys a Gaussian distribution. The main source of Gaussian noise in digital images occurs during acquisition. Due to poor lighting or sensor noise caused by high temperature, we adopted values of 0.001, 0.005, and 0.01 four different variances to evaluate the anti-Gaussian noise performance of the model. Combining the Table 4 and Fig. 3 analysis, it is concluded that since the Gaussian noise damages the image more and presents a Gaussian distribution, the encoder is more inclined to regularly embed information, the embedded information presents a regular point-like distribution, and the changed position is more obvious. At the same time, due to the large damage to the image by Gaussian noise, the adaptor also selects a value greater than 1 for adjustment when selecting S.

The space for the model to be adjusted also becomes limited and the imperceptibility is only slightly improved. Median blurring means that for each pixel, in the window centered on it, the median pixel value of the neighboring pixel is taken to replace the pixel value of the position. For median blur, due to the smoothing attack method of median filtering sliding window, the encoder chooses the embedding method of block embedding and the size of the block is related to the size of the filter. The adaptor of our scheme chooses the watermarking strength with an average value of about 0.9, which makes the model performance more excellent. Compared with MBRS [19], SSIM and PSNR value are improved by 0.1 and 2 on average. Greatly improved imperceptibility in the event of a drop in BER. This method is median smoothing, also known as median filtering. We selected different window sizes, the filtering windows of 3×3, 5×5, 7×7. The specific results of the experiment are shown in Fig. 3 and Table 5.

Table 3. Comparison of experimental results of Dropout at different ratios.

Dropout	R = 0.3				R = 0.5				R = 0.7			
Metric	BER	SSIM	PSNR	S	BER	SSIM	PSNR	S	BER	SSIM	PSNR	S
HiDDeN [17]	40.60%	0.937	34.82	1	26.1%	0.923	34.69	1	23.5%	0.902	32.58	1
MBRS [19]	0.0052%	0.961	41.39	1	0.0021%	0.977	44.45	1	0.00051%	0.983	46.64	1
Ours	0.0052%	**0.971**	**43.20**	0.87	**0.0018%**	**0.989**	**48.47**	0.79	**0.00050%**	**0.993**	**48.89**	0.76

Table 4. Comparison of experimental results of Gaussian noise under different σ^2.

Gaussian noise	$\sigma^2 = 0.001$				$\sigma^2 = 0.005$				$\sigma^2 = 0.010$			
Metric	BER	SSIM	PSNR	S	BER	SSIM	PSNR	S	BER	SSIM	PSNR	S
HiDDeN [17]	23.2%	0.910	34.60	1	28.1%	0.930	33.47	1	30.3%	0.908	32.86	1
MBRS [19]	0.031%	0.957	41.08	1	0.052%	0.923	38.03	1	0.10%	0.911	37.25	1
Ours	**0.016%**	**0.970**	**43.56**	0.77	**0.052%**	**0.937**	**39.30**	0.84	**0.084%**	**0.924**	**38.63**	0.91

4.3   Combined Noise

In addition to specific encoders, we also experiment with a combination of various noises We add several differentiable and non-differentiable attacks used above to the noise layer, and perform random combined attacks on each image. Combined noises include: Crop (R = 0.3), Dropout (R = 0.3), Gaussian noise ($\sigma^2 = 0.01$), Median blur (W = 30), JPEG compression (Q = 50). The experimental results are shown in Table 6. The adaptor selects an average value of 0.9 as the best S for watermark embedding in the face of a combination of various noises. Although the effect is not as good as the 18 specific decoders described above, it also shows that compared with MBRS [19] for better results.

4.4   Ablation Experiment

To further validate our idea, we will conduct ablation experiments. One option is training without stages. In the first 100 stages of training, we still choose 1 as the value of S. In the second stage, we leave the model unchanged to continue training for 100 stages and add the staged training of the adaptor, respectively. Another option is to train with a fixed strength factor in stages. We take the average value of each image strength factor output by the adaptor as a fixed strength factor and put it into the model without an adaptor for 100 stages of training.

The experimental results are shown in Table 7. We found that after continuing to use 1 for 100 training sessions, the performance of the model was not improved because the model had converged. When we use a fixed S for each image to perform fixed S training in stages, although the model has been improved to a certain extent, different images should choose different optimal S, and the fixed S will The watermarking strength of the actual watermark is slightly deviated from the optimal strength, making its final effect inferior to the experimental results of our staged and adaptive training scheme.

Table 5. Comparison of experimental results of median smoothing under different window sizes.

Median blur	W = 3				W = 5				W = 7			
Metric	BER	SSIM	PSNR	S	BER	SSIM	PSNR	S	BER	SSIM	PSNR	S
HiDDeN [17]	23.00%	0.892	32.74	1	27.6%	0.900	33.66	1	28.57%	0.888	31.33	1
MBRS [19]	0.0015%	0.963	39.55	1	0.17%	0.952	37.76	1	0.20%	0.941	35.60	1
Ours	**0.0010%**	**0.977**	**42.03**	0.88	**0.14%**	**0.965**	**39.16**	0.90	**0.14%**	**0.952**	**37.76**	0.91

Table 6. Comparison of experimental results against each noise under combined noise. Among them, MBRS [19]: SSIM = 0.905, PSNR = 34.94, S = 1.00, **Ours: SSIM = 0.925, PSNR = 38.55**, S = 0.92

Noise	Model	BER
JPEG	MBRS [19]	0.42%
(Q = 50)	**Ours**	**0.26%**
Crop	MBRS [19]	27.8%
(R = 0.3)	**Ours**	**26.4%**
Dropout	MBRS [19]	0.60%
(R = 0.3)	**Ours**	**0.090%**
Gaussian noise	MBRS [19]	0.87%
(σ^2 = 0.01)	**Ours**	**0.72%**
Median blur	MBRS [19]	0.096%
(W = 3)	**Ours**	**0.068%**

4.5   Disadvantages of the Model

Our model adopts a phased training mode, which will increase the training time. We compare the time complexity of the algorithm by training the average time spent(s) for an epoch of 10000 images on NVIDIA RTX 4000. Because the time spent in different noises is different, we only show the average training time in JPEG compression (Q = 50). It can be seen from the Table 8 that our model takes longer than other models. And because the encoder parameters are frozen in the second stage of training, the training time in the second stage is lower than that in the first stage.

Table 7. Comparison of experimental results of different training methods.

Noise	Metric	No staged training (S = 1)	Staged Fixed Strength Factor Training	Staged and adaptive training
JPEG (Q = 50)	BER	0.029%	0.019%	**0.016%**
	SSIM	0.944	0.954	**0.963**
	PSNR	36.51	37.52	**38.42**
Crop (R = 0.7)	BER	0.90%	0.89%	**0.86%**
	SSIM	0.962	0.971	**0.972**
	PSNR	40.24	41.54	**41.92**
Dropout (R = 0.7)	BER	0.00052%	0.00052%	**0.00050%**
	SSIM	0.982	0.992	**0.993**
	PSNR	46.60	48.19	**48.89**
Gaussian noise ($\sigma^2 = 0.5$)	BER	0.0048%	0.0048%	**0.0047%**
	SSIM	0.879	0.880	**0.880**
	PSNR	25.17	25.71	**25.74**
Median blur (W = 5)	BER	0.20%	0.16%	**0.14%**
	SSIM	0.938	0.960	**0.965**
	PSNR	35.28	38.30	**39.16**

Table 8. Time complexity comparison of different models

Model	HiDDeN [17]	MBRS [19]	Ours (step1)	Ours (step2)	Ours (step1+step2)
Time spent	583	870	708	474	1182

5   Conclusion

In this paper, we propose an adaptive watermarking strength factor embedding scheme with a two-stage training scheme. The training scheme consists of two stages: the no-adapter training stage and the adaptive factor overall fine-tuning stage. The first stage is responsible for training the overall network framework, adding the noise layer to the training to obtain images with higher robustness. In the second stage, the scheme introduces an adaptor into the component to adjust the model and improve the imperceptibility by selecting different S for each image. A large number of experiments show that the proposed watermark embedding scheme has excellent robustness and imperceptibility and stands out among various current excellent watermark embedding algorithms. However, due to the staged training method, the cost of training has also increased.

References

1. Van Schyndel, R.G., Tirkel, A.Z., Osborne, C.F.: A digital watermark. In: Proceedings of 1st International Conference on Image Processing, vol. 2, pp. 86–90. IEEE (1994)

2. Zong, T., Xiang, Y., Natgunanathan, I., Guo, S., Zhou, W., Beliakov, G.: Robust histogram shape-based method for image watermarking. IEEE Trans. Circuits Syst. Video Technol. **25**, 717–729 (2014)

3. Hua, G., Xiang, Y., Zhang, L.Y.: Informed histogram-based watermarking. IEEE Signal Process. Lett. **27**, 236–240 (2020)

4. Cox, I.J., Kilian, J., Leighton, T., Shamoon, T.: Secure spread spectrum watermarking for images, audio and video. In: Proceedings of 3rd IEEE International Conference on Image Processing, vol. 3, pp. 243–246. IEEE (1996)

5. Ruanaidh, J., Dowling, W., Boland, F.M.: Phase watermarking of digital images. In: Proceedings of 3rd IEEE International Conference on Image Processing, vol. 3, pp. 239–242. IEEE (1996)

6. Hamidi, M., Haziti, M.E., Cherifi, H., Hassouni, M.E.: Hybrid blind robust image watermarking technique based on dft-dct and arnold transform. Multimed. Tools Appl. **77**, 27181–27214 (2018)

7. Guo, H., Georganas, N.D.: Digital image watermarking for joint ownership verification without a trusted dealer. In: 2003 International Conference on Multimedia and Expo. ICME'03. Proceedings (Cat. No. 03TH8698), vol. 2, p. II-497. IEEE (2003)

8. Rawat, S., Raman, B.: A blind watermarking algorithm based on fractional fourier transform and visual cryptography. Signal Process. **92**, 1480–1491 (2012)

9. Mishra, A., Agarwal, C., Sharma, A., Bedi, P.: Optimized gray-scale image watermarking using dwt-svd and firefly algorithm. Expert Syst. Appl. **41**, 7858–7867 (2014)

10. Meng, F., Peng, H., Pei, Z., Wang, J.: A novel blind image watermarking scheme based on support vector machine in dct domain. In: 2008 International Conference on Computational Intelligence and Security, vol. 2, pp. 16–20. IEEE (2008)

11. Lin, W.H., Wang, Y.R., Horng, S.J., Kao, T.W., Pan, Y.: A blind watermarking method using maximum wavelet coefficient quantization. Expert Syst. Appl. **36**, 11509–11516 (2009)

12. Piao, C.R., Beack, S., Woo, D.M., Han, S.S.: A blind watermarking algorithm based on hvs and rbf neural network for digital image. In: International Conference on Natural Computation, pp. 493–496. Springer (2006)

13. Ali, M., Ahn, C.W., Pant, M.: A robust image watermarking technique using svd and differential evolution in dct domain. Optik **125**, 428–434 (2014)

14. Lai, C.C.: An improved svd-based watermarking scheme using human visual characteristics. Optics Commun. **284**, 938–944 (2011)

15. Kang, X.B., Zhao, F., Lin, G.F., Chen, Y.J.: A novel hybrid of dct and svd in dwt domain for robust and invisible blind image watermarking with optimal embedding strength. Multimedia Tools and Applications **77**, 13197–13224 (2018)

16. Ariatmanto, D., Ernawan, F.: Adaptive scaling factors based on the impact of selected dct coefficients for image watermarking. J. King Saud Univ.-Comput. Inf. Sci. (2020)

17. Zhu, J., Kaplan, R., Johnson, J., Fei-Fei, L.: HiDDeN: hiding data with deep networks. In: Ferrari, V., Hebert, M., Sminchisescu, C., Weiss, Y. (eds.) ECCV 2018. LNCS, vol. 11219, pp. 682–697. Springer, Cham (2018). https://doi.org/10.1007/978-3-030-01267-0_40

18. Ahmadi, M., Norouzi, A., Karimi, N., Samavi, S., Emami, A.: Redmark: framework for residual diffusion watermarking based on deep networks. Expert Syst. Appl. **146**, 113157 (2020)

19. Jia, Z., Fang, H., Zhang, W.: Mbrs: Enhancing robustness of dnn-based water-marking by mini-batch of real and simulated jpeg compression. In: Proceedings of the 29th ACM International Conference on Multimedia, pp. 41–49 (2021)
20. Kandi, H., Mishra, D., Gorthi, S.R.S.: Exploring the learning capabilities of convolutional neural networks for robust image watermarking. Comput. Secur. **65**, 247–268 (2017)
21. Tancik, M., Mildenhall, B., Ng, R.: Stegastamp: invisible hyperlinks in physical photographs. In: Proceedings of the IEEE/CVF Conference on Computer Vision and Pattern Recognition, pp. 2117–2126 (2020)
22. Liu, Y., Guo, M., Zhang, J., Zhu, Y., Xie, X.: A novel two-stage separable deep learning framework for practical blind watermarking. In: Proceedings of the 27th ACM International Conference on Multimedia, pp. 1509–1517 (2019)
23. Luo, X., Zhan, R., Chang, H., Yang, F., Milanfar, P.: Distortion agnostic deep watermarking. In: Proceedings of the IEEE/CVF Conference on Computer Vision and Pattern Recognition, pp. 13548–13557 (2020)
24. Almohammad, A., Ghinea, G.: Stego image quality and the reliability of psnr. In: 2010 2nd International Conference on Image Processing Theory, Tools and Applications, pp. 215–220. IEEE (2010)
25. Wang, Z., Bovik, A.C., Sheikh, H.R., Simoncelli, E.P.: Image quality assessment: from error visibility to structural similarity. IEEE Trans. Image Process. **13**, 600–612 (2004)

AFF-CAM: Adaptive Frequency Filtering Based Channel Attention Module

DongWook Yang⬤, Min-Kook Suh⬤, and Seung-Woo Seo$^{(\boxtimes)}$⬤

Seoul National University, Seoul, Korea
{ab3.yang,bluecdm,sseo}@snu.ac.kr

Abstract. Locality from bounded receptive fields is one of the biggest problems that needs to be solved in convolutional neural networks. Meanwhile, operating convolutions in frequency domain provides complementary viewpoint to this dilemma, as a point-wise update in frequency domain can globally modulate all input features involved in Discrete Cosine Transform. However, Discrete Cosine Transform concentrates majority of its information in a handful of coefficients in lower regions of frequency spectrum, often discarding other potentially useful frequency components, such as those of middle and high frequency spectrum. We believe valuable feature representations can be learned not only from lower frequency components, but also from such disregarded frequency distributions. In this paper, we propose a novel **A**daptive **F**requency **F**iltering based **C**hannel **A**ttention **M**odule (AFF-CAM), which exploits non-local characteristics of frequency domain and also adaptively learns the importance of different bands of frequency spectrum by modeling global cross-channel interactions, where each channel serves as a distinct frequency distribution. As a result, AFF-CAM is able to re-calibrate channel-wise feature responses and guide feature representations from spatial domain to reason over high-level, global context, which simply cannot be obtained from local kernels in spatial convolutions. Extensive experiments are conducted on ImageNet-1K classification and MS COCO detection benchmarks to validate our AFF-CAM. By effectively aggregating global information of various frequency spectrum from frequency domain with local information from spatial domain, our method achieves state-of-the-art results compared to other attention mechanisms.

1 Introduction

Recently, convolutional neural networks (CNN) have achieved remarkable progress in a broad range of vision tasks, e.g. image classification, object detection, and semantic segmentation, based on their powerful feature representation abilities. The success has mainly been fueled by strong prior by inductive bias and ability to model local relationship through large number of kernels in convolutional layers. To further enhance the performance of CNNs, recent researches have investigated to create networks that are *deeper* [1,2], *wider* [3], and also to contain more *cardinality* [4,5] by creatively stacking multiple convolutional

L. Wang et al. (Eds.): ACCV 2022, LNCS 13846, pp. 373–388, 2023.
https://doi.org/10.1007/978-3-031-26351-4_23

layers. Even with the increase in performance with aforementioned attempts, there still exists a limitation of *locality* inherited in nature of CNNs that roots from localized receptive fields (RF) due to small kernels, e.g., 3×3 kernels [2] in most image-oriented tasks. Thus, it is of the utmost importance that we guide CNN to better extract global information, also known as *long-range* dependency. Theoretically, long-range dependencies can be acquired from deeper networks. Deeper networks allow the buildup of larger and more complex RFs because stacking multiple layers increases RFs linearly or exponentially. However, recent study [6] has proven that not all pixels in a RF contribute equally to an output unit's response and that effective RF only occupies a fraction of the full theoretical RF.

To efficiently and effectively implement non-local RFs to better acquire long-range dependencies, we introduce spectral transform theory, in particular Discrete Cosine Transform (DCT). We propose to adopt DCT in our network for the following reasons. First, as stated in spectral convolution theorem in Fourier Theory, updating a single value in frequency domain globally influences all the input features associated in Fourier Transform. We take advantage of this fact and enable CNN to implement the effect of having non-local RFs even from earlier layers that have localized RFs. Second, from 2D image perspective, DCT expresses a finite sequence of data points by the series of harmonic cosine functions wavering at distinct frequencies. In other words, DCT expresses the phenomena of an image in terms of different bands, e.g., low, middle, or high, of frequency components. For example, removing high frequency components blurs the image and eliminating low frequency components leaves us with edges. This indicates that by adequately modulating the amount of different frequency details through DCT, we are able to pick the most important frequency components and discard the rest. We link this to a well-known concept known as *attention* mechanism. Attention is a tool that permits the network to utilize the most relevant parts of a given input feature in a flexible manner. By fusing the characteristics of DCT and attention mechanism, we formulate the network to give distinct attention to different bands of frequency components. Although majority of the information is stored in just a few DCT coefficients, particularly those of lower frequencies, we believe useful information can be found not only in lower frequencies but also in middle or high frequency spectrum.

With aforementioned motivations, we introduce a novel **A**daptive **F**requency **F**iltering based **C**hannel **A**ttention **M**odule (AFF-CAM), that leverages non-local characteristics of frequency domain through DCT and formulates channel-wise attention map, which explores and learns the importance of distinct frequency distributions, to modulate the local feature representations from spatial domain. As depicted in Fig. 1, AFF-CAM is composed of three main sub-modules after going through DCT: i) **G**lobal **U**pdate **M**odule (GUM) that targets feature maps to acquire long-range dependencies with its non-local RFs. The effects of non-local RFs are implemented by 1×1 convolutional layers in frequency domain because, as mentioned above, point-wise update in frequency domain globally affects input features associated in DCT. ii) **F**requency **D**istribution **L**earner

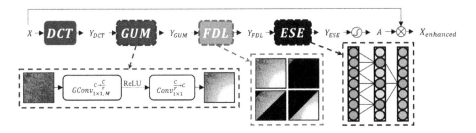

Fig. 1. General overview of AFF-CAM. AFF-CAM is composed of three sub-modules: i) Global Update Module (GUM), which gathers long-range dependencies with non-local receptive fields and globally updates input feature representations, ii) Frequency Distribution Learner (FDL), which allows the network to learn the importance of different bands of frequency spectrum through mask filtering, and iii) Enhanced Squeeze-and-Excitation (ESE) that efficiently acquires global cross-channel interactions to re-weigh channel responses.

(FDL) that partitions input feature maps in frequency domain into M different distributions/bands of frequency spectrum with a set of learnable frequency filters so that various kinds of advantageous information can be aggregated from M different distributions. We adopt this idea because DCT concentrates majority of its information in a handful of coefficients, mainly lowest frequency (DC) component, often ignoring information from other frequency distributions (e.g. middle, and high). FcaNet [7], which most resembles our method, also exploits DCT to construct multi-spectral channel attention map. However, FcaNet only uses a few pre-selected (e.g. 1, 2, 4, 8, 16, or 32) DCT coefficients that are considered profitable. By doing so, FcaNet cannot flexibly learn richer feature representations beyond fixed frequency components. With FDL, our network is not limited to specific, prefixed frequency components but provies more adaptation to learn useful details from different frequency distributions. iii) **E**nhanced **S**queeze-and-**E**xication (ESE) that produces a channel descriptor by aggregating feature maps across their spectral dimensions ($height \times width$) by "*squeeze*" operation and outputs a collection of per-channel modulation weights via "*excitation*" operation. While squeeze operation was originally conducted with Global Average Pooling (GAP) in SENet [8], we utilize combination of GAP and Global Max Pooling (GMP) operations to extract richer feature representations like in CBAM [9]. Excitation operation is generally implemented with two fully-connected (FC) layers to capture non-linear cross-channel interactions and also to control model complexity through dimension reduction. However, according to ECANet [10], using mutliple FC layers is not only memory intensive but also dimension reduction in FC layers destroys the direct correspondence between channel and its weight. ECANet proposes to replace FC layers with a single lightweight 1D convolution with adaptive kernel size k and captures *local* cross-channel interaction. Inspired by this, ESE also adopts 1D convolution layer but enhances the idea by introducing **1D-D**ilated **C**onvolution **P**yramid (1D-DCP), which stacks multiple dilated [11] 1D convolutional layers with different dilation rates and successfully obtains *global* cross-channel interactions. This way, 1D-DCP is able to implement the effect of a FC layer with the model complexity of a 1D convolution.

Contributions. To recap, main contributions of our AFF-CAM can be summarized as follows:

1. From GUM, we are able to obtain long-range dependencies that conventional convolutional layers cannot acquire through simply stacking multiple layers.
2. From FDL, we are not limited to a few, pre-defined frequency components but able to adaptively learn richer feature representations from wide range of frequency distributions.
3. From ESE, we attain global cross-channel interactions with substantially low computational complexity.

2 Related Work

2.1 Attention

By proposing to model the importance of features, attention mechanism has been a promising tool in enhancing the performance of CNNs. Attention modules facilitate the networks to learn *"what"* and *"where"* to look in spatial and channel dimensions, respectively, by focusing on important features and suppressing non-useful details through activations. **SENet** [8] first introduces *"Squeeze-and-Excitation"* (SE) block that adaptively re-calibrates channel-wise feature responses by explicitly modeling inter-dependencies between channels. With channel attention, SE block facilitates network to realize *"what"* is more meaningful representation in a given image. **ECANet** [10] reinstates the importance of efficient channel attention proposed by SENet and proposes cheaper alternative. ECANet further explains that because of channel reduction ratio r in Multi-Layer Perceptron (MLP) of SE block, relationship mapping between channels is indirect and thus, non-optimal. To alleviate such problems, ECA block replaces MLP with 1D convolution with an adaptive kernel size, k. Inspired by this, our AFF-CAM also replaces MLP with 1D convolution with additional improvements (*"1D-Dilated Convolution Pyramid"* of Sect. 3.2). **CBAM** [9] enhances SE block with *"Channel Attention Module"* (CAM) by replacing GAP with combination of GAP and GMP to preserve richer contextual information, leading to finer channel attention. Our AFF-CAM's *"squeeze"* operation shares similar architecture, as frequency feature representations are compressed with combination of GAP and GMP pooling operations (*"Enhanced Squeeze-and-Excitation"* of Sect. 3.2). CBAM also introduces *"Spatial Attention Module"* (SAM) by using 2D convolutions of kernel size $k \times k$ to guide network *"where"* to focus, which is complementary to the channel attention. Our method does not follow up on spatial-wise attention because conducting DCT destroys the pixel-to-pixel correspondence. For example, whereas first pixel of a spatial image might represent a sky, first pixel in a DCT image represents low frequency details of a whole image, and not just a sky. Thus, re-weighing feature response of each pixel position in DCT produces meaningless results. **AANet** [12] mixes *"self-attention"* [13] with

SE block. AANet does not re-calibrate the channel-wise feature responses, but creates completely new feature maps through self-attention mechanism, which simultaneously exploits spatial and feature sub-spaces, and then goes through channel-wise compression. **GCNet** [14] mixes SENet with simplified Non-local Network (NLN) [15], where NLN aggregates query-specific global context to each query position to capture long-range spatial dependencies. Simply put, GCNet models global context of a single pixel by aggregating the relational information of every other pixels in a given image, which is computationally intensive. Our proposed method eliminates this computation burden by acquiring long-range dependencies through modulating different frequency components globally with lightweight 1×1 convolution operations (*"Global Update Module"* of Sect. 3.2).

2.2 Frequency Analysis

With eminent breakthroughs of CNN, there have been wide range of works [7, 16–18] that tried to incorporate frequency analysis, more specifically Fourier Transform, into deep learning frameworks. Because of the duality between convolution in spatial domain and element-wise multiplication in frequency domain, computing convolution in frequency domain has been considered as a replacement for vanilla convolution in spatial domain to solve an issue of heavy computational expense. Simply put, properties of Fourier Transform for CNN can be denoted as $F(x * y) = F(x) \odot F(y)$, where x and y represent two spatial signals (e.g. images) and $*$ and $\odot$ the operators of the convolution and the Hadamard product, respectively. Mathieu et al. [16] first carries out the convolutional operations in frequency domain with discrete Fourier Transform (DFT) and discovers that Fourier Transform of filters and the output gradients can be reused, leading to faster training and testing process. Additionally, operating convolutions in spectral domain can alleviate the problem of *"locality"* presented in vanilla convolutions due to their local receptive fields, as point-wise modulation in frequency domain globally updates input features associated in Fourier Transform. **FFC** [17] is inspired to capsulate both local context and long-range context with a local branch that conducts ordinary small-kernel convolution and a semi-global/global branch that manipulates image-level spectrum via DFT, respectively. However, FFC naively adds responses from local and semi-global/global branches. Concept of merging local and global information through frequency analysis is similar to our AFF-CAM. However, because outputs of spatial domain and frequency domain encode different levels of feature representation, our method does not simply add but utilizes output of frequency domain as a guidance to enhance low-level details captured in spatial domain via attention mechanism. **FcaNet** [7] utilizes DCT to construct multi-spectral channel attention. FcaNet adopts DCT, rather than DFT, for computational efficiency with its ability to pre-compute basis function (Eq. 2) from real-valued cosine functions. The idea of updating channel features through DCT is similar to our AFF-CAM. However, N number of DCT weights/filters in FcaNet are hand-picked and fixed before training, thus cannot be learned and optimized. We believe useful information can be found and learned in different bands of frequencies. Therefore, we add learnable filters to fixed base filters to learn and provide more adaptation to select the frequency of interest beyond the fixed base filters ("*Frequency Distribution Learner*" of Sect. 3.2). **FNet** [18] replaces transformers' self-attention sublayers with Fourier Transform. While incorporating DFT to create attention maps is similar to our AFF-CAM, the way such attention maps are used differs. AFF-CAM utilizes attention maps to modulate the local descriptors of spatial feature representations to reason over high-level, global context. However, FNet disregards local information, but primarily considers long-range dependencies that is modeled via Fourier Transform.

3 Method

In this section, we demonstrate the core concepts of our proposed AFF-CAM. The main contributions are threefold: i) Global Update Module (GUM), which obtains long-range dependencies by globally updating feature representations associated in DCT, ii) Frequency Distribution Learner (FDL), which learns importance of different frequency distributions, and iii) Enhanced Squeeze-and-Excitation (ESE) that efficiently acquires global cross-channel interactions to re-calibrate channel-wise feature responses. The general overview of our proposed AFF-CAM is shown in Fig. 1.

3.1 Preliminaries: Discrete Cosine Transform

We begin by introducing DCT. DCT is a powerful tool used in field of digital signal processing for transforming a spatial-temporal signal or an image into spectral sub-bands of different importance. Simply put, it is a linear transformation of measurements in time/spatial domain to the frequency domain. DCT has the property that most of the visually significant information about a given image is concentrated and stored in just a few coefficients. For this reason, DCT is often used in image compression application. Even though all the properties can be extended to higher input dimensions, we constrain ourselves to the 2D DCT for simplicity. Like any Fourier-related transform, DCT expresses a signal in terms of a sum of sinusoids with different frequencies and amplitudes. The general equation for 2D DCT F for a given input feature map $f_{x,y} \in \mathbb{R}^{H \times W \times C}$, where $f_{x,y}$ represents the pixel value of $H \times W$ image at point (x, y), is defined as:

$$F_{u,v} = C(u)C(v) \sum_{x=0}^{W-1} \sum_{y=0}^{H-1} f_{x,y} B_{u,v}^{x,y} \tag{1}$$

$$\text{s.t.} \quad C(u) = \begin{cases} \sqrt{\frac{1}{W}} & \text{if } u = 0 \\ \sqrt{\frac{2}{W}} & \text{otherwise} \end{cases} \quad C(v) = \begin{cases} \sqrt{\frac{1}{H}} & \text{if } v = 0 \\ \sqrt{\frac{2}{H}} & \text{otherwise} \end{cases}$$

$$B_{u,v}^{x,y} = cos(\frac{\pi u}{2W}(2x + 1))cos(\frac{\pi v}{2H}(2y + 1)) \tag{2}$$

where $B_{u,v}^{x,y}$ is a basis function of DCT. In terms of CNN, basis function can be regarded as filters/weights for convolution operations. Basis function can be pre-computed and simply looked up in DCT computation.

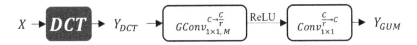

Fig. 2. Overview of GUM.

3.2 Adaptive Frequency Filtering Based Channel Attention Module (AFF-CAM)

Channel Attention. Channel attention mechanism attempts to assign different significance to the channels and reduce channel redundancy of given feature map by capturing inter-channel relationship. General equation for acquiring channel-wise attention map A, given a feature map f, can be denoted as:

$$A = \sigma(Network(compress(f))) \tag{3}$$

where σ is a sigmoid activation function, $compress$ is a operation to aggregate spatial information into a single global value, i.e., $\mathbb{R}^{H \times W \times C} \longmapsto \mathbb{R}^{1 \times 1 \times C}$, and $Network$ is a mapping function, i.e., fully-connected layer or 1D convolutional layer. There have been studies [7,18] that tried to acquire channel attention map using Fourier Transform. FcaNet is most similar to our proposed AFF-CAM, as it utilizes DCT to construct multi-spectral channel attention map. However, FcaNet exhibits three drawbacks: i) DCT feature representations are not updated globally using non-local RFs, ii) fixed number of "hand-picked" DCT filters that cannot be learned and optimized through training, and iii) large number of network parameters due to two fully-connected layers as $Network$ in Eq. 3. In the subsequent subsections, we discuss how each of our proposed submodules in AFF-CAM irons out such drawbacks.

Global Update Module (GUM). To alleviate the first issue, we propose GUM as shown by Fig. 2. Given a spatial feature map $X \in \mathbb{R}^{H \times W \times C}$, we first transform it into frequency domain by performing 2D DCT along the spatial dimensions:

$$Y_{DCT} = F[X] \in \mathbb{R}^{H \times W \times C} \tag{4}$$

where $F[\cdot]$ denotes the 2D DCT (Eq. 1). As Y_{DCT} represents the frequency spectrum of X, we then globally modulate the spectrum by performing 1×1 grouped convolution [19] with a group size of M ($GConv_{1 \times 1, M}^{c \to \frac{c}{r}}$), ReLU activation function, and 1×1 convolution operation ($Conv_{1 \times 1}^{\frac{c}{r} \to c}$):

$$Y_{GUM} = Conv_{1 \times 1}^{\frac{C}{r} \to C}(ReLU(GConv_{1 \times 1, M}^{C \to \frac{C}{r}}(Y_{DCT}))) \in \mathbb{R}^{H \times W \times C} \tag{5}$$

We control the number of parameters by adopting $C \to \frac{C}{r}$ and $\frac{C}{r} \to C$, which indicate channel reduction and channel restoration by ratio r, respectively. We set $r = 16$ for larger models, e.g., ResNet50 [2], and $r = 8$ for smaller models,

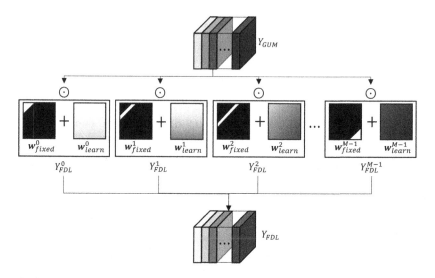

Fig. 3. Detailed overview of FDL.

e.g., ResNet-18/34 [2]. Global modulation can be implemented with 1×1 convolutional layers because point-wise update of spectrum Y_{DCT} can globally affect input feature representations X involved in DCT. We use grouped convolution with a group size of M for the first convolution operation $GConv_{1 \times 1, M}^{C \to \frac{C}{r}}$, as we will partition frequency spectrum into M different bands of frequency components in Frequency Distribution Learner. This way, each of the M different frequency distributions can be globally updated separately. Second convolution operation $Conv_{1 \times 1}^{\frac{C}{r} \to C}$ is achieved by conventional 1×1 convolutional layer as sole purpose of this operation is to restore channel dimension back to C. As a result, Y_{GUM} is able to attain long-range dependencies through the effect of using non-local RFs.

Frequency Distribution Learner (FDL). To solve the second issue, we propose FDL as demonstrated by in Fig. 3. It has been established that spectral distribution of DCT is non-uniform and most of the energy are concentrated in just a few coefficients in low frequency area. While the general consensus is to utilize low frequency components to compress and represent an image, we believe useful details can be found and learned from other frequency distributions.

To carry out this task, we first construct M different binary fixed filters $[w_{fixed}^i]_{i=1}^M$, where $w_{fixed}^i \in \mathbb{R}^{H \times W \times 1}$. As low-frequency components are placed in top-left corner and higher frequency components in the bottom-right corner of DCT spectrum, each of the M binary fixed filters are split diagonally to exploit different frequency distribution. We then add learnable filters $[w_{learn}^i]_{i=1}^M$, where $w_{learn}^i \in \mathbb{R}^{H \times W \times 1}$, to the binary fixed filters to grant more access to select the frequency of interest beyond the fixed filters. By doing so, we obtain

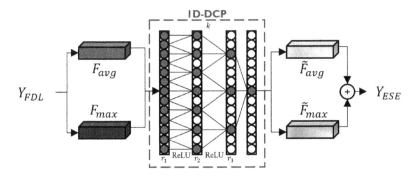

Fig. 4. Detailed overview of ESE. (Color figure online)

$w^i = [w^i_{fixed} + w^i_{learn})]^M_{i=1}$, in which we clip w^i_{learn} using Hyperbolic Tangent (tanh) to keep w^i_{learn} in a range of –1 to 1.

To apply each of obtained w^i to Y_{GUM}, we split Y_{GUM} into M parts along the channel dimension. Each of the split feature maps is denoted as:

$$Y_{GUM} = [Y^0_{GUM}; Y^1_{GUM}; \cdots, Y^{M-1}_{GUM}] \tag{6}$$

where $Y^i_{GUM} \in \mathbb{R}^{H \times W \times \frac{C}{M}}, i \in \{0, 1, \cdots, M-1\}$ and C should be divisible by M. For each Y^i_{GUM}, corresponding w^i is assigned as:

$$Y^i_{FDL} = Y^i_{GUM} \odot w^i \in \mathbb{R}^{H \times W \times \frac{C}{M}} \tag{7}$$

where $\odot$ represents element-wise multiplication. Each of the Y^i_{FDL} is then concatenated to produce the final output:

$$Y_{FDL} = concat([Y^0_{FDL}, Y^1_{FDL}, \cdots, Y^{M-1}_{FDL}]) \in \mathbb{R}^{H \times W \times C} \tag{8}$$

As a result, each $Y^i_{FDL} \in \mathbb{R}^{H \times W \times \frac{C}{M}}$ holds different information from M distinct frequency distributions.

Enhanced Squeeze-and-Excitation (ESE). To make use of the information from different frequency distributions, we introduce ESE, as depicted by Fig. 4. ESE first aggregates, or so called "squeezes", different frequency bands (e.g. low, middle, high) information of Y_{FDL} along its spectral dimensions ($height \times width$) via GAP and GMP to produce two channel context descriptors: $F_{avg} \in \mathbb{R}^{1 \times 1 \times C}$ and $F_{max} \in \mathbb{R}^{1 \times 1 \times C}$.

After, F_{avg} and F_{max} are separately forwarded to a shared network to capture cross-channel interactions and produce enhanced descriptors: $\tilde{F}_{avg}$ and $\tilde{F}_{max}$. While two FC layers are most widely used to implement a shared network, they are computationally expensive, which is our third issue. ECANet replaces two FC layer with a single 1D convolution to avoid high computation and dimension reduction that occur in typical FC frameworks [7–9,12,14,20]. While ECANet

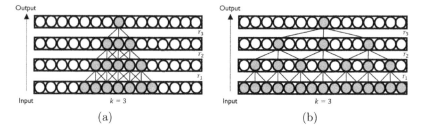

Fig. 5. Illustrations of *conventional* 1D convolution and *dilated* convolution with kernel size of $k = 3$. (a) Three-layer network using *conventional* 1D convolution operation with dilation rates $r_1 = r_2 = r_3 = 1$. (b) Three-layer network using *dilated* convolution operation with exponentially increasing dilation rates of $r_1 = 1, r_2 = 2, r_3 = 4$.

solves the computation issue, it can only capture *local* cross-channel interaction. So it can be viewed as a "partial" FC layer. We propose 1D-Dilated Convolution Pyramid (1D-DCP), as shown in orange dashed box in Fig. 4, which stacks multiple 1D convolutional layers with different dilation rates r_1, r_2, r_3 to capture *global* cross-channel interaction. Except for the last layer, each 1D convolutional layer is followed by ReLU activation function. Dilation convolution grants larger RF size by inserting spaces, i.e. zeros, between the kernel elements. For a 1D input signal $x[i]$, the output $x_{dilated}[i]$ of dilated convolution with filter $w[k]$ of length K is defined as $x_{dilated}[i] = \sum_{k=1}^{K} x[i + r \cdot k]w[k]$ where r is the dilation rate. It can be seen that when $r = 1$, dilated convolution is identical to the conventional 1D convolution operation. Figure 5 demonstrates the difference between conventional convolution and dilated convolution operated on 1D signals. Like our proposed 1D-DCP, Fig. 5 is constructed with a 3-layer structure with kernel size $k = 3$ and dilation rates r_1, r_2, r_3. Figure 5a shows that RFs of conventional 1D convolution increase linearly with the number of layers, resulting in RF of 7. However, Fig. 5b indicates that using exponentially increasing dilated rates, i.e., $r_1 = 1, r_2 = 2, r_3 = 4$, the RFs also increases exponentially to 15. Thus, by stacking multiple 1D convolutional layers with different dilation rates, our 1D-DCP can successfully capture global cross-channel interaction like a FC layer without its computation overhead. $\tilde{F}_{avg} \in \mathbb{R}^{1 \times 1 \times C}$ and $\tilde{F}_{max} \in \mathbb{R}^{1 \times 1 \times C}$ are then merged using element-wise summation to produce the output:

$$\tilde{F}_{avg} = DCP_{1D}(F_{avg}), \ \tilde{F}_{max} = DCP_{1D}(F_{max}) \tag{9}$$

$$Y_{ESE} = \tilde{F}_{avg} + \tilde{F}_{max} \in \mathbb{R}^{1 \times 1 \times C} \tag{10}$$

Channel Attention Map. Obtained Y_{ESE} then goes through sigmoid activation function σ to provide final channel attention map A:

$$A = \sigma(Y_{ESE}) \tag{11}$$

It is clearly presented that our input spatial feature map X and resulting attention map A of AFF-CAM accommodate complementary feature information; X contains low-level details, whereas A encompasses high-level semantics. By enabling effective communication between those two feature representations, our proposed AFF-CAM can simultaneously capture short-range and long-range dependencies. AFF-CAM accomplishes this by multiplying input spatial feature representation X with acquired attention map A. This lets frequency information to be a guide and modulates spatial feature representation to reason over high-level, global context. In essence, the communication between X and A is formulated as:

$$X_{enhanced} = A \otimes X \in \mathbb{R}^{H \times W \times C} \tag{12}$$

where $A \in \mathbb{R}^{1 \times 1 \times C}$, $X \in \mathbb{R}^{H \times W \times C}$, and $\otimes$ denotes element-wise product.

Table 1. Ablation study on effectiveness of M.

Model	M	Top-1 (%)	Params (M)
ResNet50	-	75.44	25.56
A	1	76.87 (+1.43)	28.12
B	4	**77.62** (+2.18)	27.22
C	8	76.36 (+0.92)	27.12
D	16	76.16 (+0.72)	27.15

Table 2. Ablation study on GUM. The results of utilizing different variations of $GConv$ and $Conv$.

Model	Method	Top-1 (%)	Params (M)
B_{GRC}	**GConv-ReLU-Conv**	**77.62**	27.22
B_{CRC}	**Conv-ReLU-Conv**	77.03	28.16
B_{GRG}	**GConv-ReLU-GConv**	75.98	26.27

4 Experiments

In this subsection, we evaluate our AFF-CAM on the widely used benchmarks: ImageNet-1k for image classification and MS COCO for object detection. We compare AFF-CAM with several state-of-the-art attention baselines built upon ResNet [2], including SENet, CBAM, GCNet, AANet, ECANet, FFC, and FcaNet.

4.1 Ablation Studies

We begin by conducting several ablation studies on ImageNet-1k dataset to empirically demonstrate the effectiveness of our network design with ResNet-50 as a baseline architecture. Initially, we experiment on how different number of partitions of frequency spectrum M in Eq. 6 affects our network in terms of accuracy and number of parameters in Table 1. For this experiment, we do not adopt our 1D-DCP sub-module into the network, as we solely want to see the effect of M. Instead, we use a single 1D convolutional layer like in ECANet. We test with $M=1$, 4, 8, and 16. Maximum value of M is 16 because of channel reduction ratio r and grouped convolution operation $GConv_{1 \times 1, M}^{C \to \frac{C}{r}}$ in Eq. 5, where $\frac{C}{r}$ needs to be divisible by M with $r = 16$. Even with added parameters from learnable filters w^i in Eq. 7, total number of parameters decreases when $M > 1$ because of the grouped convolution operation with a group size M in Eq. 5. We yield the best result of 77.62% when using $M = 4$, which significantly improves baseline ResNet50 by 2.18%. This indicates that commonly disregarded frequency distributions, such as those of middle or high frequencies, do provide meaningful feature representations and are worth giving attention to.

With obtained $M = 4$, we conduct the next experiment, where different variations of 1×1 convolution operations are adopted for GUM (Eq. 5). As demonstrated in Table 2, Model B_{GRC} outputs the best result of 77.62%. This proves that i) separately updating M different frequency components is superior to updating the whole frequency spectrum (Model B_{CRC}), and ii) sole purpose of the second convolution operation is to restore channel dimension, thus depth-wise separable convolution is not needed (Model B_{GRG}).

Next, we analyze how using different dilation rates r_1, r_2, r_3 in 1D-DCP of ESE influences our network. For this experiment, we bring the best Model B_{GRC} from above ablation study (Table 2) to be the baseline. Model $\mathrm{B}_{GRC}^{1,1,1}$ introduces the idea of stacking multiple 1D convolutional layers on top of Model B_{GRC} but does not use any dilations. Models $\mathrm{B}_{GRC}^{1,2,4}$, $\mathrm{B}_{GRC}^{1,3,9}$ and $\mathrm{B}_{GRC}^{1,4,16}$ apply exponentially increasing dilation rates. Each model's superscript indicates the applied dilation rates r_1, r_2, r_3 on to the baseline Model B_{GRC}. We generate the best result of 78.09% with Model $\mathrm{B}_{GRC}^{1,3,9}$, which improves baseline Model B_{GRC} by 0.47% without adding any trainable parameters. The result implies that stacking multiple 1D convolutions with different dilation rates enables the network to capture *global* cross-channel interactions just like a FC layer without its computation overhead.

Table 3. Ablation study on 1D-DCT. The effectiveness of different dilation rates r_1, r_2, r_3.

Model	r_1	r_2	r_3	Top-1 (%)	Params (M)
B_{GRC}	1	-	-	77.62	27.22
$\mathrm{B}_{GRC}^{1,1,1}$	1	1	1	77.77 (+0.15)	27.22
$\mathrm{B}_{GRC}^{1,2,4}$	1	2	4	77.98 (+0.36)	27.22
$\mathrm{B}_{GRC}^{1,3,9}$	1	3	9	**78.09** (+0.47)	27.22
$\mathrm{B}_{GRC}^{1,4,16}$	1	4	16	77.84 (+0.22)	27.22

Table 4. Ablation study on AFF-CAM. The effectiveness of each sub-module.

GUM	FDL	ESE	Top-1 (%)	Params (M)
-	-	-	75.44	25.56
		✓	75.91 (+0.47)	25.56
	✓	✓	76.46 (+1.02)	25.61
✓	✓	✓	78.09 (+2.65)	27.22

Finally, with selected hyper-parameters $M = 4$ (Table 1) and $r_1 = 1, r_2 = 3, r_3 = 9$ (Table 3) from above ablation studies, we establish the strength of three sub-modules of our proposed AFF-CAM in Table 4. The result indicates that the largest performance gain of 1.63% (76.46% → 78.09%) comes from adding GUM, which enables the effect of having non-local RFs and acquires long-range dependencies. With biggest performance gain, GUM is also responsible for most of the added parameters in AFF-CAM. For future works, we plan on developing a more efficient module that obtains long-range dependencies. Second biggest performance gain of 0.55% (75.91% → 76.46%) comes from adding FDL, which exploits and gives attention to commonly discarded frequency distributions. This also matches our proposed motivation that profitable feature representations can be learned not only from low frequency distribution, where majority of the information is held, but also from commonly discarded frequency distributions (Fig. 6).

Table 5. Classification results on ImageNet-1K dataset. The best Top-1/5 accuracy scores across all baselines are written in bold.

Method	Backbone	Top-1 (%)	Top-5 (%)	Params (M)	FLOPs (G)
ResNet [2]		70.40	89.45	11.69	1.814
SENet [8]	ResNet-18	70.59	89.78	11.78	1.814
CBAM [9]		70.73	89.91	11.78	1.815
AFF-CAM		**71.52**	**90.36**	11.84	1.84
ResNet [2]		73.31	91.40	21.80	3.66
SENet [8]		73.87	91.65	21.95	3.66
CBAM [9]		74.01	91.76	21.96	3.67
AANet [12]	ResNet-34	74.70	92.00	20.70	3.56
ECANet [10]		74.21	91.83	21.80	3.68
FcaNet† [7]		74.29	91.92	21.95	3.68
AFF-CAM		**74.88**	**92.27**	22.06	3.71
ResNet [2]		75.44	92.50	25.56	3.86
SENet [8]		76.86	93.30	28.09	3.86
CBAM [9]		77.34	93.69	28.09	3.86
GCNet [14]		77.70	93.66	28.11	4.13
AANet [12]	ResNet-50	77.70	93.80	25.80	4.15
ECANet [10]		77.48	93.68	25.56	3.86
FFC [17]		77.80	-	27.70	4.50
FcaNet† [7]		77.29	93.67	28.07	4.13
AFF-CAM		**78.09**	**93.82**	27.22	4.39

*All results are reproduced with the same training settings.
FcaNet† is reproduced as official code utilizes different training strategies.

4.2   Image Classification on ImageNet-1K

To evaluate the results of the proposed AFF-CAM framework on ImageNet, we employ three ResNet backbone architectures, e.g. ResNet-18, ResNet-34, and ResNet-50. We adopt the same data augmentation scheme as ResNet for training and apply single cropping with the size of 224×224 for testing. The optimizer is performed by Stochastic Gradient Descent (SGD) with momentum of 0.9 and weight decay of 1e−4. The learning rate starts with 0.1 and drops every 30 epochs. All models are trained for 90 epochs with mini-batch size of 1024 for smaller models (e.g. ResNet-18/34) and 512 for bigger models (e.g. ResNet-50) on each of the 4 A100-SXM GPUs. Table 5 summarizes the experimental results.

When using **ResNet-18** as backbone architecture, AFF-CAM outperforms the baseline ResNet-18 by 1.12% and surpasses current state-of-the-art CBAM by 0.79% for Top-1 accuracy. When using **ResNet-34** as backbone architecture, AFF-CAM outperforms the baseline ResNet-34 by 1.57% and surpasses current state-of-the-art AANet by 0.18% for Top-1 accuracy. When using **ResNet-50**as backbone architecture, AFF-CAM outperforms the baseline ResNet-50 by 2.65% and surpasses current state-of-the-art FFC by 0.29% for Top-1 accuracy.

4.3   Object Detection on MS COCO

In this subsection, we evaluate our AFF-CAM framework on object detection task to verify its general applicability across different tasks. We utilize Faster R-CNN [21] as baseline detector and ResNet-50 with Feature Pyramid Network (FPN) [22] as backbone architecture. For training implementation, we adopt MMDetection [23] toolkit and use its default settings as choice of hyper-parameters. Optimizer is executed with SGD with momentum of 0.9 and weight decay of 1e−4. The learning rate is initialized to 0.01 and drops by the factor of 10 at 8th and 11th epochs. All models are trained for 12 epochs with mini-batch size of 4 on each of the 4 A100-SXM GPUs. As shown in Table 6, our AFF-CAM framework proves its generalization ability. Without bells and whistles, our AFF-CAM outperforms baseline ResNet-50 by 3.4% and surpasses current state-of-the-art FcaNet by 0.8% for Average Precision (AP).

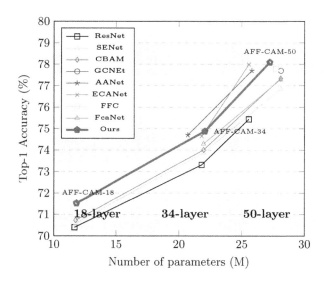

Fig. 6. ImageNet-1K Top-1 Accuracy vs. Model Complexity.

Table 6. Object detection results on MS COCO val 2017 dataset. The best Average Precision score is written in bold.

Method	Backbone	Detector	AP (%)	AP_{50} (%)	AP_{75} (%)	AP_S (%)	AP_M (%)	AP_L (%)
ResNet [2]			36.4	58.2	39.2	21.8	40.0	46.2
SENet [8]			37.7	60.1	40.9	22.9	41.9	48.2
ECANet [10]	ResNet-50	Faster-RCNN [21]	38.0	60.6	40.9	23.4	42.1	48.0
FcaNet [7]			39.0	60.9	42.3	23.0	42.9	49.9
AFF-CAM			**39.8**	60.7	43.6	22.8	42.4	51.0

*All results are reproduced with the same training settings.

5   Conclusions

In this paper, we propose a novel AFF-CAM that effectively explores the details of different frequency bands through DCT. While most information is stored in lower DCT coefficients, our method exploits other discarded frequency spectrum and adaptively re-calibrates channel-wise feature responses by efficiently modeling global inter-dependencies between channels. Furthermore, our method takes advantage of the fact that point-wise update in frequency domain globally affects input features associated in DCT. As a result, our method is able to implement the ensemble of local and non-local receptive fields in a single unit. Comprehensive experiments are conducted on ImageNet-1K classification and MS COCO detection datasets to demonstrate the applicability of AFF-CAM across different architectures, as well as different tasks. The results display consistent performance improvements that are clearly attributed to our proposed motivations.

Acknowledgement. This research was supported by the Challengeable Future Defense Technology Research and Development Program through the Agency For Defense Development (ADD) funded by the Defense Acquisition Program Administration (DAPA) in 2022 (No. 915034201).

References

1. Szegedy, C., et al.: Going deeper with convolutions. In: Proceedings of the IEEE Conference on Computer Vision and Pattern Recognition, pp. 1–9 (2015)
2. He, K., Zhang, X., Ren, S., Sun, J.: Deep residual learning for image recognition. In: Proceedings of the IEEE Conference on Computer Vision and Pattern Recognition, pp. 770–778 (2016)
3. Zagoruyko, S., Komodakis, N.: Wide residual networks. arXiv preprint arXiv:1605.07146 (2016)
4. Chollet, F.: Xception: deep learning with depthwise separable convolutions. In: Proceedings of the IEEE Conference on Computer Vision and Pattern Recognition, pp. 1251–1258 (2017)

5. Xie, S., Girshick, R., Dollár, P., Tu, Z., He, K.: Aggregated residual transformations for deep neural networks. In: Proceedings of the IEEE Conference on Computer Vision and Pattern Recognition, pp. 1492–1500 (2017)
6. Luo, W., Li, Y., Urtasun, R., Zemel, R.: Understanding the effective receptive field in deep convolutional neural networks. In: Proceedings of the 30th International Conference on Neural Information Processing Systems, pp. 4905–4913 (2016)
7. Qin, Z., Zhang, P., Wu, F., Li, X.: Fcanet: frequency channel attention networks. In: Proceedings of the IEEE/CVF International Conference on Computer Vision, pp. 783–792 (2021)
8. Hu, J., Shen, L., Sun, G.: Squeeze-and-excitation networks. In: Proceedings of the IEEE Conference on Computer Vision and Pattern Recognition, pp. 7132–7141 (2018)
9. Woo, S., Park, J., Lee, J.-Y., Kweon, I.S.: CBAM: convolutional block attention module. In: Ferrari, V., Hebert, M., Sminchisescu, C., Weiss, Y. (eds.) ECCV 2018. LNCS, vol. 11211, pp. 3–19. Springer, Cham (2018). https://doi.org/10.1007/978-3-030-01234-2_1
10. Wang, Q., Wu, B., Zhu, P., Li, P., Zuo, W., Hu, Q.: Eca-net: efficient channel attention for deep convolutional neural networks (2020)
11. Yu, F., Koltun, V.: Multi-scale context aggregation by dilated convolutions. arXiv preprint arXiv:1511.07122 (2015)
12. Bello, I., Zoph, B., Vaswani, A., Shlens, J., Le, Q.V.: Attention augmented convolutional networks. In: Proceedings of the IEEE/CVF International Conference on Computer Vision, 3286–3295 (2019)
13. Vaswani, A., et al.: Attention is all you need. Advances in neural information processing systems 30 (2017)
14. Cao, Y., Xu, J., Lin, S., Wei, F., Hu, H.: Gcnet: non-local networks meet squeeze-excitation networks and beyond. In: Proceedings of the IEEE/CVF International Conference on Computer Vision Workshops (2019)
15. Wang, X., Girshick, R., Gupta, A., He, K.: Non-local neural networks. In: Proceedings of the IEEE Conference on Computer Vision and Pattern Recognition, pp. 7794–7803 (2018)
16. Mathieu, M., Henaff, M., LeCun, Y.: Fast training of convolutional networks through ffts. arXiv preprint arXiv:1312.5851 (2013)
17. Chi, L., Jiang, B., Mu, Y.: Fast fourier convolution. Advances in Neural Information Processing Systems 33 (2020)
18. Lee-Thorp, J., Ainslie, J., Eckstein, I., Ontanon, S.: Fnet: Mixing tokens with fourier transforms. arXiv preprint arXiv:2105.03824 (2021)
19. Krizhevsky, A., Sutskever, I., Hinton, G.E.: Imagenet classification with deep convolutional neural networks. Advances in neural information processing systems 25 (2012)
20. Zhang, H., Zu, K., Lu, J., Zou, Y., Meng, D.: Epsanet: an efficient pyramid squeeze attention block on convolutional neural network. arXiv preprint arXiv:2105.14447 (2021)
21. Ren, S., He, K., Girshick, R., Sun, J.: Faster R-CNN: towards real-time object detection with region proposal networks. Advances in neural information processing systems 28 (2015)
22. Lin, T.Y., Dollár, P., Girshick, R., He, K., Hariharan, B., Belongie, S.: Feature pyramid networks for object detection. In: Proceedings of the IEEE Conference on Computer Vision and Pattern Recognition, pp. 2117–2125 (2017)
23. Chen, K., et al.: Mmdetection: open mmlab detection toolbox and benchmark. arXiv preprint arXiv:1906.07155 (2019)

Inverting Adversarially Robust Networks for Image Synthesis

Renan A. Rojas-Gomez[1]([✉]), Raymond A. Yeh[2], Minh N. Do[1], and Anh Nguyen[3]

[1] University of Illinois at Urbana -Champaign, Champaign, USA
{renanar2,minhdo}@illinois.edu
[2] Purdue University, West Lafayette, USA
rayyeh@purdue.edu
[3] Auburn University, Auburn, USA
anh.ng8@gmail.com

Abstract. Despite unconditional feature inversion being the foundation of many image synthesis applications, training an inverter demands a high computational budget, large decoding capacity and imposing conditions such as autoregressive priors. To address these limitations, we propose the use of adversarially robust representations as a perceptual primitive for feature inversion. We train an adversarially robust encoder to extract disentangled and perceptually-aligned image representations, making them easily invertible. By training a simple generator with the mirror architecture of the encoder, we achieve superior reconstruction quality and generalization over standard models. Based on this, we propose an adversarially robust autoencoder and demonstrate its improved performance on style transfer, image denoising and anomaly detection tasks. Compared to recent ImageNet feature inversion methods, our model attains improved performance with significantly less complexity. Code available at https://github.com/renanrojasg/adv_robust_autoencoder.

1 Introduction

Deep classifiers trained on large-scale datasets extract meaningful high-level features of natural images, making them an essential tool for manipulation tasks such as style transfer [1–3], image inpainting [4,5], image composition [6,7], among others [8–10]. State-of-the-art image manipulation techniques use a decoder [5,10], *i.e.*, an *image generator*, to create natural images from high-level features. Extensive work has explored how to train image generators, leading to models with photorealistic results [11]. Moreover, by learning how to invert deep features, image generators enable impressive synthesis use cases such as anomaly detection [12,13] and neural network visualization [7,14–16].

Supplementary Information The online version contains supplementary material available at https://doi.org/10.1007/978-3-031-26351-4_24.

Inverting ImageNet features is a challenging task that often requires the generator to be more complex than the encoder [5,17–19], incurring in a high computational cost. Donahue et al. [17] explained this shortcoming by the fact that the encoder bottleneck learns entangled representations that are hard to invert. An alternative state-of-the-art technique for inverting ImageNet features requires, in addition to the encoder and decoder CNNs, *an extra* autoregressive model and vector quantization [20,21] or a separate invertible network [16].

In this paper, we propose **a novel mechanism for training effective ImageNet autoencoders that do not require extra decoding layers or networks besides the encoder and its mirror decoder**. Specifically, we adopt a pre-trained classifier as encoder and train an image generator to invert its features, yielding an autoencoder for real data. Unlike existing works that use feature extractors trained on natural images, we train the encoder on adversarial examples [22]. This fundamental difference equips our *adversarially robust* (AR) autoencoder with representations that are perceptually-aligned with human vision [9,23], resulting in favorable inversion properties.

To show the advantages of learning how to invert AR features, our generator corresponds to the *mirror* architecture of the encoder, without additional decoding layers [6,17] or extra components [16,20,21,24,25]. To the best of our knowledge, we are the first to show the benefits of training an autoencoder on both adversarial and real images. Our main findings are as follows:

- A generator trained to invert AR features has a substantially higher reconstruction quality than those trained on standard features. Our method generalizes to different models (AlexNet [26], VGG-16 [27], and ResNet [28]) and datasets (CIFAR-10 [29] and ImageNet [30]) (Sect. 5.1).
- Our proposed AR autoencoder is remarkably robust to resolution changes, as shown on natural and upscaled high-resolution images (Fig. 8). Experiments on DIV2K [31] show it accurately reconstructs high-resolution images without any finetuning, despite being trained on low-resolution images (Sect. 5.3).
- Our generator outperforms state-of-the-art inversion methods based on iterative optimization techniques [23] in terms of PSNR, SSIM, and LPIPS [10]. It also attains comparable accuracy to the well-established DeepSiM model [32] with a much lower model complexity (Sect. 5.4).
- Our AR model outperforms standard baselines on three downstream tasks: style transfer [2], image denoising [5] (Sect. 6) and anomaly detection [12]. The latter is covered in detail in the Appendix (Sect. A1).

2   Related Work

Inverting Neural Networks. Prior work exploring deep feature inversion using optimization approaches are either limited to per-pixel priors or require multiple steps to converge and are sensitive to initialization [9,23,33,34]. Instead, we propose to map contracted features to images via a generator, following the work by Dosovitskiy et al. [19] and similar synthesis techniques [5–7]. By combining natural priors and AR features, we get a significant reconstruction improvement with much less trainable parameters.

Our results are consistent to prior findings on AR features being more invertible via optimization [23] and more useful for transfer learning [35]. As part of our contribution, we complement these by showing that (i) learning a map from the AR feature space to the image domain largely outperforms the original optimization approach, (ii) such an improvement generalizes to models of different complexity, and (iii) inverting AR features shows remarkable robustness to scale changes. We also show AR encoders with higher robustness can be more easily decoded, revealing potential security issues [36].

Regularized Autoencoders. Prior work requiring data augmentation to train generative and autoencoding models often requires learning an invertible transformation that maps augmented samples back to real data [37]. Instead, our approach can be seen as a novel way to regularize bottleneck features, providing an alternative to contractive, variational and sparse autoencoders [11,38,39].

3   Preliminaries

Our model exploits AR representations to reconstruct high-quality images, which is related to the feature inversion framework. Specifically, we explore AR features as a strong prior to obtain photorealism. For a clear understanding of our proposal, we review fundamental concepts of feature inversion and AR training.

Feature Inversion. Consider a target image $x_0 \in \mathbb{R}^{W \times H \times C}$ and its contracted representation $f_0 \triangleq F_\theta(x_0) \in \mathbb{R}^{W' \times H' \times C'}$. Here, F_θ denotes the target model, *e.g.* AlexNet, with parameters $\theta \in \mathbb{R}^T$ and $W'H'C' \ll WHC$. Features extracted by F_θ encapsulate rich input information that can either be used for the task it was trained on, transferred to a related domain [40] or used for applications such as image enhancement and manipulation [1,41].

An effective way to leverage these representations is by training a second model, a generator, to map them to the pixel domain. This way, deep features can be manipulated and transformed into images [19,32]. Also, since deep features preserve partial input information, inverting them elucidates what kind of attributes they encode. Based on these, *feature inversion* [32,33,42] has been extensively studied for visualization and understanding purposes as well as for synthesis and manipulation tasks. Typically, feature inversion is formulated as an optimization problem:

$$\hat{x} = \arg\min_x \mathcal{F}(F_\theta(x), f_0) + \lambda \mathcal{R}(x), \tag{1}$$

where $\hat{x}$ is the estimated image and $\mathcal{F}(F_\theta(x), f_0)$ the fidelity term between estimated and target representations, $F_\theta(x)$ and f_0 respectively. $\mathcal{R}(x)$ denotes the regularization term imposing *apriori* constraints in the pixel domain and $\lambda \in \mathbb{R}_{++}$ balances between fidelity and regularization terms.

Adversarial Robustness. Adversarial training adds perturbations to the input data and lets the network learn how to classify in the presence of such adversarial attacks [22,43,44]. Consider the image classification task with annotated dataset $\mathcal{K}$. Let an annotated pair correspond to image $x \in \mathbb{R}^{W \times H \times C}$ and

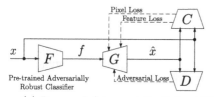

(a) Proposed Adversarially Robust Model

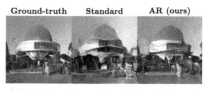

(b) Feature Inversion (224 × 224 px.)

Fig. 1. By training it to invert adversarially robust features, our proposed autoencoder obtains better reconstructions than models trained on standard features.

its one-hot encoded label $y \in \{0,1\}^{|\mathcal{C}|}$, where $\mathcal{C}$ is the set of possible classes. From the definition by Madry et al. [22], a perturbed input is denoted by $x' = x + \delta$, where x' is the perturbed sample and δ the perturbation. Let the set of perturbations be bounded by the ℓ_p ball for $p \in \{2, \infty\}$, $\mathcal{S} : \{\delta, \|\delta\|_p \le \varepsilon\}$. Then, the AR training corresponds to an optimization problem:

$$\tilde{\theta} = \arg \min_{\theta} \mathbb{E}_{(x,y) \sim \mathcal{K}} \left[\max_{\delta \in \mathcal{S}} \mathcal{L}_{x',y}(\theta) \right], \tag{2}$$

where $\tilde{\theta} \in \mathbb{R}^T$ are the optimal weights and $\mathcal{L}_{x',y}(\theta)$ the negative log-likelihood. The goal is to minimize $\mathcal{L}_{x',y}(\theta)$ in the presence of the worst possible adversary.

4   Proposed Method

4.1   Adversarially Robust Autoencoder

We propose an autoencoder architecture (Fig. 1) to extract bottleneck AR features of arbitrary input images, manipulate them for a given synthesis task, and map the results back to images. We denote the AR feature extractor as $F_{\tilde{\theta}}$, where $\tilde{\theta}$ are the AR model weights, as explained in Sect. 3. Robust features are transformed into images using a CNN-based generator denoted as $G_{\tilde{\phi}}$. Here, $\tilde{\phi}$ are the generator weights learned by inverting AR features.

Following prior works [19,45], we use AlexNet as the encoder and extract AR features from its conv5 layer. We also explore more complex encoders from the VGG and ResNet families and evaluate their improvement over standard encoders (See Sect. A4.1 for architecture details).

4.2   Image Decoder: Optimization Criteria

Given a pre-trained AR encoder $F_{\tilde{\theta}}$, the generator $G_{\tilde{\phi}}$ is trained using ℓ_1 pixel, ℓ_2 feature and GAN losses, where the feature loss matches AR representations, known to be *perceptually aligned* [23].

In more detail, we denote $\hat{x} = G_{\tilde{\phi}}(f)$ to be the reconstruction of image x, where $f = F_{\tilde{\theta}}(x)$ are its AR features. Training the generator with fixed encoder's weights $\tilde{\theta}$ corresponds to the following optimization problem:

$$\tilde{\phi} = \arg \min_{\phi} \lambda_{\text{pix}} \mathcal{L}_{\text{pix}}(\phi) + \lambda_{\text{feat}} \mathcal{L}_{\text{feat}}(\phi, \tilde{\theta}) + \lambda_{\text{adv}} \mathcal{L}_{\text{adv}}(\phi, \psi), \tag{3}$$

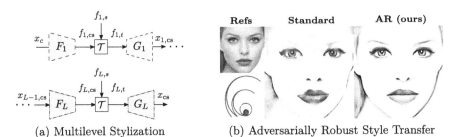

(a) Multilevel Stylization

(b) Adversarially Robust Style Transfer

Fig. 2. Example-based Style Transfer using adversarially robust features.

$$\mathcal{L}_{\text{pix}}(\phi) \triangleq \mathbb{E}_{x \sim \tilde{\mathcal{K}}} \|x - G_{\phi}(f)\|_1, \tag{4}$$

$$\mathcal{L}_{\text{feat}}(\phi, \tilde{\theta}) \triangleq \mathbb{E}_{x \sim \tilde{\mathcal{K}}} \|f - F_{\tilde{\theta}} \circ G_{\phi}(f)\|_2^2, \tag{5}$$

$$\mathcal{L}_{\text{adv}}(\phi, \psi) \triangleq \mathbb{E}_{x \sim \tilde{\mathcal{K}}} \left[-\log D_{\psi} \circ G_{\phi}(f) \right], \tag{6}$$

where $\lambda_{\text{pix}}, \lambda_{\text{feat}}, \lambda_{\text{adv}} \in \mathbb{R}_{++}$ are hyperparameters, $D_{\psi} : \mathbb{R}^{W \times H \times C} \mapsto [0,1]$ denotes the discriminator with weights ψ and predicts the probability of an image being real. The pixel loss $\mathcal{L}_{\text{pix}}(\phi)$ is the ℓ_1 distance between prediction $G_{\phi}(f)$ and target x. The feature loss $\mathcal{L}_{\text{feat}}(\phi, \theta)$ is the ℓ_2 distance between the AR features of prediction and target. The adversarial loss $\mathcal{L}_{\text{adv}}(\phi, \psi)$ maximizes the discriminator score of predictions, *i.e.*, it increases the chance the discriminator classifies them as real. On the other hand, the discriminator weights are trained via the cross-entropy loss, *i.e.*,

$$\min_{\psi} \mathcal{L}_{\text{disc}}(\phi, \psi) \triangleq \mathbb{E}_{x \sim \tilde{\mathcal{K}}} \left[-\log D_{\psi}(x) - \log(1 - D_{\psi} \circ G_{\phi}(f)) \right]. \tag{7}$$

This discriminative loss $\mathcal{L}_{\text{disc}}(\phi, \psi)$ guides D_{ψ} to maximize the score of real images and minimize the score of reconstructed (fake) images. Similar to traditional GAN algorithms, we alternate between the generator and discriminator training to reach the equilibrium point.

4.3   Applications

The trained AR autoencoder can be used to improve the performance of tasks such as style transfer [2], image denoising [46], and anomaly detection [12]. In what follows, we describe the use of our model on style transfer and image denoising. The task of anomaly detection is covered in the Appendix (Sect. A1).

Example-Based Style Transfer. Style transfer [1] aligns deep features to impose perceptual properties of a style image x_s over semantic properties of a content image x_c. This is done by matching the content and style distributions in the latent space of a pre-trained encoder to then transform the resulting features back into images. We adopt the Universal Style Transfer framework [2] to show the benefits of using our AR model for stylization (Fig. 2).

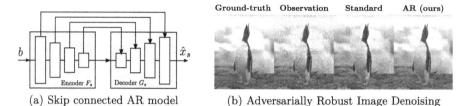

(a) Skip connected AR model   (b) Adversarially Robust Image Denoising

Fig. 3. Image denoising using our adversarially robust autoencoder.

Table 1. AlexNet feature inversion on ImageNet. Under distinct training losses, inverting AR features via our proposed generator is consistently more accurate than inverting standard features.

Losses	Model	PSNR (dB)↑	SSIM↑	LPIPS↓
Pixel	Standard	17.562 ± 2.564	0.454 ± 0.167	0.624 ± 0.099
	AR (ours)	$\mathbf{19.904 \pm 2.892}$	$\mathbf{0.505 \pm 0.169}$	$\mathbf{0.596 \pm 0.104}$
Pixel, Feature	Standard	14.462 ± 1.884	0.103 ± 0.044	0.713 ± 0.046
	AR (ours)	$\mathbf{17.182 \pm 2.661}$	$\mathbf{0.284 \pm 0.111}$	$\mathbf{0.601 \pm 0.034}$
Pixel, Feature, GAN	Standard	15.057 ± 2.392	0.307 ± 0.158	$\mathbf{0.547 \pm 0.055}$
	AR (ours)	$\mathbf{17.227 \pm 2.725}$	$\mathbf{0.358 \pm 0.163}$	0.567 ± 0.056

We train three AR AlexNet autoencoders $\{F_{l,\tilde{\theta}}, G_{l,\tilde{\phi}}\}_{l=1}^{L=3}$ and use them to sequentially align features at each scale. $F_{1,\tilde{\theta}}$, $F_{2,\tilde{\theta}}$ and $F_{3,\tilde{\theta}}$ extract AR conv5, conv2 and conv1 features, respectively. First, style features $f_{l,s} = F_{l,\tilde{\theta}}(x_s)$ are extracted at each stage. We then use the content image as initialization for the stylized output $x_{0,cs} \triangleq x_c$ and extract its conv5 features $f_{1,cs} = F_{1,\tilde{\theta}}(x_{0,cs})$.

At stage $l = 1$, the style distribution is imposed over the content features by using the whitening and coloring transform [2,47] denoted by $\mathcal{T}$. The resulting representation $f_{1,t} = \mathcal{T}(f_{1,s}, f_{1,cs})$ is characterized by the first and second moments of the style distribution. An intermediate stylized image $x_{1,cs}$ incorporating the style at the first scale is then generated as $x_{1,cs} = G_{1,\tilde{\phi}}(f_{1,t})$.

The process is repeated for $l \in \{2,3\}$ to incorporate the style at finer resolutions, resulting in the final stylized image $x_{cs} = x_{3,cs}$.

Image Denoising. Motivated by denoising autoencoders (DAE) [46] where meaningful features are extracted from distorted instances, we leverage AR features for image enhancement tasks. Similarly to deep denoising models [48], we incorporate skip connections in our pre-trained AR AlexNet autoencoder to extract features at different scales, complementing the information distilled at the encoder bottleneck (Fig. 3). Skip connections correspond to Wavelet Pooling [3], replacing pooling and upsampling layers by analysis and synthesis Haar wavelet operators, respectively. Our skip-connected model is denoted by $\{F_{s,\tilde{\theta}}, G_{s,\tilde{\phi}}\}$.

Similarly to real quantization scenarios [49–51], we assume images are corrupted by clipped additive Gaussian noise. A noisy image is denoted by $b = \rho(x + \eta) \in \mathbb{R}^{W \times H \times C}$, where $\eta \sim \mathcal{N}(0, \sigma)$ is the additive white Gaussian noise term and $\rho(x) = \max[0, \min(1, x)]$ a pointwise operator restricting the range between 0 and 1. Denoised images are denoted by $\hat{x}_s = G_{s, \tilde{\phi}} \circ F_{s, \tilde{\theta}}(b)$.

$G_{s, \tilde{\phi}}$ is trained to recover an image x from the features of its corrupted version $F_{s, \tilde{\theta}}(b)$. The training process uses the optimization criteria described in Sect. 4.2.

5   Experiments on Feature Inversion

We begin analyzing the reconstruction accuracy achieved by inverting features from different classifiers and empirically show that learning how to invert AR features via our proposed generator improves over standard feature inversion. Refer to Sect. A2 and Sect. A4 for additional inversion results and training details.

G. truth	Standard Pix.	AR (ours) Pix.	Standard Pix., Feat.	AR (ours) Pix., Feat.	Standard Pix., Feat., GAN	AR (ours) Pix., Feat., GAN

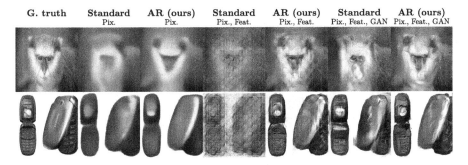

Fig. 4. AlexNet feature inversion on ImageNet. Conv5 features are inverted using our proposed generator under three different training criteria. Reconstructions from AR features are more faithful to the ground-truth image.

5.1   Reconstruction Accuracy of AR Autoencoders

Inverting AlexNet features. Standard and AR AlexNet autoencoders are trained as described in Sect. 4.1 on ImageNet for comparison purposes. The AR AlexNet classifier is trained via ℓ_2-PGD attacks [22] of radius $\varepsilon = \frac{3}{255}$ and 7 steps of size 0.5. Training is performed using 90 epochs via SGD with a learning rate of 0.1 reduced 10 times every 30 epochs. On the other hand, the standard AlexNet classifier is trained on natural images via cross-entropy (CE) loss with the same SGD setup as in the AR case.

Next, generators are trained using pixel, feature and GAN losses to invert AlexNet conv5 features (size $6 \times 6 \times 256$). Both AR and standard models use the same generator architecture, which corresponds to the mirror network of the encoder. We deliberately use a simple architecture to highlight the reconstruction

Table 2. AR VGG-16 [52] feature inversion on ImageNet. Training our generator via pixel and feature losses, reconstruction largely improves by inverting AR representations.

	Standard model	AR model (ours)
Standard accuracy	65.0	48.7
ℓ_∞ PGD Accuracy	0	23.0
PSNR (dB) ↑	18.35 ± 2.471	**21.063 ± 3.132**
SSIM ↑	0.466 ± 0.2	**0.538 ± 0.165**
LPIPS ↓	0.327 ± 0.101	**0.225 ± 0.057**

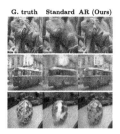

G. truth   Standard   AR (Ours)

Fig. 5. AR VGG-16 reconstruction on ImageNet.

improvement is due to inverting AR features and not the generator capacity. We also train generators using (i) pixel and (ii) pixel and feature losses to ablate their effect. Reconstruction quality is evaluated using PSNR, SSIM and LPIPS.

Under all three loss combinations, reconstructions from AR AlexNet features obtain better PSNR and SSIM than their standard counterparts (Table 1). Specifically, inverting AR AlexNet features gives an average PSNR improvement of over 2 dB in all three cases. LPIPS scores also improve, except when using pixel, feature and GAN losses. Nevertheless, inverting AR features obtain a strong PSNR and SSIM improvement in this case as well. Qualitatively, inverting AR features better preserves the natural appearance in all cases, reducing the checkerboard effect and retaining sharp edges (Fig. 4).

Inverting VGG Features. We extend the analysis to VGG-16 trained on ImageNet-143 and evaluate the reconstruction improvement achieved by inverting its AR features. We use the AR pre-trained classifier from the recent work by Liu et al. [52] trained using ℓ_∞-PGD attacks of radius $\varepsilon = 0.01$ and 10 steps of size $\frac{1}{50}$. Training is performed using 80 epochs via SGD with a learning rate of 0.1 reduced 10 times every 30, 20, 20 and 10 epochs. On the other hand, its standard version is trained on natural images via CE loss with the same SGD setup as in the AR case.

Generators are trained on pixel and feature losses to invert VGG-16 conv5_1 features (size $14 \times 14 \times 512$). Similarly to the AlexNet analysis, generators inverting both standard and AR features correspond to the mirror network of the encoder. We evaluate the reconstruction accuracy of both models and report their level of adversarial robustness (Table 2 and Fig. 5).

Quantitatively, reconstructions from AR VGG-16 features are more accurate than those of standard features in PSNR, SSIM and LPIPS by a large margin. Specifically, inverting AR VGG-16 features gives an average PSNR improvement of 2.7 dB. Qualitatively, reconstructions from AR VGG-16 features are more similar to the original images, reducing artifacts and preserving object boundaries.

Furthermore, the reconstruction accuracy attained by the AR VGG-16 autoencoder improves over that of the AR AlexNet model. This suggests that

Table 3. AR WideResNet-28-10 [53] feature inversion on CIFAR-10. Inverting AR features via our generator trained on pixel and feature losses significantly improves reconstruction.

	Standard model	AR Model (ours)
Standard accuracy	93.8	89.36
Autoattack [54]	0	59.64
PSNR (dB) ↑	17.38 ± 2.039	$\mathbf{22.14 \pm 1.626}$
SSIM ↑	0.59 ± 0.1	$\mathbf{0.81 \pm 0.067}$
LPIPS ↓	0.2547 ± 0.055	$\mathbf{0.2318 \pm 0.0833}$

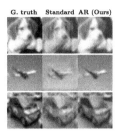

G. truth   Standard   AR (Ours)

Fig. 6. AR WideResNet-28-10 reconstruction on CIFAR-10.

the benefits of inverting AR features are not constrained to shallow models such as AlexNet, but generalize to models with larger capacity.

Inverting ResNet Features. To analyze the effect of inverting AR features from classifiers trained on different datasets, we evaluate the reconstruction accuracy obtained by inverting WideResNet-28-10 trained on CIFAR-10. We use the AR pre-trained classifier from the recent work by Zhang et al. [53]. This model obtains State-of-the-art AR classification accuracy via a novel weighted adversarial training regime. Specifically, the model is adversarially trained via PGD by ranking the importance of each sample based on how close it is to the decision boundary (how *attackable* the sample is).

AR training is performed using ℓ_∞ attacks of radius $\varepsilon = \frac{8}{255}$ and 10 steps of size $\frac{2}{255}$. Classification training is performed using 100 epochs (with a burn-in period of 30 epochs) via SGD with a learning rate of 0.1 reduced 10 times every 30 epochs. On the other hand, its standard version is trained on natural images via CE loss using the same SGD setup as in the AR case.

Generators for standard and AR WideResNet-28-10 models are trained to invert features from its 3rd residual block (size $8 \times 8 \times 640$) via pixel and feature losses. Similarly to our previous analysis, both generators correspond to the mirror architecture of the encoder. We evaluate their reconstruction via PSNR, SSIM and LPIPS, and their robustness via AutoAttack [54] (Table 3 and Fig. 6).

Similarly to previous scenarios, inverting WideResNet-28-10 AR features shows a large improvement over standard ones in all metrics. Specifically, inverting AR features increases PSNR in 4.8 dB on average over standard features. Visually, the AR WideResNet-28-10 autoencoder reduces bogus components and preserves object contours on CIFAR-10 test samples.

Overall, results enforce our claim that the **benefits of inverting AR features extend to different models, datasets and training strategies**.

Table 4. Reconstruction vs. Robustness. Experiments on ImageNet show that learning to invert AlexNet features with different AR levels can significantly improve the reconstruction accuracy.

	ℓ_2 PGD attack (ε)				
	0	0.5	2	3	4
Standard accuracy	53.69	49.9	43.8	39.83	36.31
AutoAttack [54]	8.19 ($\varepsilon = 0.5$)	48.0 ($\varepsilon = 0.5$)	28.0 ($\varepsilon = 2$)	22.27 ($\varepsilon = 3$)	14.9 ($\varepsilon = 4$)
PSNR (dB) ↑	13.12	14.41	15.5	15.53	**15.61**
SSIM ↑	0.20	0.26	**0.3**	0.26	0.25
LPIPS ↓	0.657	0.625	**0.614**	0.629	0.644

Table 5. Reconstructing upscaled ImageNet samples. Images upscaled by a factor L are reconstructed from their standard and AR AlexNet features. In contrast to the degraded standard reconstructions, AR reconstructions show an outstanding accuracy that improves for large scaling factors.

L	Standard AlexNet			Robust AlexNet		
	PSNR (dB)↑	SSIM↑	LPIPS↓	PSNR (dB)↑	SSIM↑	LPIPS↓
1	15.057	0.3067	0.5473	17.2273	0.3580	0.5665
4	15.4258	0.4655	0.4136	22.575	0.5892	0.4012
7	13.8922	0.4852	0.4587	23.5778	0.6588	0.3898
10	13.1013	0.4969	0.486	23.9566	0.7244	0.3892

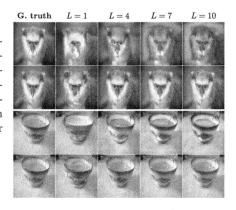

G. truth $L = 1$ $L = 4$ $L = 7$ $L = 10$

Fig. 7. Upscaled ImageNet samples reconstructed from their standard (top row) and AR (bottom row) features.

Table 6. High-resolution images inverted using our AR AlexNet model (trained on low resolution images) show improved quality over standard inversions.

Encoder	PSNR (dB)↑	SSIM↑	LPIPS↓
Standard	14.266 ± 1.9015	0.3874 ± 0.151	0.5729 ± 0.0465
AR (ours)	**18.3606 ± 2.6012**	**0.4388 ± 0.1508**	**0.5673 ± 0.0337**

5.2   Robustness Level vs. Reconstruction Accuracy

We complement the reconstruction analysis by exploring the relation between adversarial robustness and inversion quality. We train five AlexNet classifiers on ImageNet, one on natural images (standard) and four via ℓ_2-PGD attacks with $\varepsilon \in \{0.5, 2, 3, 4\}/255$. All other training parameters are identical across models.

For each classifier, an image generator is trained on an ImageNet subset via pixel, feature and GAN losses to invert conv5 features. Similar to Sect. 5.1, all five generators correspond to the mirror network of the encoder. To realiably measure the impact of adversarial robustness, reconstruction accuracy is evaluated in terms of PSNR, SSIM and LPIPS. We also report the effective robustness level achieved by each model via AutoAttack (Table 4).

Ground-truth   Standard   AR (Ours)   Ground-truth   Standard   AR (Ours)

Fig. 8. At a resolution of 2040 × 1536 px., 10 times larger than training samples, standard reconstructions on DIV2K show color and structure degradation. In contrast, reconstructions from our AR model do not suffer from distortions.

Results show LPIPS and SSIM improve almost monotonically until a maximum value is reached at $\varepsilon = 2$, while PSNR keeps increasing. This implies that just by changing ε from 0.5 to 4 while keeping the exact same architecture and training regime, a reconstruction improvement of 1.2 dB PSNR is obtained.

Based on this, we use an AR AlexNet model trained with $\varepsilon = 3$ in our experiments, which gives the best tradeoff between PSNR, SSIM and LPIPS. Overall, our analysis suggests that, while all four AR models outperform the inversion accuracy of the standard model, the reconstruction improvement is not proportional to the robustness level. Instead, it is maximized at a particular level. Please refer to Sect. A2.3 for additional robustness level vs. reconstruction accuracy experiments on ResNet-18 pointing to the same conclusion.

5.3 Reconstructing Images at Unseen Resolutions

Unlike extracting shift-invariant representations, image scaling is difficult to handle for standard CNN-based models [55,56]. Following previous work suggesting AR features are more generic and transferable than standard ones [35,57], we test whether our proposed AR autoencoder generalizes better to scale changes. We explore this property and show that our model trained on low-resolution samples improves reconstruction of images at unseen scales without any fine-tuning.

Scenario 1: Reconstructing Upscaled Images. Upscaled ImageNet samples are reconstructed from their AR AlexNet conv5 representations. For a fair comparison across scales, each image is normalized to 224 × 224 px. and then enlarged by an integer factor $L > 1$. Experiments show a higher accuracy obtained from AR features in terms of PSNR, SSIM and LPIPS (Table 5). All metrics improve almost monotonically with L. In contrast, accuracy using standard features degrades with L. Inversion from AR features show almost perfect reconstruction for large scales, while those of standard features show severe distorsions (Fig. 7).

Scenario 2: Reconstructing High-Resolution Images. Standard and AR feature inversion is performed on the DIVerse 2K resolution dataset (DIV2K) [31], containing objects at multiple scales. AR feature reconstructions show a

Table 7. Comparison against state-of-the-art inversion techniques. By inverting AR features, our autoencoder outperforms the optimization-based RI method by a large margin. Despite having 63% less parameters, we also obtain favorable results against DeepSiM, showing a significant PSNR improvement.

Algorithm	Encoder	Trainable Pars	PSNR (dB)↑	SSIM↑	LPIPS↓
RI [23]	AR AlexNet	–	16.724 ± 2.434	0.181 ± 0.071	0.63 ± 0.04
Standard autoencoder	Standard AlexNet	$4,696,026$	15.057 ± 2.392	0.307 ± 0.158	$\mathbf{0.547 \pm 0.055}$
AR autoencoder (ours)	AR AlexNet	$4,696,026$	$\mathbf{17.227 \pm 2.725}$	$\mathbf{0.358 \pm 0.163}$	0.567 ± 0.056
DeepSiM [19]	Standard CaffeNet	$12,702,307$	15.321 ± 2.011	0.417 ± 0.158	0.531 ± 0.059

significant PSNR, SSIM and LPIPS improvement over standard ones, despite not being explicitly trained to handle such large-scale objects (Table 6).

Qualitatively, reconstructions from AR AlexNet features preserve sharp edges, reduces color degradation and diminishes checkerboard effects induced by standard inversion (Fig. 8). Thus, for unseen scales and without finetuning, AR features better preserve structure without penalizing the perceptual similarity.

5.4   Comparison Against State-of-the-Art Inversion Techniques

The inversion accuracy of our AR autoencoder is compared against two alternative techniques: Optimization-based robust representation inversion (RI) [23] and DeePSiM [32]. For a fair comparison, all methods reconstruct images from AlexNet features. We begin by highlighting the differences between them.

While RI is a model-based approach that searches in the pixel domain for an image that matches a set of target AR features, we use a CNN-based generator trained on a combination of natural-image priors (Sect. 4.2). On the other hand, while DeePSiM is also a CNN-based technique trained under multiple priors, its generator has approximately 63% more trainable parameters than ours (Table 7).

Experimental Setup. All inversion methods are evaluated on ImageNet. Our standard and AR models are trained using pixel, feature and GAN losses using the training setup described in Sect. A4. DeePSiM is evaluated using its official Caffe implementation without any changes. RI is evaluated using its official PyTorch implementation modified to invert conv5 AR features. Input samples are rescaled to 224×224 px. (227×227 px. for DeepSiM).

Results. Our AR AlexNet autoencoder obtains the best accuracy in terms of PSNR and the second best in terms of SSIM (Table 7). While it outperforms its standard version in PSNR and SSIM, it gets a marginally worse LPIPS. Moreover, our AR model outperforms RI in all metrics. Also, despite DeePSiM having more layers and using larger inputs, our model achieves a large PSNR improvement over it. Results highlight the improvement obtained by inverting

Table 8. Universal Style Transfer. Our AR AlexNet autoencoder outperforms both its standard counterpart and the original VGG-19 model in terms of Gram loss, the latter using more layers, larger feature maps and feature blending.

Encoder	Stylization levels	Smallest feature map	Feature blending	Gram loss↓ (x_{cs}, x_s)	SSIM↑ (x_{cs}, x_c)
Standard AlexNet	3	$6 \times 6 \times 256$	✗	1.694	0.226
AR AlexNet (ours)	3	$6 \times 6 \times 256$	✗	**1.186**	**0.259**
VGG-19 [27]	5	$14 \times 14 \times 512$	✓	1.223	0.459

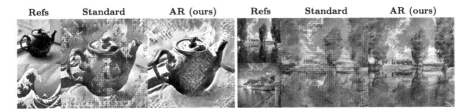

Fig. 9. Universal style transfer: By inverting AR features, our autoencoder improves both content and style preservation, obtaining a better image stylization.

AR features and how this fundamental change allows competitive reconstruction quality using three times less trainable parameters.

6   Downstream Tasks

We further evaluate the benefits of incorporating AR autoencoders into two downstream tasks: style transfer and image denoising. To assess the benefits of AR autoencoders, in each task, we simply replace the standard autoencoders by the AR versions without incorporating any additional task-specific priors or tuning. Despite not tailoring our architecture to each scenario, it obtains on-par or better results than well-established methods. Refer to Sect. A3 and Sect. A4 for more results and full implementation details.

6.1   Style Transfer via Robust Feature Alignment

Motivated by the perceptual properties of AR features [23], we analyze their impact on style transfer using our AR AlexNet autoencoder as backbone and measure their improvement in both structure and texture preservation.

Experimental Setup. Stylization is evaluated on 75 random content images and 100 random style images, leading to $7,500$ image pairs. Content and style preservation is evaluated via the SSIM between content and stylized images and the VGG-19 g loss between style and stylized images, respectively. Conv1 and

Table 9. Image denoising ($\sigma = \frac{50}{255}$): Our AR denoiser outperforms its standard version on multiple datasets. On the largest one (CBSD68), it also outperforms alternative learn-based techniques. On smaller sets (Kodak24, McMaster), it improves in SSIM and gets comparable PSNR and LPIPS performance.

Encoder	PSNR (dB)↑	SSIM↑	LPIPS↓	PSNR (dB)↑	SSIM↑	LPIPS↓	PSNR (dB)↑	SSIM↑	LPIPS↓
	CBSD68			Kodak24			McMaster		
TNRD [59]	24.75	0.662	0.445	25.994	0.695	0.461	25.01	0.66	**0.387**
MLP [60]	25.184	0.663	0.46	**26.31**	0.691	0.478	**26.039**	**0.693**	0.402
Standard	22.6297	0.6178	0.567	23.1868	0.6001	0.4968	23.1493	0.6072	0.4458
AR (ours)	**25.258**	**0.7095**	**0.4043**	25.4946	**0.701**	**0.447**	25.3527	0.6914	0.3965

conv2 models use nearest neighbor interpolation instead of transposed convolution layers to improve reconstruction and avoid checkerboard effects, while the conv5 model remains unaltered. We also include results using Universal Style Transfer's (UST) official implementation, using a VGG-19 backbone.

Results. Our AR autoencoder improves both texture and structure preservation over its standard version (Table 8). Stylization via AR features removes artifacts in flat areas, reducing blurry outputs and degraded structure (Fig. 9). Besides, our AR model gets a lower Gram loss with respect to UST. This implies that, despite matching less feature maps than the VGG-19 model (three instead of five), stylizing via our AR AlexNet autoencoder better preserves the style.

As expected, UST obtains a better SSIM since VGG-19 has more complexity and uses less contracted feature maps than our AlexNet model (e.g. $14 \times 14 \times 512$ vs. $6 \times 6 \times 256$). Also, UST *blends* stylized and content features to better preserve shapes. Overall, a comparison between our AR model and UST shows a tradeoff between content and style preservation.

6.2   Image Denoising via AR Autoencoder

Similarly to the robustness imposed by regularized autoencoders [38,46,58], we harness the manifold learned by AR models to obtain noise-free reconstructions. We evaluate our AR AlexNet denoising model and compare its restoration properties with alternative learn-based methods.

Experimental Setup. Our image denoising model consists of an AR autoencoder equipped with skip connections in conv1, conv2 and conv5 layers to better preserve image details. Skip connections follow the Wavelet Pooling approach [3]. Generators are trained on ImageNet via pixel and feature losses.

Accuracy is evaluated on the Kodak24, McMaster [61] and Color Berkeley Segmentation Dataset 68 (CBSD68) [62] for clipped additive Gaussian noise ($\sigma = 50/255$). We compare our AR model against two learn-based methods, Trainable Nonlinear Reaction Diffusion (TNRD) [59] and Multi Layer Perceptron-based model (MLP) [60], often included in real-noise denoising benchmarks [63,64].

Ground-truth	Observation	Standard	AR (ours)

Fig. 10. Image denoising ($\sigma = \frac{50}{255}$): While inverting standard features introduces artifacts and degrades color, limiting their use for restoration tasks, our AR denoiser reduces the artifacts and better preserves the original texture.

Results. Our AR model improves over its standard version in all metrics across all datasets (Table 9). While standard predictions include color distortions and texture artifacts, AR predictions show a better texture preservation and significantly reduce the distorsions introduced by the denoising process (Fig. 10).

Our AR model obtains the best PSNR, SSIM and LPIPS scores on CBSD68, the most diverse of all datasets. While it is outperformed in PSNR by MLP in the two remaining datasets, it improves in SSIM and LPIPS, getting best or second best performance. For the McMaster dataset, SSIM and LPIPS values obtained by our model are slightly below the best values. Overall, our model consistently preserves the perceptual and structural similarity across all datasets, showing competitive results with alternative data-driven approaches.

7 Conclusions

A novel encoding-decoding model for synthesis tasks is proposed by exploiting the perceptual properties of AR features. We show the reconstruction improvement obtained by generators trained on AR features and how it generalizes to models of different complexity. We showcase our model on style transfer and image denoising tasks, outperforming standard approaches and attaining competitive performance against alternative methods. A potential limitation of our model is the loss of details due to its contracted features. Yet, experiments show that using shortcut connections allow preserving these, enabling enhancement and restoration tasks. Our method also requires pre-training an AR encoder prior to training the generator, which may increase its computational requirements.

Learning how to invert AR features may be interestingly extended to conditional GANs for image-to-image translation tasks [65] and to VAEs as a latent variable regularizer [19]. Our AR autoencoder can also be seen as an energy-based model [5] for artificial and biological neural networks vizualization [7,14,15].

Acknowledgements. AN was supported by NSF Grant No. 1850117 & 2145767, and donations from NaphCare Foundation & Adobe Research. We are grateful for Kelly Price's tireless assistance with our GPU servers at Auburn University.

References

1. Gatys, L.A., Ecker, A.S., Bethge, M.: Image style transfer using convolutional neural networks. In: Proceedings of the IEEE Conference on Computer Vision and Pattern Recognition, pp. 2414–2423 (2016)
2. Li, Y., Fang, C., Yang, J., Wang, Z., Lu, X., Yang, M.H.: Universal style transfer via feature transforms. In: Proceedings of the 31st International Conference on Neural Information Processing Systems, pp. 385–395 NIPS'17, Red Hook, NY, USA, Curran Associates Inc. (2017)
3. Yoo, J., Uh, Y., Chun, S., Kang, B., Ha, J.W.: Photorealistic style transfer via wavelet transforms. In: Proceedings of the IEEE International Conference on Computer Vision, pp. 9036–9045 (2019)
4. Yang, C., Lu, X., Lin, Z., Shechtman, E., Wang, O., Li, H.: High-resolution image inpainting using multi-scale neural patch synthesis. In: Proceedings of the IEEE Conference on Computer Vision and Pattern Recognition, pp. 6721–6729 (2017)
5. Nguyen, A., Clune, J., Bengio, Y., Dosovitskiy, A., Yosinski, J.: Plug & play generative networks: Conditional iterative generation of images in latent space. In: Proceedings of the IEEE Conference on Computer Vision and Pattern Recognition, pp. 4467–4477 (2017)
6. Shocher, A., et al.: Semantic pyramid for image generation. In: Proceedings of the IEEE/CVF Conference on Computer Vision and Pattern Recognition, pp. 7457–7466 (2020)
7. Nguyen, A., Dosovitskiy, A., Yosinski, J., Brox, T., Clune, J.: Synthesizing the preferred inputs for neurons in neural networks via deep generator networks. In: Advances in Neural Information Processing Systems, pp. 3387–3395 (2016)
8. Rombach, R., Esser, P., Ommer, B.: Network-to-network translation with conditional invertible neural networks. Adv. Neural. Inf. Process. Syst. **33**, 2784–2797 (2020)
9. Santurkar, S., Ilyas, A., Tsipras, D., Engstrom, L., Tran, B., Madry, A.: Image synthesis with a single (robust) classifier. In: Advances in Neural Information Processing Systems, pp. 1262–1273 (2019)
10. Zhang, R., Isola, P., Efros, A.A., Shechtman, E., Wang, O.: The unreasonable effectiveness of deep features as a perceptual metric. In: Proceedings of the IEEE Conference on Computer Vision and Pattern Recognition, 586–595 (2018)
11. Goodfellow, I., Bengio, Y., Courville, A.: Deep Learning Book, MIT Press, 521, 800 (2016)
12. Deecke, L., Vandermeulen, R., Ruff, L., Mandt, S., Kloft, M.: Image anomaly detection with generative adversarial networks. In: Berlingerio, M., Bonchi, F., Gärtner, T., Hurley, N., Ifrim, G. (eds.) ECML PKDD 2018. LNCS (LNAI), vol. 11051, pp. 3–17. Springer, Cham (2019). https://doi.org/10.1007/978-3-030-10925-7_1
13. Golan, I., El-Yaniv, R.: Deep anomaly detection using geometric transformations. arXiv preprint arXiv:1805.10917 (2018)
14. Nguyen, A., Yosinski, J., Clune, J.: Understanding neural networks via feature visualization: a survey. In: Samek, W., Montavon, G., Vedaldi, A., Hansen, L.K., Müller, K.-R. (eds.) Explainable AI: Interpreting, Explaining and Visualizing Deep

Learning. LNCS (LNAI), vol. 11700, pp. 55–76. Springer, Cham (2019). https://doi.org/10.1007/978-3-030-28954-6_4

15. Ponce, C.R., Xiao, W., Schade, P.F., Hartmann, T.S., Kreiman, G., Livingstone, M.S.: Evolving images for visual neurons using a deep generative network reveals coding principles and neuronal preferences. Cell **177**, 999–1009 (2019)

16. Rombach, R., Esser, P., Blattmann, A., Ommer, B.: Invertible neural networks for understanding semantics of invariances of cnn representations. In: Deep Neural Networks and Data for Automated Driving. Springer, pp. 197–224 (2022). https://doi.org/10.1007/978-3-031-01233-4_7

17. Donahue, J., Simonyan, K.: Large scale adversarial representation learning. In: Advances in Neural Information Processing Systems (2019)

18. Dosovitskiy, A., T.Brox: Inverting visual representations with convolutional networks. In: CVPR (2016)

19. Dosovitskiy, A., Brox, T.: Generating images with perceptual similarity metrics based on deep networks. In: Advances in Neural Information Processing Systems, pp. 658–666 (2016)

20. Esser, P., Rombach, R., Ommer, B.: Taming transformers for high-resolution image synthesis. In: Proceedings of the IEEE/CVF Conference on Computer Vision and Pattern Recognition, pp. 12873–12883 (2021)

21. Esser, P., Rombach, R., Blattmann, A., Ommer, B.: Imagebart: bidirectional context with multinomial diffusion for autoregressive image synthesis. Adv. Neural. Inf. Process. Syst. **34**, 3518–3532 (2021)

22. Madry, A., Makelov, A., Schmidt, L., Tsipras, D., Vladu, A.: Towards deep learning models resistant to adversarial attacks. iclr. arXiv preprint arXiv:1706.06083 (2018)

23. Engstrom, L., Ilyas, A., Santurkar, S., Tsipras, D., Tran, B., Madry, A.: Adversarial robustness as a prior for learned representations. arXiv preprint arXiv:1906.00945 (2019)

24. Razavi, A., van den Oord, A., Vinyals, O.: Generating diverse high-fidelity images with vq-vae-2. In: Advances in Neural Information Processing Systems, pp. 14866–14876 (2019)

25. Van Den Oord, A., Vinyals, O., et al.: Neural discrete representation learning. In: Advances in Neural Information Processing Systems, vol. 30 (2017)

26. Krizhevsky, A., Sutskever, I., Hinton, G.E.: Imagenet classification with deep convolutional neural networks. In: Advances in Neural Information Processing Systems, pp. 1097–1105 (2012)

27. Simonyan, K., Zisserman, A.: Very deep convolutional networks for large-scale image recognition. arXiv preprint arXiv:1409.1556 (2014)

28. He, K., Zhang, X., Ren, S., Sun, J.: Deep residual learning for image recognition. In: Proceedings of the IEEE Conference on Computer Vision and Pattern Recognition, pp. 770–778 (2016)

29. Krizhevsky, A., Hinton, G., et al.: Learning multiple layers of features from tiny images (2009)

30. Russakovsky, O., et al.: Imagenet large scale visual recognition challenge. Int. J. Comput. Vision **115**, 211–252 (2015)

31. Agustsson, E., Timofte, R.: Ntire 2017 challenge on single image super-resolution: Dataset and study. In: Proceedings of the IEEE Conference on Computer Vision and Pattern Recognition Workshops, pp. 126–135 (2017)

32. Dosovitskiy, A., Brox, T.: Inverting convolutional networks with convolutional networks. arXiv preprint arXiv:1506.02753 4 (2015)

33. Mahendran, A., Vedaldi, A.: Understanding deep image representations by inverting them. In: Proceedings of the IEEE Conference on Computer Vision and Pattern Recognition, pp. 5188–5196 (2015)
34. Mahendran, A., Vedaldi, A.: Visualizing deep convolutional neural networks using natural pre-images. Int. J. Comput. Vision **120**, 233–255 (2016)
35. Salman, H., Ilyas, A., Engstrom, L., Kapoor, A., Madry, A.: Do adversarially robust imagenet models transfer better? arXiv preprint arXiv:2007.08489 (2020)
36. Zhang, Y., Jia, R., Pei, H., Wang, W., Li, B., Song, D.: The secret revealer: Generative model-inversion attacks against deep neural networks. In: Proceedings of the IEEE/CVF Conference on Computer Vision and Pattern Recognition, pp. 253–261 (2020)
37. Jun, H., et al.: Distribution augmentation for generative modeling. In: International Conference on Machine Learning, pp. 5006–5019 PMLR (2020)
38. Kingma, D.P., Welling, M.: Auto-encoding variational bayes. arXiv preprint arXiv:1312.6114 (2013)
39. Ng, A., et al.: Sparse autoencoder. CS294A Lecture notes **72**, 1–19 (2011)
40. Pan, S.J., Yang, Q.: A survey on transfer learning. IEEE Trans. Knowl. Data Eng. **22**, 1345–1359 (2009)
41. Johnson, J., Alahi, A., Fei-Fei, L.: Perceptual losses for real-time style transfer and super-resolution. In: Leibe, B., Matas, J., Sebe, N., Welling, M. (eds.) ECCV 2016. LNCS, vol. 9906, pp. 694–711. Springer, Cham (2016). https://doi.org/10.1007/978-3-319-46475-6_43
42. Simonyan, K., Vedaldi, A., Zisserman, A.: Deep inside convolutional networks: Visualising image classification models and saliency maps. arXiv preprint arXiv:1312.6034 (2013)
43. Goodfellow, I.J., Shlens, J., Szegedy, C.: Explaining and harnessing adversarial examples. arXiv preprint arXiv:1412.6572 (2014)
44. Athalye, A., Carlini, N., Wagner, D.: Obfuscated gradients give a false sense of security: Circumventing defenses to adversarial examples. arXiv preprint arXiv:1802.00420 (2018)
45. Ulyanov, D., Vedaldi, A., Lempitsky, V.: Deep image prior. In: Proceedings of the IEEE Conference on Computer Vision and Pattern Recognition, pp. 9446–9454 (2018)
46. Vincent, P., Larochelle, H., Lajoie, I., Bengio, Y., Manzagol, P.A., Bottou, L.: Stacked denoising autoencoders: Learning useful representations in a deep network with a local denoising criterion. J. Mach. Learn. Res. **11**(12), 3371–3408 (2010)
47. Kessy, A., Lewin, A., Strimmer, K.: Optimal whitening and decorrelation. Am. Stat. **72**, 309–314 (2018)
48. Mao, X.J., Shen, C., Yang, Y.B.: Image restoration using very deep convolutional encoder-decoder networks with symmetric skip connections. arXiv preprint arXiv:1603.09056 (2016)
49. El Helou, M., Süsstrunk, S.: Blind universal bayesian image denoising with gaussian noise level learning. IEEE Trans. Image Process. **29**, 4885–4897 (2020)
50. Zhang, K., Zuo, W., Zhang, L.: Ffdnet: toward a fast and flexible solution for cnn-based image denoising. IEEE Trans. Image Process. **27**, 4608–4622 (2018)
51. Moeller, M., Diebold, J., Gilboa, G., Cremers, D.: Learning nonlinear spectral filters for color image reconstruction. In: Proceedings of the IEEE International Conference on Computer Vision, pp. 289–297 (2015)
52. Liu, X., Li, Y., Wu, C., Hsieh, C.J.: Adv-bnn: Improved adversarial defense through robust bayesian neural network. arXiv preprint arXiv:1810.01279 (2018)

53. Zhang, J., Zhu, J., Niu, G., Han, B., Sugiyama, M., Kankanhalli, M.: Geometry-aware instance-reweighted adversarial training. arXiv preprint arXiv:2010.01736 (2020)
54. Croce, F., Hein, M.: Reliable evaluation of adversarial robustness with an ensemble of diverse parameter-free attacks. In: International Conference on Machine Learning, pp. 2206–2216 PMLR (2020)
55. Sosnovik, I., Szmaja, M., Smeulders, A.: Scale-equivariant steerable networks. arXiv preprint arXiv:1910.11093 (2019)
56. Fan, Y., Yu, J., Liu, D., Huang, T.S.: Scale-wise convolution for image restoration. Proc. AAAI Conf. Artif. Intell. **34**, 10770–10777 (2020)
57. Chen, P., Agarwal, C., Nguyen, A.: The shape and simplicity biases of adversarially robust imagenet-trained cnns. arXiv preprint arXiv:2006.09373 (2020)
58. Rifai, S., Vincent, P., Muller, X., Glorot, X., Bengio, Y.: Contractive auto-encoders: Explicit invariance during feature extraction. In: Icml (2011)
59. Chen, Y., Pock, T.: Trainable nonlinear reaction diffusion: a flexible framework for fast and effective image restoration. IEEE Trans. Pattern Anal. Mach. Intell. **39**, 1256–1272 (2016)
60. Burger, H.C., Schuler, C.J., Harmeling, S.: Image denoising: Can plain neural networks compete with bm3d? In: 2012 IEEE Conference on Computer Vision and Pattern Recognition, pp. 2392–2399 IEEE (2012) 2392–2399
61. Zhang, L., Wu, X., Buades, A., Li, X.: Color demosaicing by local directional interpolation and nonlocal adaptive thresholding. J. Electron. Imaging **20**, 023016 (2011)
62. Martin, D., Fowlkes, C., Tal, D., Malik, J.: A database of human segmented natural images and its application to evaluating segmentation algorithms and measuring ecological statistics. In: Proceedings of the 8th International Conference Computer Vision. Vol. 2, pp. 416–423 (2001)
63. Anwar, S., Barnes, N.: Real image denoising with feature attention. In: Proceedings of the IEEE/CVF International Conference on Computer Vision, pp. 3155–3164 (2019)
64. Guo, S., Yan, Z., Zhang, K., Zuo, W., Zhang, L.: Toward convolutional blind denoising of real photographs. In: Proceedings of the IEEE/CVF Conference on Computer Vision and Pattern Recognition, pp. 1712–1722 (2019)
65. Isola, P., Zhu, J.Y., Zhou, T., Efros, A.A.: Image-to-image translation with conditional adversarial networks. In: Proceedings of the IEEE Conference on Computer Vision and Pattern Recognition, pp. 1125–1134 (2017)
66. Ruff, L., Vandermeulen, R.A., Görnitz, N., Binder, A., Müller, E., Müller, K.R., Kloft, M.: Deep semi-supervised anomaly detection. arXiv preprint arXiv:1906.02694 (2019)
67. Wang, S., et al.: Effective end-to-end unsupervised outlier detection via inlier priority of discriminative network. In: NeurIPS, pp. 5960–5973 (2019)
68. Parkhi, O.M., Vedaldi, A., Zisserman, A., Jawahar, C.: Cats and dogs. In: 2012 IEEE Conference on Computer Vision and Pattern Recognition, pp. 3498–3505. IEEE (2012)
69. Engstrom, L., Ilyas, A., Salman, H., Santurkar, S., Tsipras, D.: Robustness (python library) (2019)
70. Miyato, T., Kataoka, T., Koyama, M., Yoshida, Y.: Spectral normalization for generative adversarial networks. arXiv preprint arXiv:1802.05957 (2018)

Rethinking Online Knowledge Distillation with Multi-exits

Hojung Lee [ID] and Jong-Seok Lee[(✉)] [ID]

School of Integrated Technology, Yonsei University, Incheon 21983, South Korea
{hjlee92,jong-seok.lee}@yonsei.ac.kr

Abstract. Online knowledge distillation is a method to train multiple networks simultaneously by distilling the knowledge among each other from scratch. An efficient way for this is to attach auxiliary classifiers (called exits) to the main network. However, in this multi-exit approach, there are important questions that have not been answered in previous studies: *What structure should be used for exits? What can be a good teacher for distillation? How should the overall training loss be constructed?* In this paper, we propose a new online knowledge distillation method using multi-exits by answering these questions. First, we examine the influence of the structure of the exits on the performance of the main network, and propose a bottleneck structure that leads to improved performance for a wide range of main network structures. Second, we propose a new distillation teacher using an ensemble of all the classifiers (main network and exits) by exploiting the diversity in the outputs and features of the classifiers. Third, we propose a new technique to form the overall training loss, which balances classification losses and distillation losses for effective training of the whole network. Our proposed method is termed balanced exit-ensemble distillation (BEED). Experimental results demonstrate that our method achieves significant improvement of classification performance on various popular convolutional neural network (CNN) structures. Code is available at https://github.com/hjdw2/BEED.

Keywords: Online knowledge distillation · Multi-exits · Ensemble

1 Introduction

Deep neural networks have made remarkable achievements in the field of image classification with the advancement of convolutional neural networks. These achievements are often based on deep and wide networks [11]. In order to successfully use deep learning in resource-limited environments such as mobile or embedded systems, model compression approaches have been studied. Knowledge distillation [10,13] is one such approach, which transfers learned knowledge,

Supplementary Information The online version contains supplementary material available at https://doi.org/10.1007/978-3-031-26351-4_25.

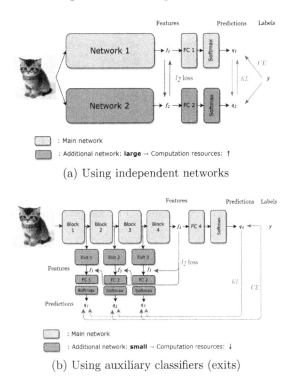

(a) Using independent networks

(b) Using auxiliary classifiers (exits)

Fig. 1. Comparison of online distillation methods using additional networks. A black arrow indicates the forward path; a red arrow indicates the cross-entropy loss; a green arrow implies the prediction distillation; and a blue arrow implies the feature distillation. (Color figure online)

such as predictions or intermediate feature maps, from a large pre-trained teacher network to a smaller student network. The student network tries to mimic the teacher's knowledge, which improves the performance of the student network. Then, the student network can be deployed instead of the teacher network for a resource-constrained environment. However, pre-training a large teacher network is a significant burden, and this issue becomes even worse when an ensemble model is used as a teacher [1].

Knowledge distillation can also be used without a pre-trained model, which is called online distillation. Online distillation trains multiple networks simultaneously by distilling the knowledge with each other from scratch. There are generally two ways to configure the networks as shown in Fig. 1. One is to use multiple independent networks in addition to the main network [4,15,42], and the other is to attach auxiliary classifiers (called exits) in the middle of the main network [23,27,40]. In the former case, independent networks are used and thus

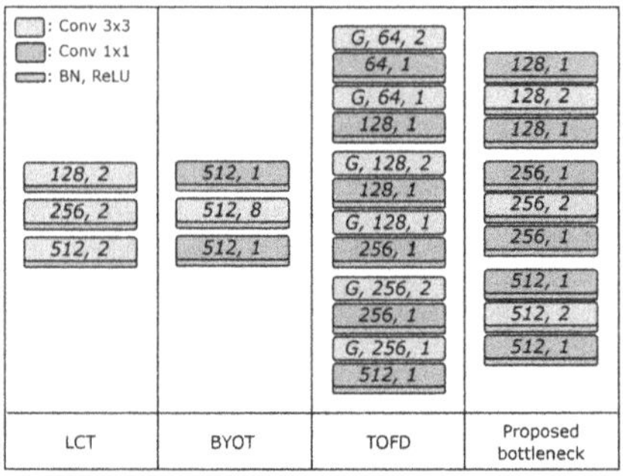

Fig. 2. Structures of the exits (the first exit in ResNet18) in the previous studies (LCT [21], BYOT [40], TOFD [39]) and this paper. G means group convolution. (Color figure online)

computational complexity is high, which reduces the advantage of online distillation. In the latter case, on the other hand, the exits are usually small and the complexity can be effectively decreased. For example, when ResNet34 is trained for CIFAR-100 [18] using two independent networks, the total number of parameters is 42.96M; when three exits are used, however, only 31.30M parameters are required (and four classifiers are obtained). Therefore, the approach using exits has the advantages of involving reduced complexity and obtaining more outputs that can be used for distillation.

While the success of online distillation using multi-exits was shown in the previous studies [23,27,40], we note that there are three important questions that have not been answered. In this paper, we offer solutions for the questions and propose a new online distillation method using multi-exits.

Q1. What structure should be used for exits? In most previous studies [27,39,40], the structure of an exit is determined mainly to match the resolution of the final feature maps to that of the main network without much consideration about its influence on the performance (Fig. 2). However, our analysis reveals that the performance of the main network can be significantly changed depending on which structure is used for exits in the same main network. In particular, we show that it is beneficial to use a different block type from the main network for exits. In addition, we present a bottleneck structure for exits, which has a simple structure but yields higher performance than other previously proposed bottleneck structures.

Q2. What can be a good teacher for distillation? The previous distillation methods using multi-exits [23,27,40] consider the exists as students and the main network as a teacher, and expect that distillation of the teacher's knowledge to the students eases learning of the network, especially for the early layers. However, we rethink this typical role assignment: Since the multi-exits inherently provide multiple outputs, we can use them to constitute a better teacher. Thus, we propose a new ensemble distillation teacher using an ensemble of all the classifiers in the network, which allows us to exploit diversity in the outputs and features of the classifiers. In particular, we apply an importance coefficient to adjust the relative contribution of each exit in the ensemble, which maximizes the advantage of the ensemble.

Q3. How should the overall training loss be constructed? After the distillation losses and the classification losses are obtained, how to properly reflect them in the overall training loss is still an open problem. In general, the learning ability of a network is closely related to its size. Thus, it is difficult for early exits having small sizes to learn properly only with the classification loss using the one-hot labels, and they often find a shortcut for classification criteria [9]. The distillation loss can alleviate this limitation, but applying the distillation loss at the same rate to all exits, as in the previous studies [23,27,40], does not consider the size-dependent learning ability of each exit. Thus, we propose a new loss-balancing technique, which adjusts the weights of the classification loss and the distillation loss for each exit. This technique can improve the performance of the main network by helping the exits learn appropriate features.

To sum up, our contributions are as follows: 1) We propose a new online knowledge distillation method using multi-exits. 2) We investigate the effect of the structure of the exits and present a simple but effective structure. 3) We propose a method to form an ensemble of the classifiers as a teacher for distillation. 4) We propose a loss-balancing technique to combine classification losses and distillation losses.

2   Related Work

Knowledge distillation is a method to use a pre-trained network as a teacher network and distill its learned knowledge to a smaller student network [13]. The teacher's knowledge can be extracted at different levels, including logits [13] and features [28], which can be used directly or after transformation using another network or a kernel function [3,12,17,43]. In addition, a teacher can be a single pre-trained network or an ensemble of multiple pre-trained networks [1].

Online distillation trains multiple networks simultaneously by distilling the knowledge with each other without a pre-trained teacher. To this end, several independent networks can be used [4,15,24,30,31,35,42] or auxiliary classifiers (i.e., exits) attached to the main network can be used [23,27,40]. The latter approach is preferable in terms of complexity, since the former approach requires higher complexity due to the large network size. In a multi-exit architecture [23,27,40], the exits can be used as paths to deliver the information at the main network's output to its early layers via distillation. Through this, each exit and shared parts of the main network can learn more general features, by not only following the true label but also receiving the knowledge of the main network from the final output. Consequently, the performance of not only the exits but also the main network is enhanced. While these studies have shown the success of online distillation using multi-exits, we focus on the research questions mentioned in the introduction, which have not been addressed yet. We show that careful consideration of the questions can significantly improve the classification performance of the trained network.

The on-the-fly native ensemble (ONE) method in [19] attaches multiple exits at a certain location of the main network, where the exits have the same structure to the main network and the ensemble of the exits form a teacher. However, since the exits are attached at the same location and have the same structure, the added value of using them for an ensemble is limited. Our experiments show that this method is outperformed by our proposed method.

3   Structure of Auxiliary Classifiers

In the previous studies, the structure of the exits is usually designed heuristically. More specifically, in an exit, the number of convolutional layers having a stride of two is determined so that the dimension of the features at the penultimate layer of the exit becomes the same to that of the main network. However, it is well known that the network structure is important in determining its performance [16]. From the same point of view, we can infer that the structure of the exits can also have a significant impact on the performance, which is investigated in this section.

The role of the exits is to provide additional training objectives to the network other than the classification loss at the final output. These additional objectives act as regularizers to prevent overfitting, which improves the generalization performance of the main network [34]. Considering this, we can hypothesize as follows: It is beneficial to use exit structures different from that of the main network so that the exits produce features and outputs that are distinguished from those of the main network, and this diversity in turn can result in informative regularizers.

Most popular CNNs are constructed based on the ResNet structure, which consist of either *basic blocks* or *bottleneck blocks*. Therefore, as a way of using a different structure for exits from the main network, we suggest using bottleneck blocks for an exit if the main network consists of basic blocks, and using basic blocks for an exit if the main network consists of bottleneck blocks.

To verify our argument, we train multi-exit architectures using different exit structures shown in Fig. 2. When we build a multi-exit architecture by inserting $k-1$ exits into a CNN (e.g., $k = 4$ in Fig. 1b), the exits, denoted as c_i ($i = 1, ..., k-1$), divide the CNN (main network) into k blocks, which are denoted as g_i ($i = 1, ..., k$). Then, the input data x produces k predictions (logits), denoted as z_i ($i = 1, ..., k$), by a single feedforward process, i.e.,

$$z_i = \begin{cases} c_i(g_i(\cdots g_1(x))) & \text{if } i < k \\ g_i(\cdots g_1(x)) & \text{if } i = k \end{cases} \qquad (1)$$

In addition, the feature information right before the fully connected layer of each exit or the main network is denoted as f_i ($i = 1, ..., k$). Then, the basic way to train the multi-exit architecture is to use the joint classification loss L_C with cross entropy (CE) for true label y, i.e.,

$$L_C = \sum_{i=1}^{k} CE(q_i, y), \tag{2}$$

where $q_i = \frac{\exp(z_i/T)}{\sum_j \exp(z_j/T)}$ is the softmax output and T is the temperature.

Table 1. Test accuracy (%) of the main network trained with different multi-exit structures (LCT [21], BYOT [40], TOFD [39]) for CIFAR-100. 'Baseline' indicates the case without multi-exits and 'Self' indicates the case where the structure of each exit is the same as the remaining main network. Basic block-based networks are marked in red and bottleneck block-based networks are marked in blue. The best results are marked in bold.

Network \ Exit	Baseline	LCT	BYOT	TOFD	Self	Proposed
ResNet18	77.70	78.22	78.51	79.01	78.79	**79.39**
ResNet34	78.01	79.80	79.41	79.92	79.41	**80.22**
WRN16-4	76.42	75.71	76.61	76.81	77.31	**77.49**
WRN28-4	78.50	78.19	78.56	79.02	79.48	**80.05**
MobileNet-V2	71.92	**74.31**	74.10	73.51	72.91	73.73
EfficientNetB0	72.01	**75.01**	74.51	74.38	73.52	74.21

The test accuracy of the main network trained for CIFAR-100 is shown in Table 1 for various main network architectures (see Sect. 6 for more details of the experimental setup). Significant differences in performance are observed depending on the combination of the main network structure and the exit structure. When the results of the previous exit structures are compared (LCT, BYOT, and TOFD), the exits consisting of a different kind of blocks from the main network lead to higher accuracy than the exits consisting of the same kind of blocks in most cases. For the main networks composed of basic blocks (i.e., ResNets and WRNs), the exit structures using bottleneck blocks are beneficial, including BYOT and TOFD. On the other hand, even though LCT uses a very shallow structure, it shows the best performance among the exit structures when MobileNet-V2 and EfficientNetB0 are used as the main network. These demonstrate that an exit structure using a different type of blocks from that of the main network is preferable as a regularizer.

However, BYOT uses only one bottleneck block, which is too simple to obtain sufficiently high performance. TOFD uses a complex structure, but the rationale for selecting such a structure is not clear. Thus, we propose to use the standardized bottleneck structure employed in the original ResNet [11] for exits as shown in Fig. 2. We make slight modifications by excluding channel expansion in the last convolution layer in the block (in order to match the dimension of the penulti-mate layer's features to that of the main network) and the residual connection (to reduce the computational burden as discussed in [22]). As shown in Table 1, our proposed bottleneck exit achieves better performance than the other bottleneck-based exit structures for the main networks based on basic blocks. In addition, our bottleneck achieves the best performance also for MobileNet-V2 and Effi-cientNetB0 when distillation is applied, which is shown in the supplementary material.

It is possible to use the exits having the same structure to the main net-work but initialize them differently to impose diversity in the additional training objectives through the exits. This case is denoted as 'Self' in Table 1, which is outperformed by the existing exit structures for several main networks and by

Table 2. Test accuracy (%) of each classifier (main network or exit) and diversity (prediction disagreement/cosine similarity) between the main network and each exit when ResNet18 is used as the main network for CIFAR-100. The exit structure is denoted as (Exit1 structure)-(Exit2 structure)-(Exit3 structure). For example, 'C-B-B' means that Exit1 uses the LCT structure and Exit2 and Exit3 use the proposed bottleneck structure. 'X' means that Exit1 is not attached.

Exit structure	Exit1 Acc. (Div.)	Exit2 Acc. (Div.)	Exit3 Acc. (Div.)	Main Acc.
LCT (C-C-C)	70.90 (0.2731/0.7914)	75.20 (0.2016/0.8577)	77.72 (0.0547/0.9831)	78.22
BYOT	66.88 (0.3146/0.7578)	73.33 (0.2176/0.8433)	77.37 (0.0766/0.9671)	78.51
TOFD	72.17 (0.2590/0.8009)	75.30 (0.2119/0.8447)	77.82 (0.0952/0.9577)	79.01
Proposed Bottleneck (B-B-B)	74.55 (0.2376/0.8263)	77.19 (0.1897/0.8670)	78.84 (0.1017/0.9485)	79.39
B-B-C	74.12 (0.2456/0.8160)	76.90 (0.1970/0.8613)	77.71 (0.0637/0.9805)	78.18
C-C-B	71.58 (0.2663/0.8014)	75.24 (0.2012/0.8612)	78.09 (0.0964/0.9545)	79.12
C-C-ResNet50	70.79 (0.2776/0.7951)	74.48 (0.2107/0.8518)	78.68 (0.1061/0.9408)	79.35
B-C-C	73.80 (0.2435/0.8179)	74.73 (0.2102/0.8497)	77.36 (0.0560/0.9485)	78.20
C-B-B	70.85 (0.2714/0.7942)	77.19 (0.1860/0.8692)	78.75 (0.1059/0.9450)	79.30
ResNet50-C-C	78.17 (0.2068/0.8437)	73.36 (0.2296/0.8333)	76.87 (0.0629/0.9784)	77.31
X-C-C	–	74.05 (0.2188/0.8474)	77.42 (0.0626/0.9813)	77.82
X-B-B	–	76.55 (0.1989/0.8605)	78.58 (0.1138/0.9395)	79.11

our proposed structure for all main networks. Thus, different initializations do not provide a sufficient regularization effect. In addition, the structure of the exits becomes excessively large, which is inefficient in terms of memory complexity and computational complexity.

3.1   Diversity of Exits

We perform further analysis on how the diversity of exits, achieved by their structures, influences the classification performance. We employ two measures for diversity of each exit. One is the prediction disagreement, which is defined as the ratio of the number of test samples that the exit classifier and the main network classifier classify differently [8]. The other is the cosine similarity between the predictions of the exit classifier and the main network classifier [7]. Table 2 shows the test accuracy and the diversity of each classifier when different exit structures are used with ResNet18 as the main network for CIFAR-100. Rows 1 to 4 compare the existing and proposed structures. In addition, we examine several variations on the block type of Exit3 (rows from 5 to 7) or Exit1 (rows from 8 to 12).

When the existing and proposed exit structures are compared, it is observed that high diversity of Exit3 leads to improving the accuracy of the main network (rows 1 to 4). The classifier obtained by Exit3 shares most of the layers with the main network, thus they inherently tend to produce highly similar outputs. Therefore, in order for Exit3 to act as a proper regularizer, its structure needs to be different from that of the main network so that it can provide meaningful additional information to improve the performance of the main network. Even though when we use the bottleneck structure for Exit1 and Exit2, if Exit3 uses the basic block structure (B-B-C), the accuracy of the main network becomes lower due to the low diversity of Exit3. In contrast, even if Exit1 and Exit2 use the basic block structure, using the bottleneck block (C-C-B) or even a large ResNet (C-C-ResNet50) allows Exit3 to have relatively high diversity and thus can improve the performance of the main network.

In the case of the earlier exits (Exit1 and Exit2), their diversity is already high since they share only small numbers of layers with the main network. Thus, their diversity is not necessarily correlated to the performance of the main network. For instance, when different structures for Exit1 are used while Exit2 and Exit3 are kept as the basic block structure (B-C-C and ResNet50-C-C), the accuracy of the main network does not change much. And, changing the structure of Exit1 (from C-C-C to B-C-C or B-B-B to C-B-B) does not change the accuracy of the main network much, either. Nevertheless, without Exit1, the main network does not achieve high performance (X-C-C and X-B-B).

In summary, the key to improving the performance of the main network is to set the structure of the exit at the later stage different from that of the main network (e.g., bottleneck structure for ResNet18). And, the proposed bottleneck exit is a reasonable choice for all exits when the performance and compactness are considered.

4   Ensemble Classifier Distillation

For online distillation using a multi-exit architecture, distillation losses are used together with the classification loss given by (2). The predictions (q_k) and/or feature information (f_k) can be used as teacher signals. Thus, the joint distillation loss L_D is generally written as

$$L_D = \sum_{i=1}^{k-1} \left\{ \alpha KL(q_i, q_k) + \beta \| f_i - f_k \|_2^2 \right\}, \tag{3}$$

where KL is the Kullback-Leibler (KL) divergence and α and β are coefficients. Thus, the overall loss is given by

$$L = \sum_{i=1}^{k} CE(q_i, y) + \sum_{i=1}^{k-1} \left\{ \alpha KL(q_i, q_k) + \beta \| f_i - f_k \|_2^2 \right\}. \tag{4}$$

The joint distillation loss (3) assumes that the outputs of the main network can act as a teacher for the exits because the performance of the main network is usually higher than that of the exits.

However, we pay attention to the potential advantage of an ensemble teacher [1]. In the multi-exit architecture, we can inherently obtain multiple outputs (from the exit classifiers and the main network) simultaneously, which can form an ensemble teacher. Moreover, the classifiers in the multi-exit architecture have significant diversity as shown in the previous section due to their structural differences, which maximizes the infomativeness of the ensemble [41]. Thus, we exploit this superior ensemble knowledge, which can be transferred to not only the exits but also the main network.

To construct an effective ensemble teacher, we propose a non-uniform strategy using an importance coefficient λ to reflect the logit of each exit at a different rate, i.e.,

$$z_E = \frac{1}{\sum_{i=1}^{k} \lambda^{i-1}} \sum_{i=1}^{k} \left(\lambda^{i-1} \cdot z_i \right), \tag{5}$$

where $\lambda > 1$. The idea is to allow high-performing exits at the later stage to contribute more in order to obtain a teacher of good quality while the exits at the earlier stage mainly enhance diversity in the ensemble teacher at appropriate levels.

Using z_E, the prediction ensemble teacher is defined as

$$q_E = \frac{\exp(z_E/T)}{\sum_j \exp(z_E/T)}. \tag{6}$$

Similarly, we define an ensemble teacher for feature distillation as

$$f_E = \frac{1}{\sum_{i=1}^{k} \lambda^{i-1}} \sum_{i=1}^{k} \left(\lambda^{i-1} \cdot f_i \right). \tag{7}$$

Thus, our new joint distillation loss is written as

$$L_D = \sum_{i=1}^{k} \left\{ \alpha KL(q_i, q_E) + \beta \|f_i - f_E\|_2^2 \right\}, \tag{8}$$

which applies the distillation mechanism to both the exits and the main network. Finally, the overall loss becomes

$$L = \sum_{i=1}^{k} \left\{ CE(q_i, y) + \alpha KL(q_i, q_E) + \beta \|f_i - f_E\|_2^2 \right\}. \tag{9}$$

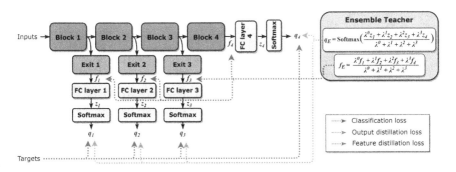

Fig. 3. Illustration of the proposed method. f_i, z_i, and q_i mean the features, logits, and predictions, respectively. (Color figure online)

The whole network including the main network and the attached exits is trained using this training loss from scratch as depicted in Fig. 3. We call this ensemble distillation *Exit-Ensemble Distillation* (EED), which will be further improved in the following section.

5   Loss-Balancing

In general, if the size of the network is not sufficiently large, the characteristics of the data cannot be learned properly through the classification loss, and instead, shortcuts are learned [9], which yield degraded generalization performance. Therefore, in multi-exit architectures, since the sizes of the early exits are relatively small, they are more difficult to learn proper features if they depend more on the classification loss during training. In this case, a distillation loss can be of help since it additionally provides the information of the non-true classes [33].

In particular, we propose to control relative contributions of the classification loss and the distillation loss for each classifier in a way that an exit at the early stage is trained more with the distillation loss than the classification loss. Therefore, the total loss using this loss-balancing method can be expressed as

$$L = \sum_{i=1}^{k} \left\{ (1 + \alpha - \gamma^{k-i}) \cdot CE(q_i, y) + \gamma^{k-i} \cdot KL(q_i, q_E) + \beta \| f_i - f_E \|_2^2 \right\} \quad (10)$$

where γ is a balancing constant satisfying $\gamma > 1$ and $\gamma^{k-1} < 1 + \alpha$. We call this *Balanced EED* (BEED), which is the final proposed method. Note that the coefficient for feature distillation (β) is fixed as a small value for simplicity, since we found that its contribution to the overall learning is only secondary.

Table 3. Test accuracy (%) of the main network trained by different methods using multi-exits for CIFAR-100.

Network	CE	KD	EED	BEED
ResNet18	79.39	79.21	80.03	**80.58**
ResNet34	80.22	80.17	81.61	**81.62**
WRN16-4	77.49	77.75	78.26	**78.51**
WRN28-4	80.05	80.06	80.55	**80.93**
MobileNet-V2	73.73	73.68	76.63	**76.74**
EfficientNetB0	74.21	74.44	77.47	**77.62**
MSDNet	74.44	75.13	74.63	**75.79**

Table 4. Test accuracy (%) (top-1/top-5) of the main network trained by different methods using multi-exits for ImageNet.

Network	CE	KD	BEED
ResNet18	69.91/88.75	70.12/89.14	70.28/89.50
ResNet34	73.13/91.30	73.75/91.66	73.96/91.75

6   Experiments

We evaluate our proposed BEED in comparison to existing methods for multi-exits and other online distillation methods using the CIFAR-100 [18] and ImageNet [5] datasets. We use several different CNN architectures composed of residual blocks as main networks such as ResNet [11], WideResNet (WRN) [37], MobileNet-V2 [29], and EfficientNetB0 [32]. MSDNet [14] is also considered, which was specially designed for anytime prediction.

We divide the main network before each residual block containing the convolutional layer having a stride of two, resulting in three or four parts. Then, we insert our proposed bottleneck structure as an exit network between the residual blocks. We use the same number of bottlenecks for an exit as the remaining residual blocks in the main network in order to match the dimension of the feature map for feature distillation. For ResNet, as an example, we use three bottlenecks for the first exit, two for the second exit, and one for the third exit. The number of channels of the bottleneck is the same to that of the corresponding residual block in the main network.

We set α to 1.0, β to 0.1, γ to 1.15, and λ to 1.6 by default. We conduct all experiments three times with different random seeds and report the average accuracy. Other implementation details and the ablation study of the hyper-parameters tuning are given in the supplementary material.

6.1 Main Network

To prove the effectiveness of our method for training the main network, we compare the test performance of the methods using multi-exits, including the method in [34] using (2) (denoted by CE), the method in [40] using (4) (denoted by KD), and the proposed BEED method using (10). We also show the performance of EED using (9) to verify the effectiveness of our loss-balancing.

Table 5. Test accuracy (%) of the main network trained for CIFAR-100 using online distillation methods.

Network	DML	ONE	DCL	OKDDip	BEED
ResNet18	78.97	78.89	79.58	79.83	**80.58**
ResNet34	78.98	78.84	79.71	79.54	**81.62**
WRN16-4	78.10	78.23	78.25	78.49	**78.51**
WRN28-4	80.35	80.67	80.71	80.89	**80.93**

Table 6. Test accuracy (%) (and GFLOPs required for one feedforward pass) of ensemble inference for CIFAR-100. The ensemble of the four classifiers (three exits and main network) trained by our BEED is compared to the case when four independent networks having the same structure are trained and used for ensembling.

Network	Indep. ens.	BEED ens.
ResNet18	80.56 (2.24)	81.45 (0.86)
ResNet34	80.80 (4.64)	82.50 (1.47)
MobileNet-V2	75.94 (0.40)	78.86 (0.27)
EfficientNetB0	76.58 (0.48)	79.36 (0.32)

The results for CIFAR-100 are shown in Table 3. Our BEED method achieves the best performance for all networks. The KD method is not always better than CE, but using an ensemble teacher on top of KD (i.e., EED) brings clear performance improvement. Especially, the performance of MoblieNet-V2 and EfficientNetB0 is greatly enhanced by the ensemble teacher (73.68% → 76.63% and 74.44% → 77.47%, respectively). In addition, our loss-balancing strategy with EED (i.e., BEED) enhances the performance further. With MSDNet, EED does not yield performance gain compared to KD, but by using BEED for proper loss-balancing, performance improvement is obtained (75.13% → 75.79%). Our BEED also achieves better performance than CE and KD for ImageNet as shown in Table 4.

In addition, we compare the performance of our BEED with that of the representative online distillation methods for image classification [4] (deep mutual learning (DML) [42] and on-the-fly native ensemble (ONE) [19]) and recent methods (deep collaborative learning (DCL) [26] and online knowledge distillation with diverse peers (OKDDip) [2]). As shown in Table 5, BEED achieves better performance than all methods with large performance gaps.

6.2   Ensemble Inference

Although we originally used the multi-exits to improve the performance of the main network, we can also use them to perform ensemble inference. As discussed in Sect. 3, our design of the structure of the exits aimed to enhance diversity. We can also make good use of this diversity to form a strong ensemble for ensemble inference.

Table 7. Test accuracy (%) of the main network with data augmentation for CIFAR-100.

Network	Aug.	KD	FRSKD	BEED
ResNet18	No aug.	79.21	77.88	80.58
	Mixup	80.32	78.83	81.12
	Cutout	80.16	79.80	80.89
	CutMix	**80.81**	81.22	**81.37**
	SLA	80.68	**81.25**	80.75
ResNet34	No aug.	80.17	77.02	81.62
	Mixup	81.01	78.37	81.57
	Cutout	81.82	80.08	82.75
	CutMix	**82.47**	81.16	**83.13**
	SLA	82.12	**81.54**	82.14

Table 6 compares the performance of the ensemble formed by all classifiers (exits and main network) in the mult-exit structure trained by BEED and the ensemble of independently trained main networks, showing that our BEED achieves better ensemble performance. Note that the performance of BEED in this case is significantly higher than that in Table 3 (e.g., 77.62% → 79.36% for

EfficientNetB0); in other words, when a multi-exit structure is trained by our BEED, ensembling the obtained classifiers further enhances the classification performance. Besides, the FLOPs required for ensemble inference is significantly reduced in BEED because the exit classifiers are smaller than the main network. In addition, even when we compare the ensemble performance of BEED to that of CE and KD, our method achieves better performance, which is shown in the supplementary material. Thus, our BEED is a good option even when ensemble inference is considered.

6.3   Performance with Data Augmentation

The recent online distillation method, feature refinement via self-knowledge distillation (FRSKD) [15], showed that data augmentation can improve performance of online distillation. Thus, we evaluate the performance of our BEED when applying the popular data augmentation methods, including Mixup [38], Cutout [6], CutMix [36], and self-supervised label augmentation (SLA) [20]. For Mixup, Cutout, and CutMix, we apply them to all exits, but SLA is applied only to the main network due to the excessive complexity of applying it to all exits.

The results in Table 7 show that CutMix is effective for KD and BEED, and SLA is effective for FRSKD. When the performance of the best data augmentation strategy in each method is compared, our BEED with CutMix outperforms the other methods for both ResNet18 and ResNet34.

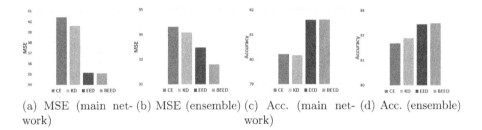

(a) MSE (main network) (b) MSE (ensemble) (c) Acc. (main network) (d) Acc. (ensemble)

Fig. 4. MSE and test accuracy (%) of different methods with ResNet34 for CIFAR-100. (Color figure online)

6.4   Good Teacher

In a recent study [25], it was found that teachers with low mean square error (MSE) between the output probabilities and the one-hot labels produce better students via distillation. Thus, we compare the MSE of the teacher in each method to verify whether our ensemble teacher is good in this criterion.

In Fig. 4, we show the MSE of the main network output (a) and ensemble output (b) with their accuracy (c and d). Overall, there exists a tendency that the lower the MSE is, the higher the accuracy is. The teacher in KD is the main network and the teacher in BEED is the ensemble output. Thus, when we compare the MSE for KD in Fig. 4a and the MSE for BEED in Fig. 4b, the latter (32.80) is much lower than the former (39.62). The ensemble teacher in BEED is the best teacher showing the smallest MSE among all cases (Figs. 4a and 4b), which results in the highest accuracy in Figs. 4c and 4d.

7   Conclusion

We proposed a new online knowledge distillation method using auxiliary classifiers (exits), called BEED. Our method is based on the selection of the structure of the exits to promote diversity, the newly proposed ensemble distillation method to obtain an improved teacher signal, and the new loss-balancing strategy to control the contributions of different losses. The experimental results showed that our method outperforms the existing online distillation methods. Further improvement was achieved by ensemble inference and data augmentation.

Acknowledgements. This work was supported by the Artificial Intelligence Graduate School Program, Yonsei University under Grant 2020-0-01361.

References

1. Asif, U., Tang, J., Harrer, S.: Ensemble knowledge distillation for learning improved and efficient networks. In: Proceedings of the European Conference on Artificial Intelligence (ECAI) (2020)
2. Chen, D., Mei, J.P., Wang, C., Feng, Y., Chen, C.: Online knowledge distillation with diverse peers. In: Proceedings of the Association for the Advancement of Artificial Intelligence (AAAI), pp. 3430–3437 (2020)
3. Chen, P., Liu, S., Zhao, H., Jia, J.: Distilling knowledge via knowledge review. In: Proceedings of the IEEE/CVF Conference on Computer Vision and Pattern Recognition (CVPR), pp. 5006–5015 (2021)
4. Chung, I., Park, S., Kim, J., Kwak, N.: Feature-map-level online adversarial knowledge distillation. In: Proceedings of the International Conference on Machine Learning (ICML), vol. 119, pp. 2006–2015 (2020)
5. Deng, J., Dong, W., Socher, R., Li, L.J., Li, K., Fei-Fei, L.: Imagenet: a large-scale hierarchical image database. In: Proceedings of the IEEE/CVF Conference on Computer Vision and Pattern Recognition (CVPR) (2009)
6. DeVries, T., Taylor, G.W.: Improved regularization of convolutional neural networks with cutout. arXiv preprint arXiv:1708.04552 (2017)
7. Dvornik, N., Mairal, J., Schmid, C.: Diversity with cooperation: ensemble methods for few-shot classification. In: Proceedings of the IEEE/CVF International Conference on Computer Vision (ICCV), pp. 3722–3730 (2019)
8. Fort, S., Hu, H., Lakshminarayanan, B.: Deep ensembles: a loss landscape perspective. arXiv preprint arXiv:1912.02757 (2019)
9. Geirhos, R., et al.: Shortcut learning in deep neural networks. Nat. Mach. Intell. **2**, 665–673 (2020)
10. Gou, J., Yu, B., Maybank, S.J., Tao, D.: Knowledge distillation: a survey. Int. J. Comput. Vision **129**, 1789–1819 (2021)

11. He, K., Zhang, X., Ren, S., Sun, J.: Deep residual learning for image recognition. In: Proceedings of the IEEE/CVF Conference on Computer Vision and Pattern Recognition (CVPR), Las Vegas, Nevada, pp. 770–778 (2016)
12. Heo, B., Kim, J., Yun, S., Park, H., Kwak, N., Choi, J.Y.: A comprehensive overhaul of feature distillation. In: Proceedings of the IEEE/CVF International Conference on Computer Vision (ICCV), pp. 1921–1930 (2019)
13. Hinton, G., Vinyals, O., Dean, J.: Distilling the knowledge in a neural network. In: Proceedings of the Neural Information Processing Systems (NeurIPS) Workshop (2014)
14. Huang, G., Chen, D., Li, T., Wu, F., van der Maaten, L., Weinberger, K.Q.: Multi-scale dense networks for resource efficient image classification. In: Proceedings of the International Conference on Learning Representations (ICLR) (2018)
15. Ji, M., Shin, S., Hwang, S., Park, G., Moon, I.C.: Refine myself by teaching myself: feature refinement via self-knowledge distillation. In: Proceedings of the IEEE/CVF Conference on Computer Vision and Pattern Recognition (CVPR), pp. 10659–10668 (2021)
16. Khan, A., Sohail, A., Zahoora, U., Qureshi, A.S.: A survey of the recent architectures of deep convolutional neural networks. Artif. Intell. Rev. 1–62 (2020)
17. Kim, Y., Park, J., Jang, Y., Ali, M., Oh, T.H., Bae, S.H.: Distilling global and local logits with densely connected relations. In: Proceedings of the IEEE/CVF International Conference on Computer Vision (ICCV), pp. 6290–6300 (2021)
18. Krizhevsky, A.: Learning multiple layers of features from tiny images. Master's thesis, Department of Computer Science, University of Toronto (2009)
19. Lan, X., Zhu, X., Gong, S.: Knowledge distillation by on-the-fly native ensemble. In: Proceedings of the Neural Information Processing Systems (NeurIPS), pp. 7528–7538 (2018)
20. Lee, H., Hwang, S.J., Shin, J.: Self-supervised label augmentation via input transformations. In: Proceedings of the International Conference on Machine Learning (ICML), vol. 119, pp. 5714–5724 (2020)
21. Lee, H., Lee, J.S.: Local critic training of deep neural networks. In: Proceedings of the International Joint Conference on Neural Networks (IJCNN) (2019)
22. Li, G., et al.: Residual distillation: towards portable deep neural networks without shortcuts. In: Proceedings of the Neural Information Processing Systems (NeurIPS), vol. 33, pp. 8935–8946 (2020)
23. Li, H., Zhang, H., Qi, X., Ruigang, Y., Huang, G.: Improved techniques for training adaptive deep networks. In: Proceedings of the IEEE/CVF International Conference on Computer Vision (ICCV), pp. 1891–1900 (2019)
24. Liu, B., Rao, Y., Lu, J., Zhou, J., Hsieh, C.-J.: MetaDistiller: network self-boosting via meta-learned top-down distillation. In: Vedaldi, A., Bischof, H., Brox, T., Frahm, J.-M. (eds.) ECCV 2020. LNCS, vol. 12359, pp. 694–709. Springer, Cham (2020). https://doi.org/10.1007/978-3-030-58568-6_41
25. Menon, A.K., Rawat, A.S., Reddi, S., Kim, S., Kumar, S.: A statistical perspective on distillation. In: Proceedings of the International Conference on Machine Learning (ICML), vol. 139, pp. 7632–7642 (2021)
26. Minami, S., Hirakawa, T., Yamashita, T., Fujiyoshi, H.: Knowledge transfer graph for deep collaborative learning. In: Ishikawa, H., Liu, C.-L., Pajdla, T., Shi, J. (eds.) ACCV 2020. LNCS, vol. 12625, pp. 203–217. Springer, Cham (2021). https://doi.org/10.1007/978-3-030-69538-5_13
27. Phuong, M., Lampert, C.: Distillation-based training for multi-exit architectures. In: Proceedings of the IEEE/CVF International Conference on Computer Vision (ICCV), pp. 1355–1364 (2019)

28. Romero, A., Ballas, N., Kahou, S.E., Chassang, A., Gatta, C., Bengio, Y.: Fit-Nets: hints for thin deep nets. In: Proceedings of the International Conference on Learning Representations (ICLR) (2015)
29. Sandler, M., Howard, A., Zhu, M., Zhmoginov, A., Chen, L.C.: MobileNetV2: inverted residuals and linear bottlenecks. In: Proceedings of the IEEE/CVF Conference on Computer Vision and Pattern Recognition (CVPR), pp. 4510–4520 (2018)
30. Song, J., Chen, Y., Ye, J., Song, M.: Spot-adaptive knowledge distillation. IEEE Trans. Image Process. **31**, 3359–3370 (2022)
31. Song, J., et al.: Tree-like decision distillation. In: Proceedings of the IEEE/CVF Conference on Computer Vision and Pattern Recognition (CVPR), pp. 13488–13497 (2021)
32. Tan, M., Le, Q.: EfficientNet: rethinking model scaling for convolutional neural networks. In: Proceedings of the International Conference on Machine Learning (ICML), vol. 97, pp. 6105–6114 (2019)
33. Tang, J., et al.: Understanding and improving knowledge distillation. arXiv preprint arXiv:2002.03532 (2020)
34. Teerapittayanon, S., McDanel, B., Kung, H.T.: BranchyNet: fast inference via early exiting from deep neural networks. In: Proceedings of the International Conference on Pattern Recognition (ICPR), pp. 2464–2469 (2016)
35. Yao, A., Sun, D.: Knowledge transfer via dense cross-layer mutual-distillation. In: Vedaldi, A., Bischof, H., Brox, T., Frahm, J.-M. (eds.) ECCV 2020. LNCS, vol. 12360, pp. 294–311. Springer, Cham (2020). https://doi.org/10.1007/978-3-030-58555-6_18
36. Yun, S., Han, D., Chun, S., Oh, S.J., Yoo, Y., Choe, J.: Cutmix: regularization strategy to train strong classifiers with localizable features. In: Proceedings of the IEEE/CVF International Conference on Computer Vision (ICCV), pp. 6022–6031 (2019)
37. Zagoruyko, S., Komodakis, N.: Wide residual networks. In: Proceedings of the British Machine Vision Conference (BMVC) (2016)
38. Zhang, H., Cisse, M., Dauphin, Y.N., Lopez-Paz, D.: Mixup: beyond empirical risk minimization. In: Proceedings of the International Conference on Learning Representations (ICLR) (2018)
39. Zhang, L., Shi, Y., Shi, Z., Ma, K., Bao, C.: Task-oriented feature distillation. In: Proceedings of the Neural Information Processing Systems (NeurIPS), vol. 33, pp. 14759–14771 (2020)
40. Zhang, L., Song, J., Gao, A., Chen, J., Bao, C., Ma, K.: Be your own teacher: improve the performance of convolutional neural networks via self distillation. In: Proceedings of the IEEE/CVF International Conference on Computer Vision (ICCV), pp. 3712–3721 (2019)
41. Zhang, S., Liu, M., Yan, J.: The diversified ensemble neural network. In: Proceedings of the Neural Information Processing Systems (NeurIPS), vol. 33, pp. 16001–16011 (2020)
42. Zhang, Y., Xiang, T., Hospedales, T.M., Lu, H.: Deep mutual learning. In: Proceedings of the IEEE/CVF Conference on Computer Vision and Pattern Recognition (CVPR) (2018)
43. Zhu, Y., Wang, Y.: Student customized knowledge distillation: bridging the gap between student and teacher. In: Proceedings of the IEEE/CVF International Conference on Computer Vision (ICCV), pp. 5057–5066 (2021)

Layout-Guided Indoor Panorama Inpainting with Plane-Aware Normalization

Chao-Chen Gao, Cheng-Hsiu Chen, Jheng-Wei Su,
and Hung-Kuo Chu[✉]

National Tsing Hua University, Hsinchu, Taiwan
hkchu@cs.nthu.edu.tw

Abstract. We present an end-to-end deep learning framework for indoor panoramic image inpainting. Although previous inpainting methods have shown impressive performance on natural perspective images, most fail to handle panoramic images, particularly indoor scenes, which usually contain complex structure and texture content. To achieve better inpainting quality, we propose to exploit both the global and local context of indoor panorama during the inpainting process. Specifically, we take the low-level layout edges estimated from the input panorama as a prior to guide the inpainting model for recovering the global indoor structure. A plane-aware normalization module is employed to embed plane-wise style features derived from the layout into the generator, encouraging local texture restoration from adjacent room structures (i.e., ceiling, floor, and walls). Experimental results show that our work outperforms the current state-of-the-art methods on a public panoramic dataset in both qualitative and quantitative evaluations. Our code is available online (https://ericsujw.github.io/LGPN-net/).

1 Introduction

Image inpainting is a widely investigated topic in computer graphics and vision communities, which aims at filling in missing regions of an image with photorealistic and fine detailed content. It plays a crucial step toward many practical applications, such as image restoration, object removal, etc. With the rapid development of deep learning, image inpainting has been revisited and improved significantly in the past few years. A considerable body of researches has been explored to generate impressive results on perspective datasets.

In this work, we address the image inpainting problem in the context of indoor panoramas. Indoor panoramas provide excellent media for the holistic scene understanding [40] that would further benefit several applications such as object detection, depth estimation, furniture rearrangement, etc. In particular, removing foreground objects and filling the missing regions in an indoor panorama is essential for the interior redesign task. However, the complex structures and textures presented in the indoor scenes make the inpainting problem non-trivial and challenging for previous methods. As shown in Fig. 2(EC),

© The Author(s), under exclusive license to Springer Nature Switzerland AG 2023
L. Wang et al. (Eds.): ACCV 2022, LNCS 13846, pp. 425–441, 2023.
https://doi.org/10.1007/978-3-031-26351-4_26

(a) Synthetic empty scene (b) Synthetic furnished scene (c) Real-world empty scene (d) Real-world furnished scene

Fig. 1. Indoor panorama inpainting. We present a learning-based indoor panorama inpainting method that is capable of generating plausible results for the tasks of hole filling (a)(c) and furniture removal (b)(d) in both synthetic (a)(b) and real-world (c)(d) scenes.

results generated by a state-of-the-art deep learning method fail to align the image structure along the layout boundaries and produce inconsistent blurry image contents.

Recently, Gkitsas et al. [9] introduced PanoDR, a diminished reality-oriented inpainting model for indoor panorama. The main idea is to translate a furnished indoor panorama into its empty counterpart via a network that leverages both a generator and an image-to-image translation module. The inpainting result is then obtained by compositing the predicted empty panorama and input panorama using the object mask. However, there are still obvious artifacts near the boundaries of masked regions as shown in Fig. 2.

To achieve better inpainting quality, we present an end-to-end deep generative adversarial framework that exploits both the global and local context of indoor panoramas to guide the inpainting process. Specifically, we take the low-level layout boundaries estimated from input panorama as a conditional input to guide the inpainting model, encouraging the preservation of sharp boundaries in the filled image. A plane-aware normalization module is then employed to embed local plane-wise style features derived from the layout into the image decoder, encouraging local texture restoration from adjacent room structures (i.e., ceiling, floor, and individual walls). We train and evaluate our model on a public indoor panorama dataset, Structured3D [41]. Experimental results show that our method produces results superior to several state-of-the-art methods (see Fig. 1, Fig. 2 and Fig. 5). The main contributions are summarized as follows:

– We present an end-to-end generative adversarial network that incorporates both the global and local context of indoor panoramas to guide the inpainting process.
– We introduce a plane-aware normalization module that guides the image decoder with spatially varying normalization parameters per structural plane (i.e., ceiling, floor, and individual walls).
– Our method achieves state-of-the-art performance and visual quality on synthetic and real-world datasets.

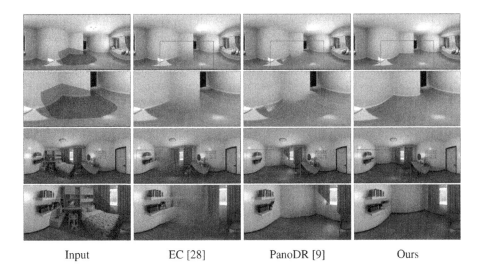

Input   EC [28]   PanoDR [9]   Ours

Fig. 2. Limitations of existing methods. EC [28] and PanoDR [9] fail to align the image structure along the layout boundaries and produce inconsistent blurry image contents in the inpainted regions (red mask). (Color figure online)

2   Related Work

Traditional Image Inpainting. There are two main genres among traditional image inpainting works: diffusion-based methods and patch-based methods. Diffusion-based methods [1,2,4,6,23,36] propagate pixels from neighboring regions to the missing ones to synthesize the image content. On the other hand, patch-based methods [3,7,11,19,26,27,32] fill the missing regions by searching for and copying similar image patches from the rest of the image or existing image datasets. Without a high-level understanding of the image contents, these methods easily fail on images with complex structures.

Learning-Based Image Inpainting. With the rapid development of deep learning, several image inpainting techniques based on convolutional neural networks (CNN) have been proposed. These methods aim to learn a generator from a large dataset to produce photorealistic image contents in the missing regions effectively. Context Encoders [30] pioneers CNN-based image inpainting by proposing an adversarial network with an encoder-decoder architecture. However, due to the information bottleneck layer of the autoencoder, the results are often blurry, incoherent, and can not work on irregular masks. Yu et al. [39] proposed a coarse-to-fine network and a context-aware mechanism to reduce blurriness. Iizuka et al. [14] adopted local and global discriminators and used dilated convolutions to increase the model's receptive field and enhance coherence. Liu et al. [25] proposed partial convolutions, which only consider valid pixels during convolution, to handle irregular masks. Yu et al. [38] further extends the partial convolutions by introducing a dynamic feature gating mechanism, named gated convolutions, to deal with free-from masks. Both Liu et al. [25] and Yu et al. [38] adopt PatchGAN discriminator [15] to improve the coherence further. Recently, several models were proposed to significantly improve the image painting quality by incorporating the structure knowledge in a different context, including image edges [22,28], object contours [37], smooth edge-preserving map [31], and gradient map [17]. Nazeri et al. [28] introduced a two-stage network named EdgeConnect, which firstly recovers the missing edges in the masked regions, followed by a generator conditioned on the reconstructed edge map. The authors prove that the structure-to-content approach can effectively preserve the structure information in the inpainting results. However, EdgeConnect uses canny edges to represent structure features, which might be suitable for natural images but may lead to complex local edges in indoor scenes. In contrast, our work exploits the Horizon-Net [34] to estimate layout edges, representing the global room structure, which is suitable for our indoor inpainting task. In addition, our model is an end-to-end architecture instead of a two-stage network. Yang et al. [17] developed a multi-task learning framework to jointly learn the completion of image contents and structure map (edges and gradient). A structure embedding scheme is employed to embed the learned structure features while inpainting explicitly. The model further learns to exploit the recurrent structures and contents via an attention mechanism. While demonstrating impressive performance in generating realistic results, these structure-aware methods still fail to model long-range structure correspondence such as the layout in the indoor scenes. On the other hand, some works have successfully recovered a single partially occluded object [5,20]. However, their architecture does not handle multiple object instances of the same class and is thus not suitable for our context where the plane-wise segmentation consists of different numbers of wall planes.

Image-to-Image Translation. The image inpainting is essentially a constrained image-to-image translation problem. Significant efforts have been made to tackle various problems based on image-to-image translation architectures [15,18,42]. Here we focus on the ones that are closely related to our work. Park et al. [29] introduced SPADE, which utilizes a spatial adaptive normalization layer for synthesizing photorealistic images given an input semantic segmentation map. Specifically, a spatially-adaptive learned transform modulates the activation layer with a semantic segmentation map and effectively propagates the semantic information throughout the network. In contrast to SPADE, which uses only one style code to control the image synthesis, Zhu et al. [43] presents SEAN by extending the SPADE architecture with per-region style encoding. By embedding one style code for individual semantic classes, SEAN shows significant improvement over SPADE and generates the highest quality results. In the context of indoor scenes, Gkitsas et al. [9] introduce PanoDR that combines image-to-image translation with a generator to constrain the image inpainting with the underlying scene structure. Percisely, to convert a furnished indoor panorama into its empty counterpart, PanoDR exploits a generator for synthesizing photorealistic image contents where the global layout structure is preserved via an image-to-image translation module. The empty indoor panorama

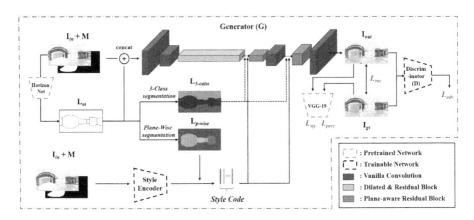

Fig. 3. Architecture overview. Our network architecture follows the conventional generative adversarial network with an encoder-decoder scheme supervised by low- and high-level loss functions and a discriminator. Given a masked indoor panoramic image $\mathbf{I}_{in}$ with a corresponding mask $\mathbf{M}$, our system uses an off-the-shelf layout prediction network to predicts a layout map. The low-level boundary lines in $\mathbf{L}_m$ serve as a conditional input to our network to assist the inpainting. Then, we compute two semantic segmentation maps from the layout map $\mathbf{L}_m$, declared $\mathbf{L}_{3-class}$ and $\mathbf{L}_{p-wise}$, where the latter is used to generate plane-wise style codes for ceiling, floor, and individual walls. Finally, these per plane style codes, together with $\mathbf{L}_{3-class}$, are fed to a structural plane-aware normalization module to constrain the inpainting.

is then used to complete the masked regions in the input panorama via a simple copy-and-paste process. Gkitsas et al. [10] extend the architecture of PanoDR to make the model end-to-end trainable. However, the quantitative evaluation indicates that the performance improvement is marginal compared with PanoDR. Our system also combines a generator with image-to-image translation as PanoDR does. However, we obtain superior results than PanoDR by exploiting the global layout edges as a prior and adapting SEAN blocks in a local plane-wise manner to guide the inpainting. Moreover, in contrast to PanoDR performs the inpainting task via an indirect way, our system performs the inpainting task in an end-to-end fashion, directly completing the mask areas instead of hallucinating an empty scene, thus resulting in better visual quality and consistency.

3   Overview

Figure 3 illustrates an overview of our architecture. Our system takes a masked panoramic image $\mathbf{I}_{in}$ and the corresponding binary mask $\mathbf{M}$ as inputs and generates the inpainted panoramic image $\mathbf{I}_{out}$. The masked panoramic image is generated by $\mathbf{I}_{in} = \mathbf{I}_{gt} \odot (\mathbf{1} - \mathbf{M})$, where $\mathbf{I}_{gt}$ represents the ground-truth panoramic image and $\odot$ denotes the Hadamard product. Our system first utilizes an off-the-shelf model to estimate the room layout $\mathbf{L}_m$ from input masked panoramic image. This layout map is then concatenated with $\mathbf{I}_{in}$ and $\mathbf{M}$ to obtain a five-channel input map fed into the generator $\mathbf{G}$. We further derive two semantic

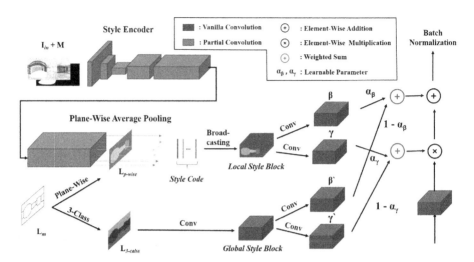

Fig. 4. Plane-aware normalization. Given an incomplete indoor panoramic image $\mathbf{I}_{in}$ with mask $\mathbf{M}$, we first predict two normalization values β and γ through several partial convolution [25] blocks and a plane-wise average pooling based on the plane-wise segmentation map $\mathbf{L}_{p-wise}$. Second, we predict another set of normalization values β' and γ' through several vanilla convolution blocks based on the 3-class segmentation map $\mathbf{L}_{3-class}$. The final normalization values are thus computed using the weighted sum weighted by learnable parameters α_β and α_γ.

segmentation maps $\mathbf{L}_{3-class}$ and $\mathbf{L}_{p-wise}$ using the layout map for the subsequent normalization module (Sect. 4.1). The image generation model follows the conventional generative adversarial architecture with one content encoder and one image decoder with one discriminator (Sect. 4.2). To impose structure information during inpainting, we introduce a plane-aware normalization that modifies the SEAN [43] block with two semantic segmentation maps to guide the decoder with spatially varying normalization parameters per structural plane (i.e., ceiling, floor, and individual walls). Such a plane-aware normalization provides useful guidance for global structure preservation as well as consistent local image content generation (Sect. 4.3). Finally, common loss functions in image inpainting, including the reconstruction loss, the perceptual loss, the style loss, and the adversarial loss are employed to train our model (Sect. 4.4).

4   Method

4.1   Layout Guidance Map

We employ an off-the-shelf model, HorizonNet [34], to estimate a layout map from input masked panorama. Through a recurrent neural network, the HorizonNet predicts a 3-dimensional vector representing ceiling, ground, and corner location. We further process the output vector to generate a layout map $\mathbf{L}_m$ comprising low-level boundary lines. This layout map serves as a conditional input to encourage the preservation of global layout structure while inpainting. Moreover, we extract two semantic segmentation maps from the layout map that depict (i) the segmentation mask $\mathbf{L}_{3-class}$ with three semantic labels of indoor scene, i.e., ceiling, floor, and wall; and (ii) a plane-wise segmentation mask $\mathbf{L}_{p-wise}$ where pixels are indexed in a per structural plane basis (i.e., ceiling, floor, or individual walls). These semantic segmentation maps are generated using conventional image processing operations (i.e., flood-fill) and will be used in the later normalization module.

4.2 Image Inpainting Backbone

As shown in Fig. 3, our network architecture consists of one generator and one discriminator. The generator $\mathbf{G}$ follows a conventional scheme with one content encoder and one image decoder. The content encoder consists of two down-sampling convolution blocks followed by eight residual blocks using dilated convolution [12]. The image decoder uses a cascade of our proposed plane-aware residual blocks and two up-sampling blocks. Motivated by EdgeConnect [28], we use PatchGAN [16] as our discriminator to determine the real or fake sample by dividing the input image into several patches. In the following sections, we will elaborate plane-aware residual block, loss functions, and discriminator in more detail.

4.3 Plane-Aware Normalization

Considering the different styles among wall planes is very common in real-world indoor scenes. We follow the architecture of SEAN [43] and propose leveraging two kinds of segmentation maps $\mathbf{L}_{p-wise}$ and $\mathbf{L}_{3-class}$ to establish our plane-aware normalization (see Fig. 4). Our plane-aware normalization consists of one style encoder and two style blocks, which enhance the global style semantics and local style consistency of the generated results. The inputs of the style encoder include masked panoramic image $\mathbf{I}_{in}$ and mask image $\mathbf{M}$. We use partial convolution blocks in style encoder instead of vanilla convolution to make feature extraction conditioned only valid pixels. We first adopt the plane-wise average pooling on the output features to generate style codes for each plane based on $\mathbf{L}_{p-wise}$. Second, we spatially broadcast each style code on the corresponding area and output the local style block. On the other side, we predict the global style block by passing the 3-class segmentation map $\mathbf{L}_{3-class}$ through several convolution layers. Finally, the remaining part of our plane-aware normalization follows the same architecture of SEAN [43], and combines global and local style blocks into the downstream β and γ parameters of the final batch normalization.

4.4 Loss Functions

Here we elaborate on the low- and high-level loss functions and the discrimination used for training our image generator.

Reconstruction Loss measures the low-level pixel-based loss between the predicted and ground-truth images. To encourage the generator to pay more attention to the missing regions, we additionally calculate the L_1 loss in the missing regions. The reconstruction loss L_{rec} is defined as follows:

$$L_{rec} = \|\mathbf{M} \odot \mathbf{I}_{gt} - \mathbf{M} \odot \mathbf{I}_{out}\|_1 + \|\mathbf{I}_{gt} - \mathbf{I}_{out}\|_1, \tag{1}$$

where $\mathbf{I}_{gt}$ and $\mathbf{I}_{out}$ represent the ground-truth image and the generator's output, respectively, and $\mathbf{M}$ is a binary mask.

Perceptual Loss encourages the predicted and ground-truth images to have similar representation in high-level feature space extracted via a pre-trained VGG-19 [33], and is defined as follows:

$$L_{perc} = \sum_i \|\phi_i (\mathbf{I}_{gt}) - \phi_i (\mathbf{I}_{out})\|_1, \tag{2}$$

where ϕ_i is the activation map of the ith layer of the pre-trained feature extraction network.

Style Loss calculates the co-variance difference between the activation maps. For the activation map ϕ_i of size $C_i \times H_i \times W_i$, the style loss is defined as follows:

$$L_{sty} = \left\| G_i^\phi (\mathbf{I}_{gt}) - G_i^\phi (\mathbf{I}_{out}) \right\|_1, \tag{3}$$

where G_i^ϕ is a $C_i \times C_i$ gram matrix [8] constructed by the activation map ϕ_i.

Adversarial Loss is implemented with the patch-based discriminator [16], which outputs the feature map divided into several feature patches and uses hinge loss [24] to optimize the generator G and the discriminator D. The adversarial loss for generator G and discriminator D are defined as follows:

$$L_G = -D (\mathbf{I}_{out}), \tag{4}$$

$$L_D = \lambda_D (max (0, 1 + D (\mathbf{I}_{out})) + max (0, 1 - D (\mathbf{I}_{gt}))); \tag{5}$$

The overall loss function used in the generator G is defined as follows:

$$L_{total} = \lambda_{rec} L_{rec} + \lambda_{perc} L_{perc} + \lambda_{sty} L_{sty} + \lambda_G L_G, \tag{6}$$

where λ_{rec}, λ_{perc}, λ_{sty}, λ_G, and λ_D are the hyperparameters for weighting the loss functions.

5   Experiments

In this section, we evaluate the performance of our model by comparing it with several state-of-the-art image inpainting approaches and conducting ablation studies to verify the necessity of individual components in the proposed architecture. Please refer to our online webpage for other experiments and more results[1].

---

[1] https://ericsujw.github.io/LGPN-net/.

Input / Layout   EC [28]   LISK [17]   PanoDR [9]   Ours   GT

Fig. 5. Qualitative comparisons with state-of-the-arts. Top 8 rows: the inpainting results of the empty indoor scenes. Bottom 8 rows: the inpainting results of the furnished indoor scenes. Our method produces superior results in generating image contents that align the layout structure well and are consistent with the surrounding of the masked regions.

5.1   Experimental Settings

Dataset and Baselines. We compare our model with the following state-of-the-art structure-aware image inpainting models:

- EC [28]: a two-stage adversarial network that comprises an edge completion model followed by a generator.
- LISK [17]: a multi-task learning framework that exploits image structure embedding and an attention mechanism in the generator.
- PanoDR [9]: a deep learning framework that combines image-to-image translation with generator to condition the inpainting on the indoor scene structure.

The experiments were conducted on a public indoor panorama dataset, Structured3D [41], which contains 21,835 indoor panoramas. The official data split is adopted for training(18,362), validation(1,776), and testing(1,697). We follow the same procedure as PanoDR to generate mask images using contours of foreground furniture (see Sect. 3.1). We use the officially released implementation of baselines for training from scratch and testing. Note that each indoor panorama in Structured3D has two representations of the same scene (i.e., empty and furnished). Therefore, the experiments were conducted in two phases to evaluate our model and baselines in different application scenarios (i.e., structural inpainting vs. furniture removal).

Evaluation Metrics. We take several commonly used image quality assessment metrics in previous inpainting approaches for quantitative evaluation. Specifically, we used the low-level feature metrics, including Mean Absolute Error (MAE), Peak Signal-to-Noise (PSNR), Structural Similarity Index (SSIM) [35], and Fréchet Inception Distance (FID) [13].

Implementation Details. We implement our model in PyTorch and conduct the experiments on a single NVIDIA V100 with 32G VRAM. The resolution of the panoramic images is resized to 512×256. We use Adam [21] optimizer in the training process with the hyper-parameters setting of $b_1 = 0.0$ and $b_2 = 0.9$, a learning rate of 0.0001, and a batch size of 8. We empirically set $\lambda_{rec} = 1$, $\lambda_{perc} = 0.1$, $\lambda_{sty} = 250$, $\lambda_G = 0.1$, and $\lambda_D = 0.5$ in the total loss function (Eq. 6). For HorizonNet [34], we use the official pre-trained model for layout estimation.

5.2   Evaluation on the Empty Scenes

In this experiment, we evaluate both the qualitative and quantitative performance of our model on the image inpainting task by comparing it with baselines. The qualitative comparisons are shown in Fig. 5 (top 8 rows). In contrast to EC and LISK, which fail to restore image structures in the masked regions, our method faithfully generates image contents adhering to the underlying layout structure. While PanoDR shows slightly better structure preservation than

Table 1. Quantitative comparisons with state-of-the-arts. The top and bottom tables summarize the performance of our model and baselines on the empty and furnished scenes, respectively.

Dataset	Method	PSNR ↑	SSIM ↑	MAE ↓	FID ↓
Empty scene	EC [28]	38.6936	0.9892	0.0039	3.9480
	LISK [17]	41.3761	0.9895	0.0055	4.1660
	PanoDR [9]	37.2431	0.9884	0.0040	4.3591
	Ours	**41.8444**	**0.9919**	**0.0030**	**2.5265**
Furnished scene	EC [28]	31.4439	0.9493	0.0076	11.9955
	LISK [17]	34.7325	0.9553	0.0068	14.2676
	PanoDR [9]	34.3340	0.9641	0.0051	7.8399
	Ours	**35.3923**	**0.9672**	**0.0047**	**7.2328**

EC and LISK, it fails to generate image contents consistent with the surrounding of masked regions as our method does. Therefore, our method achieves the best performance against all the baselines across all evaluation metrics as shown in Table 1 (top).

5.3   Evaluation on the Furnished Scenes

Furniture of irregular shape will more or less obscure the layout of the indoor scene, making it more challenging to restore the regular structure in the missing area. Therefore, in this experiment, we would like to evaluate how well our model learned from empty scenes can generalize to the furnished scenes. Since the inpainting task setup here exactly matches the one defined in the PanoDR, we use the pre-trained model of PanoDR in this experiment for a fair comparison. As shown in Fig. 5 (bottom 8 rows), our method still clearly outperforms baselines in generating image contents that align the layout structure well and are consistent with the surrounding of the masked regions. The quantitative results are shown in Table 1 (bottom). It is worth noting that the way PanoDR performs image completion via compositing the predicted empty image and input image using the object mask will lead to severe artifacts where occlusion occurred between foreground objects (see Fig. 2(PanoDR)).

5.4   Ablation Study

Here, we conduct ablation studies to validate our model from different perspectives. First, we evaluate the necessity of individual design choices in our architecture. Then, we conduct two experiments to evaluate how sensitive our model is to the size of input masks and the quality of input layout maps.

Ablation on Network Architecture. In this experiment, we start with the backbone model (**Backbone**) as the baseline, then progressively adding only

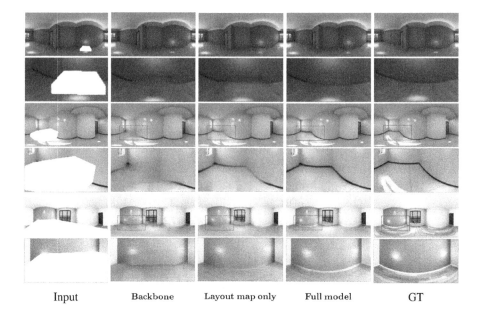

Input   Backbone   Layout map only   Full model   GT

Fig. 6. Qualitative results of the ablation study. Side-by-side comparisons of inpainting results generated using our method by gradually adding individual components. From left to right, input images and masks, our baseline model (**Backbone**), adding the layout guidance map (**Layout map only**), full model with our plane-aware normalization (**Full model**), and ground truth images.

Table 2. Quantitative results of the ablation study. We evaluate the effectiveness of our design choices by gradually adding the individual components into the architecture.

	PSNR ↑	SSIM ↑	MAE ↓	FID ↓
Baackbone	40.6449	0.9911	0.0034	3.3915
Layout map only	41.2884	0.9916	0.0033	2.8105
Full model	**41.8444**	**0.9919**	**0.0030**	**2.5265**

layout guidance map (**Layout map only**), and our plane-aware normalization (**Full model**). As shown in Table 2, we obtain the best performance with the full model on all the metrics. The qualitative comparisons shown in Fig. 6 indicate that adding layout guidance map generates clear structure boundaries in the final result (2nd and 3rd columns), while our full model with plane-aware normalization can constrain the image generation to the adjacent structural planes and obtain visually consistent results (3rd and 4th columns).

Sensitivity to the Mask Size. In this experiment, we analyze the testing dataset and classify the images into different categories according to the area proportions of input masks. Table 3 shows the inpainting performance for each

Table 3. Mask size vs. inpainting quality.

Mask size (%)	Count	Content		
		PSNR ↑	SSIM ↑	MAE ↓
0–10	1045	44.3921	0.9967	0.0011
10–20	163	34.2823	0.9841	0.0055
20–30	48	30.4371	0.9726	0.0111
30–40	39	25.0731	0.9386	0.0266
40+	13	24.2958	0.9345	0.0305
Total	1308	41.8444	0.9919	0.0030

Table 4. Accuracy of layout estimation vs. inpainting quality.

Structure	Content			
mIOU ↑	PSNR ↑	SSIM ↑	MAE ↓	FID ↓
0.9603	42.3212	0.9925	0.0028	2.4322
0.9561	42.2871	0.9925	0.0028	2.4441
0.9175	42.0682	0.9923	0.0029	2.5624
0.8489	41.7300	0.9919	0.0030	2.8455

category. We can tell that the inpainting quality degrades with the increasing mask size. A significant drop occurs where the ratio of input mask is greater than 30%.

Sensitivity to the Layout Estimation. In order to explore the effect of the accuracy of layout estimation on the inpainting quality, we first devise a mechanism to generate layout maps with different levels of accuracy. Specifically, we feed masked images of different mask sizes into HorizonNet. We start by generating randomly located rectangle masks of 5% image size and increase the mask ratio to 10%, 30% and 50% to deliberately produce layout structures with decreasing quality. Then we take these layout maps as conditional inputs of our model and compare the inpainting performance empty-room testing dataset. As shown in Table 4, our model degrades marginally when the quality of estimated layouts decreases from 0.96 to 0.84, indicating our model is robust to the varying input layout maps.

5.5 Qualitative Results on Real-World Scene

Real-world scenes have complex lighting and layout structure. However, the amount of data in the real-world scene dataset and the quality of furniture category annotations are insufficient for training our model, so we choose to train on the synthetic dataset Structured3D [41]. Nevertheless, we still compare our results with PanoDR [9], which also implements the furniture removal task, on

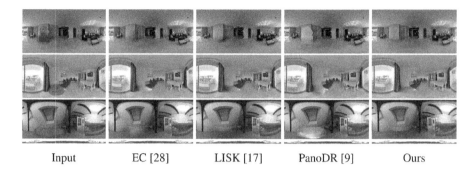

Input	EC [28]	LISK [17]	PanoDR [9]	Ours

Fig. 7. Qualitative comparisons with state-of-the-arts on real-world scenes. Our model clearly outperforms baselines by preserving layout boundary and restoring local texture from adjacent room structures (i.e., floor and walls).

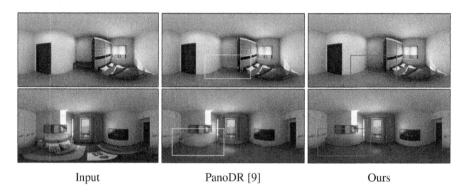

Input	PanoDR [9]	Ours

Fig. 8. Limitation. Both the state-of-the-art method and our model produce visual artifacts in the scenes presenting strong shading effect surrounding the removed furniture.

the real-world scene dataset. Since the real-world scene dataset does not contain paired data (i.e., scenes before and after furniture removal), quantitative evaluation is infeasible and we can only provide qualitative comparisons here. Figure 7 shows that our inpainted results have a higher quality of structural maintenance and color restoration. Moreover, compared with PanoDR, we can still exert more stable performance in real-world scenes. Please refer to our online webpage for more results[2].

6   Conclusions

We proposed an end-to-end structural inpainting network for the indoor scene. We introduce layout boundary line conditions the output structure and utilize the plane-aware normalization to enhance planar style consistency. Experiment

---

[2] https://ericsujw.github.io/LGPN-net/.

results show the outstanding performance of our model in both structural inpainting and furniture removal on the indoor scene.

Limitations. In the real-world application of furniture removal, we can often see residuals of shading effect caused by the removed furniture. These residuals are hard to segment and even harder to model. As shown in Fig. 8, our model is slightly affected by these residuals but still produces more realistic results than PanoDR [9].

Future Work. We plan to adopt a more reasonable segmentation mask of the indoor scene inpainting which can cover the shading area and thus improve our results in those shaded scenes.

Acknowledgements. The project was funded in part by the National Science and Technology Council of Taiwan (110-2221-E-007-060-MY3, 110-2221-E-007-061-MY3).

References

1. Ashikhmin, M.: Synthesizing natural textures. In: Proceedings of the 2001 Symposium on Interactive 3D Graphics. I3D 2001, pp. 217–226. Association for Computing Machinery, New York (2001). https://doi.org/10.1145/364338.364405
2. Ballester, C., Bertalmio, M., Caselles, V., Sapiro, G., Verdera, J.: Filling-in by joint interpolation of vector fields and gray levels. IEEE Trans. Image Process. **10**(8), 1200–1211 (2001). https://doi.org/10.1109/83.935036
3. Barnes, C., Shechtman, E., Finkelstein, A., Goldman, D.B.: Patchmatch: a randomized correspondence algorithm for structural image editing. ACM Trans. Graph. (TOG) (2009)
4. Drori, I., Cohen-Or, D., Yeshurun, Y.: Fragment-based image completion. In: ACM SIGGRAPH 2003 Papers (2003)
5. Ehsani, K., Mottaghi, R., Farhadi, A.: Segan: segmenting and generating the invisible. In: 2018 IEEE/CVF Conference on Computer Vision and Pattern Recognition, pp. 6144–6153 (2018). https://doi.org/10.1109/CVPR.2018.00643
6. Esedoglu, S.: Digital inpainting based on the Mumford-Shah-Euler image model. Eur. J. Appl. Math. **13** (2003). https://doi.org/10.1017/S0956792502004904
7. Fan, Q., Zhang, L.: A novel patch matching algorithm for exemplar-based image inpainting. Multimedia Tools Appl. **77**(9), 10807–10821 (2017). https://doi.org/10.1007/s11042-017-5077-z
8. Gatys, L.A., Ecker, A.S., Bethge, M.: Image style transfer using convolutional neural networks. In: Proceedings of the IEEE Conference on Computer Vision and Pattern Recognition (CVPR), June 2016
9. Gkitsas, V., Sterzentsenko, V., Zioulis, N., Albanis, G., Zarpalas, D.: Panodr: spherical panorama diminished reality for indoor scenes. In: Proceedings of the IEEE/CVF Conference on Computer Vision and Pattern Recognition, pp. 3716–3726 (2021)
10. Gkitsas, V., Zioulis, N., Sterzentsenko, V., Doumanoglou, A., Zarpalas, D.: Towards full-to-empty room generation with structure-aware feature encoding and soft semantic region-adaptive normalization. In: Farinella, G.M., Radeva, P., Bouatouch, K. (eds.) Proceedings of the 17th International Joint Conference on Computer Vision, Imaging and Computer Graphics Theory and Applications, VISIGRAPP 2022, Volume 4: VISAPP, Online Streaming, 6–8 February 2022, pp. 452–461. SCITEPRESS (2022). https://doi.org/10.5220/0010833100003124

11. Guo, Q., Gao, S., Zhang, X., Yin, Y., Zhang, C.: Patch-based image inpainting via two-stage low rank approximation. IEEE Trans. Vis. Comput. Graph. **24**(6), 2023–2036 (2018). https://doi.org/10.1109/TVCG.2017.2702738

12. He, K., Zhang, X., Ren, S., Sun, J.: Deep residual learning for image recognition. In: 2016 IEEE Conference on Computer Vision and Pattern Recognition (CVPR), pp. 770–778 (2016). https://doi.org/10.1109/CVPR.2016.90

13. Heusel, M., Ramsauer, H., Unterthiner, T., Nessler, B., Hochreiter, S.: GANs trained by a two time-scale update rule converge to a local Nash equilibrium (2018)

14. Iizuka, S., Simo-Serra, E., Ishikawa, H.: Globally and locally consistent image completion. ACM Trans. Graph. (Proc. SIGGRAPH) **36**(4), 107:1–107:14 (2017)

15. Isola, P., Zhu, J.Y., Zhou, T., Efros, A.A.: Image-to-image translation with conditional adversarial networks. In: CVPR (2017)

16. Isola, P., Zhu, J.Y., Zhou, T., Efros, A.A.: Image-to-image translation with conditional adversarial networks (2018)

17. Jie Yang, Zhiquan Qi, Y.S.: Learning to incorporate structure knowledge for image inpainting. In: Proceedings of the AAAI Conference on Artificial Intelligence, vol. 34, pp. 12605–12612 (2020)

18. Karras, T., Laine, S., Aila, T.: A style-based generator architecture for generative adversarial networks (2019)

19. Kawai, N., Sato, T., Yokoya, N.: Diminished reality based on image inpainting considering background geometry. IEEE Trans. Vis. Comput. Graph. **22**(3), 1236–1247 (2016). https://doi.org/10.1109/TVCG.2015.2462368

20. Ke, L., Tai, Y., Tang, C.: Occlusion-aware video object inpainting. In: 2021 IEEE/CVF International Conference on Computer Vision (ICCV), pp. 14448–14458. IEEE Computer Society, Los Alamitos, October 2021. https://doi.org/10.1109/ICCV48922.2021.01420, https://doi.ieeecomputersociety.org/10.1109/ICCV48922.2021.01420

21. Kingma, D.P., Ba, J.: Adam: a method for stochastic optimization (2017)

22. Li, J., He, F., Zhang, L., Du, B., Tao, D.: Progressive reconstruction of visual structure for image inpainting. In: Proceedings of the IEEE/CVF International Conference on Computer Vision (ICCV), October 2019

23. Liang, Z., Yang, G., Ding, X., Li, L.: An efficient forgery detection algorithm for object removal by exemplar-based image inpainting. J. Vis. Commun. Image Represent. **30**, 75–85 (2015)

24. Lim, J.H., Ye, J.C.: Geometric GAN (2017)

25. Liu, G., Reda, F.A., Shih, K.J., Wang, T.-C., Tao, A., Catanzaro, B.: Image inpainting for irregular holes using partial convolutions. In: Ferrari, V., Hebert, M., Sminchisescu, C., Weiss, Y. (eds.) ECCV 2018. LNCS, vol. 11215, pp. 89–105. Springer, Cham (2018). https://doi.org/10.1007/978-3-030-01252-6_6

26. Liu, J., Yang, S., Fang, Y., Guo, Z.: Structure-guided image inpainting using homography transformation. IEEE Trans. Multimedia **20**(12), 3252–3265 (2018). https://doi.org/10.1109/TMM.2018.2831636

27. Lu, H., Liu, Q., Zhang, M., Wang, Y., Deng, X.: Gradient-based low rank method and its application in image inpainting. Multimedia Tools Appl. **77**(5), 5969–5993 (2017). https://doi.org/10.1007/s11042-017-4509-0

28. Nazeri, K., Ng, E., Joseph, T., Qureshi, F., Ebrahimi, M.: Edgeconnect: generative image inpainting with adversarial edge learning (2019)

29. Park, T., Liu, M.Y., Wang, T.C., Zhu, J.Y.: Semantic image synthesis with spatially-adaptive normalization. In: Proceedings of the IEEE Conference on Computer Vision and Pattern Recognition (2019)

30. Pathak, D., Krähenbühl, P., Donahue, J., Darrell, T., Efros, A.: Context encoders: feature learning by inpainting. In: Computer Vision and Pattern Recognition (CVPR) (2016)
31. Ren, Y., Yu, X., Zhang, R., Li, T.H., Liu, S., Li, G.: Structureflow: image inpainting via structure-aware appearance flow (2019)
32. Ružić, T., Pižurica, A.: Context-aware patch-based image inpainting using Markov random field modeling. IEEE Trans. Image Process. **24**(1), 444–456 (2015). https://doi.org/10.1109/TIP.2014.2372479
33. Simonyan, K., Zisserman, A.: Very deep convolutional networks for large-scale image recognition (2015)
34. Sun, C., Hsiao, C., Sun, M., Chen, H.: Horizonnet: learning room layout with 1D representation and pano stretch data augmentation. In: IEEE Conference on Computer Vision and Pattern Recognition, CVPR 2019, Long Beach, 16–20 June 2019, pp. 1047–1056 (2019)
35. Wang, Z., Bovik, A., Sheikh, H., Simoncelli, E.: Image quality assessment: from error visibility to structural similarity. IEEE Trans. Image Process. **13**(4), 600–612 (2004). https://doi.org/10.1109/TIP.2003.819861
36. Wei, Y., Liu, S.: Domain-based structure-aware image inpainting. SIViP **10**(5), 911–919 (2016). https://doi.org/10.1007/s11760-015-0840-y
37. Xiong, W., Yu, J., Lin, Z., Yang, J., Lu, X., Barnes, C., Luo, J.: Foreground-aware image inpainting. In: The IEEE Conference on Computer Vision and Pattern Recognition (CVPR), June 2019
38. Yu, J., Lin, Z., Yang, J., Shen, X., Lu, X., Huang, T.S.: Free-form image inpainting with gated convolution. arXiv preprint arXiv:1806.03589 (2018)
39. Yu, J., Lin, Z., Yang, J., Shen, X., Lu, X., Huang, T.S.: Generative image inpainting with contextual attention. arXiv preprint arXiv:1801.07892 (2018)
40. Zhang, Y., Song, S., Tan, P., Xiao, J.: PanoContext: a whole-room 3D context model for panoramic scene understanding. In: Fleet, D., Pajdla, T., Schiele, B., Tuytelaars, T. (eds.) ECCV 2014. LNCS, vol. 8694, pp. 668–686. Springer, Cham (2014). https://doi.org/10.1007/978-3-319-10599-4_43
41. Zheng, J., Zhang, J., Li, J., Tang, R., Gao, S., Zhou, Z.: Structured3D: a large photo-realistic dataset for structured 3D modeling. In: Vedaldi, A., Bischof, H., Brox, T., Frahm, J.-M. (eds.) ECCV 2020. LNCS, vol. 12354, pp. 519–535. Springer, Cham (2020). https://doi.org/10.1007/978-3-030-58545-7_30
42. Zhu, J.Y., Park, T., Isola, P., Efros, A.A.: Unpaired image-to-image translation using cycle-consistent adversarial networks. In: 2017 IEEE International Conference on Computer Vision (ICCV) (2017)
43. Zhu, P., Abdal, R., Qin, Y., Wonka, P.: Sean: image synthesis with semantic region-adaptive normalization. In: IEEE/CVF Conference on Computer Vision and Pattern Recognition (CVPR) (2020)

QS-Craft: Learning to Quantize, Scrabble and Craft for Conditional Human Motion Animation

Yuxin Hong[1], Xuelin Qian[1(✉)], Simian Luo[1], Guodong Guo[3],
Xiangyang Xue[1,2], and Yanwei Fu[1]

[1] School of Data Science, and MOE Frontiers Center for Brain Science, Shanghai
Key Lab of Intelligent Information Processing, Fudan University, Shanghai, China
{20210980140,xlqian,18300180157,yanweifu}@fudan.edu.cn
[2] School of Computer Science, Shanghai Key Lab of Intelligent Information
Processing, Fudan University, Shanghai, China
xyxue@fudan.edu.cn
[3] Department of CSEE, West Virginia University, Morgantown, USA
guodong.guo@mail.wvu.edu

Abstract. This paper studies the task of conditional Human Motion
Animation (cHMA). Given a source image and a driving video, the model
should animate the new frame sequence, in which the person in the source
image should perform a similar motion as the pose sequence from the
driving video. Despite the success of Generative Adversarial Network
(GANs) methods in image and video synthesis, it is still very challenging to conduct cHMA due to the difficulty in efficiently utilizing the
conditional guided information such as images or poses, and generating images of good visual quality. To this end, this paper proposes a
novel model of learning to Quantize, Scrabble, and Craft (QS-Craft) for
conditional human motion animation. The key novelties come from the
newly introduced three key steps: quantize, scrabble and craft. Particularly, our QS-Craft employs transformer in its structure to utilize the
attention architectures. The guided information is represented as a pose
coordinate sequence extracted from the driving videos. Extensive experiments on human motion datasets validate the efficacy of our model.

1 Introduction

The task of conditional Human Motion Animation (cHMA) has attracted
increasing attention in the vision community, as it can be utilized in many
industrial applications such as computer games, advertisement, and animation
industry [4,17,18]. In this work, we aim to solve the cHMA problem by transferring driving videos to animate the humans in the source. Particularly, given

---

Supplementary Information The online version contains supplementary material
available at https://doi.org/10.1007/978-3-031-26351-4_27.

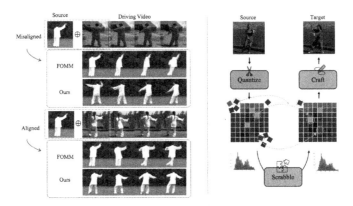

Fig. 1. Left: Examples of cHMA task. Right: idea illustration of our QS-Craft. Our method learns to quantize source image, scrabble quantized representation conditioned on driving video, and finally craft the synthesis of target images. Notice that when pose misalignment occurs (left-top), FOMM [27] fails to generate realistic motion transfer images, while our method accomplishes the task well and preserves finer details. Two histograms (right-bottom) indicate quite similar visual features of the source and target, producing intuition to play the *Scrabble* game.

a source image and a driving video, the cHMA model should animate the new frame sequence, in which the person in the source image should perform similar motion as pose sequence from the driving video.

To tackle this task, some classical approaches [3,5,30] are very domain-specific and rely on parametric models to represent humans. Generative models, such as Variational Auto-Encoders (VAE) [14,29] and Generative Adversarial Networks (GANs) [2,19,21,23], have shown good capacity on the image generation task, which could be the alternative ways to address our cHMA task. Unfortunately, these models typically demand expensive training from large collection of data in an *unconditioned* manner. On the other hand, motion flow based approaches [26–28] have received more and more attention due to its remarkable performance. The key idea of these methods is to learn motion flows between the source image and the driving frames, such that the target image features can be synthesized by wrapping. For cHMA, authors [26–28] proposed to use keypoints to produce flow maps, but these works additionally require modules to map the flow from sparse to dense. This is not only difficult to be learned but also may introduce lots of artifacts. For example, the misalignment of human motion in [27] in the source image and the first driving video frame may lead to an unreasonable animated result as shown in the left of Fig. 1.

In this paper, we advocate the way of motion flow yet from a different and novel perspective. As illustrated in Fig. 1, we propose to generate the target image by only rearranging the order of patches in the source image, on account of the observation that the source and the target images have very similar distribution. This is similar to a game of 'Scrabble' using the same letters to spell different words but following different rules. So, the key question is *how to learn the rule of Scrabble?* We argue that it should satisfy three requirements: (i) rules should be objective and independent of input; (ii) the order of patches should be reasonable, including the texture of background and the identity of foreground; (iii) obviously it should be conditioned on the driving videos. To this end, we present a novel paradigm of learning to **Q**uantize, **S**crabble and **C**raft for conditional human motion animation (cHMA), thus dubbed QS-Craft.

Formally, given the input source image and the driving video, our QS-Craft model should have the following three key steps, as illustrated in the right of Fig. 1. (1) *Quantize.* Train an encoder to get the latent feature of the source image and then quantize it to produce a bag of discrete feature pixels by referring to the global codebook, which is trained in an end-to-end manner. (2) *Scrabble.* Conditioned on motion information from driving video, our QS-Craft trains a decoder-only transformer to rearrange the feature pixels computed in (1) to produce the corresponding feature pixels for the targets. By virtue of such a way, we can effectively exploit the distribution of visual features, to help synthesize the latent features of the target images. (3) *Craft*[1]. Finally, the reordered feature pixels will be passed to a decoder layer to produce the animated target images. Extensive experiments on benchmarks validate the efficacy of our model, and the quantitative and qualitative results show that our method outperforms the state-of-the-art competitors.

Contributions. The main contribution of this paper is to propose a novel paradigm for the conditional human motion animation: learning to Quantize, Scrabble and Craft (QS-Craft). The quantize step is first introduced to encode the input source image and driving videos into a discrete representation. Next, we employ transformer to learn to *scrabble* by mixing up pixel distributions and exploiting the known distribution of the source image to fit those in driving videos. The reordered feature pixels are decoded to *craft* the human motion animation. Based on this novel model framework, we can not only address motion transfer when pose misalignment occurs (in Fig. 1) but achieve better quantitative scores in video reconstruction compared to other state-of-the-art methods.

2   Related Works

Image Animation. Image animation and video re-targeting have drawn attention of computer vision researchers in recent years. Some of the previous approaches [3,5,30] are heavily domain-specific, which means they can only tackle animation of human faces, etc. When transferred to other situations, these methods might fail and are ineffective. Recycle-GAN [1] incorporates Spatio-temporal cues into a conditional GAN architecture to translate from one domain to another. However, it has to be trained with a strong prior of specific domains and cannot be generalized to even another individual. Similarly, the model in

---

[1] The name of Craft is inspired by the game of Minecraft.

[33] aiming to address the motion transfer task is also exposed to the same problem. Compared to these works, our method does not need any prior during the training phase and can be domain-agnostic in the inference time.

X2Face [34] employs reference poses to warp a given image and obtain the final transferred video. It does not require priors but is better to face animations than cHMA. Siarohin *et al.* introduced Monkey-Net [26]. This network can indeed animate arbitrary objects guided by detected key points, but it is only effective on lower resolution images. The authors in [27] and [28] proposed an affine transformation and a PCA-based motion estimation respectively to transfer driving motions into the target images with higher resolution. Note that both of them are based on warping motion flow in order to encode images in feature space then decoding to get the targets. It suggests that the latent feature in target images has to be encoded from scratch whilst our proposed model can rearrange the quantized feature sequences conditioned on driving videos for the motion transfer task. This discretization method ensures better quality of our generated images. Moreover, the main structure of our model is transformer, which is quite different from other methods mentioned above. And both the quantitative and qualitative results show the efficacy of this prominent block.

Visual Transformer. Since the introduction of the self-attention module [32], many transformer-based methods have achieved impressive performance in numerous Natural Language Processing (NLP) and vision tasks [8,10,11,16,24]. Autoregressively generating pixels by transformer can only be applied to low-resolution images due to costly computation and huge memory footprint [9,15]. Many recent works, such as dVAE [25] and VQ-VAE [20], attempt to model discrete representation of images to reduce the total sequence length. Besides, VQ-GAN [12] added Generative Adversarial Networks (GANs) into VQ-VAE to improve training efficiency. Both VQ-VAE and VQ-GAN quantize an image according to a global codebook. In the second stage of [12], its transformer module has to look up in the whole codebook to generate latent features of targets, which may lead to accumulated errors and unreasonable generated results. Hence constructing a local dynamic codebook for each conditions-target pair can enhance the searching ability of the transformer; and thus the target images generated by the decoder will be more realistic. To achieve this goal, we propose to quantize one image twice to rearrange conditions for the target one. And this scrabbling also speed up convergence of the model.

3 Methodology

The purpose of this paper is to animate the human in a source image $x_s \in \mathbb{R}^{H \times W \times 3}$ conditioned on the motion in a driving video. For the target image $x_t \in \mathbb{R}^{H \times W \times 3}$, it should be semantically consistent with the source image, including the information of background and the content of the human texture. More importantly, it demands natural and realistic motion changes, which are guided by a series of driving frames (*i.e.*, the condition c). Following our inspiration,

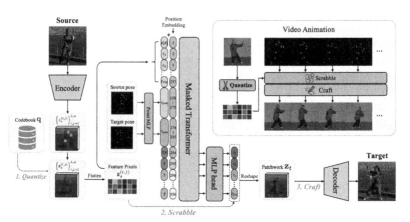

Fig. 2. The overall pipeline of QS-Craft. We first train an encoder-decoder based framework to quantize both source and target images. Then, a conditional transformer is designed to learn the scrabble game under the given driving videos. Finally, the decoder crafts the reordered features as output.

we assume that the target image x_t can be generated by reordering the latent features z_s of the source image in spatial dimensions, which can be expressed as,

$$x_t = G\left(T\left(z_s, c\right)\right) = G\left(T\left(E\left(x_s\right), c\right)\right) \tag{1}$$

where $E\left(\cdot\right)$ and $G\left(\cdot\right)$ denote the encoder and the decoder layer; $T\left(\cdot\right)$ means the operation of 'scrabble', i.e., putting latent features z_s together following a specific rule.

The overall of our framework is illustrated in Fig. 2, which is composed of three steps, *Quantize, Scrabble* and *Craft*. First, we perform the vector quantization mechanism [20] on the encoded latent features z_s of the source image, resulting in a bag of feature pixels $\left\{\mathbf{z}_s^{(i,j)}\right\}_{i,j=1}^{h,w}$, where h and w indicate the height and width of the latent features, respectively. Then, we play a Scrabble game by selecting pixels from the bag and mixing them together, $\hat{z}_t = T\left(\mathbf{z}_s, c\right)$. This process must be meaningful and also be conditioned on the motions from driving videos. Finally, the patchwork $\hat{z}_t$ is fed to the decoder to craft the image, which is realistic with natural motion changes.

Considering that $T\left(\cdot\right)$ is operated on index-based representation, we divide the training procedure of our model into two stages, *image reconstruction with scrabble* and *learning scrabble rules with transformer*. For the rest of this section, we will follow these two training stages to elaborate our framework in Sect. 3.1 and Sect. 3.2, respectively. The objective functions will be elaborated in the supplementary material.

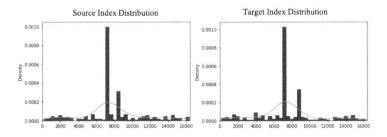

Fig. 3. Index distribution of a random sample pair $\mathbf{z}_s$ and $\mathbf{z}_t$.

3.1   Image Reconstruction with Scrabble

In the first stage, we aim to teach the decoder G to generate a natural target image x_t from a known patchwork $\hat{z}_t$. We first utilize the encoder E to extract latent features from both source and target images, denoted as z_s and z_t. Considering the correlations between each feature pixel in z_s, we adopt one more step of vector quantization before fitting them together. Specifically, a learnable codebook $\mathbf{q} \in \mathbb{R}^{m \times c_q}$ is introduced, where m and c_q are the number and dimension of codes, respectively. For each pixel $\left\{ z_s^{(i,j)} \right\}_{i,j=1}^{h,w}$, we do quantization $\mathcal{Q}(\cdot)$ by replacing it with the closest codebook entry q_k in $\mathbf{q}^2$,

$$\mathbf{z}_s = \mathcal{Q}(z_s) := \arg\min_{q_k \in \mathbf{q}} \| z_s^{(i,j)} - q_k \| \tag{2}$$

where $\mathbf{z}_s \in \mathbb{R}^{h \times w \times c_q}$. After that, we obtain a bag of quantized feature pixels $\left\{ \mathbf{z}_s^{(i,j)} \right\}_{i,j=1}^{h,w}$.

In order to reconstruct the target image x_t, we utilize the latent feature z_t as a reference to play scrabble with pixels (words) in $\mathbf{z}_s$. More concretely, we compute the distance between feature pixels in z_t and $\mathbf{z}_s$, and select the closest ones to fit a patchwork $\hat{z}_t \in \mathbb{R}^{h \times w \times c_q}$. The formulation can be written as,

$$x_t = G(\hat{z}_t), \quad \hat{z}_t := \arg\min_{z_k \in \mathbf{z}_s} \| z_t^{(i,j)} - z_k \| \tag{3}$$

To encourage the fidelity of the synthesized images, we reverse the generation flow in Eq. 3, that is, using a bag of quantized target feature pixels $\left\{ \mathbf{z}_t^{(i,j)} \right\}_{i,j=1}^{h,w}$ to fit a patchwork of the source $\hat{z}_s$. Furthermore, we also introduce a perceptual loss [31,35] and a Discriminator D [17,36] to highly maintain the perceptual quality during training. Details of structures about the Encoder E, the Decoder G and the Discriminator D can be found in the supplementary.

Remark. Different from Eq. 2, Eq. 3 is much more important here. A straightforward explanation of Eq. 3 is to narrow down the search space in Eq. 2. Experiments in Sect. 4.2 empirically show that this constraint will not degrade the

---

^{2} We refer the readers to [12] for details of the codebook learning.

expressive power of the representation $\hat{z}_s$ or $\hat{z}_t$. Even better, it is efficient and keeps more fidelity in background and foreground. Furthermore, to simply validate our explanation, we randomly choose a sample pair and plot their index distribution in Fig. 3. As we can see, the index distribution of $\mathbf{z}_s$ and $\mathbf{z}_t$ are quite similar; therefore, by scrabbling the indices in the source, we are able to reconstruct the target image.

3.2   Learning Scrabble Rules with Transformer

Through the process described in Sect. 3.1, the Decoder G now can synthesize realistic images according to the given patchwork. Nevertheless, the patchwork is generated with the reference of target image, which is not available during inference. To this end, we propose learning the rule of Scrabble, such that the desired patchwork $\hat{z}_t$ can be successfully produced *only with* a bag of source feature pixels $\mathbf{z}_s$ and the condition motion information c.

Here, the condition c refers to the information of pose coordinates. We claim that directly utilizing RGB images as condition may cause the information leakage [6] when both the source and driving frames are from the same video. Empirical results in Sect. 4.3 suggest that pose coordinates can not only provide effective and straightforward condition, but also save lots of computational costs compared with using pose image [12]. More precisely, an off-the-shelf open pose detector is applied to detect and localize n keypoints of an object. Each point is represented by x-y coordinates. If a point is occluded or undetectable, we set $x = y = -1$ for indication. Then, we attach three fully-connected layers with ReLU activation to encode the 2D pose coordinates $p \in \mathbb{R}^{n \times 2}$, which can be expressed as,

$$c = \mathcal{F}(p) \in \mathbb{R}^{n \times n_c} \qquad (4)$$

where $\mathcal{F}(\cdot)$ denotes the stacked fully-connected layers, n_c means the output dimension. We flatten the pose condition c as a sequence $\{c_i\}_{i=1}^{n}$, which is further incorporated with our transformer.

Speaking of the transformer, we adopt a decoder-only structure[3] and first convert the feature representation of $\mathbf{z}_s \in \mathbb{R}^{h \times w \times c_q}$ and $\hat{z}_t \in \mathbb{R}^{h \times w \times c_q}$ to the sequence of index representation, *i.e.*, $\{s_i\}_{i=1}^{l}$ and $\{t_i\}_{i=1}^{l}$, where its value ranges from 0 to $m - 1$, indicating the index of each feature pixel in the codebook $\mathbf{q}$, and $l = h \times w$. Two embedding layers with the dimension of n_c are subsequently followed for $\{s_i\}$ and $\{t_i\}$, respectively[4]. During training phase, we concatenate the source embedding $\{s_i\}$ and the condition sequence $\{c_i\}$ as input. Note that the previous ground-truth target embedding $\{t_i\}_{i=1}^{j-1}$ are progressively attached to the input to predict the likelihood of the next target index t_j. The overall formulation can be written as,

---

[3] Please refer to the supplementary for the transformer structure.
[4] We reuse the symbols of $\{s_i\}$ and $\{t_i\}$ after embedding for simplicity.

$$p(t|s,c) = \prod_{j=1}^{l} p\left(t_j|s,c,t_{[s]},t_{<j}\right) \tag{5}$$

where $t_{[s]} \in \mathbb{R}^{1 \times c_q}$ denotes a learnable start token, which is added after the condition sequence for the case of predicting the first target index t_1, as shown in Fig. 2. For inference, we use the previously predicted index to replace the ground-truth ones. With regard to the multi-head self-attention in the transformer, we design a new attention mask $\mathbf{M}$ with four sub-masks,

$$\mathbf{M} = \begin{bmatrix} \mathbf{A} & \mathbf{B} \\ \mathbf{C} & \mathbf{D} \end{bmatrix} = \begin{bmatrix} 1 & 0 \\ 1 & \mathbf{M}_{tril} \end{bmatrix} \tag{6}$$

where $\mathbf{B} \in \mathbb{R}^{(l+n) \times (l)}$ is a zero matrix, $\mathbf{A} \in \mathbb{R}^{(l+n) \times (l+n)}$ and $\mathbf{C} \in \mathbb{R}^{l \times (l+n)}$ are all-ones matrices, designed to learn the relationship among the source embedding $\{s_i\}$, the conditional information $\{c_i\}$ and the target embedding $\{t_i\}$; $\mathbf{M}_{tril} \in \mathbb{R}^{l \times l}$ means a standard lower triangular matrix filled with 1, so that the next target index can be deduced from the previous known information.

Recall the key idea of 'Scrabble' in the transformer, a patchwork $\hat{z}_t$ is acquired *only with* feature pixels from $\mathbf{z}_s$, thus we apply a mask constraint to the output of index probabilities. Specifically, denote the output of the j-th target index from transformer as $v_j \in \mathbb{R}^m$, we mask out some elements if their indices are out of the bag of source index $\{s_i\}_{i=1}^{l}$,

$$v_j^k = -\inf \quad if \quad k \notin \{s_i\}_{i=1}^{l} \tag{7}$$

where $k \in [0, m-1]$ and v_j^k indicates the k-th element in v_j. We feed masked v_j into *Softmax* operation to obtain final probability of the j-th target index. Furthermore, in order to improve the fidelity and consistency of the synthesized images, especially for the foreground objects, we encourage the model to learn more correlations between target indices by re-weighting the loss of each predicted index. Since we intuitively strengthen the learning of the foreground area, we call this strategy as RoI (regions of interest) weight. Formulations are elaborated in the supplementary materials.

4   Experiments

Datasets. We evaluate our model on two widely-used benchmarks. (1) Tai-Chi-HD, collected from YouTube following [31], is a dataset of human bodies performing Tai Chi actions, consisting of 252 videos for training and 28 videos for testing. Following MRAA [28] preprocessing method, we finally obtain $3,049$ and 285 video chunks for training and testing. All video frames are resized to 256×256. (2) Penn Action (PA) dataset [37] contains $2,326$ video sequences of 15 action classes. All video frames are resized to 256×256 after preprocessing.

Metrics. In our experiments, we use the following metrics to provide an in-depth comparisons with other competitors. (1) *Average Keypoint Distance (AKD),*

Fig. 4. Visualization of image animation on Tai-Chi-HD. Given the source image and driving videos, our animated images are better than those from competitors. Best viewed in color and zoom in.

which means the average distance between the detected keypoints of the ground truth image sequences and the generated ones. For both two datasets, we employ the human-pose estimator in [7] (2) *Missing Keypoint Rate (MKR)*, Another metric evaluating the difference between the poses in the real images and the reconstructed, is the proportion of keypoints detected in ground truth but missing in the reconstruction. (3) *Fréchet Inception Distance (FID)* [13], which measures the quality of generated images. In this paper, we concentrate more on the foreground area (*i.e.*, human bodies) to evaluate the fidelity and consistency.

Implementation Details. On all datasets, we train our model in two stages. (1) for the reconstruction training, our generative model is finetuned on ImageNet datasets [12]. In each training iteration, we randomly select 2 frames from the same video for training. Adam optimizer is applied with $\beta_1 = 0.5, \beta_2 = 0.9$, batch size 2 and the initial learning rate of $5e-5$. We drop the learning rate by half for every 70K steps. The total training iteration for the first stage is about 210K. (2) For the transformer training, we use Adam optimizer with $\beta_1 = 0.9, \beta_2 = 0.95$ and batch size 12. We do not change the initial learning rate but add the warmup strategy within the first 10K steps. The learning rate is linearly decayed to 0 gradually. We train the second stage 280K for Tai-Chi-HD and 270K for PA.

Competitors. Several related models are listed as competitors. For Tai-Chi-HD dataset, we compare our QS-Craft with three state-of-the-art models for animating, namely, Monkey-Net [26], FOMM [27] and MRAA and report both qualitative and quantitative results. For PA dataset, as for its complexity and variety of human motions, it is not suitable for the animation task whereas tends to be a dataset of pose-guiding. Hence, we compare with four pose-guided generative models, including PG^2 [17], PATN [38], PN-GAN [22] and MR-Net [35].

4.1 Qualitative Results

Note that the objective metrics used in our cMHA task can only reflect the general quality of synthesized images, while it is difficult for these metrics to

Fig. 5. More animation results on Tai-Chi-HD. Best viewed in color and zoom in.

Table 1. Video reconstruction results on Tai-Chi-HD.

Methods	Tai-Chi-HD		
	AKD ↓	MKR ↓	FID ↓
Monkey-Net [26]	13.77	0.061	32.223
FOMM [27]	7.02	0.031	25.910
MRAA [28]	5.73	0.025	35.794
Ours	**4.61**	**0.017**	**25.064**

Table 2. Quantitative ablation study for pose-guided generation on PA dataset.

Methods	Penn action		
	AKD ↓	MKR ↓	FID ↓
w/o Scrabble	31.878	0.326	42.721
w/o RoI weight	17.819	**0.121**	33.066
Full model	**16.358**	0.121	**30.136**

directly evaluate whether the synthesized images are mimicking the human motion sequences from driving video. In that case, qualitative evaluations are much more important in cMHA task to directly reflect whether our model works well.

Human Animation. Figures 4 and 5 show animation results on Tai-Chi-HD dataset. It can be noticed that our method can generate more realistic images with accurate motion according to driving videos on the four randomly selected samples. As these competitors all highly rely on flow information and warping operations, once the source image is not aligned with the first frame of the given driving video, it will introduce either wrong poses or twisted human bodies in the following generated animation results. For example, in the left subfigure of Fig. 4, results of Monkey-Net in the first row indicate the failure of motion animation: it only copies the source image. In contrast, our QS-Craft introduces the *Scrabble* step to rearrange the discrete pixel representations from the source image conditioned on the driving motion, thus facilitating the large human poses between the source and driving videos. Moreover, FOMM can sometimes capture action information in the driving but collapses in most cases. For MRAA, it can indeed generate the animated human bodies with roughly correct poses but details such as "raising left foot" are missing. It should be emphasized that FOMM tends to fail in the case of misalignment between human motion in the

Table 3. Pose-guided generation results on PA dataset.

Methods	Penn action		
	AKD ↓	MKR ↓	FID ↓
PG2 [17]	20.577	0.279	78.615
PN-GAN [22]	19.637	0.167	47.096
PATN [38]	19.288	0.267	51.583
MR-Net [35]	**13.663**	0.169	58.796
Ours	16.358	**0.121**	**30.136**

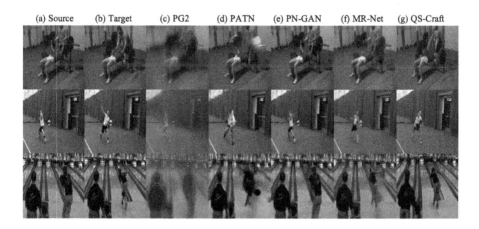

(a) Source   (b) Target   (c) PG2   (d) PATN   (e) PN-GAN   (f) MR-Net   (g) QS-Craft

Fig. 6. Visualization of pose-guided generation on PA dataset. Our method is better than the competitors.

source image and the first frame of driving video, which has been discussed in the limitation of its original paper. As for MRAA, it alleviates the misalignment problem to a certain extent but at the cost of losing a lot of details. Compared to these methods, our proposed QS-Craft can transfer source images accurately as well as retain most important details. More results about face animation can be found in the supplementary materials.

Pose Guidance. We further provide results on PA dataset, which is a more challenging and large dataset. The qualitative results are present in Fig. 6. We compare the competitors of PG^2, PATN, PN-GAN and MR-Net. Particularly, we show that PG^2 tends to generate blur results in most cases. Besides, PN-GAN is inclined to copy the source image as target ones. Human body parts in results of PATN are twisted, resulting in unreasonable artifacts. For MR-Net, the area around the human is blurred, making the synthesized images unrealistic. Compared to these models, our QS-Craft demonstrates its efficiency in generating the accurate human poses guided by conditions.

Table 4. Ablation study on different usages of pose conditions (report w/o RoI weight).

Methods	Tai-Chi-HD		
	AKD ↓	MKR ↓	FID ↓
Pose flow	22.939	0.065	70.117
Pose image	10.676	0.025	32.324
Pose VQ	19.194	0.052	56.285
Pose coord	**6.289**	**0.020**	**25.629**

Table 5. User study results on Tai-Chi-HD: user preferences in favour of our approach.

Methods	Tai-Chi-HD	
	Test 1	Test 2
FOMM [27]	19.87%	25.29%
Ours	80.13%	74.71%

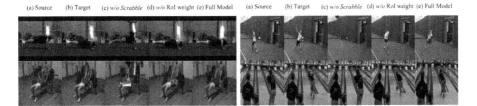

Fig. 7. Qualitative results in ablation study on PA dataset

4.2 Quantitative Results

We also give the general measurement of the image quality. Thus we compare the quantitative results on PA dataset of our proposed QS-Craft and other competitors in Table 3. As for Tai-Chi-HD dataset, since there is no ground truth according to the animation results to get quantitative scores, a sanity check by video reconstruction is conducted to demonstrate the effectiveness of our QS-Craft. Here we employ three metrics described above, Average Keypoint Distance (AKD), Missing Keypoint Rate (MKR) and Fréchet Inception Distance (FID) to measure the quality of generated results.

Note that for Monkey-Net, FOMM, and MRAA are not designed to tackle the complex images from PA dataset; and thus there is no available model for the direct comparison. Thus, the methods of PG^2, PATN, PN-GAN and MR-Net are compared here. We note that our QS-Craft outperforms all the baselines in AKD, MKR and FID. This intuitively reflects that our QS-Craft can deal with the complicated background with human motion, producing visually good synthesized results.

Sanity Check by Video Reconstruction. We take this task as the sanity check of our model, as it is designed for animation in transferring settings. That is, source image and driving video are different. In particular, we give results of video reconstruction in Fig. 10. Image frames reconstructed by Monkey-Net suffer from the wrong motion compared against the ground truth. Furthermore, FOMM and MRAA can capture the general motion information whilst ignoring some body parts such as hand movements in the third column. In a word, our reconstructed images demonstrate the superiority to the quality and detailed texture, which highly supports the efficacy of our QS-Craft framework in addressing the cMHA task. The quantitative results on Tai-Chi-HD dataset are shown in Table 1. We observe that our QS-Craft outperforms other methods in all metrics, which indicated the superiority of our method.

User Study. To complete our evaluation, a user study is conducted on Tai-Chi-HD dataset. We provide 32 users with two test sets of randomly selected animation results and ask them to select the most realistic and reasonable generation. Specifically, both test sets contain 25 different image animations, each of which involves one source image, one driving video and two animated generations. Results in Table 5 show that our QS-Craft is preferred over the competitor.

4.3   Ablation Study

Generalizablity of Model. The first ablation study is to evaluate the generalizablity of our method. We download some online videos to be the target driving. These online videos have complete novel driving poses, which are quite different from Tai-Chi-HD dataset. Qualitative results of this experiment demonstrate our method generalizes well in Fig. 8. Even for such challenging cases, Our method can still get good results, clearly beats MRAA.

Variants of Pose Conditions. In our framework, we particularly use pose coordinates, encoded by multilayer perceptrons, as conditional features. In order to verify the effectiveness of this design (termed *Pose Coord*), we conduct three variants: (1) *Pose Flow*: we follow [26] to build a motion net with five convolution layers to encode flow information. Differently, the flow features are further applied as a sequence in our transformer model, rather than warping source features [26]. (2) *Pose Image*: Similar to other studies [17,22,35], we use pose skeleton RGB images as condition information. Pose image features are extracted with five convolution layers. (3) *Pose VQ*: We use pose images to train a VQ-VAE model [20] and then the quantized pose embeddings are applied as conditions, which is the same as [12].

   As illustrated in Fig. 9, the results achieved by our QS-Craft are apparently more natural than other variants. Particularly, our results are authentic with richer accurate motion information from the driving videos. Besides, quantitative results in Table 4 also validate the same conclusion. For all the metrics, our *Pose Coord* outperforms others apparently.

Efficacy of the Proposed Modules. We further conduct studies to demonstrate the effectiveness of our proposed *Scrabble* step and RoI weight in Fig. 7 and Table 2. As we can find in Fig. 7, model trained without *Scrabble* step fails to generate reasonable target images with accurate pose information as it do not take into account the strong connection between the source and target and then accumulates prediction errors in inference. Additionally, model lack of RoI weight pays less attention to foregrounds compared to QS-Craft so it is inclined to generate blurred human motion or different clothes colors. And quantitative

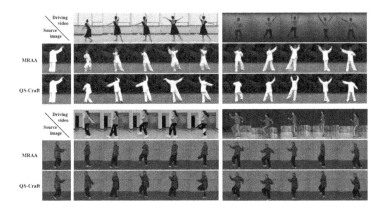

Fig. 8. Online driving videos with source Tai-Chi-HD images.

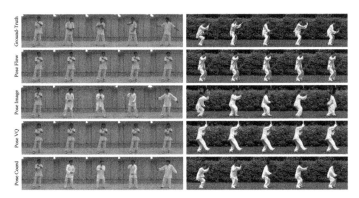

Fig. 9. Qualitative comparisons of image reconstruction with different conditions.

Fig. 10. Reconstruction results on Tai-Chi-HD. The synthesized results are compared among different methods.

results of our QS-Craft in Table 2 outperform other variants, which indicates the superiority of our full model.

5   Conclusion

In this paper, we propose a novel method to animate objects conditioned on driving videos through three phases: *Quantize, Scrabble* and *Craft*. This transformer-based model can effectively generate semantically consistent and realistic results as we demonstrate above. Besides, especially compared to other methods, our QS-Craft do not need the source given to be aligned with the first frame of the driving video as the simple pose keypoints are enough for QS-Craft.

Limitation. Our QS-Craft also encounters some challenges, including smoothness in video animation, since no temporal information are involved. Besides, we utilize information in the source to generate the target which may cause failure in some extreme cases. For example, when the person's body is frontal in the source and another person is back to camera in the driving, we cannot generate accurate faces according to the identity in the source. Hence involving more information about the source person is pretty important.

Acknowledgements. This work was supported by China Postdoctoral Science Foundation (2022M710746), the Science and Technology Major Project of Commission of Science and Technology of Shanghai (No. 21XD1402500).

References

1. Bansal, A., Ma, S., Ramanan, D., Sheikh, Y.: Recycle-GAN: unsupervised video retargeting. In: Ferrari, V., Hebert, M., Sminchisescu, C., Weiss, Y. (eds.) ECCV 2018. LNCS, vol. 11209, pp. 122–138. Springer, Cham (2018). https://doi.org/10.1007/978-3-030-01228-1_8
2. Berthelot, D., Schumm, T., Metz, L.: Began: boundary equilibrium generative adversarial networks. arXiv preprint arXiv:1703.10717 (2017)
3. Blanz, V., Vetter, T.: A morphable model for the synthesis of 3D faces. In: Proceedings of the 26th Annual Conference on Computer Graphics and Interactive Techniques, pp. 187–194 (1999)
4. Cai, H., Bai, C., Tai, Y.-W., Tang, C.-K.: Deep video generation, prediction and completion of human action sequences. In: Ferrari, V., Hebert, M., Sminchisescu, C., Weiss, Y. (eds.) ECCV 2018. LNCS, vol. 11206, pp. 374–390. Springer, Cham (2018). https://doi.org/10.1007/978-3-030-01216-8_23
5. Cao, C., Hou, Q., Zhou, K.: Displaced dynamic expression regression for real-time facial tracking and animation. ACM Trans. graph. (TOG) **33**(4), 1–10 (2014)
6. Cao, C., et al.: The image local autoregressive transformer. In: NeuPIS (2021)
7. Cao, Z., Simon, T., Wei, S.E., Sheikh, Y.: Realtime multi-person 2D pose estimation using part affinity fields. In: Proceedings of the IEEE Conference on Computer Vision and Pattern Recognition, pp. 7291–7299 (2017)
8. Carion, N., Massa, F., Synnaeve, G., Usunier, N., Kirillov, A., Zagoruyko, S.: End-to-end object detection with transformers. In: Vedaldi, A., Bischof, H., Brox, T., Frahm, J.-M. (eds.) ECCV 2020. LNCS, vol. 12346, pp. 213–229. Springer, Cham (2020). https://doi.org/10.1007/978-3-030-58452-8_13
9. Chen, M., et al.: Generative pretraining from pixels. In: International Conference on Machine Learning, pp. 1691–1703. PMLR (2020)

10. Devlin, J., Chang, M.W., Lee, K., Toutanova, K.: BERT: pre-training of deep bidirectional transformers for language understanding. arXiv preprint arXiv:1810.04805 (2018)
11. Dosovitskiy, A., et al.: An image is worth 16x16 words: transformers for image recognition at scale. arXiv preprint arXiv:2010.11929 (2020)
12. Esser, P., Rombach, R., Ommer, B.: Taming transformers for high-resolution image synthesis. In: Proceedings of the IEEE/CVF Conference on Computer Vision and Pattern Recognition, pp. 12873–12883 (2021)
13. Heusel, M., Ramsauer, H., Unterthiner, T., Nessler, B., Hochreiter, S.: GANs trained by a two time-scale update rule converge to a local Nash equilibrium. arXiv preprint arXiv:1706.08500 (2017)
14. Kingma, D.P., Welling, M.: Auto-encoding variational Bayes. arXiv preprint arXiv:1312.6114 (2013)
15. Kumar, M., Weissenborn, D., Kalchbrenner, N.: Colorization transformer. arXiv preprint arXiv:2102.04432 (2021)
16. Liu, Z., et al.: Swin transformer: hierarchical vision transformer using shifted windows. arXiv preprint arXiv:2103.14030 (2021)
17. Ma, L., Jia, X., Sun, Q., Schiele, B., Tuytelaars, T., Van Gool, L.: Pose guided person image generation. arXiv preprint arXiv:1705.09368 (2017)
18. Ma, L., Sun, Q., Georgoulis, S., Van Gool, L., Schiele, B., Fritz, M.: Disentangled person image generation. In: Proceedings of the IEEE Conference on Computer Vision and Pattern Recognition, pp. 99–108 (2018)
19. Mao, X., Li, Q., Xie, H., Lau, R.Y., Wang, Z., Paul Smolley, S.: Least squares generative adversarial networks. In: Proceedings of the IEEE International Conference on Computer Vision, pp. 2794–2802 (2017)
20. van den Oord, A., Vinyals, O., Kavukcuoglu, K.: Neural discrete representation learning. arXiv preprint arXiv:1711.00937 (2017)
21. Qi, G.J.: Loss-sensitive generative adversarial networks on Lipschitz densities. Int. J. Comput. Vision **128**(5), 1118–1140 (2020)
22. Qian, X., et al.: Pose-normalized image generation for person re-identification. In: Ferrari, V., Hebert, M., Sminchisescu, C., Weiss, Y. (eds.) ECCV 2018. LNCS, vol. 11213, pp. 661–678. Springer, Cham (2018). https://doi.org/10.1007/978-3-030-01240-3_40
23. Radford, A., Metz, L., Chintala, S.: Unsupervised representation learning with deep convolutional generative adversarial networks. arXiv preprint arXiv:1511.06434 (2015)
24. Radford, A., Narasimhan, K., Salimans, T., Sutskever, I.: Improving language understanding by generative pre-training (2018)
25. Ramesh, A., et al.: Zero-shot text-to-image generation. arXiv preprint arXiv:2102.12092 (2021)
26. Siarohin, A., Lathuilière, S., Tulyakov, S., Ricci, E., Sebe, N.: Animating arbitrary objects via deep motion transfer. In: Proceedings of the IEEE/CVF Conference on Computer Vision and Pattern Recognition, pp. 2377–2386 (2019)
27. Siarohin, A., Lathuilière, S., Tulyakov, S., Ricci, E., Sebe, N.: First order motion model for image animation. Adv. Neural. Inf. Process. Syst. **32**, 7137–7147 (2019)
28. Siarohin, A., Woodford, O.J., Ren, J., Chai, M., Tulyakov, S.: Motion representations for articulated animation. In: Proceedings of the IEEE/CVF Conference on Computer Vision and Pattern Recognition, pp. 13653–13662 (2021)
29. Sønderby, C.K., Raiko, T., Maaløe, L., Sønderby, S.K., Winther, O.: Ladder variational autoencoders. arXiv preprint arXiv:1602.02282 (2016)

30. Thies, J., Zollhofer, M., Stamminger, M., Theobalt, C., Nießner, M.: Face2Face: real-time face capture and reenactment of RGB videos. In: Proceedings of the IEEE Conference on Computer Vision and Pattern Recognition, pp. 2387–2395 (2016)
31. Tulyakov, S., Liu, M.Y., Yang, X., Kautz, J.: MOCOGAN: decomposing motion and content for video generation. In: Proceedings of the IEEE Conference on Computer Vision and Pattern Recognition, pp. 1526–1535 (2018)
32. Vaswani, A., et al.: Attention is all you need. arXiv preprint arXiv:1706.03762 (2017)
33. Wang, T.C., et al.: Video-to-video synthesis. arXiv preprint arXiv:1808.06601 (2018)
34. Wiles, O., Koepke, A.S., Zisserman, A.: X2Face: a network for controlling face generation using images, audio, and pose codes. In: Ferrari, V., Hebert, M., Sminchisescu, C., Weiss, Y. (eds.) ECCV 2018. LNCS, vol. 11217, pp. 690–706. Springer, Cham (2018). https://doi.org/10.1007/978-3-030-01261-8_41
35. Xu, C., Fu, Y., Wen, C., Pan, Y., Jiang, Y.G., Xue, X.: Pose-guided person image synthesis in the non-iconic views. IEEE Trans. Image Process. **29**, 9060–9072 (2020)
36. Yang, C., Wang, Z., Zhu, X., Huang, C., Shi, J., Lin, D.: Pose guided human video generation. In: Ferrari, V., Hebert, M., Sminchisescu, C., Weiss, Y. (eds.) ECCV 2018. LNCS, vol. 11214, pp. 204–219. Springer, Cham (2018). https://doi.org/10.1007/978-3-030-01249-6_13
37. Zhang, W., Zhu, M., Derpanis, K.G.: From actemes to action: a strongly-supervised representation for detailed action understanding. In: 2013 IEEE International Conference on Computer Vision, pp. 2248–2255 (2013). https://doi.org/10.1109/ICCV.2013.280
38. Zhu, Z., Huang, T., Shi, B., Yu, M., Wang, B., Bai, X.: Progressive pose attention transfer for person image generation. In: Proceedings of the IEEE/CVF Conference on Computer Vision and Pattern Recognition, pp. 2347–2356 (2019)

RaftMLP: How Much Can Be Done Without Attention and with Less Spatial Locality?

Yuki Tatsunami[1,2(✉)] [ID] and Masato Taki[1] [ID]

[1] Rikkyo University, Tokyo, Japan
{y.tatsunami,taki_m}@rikkyo.ac.jp
[2] AnyTech Co., Ltd., Tokyo, Japan

Abstract. For the past ten years, CNN has reigned supreme in the world of computer vision, but recently, Transformer has been on the rise. However, the quadratic computational cost of self-attention has become a serious problem in practice applications. There has been much research on architectures without CNN and self-attention in this context. In particular, MLP-Mixer is a simple architecture designed using MLPs and hit an accuracy comparable to the Vision Transformer. However, the only inductive bias in this architecture is the embedding of tokens. This leaves open the possibility of incorporating a non-convolutional (or non-local) inductive bias into the architecture, so we used two simple ideas to incorporate inductive bias into the MLP-Mixer while taking advantage of its ability to capture global correlations. A way is to divide the token-mixing block vertically and horizontally. Another way is to make spatial correlations denser among some channels of token-mixing. With this approach, we were able to improve the accuracy of the MLP-Mixer while reducing its parameters and computational complexity. The small model that is RaftMLP-S is comparable to the state-of-the-art global MLP-based model in terms of parameters and efficiency per calculation. Our source code is available at https://github.com/okojoalg/raft-mlp.

Keywords: Image classification · Network architecture · Multilayer perceptron

1 Introduction

In the past decade, CNN-based deep architectures have been developed in the computer vision domain. The first of these models was AlexNet [24], followed by other well-known models such as VGG [34], GoogLeNet [35], and ResNet [15]. These CNN-based models have exhibited high accuracy in various tasks, including image classification, object detection, semantic segmentation, and image generation. Adopting convolution, they employ the inherent inductive bias of

Supplementary Information The online version contains supplementary material available at https://doi.org/10.1007/978-3-031-26351-4_28.

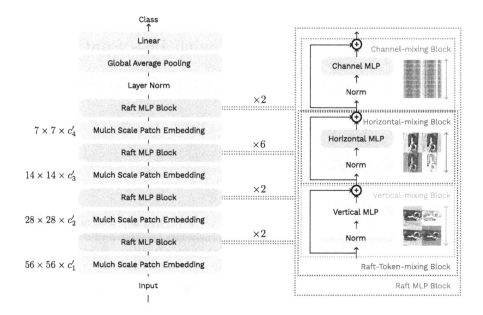

Fig. 1. The whole architecture of RaftMLP

images. Meanwhile, Transformer [45] has been winning success in recent years in the field of Natural Language Processing (NLP). Inspired by this success, Vision Transformer (ViT) [11] has been proposed. ViT is a Transformer-based visual model that replaces CNN with the self-attention mechanism. The main idea of ViT is to divide the image into patches based on their spatial locations and apply the Transformer using these patches as tokens. Immediately after the ViT paper appeared, various related works [1,4,10,12,13,29,46,52,55,56] have been done. They have shown that Transformer-based models are competitive with or even exceed CNN-based models in various image recognition and generation tasks. Although Transformer-based models have a reduced inductive bias for images compared to CNN-based models, they compensate for this lack by using a vast array of parameters and computational complexity instead. Moreover, it is successful because it can capture global correlations due to replacing the local receptive fields of convolution with global attention.

More recently, there has been a growing interest in improving the computational complexity of computationally intensive self-attention. Some works [31,40, 41] claim that Multi Layer Perceptron (MLP) alone is sufficient for image tasks without self-attention. In particular, MLP-Mixer [40] has performed a wide variety of MLP-based experiments, and the accuracy of image classification is not better than ViT, but the results are comparable. The MLP-based model, like ViT, first decomposes an image into tokens. A combined operation of MLP, transposition, and activation functions follows the tokenization. The significant point to note is that the transposition operation switches from token-mixing block to channel-mixing block and vice versa. While the channel-mixing block is equivalent to 1×1 convolution in CNN, the token-mixing block is a module that can capture the global correlations between tokens.

The wonderful thing about the MLP-Mixer is that it exhibited the possibility of competing with the existing models with a simple architecture without convolution nor self-attention. In particular, the fact that a simple MLP-based model could compete with current models leads us to think about successors to convolution. This idea has triggered the interest of many researchers on whether computer vision tasks can outgrow the classical convolution paradigm that has been in the mainstream for ten years. Motivated by the MLP-Mixer, some architectures have been proposed that inject convolutional local structures in pursuit of accuracy. We call the models with such structures local MLP-based models. In contrast, models such as MLP-Mixer, which adopt a design to capture global correlations without local operation, are called global MLP-based models. The global MLP-based model, including MLP-Mixer, has a shortcoming with the models. Unlike convolution, the resolution of the images used for training and inference is fixed, and thwarts the application to downstream tasks such as object detection and semantic segmentation. This paper aims to achieve cost-effectiveness with fewer resources in developing a global MLP-based model. The contributions of this study are as follows.

Spatial Structure. As shown in Fig. 1, we propose a module in which the token mixing block is divided into vertical and horizontal mixing blocks in series. In the standard MLP-Mixer, the relevance of patches has no inductive bias in the vertical and horizontal directions in the original two-dimensional image. In our proposed model, we implicitly assume as an inductive bias that patch sequences aligned horizontally have similar correlations with other horizontally aligned patch sequences. The same can be said for vertically aligned patch sequences-additionally, groups of channels are jointed in tensors before inputting into vertical-mixing and horizontal-mixing blocks. Jointed channels are shared with both mixing blocks. Thus, we assume that there are objects and their visual patterns are often distributed linearly over an image and geometrical relation among some channels.

Multi-scale Patch Embedding. While ViT and MLP-Mixer patch embedding was a simple method; we added a hierarchical structure. That is multi-scale patch embedding, which embeds information around the patch in the original patch embedding, as shown in Fig. 3. The multi-scale patch embedding method, which also embeds information around the patch in the embedding of the original patch, helped us increase the accuracy at the cost of a small amount of computation and memory consumption.

We will demonstrate that the proposed model with a simple inductive bias without excessive spatial locality as convolution is superior to MLP-Mixer and comparable to global MLP-based models. In addition, we will mention that the proposed method is a model that can achieve accuracy at a reduced cost compared to previous studies. In the appendix, we will study the applicability of the proposed model to downstream tasks such as semantic segmentation, instance segmentation, and object detection. The results will encourage the future possibilities of architectures without self-attention and with less spatial locality.

2   Related Work

Transformer-Based Models. Originally proposed for NLP, Transformer [45] soon began to be applied to other domains, including visual tasks. In particular, in image recognition, the attention-augmented convolution has been introduced in [3,19,48]. Stand-alone attention for visual task, rather than an augmentation to convolution, is studied in [33], where it was shown that fully self-attentional version of ResNet-50 outperforms the original ResNet in ImageNet classification task.

More Transformer-like architectures, process input tokens by self-attention, rather than augmenting CNNs by attention, were studied in [6] and [11]. In particular, in [11], ViT based on a BERT-type pure Transformer was proposed to deal with high-resolution inputs such as the ImageNet dataset. ViT was pre-trained using a large-scale dataset and transferred to ImageNet, which gave superior results compared to state-of-the-art CNNs.

Inspired by ViT, various transformer-like architectures have been proposed. The most relevant one to our study is CrossFormer [47], which includes a hierarchical structure and Cross-scale Embedding for patch embedding at each level. Cross-scale Embedding effectively injects inductive biases for image domain by using convolution with multiple kernel sizes to perform patch embedding, and it resembles our proposed Multi-scale Patch Embedding in the basic idea. In addition, CrossFormer also proposes a method called Long Short Distance Attention, in which self-attention is divided into two parts, one for long-distance and one for short-distance.

Grobal MLP-Based Models. Recently, several alternatives to CNN-based architectures have been proposed that are simple, yet competitive with CNN despite not using convolution or self-attention [31,40,41]. MLP-Mixer [40] replaces the self-attention layer of ViT with simple cross-tokens MLP. Despite its simplicity, MLP-Mixer achieves results that are competitive with ViT. gMLP [28] which consists of an MLP-based module with multiplicative gating is an alternative to MLP-Mixer, achieves higher accuracy than MLP-Mixer with fewer parameters. Vision Permutator [17] focused on mixing in vertical and horizontal directions like our work. Unlike ours, which employs a serialized structure, the Vision Permutator incorporates a parallelized structure, which results in higher accuracy with fewer parameters than the MLP-Mixer. sMLP [39] also shares the idea of decomposing token mixing into vertical and horizontal information mixing. These mixings are performed in parallel and the results are added and output from the module. Another direction of global mixing is CCS-MLP [49] as an example. To achieve translation invariance, CCS-MLP introduces circulant token mixing instead of vanilla token mixing MLP.

Local MLP-Based Models. Moving to a generic inductive bias like Transformer and MLP has attractive possibilities, but its lack of an inductive bias like convolution means that its pre-training requires vast amounts of data compared to CNNs. In order to achieve good performance without large datasets, MLP-based architectures have been proposed as an alternative to MLPs such as S^2-MLP [50], S^2-MLPv2 [51], AS-MLP [26], CycleMLP [5], and ConvMLP [25], which incorporate local structures. Although these models have the name of MLP, their essential motivation is the same as CNN in that they use the local structure of the models to extract patterns efficiently. Hence, we call these MLP-based architectures local MLP-based models. In contrast, architectures that mainly utilize MLPs to capture global correlations, such as MLP-Mixer and our study, are called global MLP-based models.

3 RaftMLP

In this section, we describe MLP-Mixer on which RaftMLP is based and the method adopted for RaftMLP.

3.1 Background

MLP-Mixer [40] splits an inputted image into patches of the same size immediately after input and is followed by MLPs that maintain the patch structure. There are two types of MLP: The first one is the token-mixing block, another is the channel-mixing block. We split an image with height h and width w into tokens with height and width p. If h and w are divisible by p, by viewing this image as a collection of these tokens, we can regard the image as an data array of height $h' = h/p$, width $w' = w/p$ and channel cp^2 where c denotes channel of the inputted image. The number of a token is then $s = hw/p^2$. The token-mixing block is map $\mathbb{R}^s \to \mathbb{R}^s$ that acts across axes of a token. In contrast, the channel-mixing block is map $\mathbb{R}^c \to \mathbb{R}^c$ that acts across axes of a channel as well where c is the number of channels. Both blocks contain the same modules: Layer Normalization (LN) [2] for each channel, Gaussian Error Linear Units (GELU) [16] and MLP. Concretely, the following equation gives the blocks

$$\mathbf{X}_{\text{output}} = \mathbf{X}_{\text{input}} + W_2\text{GELU}(W_1\text{LN}(\mathbf{X}_{\text{input}})), \tag{1}$$

where $\mathbf{X}_{\text{input}}$ denotes input tensor, $\mathbf{X}_{\text{output}}$ denotes output tensor, $W_1 \in \mathbb{R}^{a \times ae_a}$, $W_2 \in \mathbb{R}^{ae_a \times a}$ denote matrices of MLP layer, and e_a denotes expansion factor. For simplicity, the bias term in MLP was omitted. In token-mixing block, $a = s$ and in channel-mixing block, $a = c$. Moreover, the token-axis and channel-axis are permuted between both mixings. In this way, MLP-Mixer [40] is composed of transposition and two types of mixing blocks.

3.2 Vertical-Mixing and Horizontal-Mixing Block

In the previous subsection, we discussed the token-mixing block. The original token-mixing block does not reflect any two-dimensional structure of an input image, such as height or width direction. In other words, the inductive bias for images is not included in the token-mixing block. MLP-Mixer [40] therefore has no inductive bias for images except for how the first patches are made. We decompose this token-mixing block into two blocks that mix vertical and horizontal axes respectively and incorporate inductive bias for image domain. The following describes our method.

The vertical-mixing block is map $\mathbb{R}^{h'} \to \mathbb{R}^{h'}$ that acts across the vertical axis. Precisely, this map captures correlations along the horizontal axis, utilizing the same MLP along the channel and horizontal dimensions. The map also applies layer normalization for each channel, GELU, and the residual connection. The components of this mixing block are the same as the original token-mixing block.

Similarly, the horizontal-mixing block is map $\mathbb{R}^{w'} \to \mathbb{R}^{w'}$, and shuffle the horizontal axis. The structure is dual, only replacing vertical and horizontal axes. We propose replacing token-mixing with a successive application of vertical-mixing and horizontal-mixing, assuming meaningful correlations along vertical and horizontal directions of 2D images. This structure is shown in Fig. 1. The formula is as follows:

$$\mathbf{U}_{*,j,k} = \mathbf{X}_{*,j,k} + W_{2,\text{ver}}\text{GELU}(W_{1,\text{ver}}\text{LN}(\mathbf{X}_{*,j,k})),$$
$$\forall j = 1, \ldots, w', \ \forall k = 1, \ldots, c, \tag{2}$$
$$\mathbf{Y}_{i,*,k} = \mathbf{U}_{i,*,k} + W_{2,\text{hor}}\text{GELU}(W_{1,\text{hor}}\text{LN}(\mathbf{U}_{i,*,k})),$$
$$\forall i = 1, \ldots, h', \ \forall k = 1, \ldots, c, \tag{3}$$

where $W_{1,\text{ver}} \in \mathbb{R}^{h' \times h'e}$, $W_{2,\text{ver}} \in \mathbb{R}^{h'e \times h'}$, $W_{1,\text{hor}} \in \mathbb{R}^{w' \times w'e}$, and $W_{2,\text{hor}} \in \mathbb{R}^{w'e \times w'}$ denote MLP weight matrices and $\mathbf{U}, \mathbf{X},$ and $\mathbf{Y}$ denote feature tensors.

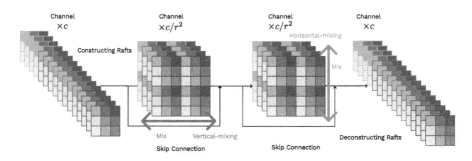

Fig. 2. The architecture of the raft-token-mixing block. Channels are rearranged with raft-like structure, and then vertical and horizontal mixed.

3.3   Channel Raft

Let us assume that several groups of feature map channels have correlations originating from spatial properties. Under this assumption, some feature maps would have some patterns across vertical or horizontal directions. To capture

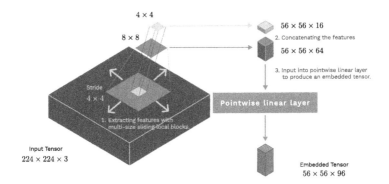

Fig. 3. A visualization of the concept of multi-scale-embedding.

such spatial correlations, we integrate feature maps into the vertical and horizontal shuffle. As shown in Fig. 2, this can be carried out by arranging the feature maps in $h'r \times w'r$, which is reshaping the $h' \times w' \times c$ tensor into a $h'r \times w'r \times c'$ tensor with $c' = c/r^2$ channels. We then perform the vertical-mixing and the horizontal-mixing blocks for this new tensor. In this case, the layer normalization done in each mixing is for the original channel. We refer to this structure as channel raft. The combination of vertical- and horizontal-mixing blocks and the channel raft is called raft-token-mixing block in this paper. The pseudocode for the raft-token-mixing block is given in Listing 1.1. The combination of raft-token-mixing block and the channel-mixing block is referred to as RaftMLP block.

```
1  # b: size of mini -batch, h: height, w: width,
2  # c: channel, r: size of raft, o: c//r,
3  # e: expansion factor,
4  # x: input tensor of shape (h, w, c)
5
6  def __init__(self):
7      self.lnv = nn.LayerNorm(c)
8      self.lnh = nn.LayerNorm(c)
9      self.fnv1 = nn.Linear(r * h, r * h * e)
10     self.fnv2 = nn.Linear(r * h * e, r * h)
11     self.fnh1 = nn.Linear(r * w, r * w * e)
12     self.fnh2 = nn.Linear(r * w * e, r * w)
13
14 def forward(self, x):
15     y = self.lnv(x)
16     y = rearrange(y, 'b (h w) (r o) -> b (o w) (r h)')
17     y = self.fcv1(y)
18     y = F.gelu(y)
19     y = self.fcv2(y)
20     y = rearrange(y, 'b (o w) (r h) -> b (h w) (r o)')
21     y = x + y
22     y = self.lnh(y)
```

```
23    y = rearrange(y, 'b (h w) (r o) -> b (o h) (r w)')
24    y = self.fch1(y)
25    y = F.gelu(y)
26    y = self.fch2(y)
27    y = rearrange(y, 'b (o h) (r w) -> b (h w) (r o)')
28    return x + y
```

Listing 1.1. Pseudocode of raft-token-mixing block (Pytorch-like)

3.4   Multi-scale Patch Embedding

The majority of both Transformer-based models and MLP-based models are based on patch embedding. We propose an extension of this method named multi-scale patch embedding, which is a patch embedding method that better represents the layered structure of an image. The main idea of the proposed method is twofold. The first is to cut out patches in such a way that the regions overlap. The second is to concatenate the channels of multiple-size patches and then project them by a linear embedding layer. The outline of the method is shown in Fig. 3, and the details are explained below. First, let r be an arbitrary even number. The method performs zero-padding of $(2^m - 1)r/2$ width on the top, bottom, left, and right sides then cut out the patch with $2^m r$ on one side and r stride. In the case of $m = 0$, the patch is cut out the same way as in conventional patch embedding. After this patch embedding, the height $h' = h/p$ and width $w' = w/p$ of the tensor is the same, and the output channel is $2^{2m}r^2$. Here, we describe the implementation of multi-scale patch embedding.

Multi-scale patch embedding is a generalization of conventional patch embedding, but it is also slightly different from convolution. However, by injecting a layered structure into the embedding, it can be said to incorporate the inductive bias for images. As the m increases, the computational complexity increases, so we should be careful to decide which m patch cutout to use. Our method is similar to convolutional embedding, but it slightly differs because it uses a linear layer projection after concatenating. See the appendix for code details.

3.5   Hierarchical Design

In the proposed method, hierarchical design is introduced. Our architecture used a four-level hierarchical structure with channel raft and multi-scale patch embedding to effectively reduce the number of parameters and improve the accuracy. The hierarchical design is shown in Fig. 1. In this architecture, the number of levels is $L = 4$, and at level l, after extracting a feature map of $h/2^{l+1} \times w/2^{l+1} \times c_l$ by multi-scale patch embedding, the RaftMLP block is repeated k_l times. The embedding is done using multi-scale patch embedding, but for $l = 1, 2, 3$, the feature maps for $m = 0, 1$ are concatenated, and for $l = 4$, conventional patch embedding is used. We prepared a hierarchical RaftMLP model with multiple scales. By settling c'_l, the number of channels for the level l, and N_l, the number of

RaftMLP blocks for the level, we developed models for three scales: **RaftMLP-S**, **RaftMLP-M**, and **RaftMLP-L**. The common settings for all three models are vertical dilation expansion factor $e_{\text{ver}} = 2$, horizontal dilation expansion factor $e_{\text{hor}} = 2$, channel dilation expansion factor $e_{\text{can}} = 4$, and channel raft size $r = 2$. For patch embedding at each level, multi-scale patch embedding is utilized, but for the $l = 1, 2, 3$ level, patch cutting is performed for $m = 0, 1$ and then concatenated. For the final level, conventional patch embedding to reduce parameters and computational complexity is utilized. For the output head, a classifier with linear layers and softmax is applied after global average pooling. Refer to the appendix for other settings. Our experiments show that the performance of image classification improves as the scale is increased.

3.6 Impact of Channel Raft on Computational Costs

We will discuss the computational complexity of channel raft, ignoring normalization and activation functions. Here, let h' denote the height of the patch placement, w' the width of the patch placement, and e the expansion factor.

Number of Parameters. The MLPs parameter for a conventional token-mixing block is

$$h'w'(2eh'w' + e + 1). \tag{4}$$

In contrast, the parameter used for a vertial-mixing block is

$$h'r(2eh'r + e + 1), \tag{5}$$

and the parameter used for a holizonal-mixing block is

$$w'r(2ew'r + e + 1). \tag{6}$$

In other words, the total number of parameters required for a raft-token-mixing block is

$$h'r(2eh'r + e + 1) + w'r(2ew'r + e + 1). \tag{7}$$

This means that if we assume $h' = w'$ and ignore $e + 1$, the parameters required for a conventional token-mixing block in the proposed method are $2(r/h')^2$ times for a conventional token-mixing. In short, if we choose r to satisfy $r < h'/\sqrt{2}$, the memory cost can be reduced.

Number of Multiply-Accumulate. If we ignore the bias term, the MLPs used for a conventional token-mixing block require $e(h'w')^4$ multiply-accumulates. By contrast, a raft-token-mixing block requires only $er^4(h'^4 + w'^4)$. Assuming $h' = w'$, a raft-token-mixing requires only multiply-accumulate of $2r^4/h'^4$ ratio to conventional token-mixing block. To put it plainly, if r is chosen so that $r < h'/2^{\frac{1}{4}}$, then multiply-accumulation has an advantage over a conventional token-mixing block.

Table 1. Accuracy of the models to be compared with the accuracy of the models derived from the experiments with ImageNet-1k. The throughput measurement infers 16 images per batch using a single V100 GPU. Performance have been not measured for S^2-MLP-deep because the code is not publicly available.

Backbone	Model	#params (M)	FLOPs (G)	Top-1 Acc. (%)	Top-5 Acc. (%)	Throughput (image/s)
Low-resource Models						
(#params × FLOPs less than 50P)						
CNN	ResNet-18 [15]	11.7	1.8	69.8	89.1	4190
	MobileNetV3 [18]	5.4	0.2	75.2	-	1896
	EfficientNet-B0 [37]	5.3	0.4	77.1	-	1275
Local MLP	CycleMLP-B1 [5]	15.2	2.1	78.9	-	904
	ConvMLP-S [25]	9.0	2.4	76.8	-	1929
Global MLP	ResMLP-S12 [41]	15.4	3.0	76.6	-	2720
	gMLP-Ti [28]	6.0	1.4	72.3	-	1194
	RaftMLP-S (ours)	9.9	2.1	76.1	93.0	875
Middle-Low-resource Models						
(#params × FLOPs more than 50P and less than 150P)						
CNN	ResNet-50 [15]	25.6	3.8	76.3	92.2	1652
	EfficientNet-B4 [37]	19.0	4.2	82.6	96.3	465
Transformer	DeiT-S [42]	22.1	4.6	81.2	-	1583
	T2T-ViT$_t$-14 [52]	21.5	6.1	81.7	-	849
	TNT-S [13]	23.8	5.2	81.5	95.7	395
	CaiT-XS24 [43]	26.6	5.4	81.8	-	560
	Nest-T [55]	17.0	5.8	81.5	-	796
Local MLP	AS-MLP-Ti [26]	28.0	4.4	81.3	-	805
	ConvMLP-M [25]	17.4	3.9	79.0	-	1410
Global MLP	Mixer-S/16 [40]	18.5	3.8	73.8	-	2247
	gMLP-S [28]	19.4	4.5	79.6	-	863
	ViP-Small/7 [17]	25.1	6.9	81.5	-	689
	RaftMLP-M (**ours**)	21.4	4.3	78.8	94.3	758
Middle-High-resource Models						
(#params × FLOPs more than 150P and less than 500P)						
CNN	ResNet-152 [15]	60.0	11.0	77.8	93.8	548
	EfficientNet-B5 [37]	30.0	9.9	83.7	-	248
	EfficientNetV2-S [38]	22.0	8.8	83.9	-	549
Transformer	PVT-M [46]	44.2	6.7	81.2	-	742
	Swin-S [29]	50.0	8.7	83.0	-	559
	Nest-S [55]	38.0	10.4	83.3	-	521
Local MLP	S^2-MLP-deep [50]	51.0	9.7	80.7	95.4	—
	CycleMLP-B3 [5]	38.0	6.9	82.4	-	364
	AS-MLP-S [26]	50.0	8.5	83.1	-	442
	ConvMLP-L [25]	42.7	9.9	80.2	-	928
Global MLP	Mixer-B/16 [40]	59.9	12.6	76.4	-	977
	ResMLP-S24 [41]	30.0	6.0	79.4	-	1415
	RaftMLP-L (**ours**)	36.2	6.5	79.4	94.3	650
High-resource Models						
(Models with #params × FLOPs more than 500P)						
Transformer	ViT-B/16 [11]	86.6	55.5	77.9	-	762
	DeiT-B [42]	86.6	17.6	81.8	-	789
	CaiT-S36 [43]	68.2	13.9	83.3	-	335
	Nest-B [55]	68.0	17.9	83.8	-	412
Global MLP	gMLP-B [28]	73.1	15.8	81.6	-	498
	ViP-Medium/7 [17]	55.0	16.3	82.7	-	392

4   Experimental Evaluation

In this section, we exhibit experiments for image classification with RaftMLP. In the principal part of this experiment, we utilize the Imagenet-1k dataset [8] to train three types of RaftMLP and compare them with MLP-based models and Transformers-based models mainly. We also carry out an ablation study to demonstrate the effectiveness of our proposed method, and as a downstream task, we evaluate transfer learning of RaftMLP for image classification. Besides, We conduct experiments employing RaftMLP as the backbone for object detection and semantic segmentation.

4.1   ImageNet-1k

To evaluate the training results of our proposed classification models, RaftMLP-S, RaftMLP-M and RaftMLP-L, we train them on ImagNet-1k dataset [8]. This dataset consists of about 1.2 million training images and about 50,000 validation images assigned 1000 category labels. We also describe how the training is set up below. We employ AdamW [30] with weight decay 0.05 and learning schedule: maximum learning rate $\frac{\text{batch size}}{512} \times 5 \times 10^{-4}$, linear warmup on first 5 epochs, and after cosine decay to 10^{-5} on the following 300 epochs to train our models. Moreover, we adopt some augmentations and regularizations; random horizontal flip, color jitter, Mixup [54] with $\alpha = 0.8$, CutMix [53] with $\alpha = 1.0$, Cutout [9] of rate 0.25, Rand-Augment [7], stochastic depth [20] of rate 0.1, and label smoothing [36] 0.1. These settings refer to the training strategy of DeiT [42]. The other settings are changed for each experiment. Additionally, all training in this experiment is performed on a Linux machine with 8 RTX Quadro 8000 cards. The results of trained models are showed in Table 1. In Fig. 4, we compare our method with other global MLP-based models in terms of accuracy against the number of parameters and computational complexity. Figure 4 reveals that RaftMLP-S is a cost-effective method.

4.2   Ablation Study

In order to verify the effectiveness of the two methods we propose, we carry out ablation studies. The setup for these experiments is the same as in Subsect. 4.1.

Channel Raft (CR). We have carried out experiments to verify the effectiveness of channel rafts. Table 2 compares and verifies MLP-Mixer and MLP-Mixer with the token mixing block replaced by channel rafts. Although we have prepared architectures for $r = 1, 2, 4$ cases, $r = 1$ case has no raft structure but is just a conventional token-mixing block vertically and horizontally separated. Table 2 has shown that channel rafts effectively improve accuracy and costless channel raft structure such as $r = 2$ is more efficient for training than increasing r.

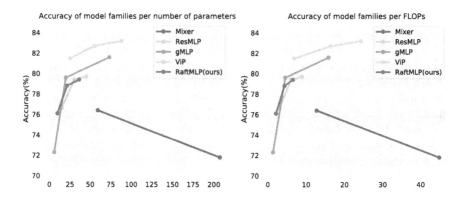

Fig. 4. Accuracy per parameter and accuracy per FLOPs for the family of global MLP-based models

Table 2. An ablation experiment of channel raft. Note that Mixer-B/16 is experimented with our implementation

Model	r	#Mparams	GFLOPs	Top-1 Acc.
Mixer-B/16	–	59.9	12.6	74.3%
Mixer-B/16 with CR	1	58.1	11.4	77.0%
	2	58.2	11.6	78.3%
	4	58.4	12.0	78.0%

Multi-scale Patch Embedding (MSPE). RaftMLP-M is composed of three multi-scale patch embeddings and a conventional patch embedding. To evaluate the effect of multi-scale patch embedding, we compared RaftMLP-M with the model with multi-scale patch embeddings replaced by conventional patch embeddings in RaftMLP-M. The result is shown on Table 3. As a result of comparing the models with and without multi-scale patch embedding, RaftMLP-M with multi-scale patch embedding improves the accuracy by 0.7% compared to the model without multi-scale patch embedding.

Table 3. An ablation experiment of multi-scale patch embedding

Model	#Mparams	GFLOPs	Top-1 Acc.
RaftMLP-M	21.4	4.3	78.8%
RaftMLP-M without MSPE	20.0	3.8	78.1%

4.3   Transfer Learning

The study of transfer learning is conducted on CIFAR-10/CIFAR-100 [23], Oxford 102 Flowers [32], Stanford Cars [22] and iNaturalist [44] to evaluate the transfer capabilities of RaftMLP pre-trained on ImageNet-1k [8]. The fine-tuning experiments adopt batch size 256, weight decay 10^{-4} and learning schedule: maximum learning rate 10^{-4}, linear warmup on first 10 epochs, and after cosine decay to 10^{-5} on the following 40 epochs. We also do not use stochastic depth [20] and Cutout [9] in this experiment. The rest of the settings are equivalent to Subsect. 4.1. In our experiments, we also resize all images to the exact resolution 224×224 as ImageNet-1k. The experiment is shown in Table 4. We achieve that RaftMLP-L is more accurate than Mixer-B/16 in all datasets.

Table 4. The accuracy of transfer learning with each dataset

Dataset	Mixer-B/16	RaftMLP-S	RaftMLP-M	RaftMLP-L
CIFAR-10	97.7%	97.4%	97.7%	98.1%
CIFAR-100	85.0%	85.1%	86.8%	86.8%
Oxford 102 Flowers	97.8%	97.1%	97.9%	98.4%
Stanford Cars	84.3%	84.7%	87.6%	89.0%
iNaturalist18	55.6%	56.7%	61.7%	62.9%
iNaturalist19	64.1%	65.4%	69.2%	70.1%

5   Discussion

The above experimental results show that even an architecture that does not use convolution but has a simple inductive bias for images like vertical and horizontal decomposition can achieve performance competing with Transformers. This is a candidate for minimal inductive biases to improve MLP-based models without convolution. Also, Our method does not require as much computational cost as Transformer. In addition, the computational cost is as expensive as or less than that of CNN. The main reason for the reduced computational cost is that it does not require self-attention. The fact that only simple operations such as MLP are needed without self-attention nor convolution means that MLP-based models will be widely used in applied fields since they do not require special software or hardware carefully designed to reduce computational weight. Furthermore, the raft-token-mixing block has the lead over the token-mixing block of MLP-Mixer in terms of computational complexity when the number of patches is large. As we described in Sect. 3, substituting the token-mixing block as the raft-token-mixing block reduces parameters from the square of the patches to several times patches. In other words, the more the resolution of images is, the more dramatically parameters are reduced with RaftMLP. The hierarchical design adopted in this paper contributes to the reduction of parameters and computational complexity. Since multi-scale embedding leads to better performance with less cost, our proposal will make it realistic to compose architectures that do not depend on convolution. Meanwhile, the experimental results in the appendix suggest that the proposed model is not very effective for some downstream tasks. As shown in the appendix, the feature map of global MLP-based models differs from the feature map of CNNs in that it is visualized as a different appearance from the input image. Such feature maps are not expected to work entirely in convolution-based architectures such as RetinaNet [27], Mask R-CNN [14], and Semantic FPN [21]. Global MLP-based models will require their specialized frameworks for object detection, instance segmentation, and semantic segmentation.

6   Conclusion

In conclusion, the result has demonstrated that the introduction of the raft-token-mixing block improves accuracy when trained on the ImageNet-1K dataset [8], as compared to plain MLP-Mixer [40]. Although the raft-token-mixing decreases the number of parameters and FLOPs only lightly compared to MLP-Mixer [40], it contributes to the improvement in accuracy in return. We conclude that adding a non-convolutional and non-self-attentional inductive bias to the token-mixing block of MLP-Mixer can improve the accuracy of the model. In addition, due to the introduction of hierarchical structures and multi-scale patch embedding, RaftMLP-S with lower computational complexity and number of parameters have achieved accuracy comparable to the state-of-the-art global MLP-based model with similar computational complexity and number of parameters. We have explicated that it is more cost-effective than the Transformer-based models and well-known CNNs.

However, global MLP-based models have not yet fully explored their potential. Inducing other utilitarian inductive biases, e.g., parallel invariance, may improve the accuracy of global MLP-based models. Further insight into these aspects is left to future work.

Acknowledgements. We thank the people who support us, belonging to Graduate School of Artificial Intelligence and Science, Rikkyo University.

References

1. Arnab, A., Dehghani, M., Heigold, G., Sun, C., Lučić, M., Schmid, C.: ViViT: a video vision transformer. In: ICCV (2021)
2. Ba, J.L., Kiros, J.R., Hinton, G.E.: Layer normalization. In: NeurIPS (2016)
3. Bello, I., Zoph, B., Vaswani, A., Shlens, J., Le, Q.V.: Attention augmented convolutional networks. In: ICCV, pp. 3286–3295 (2019)
4. Chen, C.F., Fan, Q., Panda, R.: CrossViT: cross-attention multi-scale vision transformer for image classification. In: ICCV (2021)
5. Chen, S., Xie, E., Ge, C., Liang, D., Luo, P.: CycleMLP: a MLP-like architecture for dense prediction. arXiv preprint arXiv:2107.10224 (2021)

6. Cordonnier, J.B., Loukas, A., Jaggi, M.: On the relationship between self-attention and convolutional layers. In: ICLR (2019)

7. Cubuk, E.D., Zoph, B., Shlens, J., Le, Q.V.: RandAugment: practical automated data augmentation with a reduced search space. In: CVPR Workshops, pp. 702–703 (2020)

8. Deng, J., Dong, W., Socher, R., Li, L.J., Li, K., Fei-Fei, L.: Imagenet: a large-scale hierarchical image database. In: CVPR, pp. 248–255 (2009)

9. DeVries, T., Taylor, G.W.: Improved regularization of convolutional neural networks with cutout. arXiv preprint arXiv:1708.04552 (2017)

10. Ding, M., et al.: Cogview: mastering text-to-image generation via transformers. In: NeurIPS (2021)

11. Dosovitskiy, A., et al.: An image is worth 16x16 words: transformers for image recognition at scale. In: ICLR (2021)

12. El-Nouby, A., et al.: XCIT: cross-covariance image transformers. arXiv preprint arXiv:2106.09681 (2021)

13. Han, K., Xiao, A., Wu, E., Guo, J., Xu, C., Wang, Y.: Transformer in transformer. In: NeurIPS (2021)

14. He, K., Gkioxari, G., Dollár, P., Girshick, R.: Mask R-CNN. In: ICCV, pp. 2961–2969 (2017)

15. He, K., Zhang, X., Ren, S., Sun, J.: Deep residual learning for image recognition. In: CVPR, pp. 770–778 (2016)

16. Hendrycks, D., Gimpel, K.: Gaussian error linear units (GELUs). arXiv preprint arXiv:1606.08415 (2016)

17. Hou, Q., Jiang, Z., Yuan, L., Cheng, M.M., Yan, S., Feng, J.: Vision permutator: a permutable MLP-like architecture for visual recognition. arXiv preprint arXiv:2106.12368 (2021)

18. Howard, A., et al.: Searching for MobileNetV3. In: ICCV, pp. 1314–1324 (2019)

19. Hu, J., Shen, L., Albanie, S., Sun, G., Vedaldi, A.: Gather-excite: exploiting feature context in convolutional neural networks. In: NeurIPS (2018)

20. Huang, G., Sun, Yu., Liu, Z., Sedra, D., Weinberger, K.Q.: Deep networks with stochastic depth. In: Leibe, B., Matas, J., Sebe, N., Welling, M. (eds.) ECCV 2016. LNCS, vol. 9908, pp. 646–661. Springer, Cham (2016). https://doi.org/10.1007/978-3-319-46493-0_39

21. Kirillov, A., Girshick, R., He, K., Dollár, P.: Panoptic feature pyramid networks. In: CVPR, pp. 6399–6408 (2019)

22. Krause, J., Stark, M., Deng, J., Fei-Fei, L.: 3D object representations for fine-grained categorization. In: ICCV Workshops, pp. 554–561 (2013)

23. Krizhevsky, A., Hinton, G., et al.: Learning multiple layers of features from tiny images. Technical report, University of Toronto (2009)

24. Krizhevsky, A., Sutskever, I., Hinton, G.E.: Imagenet classification with deep convolutional neural networks. In: NeurIPS, vol. 25, pp. 1097–1105 (2012)

25. Li, J., Hassani, A., Walton, S., Shi, H.: ConvMLP: hierarchical convolutional MLPs for vision. arXiv preprint arXiv:2109.04454 (2021)

26. Lian, D., Yu, Z., Sun, X., Gao, S.: AS-MLP: an axial shifted MLP architecture for vision. arXiv preprint arXiv:2107.08391 (2021)

27. Lin, T.Y., Goyal, P., Girshick, R., He, K., Dollár, P.: Focal loss for dense object detection. In: ICCV, pp. 2980–2988 (2017)

28. Liu, H., Dai, Z., So, D.R., Le, Q.V.: Pay attention to MLPs. arXiv preprint arXiv:2105.08050 (2021)

29. Liu, Z., et al.: Swin transformer: hierarchical vision transformer using shifted windows. In: ICCV (2021)

30. Loshchilov, I., Hutter, F.: Decoupled weight decay regularization. In: ICLR (2019)
31. Melas-Kyriazi, L.: Do you even need attention? A stack of feed-forward layers does surprisingly well on imagenet. arXiv preprint arXiv:2105.02723 (2021)
32. Nilsback, M.E., Zisserman, A.: Automated flower classification over a large number of classes. In: ICVGIP, pp. 722–729 (2008)
33. Ramachandran, P., Parmar, N., Vaswani, A., Bello, I., Levskaya, A., Shlens, J.: Stand-alone self-attention in vision models. In: NeurIPS (2019)
34. Simonyan, K., Zisserman, A.: Very deep convolutional networks for large-scale image recognition. In: ICLR (2015)
35. Szegedy, C., et al.: Going deeper with convolutions. In: CVPR, pp. 1–9 (2015)
36. Szegedy, C., Vanhoucke, V., Ioffe, S., Shlens, J., Wojna, Z.: Rethinking the inception architecture for computer vision. In: CVPR, pp. 2818–2826 (2016)
37. Tan, M., Le, Q.: EfficientNet: rethinking model scaling for convolutional neural networks. In: ICML, pp. 6105–6114 (2019)
38. Tan, M., Le, Q.V.: EfficientNetV2: smaller models and faster training. In: ICML (2021)
39. Tang, C., Zhao, Y., Wang, G., Luo, C., Xie, W., Zeng, W.: Sparse MLP for image recognition: is self-attention really necessary? arXiv preprint arXiv:2109.05422 (2021)
40. Tolstikhin, I., et al.: MLP-mixer: an all-MLP architecture for vision. arXiv preprint arXiv:2105.01601 (2021)
41. Touvron, H., et al.: ResMLP: feedforward networks for image classification with data-efficient training. arXiv preprint arXiv:2105.03404 (2021)
42. Touvron, H., Cord, M., Douze, M., Massa, F., Sablayrolles, A., Jégou, H.: Training data-efficient image transformers & distillation through attention. In: ICML (2021)
43. Touvron, H., Cord, M., Sablayrolles, A., Synnaeve, G., Jégou, H.: Going deeper with image transformers. In: ICCV, pp. 32–42 (2021)
44. Van Horn, G., et al.: The iNaturalist species classification and detection dataset. In: CVPR, pp. 8769–8778 (2018)
45. Vaswani, A., et al.: Attention is all you need. In: NeurIPS (2017)
46. Wang, W., et al.: Pyramid vision transformer: a versatile backbone for dense prediction without convolutions. In: ICCV (2021)
47. Wang, W., Yao, L., Chen, L., Cai, D., He, X., Liu, W.: CrossFormer: a versatile vision transformer based on cross-scale attention. arXiv preprint arXiv:2108.00154 (2021)
48. Wang, X., Girshick, R., Gupta, A., He, K.: Non-local neural networks. In: CVPR, pp. 7794–7803 (2018)
49. Yu, T., Li, X., Cai, Y., Sun, M., Li, P.: Rethinking token-mixing MLP for MLP-based vision backbone. arXiv preprint arXiv:2106.14882 (2021)
50. Yu, T., Li, X., Cai, Y., Sun, M., Li, P.: S^2-MLP: spatial-shift MLP architecture for vision. arXiv preprint arXiv:2106.07477 (2021)
51. Yu, T., Li, X., Cai, Y., Sun, M., Li, P.: S^2-mlpv2: improved spatial-shift MLP architecture for vision. arXiv preprint arXiv:2108.01072 (2021)
52. Yuan, L., et al.: Tokens-to-Token ViT: training vision transformers from scratch on ImageNet. In: ICCV, pp. 558–567 (2021)
53. Yun, S., Han, D., Oh, S.J., Chun, S., Choe, J., Yoo, Y.: Cutmix: regularization strategy to train strong classifiers with localizable features. In: ICCV, pp. 6023–6032 (2019)
54. Zhang, H., Cisse, M., Dauphin, Y.N., Lopez-Paz, D.: Mixup: beyond empirical risk minimization. In: ICLR (2018)

55. Zhang, Z., Zhang, H., Zhao, L., Chen, T., Pfister, T.: Aggregating nested trans-formers. arXiv preprint arXiv:2105.12723 (2021)
56. Zhou, D., et al.: DeepViT: towards deeper vision transformer. arXiv preprint arXiv:2103.11886 (2021)

Generalized Person Re-identification by Locating and Eliminating Domain-Sensitive Features

Wendong Wang, Fengxiang Yang, Zhiming Luo$^{(\boxtimes)}$, and Shaozi Li

Department of Artificial Intelligence, Xiamen University, Xiamen, China
{wendongwang,yangfx}@stu.xmu.edu.cn, {zhiming.luo,szlig}@xmu.edu.cn

Abstract. In this paper, we study the problem of domain generalization for person re-identification (re-ID), which adopts training data from multiple domains to learn a re-ID model that can be directly deployed to unseen target domains without further fine-tuning. One promising idea is removing the subsets of features that are not beneficial to the generalization of models. This can be achieved by muting the subset features that correspond to high back-propagated gradients as these subsets are easy for the model to overfit. But this method ignores the interaction of multiple domains. Therefore, we propose a novel method to solve this problem by comparing the gradients from two different training schemes. One of the training schemes discriminates input data from their corresponding domain to obtain back-propagated temporary gradients in the intermediate features. At the same time, another scheme discriminates input data from all domains to obtain the temporary gradients. By comparing the temporary gradient between the two schemes, we can identify the domain-generalizable subset features from those domain-specific subset features. We thus mute them in the subsequent training process to enforce the model to learn domain-generalizable information and improve its generalization. Extensive experiments on four large-scale re-ID benchmarks have verified the effectiveness of our method. Code is available at https://github.com/Ssd111/LEDF.git.

1 Introduction

Person re-identification (re-ID) aims at retrieving the target person in a non-overlapped camera system, which is a crucial technique for public security. Although person re-ID algorithms have achieved remarkable success [28,30,33, 35,37,46] with the help of deep neural networks [7,9], most of them still suffer from the problem of generalization. Concretely, the re-ID model trained on a labeled source domain may perform well but fails to achieve high accuracy when transferred to another unseen target domain. Moreover, optimizing the re-ID model requires a large number of labeled samples, which is not an economical way in real-world applications. Recent advances adopt unsupervised domain adaptation [1,4,26,32,42] or fully unsupervised re-ID [3,5,34,36] to

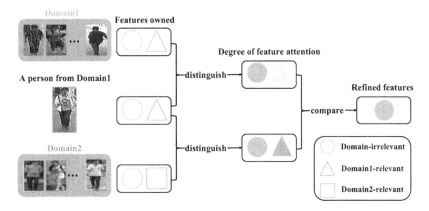

Fig. 1. Illustration of motivation and our idea. We use different shapes to represent different features, and the depth of color to indicate the degree of feature attention. We compare the degree of feature attention to eliminate domain-relevant features.

address the problem efficiently with the unlabeled data. However, these methods may not be applicable to the unseen target domains with strict privacy-preserving regulations since training data is not available. That's the domain generalization (DG) problem, which requires the model to perform well in the unseen target domains. Therefore, we consider studying the domain generalized re-ID algorithm in this paper. Prevailing generalization methods can be roughly categorized into three types: (1) data augmentation [10,16,17,44,45], (2) domain-invariant feature learning [12,13,15,20,22,23], and (3) gradient calibration [14,21,27,38]. Specifically, (1) improves the generalization by generating more diverse samples for optimization, (2) tries to use distributional metrics to narrow down the domain gaps of training domains for better representation learning, and (3) calibrates the training gradients for better learning of models. Recently, some methods like RSC [11] consider fine-grained constraints in representation learning. Specifically, RSC identifies the most predictive subsets of features through their associated gradients. The subsets with higher gradients are more likely to contain information that can mislead the model to overfit on the specific source domain and thus should be muted during the optimization. Although RSC has achieved great success, it ignores the interaction among source domains, hindering the further improvement in domain generalized re-ID.

Inspired by the idea of finding usable subsets of features during the optimization, we try to solve the DG problem in re-ID by locating and eliminating the domain-sensitive features (LEDF). This is achieved by comparing the gradients from two different training schemes for the same inputs, which fully considers the interaction among source domains. We compare two types of training schemes to locate domain-sensitive subsets. They are ① discriminating the sample from IDs of the same domain (domain-specific scheme), and ② identifying the sample from IDs of other source domains (hybrid scheme). Since the large domain discrepancy is much easier for the model to recognize, the back-propagated gradients from ② will focus more on the domain-sensitive parts of intermediate features than ① does. We can locate the domain-sensitive subset by comparing the gradients from both training schemes for better subsequent optimization. As shown in Fig. 1, due to the extremely different contrast between domain1 and domain2, the model can distinguish pedestrians in domain1 from domain2 only based on the contrast. However, the model learns the contrast feature may not be useful in other domains. This is harmful to the generalization ability of the model.

Our LEDF consists of three steps: (1) Constructing domain-specific & hybrid memory (2) Locating domain-sensitive features (3) Optimizing the generalized model. In step (1), we adopt the commonly used memory bank [42] to compute the classification losses. The "domain-specific memory" stores the class centroids of each ID for each domain, enabling us to compute the classification loss. The "hybrid memory" is the concatenation of all "domain-specific memories", which can be utilized to discriminate input samples under the training scheme ②. In step (2), we locate the domain-sensitive part of features by comparing gradients from two training schemes. Since the gradient from scheme ② will focus more on the domain-sensitive subsets of features (i.e., higher response), which is different from ①, we can compare the gradient of ① with the gradient of ② for better localization of these subsets. The located subsets will be muted in step (3) to train a generalized re-ID model.

Our main contributions are three-fold:

- We propose a novel domain generalization method for person re-ID by locating and eliminating the domain-sensitive subsets of features. After removing these features, the model can focus more on the generalized information in datasets and achieve better generalization.
- We design a novel strategy to locate domain-sensitive subsets of features by comparing the gradients from two different training schemes. As large domain discrepancy is easier for the model to recognize, the back-propagated gradients from the "hybrid scheme" will focus more on the domain-sensitive subsets of intermediate features than the "domain-specific scheme" does, enabling us to locate them in each back-propagation.
- Extensive experiments on four large-scale benchmarks verify the effectiveness of our method in multi-source domain generalization.

2   Related Work

2.1   Person Re-ID

With the rapid development of deep learning, person re-ID has made great progress in recent years [2,6,31–33,35,37,41]. However, the performance of these methods in unseen domain testing is not satisfactory. Unsupervised Domain Adaptation (UDA) uses unlabelled target domain data to improve the model's performance in the unseen domains. ECN [42] pays more attention to the intra-domain variations of the target domain. MCD [26] uses adversarial learning to maximize the difference between the two different classifiers to detect the samples in the target domain far from the source domain. Then the feature generator is used to generate features similar to the source domain. AutoDIAL [1] proposes the domain alignment layer to automatically align the feature representation of different domains. MMT [4] is trained by two network mutual teaching methods to generate reliable pseudo labels, which solves the problem of pseudo labels noise in the target domain. ACT [32] uses two asymmetric models for collaborative training. The training samples of one model are as diverse as possible, and the training of the other model is as pure as possible. The two models give reliable samples to each other to avoid label noise.

2.2 Domain Generalization

Most DG methods are based on data augmentation, domain-invariant features learning, and gradient calibration. Data augmentation means generating data different from the source domain, learning more unprecedented features, and preventing over-fitting of the source domain. Domain-invariant features learning means learning more identify-relevant features. Gradient Calibration means using the gradient to design appropriate learning strategies to improve the generalization ability of the model.

Data Augmentation. L2A-OT [44] uses Optimal Transport (OT) to make the distribution between the generated image and the source domain image very different. MixStyle [45] combines the style features at the bottom layer of the network to generate new style features and enrich the diversity of training data. PDEN [16] simulates the unseen domain by constantly changing the brightness and geometry of the data on the source domain. FSDR [10] augments the image in frequency space. It keeps the domain-invariant frequency components as much as possible and randomizes the domain-variant frequency components in the frequency space. SFA [17] uses Gaussian noise to interfere with feature embedding in the training process, which improves the performance of the classifier in the unseen domain.

Domain-Invariant Features Learning. DICA [22] minimizes dissimilarity across domains to learn domain-invariant features. MMD-AAE [15] learns domain-invariant features through adversarial autoencoders. SNR [13] uses Instance Normalization to eliminate style features and restitutes the features to ensure that effective information is not filtered. IBN [23] points out that the low-level feature representation reflects more texture information, while the high-level feature representation reflects more semantic information. IBN uses the advantages of Instance Normalization and batch normalization to improve the generalization of models. MatchDG [20] makes use of the causal influence to provide an object-conditional objective to highlight the advantage of learning domain-invariant features. FAR [12] aligns the features of different domains by adjusting the moment modulation of feature distribution, then extracts useful features from the remaining information and uses them to compensate for the aligned features.

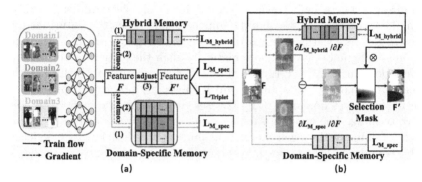

Fig. 2. Illustration of our proposed LEDF. (a) The overall framework of LEDF. (b) The detailed process of feature adjustment.

Gradient Calibration. Some methods solve DG problems through meta learning [14,38]. MLDG [14] divides the data from the source domains into a meta-training set and meta-testing set to simulate the unseen domain. It lays a foundation for the later meta-DG methods. M³L [38] uses the meta-test phase of meta-learning to simulate the unseen domain and uses metaBN to increase the diversity of meta-test features. Some methods use the gradient to further propose novel strategies [11,21,27]. Fish [27] points out that the learning ability of general features can be improved only if the gradient descent directions on the two domains are consistent. They improve the generalization ability by maximizing the inner product of the gradient descent directions of different domains. Gradient surgery [21] points out that intra-domain gradients often show higher similarity than inter-domain gradients. Consistency constraints on inter-domain gradients can encourage the learning of distinctive features common to all domains and improve the generalization performance across domains. RSC [11] points out that the model will over-rely on easy features, and improve the generalization ability of the model by filtering out features with large gradients.

3   Method

Problem Definition. Suppose we have N_S labeled source domains $\mathcal{D}_S = \{\mathcal{D}_1, ..., \mathcal{D}_{N_S}\}$, where $\mathcal{D}_i = \{\mathcal{X}_i, \mathcal{Y}_i\}$ is the i-th domain with training images $\mathcal{X}_i$ and their corresponding ID labels $\mathcal{Y}_i$. The goal of multi-domain generalized re-ID is optimizing re-ID model that can perform well on another unseen target domain $\mathcal{T}$ without using $\mathcal{T}$'s training images.

3.1   Overview

Our overall training framework is shown in Fig. 2-(a), which contains three steps. (1) designing domain-specific & hybrid training schemes (2) locating domain-sensitive features (3) generalized optimization. In step (1), we design two different training schemes for the same inputs and adopt memory banks to compute different losses. The first type of scheme (domain-specific scheme, also noted as scheme ①) aims at discriminating the inputs from their corresponding domain, while the second (hybrid scheme, also noted as scheme ②) tries to classify the given samples from IDs of all source domains. Since domain shift is much easier for the model to recognize due to the change of illumination and viewpoint [27], the back-propagated gradient from the hybrid scheme will focus more on the domain-specific subsets of features. Therefore, in step (2), we compare the back-propagated gradients of the two schemes to locate the domain-sensitive subsets. In step (3), we mute these subsets during the training process to improve the generalization of re-ID models. Figure 2-(b) shows the process of feature adjustment in detail. Next, we will introduce our method in detail.

3.2   Domain-Specific and Hybrid Scheme

In this section, we introduce the two training schemes used in our method. The two training schemes are "domain-specific scheme" and "hybrid scheme". Given a batch of samples $\{\mathcal{X}_i, \mathcal{Y}_i\}$ with N_b images $\mathcal{X}_i = \{x_{i,1}, ..., x_{i,N_b}\}$ and labels $\mathcal{Y}_i = \{y_{i,1}, ..., y_{i,N_b}\}$ of domain i, the former discriminates them from IDs of their corresponding domain while the latter classifies them in IDs of all source domains. Generally speaking, we can simply adopt the fully-connected layer to compute the classification loss for these two schemes. However, as discussed in [38], re-ID is an open-set problem [24] where each domain has completely different IDs. We thus use the parametric classifier like memory bank [42] for optimization.

Memory Initialization. In our method, we construct N_S memory banks for each domain's domain-specific training. The memory bank for domain i is denoted as $\mathcal{M}_i \in \mathbb{R}^{N_i \times d}$, which is a $N_i \times d$ matrix and stores the L2-normed class centroids in each row of it. N_i is the number of IDs in the domain i while d is the dimension of features. We use imagenet-pretrained ResNet-50 model $f(\cdot)$ to extract features and class centroids for each domain. These class centroids are then L2-normalized to initialize the memories. Moreover, we concatenate all memories to form the hybrid memory $\mathcal{M}$ for our "hybrid scheme".

Loss Functions. We conduct our domain-specific and hybrid training schemes with all memories. Specifically, for a sample $\{x_{i,j}, y_{i,j}\}$ in the given batch $\{\mathcal{X}_i, \mathcal{Y}_i\}$, we compute domain-specific classification loss with its corresponding memory $\mathcal{M}_i$, formulated as:

$$L_{M\_spec} = -\log \frac{\exp(\mathcal{M}_i[y_{i,j}]^\mathrm{T} f(x_{i,j})/\tau)}{\sum_{k=1}^{N_i} \exp(\mathcal{M}_i[k]^\mathrm{T} f(x_{i,j})/\tau)} , \tag{1}$$

where $x_{i,j}$ is the j-th sample in the batch. $f(x_{i,j})$ denotes the L2-normalized intermediate feature of input image $x_{i,j}$. $\mathcal{M}_i[y_{i,j}]$ is the $y_{i,j}$-th class centroid in memory $\mathcal{M}_i$. τ is the temperature factor that controls the scale of distribution. N_i denotes the total number of IDs in the i-th domain. By using L_{M_spec} for domain-specific training, we enforce the model to classify the given sample into its own class as traditional re-ID methods do.

The motivation for designing the hybrid scheme is to discriminate the given sample from IDs of all source domains. Therefore, we concatenate all memory banks to form the hybrid memory $\mathcal{M} \in \mathbb{R}^{N \times d}$. $N = \sum_{i=1}^{N_S} N_i$ is the number of IDs in all domains. The training loss for the hybrid scheme is defined based on the hybrid memory:

$$L_{M\_hybrid} = -\log \frac{\exp(\mathcal{M}[y_{i,j}]^{\mathrm{T}} f(x_{i,j})/\tau)}{\sum_{k=1}^{N} \exp(\mathcal{M}[k]^{\mathrm{T}} f(x_{i,j})/\tau)} . \tag{2}$$

When discriminating the given sample from all centroids of source domains, it is usually easier for the model to focus on the domain-sensitive subsets of features. That is because the images in different domains may have conspicuous differences (e.g., illumination and change of colors [34]), which is easier for the model to recognize than the fine-grained ID-related information [27]. Therefore, the back-propagated gradients from the two training schemes will be slightly different. We thus design a novel algorithm to locate this domain-sensitive information in the intermediate features by comparing gradients of two training schemes.

3.3   Locating Domain-Sensitive Features

We adopt the gradients from two training schemes to find the domain-sensitive subsets of features for subsequent generalization training. In detail, after computing the L_{M_spec} and L_{M_hybrid} for all samples in the training batch, we compute the derivative of these two losses respected to the intermediate features **F**

$$g_{spec} = \partial L_{M\_spec}/\partial \mathbf{F}, \quad g_{hybrid} = \partial L_{M\_hybrid}/\partial \mathbf{F} , \tag{3}$$

where g_{spec} and g_{hybrid} are temporary back-propagated gradients of L_{M_spec} and L_{M_hybrid} for the training batch. As the hybrid training scheme focuses more on the domain-sensitive subsets of features, the gradient in these subsets will be higher than that gradient of the domain-specific scheme, while keeping the basic focus on generalized subsets to maintain the basic discrimination [11]. We thus compare g_{spec} with g_{hybrid} to obtain a response map and highlight these subsets:

$$\Delta rank(g_{\mathbf{F}}) = rank(g_{hybrid}) - rank(g_{spec}) , \tag{4}$$

where $rank$ means calculating the ranking value and $\Delta rank(g_{\mathbf{F}})$ is the response map. The subsets with higher values in $\Delta rank(g_{\mathbf{F}})$ indicate the higher possibility of being domain-sensitive. Based on the response map $\Delta rank(g_{\mathbf{F}})$, we find domain-sensitive subsets of features by locating the regions with higher response values. In detail, we sort all the values in $\Delta rank(g_{\mathbf{F}})$ in descent order and set a threshold q based on the top $r\%$ highest values of $\Delta rank(g_{\mathbf{F}})$. $r\%$ is the dropping rate. Subset features will be considered as the domain-sensitive parts if their corresponding response value in $\Delta rank(g_{\mathbf{F}})$ is greater than q. To formulate the selection process, we define a selection mask **m** that has the same size as intermediate feature **F**. Each element in **m** can be computed with the following rule:

$$\mathbf{m}_o = \begin{cases} 0, & \text{if} \quad \varDelta rank(g_{\mathbf{F},o}) \geq q \\ 1, & \text{otherwise} \end{cases} \tag{5}$$

where $\mathbf{m}_o$ and $rank(g_{\mathbf{F},o})$ are the o-th element in $\mathbf{m}$ and $rank(g_{\mathbf{F}})$, respectively. q is the threshold for selection. The obtained mask is then used to filter out domain-sensitive subsets in $\mathbf{F}$ through element-wise product:

$$\mathbf{F}' = \mathbf{F} \odot \mathbf{m} , \tag{6}$$

where $\mathbf{F}'$ is the intermediate features that have muted the domain-sensitive subsets.

3.4   Generalized Optimization

The obtained $\mathbf{F}'$ is then sent to global average pooling and L2-norm layers through forward propagation to obtain adjusted features $\mathbf{f}' \in \mathbb{R}^{N_b \times d}$. We use $\mathbf{f}'$ to optimize the re-ID model with the following two losses:

$$L_{ce}(\mathbf{f}', \mathcal{Y}_i) = -\frac{1}{N_b} \sum_{j=1}^{N_b} \log \frac{\exp(\mathcal{M}_i[y_{i,j}]^\mathsf{T} \mathbf{f}'_j / \tau)}{\sum_{k=1}^{N_i} \exp(\mathcal{M}_i[k]^\mathsf{T} \mathbf{f}'_j / \tau)} , \tag{7}$$

$$L_{tri}(\mathbf{f}') = \frac{1}{N_b} \sum_{j=1}^{N_b} \left[||\mathbf{f}'_{+,j} - \mathbf{f}'_j||_2 - ||\mathbf{f}'_{-,j} - \mathbf{f}'_j||_2 + m \right]_+ , \tag{8}$$

where $\mathbf{f}'_j$ is the j-th feature in $\mathbf{f}'$. $\mathbf{f}'_{+,j}$ and $\mathbf{f}'_{-,j}$ are hard positive and negative samples within the batch. m is the margin for triplet loss. The final loss for optimizing re-ID model is defined as:

$$\mathcal{L}_{all} = \mathcal{L}_{ce}(\mathbf{f}', \mathcal{Y}_i) + \mathcal{L}_{tri}(\mathbf{f}') . \tag{9}$$

At the end of optimization, we update the memory of domain i to prepare for the training with next batch of samples. Specifically, the corresponding class centroids in the i-th memory bank will be updated with the exponential moving average strategy, which is commonly used in memory-based domain generalization methods [38]:

$$\mathcal{M}_i[z] \leftarrow \mu \cdot \mathcal{M}_i[z] + (1 - \mu) \cdot \frac{1}{|\mathcal{B}_z|} \sum_{x_{i,j} \in \mathcal{B}_z} f(x_{i,j}) , \tag{10}$$

where $\mathcal{B}_z$ denotes the samples belonging to the z-th ID and $|\mathcal{B}_z|$ denotes the number of samples for the z-th ID in the current mini-batch. $\mu \in [0, 1]$ controls the updating rate. The previous three steps (step (1)-(3)) are iterated for several epochs to improve the model's generalization. The overall training process has been demonstrated in Algorithm 1.

Algorithm 1: Procedure of Our Algorithm.

Inputs: N_S Labeled source domains $\mathcal{D}_S = \{\mathcal{D}_1, ..., D_{N_S}\}$, learning rate β, batch size N_b, training epochs *epoch*.

Outputs: Generalized re-ID model.

 1: Initialize all memories.
 2: **for** s in *epoch* **do**
 3:    **for** i in N_S **do**
 4:       Sample a mini-batch $\{\mathcal{X}_i, \mathcal{Y}_i\}$ with N_b images and labels from domain i;
 5:       Compute temporary gradient g_{spec} and g_{hybrid} with Eq. 3;
 6:       Locate domain-sensitive subsets with Eq. 4;
 7:       Generate $\mathbf{F}'$ with Eq. 6;
 8:       Optimize re-ID model with Eq. 9;
 9:       Update memory with Eq. 10;
10:    **end for**
11: **end for**
12: Return generalized re-ID model.

Further Discussion. Our method is inspired by the gradient-based generalization algorithm RSC [11]. However, our approach is fundamentally different from it. Specifically, our method considers the interaction among source domains by simultaneously using domain-specific and hybrid memory, while RSC does not have such interaction. The interaction of source domains enables us to define a more specific meaning of domain-shift, and make the assumption that when compared with the domain-specific scheme, the subsets of features with higher predictability in the hybrid scheme have a higher possibility of being domain-sensitive. The domain-sensitive subsets can be readily located when comparing the back-propagated gradients of the two schemes. However, RSC considers the most predictive subsets of features as the easiest part and mutes them during the optimization for generalized training. They do not explicitly consider the domain shift problem. Therefore, our method is different from RSC and we design a non-trivial solution for generalized re-ID learning.

4   Experiments

4.1   Experiment Settings

Datasets. We selected four large-scale person re-identification benchmarks for experiments, *i.e.*, Market-1501 [39], CUHK03 [19], CUHK02 [18], and MSMT-17 [29]. Market-1501 was collected by 6 cameras, of which $32,668$ labeled data composed of 1501 IDs. CUHK03 and CUHK02 have $1,467$ and $1,816$ IDs, $28,193$ and $7,264$ pedestrian images respectively. And they have five pairs of different outdoor cameras. MSMT-17 is an extra-large pedestrian dataset, including $126,441$ pedestrian images collected by 15 cameras, with a total of $4,101$ IDs. Note that, we do not take DukeMTMC-reID [25,40] into our evaluation since it has been taken down by its creators.

Evaluation Metrics. We evaluated the performance based on the cumulative matching characteristics (CMC) at Rank-1 and mean average precision (mAP).

Implementation Details. We conduct our experiments on two commonly used backbones, *i.e.*, ResNet-50 [7] and IBN-Net50 [23]. We apply our method in the intermediate feature maps. We set the total training epochs to 60. We choose Adam as the optimizer and the initial learning rate is set to 3.5×10^{-5}. We multiply the learning rate by 0.1 at the 30-th and 50-th training epoch. For the loss function, we set the margin of triple loss $m=0.3$. The temperature factor of memory-based identification loss $\tau=0.05$ and updating rate μ in memory update is set to 0.2. We set the training batch-size N_b to 64. All images are resized to 256×128, followed by random flipping and random clipping for data augmentation. We adopt the re-ID model trained with all source domains and vanilla memory-based identification loss and triplet loss [8] as the baseline.

4.2   Comparison with State-of-the-Arts Methods

We compare our method with state-of-the-art methods and report the results in Table 1. The included methods are SNR [13], RSC [11], and M³L [38]. We evaluate the generalization of the trained re-ID model with the "leave-one protocol", *i.e.*, testing the model on one of the four benchmarks and using other datasets as source domains. As shown in the table, our method outperforms other methods by a large margin in both mAP and rank-1 scores. Specifically, the experiments with ResNet-50 achieve 53.8%, 50.6%, 89.6%, and 15.7% mAP scores when using Market1501, CUHK03, CUHK02, and MSMT17 as the testing set. These results outperform M³L [38] by 3.9%, 5.5%, 2.7%, and 4.6% on the previous four generalization tasks, respectively. Moreover, when applying our method to IBN-Net50, our method also achieves the best re-ID accuracies. The mAP scores of the re-ID model are 58.6%, 53.8%, 90.0%, and 18.9%, which is higher than that of M³L by 6.9%, 3.6%, 1.8%, and 4.9% when being evaluated on Market1501, CUHK03, CUHK02, and MSMT17. Similar results can also be found in another state-of-the-art method RSC [11], which is originally designed for the classification task. Based on these results, we claim that our method is effective in handling the generalized re-ID model training problem.

4.3   Ablation Studies

To further explore the effectiveness of each component in our method, we design three ablation experiments. In these experiments, we aim to: (1) show the necessity of eliminating domain-sensitive subsets of features during the optimization; (2) prove the necessity of locating domain-sensitive subsets by subtracting $rank(g_{spec})$ from $rank(g_{hybrid})$; (3) prove the effectiveness of eliminating domain-sensitive subsets with our method.

Table 1. Comparison with State-of-the-arts. M: Market-1501, CUHK02: C2, CUHK03: C3, MS: MSMT-17.

Methods	Sources	Market		Sources	CUHK03	
		mAP	Rank-1		mAP	Rank-1
OSNet [43]	MS+C2+C3	41.7	65.5	MS+M+C2	39.4	41.1
SNR [13]		44.2	70.1		41.2	45.5
RSC [11]		50.8	76.7		46.5	51.5
M^3L [38]		49.9	75.7		45.1	50.5
Ours		53.8	79.0		50.6	56.0
M^3L (IBN-Net50)		51.7	78.0		50.2	57.5
Ours (IBN-Net50)		**58.6**	**81.8**		**53.8**	**59.8**
Methods	Sources	CUHK02		Sources	MSMT	
		mAP	Rank-1		mAP	Rank-1
OSNet [43]	MS+C2+C3	75.5	76.1	MS+M+C2	10.2	26.7
SNR [13]		78.5	79.5		14.4	37.3
RSC [11]		88.2	87.7		13.1	33.1
M^3L [38]		86.9	87.4		11.1	28.8
Ours		89.6	**90.6**		15.7	39.5
M^3L (IBN-Net50)		88.2	87.6		14.0	34.2
Ours (IBN-Net50)		**90.0**	89.1		**18.9**	**44.2**

Table 2. Ablation studies on Locating strategy. H-S: computing response map by subtracting $rank(g_{spec})$ from $rank(g_{hybrid})$. S-H: computing response map by subtracting $rank(g_{hybrid})$ from $rank(g_{spec})$. Abs: Using the absolute values of the difference between $rank(g_{hybrid})$ and $rank(g_{spec})$ to compute response map. ResNet: ResNet-50. IBN-Net: IBN-Net50.

Backbone	Strategy			MS+C2+ C3→M		M+C2+ C3→MS		Backbone	MS+C2+ C3→M		M+C2+ C3→MS	
	Abs	S-H	H-S	mAP	Rank-1	mAP	Rank-1		mAP	Rank-1	mAP	Rank-1
ResNet	×	×	×	46.1	72.3	9.5	25.0	IBN-Net	50.5	75.7	12.6	32.3
	✓	×	×	53.0	78.4	14.7	38.1		57.8	80.9	17.9	42.7
	×	✓	×	52.9	78.1	14.4	37.6		57.2	79.5	17.2	41.3
	×	×	✓	**53.8**	**79.0**	**15.7**	**39.5**		**58.6**	**81.8**	**18.9**	**44.2**

The Necessity of Eliminating Domain-Sensitive Subsets. We evaluate the re-ID model that does not use any strategy to eliminate domain-sensitive subsets during the optimization and report the results in Table 2. In ResNet-50, the model trained with vanilla multi-domain training (baseline) achieves 46.1% and 9.5% mAP scores on "MS+C2+C3→M" and "M+C2+C3→MS" tasks, respectively. The results are lower than our method in these two tasks. Similarly, in IBN-Net50, our experiment also achieved the same conclusion. This experiment indicates that eliminating the domain-sensitive subsets of features during the optimization is necessary.

Table 3. Ablation studies of dropping strategies.

Backbone	Method	MS+C2+C3 → M		M+C2+C3 → MS	
		mAP	Rank-1	mAP	Rank-1
ResNet-50	Random	48.5	73.9	9.3	25.2
	RSC	50.8	76.7	13.1	33.1
	Ours	**53.8**	**79.0**	**15.7**	**39.5**

The Necessity of Subtracting $rank(g_{spec})$ **from** $rank(g_{hybrid})$. In Eq. 4, we generate the response map by subtracting $rank(g_{spec})$ from $rank(g_{hybrid})$. Intuitively, there are also other strategies to highlight the domain-sensitive subsets of features, like using the absolute value of the difference between $rank(g_{spec})$ and $rank(g_{hybrid})$ (*i.e.*, $\Delta rank(g_{\mathbf{F}}) = |rank(g_{hybrid}) - rank(g_{spec})|$). To explore the best form of highlighting these domain-sensitive subsets of features, we conduct experiments by using different strategies to compute response map $\Delta rank(g_{\mathbf{F}})$ in Table 2. As shown in the table, the strategy define in Eq. 4 achieves the best performance when compared with other strategies. This suggests that subtracting $rank(g_{spec})$ from $rank(g_{hybrid})$ is a more plausible way of highlighting the domain-sensitive subsets during the optimization.

The Necessity of Using Our Dropping Strategy. We evaluate the re-ID model by randomly dropping features. The random dropout strategy adopts the same settings as our method, such as the same feature dropping rate, etc. As shown in Table 3, The random dropout strategy achieves 48.5% and 9.3% mAP scores on "MS+C2+C3→M" and "M+C2+C3→MS" tasks, respectively. The results are lower than RSC and our method, and our method achieves the best. This shows that our method is most effective in eliminating domain-sensitive features.

4.4 Sensitivity Analysis

Feature Dropping Rate. We explore the influence of using different dropping rates during the optimization. The higher dropping rate r may inevitably drop some decisive features while lower r may not be effective enough to improve the generalization of models. In Table 4, we vary r from 10% to 66.7% on "MS+C2+C3→M" and "MS+C2+M→C3" to find how the dropping rate will influence the final results. From Table 4, we find that: (1) When the dropping rate r increases from 10% to 50%, the re-ID accuracies in generalization tasks also improved. This is caused by the elimination of domain-sensitive subsets of features. (2) When continuously increasing the dropping rate r from 50% to 66.7%, the re-ID accuracies decreases. The results indicate that we should not set the dropping rate to a very high value. Generally speaking, setting r to a value less than 50% would be sufficient for improving the model's generalization.

Table 4. Sensitivity analysis of dropping rate.

Rate	MS+C2+C3 → M		MS+M+C2 → C3		Average	
	mAP	Rank-1	mAP	Rank-1	mAP	Rank-1
10.0%	52.3	77.9	48.7	53.0	50.5	65.45
20.0%	53.0	78.4	48.6	52.5	50.8	65.45
25.0%	53.6	78.9	48.8	55.5	51.2	67.20
33.3%	53.4	78.8	**50.8**	54.0	52.1	66.40
50.0%	**53.8**	**79.0**	50.6	**56.0**	**52.2**	**67.50**
66.7%	53.3	78.1	46.5	54.0	49.9	66.05

Table 5. Sensitivity analysis of the number of source domains.

Backbone	Method	MS+C3 → M		MS+M → C3		M+C3 → MS	
		mAP	Rank-1	mAP	Rank-1	mAP	Rank-1
ResNet-50	Baseline	38.5	64.6	29.9	34.5	6.8	18.8
	RSC	44.0	68.6	35.7	42.3	9.9	26.0
	Ours	**46.5**	**73.0**	**36.8**	**43.5**	**13.0**	**33.4**

Table 6. Sensitivity analysis of Channel-wise LEDF verse Spatial+Channel LEDF.

Backbone	Method	MS+C2+C3 → M		MS+M+C2 → C3	
		mAP	Rank-1	mAP	Rank-1
ResNet-50	Channel	50.7	77.6	46.5	54.0
	Channel+Spatial	**53.8**	**79.0**	**50.6**	**56.0**

Number of Source Domains. We also conduct experiments using fewer source domains to check the effectiveness of our method. In detail, we alternately use two of the three source domains for training and evaluate the trained model on the testing set. The results are shown in Table 5. We report the re-ID accuracies of re-ID models on "MS+C3→M", "MS+M→C3", and "M+C3→MS" tasks. For simplicity, in addition to baseline, we also compare it with RSC, which has the best average performance in previous experiments among many state-of-the-art methods. As shown in the table, we achieve 46.5%, 36.8%, and 13% mAP scores on "MS+C3→M", "MS+M→C3", and "M+C3→MS" tasks, respectively. These results outperform RSC [11] and the vanilla generalized re-ID training method, which proves the effectiveness of our method on generalization tasks with fewer source training domains.

Channel-Wise and Spatial-Wise Dropping. We also design some experiments to find the optimal strategy for dropping intermediate features. Intuitively, there are two types of dropping strategies. The first is channel-wise dropping, which means using the global average pooling to gradient tensor along the spa-

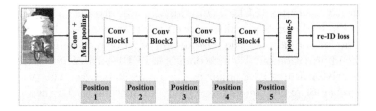

Fig. 3. Our LEDF module can be inserted into the position of ResNet-50.

Table 7. Sensitivity analysis of LEDF inserts position.

Position	MS+C2+C3 → M		MS+M+C2 → C3		Average	
	mAP	Rank-1	mAP	Rank-1	mAP	Rank-1
Position1	**53.8**	**79.0**	**50.6**	**56.0**	**52.2**	**67.50**
Position2	51.5	77.0	45.7	47.0	48.6	62.00
Position3	46.8	73.8	43.6	49.5	45.2	61.65
Position4	42.1	69.5	40.5	48.5	41.3	59.00
Position5	36.4	64.0	37.6	46.0	37.0	55.00

tial dimension and carrying out feature dropping at the channel level. And the second is spatial-wise dropping. Because ResNet uses global average pooling at the end, the values of applying global average pooling to gradient tensor along the channel dimension are all the same. Therefore, we use the same spatial-wise dropping as RSC [11], which is transformed on the basis of channel-wise dropping. As shown in Table 6, the combination of channel-wise dropping and spatial-wise dropping performs best (we use 50% of channel-wise dropping and spatial-wise dropping respectively in the training stage).

What Stage to Add Our Method? It naturally raises the question that how about adding our method to other intermediate features. To answer this question, we take the ResNet-50 model as an example and insert our method in different stages of the model to check its effectiveness. Generally speaking, ResNet-50 has four blocks, and we can insert our method at the beginning or end of each block. Therefore, we apply our method in the position depicted in Fig. 3 and report the results in Table 7. We conclude that our method achieves the best performance when being deployed in the shallow layer while performing poorly when being deployed in deeper layers. We conjecture that style information is stored in the shallow layers of deep networks while deep layers are responsible for learning semantic information. As our method aims at eliminating the domain-shift of features, it is better to deploy our method in the shallow layers of deep neural networks.

5   Conclusion

In this paper, we propose a novel domain generalization method to enhance the generalization of the model in the unseen domain by locating and eliminating domain-sensitive features (LEDF). In addition, we introduced domain-specific memory and hybrid memory, which respectively represent two different training schemes. The former only has the information of its own domain, and the latter contains the information of all source domains. LEDF locates and eliminates the domain-sensitive features by comparing the gradient between the two schemes. A large number of experiments prove that our method LEDF can effectively improve the generalization ability of the model in person re-identification.

Acknowledgement. This work is supported by the National Nature Science Foundation of China (No. 61876159, 62276221), the Natural Science Foundation of Fujian Province of China (No. 2022J01002), the Science and Technology Plan Project of Xiamen (No. 3502Z20221025).

References

1. Carlucci, F.M., Porzi, L., Caputo, B., Ricci, E., Bulo, S.R.: Autodial: automatic domain alignment layers. In: ICCV (2017)
2. Ding, C., Wang, K., Wang, P., Tao, D.: Multi-task learning with coarse priors for robust part-aware person re-identification. TPAMI (2020)
3. Fan, H., Zheng, L., Yan, C., Yang, Y.: Unsupervised person re-identification: clustering and fine-tuning. TOMM (2018)
4. Ge, Y., Chen, D., Li, H.: Mutual mean-teaching: pseudo label refinery for unsupervised domain adaptation on person re-identification. In: ICLR (2020)
5. Ge, Y., Zhu, F., Chen, D., Zhao, R., et al.: Self-paced contrastive learning with hybrid memory for domain adaptive object re-id. In: NIPS (2020)
6. Gong, X., Yao, Z., Li, X., Fan, Y., Luo, B., Fan, J., Lao, B.: LAG-Net: multi-granularity network for person re-identification via local attention system. TMM (2021)
7. He, K., Zhang, X., Ren, S., Sun, J.: Deep residual learning for image recognition. In: CVPR (2016)
8. Hermans, A., Beyer, L., Leibe, B.: In defense of the triplet loss for person re-identification. arXiv preprint arXiv:1703.07737 (2017)
9. Huang, G., Liu, Z., Van Der Maaten, L., Weinberger, K.Q.: Densely connected convolutional networks. In: CVPR (2017)
10. Huang, J., Guan, D., Xiao, A., Lu, S.: FSDR: frequency space domain randomization for domain generalization. In: CVPR (2021)
11. Huang, Z., Wang, H., Xing, E.P., Huang, D.: Self-challenging improves cross-domain generalization. In: ECCV (2020)
12. Jin, X., Lan, C., Zeng, W., Chen, Z.: Feature alignment and restoration for domain generalization and adaptation. arXiv preprint arXiv:2006.12009 (2020)
13. Jin, X., Lan, C., Zeng, W., Chen, Z., Zhang, L.: Style normalization and restitution for generalizable person re-identification. In: CVPR (2020)
14. Li, D., Yang, Y., Song, Y.Z., Hospedales, T.M.: Learning to generalize: meta-learning for domain generalization. In: AAAI (2018)
15. Li, H., Pan, S.J., Wang, S., Kot, A.C.: Domain generalization with adversarial feature learning. In: CVPR (2018)
16. Li, L., et al.: Progressive domain expansion network for single domain generalization. In: CVPR (2021)

17. Li, P., Li, D., Li, W., Gong, S., Fu, Y., Hospedales, T.M.: A simple feature augmentation for domain generalization. In: ICCV (2021)
18. Li, W., Wang, X.: Locally aligned feature transforms across views. In: CVPR (2013)
19. Li, W., Zhao, R., Xiao, T., Wang, X.: Deepreid: deep filter pairing neural network for person re-identification. In: CVPR (2014)
20. Mahajan, D., Tople, S., Sharma, A.: Domain generalization using causal matching. In: ICML (2021)
21. Mansilla, L., Echeveste, R., Milone, D.H., Ferrante, E.: Domain generalization via gradient surgery. In: ICCV (2021)
22. Muandet, K., Balduzzi, D., Schölkopf, B.: Domain generalization via invariant feature representation. In: ICML (2013)
23. Pan, X., Luo, P., Shi, J., Tang, X.: Two at once: enhancing learning and generalization capacities via ibn-net. In: ECCV (2018)
24. Panareda Busto, P., Gall, J.: Open set domain adaptation. In: ICCV (2017)
25. Ristani, E., Solera, F., Zou, R., Cucchiara, R., Tomasi, C.: Performance measures and a data set for multi-target, multi-camera tracking. In: ECCV Workshop (2016)
26. Saito, K., Watanabe, K., Ushiku, Y., Harada, T.: Maximum classifier discrepancy for unsupervised domain adaptation. In: CVPR (2018)
27. Shi, Y., et al.: Gradient matching for domain generalization. In: ICLR (2022)
28. Sun, Y., Zheng, L., Yang, Y., Tian, Q., Wang, S.: Beyond part models: person retrieval with refined part pooling (and a strong convolutional baseline). In: ECCV (2018)
29. Wei, L., Zhang, S., Gao, W., Tian, Q.: Person transfer GAN to bridge domain gap for person re-identification. In: CVPR (2018)
30. Xiang, W., Huang, J., Hua, X.S., Zhang, L.: Part-aware attention network for person re-identification. In: ACCV (2020)
31. Yan, C., et al.: Beyond triplet loss: person re-identification with fine-grained difference-aware pairwise loss. TMM (2021)
32. Yang, F., et al.: Asymmetric co-teaching for unsupervised cross-domain person re-identification. In: AAAI (2020)
33. Yang, F., et al.: Learning to attack real-world models for person re-identification via virtual-guided meta-learning. In: AAAI (2021)
34. Yang, F., et al.: Joint noise-tolerant learning and meta camera shift adaptation for unsupervised person re-identification. In: CVPR (2021)
35. Ye, M., Shen, J., Lin, G., Xiang, T., Shao, L., Hoi, S.C.: Deep learning for person re-identification: a survey and outlook. TPAMI (2021)
36. Yu, H.X., Zheng, W.S., Wu, A., Guo, X., Gong, S., Lai, J.H.: Unsupervised person re-identification by soft multilabel learning. In: CVPR (2019)
37. Zhang, Z., Lan, C., Zeng, W., Jin, X., Chen, Z.: Relation-aware global attention for person re-identification. In: CVPR (2020)
38. Zhao, Y., et al.: Learning to generalize unseen domains via memory-based multi-source meta-learning for person re-identification. In: CVPR (2021)
39. Zheng, L., Shen, L., Tian, L., Wang, S., Wang, J., Tian, Q.: Scalable person re-identification: a benchmark. In: ICCV (2015)
40. Zheng, Z., Zheng, L., Yang, Y.: Unlabeled samples generated by GAN improve the person re-identification baseline in vitro. In: ICCV (2017)
41. Zhong, Z., Zheng, L., Cao, D., Li, S.: Re-ranking person re-identification with k-reciprocal encoding. In: CVPR (2017)
42. Zhong, Z., Zheng, L., Luo, Z., Li, S., Yang, Y.: Invariance matters: exemplar memory for domain adaptive person re-identification. In: CVPR (2019)

43. Zhou, K., Yang, Y., Cavallaro, A., Xiang, T.: Learning generalisable omni-scale representations for person re-identification. TPAMI (2021)
44. Zhou, K., Yang, Y., Hospedales, T., Xiang, T.: Learning to generate novel domains for domain generalization. In: ECCV (2020)
45. Zhou, K., Yang, Y., Qiao, Y., Xiang, T.: Domain generalization with mixstyle. In: ICLR (2021)
46. Zhu, Z., et al.: Aware loss with angular regularization for person re-identification. In: AAAI (2020)

ST-CoNAL: Consistency-Based Acquisition Criterion Using Temporal Self-ensemble for Active Learning

Jae Soon Baik[ID], In Young Yoon[ID], and Jun Won Choi[(✉)][ID]

Hanyang University, Seoul, Korea
{jsbaik,inyoungyoon}@spa.hanyang.ac.kr, junwchoi@hanyang.ac.kr

Abstract. Modern deep learning has achieved great success in various fields. However, it requires the labeling of huge amounts of data, which is expensive and labor-intensive. Active learning (AL), which identifies the most informative samples to be labeled, is becoming increasingly important to maximize the efficiency of the training process. The existing AL methods mostly use only a single final fixed model for acquiring the samples to be labeled. This strategy may not be good enough in that the structural uncertainty of a model for given training data is not considered to acquire the samples. In this study, we propose a novel acquisition criterion based on temporal self-ensemble generated by conventional stochastic gradient descent (SGD) optimization. These self-ensemble models are obtained by capturing the intermediate network weights obtained through SGD iterations. Our acquisition function relies on a *consistency measure* between the student and teacher models. The student models are given a fixed number of temporal self-ensemble models, and the teacher model is constructed by averaging the weights of the student models. Using the proposed acquisition criterion, we present an AL algorithm, namely *student-teacher consistency-based AL* (ST-CoNAL). Experiments conducted for image classification tasks on CIFAR-10, CIFAR-100, Caltech-256, and Tiny ImageNet datasets demonstrate that the proposed ST-CoNAL achieves significantly better performance than the existing acquisition methods. Furthermore, extensive experiments show the robustness and effectiveness of our methods.

Keywords: Active learning · Consistency · Temporal self-ensemble · Image classification

1 Introduction

Deep neural networks (DNNs) require a large amount of training data to optimize millions of weights. In particular, for supervised-learning tasks, labeling of training data by human annotators is expensive and time-consuming. The labeling cost can be a major concern for machine learning applications, which requires

Supplementary Information The online version contains supplementary material available at https://doi.org/10.1007/978-3-031-26351-4_30.

a collection of real-world data on a massive scale (e.g., autonomous driving) or the knowledge of highly trained experts for annotation (e.g., automatic medical diagnosis). Active learning (AL) is a promising machine learning framework that maximizes the efficiency of labeling tasks within a fixed labeling budget [35].

This study focuses on the pool-based AL problem, where the data instances to be labeled are selected from a pool of unlabeled data. In a pool-based AL method, the decision to label a data instance is based on a *sample acquisition function*. The acquisition function, $a(x, f)$, takes the input instance x and the currently trained model f and produces a score to decide if x should be labeled. Till date, various types of AL methods have been proposed [9–11, 20, 35–37, 45, 46]. The predictive uncertainty-based methods [9, 10, 36, 45] used well-studied theoretic measures such as entropy and mutual information. Recently, representation-based methods [20, 34, 37, 46] have been widely used as a promising AL approach to exploit high-quality representation of DNNs. However, the acquisition used for these methods rely on a single trained model f, failing to account for model uncertainty arising given a limited labeled dataset. To solve this problem, several AL methods [2, 35] attempted to utilize an ensemble of DNNs and design acquisition functions based on them. However, these methods require significant computational costs to train multiple networks.

When the amount of labeled data is limited, semi-supervised learning (SSL) is another promising machine learning approach to improve performance with low labeling costs. SSL improves the model performance by leveraging a large number of unlabeled examples [31]. *Consistency regularization* is one of the most successful approach to SSL [11, 22, 30, 39]. In a typical semi-supervised learning, the model is trained using the consistency-regularized loss function $\mathcal{E}_{ce} + \lambda \mathcal{E}_{con}$, where $\mathcal{E}_{ce}$ denotes the cross-entropy loss and $\mathcal{E}_{con}$ denotes the consistency-regularized loss. Minimization of $\mathcal{E}_{con}$ regularizes the model to produce consistent predictions over the training process, improving the performance for a given task. Π model [22] applied a random perturbation to the input of the DNN and measured the consistency between the model outputs. Mean Teacher (MT) [39] produced the temporal self-ensemble through SGD iterations and measured the consistency between the model being trained and the teacher model obtained by taking the exponential moving average (EMA) of the self-ensemble. These methods successfully regularized the model to produce consistent predictions while using perturbed predictions on unlabeled samples.

The objective of this study is to improve the sample acquisition criterion for pool-based AL methods. Inspired by the consistency regularization for SSL, we build a new sample acquisition criterion that measures consistency between multiple ensemble models obtained during the training phase. The proposed acquisition function generates the temporal self-ensemble by sampling the models at the intermediate check-points of the weight trajectory formed by the SGD optimization. This provides a better acquisition performance and eliminates the additional computational cost required by previous ensemble-based AL methods. In [1, 17, 27], the aforementioned method has shown to produce good and diverse self-ensembles, where were used to improve the inference model via *stochastic*

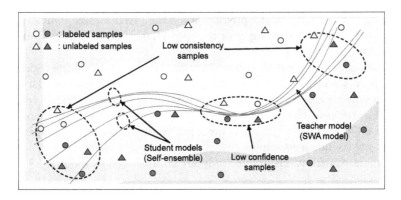

Fig. 1. Acquisition criterion: Both labeled and unlabeled samples are represented in the feature space in the binary classification problem. *Low consistency samples* produce the predictions which significantly differ between the student and teacher models. *Low confidence samples* are found near the decision boundaries of the student models. The proposed ST-CoNAL evaluates the consistency measure for each data sample and selects those with the highest consistency score.

weight averaging (SWA) [1,17,27]. We derive the acquisition criterion based on the temporal self-ensemble models used in SWA. We present the AL method, referred to as *student-teacher consistency-based AL (ST-CoNAL)*, which measures the consistency between the student and teacher models. The self-ensemble model constitutes a student model, and a teacher model is formed by taking an equally-weighted average (EWA) of the parameters of the student models. Treating the output of the teacher model as a desired supervisory signal, ST-CoNAL measures the Kullback-Leibler (KL) divergence of each teacher-student output pairs. The acquisition function of ST-CoNAL acquires the samples to be labeled that yield the highest inconsistency.

Though ST-CoNAL was inspired by the consistency regularization between student and teacher models of the MT, these two methods are quite different in the following aspects. MT constructs the teacher model by assigning larger weights to more recent model weights obtained through SGD iterations. Due to this constraint, as training progresses, the teacher model in MT tends to be correlated with the student models, making it difficult to measure good enough consistency measure for AL acquisition. To address this problem, ST-CoNAL generates a better teacher model by taking an equally-weighted averaging (EWA) of the weights of the student models instead of EMA used in MT. Similar to previous AL methods [9,10] that utilize ensemble models to capture the posterior distribution of model weights for a given data set, the use of student model weights allows our acquisition criterion to account for model uncertainty.

We further improve our ST-CoNAL method by adopting the principle of entropy minimization used for SSL [3,4,12,24,38,43]. We apply one of the entropy minimization methods, sharpening to the output of the teacher model. When the sharpened output is used for our KL divergence, our acquisition criterion can measure the uncertainty of the prediction for the given sample. Our evaluation shows that the ST-CoNAL is superior to other AL methods on various image classification benchmark datasets.

Figure 1 illustrates that these low consistency samples lie in the region of the feature space where the student models produce the predictions of a larger variation. Note that these samples are not necessarily identical to the low confidence samples located near the decision boundary specified by the teacher model. The proposed ST-CoNAL prefers the acquisition of the inconsistent samples rather than the low-confidence samples.

The main contributions of our study are summarized as follows:

- We propose a new acquisition criterion based on the temporal self-ensemble. Temporal self-ensemble models are generated by sampling DNN weights through SGD optimization. ST-CoNAL measures the consistency between these self-ensemble models and acquires the most inconsistent samples for labeling. We evaluated the performance of ST-CoNAL on four different public datasets for multi-class image classification tasks. We observe that the proposed ST-CoNAL method achieves the significant performance gains over other AL methods.
- We identified a work relevant to ours [11]. While both ours and their work aim to exploit consistency regularization for AL, our work differs from theirs in the following aspects. While CSSAL [11] relies on the input perturbation to a single fixed model, ST-CoNAL utilizes the self-ensemble models to measure the consistency. Note that the benefits of using model ensembles for AL have been demonstrated in [2] and our findings about the superior performance of ST-CoNAL over CSSAL are consistent with the results of these studies.

2   Related Work

2.1   Acquisition for AL

The acquisition methods for pool-based AL can be roughly categorized into three classes: 1) *uncertainty-based*, 2) *representation-based* and 3) *consistency-based methods*. The uncertainty-based methods [2,9,10,19,26,41] estimate the prediction uncertainty for the given data instances. Max-entropy [26,36], least confidence [26] and variation ratio [18] are the widely used criteria. Recently, the representation-based method [20,34,37,46] significantly improved the acquisition performance. VAAL [37] performed adversarial learning to find informative unlabeled data in the task-agnostic latent representation of the data. TA-VAAL [20] is the latest state-of-the-art method, which incorporated a task-aware uncertainty-based approach to the VAAL baseline. The consistency-based methods measure the disagreement among the predictions of the ensemble models [9–11,15]. TOD-Semi [16], *Query-by-committee* [35], and DBAL [10] are the well known criteria used in these methods.

2.2   Consistency Regularization for SSL

One of the most successful approaches to SSL is *consistency regularization*. The Π model [22,33] enforces consistency for model $f_\theta(x)$ by minimizing $d(f_\theta(x), f_\theta(\hat{x}))$, where $\hat{x}$ denotes the data perturbed by noise and augmentation, and $d(a, b)$ measures the distance between a and b. While Π model uses the predictions as a target, the consistency loss for regularizing the consistent behavior between an ensemble prediction and the model prediction was shown to be effective. *Mean teacher* method [39] generates the weights of the teacher model with EMA of the student weights over SGD iterations. ICT [42] and MixMatch [4] enforce consistency between linearly interpolated inputs and model predictions.

2.3   Temporal Self-ensemble via Stochastic Weight Averaging

Several studies have attempted to use temporal self-ensemble obtained through model optimization to improve the inference performance [6,17,22,25]. Izmailov et al. [17] proposed SWA method, which determines an improved inference model using the equally weighted average of the intermediate model weights traversed via SGD iterates. Using cyclical learning rate scheduling [27], SGD can yield the weights in the flat regions in the loss surface. By averaging the weights found at SGD trajectory, SWA can find the weight solution that can generalize well. In [1], consistency regularization and modified cyclical learning rate scheduling assisted in finding the improved weights through SWA.

2.4   Combining AL and SSL

The combination of SSL and AL was discussed in several works [8,10,11,32, 40,47]. However, most works considered applying SSL and AL independently. Only a few works considered the joint design of SSL and AL. Zhu et al. [47] used a Gaussian random field on a weighted graph to combine SSL and AL. Additionally, the authors of [11] proposed an enhanced acquisition function by adopting the variance over the data augmentation of the input image.

3   Proposed Active Learning

In this section, we present the details of the ST-CoNAL algorithm.

3.1   Consistency Measure-Based Acquisition

The proposed algorithm follows the setup of a pool-based AL for the K-image class classification task. Suppose that the labeling budget is fixed to b data samples. In the jth sample acquisition step, we are given the dataset $\mathcal{D}^j$, which consists of a set of labeled data $\mathcal{D}_L^j$ and a set of unlabeled data $\mathcal{D}_U^j$. $f_{\mathcal{D}^j}$ is the model trained with dataset $\mathcal{D}^j$. We consider two cases; 1) $f_{\mathcal{D}^j}$ is trained with only $\mathcal{D}_L^j$ via supervised learning and 2) $f_{\mathcal{D}^j}$ is trained with $\mathcal{D}_L^j \cup \mathcal{D}_U^j$ via SSL.

The AL algorithm aims to acquire the set of b data samples $\{x_1^*, ..., x_b^*\}$ from the pool of unlabeled data $\mathcal{D}_U^j$. To select the data samples to be labeled, the acquisition function $a_{\text{ST-CoNAL}}(x_i, f_{\mathcal{D}^j})$ is used to score the given data instance x_i with the currently trained model $f_{\mathcal{D}^j}$. The b samples that yield the highest score are selected as

$$\{x_1^*, ..., x_b^*\} = \operatorname*{argmax}_{\{x_1, ..., x_b\} \subset \mathcal{D}_U^j} \sum_{i=1}^{b} a_{\text{ST-CoNAL}}(x_i, f_{\mathcal{D}^j}). \tag{1}$$

The selected samples are then labeled, i.e., $\mathcal{D}_L^{j+1} \leftarrow \mathcal{D}_L^j \cup \{x_1^*, ..., x_b^*\}$ and $\mathcal{D}_U^{j+1} \leftarrow \mathcal{D}_U^j \setminus \{x_1^*, ..., x_b^*\}$, and the model is retrained using the newly labeled dataset $\mathcal{D}^{j+1} = \{\mathcal{D}_L^{j+1}, \mathcal{D}_U^{j+1}\}$. This procedure is repeated until a labeled dataset is obtained as large as required within the limited budget.

Suppose that we have Q student models $f_{\mathcal{D}^j}^{(s,1)}, ..., f_{\mathcal{D}^j}^{(s,Q)}$ and one teacher model $f_{\mathcal{D}^j}^{(t)}$ trained with the dataset $\mathcal{D}^j$. Each model produces the K dimensional output through the softmax output layer. The method for obtaining these models will be discussed in the next section. We first apply sharpening [3,4,43] to the output of the teacher model as

$$\bar{f}_{\mathcal{D}^j}^{(t)}(k) = \frac{\left(f_{\mathcal{D}^j}^{(t)}(k)\right)^{\frac{1}{T}}}{\sum_{k=1}^{K} \left(f_{\mathcal{D}^j}^{(t)}(k)\right)^{\frac{1}{T}}}, \tag{2}$$

where $f(k)$ denotes the kth element of the output produced by the function $f(\cdot)$ and T denotes the temperature hyper-parameter. Then, the acquisition function of the ST-CoNAL is obtained by accumulating the KL divergence between the predictions produced by each student model and the teacher model, i.e.,

$$a_{\text{ST-CoNAL}}(x_i, f_{\mathcal{D}^j}) = \frac{1}{Q} \sum_{q=1}^{Q} KL(\bar{f}_{\mathcal{D}^j}^{(t)}(x_i) \| f_{\mathcal{D}^j}^{(s,q)}(x_i)), \tag{3}$$

where $KL(p\|q) = \sum_i p_i \log(p_i/q_i)$. The KL divergence in this acquisition function measures the inconsistency between the student and teacher models. As the sharpening makes the prediction of teacher model to have low-entropy, the high KL divergence value reflects the uncertainty in the prediction of the student models.

3.2   Generation of Student and Teacher Models via Optimization Path

The ST-CoNAL computes the student and teacher models using the temporal self-ensemble networks. The parameters of these self-ensemble networks are obtained by capturing the network weights at the intermediate check points of the weight trajectory. The study in [1] revealed that the average of the weights

---

Algorithm 1: ST-CoNAL

Input:
Initial Dataset: $\mathcal{D}^1 = (\mathcal{D}_L^1, \mathcal{D}_U^1)$
Total number of acquisition steps: J
Labeling budget: b
Temperature parameter: T
for $j = 1$ **to** J **do**
    Training:
    Generate the student models $f_{\mathcal{D}^j}^{(s,1)}, ..., f_{\mathcal{D}^j}^{(s,Q)}$ using SGD with the
    modified LR schedule in (4).
    Sample acquisition:
    Compute the teacher model $f_{\mathcal{D}^j}^{(t)}$ via weight averaging.
    $\bar{f}_{\mathcal{D}^j}^{(t)} = \text{Sharpen}(f_{\mathcal{D}^j}^{(t)}, T)$.
    Evaluate $a_{\text{ST-CoNAL}}(x_i, f_{\mathcal{D}^j})$ for all $x_i \in \mathcal{D}_U^j$.
    Acquire b samples according to (1).
    Dataset update:
    $\{(x_1^*, y_1^*), ..., (x_b^*, y_b^*)\} = \text{Annotate}(\{x_1^*, ..., x_b^*\})$
    $\mathcal{D}_L^{j+1} \leftarrow \mathcal{D}_L^j \cup \{x_1^*, ..., x_b^*\}$
    $\mathcal{D}_U^{j+1} \leftarrow \mathcal{D}_U^j \setminus \{x_1^*, ..., x_b^*\}$
    $\mathcal{D}^{j+1} \leftarrow (\mathcal{D}_L^{j+1}, \mathcal{D}_U^{j+1})$
end
Train the model using $\mathcal{D}^{J+1}$ for SSL or $\mathcal{D}_L^{J+1}$ for supervised learning.
return Trained model

---

obtained through the SGD iterates can yield the weights corresponding to the flat minima of the loss surface, which are known to generalize well [29,44]. In ST-CoNAL, the average of these weights forms a teacher model. To obtain the diverse student models, we adopt the learning rate (LR) schedule used for SWA [17,29,44]. The learning rate l used for our method is given by

$$l = \begin{cases} l_0, & \text{if } t < T_0 \\ \gamma l_0, & \text{otherwise} \end{cases} \tag{4}$$

where l_0 denotes the initial learning rate, $\gamma < 1$ denotes the parameter for learning rate decay, t is the current training epoch, and T_0 denotes the training epoch at which the learning rate will be switched to a smaller value. After running T_0 epochs (i.e., $t \geq T_0$), the Q intermediate network weights are stored every c epoch, which constitute the weights of the student networks. We obtain Q self-ensemble networks $f_{\mathcal{D}^j}^{(s,1)}, ..., f_{\mathcal{D}^j}^{(s,Q)}$ and these models are treated as the student models. The teacher model $f_{\mathcal{D}^j}^{(t)}$ is then obtained by taking the equally weighted average of the parameters of $f_{\mathcal{D}^j}^{(s,1)}, ..., f_{\mathcal{D}^j}^{(s,Q)}$. Note that this learning rate schedule does not require any additional training cost for obtaining the temporal self-ensemble.

3.3 Summary of Proposed ST-CoNAL

Algorithm 1 presents the summary of the ST-CoNAL algorithm.

4 Experiments

In this section, we evaluate the performance of ST-CoNAL via experiments conducted on four public datasets, CIFAR-10 [21], CIFAR-100 [21], Caltech-256 [13] and Tiny ImageNet [23].

4.1 Experiment Setup

Datasets. We evaluated ST-CoNAL on four benchmarks: CIFAR-10 [21], CIFAR-100 [21], Caltech-256 [13] and Tiny ImageNet [23]. CIFAR-10 contains $50k$ training examples with 10 categories and CIFAR-100 contains $50k$ training examples with 100 categories. Caltech-256 has $24,660$ training examples with 256 categories and Tiny ImageNet has $100k$ training examples with 200 categories.

To see how ST-CoNAL performed on class-imbalanced scenarios, we additionally used the synthetically imbalanced CIFAR-10 datasets; *the step imbalanced CIFAR-10* [7,20] and the *long-tailed CIFAR-10* [5,7]. The step imbalance CIFAR-10 has 50 samples for the first five smallest classes and 5,000 samples for the last five largest classes. Long-tailed CIFAR-10 followed the configuration used in [5], where 12,406 training images were generated with 5,000 samples from the largest class and 50 samples from the smallest class. The imbalance ratio of 100 is the widely used setting adopted in the literature [5,20].

Implementation Details. In all experiments, an 18-layer residual network (ResNet-18) was used as the backbone network. The detailed structure of this network was provided in [14]. For CIFAR-10 and CIFAR-100 datasets, models were trained with standard data augmentation operations including random translation and random horizontal flipping [14]. For Caltech-256 and Tiny-ImageNet datasets, we applied the data augmentation operations including resizing to 256×256, random cropping to 224×224, and horizontal flipping. In the inference phase, we applied the image resizing method followed by the center cropping to generate 224×224 input images [14]. We also applied our ST-CoNAL method to SSL setup. We used the mean teacher method using the detailed configurations described in [39]. We conducted all experiments with a TITAN XP GPU for training.

Configurations for AL. According to [34,35], selection of b samples from a large pool of unlabeled samples requires computation of the acquisition function for all unlabeled samples in the pool, yielding considerable computational overhead. To mitigate this issue, the subset of unlabeled samples $\mathcal{S}$ was randomly drawn from the unlabeled pool $\mathcal{D}_U$ [2,20,45]. Then, acquisition functions were used to acquire the best b samples from $\mathcal{S}$.

In all experiments, the temperature parameter T was set to 0.7, which was determined through empirical optimization. For CIFAR-10, we set $\gamma = 1.0, c =$

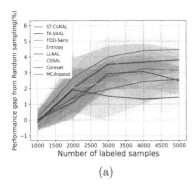
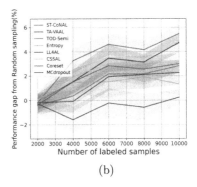

(a)   (b)

Fig. 2. Average accuracy improvement from random sampling versus the number of labeled samples on (a) CIFAR-10 and (b) CIFAR-100 datasets.

$10, b = 1k$ and $|\mathcal{S}| = 10k$, and for CIFAR-100, we set $\gamma = 0.5, c = 10, b = 2k$ and $|\mathcal{S}| = 10k$. For Tiny ImageNet, we set $\gamma = 0.5, c = 10, b = 2k$ and $|\mathcal{S}| = 20k$. For Caltech-256, we set $\gamma = 0.3, c = 10, b = 1k$ and $|\mathcal{S}| = 10k$. These configurations followed the convention adopted in the existing methods. The parameter T_0 used for the learning rate scheduling was set to 160 epochs for all datasets except Tiny ImageNet. We used T_0 of 60 epochs for Tiny ImageNet.

Baselines We compared our method with the existing AL methods including Core-set [34], MC-Dropout [9], LL4AL [45], Entropy [36], CSSAL [11], TOD-Semi [16], TA-VAAL [20], and random sampling. We adopted the average classification accuracy as a performance metric. We report the mean and standard deviation of the classification accuracy measured 5 times with different random seeds. In our performance comparison, we kept the network optimization and inference methods the same and only changed the acquisition criterion. TOD-Semi, TA-VAAL and LL4AL are exceptions because we used the optimization and inference methods proposed in their original paper. In Fig. 2 to Fig. 5, the performance difference of the target method from the random sampling baseline was used as a performance indicator.

4.2   Performance Comparison

CIFAR-10 and CIFAR-100: Figure 2 (a) and (b) show the performance of ST-CoNAL with respect to the number of labeled samples evaluated on CIFAR-10 and CIFAR-100 datasets, respectively. As mentioned earlier, we use the performance difference obtained compared to the classification accuracy of random sampling as a performance indicator. We observe that the proposed ST-CoNAL outperforms other AL methods on both CIFAR-10 and CIFAR-100. After the last acquisition step, our method achieves a performance improvement of 4.68% and 5.47% compared to the random sampling baseline on CIFAR-10 and CIFAR-100 datasets, respectively. It should be noted that ST-CoNAL achieves performance comparable to TA-VAAL, a state-of-the-art method that requires the addition of

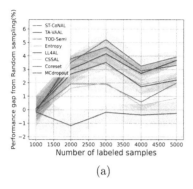 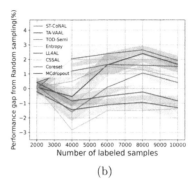

(a)   (b)

Fig. 3. Average accuracy improvement from random sampling versus the number of labeled samples on (a) Caltech-256 and (b) Tiny ImageNet datasets.

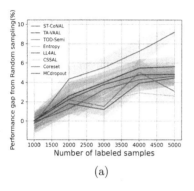 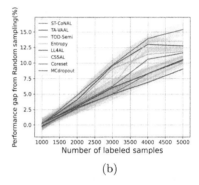

(a)   (b)

Fig. 4. Average accuracy improvement from random sampling versus the number of labeled samples on (a) the step imbalanced CIFAR-10 and (b) the long-tailed CIFAR-10. The imbalance ratio was set to 100 for both experiments.

subnetworks and complex training optimization. Entropy shows a good performance at the beginning acquisition steps but the performance improves slowly as compared to other methods. After the last acquisition, ST-CoNAL achieves 1.37% and 4.15% higher accuracy than Entropy on CIFAR-10 and CIFAR-100, respectively. Our method outperforms CSSAL, another consistency-based AL method that only considers data uncertainty, not model uncertainty.

Caltech-256 and Tiny ImageNet: Figure 3 (a) and (b) show the performance of several AL methods on Caltech-256 and Tiny ImageNet, respectively. The ST-CoNAL also achieves significant performance gain on these datasets. After the last acquisition step, ST-CoNAL achieves 3.92% higher accuracy than the random sampling baseline on Caltech-256 while it achieves 1.92% gain on Tiny-Imagenet dataset. Note that the proposed method far outperforms the CSSAL and performs comparable to more sophisticated representation-based methods, Coreset and TA-VAAL.

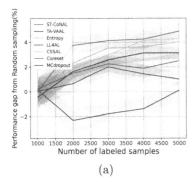
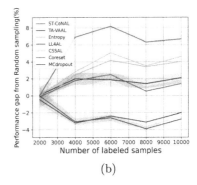

(a)   (b)

Fig. 5. Average accuracy improvement from random sampling versus the number of labeled samples on (a) CIFAR-10 and (b) CIFAR-100 dataset. The model was trained by the mean teacher [39], one of SSL methods.

4.3   Performance Comparison on Other Setups

Class-Imbalanced Datasets. We also evaluate ST-CoNAL on class imbalanced datasets. Figure 4 (a) and (b) present the performance of ST-CoNAL on (a) the step imbalanced CIFAR-10 [20] and (b) the long-tailed CIFAR-10 [5]. We see that ST-CoNAL achieves remarkable performance improvements compared to random sampling on the class imbalanced datasets. Specifically, after the last acquisition step, ST-CoNAL achieves a 9.2% performance improvement on the step-imbalanced CIFAR-10 and a 15.41% improvement on the long-tailed CIFAR-10. Furthermore, ST-CoNAL achieves larger performance gain over the current state-of-the-art, TA-VAAL. It achieves 3.58% and 4.86% performance gains over TA-VAAL on the step imbalanced CIFAR-10 and the long-tailed CIFAR-10, respectively. Note that the consistency-based method CSSAL does not perform well under this class-imbalanced setup.

SSL Setups. Figure 5 (a) and (b) show the performance evaluated on CIFAR-10 and CIFAR-100 datasets when ST-CoNAL is applied to SSL. ST-CoNAL maintains performance gains even in SSL settings and outperforms other AL methods by a larger margin than in supervised learning settings. After the last acquisition step, ST-CoNAL achieves the 4.87% and 6.66% performance gains over the random sampling baseline on CIFAR-10 and CIFAR-100, respectively. In particular, Fig. 5 (b) shows that ST-CoNAL achieves substantial performance gains over the existing methods in CIFAR-100.

4.4   Performance Analysis

In this subsection, we investigate the benefit of using self-ensemble for an acquisition criterion through some experiments.

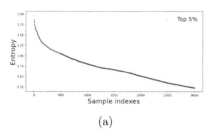
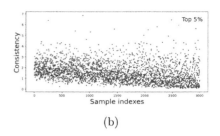

(a)   (b)

Fig. 6. The entropy and consistency measure are evaluated based on $10k$ unlabeled samples. The model is trained after $4k$ samples are acquired on CIFAR-10 dataset. (a) Entropy evaluated for the samples sorted in descending order by entropy and (b) consistency measure evaluated for the samples sorted in the same order. Top 5% of samples are marked in red. (Color figure online)

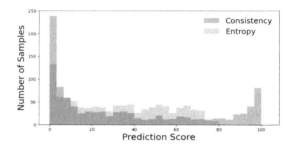

Fig. 7. Histogram of prediction scores produced by the samples selected by the proposed acquisition criterion and entropy-based one.

Comparison Between Consistency Measure Versus Uncertainty Measure. To understand the behavior of the proposed consistency measure, we compare it with the popularly used uncertainty measure, Entropy [36]. The sample acquisition process was conducted with the setup described in *Experiment Setup* section. We stopped the acquisition when $4k$ samples are labeled. Then, we evaluated both the entropy measure and the consistency measure of ST-CoNAL with 10k samples randomly selected from the remaining unlabeled samples. The 10k samples were sorted in descending order according to entropy and sample indexes were assigned in order. Figure 6 (a) shows the plot of entropy value versus the sample index. Obviously, due to sorting operation, the entropy value decreases with the sample index. Figure 6 (b) presents the plot of the consistency measure over the samples sorted in the same order. The samples ranked in the top 5% by each measure are marked in red in each figure. We observe that quite different samples were identified in the top 5% according to two criteria. From this, we can conclude that the consistency measure offers the quite different standard for acquisition from the entropy measure.

Figure 7 shows the distribution of the prediction scores produced by the samples selected by the proposed acquisition criterion and the conventional entropy-

Table 1. Ablation study on the equally-weighted average (EWA) strategy compared to exponential moving average (EMA) of MT [39].

CIFAR-10	$1k$ samples labeled	$2k$ samples labeled	$3k$ samples labeled	$4k$ samples labeled	$5k$ samples labeled
EMA	46.36	60.73	69.10	77.49	81.51
Our EWA	47.13	**61.48**	**71.85**	**79.61**	**83.05**
CIFAR-100	$2k$ samples labeled	$4k$ samples labeled	$6k$ samples labeled	$8k$ samples labeled	$10k$ samples labeled
EMA	20.34	32.96	42.75	51.77	55.49
Our EWA	20.35	**34.70**	**44.87**	**52.47**	**57.49**

based one [36]. We use a prediction score that corresponds to the true class index for the given sample. We used the same setup in Fig. 6. Obviously, the entropy-based criterion tends to select the samples with low confidence. It does not select the samples whose prediction score is above 80%. On the contrary, the proposed acquisition criterion selects samples with widely spread prediction scores. Note that it even selects samples for which predictions were made with near 100% confidence because they yielded the low consistency measure. The fact that the proposed method outperforms entropy-based acquisitions indicates that selecting samples with the lowest confidence is not necessarily the best strategy, and consistency-based acquisitions could promise a better solution by leveraging the advantage of various temporal self-ensemble models.

Comparison Between Equally-Weighted Average versus Exponential Moving Average. Table 1 compares two acquisition functions that construct a teacher model using the equally-weighted average (EWA) of the proposed method versus the exponential moving average (EMA) of the MT method. For fair comparison, only the teacher models were differently constructed while all other configurations were set equally for both training and inference. Table 1 shows that EWA achieves higher performance gains over EWA as the acquisition step proceeds on both CIFAR-10 and CIFAR-100 datasets. This shows that the proposed method can construct more effective teacher model for sample acquisition than EMA.

T-SNE Visualization. We also visualize the samples acquired according to the entropy and the proposed consistency measure using T-SNE [28]. T-SNE projects the feature vectors onto the embedding space of lower dimension for visualization. The setup used in Fig. 6 was also used to perform T-SNE. In Fig. 8, the colored dots correspond to the unlabeled sample points projected in the embedding space. The samples selected by the entropy and by the consistency measure are marked by black cross in Fig. 8 (a) and (b), respectively. We observe from Fig. 8 that the samples selected by two acquisition criteria have different distribution, which is consistent with our finding in previous section. Samples selected by entropy tend to gather near the boundary, while samples selected by consistency measure tend to spread further. This shows that more diverse samples are selected according to consistency measure than entropy.

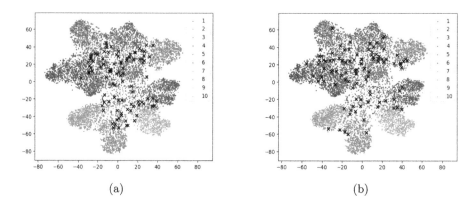

Fig. 8. T-SNE [28] visualizes the feature at the penultimate layer of the teacher model. The model is trained by $4k$ samples on CIFAR-10 dataset. The colored dots correspond to the unlabeled samples assigned to each true class and the black cross marks in (a) and (b) correspond to the top 1% sample selected by the entropy and the consistency measure, respectively. (Color figure online)

5 Conclusions

In this study, we proposed a new acquisition function for pool-based AL, which used the temporal self-ensemble generated during the SGD optimization. The proposed sample acquisition criterion measures the discrepancy between the predictions from the student model and the teacher model, where the Q student models are provided as the self-ensemble models and the teacher model is obtained through a weighted average of the student models. Using the consistency measure based on KL divergence, the proposed ST-CoNAL can acquire better samples for AL. We also showed that the sharpening operation applied to the logits of the teacher model can further improve the AL performance. The experiments conducted on CIFAR-10, CIFAR-100, Caltech-256 and Tiny ImageNet datasets demonstrated that ST-CoNAL achieved the significant performance gains over the existing AL methods. Furthermore, our numerical analysis indicated that our ST-CoNAL performs better than other AL baselines in class-imbalanced and semi-supervised learning scenarios.

Acknowledgments. This work has supported by the National Research Foundation of Korea (NRF) grant funded by the Korea government (MSIT) (No. 2020R1 A2C2012146) and Institute of Information & communications Technology Planning & Evaluation (IITP) grant funded by the Korea government (MSIT) (No. 2020-0-01373, Artificial Intelligence Graduate School Program (Hanyang University)).

References

1. Athiwaratkun, B., Finzi, M., Izmailov, P., Wilson, A.G.: There are many consistent explanations of unlabeled data: why you should average. In: International Conference on Learning Representations (ICLR) (2019)

2. Beluch, W.H., Genewein, T., Nürnberger, A., Köhler, J.M.: The power of ensembles for active learning in image classification. In: Proceedings of the IEEE/CVF Conference on Computer Vision and Pattern Recognition (CVPR), pp. 9368–9377 (2018)

3. Berthelot, D., et al.: Remixmatch: semi-supervised learning with distribution alignment and augmentation anchoring. In: International Conference on Learning Representations (ICLR) (2019)

4. Berthelot, D., Carlini, N., Goodfellow, I., Papernot, N., Oliver, A., Raffel, C.A.: Mixmatch: a holistic approach to semi-supervised learning. In: Advances in Neural Information Processing Systems (NeurIPS), pp. 5049–5059 (2019)

5. Cao, K., Wei, C., Gaidon, A., Arechiga, N., Ma, T.: Learning imbalanced datasets with label-distribution-aware margin loss. In: Advances in Neural Information Processing Systems (NeurIPS), vol. 32 (2019)

6. Chen, C., Dong, S., Tian, Y., Cao, K., Liu, L., Guo, Y.: Temporal self-ensembling teacher for semi-supervised object detection. IEEE Trans. Multimedia (2021)

7. Cui, Y., Jia, M., Lin, T.Y., Song, Y., Belongie, S.: Class-balanced loss based on effective number of samples. In: Proceedings of the IEEE/CVF Conference on Computer Vision and Pattern Recognition (CVPR), pp. 9268–9277 (2019)

8. Drugman, T., Pylkkönen, J., Kneser, R.: Active and semi-supervised learning in ASR: benefits on the acoustic and language models. In: Interspeech, pp. 2318–2322 (2016)

9. Gal, Y., Ghahramani, Z.: Dropout as a Bayesian approximation: representing model uncertainty in deep learning. In: Proceedings of the International Conference on Machine Learning (ICML), pp. 1050–1059 (2016)

10. Gal, Y., Islam, R., Ghahramani, Z.: Deep Bayesian active learning with image data. In: Proceedings of the International Conference on Machine Learning (ICML), vol. 70, pp. 1183–1192 (2017)

11. Gao, M., Zhang, Z., Yu, G., Arık, S.Ö., Davis, L.S., Pfister, T.: Consistency-based semi-supervised active learning: towards minimizing labeling cost. In: Vedaldi, A., Bischof, H., Brox, T., Frahm, J.-M. (eds.) ECCV 2020. LNCS, vol. 12355, pp. 510–526. Springer, Cham (2020). https://doi.org/10.1007/978-3-030-58607-2_30

12. Grandvalet, Y., Bengio, Y.: Semi-supervised learning by entropy minimization. In: Advances in Neural Information Processing Systems (NeurIPS), pp. 529–536 (2005)

13. Griffin, G., Holub, A., Perona, P.: Caltech-256 object category dataset. In: California Institute of Technology (2007)

14. He, K., Zhang, X., Ren, S., Sun, J.: Deep residual learning for image recognition. In: Proceedings of the IEEE/CVF Conference on Computer Vision and Pattern Recognition (CVPR), pp. 770–778 (2016)

15. Houlsby, N., Ferenc, H., Zoubin, G., Lengyel, M.: Bayesian active learning for classification and preference learning. arXiv preprint arXiv:1112.5745 (2011)

16. Huang, S., Wang, T., Xiong, H., Wen, B., Huan, J., Dou, D.: Temporal output discrepancy for loss estimation-based active learning. IEEE Trans. Neural Netw. Learn. Syst. (2022)

17. Izmailov, P., Podoprikhin, D., Garipov, T., Vetrov, D., Wilson, A.G.: Averaging weights leads to wider optima and better generalization. In: Proceedings of the Thirty-Fourth Conference on Uncertainty in Artificial Intelligence (UAI), pp. 876–885 (2018)

18. Johnson, E.H.: Elementary applied statistics: for students in behavioral science. Soc. Forces **44**(3), 455–456 (1966)

19. Joshi, A.J., Porikli, F., Papanikolopoulos, N.: Multi-class active learning for image classification. In: Proceedings of the IEEE/CVF Conference on Computer Vision and Pattern Recognition (CVPR), pp. 2372–2379 (2009)
20. Kim, K., Park, D., Kim, K.I., Chun, S.Y.: Task-aware variational adversarial active learning. In: Proceedings of the IEEE/CVF Conference on Computer Vision and Pattern Recognition (CVPR), pp. 8166–8175 (2021)
21. Krizhevsky, A.: Learning multiple layers of features from tiny images. Technical report, Department of Computer Science, University of Toronto (2009)
22. Laine, S., Aila, T.: Temporal ensembling for semi-supervised learning. In: International Conference on Learning Representations (ICLR) (2017)
23. Le, Y., Yang, X.: Tiny imagenet visual recognition challenge. CS 231N **7**(7), 3 (2015)
24. Lee, D.H.: Pseudo-label: The simple and efficient semi-supervised learning method for deep neural networks. In: Proceedings of the International Conference on Machine Learning Workshop on Challenges in Representation Learning, vol. 3, p. 2 (2013)
25. Lee, J., Chung, S.Y.: Robust training with ensemble consensus (2020)
26. Lewis, D.D., Gale, W.A.: A sequential algorithm for training text classifiers. In: Croft, B.W., van Rijsbergen, C.J. (eds.) SIGIR 1994, pp. 3–12. Springer, London (1994). https://doi.org/10.1007/978-1-4471-2099-5_1
27. Loshchilov, I., Hutter, F.: SGDR: stochastic gradient descent with warm restarts. In: International Conference on Learning Representations (ICLR) (2017)
28. van der Maaten, L., Hinton, G.: Visualizing data using t-SNE. J. Mach. Learn. Res. **9**(Nov), 2579–2605 (2008)
29. Maddox, W.J., Izmailov, P., Garipov, T., Vetrov, D.P., Wilson, A.G.: A simple baseline for Bayesian uncertainty in deep learning. In: Advances in Neural Information Processing Systems (NeurIPS), pp. 7026–7037 (2019)
30. Miyato, T., Maeda, S., Koyama, M., Ishii, S.: Virtual adversarial training: a regularization method for supervised and semi-supervised learning. IEEE Trans. Pattern Anal. Mach. Intell. **41**, 1979–1993 (2018)
31. Oliver, A., Odena, A., Raffel, C.A., Cubuk, E.D., Goodfellow, I.: Realistic evaluation of deep semi-supervised learning algorithms. In: Advances in Neural Information Processing Systems (NeurIPS), pp. 3235–3246 (2018)
32. Rhee, P., Erdenee, E., Shin, D.K., Ahmed, M., Jin, S.: Active and semi-supervised learning for object detection with imperfect data. Cogn. Syst. Res. **45**, 109–123 (2017)
33. Sajjadi, M., Javanmardi, M., Tasdizen, T.: Regularization with stochastic transformations and perturbations for deep semi-supervised learning. In: Advances in Neural Information Processing Systems (NeurIPS), pp. 1163–1171 (2016)
34. Sener, O., Savarese, S.: Active learning for convolutional neural networks: a coreset approach. In: International Conference on Learning Representations (ICLR) (2018)
35. Settles, B.: Active learning literature survey. Technical report, Department of Computer Sciences, University of Wisconsin-Madison (2009)
36. Shannon, C.E.: A mathematical theory of communication. Bell Syst. Tech. J. **27**(3), 379–423 (1948)
37. Sinha, S., Ebrahimi, S., Darrell, T.: Variational adversarial active learning. In: Proceedings of the IEEE International Conference on Computer Vision (ICCV), pp. 5972–5981 (2019)

38. Sohn, K., et al.: Fixmatch: simplifying semi-supervised learning with consistency and confidence. In: Advances in Neural Information Processing Systems (NeurIPS) (2020)

39. Tarvainen, A., Valpola, H.: Mean teachers are better role models: weight-averaged consistency targets improve semi-supervised deep learning results. In: Advances in Neural Information Processing Systems (NeurIPS), pp. 1195–1204 (2017)

40. Tomanek, K., Hahn, U.: Semi-supervised active learning for sequence labeling. In: Proceedings of the Joint Conference of the 47th Annual Meeting of the ACL and the 4th International Joint Conference on Natural Language Processing of the AFNLP, vol. 2, pp. 1039–1047. Association for Computational Linguistics (2009)

41. Tong, S., Koller, D.: Support vector machine active learning with applications to text classification. J. Mach. Learn. Res. **2**, 45–66 (2001)

42. Verma, V., Lamb, A., Kannala, J., Bengio, Y., Lopez-Paz, D.: Interpolation consistency training for semi-supervised learning. In: Proceedings of the International Joint Conference on Artificial Intelligence (IJCAI), pp. 3635–3641. IJCAI.org (2019)

43. Xie, Q., Dai, Z., Hovy, E., Luong, T., Le, Q.: Unsupervised data augmentation for consistency training. In: Advances in Neural Information Processing Systems (NeurIPS), vol. 33, pp. 6256–6268 (2020)

44. Yang, G., Tianyi, C., Kirichenko, P., Wilson, A.G., De Sa, C.: Swalp: stochastic weight averaging in low precision training. In: Proceedings of the International Conference on Machine Learning (ICML) (2019)

45. Yoo, D., Kweon, I.S.: Learning loss for active learning. In: Proceedings of the IEEE/CVF Conference on Computer Vision and Pattern Recognition (CVPR), pp. 93–102 (2019)

46. Zhang, B., Li, L., Yang, S., Wang, S., Zha, Z.J., Huang, Q.: State-relabeling adversarial active learning. In: Proceedings of the IEEE/CVF Conference on Computer Vision and Pattern Recognition (CVPR), pp. 8756–8765 (2020)

47. Zhu, X., Lafferty, J.D., Ghahramani, Z.: Combining active learning and semi-supervised learning using Gaussian fields and harmonic functions. In: Proceedings of the International Conference on Machine Learning Workshop on the Continuum from Labeled to Unlabeled Data, pp. 58–65 (2003)

Decoupling Identity and Visual Quality for Image and Video Anonymization

Maxim Maximov$^{(\boxtimes)}$, Ismail Elezi, and Laura Leal-Taixé

Technical University of Munich, Arcisstraße 21, 80333 Munich, Germany
maxim.maximov@tum.de

Abstract. The widespread usage of computer vision applications in the public domain has opened the delicate question of image data privacy. In recent years, computer vision researchers have proposed technological solutions to anonymize image and video data so that computer vision systems can still be used without compromising data privacy. While promising, these methods come with a range of limitations, including low diversity of outputs, low-resolution generation quality, the appearance of artifacts when handling extreme poses, and non-smooth temporal consistency. In this work, we propose a novel network based on generative adversarial networks (GANs) for face anonymization in images and videos. The key insight of our approach is to decouple the problems of image generation and image blending. This allows us to reach significant improvements in image quality, diversity, and temporal consistency while making possible to train the network in different tasks and datasets. Furthermore, we show that our framework is able to anonymize faces containing extreme poses, a long-standing problem in the field.

Keywords: Anonymization · Image synthesis

1 Introduction

The increase of cameras in the real world offers the possibility of widespread usage for computer vision tools, with applications ranging from autonomous robots and cars to automatic monitoring of public spaces. The question of personal privacy is becoming more prominent, especially since people are often the subject of observation by these cameras. The European Union has passed laws on data protection such as the General Data Protection Regulations (GDPR) [6]. The research community has also accepted responsibility, from taking offline one of the most popular re-identification datasets [11] to making mandatory for one of the leading machine learning conferences to consider the ethical issues of scientific publications. From a technical point of view, as researchers, we can also contribute to the solution by proposing novel computer vision tools.

For many vision tasks such as person detection, person tracking, or action recognition, we do not need to *identify* the people in the videos, we only need to

---

Supplementary Information The online version contains supplementary material available at https://doi.org/10.1007/978-3-031-26351-4_31.

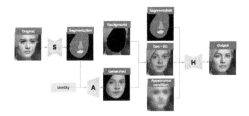

Fig. 1. The inference pipeline of our method. We use as input segmentation masks, given by a segmentation network (S). We use AnonymizationNet (A) to generate an anonymized version of the original image, and then use HarmonizationNet (H) to blend the generated image with the background.

detect them [24]. Recent works proposed to use computer vision tools to remove identity information from people's faces in videos [7,24,29,35], while still trying to preserve the accuracy of the computer vision algorithms for the final task, e.g., face detection. These methods anonymize identities by replacing or altering the input faces, achieving overall good de-identification results. While a valuable first step, these methods come with several weaknesses.

First, the visual quality of the generated images is lacking [24,29]. This is often due to the lack of high-quality datasets suitable for training anonymization methods. In other cases, there is a trade-off between image quality and anonymization results, leading to photorealistic images that are still identifiable by humans [7]. Second, output diversity is low, i.e., for the same input identity, only a few types of anonymizations are produced. If every input identity is mapped to one anonymized version, then it is straightforward to de-anonymize all faces and establish correspondences to the original identity.

In this work, we propose to overcome these issues by decoupling the anonymization task from the image generation task. We argue that it is not efficient for a single network to focus on both diversity as well as producing realistically looking results. Our pipeline is therefore separated into two networks. The job of the first network is to generate anonymized and diverse versions of the original face, while preserving its pose, without focusing on integrating it with the background information. The second network receives the anonymized face and performs image blending, i.e., changing the appearance of the generated image according to external conditioning, such as illumination or background appearance. Overall, the second network is responsible for generating high-quality realistically looking images. We show how to train the second network on a proxy task not related to image anonymization. Interestingly, this allows us to separately train the second network on datasets that do not contain information about face identities. This is the key towards generating high-quality outputs, given high-resolution face datasets do not contain identity information. It is therefore challenging for single-stage anonymization methods [7,24,29] to make use of them, and consequently, they are limited to low-resolution datasets such as CelebA [23].

In the experimental section, we show that our decoupled formulation achieves state-of-the-art results on output diversity and quality. We further compare the performance of state-of-the-art methods under extreme poses, an underestimated problem in the field [24], and evaluate the temporal consistency of the output when moving towards video anonymization. Finally, we show that our method can be intuitively extended to other domains, e.g., full-body anonymization.

Our **contribution** in this work is three-fold:

– We propose a novel two-step framework that decouples image generation from image blending. We show how to train the second step on a proxy task unrelated to image anonymization, which allows us to leverage high-resolution datasets designed for different tasks. This allows us to generate overall more diverse and high-quality outputs.
– We analyze the drawbacks of current anonymization methods with a comprehensive study on output diversity, quality, anonymization and detection rates, temporal consistency and performance on extreme poses.
– We present state-of-the-art results on six public datasets.

2   Related Work

GANs for Face Generation and Translation. The advent of Generative Adversarial Networks [9,28] brought a lot of research interest in the field of face generation [16,17,22]. Recent methods [17,18] are able to generate realistically looking high-resolution face images and provide high diversity. However, these methods have no mechanism for conditioning their output on the original face, making the blending of the generated face with the other parts of the body challenging. Additionally, they cannot keep the stature and the direction of the face, making their usability in face anonymization limited. More successful have been the methods based on temporal consistency [38]. While the method provides a simple image and video translation method, the generated faces are similar to the original identities, making it not usable for anonymization.

Face Anonymization. Traditionally, face anonymization has been achieved by heuristic methods, such as pixelization, blurring, masking or segmentation [32]. The pioneering work of [10] used for the first time model-based learning for face de-identification. Recently, deep learning models have been used for the same problem [7,14,24,29,34,35]. In particular, [14,29] are one of the first methods to use GANs that reach promising de-identification results. However, the generated outputs are not naturally blended with the rest of the image, and [29] maps every identity to a unique fake identity, not allowing the generation of diverse images. The work of [34] uses a different GAN scheme to further improve the results, but the generated images still remain unnatural looking and provide no explicit way of controlling the generated appearance. Some of these problems were remedied in [35], providing a method for generating faces that are more de-identifiable and natural-looking. However, the method is based on a parametric face model with an additional alignment procedure that does not offer a direct way of extending it to other domains such as full bodies and works only on images.

Current state-of-the-art models [7,24] mitigate some of the issues mentioned above. The work of [7] generates high-quality looking images, temporally consistent videos, and reaches high de-identification results. However, as argued in

[24], the generated images can be recognized by humans and the method does not provide a way to generate diverse images. On the other hand, [24] reaches state-of-the-art de-identification results, and the generated images are not easily identifiable by humans. At the same time, the images do not look natural and video results are not as temporally consistent as in [7]. Finally, both methods can be only trained on datasets that provide multiple images for each identity, thus making it harder to use many high-quality datasets.

In this work, by decoupling the anonymization from the blending process, our method allows higher control over the de-identification process and can be used with datasets that provide only one image per identity.

3   Methodology

Most image translation methods typically take input representations, e.g., semantic segmentation, landmarks, or a background image, and use a network to encode the input information into a low-dimensional latent space. A decoder then translates the information into a new image, which, in the case of anonymization, is a face with a new identity. The decoder is optimized for two tasks: (i) image anonymization: generating image parts that form a new identity; (ii) image blending: changing the appearance of the generated image according to external conditioning, such as illumination or background appearance. Considering that these networks are trained with a single adversarial loss, often one of the tasks is neglected in favor of the other. Neglecting image anonymization results in low diversity of the outputs, i.e., the network only generates a few types of anonymizations, thus compromising privacy. Neglecting image blending results in artifacts and unrealistically looking faces, which often leads to computer vision algorithms not being able to perform face detection. Our proposed decoupling architecture allows us to create diverse outputs and high-quality outputs.

Overview of Our Method. In this section, we describe in depth the methodology of our proposed framework. Our model includes: (i) a pre-trained segmentation network, (ii) AnonymizationNet, a network that anonymizes the face and is based on a GAN and an identity network (see Fig. 2.1), and (iii) HarmonizationNet, a network that blends the produced face with the rest of the image (see Fig. 2.2). We first explain each of the networks' tasks and analyze why decoupling is the key element that allows us to generate high-quality diverse outputs. We then discuss which elements of our pipeline allow for identity control during anonymization, pose preservation, and temporal consistency.

3.1   Decoupling Anonymization and Visual Quality

Inspired by rendering pipelines, where geometry creation and the shading process are divided, we advocate for the idea that the image generation should be separated from image blending, thus, we use two networks.

AnonymizationNet. The goal of AnonymizationNet (see Fig. 2.1) is to define the facial geometry and the characteristics of the face. We train a conditional

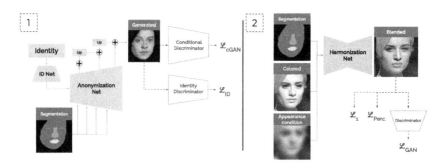

Fig. 2. The training pipeline of our model. Our model consists of two networks trained separately. 1) AnonymizationNet takes a segmentation mask and an identity condition to generate a face without any appearance conditioning. It uses losses from a conditional discriminator, and from an identity discriminator to guide generation to the desired identity. 2) HarmonizationNet is an encoder-decoder network where the encoder embeds the image information into a low dimensional space. It takes a triplet of segmentation mask, a colored face image, and an appearance condition. The appearance condition is given as a heavily blurred version of the original face, while the segmentation mask is given to indicate the image region that needs to be blended. The network learns to blend the input face to the given background by using information from the appearance condition. (Color figure online)

GAN [15] to generate an anonymized version of the input face, without considering how the face fits with the other part of the image, e.g., the background. We achieve that by conditioning the generation process only on a semantic map of the original image. By doing so, we ensure that the pose of the face is preserved and prevents identity leakage. Similar to [24], the network collaborates with an identity network that guides the generator towards generating a face with different identifying characteristics.

HarmonizationNet. The task of HarmonizationNet (see Fig. 2.2) is to blend the generated face in order to naturally fit with the background and overall illumination. We use a conditional GAN to generate a realistic-looking version of the image produced by AnonymizationNet. Importantly, we do not train the network together with AnonymizationNet. Instead, we train on a *proxy task*, which greatly simplifies the training procedure and allows us to achieve high-quality and diverse image generation. During inference, the network takes the anonymized version of a face and blends it with the rest of the image, (Fig. 1).

Advantages of Decoupling. In the experimental section, we validate that the presented decoupling achieves a higher image quality and output diversity, and has a higher degree of control over the blending process. A clear advantage of decoupling anonymization from visual quality is that it allows HarmonizationNet to be trained on a different dataset. AnonymizationNet needs to be trained on a dataset that contains multiple images per identity, with its goal being to provide anonymized versions of the images. Single-stage methods [7,24,29] are therefore limited to such datasets, e.g., CelebA, to train their anonymization pipeline. In contrast, our method can be additionally trained in high-resolution datasets, such as CelebA-MaskHQ, and consequently we are able to generate high-resolution images (see Fig 3).

3.2   Proxy Training

As mentioned before, we propose to train the networks separately, as opposed to training our entire model in an end-to-end fashion. By training the networks separately, we ensure that the second network never sees the original image, which could be a cause for identity leakage. Furthermore, we can train our second network in parallel on datasets that provide images without identity information [23]. Last, but not least, we simplify the training and as shown in the ablation studies, the model trained with the proxy task reaches higher results compared to training the networks jointly.

We propose to train HarmonizationNet on a *proxy task*, which we design to be a relaxed version of the blending task. More concretely, we use a colored foreground image as an input, see Fig. 2.2, during training. The task of HarmonizationNet is to reconstruct the original image color. In other words, we train the network to change the appearance of the foreground in the input image to match the appearance of the overall image. The model takes as input: (i) a semantic segmentation map of the foreground, i.e., the face, (ii) the altered colored image, and (iii) a blurred version of the original image. The motivation for the third input is to provide some guidance to the blending network instead of allowing it to blindly reconstruct the image from the semantic input. As we show in Table 1 of experiments, the heavily blurred image removes identity information.

Our intuition is that the proxy task is teaching HarmonizationNet two functions: to disassociate the general facial (shape) details from the rest of the input appearance in the encoder and to inpaint the missing textures on top of those details in the decoder. During the inference, encoder activates on any high-level shape details despite the domain gap and embeds them in the bottleneck. In our evaluation and supplementary, we show a robust generalization of HarmonizationNet to the output of AnonymizationNet regardless of datasets used.

3.3   Identity Guidance

The goal of AnonymizationNet is to generate a new anonymized image, given the segmentation map of the original face as input. Note, the semantic map allows us to preserve the pose of the face without allowing identity leakage. In order to control the anonymization output, we make use of a *control identity*.

For any given image, we randomly choose a control identity, parameterized by a one-hot vector. This information is fed into the generator of AnonymizationNet, with its goal being to embed identifying features of the control identity to the original semantic mask. This process is achieved with the use of an identity discriminator that provides a guiding signal to AnonymizationNet so that the generated image has similar characteristics to the control identity. The identity discriminator is a siamese neural network pre-trained on the real images using Proxy-NCA loss [25] and finetuned using the contrastive loss [1]. During finetuning, the network learns to bring together the identity representation of the fake images and the real images. We note that the identity discriminator is trained with AnonymizationNet in a collaborative (not adversarial) manner. As a result, the generator mixes the semantic segmentation map of the original identity, with the identifying features of the control identity, thereby creating a new non-identifiable identity.

Is attribute preservation desirable? We argue that preserving the attributes of the original identity is not desirable when it comes to face anonymization, and makes the pipeline less robust to identity attacks. For example, knowing the gender reduces the search space by half. Preserving other attributes, e.g., age, skin color, or specific attributes for eyes, nose, forehead, lowers the search space significantly and makes it easier to *guess* the identity. In our work, preserving attributes, e.g., gender, would be as simple as giving as control identity an identity that contains the same attribute. However, considering that some face verification methods [20,36] rely on facial attributes, we decide to not force any attribute preservation. The only exception is skin tone, considering that we generate only the facial region, and therefore need to match the face skin to the neck and the other exposed body skin areas.

3.4   Pose Preservation and Temporal Consistency

Previous works rely on facial landmarks [24], faces [29] or statistical 3D shade models [35]. While a landmark representation is simple and easy-to-use, it fails on extreme poses and cannot properly represent certain body parts such as hair [24]. Statistical 3D shade models are quite robust, but add additional computation complexity and are domain-specific. Due to privacy reasons, we avoid working directly on faces. In our work, we use face segmentation as input representation. Using segmentation allows us to outline the area we want to modify, and we are able to estimate specific occlusions. Furthermore, we can use the same framework on other domains, e.g., for full-body anonymization, with few changes on the expected input type.

Additionally, to improve temporal consistency for video sequences, we transform HarmonizationNet into a frame recurrent network by concatenating the output of the previous frame to the input of the current frame and replacing a spatial discriminator with a temporal one. The temporal discriminator [4] takes three consecutive frames as an input and judges both temporal smoothness and visual quality. This simple change to HarmonizationNet leads to less color jittering in the final video.

3.5   Architectures and Training

AnonymizationNet. We use spatially-adaptive denormalization (SPADE) [27] residual blocks as building blocks of the network. We give the same segmentation map as input to every SPADE block, and each block produces an RGB image.

The control identity, represented as one hot-vector, is given as input to a transposed convolutional neural network. The network then produces a parametrized version of the identity and gives it as input to the generator. We also use a simplified design of upsampling and summing RGB outputs to avoid progressive GAN training, leading to a more stable and efficient training in higher resolutions. We sum all RGB outputs in order to get the final result. These two changes lead to a more robust training, while achieving higher quality compared to the regular encoder-decoder architecture used in image translation [24].

HarmonizationNet. We base the network's architecture on a U-Net composed of residual blocks [30]. We give the detailed architecture of both networks in the supplementary.

Loss Functions. We use LSGAN loss function to train the networks. The loss of AnonymizationNet (A) generator is defined as:

$$\min_{G_A} V(G_A) = \frac{1}{2}\mathbb{E}_{i \sim p_{data}(i)}[(D_A(G_A(i)) - b)^2] + L_{id} \tag{1}$$

where L_{id} is the loss of the identity discriminator as explained in Sect. 3.3, b is the label for the real data, i is the input to the generator G_A, and D_A is the discriminator.

The loss of HarmonizationNet (H) generator is defined as:

$$\min_{G_H} V(G_H) = \frac{1}{2}\mathbb{E}_{i \sim p_{data}(i)}[(D_H(G_H(i)) - b)^2]$$
$$+ VGG_P(I, I') + L1(I, I') \tag{2}$$

where G_H and D_H represent the generator and the discriminator of HarmonizationNet, VGG_P represents the perceptual loss of VGG network [8], I and I' represent the original and the generated image.

The loss function for the discriminators A and H is given below:

$$\min_{D} V(D) = \frac{1}{2}\mathbb{E}_{x \sim p_{data}(x)}[(D(x) - b)^2]$$
$$+ \frac{1}{2}\mathbb{E}_{i \sim p_{data}(i)}[(D(G(i)) - a)^2] \tag{3}$$

where a is the label for the fake data, x is the real data and D is valid for both discriminator D_A and D_H.

4   Experiments

In this section, we compare our method with several classic and learning-based methods commonly used for identity anonymization. We analyze the drawbacks of current anonymization methods in terms of diversity, image quality, anonymization and detection rates, temporal consistency, performance on extreme poses, and show state-of-the-art qualitative and quantitative results.

We also present a set of comprehensive ablation studies to demonstrate the effect of our design choices. We detail the implementation details in the supplementary material.

Datasets. We perform experiments on 6 public datasets: two face datasets with annotated identities: CelebA [23] and Labeled Faces in the Wild (LFW) [13], a high-quality face dataset without identity information: CelebA-MaskHQ [23], a video dataset: FaceForensics++ [31], a dataset on extreme poses: AFLW2000 [19], and a dataset with annotated body segmentations: MOTS [37].

Baselines. We follow previous works [24] to use simple anonymization baselines such as pixelization or blurring and compare them with our method. We also compare with state-of-the-art learning-based methods [7, 24].

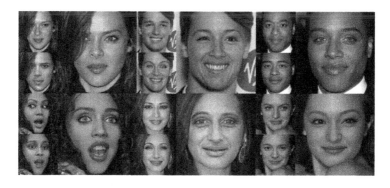

Fig. 3. A set of triplet images generated by our framework. In every triplet, the left-upper image is the original image in 128×128 resolution, the left-lower image is the anonymized version of it in 128×128 resolution, and the large image in the right is its anonymized version in 512×512 resolution. We present cases of different gender, skin-color, pose, and illumination.

4.1   Ablation Study

To validate our two-step training concept, we do an ablation study measuring the importance of each component of our model.

Setup. We investigate how our proposed decoupled pipeline affects the quality and diversity of the generated images. We use FID [12] as a quality metric and Re-ID as a diversity metric. In Table 1, we present the results of three different configurations of our method: (1) a regular model without decoupling, (2) a decoupled model where the pipeline is jointly trained instead of proxy training, and (3) our model with decoupling of the task and proxy training.

We perform this ablation on two datasets: CelebA and CelebA-MaskHQ [23]. There is a domain gap between the datasets, as CelebA-MaskHQ consists of higher quality and sharper images compared to CelebA. Most importantly,

CelebA-MaskHQ does not contain identity information by itself, hence we combine it with CelebA to be able to train AnonymizationNet. For the CelebA-MaskHQ evaluation, we train only HarmonizationNet on the CelebA-MaskHQ for decoupled configurations (networks (2) and (3)) and do simultaneous training on both datasets for the single model configuration (network (1)).

Table 1. Ablation study of our model. We measure the generation quality and diversity for different versions of our model. Lower (↓) results for FID imply a higher generation quality. Higher (↑) results for diversity imply a higher diversity in generation. Higher (↑) results for detection imply a higher detection rate.

Models	CelebA			CelebA + HQ		
	FID (↓)	Re-ID (↑)	Detection (↑)	FID (↓)	Re-ID (↑)	Detection (↑)
1) w/o decoupling	**3.05**	33.4	.993	16.25	17.3	.903
2) w/o proxy training	3.15	88.6	.992	16.75	**170.5**	.917
3) Two-step framework	4.17	**96.1**	**.999**	**10.49**	124.1	**.994**

Fig. 4. Qualitative results of diversity on CelebA-MaskHQ dataset. *Top row:* The model trained without decoupling (1). *Middle row:* The model trained without the proxy task (2) produces anonymized faces, but they are not well-blended with the rest of the image. *Bottom row:* In contrast, our model (3) produces realistic anonymized faces that are diverse and blended with the other parts of the image.

Results. As shown in Table 1, our decoupled model reaches best results in Re-ID and detection rate on CelebA. More interestingly, we significantly outperform networks (1) and (2) when working on CelebA-MaskHQ, where there is a domain gap. As we show in the qualitative example in Fig. 4, simultaneously training with two different datasets leads to artifacts in (1) and a lack of blending in (2), which explains the high diversity and decline in quality in Table 1. The separately trained model (3) achieves the most balanced results in terms of quality and diversity across both datasets. It maintains a high diversity while properly blending the output faces. It is also easier to train and can be parallelized due to the separate nature of the training. In supplementary, we provide more qualitative analysis and a discussion of each model.

4.2   Comparison to SOTA

Table 2. Results of existing detection, recognition and diversity pre-trained methods. Lower (↓) results imply a better anonymization. Upper (↑) results imply a better detection and diversity. Diversity metric is not applicable to classic methods since they can only produce a single output.

Models	Detection (↑)		Identif. (↓)	Diversity (↑)	
	Dlib	SSH	PNCA	LPIPS	Re-ID
Original	100	100	70.7	-	–
Pixelization 8 by 8	0.0	0.0	0.4	–	–
Pixelization 16 by 16	0.0	0.0	**0.3**	–	–
Blur 9 by 9	90.6	38.6	16.9	–	–
Blur 17 by 17	68.4	0.3	1.9	–	–
CIAGAN	97.8	97.4	1.3	0.032	64.5
Ours	**98.9**	**99.9**	2.2	**0.036**	**96.1**

Anonymization on CelebA. Following [24], we present in Table 2 the detection and identification results of our method compared to the other methods on the CelebA dataset. For detection, we use the classical HOG detector [5] and the deep learning-based SSH [26]. Pixelization methods, while having a higher de-identification rate, generate faces that cannot be detected by either detector, making the anonymized images unusable for computer vision applications. The low-blurring method has both a significantly lower detection rate and a lower de-identification rate. The high-blurring has a slightly better de-identification rate, but it comes at the cost of a very low detection rate, e.g., the SSH detector cannot detect virtually any of the faces. Our main competitor, CIAGAN [24], has a better de-identification rate, 1.3 for them compared to 2.2 for us, but it comes at the cost of generating less realistic images, many of which cannot be detected by the detectors. For example, HOG detector misses 2.2% of the faces generated by CIAGAN compared to 1.1% of the faces generated by our method. Even more extremely, deep-learning based SSH misses 2.6% of the faces generated by CIAGAN, but it misses less than 0.1% of the faces from our method. We qualitatively compare with [24] in Fig. 5.2. It can be seen that the images generated by our method are more realistic. An interesting case is the first image that contains an extreme pose. Our method is able to anonymize it in a realistic manner, while [24] generates an undetectable face.

Anonymization on LWF Dataset. We do a similar experiment on the LWF dataset. We follow the standard protocol, where the dataset is divided into 10 different splits, each containing 600 pairs. A pair is defined as positive if both elements share the same identity, otherwise as negative. In every split, the first 300 pairs are positive, and the remaining 300 pairs are negative. Following [7], we anonymize the second image of every pair. We use FaceNet [33] identification

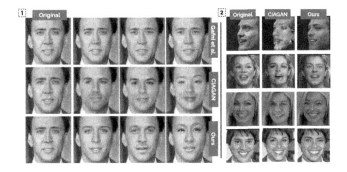

Fig. 5. Left: Qualitative comparisons with [7] and [24]. Right: Qualitative comparisons with [24], where the first two faces are extreme poses.

model, pre-trained on two public datasets: VGGFace2 [2] and CASIA-Webface [23]. The main evaluation metric is the true acceptance rate, i.e., the ratio of true positives for a maximum 0.001 ratio of false positives. We present our results in Table 3. As shown, we reach state-of-the-art results with the network trained on VGGFace2, outperforming the other two methods [7,24]. When evaluated with the network trained on CASIA-Webface, we outperform [7] but do not reach as good de-identification rate as [24]. However, we also check the detection rate of the methods; after all, it is easy to reach a very good de-identification rate if the generated faces look extremely unnatural and are not detectable. As we can see, 98.4% of the faces generated by our method can be detected by SSH, compared to 95.4% of the faces generated by [24], showing that our method has a 65% lower error in detection rate. We conclude that our method has the best trade-off between the de-identification and the detection rates. We qualitatively compare with [7,24] in Fig. 5.1. We show that the visual quality of the generated images is high for our method and [7], while the images generated by [24] are less realistic. At the same time, we observe that the images generated by our method and [24] are both anonymized and diverse, while the images generated by [7] are easily identifiable. We argue that our method combines the best of both worlds, generating images that are non-identifiable, diverse, and realistic. Unfortunately, the code for [7] has not been released, hence, we cannot compute the detection rate for their method.

Table 3. Comparisons with SOTA in LWF dataset. Lower (↓) identification rates imply better anonymization. Higher (↑) detection rate implies better generation quality.

De-ID method	VGGFace2 (↓)	CASIA (↓)	Detec. (↑)
Original	0.986 ± 0.01	0.965 ± 0.02	100
Gafni [7]	0.038 ± 0.02	0.035 ± 0.01	–
CIAGAN [24]	0.034 ± 0.02	**0.019 ± 0.01**	95.4
Ours	**0.032 ± 0.02**	0.032 ± 0.01	**98.4**

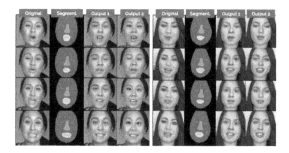

Fig. 6. Results of our model on FaceForensics++ dataset. For each sequence we show input faces, segmentation masks, and two different anonymizations results.

Diversity. We test the diversity of our metric by generating 500 anonymized versions of 100 randomly chosen input images. For each image, we randomly sample 500 pairs, where the number of possible pairs is $\frac{500 \times 499}{500}$, and measure the LPIPS score [39] between all pairs. LPIPS score measures the similarity between two images, the higher it is, the more different the two images are. As we show in Table 2, we reach a 12.5% relative higher score than CIAGAN. This means that the images our method generates look more diverse compared to the ones generated by CIAGAN. Furthermore, for every generated image, we compute the nearest neighbor in the training set (Re-ID). Intuitively, considering that for every generated image, we use 500 identities, a method that generates perfectly diverse images would result in every generated image having a different nearest identity in the training set. In this upper bound case, the number of unique identities for every image would be 500. As we show in Table 2, CIAGAN shows an average of 64.5 identities, while our method shows an average of 96.1 identities, for a 49% relative improvement, showing again that our method generates more diverse images.

Temporal Consistency. We show a quantitative evaluation of the temporal consistency in Fig. 6. We use FaceForensics++ [31] dataset and we measure tLP, as defined in [4], in addition to visual quality. tLP measures the similarity between all consecutive frames in a video. Intuitively, the better the temporal consistency is, the more similar two consecutive frames are, hence, the lower the tLP metric is. Our method reaches 0.023 tLP, better than CIAGAN which reaches 0.047 score. Additionally, our method reaches a significantly better FID score (14.7 for our method compared to 62.7 for CIAGAN), indicating its higher visual quality. Furthermore, if we finetune HarmonizationNet on FaceForensics++, the temporal consistency improves to 0.016 tLP and FID to 8.3.

Extreme Poses. We check the detection rate in the challenging AFLW dataset [19], which contains extreme poses. We run a landmark detector to generate the landmarks which are needed for CIAGAN [24]. We remove every face that the

Table 4. Results on the different resolutions of HQ. Lower (↓) results imply better.

Models	Time sec (↓)		
	x128	x256	x512
CIAGAN + SR method	35.89	38.82	37.98
Ours	**10.49**	**8.41**	**11.60**

detector cannot find in order to have the same number of generated faces as CIA-GAN which needs landmarks. We use the same detector on the anonymized versions of the faces generated by our method and CIAGAN. The detector detects 90.99% of the faces generated by our method, but only 72.58% of the faces generated by CIAGAN, showing that our method is more robust.

Different Domain. We train our method on MOTS dataset [37]. We use whole-body segmentation masks and estimated body joints, using OpenPose [3], as an input to AnonymizationNet. We provide qualitative results and additional details in the supplementary.

Super-Resolution. In order to show the potential of our two-step framework, we re-train HarmonizationNet to output a higher resolution image compared to the original image. The first step remains the same with Anonymization-Net generating images of size 128×128. We train HarmonizationNet separately on CelebA-MaskHQ dataset. It takes an input with dimensions 128×128 and outputs images of resolution 256×256 and 512×512. We compare with CIA-GAN, which is trained with 128×128 resolution. Due to its nature, we cannot re-train it on a dataset that has no identity information, as is the case for the CelebA-MaskHQ dataset. Therefore, we upscale its output to higher resolution using off-the-shelf super-resolution method [21]. We evaluate the quality of output on different resolution levels using the FID metric. As shown in Table 4, our method achieves significantly better results in all cases. We show qualitative results in Fig. 3 and in the supplementary.

5 Conclusions

The exponential increase in the deployment of cameras in public spaces and its subsequent use in computer vision applications has raised the difficult question of how to deal with data privacy. In this work, we proposed a framework to anonymize faces and bodies based on conditional generative adversarial networks. The key contribution of our approach is to separate two important concepts in face anonymization: generation and blending. We showed the benefits of our decoupled formulation, reaching state-of-the-art results in quality, diversity, and temporal consistency. We also showed the benefits of the training procedure, which can leverage datasets that do not contain identity annotations. Finally, we show how our method can be easily adapted to other tasks like full-body anonymization and can also be used to produce high-resolution images.

Acknowledgements. This research was partially funded by the Humboldt Foundation through the Sofja Kovalevskaja Award.

References

1. Bromley, J., Guyon, I., LeCun, Y., Säckinger, E., Shah, R.: Signature verification using a "Siamese" time delay neural network. In: Advances in Neural Information Processing Systems (NIPS), pp. 737–744 (1994)
2. Cao, Q., Shen, L., Xie, W., Parkhi, O.M., Zisserman, A.: Vggface2: a dataset for recognising faces across pose and age. In: International Conference on Automatic Face and Gesture Recognition, pp. 67–74 (2018)
3. Cao, Z., Hidalgo Martinez, G., Simon, T., Wei, S., Sheikh, Y.A.: Openpose: real-time multi-person 2D pose estimation using part affinity fields. IEEE Trans. Pattern Anal. Mach. Intell. (2019)
4. Chu, M., Xie, Y., Mayer, J., Leal-Taixé, L., Thuerey, N.: Learning temporal coherence via self-supervision for GAN-based video generation. ACM Trans. Graph. **39**(4), 75 (2020)
5. Dalal, N., Triggs, B.: Histograms of oriented gradients for human detection. In: Conference on Computer Vision and Pattern Recognition (CVPR), pp. 886–893 (2005)
6. 2018 reform of EU data protection rules (2018). https://gdpr-info.eu
7. Gafni, O., Wolf, L., Taigman, Y.: Live face de-identification in video. In: International Conference on Computer Vision (ICCV) (2019)
8. Gatys, L.A., Ecker, A.S., Bethge, M.: Image style transfer using convolutional neural networks. In: Conference on Computer Vision and Pattern Recognition, (CVPR), pp. 2414–2423 (2016)
9. Goodfellow, I.J., et al.: Generative adversarial nets. In: Advances in Neural Information Processing Systems (NIPS), pp. 2672–2680 (2014)
10. Gross, R., Sweeney, L., la Torre, F.D., Baker, S.: Model-based face de-identification. In: Conference on Computer Vision and Pattern Recognition Workshops (CVPRW), p. 161. IEEE Computer Society (2006)
11. Harvey, A., LaPlace, J.: Megapixels: origins, ethics, and privacy implications of publicly available face recognition image datasets (2019)
12. Heusel, M., Ramsauer, H., Unterthiner, T., Nessler, B., Hochreiter, S.: GANs trained by a two time-scale update rule converge to a local Nash equilibrium. In: Advances in Neural Information Processing Systems NIPS, Long Beach, CA, USA, pp. 6626–6637 (2017)
13. Huang, G.B., Ramesh, M., Berg, T., Learned-Miller, E.: Labeled faces in the wild: a database for studying face recognition in unconstrained environments. Technical report, 07–49, University of Massachusetts, Amherst, October 2007
14. Hukkelås, H., Mester, R., Lindseth, F.: Deepprivacy: a generative adversarial network for face anonymization. CoRR abs/1909.04538 (2019)
15. Isola, P., Zhu, J., Zhou, T., Efros, A.A.: Image-to-image translation with conditional adversarial networks. In: Conference on Computer Vision and Pattern Recognition (CVPR), pp. 5967–5976 (2017)
16. Karras, T., Aila, T., Laine, S., Lehtinen, J.: Progressive growing of GANs for improved quality, stability, and variation. In: International Conference on Learning Representations (ICLR) (2018)
17. Karras, T., Laine, S., Aila, T.: A style-based generator architecture for generative adversarial networks. CoRR abs/1812.04948 (2018)

18. Karras, T., Laine, S., Aittala, M., Hellsten, J., Lehtinen, J., Aila, T.: Analyzing and improving the image quality of styleGAN. In: Conference on Computer Vision and Pattern Recognition (CVPR), pp. 8107–8116 (2020)

19. Köstinger, M., Wohlhart, P., Roth, P.M., Bischof, H.: Annotated facial landmarks in the wild: a large-scale, real-world database for facial landmark localization. In: International Conference on Computer Vision Workshops (ICCVW), pp. 2144–2151 (2011)

20. Kumar, N., Berg, A.C., Belhumeur, P.N., Nayar, S.K.: Attribute and simile classifiers for face verification. In: International Conference on Computer Vision (ICCV), pp. 365–372 (2009)

21. Ledig, C., et al.: Photo-realistic single image super-resolution using a generative adversarial network. In: Conference on Computer Vision and Pattern Recognition (CVPR), pp. 105–114 (2017)

22. Liu, M., Tuzel, O.: Coupled generative adversarial networks. In: Advances in Neural Information Processing Systems (NIPS), pp. 469–477 (2016)

23. Liu, Z., Luo, P., Wang, X., Tang, X.: Deep learning face attributes in the wild. In: International Conference on Computer Vision (ICCV) (2015)

24. Maximov, M., Elezi, I., Leal-Taixé, L.: CIAGAN: conditional identity anonymization generative adversarial networks. In: Conference on Computer Vision and Pattern Recognition (CVPR), pp. 5446–5455 (2020)

25. Movshovitz-Attias, Y., Toshev, A., Leung, T.K., Ioffe, S., Singh, S.: No fuss distance metric learning using proxies. In: International Conference on Computer Vision (ICCV), pp. 360–368 (2017)

26. Najibi, M., Samangouei, P., Chellappa, R., Davis, L.S.: SSH: single stage headless face detector. In: International Conference on Computer Vision (ICCV), pp. 4885–4894 (2017)

27. Park, T., Liu, M., Wang, T., Zhu, J.: Semantic image synthesis with spatially-adaptive normalization. In: Conference on Computer Vision and Pattern Recognition (CVPR), pp. 2337–2346 (2019)

28. Radford, A., Metz, L., Chintala, S.: Unsupervised representation learning with deep convolutional generative adversarial networks. In: International Conference on Learning Representations (ICLR) (2016)

29. Ren, Z., Lee, Y.J., Ryoo, M.S.: Learning to anonymize faces for privacy preserving action detection. In: Ferrari, V., Hebert, M., Sminchisescu, C., Weiss, Y. (eds.) ECCV 2018. LNCS, vol. 11205, pp. 639–655. Springer, Cham (2018). https://doi.org/10.1007/978-3-030-01246-5_38

30. Ronneberger, O., Fischer, P., Brox, T.: U-net: convolutional networks for biomedical image segmentation. In: Navab, N., Hornegger, J., Wells, W.M., Frangi, A.F. (eds.) MICCAI 2015. LNCS, vol. 9351, pp. 234–241. Springer, Cham (2015). https://doi.org/10.1007/978-3-319-24574-4_28

31. Rössler, A., Cozzolino, D., Verdoliva, L., Riess, C., Thies, J., Nießner, M.: Faceforensics++: learning to detect manipulated facial images. In: International Conference on Computer Vision (ICCV), pp. 1–11 (2019)

32. Ryoo, M.S., Kim, K., Yang, H.J.: Extreme low resolution activity recognition with multi-Siamese embedding learning. In: Conference on Artificial Intelligence (AAAI), pp. 7315–7322 (2018)

33. Schroff, F., Kalenichenko, D., Philbin, J.: Facenet: a unified embedding for face recognition and clustering. In: Conference on Computer Vision and Pattern Recognition (CVPR), pp. 815–823 (2015)

34. Sun, Q., Ma, L., Oh, S.J., Gool, L.V., Schiele, B., Fritz, M.: Natural and effective obfuscation by head inpainting. In: Conference on Computer Vision and Pattern Recognition (CVPR), pp. 5050–5059 (2018)
35. Sun, Q., Tewari, A., Xu, W., Fritz, M., Theobalt, C., Schiele, B.: A hybrid model for identity obfuscation by face replacement. In: Ferrari, V., Hebert, M., Sminchisescu, C., Weiss, Y. (eds.) ECCV 2018. LNCS, vol. 11205, pp. 570–586. Springer, Cham (2018). https://doi.org/10.1007/978-3-030-01246-5_34
36. Taherkhani, F., Nasrabadi, N.M., Dawson, J.M.: A deep face identification network enhanced by facial attributes prediction. In: Conference on Computer Vision and Pattern Recognition Workshops (CVPRW), pp. 553–560 (2018)
37. Voigtlaender, P., et al.: MOTS: multi-object tracking and segmentation. In: Conference on Computer Vision and Pattern Recognition (CVPR), pp. 7942–7951 (2019)
38. Wang, T., et al.: Video-to-video synthesis. In: Advances in Neural Information Processing Systems (NeurIPS), pp. 1152–1164 (2018)
39. Zhang, R., Isola, P., Efros, A.A., Shechtman, E., Wang, O.: The unreasonable effectiveness of deep features as a perceptual metric. In: Conference on Computer Vision and Pattern Recognition (CVPR), pp. 586–595 (2018)

Unified Energy-Based Generative Network for Supervised Image Hashing

Khoa D. Doan[1,3(✉)], Sarkhan Badirli[2], and Chandan K. Reddy[3]

[1] College of Engineering and Computer Science, VinUniversity, Hanoi, Vietnam
khoadoan106@gmail.com
[2] Eli Lilly and Company, Indianapolis, IN, USA
[3] Department of Computer Science, Virginia Tech, Arlington, VA, USA
reddy@cs.vt.edu

Abstract. Hashing methods often face critical efficiency challenges, such as generalization with limited labeled data, and robustness issues (such as changes in the data distribution and missing information in the input data) in real-world retrieval applications. However, it is non-trivial to learn a hash function in existing supervised hashing methods with both acceptable efficiency and robustness. In this paper, we explore a unified generative hashing model based on an explicit energy-based model (EBM) that exhibits a better generalization with limited labeled data, and better robustness against distributional changes and missing data. Unlike the previous implicit generative adversarial network (GAN) based hashing approaches, which suffer from several practical difficulties since they simultaneously train two networks (the generator and the discriminator), our approach only trains one single generative network with multiple objectives. Specifically, the proposed generative hashing model is a bottom-up multipurpose network that simultaneously represents the images from multiple perspectives, including explicit probability density, binary hash code, and category. Our model is easier to train than GAN-based approaches as it is based on finding the maximum likelihood of the density function. The proposed model also exhibits significant robustness toward out-of-distribution query data and is able to overcome missing data in both the training and testing phase with minimal retrieval performance degradation. Extensive experiments on several real-world datasets demonstrate superior results in which the proposed model achieves up to 5% improvement over the current state-of-the-art supervised hashing methods and exhibits a significant performance boost and robustness in both out-of-distribution retrieval and missing data scenarios.

Keywords: Image hashing · Generative energy-based models · Retrieval

Supplementary Information The online version contains supplementary material available at https://doi.org/10.1007/978-3-031-26351-4_32.

1   Introduction

Searching for similar items (such as images) is an important yet challenging problem in this digital world. Accurate retrieval within a constrained response time is crucial, especially in large databases with several millions of images. This motivates the need for approximate nearest-neighbor (ANN) methods instead of using an intractable linear scan of all the images for such massive datasets. Hashing is a widely used ANN method with a principled retrieval approach for web-scale databases. In hashing, high-dimensional data points are projected onto a much smaller locality-preserving *binary* space. Searching for similar images is reduced to searching for similar discrete vectors in this binary space using computationally-efficient Hamming distance [1]. Searching for an item in the binary space is extremely fast because each Hamming distance calculation (e.g., for 64-bit vectors) only needs 2 CPU instructions in most modern hardware. Furthermore, the compact binary codes are storage-efficient, thus the entire index of items can be kept in fast-access memory; for example, a million 64-bit vectors only occupy approximately 8 megabytes. This paper focuses on the learning-to-hash methods that "learn" hash functions for efficient image retrieval.

The mapping between the original image x and the k-bit discrete vectors is expressed through a hash function $f : x \rightarrow \{-1, 1\}^k$. Learning and deploying such a hash function in real-world applications face many challenges. First, the hash function should capture the similarity relationship between images in the binary space, for example, represented in the annotated similarity between items. However, with a massive amount of data, the annotated similarity is scarce. This leads to a poor generalization in methods that exclusively rely on such annotated information. Furthermore, real-world data contains amendable missing information (e.g., a part of an image is corrupted during lossy compression or transmission between systems) and gradually changes over time (i.e., the underlying data distribution changes). A hash function that is not robust to such scenarios is not suitable for real-world applications because its expected retrieval performance will quickly degrade.

Several learning-to-hash methods, especially the supervised ones, have been proposed for efficient ANN search [2–11]. However, subject to the scarcity of similarity information, these methods run into problems such as overfitting and train/test distribution mismatch, resulting in a significant loss in retrieval performance. Recently, some methods employ generative models, specifically generative adversarial networks (GAN), to synthesize additional training data for improving the generalization of the learned hash functions. Nevertheless, these GAN-based methods do not take full advantage of generative models beyond synthetically generating the data. The main reason is that GAN is an implicit generative model that does not directly estimate the density function of the data. On the other hand, explicit generative models, specifically energy-based models (EBMs), can synthesize images and recover the missing information in those images through the inference of the EBMs. For example, when the EBM explicitly models the density of the data $p(x)$, we can recover the missing information in a data point x by revising x through the MCMC inference of the EBM to find the most probable version of x in the data distribution, thus effectively recovering x. Such ability of explicit generative models is extremely useful for real-world retrieval applications, especially when data loss or corruption can happen at any stage during the data collection or transmission process in these applications. By recovering the corrupted data, we hope to preserve much of the retrieval performance of the model.

In this paper, we propose a unified energy-based generative hashing framework (GENHASH) that simultaneously learns the representation of the images and the hash function. Our hashing network consists of a shared representation network. This network learns shared representation of the images that are useful to solve multiple objectives. Each objective is modeled as a lightweight head (a multi-layer perceptron) on top of the shared network and solves a specific task. The tasks include: 1) an explicit joint probability density estimation of an image and its semantic labels (energy head), 2) a contrastive hash-function learning (hash head) and 3) semantic label prediction (classification head). Consequently, this multipurpose network simultaneously learns to represent the images from multiple perspectives and allows the training process to develop a shared set of features as opposed to developing them redundantly in separate networks such as the GAN-based methods. Finally, since our model only trains the EBM for data synthesis, it requires fewer model parameters than approaches that use multiple networks (e.g., a generator and discriminator in GAN-based approaches). The main contributions of our paper are summarized below:

- We propose a unified generative, supervised learning-to-hash framework that takes complete advantage of generative energy-based models and enjoys better generalization and robustness towards missing data and-out-of distribution retrieval. The core component of this unified framework is the multi-headed or multipurpose hashing network, which combines density estimation (i.e., MCMC teaching process) and hash coding (i.e., contrastive loss).
- We propose a simple yet efficient training procedure to train the multipurpose hashing network. Specifically, we propagate the MCMC chains during training with two persistent contrastive divergence (PCD) buffers. One PCD buffer "explores" different modes of the model during training while the other PCD buffer is responsible for "exploiting" the learned modes to assist the contrastive hash function learning. The two PCD buffers jointly improve the efficiency of the MCMC teaching, thus allowing the training process to converge faster in practice.
- We demonstrate the advantages of our model over several state-of-the-art hashing techniques through an extensive set of experiments on various benchmark retrieval datasets.

The rest of the paper is organized as follows. We discuss the related work in Sect. 2. In Sect. 3, we describe the details of the proposed generative hashing network. We present quantitative and qualitative experimental results in Sect. 4 and conclude our discussion in Sect. 5.

2   Related Works

In this section, we review the previous research works related to two topics, namely, image hashing and energy-based generative models.

2.1   Image Hashing

Learning to hash, and especially image hashing, has been heavily investigated in both theory and practice. The existing image hashing methods can be organized into two categories: shallow hashing and deep hashing. Shallow hashing methods learn linear hash functions and rely on carefully-constructed discriminative features that are extracted from any hand-crafted feature extraction techniques or any representation-learning algorithms. On the other hand, the deep hashing methods combine the feature representation learning phase and the hashing phase into an end-to-end model and have demonstrated significant performance improvements over the hand-crafted feature-based hashing approaches [5–8,12–16].

Hashing methods can also be divided into unsupervised [2,8,17–19] and supervised hashing [4,20–27]. The works in [2,28] regress from the hash code of an image to its semantic label. Li et al. [14,15] predict the class label of an image given its hash code. On the other hand, the works in [3,8] preserve the consistency between the hash codes approximated from the similarity matrix and the hash codes approximated from the deep networks. A pairwise similarity objective or triplet ranking objective can also be formulated by randomly drawing the similar and dissimilar examples of an image from the dataset [6,7]. Our work, GENHASH, also models the relationship between the hash code of an image and its semantic label. However, GENHASH ensures that the hash codes of the synthetic samples are also consistent with their sampled labels. Furthermore, different from the previous triplet-ranking-based hashing methods, the contrastive samples (similar and dissimilar images) in our triplet-ranking objective (in Sect. 3) are synthetic (i.e., generated from a generative model) instead of being drawn from the same empirical datasets. The primary reason is to improve the generalization of the learned hash function. GENHASH is also orthogonal to OrthoHash [29] and the works in [9,10,30], all of which focus on improving the quantization aspect of learning the hash function.

Generative Supervised Hashing: Supervised methods can easily overfit with limited labeled data. Some methods overcome such a limitation by synthesizing additional training data to improve the generalization of the hash functions [31, 32]. These methods employ the popular Generative Adversarial Network (GAN) to synthesize the contrastive images. The use of generative models in hashing is currently limited to only data synthesis. Yet, generative models can benefit other downstream problems such as data imputation and out-of-distribution robustness. Our work belongs to the deep, supervised hashing category and we aim to jointly learn an energy-based generative model and the hash function in an end-to-end manner. Borrowing the strengths of EBM, we improve the retrieval performance over the GAN-based approaches and significantly improve the robustness of the hash function in terms of handling missing data and out-of-distribution retrieval.

2.2   Energy-Based Generative Models

The works in [33,34] propose a powerful generative model, called generative cooperative network (CoopNets), which can generate realistic image and video patterns. The CoopNets framework jointly trains an energy-based model (i.e., descriptor network) and a latent variable model (i.e., generator network) via a cooperative learning scheme, where the bottom-up descriptor network is trained by MCMC-based maximum likelihood estimation [35], while the top-down generator learns from the descriptor and serves as a fast initializer for the MCMC of the descriptor. While the CoopNets framework avoids mode collapse and the bottom-up descriptor is a valid model for both representation and generation, it still employs two separate networks that must be carefully designed together to ensure the model converges to a good local minima [33]. This problem also exists in GANs.

Du et al. [36] propose a scalable single-network EBM for the image generation task. The EBM can generate a realistic image and exhibits attractive properties of EBM such as out-of-distribution and adversarial robustness. Grathwohl et al. [37] reinterpreted the discriminative classification task, which estimate the conditional probability $p(x|y)$, with an energy-based model for the joint probability $p(x, y)$. To estimate the intractable partition function, the authors use MCMC sampling through the Langevin dynamics. Specifically, they build upon the persistent contrastive divergence (PCD) [38] and maintain a replay buffer to propagate the MCMC chains during training. This allows shorter mixing times than initialization of the chains from random noise, while occasionally re-initializing samples from random noise in the buffer allows the training process to explore different modes of the model. Our paper studies generative hashing based on the framework of a single EBM with multipurpose objectives. However, as we shall see later, the current PCD training procedure of existing EBM works does not work well for contrastive hash function learning where the loss function involves data synthesis of similar and dissimilar examples. Instead, we propose to train the EBMs by mixing between an exploration buffer and an exploitation buffer.

3   Multipurpose Generative Hashing Network

The proposed Multipurpose Generative Hashing Network consists of a shared representation network and multiple lightweight heads. They are jointly trained by an MCMC-based learning algorithm, as described in Fig. 1.

3.1   Problem Statement

Given a dataset $\mathcal{X} = \{x_1, x_2, ..., x_n\}$ of n images, the goal of a hashing method is to learn a discrete-output, nonlinear mapping function $\mathcal{H} : x \rightarrow \{-1, 1\}^K$, which encodes each image x into a K-bit binary vector such that the similarity structure between the images is preserved in the discrete space. In the supervised

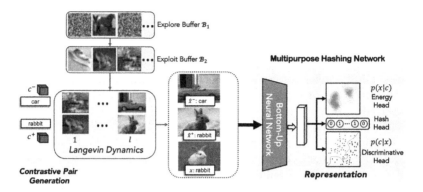

Fig. 1. GENHASH is a multipurpose hashing network (light blue block) that describes the images in multiple ways, including an explicit density model $p(x|c)$, a discriminative model $p(c|x)$, and a hashing model, all of which share a base bottom-up representational network. The multipurpose hashing network is trained by a loss including negative maximum likelihood, triplet-ranking loss, and classification loss. To compute the triplet-ranking loss, GENHASH relies on the Contrastive Pair Generation process (light yellow block) that takes a label c^+ as input and synthesizes (i.e., samples from the replay buffer $\mathcal{B}_2$) a contrastive image pair $\{\hat{x}^+, \hat{x}^-\}$ from the same class c^+ and a different class c^-. (Color figure online)

hashing setting, each example $x_i \in \mathcal{X}$ is associated with a label c_i. Note that this is a point-wise label of an image. Another common supervised scenario has the pairwise similarity label for each pair of images. However, for most image applications, pair-wise labeling is significantly labor-intensive because a dataset of n images requires n^2 pairwise labelings.

3.2   Multipurpose Energy-Based Model

The multipurpose EBM aims at representing the images from different perspectives. We propose to parameterize this network by a multi-headed bottom-up neural network, where each branch accounts for one different representation of the image. The proposed network assembles three types of representational models of data in a single network in the sense that all models share a base network but have separate lightweight heads built on top of the base network for different representational purposes. Let $f_0(x; \theta_0)$ be the shared base network with parameters θ_0. Next, we will describe the purpose of each head in more detail.

Conditional Energy head: The energy head h_E along with the base network f_0 specifies an energy function $f_E(x, c; \Theta_E)$, where observed image-label pairs (which come from the real data distribution) are assigned lower energy values than unobserved ones. For notational simplicity, let the parameters be $\Theta_E = (\theta_0, \theta_E)$ and the energy function be $f_E(x, c; \Theta_E) = h_E(c, f_0(x, \theta_0); \theta_E)$. With the energy function f_E, the energy head explicitly defines a probability distribution of x given its label c in the form of an energy-based model as follows:

$$p(x|c;\Theta_E) = \frac{p(x,c;\Theta_E)}{\int p(x,c;\Theta_E)dx} = \frac{\exp[-f_E(x,c;\Theta_E)]}{Z(c;\Theta_E)}, \qquad (1)$$

where $Z(c;\Theta_E) = \int \exp[-f_E(x,c;\Theta_E)]dx$ is the intractable normalizing constant. Equation (1) is also called generative modeling of neural network f_E [35]. Specifically, fixing the label c, $f_E(x,c;\Theta_E)$ defines the value of the compatible solution x and $-f_E(x,c;\Theta_E)$ defines the conditional energy function. Note that, for each value c, there are many compatible solutions x, i.e., there are several x's with similar, low conditional energies.

The training of θ_E in this context can be achieved by maximum likelihood estimation, which will lead to the "analysis by synthesis" algorithm [39]. Given a set of training images with labels $\{(c_i, x_i)\}_{i=1}^n$, we train Θ_E by minimizing the negative log-likelihood (NLL):

$$\mathcal{L}_E(\Theta_E) = -\frac{1}{n}\sum_{i=1}^n \log p(x_i|c_i;\Theta_E), \qquad (2)$$

The gradient of the above loss function is given by

$$\frac{1}{n}\sum_{i=1}^n \left\{ \mathbb{E}_{p(x|c_i;\Theta_E)} \left[\frac{\partial f_E(x,c_i;\Theta_E)}{\partial \Theta_E} \right] - \frac{\partial f_E(x_i,c_i;\Theta_E)}{\partial \Theta_E} \right\}, \qquad (3)$$

where the $\mathbb{E}_{p(x|c_i;\Theta_E)}$ denotes the intractable expectation with respect to $p(x|c_i;\Theta_E)$.

Following the works in [36,37], we use persistent contrastive divergence (PCD) [38] to estimate the intractable expectation since it only requires short-run MCMC chains. This gives an order of magnitude savings in computation compared to initializing new chains with a long mixing time at each iteration. Intuitively, the PCD supplies the learning process with initial solutions from a replay buffer of past generated samples. The learning process then refines these solutions at high-value region around a mode of the objective function. The model's parameters are then updated so that the objective function shifts its high-value region around the mode towards the observed solution. In the next iteration, the refined solution will (hopefully) get closer to the observed solution.

The MCMC sampling strategy with the replay buffer can be summarized in two steps: (i) the algorithm first samples $\hat{x}$ from a replay buffer $\mathcal{B}_1$ with a probability $p_{\mathcal{B}_1}$ and from uniform noise with a probability $1 - p_{\mathcal{B}_1}$, and then (ii) it refines $\hat{x}$ by finite steps of Langevin updates [40], which is an example of MCMC, to obtain final $\tilde{x}$, as follows:

$$\tilde{x}_{t+1} = \tilde{x}_t - \frac{\delta^2}{2}\frac{\partial f(\tilde{x}_t,c;\Theta_E)}{\partial \tilde{x}} + \delta\mathcal{N}(0,I_D), \tilde{x}_0 = \hat{x}, \qquad (4)$$

where t indexes the Langevin time steps, and δ is the step size. The Langevin dynamics in Eq. (4) is a gradient-based MCMC, which is equivalent to a stochastic gradient descent algorithm that seeks to find the minimum of the objective function defined by $f_E(x,c;\Theta_E)$. The replay buffer $\mathcal{B}_1$ stores past generated samples. Occasionally re-sampling from random uniform noise is crucial to the learning process since different modes of the model can be explored in training. On the other hand, between the parameters' update steps, the model only slightly changes, thus sampling from past samples, which should be reasonably close to the model distribution, allows the algorithm to simulate longer MCMC chains on the samples. However, we call $\mathcal{B}_1$ an explore buffer because of its primary function, which is to seek and cover possible modes of the model.

With the MCMC examples, we can compute the gradient of the negative log-likelihood objective by

$$\nabla(\Theta_E) \approx \frac{1}{n} \sum_{i=1}^{n} \left[\frac{\partial f_E(\tilde{x}_i, c_i; \Theta_E)}{\partial \Theta_E} - \frac{\partial f_E(x_i, c_i; \Theta_E)}{\partial \Theta_E} \right]. \tag{5}$$

Contrastive Hashing head: The head h_H learns to represent the input images as binary codes. The hash head h_H and the base network f_0 form a hash function $f_H(x; \Theta_H) = h_H(f_0(x; \theta_0); \theta_H)$, where $\Theta_H = (\theta_0, \theta_H)$. The hash function aims at mapping images with similar high-level concepts to similar hash codes and those of unrelated concepts to dissimilar codes. With a generative model, one effective way to learn such hash function is: for each image x, we "draw" a positive sample x^+ that is conceptually similar to x and a negative sample x^- that is conceptually dissimilar to x, and train the hash function to produce similar hash codes for x and x^+, and dissimilar hash codes for x and x^-.

Such contrastive learning can be achieved by recruiting labeled generated samples from the inference of the conditional EBM. These synthetic samples from each class can be similarly generated using MCMC sampling. To avoid a long mixing time where the MCMC chains are initialized from random noise, we can reuse past generated samples from the replay buffer $\mathcal{B}_1$. However, $\mathcal{B}_1$ may contain several past samples that have been less rigorously refined through the Langevin dynamics (i.e., only refined a few times). These "young" samples can still be closer to random noise. Therefore, when being selected for contrastive hash learning, there is not a useful difference between samples from a different class. That is, the current sample x and their similar and dissimilar synthetic samples x^+ and x^-, respectively, do not form an informative contrastive triplet. Empirically, we observe that only relying on $\mathcal{B}_1$ for contrastive samples learn a hash function whose performance is significantly worse than desired.

This problem is further illustrated in Fig. 2, where some samples from each class are similar to random noise. There are more of these samples in CIFAR10 than in MNIST because the generation of natural images in CIFAR10 requires a significantly more complex model than the generative model of MNIST. Even further into training, we observe that there are still similar MCMC samples due to the occasional sampling from random noise that requires longer MCMC chains when the data distribution is complex (as in the case of CIFAR10). One naive solution is to increase the number of Langevin steps; however, larger chains make the EBM significantly more computationally expensive to train.

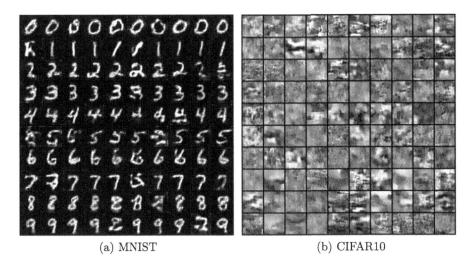

(a) MNIST   (b) CIFAR10

Fig. 2. Samples from the explore buffer $\mathcal{B}_1$. Images on each row are from the same semantic class. Some CIFAR10 images in this buffer are far from real images because $\mathcal{B}_1$ is a mixture of (i) *newly-initialized or younger samples* from the MCMC chain and (ii) *those samples that have been revised several times.*

We propose a simple, yet effective sampling strategy to solve this problem. First, we introduce a second replay buffer $\mathcal{B}_2$, where a sample $x \in \mathcal{B}_2$ is required to be initialized from supposedly longer MCMC chains. To avoid explicitly increasing the number of Langevin steps to achieve such longer MCMC chains, we leverage the existing replay buffer $\mathcal{B}_1$ by "copying" samples that have been revised several times in $\mathcal{B}_1$. Intuitively, while sampling from $\mathcal{B}_1$ allows the training process to explore different modes of the models, sampling from $\mathcal{B}_2$ exploits the learned modes. However, since we regularly copy the samples from $\mathcal{B}_1$ to $\mathcal{B}_2$ when they are "matured", sampling from $\mathcal{B}_2$ also explores all previously learned modes in for the contrastive hash learning.

Under this sampling strategy, to learn the contrastive hash function, for each observed image x and its label c, we sample a synthetic image x^+, conditioned on the label c, and a synthetic image x^-, conditioned on a different label $c^- \neq c$ using the replay buffer $\mathcal{B}_2$. The three examples form a real-synthetic triplet (x, x^+, x^-). The hash function f_H can be trained to minimize the Hamming distance (a discrete distance function that is typically approximated by the continuous L_2 distance) between $f_H(x)$ and $f_H(x^+)$ and maximize the distance between $f_H(x)$ and $f_H(x^-)$. This triplet-ranking loss is defined as follows:

$$\mathcal{L}_{\mathrm{H}}(\Theta_H) = ||f_H(x) - f_H(x^+)||_H + max(m - ||f_H(x) - h(x^-)||_H, 0) \quad (6)$$
$$s.t. \ f_H(x) \in \{-1, 1\}, f_H(x^+) \in \{-1, 1\}, f_H(x^-) \in \{-1, 1\}$$

where $||.||_H$ denotes the Hamming distance. The first term preserves the similarity between images with similar semantic concepts, while the second term penalizes the mapping of semantically dissimilar images to similar hash codes if their distance is within a margin m. Essentially, this is a contrastive objective that avoids collapsed solutions because it only considers the dissimilar pairs having distances within a certain margin to contribute to the loss.

The objective of $\mathcal{L}_h$ is a discrete optimization problem, hence it is computationally intractable to solve and is not suitable for a gradient-based backpropagation algorithm. A natural solution is to approximate the discrete constraints with real-valued output and replace the Hamming distance with Euclidean distance. For the thresholding procedure, a commonly-used trick is to employ the *tanh* or *sigmoid* function. However, we find that *tanh* or *sigmoid* makes the learning process more difficult to converge to good local optima. To overcome this, we propose to directly regularize the real-valued output of the hash function to the desired discrete values. The final triplet-ranking loss is as follows:

$$\mathcal{L}_H(\Theta_H) = ||f_H(x) - f_H(x^+)||_2 + \max(m - ||f_H(x) - f_H(x^-)||_2, 0) \\ + \lambda(|||f_H(x)| - 1||_2 \quad + \quad |||f_H(x^+)| - 1||_2 + |||f_H(x^-)| - 1||_2) \tag{7}$$

where $f_H(.)$ is now the relaxed function with real-valued vector outputs and $|.|$ is element-wise absolute operation. The first and second terms in the objective function approximate the Hamming distances in Eq. (7). The last term minimizes the quantization error of approximating the discrete solution with the real-value relaxation. Intuitively, it centers the relaxed, continuous output of the hash function around the desired binary value of -1 or 1. Note that the *max* operation is non-differentiable; however, we can define the subgradient of the *max* function to be 1 at the non-differential points.

Discriminative head: Image labels provide not only knowledge for training a classification model but also a supervised signal for extracting high-level information of the images. On the other hand, the learned hash codes should also capture high-level abstractions of the images, therefore should be predictive of the image labels. This relationship can be modeled through a multi-class classification problem. Specifically, we propose a classification head h_C that predicts the class label of an image given its hash code. For each image x_i, let $\hat{c}_i$ be the predicted label. The multi-class classification loss can be defined as follows:

$$\mathcal{L}_C(\Theta_C) = -\frac{1}{n}\sum_{i=1}^{n} c_i \log \frac{e^{\theta_{c_i,:}^T h(x)}}{\sum_j e^{\theta_{j,:}^T h(x_i)}} \tag{8}$$

where $\theta_C \in \mathbb{R}^{K \times L}$ is the parameter of the linear layer that maps each hash code into the class labels. We additionally denote $\Theta_C = (\theta_0, \theta_C)$ as the parameters of this classification network. This objective function is optimal when the discrete space is approximately linear separable with respect to the class labels. In other words, the hash codes of the images from the same semantic class have small Hamming distances between them, while the hash codes of the images from different classes have larger Hamming distances.

3.3   Optimization

At each iteration, the energy-based model $p(x|c; \Theta_E)$ samples synthetic contrastive image pairs by following the strategy described in the previous section.

With synthetic images, we train the multipurpose hashing network to simultaneously describe the images from multiple representational perspectives. The overall training objective of the network, which combines the negative log-likelihood $\mathcal{L}_E(\Theta_E)$, the triplet-ranking loss $\mathcal{L}_H(\Theta_H)$, and the classification loss $\mathcal{L}_C(\Theta_C)$, is given by:

$$\mathcal{L}(\Theta_E, \Theta_H, \Theta_C) = \mathcal{L}_E(\Theta_E) + \beta_H \mathcal{L}_H(\Theta_H) + \beta_C \mathcal{L}_C(\Theta_C) \tag{9}$$

where β_H and β_C are parameters to balance the weight between different losses.

In general, EBMs are less computationally efficient than GAN-based models [36]. However, the increased computational cost (compared to GAN-based methods) is only in the training phase, which can be mitigated with larger hardware and distributed training. With short-run MCMCs (typically only 15–20 Langevin steps in our experiments), we can already significantly reduce the training time of the EBM component. During the testing phase, since we only use the hash function and discard the remaining components (Fig. 1b), the computation is similar to the computation of the models in other hashing methods.

4   Experiments

In this section, we present the evaluation results on several real-world datasets to demonstrate the effectiveness of the proposed method.

4.1   Experimental Setup

Datasets: We evaluate our method on three widely-used datasets in the image hashing domain: **NUS-WIDE**, **COCO** and **CIFAR-10**.
Evaluation Metrics: We evaluate the retrieval performance of the methods using the standard retrieval metrics in image hashing: Mean Average Precision at K (mAP@K) and Precision at K (P@K).
Baselines: We compare our method against several representative approaches from image hashing. ITQ [4], BRE [3], and KSH [41]) are shallow supervised hashing approaches. CNNH [8], SDH [2], DNNH [7], FastHash [28], DHN [6], DSDH [14], DVStH [42], HashNet [5], CSQ [43], and the state-of-the-art generative method, HashGAN [19] are deep supervised hashing approaches. Additionally, we include the results of HashGAN-1, which is the HashGAN method where the GAN model and the hash function are jointly learned in one stage.

The complete experimental setup, including the dataset details, evaluation metric calculations, and implementation details, are provided in the Supplement.

4.2   Retrieval Results

In this section, we present the results of querying for similar images. Table 1 shows the mAP results for all the methods. Compared to the shallow hashing methods, GENHASH improves at least 14% on NUS-WIDE, 13% on CIFAR-10,

Table 1. Mean Average Precision (mAP) for different number of bits.

Method	NUS-WIDE			CIFAR-10			COCO		
	16 bits	32 bits	48 bits	16 bits	32 bits	48 bits	16 bits	32 bits	48 bits
ITQ [4]	0.460	0.405	0.373	0.354	0.414	0.449	0.566	0.562	0.530
BRE [3]	0.503	0.529	0.548	0.370	0.438	0.468	0.592	0.622	0.630
KSH [41]	0.551	0.582	0.612	0.524	0.558	0.567	0.521	0.534	0.534
SDH [2]	0.588	0.611	0.638	0.461	0.520	0.553	0.555	0.564	0.572
CNNH [8]	0.570	0.583	0.593	0.476	0.472	0.489	0.564	0.574	0.571
DNNH [7]	0.598	0.616	0.635	0.559	0.558	0.581	0.593	0.603	0.605
FastHash [28]	0.502	0.515	0.516	0.524	0.566	0.597	0.601	0.609	0.612
DHN [6]	0.637	0.664	0.669	0.568	0.603	0.621	0.677	0.701	0.695
DSDH [14]	0.650	0.701	0.705	0.655	0.660	0.682	0.659	0.688	0.710
DVStH [42]	0.661	0.680	0.698	0.667	0.695	0.708	0.689	0.709	0.713
HashNet [5]	0.662	0.699	0.711	0.643	0.667	0.675	0.687	0.718	0.730
CSQ [43]	0.701	0.713	0.720	0.646	0.699	0.709	0.679	0.699	0.714
HashGAN [19]	0.715	0.737	0.744	0.668	0.731	0.735	0.697	0.725	0.741
GENHASH	**0.742**	**0.754**	**0.773**	**0.711**	**0.739**	**0.778**	**0.747**	**0.768**	**0.775**

Table 2. Precision@1000 for different number of bits.

Method	NUS-WIDE			CIFAR-10			COCO		
	16 bits	32 bits	48 bits	16 bits	32 bits	48 bits	16 bits	32 bits	48 bits
ITQ [4]	0.489	0.572	0.590	0.289	0.271	0.305	0.489	0.518	0.545
BRE [3]	0.521	0.603	0.627	0.398	0.445	0.471	0.520	0.535	0.559
KSH [41]	0.598	0.656	0.667	0.580	0.612	0.641	0.519	0.540	0.558
SDH [2]	0.640	0.702	0.712	0.655	0.671	0.651	0.696	0.695	0.710
CNNH [8]	0.601	0.651	0.672	0.533	0.545	0.578	0.671	0.690	0.718
DNNH [7]	0.620	0.689	0.707	0.651	0.678	0.691	0.713	0.701	0.728
DHN [6]	0.655	0.713	0.726	0.659	0.701	0.725	0.703	0.731	0.750
DSDH [14]	0.658	0.728	0.752	0.678	0.710	0.729	0.721	0.735	0.754
HashNet [5]	0.680	0.729	0.741	0.720	0.721	0.741	0.745	0.746	0.753
CSQ [43]	0.701	0.741	0.750	0.725	0.735	0.741	0.749	0.742	0.749
HashGAN [19]	0.720	0.759	0.772	0.735	0.751	0.762	0.755	0.768	0.783
GENHASH	**0.749**	**0.780**	**0.808**	**0.780**	**0.799**	**0.823**	**0.789**	**0.795**	**0.811**

and 20% on COCO. Compared to the state-of-the-art deep hashing method that does not have data synthesis (i.e., HashNet), GENHASH improves at least 9%, 9%, and 5% on NUS-WIDE, CIFAR-10, and COCO, respectively. GENHASH outperforms HashGAN, the state-of-the-art supervised, data-synthesis method by statistically significant margins in all the datasets.

The mAP results provide empirical evidence to support our discussion in Sects. 1 and 2. **First**, generating synthetic data improves the performance of a supervised hashing method. This could be explained by the fact that generative models improve the amount of "labeled" training data and increase its diversity, both of which improve the method's generalization capacity. **Second**, we can observe that the performance of HashGAN significantly decreases without the fine-tuning step (HashGAN-1's results). Training GAN-based models is difficult with problems such as mode collapse; thus in GAN-based models such as Hash-GAN, a second fine-tuning step, where only the hash function is trained with the synthetic data while the other components are fixed, is needed to avoid difficulties in simultaneously training the generator and discriminator. This increases the computational requirement of the GAN-based methods. Finally, GENHASH, which simultaneously trains the generative model and the hash function, has better retrieval performance than the state-of-the-art, two-stage HashGAN. This supports our claim that the one-stage scheme learns better similarity-preserving hash codes of the images.

In addition, we present the Precision@1000 results in Table 2. The Precision@1000 is calculated at the common retrieval threshold (1000) in image applications. Similarly, the proposed GENHASH significantly outperforms all the compared methods.

4.3   Out-of-Distribution Retrieval

In this section, we show that GENHASH, which is a multipurpose EBM, exhibits better out-of-distribution (OOD) robustness in retrieval than other methods. In real-world retrieval applications, the arrival of new data instances or new data format are common. This results in conceptual drift or change in the underlying data distribution where the hashing methods are trained on. A hashing method that is robust (i.e., its performance is not significantly worse) to slight changes in such underlying distributional change in the data is preferred because it takes a longer time for the trained model to become obsolete.

Table 3. OOD Retrieval.

Train/Test	HashNet	CSQ	HashGAN	GENHASH
SVHN/*MNIST*	0.181	_0.517_	0.354	**0.609**
SVHN/*SVHN*	0.837	0.854	_0.889_	**0.895**
MNIST/*SVHN*	0.193	0.273	_0.280_	**0.498**
MNIST/*MNIST*	0.957	_0.991_	0.990	**0.991**

Table 4. Data-corruption Retrieval.

	Type	HashNet	HashGAN	GENHASH
SnP	Clean	0.513	0.608	0.680
	Corrupted	0.223	0.281	0.652
RRM	Clean	0.471	0.615	0.654
	Corrupted	0.243	0.298	0.607

We propose to simulate a minor but realistic distributional change in the data as follows. In the learning phase, each hashing method is trained on a source dataset. In the testing or evaluation phase, we use a different test dataset that is conceptually similar to the source dataset but comes from a (slightly) different data distribution. We choose MNIST and SVHN as conceptually-related datasets. One dataset is selected as both the train and retrieval sets, while the test queries are sampled from the other dataset.

Table 3 shows the retrieval results of GENHASH, HashNet (a deep hashing method), HashNet and HashGAN (a GAN-based hashing method). As can be observed, GENHASH significantly outperforms both HashNet and HashGAN in OOD retrieval, with more than 25% when using MNIST for querying, and 20% when using SVHN for querying. GENHASH's mAP performance is still roughly more than 50% when the test data distribution changes. This makes GENHASH still useful in practice, while in other methods, the retrieval performance significantly drops closer to the performance of a random retrieval.

While the OOD retrieval performance falls significantly, compared to the retrieval performance using data from the same distribution as that of the training data, data-synthesis methods (HashGAN and GENHASH) are more robust toward distributional changes, compared to the conventional deep hashing methods HashNet and CSQ. In addition, when being trained on a more complex dataset (SVHN), the retrieval performance of GENHASH significantly improves in our OOD tests, while the OOD retrieval performances of the other methods only slightly improve.

4.4   Missing-Data Robustness in Retrieval

GENHASH is a multipurpose EBM. Similar to other explicit generative EBMs [36, 37], we can additionally model the energy function of x. This provides us with an important advantage over other generative models: we can revise (or reconstruct) a sample with corruption by initializing the input chain into the Langevin dynamics with the corrupted samples. Through the Langevin revision, the corrupted samples can be re-constructed. Note that, this feature of the EBM is not immediately available in other generative hashing methods, such as HashGAN.

We perform the missing data experiments as follows. First, we assume that both training data and test data may contain corrupted input images. During training of GENHASH, we train on the clean input as mentioned previously. For corrupted input we initialize the MCMC chains with the corrupted samples and revise these samples through the Langevin dynamics. We corrupt the images in both the training and test sets of the CIFAR10 dataset. We corrupt 20% of the data using salt-and-pepper noise (denoted by SnP) or random rectangular mask (denoted by RRM, where the rectangles randomly cover approximately 10–20% of the images at random locations) on the images for both training and query sets. Then, the model in each hashing method is trained with the corrupted training set and the evaluation is performed on the corrupted test set.

In Table 4, we show the results for the missing-data robustness experiments. As can be observed, the performances of the baseline methods, including the generative hashing HashGAN method, are significantly degraded when there are corruptions in the data. On the other hand, GENHASH's retrieval performance only slightly drops when the data is corrupted. This shows the advantages of the proposed EBM-based multipurpose generative hashing network.

5   Conclusion

This paper proposes a unified generative framework, called GENHASH to solve the image hashing problem. The framework learns a multipurpose hashing network to represent images from multiple perspectives, including classification, hashing, and probability density estimation. This approach learns high-quality binary hash codes and achieves state-of-the-art retrieval performance on several benchmark datasets. Furthermore, GENHASH is significantly more robust to out-of-distribution retrieval compared to the existing methods and can handle significant corruption in the data with trivial drops in the retrieval performance. In GENHASH, we also train a single EBM-based network, which makes it easier for the practitioner to design better architectures. This is preferred compared to other GAN-based approaches because designing the discriminator and generator networks is not a trivial task with various problems when one network has more capacity than the other.

References

1. Leskovec, J., Rajaraman, A., Ullman, J.D.: Mining of Massive Datasets. Cambridge University Press, Cambridge (2014)
2. Shen, F., Shen, C., Liu, W., Tao Shen, H.: Supervised discrete hashing. In: Proceedings of the IEEE Conference on Computer Vision and Pattern Recognition, pp. 37–45 (2015)
3. Kulis, B., Darrell, T.: Learning to hash with binary reconstructive embeddings. In: Advances in Neural Information Processing Systems, pp. 1042–1050 (2009)
4. Gong, Y., Lazebnik, S., Gordo, A., Perronnin, F.: Iterative quantization: a procrustean approach to learning binary codes for large-scale image retrieval. IEEE Transactions on Pattern Analysis and Machine Intell. **35**, 2916–2929 (2012)
5. Cao, Z., Long, M., Wang, J., Yu, P.S.: HashNet: deep learning to hash by continuation. In: Proceedings of the IEEE International Conference on Computer Vision, pp. 5608–5617 (2017)
6. Zhu, H., Long, M., Wang, J., Cao, Y.: Deep hashing network for efficient similarity retrieval. In: Thirtieth AAAI Conference on Artificial Intelligence (2016)
7. Lai, H., Pan, Y., Liu, Y., Yan, S.: Simultaneous feature learning and hash coding with deep neural networks. In: Proceedings of the IEEE Conference on Computer Vision and Pattern Recognition, pp. 3270–3278 (2015)
8. Xia, R., Pan, Y., Lai, H., Liu, C., Yan, S.: Supervised hashing for image retrieval via image representation learning. In: Proceedings of the Twenty-Eighth AAAI Conference on Artificial Intelligence, pp. 2156–2162. AAAI 2014, AAAI Press (2014)
9. Doan, K.D., Reddy, C.K.: Efficient implicit unsupervised text hashing using adversarial autoencoder. In: Proceedings of The Web Conference 2020. WWW 2020, New York, NY, USA, Association for Computing Machinery, pp. 684–694 (2020)
10. Doan, K.D., Manchanda, S., Badirli, S., Reddy, C.K.: Image hashing by minimizing discrete component-wise wasserstein distance. arXiv preprint arXiv:2003.00134 (2020)
11. Doan, K.D., Yadav, P., Reddy, C.K.: Adversarial factorization autoencoder for look-alike modeling. In: Proceedings of the 28th ACM International Conference on Information and Knowledge Management (CIKM), Beijing, China, pp. 2803–2812 (2019)
12. Erin Liong, V., Lu, J., Wang, G., Moulin, P., Zhou, J.: Deep hashing for compact binary codes learning. In: Proceedings of the IEEE Conference on Computer Vision and Pattern Recognition, pp. 2475–2483 (2015)
13. Cao, Y., Long, M., Wang, J., Zhu, H., Wen, Q.: Deep quantization network for efficient image retrieval. In: Proceedings of the AAAI Conference on Artificial Intelligence, vol. 30 (2016)
14. Li, Q., Sun, Z., He, R., Tan, T.: Deep supervised discrete hashing. In: Proceedings of the 31st International Conference on Neural Information Processing Systems, 2479–2488 (2017)
15. Gui, J., Li, P.: R2SDH: robust rotated supervised discrete hashing. In: Proceedings of the 24th ACM SIGKDD International Conference on Knowledge Discovery & Data Mining, 1485–1493 (2018)

16. Jiang, Q.Y., Li, W.J.: Asymmetric deep supervised hashing. In: Proceedings of the AAAI Conference on Artificial Intelligence, vol. 32 (2018)
17. Yang, H.F., Lin, K., Chen, C.S.: Supervised learning of semantics-preserving hash via deep convolutional neural networks. IEEE Trans. Pattern Anal. Mach. Intell. **40**, 437–451 (2018)
18. Ge, T., He, K., Sun, J.: Graph cuts for supervised binary coding. In: Fleet, D., Pajdla, T., Schiele, B., Tuytelaars, T. (eds.) ECCV 2014. LNCS, vol. 8695, pp. 250–264. Springer, Cham (2014). https://doi.org/10.1007/978-3-319-10584-0_17
19. Cao, Y., Liu, B., Long, M., Wang, J.: HashGAN: deep learning to hash with pair conditional wasserstein GAN. In: Proceedings of the IEEE Conference on Computer Vision and Pattern Recognition, pp. 1287–1296 (2018)
20. Huang, S., Xiong, Y., Zhang, Y., Wang, J.: Unsupervised triplet hashing for fast image retrieval. In: Proceedings of the on Thematic Workshops of ACM Multimedia 2017, pp. 84–92. ACM (2017)
21. Lin, K., Lu, J., Chen, C.S., Zhou, J.: Learning compact binary descriptors with unsupervised deep neural networks. In: Proceedings of the IEEE Conference on Computer Vision and Pattern Recognition, pp. 1183–1192 (2016)
22. Huang, C., Change Loy, C., Tang, X.: Unsupervised learning of discriminative attributes and visual representations. In: Proceedings of the IEEE Conference on Computer Vision and Pattern Recognition, pp. 5175–5184 (2016)
23. Do, T.-T., Doan, A.-D., Cheung, N.-M.: Learning to hash with binary deep neural network. In: Leibe, B., Matas, J., Sebe, N., Welling, M. (eds.) ECCV 2016. LNCS, vol. 9909, pp. 219–234. Springer, Cham (2016). https://doi.org/10.1007/978-3-319-46454-1_14
24. Weiss, Y., Torralba, A., Fergus, R.: Spectral hashing. In: Advances in neural information processing systems, pp. 1753–1760 (2009)
25. Salakhutdinov, R., Hinton, G.: Semantic hashing. Int. J. Approximate Reasoning **50**, 969–978 (2009)
26. Yang, E., Liu, T., Deng, C., Liu, W., Tao, D.: DistillHash: unsupervised deep hashing by distilling data pairs. In: Proceedings of the IEEE Conference on Computer Vision and Pattern Recognition, pp. 2946–2955 (2019)
27. Dizaji, K.G., Zheng, F., Nourabadi, N.S., Yang, Y., Deng, C., Huang, H.: Unsupervised deep generative adversarial hashing network. In: CVPR 2018 (2018)
28. Gui, J., Liu, T., Sun, Z., Tao, D., Tan, T.: Fast supervised discrete hashing. IEEE Trans. Pattern Anal. Mach. Intell. **40**, 490–496 (2017)
29. Hoe, J.T., Ng, K.W., Zhang, T., Chan, C.S., Song, Y.Z., Xiang, T.: One loss for all: deep hashing with a single cosine similarity based learning objective. In: Advances in Neural Information Processing Systems (2021)
30. Doan, K.D., Yang, P., Li, P.: One loss for quantization: Deep hashing with discrete wasserstein distributional matching. In: Proceedings of the IEEE/CVF Conference on Computer Vision and Pattern Recognition, pp. 9447–9457 (2022)
31. Qiu, Z., Pan, Y., Yao, T., Mei, T.: Deep semantic hashing with generative adversarial networks. In: Proceedings of the 40th International ACM SIGIR Conference on Research and Development in Information Retrieval, pp. 225–234 (2017)
32. Gao, R., Lu, Y., Zhou, J., Zhu, S.C., Nian Wu, Y.: Learning generative convnets via multi-grid modeling and sampling. In: Proceedings of the IEEE Conference on Computer Vision and Pattern Recognition, pp. 9155–9164 (2018)
33. Xie, J., Lu, Y., Gao, R., Zhu, S.C., Wu, Y.N.: Cooperative training of descriptor and generator networks. IEEE Trans. Pattern Anal. Mach. Intell. **42**, 27–45 (2018)

34. Xie, J., Zheng, Z., Fang, X., Zhu, S.C., Wu, Y.N.: Cooperative training of fast thinking initializer and slow thinking solver for conditional learning. IEEE Trans. Pattern Anal. Mach. Intell. (TPAMI) (2021)
35. Xie, J., Lu, Y., Zhu, S.C., Wu, Y.: A theory of generative convnet. In: International Conference on Machine Learning, pp. 2635–2644 (2016)
36. lun Du, Y., Mordatch, I.: Implicit generation and modeling with energy based models. In: NeurIPS (2019)
37. Grathwohl, W., Wang, K., Jacobsen, J., Duvenaud, D., Norouzi, M., Swersky, K.: Your classifier is secretly an energy based model and you should treat it like one. In: 8th International Conference on Learning Representations, ICLR 2020, Addis Ababa, Ethiopia, April 26–30, 2020, OpenReview.net (2020)
38. Tieleman, T.: Training restricted boltzmann machines using approximations to the likelihood gradient. In: Proceedings of the 25th International Conference on Machine Learning, pp. 1064–1071 (2008)
39. Grenander, U., Miller, M.I., Miller, M., et al.: Pattern theory: from representation to inference. Oxford University Press, Oxford (2007)
40. Zhu, S.C., Mumford, D.: Grade: gibbs reaction and diffusion equations. In: International Conference on Computer Vision (ICCV), pp. 847–854 (1998)
41. Liu, W., Wang, J., Ji, R., Jiang, Y.G., Chang, S.F.: Supervised hashing with kernels. In: 2012 IEEE Conference on Computer Vision and Pattern Recognition, pp. 2074–2081. IEEE (2012)
42. Liong, V.E., Lu, J., Duan, L.Y., Tan, Y.P.: Deep variational and structural hashing. IEEE Trans. Pattern Anal. Mach. Intell. **42**, 580–595 (2018)
43. Yuan, L., et al.: Central similarity quantization for efficient image and video retrieval. In: Proceedings of the IEEE/CVF Conference on Computer Vision and Pattern Recognition, pp. 3083–3092 (2020)

Learning and Transforming General Representations to Break Down Stability-Plasticity Dilemma

Kengo Murata$^{(\boxtimes)}$(ID), Seiya Ito(ID), and Kouzou Ohara(ID)

Aoyama Gakuin University, Kanagawa, Japan
d5621007@aoyama.jp, {s.ito,ohara}@it.aoyama.ac.jp

Abstract. In the Class Incremental Learning (CIL) setup, a learning model must have the ability to incrementally update its knowledge to recognize newly appeared classes (plasticity) while maintaining the knowledge to recognize the classes it has already learned (stability). Such conflicting requirements are known as the stability-plasticity dilemma, and most existing studies attempt to achieve a good balance between them by stability improvements. Unlike those attempts, we focus on the generality of representations. The basic idea is that a model does not need to change if it has already learned such general representations that they contain enough information to recognize new classes. However, the general representations are not optimal for recognizing the classes a model has already learned because the representations must contain unrelated and noisy information for recognizing them. To acquire representations suitable for recognizing known classes while leveraging general representations, in this paper, we propose a new CIL framework that learns general representations and transforms them into suitable ones for the target classification tasks. In our framework, we achieve the acquisition of general representations and their transformation by self-supervised learning and attention techniques, respectively. In addition, we introduce a novel knowledge distillation loss to make the transformation mechanism stable. Using benchmark datasets, we empirically confirm that our framework can improve the average incremental accuracy of four types of CIL methods that employ knowledge distillation in the CIL setting.

1 Introduction

Deep neural network models can provide superior performance in image recognition tasks [17,24,49] if all the classes to be recognized are available when training them. However, this prerequisite is unrealistic in most practical situations. To overcome this limitation, many studies have tackled the problem of Class Incremental Learning (CIL) [6,38], in which a model learns new classes incrementally through multiple classification tasks that are sequentially provided. In the CIL setup, a learning model needs to update its knowledge to recognize

---

Supplementary Information The online version contains supplementary material available at https://doi.org/10.1007/978-3-031-26351-4_33.

newly emerged classes (plasticity), while maintaining the knowledge to recognize the classes it has already learned (stability). Such conflicting requirements are known as the stability-plasticity dilemma [40], which is the major issue in CIL.

In general, deep neural network models tend to learn task-oriented knowledge and overwrite the knowledge learned for the previous tasks with the one for the new task in CIL. This problem is known as catastrophic forgetting [32,39], which implies that the balance of the two conflicting requirements is biased toward plasticity. Thus, most existing studies attempt to achieve a good balance between stability and plasticity by improving stability. For instance, regularization methods [9] prevent important parameters of a neural network model from moving. Knowledge distillation [25,35] attempts to preserve features a model has already acquired. However, all those approaches achieve improvement in stability in exchange for the plasticity of a learning model, which implies their performance degrades for the new tasks when the model needs to be highly plastic to adapt to the new tasks.

The above observation indicates that the CIL methods with knowledge distillation cannot achieve high performance both for the new and learned tasks simultaneously without a mechanism to decrease the required plasticity for adapting to the new tasks. Therefore, in this paper, we focus on the generality of learned representation because the model does not need to change if the representations it has already learned are so general that they contain enough information to recognize new classes. The existing approaches cannot learn such general representations because they optimize model parameters with the cross-entropy loss to solve the classification task. The cross-entropy loss encourages learning task-oriented representations, but it does not ensure the model acquires representations not directly related to the current and previous tasks, even if they may be helpful for the subsequent tasks. Thus, we propose a new CIL framework and adopt the self-supervised learning technique [14] to learn general representations that could be useful for classes involved in future tasks. Here, it is noted that the general representations are not optimal for recognizing the classes a model has already learned because they must contain unrelated and noisy information for the known classes to be recognized. Thus, we further introduce into our framework a mechanism based on attention techniques [27,44] to transform the general representations into suitable ones for the target classification tasks. Furthermore, we introduce a novel knowledge distillation loss to improve the stability of our transformation mechanism.

Our contributions are summarized as follows:

1. We propose a novel CIL framework that makes a model learn general representations and transforms them into suitable ones for the target classification tasks.
2. We design a novel knowledge distillation loss that improves the stability of our transformation mechanism.
3. Through the experiments on benchmark datasets in the CIL setting, we empirically confirm that our framework improves the average incremental accuracy of existing CIL models employing knowledge distillation.

2 Related Work

2.1 Class Incremental Learning

A straightforward solution to the problem of CIL is to learn classes involved in the current task with all the classes the model has already learned in the past tasks. However, this solution is unrealistic because of the considerable training time and the huge memory space. Experience replay [11] achieves this ideal solution within a reasonable training time by memorizing only a few exemplars used in the previous tasks and replaying them while learning the current task. Thanks to its simplicity and good performance in the CIL setting, experience replay has been one of the standard methods in CIL to date.

Even if using experience replay, the model is still unstable through the process of a CIL scenario and does not perform well for classes in the previous tasks because the number of memorized exemplars is very limited. For stability improvements, many CIL methods [18,26,34,47,48,50] employ knowledge distillation, which preserves the input-output relations the model has already learned. For instance, while learning the t-th task, the less-forget constraint proposed in [26] forces a model to minimize the distance between its output feature vector and the one of the latest previous model, which has just finished learning the $(t-1)$-th task.

The other issue involved in experience replay is the class-imbalance problem between the previous and current tasks. This class-imbalance problem causes predictions biased toward the classes in the current task [54]. To tackle this problem, several studies propose the bias correction methods such as the bias correction layer [54], the normalization of weight vectors in the classification layer [4,5,26,58], and the imbalance-aware loss functions [1,30,41].

2.2 Representation Learning in CIL

A few studies on CIL focus on representation learning of deep neural network models. We categorize them into three groups: contrastive learning methods [8,37,42], meta-learning methods [3,28,46], and self-supervised learning methods [20,29,57,59]. Firstly, contrastive learning methods optimize a model with respect to supervised contrastive loss [31], which encourages the model to acquire intra-class concentrated and inter-class separated features. Secondly, meta-learning methods learn features that accelerate future learning via meta-learning frameworks [19]. However, due to the nature of the meta-learning framework, each task must be explicitly identified when using the model for prediction. This necessity for task identification leads to the requirements of the additional task prediction system [46], which should be continually updatable without forgetting. Thirdly, self-supervised learning methods utilize the self-supervised learning approaches [36] as with our framework. For instance, the existing studies [57,59] use the angle of training data as self-supervision. They optimize one feature space with respect to original and self-supervised labels. In contrast, our framework optimizes two kinds of feature space with respect to each label. To our best knowledge, DualNet [45] is the most similar method to our framework. In DualNet, two completely different networks are optimized with each label, interacting with each other. In contrast to DualNet, our framework works with a single neural network, so the number of parameters is lower than the one used in DualNet. We note that DualNet is specialized in online continual learning [2], which is similar but different to the CIL scenario targeting in our work. Therefore, we do not compare our framework to DualNet in this paper.

2.3 Self-supervised Learning

Recently, self-supervised learning has been shown effective in learning general representations without label supervision [12,14,23]. The earlier studies propose the proxy task, e.g., prediction rotations [21], patch permutation [43], image colorization [56], and clustering [7], which enables a model to learn the general representations. More recently, contrastive self-supervised learning has shown great success [36]. It encourages a model to learn the features that can identify one view of an image with the other view and distinguish the image from any other images. For instance, SimCLR [12] produces two types of views by sophisticated data augmentations, and the variants of MoCo [13,15,23] introduce a momentum encoder to produce the different views. The key issue of contrastive self-supervised learning methods is the necessity of the vast amount of negative samples. BYOL [22], SimSiam [14], and Barlow Twins [55] are representative methods that only rely on two distinct views of the same image. In our methods, we use SimSiam as a self-supervised learning method because of its simplicity and the unnecessity of negative samples.

3   Problem Setup and Preliminaries

In this section, we firstly introduce the problem setup of CIL and then briefly describe CIL methods with knowledge distillation, the baseline methods for our framework. Let $\{\mathcal{T}_1, \mathcal{T}_2, \cdots, \mathcal{T}_N\}$ be a sequence of N tasks. For the t-th task $\mathcal{T}_t$, there is a training dataset $\mathcal{D}_t$ and a memorized exemplar set $\mathcal{M}_t$. More specifically, $\mathcal{D}_t = \{(x_t^i, y_t^i)\}_{i=1}^{n_t}$ is composed of pairs of an image $x_t^i \in \mathcal{X}_t$ and its corresponding label $y_t^i \in \mathcal{Y}_t$. The memorized exemplar set $\mathcal{M}_t = \{(x_{\mathrm{mem}}^i, y_{\mathrm{mem}}^i)\}_{i=1}^{M}$ is composed of M previously learned instances $(x_{\mathrm{mem}}^i, y_{\mathrm{mem}}^i) \in \bigcup_{j=1}^{t-1} \mathcal{D}_j$. Note that the label sets of different tasks do not overlap, meaning $\mathcal{Y}_i \cap \mathcal{Y}_j = \emptyset$ if $i \neq j$. We consider a deep neural network model with two components: a feature extractor f and a classifier g. While learning the t-th task, the model updates its parameters with both the training dataset $\mathcal{D}_t$ and the exemplar set $\mathcal{M}_t$ to achieve correct prediction for any instance $x \in \bigcup_{j=1}^{t} \mathcal{X}_j$. We refer to the model that is being updated for the current task $\mathcal{T}_t$ as the current model and call its components the current feature extractor f_t and the current classifier g_t. Similarly, the model that has already been updated for the task $\mathcal{T}_{t-1}$ is referred to as the previous model, whose components are the previous feature extractor f_{t-1} and classifier g_{t-1}.

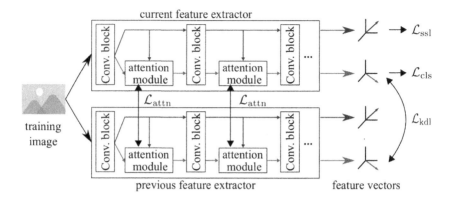

Fig. 1. Illustration of our framework. The feature extractor consists of the attention modules and convolutional blocks, e.g., Residual blocks. It outputs two feature vectors: one for the calculation of the self-supervised loss $\mathcal{L}_{ssl}$ and the other for the calculation of the loss term $\mathcal{L}_{cls}$ for classification in addition to knowledge distillation loss $\mathcal{L}_{kdl}$. The attention-wise knowledge distillation loss $\mathcal{L}_{attn}$ keeps each attention module stable. For simplicity, we omit the other network components, e.g., the classifier.

The CIL methods with knowledge distillation optimize parameters with the loss function defined as:

$$\mathcal{L}_{kd} = \beta_t^{cls}\mathcal{L}_{cls} + \beta_t^{kdl}\mathcal{L}_{kdl} + \mathcal{L}_{other} , \tag{1}$$

where $\mathcal{L}_{cls}$, $\mathcal{L}_{kdl}$, and $\mathcal{L}_{other}$ denote the loss terms for classification, knowledge distillation, and other purposes, respectively. In addition, β_t^{cls} and β_t^{kld} are the scalar values that control the impact of each loss term depending on the number of classes the model learned. The implementation of loss terms depends on individual CIL methods. For instance, UCIR [26] uses cross-entropy loss as the loss term $\mathcal{L}_{cls}$ and the cosine distance between output vectors of the previous and current feature extractors as the loss term $\mathcal{L}_{kdl}$. However, the fundamental purpose of the loss terms is the same; $\mathcal{L}_{cls}$ and $\mathcal{L}_{kdl}$ evaluate the classification performance of the current model and the dissimilarity between the current and previous models, respectively.

4   Methodology

Figure 1 shows an overview of our framework combined with CIL methods employing knowledge distillation. In our framework, the feature extractor outputs two kinds of feature vectors from an image. One vector derived through convolutional blocks (blue line in Fig. 1) is used for the calculation of the self-supervised loss $\mathcal{L}_{ssl}$. Through the optimization of the self-supervised loss, the parameters of convolutional blocks are updated to extract less task-oriented but more general features. The other vector (red line in Fig. 1) affected by attention modules is used for the calculation of the loss term for classification $\mathcal{L}_{cls}$. The

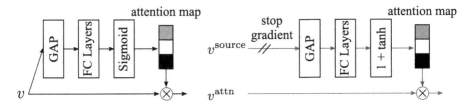

Fig. 2. The schemas of the original SE block (left) and our modified SE block (right). In our block, an attention map is generated from the intermediate feature vector v^{source} derived from the convolutional blocks. The attention map acts on the other intermediate feature vector v^{attn} derived from the convolutional blocks and attention modules.

optimization of the loss term $\mathcal{L}_{\text{cls}}$ enables the attention modules to transform general representations extracted by convolutional blocks into suitable ones for classification. Moreover, a new knowledge distillation loss $\mathcal{L}_{\text{attn}}$ improves the stability of our transformation mechanism. To sum up, our framework consists of three components: representation learning with self-supervision, the transformation mechanism with attention modules, and knowledge distillation for the transformation mechanism.

4.1 Representation Learning with Self-supervision

To encourage the model to acquire the general representation, we introduce the loss function used on SimSiam [14]. More specifically, for a training image x, we first generate two views of the image denoted as $\dot{x}$ and $\ddot{x}$ through random data augmentation. Then, we produce the two types of vectors for each view through the feature extractor f_t, the projector $proj_t$, and the predictor $pred_t$. More precisely, these vectors are denoted as $\dot{p} = (pred_t \circ proj_t \circ f_t)(\dot{x})$ and $\dot{q} = (proj_t \circ f_t)(\dot{x})$, respectively. Finally, we calculate $\mathcal{L}_{\text{ssl}}$ as below:

$$\mathcal{L}_{\text{ssl}} = \frac{1}{2}(\mathcal{D}_{\cos}(\dot{p}, \text{stopgrad}(\ddot{q})) + \mathcal{D}_{\cos}(\ddot{p}, \text{stopgrad}(\dot{q}))) , \qquad (2)$$

where stopgrad denotes the stop-gradient operation, and $\mathcal{D}_{\cos}(p, q)$ denotes the cosine distance between two vectors p and q. With the optimization of self-supervised loss $\mathcal{L}_{\text{ssl}}$, the parameters of the convolutional layers are updated so as to extract meaningful features from an image belonging to not only the learned classes but also the new upcoming classes.

4.2 Attention Module

Thanks to the optimization of self-supervised loss, the representations extracted from the convolutional layers are general. However, they definitely contain unrelated information to recognize the classes involved in the current and previous tasks. Thus, we introduce a transformation mechanism that weakens such unrelated information and strengthens the useful one for classification. We realize such transformation by introducing the attention module similar to the SE block [27]. As shown in Fig. 2, we change the original SE block with respect to the generation process of an attention map and the activation function. This modification is intended to mitigate the potential stability decrease caused by the attention modules, enable strengthening of information, and avoid unnecessary transformations.

The original SE block generates an attention map from an intermediate feature vector, so the attention map changes with the fluctuation of the intermediate vector even if the parameters of the SE block do not change while learning new tasks. In addition, the fluctuation of the intermediate vector further enlarges due to the multiplication with fluctuated attention map. Such property indicates that the fluctuation of parameters in a convolutional layer or an SE block could significantly fluctuate the final output vector even if the parameters of their succeeding layers do not change. We experimentally confirmed that SE-ResNet [27] was less stable than ResNet [24], which does not have any attention mechanism (as for the detailed experimental results, please see the supplementary materials). To mitigate the potential stability decrease, we use the intermediate feature vector derived through only convolutional blocks for the generation of the attention map. With this modification, the procedure to generate attention maps in our SE block is not affected by its proceeding attention modules. Additionally, we introduce a stop-gradient operation because this gradient could prevent the optimization with self-supervision.

We alter the activation function from sigmoid function to $1 + \tanh(\cdot)$. This altered function has two desirable properties which the sigmoid function does not have. First, the range of $1 + \tanh(\cdot)$ is from 0 to 2, so the attention module with our activation function can strengthen or weaken the values of intermediate feature vectors, while the one with a sigmoid function can only weaken the values. Second, the attention module with the activation function of $1 + \tanh(\cdot)$ becomes an identity mapping if all the values of its parameters are 0. Owing to this property, our attention modules can avoid generating unnecessary attention maps which lead to destructive transformations of general representations.

4.3   Knowledge Distillation for Attention Mechanism

Formally, the l-th attention module generates the attention map $a_t^l = 1 + \tanh(h_t^l(z_t^l))$ by applying the calculation on the FC layers h_t^l contained in the attention module to the pooled intermediate feature vector z_t^l. In addition, let $a_{t-1}^l = 1 + \tanh(h_{t-1}^l(z_{t-1}^l))$ be the attention map generated by the l-th attention module in the previous feature extractor, where h_{t-1}^l is its FC layers and z_{t-1}^l is the pooled intermediate feature vector derived from its preceding layers. To stabilize the process of generating attention maps, the input vector to each attention module should less fluctuate in addition to preserving the input-output relations defined by each attention module. More specifically, the pooled intermediate feature vector z_t^l should be close to the vector z_{t-1}^l derived through the previous feature extractor, and the l-th attention module should preserve its input-output relations. To achieve such preservation, we design the attention-wise knowledge distillation loss composed of two types of loss terms; one preserves the input-output relations, and the other prevents the fluctuation of the intermediate feature vectors.

We implement the loss term for the retention of the input-output relations as the weighted sum of the distances between the output attention maps generated by the current and previous attention modules from pooled intermediate feature vectors z_t^l and z_{t-1}^l. For the l-th attention module, we define the loss term as:

$$\mathcal{L}_{\text{attn}}^{\text{map},l} = \lambda_{\text{attn}}^{\text{map,new}} \mathcal{L}_{\text{attn}}^{\text{map,new},l} + \lambda_{\text{attn}}^{\text{map,old}} \mathcal{L}_{\text{attn}}^{\text{map,old},l} , \tag{3}$$

$$\mathcal{L}_{\text{attn}}^{\text{map,new},l} = \| \tanh(h_t^l(z_t^l)) - \tanh(h_{t-1}^l(z_t^l)) \|_2 , \tag{4}$$

$$\mathcal{L}_{\text{attn}}^{\text{map,old},l} = \| \tanh(h_t^l(z_{t-1}^l)) - \tanh(h_{t-1}^l(z_{t-1}^l)) \|_2 , \tag{5}$$

where $\lambda_{\text{attn}}^{\text{map,new}}$ and $\lambda_{\text{attn}}^{\text{map,old}}$ are the hyperparameters controlling the impact of each distance regularization.

To prevent the fluctuation of the intermediate feature vectors, we minimize the weighted distance between the intermediate feature vectors derived from the current and previous feature extractor. Formally, for the l-th attention module, we define the loss term as:

$$\mathcal{L}_{\text{attn}}^{\text{source},l} = \lambda_{\text{attn}}^{\text{source}} \hat{\omega}_l \left\| \overline{z_t^l} - \overline{z_{t-1}^l} \right\|_2 , \tag{6}$$

$$\hat{\omega}_l = \frac{\omega_l}{\sum_{j=1}^{L} \omega_j} , \tag{7}$$

where $\overline{z} = z/\|z\|_2$ denotes the l_2-normalized vector, L denotes the number of attention modules, $\lambda_{\text{attn}}^{\text{source}}$ is the hyperparameter controlling the impact of this loss term, and ω_l denotes the weighting factor. We consider the sensitivity to change in the values of the attention map with respect to change in the source vector as the weighting factor, which is calculated and updated when each task $\mathcal{T}_{t'}$ has been learned as:

$$\omega_l \leftarrow \frac{1}{2} \left(\omega_l + \mathbb{E}_{\mathcal{D}_{t'}} \left[\frac{1}{D^2} \sum_{d=1}^{D} \sum_{d'=1}^{D} \frac{\partial \tanh(h_{t'}^l(z_{t'}^l))_d^2}{\partial(z_{t'}^l)_{d'}} \right] \right) , \tag{8}$$

where D denotes the dimension of the source vector. With the introduction of this weighting factor, the fluctuation of the intermediate feature vector is highly prevented when it causes a large fluctuation of the corresponding attention map.

To sum up, we define the attention-wise knowledge distillation loss $\mathcal{L}_{attn}$ as:

$$\mathcal{L}_{\text{attn}} = \sum_{l=1}^{L} \mathcal{L}_{\text{attn}}^{\text{map},l} + \mathcal{L}_{\text{attn}}^{\text{source},l} . \tag{9}$$

4.4   Overall Loss

When the proposed framework is introduced to CIL methods with knowledge distillation, the loss function is defined as:

$$\mathcal{L} = \beta_t^{\text{cls}}(\alpha \mathcal{L}_{\text{cls}} + (1 - \alpha)\mathcal{L}_{\text{ssl}}) + \beta_t^{\text{kdl}}(\mathcal{L}_{\text{kdl}} + \mathcal{L}_{\text{attn}}) + \mathcal{L}_{\text{other}} , \tag{10}$$

where $\alpha \in [0, 1]$ is the hyperparameter that controls the balance between $\mathcal{L}_{\mathrm{cls}}$ and $\mathcal{L}_{\mathrm{ssl}}$. We note that the self-supervised loss $\mathcal{L}_{\mathrm{ssl}}$ is calculated from two views of an image generated by complex data augmentation techniques, while the others are calculated from another view generated by the other simple data augmentation techniques. The reason why we utilize these two types of data augmentation is that complex data augmentation is unsuitable for classification learning. We describe the entire learning process and learning tips in supplementary materials.

5 Experiments

5.1 Experimental Settings

Datasets and Task Configurations. We employed two image datasets for our experiments: CIFAR100 [33] and ImageNet100 [16, 26]. CIFAR100 contains 60,000 images of size 32×32 from 100 classes, and each class includes 500 training samples and 100 test samples. ImageNet100 is a subset of the original ImageNet1000 [16] with 100 classes randomly selected from the original one. According to the common CIL setting [47], the arrangement of all classes was shuffled with Numpy random seed 1993. We used the first 50 classes for the first task and the rest for subsequent tasks by dividing them into K sets. We constructed two kinds of CIL scenarios for each dataset by setting K to 5 and 10. Each CIL scenario is referred to as a K-phase setup.

Baselines. We used the following four knowledge distillation-based methods as baselines of our framework:

- IL-Baseline [30]: IL-Baseline optimizes the parameters of a model through the cross-entropy loss and the original knowledge distillation loss [25], which restricts the output probability of the model from moving.
- UCIR [26]: UCIR introduces cosine normalization in a classification layer to deal with the class-imbalance problem. Its implementation of knowledge distillation loss is the cosine similarity between the output vectors of the previous and current feature extractors.
- PODNet [18]: PODNet constrains the intermediate feature vectors of a feature extractor in addition to its output vector. In addition, it employs the local similarity classifier, which is the extended version of the classification layer used in UCIR.
- BSCE [30]: BSCE has the same learning procedure as IL-Baseline except for introducing the balanced softmax cross-entropy loss instead of the standard cross-entropy loss.

The detailed learning procedure of each baseline method is described in supplementary materials. We evaluated all of the methods through the average incremental accuracy (AIA) [47], defined as the average taken over accuracies of the model for test data after training for each task.

Table 1. Average incremental accuracy of four baselines *w/* and *w/o* our framework. Each result is in the form of the average ± standard deviation obtained from three independent trials using different random seeds. On ImageNet100, the scores of the baselines are reported from their respective papers.

Method	CIFAR100				ImageNet100			
	5-phase		10-phase		5-phase		10-phase	
IL-Baseline [30]	52.92	±0.15	43.14	±0.31	51.52		42.22	
w/ Ours	56.49	±0.20	48.13	±0.51	61.57	±0.05	59.13	±0.09
UCIR [26]	69.29	±0.15	63.16	±0.12	70.47		68.09	
w/ Ours	71.03	±0.28	66.24	±0.42	76.80	±0.08	76.06	±0.19
PODNet [18]	68.99	±0.36	66.64	±0.15	75.54		74.33	
w/ Ours	70.61	±0.12	69.02	±0.05	**78.05**	±0.19	**76.66**	±0.10
BSCE [30]	71.64	±0.16	64.87	±0.39	72.57		68.25	
w/ Ours	**74.09**	±0.24	**70.30**	±0.38	74.96	±0.39	72.32	±0.23

Implementation Details. We used ResNet18 [24] as the CNN backbone. Our attention modules were attached to residual blocks in a similar manner to the SE blocks [27]. In addition, we used the same architectures of the projector and predictor as the ones of SimSiam [14]. All parameters were optimized through stochastic gradient descent (SGD) with a momentum of 0.9. For the first task of CIFAR100, the network was trained with 400 epochs using a cosine learning rate decay for the base learning rate of 0.2 and weight decay of 5e-4. Then, it was further optimized using the remaining tasks one by one with 200 epochs per task. For ImageNet100, we set the number of epochs and the base learning rate to 150 and 0.2 for the first task. For the other tasks, the number of epochs was set to 90. We adopted 1e-4 as the weight decay for all the tasks of ImageNet100. For all the experiments, the batch size was set to 128, and the number of exemplars was set to 20 per class. The exemplars were sampled based on the herd selection method [47,52]. We employed the same data augmentation technique used in SimSiam for self-supervised learning, while using image flipping, random cropping, and color jittering for calculating the loss functions other than the self-supervised loss. Based on the hyperparameter tuning process in the existing work [10], we tuned the other hyperparameters through the three-task CIL setting constructed from the training data belonging to the first task. We describe the detailed hyperparameter tuning process and resulting hyperparameters in the supplementary materials.

5.2   Main Results

Table 1 shows the AIA of four baselines with and without our framework on CIFAR100 and ImageNet100. As shown in Table 1, our framework increases the AIA of all baselines on every dataset and setup. More precisely, the minimum increase of AIA is 1.62 points, and the maximum is 5.43 points on CIFAR100.

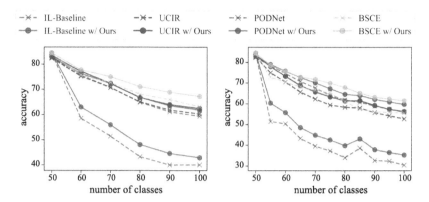

Fig. 3. The curve of accuracy over the classes on CIFAR100 (left: 5-phase, right: 10-phase). Each point indicates the average accuracy obtained from three independent trials using different random seeds.

Table 2. Three types of the average accuracies of BSCE with a part of our framework on CIFAR100 under the 5-phase setup. The first three columns indicate whether self-supervised learning, attention mechanism, and attention-wise knowledge distillation are introduced, respectively. Each result is in the form of the average ± standard deviation obtained from three independent trials using different random seeds.

SSL	AM	AwKD	AIA	Avg. Acc. (the first task)	Avg. Acc. (the new tasks)
			71.64 ±0.16	68.94 ±0.50	78.26 ±0.18
✓			71.76 ±0.53	68.68 ±1.02	76.78 ±0.21
	✓		70.34 ±0.14	66.30 ±0.43	**79.16** ±0.22
✓	✓		71.32 ±0.43	67.23 ±0.33	78.74 ±0.48
	✓	✓	72.54 ±0.51	73.11 ±0.45	72.48 ±1.17
✓	✓	✓	**74.09** ±0.24	**74.17** ±0.57	74.35 ±0.20

On ImageNet100, the increase of AIA is from 2.33 to 16.91 points. This common tendency of increase in AIA indicates the high flexibility of our framework. We also show the curve of accuracy over the classes on CIFAR100 in Fig. 3. As shown in Fig. 3, our framework consistently exceeds the accuracy of any baseline method. This result implies that the increase in AIA is not by chance.

5.3   Ablation Study

In this section, we present the results of several ablation experiments to clarify the effect of our framework. We report the AIA on CIFAR100 with the 5-phase setup in all the ablation experiments. Following the existing work [18], we use the average accuracy on the first task and the one on the new tasks as the additional evaluation metrics to analyze the effect of our framework in detail.

Table 3. Three types of the average accuracies on CIFAR100 with the 5-phase setup for different implementations of the transformation mechanism. "Original" means the implementation of the transformation mechanism is the original SE block, and "Ours" means the implementation is our modified SE block. The second column denotes whether attention-wise knowledge distillation is introduced. Note that all the methods optimize a model through the learning procedure of BSCE and self-supervision. Each result is in the form of the average ± standard deviation obtained from three independent trials using different random seeds.

AM	AwKD AIA		Avg. Acc. (the first task)	Avg. Acc. (the new tasks)
Original		$71.09_{\pm0.23}$	$67.13_{\pm0.50}$	$77.20_{\pm0.10}$
Ours		$71.32_{\pm0.43}$	$67.23_{\pm0.33}$	$78.74_{\pm0.48}$
Original	✓	$72.99_{\pm0.34}$	$72.98_{\pm0.66}$	$71.62_{\pm0.51}$
Ours	✓	$\mathbf{74.09}_{\pm0.24}$	$\mathbf{74.17}_{\pm0.57}$	$74.35_{\pm0.20}$

Intuitively, the former accuracy gets a high value if the model is stable without the influence of forgetting, while the latter gets high if the model is plastic enough to learn the new tasks. We give the definition of each additional metric in supplementary materials. The baseline method is BSCE because it shows the highest AIA on CIFAR100 with the 5-phase setup regardless of whether our framework is introduced.

First, we verify the effect of the components of our framework, namely, self-supervised learning, attention mechanism, and attention-wise knowledge distillation. Table 2 shows the scores of the three evaluation metrics for the six types of methods that differ with the existence of each component. We summarize the comparing results as follows:

- The results on the first two rows show that self-supervised learning only increases AIA slightly (71.64 to 71.76) when the self-supervised loss is simply added as with the existing work [57].
- From the comparison between the results on the first and third rows, we can confirm that the attention mechanism boosts the accuracy for the new tasks while decreasing the accuracy for the first task and AIA. The results on the second and fourth rows indicate that the same tendency appears when introducing self-supervised learning.
- Even if self-supervised learning is not introduced (the fifth row), its AIA is higher than the baseline (the first row), however, the difference is only 0.9 points because of the low accuracy for the new tasks.
- Our framework (the sixth row) increases the AIA of the baseline by 2.45 points by improving the accuracy for the first task while mitigating the decrease in the accuracy for the new tasks.

The above findings suggest that the increase of AIA with our framework results from the synergistic effect of the components, but not from an independent one of each component.

Table 4. Three types of average accuracies on CIFAR100 with the 5-phase setup for different implementation of attention-wise knowledge distillation when the baseline method is BSCE. In the first column, "None", "w/o weight", and "w/ weight" mean the loss term $\mathcal{L}_{\text{attn}}^{\text{source},l}$ is not introduced, introduced without weighting, and introduced with weighting, respectively. The second column denotes whether the loss term $\mathcal{L}_{\text{attn}}^{\text{map},l}$ is introduced. Each result is in the form of the average $\pm$ standard deviation obtained from three independent trials using different random seeds.

Source	Map	AIA	Avg. Acc. (the first task)	Avg. Acc. (the new tasks)
None		71.32 ± 0.43	67.23 ± 0.33	$\mathbf{78.74} \pm 0.48$
w/o weight		73.57 ± 0.35	73.99 ± 0.35	72.52 ± 0.35
w/ weight		73.68 ± 0.36	74.04 ± 0.47	72.61 ± 0.47
None	✓	71.46 ± 0.22	67.50 ± 0.32	78.09 ± 0.17
w/o weight	✓	73.84 ± 0.24	$\mathbf{74.31} \pm 0.18$	72.55 ± 0.46
w/ weight	✓	$\mathbf{74.09} \pm 0.24$	74.17 ± 0.57	74.35 ± 0.20

Next, we compare the original SE block [27] and our modified SE block to clarify the effect of our modification on the transformation mechanism. Table 3 shows the scores of the three evaluation metrics for the methods whose transformation mechanism is implemented by the original SE block or our modified SE block. Without attention-wise knowledge distillation (the first and second rows), AIA slightly increases (71.09 to 71.32) with our modification of the SE block. However, with attention-wise knowledge distillation (the last two rows), the increase of AIA by our modification becomes 1.10 points. In addition, the accuracy for the first task and the one for the new tasks both increase through the modification of the transformation mechanism. These results indicate that our modification only has a negligible impact on the performance of the model if the attention-wise knowledge distillation is not applied, however, the impact becomes relatively large when it is introduced.

Finally, we clarify the effect of the attention-wise knowledge distillation loss by the comparing results in Table 4. From the result on the first three rows, we can verify that the constraints on the input vector to the attention modules imposed by the loss term $\mathcal{L}_{\text{attn}}^{\text{source},l}$ increase AIA by improving the stability of a model, whether with or without weighting. The effect of weighting is very limited without the loss term $\mathcal{L}_{\text{attn}}^{\text{map},l}$. Similarly, the comparison between the results on the first and fourth rows shows that introducing the loss term $\mathcal{L}_{\text{attn}}^{\text{map},l}$ increases AIA by only 0.14 points when the loss term $\mathcal{L}_{\text{attn}}^{\text{source},l}$ is not employed. However, when the weighting and the loss term $\mathcal{L}_{\text{attn}}^{\text{map},l}$ are introduced (the sixth row), the accuracy for the new tasks is 2.17 points higher than the accuracy of the method employing only the loss term $\mathcal{L}_{\text{attn}}^{\text{source},l}$ without weighting (the second row). Thus, introducing the weighting and the loss term $\mathcal{L}_{\text{attn}}^{\text{map},l}$ is effective in improving the plasticity of a model. This is because they control the power of constraints for each attention module. In fact, the weighting procedure controls the power of the constraints on the input vector to each attention module. In

Table 5. Average incremental accuracy and the last accuracy (LA) of Co2L $w/$ and w/o our framework on CIFAR10 [33] with 200 exemplars. The experimental configurations are all the same as the ones described in the original paper [8]. Each result is in the form of the average $\pm$ standard deviation obtained from three independent trials using different random seeds.

Method	AIA	LA
Co2L	79.17 ± 0.15	64.46 ± 0.33
$w/$ Ours	**80.69** ± 0.21	**66.76** ± 0.79

addition, the constraints imposed by the loss term $\mathcal{L}_{\mathrm{attn}}^{\mathrm{map},l}$ affect the parameter of each attention module only when its input-output relation changes. Such selective constraint strongly regularizes a part of the parameters, which means the other parameters are relatively free to adapt to new tasks.

5.4 The Effect on Contrastive Learning Methods

To show the effect on the contrastive learning methods, we conducted the comparative experiment using Co2L [8] as the baseline method, which learned classification through the supervised contrastive loss. We followed the experimental settings reported in the original paper [8] on CIFAR10 [33] with 200 exemplars. Table 5 shows the results in AIA and the last accuracy (LA), the accuracy of a model having learned all the tasks. Note that we compare the methods in terms of LA because it is the evaluation metric in [8]. The experimental results show that our framework increases AIA by 1.52 points and LA by 2.3 points. This indicates that our framework can improve the performance of not only methods that learn classification with the cross-entropy loss but also those which learn it with supervised contrastive loss.

6   Conclusion

In this paper, we proposed a novel CIL framework that incorporates the representation learning with self-supervision, the transformation mechanism with attention modules, and the attention-wise knowledge distillation. We empirically confirmed our framework can improve the average incremental accuracy of four types of knowledge distillation-based methods using benchmark datasets. In addition, we showed that our framework can also improve the average incremental accuracy and the last accuracy of Co2L, a contrastive learning method. These results assure the high generality of our framework. For future work, we plan to verify the effect of our framework in the other continual learning scenarios, including the CIL scenario without any exemplar [53], few-shot CIL [51], and online continual learning [2].

Acknowledgement. This work was partially supported by JSPS KAKENHI Grant Number JP21J21785.

References

1. Ahn, H., Kwak, J., Lim, S., Bang, H., Kim, H., Moon, T.: SS-IL: separated softmax for incremental learning. In: ICCV, pp. 844–853 (2021)
2. Aljundi, R., Kelchtermans, K., Tuytelaars, T.: Task-free continual learning. In: CVPR, pp. 11254–11263 (2019)
3. Beaulieu, S., et al.: Learning to continually learn. arXiv preprint arXiv:2002.09571 (2020)
4. Belouadah, E., Popescu, A.: Scail: Classifier weights scaling for class incremental learning. In: WACV, pp. 1266–1275 (2020)
5. Belouadah, E., Popescu, A., Kanellos, I.: Initial classifier weights replay for memoryless class incremental learning. In: BMVC (2020)
6. Belouadah, E., Popescu, A., Kanellos, I.: A comprehensive study of class incremental learning algorithms for visual tasks. Neural Netw. **135**, 38–54 (2021)
7. Caron, M., Bojanowski, P., Joulin, A., Douze, M.: Deep clustering for unsupervised learning of visual features. In: ECCV, pp. 132–149 (2018)
8. Cha, H., Lee, J., Shin, J.: Co2l: contrastive continual learning. In: ICCV, pp. 9516–9525 (2021)
9. Chaudhry, A., Dokania, P.K., Ajanthan, T., Torr, P.H.: Riemannian walk for incremental learning: Understanding forgetting and intransigence. In: ECCV, pp. 532–547 (2018)
10. Chaudhry, A., Ranzato, M., Rohrbach, M., Elhoseiny, M.: Efficient lifelong learning with A-GEM. In: ICLR (2019)
11. Chaudhry, A., et al.: On tiny episodic memories in continual learning. arXiv preprint arXiv:1902.10486 (2019)
12. Chen, T., Kornblith, S., Norouzi, M., Hinton, G.: A simple framework for contrastive learning of visual representations. In: ICML, pp. 1597–1607 (2020)
13. Chen, X., Fan, H., Girshick, R., He, K.: Improved baselines with momentum contrastive learning. arXiv preprint arXiv:2003.04297 (2020)
14. Chen, X., He, K.: Exploring simple siamese representation learning. In: CVPR, pp. 15750–15758 (2021)
15. Chen, X., Xie, S., He, K.: An empirical study of training self-supervised vision transformers. In: ICCV, pp. 9640–9649 (2021)
16. Deng, J., Dong, W., Socher, R., Li, L.J., Li, K., Fei-Fei, L.: ImageNet: a large-scale hierarchical image database. In: CVPR, pp. 248–255 (2009)
17. Dosovitskiy, A., et al.: An image is worth 16×16 words: transformers for image recognition at scale. In: ICLR (2020)
18. Douillard, A., Cord, M., Ollion, C., Robert, T., Valle, E.: PodNet: pooled outputs distillation for small-tasks incremental learning. In: ECCV, pp. 86–102 (2020)
19. Finn, C., Abbeel, P., Levine, S.: Model-agnostic meta-learning for fast adaptation of deep networks. In: ICML, pp. 1126–1135 (2017)
20. Gallardo, G.J., Hayes, T.L., Kanan, C.: Self-supervised training enhances online continual learning. In: BMVC (2021)
21. Gidaris, S., Singh, P., Komodakis, N.: Unsupervised representation learning by predicting image rotations. In: ICLR (2018)
22. Grill, J.B., et al.: Bootstrap your own latent - a new approach to self-supervised learning. In: NeurIPS, vol. 33, pp. 21271–21284 (2020)
23. He, K., Fan, H., Wu, Y., Xie, S., Girshick, R.: Momentum contrast for unsupervised visual representation learning. In: CVPR, pp. 9729–9738 (2020)

24. He, K., Zhang, X., Ren, S., Sun, J.: Deep residual learning for image recognition. In: CVPR, pp. 770–778 (2016)
25. Hinton, G., Vinyals, O., Dean, J.: Distilling the knowledge in a neural network. arXiv preprint arXiv:1503.02531 (2015)
26. Hou, S., Pan, X., Loy, C.C., Wang, Z., Lin, D.: Learning a unified classifier incrementally via rebalancing. In: CVPR, pp. 831–839 (2019)
27. Hu, J., Shen, L., Sun, G.: Squeeze-and-excitation networks. In: CVPR, pp. 7132–7141 (2018)
28. Javed, K., White, M.: Meta-learning representations for continual learning. In: NeurIPS, vol. 32 (2019)
29. Ji, Z., Li, J., Wang, Q., Zhang, Z.: Complementary calibration: boosting general continual learning with collaborative distillation and self-supervision. arXiv preprint arXiv:2109.02426 (2021)
30. Jodelet, Q., Liu, X., Murata, T.: Balanced softmax cross-entropy for incremental learning. In: ICANN, vol. 12892, pp. 385–396 (2021)
31. Khosla, P., et al.: Supervised contrastive learning. In: NeurIPS, vol. 33, pp. 18661–18673 (2020)
32. Kirkpatrick, J., et al.: Overcoming catastrophic forgetting in neural networks. Proc. National Acad. Sci. **114**(13), 3521–3526 (2017)
33. Krizhevsky, A.: Learning multiple layers of features from tiny images. University of Toronto, Tech. rep. (2009)
34. Kurmi, V.K., Patro, B.N., Subramanian, V.K., Namboodiri, V.P.: Do not forget to attend to uncertainty while mitigating catastrophic forgetting. In: WACV, pp. 736–745 (2021)
35. Li, Z., Hoiem, D.: Learning without forgetting. IEEE TPAMI **40**(12), 2935–2947 (2017)
36. Liu, X., Zhang, F., Hou, Z., et al.: Self-supervised learning: generative or contrastive. IEEE TKDE (2021). https://doi.org/10.1109/TKDE.2021.3090866
37. Mai, Z., Li, R., Kim, H., Sanner, S.: Supervised contrastive replay: revisiting the nearest class mean classifier in online class-incremental continual learning. In: CVPR, pp. 3589–3599 (2021)
38. Masana, M., Liu, X., Twardowski, B., Menta, M., Bagdanov, A.D., van de Weijer, J.: Class-incremental learning: survey and performance evaluation on image classification. arXiv preprint arXiv:2010.15277 (2020)
39. McCloskey, M., Cohen, N.J.: Catastrophic interference in connectionist networks: the sequential learning problem. In: Psychology of learning and motivation, vol. 24, pp. 109–165. Elsevier (1989)
40. Mermillod, M., Bugaiska, A., Bonin, P.: The stability-plasticity dilemma: investigating the continuum from catastrophic forgetting to age-limited learning effects. Front. Psychol. **4**, 504 (2013)
41. Mittal, S., Galesso, S., Brox, T.: Essentials for class incremental learning. In: CVPR, pp. 3513–3522 (2021)
42. Ni, Z., Shi, H., Tang, S., Zhuang, Y.: Alleviate representation overlapping in class incremental learning by contrastive class concentration. arXiv preprint arXiv:2107.12308 (2021)
43. Noroozi, M., Favaro, P.: Unsupervised learning of visual representations by solving jigsaw puzzles. In: ECCV, pp. 69–84 (2016)
44. Pei, W., Mayer, A., Tu, K., Yue, C.: Attention please: your attention check questions in survey studies can be automatically answered. In: WWW, pp. 1182–1193 (2020)

45. Pham, Q., Liu, C., Hoi, S.: DualNet: continual learning, fast and slow. In: NeurIPS, vol. 34, pp. 16131–16144 (2021)
46. Rajasegaran, J., Khan, S., Hayat, M., Khan, F.S., Shah, M.: iTAML: an incremental task-agnostic meta-learning approach. In: CVPR, pp. 13588–13597 (2020)
47. Rebuffi, S.A., Kolesnikov, A., Sperl, G., Lampert, C.H.: iCARL: incremental classifier and representation learning. In: CVPR, pp. 2001–2010 (2017)
48. Simon, C., Koniusz, P., Harandi, M.: On learning the geodesic path for incremental learning. In: CVPR, pp. 1591–1600 (2021)
49. Simonyan, K., Zisserman, A.: Very deep convolutional networks for large-scale image recognition. In: ICLR (2015)
50. Tao, X., Chang, X., Hong, X., Wei, X., Gong, Y.: Topology-preserving class-incremental learning. In: ECCV, pp. 254–270 (2020)
51. Tao, X., Hong, X., Chang, X., Dong, S., Wei, X., Gong, Y.: Few-shot class-incremental learning. In: CVPR, pp. 12183–12192 (2020)
52. Welling, M.: Herding dynamical weights to learn. In: ICML, pp. 1121–1128 (2009)
53. Wu, G., Gong, S., Li, P.: Striking a balance between stability and plasticity for class-incremental learning. In: ICCV, pp. 1124–1133 (2021)
54. Wu, Y., et al.: Large scale incremental learning. In: CVPR, pp. 374–382 (2019)
55. Zbontar, J., Jing, L., Misra, I., LeCun, Y., Deny, S.: Barlow twins: self-supervised learning via redundancy reduction. In: ICML, pp. 12310–12320 (2021)
56. Zhang, R., Isola, P., Efros, A.A.: Colorful image colorization. In: ECCV, pp. 649–666 (2016)
57. Zhang, S., Shen, G., Huang, J., Deng, Z.H.: Self-supervised learning aided class-incremental lifelong learning. arXiv preprint arXiv:2006.05882 (2020)
58. Zhao, B., Xiao, X., Gan, G., Zhang, B., Xia, S.T.: Maintaining discrimination and fairness in class incremental learning. In: CVPR, pp. 13208–13217 (2020)
59. Zhu, F., Zhang, X.Y., Wang, C., Yin, F., Liu, C.L.: Prototype augmentation and self-supervision for incremental learning. In: CVPR, pp. 5871–5880 (2021)

Exploring Adversarially Robust Training for Unsupervised Domain Adaptation

Shao-Yuan Lo$^{(\boxtimes)}$ and Vishal M. Patel

Department of Electrical and Computer Engineering, Johns Hopkins University,
Baltimore, USA
{sylo,vpatel36}@jhu.edu

Abstract. Unsupervised Domain Adaptation (UDA) methods aim to transfer knowledge from a labeled source domain to an unlabeled target domain. UDA has been extensively studied in the computer vision literature. Deep networks have been shown to be vulnerable to adversarial attacks. However, very little focus is devoted to improving the adversarial robustness of deep UDA models, causing serious concerns about model reliability. Adversarial Training (AT) has been considered to be the most successful adversarial defense approach. Nevertheless, conventional AT requires ground-truth labels to generate adversarial examples and train models, which limits its effectiveness in the unlabeled target domain. In this paper, we aim to explore AT to robustify UDA models: How to enhance the unlabeled data robustness via AT while learning domain-invariant features for UDA? To answer this question, we provide a systematic study into multiple AT variants that can potentially be applied to UDA. Moreover, we propose a novel Adversarially Robust Training method for UDA accordingly, referred to as ARTUDA. Extensive experiments on multiple adversarial attacks and UDA benchmarks show that ARTUDA consistently improves the adversarial robustness of UDA models. Code is available at https://github.com/shaoyuanlo/ARTUDA.

1 Introduction

Recent advances in image recognition have enjoyed remarkable success via deep supervised learning [12,17,41]. However, the domain shift problem is very common in real-world applications, *i.e.*, source and target domains have different data characteristics. Furthermore, it is costly and labor-intensive to collect the ground-truth labels of target data. To address this issue, Unsupervised Domain Adaptation (UDA) methods have been developed in which the objective is to transfer the knowledge from a labeled source dataset to an unlabeled target dataset. Most existing UDA approaches rely on minimizing distribution discrepancy between source and target domains to learn domain-invariant representations [7,8,22–24,34]. Although these approaches achieve impressive performance, they do not consider the robustness against adversarial attacks [3,32], which causes critical concerns.

Supplementary Information The online version contains supplementary material available at https://doi.org/10.1007/978-3-031-26351-4_34.

L. Wang et al. (Eds.): ACCV 2022, LNCS 13846, pp. 561–577, 2023.
https://doi.org/10.1007/978-3-031-26351-4_34

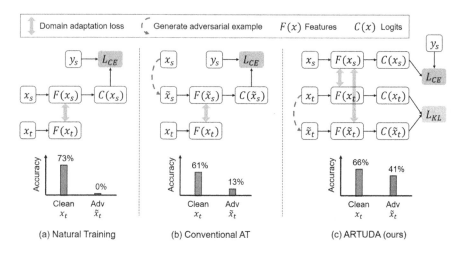

Fig. 1. Overview of the proposed ARTUDA and its importance. L_{CE}: Cross-entropy loss. L_{KL}: KL divergence loss. Compared to conventional AT [26], ARTUDA significantly improves adversarial robustness while maintaining decent clean accuracy. We use DANN [8] with ResNet-50 [12] backbone, the VisDA-2017 [29] dataset, and the PGD-20 [26] attack for this experiment.

Adversarial attacks pose serious security risks to deep networks. In other words, deep networks could suffer from dramatic performance degradation in the presence of carefully crafted perturbations. To defend against adversarial attacks, various defense mechanisms have been proposed [10,11,16,20,26,30,42]. Currently, Adversarial Training (AT) based defenses [10,16,26,42] have been considered the most effective, especially under the white-box setting [1]. The core idea is to train a model on adversarial examples that are generated on the fly according to the model's current parameters. Nevertheless, conventional AT requires ground-truth labels to generate adversarial examples. This makes it not applicable to the UDA problem since UDA considers the scenario that label information is unavailable to a target domain. A nearly contemporary work [2] resorts to external adversarially pre-trained ImageNet models as teacher models to distill robustness knowledge. However, its performance is highly sensitive to the teacher models' perturbation budget, architecture, *etc.*, which limits the flexibility in a wide range of uses. Another very recent work [40] uses an external pre-trained UDA model to produce pseudo labels for doing AT on target data. Unfortunately, we show that it suffers from suboptimal accuracy and robustness against white-box attacks.

Given the above observations, intuitive questions emerge: *Can we develop an AT algorithm specifically for the UDA problem? How to improve the unlabeled data robustness via AT while learning domain-invariant features for UDA?* In this paper, we seek to answer these questions by systematically studying multiple AT variants that can potentially be applied to UDA. First, we apply a conventional AT [26] to an UDA model to see its effectiveness. In other words, the AT is performed on only the labeled source data. Second, inspired by [16,42], we attempt to train models by minimizing the difference between the output logits of clean target data and the corresponding adversarial examples. With this, we can conduct a kind of AT directly on the target data in a self-supervised manner. We call it *Self-Supervised Adversarial Training* or *Self-Supervised AT*. Next, we look into the effects of clean images and adversarial examples in the AT for UDA. We present the trade-off behind different AT variants. Last, we observe that Batch Normalization (BN) [13] plays an important role in the AT for UDA. The feature statistic estimations at training time would affect an UDA model's robustness.

Through these investigations, we propose a novel Adversarially Robust Training method for UDA accordingly, referred to as ARTUDA. It uses both source and target data for training and does not require target domain labels, so it is feasible for UDA. Moreover, it does not need guidance from external models such as adversarially pre-trained models and pre-trained UDA models. Figure 1 illustrates an overview and the importance of the proposed ARTUDA. The naturally trained (*i.e.*, train with only clean data) model's accuracy decreases to 0% under an adversarial attack. Conventional AT [26] improves robust accuracy to 13% but sacrifices clean accuracy. As can be seen, ARTUDA significantly increases robust accuracy to 41% while maintaining better clean accuracy. This shows that our method can improve unlabeled data robustness and learn domain-invariant features simultaneously for UDA. To the best of our knowledge, ARTUDA is the first AT-based UDA defense that is robust against white-box attacks. In Sect. 5, we extensively evaluate ARTUDA on five adversarial attacks, three datasets and three different UDA algorithms. The results demonstrate its wide range of effectiveness.

Our main contributions can be summarized as follows: (i) We provide a systematic study into various AT methods that are suitable for UDA. We believe that such experimental analysis would provide useful insight into this relatively unexplored research direction. (ii) We propose ARTUDA, a new AT method specifically designed for UDA. To the best of our knowledge, it is the first AT-based UDA defense method that is robust against white-box attacks. (iii) Comprehensive experiments show that ARTUDA consistently improves UDA models' adversarial robustness under multiple attacks and datasets.

2   Related Work

Unsupervised Domain Adaptation. UDA considers the scenario that a source dataset contains images with category labels, while label information is unavailable to a target dataset. Most popular approaches attempt to transfer knowledge from the labeled source domain to the unlabeled target domain [7,8,22–24,34]. DANN [8] proposes to use a domain discriminator that distinguishes between source and target features, and the feature extractor is trained to fool it via GAN [9] learning scheme. ADDA [34] combines DANN with discriminative feature learning. CDAN [23] extends DANN using a class-conditional adversarial game. JAN [24] aligns the joint distributions of domain-specific layers between two domains. Nevertheless, these works do not take adversarial robustness into consideration.

RFA [2] and ASSUDA [40] are the most related works in the literature, which are nearly contemporary with our work. They are the first to focus on UDA's adversarial robustness, but we would like to point out the clear differences from our work. RFA leverages external adversarially pre-trained ImageNet models as teacher models to distill robustness knowledge. Its performance is highly sensitive to the teacher models' setup, such as perturbation budget, architecture and the number of teachers. AT on ImageNet is very expensive, so it is not always easy to obtain the preferred teacher models. In contrast, we propose a method that directly performs AT on a given UDA task, enjoying maximum flexibility. ASSUDA aims at semantic segmentation and considers only weak black-box attacks. It employs an external pre-trained UDA model to produce pseudo labels for target data, then uses the pseudo labels to do AT. However, we show that this approach has suboptimal accuracy and robustness against white-box attacks. In contrast, our method is robust under both black-box and white-box settings.

Adversarial Attack and Defense. Previous studies reveal that deep networks are vulnerable to adversarial examples [3,32]. Many adversarial attack algorithms have been proposed, such as Fast Gradient Sign Method (FGSM) [10], Projected Gradient Descent (PGD) [26], Momentum Iterative FGSM (MI-FGSM) [6] and Multiplicative Adversarial Example (MultAdv) [21].

Various adversarial defense mechanisms have also been introduced, where AT-based defenses [10,16,26,42] are considered the most effective, especially under the white-box setting [1]. AT trains a model on adversarial examples that are generated on the fly according to the model's current parameters. The most commonly used AT approaches include Madry's AT scheme (PGD-AT) [26] and TRADES [42]. PGD-AT formulates AT as a min-max optimization problem and trains a model with only adversarial examples. TRADES minimizes a regularized surrogate loss to obtain a better trade-off between robustness and performance, where both clean data and adversarial examples are used for training. However, AT requires the labels of input images to generate the corresponding adversarial examples, which can not be directly applied to the UDA problem. In this work, we propose a new AT method specifically designed for UDA.

3   Preliminary

UDA. Given a labeled source dataset $\mathbb{D}_s = \{(x_s^i, y_s^i)\}_{i=1}^{n_s}$ and an unlabeled target dataset $\mathbb{D}_t = \{x_t^i\}_{i=1}^{n_t}$ with n_s and n_t number of samples, respectively, a typical UDA model learns a feature extractor F and a classifier C on top of F. Given an input image x, we express its feature space representation as $F(x)$ and its output logits as $C(x)$, where we use $C(x)$ as a simplification of the formal expression $C(F(x))$. The objective function of an UDA model can be written as:

$$\mathcal{L}_{CE}\big(C(x_s), y_s\big) + \mathcal{L}_{DA}\big(x_s, x_t\big), \tag{1}$$

where $\mathcal{L}_{CE}$ is the standard cross-entropy loss, and $\mathcal{L}_{DA}$ is the domain adaptation loss defined by each UDA approach. One of the most common $\mathcal{L}_{DA}$ is the adversarial loss introduced by DANN [8], which is defined as:

$$\mathcal{L}_{DA}(x_s, x_t) = \mathbb{E}[log D(F(x_s))] + \mathbb{E}[1 - (log D(F(x_t)))], \tag{2}$$

where D is a domain discriminator used to encourage domain-invariant features.

AT. PGD-AT [26] is one of the most commonly-used AT algorithm. It formulates AT as a min-max optimization problem and trains models on adversarial examples exclusively:

$$\min_{F,C} \mathbb{E}\left[\max_{\|\delta\|_p \leq \epsilon} \mathcal{L}(C(\tilde{x}), y)\right], \tag{3}$$

where $\tilde{x} = x + \delta$ is the generated adversarial example of x, and ϵ denotes an L_p-norm perturbation budget. Here, δ corresponds to the adversarial noise which is added to x to make it adversarial. For image classification tasks, $\mathcal{L}$ is the cross-entropy loss $\mathcal{L}_{CE}$. PGD [26] is the most widely-used attack approaches. It generates $\tilde{x}$ in an iterative way:

$$x^{j+1} = \Pi_{\|\delta\|_p \leq \epsilon}\left(x^j + \alpha \cdot sign(\nabla_{x^j}\mathcal{L}(C(x^j), y))\right); \tag{4}$$

and $\tilde{x} = x^{j_{max}}$, where j_{max} denotes the maximum number of attack iterations. FGSM [10] can be treated as a single-step and non-random start version of PGD.

4   Exploring at for UDA

In this section, we systematically study multiple variants of AT to explore suitable AT methods for UDA. Then we finalize the proposed ARTUDA accordingly. Here we conduct a set of experiments on the VisDA-2017 [29] dataset. We employ DANN [8] as the UDA algorithm with ResNet-50 [12] backbone. The white-box FGSM [10] attack with perturbation budget of $\epsilon = 3$ is used for both AT and testing. Following the practice of [2,40], we assume that attackers have the labels of the target dataset to generate adversarial examples. The rationale behind these settings is that (i) most existing UDA approaches [23,34] are based on DANN's key idea, so DANN is a fair representative; (ii) the white-box threat model is the strongest attack setting, which has been considered a standard evaluation protocol for defenses [1,26,39,42].

4.1   Conventional at on UDA

We start with applying a conventional AT [26] to DANN to see its effectiveness. That is, the AT is performed on only the labeled source data, *i.e.*, apply Eq. (3) on source dataset $\mathbb{D}_s$. Therefore, the objective of the DANN model becomes:

$$\mathcal{L}_{CE}(C(\tilde{x}_s), y_s) + \mathcal{L}_{DA}(\tilde{x}_s, x_t). \tag{5}$$

Table 1. Results (%) of Conventional AT and our Self-Supervised AT on the VisDA-2017 dataset.

Training method	Clean	FGSM
Natural Training	73.2	21.2
Conventional AT [26]	62.9 (−10.3)	27.1 (+5.9)
Pseudo Labeling	33.1 (−40.1)	27.1 (+5.9)
Self-Supervised AT-L1	56.2 (−17.0)	15.8 (−5.4)
Self-Supervised AT-L2	51.3 (−21.9)	26.0 (+4.8)
Self-Supervised AT-KL	67.1 (**−6.1**)	**35.0 (+13.8)**

It is reasonable to expect that Conventional AT cannot fully benefit target domain robustness, as source domain robustness may not perfectly transfer to the target domain due to domain shift. As reported in Table 1, compared to the Natural Training baseline (*i.e.*, train with only clean data), Conventional AT indeed improves robustness to a certain extent but is not significant. Also, the clean accuracy is largely decreased. Hence, we argue that applying AT directly on the target data is important.

A naive way of applying AT on the target data is to produce pseudo labels y'_t using an external pre-trained UDA model. ASSUDA [40] resorts to this idea and applies it to the UDA semantic segmentation problem. Note that ASSUDA only evaluates black-box robustness. Here we implement the *Pseudo Labeling* idea on image classification and observe its white-box robustness. We use a naturally trained DANN as the pseudo labeler. The objective of Pseudo Labeling approach is as follows:

$$\mathcal{L}_{CE}\big(C(x_s), y_s\big) + \mathcal{L}_{CE}\big(C(\tilde{x}_t), y'_t\big) + \mathcal{L}_{DA}\big(x_s, \tilde{x}_t\big). \tag{6}$$

In Table 1, we find that Pseudo Labeling's robustness is not better than Conventional AT, and the clean accuracy drops dramatically. We believe that the label noise problem is inevitable in pseudo labels y'_t and limits model performance. This motivates us to explore a new AT method that can be directly performed on the target domain.

4.2 Self-supervised AT

Inspired by [16,42], we seek to use clean target data's logits $C(x_t)$ as a self-supervision signal to generate adversarial examples $\tilde{x}_t$. Based on the min-max optimization for AT [26], we generate $\tilde{x}_t$ by maximizing the difference between $C(x_t)$ and $C(\tilde{x}_t)$, and minimize that difference to train a model. With this idea, we can generate adversarial examples via self-supervision and perform a kind of AT for the target domain. We call it *Self-Supervised Adversarial Training* or *Self-Supervised AT*. In other words, to generate $\tilde{x}_t$, Self-Supervised AT changes Eq. (4) to:

$$x_t^{j+1} = \Pi_{\|\delta\|_p \le \epsilon} \left(x_t^j + \alpha \cdot sign(\nabla_{x_t^j} \mathcal{L}(C(x_t^j), C(x_t))) \right), \tag{7}$$

Table 2. Results (%) of SS-AT variants on VisDA-2017. (x_s, x_t) denotes $\mathcal{L}_{DA}(x_s, x_t)$. •: selected. —: not applicable.

Training method	x_s	$\tilde{x}_s$	x_t	$\tilde{x}_t$	(x_s,x_t)	$(x_s,\tilde{x}_t)$	$(\tilde{x}_s,x_t)$	$(\tilde{x}_s,\tilde{x}_t)$	Clean	FGSM
Natural Training	•		•		•	—	—	—	73.2	21.2
Conventional AT [26]		•	•		—	—	•	—	62.9	27.1
SS-AT-KL	•			•	—	•	—	—	67.1	35.0
SS-AT-s-t-$\tilde{t}$-1	•		•	•	•	—	—		67.3	27.5
SS-AT-s-t-$\tilde{t}$-2	•		•	•	•	•	—	—	73.0	39.4
SS-AT-s-$\tilde{s}$-t-$\tilde{t}$-1	•	•	•	•	•			•	63.4	41.6
SS-AT-s-$\tilde{s}$-t-$\tilde{t}$-2	•	•	•	•		•	•		62.8	42.3
SS-AT-s-$\tilde{s}$-t-$\tilde{t}$-3	•	•	•	•	•	•	•	•	61.3	41.6

and $\tilde{x}_t = x_t^{j_{max}}$. To adversarially train an UDA model, Self-Supervised AT changes Eq. (3) to:

$$\min_{F,C} \mathbb{E} \left[\max_{\|\delta\|_p \le \epsilon} \mathcal{L}\big(C(\tilde{x}_t), C(x_t)\big) \right]. \tag{8}$$

$\mathcal{L}$ is a loss function that encourages the logits to be similar. Possible choices include L1 loss, L2 loss, Kullback-Leibler (KL) divergence loss, *etc.* Taking KL divergence loss as an example, the objective of Self-Supervised AT for UDA can be written as follows:

$$\mathcal{L}_{CE}\big(C(x_s), y_s\big) + \mathcal{L}_{KL}\big(C(\tilde{x}_t), C([x_t]_{sg})\big) + \mathcal{L}_{DA}\big(x_s, \tilde{x}_t\big), \tag{9}$$

where $[\cdot]_{sg}$ denotes the stop-gradient operator [35] constraining its operand to be a non-updated constant. We do not expect that Self-Supervised AT is as robust as conventional supervised AT since the ground-truth labels y are always the strongest supervision. However, given that target domain labels y_t are unavailable, we believe that the clean logits $C(x_t)$ could be a good self-supervision signal.

Table 1 shows that Self-Supervised AT-L1 and Self-Supervised AT-L2 are not effective, while Self-Supervised AT-KL achieves excellent results. Self-Supervised AT-KL increases robust accuracy over Natural Training by 13.8%, which is much better than Conventional AT. It also maintains decent clean accuracy. These results demonstrate that our Self-Supervised AT strategy is effective, but the choice of the loss function is critical, where KL divergence loss is the preferred one.

4.3 On the Effects of Clean and Adversarial Examples in Self-supervised AT

Let us revisit the results of the last experiment from another perspective. We observe a trade-off between clean performance and robustness, and the upper part of Table 2 illustrates this point more clearly. Specifically, from Natural

Training and Conventional AT, we can see that replacing clean images x_s by adversarial examples $\tilde{x}_s$ increases robust accuracy but decreases clean accuracy. A similar trade-off can be found between Natural Training and Self-Supervised AT-KL, which train with x_t and $\tilde{x}_t$, respectively. This interests us to further investigate the usage of the four data types $\{x_s, \tilde{x}_s, x_t, \tilde{x}_t\}$ in the AT for UDA. Self-Supervised AT-KL outperforms Conventional AT in terms of both clean and robust accuracies, indicating that using $\tilde{x}_t$ is more efficient than $\tilde{x}_s$, so we start with Self-Supervised AT-KL as a baseline.

First, we add x_t to Self-Supervised AT-KL. This turn out SSAT-s-t-$\tilde{t}$-1 and SSAT-s-t-$\tilde{t}$-2, where SSAT-s-t-$\tilde{t}$-1's domain adaptation loss is $\mathcal{L}_{DA}(x_s, x_t)$, while SSAT-s-t-$\tilde{t}$-2 involves another term and becomes $\mathcal{L}_{DA}(x_s, x_t) + \mathcal{L}_{DA}(x_s, \tilde{x}_t)$. In other words, SSAT-s-t-$\tilde{t}$-1 explicitly transfers the supervised knowledge from x_s to only x_t, while SSAT-s-t-$\tilde{t}$-2 transfers to both x_t and $\tilde{x}_t$. We expect that SSAT-s-t-$\tilde{t}$-1 and SSAT-s-t-$\tilde{t}$-2 enjoy higher clean accuracy than Self-Supervised AT-KL because they involve x_t.

The lower part of Table 2 reports the results. We find that SSAT-s-t-$\tilde{t}$-1's robust accuracy drops significantly, but the clean accuracy does not improve much. In contrast, SSAT-s-t-$\tilde{t}$-2 largely increases both clean and robust accuracies by 5.9% and 4.4%, respectively. The improvement of clean performance matches our expectations, but we are surprised at that of robustness. We see this is due to our Self-Supervised AT's specific property. Self-Supervised AT leverages the objective $\mathcal{L}_{KL}\big(C(\tilde{x}_t), C(x_t)\big)$ to do AT, so $C(x_t)$'s quality is critical. Given that the labels y_t is unavailable, $\mathcal{L}_{DA}(x_s, x_t)$ can transfer the supervised knowledge to x_t and thus enhance $C(x_t)$'s quality. Therefore, adding x_t to Self-Supervised AT benefits robustness as well. This observation is different from the conventional supervised AT that exists the trade-off between performance and robustness [33, 39, 42]. We conclude that involving x_t into training does help, but an explicit supervised knowledge transfer to $\tilde{x}_t$ is needed. This is rational since $\tilde{x}_t$ plays the most important role in Self-Supervised AT, giving firm guidance to it is essential.

Second, we look into the effects of $\tilde{x}_s$ in Self-Supervised AT. We add $\tilde{x}_s$ and study three variants: SSAT-s-$\tilde{s}$-t-$\tilde{t}$-1, SSAT-s-$\tilde{s}$-t-$\tilde{t}$-2 and SSAT-s-$\tilde{s}$-t-$\tilde{t}$-3. Their differences are in their domain adaptation loss, which is also illustrated in Table 2. Intuitively, we expect that adding $\tilde{x}_s$ falls into the trade-off that leads to lower clean performance but better robustness, as $\tilde{x}_s$ is the conventional supervised adversarial example.

As shown in Table 2, all the three variants obtain lower clean accuracy and higher robust accuracy than SSAT-s-t-$\tilde{t}$-1 and SSAT-s-t-$\tilde{t}$-2, which matches our assumption. The results among these three are very close. Compared to SSAT-s-t-$\tilde{t}$-2, their clean accuracy drops 9.6%–11.7%, but robust accuracy only improves 2.2%–2.9%. This is consistent with Conventional AT's result, *i.e.*, source domain robustness is not easy to transfer to the target domain. Because training without $\tilde{x}_s$ achieves a better trade-off between performance and robustness, we use SSAT-s-t-$\tilde{t}$-2 as a baseline for the next investigation. To present our experiments more clear, in the following, we summarize the objective functions of each Self-Supervised AT variant discussed in this part:

– SSAT-s-t-$\tilde{t}$-1:

$$\mathcal{L}_{CE}\big(C(x_s), y_s\big) + \mathcal{L}_{KL}\big(C(\tilde{x}_t), C([x_t]_{sg})\big) + \mathcal{L}_{DA}\big(x_s, x_t\big). \tag{10}$$

– SSAT-s-t-$\tilde{t}$-2:

$$\begin{aligned}
&\mathcal{L}_{CE}\big(C(x_s), y_s\big) + \mathcal{L}_{KL}\big(C(\tilde{x}_t), C([x_t]_{sg})\big) \\
&+ \mathcal{L}_{DA}\big(x_s, x_t\big) + \mathcal{L}_{DA}\big(x_s, \tilde{x}_t\big).
\end{aligned} \tag{11}$$

– SSAT-s-$\tilde{s}$-t-$\tilde{t}$-1:

$$\begin{aligned}
&\mathcal{L}_{CE}\big(C(x_s), y_s\big) + \mathcal{L}_{KL}\big(C(\tilde{x}_t), C([x_t]_{sg})\big) \\
&+ \mathcal{L}_{CE}\big(C(\tilde{x}_s), y_s\big) + \mathcal{L}_{DA}\big(x_s, x_t\big) + \mathcal{L}_{DA}\big(\tilde{x}_s, \tilde{x}_t\big).
\end{aligned} \tag{12}$$

– SSAT-s-$\tilde{s}$-t-$\tilde{t}$-2:

$$\begin{aligned}
&\mathcal{L}_{CE}\big(C(x_s), y_s\big) + \mathcal{L}_{KL}\big(C(\tilde{x}_t), C([x_t]_{sg})\big) \\
&+ \mathcal{L}_{CE}\big(C(\tilde{x}_s), y_s\big) + \mathcal{L}_{DA}\big(x_s, \tilde{x}_t\big) + \mathcal{L}_{DA}\big(\tilde{x}_s, x_t\big).
\end{aligned} \tag{13}$$

– SSAT-s-s-'t-$\tilde{t}$-3:

$$\begin{aligned}
&\mathcal{L}_{CE}\big(C(x_s), y_s\big) + \mathcal{L}_{KL}\big(C(\tilde{x}_t), C([x_t]_{sg})\big) + \mathcal{L}_{CE}\big(C(\tilde{x}_s), y_s\big) \\
&+ \mathcal{L}_{DA}\big(x_s, x_t\big) + \mathcal{L}_{DA}\big(x_s, \tilde{x}_t\big) + \mathcal{L}_{DA}\big(\tilde{x}_s, x_t\big) + \mathcal{L}_{DA}\big(\tilde{x}_s, \tilde{x}_t\big).
\end{aligned} \tag{14}$$

4.4   On the Effects of BN in Self-supervised AT

It has been well-known that the statistic estimation of BN [13] plays an important role in both the UDA [4,18] and the adversarial machine learning [19,37,39] fields. It is worth investigating the effects of BN given these two research fields meet together in this paper.

Recall that during training, BN computes the mean and variance of the feature space for each mini-batch, referred to as *batch statistics* [39]. Each mini-batch is normalized by its batch statistics at training time. Hence, the composition of a mini-batch defines its batch statistics, thereby affecting the normalized values of each data point's features. To observe the effects on Self-Supervised AT, we create four variants of SSAT-s-t-$\tilde{t}$-2. They involve the same data types $\{x_s, x_t, \tilde{x}_t\}$ into training but with different mini-batch compositions. Specifically, at each training step, Batch-st-$\tilde{t}$ has two mini-batches, $[x_s, x_t]$ and $[\tilde{x}_t]$; Batch-s-t$\tilde{t}$ has two mini-batches, $[x_s]$ and $[x_t, \tilde{x}_t]$; Batch-s-t-$\tilde{t}$ has three mini-batches, $[x_s]$, $[x_t]$ and $[\tilde{x}_t]$; and Batch-st$\tilde{t}$ has one mini-batch, $[x_s, x_t, \tilde{x}_t]$. Batch-st-$\tilde{t}$ is the original SSAT-s-t-$\tilde{t}$-2, which follows the setting of [15]. We expect that their batch statistics differences would cause different results.

Table 3 shows the results. As can be seen, Batch-st-$\tilde{t}$ achieves the highest clean accuracy, while Batch-st$\tilde{t}$ achieves the highest robust accuracy. We argue that in Batch-st$\tilde{t}$, x_s is with the same mini-batch as x_t and $\tilde{x}_t$, so it can also

Table 3. Results (%) of different mini-batch combinations on the VisDA-2017 dataset.

Method	Mini-batches	Clean	FGSM
Batch-st-$\tilde{t}$	$[x_s, x_t], [\tilde{x}_t]$	73.0	39.4
Batch-s-t$\tilde{t}$	$[x_s], [x_t, \tilde{x}_t]$	68.2	37.0
Batch-s-t-$\tilde{t}$	$[x_s], [x_t], [\tilde{x}_t]$	68.2	35.5
Batch-st$\tilde{t}$	$[x_s, x_t, \tilde{x}_t]$	69.0	41.4

transfer the supervised knowledge through batch statistics. In other words, the batch statistics used to normalize x_t and $\tilde{x}_t$ contain x_s's information. This shares a similar spirit with the domain adaptation loss $\mathcal{L}_{DA}(x_s, x_t) + \mathcal{L}_{DA}(x_s, \tilde{x}_t)$ discussed in Sect. 4.3, and we have known that it can improve robustness. For Batch-st-$\tilde{t}$, we see its high performance is due to the separation of x_t and $\tilde{x}_t$. Recall that clean and robust features have distinct characteristics [14,33], so putting them into the same mini-batch leads to suboptimal results [39]. Batch-s-t-$\tilde{t}$, however, achieves lower performance than Batch-st-$\tilde{t}$ though it has that separation as well. The reason is that in Batch-st-$\tilde{t}$, x_s and x_t are with the same mini-batch. This encourages the knowledge transfer from x_s to x_t, similar to the spirit of the domain adaptation loss $\mathcal{L}_{DA}(x_s, x_t)$.

Both Batch-st-$\tilde{t}$ and Batch-st$\tilde{t}$ achieve a good trade-off between performance and robustness. We can choose according to the downstream application's focus.

4.5 Summary

In this section, we explore four main aspects of AT for UDA, including Conventional AT, our Self-Supervised AT, the effects of clean and adversarial examples in Self-Supervised AT, and the effects of BN statistics. We progressively derive the best method from each investigation, then we take Batch-st$\tilde{t}$ as our final method, referred to as Adversarially Robust Training for UDA (ARTUDA). ARTUDA's training objective is Eq.(11), and Fig. 1 offers a visualized illustration. Note that some of the other variants also have their advantages, e.g., Batch-st-$\tilde{t}$, so they are still useful for certain focusses.

5 Experiments

We extensively evaluate the proposed ARTUDA on five adversarial attacks, three datasets and three different UDA algorithms. We further compare ARTUDA with the nearly contemporary work, RFA [2]. An analysis of feature space is also presented.

5.1 Experimental Setup

Datasets. We use three UDA datasets for evaluation: VisDA-2017 [29], Office-31 [31] and Office-Home [36]. VisDA-2017 contains two domains: Synthetic and

Real. There are 152,409 Synthetic and 55,400 Real images from 12 object categories in this large-scale dataset. Office-31 has three domains with 31 object categories. These are Amazon (A) with 2,817 images, Webcam (W) with 795 images, and DSLR (D) with 498 images. We employ the D $\rightarrow$ W task for our experiment. Office-Home includes four domains with 65 categories: Art (Ar) with 2,427 images, Clipart (Cl) with 4,365, Product (Pr) with 4,439 images, and Real-World (Rw) with 4,375 images. We employ the Ar $\rightarrow$ Cl task for our experiment.

Attack Setting. We test UDA models' adversarial robustness against four white-box attacks, including FGSM [10], PGD [26], MI-FGSM [6] and MultAdv [21], where PGD is the default attack unless stated otherwise. A black-box attack [27] is also considered. For AT, we use the PGD attack with $j_{max} = 3$ and $\epsilon = 3$ of L_∞-norm. If not otherwise specified, we set the same for all the attacks at testing time except that FGSM's j_{max} is 1.

Benchmark UDA Algorithms. We apply ARTUDA to three common UDA algorithms, including DANN [8], JAN [24] and CDAN [23]. We use ResNet-50 [12] as a backbone for all of them. If not otherwise specified, DANN is the default UDA algorithm in our experiments.

Baseline Defenses. We employ two commonly-used conventional AT algorithms, PGD-AT [26] and TRADES [42], to be our baseline defenses. To the best of our knowledge, RFA [2] might be the only approach aiming at the same problem as ours, and we also compare with it.

Implementation Details. Our implementation is based on PyTorch [28]. We adopt Transfer-Learning-library [15] to set up UDA's experimental environment and follow the training hyper-parameters used in [15]. We also use the widely-used library, AdverTorch [5], to perform adversarial attacks. We will release our source code if the paper gets accepted.

5.2 Evaluation Results

White-box Robustness. The robustness of multiple training methods against various white-box attacks is reported in Table 4. Without a defense, Natural Training's accuracy drops to almost 0% under the strong iterative attacks. PGD-AT and TRADES improve adversarial robustness though they are originally designed for the traditional classification task. However, they also reduce clean accuracy. The proposed method, ARTUDA, significantly increases robust accuracy. Specifically, on VisDA-2017, it achieves more than 10% and 20% higher robustness than TRADES and PGD-AT, respectively. On Office-31, its robust accuracy is higher than PGD-AT and TRADES by 25%–48% under white-box iterative attacks. On Office-Home, although TRADES is slightly more robust to white-box iterative attacks, ARTUDA has higher accuracy under clean data, FGSM and black-box attacks, leading by a decent margin. In general, ARTUDA is effective across all the five attacks on three datasets. ARTUDA's clean accuracy drops but is still the best among the defenses. It can greatly improve robustness and maintain decent clean performance simultaneously.

Table 4. Results (%) of UDA models on multiple datasets under various adversarial attacks.

Dataset	Training method	Clean	FGSM	PGD	MI-FGSM	MultAdv	Black-box
VisDA-2017	Natural Training	73.2	21.2	0.9	0.5	0.3	58.3
[29]	PGD-AT [26]	60.5	34.6	21.3	22.7	7.8	59.1
	TRADES [42]	64.0	42.1	29.7	31.2	16.4	62.6
	ARTUDA (ours)	65.5	**52.5**	**44.3**	**45.0**	**27.3**	**65.1**
Office-31	Natural Training	98.0	52.7	0.9	0.6	0.1	95.0
D → W [31]	PGD-AT [26]	95.3	91.8	68.2	66.5	31.4	95.3
	TRADES [42]	88.4	85.3	66.4	67.0	28.2	88.2
	ARTUDA (ours)	96.5	**95.2**	**92.5**	**92.5**	**77.1**	**96.5**
Office-Home	Natural Training	54.5	26.4	4.7	2.8	2.0	53.1
Ar → Cl [36]	PGD-AT [26]	42.5	38.8	36.0	35.8	21.7	43.0
	TRADES [42]	49.3	45.1	**41.6**	**41.6**	**22.5**	49.4
	ARTUDA (ours)	54.0	**49.5**	41.3	39.9	21.6	**53.9**

Table 5. Results (%) of UDA models on the VisDA-2017 dataset under the PGD attack. Three UDA algorithms are considered.

UDA algorithm →	DANN [8]			JAN [24]			CDAN [23]		
Training method ↓	Clean	PGD	Drop	Clean	PGD	Drop	Clean	PGD	Drop
Natural Training	73.2	0.0	−73.2	64.2	0.0	−64.2	75.1	0.0	−75.1
PGD-AT [26]	60.5	13.3	−47.2	47.7	5.8	−41.9	58.2	11.7	−46.5
TRADES [42]	64.0	19.4	−44.6	48.7	8.5	−40.2	64.6	15.7	−48.9
Robust PT [2]	65.8	38.2	−27.6	55.1	32.2	**−22.9**	68.0	41.7	−26.3
RFA [2]	65.3	34.1	−31.2	63.0	32.8	−30.2	72.0	43.5	−28.5
ARTUDA (ours)	65.5	**40.7**	**−24.8**	58.5	**34.4**	−24.1	68.0	**43.6**	**−24.4**

Black-box Robustness. The robustness against black-box attacks is shown in the last column of Table 4. Here we consider a naturally trained DANN with ResNet-18 as a substitute model and use MI-FGSM, which has better transferability, to generate black-box adversarial examples for target models. In general, the black-box attacks hardly fool the target models. However, we find that the conventional AT approaches have lower black-box accuracy than Natural Training in some cases. This is due to their lower clean accuracy. In contrast, ARTUDA has better clean accuracy and consistently achieves the best black-box robustness across all the datasets.

Generalizability. To compare with the results of [2], in this part, we evaluate robustness against the white-box PGD attack with $j_{max} = 20$ that used in [2]. Table 5 reports the adversarial robustness of multiple popular UDA algo-

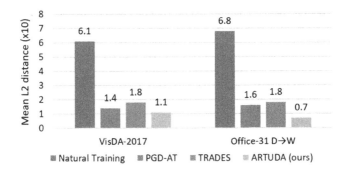

Fig. 2. Mean L_2-norm distance between the feature space of clean images and that of their adversarial examples. The values are the mean over an entire dataset.

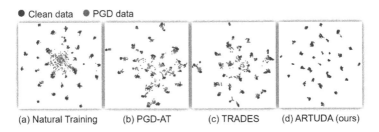

Fig. 3. The t-SNE visualization of the feature space on the Office-31 D→W task.

rithms. All of them are vulnerable to adversarial attacks. The state-of-the-art approaches, Robust PT and RFA, show excellent effectiveness in improving robustness. We apply our ARTUDA training method to these UDA models to protect them as well. As can be seen, ARTUDA uniformly robustfies all of these models. It consistently achieves low accuracy drops and the highest robust accuracy, which outperforms both Robust PT and RFA. This demonstrates that ARTUDA is generic and can be applied to multiple existing UDA algorithms.

In terms of clean data accuracy, all the defenses lose clean accuracy to a certain extent. Still, the proposed ARTUDA achieves the best or the second-best clean accuracy among these defenses. Overall, it can significantly improve robustness and maintain decent clean performance simultaneously.

5.3   Analysis

Stability of Feature Space. Small adversarial perturbations on image space are enlarged considerably in feature space [38]. Hence, the stability of the feature space can reflect a model's robustness [20]. In other words, a robust model's feature space would hardly change under an adversarial example. We compute the mean L_2-norm distance between the feature space of clean images and that of their PGD examples for our models: $\| F(x_t) - F(\tilde{x}_t) \|_2$. The features from the last conv layer of the ResNet-50 backbone are used. As can be seen in

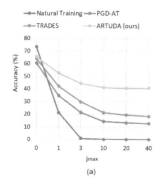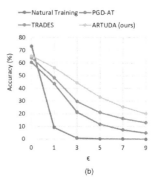

Fig. 4. Accuracy of models under PGD attacks (a) with varied numbers of attack iterations j_{max} and (b) with varied perturbation sizes ϵ.

Fig. 2, Natual Training has the largest distance, which means that its features are greatly changed when images are adversarially perturbed and thus cause wrong predictions. PGD-AT and TRADES can reduce the distance. ARTUDA attains the smallest distance on both datasets, showing that its feature space is not easily affected by adversarial perturbations.

Visualization of Feature Space. Figure 3 visualizes the different methods' feature space on the Office-31 D→W task using t-SNE [25]. The features are from the last conv layer of the ResNet-50 backbone. The PGD data in the Natural Training model are disorderly scatter and do not align with clean data. PGD-AT and TRADES narrow the distribution gap to a certain extent. ARTUDA impressively align the feature space of PGD and clean data in which they almost overlap with each other. This implies that ARTUDA is effective in learning adversarially robust features. This result is consistent with the above stability analysis.

Attack Budgets. We test our ARTUDA's scalability to various attack budgets. We vary the attack budgets by two aspects: the number of attack iterations j_{max} and the perturbation size ϵ. Figure 4 shows the results. First, we can find that the attack strength does not increase apparently along with the increase of j_{max} when $j_{max} > 3$. This observation is consistent with that of [26]. The proposed ARTUDA demonstrates stable adversarial robustness and consistently performs better than Natural Training, PGD-AT [26] and TRADES [42] under varied j_{max}. On the other hand, the attack strength dramatically increases along with the increase of ϵ. It can be seen that ARTUDA consistently shows better robustness under varied ϵ. Obviously, ARTUDA is scalable to various attack budgets.

6   Conclusion

This paper explores AT methods for the UDA problem. Existing AT approaches require labels to generate adversarial examples and train models, but this does not apply to the unlabeled target domain. We provide a systematic study into multiple AT variants that may suitable for UDA. This empirical contribution could offer useful insight to the research community. Based on our study, we propose ARTUDA, a novel AT method specifically designed for UDA. Our comprehensive experiments show that ARTUDA improves robustness consistently across multiple attacks and datasets, and outperforms the state-of-the-art methods.

Acknowledgements. This work was supported by the DARPA GARD Program HR001119S0026-GARD-FP-052.

References

1. Athalye, A., Carlini, N., Wagner, D.: Obfuscated gradients give a false sense of security: circumventing defenses to adversarial examples. In: International Conference on Machine Learning (2018)
2. Awais, M., et al.: Adversarial robustness for unsupervised domain adaptation. In: IEEE International Conference on Computer Vision (2021)
3. Biggio, B., et al.: Evasion attacks against machine learning at test time. In: Blockeel, H., Kersting, K., Nijssen, S., Železný, F. (eds.) ECML PKDD 2013. LNCS (LNAI), vol. 8190, pp. 387–402. Springer, Heidelberg (2013). https://doi.org/10.1007/978-3-642-40994-3_25
4. Chang, W.G., You, T., Seo, S., Kwak, S., Han, B.: Domain-specific batch normalization for unsupervised domain adaptation. In: IEEE Conference on Computer Vision and Pattern Recognition (2019)
5. Ding, G.W., Wang, L., Jin, X.: AdverTorch v0.1: an adversarial robustness toolbox based on pyTorch. arXiv preprint arXiv:1902.07623 (2019)
6. Dong, Y., et al.: Boosting adversarial attacks with momentum. In: IEEE Conference on Computer Vision and Pattern Recognition (2018)
7. Ganin, Y., Lempitsky, V.: Unsupervised domain adaptation by backpropagation. In: International Conference on Machine Learning (2015)
8. Ganin, Y., et al.: Domain-adversarial training of neural networks. J. Mach. Learn. Res. **17**, 1–35 (2016)
9. Goodfellow, I., et al.: Generative adversarial nets. In: Conference on Neural Information Processing Systems (2014)
10. Goodfellow, I.J., Shlens, J., Szegedy, C.: Explaining and harnessing adversarial examples. In: International Conference on Learning Representations (2015)
11. Guo, C., Rana, M., Cisse, M., Van Der Maaten, L.: Countering adversarial images using input transformations (2018)
12. He, K., Zhang, X., Ren, S., Sun, J.: Deep residual learning for image recognition. In: IEEE conference on Computer Vision and Pattern Recognition (2016)
13. Ioffe, S., Szegedy, C.: Batch normalization: accelerating deep network training by reducing internal covariate shift. In: International Conference on Machine Learning (2015)

14. Itazuri, T., Fukuhara, Y., Kataoka, H., Morishima, S.: What do adversarially robust models look at? arXiv preprint arXiv:1905.07666 (2019)
15. Jiang, J., Chen, B., Fu, B., Long, M.: Transfer-learning-library. https://github.com/thuml/Transfer-Learning-Library (2020)
16. Kannan, H., Kurakin, A., Goodfellow, I.: Adversarial logit pairing. In: Conference on Neural Information Processing Systems (2018)
17. Krizhevsky, A., Sutskever, I., Hinton, G.E.: ImageNet classification with deep convolutional neural networks. In: Conference on Neural Information Processing Systems (2012)
18. Li, Y., Wang, N., Shi, J., Liu, J., Hou, X.: Revisiting batch normalization for practical domain adaptation. In: International Conference on Learning Representations Workshop (2017)
19. Lo, S.Y., Patel, V.M.: Defending against multiple and unforeseen adversarial videos. IEEE Transactions on Image Processing (2021)
20. Lo, S.Y., Patel, V.M.: Error diffusion halftoning against adversarial examples. In: IEEE International Conference on Image Processing (2021)
21. Lo, S.Y., Patel, V.M.: MultAV: multiplicative adversarial videos. In: IEEE International Conference on Advanced Video and Signal-based Surveillance (2021)
22. Long, M., Cao, Y., Wang, J., Jordan, M.: Learning transferable features with deep adaptation networks. In: International Conference on Machine Learning (2015)
23. Long, M., Cao, Z., Wang, J., Jordan, M.I.: Conditional adversarial domain adaptation. In: Conference on Neural Information Processing Systems (2018)
24. Long, M., Zhu, H., Wang, J., Jordan, M.I.: Deep transfer learning with joint adaptation networks. In: International Conference on Machine Learning (2017)
25. Van der Maaten, L., Hinton, G.: Visualizing data using T-SNE. J. Mach. Learn. Res. **9**, 2579–2605 (2008)
26. Madry, A., Makelov, A., Schmidt, L., Tsipras, D., Vladu, A.: Towards deep learning models resistant to adversarial attacks. In: International Conference on Learning Representations (2018)
27. Papernot, N., McDaniel, P., Goodfellow, I., Jha, S., Celik, Z.B., Swami, A.: Practical black-box attacks against machine learning. In: ACM Asia Conference on Computer and Communications Security (2017)
28. Paszke, A., et al.: PyTorch: an imperative style, high-performance deep learning library. In: Conference on Neural Information Processing Systems (2019)
29. Peng, X., Usman, B., Kaushik, N., Hoffman, J., Wang, D., Saenko, K.: VisDA: the visual domain adaptation challenge. arXiv preprint arXiv:1710.06924 (2017)
30. Raff, E., Sylvester, J., Forsyth, S., McLean, M.: Barrage of random transforms for adversarially robust defense. In: IEEE Conference on Computer Vision and Pattern Recognition (2019)
31. Saenko, K., Kulis, B., Fritz, M., Darrell, T.: Adapting visual category models to new domains. In: Daniilidis, K., Maragos, P., Paragios, N. (eds.) ECCV 2010. LNCS, vol. 6314, pp. 213–226. Springer, Heidelberg (2010). https://doi.org/10.1007/978-3-642-15561-1_16
32. Szegedy, C., et al.: Intriguing properties of neural networks. In: International Conference on Learning Representations (2014)
33. Tsipras, D., Santurkar, S., Engstrom, L., Turner, A., Madry, A.: Robustness may be at odds with accuracy. In: International Conference on Learning Representations (2019)
34. Tzeng, E., Hoffman, J., Saenko, K., Darrell, T.: Adversarial discriminative domain adaptation. In: IEEE Conference on Computer Vision and Pattern Recognition (2017)

35. Van Den Oord, A., Vinyals, O., et al.: Neural discrete representation learning. In: Conference on Neural Information Processing Systems (2017)

36. Venkateswara, H., Eusebio, J., Chakraborty, S., Panchanathan, S.: Deep hashing network for unsupervised domain adaptation. In: IEEE Conference on Computer Vision and Pattern Recognition (2017)

37. Xie, C., Tan, M., Gong, B., Wang, J., Yuille, A., Le, Q.V.: Adversarial examples improve image recognition. In: IEEE Conference on Computer Vision and Pattern Recognition (2020)

38. Xie, C., Wu, Y., van der Maaten, L., Yuille, A., He, K.: Feature denoising for improving adversarial robustness. In: IEEE Conference on Computer Vision and Pattern Recognition (2019)

39. Xie, C., Yuille, A.: Intriguing properties of adversarial training at scale. In: International Conference on Learning Representations (2020)

40. Yang, J., et al.: Exploring robustness of unsupervised domain adaptation in semantic segmentation. In: IEEE International Conference on Computer Vision (2021)

41. Zagoruyko, S., Komodakis, N.: Wide residual networks. In: British Machine Vision Conference (2016)

42. Zhang, H., Yu, Y., Jiao, J., Xing, E.P., Ghaoui, L.E., Jordan, M.I.: Theoretically principled trade-off between robustness and accuracy. In: International Conference on Machine Learning (2019)

Learning Common and Specific Visual Prompts for Domain Generalization

Aodi Li[1], Liansheng Zhuang[1(✉)], Shuo Fan[1], and Shafei Wang[2]

[1] University of Science and Technology of China, Hefei 230026, China
aodi8055@mail.ustc.edu.cn, lszhuang@ustc.edu.cn
[2] Peng Cheng Laboratory, Shenzhen 518000, China

Abstract. Although fine-tuning a pre-trained large-scale model has become an effective method for domain generalization, domain shifts still issue a huge challenge for successfully transferring models to unseen test domains. In this paper, we study how to effectively adapt pre-trained vision Transformers for domain generalization problems in image classification. To this end, this paper proposes a novel Common-Specific Visual Prompt Tuning (CSVPT) method to transfer large-scale vision Transformer models to unknown test domains. Different from existing methods which learn fixed visual prompts for each task, CSVPT jointly learns domain-common prompts to capture the task context and sample-specific prompts to capture information about data distribution, which are generated for each sample through a trainable prompt-generating module (PGM). Combining the domain-common prompts and the sample-specific prompts, visual prompts learned by CSVPT are conditioned on each input sample rather than fixed once learned, which helps out-of-distribution generalization. Extensive experimental results show the effectiveness of CSVPT, and CSVPT with the backbone ViT-L/14 achieves state-of-the-art (SOTA) performance on five widely used benchmark datasets.

1 Introduction

Though deep learning has achieved remarkable success in many areas [1–4], it relies on the i.i.d. assumption that training and testing data are independent and identically distributed [5]. However, this assumption does not always hold in real applications. When collecting data under different conditions or from different sources, test data is often out of the distributions of training data. The out-of-distribution (OOD) problem significantly degrades the performance of deep models [6]. To tackle this problem, lots of *domain generalization* (DG) methods aim to learn a model from multiple training domains that will generalize well on unseen testing domains [6].

The past few years have witnessed the advance of DG algorithms [6,7]. Among them, learning feature representations that were invariant across domains [8–12] and decomposing model parameters into shared and domain-specific components [13,14] are the two most common methods. However, some

L. Wang et al. (Eds.): ACCV 2022, LNCS 13846, pp. 578–593, 2023.
https://doi.org/10.1007/978-3-031-26351-4_35

researchers have revealed that none of the existing DG methods greatly out-perform simple baselines on the diverse DG benchmarks [15]. This is because the training and test distributions are too different to learn domain-invariant features or obtain excellent common-specific decomposition from the training domains alone.

Inspired by the great success of Transformers [16–19], a line of works such as [20–22] turned to large-scale pre-trained models for help. Benefiting from massive labeled and unlabeled data, pre-training models on diverse data can efficiently capture rich prior knowledge and improve OOD generalization [23]. By fine-tuning on specific tasks, the rich knowledge implicitly encoded in the pre-trained models can benefit a variety of downstream tasks. Full fine-tuning is one of the most common practices, which updates all parameters on the downstream tasks. However, storing a separate copy of the whole backbone parameters for each task is an expensive and infeasible proposal, especially for large-scale Trans-former models. Moreover, full fine-tuning may distort pre-trained features and thus harm the robustness against distribution shifts [24]. Instead of fine-tuning the pre-trained Transformer itself, visual prompt tuning (VPT) [25] modifies the input to the Transformer. It introduces a small amount of task-specific trainable parameters (namely visual prompts) into the input space while keeping the whole pre-trained backbone frozen. Since only a few parameters (1% of model param-eters) requires to be updated, VPT not only greatly reduces computational and storage costs but also prevents overfitting and feature distortion. Although a proper prompt that matches with data distribution could improve the perfor-mance, it is difficult to design an appropriate visual prompt for an unknown domain to address the domain shift problem.

In this paper, we investigate how to effectively adapt pre-trained vision Trans-former models for domain generalization in image classification. Taking inspira-tion from VPT [25] and traditional DG methods [13,14], this paper proposes a novel Common-Specific Visual Prompt Tuning (CSVPT) method to transfer the pre-trained vision Transformer models to unknown testing domains for bet-ter OOD generalization. To our best knowledge, it is the first work to design a DG algorithm based on visual prompts. Different from existing prompt-based methods [25,26] which only learn task-specific prompts, our proposed CSVPT jointly learns domain-common prompts and sample-specific prompts to modify the input to the pre-trained vision Transformer models. The domain-common prompts capture the task context and are fixed once learned, thus easy to over-fit the training domains. To generalize the prompts to wider unseen domains within the same task, CSVPT learns a lightweight neural network (namely prompt-generating module, PGM) to generate the sample-specific prompts for each sample so as to capture information about data distribution. Combining the domain-common prompts and the sample-specific prompts, our visual prompts are conditioned on each input sample rather than fixed once learned, which helps out-of-distribution generalization. To validate the effectiveness of our proposed CSVPT method, we perform extensive experiments on five popular datasets of DomainBed [15], including PACS [27], VLCS [28], OfficeHome [29], TerraIncognita [30] and DomainNet [31]. Experimental results demonstrate that CSVPT consistently performs better on these datasets than the vanilla VPT methods and other DG methods based on pre-trained models. Moreover, CSVPT with ViT-L/14 pre-trained on CLIP [32] achieves new state-of-the-art performances on the five datasets.

In summary, our key contributions are as follows:

– A novel CSVPT method is proposed to efficiently adapt large-scale vision Transformers for the DG problem. Instead of learning fixed visual prompts as VPT does, CSVPT generates the visual prompts conditioned on each input sample, and thus achieves better OOD generalization.
– Extensive experiments on five public datasets demonstrate that our proposed CVSVPT consistently outperforms existing fine-tuning methods for domain generalization in image classification. Especially, CSVPT with the backbone ViT-L/14 achieves new SOTA performance.

2   Related Work

Invariance learning and decomposition learning are two mainstream methods for DG. These conventional DG methods usually fail to learn domain-invariant features or obtain excellent common-specific decomposition from the training distributions alone. To solve this problem, we propose a novel CSVPT method, which is mainly inspired by decomposition learning and pre-trained model-based methods. In this section, we will introduce these related works concisely.

2.1   Decomposition Learning Method

Decomposition learning, which supposes that features, model parameters, or gradients are composed of domain-specific components and domain-common components, is one of the most popular methods for DG. Decomposition learning can be divided into three categories as follows. The first type is feature decomposition learning. Feature decomposition learning tries to disentangle the feature representation into two parts, i.e., domain-specific parts and domain-common parts. Afterward, we can either use the domain-common feature only or combine the domain-common features with augmented domain-specific features for prediction [33]. The second category is predictor decomposition learning, such as CSD [14]. It learns a domain-common predictor (which helps generalization) and a domain-specific predictor (which may harm generalization). The domain-specific predictors are discarded after training and only the common predictor is used for prediction. The last one is gradient decomposition learning. For example, AndMask [34] updates weights only when gradients from different domains point to the same direction, i.e., retaining the domain-common gradient component. Similarly, we assume prompts are composed of domain-common and sample-specific components in this paper. Domain-common components learned from the training data are shared by the test data, but sample-specific components are generated from the input data via a simple linear PGM. Combining the domain-common and sample-specific prompts, we can obtain more appropriate prompts for samples from unseen testing domains, which helps out-of-distribution generalization.

2.2 Pre-trained Model-Based Method

As we all know, full fine-tuning and linear probing are two popular methods when transferring a pre-trained model to a downstream task. All the model parameters are trainable for full fine-tuning, while only the parameters of the last fully connected layer are for linear probing. When training and testing data are independent and identically distributed, full fine-tuning usually outperforms linear probing. However, some researchers [24] pointed out full fine-tuning may distort pre-trained features and underperform out-of-distribution, because the features of in-distribution training data are updated greatly while those of out-of-distribution data change less. Ananya Kumar et al. [24] proposed a two-step approach (linear probing then full fine-tuning) to solve the problem. Besides, some researchers [21] utilized a mutual information regularization with the pre-trained model, called Mutual Information Regularization with Oracle (MIRO), to prevent overfitting and feature distortion. Although MIRO achieved SOTA performance on several DG benchmarks, updating all parameters and calculating the above loss consume a lot of computation and storage resources. Instead of fine-tuning the pre-trained Transformer itself, visual prompt tuning (VPT) [25] modifies the input to the Transformer models. It introduces a small amount of task-specific trainable parameters (namely visual prompts) into the input space while keeping the whole pre-trained backbone frozen. It not only greatly saves the computation and storage resources but also prevents the feature distortion brought by full fine-tuning. Inspired by VPT, we propose a novel visual prompt tuning method named CSVPT for domain generalization.

3   Methodology

We propose a novel CSVPT method to effectively adapt pre-trained vision Transformers for domain generalization problems in image classification. In this section, we will first define the problem of domain generalization formally and then elaborate on the proposed CSVPT method.

3.1   Problem

This paper mainly studies the problem of domain generalization. In this subsection, we give the formal definition of domains and domain generalization in the following.

Definition 1 (Domain) [6]. To be simple, a domain is a set of data sampled from a distribution, denoted as $\mathcal{S} = \{(\mathbf{x}_i, y_i)\}_{i=1}^{n} \sim P_{XY}$, where $\mathbf{x}_i \in \mathcal{X}$ denotes an input sample in the input space, $y_i \in \mathcal{Y}$ denotes corresponding label in the output space, n denotes number of samples in domain $\mathcal{S}$, and P_{XY} denotes the joint distribution of random variable X (which means the input sample) and random variable Y (which means the output label).

Definition 2 (Domain Generalization) [6]. In the setting of DG problem, we have M training domains $\mathcal{S}_{train} = \{\{(\mathbf{x}_i^{(d)}, y_i^{(d)}\}_{i=1}^{n_d}\}_{d=1}^{M}$ and one testing domain $\mathcal{S}_{test} = \{(\mathbf{x}_i^{(M+1)}, y_i^{(M+1)}\}_{i=1}^{n_{M+1}}$. The joint distributions between every two above domains are different: $P_{XY}^{(i)} \neq P_{XY}^{(j)}$, $1 \leq i \neq j \leq M+1$. DG aims to learn a mapping function $f : \mathcal{X} \rightarrow \mathcal{Y}$ (using $\mathcal{S}_{train}$ only) such that f minimizes the generalization error on domain $\mathcal{S}_{test}$:

$$\min_{f} \mathbb{E}_{(\mathbf{x},y)\in\mathcal{S}_{test}}[l(f(\mathbf{x}),y)]. \tag{1}$$

Note that the testing domain $\mathcal{S}_{test}$ is not available during training, which differs from the problem of domain adaptation [35].

3.2 Our CSVPT Algorithm

We propose a novel Common-Specific Visual Prompt Tuning (CSVPT) method to adapt large-scale vision Transformer models for domain generalization (Fig. 1). It tunes the pre-trained vision Transformer by appending N trainable prompt tokens to the input of the Transformer layers. Different from existing prompt-based methods [25,26] which only learn task-specific prompts, our proposed CSVPT jointly learns domain-common prompts and sample-specific prompts to modify the input to the pre-trained vision Transformer models. The domain-common prompts capture the task context and are fixed once learned, while the sample-specific prompts capture information about data distribution and are generated through a lightweight neural network (PGM). Combining the two types of prompts above, we can make more appropriate prompts for test data from unseen domains, which helps out-of-distribution generalization. Before elaborating on our CSVPT algorithm, let us review the vanilla vision Transformer (ViT) first.

For a vision Transformer [18], an input image $\mathbf{x}$ is divided into M patches first: $P = \{I_i | I_i \in \mathbb{R}^{3 \times h \times w}, 1 \leq i \leq M\}$, where h and w denote the height and width of an image patch, respectively. Then, each image patch is mapped to a d-dimension vector, a.k.a, the context token, by a feature embedding module (usually a 2D convolution layer):

$$t_i^{(0)} = \text{Embed}(I_i), \tag{2}$$

where $I_i \in P$ and $t_i^{(0)} \in \mathbb{R}^d$. After that, the class token $c^{(0)} \in \mathbb{R}^d$ and all d-dimensional context tokens are concatenated as the input of the first Transformer layer:

$$(c^{(1)}, t_1^{(1)}, \ldots, t_M^{(1)}) = \text{L}_1(c^{(0)}, t_1^{(0)}, \ldots, t_M^{(0)}), \tag{3}$$

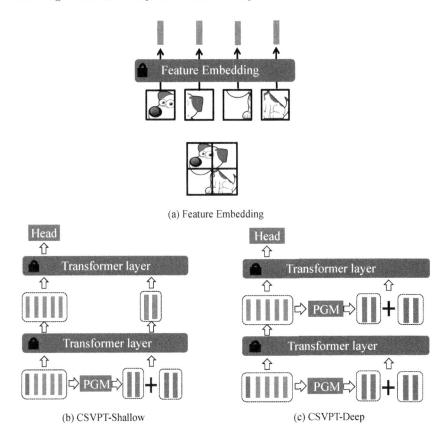

(a) Feature Embedding

(b) CSVPT-Shallow

(c) CSVPT-Deep

Fig. 1. Overview of the proposed Common-Specific Visual Prompt Tuning (CSVPT). (a) We first utilize a feature embedding module to embed input image patches into several context tokens (marked gray). (b) Mapping the class token (marked blue, pretrained) and input context tokens to several prompt tokens (sample-specific prompts, marked green) through a prompt-generating module (PGM). Then, initialize domain-common prompts (marked red) to zeros and add domain-common prompts and sample-specific prompts together as total prompts. Finally, concatenate the class token, input context tokens and total prompt tokens as the input of the frozen Transformer Layer (CSVPT-Shallow). (c) Use PGM to generate sample-specific prompt tokens and initialize domain-common prompt tokens at each Transformer encoder layer (CSVPT-Deep). During training on downstream DG tasks, only the parameters (marked red) of domain-common prompts, PGMs and the linear head are updated, while keeping the whole Transformer encoder frozen. (Color figure online)

where the superscripts "(1)" and "(0)" denote the output and input of the first Transformer layer, respectively. For a vision Transformer with L layers, we have

$$(c^{(l)}, t_1^{(l)}, \ldots, t_M^{(l)}) = L_l(c^{(l-1)}, t_1^{(l-1)}, \ldots, t_M^{(l-1)}), \tag{4}$$

where $l \in \{1, 2, \ldots, L\}$. Finally, $c^{(L)}$ is used for classification through the head module:

$$\hat{y} = \text{Head}(c^{(L)}). \tag{5}$$

As mentioned above, our proposed CSVPT algorithm (Fig. 1) attempts to learn common-specific visual prompts to tune the pre-trained ViTs for better OOD generalization. Specifically, we first utilize a feature embedding module to embed input image patches into several context tokens (Fig. 1(a)) as in (2). Then, CSVPT utilizes a Prompt-generating Module (PGM) to generate sample-specific prompt tokens from the input context tokens to adapt to changes of data distributions:

$$(p_{s,1}^{(k)}, \ldots, p_{s,N}^{(k)}) = \text{PGM}(c^{(k)}, t_1^{(k)}, \ldots, t_M^{(k)}), \tag{6}$$

where k represents the input prompts of the $(k+1)$th layer, and the subscript "s" in $p_{s,i}^{(k)}$ means specific prompts. For the sake of simplicity, we apply a linear module as PGM:

$$[p_{s,1}^{(k)}, \ldots, p_{s,N}^{(k)}] = [c^{(k)}, t_1^{(k)}, \ldots, t_M^{(k)}]\mathbf{W^T}, \tag{7}$$

where $\mathbf{W} \in \mathbb{R}^{N \times (M+1)}$ denotes the weights of the PGM. Next, we add specific and common prompt tokens (which are initialized to zeros and updated during training like other prompt tuning methods) together:

$$p_i^{(k)} = p_{s,i}^{(k)} + p_{c,i}^{(k)}, \tag{8}$$

where $i \in \{1, 2, \ldots, N\}$ and the subscript "c" in $p_{c,i}^{(k)}$ means common prompts. Similar to VPT, we propose two specific implementations: CSVPT-Shallow and CSVPT-Deep. In the setting of CSVPT-Shallow (Fig. 1(b)), sample-specific prompt tokens generated by PGM and domain-common prompt tokens are used only in the input space of the first Transformer layer (i.e., $k \in \{0\}$), while at each Transformer layer (i.e., $k \in \{0, 1, \ldots, L-1\}$) in the setting of CSVPT-Deep (Fig. 1(c). Finally, the total prompt tokens are used to modify the input to the pre-trained vision Transformer models. Specifically, for CSVPT-Shallow, we have

$$(c^{(l)}, t_1^{(l)}, \ldots, t_M^{(l)}, p_1^{(l)}, \ldots, p_N^{(l)})$$
$$= L_l(c^{(l-1)}, t_1^{(l-1)}, \ldots, t_M^{(l-1)}, p_1^{(l-1)}, \ldots, p_N^{(l-1)}), \tag{9}$$

where $\{p_i^{(0)}\}_{i=1}^N$ is obtained from (8). But for VPT-Deep, we have

$$(c^{(l)}, t_1^{(l)}, \ldots, t_M^{(l)}, \widetilde{p}_1^{(l)}, \ldots, \widetilde{p}_N^{(l)})$$
$$= L_l(c^{(l-1)}, t_1^{(l-1)}, \ldots, t_M^{(l-1)}, p_1^{(l-1)}, \ldots, p_N^{(l-1)}), \tag{10}$$

where $\{p_i^{(l-1)}\}_{i=1}^N$ is obtained from (8) and $\widetilde{p}_i^{(j)}$ is discarded in the next layer's input in order to prevent the number of tokens from gradually increasing with layers. During training on downstream DG tasks, only parameters of common prompt tokens, PGMs and the linear head are updated while the whole Transformer encoder is frozen, simply using the cross entropy loss.

4   Experiments

In this section, we conduct extensive experiments to compare the performance of the proposed CSVPT algorithm and other pre-trained model-based DG methods on different challenging and widely used datasets via DomainBed [15], a testbed for domain generalization.

4.1   Datasets and Implementation Details

Datasets. We evaluate our method on five challenging benchmark datasets, including PACS [27] (4 domains, 7 classes, and 9, 991 examples), VLCS [28] (4 domains, 5 classes, and 10, 729 examples), OfficeHome [29] (4 domains, 65 classes, and 15, 588 images), TerraIncognita [30] (4 domains, 10 classes, and 24, 788 examples), and DomainNet [31] (6 domains, 345 classes, and 586, 575 examples).

Implement Details. Two backbones, ViT-B/16 [18] and ViT-L/14, are used on these five datasets to explore the influence of backbone scale on the performance of downstream DG tasks. Without further explanation, ViT-B/16 is used in the next experiments. In general, the number of training iterations is 5,000, and the batch size is 16 times the number of domains. But more training iterations are implemented for large datasets like DomainNet, and we reduce the batch size by half when using a larger backbone ViT-L/14. In our experiments, we uniformly use the Adam optimizer and determine the optimal learning rate through a model selection process. We follow the same training, validation and testing split scheme as in MIRO [21]. For each domain, twenty percent of the data is set aside as a validation set, that is, the holdout fraction is 0.2.

As Ishaan Gulrajani and David Lopez-Paz [15] put it, any DG algorithm without model selection is incomplete. We use two model selection criteria in our experiments:

– **Training-domain validation set**. We split every training domain into two subsets used for training and validation respectively. Then, we aggregate the validation subsets of all training domains to obtain the final validation set. Finally, the model maximizing the top-1 accuracy on the validation set is chosen as the best model.
– **Testing-domain validation set**. We split the testing domain into testing and validation subsets. The model maximizing the top-1 accuracy on this validation set is chosen as the best model.

Note that the leave-one-domain-out validation experiments are conducted just like previous work [27]. We select one domain for testing and the remaining domains for training every time. Finally, the average top-1 accuracy of classification is calculated as the evaluation metric for each dataset.

4.2   Main Results and Discussion

Comparison with Other Methods. In our experiments, we choose the vanilla VPT [25] method and popular DG methods (including ERM [15], DANN [8],

Table 1. Experimental Results of ViT-B/16.

Model selection method: training-domain validation set						
Algorithm	PACS	VLCS	OH	TI	DN	Avg
ERM [15]	92.9	81.4	78.9	53.6	56.1	72.6
DANN [8]	92.2	80.1	78.0	47.9	57.5	71.1
CORAL [11]	92.6	79.6	78.5	51.7	56.4	71.8
MIRO [21]	95.2	81.1	82.5	52.9	56.6	73.7
VPT-Shallow [25]	**97.0**	81.7	83.6	53.1	58.7	74.8
CSVPT-Shallow (Ours)	96.6	**82.7**	84.2	**56.3**	**59.2**	**75.8**
VPT-Deep [25]	**96.6**	**82.9**	85.0	57.0	59.6	76.2
CSVPT-Deep (Ours)	**96.6**	82.7	**85.5**	**57.7**	**59.8**	**76.5**
Model selection method: testing-domain validation set						
ERM [15]	90.8	79.1	74.9	54.2	56.2	71.0
DANN [8]	90.6	81.4	76.2	50.7	57.7	71.3
CORAL [11]	90.6	80.2	76.8	52.0	56.0	71.1
MIRO [21]	95.8	83.6	82.3	58.8	57.2	75.5
VPT-Shallow [25]	**96.8**	83.2	83.6	56.7	59.0	75.9
CSVPT-Shallow (Ours)	96.6	**83.5**	84.5	**60.1**	59.5	76.8
VPT-Deep [25]	97.2	**84.9**	85.2	59.9	59.8	77.4
CSVPT-Deep (Ours)	**97.3**	**84.9**	85.0	**60.1**	**60.0**	**77.5**

CORAL [11], MIRO [21]) as our baselines. We provide extensive performance on five DG benchmarks in Table 1. For the sake of fairness, all the experiments in Table 1 are conducted with the same backbone, ViT-B/16 for CLIP [32], keeping other experimental conditions as consistent as possible. As said in the last subsection, we use two model selection criteria in our experiments: training-domain validation set and testing-domain validation set. We show the corresponding experimental results at the top and bottom of Table 1. Experimental results in Table 1 show that popular full fine-tuning DG methods (e.g., ERM [15], DANN [8], CORAL [11]) are prone to overfitting training data and often have inferior DG performances. MIRO that utilizes a mutual information regularization significantly improves performance on every dataset, resulting in +0.9pp average improvement (72.6% → 73.7%) with training domain validation set and +4.2pp average improvement (71.3% → 75.5%) with testing domain validation set, which achieved SOTA performance with the backbone of ViT-B/16 for CLIP before VPT. Compared to MIRO, the vanilla VPT algorithm further improves performance on almost every benchmark dataset. We obtain 74.8% average top-1 accuracy with VPT-Shallow and 76.2% with VPT-Deep using the first model selection criterion, while VPT-Shallow achieves 75.9% average top-1 accuracy and VPT-Deep 77.4% using the second model selection criterion. VPT-Deep slightly outperforms VPT-Shallow, because VPT-Shallow only tunes the input of the first Transformer layer, and VPT-Deep tunes that of each layer. Most

Table 2. Experimental Results of ViT-L/14.

Algorithm	PACS	VLCS	OH	TI	DN	Avg
Model selection method: training-domain validation set						
VPT-Shallow [25]	98.5	81.6	88.5	60.0	63.6	78.4
CSVPT-Shallow (Ours)	**98.6**	**81.8**	**89.0**	**61.5**	**63.7**	**78.9**
VPT-Deep [25]	98.4	82.3	90.8	**65.4**	65.0	80.4
CSVPT-Deep (Ours)	**98.5**	**83.0**	**90.9**	65.3	**65.3**	**80.6**
Model selection method: testing-domain validation set						
VPT-Shallow [25]	**98.5**	81.7	88.3	62.9	**64.3**	79.1
CSVPT-Shallow (Ours)	**98.5**	**82.1**	**88.9**	**66.1**	64.1	**79.9**
VPT-Deep [25]	98.5	84.3	90.3	**67.3**	65.5	81.2
CSVPT-Deep (Ours)	**98.7**	**85.3**	**90.7**	67.1	**65.7**	**81.5**

importantly, our proposed CSVPT further improves the performance on the five benchmark datasets, especially in the setting of "Shallow": +1.0pp average improvement (74.8% → 75.8%) with the training domain validation set and +0.9pp average improvement (75.9% → 76.8%) with the testing domain validation set. However, in the setting of "Deep", the improvement of CSVPT is not so remarkable: +0.3pp average improvement (76.2% → 76.5%) with the training domain validation set and +0.1pp average improvement (77.4% → 77.5%) with the testing domain validation set. Anyway, the experimental results have shown the superior performance of CSVPT over popular DG methods and the vanilla VPT, which validates the effectiveness of the CSVPT algorithm.

CSVPT on Various Backbone Scales. In this part, we explore how different backbone scales influence the performance of our proposed CSVPT. We choose two different backbones for comparison: ViT-B/16 and ViT-L/14 for CLIP. The experimental results are listed in Tables 1 and 2, respectively. Similarly, in Table 2, CSVPT also achieves superior performances over VPT, especially in the setting of "Shallow": +0.5pp average improvement (78.4% → 78.9%) with the training domain validation set and +0.8pp average improvement (79.1% → 79.9%) with the testing domain validation set. Besides, we can find that there is a remarkable performance improvement on the five benchmarks when using larger Transformer backbones ViT-L/14: +4.0pp average improvement (77.5% → 81.5%), which achieves new SOTA performances.

CSVPT with Different Dataset Scales. As we know, the VPT method [25] consistently outperforms other tuning methods across different training dataset scales. In order to explore whether our proposed CSVPT algorithm could handle domain generalization problems with different dataset scales, we gradually reduce the training data in the next experiments. Detailed experimental results are presented in Fig. 2. From Fig. 2, we can find that the average accuracy decreases gradually as the size of the training set decreases, but our proposed CSVPT always outperforms VPT and MIRO in this process. Surprisingly,

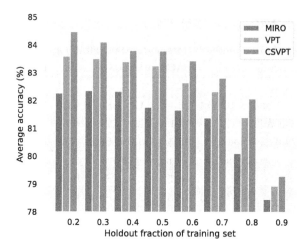

Fig. 2. DG performances with different dataset scales on the OfficeHome benchmark. We change the holdout fraction of the training set from 0.2 to 0.9, that is, we gradually reduce the training data from 80% to 10% of all training domain datasets. The variation of the average accuracy on the four domains that are alternately used as the testing domain with the size of the training set is shown in the histogram.

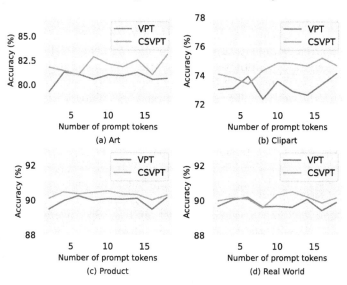

Fig. 3. Performances of VPT (without PGMs) and VPT (with PGMs) with different numbers of prompt tokens N. In this experiment, we also adopt the leave-one-domain-out scheme, which chooses one domain as the testing domain and aggregates the remaining domains as training domains. We show experimental results on the four domains of OfficeHome benchmark in this figure: (a) Art; (b) Clipart; (c) Product; (d) Real World. The caption represents the testing domain at each time.

CSVPT with less than 40% of training data (i.e., the holdout fraction is 0.6) could achieve the performance of VPT with 80% of training data (i.e., the holdout fraction is 0.2), while CSVPT with only 20% of training data achieves the performance of MIRO with 80% of training data. Besides, when training data is extremely scarce, the performance of CSVPT deteriorates rapidly. We believe that the reason for this phenomenon is that training data is too scarce to train PGMs well enough to generate meaningful specific prompts.

CSVPT with Different Numbers of Prompt Tokens N. The difference between the vanilla VPT and our proposed CSVPT lies in whether PGMs are used to generate specific prompts. We conduct more experiments to illustrate the difference with and without the PGMs. In this part, different numbers of prompt tokens N are used in our experiments to show the consistency of CSVPT's superiority over VPT methods. Specially, we only change the number of prompt tokens N from 2 to 18, keeping other experimental conditions the same. We show detailed experimental results on the OfficeHome benchmark in Fig. 3. Observing the curves in Fig. 3, we can find that the CSVPT method achieves the highest performance when using different numbers of prompt tokens for different datasets. For Art, CSVPT achieved the highest performance of 83.2% when N equals 18. But for Clipart, Product and Real World, N equals 18, 10 and 12, respectively. Yet despite all that, the orange curve almost always lies on top of the blue curve in each subfigure, which means CSVPT (with PGMs) almost always outperforms VPT (without PGMs) on each testing domain of OfficeHome benchmark. This observation is violated only at some special points, e.g., when N equals 6 or 8. However, CSVPT always achieves higher optimal performance than VPT.

More Ablations on Common and Specific Prompts. The above experiments mainly focus on the comparison between VPT (which only uses common prompts) and CSVPT (which uses both common prompts and specific prompts). To further show the necessity of both kinds of prompts, we conduct an ablation study to compare results with common prompts only (VPT), specific prompts only (SVPT), and a combination of both (CSVPT). Experimental results in Table 3 show that CSVPT achieves the best performance, which also justifies both the necessity of common prompts and that of specific prompts in CSVPT.

Table 3. Ablation Experiments on Common and Specific Prompts.

Algorithm	PACS	VLCS	OH	TI	DN	Avg.
VPT	97.0	81.7	83.6	53.1	58.7	74.8
SVPT	95.8	81.5	82.8	50.7	58.0	73.8
CSVPT	**96.6**	**82.7**	**84.2**	**56.3**	**59.2**	**75.8**

4.3   Case Study

In this part, we study three cases in detail to further illustrate how the PGMs influence the output of Transformers.

Input image   Pre-trained   VPT   CSVPT(Ours)

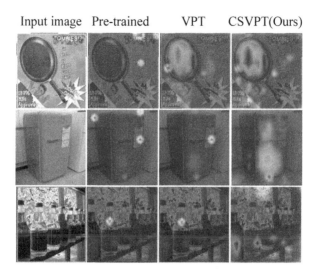

Fig. 4. We show how the attention flows from the start to the end throughout the Transformer when using the pre-trained backbone (without fine-tuning), VPT methods and our proposed CSVPT methods.

Similar to other tuning methods [36], VPT-based methods mainly influence the process of attention in this way:

$$
\begin{aligned}
&\mathrm{Attn}(\mathbf{q^T W_q}, \mathrm{concat}(\mathbf{CW_k}, \mathbf{PW_k}), \mathrm{concat}(\mathbf{CW_v}, \mathbf{PW_v})) \\
&= \lambda \mathrm{Attn}(\mathbf{q^T W_q}, \mathbf{CW_k}, \mathbf{CW_v}) + (1-\lambda)\mathrm{Attn}(\mathbf{q^T W_q}, \mathbf{PW_k}, \mathbf{PW_v}),
\end{aligned} \tag{11}
$$

where $\mathbf{q} \in \mathbb{R}^d$ denotes a query token, $\mathbf{C} = [t_1, \ldots, t_M]^T \in \mathbb{R}^{M \times d}$ denotes context tokens, $\mathbf{P} = [p_1, \ldots, p_N]^T \in \mathbb{R}^{N \times d}$ denotes prompt tokens, $\mathbf{W_q}, \mathbf{W_k}, \mathbf{W_v} \in \mathbb{R}^{d \times d'}$ denote the weights of the linear layers before attention, and

$$
\lambda = \frac{\sum_i \exp(\mathbf{q^T W_q W_k^T C^T})_i}{\sum_i \exp(\mathbf{q^T W_q W_k^T C^T})_i + \sum_i \exp(\mathbf{q^T W_q W_k^T P^T})_i}. \tag{12}
$$

In (11), the second term shows how prompt tokens influence the previous attention. In order to intuitively demonstrate the effect of (sample-specific) prompt tokens on the attention, we show how the attention flows from the start to the end in Fig. 4 using a technique called "Attention Rollout" [37]. In the first case of Fig. 4, the pre-trained model without fine-tuning focuses on pixels not on the "pan", while the models with VPT-based method focus on the right pixels. However, compared to the VPT method (without specific prompt tokens), the proposed CSVPT method (with specific prompt tokens generated by PGMs) pays more attention to the object in the image. In the second case, pre-trained models without fine-tuning and with VPT method only focus on local point-like regions of the object in the image, but our CSVPT method focuses on bigger regions of the object. Surprisingly, in the third case, the CSVPT method captures three objects in the image, while other methods only focus on the bottleneck of one bottle in that image. In a word, the success of the three cases shown in Fig. 4 further illustrates the benefit of PGMs and sample-specific prompt tokens on the DG classification tasks.

5   Conclusion

In this paper, we propose a novel Common-Specific Visual Prompt Tuning (CSVPT) method to adapt pre-trained vision Transformers for domain generalization problems in image classification. It tunes the pre-trained vision Transformer by appending several trainable prompt tokens to the input of the Transformer layers. Different from existing methods, CSVPT jointly learns domain-common prompts to capture the task context and sample-specific prompts to capture information about data distribution, which are generated for each sample through a trainable prompt-generating module (PGM). Combining the domain-common prompts and the sample-specific prompts, CSVPT makes dynamic visual prompts changing with data distributions adaptively, which helps OOD generalization. Our experimental results demonstrate the effectiveness of the proposed method. CSVPT achieves consistent superior performance over other related DG methods under different experimental settings. Furthermore, CSVPT with ViT-L/14 achieves new state-of-the-art performances on the five widely used datasets of DomainBed benchmarks. Our experimental results also illustrate that the success of CSVPT probably results from its positive influence on the attention flows in the vision Transformer models. We hope that this study will encourage more research on advanced fine-tuning approaches for domain generalization, and more theoretical analysis and technical improvement will be our future work.

Acknowledgements. This work was supported in part to Dr. Liansheng Zhuang by NSFC under contract No.U20B2070 and No.61976199.

References

1. Voulodimos, A., Doulamis, N., Doulamis, A., Protopapadakis, E.: Deep learning for computer vision: a brief review. Comput. Intell. Neurosci. **2018**, 7068349 (2018)
2. Lopez, M.M., Kalita, J.: Deep learning applied to NLP. arXiv preprint arXiv:1703.03091 (2017)
3. Zhang, Z., Geiger, J., Pohjalainen, J., Mousa, A.E.-D., Jin, W., Schuller, B.: Deep learning for environmentally robust speech recognition: an overview of recent developments. ACM Trans. Intell. Syst. Technol. (TIST) **9**(5), 1–28 (2018)
4. Kamath, U., Liu, J., Whitaker, J.: Deep Learning for NLP and Speech Recognition. Springer, Cham (2019). https://doi.org/10.1007/978-3-030-14596-5
5. Shen, Z., et al.: Towards out-of-distribution generalization: a survey. arXiv preprint arXiv:2108.13624 (2021)
6. Wang, J., et al.: Generalizing to unseen domains: a survey on domain generalization. In: IEEE Transactions on Knowledge and Data Engineering (2022)

7. Zhou, K., Liu, Z., Qiao, Y., Xiang, T., Loy, C.C.: Domain generalization in vision: a survey. arXiv preprint arXiv:2103.02503 (2021)
8. Ganin, Y., et al.: Domain-adversarial training of neural networks. J. Mach. Learn. Res. **17**(1), 2030–2096 (2016)
9. Li, H., Pan, S.J., Wang, S., Kot, A.C.: Domain generalization with adversarial feature learning. In: Proceedings of the IEEE Conference on Computer Vision and Pattern Recognition, pp. 5400–5409 (2018)
10. Li, Y., et al.: Deep domain generalization via conditional invariant adversarial networks. In: Ferrari, V., Hebert, M., Sminchisescu, C., Weiss, Y. (eds.) ECCV 2018. LNCS, vol. 11219, pp. 647–663. Springer, Cham (2018). https://doi.org/10.1007/978-3-030-01267-0_38
11. Sun, B., Saenko, K.: Deep CORAL: correlation alignment for deep domain adaptation. In: Hua, G., Jégou, H. (eds.) ECCV 2016. LNCS, vol. 9915, pp. 443–450. Springer, Cham (2016). https://doi.org/10.1007/978-3-319-49409-8_35
12. Arjovsky, M., Bottou, L., Gulrajani, I., Lopez-Paz, D.: Invariant risk minimization. arXiv preprint arXiv:1907.02893 (2019)
13. Khosla, A., Zhou, T., Malisiewicz, T., Efros, A.A., Torralba, A.: Undoing the damage of dataset bias. In: Fitzgibbon, A., Lazebnik, S., Perona, P., Sato, Y., Schmid, C. (eds.) ECCV 2012. LNCS, vol. 7572, pp. 158–171. Springer, Heidelberg (2012). https://doi.org/10.1007/978-3-642-33718-5_12
14. Piratla, V., Netrapalli, P., Sarawagi, S.: Efficient domain generalization via common-specific low-rank decomposition. In: International Conference on Machine Learning, pp. 7728–7738. PMLR (2020)
15. Gulrajani, I., Lopez-Paz, D.: In search of lost domain generalization. arXiv preprint arXiv:2007.01434 (2020)
16. Devlin, J., Chang, M.-W., Lee, K., Toutanova, K.: BERT: pre-training of deep bidirectional transformers for language understanding. arXiv preprint arXiv:1810.04805 (2018)
17. Floridi, L., Chiriatti, M.: GPT-3: Its nature, scope, limits, and consequences. Mind. Mach. **30**(4), 681–694 (2020)
18. Dosovitskiy, A., et al.: An image is worth 16x16 words: transformers for image recognition at scale. arXiv preprint arXiv:2010.11929 (2020)
19. Zhang, C., et al.: Delving deep into the generalization of vision transformers under distribution shifts. In: Proceedings of the IEEE/CVF Conference on Computer Vision and Pattern Recognition, pp. 7277–7286 (2022)
20. Li, Z., Ren, K., Jiang, X., Li, B., Zhang, H., Li, D.: Domain generalization using pretrained models without fine-tuning. arXiv preprint arXiv:2203.04600 (2022)
21. Cha, J., Lee, K., Park, S., Chun, S.: Domain generalization by mutual-information regularization with pre-trained models. arXiv preprint arXiv:2203.10789 (2022)
22. Zhang, X., Iwasawa, Y., Matsuo, Y., Gu, S.S.: Amortized prompt: guide clip to domain transfer learning. arXiv preprint arXiv:2111.12853 (2021)
23. Hendrycks, D., Liu, X., Wallace, E., Dziedzic, A., Krishnan, R., Song, D.: Pretrained transformers improve out-of-distribution robustness. arXiv preprint arXiv:2004.06100 (2020)
24. Kumar, A., Raghunathan, A., Jones, R., Ma, T., Liang, P.: Fine-tuning can distort pretrained features and underperform out-of-distribution. arXiv preprint arXiv:2202.10054 (2022)
25. Jia, M., et al.: Visual prompt tuning. arXiv preprint arXiv:2203.12119 (2022)
26. Zhou, K., Yang, J., Loy, C.C., Liu, Z.: Learning to prompt for vision-language models. arXiv preprint arXiv:2109.01134 (2021)

27. Li, D., Yang, Y., Song, Y.-Z., Hospedales, T.M.: Deeper, broader and artier domain generalization. In: Proceedings of the IEEE International Conference on Computer Vision, pp. 5542–5550 (2017)

28. Fang, C., Xu, Y., Rockmore, D.N.: Unbiased metric learning: on the utilization of multiple datasets and web images for softening bias. In: Proceedings of the IEEE International Conference on Computer Vision, pp. 1657–1664 (2013)

29. Venkateswara, H., Eusebio, J., Chakraborty, S., Panchanathan, S.: Deep hashing network for unsupervised domain adaptation. In: Proceedings of the IEEE Conference on Computer Vision and Pattern Recognition, pp. 5018–5027 (2017)

30. Beery, S., Van Horn, G., Perona, P.: Recognition in terra incognita. In: Ferrari, V., Hebert, M., Sminchisescu, C., Weiss, Y. (eds.) ECCV 2018. LNCS, vol. 11220, pp. 472–489. Springer, Cham (2018). https://doi.org/10.1007/978-3-030-01270-0_28

31. Peng, X., Bai, Q., Xia, X., Huang, Z., Saenko, K., Wang, B.: Moment matching for multi-source domain adaptation. In: Proceedings of the IEEE/CVF International Conference On Computer Vision, pp. 1406–1415 (2019)

32. Radford, A., et al.: Learning transferable visual models from natural language supervision. In: International Conference on Machine Learning, pp. 8748–8763. PMLR (2021)

33. Bai, H., et al.: DecAug: out-of-distribution generalization via decomposed feature representation and semantic augmentation. In: Proceedings of the AAAI Conference on Artificial Intelligence, vol. 35, pp. 6705–6713 (2021)

34. Parascandolo, G., Neitz, A., Orvieto, A., Gresele, L., Schölkopf, B.: Learning explanations that are hard to vary. arXiv preprint arXiv:2009.00329 (2020)

35. Wang, M., Deng, W.: Deep visual domain adaptation: a survey. Neurocomputing **312**, 135–153 (2018)

36. He, J., Zhou, C., Ma, X., Berg-Kirkpatrick, T., Neubig, G.: Towards a unified view of parameter-efficient transfer learning. arXiv preprint arXiv:2110.04366 (2021)

37. Abnar, S., Zuidema, W.: Quantifying attention flow in transformers. arXiv preprint arXiv:2005.00928 (2020)

Filter Pruning via Automatic Pruning Rate Search

Qiming Sun[1], Shan Cao[1(✉)], and Zhixiang Chen[2]

[1] Shanghai University, Shanghai 200444, China
cshan@shu.edu.cn
[2] The University of Sheffield, Sheffield S1 4DP, UK

Abstract. Model pruning is important for deploying models on devices with limited resources. However, the searching of optimal pruned model is still a significant challenge due to the large space to be exploited. In this paper, we propose an Automatic Pruning Rate Search(APRS) method to achieve automatic pruning. We reveal the connection between the model performance and Wasserstein distance to automatic searching optimal pruning rate. To reduce the search space, we quantify the sensitivity of each filter layer by layer and reveal the connection between model performance and Wasserstein distance. We introduce an end-to-end optimization method called Pareto plane to automatically search for the pruning rate to fit the overall size of the model. APRS can obtain more compact and efficient pruning models. To verify the effectiveness of our method, we conduct extensive experiments on ResNet, VGG and DenseNet, and the results show that our method outperforms the state-of-the-art methods under different parameter settings.

Keywords: Filter pruning · Pruning rate search · Pareto optimization

1 Introduction

Convolutional neural networks (CNNs) have achieved great success in computer vision applications such as image classification [12,28,31], object detection [61,62], and segmentation [60]. However, most state-of-the-art CNNs are difficult to run in real-time on resource-limited embedded terminals due to high requirements on computing power and memory footprint. Reducing the computational cost and model size is an eternal and important requirement. To achieve this, prevalent technologies include network pruning [22,32–36], weight quantization [37–41], knowledge distillation [42–46], and low-rank decomposition [47–49].

This work is supported by National Natural Science Foundation of China (No.61904101) and Shanghai Committee of Science and Technology of China (No.21ZR1422200).

Supplementary Information The online version contains supplementary material available at https://doi.org/10.1007/978-3-031-26351-4_36.

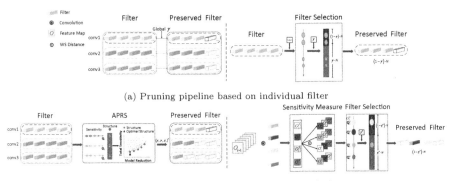

(a) Pruning pipeline based on individual filter

(b) Pruning pipieline based on feature maps before and after pruning

Fig. 1. Two pipelines for pruning tasks. γ_i is the pruning rate of i-th layer. Figure 1(a) shows a traditional pipeline based on weight attribute sorting. The left and right are the result and process of manually setting the pruning rate. (b) is our pipeline based on the information difference of feature maps before and after pruning. (Left) Determining optimal pruned structure using automatic structure redistribution. (Right) Filter selection using the wasserstein distance.

CNN pruning can be viewed as a search problem in the pruning solution space. The solution space of pruning consists of the pruning rate of each layer, and each pruning solution corresponds to a sub-net or pruned candidate. In huge search space, the task of pruning is to get a more compact and efficient model to adapt to more application scenarios and devices. Filter pruning is dedicated to searching for filters that can satisfy the accuracy under the target model size. Its process has two steps, filter sorting and pruning rate selection. In the first step, measurement criteria are usually designed based on weights or output feature maps to evaluate the importance of filters, and eliminate the weights with less importance in units of filters. Filter sorting is mainly based on experience to propose custom metrics.

Pruning Rate Selection: After sorting the importance of filters, it is necessary to find the pruning rate to prune the pre-trained model. The choice of pruning rate in CNN has a huge impact on performance [10]. When a suitable pruning rate is used, the accuracy of the pruned model can even exceed the original model [65]. The choice of pruning rate can be divided into two ways: pre-defined and automatic search [1]. Pre-defined methods manually specify the clipping rate of each layer and determine the target structure in advance. Such methods usually remove parameters in each layer with fixed pruning rate [2,6], as shown on the left side of Fig. 1(a). Despite the target model size can be achieved, each layer retains a large amount of redundancy. The pre-defined methods cannot compare the pros and cons of different pruning rates, and it is difficult to prove the correctness of the pre-defined pruning rates. Moreover, the optimal pruning rate combination will change with the requirements of the model size, so the pre-defined method requires a lot of manual labor. Automatic search for pruning rates has begun to emerge, and more suitable pruning rates are automatically obtained through theoretical guidance, enabling end-to-end fine-tuning without manual labor. A specific compression rate on a continuous space can be auto-

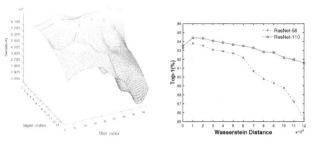

(a) Visualize the sensitivity of   (b) The effect of distance.
different layers on VGG-16.

Fig. 2. Visualization of the pruning loss. (a) is the sensitivity of some filters in convolutional layers of VGG-16. (b) reveal the connection between the model performance and wasserstein distance for ResNet-56 and ResNet-110.

matically generated using the DDPG algorithm in reinforcement learning [17]. Singh *et al.* [7] models the pruning problem as a min-max optimization problem, and control the accuracy loss by adjusting the pruning rate. Automated deep compression [8] uses reinforcement learning to learn the optimal sparsity rate for each layer according to different requirements such as guaranteeing accuracy or limiting the amount of computation. However, in general, the current automatic methods do not quantitatively analyze the importance of each filter, and cannot maximize the performance improvement brought by the pruning rate.

Inspired by automatic pruning, the sensitivity analysis of each filter is introduced in our APRS to quantitatively prune the redundancy of the model , so as to search for a more suitable pruning rate. As shown in Fig. 1(b), we use Wasserstein distance to calculate the sensitivity and reveal that there is a strong correlation between the sensitivity of the pruned structure and the accuracy after fine-tune, this can help us quickly estimate the accuracy. Figure 2(b) analyzes the relationship between the sub-network performance and sensitivity of ResNet-56 and ResNet-110. When the distance is within 7M, the sub-network accuracy exceeds the baseline, which means that the network can be more compact and efficient. The role of sensitivity can be explained in terms of the relative importance of the filters. We visualize the sensitivities of different layers and use the flatness of the sensitivity curves to characterize the relative contributions of the filters. As shown in Fig. 2(a), Layers with large curve fluctuations have high redundancy and vice versa. As the number of layers deepens, the redundancy increases greatly. APRS automatically assigns larger pruning rates to sensitive layers. The pruning rate depends on the number of filters retained in each layer. The filters retained under quantitative sensitivity analysis constituted a large number of sub-structure candidates. In this paper we attain a appropriate pruning rate by searching the sub-structure with Pareto optimization algorithm.

To sum up, our main contributions are three-fold:

1. Based on extensive statistical validation, we demonstrate that the impact of pruning can be effectively measured by Wasserstein distance. We were the first to introduce Wasserstein distance to predict model performance.
2. We propose an automatic search method to assign optimal pruning power without manual labor, which greatly saves the computational cost of automatic search for pruning rate.
3. APRS achieves state-of-the-art pruning performance compared to many more sophisticated methods. In the VGG-16 experiments, APRS can help us get 1.3% to 2.8% higher accuracy than the state-of-the-art algorithms. Meanwhile, it can greatly reduce the FLOPs of the model for computationally intensive devices.

2   Related Works

Different approaches have been proposed to obtain more compact, faster and more efficient networks, mainly including efficient neural network design [2, 12, 28, 31], pruning [13, 14, 18, 19, 21, 34], quantization [24, 39, 41], and distillation [43–46]. This paper briefly discusses related work on filter pruning and automated machine learning for pruning.

CNN pruning is mainly divided into unstructured pruning [4, 11, 69], where arbitrary parameters can be removed, and structured pruning [6, 32, 36], where a set of weights is removed. Structured pruning is divided into filter pruning and channel pruning [64], etc. Filter pruning removes filters under certain metric. Since the original convolutional structure in filter prunnnig is still preserved, no dedicated hardware is required for implementation. [5] uses $l1$-norm as an indicator for judging the importance of filters. [10] uses the rank of the feature map of each layer to judge the importance of the filter, [16] uses the geometric median to prune the model, and delete the filter with a lower median. Some works judge whether the filter contributes [14] according to the importance of the output channel, and discard the unimportant filters. [15] prunes filters using Taylor expansion as a measure of pruning criteria. Channel Pruning regards the same output channel of different filters as a group, [13] proposes to prune channels through LASSO regression-based channel selection and least squares reconstruction. [6] uses the scaling factor γ in the BN layer to measure the importance of channels. Mitsuno *et al.*. [25] analyzes the effect of channels of different convolutional layers on model performance.

AutoML Based Pruning. Traditional manual pruning methods rely heavily on expert experience to balance the amount of calculation, parameter size and accuracy, and usually cannot obtain the best pruning rate strategy. Liu *et al.* [1] proposed that pruning can be solved by automated machine learning (AutoML), which determines hyperparameters through learning. After the emergence of AutoML, it was quickly combined with the network structure search method [66], and model pruning was performed by searching for the structure of the model. Most of the previous AutoML-based pruning methods are layer-by-layer pruning.

Table 1. Comparison of APRS and other state-of-the-art methods on VGG16 with CIFAR10, "No FT" means no fine-tuning is required, "Layer-wise" stand for hierarchical reallocation. "Auto-P" means automatically assign optimal pruning substructure.

Method	No FT	Layer-wise	Auto-P	Param.↓(%)	Acc.(%)
L1 [5]	✗	✓	✗	64.0	93.40
EagleEye [23]	✓	✗	✓	-	-
Hrank [10]	✗	✓	✗	82.1	93.43
ABCPruner [22]	✗	✗	✓	88.7	93.08
AutoCompress [65]	✗	✓	✓	89.0	93.21
APRS(ours)	✓	✓	✓	**89.9**	**94.21**

The typical work [17] proposes to adaptively determine the compression rate of each layer through reinforcement learning. In addition, A platform-aware neural network adaptation (NetAdapt) method [67] was proposed to sequentially obtain suitable pruning rate through progressive compression and short-term finetune. The work of [68] uses layer-by-layer greedy search to automate compression models. Currently, some AutoML based pruning methods pay attention to the compression rate of pruning.

Table 1 shows the exploration of pruning rates by recent automatic methods. HRank [10] introduces manually predefined hierarchical pruning rates, but cannot search for more accurate pruning rates. EagleEye [23] proposes to find the relative optimal pruning rate, but it can only be selected from several candidate models. [22] supports automatic search of pruned structures, but cannot be pruned hierarchically and cannot achieve high compression rates. Due to the lack of sensitivity analysis and subsequent optimization of pruning schemes in previous AutoML based methods, it is difficult to find the optimal number of filters for each layer of convolution. Newer research shows that the essence of pruning is to determine the number of filters, not to choose the important filter/channel [1]. Cai et al. [24] proposes to measure the sensitivity of each quantization scheme to obtain a quantization scheme with less loss. Inspired by [1,24], the APRS proposed in this paper considers the total sensitivity and regards the problem of automatic pruning as searching for an appropriate number of filters. Pareto optimization is applied to model formulation for the first time, which can accurately reduce parameters size or computational cost.

3   Methodology

In this paper, our task is to automatically obtain a more compact and efficient network given a large pre-trained model, while minimizing accuracy reduction and minimizing computational cost and memory consumption. APRS will automatically find filter pruning rates for each layer, and possible pruning rate combinations $\gamma_1, \gamma_2, ..., \gamma_L$ for L layers. We focus on finding suitable structure vectors to search for sub-structures, and acquire the target pruned model after optimization in our method. As shown in Fig. 3, first we measure the Wasserstein distance

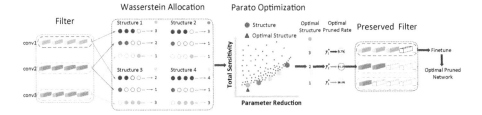

Fig. 3. Framework of our accurately filter pruning method (ASPR) for automatically optimizing pruning rates.

of all filters, which will guide us how to sort, called the sensitivity coefficient. According to the sensitivity coefficients, the unimportant filters in each layer can be roughly sorted and removed, which initially reduces the solution space in our APRS. The remaining filters are then reorganized across layers to construct as many the number of filter combinations(sub-structure vectors) as possible, and the total sensitivity of each sub-structure is calculated. All sub-structure vectors are sent into the Pareto plane, and its position on the Pareto plane can be determined according to the size and sensitivity of the sub-structure, so the sub-structure vector with the least perturbation can be intuitively locked under the constraint of model size. The sub-structure vector with the least sensitivity is output by the Pareto plane, and the pruning rate of each layer is fed back to the model to help us find the best sub-structure with minimal loss of accuracy. Finally, the sub-structure is fine-tuned end-to-end, and the fine-tuned model is used as the output of APRS. The raw optimization objective of pruning can be expressed as

$$\underset{\gamma_1, \gamma_2, \ldots, \gamma_L}{\arg\max} \; acc\left(M(\gamma_1, \gamma_2, \ldots, \gamma_L; T_{train}); T_{test}\right), \tag{1}$$

where γ_L is the pruning rate applied to the L-th layer, M is the pre-trained model with L layers. T_{train} and T_{test} represent the training dataset and test dataset respectively, acc is the model accuracy. The optimization goal is to achieve the highest accuracy acc on the test dataset. Given constraints such as targeted model size or FLOPs, a set of suitable pruning rates $\gamma_1, \gamma_2, \ldots, \gamma_L$ are automatically searched in APRS.

3.1 Notations

Assume a pre-trained CNN model consists of L convolutional layers, where $\mathbb{C}_l$ represents the l-th convolutional layer. The output channels (*i.e.*, feature maps) of the l-th layer, are denoted as $O_l = \left\{o_l^1, o_l^2, \ldots, o_l^{n_l}\right\} \; \epsilon \; \mathbb{R}^{n_l \times g \times h_l \times w_l}$, n_l represents the number of filters in $\mathbb{C}_l$, g is the size of input images. h_l and w_l are the height and width of the feature map, respectively. The parameter of the $\mathbb{C}_l$ layer can be described as a series of matries $W_{\mathbb{C}_l} = \left\{w_l^1, w_l^2, \ldots, w_l^{n_l}\right\} \; \epsilon \; \mathbb{R}^{n_l \times n_{l-1} \times a_l \times a_l}$, where the i-th filter of the l-th layer $w_l^i \; \epsilon \; \mathbb{R}^{n_{l-1} \times a_l \times a_l}$ can generate the i-th channel o_l^i. a_l refers to the kernel size. In our APRS, for the l-th layer, We get pruned output feature maps

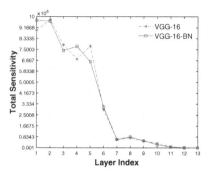

Fig. 4. Sensitivity of VGG-16 and its variant. In general, deeper convolutional layers have lower sensitivity.

$O_l^1, O_l^2, ..., O_l^{n_l}$, where $O_l^1 = \{0, o_l^2, ..., o_l^{n_l}\}$. For convenience, we assign zero to the activation value corresponding to the pruned channel. We compute the difference $\mathbb{Q}_l^i$ between the original output feature map and the output feature map after pruning the i-th filter. So we get the difference set: $\mathbb{Q}_l = \{\mathbb{Q}_l^1, \mathbb{Q}_l^2, ..., \mathbb{Q}_l^{n_l}\}$ where $\mathbb{Q}_l^i$ is the distance after removing the i-th filter o_l^i of the l-th layer. We prune filters with sequential traversal, so the number of distances is equal to the number of filters. In this paper, we call $\mathbb{Q}_l^i$ as sensitivity and use the Wasserstein distance to calculate it: $\mathbb{Q}_l^i = was\left\{O_l, O_l^i\right\}$ (Fig. 4).

3.2   Sensitivity Measurement

Wasserstein distance is used to measure the difference between two distributions, specifically, which describes the minimum cost required to transform from one distribution to the other.

$$
\begin{aligned}
was\,(O_1, O_2) &= \inf_{\gamma(x,y)\in\mathbb{Z}} \sum_{x,y} \|x - y\| \\
&= \inf_{\gamma\sim\mathbb{Z}(O_1,O_2)} E_{(x,y)\sim\gamma} \|x - y\|, \\
s.t.\ x &\in O_1, y \in O_2
\end{aligned}
\tag{2}
$$

Intuitively, $E_{(x,y)\sim\gamma} \|x - y\|$ can be understood as the consumption required to move O_1 to O_2 under the path planning of γ. $\mathbb{Z}$ is the set of all possible joint distributions that combine the O_1 and O_2 distributions. The Wasserstein distance is the minimum cost under the optimal path planning. Compared with using Kullback-Leibler(KL) divergence as the post-quantization sensitivity [24] in parameter quantization, the advantage of Wesserstein distance is that even if the support sets of the two distributions do not overlap or overlap very little, they can still reflect the distance of the two distributions. Since the activation values are relatively concentrated, to a certain extent, it is more friendly to use Wesserstein distance to calculate the distance.

So the importance of a single filter is obtained, so that we can flexibly choose the filters we need to delete according to the objective requirements, such as pre-trained model based on VGG-16 with CIFAR-10, if we need to get a 2.6M model, we can find a set of the most suitable filter pruning schemes. In this case, the accuracy of the model is up to 94.5%, which is theoretically the best. Assuming that the sensitivity measured by Wasserstein is:

$$\mathbb{Q}_i\left(\gamma_i\right) = \frac{1}{N} \sum_{j=1}^{N_{dist}} was\left(M\left(n_i, O_i\right), M'\left(n_i * \gamma_i, O_i'\right)\right) \tag{3}$$

$$s.t.\&n_i * \gamma_i \leqslant \mathbb{I}_{size}$$

where n_i is the number of filters for the i-th layer, and $\mathbb{I}_{size}$ refers to the limit of model size. The output of the sub-net is close to the output of the pre-trained model when $\mathbb{Q}_i(\gamma_i)$ is small, so it is relatively insensitive when pruning $n_i * \gamma_i$ filters for i-th layer, and vice versa.

3.3 Pareto Optimization

Pareto optimization is a scientific research method that has recently been used in mixed-precision quantization [24,26] to find the most suitable solution. The implementation principle of Pareto optimization is as follows. Given target model size $\mathbb{I}_{size}$, we measure the total sensitivity of pruned model for each combination of pruning rate. We choose the pruning rate corresponding to the smallest disturbance in Fig. 5. In detail, we solve the following optimization problem:

$$\underset{\gamma_1,\gamma_2,\dots,\gamma_L}{\arg\min} \ \mathbb{Q}_{sum} = \sum_{i=1}^{L}\sum_{n=1}^{n_i} \mathbb{Q}_i\left(\gamma_i\right) \ s.t. \ \sum_{i=1}^{L} n_i * \gamma_i \leqslant \mathbb{I}_{size} \tag{4}$$

Note that we verify the sensitivity of different filters independently (since pruning multiple channels and pruning these channels separately are very close in sensitivity). Using dynamic programming methods, we can get optimal solutions in different sets. Benefiting from the Pareto optimization algorithm, APRS can fulfill a batter balance between model size and sensitivity. Given a target model size $\mathbb{I}_{size}$, the pruning combination candidate with the smallest overall sensitivity is search as the optimal pruning scheme.

Suppose our final solution space is $\mathbb{P} = \prod_{l=1}^{L} n_l$. Here, the nominal goal is to maximize the sub-nets performance on the validation set by solving the following optimization problem: $\arg\min_{\gamma_1,\gamma_2,\dots,\gamma_L} \mathbb{Q}_{sum}$. The computational cost of the Pareto plane is reduced from $O(N\Pi_{i=1}^{L} n_i)$ to $O(N \sum_{i=1}^{L} n_i)$ by calculating the sensitivity of each layer separately. That is to say, we compute N total sensitivities $\mathbb{Q}_{sum}$ for all N different pruning choices, while the computational complexity of each sub-nets is $O(\sum_{i=1}^{L} n_i)$. The dynamic programming algorithm traverses sensitivity caused by each filter and obtains all the pruned sub-nets at the filter level, so theoretically can find the best pruning rate configuration among the set. Our experiments show that the final subnet achieves state-of-the-art accuracy with a smaller amount of parameters compared to the original pretrained model.

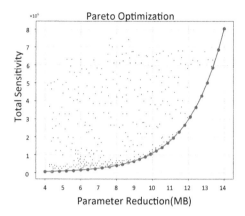

Fig. 5. The Pareto plane of VGG-16 on CIFAR-10. Each point shows a sub-structure vector setting. The x-axis is the parameter size of each configuration, and the y-axis is the total sensitivity. Then Pareto plane method chooses a sub-structure vector configuration with minimum perturbation given the model size.

APRS can also be used as a plug-and-play module, which can be combined with other filter pruning methods to bring a lot of improvement without changing the original algorithm. Further results may be found in supplementary material.

4 Experiments

4.1 Experimental Settings

Datasets and CNNs. In order to get a rigorous pruning result, we conducted experiments on the classic classification datasets CIFAR-10 [27] and ImageNet [70]. Mainstream CNN models was introduced into our ASPR experiments, including VGG-16 [31], Resnet-50/110 with residual module [28], and DenseNet-40 with a dense block [29], which is relatively simple and easy to implement in hardware. For each sub-net, we calculate the Wasserstein distance and use this as a theoretical guide for pruning rate search.

Evaluating Indicator. We adopt general evaluation indicator, *i.e.*, the number of weights and overall FLOPs (refers Float Points Operations) in the convolutional layer, to describe model size and floating-point operations of the sub-net. We adopt the variation of top-1 accuracy to compare model performance. To evaluate performance on specific tasks, we furnish top-1 and top-5 accuracy of pruned models and the pruning rate (denoted as PR) on CIFAR-10 and ImageNet.

Configurations. The implementation environment of APRS is pytorch [30]. The batch size, learning rate and momentum are set to 128, 0.01 and 0.9, respectively. We train on two NVIDIA Tesla P40 GPUs. It is worth noting that APRS

Table 2. Comparison results on VGG-16 for the CIFAR-10 dataset. Acc(%)↓ refers Top-1 accuracy decrease.

Model	Top-1(%)	Top-5(%)	Acc(%)↓	Parameters	FLOPs
VGG-16	93.87	99.47	0	14.98M	313.73M
L1 [5]	93.40	99.40	0.47	5.4M	206.00M
SFP [54]	92.08	-	0.28	5.4M	113.23M
Zhao *et al.* [51]	93.18	99.12	0.63	3.92M	190.00M
GAL-0.05 [18]	92.03	98.95	1.84	3.36M	189.49M
SSS [50]	93.02	99.40	0.85	3.93M	183.22M
Hinge [53]	93.59	-	0.28	2.98M	191.16M
APRS(ours)	**94.73**	**99.61**	**-0.86**	**2.92M**	**109.09M**
GAL-0.1 [18]	90.73	-	3.14	2.67M	171.92M
HRank [10]	92.34	-	1.53	2.64M	108.61M
Guo *et al.* [71]	93.76	-	0.11	2.85M	-
APRS(ours)	**94.49**	**99.67**	**-0.65**	**2.64M**	**91.57M**
ABCPruner [22]	93.08	-	0.79	1.67M	82.81M
HRank [10]	91.23	-	2.64	1.78M	73.70M
HAP [52]	93.66	-	0.21	1.51M	93.18M
APRS(ours)	**94.21**	**99.57**	**-0.34**	**1.51M**	**87.23M**

obtains substructure vectors based on the analysis results of one-off pruning all layers. But after getting the sub-structure vector, we employ progressive fine-tuning to restore the accuracy during the fine-tuning stage.

4.2   Results and Analysis

Results on CIFAR-10. We analyzed the performance of the mainstream network mentioned above on CIFAR-10. A variant of VGG [5] and DenseNet-40 with 3 dense blocks and 2 translation layers are used in our experiments, respectively.

Once the final sub-structure vector is determined, we immediately calculate the corresponding layer-by-layer pruning rates and guide the pruning to obtain the determined pruning model. The pruned model inherits the weights and is then fine-tuned. Take account of one-off pruning too many parameters may affect the network performance and fail to recover accuracy, we adopt a progressive fine-tune scheme, pruning a small number of filters, and fine-tuning the remaining network multiple times. In the fine-tune stage, we prune and fine-tune layer by layer to minimize the loss. We take the performance of the pre-trained model as the baseline and compare with other pruning methods. The experiment results show the accuracy of pruned sub-nets in proposed APRS outgo the original baseline.

VGG-16. VGG-16 only consists of plain layers, so we can easily calculate the sensitivity of each filter in each layer to guide pruning. We determine the number

Table 3. Pruning results of ResNet-110 on CIFAR-10. Acc(%)↓ refers Top-1 accuracy decrease. ResNet-110 denotes the baseline in our APRS. PR refers the pruning rate.

Model	Top-1(%)	Top-5(%)	Acc(%)↓	Parameters(PR)	FLOPs(PR)
ResNet-110	93.53	99.81	-	1.72M(0.0%)	252.89M(0.0%)
L1 [5]	93.55	-	-0.02	1.68M(2.3%)	213.00M(15.8%)
GAL-0.05 [18]	92.55	-	0.98	0.95M(44.7%)	130.20M(48.5%)
HRank [10]	94.23	-	-0.70	1.04M(39.5%)	148.70M(41.2%)
APRS(ours)	**94.39**	**99.82**	**-0.77**	**0.99M(42.4%)**	**139.27M(45.0%)**
ABCPruner [22]	93.58	-	-0.05	0.56M(67.4%)	89.87M(64.5%)
APRS(ours)	**93.97**	**99.29**	**-0.44**	**0.53M(69.2%)**	**87.86M(65.3%)**

of filters in each layer, then divide by the total number of filters in the current layer to get the pruning rate. The sub-network with the smallest overall sensitivity is searched through Pareto front planning until the limit of $\mathbb{I}_{size}$ is reached, so as to obtain the most accurate combination of L-layer pruning rates. Table 2 shows the performance of different methods, including filter sorting methods such as L1, and several adaptive importance-based methods [18,50]. Compared with the state-of-the-art Hessian-Aware Pruning [52] recently, APRS has achieved a very big leap. Compared to [10], we achieved a 2.11% improvement in accuracy, reaching 94.49% top-1 accuracy. For intuitive comparison, we set the similar model target size. When the model size $\mathbb{I}_{size}$ is set as 2.64M, the top-1 accuracy of APRS is 3.76% higher than that of GAL-0.01 [18], 2.15% higher than that of HRank [10], and the FLOPs almost half as those of GAL-0.01.

ResNet-110. Table 3 is the comparison result with other methods on ResNet-110. With parameter reductions and FLOPs close to the GAL [18], APRS achieves excellent top-1 accuracy (94.39% *vs.* 92.55%), which is better than the baseline model. Compared with HRank [10], APRS has advantages in all aspects (45.0% *vs.* 41.2% in FLOPs reduction, 42.4% *vs.* 39.5% in parameters reduction, 94.39% *vs.* 94.23% in top-1 accuracy). Compared with another automatic search pruned model method [22], APRS also attains better top-1 accuracy (93.97% *vs.* 93.58%) with slightly smaller parameters and FLOPs. Therefore, the Wasserstein distance can effectively reflect the relative importance of filters. Theoretically, APRS can fully remove the redundancy of the network since all channels can hypothetically be combined greedily.

DenseNet-40. Table 4 summarizes the experimental results on DenseNet-40. We observed the potential of APRS in removing FLOPs. Despite Liu *et al.* achieve a pruning performance close to the baseline [6], they only reduces FLOPs by 38.2%. In contrast, APRS can eliminate 45.7% FLOPs while maintaining high performance. Compared with GAL [18] and HRank [10], it has better compression rate in terms of parameters and FLOPs.

Table 4. Comparison on pruning approaches using DenseNet-40 on CIFAR-10. PR represents the pruning rate.

Model	Top-1(%)	Top-5(%)	Parameters(PR)	FLOPs(PR)
DenseNet-40	94.75	99.84	1.04M	0.282B
Liu *et al.*-40% [6]	94.81	-	0.66M(36.5%)	0.190B(32.6%)
HRank [10]	93.87	-	0.66M(36.5%)	0.167B(40.8%)
GAL-0.01 [18]	94.29	-	0.67M(35.6%)	0.182B(35.5%)
APRS(ours)	**94.37**	**99.85**	**0.63M(39.4%)**	**0.153B(45.7%)**

Table 5. Pruning results of ResNet-50 on ImageNet. PR represents the pruning rate.

Method	Top-1(%)	Parameters(PR)	FLOPs(PR)
Baseline	76.15	25.50M(0.0%)	4.09B(0.0%)
CP [13]	72.30	-	2.73B(33.2%)
GAL-0.5 [18]	71.95	21.20M(16.8%)	2.33B(43.0%)
SSS [50]	74.18	18.60M(27.0%)	2.82B(31.0%)
He *et al.* [54]	74.61	-	2.38B(41.8%)
HRank [10]	74.98	16.15M(36.7%)	2.30B(43.7%)
MetaP [55]	72.27	15.64M(38.7%)	2.31M(43.5%)
APRS(ours)	**75.58**	**16.17M(35.4%)**	**2.29B(44.0%)**
HAP [52]	75.12	14.13M(53.74%)	2.70B(66.1%)
GDP [56]	71.19	-	1.88B(54.0%)
APRS(ours)	**75.35**	**14.69M(57.6%)**	**1.94B(52.6%)**

Results on ImageNet. Table 5 reflects our performance for ResNet-50 on ImageNet to verify the proposed APRS. Generally, APRS outperforms other pruning methods in any aspects, including top-1 and top-5 accuracies, as well as FLOPs and parameters reduction. Specifically, our accuracy is improved by 3.31%(75.58% *vs.* 72.27%) in contrast to MetaP [55] while the parameter reduction and FLOPs are maintained. In detail, APRS removes 1.58× parameters and 1.79× FLOPs and the accuracy drops by only 0.57%, which is 0.6% better than HRank [10] under the same FLOPs and parameters, and outperforms the state-of-the-art HAP [52]. Furthermore, APRS greatly reduces model complexity compared to SSS [50] (44.0% vs. 31.0% for FLOPs). Summarily, more FLOPs can be removed in our APRS than state-of-the-art methods. Our method outperforms previous studies when removing nearly half of the parameters. Compared with HAP [52], we remove more parameters with almost the same performance.

Ablation Experiment. We conduct two ablation experiments using ResNet-50 on ImageNet to demonstrate the effectiveness of Wasserstein distance in APRS.

Table 6. Ablation studies of sensitivity indicators for ResNet-50 on the ImageNet dataset. Anti-APRS means pruning in the reverse order recommended by APRS, Random is achieved by randomly assigning channel sensitivity. $\downarrow\%$ means the percentage of the portion removed.

Method	Acc(%)	Parameters($\downarrow\%$)	FLOPs($\downarrow\%$)
ResNet-50	76.15	0.0	0.0
Random	70.68	21.6	30.42
Anti-APRS	69.47	22.8	27.53
APRS(ours)	**75.92**	**22.3**	**26.50**
Random	65.44	50.7	54.41
Anti-APRS	62.37	50.0	55.77
APRS(ours)	**74.72**	**52.9**	**57.21**

In the first ablation experiment, we apply a random constant pruning rate and demonstrate that sensitivity-based pruning is effective. The results in Table 6 show that when the pruning rate of the parameters is more than 20% , the accuracy of random pruning lags far behind APRS (less than 5.24%). In the second ablation experiment we use the reverse order of what APRS recommends, named Anti-APRS. It can be clearly observed that Anti-APRS performs poorly in all cases compared to APRS, with an accuracy of 62.37% at a pruning rate of 50% of the parameters. Random pruning is slightly better than Anti-APRS, while there is still a big gap than APRS. APRS reaches a higher top-1 accuracy, which proves that our proposed method in this paper is powerful. Table 6 confirms that using the overall Wasserstein ranking and considering the common influence of the sensitivity between the layers will bring greater benefits. The impact of each layer on the overall performance is limited in spite of every filter of the deep network can extract features. Therefore, the distribution of pruning force should be more precise and efficient. Table 6 shows that certain more representative filters can be selected to form more effective pruning networks by using APRS, resulting in higher overall performance. Further details may be found in supplementary material.

5   Conclusions

In previous AutoML based methods, we found that the redundancy between convolutional layers varies greatly and the combination of different pruning rates may lead to various accuracy with the same parameter reduction. To search for a suitable pruning rate, we introduce sensitivity analysis to evaluate the impact of filters in each layer. We can initially set the pruning rate of each layer based on sensitivity analysis, then the Pareto optimization algorithm was utilized to search for appropriate combination of pruning rates. We introduced the

Sinkhorn algorithm to help us solve the Wasserstein distance iteratively. Finally, we conducted experiments on the mainstream networks VGG-16 and ResNet-110, which proved that using sensitivity to remove the redundancy of the pre-trained model has a good effect. For VGG-16 on CIFAR-10, the top-1 accuracy reached 94.49% with 82.4% of the parameters are removed. In comparison to HRank [10], we achieve up to 2.15% higher accuracy with fewer parameters and FLOPs. Moreover, for ResNet-50 APRS achieves 75.35% top-1 accuracy (0.8% degradation) on ImageNet, after pruning 42.4% of the parameters.

References

1. Liu, Z., Sun, M., Zhou, T., Huang, G., Darrell, T.: Rethinking the value of Net-workPruning. In: ICLR (2019)
2. Howard, G., et al.: MobileNets: efficient Convolutional Neural Networks for Mobile Vision Applications. In: CVPR (2017)
3. Ta, M., Le, Q.V.: EfficientNet: rethinking Model Scaling for Convolutional Neural Networks. In: International Conference on Machine Learning, PMLR (2019)
4. Han, S., Pool, J., Tran, J., Dally, W.J.: Learning both weights and connections for efficient neural networks. In: NeurIPS (2015)
5. Li, H., Kadav, A., Durdanovic, I., Samet, H., Graf, H.P.: Pruning filters for efficient ConvNets. In: ICLR (2017)
6. Liu, Z., Li, J., Shen, Z., Huang, G., Yan, S., Zhang, C.: Learning efficient convolu-tional networks through network slimming. In: ICCV (2017)
7. Singh, P., Verma, V.K., Piyush Rai, V.P.N.: play and prune: adaptive filter pruning for deep model compression. In: IJCAI (2019)
8. He, Y., Han, S.: ADC: automated deep compression and acceleration with rein-forcement learning. In: CVPR (2018)
9. Carreira-Perpiñán, M.A., Idelbayev, Y.: "Learning-Compression" algorithms for neural net pruning. In: CVPR (2018)
10. Lin, M., et al.: HRank: filter pruning using high-rank feature map. In: CVPR (2020)
11. Han, S., Mao, H., Dally, W.J.: Deep compression: compressing deep neural net-works with pruning, trained quantization and Huffman coding. In: ICLR (2016)
12. Krizhevsky, A., Sutskever, I., Hinton, G.E.: ImageNet classification with deep con-volutional neural networks. In: NeurIPS (2012)
13. He, Y., Zhang, X., Sun, J.: Channel pruning for accelerating very deep neural networks. In: ICCV (2017)
14. Luo, J.H., Wu, J., Lin, W.: ThiNet: a filter level pruning method for deep neural network compression. In: ICCV (2017)
15. Molchanov, P., Tyree, S., Karras, T., Aila, T., Kautz, J.: Pruning convolutional neural networks for resource efficient inference. In: ICLR (2017)
16. He, Y., Liu, P., Wang, Z., Hu, Z., Yang, Y.: Filter pruning via geometric median for deep convolutional neural networks acceleration. In: CVPR (2019)
17. He, Y., Lin, J., Liu, Z., Wang, H., Li, L.-J., Han, S.: AMC: AutoML for model compression and acceleration on mobile devices. In: Ferrari, V., Hebert, M., Smin-chisescu, C., Weiss, Y. (eds.) ECCV 2018. LNCS, vol. 11211, pp. 815–832. Springer, Cham (2018). https://doi.org/10.1007/978-3-030-01234-2_48
18. Lin, S., et al.: Towards optimal structured CNN pruning via generative adversarial learning. In: ICCV (2019)

19. Lemaire, C., Achkar, A., Jodoin, P.M.: Structured pruning of neural networks with budget-aware regularization. In: CVPR (2019)
20. You, Z., Yan, K., Ye, J., Ma, M., Wang, P.: Gate decorator: global filter pruning method for accelerating deep convolutional neural networks. In: NeurIPS (2019)
21. Yu, R., et al.: NISP: pruning networks using neuron importance score propagation. In: CVPR (2018)
22. Lin, M., Ji, R., Zhang, Y., Zhang, B., Wu, Y., Tian, Y.: Channel pruning via automatic structure search. In: IJCAI (2020)
23. Li, B., Wu, B., Su, J., Wang, G.: EagleEye: fast sub-net evaluation for efficient neural network pruning. In: Vedaldi, A., Bischof, H., Brox, T., Frahm, J.-M. (eds.) ECCV 2020. LNCS, vol. 12347, pp. 639–654. Springer, Cham (2020). https://doi.org/10.1007/978-3-030-58536-5_38
24. Cai, Y., Yao, Z., Dong, Z., Gholami, A., Mahoney, M.W., Keutzer, K.: ZeroQ: a novel zero shot quantization framework. In: CVPR (2020)
25. Mitsuno, K., Kurita, T.: Filter pruning using hierarchical group sparse regularization for deep convolutional neural networks. In: ICPR (2020)
26. Dong, Z., et al.: HAWQ-V2: Hessian aware trace-weighted quantization of neural net-works. In: NeurIPS (2020)
27. Krizhevsky, A., Hinton, G.: Learning multiple layers of features from tiny images, technical report, CiteSeer (2009)
28. He, K., Zhang, X., Ren, S., Sun, J.: Deep residual learning for image recognition. In: CVPR (2016)
29. Huang, G., Liu, Z., Maaten, L.V.D., Weinberger, K.Q.: Densely connected convolutional networks. In: CVPR (2017)
30. Paszke, A., et al.: Automatic differentiation in pyTorch. In: NeurIPS (2017)
31. Simonyan, K., Zisserman, A.: Very deep convolutional networks for large-scale image recognition. In: ICLR (2015)
32. Zhang, T., Ye, S., Feng, X., Ma, X., Wang, Y.: StructADMM: achieving ultra-high efficiency in structured pruning for DNNs. In: IEEE Transactions on Neural Networks and Learning Systems, vol. 12, pp. 1–15 (2021)
33. Mingbao, L., et al.: Filter sketch for network pruning. In: IEEE Computer Society, pp. 1–10 (2020)
34. Chang, J., Lu, Y., Xue, P., Xu, Y., Wei, Z.: ACP: automatic channel pruning via clustering and swarm intelligence optimization for CNN. In: CVPR (2021)
35. Xu, P., Cao, J., Shang, F., Sun, W., Li, P.: Layer pruning via fusible residual convolutional block for deep neural networks. In: CVPR (2020)
36. Wanga, Z., Li, C., Wang, X.: Convolutional neural network pruning with structural redundancy reduction. In: CVPR (2021)
37. Zhu, F., et al.: Towards unified INT8 training for convolutional neural network. In: CVPR (2019)
38. Qin, H., Gong, R., Liu, X., Bai, X., Song, J., Sebe, N.: Binary neural networks: a survey. In: PR (2020)
39. Qin, H., et al.: Forward and backward information retention for accurate binary neural networks. In: CVPR (2020)
40. Kravchik, E., Yang, F., Kisilev, P., Choukroun, Y.: Low-bit quantization of neural networks for efficient inference. In: ICCV (2019)
41. Yao, Z., et al.: HAWQV3: dyadic neural network quantization. In: International Conference on Machine Learning, PMLR (2021)
42. Jin, Q., et al.: Teachers do more than teach: compressing image-to-image models. In: CVPR (2021)

43. Guo, J., et al.: Distilling object detectors via decoupled features. In: CVPR (2021)
44. Gou, J., Yu, B., Maybank, S.J., Tao, D.: Knowledge distillation: a survey. In: CVPR, pp. 1789–1819 (2021)
45. Mirzadeh, S., Farajtabar, M., Li, A., Levine, N., Ghasemzadeh, H.: Improved knowledge distillation via teacher assistant. In: AAAI (2020)
46. Tang, J., et al.: Understanding and improving knowledge distillation. In: CVPR (2020)
47. Sainath, T.N., Kingsbury, B., Sindhwani, V., Arisoy, E., Ramabhadran, B.: Low-rank matrix factorization for Deep Neural Network training with high-dimensional output targets. In: IEEE Computer Society (2013)
48. Swaminathan, S., Garg, D., Kannan, R., Andres, F.: Sparse low rank factorization for deep neural network compression. In: IEEE Computer Society, vol. 398, pp. 185–196 (2020)
49. Zhang, Y., Chuangsuwanich, E., Glass, J.: Extracting deep neural network bottleneck features using low-rank matrix factorization. In: IEEE Computer Society (2014)
50. Huang, Z., Wang, N.: Data-driven sparse structure selection for deep neural networks. In: Ferrari, V., Hebert, M., Sminchisescu, C., Weiss, Y. (eds.) ECCV 2018. LNCS, vol. 11220, pp. 317–334. Springer, Cham (2018). https://doi.org/10.1007/978-3-030-01270-0_19
51. Zhao, C., Ni, B., Zhang, J., Zhao, Q., Zhang, W., Tian, Q.: Variational convolutional neural network pruning. In: CVPR, pp. 304–320 (2019)
52. Yu, S., et al.: Hessian-aware pruning and optimal neural implant. In: Proceedings of the IEEE/CVF Winter Conference on Applications of Computer Vision, pp. 3880–3891 (2022)
53. Li, Y., Gu, S., Mayer, C., Gool, L.V., Timofte, R.: Group Sparsity: the hinge between filter pruning and decomposition for network compression. In: CVPR, pp. 8018–8027 (2020)
54. He, Y., Kang, G., Dong, X., Fu, Y., Yang, Y.: Soft filter pruning for accelerating deep convolutional neural networks. In: IJCAI (2018)
55. Liu, Z., et al.: MetaPruning: meta learning for automatic neural network channel pruning. In: ICCV (2019)
56. Lin, S., Ji, R., Li, Y., Wu, Y., Huang, F., Zhang, B.: Accelerating convolutional networks via global & dynamic filter pruning. In: IJCAI (2018)
57. Kurtz, M., et al.: Inducing and exploiting activation sparsity for fast inference on deep neural networks. In: International Conference on Machine Learning, PMLR, vol. 119, pp. 5533–5543. PMLR, Virtual (13–18 Jul 2020)
58. Zhang, Y., et al.: Carrying out CNN channel pruning in a white box. In: CVPR (2022)
59. Hu, H., Peng, R., Tai, Y.W., Tang, C.K.: Network trimming: a data-driven neuron pruning approach towards efficient deep architectures. In: ICCV (2019)
60. Chen, L.-C., Zhu, Y., Papandreou, G., Schroff, F., Adam, H.: Encoder-decoder with atrous separable convolution for semantic image segmentation. In: Ferrari, V., Hebert, M., Sminchisescu, C., Weiss, Y. (eds.) ECCV 2018. LNCS, vol. 11211, pp. 833–851. Springer, Cham (2018). https://doi.org/10.1007/978-3-030-01234-2_49
61. Redmon, J., Farhadi, A.: YOLOv3: an incremental improvement. In: CVPR (2018)
62. Xu, H., Yao, L., Zhang, W., Liang, X., Li, Z.: Auto-FPN: automatic network architecture adaptation for object detection beyond classification. In: ICCV (2019)
63. Mao, H., et al.: Exploring the granularity of sparsity in convolutional neural networks. In: ICCV (2017)

64. Wen, W., Wu, C., Wang, Y., Chen, Y., Li, H.: Learning structured sparsity in deep neural networks. In: Advances in Neural Information Processing Systems (2016)
65. Liu, N., Ma, X., Xu, Z., Wang, Y., Tang, J., Ye, J.: AutoCompress: an automatic DNN structured pruning framework for ultra-high compression rates. In: AAAI (2020)
66. Zoph, B., Vasudevan, V., Shlens, J., Le, Q.V.: Learning transferable architectures for scalable image recognition. In: CVPR (2018)
67. Yang, T.-J., et al.: NetAdapt: platform-aware neural network adaptation for mobile applications. In: Ferrari, V., Hebert, M., Sminchisescu, C., Weiss, Y. (eds.) ECCV 2018. LNCS, vol. 11214, pp. 289–304. Springer, Cham (2018). https://doi.org/10.1007/978-3-030-01249-6_18
68. Yu, J., Huang, T.: AutoSlim: towards one-shot architecture search for channel numbers. In: ICLR (2019)
69. Ye, S., et al.: Progressive weight pruning of deep neural networks using ADMM. In: CVPR (2018)
70. Russakovsky, O., et al.: ImageNet large scale visual recognition challenge. In: IJCV (2015)
71. Guo, Y., She, Y., Barbu, A.: Network pruning via annealing and direct sparsity control. In: IJCNN (2021)

A Lightweight Local-Global Attention Network for Single Image Super-Resolution

Zijiang Song[ID] and Baojiang Zhong[✉]

School of Computer Science and Technology, Soochow University, Suzhou 215008,
China
bjzhong@suda.edu.cn

Abstract. For a given image, the self-attention mechanism aims to capture dependencies for each pixel. It has been proved that the performance of neural networks which employ self-attention is superior in various image processing tasks. However, the performance of self-attention has extensively correlated with the amount of computation. The vast majority of works tend to use local attention to capture local information to reduce the amount of calculation when using self-attention. The ability to capture information from the entire image is easily weakened on this occasion. In this paper, a *local-global attention block* (LGAB) is proposed to enhance both the local features and global features with low calculation complexity. To verify the performance of LGAB, a lightweight *local-global attention network* (LGAN) for single image super-resolution (SISR) is proposed and evaluated. Compared with other lightweight state-of-the-arts (SOTAs) of SISR, the superiority of our LGAN is demonstrated by extensive experimental results. The source code can be found at https://github.com/songzijiang/LGAN.

1 Introduction

For a given low-resolution (LR) image, single image super-resolution (SISR) is a task aiming at generating a high-resolution (HR) one. Among the current mainstream SISR methods (e.g., [5,8–10,12,13,15,17,18,20,25]), the SwinIR [17] achieves the impressive performance, and the fundamental idea of SwinIR is self-attention. The self-attention captures *long-range dependencies* (LRDs) for each pixel in an image, and the greatest advantage of self-attention is producing large receptive fields. However, the advantage of self-attention comes with the huge computation. Therefore, lots of works (e.g., [7,16,24]) attempt to reduce the computation with less negative impact. Among them, reducing the number of

This work was supported in part by the Natural Science Foundation of the Jiangsu Higher Education Institutions of China under Grant 21KJA520007, in part by the National Natural Science Foundation of China under Grant 61572341, in part by the Priority Academic Program Development of Jiangsu Higher Education Institutions, in part by Collaborative Innovation Center of Novel Software Technology and Industrialization.

pixels involved to calculate the LRDs is the most salient means. In SwinIR [17], dividing the image into non-overlapped windows and executing the self-attention operation in each window. Next, the operation of shifting windows is performed to enlarge the receptive fields. By repeating the operations above, the receptive fields are expanded to the whole image. However, only local attention is used in SwinIR, and it is hard to acquire information efficiently from long-range targets directly. Thus, SwinIR suffers from the lack of long-range relationships to generate the image. Note that, it has been reported in [7] that calculating pixels on the specific path can also effectively reduce the amount of calculation and the receptive fields are able to be expanded to the whole image without repeating. However in CCNet [7], too much attention is paid to long-range relationships, and local relationships are neglected, it is fatal for CCNet [7]. Therefore, networks like CCNet, which reduces computation only by reducing the pixels involved to calculate LRDs, are difficult to achieve an outperforming result.

Motivated by the SwinIR [17] and CCNet [7], we aim to combine both local and global features in an efficient way and reduce the complexity of the self-attention computation. For that, we use self-attention both in the local features and global features in our proposed *local-global attention block* (LGAB). In our proposed LGAB, there are three attention parts: 1) window attention (WA), 2) shifted window attention (SWA), and 3) long-range attention (LRA). Dividing each image into non-overlapped windows is used in WA to extract the local features effectively. Due to the resolution of each window is small, the computational complexity is low in WA. The local features suffer from the lack of long-range relationships, which is expressed in the form of receptive fields. Therefore, we use SWA to build the relationship between neighbor windows and use LRA to expand the receptive fields to the whole image. LGAB can extract both local features and global features. To evaluate the performance of the LGAB we proposed, a *local-global attention network* (LGAN) using LGAB is therefore developed for SISR. For accommodating objects of multiple sizes and further enhancing information of receptive fields, multi-scale method is used in our LGAN.

The rest parts of this paper are organized as follows. Related works are described in Sect. 2 and our proposed LGAN and LGAB are described in Sect. 3. Extensive experiments are shown in Sect. 4 for the performance evaluation of our proposed LGAN. Lastly in Sect. 5, conclusion is drawn.

2   Related Work

The existing deep learning methods usually enlarge the receptive fields using self-attention for better performance. Non-local block and transformer block are two outstanding blocks using self-attention. For ease of understanding, a brief description of non-local neural networks and transformer-based networks in computer vision (CV) is given.

2.1   Non-local Neural Networks

Non-local neural network, whose basic idea is self-attention. This idea was first proposed in [29] as a generic block for capturing LRDs. The non-local operation in [29] can be seen as computing the weighted sum of other positions for each pixel. For each pixel, densely computing LRDs required by pixel-wise dot-products over the entire image has a high complexity. Therefore, multiple non-local blocks can not be added to the network, due to the unbearable amount of calculation. To address this issue, Huang *et al.* [7] suggested reducing the LRD computation by limiting the number of pixels involved. For that, *recurrent criss-cross attention* (RCCA) was proposed in [7], and it computes the LRDs at each pixel position along a specific criss-cross path. A network called *criss-cross network* (CCNet) using RCCA was then proposed for image segmentation [7]. The receptive fields can be easily expanded to the entire image without having to be repeated using non-local-based blocks. Additionally, Mei *et al.* [24] investigated the combinations of non-local operation and sparse representation, and proposed a novel *non-local sparse attention* (NLSA) with a dynamic sparse attention pattern for SISR. However, these approaches suffer from a huge computational burden and do not balance well the local and global representation capabilities.

2.2   Transformer in Computer Vision

Transformer was proposed in [27] firstly, whose outperforming results quickly swept through many tasks in natural language processing (NLP). Due to the difference in the dataset between CV and NLP, the number of pixels in the image is far greater than the number of words in the sentence. Repeating self-attention operations on each pixel in a transformer-based network causes unaffordable expenses in CV task. Therefore, dividing the image into non-overlapped 16×16 windows is used in ViT [3] for CV task. Each window is seen as a token and fed into the transformer block. With the operation above, the information of position in image is destroyed, and position embedding is therefore added to the network. ViT is effective to reduce the computation complexity compared to treating each pixel as a token. However, considering that taking each 16×16 window as a token could lose low-level information, especially for image restoration. To solve this issue, Swin [19] was proposed. The same as ViT [3], the input images are divided into non-overlapped windows. Different from ViT [3], the self-attention operation is only performed in each window. We can think of this operation as a local attention block. However, global information is lost as a result. To get the information from the entire image, a shifting window operation was proposed in [19]. With the repetition of the transformer operations, the receptive fields can be expanded to the global image. Due to the impressive performance of Swin, the network structure was applied to SISR and named SwinIR [17]. SwinIR achieved state-of-the-art (SOTA) result compared to the previous networks on the vast majority of benchmark datasets. Although the shifting operation is added in the network, SwinIR is not efficient enough at obtaining information from long-range targets.

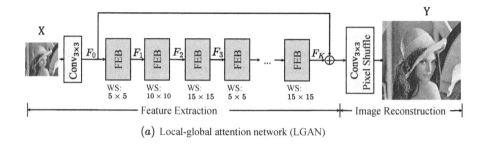

(*a*) Local-global attention network (LGAN)

(*b*) Feature extract block (FEB)

Fig. 1. The overall of the proposed LGAN. The window size of each feature extract block (FEB) is denoted by WS, and '⊕' denotes the operation of residual plus.

3   The Proposed Approach

In this section, the structures of 1) the proposed *local-global attention network* (LGAN), 2) *feature extract block* (FEB) and 3) *local-global attention block* (LGAB) are described.

3.1   Network Structure

As shown in Fig. 1, our proposed LGAN contains two stages: 1) feature extraction and 2) image reconstruction. A set of feature maps denoted by F_0 is generated by 3×3 convolution based on the given image X in the feature extraction stage as follows:

$$F_0 = \text{Conv}_{3 \times 3}(X), \tag{1}$$

where $\text{Conv}_{3 \times 3}(\cdot)$ denotes the convolution operation with 3×3 kernel size. As shown in Fig. 1, the generated F_0 is further enhanced by several FEBs. In our LGAN, it is empirically determined that the number of FEBs is 24 (i.e., $K = 24$). Finally in the image reconstruction stage, based on the 'coarse' feature maps F_0 and the residual part F_K, HR image Y will be generated via the *pixel shuffle* [26] as follows:

$$Y = \text{Conv}_{3 \times 3}(\text{U}(F_0 + F_K)), \tag{2}$$

where the pixel shuffle operator is denoted by $\text{U}(\cdot)$, which is used in LGAN for upsampling.

When training our LGAN, a set of image pairs $\{X^{(n)}, H^{(n)}\}_{n=1}^N$ is used. The $X^{(n)}$ denotes the LR image and the $H^{(n)}$ denotes the ground-truth (GT) image correspondingly. Minimizing the loss is performed for training between $Y^{(n)}$ and $H^{(n)}$; i.e.,

$$\Theta^* = \underset{\Theta}{\arg\min} \; \frac{1}{N} \sum_{n=1}^{N} \mathcal{L}\left(Y^{(n)}, H^{(n)}\right), \tag{3}$$

where Θ denotes the set of parameters to be learned in our LGAN, and $\mathcal{L}(\cdot)$ stands for the smooth ℓ_1 loss function [4].

3.2   Feature Extract Block (FEB)

Different from the existing transformer blocks, our FEBs excavate both local and global information simultaneously with low computational complexity as depicted in Fig. 1(b). In our proposed FEB, there are a local-global attention block (LGAB) and two shift-conv blocks [30]. For shift-conv blocks, smaller computational parameters are required when expanding the receptive fields compared with 3×3 convolutions. GELU is chosen to be the activation function. For F_i, the mathematical definitions in FEB are depicted as follows to generate F_{i+1}:

$$\begin{aligned} T_i &= \text{SC}(\text{GELU}(\text{SC}(F_i))) + F_i, \\ F_{i+1} &= \text{LGAB}(T_i) + T_i, \end{aligned} \tag{4}$$

where $\text{SC}(\cdot)$ denotes the shift-conv blocks [30], $\text{GELU}(\cdot)$ is the activation function, and $\text{LGAB}(\cdot)$ represents LGAB which defined as shown in the following section.

3.3   Local-Global Attention Block (LGAB)

As depicted in Fig. 2, there are three attention parts in an LGAB: 1) window attention (WA), 2) shifted window attention (SWA), and 3) long-range attention (LRA). For a given set of feature maps T_i, it is splited into three parts on the channel dimension, denoted by $x^{(1)}$, $x^{(2)}$ and $x^{(3)}$, respectively. The number of channels of $x^{(k)}$ ($k = 1, 2, 3$) is one third of the number of channels of T_i. $x^{(1)}$, $x^{(2)}$ and $x^{(3)}$ are fed into the three attention parts to achieve $\text{LGAB}(T_i)$ as follows:

$$\text{LGAB}(T_i) = \text{Conv}_{1\times1}(\text{CAT}(\text{WA}(x^{(1)}), \text{SWA}(x^{(2)}), \text{LRA}(x^{(3)}))), \tag{5}$$

where $\text{WA}(\cdot)$, $\text{SWA}(\cdot)$ and $\text{LRA}(\cdot)$ denote window attention, shifted window attention and long rang attention, respectively; concatenate operation on channel dimension is denoted by $\text{CAT}(\cdot)$.

Window Attention. Motivated by SwinIR [17], the original images are divided into non-overlapped windows. In order to adapt to objects of different scales, multi-scale resolutions of windows (i.e., 5×5, 10×10, and 15×15) are used. The reason that we not set the sizes of windows to power of 2 (e.g. 4×4, 8×8, and 16×16), is to seek larger receptive fields. For each pixel, the range capturing

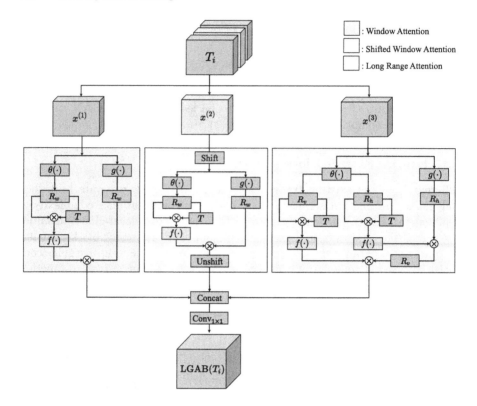

Fig. 2. The overview of our proposed LGAB. The input set of feature maps is divided on channels into 3 sets of feature maps. Three attention parts are performed on these three divided feature maps, respectively.

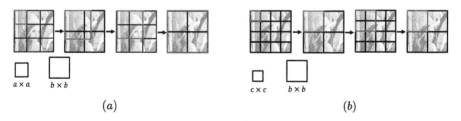

Fig. 3. Receptive fields in windows of different sizes. The windows are denoted in the big black square and the receptive fields are represented by the red box. Each small black box denotes a divided window. (Color figure online)

information is determined by the size of its corresponding receptive fields. For example, only considering WA, the size of receptive fields is determined by the least common multiple of the sizes of windows. As shown in Fig. 3(a), there are two window sizes $a \times a$ and $b \times b$, and there is $3a = 2b$. Therefore, the least common multiple of these window sizes is $2b \times 2b$, which is the same size as the

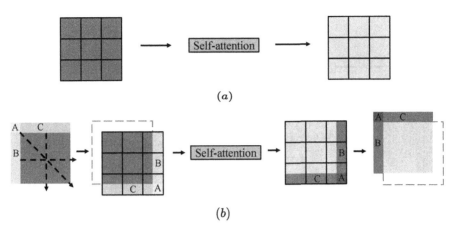

(a)

(b)

Fig. 4. A comparison of two parts in LGAB: (a) window attention and (b) shifted window attention.

entire image. On the other hand in Fig. 3(b), the window sizes are $c \times c$ and $b \times b$. The least common multiple of these window sizes is b and the receptive fields is $b \times b$. These two cases have the approximate amount of computation, but the receptive fields of case (a) are quadruple of case (b).

Let θ and g denote two 1×1 convolutions. For the given feature maps $x^{(1)}$, there are $\theta(x^{(1)}) = W_\theta x^{(1)}$ and $g(x^{(1)}) = W_g x^{(1)}$, where W_θ and W_g are weight matrices to be learned. The operation of reshaping feature maps into windows is denoted by R_w. For the given feature maps $x^{(1)}$ of shape $B \times C \times H \times W$, shape of $R_w(x^{(1)})$ is $B \cdot n \cdot n \times nh \cdot nw \times C$, where $nw \times nh$ denotes the pre-set window size; and $n = \lceil W/nw \rceil$, $n = \lceil H/nh \rceil$. The window where $x_{i,j}^{(1)}$ is located is denoted by $\Omega^{(1)}(i,j)$, and WA$(x^{(1)})_{i,j}$ is performed as follows:

$$\mathrm{WA}(x^{(1)})_{i,j} = \sum_{(s,t) \in \Omega^{(1)}(i,j)} f(\theta(x_{i,j}^{(1)}) \cdot \theta(x_{s,t}^{(1)})^T) \cdot g(x_{s,t}^{(1)}), \qquad (6)$$

where $f(\cdot)$ denotes the softmax operation. WA can fully utilize the local features with low computation complexity.

Shifted Window Attention. WA only captures information within each individual window, and the information in the neighbor window is established by SWA [17]. As shown in Fig. 4(b), the black boxes denote the windows and the shift size is set to the half of the window size to expand the receptive fields to a greater extent. As for a given set of feature maps in WA, it is divided into several windows and self-attention is executed in each window in Fig. 4(a). Comparatively speaking between Fig. 4(a) and (b), the yellow pixels in area A are shifted from top left to bottom right, and pixels in area B and area C are processed correspondingly in SWA. Following, the shifted image is divided into windows as shown in the WA part. Next, the self-attention operation is performed in

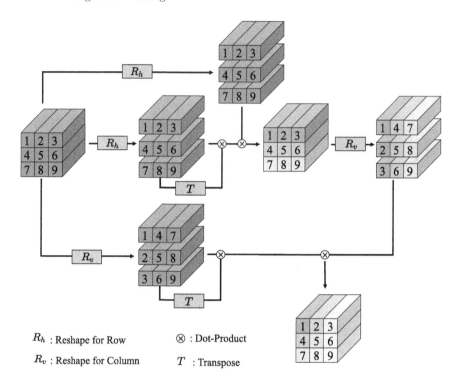

R_h : Reshape for Row   ⊗ : Dot-Product

R_v : Reshape for Column T : Transpose

Fig. 5. Operations of reshaping feature maps in LRA. There are two reshaping operations in LRA: (a) R_h, and (b) R_w. Each number denotes a pixel in the feature maps. For the convenience of presentation, the parts of convolution and softmax operation are omitted.

each shifted window. Inverse operation of shifting windows is used to restore the original image. The feature maps $x^{(2)}$ are calculated as follows:

$$\text{SWA}(x^{(2)}) = \text{UnShift}(\text{WA}(\text{Shift}(x^{(2)}))), \qquad (7)$$

where $\text{WA}(\cdot)$ denotes the window attention described in previous subsection and $\text{Shift}(\cdot)$, $\text{UnShift}(\cdot)$ denote the shifting windows, and the inverse operation of shifting windows as shown in Fig. 4(b), respectively. SWA enhances the relationship between neighbor windows, which is lacking in WA.

Long-range Attention. In both WA and SWA, self-attention is calculated densely between the current pixel and other pixels in the same window. Although receptive fields can be expanded to the entire image by shifted windows, we use LRA to enhance the ability of the network to catch information from the whole image in a more efficient way. For a given set of feature maps $x^{(3)}$, whose shape is $B \times C \times H \times W$. There are R_h and R_v denote the operation of reshaping feature maps along horizontal and vertical direction, respectively, as shown in Fig. 5. After R_h, the shape of the set of feature maps is $B \cdot W \times H \times C$ and after R_v is $B \cdot H \times W \times C$, where H and W denote the height and width of the set of the feature maps $x^{(3)}$, respectively. As depicted in Fig. 5, the set of the feature maps $x^{(3)}$ is reshaped by R_h and executed self-attention in the same row for each pixel (e.g., for pixel 1, the pixels involved to calculate are pixel 1, pixel 2, and pixel 3). Then the set of the feature maps is reshaped by R_w, and only pixels in the same column are considered into self-attention calculating (e.g., for pixel 1, pixels involved in calculating are pixel 1, pixel 4, and pixel 7 in Fig. 5). The definition of $\mathrm{LRA}(x^{(3)})$ is shown as follows:

$$M = f(R_h(\theta(x^{(3)})) \cdot R_h(\theta(x^{(3)}))^T) \cdot R_h(g(x^{(3)})), \tag{8}$$

$$\mathrm{LRA}(x^{(3)}) = f(R_v(\theta(x^{(3)})) \cdot R_v(\theta(x^{(3)}))^T) \cdot R_v(g(M)). \tag{9}$$

LRA can catch the LRDs from the entire image with low computation complexity and make up for the lack of global features in WA and SWA.

4   Experiments

In this section, the settings of the experiment and training steps are shown. To verify the outperforming structure of our LGAN, the ablation experiments are shown. Lastly, The experiments of performance are shown in indicators and visual results for a comparison between proposed LGAN and other lightweight SOTAs for SISR.

4.1   Experimental Setup

Our LGAN is trained on DIV2K [1], which is the standard benchmark dataset for SISR. Set5 [2], Set14 [31], B100 [22], Urban100 [6], and Manga109 [23] are used to evaluate the performance of LGAN. Window sizes are set to 5×5, 10×10, and 15×15 for 3 continuously FEBs. There are 24 FEBs in our proposed LGAN and the number of channels is set to 60. And 64 images are used in a batch for training fairly. Adam [11] is selected as our optimizer and smooth ℓ_1 loss [4] is selected as our loss function. All experiments were running on Nvidia Titan XP GPUs and implemented by PyTorch based on ELAN [32][1]. The results are evaluated by PSNR and SSIM metrics on the Y channel (i.e., luminance) of YCbCr space. The LR images generated from the HR images (i.e., GT images) by downsampling are fed into the network. Data augmentation including random flips and rotations is applied when training our proposed LGAN. We cut each LR image into a 60×60 patch for training. Lastly, the $\times 2$ model was trained with $1,000$ epochs, for each epoch, the training dataset are repeated 80 times. The initial learning rate was 2×10^{-4} and was reduced by half at epoch 500, 800, 900, and 950. Larger magnification factors (i.e., $\times 3$ and $\times 4$) were trained for 500 epochs from the starting based on the trained $\times 2$ network. The learning rate was reduced by half at epoch 250, 400, 450, and 475, the initial learning rate was also inited to 2×10^{-4}.

---

[1] https://github.com/xindongzhang/ELAN.

Table 1. An ablation study using PSNR and SSIM for LGAN of scale ×2 trained with 100 epochs.

Case	Attention Block	Activation Function	BSDS100 PSNR/SSIM	Urban100 PSNR/SSIM	Manga109 PSNR/SSIM
(a)	WA+SWA+LRA	GELU	**32.13**/.8994	**32.00**/.9274	**38.34**/.9764
(b)	WA	GELU	32.12/.8991	31.83/.9260	38.24/.9260
(c)	WA+SWA	GELU	**32.13**/.8992	31.91/.9262	38.29/.**9764**
(d)	LRA	GELU	32.04/.8976	31.73/.9239	38.04/.9758
(e)	WA+SWA+LRA	ReLU	32.11/.8992	31.95/.9267	38.19/.9762

Table 2. A comparison of total FLOPs in attention operations between three attention blocks in ablation experiments. For the convenience of count, the calculation of convolution and softmax are discarded. Total channels of these cases are all set to 60. The column of channels in the table is denoted by $a \times b$, where a denotes the channels of each block and b denotes the number of blocks.

Case	WA	SWA	LRA	Channels	FLOPs (M)
(a)	✓	✓	✓	20×3	506.9
(b)	✓	×	×	60×1	604.8
(c)	✓	✓	×	30×2	604.8
(d)	×	×	✓	60×1	311.0

4.2   Ablation Study

To prove that our LGAN is an effective structure, we made an ablation experiment on the scale of ×2 and the results are shown in Table 1. To save time and computational resources, all ablation experiments were trained with 100 epochs, and the LR images are cropped into 30×30 patches for training, and the batchsize is set to 64. Due to the different attention parts occupying a part of channels alone, respectively. The more attention parts are added to the LGAB, the fewer channels are distributed to each attention part. Therefore as shown in Table 2, cases with more attention parts are not necessarily more computationally expensive than cases with fewer attention parts. In Table 1, case (a) serves as the baseline and other cases are built based on case (a). In case (b), only WA part is used in block and the result of PSNR reduces from 32.00 dB to 31.83 dB on Urban100. Same, the performance also deteriorates on both BSD100 and Manga109. And then in case (c), WA part and SWA part are added to the block. Compared with case (b), performance has improved (i.e., 31.91 dB vs 31.83 dB) but there is still a certain gap with case (a) (i.e., 31.91 dB vs 32.00 dB) on Urban100. In case (d), only LRA part is added in LGAB. Compared with case (a), case (d) yields a worse result on Urban100 (i.e., 31.73 dB vs 32.00 dB). As shown in case (a), (b), (c) and (d), it is demonstrated that these three attention parts in LGAB can compensate each other for local and global relationships. To further explore

Table 3. Angles of the line segment produced by LSD [28] in five benchmark datasets and the changing PSNR and SSIM of SwinIR compared to LGAN.

	Method	Set5	Set14	BSDS100	Urban100	Manga109
$0° \pm 10°$	–	13.60%	13.86%	13.19%	19.70%	18.18%
$90° \pm 10°$		10.00%	19.71%	21.37%	19.81%	15.82%
Total		23.60%	33.57%	34.56%	39.51%	34.60%
PSNR	SwinIR	−0.04 dB	−0.06 dB	−0.02 dB	−0.16 dB	−0.15 dB
SSIM		−0.0008	−0.0006	−0.0010	−0.0042	−0.0000

higher performance, GELU is replaced by ReLU in case (e). It turns out that GELU is better than ReLU for our network (i.e., case(a) vs case (e)).

4.3 Compared with SwinIR

In this subsection, the reason LGAN outperforms SwinIR [17], which is the most effective SISR network of the currently accepted papers in mainstream opinion, is discussed.

'Local Attention Only' versus 'Local and Global Attention'. In SwinIR [17], the image is split into several non-overlapped windows, and attention operation is executed in each window. Only local information is captured and it is a fatal problem. In our LGAN, LRA is proposed to obtain the global information at the same time in one block.

Better Spatial Location. Spatial information is very important for CV tasks. However, in original ViT [3] or SwinIR [17], spatial information is handled by position embedding, which can not explore the potential of spatial information well. Our proposed LRA could utilize spatial information more effectively.

More Reasonable Organization of Blocks. Although SwinIR and LGAN both include base units window attention (WA) and shifted window attention (SWA), the ways these base units are organized are quite different. In SwinIR [17] or in transformer [27], multi-head attention (MHA) is designed to extract features. In each block, channels are split into several heads. Each head is executed by the same attention operation (e.g., WA). In our LGAN, channels are split into 3 parts to execute 3 different attention operations (i.e., WA, SWA, LRA). Experimental results demonstrated that, compared with SwinIR's single function, our LGAB has more powerful functions with fewer parameters and complexity as shown in Table 2.

Adaptivity to Object Size. Multi-scale strategy is applied in our LGAN to adapt to objects with different sizes. In the image, the size of pixels occupied by objects is different. Window sizes of $5, 10, 15$ are used in our LGAN.

Table 4. Comparison of PSNR and SSIM with other lightweight SISR methods. The results highlighted in red are the best, and the second best results are in blue. Data not given in the corresponding paper is identified using '–'.

Method	Scale	Params	Set5 PSNR/SSIM	Set14 PSNR/SSIM	BSDS100 PSNR/SSIM	Urban100 PSNR/SSIM	Manga109 PSNR/SSIM
MSICF [5]	x2	–	37.89/.9605	33.41/.9153	32.15/.8992	31.47/.9220	–/–
SRNIF [15]		–	38.05/.9607	33.65/.9181	32.19/.9002	32.14/.9286	–/–
NLRN [18]		–	38.00/.9603	33.46/.9159	32.19/.8992	31.81/.9249	–/–
LapSRN [12]		–	37.52/.9591	33.08/.9130	31.80/.8949	30.41/.9101	37.27/.9740
MSRN [13]		–	38.08/.9605	33.74/.9170	32.23/.9013	32.22/.9326	38.82/.9771
MIPN [20]		–	38.12/.9609	33.73/.9188	32.25/.9006	32.42/.9312	38.88/.9773
AMNet [10]		–	38.13/.9608	33.77/.9191	32.27/.9008	32.52/.9320	39.02/.9779
LatticeNet [21]		756 K	38.06/.9607	33.70/.9187	32.20/.8999	32.25/.9288	–/–
LAPAR-A [14]		548 K	38.01/.9605	33.62/.9183	32.19/.8999	32.10/.9283	38.67/.9772
IDN [9]		579 K	37.83/.9600	33.30/.9148	32.08/.8985	31.27/.9196	38.01/.9749
IMDN [8]		694 K	38.00/.9605	33.63/.9177	32.19/.8996	32.17/.9283	38.88/.9774
HRFFN [25]		646 K	38.12/.9608	33.80/.9192	32.24/.9005	32.52/.9319	39.05/.9797
SwinIR [17]		878 K	38.14/.9611	33.86/.9206	32.31/.9012	32.76/.9340	39.12/.9783
LGAN (Ours)		650 K	38.13/.9612	33.95/.9221	32.32/.9017	32.81/.9343	39.13/.9777
MSICF [5]	x3	–	34.24/.9266	30.09/.8371	29.01/.8024	27.69/.8411	–/–
SRNIF [15]		–	34.42/.9274	30.36/.8426	29.06/.8047	28.23/.8541	–/–
NLRN [18]		–	34.27/.9266	30.16/.8374	29.06/.8026	27.93/.8453	–/–
LapSRN [12]		–	33.82/.9227	29.87/.8320	28.82/.7973	27.07/.8270	32.21/.9343
MSRN [13]		–	34.38/.9262	30.34/.8395	29.08/.8041	28.08/.8554	33.44/.9427
MIPN [20]		–	34.53/.9280	30.43/.8440	29.15/.8061	28.38/.8573	33.86/.9460
AMNet [10]		–	34.51/.9281	30.47/.8445	29.18/.8074	28.51/.8595	34.10/.9474
LatticeNet [21]		765 K	34.40/.9272	30.32/.8416	29.10/.8049	28.19/.8513	–/–
LAPAR-A [14]		544 K	34.36/.9267	30.34/.8421	29.11/.8054	28.15/.8523	33.51/.9441
IDN [9]		588 K	34.11/.9253	29.99/.8354	28.95/.8013	27.42/.8359	32.71/.9381
IMDN [8]		703 K	34.36/.9270	30.32/.8417	29.09/.8046	28.17/.8519	33.61/.9445
HRFFN [25]		654 K	34.49/.9279	30.41/.8433	29.13/.8061	28.43/.8574	33.82/.9459
SwinIR [17]		886 K	34.62/.9289	30.54/.8463	29.20/.8082	28.66/.8624	33.98/.9478
LGAN (Ours)		658 K	34.56/.9286	30.60/.8463	29.24/.8092	28.79/.8646	34.19/.9482
MSICF [5]	x4	–	31.91/.8923	28.35/.7751	27.46/.7308	25.64/.7692	–/–
SRNIF [15]		–	32.34/.8970	28.66/.7838	27.62/.7380	26.32/.7935	–/–
NLRN [18]		–	31.92/.8916	28.36/.7745	27.48/.7306	25.79/.7729	–/–
LapSRN [12]		–	31.54/.8863	28.19/.7720	27.32/.7262	25.21/.7548	29.09/.8890
MSRN [13]		–	32.07/.8903	28.60/.7751	27.52/.7273	26.04/.7896	30.17/.9034
MIPN [20]		–	32.31/.8971	28.65/.7832	27.61/.7375	26.23/.7906	30.67/.9107
AMNet [10]		–	32.28/.8962	28.71/.7841	27.66/.7392	26.37/.7951	31.04/.9136
LatticeNet [21]		777 K	32.18/.8943	28.61/.7812	27.57/.7355	26.14/.7844	–/–
LAPAR-A [14]		569 K	32.15/.8944	28.61/.7818	27.61/.7366	26.14/.7871	30.42/.9074
IDN [9]		677 K	31.82/.8903	28.25/.7730	27.41/.7297	25.41/.7632	29.41/.8942
IMDN [8]		715 K	32.21/.8948	28.58/.7811	27.56/.7353	26.04/.7838	30.45/.9075
HRFFN [25]		666 K	32.33/.8960	28.69/.7830	27.62/.7378	26.32/.7928	30.73/.9107
SwinIR [17]		897 K	32.44/.8976	28.77/.7858	27.69/.7406	26.47/.7980	30.92/.9151
LGAN (Ours)		669 K	32.48/.8984	28.83/.7864	27.71/.7416	26.63/.8022	31.07/.9151

Higher Quality of Restoring Line Segments. At the same time, we observe that on the Urban100 dataset, our LGAN has huge superiority to restore the horizontal and vertical line segments. To evaluate the reinforcement of our LGAN of line segments, Table 3 is shown. Straight line segment detection by LSD [28]

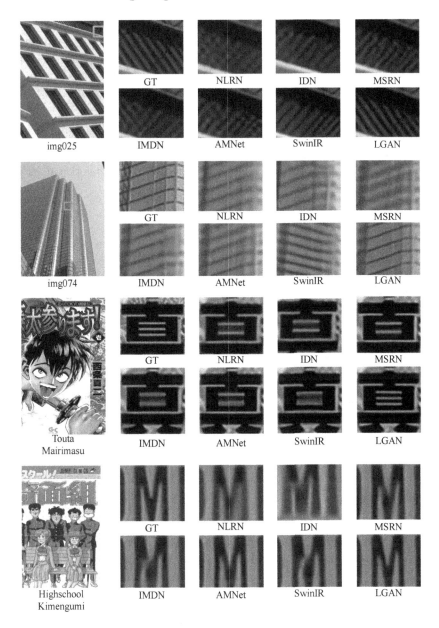

Fig. 6. A visual comparison of ×4 scale with other lightweight SISR networks on Urban100 and Manga109.

is firstly performed on the five datasets, and then the detected straight line segments are divided into from −10° to 170° according to their slopes. The line segments with slopes from −10° to 10° are considered as horizontal ones, and line segments from 80° to 100° are considered as vertical straight line segments. The percentage of horizontal and vertical line segments are 19.70% and 19.81% in Urban100 respectively, and significantly ahead of the average (percentage of per 20° is 11.11%). Comparing SwinIR and our proposed LGAN, PSNR is reduced by 0.16 dB correspondingly in Urban100. In contrast in Set5, only 13.60% and 10.00% of line segments are horizontal or vertical. As a result, PSNR has been reduced only by 0.04 dB. From this, we can speculate that our LGAN can yield outperforming results compared with SwinIR on the datasets regardless of the ratio of vertical and horizontal line segments, and if on a dataset with more vertical and horizontal line segments like Urban100, our network can achieve considerably increased performance.

4.4 Performance Evaluation

The results of indicators are shown in Table 4. We choose several lightweight SISR networks to compare, including MSICF [5], SRNIF [15], NLRN [18], Lap-SRN [12], MSRN [13], MIPN [20], AMNet [10], LatticeNet [21], LAPAR-A [14], IDN [9], IMDN [8], HRFFN [25], and SwinIR [17]. If there are multiple versions of the same network to choose from, the lightweight version is chosen to be compared in this paper fairly. Since some networks did not provide the number of parameters, only a part of parameters are listed in Table 4. Our proposed LGAN achieves impressive results on most benchmark datasets and most scales.

In Fig. 6, subjective comparisons on Urban100 and Manga109 are shown. Due to space limitations, we have only selected six networks developed in recent years for comparison, including NLRN [18], IDN [9], MSRN [13], IMDN [8], AMNet [10], and SwinIR [17]. Note that, SwinIR is the most effective of the currently accepted papers in mainstream opinion. From the visual results, the reconstructions of existing methods are of low quality and have obvious errors, while our LGAN delivers an outstanding image quality for SISR.

5 Conclusion

In this paper, a block called *local-global attention block* (LGAB) is proposed. In each LGAB, there are three different attention parts: 1) window attention (WA), 2) shifted window attention (SWA), and 3) long-range attention (LRA). Then an efficient network called *local-global attention network* (LGAN) is proposed for single image super-resolution (SISR). Extensive experiments demonstrate that our proposed LGAN can yield outperformance on the most benchmark datasets over the existing lightweight state-of-the-arts for SISR. This work focuses on the mechanism of self-attention blocks, and may enlighten some insights for further studies.

References

1. Agustsson, E., Timofte, R.: NTIRE 2017 challenge on single image super-resolution: dataset and study. In: Proceedings of the IEEE Conference on Computer Vision and Pattern Recognition Workshop, pp. 126–135 (2017)

2. Bevilacqua, M., Roumy, A., Guillemot, C., Alberi-Morel, M.L.: Low-complexity single-image super-resolution based on nonnegative neighbor embedding. In: Proceedings of the British Machine Vision Conference, pp. 1–10 (2012)
3. Dosovitskiy, A., et al.: An image is worth 16x16 words: transformers for image recognition at scale. In: International Conference on Learning Representations (2020)
4. Girshick, R.: Fast R-CNN. In: Proceedings of the IEEE Conference on Computer Vision and Pattern Recognition (2015)
5. Hu, Y., Gao, X., Li, J., Huang, Y., Wang, H.: Single image super-resolution with multi-scale information cross-fusion network. Signal Process. **179**, 107831 (2021)
6. Huang, J.B., Singh, A., Ahuja, N.: Single image super-resolution from transformed self-exemplars. In: Proceedings of the IEEE Conference on Computer Vision and Pattern Recognition, pp. 5197–5206 (2015)
7. Huang, Z., et al.: CCNet: Criss-cross attention for semantic segmentation. IEEE Transactions on Pattern Analysis and Machine Intelligence (2020)
8. Hui, Z., Gao, X., Yang, Y., Wang, X.: Lightweight image super-resolution with information multi-distillation network. In: Proceedings of the ACM International Conference on Multimedia, pp. 2024–2032 (2019)
9. Hui, Z., Wang, X., Gao, X.: Fast and accurate single image super-resolution via information distillation network. In: Proceedings of the IEEE Conference on Computer Vision and Pattern Recognition, pp. 723–731 (2018)
10. Ji, J., Zhong, B., Ma, K.K.: Single image super-resolution using asynchronous multi-scale network. IEEE Signal Process. Lett. **28**, 1823–1827 (2021)
11. Kingma, D.P., Ba, J.: Adam: a method for stochastic optimization. In: International Conference on Learning Representations (2015)
12. Lai, W.S., Huang, J.B., Ahuja, N., Yang, M.H.: Deep Laplacian pyramid networks for fast and accurate super-resolution. In: Proceedings of the IEEE Conference on Computer Vision and Pattern Recognition, pp. 624–632 (2017)
13. Li, J., Fang, F., Mei, K., Zhang, G.: Multi-scale residual network for image super-resolution. In: Proceedings of the European Conference on Computer Vision, pp. 517–532 (2018)
14. Li, W., Zhou, K., Qi, L., Jiang, N., Lu, J., Jia, J.: LAPAR: linearly-assembled pixel-adaptive regression network for single image super-resolution and beyond. In: Advances in Neural Information Processing Systems (2020)
15. Li, X., Chen, Z.: Single image super-resolution reconstruction based on fusion of internal and external features. Multimed. Tools. Appl. **81**, 1–17 (2021)
16. Li, Y., et al.: Neural architecture search for lightweight non-local networks. In: Proceedings of the IEEE Conference on Computer Vision and Pattern Recognition, pp. 10297–10306 (2020)
17. Liang, J., Cao, J., Sun, G., Zhang, K., Van Gool, L., Timofte, R.: SwinIR: Image restoration using swin transformer. In: Proceedings of the IEEE Conference on Computer Vision and Pattern Recognition, pp. 1833–1844 (2021)
18. Liu, D., Wen, B., Fan, Y., Loy, C.C., Huang, T.S.: Non-local recurrent network for image restoration. In: Advances in Neural Information Processing Systems, pp. 1673–1682 (2018)
19. Liu, Z., et al.: Swin transformer: hierarchical vision transformer using shifted windows. In: Proceedings of the IEEE International Conference on Computer Vision, pp. 10012–10022 (2021)
20. Lu, T., Wang, Y., Wang, J., Liu, W., Zhang, Y.: Single image super-resolution via multi-scale information polymerization network. IEEE Signal Process. Lett. **28**, 1305–1309 (2021)

21. Luo, X., Xie, Y., Zhang, Y., Qu, Y., Li, C., Fu, Y.: LatticeNet: towards lightweight image super-resolution with lattice block. In: Vedaldi, A., Bischof, H., Brox, T., Frahm, J.-M. (eds.) ECCV 2020. LNCS, vol. 12367, pp. 272–289. Springer, Cham (2020). https://doi.org/10.1007/978-3-030-58542-6_17

22. Martin, D., Fowlkes, C., Tal, D., Malik, J., et al.: A database of human segmented natural images and its application to evaluating segmentation algorithms and measuring ecological statistics. In: Proceedings of the IEEE International Conference on Computer Vision, pp. 416–423 (2001)

23. Matsui, Y., Ito, K., Aramaki, Y., Fujimoto, A., Ogawa, T., Yamasaki, T., Aizawa, K.: Sketch-based manga retrieval using manga109 dataset. Multimed. Tools. Appl. **76**, 21811–21838 (2017)

24. Mei, Y., Fan, Y., Zhou, Y.: Image super-resolution with non-local sparse attention. In: Proceedings of the IEEE Conference on Computer Vision and Pattern Recognition, pp. 3517–3526 (2021)

25. Qin, J., Liu, F., Liu, K., Jeon, G., Yang, X.: Lightweight hierarchical residual feature fusion network for single-image super-resolution. Neurocomputing **478**, 104–123 (2022)

26. Shi, W., et al.: Real-time single image and video super-resolution using an efficient sub-pixel convolutional neural network. In: Proceedings of the IEEE Conference on Computer Vision and Pattern Recognition, pp. 1874–1883 (2016)

27. Vaswani, A., et al.: Attention is all you need. In: Advances in Neural Information Processing Systems 30 (2017)

28. Von Gioi, R.G., Jakubowicz, J., Morel, J.M., Randall, G.: LSD: a line segment detector. Image Process. Line **2**, 35–55 (2012)

29. Wang, X., Girshick, R., Gupta, A., He, K.: Non-local neural networks. In: Proceedings of the IEEE Conference on Computer Vision and Pattern Recognition, pp. 7794–7803 (2018)

30. Wu, B., et al.: Shift: A zero flop, zero parameter alternative to spatial convolutions. In: Proceedings of the IEEE Conference on Computer Vision and Pattern Recognition, pp. 9127–9135 (2018)

31. Zeyde, R., Elad, M., Protter, M.: On single image scale-up using sparse-representations. In: Boissonnat, J.-D., et al. (eds.) Curves and Surfaces 2010. LNCS, vol. 6920, pp. 711–730. Springer, Heidelberg (2012). https://doi.org/10.1007/978-3-642-27413-8_47

32. Zhang, X., Zeng, H., Guo, S., Zhang, L.: Efficient long-range attention network for image super-resolution. In: Avidan, S., (eds.) Computer Vision – ECCV 2022. ECCV 2022. Lecture Notes in Computer Science, vol. 13677. Springer, Cham (2022). https://doi.org/10.1007/978-3-031-19790-1_39

Comparing Complexities of Decision Boundaries for Robust Training: A Universal Approach

Daniel Kienitz$^{(\boxtimes)}$, Ekaterina Komendantskaya, and Michael Lones

Heriot-Watt University, Edinburgh, UK
{dk50,e.komendantskaya,m.lones}@hw.ac.uk

Abstract. We investigate the geometric complexity of decision boundaries for robust training compared to standard training. By considering the local geometry of nearest neighbour sets, we study them in a model-agnostic way and theoretically derive a lower-bound $R^* \in \mathbb{R}$ on the perturbation magnitude $\delta \in \mathbb{R}$ for which robust training provably requires a geometrically more complex decision boundary than accurate training. We show that state-of-the-art robust models learn more complex decision boundaries than their non-robust counterparts, confirming previous hypotheses. Then, we compute R^* for common image benchmarks and find that it also empirically serves as an upper bound over which label noise is introduced. We demonstrate for deep neural network classifiers that perturbation magnitudes $\delta \geq R^*$ lead to reduced robustness and generalization performance. Therefore, R^* bounds the maximum feasible perturbation magnitude for norm-bounded robust training and data augmentation. Finally, we show that $R^* < 0.5R$ for common benchmarks, where R is a distribution's minimum nearest neighbour distance. Thus, we improve previous work on determining a distribution's maximum robust radius.

1 Introduction

The decision boundary learned by a classifier is a crucial property to study [1–3]. Its geometric complexity, i.e. its number of linear segments, is an indication of the train distribution's complexity and the difficulty of learning [4–6], its margin to the train samples defines its robustness [1,2,7] and studying its general position in input space is used for explaining model predictions [8]. Deep neural network classifiers have over the past years reached or even surpassed human-level performance in computer vision tasks [9,10]. However, despite recent progress [11] they still remain vulnerable to a large variety of distribution shifts [12–16]. In light of this brittleness [12,13,17] and the observation that robust training methods cause non-robust accuracy to deteriorate [17–22], several recent works

---

Supplementary Information The online version contains supplementary material available at https://doi.org/10.1007/978-3-031-26351-4_38.

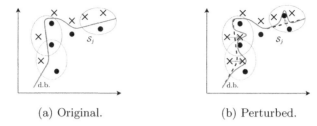

(a) Original.   (b) Perturbed.

Fig. 1. Illustration of the main idea in $d = 2$ dimensions. (a) The input distribution is separated into sets $\mathcal{S}_j$ of linearly separable nearest neighbours. (b) If $\mathcal{S}_j$ changes and is no longer linearly separable, the complexity of the decision boundary (d.b.) increases.

have hypothesized that robust training might require different, and possibly geometrically more complex, decision boundaries than standard training [1,17,23–26]. If this hypothesis is true, the need for greater capacity [26] and increased sample complexity of robust training (see Sect. 2 for overview) could partially be explained. As the decision boundary learned by a deep classifier is build on top of a largely opaque feature representation [23,27], is high-dimensional, highly non-linear and could theoretically consist of multiple disconnected decision regions [28] its study is a challenging problem.

In this paper we take a model-agnostic approach to studying decision boundaries. We assume the existence of an *accurate decision boundary*, obtained by minimizing the train loss, which perfectly separates the input data's classes and give a comparative study of the *robust decision boundary* that would be required if the data was altered by worst-case perturbations of its samples. To achieve this, we divide the input distribution into linearly separable sets $\mathcal{S}$ of nearest neighbours and investigate the perturbation magnitudes required to make them non-linearly separable. This approach allows us to make the following contributions:

- On the theoretical side, we derive a lower bound $R^* \in \mathbb{R}$ in l_2-norm on the perturbation magnitude $\delta \in \mathbb{R}$ in l_2-norm in input space for which the geometric complexity of a robust decision boundary provably increases compared to an accurate decision boundary. (See Sect. 3).
- Since R^* is efficiently computable, we show for common image benchmarks that state-of-the-art robust deep classifiers indeed learn geometrically more complex decision boundaries than their accurate counter parts and that they are better calibrated in low-density regions. (See Sect. 4).
- When computing R^* for common image benchmarks, we find that perturbation magnitudes $\delta \geq R^*$ introduce label noise and demonstrate that this leads to decreased robustness and generalization performance. (See Sect. 5).

As the geometric complexity of decision boundaries is a crucial factor for the sample complexity of a learning problem [4–6], showing under which perturbation magnitudes decision boundaries increase in complexity is important for the selection of hypothesis classes. Further, as label noise is known to be one of the reasons for the lack of robustness [27], bounding the maximum perturbation magnitude for which norm-bounded robust training and data augmentation is possible for these benchmarks, is crucial in practical applications.

Finally, we show that R^* is a more accurate approximation of a distribution's robust radius. Previous work [29] utilized the minimum nearest neighbour distance between any two samples in the dataset, $R \in \mathbb{R}$. We show that $R^* < 0.5R$ for common image benchmarks.

2   Related Work

Learned Representations of Standard Training. It has been shown that part of the adversarial vulnerability of deep classifiers stems from common image benchmarks containing highly predictive yet brittle features [30,31]. These features are usually not aligned with those used by humans for classification [32], so small-norm and non-semantic changes to inputs are often sufficient to change the classification decisions of otherwise well-performing classifiers [12,13,33]. Since neural networks were shown to rely on simple features for classification [27,34–37], even in the presence of complex ones with better predictive power [23], models were found to learn feature representations on top of superficial statistical regularities [38,39] like texture [40–42] and non-semantic pixel subsets [43,44]. As decision boundaries are functions of the learned representation, this simplicity bias and the presence of non-semantic but highly predictive features leads to boundaries that are accurate but not robust. These observations led several authors to suggested that robust training might require more complex decision boundaries than accurate training [1,17,24–26]. In this work we confirm this hypothesis and further show that in the low-density region where the decision boundary is supposed to lie [45], state-of-the-art robust classifiers are largely better calibrated than non-robust ones.

Sample Complexity. Several studies argue that adversarial training has a larger sample complexity than standard training. Bounds on the sample complexity where the data distribution is a mixture of Gaussians were first provided by Schmidt et al. [24] who showed that the increased sample complexity of adversarial training holds regardless of the training algorithm and the model family. Later, Bhagoji et al. [46] studied sample complexity with an approach from optimal transport. Dobriban et al. [47] extended prior analyses to mixtures of three Gaussians in 2- and ∞-norm and Dan et al. [48] derived general results for the case of two-mixture Gaussians for all norms. More recently, Bhattacharjee et al. [49] studied the sample complexity of robust classification for linearly separable datasets. They showed that in contrast to accurate classification, the sample complexity of robust classification has a linear dependence on the dimension d. Yin et al. [25] further showed a dependence of the sample complexity on d for neural networks. Distribution-agnostic bounds for robust classification have been provided by several authors [50–53]. As the sample complexity is also influenced by the geometric complexity of the decision boundary [4–6], we provide another reason for its increase for robust training by showing that robust models learn more complex decision boundaries compared to non-robust ones.

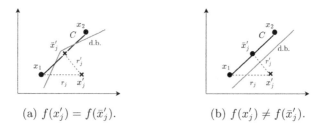

(a) $f(x_j') = f(\bar{x}_j')$.   (b) $f(x_j') \neq f(\bar{x}_j')$.

Fig. 2. Illustration of an $\mathcal{S}_j$ in $d = 2$ dimensions. (a) If classifier f does not assign a class change between x_j' and $\bar{x}_j'$, the decision boundary's (d.b.) complexity increases. (b) If f assigns a class change to $\bar{x}_j'$, $\mathcal{S}_j$ is still linearly separable, however, if $r_j' < 0.5r_j$, robust training for $\delta = r_j'$ introduces label noise.

Robust Training. Recently, several methods have been proposed to mitigate the reliance on superficial regularities by removing texture clues [40,54], improved data augmentation [55,56], pre-training [57] and utilization of unlabelled data in the training process [56,58,59]. Further, several robust training methods like adversarial training [13,17], regularization [60,61] and saliency methods [62–64] have been proposed. Nevertheless, all previously mentioned methods found reduced generalization performance with increasing robustness. In this work we hypothesize and empirically confirm that robust training for large magnitudes reduces generalization performance because it introduces label noise which biases the model towards learning non-generalizing textural features. We provide a lower bound R^* over which this provably occurs for common image benchmarks.

3   Derivation of R^*

In this section we describe how R^* is derived for an arbitrary distribution $X \in \mathbb{R}^{l \times d}$, where l is the number of samples and d is the ambient dimension[1]. Each sample $x_j' \in X$ is associated with a unique label $y_j' \in Y$, where c is the number of distinct classes in Y.

3.1   Nearest Neighbour Sets

Since determining the geometric complexity of a distribution's decision boundary is still an open problem, we study under which perturbation magnitudes sets of linearly separable nearest neighbours $\mathcal{S}$ become non-linearly separable. This approach allows us to treat the geometric complexity of the decision boundary for X as the unknown base case and only investigate the increase in complexity under the worst-case perturbation. Without loss of generality we describe the method for binary classification, so $c = 2$ classes. Later we describe how it can be extended to the multi-class case where $c > 2$.

---

[1] We assume that samples do not lie on a flat manifold, so are not perfectly collinear.

For every sample $x'_j \in X$, $j = 1, ..., l$, we consider its d nearest neighbours (according to l_2-norm) with a different class label. This results in a separation of the input distribution $X \in \mathbb{R}^{l \times d}$ into l subsets $\mathcal{S}_j = \{x_1, ..., x_d, x'_j\}$. The samples $x_1, ..., x_d$ are the ordered d-nearest neighbours with the other class label where x_1 is the closest and x_d the farthest. Since the cardinality of each $\mathcal{S}_j$ is equal to the VC-dimension of a linear classifier, so $|\mathcal{S}_j| = d + 1$, a single hyperplane is sufficient to separate x'_j from $\{x_i\}_{i=1}^d$ with perfect accuracy. With this approach we can investigate what perturbation magnitude is required so that the set $\mathcal{S}_j = \{x_1, ..., x_d, x'_j\}$ is not linearly separable any more. The linear separability property of $\mathcal{S}_j$ is violated if x'_j is projected onto the convex hull $\mathcal{C}(\{x_i\}_{i=1}^d)$ of its d nearest neighbours. We define the projection of x'_j onto $\mathcal{C}(\{x_i\}_{i=1}^d)$ as

$$\bar{x}'_j := \operatorname{argmin}_{\hat{x} \in \mathcal{C}(\{x_i\}_{i=1}^d)} ||x'_j - \hat{x}||_2 \text{ s.t.}$$
$$\hat{x} = \sum_{i=1}^d w_i x_i, \ 0 \le w_i \le 1, \ \sum_{i=1}^d w_i = 1 \tag{1}$$

Thus, replacing x'_j with $\bar{x}'_j$ in $\mathcal{S}_j$ removes the linear separability property because all samples are collinear. In Appendix A we describe how the optimization problem in Eq. 1 can be solved exactly and deterministically and show that choosing $|\mathcal{S}_j| \ne d + 1$ leads to a vacuous bound.

3.2 Properties of Nearest Neighbour Sets

We define the distance between a sample x'_j and its projection onto the convex hull of its nearest neighbours $\bar{x}'_j$ of another class as

$$r'_j := ||x'_j - \bar{x}'_j||_2 \tag{2}$$

Further,

$$r_j := ||x'_j - x_1||_2 \tag{3}$$

defines the distance between a sample x'_j and its nearest neighbour x_1 of a different class. The value $0.5r_j$ defines the same quantity as the robust radius defined by Yang et al. [29]. We illustrate these quantities in $d = 2$ dimensions in Fig. 2.

3.3 Decision Boundary of Nearest Neighbour Sets

In Fig. 3 we illustrate the main intuition behind our approach. Figuratively speaking, we require a more complex decision boundary for $\mathcal{S}_j$, so two connected hyperplanes instead of one[2], if the $(0.5r_j)$-ball $B_{0.5r_j}(x'_j) = \{x : ||x'_j - x||_2 \le 0.5r_j\}$ of sample x'_j intersects with $\mathcal{C}(\{x_i\}_{i=1}^d)$. This is the case if $r'_j < 0.5r_j$. We define the threshold

$$r_j^{\text{crit}} := \frac{r'_j}{0.5r_j} \tag{4}$$

---

[2] Note that enclosing just the point $\bar{x}'_j$ requires d hyperplanes arranged as a simplex.

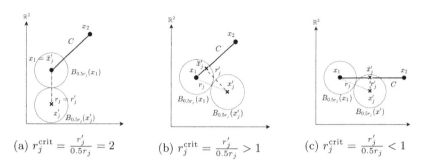

$$\text{(a) } r_j^{\text{crit}} = \frac{r_j'}{0.5r_j} = 2 \qquad \text{(b) } r_j^{\text{crit}} = \frac{r_j'}{0.5r_j} > 1 \qquad \text{(c) } r_j^{\text{crit}} = \frac{r_j'}{0.5r_j} < 1$$

Fig. 3. Illustration of nearest neighbour sets $\mathcal{S}_j$ for $d = 2$ dimensions. (a) A more complex decision boundary is not required as $||x_j' - \bar{x}_j'||_2 = ||x_j' - x_1||_2 = r_j' = r_j$. (b) A more complex decision boundary is not required as $||x_j' - \bar{x}_j'||_2 = r_j' > 0.5r_j$. (c) A more complex decision boundary is required as $||x_j' - \bar{x}_j'||_2 = r_j' < 0.5r_j$.

for a single sample x_j' and its associated $\mathcal{S}_j$. If $r_j' < 0.5r_j$ then $r_j^{\text{crit}} < 1$ and robust accuracy with perturbation magnitudes of $\delta \geq r_j'$ *provably* requires a geometrically more complex decision boundary for $\mathcal{S}_j$. Conversely, $\mathcal{S}_j$ is still linearly separable for $r_j^{\text{crit}} > 1$ for any perturbation magnitude $\delta < 0.5r_j'$.

It is important to note that while the introduction of a perturbation $\delta < 0.5r_j'$ does not result in a locally more complex decision boundary for $\mathcal{S}_j$, it might result in a globally more complex decision boundary for the entire distribution X. Therefore, r_j' is the largest lower bound. Finding the smallest lower bound that holds globally requires knowing the optimal decision boundary which is generally unknown. As illustrated in Fig. 1b, we assume that a locally more complex decision boundary for $\mathcal{S}_j$ results in a globally more complex decision boundary for X, so $\bar{x}_j'$ are not merely memorized. This assumption is reasonable as there is strong evidence that deep networks build connected decision regions encompassing all samples of a single class [3,65].

Extension to Multiple Classes. The method described above for the binary scenario can easily be extended to multi-class classification. Instead of determining the set of nearest neighbours $\mathcal{S}_j$ once for the single other class, the computation is repeated $(c - 1)$-times for all other classes. The rationale from above holds, as we simply restrict the $B_{0.5r_j}(x_j')$-ball to not intersect with any convex hull of nearest neighbours of any other class. So, the method scales linearly with the number of classes c in X. Then,

$$r_j' := \min_{i \in Y \setminus y_j'} \left(\{r_j'(y_i)\}\right) \tag{5}$$

and

$$r_j := \min_{i \in Y \setminus y_j'} \left(\{r_j(y_i)\}\right) \tag{6}$$

where $Y \setminus y_j'$ denotes the set of unique class labels without label y_j' of x_j' and $r_j'(y_i)$ and $r_j(y_i)$ denote the equivalents of r_j' and r_j defined in Eqs. 2 and 3, respectively, computed for class y_i. We always report the results for all classes in a particular dataset, unless stated otherwise.

Extension to the Entire Dataset. The quantities in Eqs. 2, 3, and 4 are defined for a single $\mathcal{S}_j$. We define the robust radius of the entire distribution as

$$R := \min_{j \in 1, \dots, l}(\{r_j\}) \tag{7}$$

which is equivalent to the definition of R by Yang et al. [29] and describes the minimum nearest neighbours distance between any two samples of different classes. Intuitively, $0.5R$ describes the maximum perturbation magnitude such that the $B_{0.5R}(\cdot)$-balls of any two samples do not intersect. We define

$$R_j^{\mathrm{crit}} := \frac{r_j'}{0.5 \cdot \min_{i \in 1, \dots, l}(\{r_i\})} = \frac{r_j'}{0.5R} \tag{8}$$

The interpretation of R_j^{crit} is equivalent to the one of r_j^{crit} in Eq. 4 with the exception that we consider the global robust radius R instead of the local robust radius r_j. For $R_j^{\mathrm{crit}} < 1$, the distance to the convex hull of a sample is smaller than the robust radius and therefore increases the complexity of the decision boundary. We further define

$$R^* := \min_{j \in 1, \dots, l}(\{r_j'\}) \tag{9}$$

which describes the perturbation magnitude over which we provably require a geometrically more complex decision boundary for the given distribution. Finally,

$$R^{\mathrm{crit}} := \frac{\min_{j \in 1, \dots, l}(\{r_j'\})}{0.5 \cdot \min_{j \in 1, \dots, l}(\{r_j\})} = \frac{R^*}{0.5R} \tag{10}$$

describes whether R is an over-approximation of a distribution's robust radius.

Definition of Critical Points. We refer to those points $\bar{x}_j'$ for which locally $r_j' < 0.5 r_j$, so $r_j^{\mathrm{crit}} < 1$, as *critical* as they require a locally more complex decision boundary under norm-bounded robustness scenarios and cause r_j to be an overestimation of the actual robust radius,

$$\{\bar{x}\}_{\mathrm{local}}^{\mathrm{crit}} := \{\bar{x}_j' : r_j^{\mathrm{crit}} < 1, \ j = 1, \dots, l\} \tag{11}$$

Conversely, we define those points for which $R_j^{\mathrm{crit}} < 1$ as

$$\{\bar{x}\}_{\mathrm{global}}^{\mathrm{crit}} := \{\bar{x}_j' : R_j^{\mathrm{crit}} < 1, \ j = 1, \dots, l\} \tag{12}$$

It follows that $|\{\bar{x}\}_{\mathrm{global}}^{\mathrm{crit}}| \leq |\{\bar{x}\}_{\mathrm{local}}^{\mathrm{crit}}|$. Note that in the multi-class case, $c > 2$, a single x_j' can have multiple associated $\bar{x}_j'$ that are elements of $\{\bar{x}\}_{\mathrm{local}}^{\mathrm{crit}}$ or $\{\bar{x}\}_{\mathrm{global}}^{\mathrm{crit}}$, possibly one for every other class in the dataset. Thus, $0 \leq |\{\bar{x}\}_{\mathrm{global}}^{\mathrm{crit}}| \leq l(c-1)$ and $0 \leq |\{\bar{x}\}_{\mathrm{local}}^{\mathrm{crit}}| \leq l(c-1)$, where l is the number of samples in X and c is the number of unique class labels.

3.4   Class Membership of $\bar{x}'$

Throughout this section we assumed that there is no change of the ground truth class between x'_j and its associated $\bar{x}'_j$. If Euclidean distance is a valid proxy for semantic similarity, then this assumption is valid. Furthermore, as only those $\bar{x}'_j$ for which its corresponding $r'_j < 0.5r_j$ (or $r'_j < 0.5R$) are of interest, the assumption of no class change is valid for such distributions. However, since it is well known that l_p-norms are not a suitable proxy for semantic similarity for real-world datasets, the class membership of $\bar{x}'_j$ cannot be inferred from a simple distance metric in input space. Thus, distinguishing between the three following possible scenarios is necessary.

No Class Change (NCC). If no change of the ground truth class label between x'_j and its corresponding $\bar{x}'_j$ occurs, then robust training for $\delta \geq r'_j$ requires a more complex decision boundary for $\mathcal{S}_j$ (see Fig. 2a).

Class Change (CC). If the ground truth class changes between x'_j and $\bar{x}'_j$, the decision boundary for $\mathcal{S}_j$ does not increase in complexity (see Fig. 2b). However, this implies that R is not the actual robust radius of that distribution as there is at least one r_j for which $r'_j < 0.5r_j$. In this case, the robust radius is over-approximated by R and R^* is the actual robust radius. Crucially, this implies that robust training for magnitudes $\delta \geq R^*$ introduces label noise.

Ambiguous Class. If $\bar{x}'_j$ cannot be assigned a ground truth class membership, it lies within the low-density region between classes. In this case r_j is again an over-approximation of the actual robust radius and robust training for $\delta \geq R^*$ introduces label noise as well.

In summary, the interpretation of R^* depends on the class membership of $\bar{x}_j$. In all cases it is a model-agnostic lower-bound on the perturbation magnitude for which a geometrically more complex decision boundary is required. Therefore, it can guide the choice of hypothesis classes required for robust training. Further, it can also upper-bound the maximum feasible perturbation magnitude for a given dataset over which label noise is introduced. As label noise is known to hurt robustness [27], R^* can guide the usage of norm-bounded robust training and data augmentation for neural networks.

4   Computation of R^* for Image Benchmarks

In this section we compute R^* for real-world image benchmarks. We show that for those datasets it indeed upper-bounds the maximum feasible perturbation magnitude and that state-of-the-art robust models exhibit geometrically more complex decision boundaries. Finally, we also show that $R^* < 0.5R$, so it improves prior work on bounding the robust radius of a distribution [29].

As norm-bounded perturbations are usually given either in the l_2-norm or the l_∞-norm, we extend R^* to the l_∞-norm as well. Finally, we also show that R^* is independent of the ambient dimension d.

Table 1. Results in l_2-norm for real image benchmarks.

	R	$0.5R$	R^*	R^{crit}	$|\{\bar{x}\}_{\mathrm{local}}^{\mathrm{crit}}|$	$\frac{|\{\bar{x}\}_{\mathrm{local}}^{\mathrm{crit}}|}{l(c-1)}$	$|\{\bar{x}\}_{\mathrm{global}}^{\mathrm{crit}}|$	$\frac{|\{\bar{x}\}_{\mathrm{global}}^{\mathrm{crit}}|}{l(c-1)}$
SVHN	1.577	0.788	0.255	0.323	132061	0.200	2501	0.004
CIFAR-10	2.751	1.375	0.578	0.421	26608	0.059	132	0.000
FASHION	1.599	0.799	0.906	1.133	811	0.002	0	0.000
MNIST	2.398	1.199	1.654	1.379	0	0.000	0	0.000

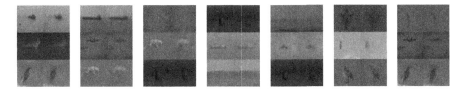

Fig. 4. Example image-pairs of $\{\bar{x}\}_{\mathrm{global}}^{\mathrm{crit}}$ (right) their associated x'_j (left) for CIFAR-10. A single x'_j can be associated with multiple $\bar{x}'_j \in \{\bar{x}\}_{\mathrm{global}}^{\mathrm{crit}}$, possibly one for all other classes. Additional example images can be found in Appendix I.

4.1 R Overestimates the Robust Radius for Real Image Benchmarks

We compute the introduced quantities for the MNIST [68], FASHION [69], SVHN [70] and CIFAR-10 [71] datasets. For all datasets we use exact nearest neighbour search over the entire original train set. SVHN contains two mislabelled samples which we remove from the dataset (see Appendix E).

In Table 1, we display all the derived quantities from Sect. 3 for all aforementioned datasets. They display intuitive results. They confirm, for instance, the common knowledge that MNIST and FASHION are well-separated. As $R^* > 0.5R$, the robust radius is accurately described by $0.5R$. However, as R^* defines a lower bound, no definitive statement can be made about increases in the geometric complexity of the decision boundaries for robust training.

For the more sophisticated benchmarks SVHN and CIFAR-10 we observe that the nearest neighbour distance R is an overestimation of the actual robust radius, as $R^* < 0.5R$ and thus $R^{\mathrm{crit}} < 1$. As a result, for both datasets $\{\bar{x}\}_{\mathrm{global}}^{\mathrm{crit}}$ are non-empty and it follows that they require a locally more complex decision boundary for perturbation magnitudes δ with $0.5R \geq \delta \geq R^*$.

$\bar{x}'_j$ *are Low-Density Samples.* In Sect. 3 we showed that the exact interpretation of R^* relies on the ground truth class label of the projections $\bar{x}'_j$. The question of class membership cannot be answered by l_p-norm distance metrics as for real-world datasets they are usually a bad proxy for semantic similarity. Thus, in Fig. 4 we display several images from $\{\bar{x}\}_{\mathrm{global}}^{\mathrm{crit}}$ with their associated x'_j from the CIFAR-10 dataset. We find that the majority of $\bar{x}'_j$ are strongly blurred versions of their corresponding x'_j and do not contain a clearly recognizable object. Therefore, those samples are part of the low-density region between classes.

Table 2. Predictions and confidences of model f for $\{\bar{x}\}_{\text{global}}^{\text{crit}}$ for CIFAR-10. Confidence values are reported as: mean $\pm$ standard deviation. NCC denotes no predicted class change by f and CC denotes a predicted class change between x'_j and $\bar{x}'_j \in \{\bar{x}\}_{\text{global}}^{\text{crit}}$. The complete table can be found in Appendix I.

Model f		$f(x'_j) = f(\bar{x}'_j)$ (NCC)		$f(x'_j) \neq f(\bar{x}'_j)$ (CC)	
		Fraction	Confidence	Fraction	Confidence
Andriushchenko et al. [66]	Non-robust	0.62	0.887 ± 0.154	0.38	0.708 ± 0.192
	Robust	0.79	0.535 ± 0.164	0.21	0.373 ± 0.098
Ding et al. [7]	Non-robust	0.52	0.913 ± 0.171	0.48	0.826 ± 0.174
	Robust	0.93	0.979 ± 0.057	0.07	0.791 ± 0.113
Rebuffi et al. [56]	Non-robust	0.50	0.844 ± 0.177	0.50	0.650 ± 0.171
	Robust	0.94	0.643 ± 0.202	0.06	0.389 ± 0.083
Rice et al. [67]	Non-robust	0.54	0.863 ± 0.168	0.46	0.677 ± 0.204
	Robust	0.92	0.635 ± 0.200	0.08	0.401 ± 0.072

4.2   Robust Models Learn More Complex Decision Boundaries

In addition to the visual investigation of $(x'_j, \bar{x}'_j)$, we gather the predictions and confidences of thirteen state-of-the-art robust models on $\{\bar{x}\}_{\text{global}}^{\text{crit}}$ from CIFAR-10. These models are obtained from Croce et al. [72] and referred to as *robust* models. In addition, we re-initialize these architectures and re-train only with the Adam optimizer [73] on the original train set to remove their robust representation. Thus, the re-trained models are their *non-robust* counterparts. In Table 2 we display, due to space constraints, four models. For all thirteen models we observe two major differences between the robust and non-robust ones. Firstly, the non-robust models assign high confidences to $\{\bar{x}\}_{\text{global}}^{\text{crit}}$. As the visual inspection shows that $\{\bar{x}\}_{\text{global}}^{\text{crit}}$ are part of the low-density region between classes, high confidence scores indicate a poorly calibrated classifier. In contrast, the robust models usually assign significantly lower confidences to these low-density samples, a result that would be expected from a well-performing classifier. Secondly, we find that robust and non-robust models differ in their predictions of whether a class change has occurred between x'_j and its corresponding $\bar{x}'_j$. Whereas the robust models predict in most of the cases that no class change occurs, the non-robust models predict class changes in half of the cases. As the addition of $\{\bar{x}\}_{\text{global}}^{\text{crit}}$ to the train set increases the geometric complexity of the decision boundary, robust models learn more complex decision boundaries. Thus, we experimentally confirm the previously made hypothesis [1,17,24–26]. These results also partially explain why robust training has a greater sample complexity than standard training, since the geometric complexity of decision boundaries is known to increase the sample complexity [4–6].

4.3   From l_2- to l_∞-Norm

Perturbation magnitudes for robust training and data augmentation are usually given in l_2- or l_∞-norm. In the previous section we computed R^* in l_2-norm so

Table 3. Number of pixels $\lceil(p - \tilde{p})\rceil$ (see Eq. 13) that need to be perturbed by ϵ in l_∞-norm to introduce perturbations $\delta > R^*$ in l_2-norm.

	$0.5R$	R^*	p	$\lceil(p - \tilde{p})\rceil$				
				$\epsilon = \frac{2}{255}$	$\epsilon = \frac{4}{255}$	$\epsilon = \frac{8}{255}$	$\epsilon = \frac{16}{255}$	$\epsilon = \frac{32}{255}$
SVHN	1.003	0.525	1024	4478	1120	280	70	18
CIFAR-10	1.375	0.578	1024	5439	1360	340	85	22
FASHION	0.799	0.906	784	13340	3335	834	209	53
MNIST	1.199	1.654	784	44461	11116	2779	695	174

here we expand the analysis to the l_∞-norm. Since the l_∞-norm is the maximum absolute change ϵ between any two vector dimensions, we compute how many dimensions in common image benchmarks need to be changed to surpass the specific R^*-value in l_2-norm. It is common practice in the robustness literature to apply the l_∞-norm on the pixel level, so to ignore the colour channel. Denoting the number of pixels in a dataset as p, with $0 \le \tilde{p} \le p$, it is easy to see that

$$||x - \tilde{x}||_2 = \sqrt{\sum_{i=1}^{p}(x_i - \tilde{x}_i)^2} = \sqrt{\sum_{i=1}^{\tilde{p}-1}(x_i - \tilde{x}_i)^2 + \sum_{j=\tilde{p}}^{p}(x_j - \tilde{x}_j)^2} > R^*$$

$$= \sqrt{\sum_{j=\tilde{p}}^{p} \epsilon^2} > R^* \Leftrightarrow (p - \tilde{p}) > \left(\frac{R^*}{\epsilon}\right)^2 \tag{13}$$

where the first sum is equal to zero because those pixels are not altered and the pixels in the second sum are all changed by ϵ due to the l_∞-norm. Thus, $(p - \tilde{p})$ is the number of pixels that need to be changed by ϵ such that the resulting perturbation magnitude in l_2-norm surpasses R^*. We round $(p - \tilde{p})$ to the nearest integer. In Table 3 we display the minimum number of pixels $\lceil(p - \tilde{p})\rceil$ that need to be changed to surpass R^* in l_2-norm when perturbations ϵ are applied in l_∞-norm. For CIFAR-10, for example, we observe that a l_∞ perturbation magnitude of $\epsilon = 4/255$ requires $1,360$ pixels to be altered. As this is more than the original number of $1,024$ pixels, R^* is not surpassed in l_2-norm. In general, we observe that for the common perturbation magnitude $\epsilon = 8/255$ only a small fraction of pixels need to be altered in both SVHN and CIFAR-10 to surpass the threshold R^* in l_2-norm. In Sect. 5 we show that including samples with perturbation magnitude $\delta \ge R^*$ leads to reduced generalization performance.

4.4   Results Are Independent of the Ambient Dimension d

The point $\bar{x}'_j$ minimizes the Euclidean distance between x'_j and the convex hull $\mathcal{C}(\{x_i\}_{i=1}^{d})$. Since the convex hull is defined by the d nearest neighbours with

Table 4. Influence of the ambient dimension d for CIFAR-10.

	d	R	$0.5R$	R^*	R^{crit}	$|\{\bar{x}\}^{\text{crit}}_{\text{local}}|$	$\frac{|\{\bar{x}\}^{\text{crit}}_{\text{local}}|}{l(c-1)}$	$|\{\bar{x}\}^{\text{crit}}_{\text{global}}|$	$\frac{|\{\bar{x}\}^{\text{crit}}_{\text{global}}|}{l(c-1)}$
34×34	3468	2.843	1.422	0.497	0.350	38827	0.086	283	0.001
32×32	3072	2.751	1.375	0.578	0.421	26608	0.059	132	0.000
30×30	2700	2.514	1.257	0.486	0.386	36167	0.080	236	0.001
28×28	2352	2.324	1.162	0.467	0.402	34784	0.077	214	0.000
26×26	2028	2.157	1.079	0.444	0.412	33066	0.073	200	0.000

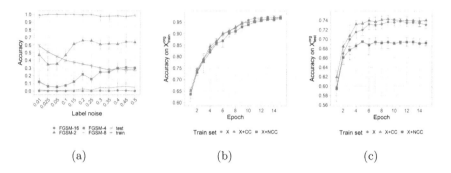

(a)   (b)   (c)

Fig. 5. Results for CIFAR-10. Error-bars denote minimum and maximum over five runs. (a) Mean accuracy on the train and test set and against FGSM-$i/255$, $i \in \{2,5,8\}$ attacks for different levels of label noise introduced by $\{\bar{x}\}^{\text{crit}}_{\text{global}}$. (b) Mean accuracy on $X^{\text{org}}_{\text{train}}$ during training with $\{\bar{x}\}^{\text{crit}}_{\text{local}}$. (c) Mean accuracy on $X^{\text{org}}_{\text{test}}$ during training with $\{\bar{x}\}^{\text{crit}}_{\text{local}}$.

another class label of x'_j, all quantities that are deducted from $\bar{x}'_j$ are functions of the ambient dimension d. Therefore, we investigate whether changes of the ambient dimension change the previously computed quantities.

We report the results for CIFAR-10 in Table 4. For image distributions an increase in their ambient dimension d, so their resolution, results in higher correlations between pixels and larger Euclidean distances between images. So, simultaneously higher values of R and R^* are expected. Further, there is no clear relationship between $|\{\bar{x}\}^{\text{crit}}_{\text{local}}|$ and $|\{\bar{x}\}^{\text{crit}}_{\text{global}}|$ with respect to d. Thus, the derived quantities are not artefacts of high dimensional spaces but dataset specific properties.

5   Training with $\delta \geq R^*$ Deteriorates Performance

In Sect. 3 we derived R^* theoretically for arbitrary datasets. We discussed that the implications of robust training for perturbation magnitudes $\delta \geq R^*$ depend on the class membership of those samples for which $r'_j < 0.5r_j$. In Sect. 4 we showed that for sophisticated real-world benchmarks $\{\bar{x}\}^{\text{crit}}_{\text{global}}$ lie within the low-density region between classes. Including these samples that do not display

Table 5. Accuracy against noise- (top) and blur-perturbations (bottom) [14] for CIFAR-10 and $\{\bar{x}\}_{\text{local}}^{\text{crit}}$. Networks trained on X+CC and X+NCC exhibit better robustness against small-norm noise-perturbations but worse robustness against large-norm blur perturbations. Example images can be found in Appendix H.

	Gaussian	Shot	Impulse	Speckle
X	0.521	0.501	0.537	0.557
X+CC	0.526	0.504	0.546	0.562
X+NCC	**0.600**	**0.581**	**0.584**	**0.621**

	Zoom	Defocus	Gaussian	Glass	Fog	Brightness	Contrast
X	**0.638**	**0.691**	0.324	0.703	**0.352**	0.694	0.328
X+CC	0.625	0.689	0.273	**0.704**	0.292	**0.709**	0.246
X+NCC	0.607	0.647	**0.423**	0.656	0.342	0.648	**0.343**

a clearly distinguishable object is equivalent to the addition of label noise which is known to hurt robustness [27]. In this section we show that the addition of samples with perturbations $\delta \geq r'_j$ for $r'_j < 0.5 r_j$ indeed hurts the performance of classifiers according to several metrics on CIFAR-10. Due to space constraints we present further affirmative results for SVHN in Appendix F.

Extension by the Globally Critical Points. As $|\{\bar{x}\}_{\text{global}}^{\text{crit}}| = 132$ for CIFAR-10 (see Table 1), their addition is not measurably impacting generalization performance (see Appendix H). Thus, to simulate different levels of label noise we add random samples from the original train set $X_{\text{train}}^{\text{org}}$ to $\{\bar{x}\}_{\text{global}}^{\text{crit}}$ to obtain train sets with different relative amounts of original and critical samples and therefore different amounts of label noise. This experimental setup roughly follows Sanyal et al. [27]. We train a neural network on these datasets and measure its accuracy on the original train and test set and against FGSM attacks [13] of different strengths.

In Fig. 5a we observe that with increasing label noise test accuracy deteriorates while adversarial accuracy against FGSM attacks increases. Although, due to the small train set, test accuracy is already low, adding samples with no visible class object further deteriorates test accuracy as the model is likely biased towards learning superficial textural clues. Train accuracy on the other hand is not hurt, as those samples can simply be memorized. As $\{\bar{x}\}_{\text{global}}^{\text{crit}}$ are defined by having $r'_j \leq 0.5R$, the distance between $\bar{x}'_j$ and x'_j is small and thus small-norm perturbations as those introduced by FGSM do not result in wrong predictions as the network interpolates between $\bar{x}'_j$ and x'_j.

Extension by the Locally Critical Points. It is common practice in adversarial training to pick a single perturbation magnitude δ for all samples under the assumption that no class change is induced by its application. However, this procedure is suboptimal and error-prone as upper-bounds on δ can be influenced by labelling errors in the original train set. Thus, more recent robust training methods work with instance-specific perturbation magnitudes [7].

To further show that the addition of samples for which $\delta \geq R^*$ leads to reduced generalization performance, we create two new train sets by appending either $\{\bar{x}\}_{\text{local}}^{\text{crit}}$ with the label of its corresponding x_j' (no class change, NCC), denoted X+NCC, or the label of its corresponding nearest neighbours $\{x_i\}_{i=1}^{d}$ (class change, CC), denoted X+CC, to the original train set $X_{\text{train}}^{\text{org}}$. We train a network on each of these three datasets and report accuracies on the original train and original test set in Figs. 5b and 5c. We observe that while train accuracy is not hurt, test accuracy deteriorates when trained on X+NCC. This is likely due to $\{\bar{x}\}_{\text{local}}^{\text{crit}}$ biasing the model towards learning superficial textural clues which does not deteriorate train but does reduce generalization performance. The addition of $\{\bar{x}\}_{\text{local}}^{\text{crit}}$ when assigned a different class label than x_j' improves generalization performance. This is likely due to the network interpolating between $\{x_i\}_{i=1}^{d}$ which appears to help for CIFAR-10. Contrary, in Appendix F we show for SVHN that both train sets X+NCC and X+CC reduce generalization performance.

Finally, we also test these models against a benchmark of common perturbations [14]. We obtain similar results to the label noise experiments above. In Table 5 we observe that accuracy against small-norm noise perturbations is increased whereas accuracy against large-norm blur perturbations is mostly decreased. Intuitively, a flat loss surface around training points or obfuscated gradients [74] help to protect against small-norm changes, whereas large-norm changes need to be defend against by learning semantic concepts.

These results show that the maximum perturbation magnitudes for robust training need to be chosen carefully as they can deteriorate the generalisation to accuracy and robustness benchmarks while train accuracy is unharmed.

6 Conclusions

Robustness and generalization behaviour of neural networks have traditionally been studied by investigating properties of their learned representation or their training methods. More recently, properties of datasets came into focus as potential causes for their generalization and robustness deficits (see Sect. 2). This work contributes to this line of work. We study the complexity of decision boundaries for robust training in a model-agnostic way and derive a lower bound on the perturbation magnitude that increase their complexity. For common image benchmarks it also bounds the introduction of label noise which we show to hurt generalization and robustness. Thus, our work shows that studying geometric properties of data distributions can yield practical insights into modern deep classifiers and can provide guidelines for the choice of architectures and training parameters.

Acknowledgements. D. Kienitz and E. Komendantskaya acknowledge support of EPSRC grant EP/T026952/1: *AI Secure and Explainable by Construction (AISEC).*

References

1. He, W., Li, B., Song, D.: Decision boundary analysis of adversarial examples. In: International Conference on Learning Representations (2018)
2. Fawzi, A., Moosavi-Dezfooli, S.M., Frossard, P., Soatto, S.: Classification regions of deep neural networks. arXiv preprint arXiv:1705.09552 (2017)
3. Ortiz-Jimenez, G., Modas, A., Moosavi, S.M., Frossard, P.: Hold me tight! influence of discriminative features on deep network boundaries. Adv. Neural. Inf. Process. Syst. **33**, 2935–2946 (2020)
4. Narayanan, H., Mitter, S.: Sample complexity of testing the manifold hypothesis. In: Advances in Neural Information Processing Systems, pp. 1786–1794 (2010)
5. Narayanan, H., Niyogi, P.: On the sample complexity of learning smooth cuts on a manifold. In: COLT (2009)
6. Kienitz, D., Komendantskaya, E., Lones, M.: The effect of manifold entanglement and intrinsic dimensionality on learning. In: 36th AAAI Conference on Artificial Intelligence 2022, AAAI Press (2021)
7. Ding, G.W., Sharma, Y., Lui, K.Y.C., Huang, R.: Mma training: direct input space margin maximization through adversarial training. In: International Conference on Learning Representations. (2019)
8. Ribeiro, M.T., Singh, S., Guestrin, C.: "Why should i trust you?" explaining the predictions of any classifier. In: Proceedings of the 22nd ACM SIGKDD International Conference on Knowledge Discovery and Data Mining, pp. 1135–1144 (2016)
9. Krizhevsky, A., Sutskever, I., Hinton, G.E.: Imagenet classification with deep convolutional neural networks. In: Advances in Neural Information Processing Systems, pp. 1097–1105 (2012)
10. Radford, A., Metz, L., Chintala, S.: Unsupervised representation learning with deep convolutional generative adversarial networks. arXiv preprint arXiv:1511.06434 (2015)
11. Geirhos, R., et al.: Partial success in closing the gap between human and machine vision. Adv. Neural. Inf. Process. Syst. **34**, 23885–23899 (2021)
12. Szegedy, C., et al.: Intriguing properties of neural networks. In: 2nd International Conference on Learning Representations, ICLR 2014 (2014)
13. Goodfellow, I.J., Shlens, J., Szegedy, C.: Explaining and harnessing adversarial examples. arXiv preprint arXiv:1412.6572 (2014)
14. Hendrycks, D., Dietterich, T.: Benchmarking neural network robustness to common corruptions and perturbations. In: International Conference on Learning Representations (2018)
15. Taori, R., Dave, A., Shankar, V., Carlini, N., Recht, B., Schmidt, L.: Measuring robustness to natural distribution shifts in image classification. Adv. Neural. Inf. Process. Syst. **33**, 18583–18599 (2020)
16. Recht, B., Roelofs, R., Schmidt, L., Shankar, V.: Do imagenet classifiers generalize to imagenet? In: International Conference on Machine Learning, PMLR, pp. 5389–5400 (2019)
17. Madry, A., Makelov, A., Schmidt, L., Tsipras, D., Vladu, A.: Towards deep learning models resistant to adversarial attacks. In: International Conference on Learning Representations (2018)
18. Raghunathan, A., Xie, S.M., Yang, F., Duchi, J.C., Liang, P.: Adversarial training can hurt generalization. arXiv preprint arXiv:1906.06032 (2019)
19. Zhang, X., Chen, J., Gu, Q., Evans, D.: Understanding the intrinsic robustness of image distributions using conditional generative models. In: International Conference on Artificial Intelligence and Statistics, PMLR, pp. 3883–3893 (2020)

20. Tsipras, D., Santurkar, S., Engstrom, L., Turner, A., Madry, A.: Robustness may be at odds with accuracy. arXiv preprint arXiv:1805.12152 (2018)
21. Stutz, D., Hein, M., Schiele, B.: Disentangling adversarial robustness and generalization. In: Proceedings of the IEEE Conference on Computer Vision and Pattern Recognition, pp. 6976–6987 (2019)
22. Yang, Y.Y., Rashtchian, C., Wang, Y., Chaudhuri, K.: Robustness for nonparametric classification: a generic attack and defense. In: International Conference on Artificial Intelligence and Statistics, PMLR, pp. 941–951 (2020)
23. Shah, H., Tamuly, K., Raghunathan, A., Jain, P., Netrapalli, P.: The pitfalls of simplicity bias in neural networks. Adv. Neural. Inf. Process. Syst. **33**, 9573–9585 (2020)
24. Schmidt, L., Santurkar, S., Tsipras, D., Talwar, K., Madry, A.: Adversarially robust generalization requires more data. In: Proceedings of the 32nd International Conference on Neural Information Processing Systems, pp. 15019–503 (2018)
25. Yin, D., Kannan, R., Bartlett, P.: Rademacher complexity for adversarially robust generalization. In: International Conference on Machine Learning, PMLR, pp. 7085–7094 (2019)
26. Nakkiran, P.: Adversarial robustness may be at odds with simplicity. arXiv preprint arXiv:1901.00532 (2019)
27. Sanyal, A., Dokania, P.K., Kanade, V., Torr, P.: How benign is benign overfitting? In: International Conference on Learning Representations (2020)
28. Nguyen, Q., Mukkamala, M.C., Hein, M.: Neural networks should be wide enough to learn disconnected decision regions. In: International Conference on Machine Learning, PMLR, pp. 3740–3749 (2018)
29. Yang, Y.Y., Rashtchian, C., Zhang, H., Salakhutdinov, R.R., Chaudhuri, K.: A closer look at accuracy vs. robustness. In: Advances in Neural Information Processing Systems 33, pp. 8588–8601 (2020)
30. Ilyas, A., Santurkar, S., Tsipras, D., Engstrom, L., Tran, B., Madry, A.: Adversarial examples are not bugs, they are features. In: Advances in Neural Information Processing Systems 32 (2019)
31. Joe, B., Hwang, S.J., Shin, I.: Learning to disentangle robust and vulnerable features for adversarial detection. arXiv preprint arXiv:1909.04311 (2019)
32. Singla, S., Feizi, S.: Salient imagenet: How to discover spurious features in deep learning? In: International Conference on Learning Representations (2021)
33. Nguyen, A., Yosinski, J., Clune, J.: Deep neural networks are easily fooled: High confidence predictions for unrecognizable images. In: Proceedings of the IEEE Conference on Computer Vision and Pattern Recognition, pp. 427–436 (2015)
34. Arpit, D., et al.: A closer look at memorization in deep networks. In: Proceedings of the 34th International Conference on Machine Learning-Volume 70, JMLR. org, pp. 233–242 (2017)
35. Hermann, K., Lampinen, A.: What shapes feature representations? exploring datasets, architectures, and training. Adv. Neural. Inf. Process. Syst. **33**, 9995–10006 (2020)
36. Ahmed, F., Bengio, Y., van Seijen, H., Courville, A.: Systematic generalisation with group invariant predictions. In: International Conference on Learning Representations (2020)
37. Valle-Perez, G., Camargo, C.Q., Louis, A.A.: Deep learning generalizes because the parameter-function map is biased towards simple functions. In: International Conference on Learning Representations. (2018)
38. Jo, J., Bengio, Y.: Measuring the tendency of CNNs to learn surface statistical regularities. arXiv preprint arXiv:1711.11561 (2017)

39. Beery, S., Van Horn, G., Perona, P.: Recognition in terra incognita. In: Ferrari, V., Hebert, M., Sminchisescu, C., Weiss, Y. (eds.) ECCV 2018. LNCS, vol. 11220, pp. 472–489. Springer, Cham (2018). https://doi.org/10.1007/978-3-030-01270-0_28
40. Geirhos, R., Rubisch, P., Michaelis, C., Bethge, M., Wichmann, F.A., Brendel, W.: Imagenet-trained CNNs are biased towards texture; increasing shape bias improves accuracy and robustness. In: International Conference on Learning Representations (2018)
41. Geirhos, R., Medina Temme, C., Rauber, J., Schütt, H., Bethge, M., Wichmann, F.: Generalisation in humans and deep neural networks. In: Thirty-second Annual Conference on Neural Information Processing Systems 2018 (NeurIPS 2018), Curran, pp. 7549–7561 (2019)
42. Hermann, K., Chen, T., Kornblith, S.: The origins and prevalence of texture bias in convolutional neural networks. Adv. Neural. Inf. Process. Syst. **33**, 19000–19015 (2020)
43. Carter, B., Jain, S., Mueller, J.W., Gifford, D.: Overinterpretation reveals image classification model pathologies. In: Advances in Neural Information Processing Systems 34 (2021)
44. Singla, S., Nushi, B., Shah, S., Kamar, E., Horvitz, E.: Understanding failures of deep networks via robust feature extraction. In: Proceedings of the IEEE/CVF Conference on Computer Vision and Pattern Recognition, pp. 12853–12862 (2021)
45. Bengio, Y., Courville, A., Vincent, P.: Representation learning: a review and new perspectives. IEEE Trans. Pattern Anal. Mach. Intell. **35**, 1798–1828 (2013)
46. Bhagoji, A.N., Cullina, D., Mittal, P.: Lower bounds on adversarial robustness from optimal transport. Adv. Neural. Inf. Process. Syst. **32**, 7498–7510 (2019)
47. Dobriban, E., Hassani, H., Hong, D., Robey, A.: Provable tradeoffs in adversarially robust classification. arXiv preprint arXiv:2006.05161 (2020)
48. Dan, C., Wei, Y., Ravikumar, P.: Sharp statistical guaratees for adversarially robust gaussian classification. In: International Conference on Machine Learning, PMLR, pp. 2345–2355 (2020)
49. Bhattacharjee, R., Jha, S., Chaudhuri, K.: Sample complexity of robust linear classification on separated data. In: International Conference on Machine Learning, PMLR, pp. 884–893 (2021)
50. Khim, J., Loh, P.L.: Adversarial risk bounds via function transformation. arXiv preprint arXiv:1810.09519 (2018)
51. Attias, I., Kontorovich, A., Mansour, Y.: Improved generalization bounds for robust learning. In: Algorithmic Learning Theory, PMLR, pp. 162–183 (2019)
52. Montasser, O., Hanneke, S., Srebro, N.: Vc classes are adversarially robustly learnable, but only improperly. In: Conference on Learning Theory, PMLR, pp. 2512–2530 (2019)
53. Ashtiani, H., Pathak, V., Urner, R.: Black-box certification and learning under adversarial perturbations. In: International Conference on Machine Learning, PMLR, pp. 388–398 (2020)
54. Hendrycks, D., et al.: The many faces of robustness: a critical analysis of out-of-distribution generalization. In: Proceedings of the IEEE/CVF International Conference on Computer Vision, pp. 8340–8349 (2021)
55. Hendrycks, D., Mu, N., Cubuk, E.D., Zoph, B., Gilmer, J., Lakshminarayanan, B.: Augmix: a simple data processing method to improve robustness and uncertainty. In: International Conference on Learning Representations (2019)
56. Rebuffi, S.A., Gowal, S., Calian, D.A., Stimberg, F., Wiles, O., Mann, T.A.: Data augmentation can improve robustness. In: Advances in Neural Information Processing Systems 34 (2021)

57. Hendrycks, D., Lee, K., Mazeika, M.: Using pre-training can improve model robustness and uncertainty. arXiv preprint arXiv:1901.09960 (2019)
58. Carmon, Y., Raghunathan, A., Schmidt, L., Liang, P., Duchi, J.C.: Unlabeled data improves adversarial robustness. In: Proceedings of the 33rd International Conference on Neural Information Processing Systems, pp. 11192–11203 (2019)
59. Alayrac, J.B., Uesato, J., Huang, P.S., Fawzi, A., Stanforth, R., Kohli, P.: Are labels required for improving adversarial robustness? Adv. Neural. Inf. Process. Syst. **32**, 12214–12223 (2019)
60. Qin, C., et al.: Adversarial robustness through local linearization. In: Advances in Neural Information Processing Systems 32 (2019)
61. Ross, A., Doshi-Velez, F.: Improving the adversarial robustness and interpretability of deep neural networks by regularizing their input gradients. In: Proceedings of the AAAI Conference on Artificial Intelligence, vol. 32 (2018)
62. Chan, A., Tay, Y., Ong, Y.S., Fu, J.: Jacobian adversarially regularized networks for robustness. In: International Conference on Learning Representations (2020)
63. Etmann, C., Lunz, S., Maass, P., Schönlieb, C.: On the connection between adversarial robustness and saliency map interpretability. In: ICML (2019)
64. Simpson, B., Dutil, F., Bengio, Y., Cohen, J.P.: Gradmask: reduce overfitting by regularizing saliency. In: International Conference on Medical Imaging with Deep Learning-Extended Abstract Track (2019)
65. Fawzi, A., Moosavi-Dezfooli, S.M., Frossard, P., Soatto, S.: Empirical study of the topology and geometry of deep networks. In: Proceedings of the IEEE Conference on Computer Vision and Pattern Recognition, pp. 3762–3770 (2018)
66. Andriushchenko, M., Flammarion, N.: Understanding and improving fast adversarial training. Adv. Neural. Inf. Process. Syst. **33**, 16048–16059 (2020)
67. Rice, L., Wong, E., Kolter, Z.: Overfitting in adversarially robust deep learning. In: International Conference on Machine Learning, PMLR, pp. 8093–8104 (2020)
68. LeCun, Y., Boser, B.E., Denker, J.S., Henderson, D., Howard, R.E., Hubbard, W.E., Jackel, L.D.: Handwritten digit recognition with a back-propagation network. In: Advances in Neural Information Processing Systems, pp. 396–404 (1990)
69. Xiao, H., Rasul, K., Vollgraf, R.: Fashion-mnist: a novel image dataset for benchmarking machine learning algorithms. arXiv preprint arXiv:1708.07747 (2017)
70. Netzer, Y., Wang, T., Coates, A., Bissacco, A., Wu, B., Ng, A.Y.: Reading digits in natural images with unsupervised feature learning. In: NIPS Workshop on Deep Learning and Unsupervised Feature Learning 2011 (2011)
71. Krizhevsky, A., Hinton, G., et al.: Learning multiple layers of features from tiny images. Technical report, University of Toronto (2009)
72. Croce, F., et al.: Robustbench: a standardized adversarial robustness benchmark. In: Thirty-Fifth Conference on Neural Information Processing Systems Datasets and Benchmarks Track (2021)
73. Kingma, D.P., Ba, J.: Adam: a method for stochastic optimization. In: ICLR (Poster) (2015)
74. Athalye, A., Carlini, N., Wagner, D.: Obfuscated gradients give a false sense of security: Circumventing defenses to adversarial examples. arXiv preprint arXiv:1802.00420 (2018)
75. Boser, B.E., Guyon, I.M., Vapnik, V.N.: A training algorithm for optimal margin classifiers. In: Proceedings of the Fifth Annual Workshop on Computational Learning Theory, pp. 144–152 (1992)
76. Moosavi-Dezfooli, S.M., Fawzi, A., Frossard, P.: Deepfool: a simple and accurate method to fool deep neural networks. In: Proceedings of the IEEE Conference on Computer Vision and Pattern Recognition, pp. 2574–2582 (2016)

77. Addepalli, S., Jain, S., Sriramanan, G., Khare, S., Radhakrishnan, V.B.: Towards achieving adversarial robustness beyond perceptual limits. In: ICML 2021 Workshop on Adversarial Machine Learning (2021)
78. Augustin, M., Meinke, A., Hein, M.: Adversarial robustness on in- and out-distribution improves explainability. In: Vedaldi, A., Bischof, H., Brox, T., Frahm, J.-M. (eds.) ECCV 2020. LNCS, vol. 12371, pp. 228–245. Springer, Cham (2020). https://doi.org/10.1007/978-3-030-58574-7_14
79. Engstrom, L., Ilyas, A., Salman, H., Santurkar, S., Tsipras, D.: Robustness (python library) (2019)
80. Kireev, K., Andriushchenko, M., Flammarion, N.: On the effectiveness of adversarial training against common corruptions. In: Uncertainty in Artificial Intelligence, PMLR, pp. 1012–1021 (2022)
81. Modas, A., Rade, R., Ortiz-Jiménez, G., Moosavi-Dezfooli, S.M., Frossard, P.: Prime: A few primitives can boost robustness to common corruptions. arXiv preprint arXiv:2112.13547 (2021)
82. Rade: Helper-based adversarial training: Reducing excessive margin to achieve a better accuracy vs. robustness trade-off. In: ICML 2021 Workshop on Adversarial Machine Learning (2021)
83. Wong, E., Rice, L., Kolter, J.Z.: Fast is better than free: Revisiting adversarial training. In: International Conference on Learning Representations (2019)
84. Ioffe, S., Szegedy, C.: Batch normalization: accelerating deep network training by reducing internal covariate shift. In: International conference on machine learning, PMLR, pp. 448–456 (2015)
85. Fukushima, K.: Visual feature extraction by a multilayered network of analog threshold elements. IEEE Trans. Syst. Sci. Cybern. 5, 322–333 (1969)
86. Fukushima, K., Miyake, S.: Neocognitron: a self-organizing neural network model for a mechanism of visual pattern recognition. In: Competition and Cooperation in Neural Nets, pp. 267–285. Springer (1982). https://doi.org/10.1007/978-3-642-46466-9_18
87. Glorot, X., Bordes, A., Bengio, Y.: Deep sparse rectifier neural networks. In: Proceedings of the Fourteenth International Conference on Artificial Intelligence and Statistics, JMLR Workshop and Conference Proceedings, pp. 315–323 (2011)
88. Paszke, A., et al.: Pytorch: an imperative style, high-performance deep learning library. In: Advances in Neural Information Processing Systems 32, pp. 8024–8035. Curran Associates, Inc. (2019)

DreamNet: A Deep Riemannian Manifold Network for SPD Matrix Learning

Rui Wang[1,2], Xiao-Jun Wu[1,2(✉)], Ziheng Chen[1,2], Tianyang Xu[1,2], and Josef Kittler[1,2,3]

[1] School of Artificial Intelligence and Computer Science, Jiangnan University, Wuxi 214122, China
cs_wr@jiangnan.edu.cn, xiaojun_wu_jnu@163.com

[2] Jiangsu Provincial Engineering Laboratory of Pattern Recognition and Computational Intelligence, Jiangnan University, Wuxi 214122, China
zh_chen@stu.jiangnan.edu.cn

[3] Centre for Vision, Speech and Signal Processing (CVSSP), University of Surrey, Guildford GU2 7XH, UK
j.kittler@surrey.ac.uk

Abstract. The methods of symmetric positive definite (SPD) matrix learning have attracted considerable attention in many pattern recognition tasks, as they are eligible to capture and learn appropriate statistical features while respecting the Riemannian geometry of SPD manifold where the data reside on. Accompanied with the advanced deep learning techniques, several Riemannian networks (RiemNets) for SPD matrix nonlinear processing have recently been studied. However, it is pertinent to ask, whether greater accuracy gains can be realized by simply increasing the depth of RiemNets. The answer appears to be negative, as deeper RiemNets may be difficult to train. To explore a possible solution to this issue, we propose a new architecture for SPD matrix learning. Specifically, to enrich the deep representations, we build a stacked Riemannian autoencoder (SRAE) on the tail of the backbone network, *i.e.*, SPDNet [23]. With this design, the associated reconstruction error term can prompt the embedding functions of both SRAE and of each RAE to approach an identity mapping, which helps to prevent the degradation of statistical information. Then, we implant several residual-like blocks using shortcut connections to augment the representational capacity of SRAE, and to simplify the training of a deeper network. The experimental evidence demonstrates that our DreamNet can achieve improved accuracy with increased depth.

Keywords: SPD matrix learning · Riemannian neural network · Information degradation · Stacked Riemannian Autoencoder (SRAE)

Supplementary Information The online version contains supplementary material available at https://doi.org/10.1007/978-3-031-26351-4_39.

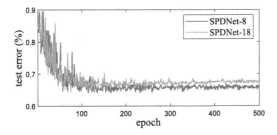

Fig. 1. Test error of SPDNets versus the number of epochs on the AFEW dataset.

1 Introduction

Covariance matrices are well-known in any statistical-related field, but their direct usage as data descriptors in the community of computer vision and pattern recognition (CV&PR) is less common. Even so, their effectiveness has been verified in a variety of applications. In medical imaging, covariance matrices are taken to classify time-series for Brain-Computer Interfaces (BCI) [3] and analyze magnetic resonance imaging (MRI) [5,8]. In visual classification, since a global covariance matrix has the capacity to characterize the spatiotemporal fluctuations of data points of different lengths, covariance features have gained remarkable progress in many practical scenarios, such as dynamic scene classification [38,46,47], facial emotional recognition [4,23,44], face recognition [19,24,26], and action recognition [18,33,51], *etc.*

However, the main difficulty of processing and classifying these matrices, which are actually SPD, is that they cannot be regarded as the Euclidean elements, as their underlying space is a curved Riemannian manifold, *i.e.*, an SPD manifold [2]. Consequently, the tools from Euclidean geometry cannot directly be applied for computation. Thanks to the well-studied Riemannian metrics, including Log-Euclidean Metric (LEM) [2] and Affine-Invariant Riemannian Metric (AIRM) [34], the Euclidean methods can be generalized to the SPD manifolds by either mapping it into an associated flat space via tangent approximation [36,40,41] or utilizing the Riemannian kernel functions to embed it into a Reproducing Kernel Hilbert Space (RKHS) [17,20,43,48]. However, these two types of approaches may lead to undesirable solutions as they distort the geometrical structure of the input data manifold by the data transformation process. To respect the original Riemannian geometry more faithfully, several geometry-aware discriminant analysis algorithms [13,19,26,54] have been developed for learning an efficient, manifold-to-manifold projection mapping. Regrettably, despite their notable success, the intrinsic shallow linear SPD matrix learning scheme, implemented on nonlinear manifolds, impede these methods from mining fine-grained geometric representations.

Motivated by the philosophy of convolutional neural networks (ConvNets) [21,37], an end-to-end Riemannian architecture for SPD matrix nonlinear learning has been proposed (SPDNet [23]). The structure of SPDNet is analogous to

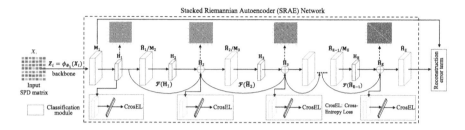

Fig. 2. Schematic diagram of the proposed Riemannian network.

a classical ConvNet (*e.g.*, with transformation and activation layers), but each layer processes the SPD manifold-valued data points. The final layer of SPDNet maps the learned feature manifold into a flat space for classification. More architectures have followed thereafter [4,33,46,51], modifying the elementary building blocks for different application scenarios. As recent evidence [21,37] reveals, the network depth is of vital importance for promoting good performance. A question therefore arises: *can the classification accuracy be improved by simply stacking more layers on top of each other in the SPD neural networks?* The following three factors make it impossible to provide ready answers: 1) existing RiemNets have a small number of layers and there is no prior experience in building very deep RiemNets; 2) there is limited research on this topic; 3) deeper SPD network may be difficult to train. A typical example is illustrated in Fig. 1. It should be noted that the classification error of SPDNet-18 is higher than that of SPDNet-8.

The above observation suggests that simply stacking more layers on top of each other does not mean that a better RiemNet can be learnt. This article proposes a new architecture for SPD matrix processing and classification that avoids the pitfalls of layer stacking in RiemNet. The overall framework of our approach is shown in Fig. 2. As a greater depth of representation is essential for many classification tasks [21,49,53,55], the purpose of the proposed network is to pursue a deeper manifold-to-manifold embedding mapping that would transform the input SPD matrices into more informative ones of lower dimensionality and the same topology. To meet this requirement, we select the original architecture proposed in [23] as the backbone of our model, in view of its demonstrable strength in SPD matrix nonlinear learning. Then, a stacked Riemannian autoencoder network (SRAE) is established at the end of the backbone to increase the depth of the structured representations. Under the supervision of a reconstruction error term associated with the input-output SPD matrices of SRAE, the embedding mechanisms of both SRAE and each RAE will asymptotically approach an identity mapping, thus being capable of preventing a degradation of statistical information during multi-stage data compressed sensing. The proposed solution ensures that the classification error produced by our deeper model would not be higher than that of the shallower backbone. To enhance the representational capacity of SRAE, we build multiple residual-like blocks within it, implemented by the shortcut connections [21] between the hidden layers of any two adjacent RAEs. This design makes the current RAE learning stage access the informative features of the previous stages easily, facilitating the reconstruction of the remaining structural details. Since the above design ensures that the SRAE network remains sensitive to the data variations in the new feature manifolds, we also append a classification module, composed of the LogEig layer (will be introduced later), FC layer, and cross-entropy loss, to each RAE to facilitate the training of a discriminative manifold-to-manifold deep transformation mapping. In this manner, a series of effective classifiers can be obtained. Finally, a simple maximum voting strategy is applied for decision making.

We demonstrate the benefits of the proposed approach on the tasks of facial emotion recognition, skeleton-based hand action recognition, and skeleton-based action recognition with UAVs, respectively. The experimental results achieved on three benchmarking datasets show that our DreamNet achieves accuracy gains from an increasing network depth, producing better results than the previous methods.

2   Related Works

To endow SPD matrix representation learning with deep and nonlinear function, Ionescu et al. [28] integrate global SPD computation layers with the proposed matrix backpropagation methodology into deep networks to capture structured features for visual scene understanding. Inspired by the paradigm of ConvNets, Huang et al. [23] design a novel Riemannian neural network for SPD matrix nonlinear learning, comprising of a stack of SPD matrix transformation and activation layers, referred to as SPDNet. To provide a better guidance for the network training, Brooks et al. [4] design a Riemannian batch normalization module for SPDNet. Considering the potential importance of the local structural information contained in the SPD matrix, Zhang et al. [51] propose an SPD matrix 2D convolutional layer for data transformation, requiring each convolutional kernel also to be SPD. Different from [51], Chakraborty et al. [5] use the weighted Fréchet Mean (wFM) operation to simulate convolution on the manifolds, considering the intrinsic Riemannian geometry of the data points like diffusion tensors. More recently, Wang et al. [46] design a lightweight cascaded neural network for SPD matrix learning and classification, which shows higher computational efficiency and competitive classification performance, especially with limited training data.

3   Proposed Method

Although the Riemannian neural network approaches for SPD matrix processing can alleviate the negative impact of data variations on the classification performance, achieving accuracy gains is not simply a matter of increasing the network depth. The main obstacle to this simplistic solution is the degradation of statistical information (degradation problem), which makes the learned deep representations unable to effectively characterize the structural information of the original imaged scene, thus resulting in lower accuracy. In this paper, we design a novel Riemannian architecture named DreamNet to solve this issue. Figure 2 provides an overview of our approach.

3.1 Preliminaries

SPD Manifold: A real-valued symmetric matrix X is called SPD if and only if $v^T X v > 0$ for all non-zero vector $v \in \mathbb{R}^d$. As studied in [2,34], when endowed with manifold structures, the set of d-by-d SPD matrices, denoted as $\mathcal{S}_{++}^d$:

$$\mathcal{S}_{++}^d := \{X \in \mathbb{R}^{d \times d} : X = X^T, v^T X v > 0, \forall v \in \mathbb{R}^d \setminus \{0_d\}\}. \tag{1}$$

forms a specific Riemannian manifold, *i.e.*, SPD manifold. This enables the use of concepts related to differential geometry to address $\mathcal{S}_{++}^d$, such as geodesic.

Data Modeling with Second-Order Statistics: Let $S_i = [s_1, s_2, ..., s_{n_i}]$ be the ith given data sequence with n_i entries, where $s_t \in \mathbb{R}^{d \times 1}$ denotes the tth vectorized instance. For S_i, its second-order representation is computed by: $X_i = \frac{1}{n_i - 1} \sum_{t=1}^{n_i} (s_t - u_i)(s_t - u_i)^T$, where $u_i = \frac{1}{n_i} \sum_{t=1}^{n_i} s_t$ signifies the mean of S_i. Considering that X_i does not necessarily satisfy the condition of positive definiteness, it is regularised, *i.e.*, $X_i \leftarrow X_i + \lambda I_d$, where I_d is an identity matrix of size $d \times d$, and λ is set to $trace(X_i) \times 10^{-3}$ in all the experiments. In this way, X_i is a true SPD manifold-valued element [34].

Basic Layers of SPDNet: Let $X_{k-1} \in \mathcal{S}_{++}^{d_{k-1}}$ be the input SPD matrix of the kth layer. The Riemannian operation layers defined in [23] are as follows:

BiMap Layer: This layer is analogous to the usual dense layer, used to transform the input SPD data points into a lower dimensional space by a bilinear mapping f_b, expressed as $X_k = f_b^{(k)}(W_k, X_{k-1}) = W_k^T X_{k-1} W_k$, where W_k is the column full-rank transformation matrix with semi-orthogonality.

ReEig Layer: This layer is similar to the classical ReLU layers, designed to inject nonlinearity into SPDNet by modifying the small positive eigenvalues of each input SPD matrix with a nonlinear rectification function f_r, formulated as $X_k = f_r^{(k)}(X_{k-1}) = U_{k-1} \max(\epsilon I, \Sigma_{k-1}) U_{k-1}^T$. Here, $X_{k-1} = U_{k-1} \Sigma_{k-1} U_{k-1}^T$ represents the eigenvalue decomposition, and ϵ is a small activation threshold.

LogEig Layer: This layer is designed to perform the following logarithmic mapping: $X_k = f_l^{(k)}(X_{k-1}) = U_{k-1} \log(\Sigma_{k-1}) U_{k-1}^T$, where $\log(\Sigma)$ represents the logarithm operation on each diagonal element of Σ, and $X_{k-1} = U_{k-1} \Sigma_{k-1} U_{k-1}^T$ denotes the eigenvalue decomposition. In the resulting flat space, the classification tasks can be realized with the conventional dense layers.

3.2 Deep Riemannian Network

As shown in Fig. 2, the designed SRAE module contains a cascade of Riemannian autoencoders (RAEs) to achieve continuous incremental reconstruction learning, in which the output feature maps of each RAE are used as the input data points of the adjacent one. To enrich the information flow in the SRAE network, we augment the sequential connections between adjacent RAEs using the shortcut connections, so that the current RAE module can effectively mine the revelant structural information with the aid of the former prediction for a better reconstruction. The network structure of each RAE is composed of three components. The first part is an encoder module, made up of the input (BiMap), nonlinear activation (ReEig), and hidden (BiMap) layers for geometry-aware dimensionality reduction of SPD matrices. The second part is the decoder module, mainly used for data reconstruction. Since it has a symmetric structure with the encoder, the RAE is defined strictly in the context of Riemannian manifolds, and so is SRAE and the whole network. Moreover, each RAE also connects to a classification network with the layers of LogEig and FC, guided by the cross-entropy loss.

Let $\mathfrak{S} = [\boldsymbol{S}_1, \boldsymbol{S}_2, ..., \boldsymbol{S}_N]$ and $\boldsymbol{L} = [l_1, l_2, ..., l_N] \in \mathbb{R}^{1 \times N}$ be the original training set and its corresponding label vector, respectively. In this article, we denote the SPD manifold-valued training set as: $\mathcal{X} = [\boldsymbol{X}_1, \boldsymbol{X}_2, ..., \boldsymbol{X}_N]$. For the ith input SPD matrix $\boldsymbol{X}_i$ of our DreamNet, the low-dimensional and compact feature matrix output by the backbone can be expressed as: $\boldsymbol{\mathcal{Z}}_i = \phi_{\boldsymbol{\theta}_1}(\boldsymbol{X}_i)$. Here, $\phi_{\boldsymbol{\theta}_1}$ represents the Riemannian network embedding from the input data manifold to the target one, realized by a stack of BiMap and ReEig layers. Besides, $\boldsymbol{\theta}_1$ indicates the to-be-learnt parameters of this backbone network. As the SRAE module consists of E RAEs, we use $\mathbf{M}_e$ ($\mathbf{M}_e = \boldsymbol{\mathcal{Z}}_i$ when $e = 1$), $\mathbf{H}_e$, and $\hat{\mathbf{H}}_e$ to denote the input, output of the hidden layer, and reconstruction of the input of the eth ($e = 1 \to \text{E}$) RAE, respectively. Thus, $\mathbf{H}_e$ and $\hat{\mathbf{H}}_e$ can be computed by:

$$\mathbf{H_e} = f_{b_e}(\boldsymbol{W}_{e_1}, \mathbf{M}_e) = \boldsymbol{W}_{e_1}^T \mathbf{M}_e \boldsymbol{W}_{e_1}, \tag{2}$$

$$\hat{\mathbf{H}}_e = f_{b_e}(\boldsymbol{W}_{e_2}, \mathbf{H}_e) = \boldsymbol{W}_{e_2} \mathbf{H}_e \boldsymbol{W}_{e_2}^T, \tag{3}$$

where f_{b_e} and $\boldsymbol{W}_{e_1} \in \mathbb{R}^{d_{e-1} \times d_e}$ ($d_e \leq d_{e-1}$), $\boldsymbol{W}_{e_2} \in \mathbb{R}^{d_{e-1} \times d_e}$ represent the bilinear mapping function and the transformation matrices of the eth RAE, respectively. Since $\mathbf{M}_e$ is actually equivalent to $\hat{\mathbf{H}}_{e-1}$, we replace $\mathbf{M}_e$ with $\hat{\mathbf{H}}_{e-1}$ in the following for clarity.

Based on the constructed SRAE architecture, the shortcut connections (SCs) and element-wise addition (EWA) enable the Riemannian residual learning to be adopted for every set of a few stacked layers. In this article, we define the building block shown in Fig. 2 as:

$$\tilde{\mathbf{H}}_e = \mathbf{H}_e + \tilde{\mathbf{H}}_{e-1} = \mathcal{F}(\tilde{\mathbf{H}}_{e-1}, \{\boldsymbol{W}_i\}) + \tilde{\mathbf{H}}_{e-1}, \tag{4}$$

where $\tilde{\mathbf{H}}_{e-1}$ and $\tilde{\mathbf{H}}_e$ respectively represent the input and output of the Riemannian residual block, $e = 3 \to \text{E}$ (when $e = 2$, $\tilde{\mathbf{H}}_{e-1}$ is replaced by $\mathbf{H}_{e-1}$ in Eq. (4)), and $\mathcal{F}(\tilde{\mathbf{H}}_{e-1}, \{\boldsymbol{W}_i\})$ denotes the Riemannian residual mapping. For example, $\mathcal{F} = \boldsymbol{W}_{3_1}^T r(\boldsymbol{W}_{2_2} \tilde{\mathbf{H}}_2 \boldsymbol{W}_{2_2}^T) \boldsymbol{W}_{3_1}$ when e is set to 3, in which r signifies the ReEig operation. In what follows, another ReEig nonlinearity is applied to the generated $\tilde{\mathbf{H}}_e$ (i.e., $\tilde{\mathbf{H}}_e \leftarrow r(\tilde{\mathbf{H}}_e)$). In Eq. (4), our fundamental considerations for utilizing EWA to implement SC between SPD matrices are threefold: 1) it introduces neither parameters to be learnt nor computational complexity; 2) it can make the resulting data points still lie on the SPD manifold; 3) although the Abelian group operation (AGO) (Definition 3.1 of [2]) is faithful to the Riemannian geometry of SPD manifolds and demonstrates strong theoretical and practical benefits in Riemannian data analysis, it requires at least $\mathcal{O}(d^3)$ to achieve SC compared with EWA. Furthermore, the experimental results (reported in Sect. 2.1 of our supplementary material) show that although the accuracy of DreamNet-27-EWA is somewhat lower than that of DreamNet-27-AGO, its superiority in computation time is significant compared to DreamNet-27-AGO.

3.3   Objective Function

Briefly speaking, our goal is to probe a discriminative deep Riemannian network embedding to transform the input SPD matrices into more efficient and compact ones for improved classification. Taking the challenge of statistical information degradation caused by increasing the network depth into account, we establish a cascaded RAE module at the end of the backbone to reconstruct the remaining structural details from the input stage-by-stage. The built residual-like blocks facilitate the reconstruction of the remaining residual by SRAE. In addition, minimizing the reconstruction error term enables SRAE to remain highly sensitive to the variations of representations in the generated new feature manifolds, rendering the classification terms to be more effective in encoding and learning the multi-view feature distribution information. Accordingly, the loss function of the proposed method is formulated as:

$$\mathcal{L}(\theta_2, \phi; \boldsymbol{\mathcal{X}}) = \sum_{e=1}^{\mathrm{E}} \sum_{i=1}^{N} \mathcal{L}_e(\boldsymbol{X}_i, l_i) + \lambda \sum_{i=1}^{N} \mathcal{L}_2(\boldsymbol{\mathcal{Z}}_i, \hat{\mathbf{H}}_E), \tag{5}$$

where $\boldsymbol{\theta}_2 = \{\boldsymbol{\theta}_1, \boldsymbol{W}_{e_1}, \boldsymbol{W}_{e_2}, \boldsymbol{\mathcal{P}}_e\}$ ($\boldsymbol{\mathcal{P}}_e$ represents the to-be-learnt projection matrix of the FC layer of the eth RAE) and λ is the trade-off parameter. In this paper, we assign a small value to λ to fine-tune the classification performance.

The first term of Eq. (5) is the cross-entropy loss used to minimize the classification error of the input-target pairs $(\boldsymbol{X}_i, l_i)$ $(i = 1 \rightarrow N)$, implemented with the aid of the LogEig and FC layers. Specifically, $\mathcal{L}_e$ is given as:

$$\mathcal{L}_e(\boldsymbol{X}_i, l_i) = -\sum_{t=1}^{c} r(l_i, t) \times \log \frac{e^{\boldsymbol{\mathcal{P}}_e^t \boldsymbol{V}_e}}{\sum_{\tau} e^{\boldsymbol{\mathcal{P}}_e^\tau \boldsymbol{V}_e}}, \tag{6}$$

where $\boldsymbol{V}_e$ denotes the vectorized form of $\tilde{\mathbf{H}}_e$ ($\mathbf{H}_e$, when $e = 1$), $\boldsymbol{\mathcal{P}}_e^t$ signifies the tth row of the projection matrix $\boldsymbol{\mathcal{P}}_e \in \mathbb{R}^{c \times (d_e)^2}$, and $r(l_i, t)$ is an indicator function, where $r(l_i, t) = 1$ if $l_i = t$, and 0 otherwise.

The second term of Eq. (5) is the reconstruction error term (RT) measuring the discrepancy between the input sample and its corresponding reconstruction, computed by:

$$\mathcal{L}_2(\boldsymbol{\mathcal{Z}}_i, \hat{\mathbf{H}}_E) = ||\boldsymbol{\mathcal{Z}}_i - \hat{\mathbf{H}}_E||_{\mathrm{F}}^2. \tag{7}$$

It is evident that the Euclidean distance (EuD) is utilized to supersede LEM for similarity measurement in Eq. (7). Our motivations for this replacement are

Table 1. Comparison of DreamNet-27 on the AFEW dataset.

Metrics	Acc. (%)	Training time (s/epoch)
RT-EuD, *i.e.*, Eq. (7)	36.59	31.32
RT-LEM	36.71	88.16

twofold: 1) matrix inversion can be shunned during backpropagation; 2) EuD can measure the 'statistical-level' similarity between SPD samples intuitively.

In theory, for a given pair of SPD matrices $(\boldsymbol{\mathcal{Z}}_i, \boldsymbol{\mathcal{Z}}_j)$, EuD is infinitesimal iff LEM is infinitesimal, thanks to the smoothness of matrix logarithm (Theorem 2.8 of [2]): $\forall \varepsilon, \exists \delta > 0, \forall \boldsymbol{\mathcal{Z}}_j : \|\boldsymbol{\mathcal{Z}}_i - \boldsymbol{\mathcal{Z}}_j\|_F^2 < \delta \Rightarrow \|\log(\boldsymbol{\mathcal{Z}}_i) - \log(\boldsymbol{\mathcal{Z}}_j)\|_F^2 < \varepsilon$. Similarly, by the smoothness of $\exp(\cdot)$ (Theorem 2.6 of [2]), the inverse map of $\log(\cdot)$, the sufficient condition of the claim mentioned above can also be proved. This theoretically indicates that the aforementioned replacement is feasible. Besides, Table 1 shows that although the use of LEM can lead to a certain improvement in accuracy, the computation time required is close to three times than that of EuD, which experimentally confirms the rationality of using EuD in Eq. (7). The experimental discussions of the role of RT are given in Sect. 2.2 of our supplementary material, please kindly refer to.

3.4 Motivation for Designing the SRAE Architecture

Considering that the weight matrices $\boldsymbol{W}_k$ are semi-orthogonal, *i.e.*, $\boldsymbol{W}_k^T \boldsymbol{W}_k = \boldsymbol{I}$ [1,11,23], inspired by the paradigm of Euclidean autoencoder, if one can design an autoencoder network with successive SPD matrix upsampling and downsampling layers in the context of SPD manifolds, its function composition would be able to asymptotically approach an identity mapping (IM) theoretically. For simplicity, we denote $\mathbf{H}_2 = \boldsymbol{W}_2^T r(\boldsymbol{W}_1 \mathbf{H}_1 \boldsymbol{W}_1^T) \boldsymbol{W}_2$ as the resulting SPD matrix after one upsampling and downsampling operation. As the ReEig operation only brings about minor perturbations to the eigenvalue space of the input data, under the supervision of the reconstruction term, the proposed SRAE could drive $\boldsymbol{W}_1$ and $\boldsymbol{W}_2$ close to each other, so that $\|\mathbf{H}_2\|_F \rightarrow \|\mathbf{H}_1\|_F$. This design makes it possible to create an IM on the SPD manifolds, thus providing a feasible path to mitigate the degradation problem caused by increasing the network depth. In this scenario, the added shortcut connections can enable the current RAE learning phase to easily access the features of the previous stages, facilitating the reconstruction of the remaining structural details.

4   Experiments

We validate the efficacy of DreamNet[1] on three typical visual classification tasks, namely facial emotion recognition using the AFEW dataset [9], skeleton-based

---

[1] The source code will be released on: https://github.com/GitWR/DreamNet.

hand action recognition using the FPHA dataset [15], and skeleton-based human action recognition using the UAV-Human dataset [30], respectively.

4.1   Implementation

In this article, we use four layers to construct the backbone: $\boldsymbol{X}_i \rightarrow f_b^{(1)} \rightarrow f_{re}^{(2)} \rightarrow f_b^{(3)} \rightarrow f_{re}^{(4)}$, where f_b and f_{re} denote the layers of BiMap and ReEig, respectively. The stacked Riemannian autoencoder network (SRAE) is constituted by E RAEs, each of which making up five layers: $\hat{\mathbf{H}}_{e-1} \rightarrow f_b$ (input) $\rightarrow f_{re} \rightarrow f_b$ (hidden) $\rightarrow f_{re} \rightarrow f_b$ (reconstruction). Besides, the hidden layer of each RAE also connects to a classification module, consisting of three layers: $\tilde{\mathbf{H}}_e$ ($\mathbf{H}_e$ when $e = 1$)$\rightarrow f_{\log} \rightarrow f_{fc} \rightarrow f_{ce}$. Wherein, $f_{\log}$, f_{fc}, and f_{ce} represent the LogEig layer, FC layer, and cross-entropy loss, respectively. In the experiments, the learning rate η is set to 0.01, the batch size B is configured as 30, and the weights of the BiMap and FC layers are initialized as random semi-orthogonal matrices and random matrices, respectively. In addition, the threshold ϵ of the ReEig layer is set to 1e-4 for the AFEW and FPHA datasets and 1e-5 for the UAV-Human dataset. To train our DreamNet, we use an i7-9700 (3.4GHz) PC with 16GB RAM. We found that using GPU (GTX 2080Ti) does not speed up network training. The main bottleneck seems to be the series of eigenvalue operations.

4.2   Dataset Description and Settings

AFEW Dataset: This dataset consists of 2118 video clips (split in 1741+371 fixed training and validation sets) of natural facial expressions collected from movies. For the evaluation, we follow the protocols of [23,46] to scale down each video clip to a set of 20×20 gray-scale images, such that a 400×400 SPD matrix can be computed for video representation. On this dataset, the filter sizes of the backbone are set to 400×200 and 200×100, and those of the eth RAE are configured as 100×50 and 50×100.

FPHA Dataset: This dataset includes 1,175 hand action videos belonging to 45 different categories, collected in the first-person view. For the evaluation, we follow the criterion of [15,46] to transfer each frame into a 63-dimensional vector using the 3D coordinates of 21 hand joints provided. Hence, a total of 1,175 SPD matrices of size 63×63 can be computed, of which 600 are designated for training and the remaining 575 are used for testing. On this dataset, the filter sizes of the backbone are configured as 63×53 and 53×43, and those of the eth RAE are set to 43×33 and 33×43.

UAV-Human: This dataset contains 22,476 video sequences representing 155 human action categories, collected by unmanned aerial vehicles (UAVs). Here, we first follow the practice of [6] to shape each frame (labeled by 17 major body

Table 2. Results on the AFEW dataset.

Networks	Acc. (%)	s/epoch	#params
DreamNet-27	36.59	31.32	0.36 M
DreamNet-47	36.98	46.98	0.53 M
DreamNet-92	37.47	80.62	0.95 M

Table 3. Results on the FPHA dataset.

Networks	Acc. (%)	s/epoch	#params
DreamNet-27	87.78	2.60	0.11 M
DreamNet-47	88.64	3.66	0.18 M
DreamNet-92	88.12	6.70	0.36 M

Table 4. Results on the UAV-Human dataset.

Networks	Acc. (%)	s/epoch	#params
DreamNet-27	44.88	49.04	0.10 M
DreamNet-47	45.57	71.33	0.16 M
DreamNet-92	46.28	129.29	0.31 M

joints with 3D coordinates) into a 51-dimensional vector. Since some actions are performed by two persons, the PCA technique is then applied to transform the 102-dimensional vectors into 51-dimensional ones, by preserving 99% energy of the data. In this case, each video can be described by an SPD matrix of size 51×51. Finally, the seventy-thirty-ratio (STR) protocol is utilized to construct the gallery and probes from the randomly picked 16,724 SPD matrices. On this dataset, the sizes of the connection weights are set to $(51 \times 43, 43 \times 37)$ and $(37 \times 31, 31 \times 37)$ for the backbone and the eth RAE, respectively.

4.3   Ablation Studies

In this subsection, we conduct experiments to study the effectiveness of the proposed method for SPD matrix nonlinear learning.

Ablation for DreamNet: To evaluate the designed model, we carry out experiments on the AFEW, FPHA, and UAV-Human datasets to measure the impact of the network depth on the learning capacity of the proposed model. Based on the experimental results reported in Fig. 3(a), we can make three main observations. Firstly, the inverse correlation between the depth and network accuracy is reversed with the embedding function proposed in this paper, *i.e.*, the 47-layer DreamNet (E = 5) performs better than the 27-layer DreamNet (E = 3). More importantly, the test error of DreamNet-47 is lower than that of DreamNet-27. This signifies that the degradation problem is alleviated under this design, and we succeed in improving accuracy with the increased depth. The consistency of these findings can be gleaned from Figs. 3(b) and (c).

Secondly, we also explore a 92-layer DreamNet by simply stacking more RAEs (E = 10 at this time). We find that compared with the 27/47-layer Dream-Nets, the 92-layer DreamNet achieves even lower test errors on the AFEW and UAV-Human datasets, demonstrating that the learning capacity of our network

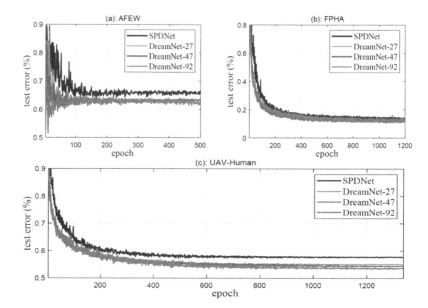

Fig. 3. The classification error of the 27/47/92-layer DreamNets versus the number of training epochs on the AFEW, FPHA, and UAV-Human datasets.

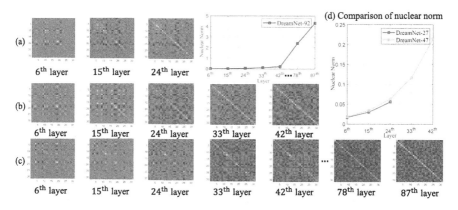

Fig. 4. The feature maps from different layers of the 27/47/92-layer DreamNets on the UAV-Human dataset are visualized in (a), (b), and (c), respectively. (d) shows the nuclear norms of these feature maps. Here, the 6th layer is actually the hidden layer of the first RAE, and the other layers are actually used to realize element-wise addition.

benefits from an extensive increase in the number of network layers. However, from Fig. 3(b) and Table 3, we note that the test error of DreamNet-92 is slightly higher than that of DreamNet-47 on the FPHA dataset. This could be caused by the relatively small size of this dataset. Although the benefits of depth are reflected in the classification accuracy reported in Tables 2, 3, 4, the increase

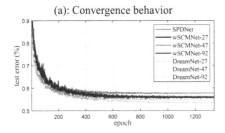

(a): Convergence behavior

(b): Classification accuracy

Methods	Acc. (%)
wSCMNet-27	43.86
wSCMNet-47	44.04
wSCMNet-92	44.40

Fig. 5. Performance on the UAV-Human dataset.

in network complexity (number of parameters, #params, and training speed, s/epoch) are detrimentally affected.

Thirdly, from Fig. 3, we can see that the 27/47/92-layer DreamNets are easy to train on all the used datasets. The convergence speed of these three networks is greater than that of the original SPDNet. Note that on the AFEW dataset, the test error of our 92-layer DreamNet first shows a degradation, but eventually it recovers and exhibits performance gains. We find that this behaviour is also mirrored by the loss function on the test set. The following two factors are the main reasons for overfitting: 1) this dataset contains only 7 categories and has large intra-class diversity and inter-class ambiguity; 2) this 92-layer network may be a bit large.

Visualization: To give the reader an intuitive feeling about the proposed method in addressing the problem of structural information degradation, we choose the UAV-Human dataset as an example to visualize the SPD feature maps learned by the different layers of the 27/47/92-layer DreamNets. From Fig. 4(a)-(c), we make two interesting observations: 1) for each DreamNet, compared to the low-level feature matrices, the magnitudes of the elements on the main diagonal of the high-level feature matrices are becoming larger, while the off diagonal ones are getting smaller; 2) with increasing the network depth, this concentration of energy becomes even more significant. Besides, the nuclear norms shown in Fig. 4(d) reflect that the deeper the learned features, the lower their redundancy. These results suggest that the continuous incremental learning on the remaining residuals can enable the proposed network to capture pivotal structural information embodied in the original data points, thus being helpful for classification.

Ablation Study for the Shortcut Connections: To verify the benefits of the shortcut connections (SCs), we make experiments to study the performance of a simplified DreamNet (named wSCMNet) obtained by removing the SCs from SRAE module. We choose the UAV-Human dataset as an example. It can be seen from Fig. 5(a) that the wSCMNet with different depths can converge to a better solution in less than 1,300 epochs, indicating that it has a good convergence behavior. However, the classification scores of 27/47/92-layer wSCMNets

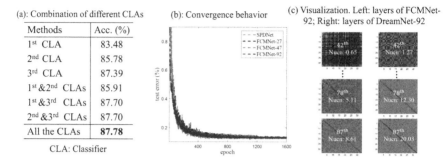

Fig. 6. Performance on the FPHA dataset, where 'Nucn' represents the nuclear norm.

tabulated in Fig. 5(b) are lower than those of 27/47/92-layer DreamNets. In spite of this, they are still better than those of the competitors listed in Table 5. From Fig. 5(a), we also find that the convergence speed of DreamNets is slightly faster than that of wSCMNets. These experimental results not only demonstrate the effectiveness of the proposed SRAE network, but also confirm that the SCs can: 1) enhance the representational capacity of SRAE module; 2) simplify the training of deeper networks. The underlying reason is that this operation facilitates the information interaction between different RAEs.

Ablation of the Classification Module: In this part, we make experiments on the FPHA dataset as an example to investigate the impact of the number of classification modules on the accuracy of DreamNet (here we take DreamNet-27 as an example) in the test phase. From Fig. 6(a), we can see that: 1) the greater the number of classifiers, the higher the accuracy; 2) the 3rd classifier are more effective than the others. This not only indicates that these classifiers are complementary to each other, but also demonstrates that the higher-level features are more informative.

Inspired by this experiment, we then investigated how the performance of DreamNet is affected by removing the first E-1 classification modules from SRAE (we name the simplified DreamNet FCMNet here). In this case, we find that the initial learning rate of 0.01 is a bit too small for the 47/92-layer FCMNets. So we respectively assign the initial learning rates of 0.02 and 0.05 to FCMNet-47 and FCMNet-92, and make them attenuate by a factor of 0.9 every 100 epochs. It is evident that the studied FCMNets converge well (Fig. 6(b)). Although the accuracy of 27/47/92-layer FCMNets (87.18%, 87.60%, and 87.30%) are somewhat inferior to that of 27/47/92-layer DreamNets, they are still better than those of the competitors listed in Table 6. These observations again certify the effectiveness of our design in overcoming the degradation problem and learning a powerful manifold-to-manifold deep transformation mapping. Besides, Fig. 6(c) not only further indicates that the residual mapping $\mathcal{F}$ is not close to a zero mapping, but also shows that the multi-classifier learning (MCL) scheme of DreamNet can

Table 5. Accuracy (%) on the AFEW and UAV-Human datasets.

Methods	AFEW	UAV-Human
GDA [16]	29.11	28.13
CDL [48]	31.81	31.11
PML [25]	28.98	10.66
HERML [24]	32.14	34.18
HRGEML [6]	35.89	36.10
SPDML [19]	26.72	22.69
GEMKML [45]	35.71	34.67
DeepO2P [28]	28.54	N/A
DARTS [31]	25.87	36.13
FairDARTS [7]	25.34	40.01
GrNet [27]	34.23	35.23
SPDNet [23]	34.23	42.31
SPDNetBN [4]	36.12	43.28
ManifoldNet [5]	23.98	N/A
SymNet [46]	32.70	35.89
DreamNet-27	36.59	44.88
DreamNet-47	36.98	45.57
DreamNet-92	**37.47**	**46.28**

Table 6. Accuracy (%) on the FPHA dataset.

Methods	Color	Depth	Pose	Acc.
Two streams [12]	✓	✗	✗	75.30
Novel View [35]	✗	✓	✗	69.21
Lie Group [42]	✗	✗	✓	82.69
HBRNN [10]	✗	✗	✓	77.40
LSTM [15]	✗	✗	✓	80.14
JOULE [22]	✓	✓	✓	78.78
Gram Matrix [52]	✗	✗	✓	85.39
TF [14]	✗	✗	✓	80.69
TCN [29]	✗	✗	✓	78.57
ST-GCN [50]	✗	✗	✓	81.30
H+O [39]	✓	✗	✗	82.43
TTN [32]	✗	✗	✓	83.10
DARTS [31]	✗	✗	✓	74.26
FairDARTS [7]	✗	✗	✓	76.87
SPDML [25]	✗	✗	✓	76.52
HRGEML [6]	✗	✗	✓	85.04
SPDNet [23]	✗	✗	✓	86.26
SPDNetBN [4]	✗	✗	✓	86.83
SymNet [46]	✗	✗	✓	82.96
DreamNet-27	✗	✗	✓	87.78
DreamNet-47	✗	✗	✓	**88.64**
DreamNet-92	✗	✗	✓	88.12

produce more efficient deep features with lower redundancy. Since the use of multiple classifiers can provide sufficient supervision information, and the increase in training time is slight (*e.g.*, one training epoch lasted on average 4.51s for FCMNet-92, and 6.70 s for DreamNet-92 on this dataset), we adopt the MCL mechanism in this article.

4.4 Comparison with State-of-the-art Methods

For a fair comparison, based on the publicy available source codes, we follow the original recommendations to tune the parameters of each comparative method, and report their best results on all three datasets. For DARTS and FairDARTS, we run their official implementations with default settings in the SPD matrix logarithmic domain. For DeepO2P, its classification accuracy on the AFEW dataset is provided by [23]. Since ManifoldNet requires SPD data points with multiple channels, it is inapplicable to the FPHA and UAV-Human skeleton datasets. From Table 5, it is evident that our 27-layer DreamNet outperforms all the involved competitors on the AFEW and UAV-Human datasets. Besides, with the network depth (the number E of the cascaded RAEs) increases, the accuracy of the 47/92-layer DreamNets is monotonically improving. Here, we also select some popular action recognition methods for better comparison on the FPHA dataset. Table 6 shows that our 27/47/92-layer DreamNets are the best performers for the hand action recognition task. For further evaluation, an aggressively deep model of over 180 layers has also been explored on the UAV-Human dataset. We set E = 20 that leads to a 182-layer DreamNet. The experimental results (reported in Sect. 2.3 of our supplementary material) show that it has no difficulty in optimization, and the classification accuracy (46.03%) achieved is still fairly good. These observations confirm that the suggested deep learning mechanism over the original SPD network is effective for improving the visual classification performance.

5 Conclusion

In this paper, we proposed an effective methodology for increasing the depth of SPD neural networks without destroying the geometric information conveyed by the input data. This is achieved by proposing a novel cascading network architecture with multiple Riemannian autoencoder learning stages appended to the backbone SPD network to enrich the deep layers of structured representations. Thanks to the insertion of innovative residual-like blocks via shortcut connections, a better incremental learning of residual structural details can be facilitated. The experimental results suggest that our Riemannian network is an effective solution against the geometric information degradation problem, with favourable performance compared to the state-of-the-art methods. For future work, we plan to develop an adaptive criterion that would enable an automatic assessment of the relative significance of the generated feature maps. This would facilitate the use of a neural architecture search (NAS) technique to adapt the proposed network to different pattern recognition tasks.

Acknowledgements. This work was supported by the National Natural Science Foundation of China (62020106012, U1836218, 61672265, 62106089, 62006097), the 111 Project of Ministry of Education of China (B12018), the Postgraduate Research & Practice Innovation Program of Jiangsu Province (KYCX21-2006), and the UK EPSRC EP/N007743/1, MURI/EPSRC/DSTL EP/R018456/1 grants.

References

1. Absil, P.A., Mahony, R., Sepulchre, R.: Optimization algorithms on matrix manifolds. Princeton University Press (2009)
2. Arsigny, V., Fillard, P., Pennec, X., Ayache, N.: Geometric means in a novel vector space structure on symmetric positive-definite matrices. SIAM J. Matrix Anal. Appl. **29**, 328–347 (2007)
3. Barachant, A., Bonnet, S., Congedo, M., Jutten, C.: Classification of covariance matrices using a riemannian-based kernel for BCI applications. Neurocomputing **112**, 172–178 (2013)
4. Brooks, D., Schwander, O., Barbaresco, F., Schneider, J.Y., Cord, M.: Riemannian batch normalization for spd neural networks. arXiv preprint arXiv:1909.02414 (2019)

5. Chakraborty, R., Bouza, J., Manton, J., Vemuri, B.C.: ManifoldNet: a deep neural network for manifold-valued data with applications. IEEE Trans. Pattern Anal. Mach. Intell. **44**, 799–810 (2022)
6. Chen, Z., Xu, T., Wu, X.J., Wang, R., Kittler, J.: Hybrid Riemannian graph-embedding metric learning for image set classification. IEEE Trans. Big Data **9**, 75–92 (2021) https://doi.org/10.1109/TBDATA.2021.3113084
7. Chu, X., Zhou, T., Zhang, B., Li, J.: Fair DARTS: eliminating unfair advantages in differentiable architecture search. In: Vedaldi, A., Bischof, H., Brox, T., Frahm, J.-M. (eds.) ECCV 2020. LNCS, vol. 12360, pp. 465–480. Springer, Cham (2020). https://doi.org/10.1007/978-3-030-58555-6_28
8. Dai, M., Zhang, Z., Srivastava, A.: Analyzing dynamical brain functional connectivity as trajectories on space of covariance matrices. IEEE Trans. Med. Imaging **39**, 611–620 (2019)
9. Dhall, A., Goecke, R., Joshi, J., Sikka, K., Gedeon, T.: Emotion recognition in the wild challenge 2014: baseline, data and protocol. In: ICMI, pp. 461–466 (2014)
10. Du, Y., Wang, W., Wang, L.: Hierarchical recurrent neural network for skeleton based action recognition. In: CVPR, pp. 1110–1118 (2015)
11. Edelman, A., Arias, T.A., Smith, S.T.: The geometry of algorithms with orthogonality constraints. SIAM J. Matrix Anal. Appl. **20**, 303–353 (1998)
12. Feichtenhofer, C., Pinz, A., Zisserman, A.: Convolutional two-stream network fusion for video action recognition. In: CVPR, pp. 1933–1941 (2016)
13. Gao, Z., Wu, Y., Harandi, M., Jia, Y.: A robust distance measure for similarity-based classification on the SPD manifold. IEEE Trans. Neural Netw. Learn. Syst. **31**, 3230–3244 (2020)
14. Garcia-Hernando, G., Kim, T.K.: Transition forests: learning discriminative temporal transitions for action recognition and detection. In: CVPR, pp. 432–440 (2017)
15. Garcia-Hernando, G., Yuan, S., Baek, S., Kim, T.K.: First-person hand action benchmark with RGB-D videos and 3D hand pose annotations. In: CVPR, pp. 409–419 (2018)
16. Hamm, J., Lee, D.D.: Grassmann discriminant analysis: a unifying view on subspace-based learning. In: ICML, pp. 376–383 (2008)
17. Harandi, M., Salzmann, M.: Riemannian coding and dictionary learning: kernels to the rescue. In: CVPR, pp. 3926–3935 (2015)
18. Harandi, M., Salzmann, M., Hartley, R.: Joint dimensionality reduction and metric learning: a geometric take. In: ICML, pp. 1404–1413 (2017)
19. Harandi, M., Salzmann, M., Hartley, R.: Dimensionality reduction on SPD manifolds: the emergence of geometry-aware methods. IEEE Trans. Pattern Anal. Mach. Intell. **40**, 48–62 (2018)
20. Harandi, M.T., Sanderson, C., Hartley, R., Lovell, B.C.: Sparse coding and dictionary learning for symmetric positive definite matrices: a Kernel approach. In: Fitzgibbon, A., Lazebnik, S., Perona, P., Sato, Y., Schmid, C. (eds.) ECCV 2012. LNCS, vol. 7573, pp. 216–229. Springer, Heidelberg (2012). https://doi.org/10. 1007/978-3-642-33709-3_16
21. He, K., Zhang, X., Ren, S., Sun, J.: Deep residual learning for image recognition. In: CVPR, pp. 770–778 (2016)
22. Hu, J.F., Zheng, W.S., Lai, J., Zhang, J.: Jointly learning heterogeneous features for RGB-D activity recognition. In: CVPR, pp. 5344–5352 (2015)
23. Huang, Z., Van Gool, L.: A Riemannian network for SPD matrix learning. In: AAAI, pp. 2036–2042 (2017)

24. Huang, Z., Wang, R., Shan, S., Chen, X.: Hybrid Euclidean-and-Riemannian metric learning for image set classification. In: ACCV, pp. 562–577 (2014)
25. Huang, Z., Wang, R., Shan, S., Chen, X.: Projection metric learning on Grassmann manifold with application to video based face recognition. In: CVPR, pp. 140–149 (2015)
26. Huang, Z., Wang, R., Shan, S., Li, X., Chen, X.: Log-Euclidean metric learning on symmetric positive definite manifold with application to image set classification. In: ICML, pp. 720–729 (2015)
27. Huang, Z., Wu, J., Van Gool, L.: Building deep networks on Grassmann manifolds. In: AAAI, pp. 1137–1145 (2018)
28. Ionescu, C., Vantzos, O., Sminchisescu, C.: Training deep networks with structured layers by matrix backpropagation. arXiv preprint arXiv:1509.07838 (2015)
29. Kim, T.S., Reiter, A.: Interpretable 3D human action analysis with temporal convolutional networks. In: CVPRW, pp. 1623–1631 (2017)
30. Li, T., Liu, J., Zhang, W., Ni, Y., Wang, W., Li, Z.: UAV-Human: a large benchmark for human behavior understanding with unmanned aerial vehicles. In: CVPR, pp. 16266–16275 (2021)
31. Liu, H., Simonyan, K., Yang, Y.: Darts: Differentiable architecture search. In: ICLR (2019)
32. Lohit, S., Wang, Q., Turaga, P.: Temporal transformer networks: joint learning of invariant and discriminative time warping. In: CVPR, pp. 12426–12435 (2019)
33. Nguyen, X.S., Brun, L., Lézoray, O., Bougleux, S.: A neural network based on SPD manifold learning for skeleton-based hand gesture recognition. In: CVPR, pp. 12036–12045 (2019)
34. Pennec, X., Fillard, P., Ayache, N.: A Riemannian framework for tensor computing. Int. J. Comput. Vis. **66**, 41–66 (2006). https://doi.org/10.1007/s11263-005-3222-z
35. Rahmani, H., Mian, A.: 3D action recognition from novel viewpoints. In: CVPR, pp. 1506–1515 (2016)
36. Sanin, A., Sanderson, C., Harandi, M.T., Lovell, B.C.: Spatio-temporal covariance descriptors for action and gesture recognition. In: WACV Workshop, pp. 103–110 (2013)
37. Simonyan, K., Zisserman, A.: Very deep convolutional networks for large-scale image recognition. arXiv preprint arXiv:1409.1556 (2014)
38. Sun, H., Zhen, X., Zheng, Y., Yang, G., Yin, Y., Li, S.: Learning deep match Kernels for image-set classification. In: CVPR, pp. 3307–3316 (2017)
39. Tekin, B., Bogo, F., Pollefeys, M.: H+O: unified egocentric recognition of 3D hand-object poses and interactions. In: CVPR, pp. 4511–4520 (2019)
40. Tosato, D., Farenzena, M., Spera, M., Murino, V., Cristani, M.: Multi-class classification on Riemannian manifolds for video surveillance. In: Daniilidis, K., Maragos, P., Paragios, N. (eds.) ECCV 2010. LNCS, vol. 6312, pp. 378–391. Springer, Heidelberg (2010). https://doi.org/10.1007/978-3-642-15552-9_28
41. Tuzel, O., Porikli, F., Meer, P.: Pedestrian detection via classification on Riemannian manifolds. IEEE Trans. Pattern Anal. Mach. Intell. **30**, 1713–1727 (2008)
42. Vemulapalli, R., Arrate, F., Chellappa, R.: Human action recognition by representing 3D Skeletons as points in a lie group. In: CVPR, pp. 588–595 (2014)
43. Vemulapalli, R., Pillai, J.K., Chellappa, R.: Kernel learning for extrinsic classification of manifold features. In: CVPR, pp. 1782–1789 (2013)
44. Wang, R., Wu, X.J., Chen, Z., Xu, T., Kittler, J.: Learning a discriminative SPD manifold neural network for image set classification. Neural Netw. **151**, 94–110 (2022)

45. Wang, R., Wu, X.J., Kittler, J.: Graph embedding multi-kernel metric learning for image set classification with Grassmann manifold-valued features. IEEE Trans. Multimedia **23**, 228–242 (2021)

46. Wang, R., Wu, X.J., Kittler, J.: SymNet: a simple symmetric positive definite manifold deep learning method for image set classification. IEEE Trans. Neural Netw. Learn. Syst. **33**, 2208–2222 (2022)

47. Wang, R., Wu, X.J., Xu, T., Hu, C., Kittler, J.: Deep metric learning on the SPD manifold for image set classification. In: IEEE Transactions on Circuits and Systems for Video Technology (2022)

48. Wang, R., Guo, H., Davis, L.S., Dai, Q.: Covariance discriminative learning: a natural and efficient approach to image set classification. In: CVPR, pp. 2496–2503 (2012)

49. Xu, T., Feng, Z.H., Wu, X.J., Kittler, J.: An accelerated correlation filter tracker. Pattern Recognit. **102**, 107172 (2020)

50. Yan, S., Xiong, Y., Lin, D.: Spatial temporal graph convolutional networks for skeleton-based action recognition. In: AAAI (2018)

51. Zhang, T., et al.: Deep manifold-to-manifold transforming network for skeleton-based action recognition. IEEE Trans. Multimedia **22**, 2926–2937 (2020)

52. Zhang, X., Wang, Y., Gou, M., Sznaier, M., Camps, O.: Efficient temporal sequence comparison and classification using gram matrix embeddings on a Riemannian manifold. In: CVPR, pp. 4498–4507 (2016)

53. Zhao, S., Xu, T., Wu, X.J., Zhu, X.F.: Adaptive feature fusion for visual object tracking. Pattern Recognit. **111**, 107679 (2021)

54. Zhou, L., Wang, L., Zhang, J., Shi, Y., Gao, Y.: Revisiting metric learning for SPD matrix based visual representation. In: CVPR, pp. 3241–3249 (2017)

55. Zhu, X.F., Wu, X.J., Xu, T., Feng, Z.H., Kittler, J.: Complementary discriminative correlation filters based on collaborative representation for visual object tracking. IEEE Trans. Circuits Syst. Video Technol. **31**, 557–568 (2020)

Augmenting Softmax Information for Selective Classification with Out-of-Distribution Data

Guoxuan Xia$^{(\boxtimes)}$ and Christos-Savvas Bouganis

Imperial College London, London, UK
{g.xia21,christos-savvas.bouganis}@imperial.ac.uk

Abstract. Detecting out-of-distribution (OOD) data is a task that is receiving an increasing amount of research attention in the domain of deep learning for computer vision. However, the performance of detection methods is generally evaluated on the task in isolation, rather than also considering potential downstream tasks in tandem. In this work, we examine selective classification in the presence of OOD data (SCOD). That is to say, the motivation for detecting OOD samples is to reject them so their impact on the quality of predictions is reduced. We show under this task specification, that existing post-hoc methods perform quite differently compared to when evaluated only on OOD detection. This is because it is no longer an issue to conflate in-distribution (ID) data with OOD data *if the ID data is going to be misclassified.* However, the conflation within ID data of correct and incorrect predictions becomes undesirable. We also propose a novel method for SCOD, Softmax Information Retaining Combination (SIRC), that augments softmax-based confidence scores with feature-agnostic information such that their ability to identify OOD samples is improved without sacrificing separation between correct and incorrect ID predictions. Experiments on a wide variety of ImageNet-scale datasets and convolutional neural network architectures show that SIRC is able to consistently match or outperform the baseline for SCOD, whilst existing OOD detection methods fail to do so. Code is available at https://github.com/Guoxoug/SIRC.

1 Introduction

Out-of-distribution (OOD) detection [49], i.e. identifying data samples that do not belong to the training distribution, is a task that is receiving an increasing amount of attention in the domain of deep learning [4,6,15,16,19,22,31–33,39,41,45,46,48–50]. The task is often motivated by safety-critical applications, such as healthcare and autonomous driving, where there may be a large cost associated with sending a prediction on OOD data downstream.

However, in spite of a plethora of existing research, there is generally a lack of focus with regards to the specific motivation behind OOD detection in the

Supplementary Information The online version contains supplementary material available at https://doi.org/10.1007/978-3-031-26351-4_40.

literature, other than it is often done as part of the pipeline of another primary task, e.g. image classification. As such the task is evaluated in isolation and formulated as binary classification between in-distribution (ID) and OOD data. In this work we consider the question *why exactly do we want to do OOD detection during deployment?* We focus on the problem setting where the primary objective is classification, and we are motivated to detect and then reject OOD data, as predictions on those samples will incur a cost. That is to say the task is selective classification [5,8] where OOD data has polluted the input samples. Kim et al. [27] term this problem setting *unknown detection.* However, we prefer to use Selective Classification in the presence of Out-of-Distribution data (SCOD) as we would like to emphasise the downstream classifier as the objective, and will refer to the task as such in the remainder of the paper.

The *key difference* between this problem setting and OOD detection is that *both* OOD data *and* incorrect predictions on ID data will incur a cost [27]. It does not matter if we reject an ID sample if it would be incorrectly classified anyway. As such we can view the task as separating correctly predicted ID samples (ID✓) from misclassified ID samples (ID✗) and OOD samples. This reveals a potential blind spot in designing approaches solely for OOD detection, as the cost of ID misclassifications is ignored. The *key contributions* of this work are:

1. Building on initial results from [27] that show poor SCOD performance for existing methods designed for OOD detection, we show novel insight into the behaviour of different post-hoc (after-training) detection methods for the task of SCOD. Improved OOD detection often comes directly at the expense of SCOD performance. Moreover, the relative SCOD performance of different methods varies with the proportion of OOD data found in the test distribution, the relative cost of accepting ID✗ vs OOD, as well as the distribution from which the OOD data samples are drawn.
2. We propose a novel method, targeting SCOD, Softmax Information Retaining Combination (SIRC), that aims to improve the OOD|ID✓ separation of softmax-based methods, whilst retaining their ability to identify ID✗. It consistently outperforms or matches the baseline maximum softmax probability (MSP) approach over a wide variety of OOD datasets and convolutional neural network (CNN) architectures, unlike existing OOD detection methods.

2   Preliminaries

Neural Network Classifier. For a K-class classification problem we learn the parameters $\boldsymbol{\theta}$ of a discriminative model $P(y|\boldsymbol{x};\boldsymbol{\theta})$ over labels $y \in \mathcal{Y} = \{\omega_k\}_{k=1}^K$ given inputs $\boldsymbol{x} \in \mathcal{X} = \mathbb{R}^D$, using finite training dataset $\mathcal{D}_{\text{tr}} = \{y^{(n)}, \boldsymbol{x}^{(n)}\}_{n=1}^N$ sampled independently from true joint data distribution $p_{\text{tr}}(y, \boldsymbol{x})$. This is done in order to make predictions $\hat{y}$ given new inputs $\boldsymbol{x}^* \sim p_{\text{tr}}(\boldsymbol{x})$ with unknown labels,

$$\hat{y} = f(\boldsymbol{x}^*) = \arg\max_{\omega} P(\omega|\boldsymbol{x}^*;\boldsymbol{\theta}) , \qquad (1)$$

where f refers to the classifier function. In our case, the parameters $\boldsymbol{\theta}$ belong to a deep neural network with categorical softmax output $\boldsymbol{\pi} \in [0,1]^K$,

$$P(\omega_i|\boldsymbol{x};\boldsymbol{\theta}) = \pi_i(\boldsymbol{x};\boldsymbol{\theta}) = \exp v_i(\boldsymbol{x}) / \sum_{k=1}^{K} \exp v_k(\boldsymbol{x}) , \tag{2}$$

where the logits $\boldsymbol{v} = \boldsymbol{W}\boldsymbol{z}+\boldsymbol{b}$ $(\in \mathbb{R}^K)$ are the output of the final fully-connected layer with weights $\boldsymbol{W} \in \mathbb{R}^{K \times L}$, bias $\boldsymbol{b} \in \mathbb{R}^K$, and final hidden layer features $\boldsymbol{z} \in \mathbb{R}^L$ as inputs. Typically $\boldsymbol{\theta}$ are learnt by minimising the cross entropy loss, such that the model approximates the true conditional distribution $P_{\text{tr}}(y|\boldsymbol{x})$,

$$\mathcal{L}_{\text{CE}}(\boldsymbol{\theta}) = -\frac{1}{N} \sum_{n=1}^{N} \sum_{k=1}^{K} \delta(y^{(n)}, \omega_k) \log P(\omega_k|\boldsymbol{x}^{(n)};\boldsymbol{\theta}) \tag{3}$$

$$\approx -\mathbb{E}_{p_{\text{tr}}(\boldsymbol{x})} \left[\sum_{k=1}^{K} P_{\text{tr}}(\omega_k|\boldsymbol{x}) \log P(\omega_k|\boldsymbol{x};\boldsymbol{\theta}) \right] = \mathbb{E}_{p_{\text{tr}}} \left[KL\left[P_{\text{tr}}||P_{\boldsymbol{\theta}}\right] \right] + A ,$$

where $\delta(\cdot,\cdot)$ is the Kronecker delta, A is a constant with respect to $\boldsymbol{\theta}$ and $KL[\cdot,\cdot]$ is the Kullback-Leibler divergence.

Selective Classification. A selective classifier [5] can be formulated as a pair of functions, the aforementioned classifier $f(\boldsymbol{x})$ (in our case given by Eq. 1) that produces a prediction $\hat{y}$, and a binary rejection function

$$g(\boldsymbol{x};t) = \begin{cases} 0 \text{ (reject prediction)}, & \text{if } S(\boldsymbol{x}) < t \\ 1 \text{ (accept prediction)}, & \text{if } S(\boldsymbol{x}) \geq t , \end{cases} \tag{4}$$

where t is an operating threshold and S is a scoring function which is typically a measure of predictive confidence (or $-S$ measures uncertainty). Intuitively, a selective classifier chooses to reject if it is uncertain about a prediction.

Problem Setting. We consider a scenario where, during deployment, classifier inputs $\boldsymbol{x}^*$ may be drawn from either the training distribution $p_{\text{tr}}(\boldsymbol{x})$ (ID) or another distribution $p_{\text{OOD}}(\boldsymbol{x})$ (OOD). That is to say,

$$\boldsymbol{x}^* \sim p_{\text{mix}}(\boldsymbol{x}), \quad p_{\text{mix}}(\boldsymbol{x}) = \alpha p_{\text{tr}}(\boldsymbol{x}) + (1-\alpha)p_{\text{OOD}}(\boldsymbol{x}) , \tag{5}$$

where $\alpha \in [0,1]$ reflects the proportion of ID to OOD data found in the wild. Here "Out-of-Distribution" inputs are defined as those drawn from a distribution with label space that does not intersect with the training label space $\mathcal{Y}$ [49]. For example, an image of a car is considered OOD for a CNN classifier trained to discriminate between different types of pets.

We now define the predictive loss on an accepted sample as

$$\mathcal{L}_{\text{pred}}(f(\boldsymbol{x}^*)) = \begin{cases} 0, & \text{if } f(\boldsymbol{x}^*) = y^*, \quad y^*, \boldsymbol{x}^* \sim p_{\text{tr}}(y,\boldsymbol{x}) \quad (\text{ID}✓) \\ \beta, & \text{if } f(\boldsymbol{x}^*) \neq y^*, \quad y^*, \boldsymbol{x}^* \sim p_{\text{tr}}(y,\boldsymbol{x}) \quad (\text{ID}✗) \\ 1-\beta, & \text{if } \boldsymbol{x}^* \sim p_{\text{OOD}}(\boldsymbol{x}) \quad (\text{OOD}) , \end{cases} \tag{6}$$

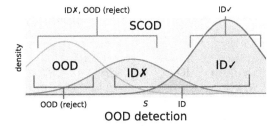

Fig. 1. Illustrative sketch showing how SCOD differs to OOD detection. Densities of OOD samples, misclassifications (ID✗) and correct predictions (ID✓) are shown with respect to confidence score S. For OOD detection the aim is to separate OOD|ID✗ID✓, whilst for SCOD the data is grouped as OOD ID✗|ID✓.

where $\beta \in [0, 1]$, and define the selective risk as in [8],

$$R(f, g; t) = \frac{\mathbb{E}_{p_{\mathrm{mix}}(x)}[g(x; t)\mathcal{L}_{\mathrm{pred}}(f(x))]}{\mathbb{E}_{p_{\mathrm{mix}}(x)}[g(x; t)]} , \qquad (7)$$

which is the average loss of the accepted samples. We are only concerned with the relative cost of ID✗ and OOD samples, so we use a single parameter β.

The objective is to find a classifier and rejection function (f, g) that minimise $R(f, g; t)$ for some given setting of t. We focus on comparing post-hoc (after-training) methods in this work, where g or equivalently S is varied with f fixed. This removes confounding factors that may arise from the interactions of different training-based and post-hoc methods, as they can often be freely combined.

In practice, both α and β will depend on the deployment scenario. However, whilst β can be set freely by the practitioner, α is outside of the practitioner's control and their knowledge of it is likely to be very limited.

It is worth contrasting the SCOD problem setting with OOD detection. SCOD aims to separate OOD, ID✗ |ID✓, whilst for OOD detection the data is grouped as OOD|ID✗, ID✓ (see Fig. 1). We note that previous work [26, 34, 35, 38, 41] refer to different types of predictive uncertainty, namely aleatoric and epistemic. The former arises from uncertainty inherent in the data (i.e. the true conditional distribution $P_{\mathrm{tr}}(y|x)$) and as such is irreducible, whilst the latter can be reduced by having the model learn from additional data. Typically, it is argued that it is useful to distinguish these types of uncertainty at prediction time. For example, epistemic uncertainty should be an indicator of whether a test input x^* is OOD, whilst aleatoric uncertainty should reflect the level of class ambiguity of an ID input. An interesting result within our problem setting is that the conflation of these different types of uncertainties may not be an issue, as there is no need to separate ID✗ from OOD, as both should be rejected.

3   OOD Detectors Applied to SCOD

As the explicit objective of OOD detection is different to SCOD, it is of interest to understand how existing detection methods behave for SCOD. Previous work [27] has empirically shown that some existing OOD detection approaches perform worse, and in this section we shed additional light as to why this is the case.

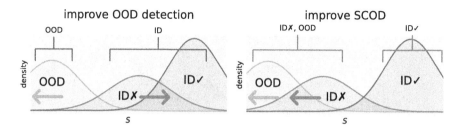

Fig. 2. Illustrations of how a detection method can improve over a baseline. Left: For OOD detection we can either have OOD further away from ID✓ or ID✗ closer to ID✓. Right: For SCOD we want both OOD and ID✗ to be further away from ID✓. Thus, we can see how improving OOD detection may in fact be at odds with SCOD.

Improving Performance: OOD Detection vs SCOD. In order to build an intuition, we can consider, qualitatively, how detection methods can improve performance over a baseline, with respect to the distributions of OOD and ID✗ relative to ID✓. This is illustrated in Fig. 2. For OOD detection the objective is to better separate the distributions of ID and OOD data. Thus, we can either find a confidence score S that, compared to the baseline, has OOD distributed further away from ID✓, and/or has ID✗ distributed closer to ID✓. In comparison, for SCOD, we want both OOD and ID✗ to be distributed further away from ID✓ than the baseline. Thus there is a conflict between the two tasks as, for ID✗, the desired behaviour of confidence score S will be different.

Existing Approaches Sacrifice SCOD by Conflating ID✓ and ID✗. Considering post-hoc methods, the baseline confidence score S used is Maximum Softmax Probability (MSP) [16]. Improvements in OOD detection are often achieved by moving away from the softmax π in order to better capture the differences between ID and OOD data. Energy [33] and Max Logit [14] consider the logits v directly, whereas the Mahalanobis detector [31] and DDU [38] build generative models using Gaussians over the features z. ViM [48] and Gradnorm [21] incorporate class-agnostic, feature-based information into their scores.

Recall that typically a neural network classifier learns a model $P(y|\boldsymbol{x};\boldsymbol{\theta})$ to approximate the true conditional distribution $P_{\mathrm{tr}}(y|\boldsymbol{x})$ of the training data (Eqs. 2, 3). As such, scores S extracted from the softmax outputs π should best reflect how likely a prediction on ID data is going to be correct or not (and this is indeed the case in our experiments in Sect. 5). As the above (post-hoc) OOD detection approaches all involve moving away from the modelled $P(y|\boldsymbol{x};\boldsymbol{\theta})$, we would expect worse separation between ID✗ and ID✓ even if overall OOD is better distinguished from ID. Figure 3 shows empirically how well different types of data are separated using MSP ($\pi_{\max}$) and Energy ($\log\sum_k \exp v_k$), by plotting false positive rate (FPR) against true positive rate (TPR). Lower FPR indicates better separation of the negative class away from the positive class. Although Energy has better OOD detection performance compared to MSP, this is actually because the separation between ID✗ and ID✓ is much less for Energy, whilst the behaviour of OOD rela-

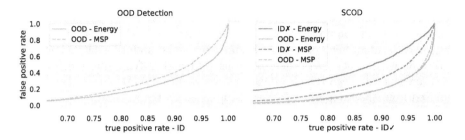

Fig. 3. Left: False positive rate (FPR) of OOD samples plotted against true positive rate (TPR) of ID samples. Energy performs better (lower) for OOD detection relative to the MSP baseline. Right: FPR of IDX and OOD samples against TPR of ID✓. Energy is worse than the baseline at separating IDX|ID✓ and no better for OOD|ID✓, meaning it is worse for SCOD. Energy's improved OOD detection performance arises from pushing IDX closer to ID✓. The ID dataset is ImageNet-200, OOD dataset is iNaturalist and the model is ResNet-50.

tive to ID✓ is not meaningfully different to the MSP baseline. Therefore, SCOD performance for Energy is worse in this case. Another way of looking at it would be that for OOD detection, MSP does worse as it conflates ID with OOD, however, this doesn't harm SCOD performance as much, as those ID samples are mostly incorrect anyway. The ID dataset is ImageNet-200 [27], OOD dataset is iNaturalist [22] and the model is ResNet-50 [13].

4   Targeting SCOD – Retaining Softmax Information

We would now like to develop an approach that is tailored to the task of SCOD. We have discussed how we expect softmax-based methods, such as MSP, to perform best for distinguishing IDX from ID✓, and how existing approaches for OOD detection improve over the baseline, in part, by sacrificing this. As such, to improve over the baseline for SCOD, we will aim to *retain* the ability to separate IDX from ID✓ whilst *increasing* the separation between OOD and ID✓.

Combining Confidence Scores. Inspired by Gradnorm [21] and ViM [48] we consider the combination of two different confidence scores S_1, S_2. We shall consider S_1 our primary score, which we wish to augment by incorporating S_2. For S_1 we investigate scores that are strong for selective classification on ID data, but are also capable of detecting OOD data – MSP and (the negative of) softmax entropy, $(-)\mathcal{H}[\boldsymbol{\pi}]$. For S_2, the score should be useful *in addition* to S_1 in determining whether data is OOD or not. We should consider scores that capture different information about OOD data to the post-softmax S_1 if we want to improve OOD|ID✓. We choose to examine the l_1-norm of the feature vector $||\boldsymbol{z}||_1$

from [21] and the negative of the Residual[1] score $-||z^{P^\perp}||_2$ from [48] as these scores capture class-agnostic information at the feature level. Note that although $||z||_1$ and Residual have previously been shown to be useful for OOD detection in [21,48], we do not expect them to be useful for identifying misclassifications. They are separate from the classification layer defined by (W, b), so they are far removed from the categorical $P(y|x; \theta)$ modelled by the softmax.

Softmax Information Retaining Combination (SIRC). We want to create a combined confidence score $C(S_1, S_2)$ that retains S_1's ability to distinguish ID✗ |ID✓ but is also able to incorporate S_2 in order to augment OOD|ID✓. We develop our approach based on the following set of *assumptions*:

- S_1 will be higher for ID✓ and lower for ID✗ and OOD.
- S_1 is bounded by maximum value $S_1^{\max}$.[2]
- S_2 is unable to distinguish ID✗ |ID✓, but is lower for OOD compared to ID.
- S_2 is useful in addition to S_1 for separating OOD|ID.

We propose to combine S_1 and S_2 using

$$C(S_1, S_2) = -(S_1^{\max} - S_1)(1 + \exp(-b[S_2 - a])) \ , \tag{8}$$

[3]where a, b are parameters chosen by the practitioner. The idea is for the accept/reject decision boundary of C to be in the shape of a sigmoid on the (S_1, S_2)-plane (See Fig. 4). As such the behaviour of only using the softmax-based S_1 is recovered for ID✗ |ID✓ as S_2 is increased, as the decision boundary tends to a vertical line. However, S_2 is considered increasingly important as it is decreased, allowing for improved OOD|ID✓. We term this approach Softmax Information Retaining Combination (SIRC).

The parameters a, b allow the method to be adjusted to different distributional properties of S_2. Rearranging Eq. 8,

$$S_1 = S_1^{\max} + C/[1 + \exp(-b[S_2 - a])] \ , \tag{9}$$

we see that a controls the vertical placement of the sigmoid, and b the sensitivity of the sigmoid to S_2. We use the empirical mean and standard deviation of S_2, μ_{S_2}, σ_{S_2} on ID data (training or validation) to set the parameters. We choose $a = \mu_{S_2} - 3\sigma_{S_2}$ so the centre of the sigmoid is below the ID distribution of S_2, and we set $b = 1/\sigma_{S_2}$, to match the ID variations of S_2. Note that other parameter settings are possible, and practitioners are free to tune a, b however they see fit (on ID data), but we find the above approach to be empirically effective.

Figure 4 compares different methods of combination by plotting ID✓, ID✗ and OOD data densities on the (S_1, S_2)-plane. Other than SIRC we consider

---

[1] $z^{P^\perp}$ is the component of the feature vector that lies outside of a principle subspace calculated using ID data. For more details see Wang et al. [48]'s paper.

[2] This holds for our chosen S_1 of $\pi_{\max}$ and $-\mathcal{H}$.

[3] To avoid overflow this is implemented using the `logaddexp` function in PyTorch [40].

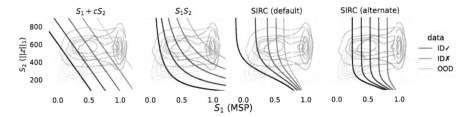

Fig. 4. Comparison of different methods of combining confidence scores S_1, S_2 for SCOD. OOD, ID✗ and ID✓ distributions are displayed using kernel density estimate contours. Graded contours for the different combination methods are then overlayed (lighter means higher combined score). We see that our method, SIRC (centre right) is able to better retain ID✗|ID✓ whilst improving OOD|ID✓. An alternate parameter setting for SIRC, with a stricter adherence to S_1, is also shown (far right). The ID dataset is ImageNet-200, the OOD dataset iNaturalist and the model ResNet-50. SIRC parameters are found using ID training data; the plotted distributions are test data.

the combination methods used in ViM, $C = S_1 + cS_2$, where c is a user set parameter, and in Gradnorm, $C = S_1 S_2$. The overlayed contours of C represent decision boundaries for values of t. We see that the linear decision boundary of $C = S_1 + cS_2$ must trade-off significant performance in ID✗ |ID✓ in order to gain OOD|ID✓ (through varying c), whilst $C = S_1 S_2$ sacrifices the ability to separate ID✗ |ID✓ well for higher values of S_1. We also note that $C = S_1 S_2$ is not robust to different ID means of S_2. For example, arbitrarily adding a constant D to S_2 will completely change the behaviour of the combined score. On the other hand, SIRC is designed to be robust to this sort of variation between different S_2. Figure 4 also shows an alternative parameter setting for SIRC, where a is lower and b is higher. Here more of the behaviour of only using S_1 is preserved, but S_2 contributes less. It is also empirically observable that the assumption that S_2 (in this case $||z||_1$) is not useful for distinguishing ID✓ from ID✗ holds, and in practice this can be verified on ID validation data when selecting S_2.

We also note that although we have chosen specific S_1, S_2 in this work, SIRC can be applied to any S that satisfy the above assumptions. As such it has the potential to improve beyond the results we present, given better individual S.

5   Experimental Results

We present experiments across a range of CNN architectures and ImageNet-scale OOD datasets. Extended results can be found in the supplemental material.

Data, Models and Training. For our ID dataset we use ImageNet-200 [27], which contains a subset of 200 ImageNet-1k [43] classes. It has separate training, validation and test sets. We use a variety of OOD datasets for our evaluation that display a wide range of semantics and difficulty in being identified. Near-ImageNet-200 (Near-IN-200) [27] is constructed from remaining ImageNet-1k classes semantically similar to ImageNet-200, so it is especially challenging to detect. Caltech-45 [27] is a subset of the Caltech-256 [12] dataset with non-overlapping classes to ImageNet-200. Openimage-O [48] is a subset of the Open Images V3 [29] dataset selected to be OOD with respect to ImageNet-1k. iNaturalist [22] and Textures [48] are the same for their respective datasets [2,47]. Colorectal [25] is a collection of histological images of human colorectal cancer, whilst Colonoscopy is a dataset of frames taken from colonoscopic video of gastrointestinal lesions [36]. Noise is a dataset of square images where the resolution, contrast and pixel values are randomly generated (for details see the supplemental material). Finally, ImageNet-O [18] is a dataset OOD to ImageNet-1k that is adversarially constructed using a trained ResNet. Note that we exclude a number of OOD datasets from [27] and [22] as a result of discovering ID examples.

We train ResNet-50 [13], DenseNet-121 [20] and MobileNetV2 [44] using hyperparameters based around standard ImageNet settings[4]. Full training details can be found in the supplemental material. For each architecture we train 5 models independently using random seeds $\{1,\ldots,5\}$ and report the mean result over the runs. The supplemental material contains results on single pre-trained ImageNet-1k models, BiT ResNetV2-101 [28] and PyTorch DenseNet-121.

Detection Methods for SCOD. We consider four variations of SIRC using the components $\{\text{MSP},\mathcal{H}\}\times\{\|\boldsymbol{z}\|_1,\text{Residual}\}$, as well as the components individually. We additionally evaluate various existing post-hoc methods: MSP [16], Energy [33], ViM [48] and Gradnorm [21]. For SIRC and ViM we use the full ID train set to determine parameters. Results for additional approaches, as well as further details pertaining to the methods, can be found in the supplemental material.

5.1   Evaluation Metrics

For evaluating different scoring functions S for the SCOD problem setting we consider a number of metrics. Arrows($\uparrow\downarrow$) indicate whether higher/lower is better. (For illustrations and additional metrics see the supplemental material.)

Area Under the Risk-Recall curve (AURR)$\downarrow$. We consider how empirical risk (Eq. 7) varies with recall of ID✓, and aggregate performance over different t by calculating the area under the curve. As recall is only measured over ID✓, the base accuracy of f is not properly taken into account. Thus, this metric is only suitable for comparing different g with f fixed. To give an illustrative example, a f, g pair where the classifier f is only able to produce a single correct prediction will have perfect AURR as long as S assigns that correct prediction the highest confidence (lowest uncertainty) score. Note that results for the AURC metric [10,27] can be found in the supplemental material, although we omit them from the main paper as they are not notably different to AURR.

Risk@Recall=0.95 (Risk@95)$\downarrow$. Since a rejection threshold t must be selected at deployment, we also consider a particular setting of t such that 95% of ID✓ is recalled. In practice, the corresponding value of t could be found on

---

[4] https://github.com/pytorch/examples/blob/main/imagenet/main.py.

a labelled ID validation set before deployment, without the use of any OOD data. It is worth noting that differences tend to be greater for this metric between different S as it operates around the tail of the positive class.

Area Under the ROC Curve (AUROC)↑. Since we are interested in rejecting both ID✗ and OOD, we can consider ID✓ as the positive class, and ID✗, OOD as separate negative classes. Then we can evaluate the AUROC of OOD|ID✓ and ID✗ |ID✓ independently. The AUROC for a specific value of α would then be a weighted average of the two different AUROCs. This is not a direct measure of risk, but does measure the separation between different empirical distributions. Note that due to similar reasons to AURR this method is only valid for fixed f.

False Positive Rate@Recall=0.95 (FPR@95)↓. FPR@0.95 is similar to AUROC, but is taken at a specific t. It measures the proportion of the negative class accepted when the recall of the positive class (or true positive rate) is 0.95.

5.2 Separation of ID✗ |ID✓ and OOD|ID✓ Independently

Table 1 shows %AUROC and %FPR@0.95 with ID✓ as the positive class and ID✗, OOD independently as different negative classes (see Sect. 5.1). In general, we see that SIRC, compared to S_1, is able to improve OOD|ID✓ whilst incurring only a small (< 0.2%AUROC) reduction in the ability to distinguish ID✗ |ID✓, across all 3 architectures. On the other hand, non-softmax methods designed for OOD detection show poor ability to identify ID✗, with performance ranging from ∼ 8 worse %AUROC than MSP to ∼ 50% AUROC (random guessing). Furthermore, they cannot consistently outperform the baseline when separating OOD|ID✓, in line with the discussion in Sect. 3.

SIRC is Robust to Weak S_2. Although for the majority of OOD datasets SIRC is able to outperform S_1, this is not always the case. For these latter instances, we can see that S_2 individually is not useful, e.g. for ResNet-50 on Colonoscopy, Residual performs *worse* than random guessing. However, in cases like this the performance is still close to that of S_1. As S_2 will tend to be higher for these OOD datasets, the behaviour is like that for ID✗ |ID, with the decision boundaries close to vertical (see Fig. 4). As such SIRC is *robust* to S_2 performing poorly, but is able to improve on S_1 when S_2 is of use. In comparison, ViM, which linearly combines Energy and Residual, is much more sensitive to when the latter stumbles. On Colonoscopy ViM has ∼ 30 worse %FPR@95 compared to Energy, whereas SIRC $(-\mathcal{H}, \text{Res.})$ loses < 1% compared to $-\mathcal{H}$.

OOD Detection Methods Are Inconsistent over Different Data. The performance of existing methods for OOD detection relative to the MSP baseline is varies considerably from dataset to dataset. For example, even though ViM is able to perform very well on Textures, Noise and ImageNet-O (>50 better %FPR@95 on Noise), it does worse than the baseline on most other OOD datasets (>20 worse %FPR@95 for Near-ImageNet-200 and iNaturalist). This

Table 1. %AUROC and %FPR@95 with ID✓ as the positive class, considering ID✗ and each OOD dataset separately. Full results are for ResNet-50 trained on ImageNet-200. We show abridged results for MobileNetV2 and DenseNet-121. **Bold** indicates best performance, <u>underline</u> 2nd or 3rd best and we show the mean over models from 5 independent training runs. Variants of SIRC are shown as tuples of their components (S_1,S_2). We also show error rate on ID data. SIRC is able to consistently match or improve over S_1 for OOD|ID✓, at a negligible cost to ID✗|ID✓. Existing OOD detection methods are significantly worse for ID✗|ID✓ and inconsistent at improving OOD|ID✓.

Model	Method	ID✗ AUROC↑	FPR@95↓	OOD mean AUROC↑	FPR@95↓	Near-IN-200 AUROC↑	FPR@95↓	Caltech-45 AUROC↑	FPR@95↓	Openimage-O AUROC↑	FPR@95↓	iNaturalist AUROC↑	FPR@95↓
ResNet-50 ID %Error: 19.01 SIRC	(MSP,‖z‖₁)	<u>90.34</u>	<u>52.70</u>	91.51	40.27	85.56	59.76	91.36	41.44	92.28	41.36	94.80	29.60
	(MSP,Res.)	**90.43**	52.10	<u>92.56</u>	<u>34.98</u>	85.52	60.03	91.19	42.27	92.57	<u>39.95</u>	94.10	33.55
	(−H,‖z‖₁)	90.00	54.26	92.24	35.85	<u>85.88</u>	<u>58.50</u>	**92.19**	36.08	<u>92.87</u>	<u>37.83</u>	95.38	**25.09**
	(−H,Res.)	90.13	54.01	**93.36**	**30.05**	85.85	58.93	<u>92.11</u>	<u>36.76</u>	**93.25**	36.36	<u>94.82</u>	<u>28.51</u>
	MSP	<u>90.41</u>	<u>52.13</u>	91.00	43.25	85.59	59.74	91.13	42.72	91.95	43.55	94.23	33.21
	−H	90.07	54.05	91.81	38.24	**85.91**	**58.47**	92.01	<u>37.20</u>	<u>92.59</u>	40.10	<u>94.90</u>	<u>28.01</u>
	‖z‖₁	48.06	94.70	78.22	58.70	52.27	94.58	70.28	77.83	72.23	71.51	85.65	49.50
	Residual	47.59	96.45	58.45	78.97	44.30	96.79	47.76	94.83	59.65	86.85	40.07	97.32
	Energy	82.05	69.79	92.06	<u>35.32</u>	81.96	68.70	<u>92.15</u>	38.62	90.92	46.28	94.13	31.70
	Gradnorm	60.17	87.88	85.22	44.41	62.90	86.89	81.11	59.23	81.09	57.80	91.00	34.46
	ViM	80.62	78.13	<u>92.34</u>	38.14	78.90	80.30	90.54	54.70	91.87	43.84	90.13	56.97

Model	Method	ID✗ AUROC↑	FPR@95↓	Textures AUROC↑	FPR@95↓	Colonoscopy AUROC↑	FPR@95↓	Colorectal AUROC↑	FPR@95↓	Noise AUROC↑	FPR@95↓	ImageNet-O AUROC↑	FPR@95↓
ResNet-50 ID %Error: 19.01 SIRC	(MSP,‖z‖₁)	<u>90.34</u>	<u>52.70</u>	93.64	32.02	95.93	25.33	95.84	24.39	90.72	49.63	83.44	58.91
	(MSP,Res.)	**90.43**	52.10	<u>96.00</u>	<u>19.81</u>	95.52	27.31	95.32	26.97	<u>98.21</u>	<u>10.97</u>	<u>84.62</u>	<u>53.99</u>
	(−H,‖z‖₁)	90.00	54.26	94.38	27.38	<u>96.97</u>	16.87	96.71	18.71	91.74	45.84	84.01	56.34
	(−H,Res.)	90.13	54.01	<u>96.68</u>	<u>15.70</u>	96.72	18.10	96.41	20.42	<u>99.02</u>	<u>4.89</u>	<u>85.33</u>	<u>50.81</u>
	MSP	<u>90.41</u>	<u>52.13</u>	92.88	36.61	95.75	26.52	94.86	30.28	89.33	56.83	83.29	59.78
	−H	90.07	54.05	93.77	30.79	<u>96.87</u>	<u>17.55</u>	95.93	23.43	90.47	51.63	83.89	57.02
	‖z‖₁	48.06	94.70	88.90	39.67	76.97	82.24	97.28	14.64	97.36	13.51	63.00	84.82
	Residual	47.59	96.45	82.84	46.63	38.09	99.64	53.93	88.78	91.31	20.92	68.04	78.98
	Energy	82.05	69.79	95.37	22.50	**97.51**	**14.19**	**99.07**	<u>5.00</u>	94.93	29.05	82.52	61.86
	Gradnorm	60.17	87.88	93.00	26.57	90.54	42.85	<u>98.98</u>	**4.98**	97.59	13.05	70.78	73.88
	ViM	80.62	78.13	**98.46**	**7.62**	94.42	44.55	<u>98.04</u>	<u>8.84</u>	**99.82**	**0.31**	**88.85**	**46.15**

Model	Method	ID✗ AUROC↑	FPR@95↓	OOD mean AUROC↑	FPR@95↓	Model	Method	ID✗ AUROC↑	FPR@95↓	OOD mean AUROC↑	FPR@95↓
MobileNetV2 ID %Error: 21.35 SIRC	(MSP,‖z‖₁)	<u>89.53</u>	<u>55.51</u>	92.27	<u>34.82</u>	DenseNet-121 ID %Error: 17.20 SIRC	(MSP,‖z‖₁)	<u>90.22</u>	<u>52.41</u>	91.68	38.83
	(MSP,Res.)	**89.67**	<u>55.10</u>	91.78	38.56		(MSP,Res.)	<u>90.20</u>	<u>52.42</u>	<u>92.81</u>	<u>32.68</u>
	(−H,‖z‖₁)	88.90	58.64	**92.92**	**32.16**		(−H,‖z‖₁)	89.95	53.96	<u>92.42</u>	<u>32.92</u>
	(−H,Res.)	89.12	57.85	<u>92.69</u>	<u>34.20</u>		(−H,Res.)	89.92	54.17	**93.45**	**27.97**
	MSP	<u>89.64</u>	<u>55.03</u>	91.54	39.73		MSP	**90.30**	**51.85**	91.44	40.44
	−H	89.02	58.43	<u>92.37</u>	36.04		−H	90.04	53.41	92.24	34.49
	‖z‖₁	53.56	93.40	81.06	53.50		‖z‖₁	36.87	98.70	63.53	80.35
	Residual	41.99	97.30	41.42	94.11		Residual	46.08	95.44	69.38	71.33
	Energy	81.87	67.98	91.68	36.68		Energy	82.12	66.54	90.92	38.87
	Gradnorm	65.27	85.73	87.25	40.67		Gradnorm	50.18	95.19	76.18	62.58
	ViM	80.21	74.36	89.46	51.97		ViM	76.63	84.73	90.50	44.71

suggests that the inductive biases incorporated, and assumptions made, when designing existing OOD detection methods may prevent them from generalising across a wider variety of OOD data. In contrast, SIRC more *consistently*, albeit modestly, improves over the baseline, due to its aforementioned robustness.

5.3   Varying the Importance of OOD Data Through α and β

At deployment, there will be a specific ratio of ID:OOD data exposed to the model. Thus, it is of interest to investigate the risk over different values of α

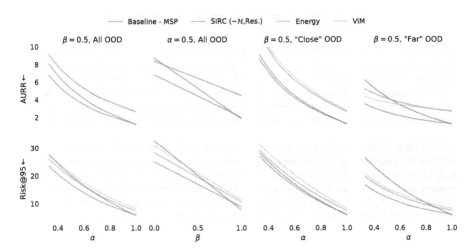

Fig. 5. AURR↓ and Risk@95↓ ($\times 10^2$) for different methods as α and β vary (Eqs. 5,6) on a mixture of all the OOD data. We also split the OOD data into qualitatively "Close" and "Far" subsets (Sect. 5.3). For high α, β, where ID✗ dominates in the risk, the MSP baseline is the best. As α, β decrease, increasing the effect of OOD data, other methods improve relative to the baseline. SIRC is able to *most consistently* improve over the baseline. OOD detection methods perform better on "Far" OOD. The ID dataset is ImageNet-200, the model ResNet-50. We show the mean over 5 independent training runs. We multiply all values by 10^2 for readability.

(Eq. 5). Similarly, an incorrect ID prediction may or may not be more costly than a prediction on OOD data so we investigate different values of β (Eq. 6). Figure 5 shows how AURR and Risk@95 are affected as α and β are varied independently (with the other fixed to 0.5). We use the full test set of ImageNet-200, and pool OOD datasets together and sample different quantities of data randomly in order to achieve different values of α. We use 3 different groupings of OOD data: All, "Close" {Near-ImageNet-200, Caltech-45, Openimage-O, iNaturalist} and "Far" {Textures, Colonoscopy, Colorectal, Noise}. These groupings are based on relative qualitative semantic difference to the ID dataset (see supplemental material for example images from each dataset). Although the grouping is not formal, it serves to illustrate OOD data-dependent differences in SCOD performance.

Relative Performance of Methods Changes with α and β. At high α and β, where ID✗ dominates the risk, the MSP baseline performs best. However, as α and β are decreased, and OOD data is introduced, we see that other methods improve relative to the baseline. There may be a *crossover* after which the ability to better distinguish OOD|ID✓ allows a method to surpass the baseline. Thus, which method to choose for deployment will depend on the practitioner's setting of β and (if they have any knowledge of it at all) of α.

SIRC Most Consistently Improves over the Baseline. SIRC $(-\mathcal{H}, \text{Res.})$ is able to outperform the baseline most consistently over the different scenarios and settings of α, β, only doing worse for ID✗ dominated cases (α, β close to 1). This is because SIRC has close to baseline ID✗ |ID✓ performance and is superior

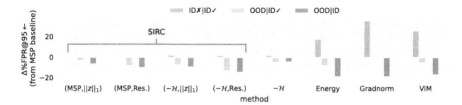

Fig. 6. The change in %FPR@95↓ relative to the MSP baseline of different methods. Different data classes are shown negative|positive. Although OOD detection methods are able to improve OOD|ID, they do so mainly at the expense of ID✗|ID✓ rather than improving OOD|ID✓. SIRC is able to improve OOD|ID✓ with minimal loss to ID✗|ID✓, alongside modest improvements for OOD|ID. Results for OOD are averaged over all OOD datasets. The ID dataset is ImageNet-200 and the model ResNet-50.

for OOD|ID✓. In comparison, ViM and Energy, which conflate ID✗ and ID✓, are often worse than the baseline for most (if not all) values of α, β. Their behaviour on the different groupings of data illustrates how these methods may be biased towards different OOD datasets, as they significantly outperform the baseline at lower α for the "Far" grouping, but always do worse on "Close" OOD data.

5.4 Comparison Between SCOD and OOD Detection

Figure 6 shows the difference in %FPR@95 relative to the MSP baseline for different combinations of negative|positive data classes (ID✗|ID✓, OOD|ID✓, OOD|ID), where OOD results are averaged over all datasets and training runs. In line with the discussion in Sect. 3, we observe that the non-softmax OOD detection methods are able to improve over the baseline for OOD|ID, but this comes mostly at the cost of inferior ID✗|ID✓ rather than due to better OOD|ID✓, so they will do worse for SCOD. SIRC on the other hand is able to retain much more ID✗|ID✓ performance whilst improving on OOD|ID✓, allowing it to have better OOD detection *and* SCOD performance compared to the baseline.

6   Related Work

There is extensive existing research into OOD detection, a survey of which can be found in [49]. To improve over the MSP baseline in [16], early post-hoc approaches, primarily experimenting on CIFAR-scale data, such as ODIN [32], Mahalanobis [31], Energy [33] explore how to extract non-softmax information from a trained network. More recent work has moved to larger-scale image datasets [14,22]. Gradnorm [21], although motivated by the information in gradients, at its core combines information from the softmax and features together. Similarly, ViM [48] combines Energy with the class-agnostic Residual score. ReAct [45] aims to improve logit/softmax-based scores by clamping the magnitude of final layer features. There are also many training-based approaches. Outlier Exposure [17] explores training networks to be uncertain on "known" existing OOD data, whilst VOS [4] instead generates virtual outliers during training for this purpose. [19,46] propose the network explicitly learn a scaling factor for the logits to improve softmax behaviour. There also exists a line of research that explores the use of generative models, $p(\boldsymbol{x}; \boldsymbol{\theta})$, for OOD detection [1,39,42,50], however, these approaches are completely separate from classification.

Selective classification, or misclassification detection, has also been investigated for deep learning scenarios. Initially examined in [8,16], there are a number of approaches to the task that target the classifier f through novel training losses and/or architectural adjustments [3,9,37]. Post-hoc approaches are fewer. DOCTOR [11] provides theoretical justification for using the l_2-norm of the softmax output $||\boldsymbol{\pi}||_2$ as a confidence score for detecting misclassifications, however, we find its behaviour similar to MSP and $\mathcal{H}$ (see supplemental material).

There also exist general approaches for uncertainty estimation that are then evaluated using the above tasks, e.g. Bayesian Neural Networks [23], MC-Dropout [7], Deep Ensembles [30], Dirichlet Networks [34,35] and DDU [38].

The two works closest to ours are [24] and [27]. [24] investigates selective classification under covariate shift for the natural language processing task of question and answering. In the case of *covariate* shift, valid predictions can still be produced on the shifted data, which by our definition is not possible for OOD data (see Sect. 2). Thus the problem setting here is different to our work. We remark that it would be of interest to extend this work to investigate selective classification with covariate shift for tasks in computer vision. [27] introduces the idea that ID✗ and OOD data should be rejected together and investigates the performance of a range of existing approaches. They examine both training and post-hoc methods (comparing different f and g) on SCOD (which they term unknown detection), as well as misclassification detection and OOD detection. They do not provide a novel approach targeting SCOD, and consider a single setting of (α, β), where the α is not specified and $\beta = 0.5$.

7 Concluding Remarks

In this work, we consider the performance of existing methods for OOD detection on selective classification with out-of-distribution data (SCOD). We show how their improved OOD detection vs the MSP baseline often comes at the cost of inferior SCOD performance. Furthermore, we find their performance is inconsistent over different OOD datasets. In order to improve SCOD performance over the baseline, we develop SIRC. Our approach aims to retain information, which is useful for detecting misclassifications, from a softmax-based confidence score, whilst incorporating additional information useful for identifying OOD samples. Experiments show that SIRC consistently matches or improves over the baseline approach for a wide range of datasets, CNN architectures and problem scenarios.

Acknowledgements. GX's PhD is funded jointly by Arm and the EPSRC.

References

1. Caterini, A.L., Loaiza-Ganem, G.: Entropic issues in likelihood-based ood detection. ArXiv abs/2109.10794 (2021)
2. Cimpoi, M., Maji, S., Kokkinos, I., Mohamed, S., Vedaldi, A.: Describing textures in the wild. In: Proceedings of the IEEE Conference on Computer Vision and Pattern Recognition (CVPR) (2014)
3. Corbière, C., THOME, N., Bar-Hen, A., Cord, M., Pérez, P.: Addressing failure prediction by learning model confidence. In: Wallach, H., Larochelle, H., Beygelzimer, A., d' Alché-Buc, F., Fox, E., Garnett, R. (eds.) Advances in Neural Information Processing Systems 32, pp. 2902–2913. Curran Associates, Inc. (2019). http://papers.nips.cc/paper/8556-addressing-failure-prediction-by-learning-model-confidence.pdf
4. Du, X., Wang, Z., Cai, M., Li, Y.: Vos: Learning what you don't know by virtual outlier synthesis. ArXiv abs/2202.01197 (2022)
5. El-Yaniv, R., Wiener, Y.: On the foundations of noise-free selective classification. J. Mach. Learn. Res. **11**, 1605–1641 (2010)
6. Fort, S., Ren, J., Lakshminarayanan, B.: Exploring the limits of out-of-distribution detection. In: NeurIPS (2021)
7. Gal, Y., Ghahramani, Z.: Dropout as a bayesian approximation: representing model uncertainty in deep learning. In: Balcan, M.F., Weinberger, K.Q. eds.) Proceedings of the 33rd International Conference on Machine Learning. Proceedings of Machine Learning Research, vol. 48, 20–22 June 2016, pp. 1050–1059. PMLR, New York. https://proceedings.mlr.press/v48/gal16.html
8. Geifman, Y., El-Yaniv, R.: Selective classification for deep neural networks. In: NIPS (2017)
9. Geifman, Y., El-Yaniv, R.: Selectivenet: a deep neural network with an integrated reject option. In: International Conference on Machine Learning, pp. 2151–2159. PMLR (2019)
10. Geifman, Y., Uziel, G., El-Yaniv, R.: Bias-reduced uncertainty estimation for deep neural classifiers. In: ICLR (2019)
11. Granese, F., Romanelli, M., Gorla, D., Palamidessi, C., Piantanida, P.: Doctor: a simple method for detecting misclassification errors. In: NeurIPS (2021)
12. Griffin, G., Holub, A., Perona, P.: Caltech-256 object category dataset (2007)
13. He, K., Zhang, X., Ren, S., Sun, J.: Deep residual learning for image recognition. In: 2016 IEEE Conference on Computer Vision and Pattern Recognition (CVPR), pp. 770–778 (2016)
14. Hendrycks, D., Basart, S., Mazeika, M., Mostajabi, M., Steinhardt, J., Song, D.X.: Scaling out-of-distribution detection for real-world settings. arXiv: Computer Vision and Pattern Recognition (2020)
15. Hendrycks, D., Dietterich, T.G.: Benchmarking neural network robustness to common corruptions and perturbations. ArXiv abs/1903.12261 (2019)
16. Hendrycks, D., Gimpel, K.: A baseline for detecting misclassified and out-of-distribution examples in neural networks. ArXiv abs/1610.02136 (2017)
17. Hendrycks, D., Mazeika, M., Dietterich, T.G.: Deep anomaly detection with outlier exposure. ArXiv abs/1812.04606 (2019)
18. Hendrycks, D., Zhao, K., Basart, S., Steinhardt, J., Song, D.X.: Natural adversarial examples. In: 2021 IEEE/CVF Conference on Computer Vision and Pattern Recognition (CVPR), pp. 15257–15266 (2021)

19. Hsu, Y.C., Shen, Y., Jin, H., Kira, Z.: Generalized odin: detecting out-of-distribution image without learning from out-of-distribution data. In: 2020 IEEE/CVF Conference on Computer Vision and Pattern Recognition (CVPR), pp. 10948–10957 (2020)

20. Huang, G., Liu, Z., Weinberger, K.Q.: Densely connected convolutional networks. In: 2017 IEEE Conference on Computer Vision and Pattern Recognition (CVPR), pp. 2261–2269 (2017)

21. Huang, R., Geng, A., Li, Y.: On the importance of gradients for detecting distributional shifts in the wild. In: NeurIPS (2021)

22. Huang, R., Li, Y.: Mos: towards scaling out-of-distribution detection for large semantic space. In: 2021 IEEE/CVF Conference on Computer Vision and Pattern Recognition (CVPR), pp. 8706–8715 (2021)

23. Jospin, L.V., Laga, H., Boussaid, F., Buntine, W., Bennamoun, M.: Hands-on bayesian neural networks-a tutorial for deep learning users. IEEE Comput. Intell. Mag. **17**(2), 29–48 (2022)

24. Kamath, A., Jia, R., Liang, P.: Selective question answering under domain shift. In: ACL (2020)

25. Kather, J.N., et al.: Multi-class texture analysis in colorectal cancer histology. Scientific Reports 6 (2016)

26. Kendall, A., Gal, Y.: What uncertainties do we need in bayesian deep learning for computer vision? In: Proceedings of the 31st International Conference on Neural Information Processing Systems, NIPS 2017, pp. 5580–5590. Curran Associates Inc., Red Hook (2017)

27. Kim, J., Koo, J., Hwang, S.: A unified benchmark for the unknown detection capability of deep neural networks. ArXiv abs/2112.00337 (2021)

28. Kolesnikov, A., Beyer, L., Zhai, X., Puigcerver, J., Yung, J., Gelly, S., Houlsby, N.: Big transfer (bit): General visual representation learning. In: ECCV (2020)

29. Krasin, I., et al.: Openimages: a public dataset for large-scale multi-label and multi-class image classification. Dataset available from https://github.com/openimages (2017)

30. Lakshminarayanan, B., Pritzel, A., Blundell, C.: Simple and scalable predictive uncertainty estimation using deep ensembles. In: NIPS (2017)

31. Lee, K., Lee, K., Lee, H., Shin, J.: A simple unified framework for detecting out-of-distribution samples and adversarial attacks. In: NeurIPS (2018)

32. Liang, S., Li, Y., Srikant, R.: Enhancing the reliability of out-of-distribution image detection in neural networks. arXiv: Learning (2018)

33. Liu, W., Wang, X., Owens, J.D., Li, Y.: Energy-based out-of-distribution detection. ArXiv abs/2010.03759 (2020)

34. Malinin, A., Gales, M.J.F.: Predictive uncertainty estimation via prior networks. In: NeurIPS (2018)

35. Malinin, A., Mlodozeniec, B., Gales, M.J.F.: Ensemble distribution distillation. ArXiv abs/1905.00076 (2020)

36. Mesejo, P., Pizarro, D., Abergel, A., Rouquette, O.Y., Béorchia, S., Poincloux, L., Bartoli, A.: Computer-aided classification of gastrointestinal lesions in regular colonoscopy. IEEE Trans. Med. Imaging **35**(9), 2051–2063 (2016)

37. Moon, J., Kim, J., Shin, Y., Hwang, S.: Confidence-aware learning for deep neural networks. In: ICML (2020)

38. Mukhoti, J., Kirsch, A., van Amersfoort, J.R., Torr, P.H.S., Gal, Y.: Deterministic neural networks with appropriate inductive biases capture epistemic and aleatoric uncertainty. ArXiv abs/2102.11582 (2021)

39. Nalisnick, E.T., Matsukawa, A., Teh, Y.W., Görür, D., Lakshminarayanan, B.: Do deep generative models know what they don't know? ArXiv abs/1810.09136 (2019)

40. Paszke, A., et al.: Pytorch: an imperative style, high-performance deep learning library. In: Wallach, H., Larochelle, H., Beygelzimer, A., d' Alché-Buc, F., Fox, E., Garnett, R. (eds.) Advances in Neural Information Processing Systems 32, pp. 8024–8035. Curran Associates, Inc. (2019)

41. Pearce, T., Brintrup, A., Zhu, J.: Understanding softmax confidence and uncertainty. ArXiv abs/2106.04972 (2021)

42. Ren, J., et al.: Likelihood ratios for out-of-distribution detection. In: Wallach, H., Larochelle, H., Beygelzimer, A., d' Alché-Buc, F., Fox, E., Garnett, R. (eds.) Advances in Neural Information Processing Systems. vol. 32. Curran Associates, Inc. (2019). https://proceedings.neurips.cc/paper/2019/file/1e79596878b2320cac26dd792a6c51c9-Paper.pdf

43. Russakovsky, O., et al.: Imagenet large scale visual recognition challenge. Int. J. Comput. Vision **115**, 211–252 (2015)

44. Sandler, M., Howard, A.G., Zhu, M., Zhmoginov, A., Chen, L.C.: Mobilenetv 2: inverted residuals and linear bottlenecks. In: 2018 IEEE/CVF Conference on Computer Vision and Pattern Recognition, pp. 4510–4520 (2018)

45. Sun, Y., Guo, C., Li, Y.: React: out-of-distribution detection with rectified activations. In: NeurIPS (2021)

46. Techapanurak, E., Suganuma, M., Okatani, T.: Hyperparameter-free out-of-distribution detection using cosine similarity. In: Proceedings of the Asian Conference on Computer Vision (ACCV), November 2020

47. Van Horn, G., et al.: The inaturalist species classification and detection dataset (2017). https://arxiv.org/abs/1707.06642

48. Wang, H., Li, Z., Feng, L., Zhang, W.: Vim: Out-of-distribution with virtual-logit matching. ArXiv abs/2203.10807 (2022)

49. Yang, J., Zhou, K., Li, Y., Liu, Z.: Generalized out-of-distribution detection: a survey. ArXiv abs/2110.11334 (2021)

50. Zhang, M., Zhang, A., McDonagh, S.G.: On the out-of-distribution generalization of probabilistic image modelling. In: NeurIPS (2021)

COLLIDER: A Robust Training Framework for Backdoor Data

Hadi M. Dolatabadi$^{(\boxtimes)}$ ⓘ, Sarah Erfani ⓘ, and Christopher Leckie ⓘ

School of Computing and Information Systems, The University of Melbourne,
Parkville, Vic, Australia
hadi.mohagheghdolatabadi@student.unimelb.edu.au

Abstract. Deep neural network (DNN) classifiers are vulnerable to
backdoor attacks. An adversary poisons some of the training data in
such attacks by installing a trigger. The goal is to make the trained
DNN output the attacker's desired class whenever the trigger is acti-
vated while performing as usual for clean data. Various approaches have
recently been proposed to detect malicious backdoored DNNs. However,
a robust, end-to-end training approach, like adversarial training, is yet to
be discovered for backdoor poisoned data. In this paper, we take the first
step toward such methods by developing a robust training framework,
COLLIDER, that selects the most prominent samples by exploiting the
underlying geometric structures of the data. Specifically, we effectively
filter out candidate poisoned data at each training epoch by solving a
geometrical coreset selection objective. We first argue how clean data
samples exhibit (1) gradients similar to the clean majority of data and
(2) low local intrinsic dimensionality (LID). Based on these criteria, we
define a novel coreset selection objective to find such samples, which
are used for training a DNN. We show the effectiveness of the proposed
method for robust training of DNNs on various poisoned datasets, reducing the backdoor success rate significantly.

Keywords: Backdoor attacks · Data poisoning · Coreset selection ·
Local intrinsic dimensionality · Efficient training

1 Introduction

Deep neural networks (DNN) have gained unprecedented attention recently and
achieved human-level performance in various tasks such as object detection [1].
Due to their widespread success, neural networks have become a promising candidate for use in safety-critical applications, including autonomous driving [2,3]
and face recognition [4,5]. Unfortunately, it has been shown that neural networks
may exhibit unexpected behavior when facing an adversary.

It has been shown that neural networks suffer from *backdoor attacks* [6].
In such attacks, the attacker has control over the training process. Usually, the

---

Supplementary Information The online version contains supplementary material
available at https://doi.org/10.1007/978-3-031-26351-4_41.

adversary poisons a portion of the training data by installing a trigger on natural inputs. Then, the neural network is trained either by the adversary or the user on this poisoned training data. The attacker may add its trigger to the inputs at inference time to achieve its desired output. However, such poisoned neural networks behave ordinarily on clean data. As such, defending neural networks against backdoor attacks can empirically be an arduous task.

In the most common setting for backdoor defense, motivated by the rise of Machine Learning as a Service (MLaaS) [7], it is assumed that the user outsources training of its desired model to a third party. The adversary then can exploit this freedom and provide a malicious, backdoored neural network to the user [8–12]. From this perspective, the status-quo defense strategies against backdoor attacks can be divided into two categories [13]. In *detection-based* methods the goal is to identify maliciously trained neural networks [11,14]. *Erasing-based* approaches, in contrast, try to effectively eliminate the backdoor data ramifications in the trained model, and hence, give a pure, backdoor-free network [8,9,15–17].

A less-explored yet realistic scenario in defending neural networks against backdoor poisonings is when the user obtains its training data from untrustworthy sources. Here, the attacker can introduce backdoors into the user's model by solely poisoning the training data [6,13,18,19]. In this setting, existing approaches have several disadvantages. First, these methods may require having access to a *clean held-out validation dataset* [18]. This assumption may not be valid in real-world applications where collecting new, reliable data is costly. Moreover, such approaches may need a *two-step training procedure*: a neural network is first trained on the poisoned data. Then, the backdoor data is removed from the training set using the previously trained network. After purification of the training set, the neural network needs to be re-trained [18,19]. Finally, some methods achieve robustness by *training multiple neural networks* on subsets of training data to enable a "majority-vote mechanism" [13,20,21]. These last two assumptions may also prove expensive in real-world applications where it is more efficient to train a *single* neural network only *once*. As a result, one can see that a standard, robust, and end-to-end training approach, like adversarial training, is still lacking for training on backdoor poisoned data.

To address these pitfalls, in this paper we leverage the theory of coreset selection [22–26] for end-to-end training of neural networks. In particular, we aim to sanitize the possibly malicious training data by training the neural network on a subset of the training data. To find this subset in an online fashion, we exploit coreset selection by identifying the properties of the poisoned data. To formulate our coreset selection objective, we argue that the *gradient space characteristics* and *local intrinsic dimensionality* (LID) of poisoned and clean data samples are different from one another. We empirically validate these properties using various case studies. Then, based on these two properties, we define an appropriate coreset selection objective and effectively filter out poisoned data samples from the training set. As we shall see, this process is done online as the neural network is being trained. As such, we can effectively eliminate the previous methods' re-training requirement. We empirically show the successful performance of our method, named COLLIDER, in training robust neural networks under various backdoor data poisonings resulting in about 25% faster training.

Our contributions can be summarized as follows:

- To the best of our knowledge, we are the first to introduce a practical algorithm for single-run training of neural networks on backdoor data by using the idea of coreset selection.
- We characterize clean data samples based on their gradient space and local intrinsic dimensionality and define a novel coreset selection objective that effectively selects them.
- We perform extensive experiments under different settings to show the excellent performance of the proposed approach in reducing the effect of backdoor data poisonings on neural networks in an online fashion.

2   Related Work

This section reviews some of the most related work to our proposed approach. For a more thorough overview of backdoor attacks and defense, please see [13,27]

2.1   Backdoor Attacks

In BadNets, Gu *et al.* [6] showed that neural network image classifiers suffer from backdoor attacks for the first time. Specifically, the training data is poisoned by installing small triggers in the shape of single pixels or checkerboard patterns on a few images. This poisoned data may come from any class. Therefore, their label needs to be modified to the target class by the adversary. As the labels are manipulated in addition to the training data, this type of backdoor data poisoning is known as *dirty-label* attacks. Similar findings have also been demonstrated on face-recognition networks using dirty-label data poisoning [28,29].

Different from dirty-label attacks, one can effectively poison the training data without changing the labels. As the adversary does not alter the labels even for the poisoned data, such attacks are called *clean-label* [30,31]. To construct such backdoor data, Turner *et al.* [31] argue that the underlying image, before attaching the trigger, needs to become "hard-to-classify." Intuitively, this choice would force the neural network to rely on the added trigger rather than the image semantics and hence, learn to associate the trigger with the target class more easily [31]. To this end, Turner *et al.* [31] first render hard-to-classify samples using adversarial perturbation or generative adversarial network interpolation and then add the trigger. To further strengthen this attack, they reduce the trigger intensity (to go incognito) and install the trigger to all four corners of the poisoned image (to evade data augmentation). Various stealthy trigger patterns can also help in constructing powerful clean-label attacks. As such, different patterns like sinusoidal strips [32], invisible noise [33,34], natural reflections [35], and imperceptible warping (WANet) [36] have been proposed as triggers.

In a different approach, Shafahi *et al.* [30] use the idea of "feature-collision" to create clean-label poisoned data. In particular, they try to find samples that are

(1) similar to a base image and (2) close to the target class in the feature space of a pre-trained DNN. This way, if the network is re-trained on the poisoned data, it will likely associate target class features to the poisoned data and hence, can fool the classifier. Saha *et al.* [37] further extend "feature-collision" to data samples that are poisoned with patch triggers. These triggers are installed at random locations in a given image.

2.2   Backdoor Defense

Existing backdoor defense techniques can be divided into several categories [13]. Some methods aim at *detecting backdoor poisoned data* [18,38–40]. Closely related to our work, Jin *et al.* [41] try to detect backdoor samples using the local intrinsic dimensionality of the data. To this end, they extract features of each image using a pre-trained neural network on clean data. In contrast, as we shall see in Sect. 4, we use the feature space of the same neural network we are training, which may have been fed with poisoned data. *Identification of poisoned models* is another popular defense mechanism against backdoor attacks. In this approach, given a DNN model, the aim is to detect if it has backdoors. Neural cleanse [9], DeepInspect [10], TABOR [42], and Universal Litmus Patterns [11] are some of the methods that fall into this category. Furthermore, some techniques aim at *removing the backdoor data effects in a trained neural network* [8,9,15–17].

Most related to this work are approaches that try to *avoid learning the triggers during training* [18,19]. To this end, they first train a neural network on poisoned data. Then, using the backdoored DNN and a clean validation set, they extract robust statistical features associated with clean samples. Next, the training set is automatically inspected, and samples that do not meet the cleanness criteria are thrown away. Finally, the neural network is re-trained on this new training dataset. In contrast, our approach does not require additional certified clean data. Moreover, our proposed method trains the neural network only once, taking less training time compared to existing methods [18,19]. Other approaches in this category, such as deep partition aggregation [20] and bagging [21], require training multiple networks to enable a "majority-vote mechanism" [13]. However, our approach focuses on the robust training of a single neural network.

3   Background

As mentioned in Sect. 1, our approach consists of a coreset selection algorithm based on the gradient space attributes and the local intrinsic dimensionality of the data. This section reviews the background related to coreset selection and local intrinsic dimensionality.

3.1   Coreset Selection

Coreset selection refers to algorithms that create weighted subsets of the original data. For deep learning, these subsets are selected so that training a model over them is approximately equivalent to fitting a model on the original data [25]. Closely related to this work, Mirzasoleiman *et al.* [26] exploit the idea of coreset selection for training with noisy labels. It is argued that data with label noise would result in neural network gradients that differ from clean data. As such, a coreset selection objective is defined to select the data with "the most centrally located gradients" [26]. The network is then trained on this selected data.

3.2   Local Intrinsic Dimensionality

Traditionally, classical expansion models such as generalized expansion dimension (GED) [43] were used to measure the intrinsic dimensionality of the data. As a motivating example, consider two equicenter balls of radii r_1 and r_2 in a d-dimensional Euclidean space. Assume the volumes of these balls are given as V_1 and V_2, respectively. Then, the space dimension can be deduced using

$$\frac{V_2}{V_1} = \left(\frac{r_2}{r_1}\right)^d \Rightarrow d = \frac{\ln (V_2/V_1)}{\ln (r_2/r_1)}.$$

To estimate the data dimension d, GED formulations approximate each ball's volume by the number of data samples they capture [43,44].

By extending the aforementioned setting into a statistical one, classical expansion models can provide a local view of intrinsic dimensionality [45,46]. To this end, the natural analogy of volumes and probability measures is exploited. In particular, instead of a Euclidean space, a statistical setting powered with continuous distance distributions is considered.

Definition 1 (Local Intrinsic Dimensionality (LID) [45,47]**).** *Let $x \in \mathbb{X}$ be a data sample. Also, let $r > 0$ denote a non-negative random variable that measures the distance of x to other data samples, and assume its cumulative distribution function is denoted by $F(r)$. If $F(r)$ is positive and continuously differentiable for every $r > 0$, then the LID of x at distance r is given by*

$$\mathrm{LID}_F(r) \triangleq \lim_{\epsilon \to 0^+} \frac{\ln(F((1+\epsilon)r)/F(r))}{\ln(1+\epsilon)} = \frac{rF'(r)}{F(r)},$$

whenever the limit exists. The LID at x is defined by taking the limit of $\mathrm{LID}_F(r)$ as $r \to 0^+$

$$\mathrm{LID}_F = \lim_{r \to 0^+} \mathrm{LID}_F(r). \tag{1}$$

Calculating Eq. (1) limit is not straightforward as it requires knowing the exact distance distribution $F(r)$. Instead, several estimators using extreme value theory (EVT) have been proposed [48,49]. Given its efficacy, here we use the following maximum likelihood estimator for LID [47,49]

$$\widehat{\mathrm{LID}}(x) = -\left(\frac{1}{k} \sum_{i=1}^{k} \log \frac{r_i(x)}{r_k(x)}\right)^{-1}, \tag{2}$$

where $r_i(\boldsymbol{x})$ is the distance between the data $\boldsymbol{x}$ and its i-th nearest neighbor from the dataset. As seen, only data samples in a local neighborhood would be considered in such an estimate. Thus, under this regime, a *local view* of the intrinsic dimensionality is obtained.

Finally, note that even computing the estimate given in Eq. (2) might become computationally prohibitive, especially for high-dimensional datasets with thousands of samples. Thus, to further make this computation straightforward, Ma *et al.* [47,50] propose an alternative approach. First, randomly sampled mini-batches of data are used to determine the set of nearest neighbors. Second, instead of working with high-dimensional data samples directly, their feature space representation given by an underlying DNN is used. We will also be using this approximator in our approach.

4   Proposed Method

In this section, we formally define the problem of training neural networks with backdoor poisoned data. Next, we argue that two critical features can characterize clean samples in a backdoor poisoned dataset. First, gradient updates for clean data differ in their magnitudes and directions from those of poisoned data [51]. Second, clean data usually has lower LID than its tampered counterparts [41,46,47]. We define a COreset selection algorithm with LocaL Intrinsic DimEnisonality Regularization based on these two criteria, called COLLIDER. Using COLLIDER, we effectively select data samples that satisfy the properties mentioned above and are likely to be clean. As such, the neural network trained on this subset of data would not be affected by the installed triggers. As we shall see, COLLIDER has several advantages over existing methods. Namely, it does not require (1) having access to clean validation data, (2) re-training the whole model, or (3) training multiple neural networks.

4.1   Problem Statement

Let $\mathcal{D} = \{(\boldsymbol{x}_i, y_i)\}_{i=1}^n \subset \mathbb{X} \times \mathbb{C}$ denote a training dataset. Each sample consists of an image $\boldsymbol{x}_i$ from domain $\mathbb{X}$ and a label y_i which takes one of the k possible values from the set $\mathbb{C} = [k] = \{1, 2, \ldots, k\}$. Suppose that $f_{\boldsymbol{\theta}} : \mathbb{X} \to \mathbb{R}^k$ denotes a neural network image classifier with parameters $\boldsymbol{\theta}$. It takes an image $\boldsymbol{x}_i \in \mathbb{X}$ and outputs a k-dimensional real-valued vector, also known as the logit. This vector gives the predicted label of the input $\boldsymbol{x}_i$ by $\hat{y}_i = \arg\max f_{\boldsymbol{\theta}}(\boldsymbol{x}_i)$. The neural network is trained to minimize an appropriately defined objective function

$$\mathcal{L}(\boldsymbol{\theta}) = \sum_{i \in V} \ell\left(f_{\boldsymbol{\theta}}(\boldsymbol{x}_i), y_i\right) = \sum_{i \in V} \ell_i(\boldsymbol{\theta}), \tag{3}$$

over the training set. Here, $\ell(\cdot)$ stands for a standard cost function such as cross-entropy, and $V = [n] = \{1, 2, \ldots, n\}$ denotes the set of all training data. Optimizing Eq. (3) using gradient descent requires finding the gradient of the loss for all the data points in V, which is costly. In practice, one usually takes random mini-batches of training data and performs stochastic gradient descent.

Here, we assume that the training dataset consists of backdoor poisoned data. In particular, let $\mathcal{B} : \mathbb{X} \to \mathbb{X}$ denote a backdoor data poisoning rule by which the data is tampered.[1] In targeted backdoor attacks, which we consider here, the adversary first replaces some training data samples $\boldsymbol{x}_i$ with their poisoned counterparts $\mathcal{B}(\boldsymbol{x}_i)$. The goal is to force the model to unintentionally learn the injection rule, so that during inference for any test sample $(\boldsymbol{x}_{\text{test}}, y_{\text{test}})$ the neural network outputs

$$y_{\text{test}} = \arg\max f_{\boldsymbol{\theta}}(\boldsymbol{x}_{\text{test}}) \quad \& \quad t = \arg\max f_{\boldsymbol{\theta}}(\mathcal{B}(\boldsymbol{x}_{\text{test}})), \qquad (4)$$

where $t \in \mathbb{C}$ denotes the attacker's intended target class. In this paper, we want to meticulously select a subset S of the entire training data V such that it only contains clean data samples. To this end, we carefully identify properties of the clean data that should be in the set S. We define a coreset selection objective based on these criteria to form the subset S at each epoch. The model is then trained on the data inside the coreset S.

4.2   Clean vs. Poisoned Data Properties

Next, we argue how the gradient space and LID differences between clean and poisoned samples can help us identify poisoned data. Based on these arguments, we will then define a coreset selection objective to effectively filter out such samples from the training set in an online fashion.

Gradient Space Properties. Recently, Hong *et al.* [51] have empirically shown that in the gradient space, poisoned data exhibit different behavior compared to clean samples. Specifically, it is shown that the gradient updates computed on poisoned data have comparably (1) larger ℓ_2 norm and (2) different orientation in contrast to clean data. Given the empirical observations of Hong *et al.* [51], we conclude that the backdoor poisoned data have different gradients compared to the clean data. Moreover, Mirzasoleiman *et al.* [26] studied neural network training with noisy labeled data and argued that in the gradient space, clean data samples tend to be tied with each other. Putting these two observations together, we deduce that the clean data samples are usually tied together in the gradient space while poisoned data is scattered in the gradient space. Thus, we can use this property to find the set of "most centrally located samples" in the gradient space and filter out poisoned data.

We empirically investigate our assumptions around gradient space properties in Fig. 1. Specifically, we visualize the gradients of a randomly initialized neural network for the CIFAR-10 dataset poisoned with the backdoor triggers of Gu *et al.* [6]. To this end, we first show the t-SNE [52] plot of the gradients in Fig. 1a.

---

[1] The adversary may also change the injected data labels. For notation brevity, we assume that the injection rule only changes the image itself, not the label.

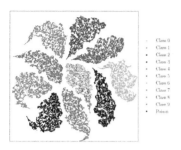
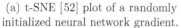

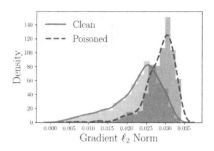

(a) t-SNE [52] plot of a randomly initialized neural network gradient.

(b) Distribution of the neural network gradient norm after 3 epochs of training.

Fig. 1. Visualization of the loss gradients for a neural network on poisoned CIFAR-10 dataset using the last layer approximation of Sect. 4.3. As seen, the gradients of the poisoned data are scattered in the gradient space and tend to exhibit a larger norm.

As can be seen, the poisoned data is scattered in the gradient space. Moreover, as seen in Fig. 1b, the ℓ_2 norm of the gradients tends to be larger for the poisoned data. This case study demonstrates how our assumptions around gradient space properties hold for poisoned data.

Unfortunately, as we will empirically see, after the first few epochs, the gradient dissimilarities between clean and poisoned samples gradually vanish. This is in line with empirical observations of Hong et al. [51]. As such, we need an additional regularizer to help us maintain the performance of data filtering throughout training. To this end, we make use of LID.

Local Intrinsic Dimensionality Properties. As discussed above, gradient space properties may not be sufficient to design a robust training algorithm against backdoor data. Thus, we look into the geometrical structure of the underlying data to further enhance the performance of our method. To this end, we utilize the LID of the data [45,53].

Empirically, Ma et al. [50] show that neural networks tend to progressively transform the data into subspaces of low local intrinsic dimensionality, such that each clean data point is surrounded by other clean samples. The LID has also been successfully applied to characterize adversarial subspaces [47]. In particular, Ma et al. [47] argue how the LID values of adversarially perturbed examples are probably higher than their underlying clean data. This is motivated by the fact that legitimate perturbed examples are likely to be found in a neighborhood where not many clean examples reside, and hence, have high intrinsic dimensionality. For k-NN classifiers, Amsaleg et al. [46] provide a rigorous theoretical analysis. It has been proved that if data samples have large LID values, the level of perturbation required to turn them into adversarial examples diminishes. This theoretical study supports the empirical observations of Ma et al. [47] that tampered examples exhibit high LID values. These results collectively indicate that manipulating clean data samples will likely increase their LID.

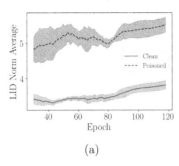 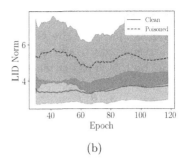

(a)   (b)

Fig. 2. The LID of clean and BadNet poisoned data samples for CIFAR-10 dataset. (a) average LID norm across 5 different seeds (b) LID distribution for a single run. As expected, benign data samples have a lower LID compared to poisoned data.

Similarly, one would expect that successful backdoor attacks effectively move a sample away from all clean data. This way, they try to eventually form a subspace secluded from the clean samples that can subvert the neural network's decision into the attacker's target class. Thus, we contemplate that a neighborhood with higher dimensionality is needed to shelter poisoned samples compared to clean data. In other words, clean data samples are expected to have low LID values. In Fig. 2, we empirically show the distribution of LID values for clean and poisoned data recorded during training a neural network on the CIFAR-10 dataset. As expected, poisoned data generally exhibit a higher LID.

4.3 COLLIDER: Coreset Selection with Local Intrinsic DimEnisonality Regularization

In this section, we exploit the properties of clean data discussed in Sect. 4.2 and define our coreset selection objective. As stated in Sect. 4.2, we need to first identify the set of most centrally located samples in the gradient space as the clean data are likely to be tied together. Thus, as our base component, we use a coreset selection objective to find clusters of data that are tied together in the gradient space [26]

$$S^*(\boldsymbol{\theta}) \in \arg\min_{S \subseteq V} \sum_{i \in V} \min_{j \in S} d_{ij}(\boldsymbol{\theta}) \quad \text{s.t.} \quad |S| \leq k. \tag{5}$$

Here, $d_{ij}(\boldsymbol{\theta}) = \|\nabla \ell_i(\boldsymbol{\theta}) - \nabla \ell_j(\boldsymbol{\theta})\|_2$ shows the ℓ_2 distance of loss gradients between samples i and j, and k denotes the number of samples in the coreset.

To add the LID to our approach, we need to ensure that the underlying neural network has reached a point where it can extract meaningful features from the data. Remember from Sect. 3 that this is important as these features are used to approximate the LID values, and thus, they need to have a meaningful structure across data. Therefore, we run our basic coreset selection objective of Eq. (5) during the first epochs until we obtain a steady validation accuracy. Afterward, we start to consider the LID values. Remember that we want to encourage the selection of samples that are likely to be clean, i.e., have low LID values. Thus, we add a regularizer to our coreset selection objective that promotes this. In particular, Eq. (5) is re-written as

$$S^*(\boldsymbol{\theta}) \in \arg\min_{S \subseteq V, |S| \leq k} \sum_{i \in V} \min_{j \in S} d_{ij}(\boldsymbol{\theta}) + \lambda \mathrm{LID}(\boldsymbol{x}_j), \tag{6}$$

where λ is a hyperparameter that determines the relative importance of LID against the gradient term. Here, $\mathrm{LID}(\cdot)$ is computed as discussed in Sec. Sect. 3 using mini-batches of data. As seen in Eq. (6), we encourage the algorithm to select data points with low LID values.

4.4 Practical Considerations

Gradient Approximation and Greedy Solvers. As pointed out in [25,26], finding the optimal solution of Eq. (5) and as a result Eq. (6) is intractable. This is since computing $d_{ij}(\boldsymbol{\theta})$ for all $i \in V$ requires backpropagation over the entire training set, which is computationally prohibitive. More importantly, finding the optimal coresets as in Eq. (5) is shown to be NP-hard [25].

To address the first issue, the following upper-bound is usually used instead of the exact $d_{ij}(\boldsymbol{\theta})$ values [25,26,54]

$$d_{ij}(\boldsymbol{\theta}) = \|\nabla\ell_i(\boldsymbol{\theta}) - \nabla\ell_j(\boldsymbol{\theta})\|_2$$
$$\leq c_1 \left\| \Sigma'_L\left(z_i^{(L)}\right) \nabla\ell_i^{(L)}(\boldsymbol{\theta}) - \Sigma'_L\left(z_j^{(L)}\right) \nabla\ell_j^{(L)}(\boldsymbol{\theta}) \right\| + c_2,$$

where $\Sigma'_L\left(z_i^{(L)}\right) \nabla\ell_i^{(L)}(\boldsymbol{\theta})$ denotes the gradient of the loss with respect to the neural network's penultimate layer, shown by $z_i^{(L)}$. Also, c_1 and c_2 are constants, and L denotes the number of DNN layers. This upper-bound can be computed efficiently, with a cost approximately equal to forward-propagation [26]. As for the NP-hardness issue, there exist efficient greedy algorithms that can solve Eq. (5) sub-optimally [55–57]. Specifically, Eq. (5) is first turned into its *submodular optimization* equivalent, and then solved. Details of this re-formulation can be found in [25,26] and Appendix A.

Repetitive Coreset Selection. As our coresets are a function of the neural network parameters $\boldsymbol{\theta}$, we need to update them as the training goes on. Thus, at the beginning of every epoch, we first select data samples S by solving Eq. (6). We then train the neural network using mini-batch gradient descent on the data that falls inside the coreset S.

LID Computation. For LID estimation, we select neighbors of each sample from the same class. This way, we ensure that clean samples have similar feature representations among themselves. As a result, our LID estimates can better capture the dimensionality differences between the clean and poisoned samples. To further stabilize LID estimates, we use a moving average of LID values taken over a few successive epochs, not a single one, as the LID estimate of a training sample. Moreover, as the training evolves, we permanently eliminate samples with the highest LID values. This is motivated by the fact that our LID estimates are the average of LID values for the past epochs. Thus, samples that exhibit a high LID value over successive training epochs are likely to be poisoned data. However, we must be careful not to remove too many samples so that the solution to Eq. (6) becomes trivial. As a result, we select the number of removals such that the coreset selection always has a non-trivial problem to solve. According to Eq. (6), this means that at the last epoch, we need to have at least k samples left in our training set. Thus, we gradually eliminate $n - k$ samples throughout the training. Also, as in Mirzasoleiman *et al.* [26], we use mix-up to enhance the quality of our coresets further. Finally, note that the computational complexity of the LID regularization is minimal. This is because for computing the $d_{ij}(\boldsymbol{\theta})$ terms in Eq. (5) we have already computed the logits. The same values can be re-used for LID calculation. The final algorithm can be found in Appendix A.

5   Experimental Results

This section presents our experimental results. We demonstrate how by using COLLIDER one can train robust neural networks against backdoor data poisonings. Furthermore, we show the role of each component in COLLIDER in our extensive ablation studies.

Settings. We use CIFAR-10 [58], SVHN [59], and ImageNet-12 [1,35] datasets in our experiments. To test our approach against various backdoor data poisonings, we use BadNets [6], label-consistent attacks [31], sinusoidal strips [32], and triggers used in HTBA [37] to poison the aforementioned datasets. We randomly select a target class for each dataset and poison it with backdoor-generated data. The ratio of poisoned samples in the target class is referred to as the *injection rate*. Samples from each backdoor poisoned dataset can be found in Appendix B. Furthermore, we use ResNet [60] as our DNN architecture. For training, we use a stochastic gradient descent (SGD) optimizer with momentum of 0.9 and weight decay 5e-4. The initial learning rate is set to 0.1, which is divided by 10 at epochs 80 and 100 for CIFAR-10 and SVHN (epochs 72 and 144 for ImageNet-12). In what follows, the *coreset size* refers to the ratio of the original data in each class that we intend to keep for training. For more details on the experimental settings and also extra experiments see Appendices B and C.

Baselines. Our approach differs significantly in its assumptions from the current backdoor defenses. Thus, for a fair comparison, we compare COLLIDER to two other baselines: (1) the usual training, denoted as "vanilla", and (2) basic coreset selection (Eq. (5)), denoted as "coresets". Furthermore, to provide a complete picture of the performance of our proposed approach, we also include Spectral Signatures (SS) [18], Activation Clustering (AC) [39], SPECTRE [19],

Table 1. Clean test accuracy (ACC) and attack success rate (ASR) in % for backdoor data poisonings on CIFAR-10 (BadNets and label-consistent) and SVHN (sinusoidal strips) datasets. The results show the mean and standard deviation for 5 different seeds. The poisoned data injection rate is 10%. For BadNets and label-consistent attacks, the coreset size is 0.3. It is 0.4 for sinusoidal strips.

Training	BadNets [6]		Label-consistent [31]		Sinusoidal Strips [32]	
	ACC	ASR	ACC	ASR	ACC	ASR
Vanilla	92.19 ± 0.20	99.98 ± 0.02	92.46 ± 0.16	100	95.79 ± 0.20	77.35 ± 3.68
SS [18]	92.05 ± 0.43	1.18 ± 0.36	92.24 ± 0.35	0.53 ± 0.09	95.38 ± 0.28	77.30 ± 2.50
AC [39]	91.78 ± 0.21	99.87 ± 0.08	91.59 ± 0.31	75.44 ± 42.53	95.45 ± 0.20	77.43 ± 4.59
SPECTRE [19]	91.28 ± 0.22	98.17 ± 1.97	91.78 ± 0.37	0.51 ± 0.15	95.41 ± 0.12	8.51 ± 7.03
NAD [17]	72.19 ± 1.73	3.55 ± 1.25	70.18 ± 1.70	3.44 ± 1.50	92.41 ± 0.34	6.99 ± 3.02
Coresets	84.86 ± 0.47	74.93 ± 34.6	83.87 ± 0.36	7.78 ± 9.64	92.30 ± 0.19	24.30 ± 8.15
COLLIDER (Ours)	80.66 ± 0.95	4.80 ± 1.49	82.11 ± 0.62	5.19 ± 1.08	89.74 ± 0.31	6.20 ± 3.69

and Neural Attention Distillation (NAD) [17] to our comparisons. It should be noted that these approaches have a different set of assumptions compared to COLLIDER, and the comparisons are not fair. This is because SS [18], AC [39], and SPECTRE [19] train the neural network *twice*, and NAD [17] is trying to erase the backdoor after the training is complete.

5.1   Clean Test Accuracy and Attack Success Rate

In Table 1 we show our experimental results. We measure the performance of each training algorithm by two quantities: (1) accuracy on the clean test set (ACC) and (2) the attack success rate (ASR), which indicates the accuracy of the installed triggers on non-target class images. As seen, using COLLIDER we can reduce the attack success rate significantly in nearly all the cases. Moreover, although the coreset selection based on the gradient space properties can improve robustness (see the "coresets" row), its performance is insufficient to provide a robust model. This, as we see, can be improved using the intrinsic dimensionality of the data that captures the geometrical structure of the training samples.

Interestingly, observe how our approach is a middle-ground between SS [18] and NAD [17] settings. Specifically, in SS [18] the entire network is re-trained to get a better performance, but this is inefficient. To show this, in Table 2 we report the total training time for our approach against SS [18] that trains the neural network twice. As seen, our approach results in an average of 22% reduction in training time compared to existing methods that need re-training.[2]

At the other end of the spectrum, NAD [17] tries to erase the backdoors from the vanilla network without re-training. In COLLIDER we are trying to prevent the network from learning the triggers in an online fashion, such that there would be no need to re-train the network. More importantly, NAD [17] shows the difficulty of this task because once the model learns the triggers, one cannot erase them without sacrificing too much of the clean accuracy.

As seen in Table 1, while COLLIDER can significantly reduce the ASR, it also exhibits a gap in terms of ACC with other methods. As a remedy, we investigate

---

[2] Note that here we measure the training time for SS [18] as a representative of techniques that need re-training, e.g., AC [39] and SPECTRE [19].

Table 2. Total training time (in minutes) for experiments of Table 1. The results show the mean and standard deviation for 5 different seeds.

Method	BadNets [6]	Label-consistent [31]	Sinusoidal Strips [32]
Coresets	61.35 ± 0.31	63.09 ± 0.36	66.04 ± 1.11
COLLIDER	62.56 ± 0.13	67.10 ± 0.95	64.53 ± 0.38
SS [18] ($\sim$AC [39]/SPECTRE [19])	85.48 ± 0.28	85.26 ± 0.26	79.46 ± 0.86

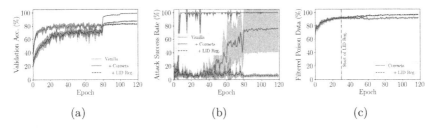

(a)   (b)   (c)

Fig. 3. Ablation study on the effect of coreset selection and LID regularization terms in COLLIDER for training robust models on BadNet poisonings. (a) validation accuracy (b) attack success rate (c) percentage of poisoned data filtered. Epoch 30 (annotated in (c)) is the start of our LID regularization. As seen, while the difference between the percentage of the filtered poison data is very close, this translates to a significant difference in ASR.

using non-coreset data in training to increase the clean accuracy gap while maintaining backdoor robustness. To this end, we use semi-supervised learning and treat the non-coreset data as unlabeled samples. As shown in Appendix C, one can enhance the ACC while decreasing ASR. For a detailed description of this version of our approach and other extensive experiments, please see Appendix C.

5.2 Ablation Studies

To clarify the role of each component in COLLIDER, we record some performance measures during training. For each algorithm, we record the accuracy on the validation set and the attack success rate on the test set. Also, to better monitor the coresets, we record the percentage of the poisoned data filtered during training. This measure is defined as the complement of the number of poisoned data in the coreset divided by the total number of poisoned data. This ratio is always between zero and one: one means that the selected coreset does not contain any poisoned data. As seen in Fig. 3c, after the first few epochs where the performance of the basic coreset selection improves, it suddenly degrades. At this point, we are ready to enable the LID regularization in COLLIDER since we have reached a point with steady validation accuracy. This addition helps the coreset selection to maintain its performance throughout the training. This slight difference is decisive when it comes to the attack success rate, which, as seen in Fig. 3b, can determine the robustness of the final model.[3]

5.3 Trade-Offs

Finally, there are some trade-offs in COLLIDER that need to be discussed. First, in Fig. 7 in Appendix C one can see that as we increase the coreset size, the clean test accuracy and the attack success rate both increase. This is inevitable as by increasing the coreset size, we are likely to let more poisoned data into the selected subset used for training. As a result, the attack success rate starts to increase. However, we can see that this trade-off is less severe in COLLIDER due to its use of LID that can capture the poisoned samples more accurately. Second, in Fig. 8 of Appendix C we show the performance of our proposed method as the injection rate is varied. For the experiments in this figure, the coreset size is fixed to 0.3 or 30%. Ideally, we should be able to train a robust model with a 70% injection rate successfully. However, as discussed in Sec. Sect. 4.2, our solutions to the coreset selection objective of Eq. (6) are always sub-optimal as finding the exact solution is NP-hard. Thus, as the injection rate increases, so does the attack success rate. Again, the rate of this trade-off is less dramatic for COLLIDER compared to gradient-based coreset selection.

6 Conclusion

We proposed a robust, end-to-end training algorithm for backdoor datasets in this paper. Our method, named COLLIDER, exploits the idea of coreset selection to purify the given data before using them for training a neural network. Specifically, we saw how clean and poisoned data samples differ in their gradient space and local intrinsic dimensionality attributes. Based on these differences, we defined a coreset selection algorithm that tries to filter out malicious data effectively. The neural network can then be trained on this carefully selected data. We showed the performance of the proposed approach in improving the robustness of neural networks against backdoor data poisonings and identified the role of each component through extensive ablation studies. While successful in decreasing the attack success rate significantly, we saw that COLLIDER also reduces the clean test accuracy slightly.

Acknowledgments. We thank Michael Houle for thoughtful discussions and comments on LID evaluation. This research was undertaken using the LIEF HPC-GPGPU Facility hosted at the University of Melbourne. This Facility was established with the assistance of LIEF Grant LE170100200. Sarah Erfani is in part supported by Australian Research Council (ARC) Discovery Early Career Researcher Award (DECRA) DE220100680.

---

[3] Note that the sudden jump observed in the validation accuracy during epochs 80 and 100 is due to the use of a multi-step learning rate scheduler discussed at the beginning of Sect. 5.

References

1. Russakovsky, O., et al.: ImageNet large scale visual recognition challenge. Int. J. Comput. Vision **115**, 211–252 (2015)
2. Geiger, A., Lenz, P., Urtasun, R.: Are we ready for autonomous driving? the KITTI vision benchmark suite. In: Proceedings of the 2012 IEEE Conference on Computer Vision and Pattern Recognition (CVPR), pp. 3354–3361 (2012)
3. Lillicrap, T.P., et al.: Continuous control with deep reinforcement learning. In: Proceedings of the 4th International Conference on Learning Representations (ICLR) (2016)
4. Deng, J., Guo, J., Xue, N., Zafeiriou, S.: ArcFace: additive angular margin loss for deep face recognition. In: Proceedings of the 2019 IEEE Conference on Computer Vision and Pattern Recognition (CVPR), pp. 4690–4699 (2019)
5. Schroff, F., Kalenichenko, D., Philbin, J.: FaceNet: a unified embedding for face recognition and clustering. In: Proceedings of the 2015 IEEE Conference on Computer Vision and Pattern Recognition (CVPR), pp. 815–823 (2015)
6. Gu, T., Dolan-Gavitt, B., Garg, S.: BadNets: identifying vulnerabilities in the machine learning model supply chain. CoRR abs/1708.06733 (2017)
7. Shokri, R., Stronati, M., Song, C., Shmatikov, V.: Membership inference attacks against machine learning models. In: Proceedings of the 2017 IEEE Symposium on Security and Privacy (SP) (2017) 3–18
8. Liu, K., Dolan-Gavitt, B., Garg, S.: Fine-Pruning: defending against backdooring attacks on deep neural networks. In: Proceedings of the 21st International Symposium Research in Attacks, Intrusions, and Defenses (RAID), pp. 273–294 (2018)
9. Wang, B., Yao, Y., Shan, S., Li, H., Viswanath, B., Zheng, H., Zhao, B.Y.: Neural Cleanse: Identifying and mitigating backdoor attacks in neural networks. In: Proceedings of the 2019 IEEE Symposium on Security and Privacy (SP), pp. 707–723 (2019)
10. Chen, H., Fu, C., Zhao, J., Koushanfar, F.: DeepInspect: a black-box trojan detection and mitigation framework for deep neural networks. In: Proceedings of the 28th International Joint Conference on Artificial Intelligence (IJCAI), pp. 4658–4664 (2019)
11. Kolouri, S., Saha, A., Pirsiavash, H., Hoffmann, H.: Universal litmus patterns: revealing backdoor attacks in CNNs. In: Proceedings of the 2020 IEEE Conference on Computer Vision and Pattern Recognition (CVPR), pp. 298–307 (2020)
12. Sikka, K., Sur, I., Jha, S., Roy, A., Divakaran, A.: Detecting trojaned DNNs using counterfactual attributions. CoRR abs/2012.02275 (2020)
13. Goldblum, M., et al.: Dataset security for machine learning: data poisoning, backdoor attacks, and defenses. CoRR abs/2012.10544 (2020)
14. Wang, R., Zhang, G., Liu, S., Chen, P.-Y., Xiong, J., Wang, M.: Practical detection of trojan neural networks: data-limited and data-free cases. In: Vedaldi, A., Bischof, H., Brox, T., Frahm, J.-M. (eds.) ECCV 2020. LNCS, vol. 12368, pp. 222–238. Springer, Cham (2020). https://doi.org/10.1007/978-3-030-58592-1_14
15. Liu, X., Li, F., Wen, B., Li, Q.: Removing backdoor-based watermarks in neural networks with limited data. In: Proceedings of the 25th International Conference on Pattern Recognition (ICPR), pp. 10149–10156 (2020)
16. Zhao, P., Chen, P., Das, P., Ramamurthy, K.N., Lin, X.: Bridging mode connectivity in loss landscapes and adversarial robustness. In: Proceedings of the 8th International Conference on Learning Representations (ICLR) (2020)

17. Li, Y., Lyu, X., Koren, N., Lyu, L., Li, B., Ma, X.: Neural attention distillation: erasing backdoor triggers from deep neural networks. In: Proceedings of the 9th International Conference on Learning Representations (ICLR) (2021)
18. Tran, B., Li, J., Madry, A.: Spectral signatures in backdoor attacks. In: Proceedings of the Advances in Neural Information Processing Systems 31: Annual Conference on Neural Information Processing Systems (NeurIPS), pp. 8011–8021 (2018)
19. Hayase, J., Kong, W., Somani, R., Oh, S.: SPECTRE: defense against backdoor attacks via robust covariance estimation. In: Proceedings of the 38th International Conference on Machine Learning (ICML), pp. 4129–4139 (2021)
20. Levine, A., Feizi, S.: Deep partition aggregation: provable defenses against general poisoning attacks. In: Proceedings of the 9th International Conference on Learning Representations (ICLR) (2021)
21. Jia, J., Cao, X., Gong, N.Z.: Intrinsic certified robustness of bagging against data poisoning attacks. CoRR abs/2008.04495 (2020)
22. Har-Peled, S., Mazumdar, S.: On coresets for k-means and k-median clustering. In: Proceedings of the 36th Annual ACM Symposium on Theory of Computing (STOC), pp. 291–300 (2004)
23. Agarwal, P.K., Har-Peled, S., Varadarajan, K.R.: Approximating extent measures of points. J. ACM **51**, 606–635 (2004)
24. Campbell, T., Broderick, T.: Bayesian coreset construction via greedy iterative geodesic ascent. In: Proceedings of the 35th International Conference on Machine Learning (ICML), pp. 697–705 (2018)
25. Mirzasoleiman, B., Bilmes, J.A., Leskovec, J.: Coresets for data-efficient training of machine learning models. In: Proceedings of the 37th International Conference on Machine Learning (ICML), pp. 6950–6960 (2020)
26. Mirzasoleiman, B., Cao, K., Leskovec, J.: Coresets for robust training of deep neural networks against noisy labels. In: Proceedings of the Advances in Neural Information Processing Systems 33: Annual Conference on Neural Information Processing Systems (NeurIPS) (2020)
27. Li, Y., Wu, B., Jiang, Y., Li, Z., Xia, S.: Backdoor learning: a survey. CoRR abs/2007.08745 (2020)
28. Chen, X., Liu, C., Li, B., Lu, K., Song, D.: Targeted backdoor attacks on deep learning systems using data poisoning. CoRR abs/1712.05526 (2017)
29. Liu, Y., et al.: Trojaning attack on neural networks. In: Proceedings of the 25th Annual Network and Distributed System Security Symposium (NDSS) (2018)
30. Shafahi, A., et al.: Poison frogs! targeted clean-label poisoning attacks on neural networks. In: Proceedings of the Advances in Neural Information Processing Systems 31: Annual Conference on Neural Information Processing Systems (NeurIPS), pp. 6106–6116 (2018)
31. Turner, A., Tsipras, D., Madry, A.: Label-consistent backdoor attacks. CoRR abs/1912.02771 (2019)
32. Barni, M., Kallas, K., Tondi, B.: A new backdoor attack in CNNS by training set corruption without label poisoning. In: Proceedings of the 2019 IEEE International Conference on Image Processing (ICIP), pp. 101–105 (2019)
33. Zhong, H., Liao, C., Squicciarini, A.C., Zhu, S., Miller, D.J.: Backdoor embedding in convolutional neural network models via invisible perturbation. In: Proceedings of the 10th ACM Conference on Data and Application Security and Privacy (CODASPY), pp. 97–108 (2020)
34. Li, S., Xue, M., Zhao, B., Zhu, H., Zhang, X.: Invisible backdoor attacks on deep neural networks via steganography and regularization. IEEE Transactions on Dependable and Secure Computing (2020)

35. Liu, Y., Ma, X., Bailey, J., Lu, F.: Reflection backdoor: a natural backdoor attack on deep neural networks. In: Vedaldi, A., Bischof, H., Brox, T., Frahm, J.-M. (eds.) ECCV 2020. LNCS, vol. 12355, pp. 182–199. Springer, Cham (2020). https://doi.org/10.1007/978-3-030-58607-2_11

36. Nguyen, T.A., Tran, A.T.: WaNet - imperceptible warping-based backdoor attack. In: Proceedings of the 9th International Conference on Learning Representations (ICLR) (2021)

37. Saha, A., Subramanya, A., Pirsiavash, H.: Hidden trigger backdoor attacks. In: Proceedings of the 34th AAAI Conference on Artificial Intelligence, pp. 11957–11965 (2020)

38. Gao, Y., Xu, C., Wang, D., Chen, S., Ranasinghe, D.C., Nepal, S.: STRIP: a defence against trojan attacks on deep neural networks. In: Proceedings of the 35th Annual Computer Security Applications Conference (ACSAC), pp. 113–125 (2019)

39. Chen, B., et al.: Detecting backdoor attacks on deep neural networks by activation clustering. In: Workshop on Artificial Intelligence Safety, 33rd AAAI Conference on Artificial Intelligence (2019)

40. Peri, N., et al.: Deep k-NN defense against clean-label data poisoning attacks. In: Bartoli, A., Fusiello, A. (eds.) ECCV 2020. LNCS, vol. 12535, pp. 55–70. Springer, Cham (2020). https://doi.org/10.1007/978-3-030-66415-2_4

41. Jin, K., et al.: A unified framework for analyzing and detecting malicious examples of DNN models. CoRR abs/2006.14871 (2020)

42. Guo, W., Wang, L., Xing, X., Du, M., Song, D.: TABOR: a highly accurate approach to inspecting and restoring trojan backdoors in AI systems. CoRR abs/1908.01763 (2019)

43. Houle, M.E., Kashima, H., Nett, M.: Generalized expansion dimension. In: 12th IEEE International Conference on Data Mining (ICDM) Workshops, pp. 587–594 (2012)

44. Karger, D.R., Ruhl, M.: Finding nearest neighbors in growth-restricted metrics. In: Proceedings of the 34th Annual ACM Symposium on Theory of Computing (STOC), pp. 741–750 (2002)

45. Houle, M.E.: Local intrinsic dimensionality I: an extreme-value-theoretic foundation for similarity applications. In: Proceedings of the 10th International Conference on Similarity Search and Applications SISAP, pp. 64–79 (2017)

46. Amsaleg, L., et al.: High intrinsic dimensionality facilitates adversarial attack: theoretical evidence. IEEE Transactions on Information Forensics Security, pp. 854–865 (2021)

47. Ma, X., et al.: Characterizing adversarial subspaces using local intrinsic dimensionality. In: Proceedings of the 6th International Conference on Learning Representations (ICLR) (2018)

48. Levina, E., Bickel, P.J.: Maximum likelihood estimation of intrinsic dimension. In: Proceedings of the Advances in Neural Information Processing Systems 17: Annual Conference on Neural Information Processing Systems (NeurIPS), pp. 777–784 (2004)

49. Amsaleg, L., et al.: Estimating local intrinsic dimensionality. In: Proceedings of the 21st ACM SIGKDD International Conference on Knowledge Discovery and Data Mining, pp. 29–38 (2015)

50. Ma, X., et al.: Dimensionality-driven learning with noisy labels. In: Proceedings of the 35th International Conference on Machine Learning (ICML), pp. 3361–3370 (2018)

51. Hong, S., Chandrasekaran, V., Kaya, Y., Dumitras, T., Papernot, N.: On the effectiveness of mitigating data poisoning attacks with gradient shaping. CoRR abs/2002.11497 (2020)
52. Van der Maaten, L., Hinton, G.: Visualizing data using t-SNE. J. Mach. Learn. Res. (JMLR) **9**, 2579–2605 (2008)
53. Houle, M.E.: Local intrinsic dimensionality II: multivariate analysis and distributional support. In: Proceedings of the 10th International Conference on Similarity Search and Applications SISAP, pp. 80–95 (2017)
54. Katharopoulos, A., Fleuret, F.: Not all samples are created equal: deep learning with importance sampling. In: Proceedings of the 35th International Conference on Machine Learning (ICML), pp. 2530–2539 (2018)
55. Minoux, M.: Accelerated greedy algorithms for maximizing submodular set functions. In: Stoer, J. (eds.) Optimization Techniques. Lecture Notes in Control and Information Sciences, vol. 7, pp. 234–243. Springer, Heidelberg (1978). https://doi.org/10.1007/BFb0006528
56. Nemhauser, G.L., Wolsey, L.A., Fisher, M.L.: An analysis of approximations for maximizing submodular set functions - I. Math. Program. **14**, 265–294 (1978)
57. Wolsey, L.A.: An analysis of the greedy algorithm for the submodular set covering problem. Combinatorica **2**, 385–393 (1982)
58. Krizhevsky, A., Hinton, G.: Learning multiple layers of features from tiny images. Master's thesis, Department of Computer Science, University of Toronto (2009)
59. Netzer, Y., Wang, T., Coates, A., Bissacco, A., Wu, B., Ng, A.Y.: Reading digits in natural images with unsupervised feature learning. In: NeurIPS Workshop on Deep Learning and Unsupervised Feature Learning (2011)
60. He, K., Zhang, X., Ren, S., Sun, J.: Deep residual learning for image recognition. In: Proceedings of the 2016 IEEE Conference on Computer Vision and Pattern Recognition (CVPR), pp. 770–778 (2016)
61. Berthelot, D., Carlini, N., Goodfellow, I.J., Papernot, N., Oliver, A., Raffel, C.: MixMatch: a holistic approach to semi-supervised learning. In: Proceedings of the Advances in Neural Information Processing Systems 32: Annual Conference on Neural Information Processing Systems (NeurIPS), pp. 5050–5060 (2019)
62. Kingma, D.P., Ba, J.: Adam: a method for stochastic optimization. In: Proceedings of the 3rd International Conference on Learning Representations (ICLR) (2015)

Synchronous Bi-directional Pedestrian Trajectory Prediction with Error Compensation

Ce Xie[1,2], Yuanman Li[1,2(✉)], Rongqin Liang[1,2], Li Dong[3], and Xia Li[1,2]

[1] College of Electronics and Information Engineering, Shenzhen University,
Shenzhen, China
{2100432087,1810262064}@email.szu.edu.cn, {yuanmanli,lixia}@szu.edu.cn
[2] Guangdong Key Laboratory of Intelligent Information Processing, Shenzhen, China
[3] Department of Computer Science, Ningbo University, Ningbo, China

Abstract. Pedestrian trajectory prediction as an essential part of reasoning human motion behaviors, has been deployed in a number of vision applications, such as autonomous navigation and video surveillance. Most existing methods adopt autoregressive frameworks to forecast the future trajectory, where the trajectory is iteratively generated based on the previous outputs. Such a process will suffer from large accumulated errors over the long-term forecast horizon. To address this issue, in this paper, we propose a Synchronous Bi-Directional framework (SBD) with error compensation for pedestrian trajectory prediction, which can greatly alleviate the error accumulation during prediction. Specifically, we first develop a bi-directional trajectory prediction mechanism, and force the predicting procedures for two opposite directions to be synchronous through a shared motion characteristic. Different from previous works, the mutual constraints inherent to our framework from the synchronous opposite-predictions can significantly prevent the error accumulation. In order to reduce the possible prediction error in each timestep, we further devise an error compensation network to model and compensate for the positional deviation between the ground-truth and the predicted trajectory, thus improving the prediction accuracy of our scheme. Experiments conducted on the Stanford Drone dataset and the ETH-UCY dataset show that our method achieves much better results than existing algorithms. Particularly, by resorting to our alleviation methodology for the error accumulation, our scheme exhibits superior performance in the long-term pedestrian trajectory prediction.

1 Introduction

Pedestrian trajectory prediction aims to forecast the future trajectory based on the observed history trajectory. As one of the most important human behavior prediction tasks, it plays an important role in many related fields, such as autonomous navigation [1,2] and video surveillance [3,4].

Although the pedestrian trajectory prediction has been analyzed and researched in a variety of ways, it remains to be a challenging task because of the inherent properties of human. First, human behaviors are full of indeterminacy,

L. Wang et al. (Eds.): ACCV 2022, LNCS 13846, pp. 699–715, 2023.
https://doi.org/10.1007/978-3-031-26351-4_42

thus there could be several plausible but distinct future trajectories under the same historical trajectory and scene. Second, pedestrians are highly affected by their neighbors. However, modeling the underlying complex inter-personal inter-actions is still challenging in real scenarios. Given the historical trajectory of the target pedestrian, a pedestrian trajectory prediction method should effectively model both the temporal motion patterns and the possible spatial interactions, and then forecast the positions or distribution of the future trajectory based on the modeled features.

The pioneering methods [5–8] mainly focus on the human motions and human-human interactions by using handcrafted features. Recently, the atten-tion mechanism and the recurrent neural networks (RNNs), which show out-standing ability in extracting temporal dependencies and spatial interactions among adjacent pedestrians, have been applied to many methods [9–15] and achieve a great success in pedestrian trajectory prediction. However, most of these methods use the single autoregressive frameworks to forecast the future trajectory. For examples, approaches like [9, 10] generate trajectory at a timestep and feed the predicted trajectory back into the model to produce the trajectory for the next timestep. Alternatively, methods like [11–13] forecast the spatial position at a future time and then feed the currently predicted position back into the model to produce the next spatial position. These frameworks would suffer from the huge accumulated errors over the long-term forecast horizon [16], and thus their performance may tend to degrade rapidly over time.

In this paper, we propose a novel Synchronous Bi-Directional framework (SBD) with error compensation for pedestrian trajectory prediction to allevi-ate the problem of error accumulation. SBD first models the spatial-temporal feature through a simple temporal motion extractor and a spatial interaction extractor. Meanwhile, SBD incorporates a conditional variational autoencoder (CVAE) module to produce the multi-modality of the future trajectory. We then propose a synchronous bi-directional trajectory generator to alleviate the error accumulation in trajectory prediction process. Specifically, we devise a shared characteristic between two opposite predictions, by resorting to which, the gen-erator performs mutually constrained synchronous bi-directional prediction to greatly prevent the error accumulation. Different from previous methods, such as [12], the trajectory generator in SBD implements predictions for two oppo-site directions synchronously, while maintaining relative independence to pre-vent from the error propagation between the two branches. Besides, to further reduce possible errors in the predicted trajectory, we design an error compensa-tion network to model and compensate for the positional deviation between the ground-truth and predicted trajectory. The main contributions of our work can be summarized as follows:

- We propose a synchronous bi-directional framework (SBD) for pedestrian trajectory prediction. Different from existing approaches, our predicting pro-cedures for two opposite directions are designed to be synchronous through a shared motion characteristic, and the mutual constraints from the synchronous opposite-predictions can significantly prevent the error accumulation.

– Through modeling the spatial deviation between the predicted trajectory and the ground-truth, we further devise an error compensation network to compensate the prediction error at each timestep, thus improving the final prediction accuracy.

– Our method achieves the state-of-the-art performance on two benchmark pedestrian trajectory prediction datasets. Particularly, thanks to the alleviation scheme for the error accumulation, our method exhibits excellent performance in the long-term pedestrian trajectory prediction.

2   Related Work

Pedestrian trajectory prediction aims to estimate the future positions base on the observed paths, which can be roughly categorized into methods based on hand-crafted features and methods based on deep learning. In this section, we give a brief review of related work.

Pedestrian Trajectory Prediction Based on Hand-Crafted Features. Traditional methods [5–8] heavily rely on the hand-crafted rules to describe human motions and human-human interactions. For examples, the Social Force [5] employs a dynamic system to model the human motions as attractive force towards a destination and repulsive forces to avoid collision. The Linear Trajectory Avoidance is proposed in [8] for short-term pedestrian trajectory prediction through jointly modeling the scene information and the dynamic social interactions among pedestrians. However, these hand-crafted methods are difficult to generalize in more complex real scenes.

Pedestrian Trajectory Prediction Based on Deep Learning. Thanks to the powerful representation of deep learning, many methods design ingenious networks for pedestrian trajectory prediction. For examples, Social-LSTM [14] extracts the motion feature for each pedestrian through individual Long Short Term Memory networks (LSTMs) and devises a social pooling layer to aggregate the interaction information among nearby pedestrians. SR-LSTM [17] refines the current states of all pedestrians in a crowd by timely capturing the changes of their neighbors and modeling the social interactions within the same moment.

The graph convolutional networks (GCNs) [18] are also introduced by many trajectory prediction methods to extract the cooperative interactions among pedestrians [10, 19–22]. For instance, Social-STGCNN [19] learns the spatial context and temporal context using a spatio-temporal graph convolution neural network. SGCN [21] introduces a sparse graph to model the sparse directed interactions among pedestrians. In addition, VDRGCN [22] devises three directed graph topologies to exploit different types of social interactions.

The attention based approaches have been devised for pedestrian trajectory prediction to model the temporal dependencies and spatial interactions among pedestrians. For examples, Social-BiGAT [20] combines the graph model and attention mechanism to model the social interactions. TPNSTA [13] adaptively extracts important information in both spatial and temporal domains through a unified spatial-temporal attention mechanism. Agentformer [9] simultaneously learns representations from the time and social dimensions and proposes a agent-aware attention mechanism for multi-agent trajectory prediction. More recently, the work CAGN [23] designs a complementary dual-path attention architecture to capture the frequent and peculiar modals of the trajectory.

Due to the inherent multi-modality of human behaviors, many stochastic prediction methods are proposed to learn the distribution of trajectory based on the deep generative model, such as generative adversarial networks (GANs) [13, 15,24,25], conditional variational autoencoders (CVAEs) [9,11,12,26–28]. For examples, Social-GAN [15] incorporates the LSTM model with the GANs to produce multiple plausible trajectories. PECNet [26] concatenates the features of historical trajectory and predicted multi-modal end-points to predict the whole trajectories. BiTraP [12] predicts future trajectories from two directions based on multi-modal goal estimation. DisDis [27] further studies the latent space and proposes to learn the discriminative personalized latent distributions to represent personalized future behaviors. In addition, SIT [29] builds a hand-craft tree and uses the branches in the tree to represent the multi-modal future trajectories.

3   Proposed Method

In this section, we introduce our SBD, which performs mutually constrained synchronous bi-directional trajectory prediction based on a shared motion characteristic to alleviate the problem of error accumulation. We describe the architecture of our method in Fig. 1, which mainly consists of three components: 1) a spatial-temporal encoder; 2) a synchronous bi-directional decoder and 3) an error compensation network.

3.1   Problem Formulation

Pedestrian trajectory prediction task aims to generate plausible future trajectory for the target pedestrian based on the historical trajectories of target and target's neighboring pedestrians. Mathematically, let $x^t \in \mathbb{R}^2$ be the spatial coordinate of a target pedestrian at the timestamp t, and denote $X = [x^{-H+1}, x^{-H+2}, ..., x^0] \in \mathbb{R}^{H \times 2}$ as the observed history trajectory, where H is observation horizon and the current location is x^0. Let $\mathcal{N}$ represent the neighbor set and $\mathbb{X}_{\mathcal{N}} = [X_{\mathcal{N}_1}, X_{\mathcal{N}_2}, ..., X_{\mathcal{N}_N}] \in \mathbb{R}^{N \times H \times 2}$ be the historical trajectories of neighbors, where the $X_{\mathcal{N}_i} \in \mathbb{R}^{H \times 2}$ belongs to the i-th neighbor. We use $Y = [y^1, y^2, ..., y^{T_f}] \in \mathbb{R}^{T_f \times 2}$ to represent the ground-truth future trajectory of the target pedestrian, where $y^t \in \mathbb{R}^2$ denotes the spatial coordinate at the future timestamp t, and T_f is the prediction horizon. Similarly, we use $\hat{Y} = [\hat{y}^1, \hat{y}^2, ..., \hat{y}^{T_f}] \in \mathbb{R}^{T_f \times 2}$ to indicate the predicted future trajectory. The overall goal is to learn a trajectory prediction model $\mathcal{F}$, which predicts a future trajectory $\hat{Y} = \mathcal{F}(X, \mathbb{X}_{\mathcal{N}})$ close to Y.

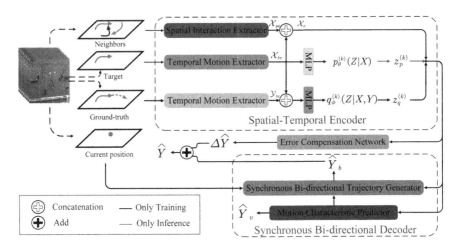

Fig. 1. The framework of SBD. The blue trajectory belongs to the target pedestrian and the orange/green trajectories are neighbours. (Color figure online)

3.2 Spatial-Temporal Encoder

Modeling Trajectories. To capture the temporal motion feature of a target pedestrian, we adopt a simple temporal motion extractor as proposed in [12]. We first embed the positions of the target pedestrian through a fully connected layer (FC) with ReLU activation as

$$e^t = FC(x^t; \Theta_e) , \tag{1}$$

where $t = -H+1, ..., 0$ and Θ_e represents the parameters of FC. The embedded feature $e^t \in \mathbb{R}^{1 \times d_{te}}$ is then fed into a GRU block to produce the hidden state at the time step t:

$$h_{te}^t = GRU(h_{te}^{t-1}, e^t) , \tag{2}$$

We obtain the temporal motion feature $\mathcal{X}_{te} \in \mathbb{R}^{1 \times d_{te}}$ as $\mathcal{X}_{te} = h_{te}^0$.

As for the modeling of social interactions among surrounding pedestrians, in this paper, we propose to capture the social influence of the neighbors to the target using the attention mechanism [30]. Specifically, we first embed the current states of all pedestrians including the target and neighbors as:

$$r = FC(x^0; \Theta_r) , \quad r_{\mathcal{N}} = FC(x_{\mathcal{N}}^0; \Theta_r) , \tag{3}$$

where $r \in \mathbb{R}^{1 \times d_{se}}$ and $r_{\mathcal{N}} \in \mathbb{R}^{N \times d_{se}}$ contains the features of the target and neighbors, respectively, and Θ_r represents the parameters of FC. According to the dot-product attention strategy [30], we calculate the spatial interaction feature as:

$$\mathcal{X}_{se} = softmax(\frac{QK^T}{\sqrt{d_{se}}})V \in \mathbb{R}^{1 \times d_{se}} . \tag{4}$$

$$Q = rW_Q , \quad K = (r \oplus r_{\mathcal{N}})W_K , \quad V = (r \oplus r_{\mathcal{N}})W_V , \tag{5}$$

where $\oplus$ serves as the concatenation operation, and $W_Q, W_K, W_V \in \mathbb{R}^{d_{se} \times d_{se}}$ represent the trainable parameters of dividual linear transformations to generate the query $Q \in \mathbb{R}^{1 \times d_{se}}$, key $K \in \mathbb{R}^{(N+1) \times d_{se}}$ and value $V \in \mathbb{R}^{(N+1) \times d_{se}}$.

Finally, we produce the spatial-temporal feature $\mathcal{X}_e$ of the target as:

$$\mathcal{X}_e = (\mathcal{X}_{te} \oplus \mathcal{X}_{se})W_e , \tag{6}$$

where $W_e \in \mathbb{R}^{(d_{te}+d_{se}) \times d_e}$ is the trainable weight matrices. In the training stage, the ground-truth Y is also encoded by another temporal motion extractor yielding $\mathcal{Y}_{te}$.

Generating Distributions of Trajectory. Considering the multi-modality of future trajectory, similar to the previous methods [9,11,12,27], SBD incorporates a conditional variational autoencoder (i.e., CVAE [31]) to estimate the future trajectory distribution $p(Y|X)$. Based on the [31], we introduce a latent variable z to represent the high-level latent intent of the target pedestrian and rewrites $p(Y|X)$ as:

$$p(Y|X) = \int p(Y|X, Z)p_\theta(Z|X)dZ , \tag{7}$$

where $p_\theta(Z|X)$ is the Gaussian distribution based on the observed trajectory.

In this work, we use a multilayer perceptron (MLP) to map the temporal feature $\mathcal{X}_{te}$ to the Gsussian parameters (μ_p, σ_p) of the distribution $p_\theta(Z|X) = N(\mu_p, \sigma_p^2)$. According to the [31], in the training stage, another MLP is adopted to produce the distribution $q_\phi(Z|X, Y) = N(\mu_q, \sigma_q^2)$ with the inputs of $\mathcal{X}_{te}$ and $\mathcal{Y}_{te}$. The latent variable z is sampled from $q_\phi(Z|X, Y)$. In the inference stage, we directly obtain different latent variables from $p_\theta(Z|X)$ to generate the multimodality of trajectory.

To produce diverse and plausible trajectories, we stack K parallel pairs of MLP to obtain the diverse latent variables. Therefore, we take the accumulation of negative evidence lower bound in the [31] as the corresponding loss function:

$$\mathcal{L}_{elbo} = \sum_{k=1}^{K} \left\{ -\mathbb{E}_{q_\phi^{(k)}(Z|X,Y)} \left[\log p^{(k)}(Y \mid X, Z) \right] \right.$$
$$\left. + KL \left(q_\phi^{(k)}(Z \mid X, Y) \| p_\theta^{(k)}(Z \mid X) \right) \right\} . \tag{8}$$

3.3   Synchronous Bi-directional Decoder

In order to alleviate the problem of error accumulation in the trajectory prediction process, we propose a novel synchronous bi-directional decoder as shown in Fig. 2. The proposed decoder is a two-phase trajectory prediction system, where the first step is to generate a series of motion characteristics shared by two opposite directions, and the second step is to perform the mutually constrained simultaneous bi-directional prediction based on the motion characteristic.

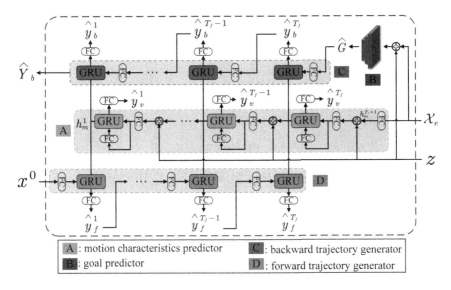

Fig. 2. The structure of the synchronous bi-directional decoder. The proposed decoder is a two-phase trajectory prediction system, where the first step is to generate motion characteristics through a motion characteristic predictor and the second step is to perform the mutually constrained simultaneous bi-directional prediction based on the motion characteristic. Finally, the decoder output the backward trajectory $\hat{Y}_b$ as the preliminary predicted result.

We should note that the existing work [12] also adopts a bi-directional trajectory prediction structure. However, it predicts two opposite directions sequentially, where it first performs forward trajectory prediction, and the results are then used as an assistance for the backward trajectory prediction. Such a sequential process can not solve the problem of error propagation. One may also use a vanilla independent bi-directional framework, which independently predicts trajectories in opposite directions. Nevertheless, the error accumulation would occur in both directions since no interactions between them.

Compared with the above strategies, our bi-directional decoder performs synchronous bi-directional prediction, where the mutual constraints from two directions can significantly prevent the error accumulation. The experiments shown in the Sect. 4 will also show the superiority of our scheme.

Motion Characteristic Predictor. In order to prevent the error propagation in each prediction direction, we devise a motion characteristic predictor, where the generated features are shared by two opposite predictions. Since the prediction procedures for two opposite predictions rely on the same feature, they would be affected by the mutual constraint from each other, thus greatly alleviating the error propagation in both directions. Intuitively, the characteristic should reflect the common real-time state of the target pedestrian in the physical space. In this paper, we specialize motion characteristic as the velocity feature of the pedestrian, and supervise the motion characteristic predictor using the real velocity.

Specifically, the spatial-temporal feature $\mathcal{X}_e$ and the latent vector z are fed into the motion characteristic predictor to generate the motion characteristics. As shown in Fig. 2, a GRU is used as the basic model of the predictor. We first adopt a FC to map $\mathcal{X}_e$ to the initial hidden state $h_m^{T_f+1}$ and produce the hidden states for the timesteps from T_f to 1:

$$r_m^{t+1} = FC(h_m^{t+1} \oplus z; \Theta_m) , \tag{9}$$

$$h_m^t = GRU\left(r_m^{t+1}, FC(r_m^{t+1}; \Theta_m^{in})\right) , \tag{10}$$

where Θ_m, Θ_m^{in} are parameters, and the hidden state h_m^t represents the motion characteristic at the time step t. Then, we propose to forecast the velocity vector $\hat{Y}_v = [\hat{y}_v^1, \hat{y}_v^2, ..., \hat{y}_v^{T_f}]$ based on the motion characteristics h_m^t $(t = 1, ..., T_f)$ as:

$$\hat{y}_v^t = FC(h_m^t; \Theta_v) , \tag{11}$$

where Θ_v are parameters to be learned. In the training stage, we force $\hat{Y}_v$ to approximate the true velocity $\widetilde{Y}_v = \frac{\partial Y}{\partial t}$, and the corresponding loss function is formulated as:

$$\mathcal{L}_{motion} = \left\| \hat{Y}_v - \widetilde{Y}_v \right\|_2 . \tag{12}$$

Synchronous Bi-directional Trajectory Generator. In order to alleviate the error accumulation in the trajectory prediction process, we devise a synchronous bi-directional trajectory generator, which consists of a goal predictor, a backward trajectory generator and a forward trajectory generator.

Goal predictor. The goal predictor aims to forecast the goal position of the trajectory based on the feature $\mathcal{X}_e$ and the latent vector z, which will be used to guide the backward trajectory generation as shown in Fig. 2. The loss of the goal predictor is defined as:

$$\mathcal{L}_{goal} = \left\| \hat{G} - \tilde{y}^{T_f+1} \right\|_2 . \tag{13}$$

Here, $\tilde{y}^{T_f+1}$ represents the next position after the endpoint of the target trajectory, which is approximately calculated as:

$$\tilde{y}^{T_f+1} \approx y^{T_f} + (y^{T_f} - y^{T_f-1}) . \tag{14}$$

Bi-directional trajectory generator. As depicted in Fig. 2, the two opposite prediction branches are synchronous at each timestep with a shared motion characteristic h_m^t $(t = 1, ..., T)$. The GRU is adopted as the basic model of two opposite trajectory generators. The current position x^0 and predicted goal $\hat{G}$ act as the initial states for the forward and backward branches, respectively. The procedure of the forward prediction is formulated as:

$$h_f^t = GRU(h_m^t, FC(\hat{y}_f^{t-1}; \Theta_f) , $$
$$\hat{y}_f^t = FC(h_f^t; \Theta_f') , \tag{15}$$

while the procedure of the backward prediction is

$$h_b^t = GRU(h_m^t, FC(\hat{y}_b^{t+1}; \Theta_b)) \,,$$
$$\hat{y}_b^t = FC(h_b^t; \Theta_b') \,,$$

$$(16)$$

Here, $t = 1, ..., T_f$; $\Theta_f, \Theta_f', \Theta_b, \Theta_b'$ are learnable parameters; h_f^t, h_b^t represent the hidden states, and $\hat{y}_f^t, \hat{y}_b^t$ denote the predicted positions at timestep t by the forward generator and the backward generator, respectively.

As illustrated in Fig. 2, the motion characteristic h_m^t plays as a shared feature, which is used to predict the position $\hat{y}_b^t$ based on the position at $t + 1$ in the backward branch while participating in the prediction of $\hat{y}_f^t$ with the input of $\hat{y}_f^{t-1}$ in the forward branch. This design lets the two opposite prediction branches mutually constrained from each other, thus preventing the error accumulation. For instance, as for the prediction of $\hat{y}_b^1$, the output of the backward generator not only relies on the previous state $\hat{y}_b^2$, but also the shared motion feature h_m^1, which is constrained by the forward generator.

Denote $\hat{Y}_f = [\hat{y}_f^1, \hat{y}_f^2, ..., \hat{y}_f^{T_f}]$ and $\hat{Y}_b = [\hat{y}_b^1, \hat{y}_b^2, ..., \hat{y}_b^{T_f}]$ as the predicted trajectory by the forward and backward trajectory generators, respectively. The loss of our synchronous bi-directional trajectory generator is defined as:

$$\mathcal{L}_{traj} = \alpha_1 \left\| \hat{Y}_f - Y \right\|_2 + \alpha_2 \left\| \hat{Y}_b - Y \right\|_2 \,,$$

$$(17)$$

where α_1 and α_2 are two hyper-parameters used to balance two prediction branches.

3.4   Error Compensation Network

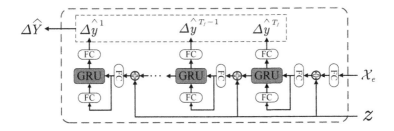

Fig. 3. The structure of the error compensation network.

Despite that our synchronous bi-directional framework can effectively prevent the error accumulation in the sequentially prediction process. However, due to the complex multi-modality property inherent to human motion behaviors, there may still exist prediction deviations for some certain contexts. In order to further reduce the possible prediction error at each time-step, we introduce an error compensation network, which aims to compensate for the spatial deviations between the ground-truth trajectory and the predicted one based on the current context.

As shown in Fig. 3, with the context of the spatial-temporal feature $\mathcal{X}_e$ and the latent vector z, the error compensation network predicts a compensation value for the target pedestrian at each timestep, which is formulated as:

$$r_e^{t+1} = FC(h_e^{t+1} \oplus z; \Theta_e) , \tag{18}$$

$$h_e^t = GRU\left(r_e^{t+1}, FC(r_e^{t+1}; \Theta_e^{in})\right) , \tag{19}$$

$$\Delta \hat{y}^t = FC(h_e^t; \Theta_e^{out})) , \tag{20}$$

where $t = 1, ..., T_f$, and the initial hidden state $h_e^{T_f+1}$ is generated by a FC based on the spatial-temporal feature $\mathcal{X}_e$. Besides, $\Theta_e, \Theta_e^{in}, \Theta_e^{out}$ are parameters, and $\Delta \hat{y}^t$ represents the compensation value at the timestep t. Letting $\Delta \hat{Y} = [\Delta \hat{y}^1, \Delta \hat{y}^2, ..., \Delta \hat{y}^{T_f}]$ be the predicted compensation value, we take the $\hat{Y}_b + \Delta \hat{Y}$ as the final predicted trajectory. The loss of error compensation network can be written as:

$$\mathcal{L}_{error} = \left\|\hat{Y}_b + \Delta \hat{Y} - Y\right\|_2 . \tag{21}$$

Finally, SBD is trained end-to-end by minimizing the following loss function:

$$\mathcal{L} = \beta_1 \mathcal{L}_{goal} + \beta_2 \mathcal{L}_{traj} + \beta_3 \mathcal{L}_{error} + \beta_4 \mathcal{L}_{motion} + \beta_5 \mathcal{L}_{elbo} , \tag{22}$$

where the $\beta_1, \beta_2, \beta_3, \beta_4$ and β_5 are used to balance different terms.

4   Experiments

In this section, we evaluate the performance of our proposed SBD, which is implemented using the PyTorch framework. All the experiments are conducted on a desktop equipped with an NVIDIA RTX 3090 GPU.

4.1   Experimental Setup

Datasets. We evaluate our method on two public trajectories datasets: the Stanford Drones Dataset (SDD) [32] and ETH-UCY [8,33].

SDD is a well established benchmark for pedestrian trajectory prediction in bird's eye view. The dataset consists of 20 scenes containing several moving agents and the coordinates of trajectory is recorded at 2.5 Hz in pixel coordinate system in pixels.

ETH-UCY contains of five sub-datasets: ETH, HOTEL, UNIV, ZARA1 and ZARA2. All the pedestrian trajectory data in these datasets are captured by fixed surveillance cameras at 2.5 Hz and recorded in world-coordinates.

Evaluation Metric. For the sake of fairness, we use the standard history-future split, which segment the first 3.2 s (8 frames) of a trajectory as historical trajectory to predict the next 4.8 s (12 frames) future trajectory. For the ETH-UCY, we follow the leave-one-out strategy [14] with 4 scenes for training and the remaining one for testing. Following prior works [8,14,22], we adopt the two widely-used error metrics to evaluate the performance of different pedestrian trajectory prediction models, including: 1) Average Displacement Error (ADE): The average Euclidean distance between the ground-truth trajectory and the predicted one; and 2) Final Displacement Error (FDE): The Euclidean distance between the endpoints of the ground-truth trajectory and the predicted one. To be consistent with previous works [9,15,23], we adopt the best-of-K (K = 20) strategy to compute the final ADE and FDE.

Implementation Details. In our experiments, the embedding dimension d_{te} and d_{se} in encoder are set to 256 and 32, respectively. The dimension of hidden dimensions in the temporal motion extractor, synchronous bi-directional decoder and error compensation network are 256. The length of the latent vector is 32. Besides, the number of prior nets and posterior nets in encoder is 20. We employ the Adam optimizer [34] to train model and use cosine annealing schedule as in [35] to adjust the learning rate. Beside, we train the entire network with the following hyper-parameter settings: initial learning rate of 10^{-3}, batch size is 128, α_1, α_2 in (17) are 0.2, 0.4, the β_1, β_2, β_3, β_4, β_5 in (21) are 3, 1, 0.6, 0.4, 0.1, and the number of epochs is 100.

4.2   Quantitative Evaluation

We compare our SBD with several generative baselines, including the GAN based methods [15,25,36–38], GCN based methods [19,21], TransFormer based methods [9,10], CVAE based methods [11,12,26], and other generative methods [23,29,39–41].

Performance on Standard Trajectory Prediction. Table 1 reports the results of our SBD and existing methods [15,25,26,29,39–41] on SDD. We observe that our method significantly outperforms all the competitive approaches under standard 20 samplings. Specifically, our method reduces the ADE from 8.59 to 7.78 compare to the previous state-of-the-art-20-samplings method, i.e., SIT [29], achieving 9.4% relative improvement. As for FDE metric, SBD is better than Y-Net with 20 samplings by 18.1%. Besides, compared with the method Y-Net [41]+Test Time Sampling Trick (TTST) with 10000 sampling, our method still achieves performance gains on the ADE metric. Notice that our method does not use any scene context, while Y-Net models the additional image information and thus suffers from huge computational costs.

   In Table 2, we summarize the results of SBD and existing methods [9–12,15, 19,21,23,26,29,36–38,41] on ETH-UCY. We can still observe that our method achieves the best or second best rank for each dataset. Besides, the proposed

Table 1. Comparison with different methods on the SDD (Lower is better). † indicates that the results are reproduced by [42] with the official released code. The values highlighted by red and blue represent the best and second best results, respectively.

Methods	SGAN	Goal-GAN	PECNet	LB-EBM	PCCSNET	Y-net†	Y-Net+TTST	SIT	SBD
Samping	20	20	20	20	20	20	10000	20	20
ADE	27.23	12.2	9.96	8.87	8.62	8.97	7.85	8.59	7.78
FDE	41.44	22.1	15.88	15.61	16.16	14.61	11.85	15.27	11.97

Table 2. Comparison with baselines on the ETH-UCY (Lower is better). The values highlighted by red and blue represent the best and second best results, respectively.

Method	Sampling	ETH	HOTEL	UNIV	ZARA1	ZARA2	AVG
SGAN	20	0.81/1.52	0.72/1.61	0.60/1.26	0.34/0.69	0.42/0.84	0.58/1.18
STGAT	20	0.65/1.12	0.35/0.66	0.52/1.10	0.34/0.69	0.29/0.60	0.43/0.83
Social-STGCNN	20	0.64/1.11	0.49/0.85	0.44/0.79	0.34/0.53	0.30/0.48	0.44/0.75
PECNet	20	0.54/0.87	0.18/0.24	0.35/0.60	0.22/0.39	0.17/0.30	0.29/0.48
STAR	20	0.36/0.65	0.17/0.36	0.31/0.62	0.26/0.55	0.22/0.46	0.26/0.53
Trajectron++	20	0.39/0.83	0.12/0.21	0.20/0.44	0.15/0.33	0.11/0.25	0.19/0.41
TPNMS	20	0.52/0.89	0.22/0.39	0.55/1.13	0.35/0.70	0.27/0.56	0.38/0.73
SGCN	20	0.63/1.03	0.32/0.55	0.37/0.70	0.29/0.53	0.25/0.45	0.37/0.65
STSF-Net	20	0.63/1.13	0.24/0.43	0.28/0.52	0.23/0.45	0.21/0.41	0.32/0.59
AgentFormer	20	0.45/0.75	0.14/0.22	0.25/0.45	0.18/0.30	0.14/0.24	0.23/0.39
BiTraP-NP	20	0.37/0.69	0.12/0.21	0.17/0.37	0.13/0.29	0.10/0.21	0.18/0.35
Y-Net+TTST	10000	0.28/0.33	0.10/0.14	0.24/0.41	0.17/0.27	0.13/0.22	0.18/0.27
CAGN	20	0.41/0.65	0.13/0.23	0.32/0.54	0.21/0.38	0.16/0.33	0.25/0.43
SIT	20	0.39/0.61	0.13/0.22	0.29/0.49	0.19/0.31	0.15/0.29	0.23/0.38
SBD	20	0.32/0.54	0.10/0.17	0.15/0.32	0.12/0.25	0.09/0.18	0.16/0.29

method outperforms competitive methods in terms of the average ADE and FDE under standard 20 samplings. Compared with the previous state-of-the-art-20-samplings method, i.e., BiTraP-NP [12], our algorithm achieves 11.1% and 17.1% relative improvements in terms of the average ADE and FDE.

Performance on Long-Term Trajectory Prediction. In order to further demonstrate the effectiveness of our scheme in alleviating the problem of error accumulation, we conduct additional experiments for the long-term trajectory prediction on ETH-UCY. Following the setting in [29], we keep the observed trajectory for 3.2 s (8 frames) and set the longer future trajectory to 6.4 s (16 frames), 8.0 s (20 frames) and 9.6 s (24 frames), respectively. As shown in Table 3, our method outperforms all baselines on all long-term prediction lengths by a big margin. For example, when the prediction horizon is extended to 9.6 s, our SBD is better than the second best rank method BiTraP-NP [12] by 26.9% in ADE, which is significant. The reason behind is that our framework benefits from the synchronous bi-directional prediction via mutual constraints from two opposite branches, endowing it capability to alleviate error accumulation in long-term trajectory prediction.

Table 3. Long-term prediction results on ETH-UCY in ADE/FDE. ‡ denotes that the results are from [29]. † represents that the results are reproduced with the official released code.

	T=16	T=20	T=24
	ADE/FDE	ADE/FDE	ADE/FDE
SGAN‡	2.16/3.96	2.40/4.52	2.79/4.66
PECNet‡	2.89/2.63	3.02/2.55	3.16/2.53
Social-STGCNN‡	0.54/1.05	0.71/1.30	0.92/1.76
BiTraP-NP†	0.29/0.57	0.38/0.74	0.52/1.07
SIT	0.49/1.01	0.55/1.12	0.68/1.22
SBD	0.22/0.41	0.30/0.54	0.38/0.71

Table 4. Ablation study of each component on the SDD dataset in ADE/FDE.

	SD	viBD	sBD	ECN	ADE	FDE
Group-1	✓	×	×	×	8.71	13.13
Group-2	×	✓	×	×	8.77	12.94
Group-3	×	×	✓	×	8.06	12.45
Group-4	×	×	✓	✓	7.78	11.97

4.3 Ablation Studies

In this subsection, we perform ablation experiments to explore the contribution of each component of our method. The results are detailed in Table 4. The "SD" denotes that model uses the single directional generator (backward trajectory generator) as the prediction module. The "viBD" indicates that using the vanilla independent bi-directional trajectory generator. The "sBD" represents the proposed synchronous bi-directional prediction based on a share motion characteristic. The "ECN" denotes the error compensation network. According to the results of group-1 and group-2 in Table 4, we observe that vanilla independent bi-directional prediction cannot effectively alleviate the error accumulation and improve pedestrian prediction. The results of group-1, group-2 and group-3 in Table 4 show that the proposed mutually constrained simultaneous bi-directional prediction by the synchronous bi-directional decoder could effectively alleviate the limitation of error accumulation and improve pedestrian prediction. Besides, the error compensation network can further reduce the positional deviation between the ground-truth and predicted trajectory as shown in group-3 and group-4 in Table 4.

4.4 Qualitative Evaluation

We conclude this section by conducting the qualitative comparisons. Due to the page limit, we only compare with the recent BiTraP-NP method [12], which also adopts a (sequential) bi-directional prediction. As shown in Fig. 4, we visualize

ETH	HOTEL	UNIV	ZARA

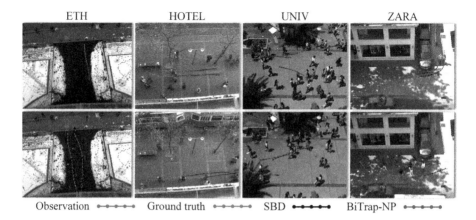

Observation •—•—•—•   Ground truth •—•—•—•   SBD •—•—•—•   BiTrap-NP •—•—•—•

Fig. 4. Visualization of predicted trajectories on the ETH-UCY Dataset by our SBD and BiTrap-NP [12]. The best one of the 20 generated trajectories are plotted.

the best-of-20 predicted trajectories of our SBD and BiTraP-NP in different real traffic scenes on the ETH-UCY datasets. We observe that our method is able to accurately predict the future trajectory in various traffic scenes. For example, the visualization results of the first row in Fig. 4 show that BiTraP-NP performs similar to SBD for short-term prediction yet a little deviates from the ground truth paths over time, and our SBD still exhibits better performance in longer prediction.

5   Conclusion

In this paper, we propose a synchronous bi-directional framework (SBD) with error compensation for pedestrian trajectory prediction. Our method performs the mutually constrained synchronous bi-directional prediction based on a shared motion characteristic, which can greatly alleviate the problem of error accumulation. Besides, we have introduced an error compensation network to reduce the spatial deviation for certain contexts in the predicted trajectory, further improving the prediction accuracy. Experimental results are provided to demonstrate the superiority of our method on Stanford Drone Dataset and ETH-UCY. Furthermore, we have also shown that our method with alleviating error accumulation performs significantly better than existing algorithms for long-term pedestrian trajectory prediction.

Acknowledgements. This work was supported in part by the Natural Science Foundation of China under Grant 62001304, Grant 61871273, Grant 61901237 and Grant 62171244; in part by the Foundation for Science and Technology Innovation of Shenzhen under Grant RCBS20210609103708014, the Guangdong Basic and Applied Basic Research Foundation under Grant 2022A1515010645 and the Shenzhen College Stability Support Plan (Key Project).

References

1. Liang, J., Jiang, L., Niebles, J.C., Hauptmann, A.G., Fei-Fei, L.: Peeking into the future: predicting future person activities and locations in videos. In: Proceedings of the IEEE Conference on Computer Vision and Pattern Recognition, pp. 5725–5734 (2019)
2. Luo, Y., Cai, P., Bera, A., Hsu, D., Lee, W.S., Manocha, D.: PORCA: modeling and planning for autonomous driving among many pedestrians. IEEE Robot. Autom. Lett. **3**(4), 3418–3425 (2018)
3. Luber, M., Stork, J.A., Tipaldi, G.D., Arras, K.O.: People tracking with human motion predictions from social forces. In: Proceedings of the IEEE International Conference on Robotics and Automation, pp. 464–469 (2010)
4. Bastani, V., Marcenaro, L., Regazzoni, C.S.: Online nonparametric bayesian activity mining and analysis from surveillance video. IEEE Trans. Image Process. **25**(5), 2089–2102 (2016)
5. Helbing, D., Molnar, P.: Social force model for pedestrian dynamics. Phys. Rev. E **51**(5), 4282 (1995)
6. Tay, M.K.C., Laugier, C.: Modelling smooth paths using gaussian processes. In: Proceedings of the International Conference on Field and Service Robotics, pp. 381–390 (2008)
7. Treuille, A., Cooper, S., Popović, Z.: Continuum crowds. ACM Trans. Graph. (TOG) **25**(3), 1160–1168 (2006)
8. Pellegrini, S., Ess, A., Schindler, K., Van Gool, L.: You'll never walk alone: modeling social behavior for multi-target tracking. In: Proceedings of the IEEE International Conference on Computer Vision, pp. 261–268 (2009)
9. Yuan, Y., Weng, X., Ou, Y., Kitani, K.M.: AgentFormer: agent-aware transformers for socio-temporal multi-agent forecasting. In: Proceedings of the IEEE International Conference on Computer Vision, pp. 9813–9823 (2021)
10. Yu, C., Ma, X., Ren, J., Zhao, H., Yi, S.: Spatio-temporal graph transformer networks for pedestrian trajectory prediction. In: Proceedings of the European Conference on Computer Vision, pp. 507–523 (2020)
11. Salzmann, T., Ivanovic, B., Chakravarty, P., Pavone, M.: Trajectron++: dynamically-feasible trajectory forecasting with heterogeneous data. In: Proceedings of the European Conference on Computer Vision, pp. 683–700 (2020)
12. Yao, Y., Atkins, E., Johnson-Roberson, M., Vasudevan, R., Du, X.: BiTraP: Bidirectional pedestrian trajectory prediction with multi-modal goal estimation. IEEE Robot. Autom. Lett. **6**(2), 1463–1470 (2021)
13. Li, Y., Liang, R., Wei, W., Wang, W., Zhou, J., Li, X.: Temporal pyramid network with spatial-temporal attention for pedestrian trajectory prediction. IEEE Trans. Netw. Sci. Eng. **9**, 1006–1019 (2021)
14. Alahi, A., Goel, K., Ramanathan, V., Robicquet, A., Fei-Fei, L., Savarese, S.: Social LSTM: human trajectory prediction in crowded spaces. In: Proceedings of the IEEE Conference on Computer Vision and Pattern Recognition, pp. 961–971 (2016)
15. Gupta, A., Johnson, J., Fei-Fei, L., Savarese, S., Alahi, A.: Social GAN: socially acceptable trajectories with generative adversarial networks. In: Proceedings of the IEEE Conference on Computer Vision and Pattern Recognition, pp. 2255–2264 (2018)
16. Fragkiadaki, K., Levine, S., Felsen, P., Malik, J.: Recurrent network models for human dynamics. In: Proceedings of the IEEE International Conference on Computer Vision, pp. 4346–4354 (2015)

17. Zhang, P., Ouyang, W., Zhang, P., Xue, J., Zheng, N.: SR-LSTM: state refinement for LSTM towards pedestrian trajectory prediction. In: Proceedings of the IEEE Conference on Computer Vision and Pattern Recognition, pp. 12085–12094 (2019)
18. Kipf, T.N., Welling, M.: Semi-supervised classification with graph convolutional networks. arXiv preprint arXiv:1609.02907 (2016)
19. Mohamed, A., Qian, K., Elhoseiny, M., Claudel, C.: Social-STGCNN: a social spatio-temporal graph convolutional neural network for human trajectory prediction. In: Proceedings of the IEEE Conference on Computer Vision and Pattern Recognition, pp. 14424–14432 (2020)
20. Kosaraju, V., Sadeghian, A., Martín-Martín, R., Reid, I., Rezatofighi, H., Savarese, S.: Social-BiGAT: multimodal trajectory forecasting using bicycle-GAN and graph attention networks. In: Proceedings of the Advances in Neural Information Processing Systems. **32** (2019)
21. Shi, L., et al.: SGCN: sparse graph convolution network for pedestrian trajectory prediction. In: Proceedings of the IEEE Conference on Computer Vision and Pattern Recognition, pp. 8994–9003 (2021)
22. Su, Y., et al.: Trajectory forecasting based on prior-aware directed graph convolutional neural network. IEEE Trans. Intell. Transp. Syst. **23**, 16773–16785 (2022)
23. Duan, J., et al.: Complementary attention gated network for pedestrian trajectory prediction (2022)
24. Sadeghian, A., Kosaraju, V., Sadeghian, A., Hirose, N., Rezatofighi, H., Savarese, S.: SoPhie: an attentive GAN for predicting paths compliant to social and physical constraints. In: Proceedings of the IEEE Conference on Computer Vision and Pattern Recognition, pp. 1349–1358 (2019)
25. Dendorfer, P., Osep, A., Leal-Taixé, L.: Goal-GAN: multimodal trajectory prediction based on goal position estimation. In: Proceedings of the Asian Conference on Computer Vision (2020)
26. Mangalam, K., et al.: It is not the journey but the destination: endpoint conditioned trajectory prediction. In: Proceedings of the European Conference on Computer Vision, pp. 759–776 (2020)
27. Chen, G., Li, J., Zhou, N., Ren, L., Lu, J.: Personalized trajectory prediction via distribution discrimination. In: Proceedings of the IEEE International Conference on Computer Vision, pp. 15580–15589 (2021)
28. Wang, C., Wang, Y., Xu, M., Crandall, D.: Stepwise goal-driven networks for trajectory prediction. IEEE Robot. Autom. Lett. **7**, 2716–2723 (2022)
29. Shi, L., et al.: Social interpretable tree for pedestrian trajectory prediction (2022)
30. Vaswani, A., et al.: Attention is all you need. In: Proceedings of the Advances in Neural Information Processing Systems, pp. 5998–6008 (2017)
31. Kingma, D.P., Welling, M.: Auto-encoding variational bayes. arXiv preprint arXiv:1312.6114 (2013)
32. Robicquet, A., Sadeghian, A., Alahi, A., Savarese, S.: Learning social etiquette: human trajectory understanding in crowded scenes. In: Proceedings of the European Conference on Computer Vision, pp. 549–565 (2016)
33. Lerner, A., Chrysanthou, Y., Lischinski, D.: Crowds by example. Comput. Graph. Forum **26**, 655–664 (2007)
34. Kingma, D.P., Ba, J.: Adam: a method for stochastic optimization. arXiv preprint arXiv:1412.6980 (2014)
35. Loshchilov, I., Hutter, F.: SGDR: stochastic gradient descent with warm restarts. arXiv preprint arXiv:1608.03983 (2016)

36. Huang, Y., Bi, H., Li, Z., Mao, T., Wang, Z.: STGAT: modeling spatial-temporal interactions for human trajectory prediction. In: Proceedings of the IEEE International Conference on Computer Vision, pp. 6272–6281 (2019)
37. Liang, R., Li, Y., Li, X., Tang, Y., Zhou, J., Zou, W.: Temporal pyramid network for pedestrian trajectory prediction with multi-supervision. In: Proceedings of the AAAI Conference on Artificial Intelligence. vol. 35, pp. 2029–2037 (2021)
38. Wang, Y., Chen, S.: Multi-agent trajectory prediction with spatio-temporal sequence fusion. IEEE Trans. Multimedia **25**, 13–23 (2021)
39. Pang, B., Zhao, T., Xie, X., Wu, Y.N.: Trajectory prediction with latent belief energy-based model. In: Proceedings of the IEEE Conference on Computer Vision and Pattern Recognition, pp. 11814–11824 (2021)
40. Sun, J., Li, Y., Fang, H.S., Lu, C.: Three steps to multimodal trajectory prediction: Modality clustering, classification and synthesis. In: Proceedings of the IEEE International Conference on Computer Vision, pp. 13250–13259 (2021)
41. Mangalam, K., An, Y., Girase, H., Malik, J.: From goals, waypoints & paths to long term human trajectory forecasting. In: Proceedings of the IEEE International Conference on Computer Vision, pp. 15233–15242 (2021)
42. Gu, T., et al.: Stochastic trajectory prediction via motion indeterminacy diffusion. In: Proceedings of the IEEE Conference on Computer Vision and Pattern Recognition, pp. 17113–17122 (2022)

Image Retrieval with Well-Separated Semantic Hash Centers

Liangdao Wang, Yan Pan$^{(\boxtimes)}$, Hanjiang Lai, and Jian Yin

School of Computer Science and Engineering, Sun Yat-sen University, Guangzhou, China
wangld5@mail2.sysu.edu.cn

Abstract. Recently, some point-wise hash learning methods such as CSQ and DPN adapted "hash centers" as the global similarity label for each category and force the hash codes of the images with the same category to get closed to their corresponding hash centers. Although they outperformed other pairwise/triplet hashing methods, they assign hash centers to each class randomly and result in a sub-optimal performance because of ignoring the semantic relationship between categories, which means that they ignore the fact that the Hamming distance between the hash centers corresponding to two semantically similar classes should be smaller than the Hamming distance between the hash centers corresponding to two semantically dissimilar classes. To solve the above problem and generate well-separated and semantic hash centers, in this paper, we propose an optimization approach which aims at generating hash centers not only with semantic category information but also distinguished from each other. Specifically, we adopt the weight of last fully-connected layer in ResNet-50 model as category features to help inject semantic information into the generation of hash centers and try to maximize the expectation of the Hamming distance between each two hash centers. With the hash centers corresponding to each image category, we propose two effective loss functions to learn deep hashing function. Importantly, extensive experiments show that our proposed hash centers and training method outperform the state-of-the-art hash models on three image retrieval datasets.

Keywords: Hash centers · Semantic category information · Image retrieval

1 Introduction

Image hashing method is popular in the field of image retrieval for its highly efficient storage ability and retrieval speed with the objective of representing an image using a binary code. Recently, depending on the development of the deep convolution neural network, deep hashing methods have great improvement in

Supplementary Information The online version contains supplementary material available at https://doi.org/10.1007/978-3-031-26351-4_43.

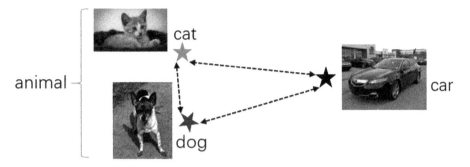

Fig. 1. an example to show that the Hamming distance between cat and dog should be smaller than that between not only dog and car, but also cat and car, because cat and dog are both animal.

terms of learning non-linear hash functions which encode tight hash codes for similar image pairs while encoding hash codes with a large Hamming distance for dissimilar image pairs.

Deep hashing methods can be grouped by how the similarity of the learned hashing codes are measured, namely point-wise hashing methods (e.g., [4,20,26, 27,30]), pairwise/triplet hashing methods (e.g., [2,11,22,24]) and listwise hashing methods [28]. Among them, pairwise/triplet hashing methods randomly sample a mini-batch training sample to learn hashing function with pairwise/triplet similarity between these training samples which suffer from three questions: low efficiency in profiling global similarity of the whole dataset, insufficient coverage of data distribution, and low effectiveness on imbalanced data. To solve these issues, some point-wise methods propose to learn hash codes for images with hash centers, by forcing the hash codes of images belonging to the same class to be as similar as the hash centers of their class.

In deep hashing methods with hash centers, we consider that there are two main challenges for learning a good hash function: 1) Firstly, it is important to construct a set of hash centers separated from each other. 2) Secondly, the assignment of hash centers for each class should not be ignored. To solve the above challenges, DPN [4] uses Bernoulli sampling to generate hash centers. CSQ [27] leverages Hadamard matrix and Bernoulli sampling to construct hash centers, considering that Hadamard matrix has a nice property that every two rows are mutually orthogonal. However, both of them choose to assign the generated hash centers randomly to each class, ignoring the fact that the Hamming distance between hash centers corresponding to two categories with similar semantic information should be smaller than that between hash centers corresponding to two categories with irrelevant semantic information. For example, as can be seen in Fig. 1, the similarity between dogs and cats should be greater than that between not only dogs and cars, but also cats and cars, because cats and dogs are both animals, but the other two pairs do not belong to the same species. The neglect of semantic relation information between categories makes them get sub-optimal performance.

To address both challenges, we propose a novel deep hashing method that employs an optimization procedure with two optimization targets. The first optimization target is to make the expectation of the Hamming distance between each two hash centers as large as possible to address the first challenge. In terms of the second optimization target, we introduce a variable called category feature that contains semantic information of category and makes the inner product between two hash centers should be close to the inner product between their corresponding category features to address the second challenge, which means that the similarity between two hash centers should be closed to that between their corresponding category features.

Our deep hashing method includes a two-stage pipeline. In the first stage, inspired by the existing retrieval/segmentation method [15, 29], we use the weight of last fully-connected layer in fine-tuned ResNet-50 model as the category features and solve the above optimization problem to obtain the semantic preserved and separated hash centers for each image class. To solve the NP-hard optimization issue, we develop an alternating optimization procedure based on the ℓ_p-box binary optimization scheme. In the second stage, with the constructed hash centers corresponding to each class, we train a deep neural network to learn the hashing function. Specifically, we define loss functions to encourage that (1) the hash code of an input image is nearby the hash center of its class but distanced from other hash centers and (2) quantization errors between continuous code and hash code are minimized during training.

To evaluate our proposed method, we experiment on three image datasets for image retrieval. The results demonstrate that the generated hash centers contain category semantic information of their corresponding class and are separated from each other. The proposed method achieves superior retrieval performance over the state-of-the-art deep hashing methods. The code is relased in https://github.com/Wangld5/SHC-IR

2   Related Work

The traditional hashing methods use hand-craft image features and shallow hash functions to learn hash codes for each input image. For example, SDH [18] presents an SVM-like formulation to minimize the quantization loss and the classification loss to learn hash function. SH [25] is a graph-based hashing method that learns hash function by spectral graph partitioning. Recently, deep hashing methods which learn hash codes for images by DNN have dominated the hashing research due to the superior learning ability of deep neural network and can be divided into point-wise hashing methods [4, 20, 26, 27, 30], pairwise/triplet hashing methods [2, 3, 11, 12, 14, 22, 24], and listwise hashing methods [28].

To keep the similarity structure of data, pairwise/triplet hashing methods learn hash function by forcing the similar pairs of images to have similar hash codes while dissimilar pairs of images to have dissimilar hash codes, or maintaining the consistency between the data triplets from the original and Hamming space. For example, CNNH [24] learn the hash function by forcing the similarity of the image pairs to that of their corresponding approximate binary code pairs.

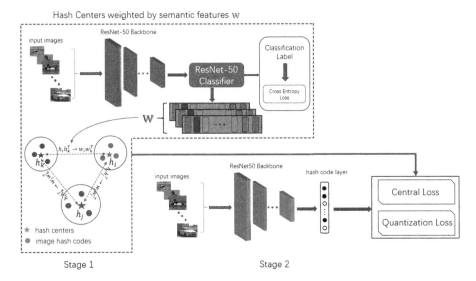

Fig. 2. Overview of the proposed method with a pipeline of two stages. Stage 1 (left) uses a carefully designed optimization procedure to generate hash centers containing semantic information with the help of category features w where each hash center corresponding to an image class and w is the weight of last fully-connected layer obtained from the fine-tuned ResNet-50 classification model. Stage 2 (**right**) uses a deep hashing network trained with two loss functions. The first loss encourages the hash code of an image to become close to its hash center and faraway from others. The second loss reduces quantization errors.

DPSH [12] adopts deep networks to learn hash function with the standard form of likelihood loss based on similarity information of the image pairs. HashNet [3] trains the hashing network by adopting maximum likelihood loss with different weights for each image pair.

To solve the three problems of pairwise/triplet hashing methods mentioned in Sect. 1. Point-wise hashing methods use a target as a guide to learn hash functions. On the one hand, some hashing methods use aware label information for each sample to guide the learning of the hash functions such as DLBHC [13], SSDH [26] and Greedy Hash [20]. On the other hand, some hashing methods generate binary codes called hash centers corresponding to each semantic class in Hamming space which are distinguished from each other and generate hash codes for input images with these separated hash centers as supervised information. For example, DPN [4] proposed to generate hash centers by Bernoulli sampling. CSQ [27] proposed to use Hadamard matrix and Bernoulli sampling to generate a set of hash centers, with the expectation that the average Hamming distance of all pairs of hash centers is half of the code length. However, both CSQ and DPN randomly allocate hash centers, ignoring the semantic relationship between their corresponding categories which may lead to inferior retrieval performance.

Inspired by some unsupervised hashing methods [9,32] using semantic information, in this work, we propose an optimization approach that generates hash centers under the guidance of semantic relationships between categories, which make the hash centers not only separated from each other but also contain semantic information.

3   Approach

For the deep hashing problem, given an input image x, hash learning aims to obtain a mapping function $f : x \rightarrow b \in \{-1,1\}^q$ that encodes the image to a binary hash code b with length q for the convenience of image retrieval, so that similar images or images belonging to the same class are mapping to similar hash codes with small Hamming distances. In deep hashing methods, f is a non-linear hashing function implemented by the deep hashing network.

As shown in Fig. 2, to achieve this goal, we propose a deep hashing method of two stages. In Stage 1, based on the initialization of hash centers with Hadamard Matrix, we propose an optimization method to optimize and generate the hash centers with semantic information to ensure that the Hamming distance between two hash centers is associated with the semantic similarity between their corresponding categories. More specifically, we try to decrease the root mean square error between the inner product of two hash centers and that of their corresponding category features in the optimization procedure to increase the semantic information of hash centers, each of which corresponds to one class, respectively. In Stage 2, we train a deep hashing network to learn f with two losses: 1) the central loss to force hash codes of the input images to not only get closed to their corresponding hash centers but also separate from other hash centers with long distance. 2) the quantization loss to decrease errors between continuous codes and binary codes. We present the details of each stage as follows.

3.1   Stage 1: Generate Hash Centers by Optimization

In this stage, we propose an optimization method to find a set of separated hash centers that contain semantic information, which adopts the category feature extracted from the pre-trained models to inject the semantic information into hash centers.

Optimization Target. For images in m classes, utilizing the category features $w_1, w_2, ..., w_m$, we try to learn m hash centers $c_1, c_2, ..., c_m$ by maximizing the following optimization target. To measure the similarity between a pair of hash centers and their corresponding category features, we simultaneously enforce the inner product of two hash centers closed to the inner product of their corresponding category features. Specifically, we formulate an optimization objective as:

$$\max_{c_1,...,c_m \in \{-1,1\}^q} \frac{1}{m(m-1)} \sum_i \sum_{j:j \neq i} (||c_i - c_j||_H - ||c_i^T c_j - w_i^T w_j||_2^2) \tag{1}$$

where $||.||_H$ represents the Hamming distance, and $||.||_2$ be the ℓ_2 norm

For two hash centers $c_i, c_j \in \{-1, 1\}^q$, the Hamming distance between them can be transform to the inner product between c_i and c_j with the following equation:

$$||c_i - c_j||_H = \frac{1}{4}||c_i - c_j||_2^2 = \frac{1}{4}(c_i^T c_i + c_j^T c_j - 2c_i^T c_j) = \frac{1}{2}(q - c_i^T c_j) \quad (2)$$

where q is the constant hash code length. Therefore, maximizing $||c_i - c_j||_H$ is equivalent to minimizing $c_i^T c_j$ and the objective in Eq. (1) can be equivalent to:

$$\min_{c_1,\ldots,c_m \in \{-1,1\}^q} \sum_i \sum_{j:j\neq i} (c_i^T c_j + ||c_i^T c_j - w_i^T w_j||_2^2) \quad (3)$$

Obtaining the Category Feature w. For the objective in Eq. (1), we need to obtain the semantic category features w for their corresponding class so that the similarity between any two hash centers c_i, c_j of their corresponding classes get closed to the similarity of their corresponding semantic category feature w_i, w_j. To address this issue, inspired by the previous work [15,29], we compare three pre-trained models including VGG16 [19], ResNet50 [7], AlexNet [1] (the comparison results can be seen in supplementary material) and choose to fine-tune ResNet-50 pre-trained model on three experiment datasets with cross-entropy loss, and the weight of last fully-connected layer is considered as the category features for each class. However, the range of the inner product of two category features w_i, w_j can not be guaranteed to be the same as the inner product hash centers c_i, c_j which is $[-q, q]$. To solve the problem, we use linear transformation to transform the range of inner products of two category features into $[-q, q]$. Specifically, for two category features w_i, w_j corresponding to hash center c_i, c_j, the transformation formula of the inner product between w_i and w_j can be defined as:

$$w_i^T w_j = -q + 2q \frac{w_i^T w_j - min(w_i^T w_{\sim i})}{max(w_i^T w_{\sim i}) - min(w_i^T w_{\sim i})} \quad (4)$$

where $w_i^T w_j$ represents the inner product between $w_i.w_j$, and $w_{\sim i} = [w_1, ..., w_{i-1}, w_{i+1}, ..., w_m]$ represents the matrix that consists of $w_j(1 \leq j \leq m, j \neq i)$. The derivation process can be seen in the supplementary material.

Alternative Optimization Procedure. Since it is NP-hard to optimize the target in Eq. 3 for the binary constraint of hash centers. Alternatively, for each hash center c_i, we adopt an optimization procedure that updates c_i by fixing other centers c_j ($1 \leq j \leq m, j \neq i$).

Specifically, with all c_j ($j \neq i$) being fixed, the sub-problem for c_i can be formulated as:

$$\min_{c_i \in \{-1,1\}^q} \sum_{j:j\neq i} (c_i^T c_j + ||h_i^T h_j - w_i^T w_j||_2^2) \quad (5)$$

Inspired by the Proposition 1 in [23], we prove that the binary constraint $z \in \{-1, 1\}^q$ is equivalent to $z \in [-1, 1]^q \bigcap \{z : ||z||_p^p = q\}$ (The proof can be found in the supplementary material) and adopt the ℓ_p-box algorithm [23] to solve the subproblem in Eq. (5). For ease of optimization, hereafter we set $p = 2$.

With this fact, the binary constraint can be replaced and Eq. 5 can be equivalent to the following form:

$$
\min_{c_i, z_1, z_2} \sum_{j: j \neq i} (c_i^T c_j + ||h_i^T h_j - w_i^T w_j||_2^2)
$$

$$
\text{s.t. } c_i = z_1, \ c_i = z_2, z_1 \in \mathcal{S}_b, \ z_2 \in \mathcal{S}_p,
$$

(6)

where $\mathcal{S}_b = \{z : -1_q < z < 1_q\}$, $\mathcal{S}_p = \{z : ||z||_2^2 = q\}$, 1_q represents a q-dimensional vector with all ones. For ease of solution, the augmented Lagrange function of Eq. (6) is:

$$
L(c_i, z_1, z_2, y_1, y_2) = \sum_{j \neq i} (c_i^T c_j + ||c_i^T c_j - w_i^T w_j||_2^2) + y_1^T (c_i - z_1) + y_2^T (c_i - z_2)
$$

$$
+ \frac{\mu}{2} ||c_i - z_1||_2^2 + \frac{\mu}{2} ||c_i - z_2||_2^2 \qquad \text{s.t. } z_1 \in \mathcal{S}_b, z_2 \in \mathcal{S}_p,
$$

(7)

where y_1, y_2 are Lagrange multipliers.

Then we will perform the following update steps for c_i, z_1, z_2, y_1, y_2 through Alternating Direction Method of Multipliers(ADMM).

Update c_i. By fixing other variables except c_i, the sub-problem in Eq. 7 is an unconstrained convex function for c_i. The gradient of Eq. 7 for h_i is

$$
\frac{\partial L(c_i)}{\partial c_i} = 2\mu c_i + 2C_{\sim i} C_{\sim i}^T c_i + \sum_{j \neq i} c_j + y_1 + y_2 - \mu(z_1 + z_2) - 2(C_{\sim i} w_{\sim i}^T w_i).
$$

where $C_{\sim i} = [c_1, ..., c_{i-1}, c_{i+1}, ..., c_m]$ represents a matrix that consists of $c_j (1 \leq j \leq m, j \neq i)$. By setting this gradient to zero, we can update c_i by

$$
c_i \leftarrow (2\mu I_q + 2C_{\sim i} C_{\sim i}^T)^{-1} (\mu(z_1 + z_2) + 2(C_{\sim i} w_{\sim i}^T w_i) - \sum_{j \neq i} c_j - y_1 - y_2).
$$

(8)

Update z_1, z_2. The subproblem of L in Eq. (7) for z_1 and z_2 are

$$
\begin{cases} L(z_1) = y_1^T (c_i - z_1) + \frac{\mu}{2} ||c_i - z_1||_2^2 \ \ s.t. z_1 \in \mathcal{S}_b \\ L(z_2) = y_2^T (c_i - z_2) + \frac{\mu}{2} ||c_i - z_2||_2^2 \ \ s.t. z_2 \in \mathcal{S}_p \end{cases}
$$

(9)

We update z_1 and z_2 by setting the gradient of Eq. 9 to be zero:

$$
\begin{cases} z_1 \leftarrow P_{\mathcal{S}_b}(c_i + \frac{1}{\mu} y_1) \\ z_2 \leftarrow P_{\mathcal{S}_p}(c_i + \frac{1}{\mu} y_2) \end{cases}
$$

(10)

Algorithm 1. Hash Centers generation process

Input: $C = [c_1, ... c_m]$ initialized by Hadamard Matrix and Bernoulli sampling.
Initialize: learning rate $\rho = 1.03$, iteration number $T = 50$, $\mu_{max} = 10^{10}$, tolerance error $\epsilon = 10^{-6}$, $w_1, ..., w_m$ obtained from ResNet-50 model.

 1: **for** $t = 1, ..., T$ **do**
 2:     **for** $i = 1, ..., c$ **do**
 3:        initialize $z_1 = z_2 = c_i$, $y_1 = y_2 = 0_q$, $\mu = 10^6$
 4:        **repeat**
 5:           update c_i^t by Eq.8
 6:           project and update z_1^t, z_2^t on S_b, S_p with Eq.11
 7:           update y_1^t, y_2^t with gradient ascent by Eq.12
 8:           update $\mu = min(\rho\mu, \mu_{max})$
 9:        **until** $max(||c_i^t - z_1^t||_\infty, ||c_i^t - z_2^t||_\infty) \leq \epsilon$
10:     **end for**
11:     t=t+1, calculate L^t by Eq.3
12:     if the relative change $\frac{L^{t-1}-L^t}{L^{t-1}} \leq \epsilon$, then break
13: **end for**
Output: hash centers $C = [c_1, ..., c_m]$

Following [23], we project z_1 and z_2 onto their corresponding space S_b and S_p and use the following closed form solutions to update them:

$$\begin{cases} z_1 \leftarrow min(1, max(-1, c_i + \frac{1}{\mu}y_1)) \\ z_2 \leftarrow \sqrt{\mu q}\dfrac{c_i + y_2}{||c_i + y_2||_2} \end{cases} \tag{11}$$

Update y_1, y_2. We use the conventional gradient ascent to update y_1 and y_2:

$$\begin{cases} y_1 \leftarrow y_1 + \mu(c_i - z_1) \\ y_2 \leftarrow y_2 + \mu(c_i - z_2) \end{cases} \tag{12}$$

The sketch of the proposed optimization procedure is shown in Algorithm 1.

3.2 Stage 2: Train a Deep Hashing Network

As shown in the right part of Fig. 2, we build a deep hashing network to learn hash functions with the generated semantic hash centers as label information. The hashing network can be divided into two blocks.

The first block is a backbone consisting of multiple convolution layers based on ResNet-50 [7] following a hashing code layer consisting of a fully connected layer and *Tanh* activation function. The goal of the first block is to generate continuous codes $v \in [-1, 1]^q$ for each input image during the training process. In the testing process, each continuous code v will be converted to binary hash code $b \in \{-1, +1\}^q$ by quantization. Specifically, we define that the training set has m hash centers $c_1, c_2, ..., c_m$, N image $I_1, I_2, ..., I_N$ whose output continuous codes are $v_1, v_2, ..., v_N$, respectively.

The second block is a two-loss function served for the training of hashing network. One is to encourage the continuous codes of images belonging to the same class nearby their corresponding hash centers while separated from other hash centers with a high distance. While another is to reduce the quantization loss between continuous codes and binary hash codes. We will introduce the details of these losses, respectively.

Central Loss. With the obtained m hash centers from Stage 1, we assign the hash center to each image class according to the category weights w. We develop a loss function that forces the continuous code of an image to approach the hash center assigned to this image's class while being faraway from the hash centers of other categories. Specifically, for the image I_j, the loss function that measures the error between the continuous code v_j of I_j and its corresponding hash center c_i can be defined as:

$$L_{C,j,i} = -(\log P_{j,i} + \frac{1}{m-1} \sum_{k \neq i}^{m} \log(1 - N_{j,k})) \tag{13}$$

with

$$P_{j,i} = \frac{e^{-S(v_j,c_i)}}{\sum_{p=1}^{m} e^{-S(v_j,c_p)}}, N_{j,k} = \frac{e^{-S(v_j,c_k)}}{\sum_{p=1}^{m} e^{-S(v_j,c_p)}} \tag{14}$$

where $S(x,y)$ represents the similarity metric between x and y, $P_{j,i}$ represents the probability that the continuous code v_j of image I_j belongs to its corresponding hash center c_i while $N_{j,k}$ represents the probability that the continuous code v_j of image I_j belongs to other hash centers of different categories which should be reduced. Following the existing hashing methods [5,8], we use the scaled cosine similarity as the similarity metric, so $P_{j,i}$ in Eq. (14) can be reformulated as:

$$P_{j,i} = \frac{e^{\sqrt{q}\cos(v_j,c_i)}}{\sum_{p=1}^{m} e^{\sqrt{q}\cos(v_j,c_p)}}, N_{j,k} = \frac{e^{\sqrt{q}\cos(v_j,c_k)}}{\sum_{p=1}^{m} e^{\sqrt{q}\cos(v_j,c_p)}}, \tag{15}$$

where $\cos(x,y) = \frac{x^T y}{||x||_2 ||y||_2}$ represents the cosine similarity between the vectors x and y, $\sqrt{q}$ is the scale factor with q being the hash code length.

Quantization Loss. To make it easy to back propagate the gradient of the loss function, the continuous outputs of the deep hashing network are used as a relaxation of the binary hash codes during training. To reduce quantization error between binary hash codes and continuous outputs, similar to existing methods (e.g. [31]), the quantization loss of continuous code v_j is defined as:

$$L_{Q,j} = |||v_j| - 1_q||_1, \tag{16}$$

where $||.||_1$ is the ℓ_1 norm, 1_q represents a q-dimensional vector with all ones.

Table 1. Comparison in mAP of Hamming Ranking for different bits on image retrieval.

Method	ImageNet (mAP@1000)			NABirds (mAP@All)			Stanford Cars (mAP@All)		
	16 bits	32 bits	64 bits	16 bits	32 bits	64 bits	16 bits	32 bits	64 bits
SH [25]	0.1705	0.2997	0.4561	0.0107	0.0200	0.0312	0.0130	0.0160	0.0210
ITQ-CCA [6]	0.1907	0.3850	0.5325	0.0135	0.0270	0.0452	0.0163	0.0235	0.0323
SDH [18]	0.3416	0.4956	0.5990	0.0102	0.0225	0.0459	0.0161	0.0231	0.0298
DSH [14]	0.7179	0.7448	0.7585	0.0820	0.1011	0.2030	0.2153	0.3124	0.4309
DPSH [12]	0.6241	0.7626	0.7992	0.1171	0.1855	0.2811	0.1764	0.2949	0.4132
HashNet [3]	0.6024	0.7158	0.8071	0.0825	0.1439	0.2359	0.2637	0.3611	0.4845
GreedyHash [20]	0.7394	0.7977	0.8243	0.3519	0.5350	0.6117	0.7312	0.8271	0.8432
DPN [4]	0.7987	0.8298	0.8394	0.6151	0.6928	0.7244	0.7287	0.8214	0.8488
CSQ [27]	0.8377	0.8750	0.8836	0.6183	0.7210	0.7491	0.7435	0.8392	0.8634
OrthoHash [8]	0.8540	0.8792	0.8936	0.6366	0.7243	0.7544	0.8012	0.8490	0.8676
Ours	**0.8616**	**0.8851**	**0.8982**	**0.6693**	**0.7381**	**0.7599**	**0.8218**	**0.8569**	**0.8771**

Combination of Loss Functions. We combine the three loss functions to form the optimization objective used in the proposed deep hashing network.

$$L = \frac{1}{N} \sum_{j=1}^{N} L_{C,j,i} + \alpha \frac{1}{N} \sum_{j=1}^{N} L_{Q,j} \qquad (17)$$

where α are trade-off hyper-parameters.

4 Experiments

4.1 Experiment Settings

Three benchmark image dataset for image retrieval are used to conducted our experiments, including, ImageNet [17], NABirds [21] and Stanford Cars [10]. Following the same settings as in [3,27], the ImageNet dataset we used consists of 143,495 images for 100 classes, including 100 images for each class as training set, 50 images for each class as test queries, and the rest images as the retrieval database. For Stanford Cars containing 16,185 images in 196 classes and NABirds containing 48,562 images in 555 classes, the training set in the official train/test split is used as the training images and the retrieval database, the test set in the official train/test split as the test queries for retrieval. The identical training set, test set and retrieval database are applied to our method and all other comparison methods for a fair comparison.

We compare the performance of the proposed method with nine baselines, including six popular deep hashing methods OrthoHash [8], CSQ [27], DPN [4], Greedy Hash [20], HashNet [3], DPSH [12] and DSH [14], three conventional hashing methods SH [25], ITQ-CCA [6] and SDH [18]. For the three conventional hashing methods, we adopt the output of the last fully-connected layer in the pre-trained ResNet-50 model as the input features. For a fair comparison, the pre-trained ResNet-50 model is used as the backbone for all deep hashing methods.

Two widely-used evaluation metrics are used to evaluate the effectiveness of our method, including Mean Average Precision (MAP) and Precision-Recall curves. Following [3,27], we use MAP@1000 as the MAP metric on ImageNet because it contains a large-scale retrieval database. On NABirds and Stanford Cars, we use MAP@ALL as the MAP metric.

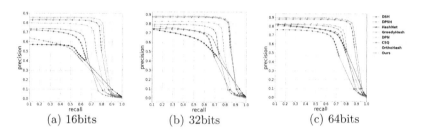

(a) 16bits   (b) 32bits   (c) 64bits

Fig. 3. Comparison results w.r.t. Precision-Recall curves on ImageNet

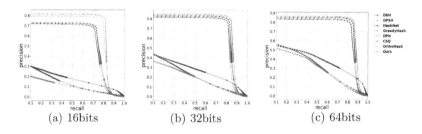

(a) 16bits   (b) 32bits   (c) 64bits

Fig. 4. Comparison results w.r.t. Precision-Recall curves on Stanford Cars

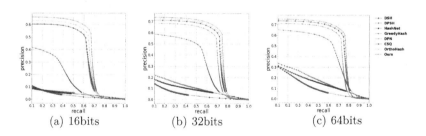

(a) 16bits   (b) 32bits   (c) 64bits

Fig. 5. Comparison results w.r.t. Precision-Recall curves on NABirds

4.2   Implementation Details

We implement our methods with Pytorch [16]. For all experiments, the optimizer of the deep hashing network in Stage 2 is RMSprop(root mean square prop) with the initial learning rate $lr = 10^{-5}$ and the batch size is set as 64. To determine the proper hyper-parameter α in the loss function, we randomly split the official training set into a validation set with 20% images and a sub-training set with the rest 80% images for each dataset. Then we determine α through the validation set after the model is trained on the sub-training set. Finally, we use the obtained α to train the model on the official training set. In the testing process, each image will be encoded into a hash code with $b = sign(v)$, where v is the output continuous code of our deep hashing network.

Table 2. Comparison results of the mean Hamming distance and minimum Hamming distance over all pairs of hash centers, for different ways to generate hash centers

Datasets	Methods	16bits		32bits		64bits	
		Min	Mean	Min	Mean	Min	Mean
ImageNet	DPN Centers	2	7.96	6	15.98	18	32.02
	CSQ Centers	2	8.04	6	16.11	32	32.23
	Ours Centers	3	8.08	10	16.15	32	32.23
Stanford Cars	DPN Centers	0	7.97	6	15.99	16	32.02
	CSQ Centers	0	8.01	6	16.03	16	32.10
	Ours Centers	3	8.05	9	16.08	22	32.15
NABirds	DPN Centers	0	7.96	4	15.95	12	31.98
	CSQ Centers	0	7.98	4	15.98	14	32.01
	Ours Centers	2	8.01	8	16.03	20	32.05

Table 3. Comparison results of the Mean Average Precision (MAP) for different ways to generate hash centers on three image datasets with the same settings of Stage 2

Datasets	Methods	16bits	32bit	64bits
ImageNet	DPN Center	0.8218	0.8501	0.8876
	CSQ Center	0.8498	0.8787	0.8982
	Ours Center	0.8616	0.8851	0.8982
Stanford Cars	DPN Center	0.7611	0.8378	0.8602
	CSQ Center	0.7790	0.8475	0.8681
	Ours Center	0.8218	0.8569	0.8771
NABirds	DPN Center	0.6309	0.7090	0.7448
	CSQ Center	0.6335	0.7136	0.7527
	Ours Center	0.6693	0.7381	0.7599

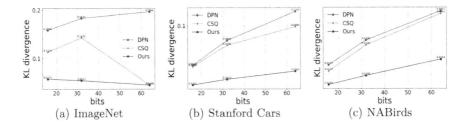

(a) ImageNet   (b) Stanford Cars   (c) NABirds

Fig. 6. The KL divergence of the distribution of similarity between hash centers relative to the distribution of similarity between category features on three experiment datasets with different length of hash centers

4.3 Results of Retrieval Accuracies

Table 1 shows the Mean Average Precision (MAP) results of retrieval performance on three datasets. On all of these datasets, the proposed method achieves superior retrieval accuracies against the baseline methods. For example, compared to the best baseline, the MAP results of the proposed method indicate a relative increase of **0.51%** ~**0.89%/1.1%** ~ **2.6%/0.73%** ~ **5.1%** on ImageNet/Stanford Cars/NABirds, respectively. Figure 3, Fig. 4, and Fig. 5 shows the retrieval performance in Precision-Recall curves (P-R curve) on three datasets. The comparison above shows that the well-separated hash centers with semantic information we generated can effectively improve the retrieval effect. Note that the proposed method makes large improvements when the number of image classes is large and the length of hash code is short. For example, when the hash code is 16-bits, on Stanford Cars with 196 classes or NABirds with 555 classes, the MAP results of the proposed method show a relative improvement of **2.6%** or **5.1%** compared to the best baseline OrthoHash, respectively. The reason may be that when the code length is short, previous methods will generate two hash centers with Hamming distance of 0 and contain no semantic information which make the performance to be sub-optimal. But, with the injection of semantic relevance, the proposed method not only generates well-separated hash centers but also contains semantic information.

4.4   Ablation Studies

Effectiveness of Hash Centers. The main contribution of this paper is the proposed optimization procedure to generate mutually separated hash centers with semantic information. To verify the effectiveness of the generated hash centers by the proposed method, we adopt two existing methods to generate hash centers as baselines. The two baselines to be compared are 1) center learning in CSQ, and 2) center learning in DPN. We train a deep hashing network with these hash centers by using the same settings as the proposed method in Stage 2. The only difference between these baselines and the proposed method lies in different ways to generate hash centers.

To explore how much category semantic relation information is contained in the hash centers generated by not only the proposed method but also baselines, we calculate the KL divergence of the distribution of similarity between hash centers relative to the distribution of similarity between category features, where the similarity between hash centers is expressed by the inner product of them, and so is the similarity between category features. The results in Fig. 6 shows that in most case, the KL divergence of the similarity distribution between hash centers generated by our method relative to the similarity distribution between category features is the smallest which means the hash centers generated by our method contains more category semantic relation information.

To explore how well the hash centers generated by different methods are separated from each other, we compare the average of the Hamming distance over all pairs of hash centers and the minimum Hamming distance between any two hash centers for both our method and two baselines. The results shown on Table 2 can be observed that (1) In most cases, the minimum Hamming distance of our method is larger than that of the two baselines, which indicates that the baselines can not generate well-separated hash centers in some cases. For example, the minimum Hamming distance between any two hash centers is 0 with 16 bits on both Stanford Cars and NABirds. (2) Compared to both the baselines, the hash centers generated by our methods have largest average Hamming distance. The comparison results show that our method can generate well-separated hash centers with the help of category features. As shown in Table 3, on all of the datasets, the proposed method outperforms the baseline with a clear gap, e.g.,

Table 4. Comparison results w.r.t. MAP for different combinations of loss functions

		ImageNet			Stanford CAR			NABirds		
L_C	L_Q	16bits	32bits	64bits	16bits	32bits	64bits	16bits	32bits	64bits
✓	✓	0.8616	0.8851	0.8982	0.8218	0.8569	0.8771	0.6693	0.7381	0.7599
✓		0.8572	0.8828	0.8958	0.8048	0.8531	0.8671	0.6526	0.7236	0.7539
CSQ-L_c		0.8543	0.8767	0.8836	0.7761	0.8481	0.8739	0.6429	0.7202	0.7464
DPN-L		0.8323	0.8573	0.8677	0.7643	0.8337	0.8503	0.6604	0.7093	0.7383

for 16-bit codes on NABirds and Stanford Cars. In summary, the ablation results in Fig. 6, Table 2 and 3 verify the hash centers obtained by our optimization approach, which not only contain category semantic information but also are well separated, can help to improve the retrieval performance.

Effectiveness of Loss Functions. To explore the individual effect of each part of the loss function, we evaluate different combinations of the central loss L_C and the quantization loss L_Q used in the proposed deep hashing network.

In Table 4, with identical hash centers and identical network architecture, we compare the MAP results of three methods. CSQ-L_C is a baseline that uses the loss L_C for hash centers proposed in CSQ [27]. DPN-L is a baseline that uses the central loss for hash centers proposed in DPN [4]. L_C represents only the central loss L_C used for experiments. Two observations can be seen from Table 4: (1) The method with the proposed central loss L_C outperforms both CSQ-L_C and DPN-L. Because we not only encourage hash codes to be close to their corresponding hash centers, but also to be far away from other hash centers. (2) The loss L_Q can also improve the retrieval performance, because we make the continuous codes get closed to the binary hash codes during training.

5   Conclusion

In this paper, we developed an optimization approach to generate well-separated hash centers with semantic information, where we adopt the weight of last fully-connected layer in fine-tuned ResNet-50 model as the category features and force the inner product between a pair of hash centers closed to the inner product between their corresponding category features. With these hash centers, each corresponding to one image class, we propose several effective loss functions to train deep hashing networks. Empirical evaluations in image retrieval show that the proposed method has superior performance gain over state-of-the-arts. In the future, we will continue to explore how to design an effective loss function that better matches the hash center to improve the effect of image retrieval.

Acknowledgements. This work was supported in part by the National Science Foundation of China under Grant U1811262, Grant 61772567.

References

1. Alex, K., Ilya, S., Hinton, G.E.: Imagenet classification with deep convolutional neural networks. In: Proceedings of the 25th International Conference on Neural Information Processing Systems (NIPS-12), pp. 1097–1105 (2012)
2. Cao, Y., Long, M., Liu, B., Wang, J.: Deep cauchy hashing for hamming space retrieval. In: Proceedings of the IEEE Conference on Computer Vision and Pattern Recognition (CVPR-18), pp. 1229–1237 (2018)
3. Cao, Z., Long, M., Wang, J., Yu, P.S.: HashNet: deep learning to hash by continuation. In: Proceedings of the IEEE International Conference on Computer Vision (ICCV-17), pp. 5608–5617 (2017)
4. Fan, L., Ng, K., Ju, C., Zhang, T., Chan, C.S.: Deep polarized network for supervised learning of accurate binary hashing codes. In: Proceedings of the Twenty-Ninth International Conference on International Joint Conferences on Artificial Intelligence (IJCAI-20), pp. 825–831 (2020)
5. Gong, Y., Kumar, S., Verma, V., Lazebnik, S.: Angular quantization-based binary codes for fast similarity search. In: Advances in Neural Information Processing Systems (NIPS-12), pp. 1196–1204 (2012)
6. Gong, Y., Lazebnik, S., Gordo, A., Perronnin, F.: Iterative quantization: a procrustean approach to learning binary codes for large-scale image retrieval. IEEE Trans. Pattern Anal. Mach. Intell. **35**(12), 2916–2929 (2013)
7. He, K., Zhang, X., Ren, S., Sun, J.: Deep residual learning for image recognition. In: Proceedings of the IEEE Conference on Computer Vision and Pattern Recognition (CVPR-16), pp. 770–778 (2016)
8. Hoe, J.T., Ng, K.W., Zhang, T., Chan, C.S., Song, Y.Z., Xiang, T.: One loss for all: deep hashing with a single cosine similarity based learning objective. In: Advances in Neural Information Processing Systems (NIPS-21) (2021)
9. Karaman, S., Lin, X., Hu, X., Chang, S.F.: Unsupervised rank-preserving hashing for large-scale image retrieval. In: Proceedings of the 2019 on International Conference on Multimedia Retrieval, pp. 192–196 (2019)
10. Krause, J., Stark, M., Deng, J., Fei-Fei, L.: 3D object representations for fine-grained categorization. In: Proceedings of the IEEE International Conference on Computer Vision Workshops (ICCV-13), pp. 554–561 (2013)
11. Li, Q., Sun, Z., He, R., Tan, T.: Deep supervised discrete hashing. In: Advances in Neural Information Processing Systems (NIPS-17), pp. 2479–2488 (2017)
12. Li, W., Wang, S., Kang, W.: Feature learning based deep supervised hashing with pairwise labels. In: Proceedings of the Twenty-Fifth International Joint Conference on Artificial Intelligence (IJCAI-16), pp. 1711–1717 (2016)
13. Lin, K., Yang, H.F., Hsiao, J.H., Chen, C.S.: Deep learning of binary hash codes for fast image retrieval. In: Proceedings of the IEEE Conference on Computer Vision and Pattern Recognition Workshops, pp. 27–35 (2015)
14. Liu, H., Wang, R., Shan, S., Chen, X.: Deep supervised hashing for fast image retrieval. In: Proceedings of the IEEE Conference on Computer Vision and Pattern Recognition (CVPR-16), pp. 2064–2072 (2016)
15. Long, J., Shelhamer, E., Darrell, T.: Fully convolutional networks for semantic segmentation. In: Proceedings of the IEEE Conference on Computer Vision and Pattern Recognition, pp. 3431–3440 (2015)
16. Paszke, A., et al.: PyTorch: an imperative style, high-performance deep learning library. In: Advances in Neural Information Processing Systems (NIPS-19), pp. 8024–8035. Curran Associates, Inc. (2019)

17. Russakovsky, O., et al.: ImageNet large scale visual recognition challenge. Int. J. Comput. Vision **115**(3), 211–252 (2015). https://doi.org/10.1007/s11263-015-0816-y
18. Shen, F., Shen, C., Liu, W., Tao Shen, H.: Supervised discrete hashing. In: Proceedings of the IEEE Conference on Computer Vision and Pattern Recognition (CVPR-15), pp. 37–45 (2015)
19. Simonyan, K., Zisserman, A.: Very deep convolutional networks for large-scale image recognition. In: ICLR (2015)
20. Su, S., Zhang, C., Han, K., Tian, Y.: Greedy hash: towards fast optimization for accurate hash coding in CNN. In: Advances in Neural Information Processing Systems (NIPS-18), pp. 806–815 (2018)
21. Van Horn, G., et al.: Building a bird recognition app and large scale dataset with citizen scientists: the fine print in fine-grained dataset collection. In: Proceedings of the IEEE Conference on Computer Vision and Pattern Recognition (CVPR-15), pp. 595–604 (2015)
22. Wang, X., Shi, Y., Kitani, K.M.: Deep supervised hashing with triplet labels. In: Asian Conference on Computer Vision (ACCV-16), pp. 70–84 (2016)
23. Wu, B., Ghanem, B.: ℓ_p-box ADMM: a versatile framework for integer programming. IEEE Trans. Pattern Anal. Mach. Intell. **41**(7), 1695–1708 (2019)
24. Xia, R., Pan, Y., Lai, H., Liu, C., Yan, S.: Supervised hashing for image retrieval via image representation learning. In: Proceedings of the AAAI conference on Artificial Intelligence (AAAI-14), pp. 2156–2162 (2014)
25. Yair, W., Antonio, T., Robert, F.: Spectral hashing. In: Advances in Neural Information Processing Systems (NIPS-08), pp. 1753–1760 (2008)
26. Yang, H.F., Lin, K., Chen, C.S.: Supervised learning of semantics-preserving hash via deep convolutional neural networks. IEEE Trans. Pattern Anal. Mach. Intell. **40**(2), 437–451 (2017)
27. Yuan, L., et al.: Central similarity quantization for efficient image and video retrieval. In: Proceedings of the IEEE Conference on Computer Vision and Pattern Recognition (CVPR-20), pp. 3083–3092 (2020)
28. Zhao, F., Huang, Y., Wang, L., Tan, T.: Deep semantic ranking based hashing for multi-label image retrieval. In: Proceedings of the IEEE Conference on Computer Vision and Pattern Recognition, pp. 1556–1564 (2015)
29. Zheng, X., Ji, R., Sun, X., Zhang, B., Wu, Y., Huang, F.: Towards optimal fine grained retrieval via decorrelated centralized loss with normalize-scale layer. In: Proceedings of the AAAI Conference on Artificial Intelligence, pp. 9291–9298 (2019)
30. Zhou, C., et al.: Angular deep supervised hashing for image retrieval. IEEE Access **7**, 127521–127532 (2019)
31. Zhu, H., Long, M., Wang, J., Cao, Y.: Deep hashing network for efficient similarity retrieval. In: Proceedings of the AAAI Conference on Artificial Intelligence (AAAI-16), pp. 2415–2421 (2016)
32. Zieba, M., Semberecki, P., El-Gaaly, T., Trzcinski, T.: BinGAN: learning compact binary descriptors with a regularized GAN. In: Advances in Neural Information Processing Systems, vol. 31 (2018)

Feature Decoupled Knowledge Distillation via Spatial Pyramid Pooling

Lei Gao and Hui Gao(✉)

University of Electronic Science and Technology of China, Chengdu, China
202021080708@std.uestc.edu.cn, huigao@uestc.edu.cn

Abstract. Knowledge distillation (KD) is an effective and widely used technique of model compression which enables the deployment of deep networks in low-memory or fast-execution scenarios. Feature-based knowledge distillation is an important component of KD which leverages intermediate layers to supervise the training procedure of a student network. Nevertheless, the potential mismatch of intermediate layers may be counterproductive in the training procedure. In this paper, we propose a novel distillation framework, termed Decoupled Spatial Pyramid Pooling Knowledge Distillation, to distinguish the importance of regions in feature maps. Specifically, we reveal that (1) spatial pyramid pooling is an outstanding method to define the knowledge and (2) the lower activation regions in feature maps play a more important role in KD. Our experiments on CIFAR-100 and Tiny-ImageNet achieve state-of-the-art results.

Keywords: Knowledge distillation · Spatial pyramid pooling

1 Introduction

In the last few years, deep neural networks have been the basis of many successes in both industry and academia, especially for computer vision [12,16] and natural language processing [11] tasks. Nevertheless, the large depth or width and numbers of parameters account for the drawback that they may demand high-speed computing power and large memory to store, limiting their availability in applications or platforms with low memory or real-time requirements, e.g., mobile phones and embedded devices. This led to a rapidly increasing interest in research on exploring smaller and faster models. Therefore, a variety of ways including explicit prudent network design [19], model binarization [10,33], network pruning [25], model compression [14] and most attractively knowledge distillation [18].

Previous works [3,5] have revealed that small networks usually have comparable representation capacity to large networks; but compared with large networks they are hard to train and find proper parameters to realise the objective function. The limitation of small networks appears to be caused by the difficulty of optimization rather than the size of networks. To better train a small network

,the distillation approach starts with a powerful teacher network or network ensemble, and then designs learning rules, i.e., elaborate loss function, to train a smaller student network mimicking the teacher. In the vanilla KD framework, the knowledge is defined as the prediction of the final layer of the teacher,i.e., response-based KD, which is an intuitive understanding of how a model generalizes [18]. However, the high abstraction of knowledge transferring from teacher to student ignores the valuable information contained in the intermediate layers.

Benefit from the techniques of representation learning [4], networks are good at acquiring multiple levels of feature representation with increasing abstraction [13], arousing an increasing interest in the research of feature-based KD. Feature-based KD exploits both the output of the last layer and the output of intermediate layers, i.e., feature maps, to supervise the training of student network. Fitnets [34] first introduced intermediate representations in KD, providing hints[1] to alleviate the difficulty of training a fast yet accuracy student network. Inspired by this work, a variety of feature-based KD methods have been proposed to match the features between teacher and student network indirectly [1,7,21,22,39,42]. Nevertheless, existing efforts mainly rely on handcrafted layer assignments, i.e., random selection or one-to-one association and may cause semantic mismatch or negative regularization effect in student's training. Cheng et al. [9] conduct a series of experiments to illustrate why KD works and reveal that the position differences of visual concepts (VCs) that reflect the larger activation regions from the teacher and the student are marginal. Therefore, we infer that non-VCs reflecting the lower activation regions play a more important role in the process of KD. Back to the feature map itself, we should further dig more information to improve the performance of KD.

In this paper, we propose Decoupled Spatial Pyramid Pooling Knowledge Distillation (DSPP) to exploit intermediate knowledge by exploring a novel method to define knowledge and decoupling feature map to optimize KD training procedure. A spatial pyramid pooling architecture [15] is applied in our approach for automatically perceiving knowledge, which effectively captures informative knowledge at various scales of feature map. Then a decoupling module is designed to analyze region-level semantic loss between student and teacher network based on the observation that the lower activation regions in feature map plays a more important role in KD, i.e., lower activation regions contain more informative knowledge cues. To align the spatial dimension of teacher and student layer pair, feature map of the student layer is projected to the same dimension of the teacher layer. By taking advantage of spatial pyramid pooling and decoupled region-level loss assignment, the student network can be effectively optimized with more sophisticated supervision. Our main contributions are as follows:

- A new method of defining knowledge named Spatial Pyramid Pooling is proposed to perceive knowledge in the last feature map at various scales.

---

[1] Hints mean the output of a teacher's hidden layers that supervise the student's training.

- Decoupled semantic loss assignment is applied to improve the weights of lower activation regions which play a more important role in KD, aiming at alleviating the difficulty of training the student network.
- Extensive experiments on CIFAR-100 and Tiny-ImageNet with a variety of settings based on popular network architectures reveal that DSPP outperforms than most of state-of-the-art approaches.

The source code is available at https://github.com/luilui97/DSPP.

2   Related Work

2.1   Knowledge Distillation

Knowledge distillation for model compression is similar to the way in which human beings perceive and learn knowledge. The distillation-based approach of model compression is first proposed by [5] and is re-popularised by [18], where soft targets from a pretrained teacher model are exploited to improve the performance of a given student model. Furthermore, recent knowledge distillation methods have extended to mutual learning [44], assistant teaching [27] and self-learning [41]. As pointed out in [28,32,41], soft targets predicted by the teacher model serve as an effective regularization to prevent the student model from making over-confident prediction. Moreover, some online KD variants have been proposed to reduce the expense of pre-training [2,6].

2.2   Response-Based Knowledge Distillation

Response-based knowledge often refers to the logits or predictions of the teacher model. The main idea of response-based KD is to mimic the final prediction of the teacher model. The response-based KD is simple yet effective for model compression, and has been widely applied in various tasks. For example, the response in object detection task may contains classification logits with offsets of bounding boxes [8]. The most fashionable response-based knowledge for image classification is proposed by [18] named soft targets, which contains the informative dark knowledge from the teacher model. Besides dark knowledge, another interpretation for the effectiveness of response-based KD is the similarity between soft targets and label smoothing [8] or regularizers [28]. However, the compact reliability of the output of last layer lead to the absence of intermediate-level supervision from the teacher model, limiting the student's supervised learning. Our proposed approach incorporates more informative guidance from the teacher's last hint layer via spatial pyramid pooling.

2.3   Feature-Based Knowledge Distillation

With the techniques of representation learning [4], both the output of last layer and the intermediate layers, i.e., feature maps, can offer informative knowledge guidance to the student model. Feature-based KD is first proposed in Fitnet

[34], in which hints are leveraged to improve the training of the student model. Inspired by Fitnet, various feature-based KD methods have been proposed to match the hint layers indirectly. Specifically, Zagoruyko et al. [42] derive an attention map from the teacher model to express knowledge and transferred it to the student model. To simplify the transfer of knowledge, Kim et al. [22] introduce factors to provide a more interpretive form of intermediate representations. Furthermore, Jin et al. [21] design a route constrained optimization to overcome the challenge of performance gap between teacher and student. Heo et al. [17] utilize activation boundary formed by hidden neurons rather than activation values to transfer knowledge. Recently, Chen et al. [7] suggest an adaptive semantic attention allocation mechanism, which matches teacher layers and student layers properly. SAKD [37] creatively proposes that distillation spots should be adaptive to training samples and distillation epochs. These feature-based KD methods pay more attention to fixing multiple potential mismatched intermediate layers, while our proposed method focuses on the last hint layer and leverages spatial pyramid pooling and decoupled semantic loss assignment to supervise the student, which relieves us from the exhausting layer matching process.

3 Method

We describe our proposed Decoupled Spatial Pyramid Pooling Knowledge Distillation (DSPP) method in this section. Firstly, we briefly recap the basic classic KD and illustrate it through additional necessary notations. Then, we provide an overview of our proposed DSPP architecture as well as the details of DSPP, e.g., loss function.

3.1 Preliminary

Firstly, we recap the procedure of classic knowledge distillations. Given a dataset $\mathcal{D} = \{(x_i, y_i)\}_{i=1}^{N}$ consisting of N samples from K categories, and a powerful teacher network Θ_T pretrained on dataset $\mathcal{D}$, the goal of KD is training a student network Θ_S on $\mathcal{D}$ with less computational demand and shorter inference time under the supervision of Θ_T. Specifically, in response-based KD, the student Θ_S learns the knowledge from the last layer of the teacher Θ_T, while the student Θ_S learns knowledge from the hint layers of the teacher Θ_T in feature-based KD.

As is known to all, the probability of class k given by a network Θ is computed as

$$p(z_i) = \frac{exp(z_i)}{\sum_{j=1}^{K} exp(z_j)} \tag{1}$$

where the logit z_i is the output of the softmax layer in Θ for the i-th class. In response-based KD, a hyperparameter T is introduced to control the importance of each soft target. Accordingly, the soft targets can be estimated by a softmax function as:

$$p(z_i, T) = \frac{exp(z_i/T)}{\sum_{j=1}^{K} exp(z_j/T)} \tag{2}$$

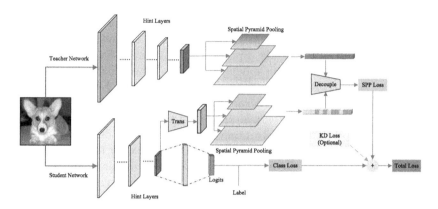

Fig. 1. The overview of Decoupled Spatial Pyramid Pooling Knowledge Distillation architecture. The last hint layer of the teacher is utilized to supervise the training of the student model via decoupled spatial pyramid pooling.

The distillation loss for response-based KD can be expressed as:

$$L_{KD}\left(p\left(\mathbf{z_t},T\right),p\left(\mathbf{z_s},T\right)\right) = D_{KL}\left(p\left(\mathbf{z_t},T\right),p\left(\mathbf{z_s},T\right)\right)$$
$$= p\left(\mathbf{z_s},T\right)\log\frac{p\left(\mathbf{z_s},T\right)}{p\left(\mathbf{z_t},T\right)} \tag{3}$$

where D_{KL} denotes Kullback Leibler (KL) Divergence. Obviously, the optimization of Eq. (3) can match logits $\mathbf{z_s}$ of student model and $\mathbf{z_t}$ of teacher model.

For feature-based KD, the target is mimicking the teacher model's intermediate layers, the distillation loss can be formulated as:

$$L_{FD}\left(f_t\left(x\right),f_s\left(x\right)\right) = \mathcal{L}_F\left(\Phi\left(f_t\left(x\right)\right),\Phi\left(f_s\left(x\right)\right)\right) \tag{4}$$

where $f_t\left(x\right)$ and $f_s\left(x\right)$ denotes the feature maps, i.e., hint layers of teacher and student models respectively. $\Phi\left(\cdot\right)$ is transformation function, which is applied when the feature maps of student and teacher model are in different shape. $\mathcal{L}_F$ indicates the similarity measurement function which is applied to match the feature maps of student and teacher model. Specifically, $\mathcal{L}_F\left(\cdot\right)$ can be l_1-norm distance, l_2-norm distance, cross-entropy loss and maximum mean discrepancy loss in different feature-based KD methods.

3.2　Network Architecture

Figure 1 illustrates our proposed DSPP architecture, which contains two subnetworks, i.e., student and teacher network, interacting with each other through decoupled spatial pyramid pooling. As mentioned earlier, the soft logits are actually the class probability distribution which is too abstract for the student to get informative knowledge. Furthermore, it's hard to find an appropriate match of hint layers of the teacher and student model. Therefore, we suggest leveraging the last hint layer to resolve the high abstraction of soft logits and avoid exhausting efforts on matching the hint layers. To align the last hint layers from the teacher and student model, a transformation operation is applied in the architecture. Inspired by [15], we introduce a new method to define knowledge in the hint layer, in which a spatial pyramid pooling is applied to capture informative knowledge in the hint layer at different scales. Besides, a decouple module is proposed to improve the importance of lower activation regions in the spatial pooling pyramid. The total loss consists of SPP loss from the Decouple module and class loss from the student network itself. Vanilla KD loss, i.e., response-based KD loss, is optional for our architecture. More details are introduced in the next part, Sect. 3.3.

3.3   Decoupled Spatial Pyramid Pooling

Spatial Pyramid Pooling. How to acquire informative knowledge from the last hint layer is a key issue for DSPP knowledge distillation. Spatial pyramid pooling is first proposed by He et al. [15] in visual recognition task, which liberates convolutional neural network from the limit of fixed input size. Considering the different architecture of the teacher and student network, we utilize spatial pyramid pooling to resolve the inconsistence issue that the student's last hint layer is of different shape from the teacher model. Moreover, contributed by hierarchical structure of spatial pyramid pooling, we can have a multi-scale receptive filed size of the last hint layer, which enables our model to perceive both global and local knowledge cue from the last hint layer. The procedure of spatial pyramid pooling can be formulated as follows:

$$f_{pyramid} = \left\{ Pooling\left(L, W\left(L\right)/k\right), \quad k = 1, 2, \cdots, n, \quad L \in \mathbb{R}^{b \times c \times h \times w} \right\} \quad (5)$$

where L denotes the input hint layer, and $W\left(\cdot\right)$ is adopted to get the width of L. Parameter k is the serial number of pyramid layer and starts from 1 to n. The function $Pooling\left(\cdot\right)$ takes 2 parameters: input feature map and the size of pooling kernel.

Why Choose the Last Hint Layer. As we know, the logits of the student model come from the fully-connected layer and are highly similar to the teacher model, i.e., their predictions are same on one dataset. However, for image classification task, the fully-connected layer is absence of spatial information of the input image which is two-dimensional or three-dimensional. As mentioned earlier, it's hard to find an appropriate match of hint layers of the teacher and student model and may reduce the interpretability of KD. These are the motivations why we choose the last hint layer. Moreover, the fully-connect layer is directly computed from the last hint layer which is theoretically and physically closest to the logits among all hint layers.

Decouple Module. To pay more attention to the lower activation regions, we propose a decouple module to handle the flattened feature from spatial pyramid

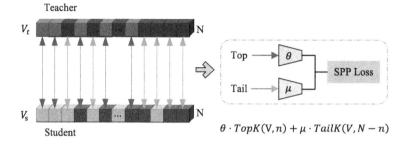

Fig. 2. An illustration of decouple module for SPP feature.

pooling. In decouple module, the flattened feature is decoupled into two components according to value of each element in the feature. As shown in Fig. 2, the student feature V_s is element-wise matched to the teacher feature V_t by a two-way arrow. The red arrows point to the top-n largest element in V_t, whose the other ends point to the corresponding position in V_s. On the contrary, the blue arrows point to the last tail-$(N-n)$ element in V_t, where N denotes the length of V_s or V_t. The loss of SPP can be calculated as:

$$
\begin{aligned}
top\,(n) &= argmax\,(V_t)\,[0:n]\,, \quad n = 0, 1, \cdots, N; \\
tail\,(m) &= argmin\,(V_t)\,[0:m]\,, \quad m = N - n; \\
\mathcal{L}_{SPP} &= \theta \mathcal{L}_2\,(V_t\,[top\,(n)]\,, V_s\,[top\,(n)]) + \\
&\quad \mu \mathcal{L}_2\,(V_t\,[tail\,(m)]\,, V_s\,[tail\,(m)])\,, \quad V_t, V_s \in \mathbb{R}^N
\end{aligned}
\tag{6}
$$

where $top(\cdot)$ denotes the indices of top-$(\cdot)$ elements in V_t and $tail(\cdot)$ denotes the indices of tail-$(\cdot)$ elements in V_t. Function $\mathcal{L}_2\,(\cdot)$ indicates l_2-norm distance. θ and μ are hyperparameters to control the weight of decoupled components. To improve the importance of lower activation regions, we let μ greater than θ. The reason why we pay more attention to the lower activation regions is that the powerful teacher models with numerous parameters may have a more sophisticated mechanism to find more details of the input which reflect on the lower activation regions. The lower activation regions contribute to improve the accuracy and generalization of the student model.

3.4 Loss and Optimization

As mentioned earlier, the loss of our proposed consist of three parts: classification loss $\mathcal{L}_{cls}$, SPP loss $\mathcal{L}_{SPP}$, and KD loss $\mathcal{L}_{KD}$ (optional). For multi-class classification, the objective function $\mathcal{L}_{cls}$ is defined as the cross entropy error between the predictions $\hat{y}$ and the correct labels y:

$$
\mathcal{L}_{cls} = -\left[y \log \hat{y} + (1 - y) \log (1 - \hat{y})\right].
\tag{7}
$$

In the end, $\mathcal{L}_{total}$ is calculated as follows:

$$
\mathcal{L}_{total} = \gamma \mathcal{L}_{cls} + \alpha \mathcal{L}_{KD} + \beta \mathcal{L}_{SPP}
\tag{8}
$$

Algorithm 1. DSPP Knowledge Distillation

Input:
Training dataset $\mathcal{D} = \{(x_i, y_i)\}_{i=1}^{N}$;
A pre-trained teacher model with parameter Θ^t;
A randomly initialized student model with parameter Θ^s
Output: A well-trained model;

1: **while** Θ^s is not converged **do**
2:    Sample a mini-batch $\mathcal{B}$ from $\mathcal{D}$.
3:    Input $\mathcal{B}$ into Θ^t and Θ^s to obtain last hint layers F_1^t and F_1^s.
4:    Align F_1^t and F_1^s then get F_2^t and F_2^s.
5:    Perform Spatial Pyramid Pooling on F_2^t and F_2^s.
6:    Backward propagate the gradients of loss by Equ. (8) and update Θ^s.
    end while

---

where hyperparameters γ, α and β are adopted to balance the weight of $\mathcal{L}_{cls}$, $\mathcal{L}_{KD}$, and $\mathcal{L}_{SPP}$ respectively. The training procedure of our proposed DSPP is summarized in Algorithm 1.

4   Experiment

To demonstrate the effectiveness of our proposed DSPP knowledge distillation, we conduct a series of experiments with a variety of teacher-student combinations on popular network architectures, including VGG [36], MobileNet [19,35] ResNet [16] and ShuffleNet [26,43]. The *CIFAR-100* [23] dataset is used in our experiments, which contains 50K training color images (32 × 32) with 0.5K images per class and 10K test images, 100 classes in total. Students and teachers of the same and different architecture style are both evaluated and compared with representative distillation approaches. Furthermore, ablation studies on the decouple module and the weights of lower activation regions are also conducted. We add our DSPP module in the KD collection established by [38] and follow their experiment settings. To evaluate the generalization of our method, we further conduct a series of experiments on Tiny-ImageNet [24].

4.1   Results

Table 1 gives the Top-1 test accuracy on CIFAR-100 based on five homogeneous network combinations and thirteen KD methods are compared with our proposed DSPP. The results of other approaches are partially cited from [38], as well as Table 2. According to Table 1, it is shown that DSPP consistently achieves higher accuracy than state-of-the-art distillation approaches with the participation of vanilla KD. Surprisingly, we found that our DSPP works well and none of the other methods except CRD consistently outperforms than vanilla KD.

Table 1. Test Top-1 accuracy (%) of homogeneous teacher-student networks on CIFAR-100 dataset of a variety of KD approaches.

Teacher	resnet56	resnet110	resnet110	resnet32x4	vgg13
Student	resnet20	resnet20	resnet32	resnet8x4	vgg8
Teacher	72.34	74.31	74.31	79.42	74.64
Student	69.06	69.06	71.14	72.50	70.36
KD [18]	70.66	70.67	73.08	73.33	72.98
FitNet [34]	69.21	68.99	71.06	73.50	71.02
AT [42]	70.55	70.22	72.31	73.44	71.43
SP [39]	69.67	70.04	72.69	72.94	72.68
CC [31]	69.63	69.48	71.48	72.97	70.71
VID [1]	70.38	70.16	72.61	73.09	71.23
PKD [29]	69.61	69.25	71.82	71.90	71.48
PKT [30]	70.34	70.25	72.61	73.64	72.88
AB [17]	69.47	69.53	70.98	73.17	70.94
FT [22]	69.84	70.22	72.37	72.86	70.58
FSP [40]	69.95	70.11	71.89	72.62	70.23
NST [20]	69.60	69.53	71.96	73.30	71.53
CRD [38]	71.16	**71.46**	73.48	**75.51**	**73.94**
DSPP(OURS)	**71.45**	71.19	**73.56**	75.31	73.59
DSPP+KD	**71.51**	**71.88**	**73.74**	**75.63**	**73.99**

Table 2. Test Top-1 accuracy (%) of heterogeneous teacher-student networks on CIFAR-100 dataset of a variety of KD approaches.

Teacher	vgg13	ResNet50	ResNet50	resnet32x4	resnet32x4
Student	MobileNetV2	MobileNetV2	vgg8	ShuffleNetV1	ShuffleNetV2
Teacher	74.64	79.34	79.34	79.42	79.42
Student	64.60	64.60	70.36	70.50	71.82
KD	67.37	67.35	73.81	74.07	74.45
FitNet	64.14	63.16	70.69	73.59	73.54
AT	59.40	58.58	71.84	71.73	72.73
SP	66.30	68.08	73.34	73.48	74.56
CC	64.86	65.43	70.25	71.14	71.29
VID	65.56	67.57	70.30	73.38	73.40
PKD	64.52	64.43	71.50	72.28	73.21
PKT	67.13	66.52	73.01	74.10	74.69
AB	66.06	67.20	70.65	73.55	74.31
FT	61.78	60.99	70.29	71.75	72.50
NST	58.16	64.96	71.28	74.12	74.68
CRD	**69.73**	69.11	**74.3**	75.11	75.65
DSPP(OURS)	67.87	68.18	73.70	74.61	75.71
DSPP+KD	68.95	**69.21**	74.13	**75.25**	**76.33**

Table 3. Test Top-1 accuracy (%) of a variety of KD approaches on Tiny-ImageNet dataset.

T→S	ResNet56→ResNet20	ResNet110→ResNet20	Vgg13→Vgg8
Teacher	58.34	58.46	60.09
Student	51.89	51.89	56.03
KD	53.04	53.40	57.33
FitNet	54.43	54.04	58.33
AT	54.39	54.57	58.85
FT	53.90	54.46	58.87
PKT	54.29	54.70	58.87
SP	54.23	54.38	58.78
VID	53.89	53.94	58.55
CC	54.22	54.26	58.18
RKD	53.95	53.88	58.58
NST	53.66	53.82	58.85
CRD	55.04	54.69	58.88
SAKD [37]+CRD	55.06	55.28	59.38
DSPP(OURS)	**55.23**	**55.56**	**59.69**

The results of five heterogeneous network combinations are shown in Table 2. Obviously, while switching the teacher-student combinations from homogeneous to heterogeneous styles, methods that constructed on multiple intermediate layers tend to perform worse than methods that distill last few layers or logits. Even worse, some methods may play a opposed negative role in the training procedure of student network. For instance, the AT and FitNet even preform worse than the vanilla student. As mentioned earlier, the mismatch of hint layers may account for this phenomenon. Tian et al. [38] gives another explanation that networks of different style have their unique hyperspace and paths mapping from the input to the output and the forced mimics of intermediate layers then conflicts with these kind of misleading. This why we have a almost equal performance compared with CRD which utilizes a family of contrastive objectives.

To evaluate the generalization of our method, we conduct a series of experiments on Tiny-ImageNet on three classical teacher-student architecture as shown in Table 3. The results show that DSPP outperforms other methods including a combination of CRD and SAKD [37] and further demonstrate the effectiveness of DSPP. Images in Tiny-ImageNet are two times larger than CIFAR-100, so the feature map is two times larger which can provide more information. Consequently, the performance of DSPP on Tiny-ImageNet is better than CIFAR-100.

Table 4. Distillation (ResNet110→ResNet32) accuracy at different μ on *CIFAR-100*.

μ	0.1	0.2	0.3	0.4	0.5	0.6	0.7	0.8	0.9	1
acc	70.78	71.14	71.26	71.35	71.32	71.62	71.90	71.82	71.90	72.12
μ	1.5	2	3	4	5	6	7	8	9	10
acc	72.17	72.61	72.65	73.21	73.42	73.5	73.52	73.59	73.50	73.49

Table 5. Test Top-1 accuracy (%) of ten teacher-student networks with/without decouple module. "w" denotes with decouple module, while "w/o" denotes without decouple module.

Teacher	resnet56	resnet110	resnet110	resnet32x4	vgg13
Student	resnet20	resnet20	resnet32	resnet8x4	vgg8
w	71.45	71.19	73.56	75.31	73.59
w/o	71.44	70.34	72.56	74.21	72.24
Improvement	0.01	0.85	1.00	1.10	1.35
Teacher	vgg13	ResNet50	ResNet50	resnet32x4	resnet32x4
Student	MobileNetV2	MobileNetV2	vgg8	ShuffleNetV1	ShuffleNetV2
w	67.87	68.18	73.70	74.61	75.56
w/o	66.28	66.67	72.47	73.22	74.84
improvement	1.59	1.51	1.23	1.39	0.72

4.2 Ablation Study

Firstly, we conduct a series of experiments on ResNet110→ResNet32 architecture to demonstrate that regions of lower activation values play a more important role in KD. We set μ from 0.1 to 10 to verify whether we should pay more attention to regions of lower activation values. As shown in Table 4, the performances of DSPP are better when $\mu > 1$ compared with $\mu \leq 1$. The cases $\mu > 1$ denote that the model concentrate more on lower activation regions.

To evaluate the performance of decouple module, we conduct a series experiments on how much improvement the decouple module brings. The results in Table 5 demonstrate the effectiveness of decouple module. Obviously, the decouple module contributes a lot to the improvement of DSPP, where the largest improvement is 1.59% in (vgg13-MobileNetV2) teacher-student architecture. Another interesting observation is that teacher-student architectures of heterogeneous style benefit more from the decouple module than those of homogeneous style.

5 Conclusion

Intermediate layers of a powerful teacher model contain various informative semantic knowledge, but mismatch of hint layers may lead to a counterproductive result. An urgent challenge for knowledge distillation is to establish a mechanism of correctly leveraging logits and intermediate layers. To reduce dependence on multiple intermediate layers and improve the interpretability of KD, we propose feature decoupled knowledge distillation via spatial pyramid pooling. Decoupled spatial pyramid pooling operation is applied on aligned last hint layer of both teacher and student model to acquire multi-scale knowledge cues. Experimental results show that distillation via DSPP outperforms the compared approaches. Additional ablation studies also demonstrate the effectiveness of our decouple module. For the future work, the proposed method can be combined with other KD methods and the way to select KD spot can be also explored further.

References

1. Ahn, S., Hu, S.X., Damianou, A.C., Lawrence, N.D., Dai, Z.: Variational information distillation for knowledge transfer. In: IEEE Conference on Computer Vision and Pattern Recognition, CVPR, pp. 9163–9171 (2019). https://doi.org/10.1109/CVPR.2019.00938
2. Anil, R., Pereyra, G., Passos, A., Ormándi, R., Dahl, G.E., Hinton, G.E.: Large scale distributed neural network training through online distillation. In: 6th International Conference on Learning Representations, ICLR (2018)
3. Ba, J., Caruana, R.: Do deep nets really need to be deep? In: Advances in Neural Information Processing Systems, pp. 2654–2662 (2014)
4. Bengio, Y., Courville, A., Vincent, P.: Representation learning: a review and new perspectives. IEEE Trans. Pattern Anal. Mach. Intell. **35**(8), 1798–1828 (2013). https://doi.org/10.1109/TPAMI.2013.50
5. Buciluundefined, C., Caruana, R., Niculescu-Mizil, A.: Model compression. In: Proceedings of the 12th ACM SIGKDD International Conference on Knowledge Discovery and Data Mining, pp. 535–541, New York, NY, USA (2006). https://doi.org/10.1145/1150402.1150464
6. Chen, D., Mei, J., Wang, C., Feng, Y., Chen, C.: Online knowledge distillation with diverse peers. In: The Thirty-Fourth AAAI Conference on Artificial Intelligence, AAAI, pp. 3430–3437 (2020)
7. Chen, D., et al.: Cross-layer distillation with semantic calibration. In: Thirty-Fifth AAAI Conference on Artificial Intelligence, AAAI, pp. 7028–7036 (2021)
8. Chen, G., Choi, W., Yu, X., Han, T.X., Chandraker, M.: Learning efficient object detection models with knowledge distillation. In: Guyon, I., von Luxburg, U., Bengio, S., Wallach, H.M., Fergus, R., Vishwanathan, S.V.N., Garnett, R. (eds.) Advances in Neural Information Processing Systems, pp. 742–751 (2017)
9. Cheng, X., Rao, Z., Chen, Y., Zhang, Q.: Explaining knowledge distillation by quantifying the knowledge. In: Proceedings of the IEEE/CVF Conference on Computer Vision and Pattern Recognition, pp. 12925–12935 (2020)
10. Courbariaux, M., Bengio, Y., David, J.: Binaryconnect: training deep neural networks with binary weights during propagations. In: Advances in Neural Information Processing Systems, pp. 3123–3131 (2015)
11. Devlin, J., Chang, M.W., Lee, K., Toutanova, K.: BERT: pre-training of deep bidirectional transformers for language understanding. In: Proceedings of the 2019 Conference of the North American Chapter of the Association for Computational Linguistics: Human Language Technologies, Volume 1 (Long and Short Papers), pp. 4171–4186 (2019). https://doi.org/10.18653/v1/N19-1423
12. Dosovitskiy, A., et al.: An image is worth 16x16 words: transformers for image recognition at scale. In: International Conference on Learning Representations (2021)

13. Gou, J., Yu, B., Maybank, S.J., Tao, D.: Knowledge distillation: a survey. Int. J. Comput. Vision **129**(6), 1789–1819 (2021). https://doi.org/10.1007/s11263-021-01453-z

14. Han, S., Mao, H., Dally, W.J.: Deep compression: compressing deep neural network with pruning, trained quantization and huffman coding. In: 4th International Conference on Learning Representations, ICLR (2016)

15. He, K., Zhang, X., Ren, S., Sun, J.: Spatial pyramid pooling in deep convolutional networks for visual recognition. In: Fleet, D., Pajdla, T., Schiele, B., Tuytelaars, T. (eds.) ECCV 2014. LNCS, vol. 8691, pp. 346–361. Springer, Cham (2014). https://doi.org/10.1007/978-3-319-10578-9_23

16. He, K., Zhang, X., Ren, S., Sun, J.: Deep residual learning for image recognition. In: 2016 IEEE Conference on Computer Vision and Pattern Recognition, CVPR, pp. 770–778 (2016). https://doi.org/10.1109/CVPR.2016.90

17. Heo, B., Lee, M., Yun, S., Choi, J.Y.: Knowledge transfer via distillation of activation boundaries formed by hidden neurons. In: The Thirty-Third AAAI Conference on Artificial Intelligence, AAAI, pp. 3779–3787 (2019). https://doi.org/10.1609/aaai.v33i01.33013779

18. Hinton, G., Vinyals, O., Dean, J.: Distilling the knowledge in a neural network. Comput. Sci. **14**(7), 38–39 (2015)

19. Howard, A.G., et al.: Mobilenets: efficient convolutional neural networks for mobile vision applications. arXiv preprint arXiv:1704.04861 (2017)

20. Huang, Z., Wang, N.: Like what you like: knowledge distill via neuron selectivity transfer. arXiv preprint arXiv:1707.01219 (2017)

21. Jin, X., et al.: Knowledge distillation via route constrained optimization. In: 2019 IEEE/CVF International Conference on Computer Vision, ICCV, pp. 1345–1354 (2019). https://doi.org/10.1109/ICCV.2019.00143

22. Kim, J., Park, S., Kwak, N.: Paraphrasing complex network: Network compression via factor transfer. In: Bengio, S., Wallach, H.M., Larochelle, H., Grauman, K., Cesa-Bianchi, N., Garnett, R. (eds.) Advances in Neural Information Processing Systems, pp. 2765–2774 (2018)

23. Krizhevsky, A., Hinton, G.: Learning multiple layers of features from tiny images. Handbook of Systemic Autoimmune Diseases **1**(4), 7 (2009)

24. Le, Y., Yang, X.: Tiny imagenet visual recognition challenge. CS 231N **7**(7), 3 (2015)

25. Li, H., Kadav, A., Durdanovic, I., Samet, H., Graf, H.P.: Pruning filters for efficient convnets. In: 5th International Conference on Learning Representations, ICLR (2017)

26. Ma, N., Zhang, X., Zheng, H.-T., Sun, J.: ShuffleNet V2: practical guidelines for efficient CNN architecture design. In: Ferrari, V., Hebert, M., Sminchisescu, C., Weiss, Y. (eds.) Computer Vision – ECCV 2018. LNCS, vol. 11218, pp. 122–138. Springer, Cham (2018). https://doi.org/10.1007/978-3-030-01264-9_8

27. Mirzadeh, S., Farajtabar, M., Li, A., Levine, N., Matsukawa, A., Ghasemzadeh, H.: Improved knowledge distillation via teacher assistant. In: The Thirty-Fourth AAAI Conference on Artificial Intelligence, AAAI, pp. 5191–5198 (2020)

28. Müller, R., Kornblith, S., Hinton, G.E.: When does label smoothing help? In: Wallach, H.M., Larochelle, H., Beygelzimer, A., d'Alché-Buc, F., Fox, E.B., Garnett, R. (eds.) Advances in Neural Information Processing Systems. pp. 4696–4705 (2019)

29. Park, W., Kim, D., Lu, Y., Cho, M.: Relational knowledge distillation. In: IEEE Conference on Computer Vision and Pattern Recognition, CVPR, pp. 3967–3976 (2019). https://doi.org/10.1109/CVPR.2019.00409

30. Passalis, N., Tefas, A.: Learning deep representations with probabilistic knowledge transfer. In: Ferrari, V., Hebert, M., Sminchisescu, C., Weiss, Y. (eds.) ECCV 2018. LNCS, vol. 11215, pp. 283–299. Springer, Cham (2018). https://doi.org/10.1007/978-3-030-01252-6_17
31. Peng, B., Jin, X., Li, D., Zhou, S., Wu, Y., Liu, J., Zhang, Z., Liu, Y.: Correlation congruence for knowledge distillation. In: 2019 IEEE/CVF International Conference on Computer Vision, ICCV, pp. 5006–5015 (2019). https://doi.org/10.1109/ICCV.2019.00511
32. Pereyra, G., Tucker, G., Chorowski, J., Kaiser, L., Hinton, G.E.: Regularizing neural networks by penalizing confident output distributions. In: 5th International Conference on Learning Representations, ICLR (2017)
33. Rastegari, M., Ordonez, V., Redmon, J., Farhadi, A.: XNOR-net: Imagenet classification using binary convolutional neural networks. In: Leibe, B., Matas, J., Sebe, N., Welling, M. (eds.) ECCV 2016. LNCS, vol. 9908, pp. 525–542. Springer, Cham (2016). https://doi.org/10.1007/978-3-319-46493-0_32
34. Romero, A., Ballas, N., Kahou, S.E., Chassang, A., Gatta, C., Bengio, Y.: FitNets: hints for thin deep nets. In: 3rd International Conference on Learning Representations, ICLR (2015)
35. Sandler, M., Howard, A.G., Zhu, M., Zhmoginov, A., Chen, L.: Mobilenetv 2: inverted residuals and linear bottlenecks. In: 2018 IEEE Conference on Computer Vision and Pattern Recognition, CVPR. pp. 4510–4520 (2018). https://doi.org/10.1109/CVPR.2018.00474
36. Simonyan, K., Zisserman, A.: Very deep convolutional networks for large-scale image recognition. In: 3rd International Conference on Learning Representations, ICLR (2015)
37. Song, J., Chen, Y., Ye, J., Song, M.: Spot-adaptive knowledge distillation. IEEE Trans. Image Process. **31**, 3359–3370 (2022)
38. Tian, Y., Krishnan, D., Isola, P.: Contrastive representation distillation. In: 8th International Conference on Learning Representations, ICLR (2020)
39. Tung, F., Mori, G.: Similarity-preserving knowledge distillation. In: 2019 IEEE/CVF International Conference on Computer Vision, ICCV, pp. 1365–1374 (2019). https://doi.org/10.1109/ICCV.2019.00145
40. Yim, J., Joo, D., Bae, J., Kim, J.: A gift from knowledge distillation: fast optimization, network minimization and transfer learning. In: 2017 IEEE Conference on Computer Vision and Pattern Recognition, CVPR, pp. 7130–7138 (2017). https://doi.org/10.1109/CVPR.2017.754
41. Yuan, L., Tay, F.E.H., Li, G., Wang, T., Feng, J.: Revisiting knowledge distillation via label smoothing regularization. In: 2020 IEEE/CVF Conference on Computer Vision and Pattern Recognition, CVPR, pp. 3902–3910 (2020). https://doi.org/10.1109/CVPR42600.2020.00396
42. Zagoruyko, S., Komodakis, N.: Paying more attention to attention: improving the performance of convolutional neural networks via attention transfer. In: 5th International Conference on Learning Representations, ICLR (2017)
43. Zhang, X., Zhou, X., Lin, M., Sun, J.: ShuffleNet: an extremely efficient convolutional neural network for mobile devices. In: 2018 IEEE Conference on Computer Vision and Pattern Recognition, CVPR, pp. 6848–6856 (2018). https://doi.org/10.1109/CVPR.2018.00716
44. Zhang, Y., Xiang, T., Hospedales, T.M., Lu, H.: Deep mutual learning. In: 2018 IEEE Conference on Computer Vision and Pattern Recognition, CVPR, pp. 4320–4328 (2018). https://doi.org/10.1109/CVPR.2018.00454

Few-shot Adaptive Object Detection with Cross-Domain CutMix

Yuzuru Nakamura[1]($\boxtimes$)(iD), Yasunori Ishii[1](iD), Yuki Maruyama[1](iD), and Takayoshi Yamashita[2](iD)

[1] Panasonic Holdings Corporation, 3-1-1 Yagumo-naka-machi, Moriguchi, Osaka 570-8501, Japan
{nakamura.yuzuru,ishii.yasunori,maruyama.yuuki}@jp.panasonic.com
[2] Chubu University, 1200 Matsumoto-cho, Kasugai, Aichi 487-8501, Japan
takayoshi@isc.chubu.ac.jp

Abstract. In object detection, data amount and cost are a trade-off, and collecting a large amount of data in a specific domain is labor-intensive. Therefore, existing large-scale datasets are used for pre-training. However, conventional transfer learning and domain adaptation cannot bridge the domain gap when the target domain differs significantly from the source domain. We propose a data synthesis method that can solve the large domain gap problem. In this method, a part of the target image is pasted onto the source image, and the position of the pasted region is aligned by utilizing the information of the object bounding box. In addition, we introduce adversarial learning to discriminate whether the original or the pasted regions. The proposed method trains on a large number of source images and a few target domain images. The proposed method achieves higher accuracy than conventional methods in a very different domain problem setting, where RGB images are the source domain, and thermal infrared images are the target domain. Similarly, the proposed method achieves higher accuracy in the cases of simulation images to real images.

Keywords: Object detection · Domain adaptation · Few-shot learning

1 Introduction

Systems used in various environments throughout the day, such as autonomous driving and surveillance robots, are being put to practical use. These systems require high accuracy throughout the day. Infrared cameras can capture visible images even in such situations, and they can robustly detect objects. To achieve high accuracy, object detection models require a large amount of labeled training data. It is easy to use a large amount of labeled training data of RGB images [4,7, 20,22,24,34]. However, most of the images are captured using an RGB camera,

---

Y. Nakamura and Y. Ishii—Equal contribution.

Supplementary Information The online version contains supplementary material available at https://doi.org/10.1007/978-3-031-26351-4_45.

and a few images are captured using an infrared camera (hereinafter infrared images). Therefore, to achieve high accuracy, detection models need to train with a few labeled infrared images.

One of the methods for training high accuracy detection model is transfer learning using pre-trained model trained with RGB images. However, it is difficult to improve the accuracy if the domain gap between RGB and infrared images is large [30,40]. This phenomenon, called negative transfer, occurred under the large domain gap between the training images for pre-trained model and the ones for fine-tuning model. As one of the conventional methods for overcoming the domain gap, there are style transformation methods such as CycleGAN [33,51]. GAN-based style transformations can easily convert between images with similar spectra. However, the style transformation is difficult when the spectral distributions are significantly different, such as in RGB and infrared images. A method using GRL [2,8,29] is proposed as a training method for domain adaptation in the feature space. However, if the spectral distributions between the input images are significantly different, it is difficult to align the distributions of different domains because the feature distributions are extremely different. The methods for training features that interpolate between two images are as follows: Mixup [46], BC-learning [37], CutMix [45], and CutDepth [16]. These methods train features located between two images by mixing the two images or by replacing a portion of the image with the other image. These data augmentation methods synthesize features with a mixture of different domains.

We propose a few shot adaptive object detection with cross-domain CutMix. We take advantage of the fact that data augmentation can reduce the domain gap by mixing features of domains with a large domain gap. Our method enables highly accurate object detection even for a few annotated infrared images based on a pre-trained model of RGB images. We paste a part of one domain's image onto a part of another domain's image, such as CutMix, because we overcome large domain gap. Particularly, in object detection task, the size of detection targets is smaller than that of the background. Therefore, to perform domain adaptation of small detection object, we cut out the detection object and paste it onto the other domain instead of randomly cutting out the image. Even if there is a significant difference in appearance between domains, the features of the detected objects between domains are trained to be similar to each other.

Additionally, we adapt the domain using feature-based adversarial learning. In conventional methods, the discriminator of the domain identification label does not change during training. However, the domain identification label also needs to change the label according to the pasted area because our CutMix-based method changes the pasting area during training. The conventional domain identification label cannot be used by pasting an image of another domain. Therefore, the domain identification label should be the same domain label as the input image to which the image of another domain is pasted. Since the correct domain label can be assigned according to the pasting position of the object, feature-level domain alignment can be performed even when the input image is changed, as in the proposed method.

Our contributions are as follows: we propose a few shot adaptive object detection with cross-domain CutMix so that we can adapt the domain, which looks significantly different. Furthermore, we propose an input image synthesizing method based on CutMix for cross-domains and domain identification label in discriminator for that. Through experiments, we show the effectiveness of the proposed method using RGB images as a pre-trained model and data from multiple domains such as RGB and thermal infrared images.

2   Related Work

2.1   Object Detection for Each Domain

Most object detection methods have been studied for RGB images [18,26,41]. These methods can be roughly divided into two-stage and one-stage detection methods. R-CNN and its extended technologies [10,11,32] represent the two-stage methods. YOLO [31], SSD (Single Shot Multi-box Detector) [27], and their extended technologies represent the one-stage methods. Additionally, object detection techniques that use transformer have been proposed [3,6,28,44,52], and they are expected that it will be applied to various environments.

There is research on applications in the real environment such as robots [19,36], drones [13,42], object detection for in-vehicle cameras [23,49], and license plate detection [43]. Many datasets [4,7,20,22,24,34] that can be used to train object detection are available to the public. The night scenes on these datasets are fewer than daytime scenes. Furthermore, visibility is poor because the pixel value of the subject in the RGB image captured at night is small. Thus, it is difficult to achieve high detection performance using RGB images both day and night.

Highly accurate object detection with in-vehicle cameras and outdoor drones is required for both day and night. Some methods for detecting objects using spectra information other than RGB images were proposed to detect objects with high accuracy on both day and night. Lu et al. [47] proposed object detection using RGB and infrared images in the framework of weakly supervised learning. This method focuses on the use of multispectral information, and it detects objects using a roughly aligned RGB image and an infrared image. Liu et al. [25] and Konig et al. [21] proposed methods for inputting RGB and thermal infrared images into a deep learning model and fusing their features. Highly accurate object detection is possible under various lighting conditions using RGB and infrared images simultaneously. These methods are algorithms that assume that there are numerous RGB and infrared images. Thus, they can be used if the RGB and the infrared images can be photographed in large quantities and annotated in the same environment as the inference scene. However, the cost of collecting data and annotating in each application environment is high in reality.

2.2   Knowledge Transfer to Different Domain

To reduce the cost of preparing infrared images and training high accurate object detection models, domain adaptation and transfer learning use a pre-trained model with a small number of labeled infrared and RGB images.

Akkaya et al. [1] proposed unsupervised domain adaptation between a model taken from numerous RGB and thermal infrared images for image classification. Vibashan et al. [38] used paired RGB and thermal infrared images to perform domain adaptation for object detection. When only the recognized object is displayed as in the image classification, the domains of both the difference in the sensor and shooting scene can be applied. However, when the background area without objects occupies a large area in object detection, it is difficult to adapt the domain of both the sensor difference and the shooting scene difference without using a pair of datasets. Thus, it is still a problem to adapt between different sensors and scenes for object detection.

There is a knowledge transfer method, which is by fine-tuning infrared images, using a model trained with RGB images as pre-trained model. For fine-tuning to be effective, the feature of training data between source domain and target domain must be similar. RGB and infrared images have extremely different spectrum to be imaged, and they look very different even if they have the same object and color. Negative transfer [30,40] occurs because of the difference in the distribution of these data. Therefore, knowledge transfer using a small number of labeled infrared images is difficult. In both domain adaptation and fine-tuning, the key to improving performance is transferring knowledge while making the differences between domains closer.

3   Proposed Method

3.1   Overview

In this paper, we propose high-accuracy object detection on infrared images using a large number of labeled RGB images and a small number of labeled infrared images. RGB and infrared images receive different spectra; thus, there is a significant difference in appearance, which is a large gap between domains. Therefore, we not only align the gaps between domains at the feature level using methods such as adversarial learning but also explicitly reduce the gaps between domains at the image level. This improves the accuracy of domain adaptation by converting the input image to conditions that make it adapt the domain easier.

We propose Object aware Cross-Domain CutMix (OCDC) and OCDC-based Discriminator Label (OCDCDL) based on the domain for each location. Figure 1 shows our proposed framework. We explain the outline of the proposed method using the model of the domain adaptation method based on adversarial learning proposed by Han-Kai et al. [14] as an example. This method trais using the loss of both object detection and adversarial learning to reduce the difference between domains. This proposed method is simple and easy to incorporate into the type of domain adaptation that uses adversarial learning in object detection problems, which uses few labeled images.

OCDC (Fig. 1 (a)) is a method for cutting out an object area and pasting a part of the image between domains to reduce the gap between the source and the target domains. Zhou et al. showed that there is a domain generalization effect by mixing images with different domains in a batch [50]. Inspired by that

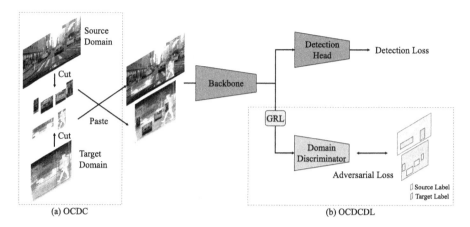

Fig. 1. The framework of our proposed method; (a) OCDC mitigates the image-level domain gap by cutting out the object area and pasting them in each other domain. (b) We adaptively determine the domain identification label based on the area pasted by the OCDC. The pasted object, which serve areas as new ground truth, are input into the detection network, and the detection and the adversarial losses are calculated.

study, we focused on mixing object units, which is important for object detection. When the entire image is mixed, it is trained to reduce the distance between the background domains that occupy most of the image. In the proposed method, the distance between domains is emphasized rather than the background features, so the object detection performance is expected to improve.

OCDCDL (Fig. 1 (b)) is a method for adaptively changing the domain label of the discriminator based on the pasting position of other domain images. By converting the input image using OCDC, the domain identification label is no longer one value. The output feature using the input image includes information from multiple domains by pasting an image of another domain on the input image using OCDC. Thus, the conventional single identification label cannot correctly discriminate the domain. By adaptively changing the label based on the OCDC, the discriminator makes it possible to discriminate the domain even if there is information on different domains in the image.

3.2   Object Aware Cross-Domain CutMix (OCDC)

For domain adaptation to data with a large gap between domains such as RGB and infrared images, we propose a method of aligning domains at the image level in addition to the conventional method of aligning domains using features. A method based on data augmentation called DomainMix augmentation [39] was proposed: as a method for reducing the domain gap at the image level. This method reduces the difference in appearance between images by simply connecting different domains without using a deep generative model. Mixup [46], BC-learning [37], CutMix [45], and CutDepth [16] are data augmentation methods to be mixed at the image level. These studies mention that mixing images can generate features that interpolate two images. By mixing them at the image level, the features between the domains in the input image can be brought closer to each other.

However, the background area without objects occupies most of the image, and the objects that should align the domains are only part of the image. Thus, in Mixup or CutMix, which uses the entire image or mixes random regions, respectively, the gap in the background domain is small, but the gap in the domain of the object to be detected is not always small. Therefore, we propose an OCDC to cut out the object area existing in one domain and paste it onto the other domain. The domain gap is reduced at the image level by cutting out the object area from the source and target and pasting them together.

The pasting process is performed for each training iteration. The images of the source domain and that of the target domain included in the batch are used. The object to be detected is cut out from those images based on the ground truth coordinates. The object image cut out from the image of the source domain is pasted onto the image of the target domain selected at random. On the other hand, the image cut out from the object image of the target domain is pasted onto the image of the source domain selected at random. The ground truth labels for detection loss are updated by adding the ground truth label of the pasted image of another domain to that of the image where the image of another domain is pasted.

If the object images are pasted while the objects already exist, the originally existing objects will be hidden. The loss of object detection becomes large because it is difficult to detect such hidden objects. Therefore, we decide the pasting position of the image based on the overlap between the image to be pasted and the object of the image to which the object image is pasted. If the area where the object is hidden increases more than a certain percentage after pasting the image, the pasting position is reselected when deciding the pasting position. This prevents the original object from being hidden after pasting.

Additionally, to train the position and label of an object, the object detection model pastes an object image to a real-world location. For example, if the domain is adapted between the images of the in-vehicle camera, which is installed at almost the same position, the coordinates before and after pasting do not change significantly. Alternatively, the object image is pasted at the same position as the position before pasting or at a slightly shifted position.

The domain adaptation for object detection that has been used so far has insufficient consideration for object detection. On the other hand, our method using cutting out the position of objects is a new point of view that the domain gap of the object to be recognized can be reduced. In addition, we argue that it causes problems in adversarial learning and propose a solution. In the following subsections, each proposed method is explained concretely.

3.3 OCDC-based Discriminator Label (OCDCDL)

In domain adaptation using adversarial learning such as a method [14], features calculated from the source or target domains are input into the discriminator.

In our proposed OCDC, the information of another domain is included in a part of the feature because the image of another domain is pasted on the part of the input image. Therefore, when one value is used for the domain identification label of the discriminator as in the conventional method, the loss of the area where the image of another domain is pasted cannot be calculated correctly.

The discriminator is trained so that neither of the two domains can be discriminated. We append the discriminator D after the backbone F. The input image of the source domain and the target domain are I_S and I_T, respectively. D outptus a domain prediction map of each pixel $D(\cdot)_{h,w}$. The source domain identification label and target domain identification label are $d = 0$ and $d = 1$, respectively. Equation 1 is a adversarial loss $\mathcal{L}_{adv}$ and Eq. 2 is an overall loss $\mathcal{L}$.

$$\mathcal{L}_{adv}(F(I)) = -\Sigma_{h,w}[d \log D(F(I))_{h,w} + (1-d) \log(1 - D(F(I))_{h,w})], \quad (1)$$

$$\min_F \max_D \mathcal{L}(I_S, I_T) = \mathcal{L}_{det}(I_S) + \mathcal{L}_{det}(I_T) + \lambda_{adv}[\mathcal{L}_{adv}(F(I_S)) + \mathcal{L}_{adv}(F(I_T))], \quad (2)$$

where $\mathcal{L}_{det}(\cdot)$ is the detection loss, and λ_{adv} is a weight that determines the loss balance. We set λ_{disc} is 0.1 in our experiments.

However, because the features near the boundary of the area where the object of another domain is pasted using OCDC are a mixture of the features of the two domains, it is difficult to distinguish which domain is near this boundary. Thus, the loss near the boundary of the trained discriminator is smaller than that in other regions. However, information from different domains is rarely mixed at a position far from the boundary of the pasted object. Therefore, the loss of discriminator in the feature is large in that area.

Furthermore, we adaptively determine the domain identification label based on the position and domain of the image pasted by OCDC. After the pasting process, the RGB domain label is replaced with the domain identification label corresponding to the infrared image region, and the infrared domain label is replaced with the domain identification label corresponding to the RGB image region.

4   Experiments

We evaluate the effectiveness of the proposed methods using RGB images [5, 20] and thermal infrared images [12, 15] with a large domain gap. In these experiments, there are differences in both the spectrum and the captured scene. We compare the performance with a large amount of RGB images and a small amount of thermal infrared images. All datasets are labeled. Additionally, to verify the generalization performance of the proposed method, we evaluate the performance using real images [4] and simulation images [17].

4.1   Comparison Methods

We explain the comparison method used for each experimental setting. In our experiment, images of the target domain are used for evaluation. Source-only and target-only labels in the tables of experimental results show the evaluation results when the model is trained using only the image of the source or target domains, respectively. The fine-tuning label shows the results using a pre-trained model and fine-tuning using target domain data. The target samples label shows the number of target domain data using fine-tuning. The Domain-Adversarial Training of Neural Networks (DANN) [9], one of the adversarial learning methods, is used as the baseline of the adversarial learning method. DANN label shows the detection results using domain adaptation with DANN. We use Faster R-CNN [32] as the detection network and VGG16 [35] for the backbone. In domain adaptation, the model parameters are pre-trained in the source domain. The height size is 600 of the image resolution, but if the maximum width size is more than 1,000, we set it to 1,000 while maintaining the aspect ratio. Ours label shows the result using the proposed method, which uses the OCDC and OCDCDL. The optimizer is SGD; the learning rate, the weight decay, and the momentum are 0.001, 0.0005, and 0.9, respectively. The batch size is one. The evaluation metrics are the average precision at an intersection over union (IoU), which threshold is 0.5. The front of the arrow indicates the source domain, and the tip of the arrow indicates the target domain. The results of each experiment are shown in Table 1.

BDD100k $\rightarrow$ FLIR: The BDD100k dataset [20] is collected based on six types of weather conditions, six different scenes, and three categories of time of data; the number of images is 100,000. This dataset is annotated in ten categories. FLIR ADAS dataset [12] is an image captured by a FLIR Tau2 camera, and the number of images is 10,228. Only thermal infrared images from this dataset are used. In our experiment, the training data includes 36,728 images labeled as daytime from the BDD100k dataset as the source domain data and 8,862 thermal infrared images used as training splits from the FLIR ADAS dataset. The categories person, bicycle, and car, which are common categories.

The detection accuracy of source-only is the lowest because this does not use knowledge of the target domain. In target-only, mAP is 72.1% using all target data named Full. However, performances considerably deteriorates when the amount of data decreased. In fine-tuning, performances are higher than the performances of target-only because fine-tuning models had a knowledge that performance improves somewhat even in different domains. The performances of DANN are higher than fine-tuning because of the effects of domain adaptation. There is no significant performance degradation due to negative transfer, but the effect of domain adaptation can be confirmed. The performances of the proposed method tend to improve overall, but in particular, the performance of the person label outperformed DANN.

When the target samples are Full, the number of each object is large, so even if the object areas are small, there are enough numbers to improve the performance by domain adaptation. However, in the case of Full, there is only a difference of 0.3 points, so the conventional domain adaptation does not have a difference drastically. In particular, in this experimental result, it should be noted that the target samples, which are our targets, are smaller than $1/2$,

Table 1. Results on BDD100k → FLIR, Caltech → KAIST, and SIM10K → Cityscapes

Method	Target Samples	FLIR				KAIST	Cityscapes
		Person	Bicycle	Car	mAP	Person	Car
Source-only	—	39.9	24.9	68.2	44.4	2.8	43.1
Target-only	Full	74.2	57.9	84.1	72.1	67.0	60.3
	1/2	71.5	56.0	82.3	69.9	67.6	58.1
	1/4	66.7	48.7	78.5	64.6	63.0	54.3
	1/8	61.4	41.4	75.4	59.4	58.7	52.0
	1/16	57.0	42.5	71.8	57.1	57.1	48.3
	1/32	51.3	34.9	67.3	51.2	51.3	45.2
	1/64	44.4	32.0	63.6	46.7	47.4	41.1
Fine-tuning	Full	75.0	60.5	86.3	73.9	63.4	58.1
	1/2	74.8	58.3	86.1	73.1	63.4	58.1
	1/4	72.4	53.1	85.4	70.1	63.5	57.8
	1/8	69.1	47.8	82.9	66.6	63.2	56.8
	1/16	64.6	45.4	79.5	63.2	61.7	55.7
	1/32	65.9	46.7	**83.3**	65.3	**59.5**	52.5
	1/64	64.5	41.2	82.0	62.6	**57.1**	49.8
DANN	Full	**78.1**	**63.8**	**87.0**	**76.3**	**69.4**	62.0
	1/2	77.6	**63.1**	**87.2**	76.0	71.7	61.0
	1/4	75.2	56.5	86.2	72.6	70.4	58.6
	1/8	72.4	58.8	84.5	71.9	69.1	**59.6**
	1/16	70.6	55.8	83.8	70.1	66.9	55.2
	1/32	69.4	**53.8**	82.3	68.5	57.0	54.1
	1/64	67.7	**51.8**	81.9	67.1	54.5	52.3
Ours	Full	77.8	63.5	86.9	76.1	68.4	**63.6**
	1/2	**78.3**	62.6	**87.2**	76.1	**73.3**	61.8
	1/4	**76.9**	59.9	86.9	74.5	72.4	60.0
	1/8	**75.4**	60.9	85.7	74.0	69.7	59.6
	1/16	**72.2**	57.9	84.5	71.5	67.5	57.4
	1/32	**71.1**	53.8	82.0	69.3	59.1	56.5
	1/64	**68.5**	51.6	**82.3**	67.5	**57.1**	54.2

rather than the detection result of Full. Under these conditions, the our method has higher performance than the conventional method in almost all cases. We confirmed about 4 point improvements over DANN even if there is a few data. For example, if we consider person label, this is because the percentage of people in the dataset was high, and the overall percentage of pasting person's images onto another domain based on the input image was high.

Caltech → KAIST: The Caltech Pedestrian dataset [5] is a dataset that contains labeled images of pedestrians captured using an in-vehicle camera. 42,782 images from this dataset are used for the images. The KAIST Multispectral Pedestrian dataset [15] is a dataset captured using the FLIR A35 microbolometer LWIR camera and contains 95,000 images labeled for pedestrians. The thermal infrared image of this dataset is used. In KAIST, 7,688 thermal infrared images are used for training, and 2,252 thermal infrared images are used for testing. This is based on the procedure in the paper [48]. In this experiment, only person is used as the category.

Source-only detection accuracy is extremely low because the appearance of RGB and thermal infrared images differs significantly. Target-only and fine-tuning detection accuracy deteriorated as the target sample decreased, as demonstrated in the FLIR experiment. Particularly, fine-tuning detection accuracy was lower than target-only detection accuracy by pre-training in the source domain. However, the performance degradation is suppressed when the target samples decrease. DANN and the proposed method perform better than target-only when there are many target samples. Performance is higher than fine-tuning when the number of samples decreased. The proposed method showed more than two points higher performance than DANN when target samples are $1/32$ and $1/64$. This experiment shows that the proposed method is more effective in single-class object detection than in multi-class object detection. In single-class object detection, when an image of another domain is pasted on an image of another domain, the image is rarely pasted to the detected object. Therefore, few occlusion problems due to pasting occurred in the BDD100k → FLIR experiment. Since the proposed method has a remarkable effect when the number of targets is small, it is expected to be effective in applications that are often used, such as pedestrian detection.

SIM10K → Cityscapes: The SIM10K dataset [17] is a composite of 10,000 images generated by the Grand Theft Auto (GTA) game engine and is annotated with cars and other similar images. The Cityscapes dataset [4] consists of real images captured in multiple urban areas and segmentation labels. We used the circumscribed rectangle of the object segmentation label as the bounding box for evaluation in the car categories. Furthermore, we used 10,000 composite images from SIM10K as a training set. Note that 2,975 images, which are training splits from Cityscapes, are used as training data, and 500 images, which are validation splits, are used as evaluation data. The evaluation is performed using the common category of car.

Similar to the previous results, the source-only detection accuracy is the lowest. If the target domain detection accuracy has a large amount of data, the target-only detection performance is high, but when the amount of data is small, the performance is significantly reduced. Fine-tuning detection accuracy reduces performance degradation when the amount of data is small. However, when the amount of data is small, the performance of DANN improves, so the effect of domain adaptation can be confirmed. When the target samples were $1/8$, the proposed method and DANN had the same accuracy. Cityscapes are in-vehicle camera images, and the size of the car in the image is much larger than that of a person. Therefore, even if the number of data is reduced a little, the vehicle area can be used for domain adaptation in the same area as the background, so the accuracy is not so decrease. In this experiment, we confirmed that the proposed method is effective not only for domain adaptation between RGB and infrared images but also for conventional problem settings. This experiment showed that the proposed method is a general-purpose technique that can be used in various source and target data domains.

4.2 Ablation Study

This section shows the comparison results under different experimental conditions. In either case, a comparison is made under the evaluation conditions of BDD → FLIR.

Contribution of Components: We evaluate the effect of OCDC and OCDCDL. Table 2 shows the results. For Person, the method using both OCDC and OCDCDL had high performance. On the other hand, Bicycle and Car have high performance even with OCDC alone. Our experiment do not consider labels near the boundaries of objects. Thus, even if a person with a small area makes a mistake in the discriminator label near the object boundary, the effect on detection accuracy is small. However, Bicycle and Car have a large area. Therefore, the performance decrease if the discriminator label near the object boundary is mistaken. However, in comparison with mAP, our proposed methods have the highest accuracy and effectiveness.

Region Selection Strategies: We compare the accuracy of whether the pasting position and scale are the same before and after pasting in OCDC. Table 3 shows the experimental results. A fixed label indicates position or scale are the same before and after pasting, and a random label indicates that the position and scale are set randomly. The detection accuracy in many cases is higher if the same position is maintained before and after pasting. For example, in the case of an in-vehicle camera, objects are concentrated on the lower side of the image. The object detection model trains a set of the position and the class. To train the relationship between the position and the class, which is unlikely to occur, does not have a positive effect on the inference result. In our experiment, by making the pasting position and size the same, the detection model is able to train the positions and scales that are likely to occur during inference.

4.3 Qualitative Results

Figure 2 is object detection results of FLIR, KAIST, and Cityscapes after domain adaptation performed in Subsect. 4.1. At the top of each dataset is the result when target samples is 1/16, and at the bottom of each dataset is the result when it is 1/64. The comparison methods are (a) fine-tuning, (b) DANN, and (c) Ours, respectively, and (d) Ground Truth. The car detection result is shown in magenta, and the person detection result is shown in cyan.

Table 2. Results on contribution of components

Target samples	OCDC	OCDCDL	Person	Bicycle	Car	mAP
Full			**78.1**	**63.8**	**87.0**	**76.3**
	✓		77.8	63.2	86.9	76.0
	✓	✓	77.8	63.5	86.9	76.1
1/2			77.6	63.1	87.2	76.0
	✓		78.2	**63.2**	**87.4**	**76.3**
	✓	✓	**78.3**	62.6	87.2	76.1
1/4			75.2	56.5	86.2	72.6
	✓		76.7	**61.9**	86.8	**75.1**
	✓	✓	**76.9**	59.9	**86.9**	74.5
1/8			72.4	58.8	84.5	71.9
	✓		74.4	58.5	85.5	72.8
	✓	✓	**75.4**	**60.9**	**85.7**	**74.0**
1/16			70.6	55.8	83.8	70.1
	✓		72.1	54.9	**84.9**	70.6
	✓	✓	**72.2**	**57.9**	84.5	**71.5**
1/32			69.4	53.8	82.3	68.5
	✓		71.0	**54.0**	**82.6**	69.2
	✓	✓	**71.1**	53.8	82.0	**69.3**
1/64			67.7	51.8	81.9	67.1
	✓		68.1	**52.5**	81.8	**67.5**
	✓	✓	**68.5**	51.6	**82.3**	**67.5**

In the FLIR results, there is no difference in the car detection results, but there is a difference in the person detection results. In fine-tuning and DANN, even people with similar reflection intensities in thermal infrared images are not detected. On the other hand, the proposed method detects objects with similar reflection intensities, even if they are people far away. The proposed method adapted the domain to information about the reflection intensity of persons, which is a small area in the image. On the other hand, the conventional methods did not fully adapt the domain, so some objects could not be detected.

In the KAIST results, the conventional methods did not detect some small persons. In domain adaptation, it is difficult to adapt information on small objects because even if the information in a small object is ignored, the loss of the detection model decreases. However, the proposed method makes it easier to detect even small objects by explicitly giving information from other domains to the input image.

In the Cityscapes results, in both 1/16 and 1/64, the farthest car on the left side was not detected by conventional methods, but the proposed method could detect the car. This is because it is difficult to adapt the domain of a small

Table 3. Results on region selection strategies

Target Samples	Position	Scaling	Person	Bicycle	Car	mAP
Full	Fixed	Fixed	77.8	**63.5**	86.9	**76.1**
	Fixed	Random	**77.9**	62.8	**87.0**	75.9
	Random	Fixed	76.0	62.5	86.5	75.0
	Random	Random	76.4	62.2	86.6	75.0
1/2	Fixed	Fixed	**78.3**	62.6	87.2	76.1
	Fixed	Random	**78.3**	**63.4**	**87.4**	**76.4**
	Random	Fixed	77.2	62.5	87.0	75.5
	Random	Random	77.0	61.2	87.0	75.1
1/4	Fixed	Fixed	76.9	59.9	**86.9**	74.5
	Fixed	Random	**77.3**	**61.4**	**86.9**	**75.2**
	Random	Fixed	75.9	59.8	86.3	74.0
	Random	Random	76.1	59.4	86.3	73.9
1/8	Fixed	Fixed	**75.4**	**60.9**	**85.7**	**74.0**
	Fixed	Random	74.6	58.1	85.5	72.7
	Random	Fixed	73.4	58.6	85.2	72.4
	Random	Random	73.8	58.0	85.1	72.3
1/16	Fixed	Fixed	**72.2**	**57.9**	**84.5**	**71.5**
	Fixed	Random	72.1	56.4	84.4	71.0
	Random	Fixed	71.3	53.9	84.1	69.8
	Random	Random	70.7	56.3	84.0	70.4
1/32	Fixed	Fixed	**71.1**	**53.8**	82.0	**69.3**
	Fixed	Random	70.2	52.0	**82.9**	68.4
	Random	Fixed	70.5	53.4	82.3	68.7
	Random	Random	69.2	51.9	82.4	67.8
1/64	Fixed	Fixed	**68.5**	**51.6**	**82.3**	**67.5**
	Fixed	Random	68.4	51.1	81.9	67.1
	Random	Fixed	67.7	46.9	81.8	65.5
	Random	Random	66.8	51.1	82.1	66.6

object, which is the same reason as in the case of KAIST. In this experiment, we clarified the importance of explicitly giving information of other domains to the input image in domain adaptation of small objects as in the proposed method.

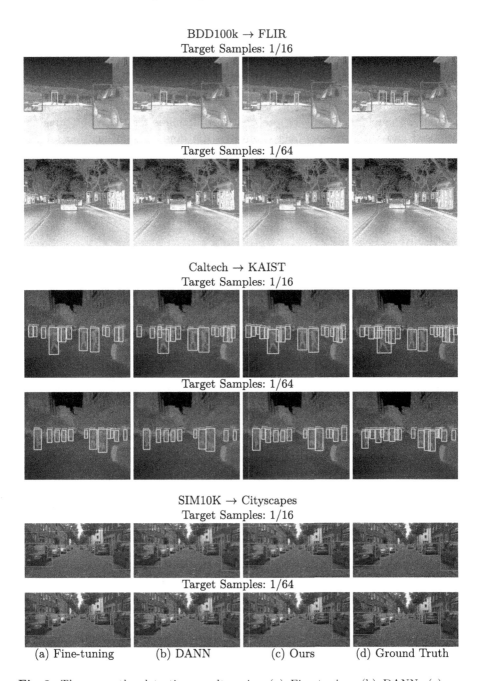

Fig. 2. There are the detection results using (a) Fine-tuning, (b) DANN, (c) our method, and (d) ground truth, respectively. The bounding box colored cyan indicates person, and the bounding box colored magenta indicates car, respectively. (Color figure online)

5   Conclusion

We proposed few-shot supervised domain adaptation for object detection in cases with large domain gaps, such as RGB and thermal infrared images. Although the number of infrared images is smaller than that of RGB images, the performance is improved compared with the conventional domain identification via OCDC method for reducing the gap between domains for the input image we proposed and the corresponding change in the domain identification label of the discriminator (OCDCDL). Furthermore, it was confirmed that the proposed method is effective by a comparative experiments in which the number of data was changed, and the versatility of the method was shown by a comparative experiments using various data.

References

1. Akkaya, I.B., Altinel, F., Halici, U.: Self-training guided adversarial domain adaptation for thermal imagery. In: Proceedings of the IEEE/CVF Conference on Computer Vision and Pattern Recognition (CVPR), pp. 4317–4326 (2021). https://doi.org/10.1109/CVPRW53098.2021.00488
2. Bolte, J.A., et al.: Unsupervised domain adaptation to improve image segmentation quality both in the source and target domain. In: Proceedings of the IEEE/CVF Conference on Computer Vision and Pattern Recognition (CVPR) Workshops, pp. 1404–1413 (2019). https://doi.org/10.1109/CVPRW.2019.00181
3. Carion, N., Massa, F., Synnaeve, G., Usunier, N., Kirillov, A., Zagoruyko, S.: End-to-end object detection with transformers. In: Vedaldi, A., Bischof, H., Brox, T., Frahm, J.-M. (eds.) ECCV 2020. LNCS, vol. 12346, pp. 213–229. Springer, Cham (2020). https://doi.org/10.1007/978-3-030-58452-8_13
4. Cordts, M., et al.: The cityscapes dataset for semantic urban scene understanding. In: Proceedings of the IEEE/CVF Conference on Computer Vision and Pattern Recognition (CVPR), pp. 3213–3223 (2016). https://doi.org/10.1109/CVPR.2016.350
5. Dollár, P., Wojek, C., Schiele, B., Perona, P.: Pedestrian detection: a benchmark. In: Proceedings of the IEEE/CVF Conference on Computer Vision and Pattern Recognition (CVPR), pp. 304–311 (2009). https://doi.org/10.1109/CVPR.2009.5206631
6. Dosovitskiy, A., et al.: An image is worth 16x16 words: transformers for image recognition at scale. In: Proceedings of the International Conference on Learning Representations (ICLR) (2020). https://doi.org/10.8550/arXiv.2010.11929
7. Everingham, M., Eslami, S.M.A., Van Gool, L., Williams, C.K.I., Winn, J., Zisserman, A.: The PASCAL visual object classes challenge: a retrospective. Int. J. Comput. Vision 111(1), 98–136 (2014). https://doi.org/10.1007/s11263-014-0733-5
8. Ganin, Y., Lempitsky, V.: Unsupervised domain adaptation by backpropagation. In: Proceedings of the International Conference on Machine Learning (ICML), vol. 37, pp. 1180–1189 (2015). https://doi.org/10.48550/arXiv.1409.7495
9. Ganin, Y., et al.: Domain-adversarial training of neural networks. J. Mach. Learn. Res. 17(59), 1–35 (2016). https://doi.org/10.48550/arXiv.1505.07818

10. Girshick, R.: Fast R-CNN. In: Proceedings of the IEEE/CVF International Conference on Computer Vision (ICCV), pp. 1440–1448 (2015). https://doi.org/10.1109/ICCV.2015.169
11. Girshick, R., Donahue, J., Darrell, T., Malik, J.: Rich feature hierarchies for accurate object detection and semantic segmentation. In: Proceedings of the IEEE/CVF Conference on Computer Vision and Pattern Recognition (CVPR), pp. 580–587 (2014). https://doi.org/10.1109/CVPR.2014.81
12. Group, F., et al.: Flir thermal dataset for algorithm training. http://www.flir.co.uk/oem/adas/adas-dataset-form/(May2019) (2018)
13. Hossain, S., Lee, D.J.: Deep learning-based real-time multiple-object detection and tracking from aerial imagery via a flying robot with GPU-based embedded devices. Sensors **19**(15), 3371 (2019). https://doi.org/10.3390/s19153371
14. Hsu, H.K., et al.: Progressive domain adaptation for object detection. In: Proceedings of the IEEE/CVF Winter Conference on Applications of Computer Vision (WACV), pp. 738–746 (2020). https://doi.org/10.1109/WACV45572.2020.9093358
15. Hwang, S., Park, J., Kim, N., Choi, Y., So Kweon, I.: Multispectral pedestrian detection: benchmark dataset and baseline. In: Proceedings of the IEEE/CVF Conference on Computer Vision and Pattern Recognition (CVPR), pp. 1037–1045 (2015). https://doi.org/10.1109/CVPR.2015.7298706
16. Ishii, Y., Yamashita, T.: Cutdepth: Edge-aware data augmentation in depth estimation. arXiv preprint arXiv:2107.07684 (2021). https://doi.org/10.48550/arXiv.2107.07684
17. Johnson-Roberson, M., Barto, C., Mehta, R., Sridhar, S.N., Rosaen, K., Vasudevan, R.: Driving in the matrix: Can virtual worlds replace human-generated annotations for real world tasks? In: Proceedings of the IEEE International Conference on Robotics and Automation (ICRA,. pp. 746–753 (2017). https://doi.org/10.1109/ICRA.2017.7989092
18. Kang, J., Tariq, S., Oh, H., Woo, S.S.: A survey of deep learning-based object detection methods and datasets for overhead imagery. IEEE Access **10**, 20118–20134 (2022). https://doi.org/10.1109/ACCESS.2022.3149052
19. Khokhlov, I., et al.: Tiny-yolo object detection supplemented with geometrical data. In: Proceedings of the IEEE Vehicular Technology Conference (VTC), pp. 1–5 (2020). https://doi.org/10.1109/VTC2020-Spring48590.2020.9128749
20. Kim, J., Rohrbach, A., Darrell, T., Canny, J., Akata, Z.: Textual explanations for self-driving vehicles. In: Ferrari, V., Hebert, M., Sminchisescu, C., Weiss, Y. (eds.) ECCV 2018. LNCS, vol. 11206, pp. 577–593. Springer, Cham (2018). https://doi.org/10.1007/978-3-030-01216-8_35
21. Konig, D., Adam, M., Jarvers, C., Layher, G., Neumann, H., Teutsch, M.: Fully convolutional region proposal networks for multispectral person detection. In: Proceedings of the IEEE/CVF Conference on Computer Vision and Pattern Recognition (CVPR) Workshops, pp. 243–250 (2017). https://doi.org/10.1109/CVPRW.2017.36
22. Krasin, I., et al.: Openimages: a public dataset for large-scale multi-label and multi-class image classification (2016). Dataset https://github.com/openimages
23. Lin, C., Lu, J., Wang, G., Zhou, J.: Graininess-aware deep feature learning for pedestrian detection. In: Ferrari, V., Hebert, M., Sminchisescu, C., Weiss, Y. (eds.) ECCV 2018. LNCS, vol. 11213, pp. 745–761. Springer, Cham (2018). https://doi.org/10.1007/978-3-030-01240-3_45
24. Lin, T.-Y., et al.: Microsoft COCO: common objects in context. In: Fleet, D., Pajdla, T., Schiele, B., Tuytelaars, T. (eds.) ECCV 2014. LNCS, vol. 8693, pp. 740–755. Springer, Cham (2014). https://doi.org/10.1007/978-3-319-10602-1_48

25. Liu, J., Zhang, S., Wang, S., Metaxas, D.N.: Multispectral deep neural networks for pedestrian detection. arXiv preprint arXiv:1611.02644 (2016). https://doi.org/10.48550/arXiv.1611.02644

26. Liu, L., et al.: Deep learning for generic object detection: a survey. Int. J. Comput. Vision **128**(2), 261–318 (2019). https://doi.org/10.1007/s11263-019-01247-4

27. Liu, W., et al.: SSD: single shot MultiBox detector. In: Leibe, B., Matas, J., Sebe, N., Welling, M. (eds.) ECCV 2016. LNCS, vol. 9905, pp. 21–37. Springer, Cham (2016). https://doi.org/10.1007/978-3-319-46448-0_2

28. Liu, Z., et al.: Swin transformer: hierarchical vision transformer using shifted windows. In: Proceedings of the IEEE/CVF International Conference on Computer Vision (ICCV), pp. 9992–10002 (2021). https://doi.org/10.1109/ICCV48922.2021.00986

29. Osumi, K., Yamashita, T., Fujiyoshi, H.: Domain adaptation using a gradient reversal layer with instance weighting. In: Proceedings of the International Conference on Machine Vision Applications (MVA), pp. 1–5 (2019). https://doi.org/10.23919/MVA.2019.8757975

30. Pan, S.J., Yang, Q.: A survey on transfer learning. IEEE Trans. Knowl. Data Eng. (TKDE) **22**(10), 1345–1359 (2009). https://doi.org/10.1109/TKDE.2009.191

31. Redmon, J., Divvala, S., Girshick, R., Farhadi, A.: You only look once: unified, real-time object detection. In: Proceedings of the IEEE/CVF Conference on Computer Vision and Pattern Recognition (CVPR), pp. 779–788 (2016). https://doi.org/10.1109/CVPR.2016.91

32. Ren, S., He, K., Girshick, R., Sun, J.: Faster R-CNN: towards real-time object detection with region proposal networks. In: Proceedings of the Advances in Neural Information Processing Systems (NeurIPS). vol. 28 (2015). https://doi.org/10.48550/arXiv.1506.01497

33. Shang, Q., Hu, L., Li, Q., Long, W., Jiang, L.: A survey of research on image style transfer based on deep learning. In: Proceedings of the International Conference on Artificial Intelligence and Advanced Manufacture (AIAM), pp. 386–391 (2021). https://doi.org/10.1109/AIAM54119.2021.00084

34. Shao, S., et al.: Objects365: a large-scale, high-quality dataset for object detection. In: Proceedings of the IEEE/CVF International Conference on Computer Vision (ICCV), pp. 8429–8438 (2019). https://doi.org/10.1109/ICCV.2019.00852

35. Simonyan, K., Zisserman, A.: Very deep convolutional networks for large-scale image recognition. In: Proceedings of the International Conference on Learning Representations (ICLR) (2015). https://doi.org/10.48550/arXiv.1409.1556

36. Szemenyei, M., Estivill-Castro, V.: Fully neural object detection solutions for robot soccer. Neural Comput. Appl. (2), 1–14 (2021). https://doi.org/10.1007/s00521-021-05972-1

37. Tokozume, Y., Ushiku, Y., Harada, T.: Between-class learning for image classification. In: Proceedings of the IEEE/CVF Conference on Computer Vision and Pattern Recognition (CVPR), pp. 5486–5494 (2018). https://doi.org/10.1109/CVPR.2018.00575

38. Vs, V., Poster, D., You, S., Hu, S., Patel, V.M.: Meta-UDA: unsupervised domain adaptive thermal object detection using meta-learning. In: Proceedings of the IEEE/CVF Winter Conference on Applications of Computer Vision (WACV), pp. 3697–3706 (2022). https://doi.org/10.1109/WACV51458.2022.00375

39. Wang, W., Liao, S., Zhao, F., Kang, C., Shao, L.: Domainmix: learning generalizable person re-identification without human annotations. In: Proceedings of the British Machine Vision Conference (BMVC) (2021). https://doi.org/10.48550/arXiv.2011.11953

40. Weiss, K., Khoshgoftaar, T.M., Wang, D.D.: A survey of transfer learning. J. Big Data **3**(1), 1–40 (2016). https://doi.org/10.1186/s40537-016-0043-6
41. Wu, X., Sahoo, D., Hoi, S.C.: Recent advances in deep learning for object detection. Neurocomputing **396**, 39–64 (2020). https://doi.org/10.1016/j.neucom.2020.01.085
42. Wu, Z., Suresh, K., Narayanan, P., Xu, H., Kwon, H., Wang, Z.: Delving into robust object detection from unmanned aerial vehicles: A deep nuisance disentanglement approach. In: Proceedings of the IEEE/CVF International Conference on Computer Vision (ICCV), pp. 1201–1210 (2019). https://doi.org/10.1109/ICCV.2019.00129
43. Xu, Z., et al.: Towards end-to-end license plate detection and recognition: a large dataset and baseline. In: Ferrari, V., Hebert, M., Sminchisescu, C., Weiss, Y. (eds.) ECCV 2018. LNCS, vol. 11217, pp. 261–277. Springer, Cham (2018). https://doi.org/10.1007/978-3-030-01261-8_16
44. Yao, Z., Ai, J., Li, B., Zhang, C.: Efficient detr: improving end-to-end object detector with dense prior. arXiv preprint arXiv:2104.01318 (2021). https://doi.org/10.48550/arXiv.2104.01318
45. Yun, S., Han, D., Chun, S., Oh, S.J., Yoo, Y., Choe, J.: Cutmix: regularization strategy to train strong classifiers with localizable features. In: Proceedings of the IEEE/CVF International Conference on Computer Vision (ICCV), pp. 6022–6031 (2019). https://doi.org/10.1109/ICCV.2019.00612
46. Zhang, H., Cisse, M., Dauphin, Y., Lopez-Paz, D.: mixup: beyond empirical risk management. In: Proceedings of the International Conference on Learning Representations (ICLR), pp. 1–13 (2018). https://doi.org/10.48550/arXiv.1710.09412
47. Zhang, L., Zhu, X., Chen, X., Yang, X., Lei, Z., Liu, Z.: Weakly aligned cross-modal learning for multispectral pedestrian detection. In: Proceedings of the IEEE/CVF International Conference on Computer Vision (ICCV), pp. 5126–5136 (2019). https://doi.org/10.1109/ICCV.2019.00523
48. Zhang, S., Benenson, R., Omran, M., Hosang, J., Schiele, B.: How far are we from solving pedestrian detection? In: Proceedings of the IEEE/CVF Conference on Computer Vision and Pattern Recognition (CVPR), pp. 1259–1267 (2016). https://doi.org/10.1109/CVPR.2016.141
49. Zhou, C., Yuan, J.: Bi-box regression for pedestrian detection and occlusion estimation. In: Ferrari, V., Hebert, M., Sminchisescu, C., Weiss, Y. (eds.) ECCV 2018. LNCS, vol. 11205, pp. 138–154. Springer, Cham (2018). https://doi.org/10.1007/978-3-030-01246-5_9
50. Zhou, K., Yang, Y., Qiao, Y., Xiang, T.: Domain generalization with mixstyle. In: Proceedings of the International Conference on Learning Representations (ICLR) (2021). https://doi.org/10.48550/arXiv.2104.02008
51. Zhu, J.Y., Park, T., Isola, P., Efros, A.A.: Unpaired image-to-image translation using cycle-consistent adversarial networks. In: Proceedings of the IEEE/CVF International Conference on Computer Vision (ICCV), pp. 2242–2251 (2017). https://doi.org/10.1109/ICCV.2017.244
52. Zhu, X., Su, W., Lu, L., Li, B., Wang, X., Dai, J.: Deformable detr: deformable transformers for end-to-end object detection. In: Proceedings of the International Conference on Learning Representations (ICLR) (2020). https://doi.org/10.48550/arXiv.2010.04159

Author Index

Printed in the United States
by Baker & Taylor Publisher Services